THE COMPLETE PLAYS OF HENRY JAMES

Henry James
as he appeared at the time of *Guy Domville*, 1895

The
Complete Plays
of
Henry James

EDITED BY

LEON EDEL

NEW YORK   OXFORD

OXFORD UNIVERSITY PRESS

1990

Oxford University Press

Oxford   New York   Toronto
Delhi   Bombay   Calcutta   Madras   Karachi
Petaling Jaya   Singapore   Hong Kong   Tokyo
Nairobi   Dar es Salaam   Cape Town
Melbourne   Auckland

and associated companies in
Berlin   Ibadan

Published by Oxford University Press, Inc.,
200 Madison Avenue, New York, New York 10016

Oxford is a registered trademark of Oxford University Press

Library of Congress Cataloging-in-Publication Data
James, Henry, 1843–1916.
[Plays. 1990]
The complete plays of Henry James / edited by Leon Edel.
p. cm.   ISBN 0–19–504379–0
I. Edel, Leon, 1907– . II. Title.
PS2111.E4   1990
812'.4—dc20   90–6754

2 4 6 8 9 7 5 3 1
Printed in the United States of America
on acid-free paper

CONTENTS

CONTENTS

THE LATER PLAYS

ILLUSTRATIONS

PREFACE

Henry James's "Second Chance"

The Complete Plays of Henry James was conceived by me long ago as a study in the psychology of genius—a study in failure—as well as a study of the influence of the novelist's "dramatic years," from 1890 to 1895, on his later novels. It thus became a book in which the reader (in addition to examining the texts of the plays, seven of which had never before been published) could determine how James converted his failure into an unusual literary success. His plays proved to be the scaffolding he used when he created his final masterpieces. James himself spoke of "the interest, at the worst, of certain sorts of failure."

The following was my hypothesis: James was in reality a dramatist who could not write plays. He accordingly made himself into a dramatist of the novel. I had originally written a small book on the subject that was published in Paris in 1932 as *Henry James: Les années dramatiques*. The hypothesis was confirmed when James's literary executor gave me permission to edit the plays and allowed me access to private James papers. In his notebooks—which (as I have described elsewhere) I found in an old sea chest at Harvard together with variant versions of some of the plays—there existed a passage in which the novelist spoke of "compensations and solutions" for his five years of struggle. This involved seeing his fictions as "scenarios." The "divine principle of the Scenario" became "a key that fitted the complicated chambers of *both* the dramatic and narrative lock."

Readers of the *Complete Plays* also found a great many details about James's apprenticeship in the theatre. He came to know Bernard Shaw and had an argument with him about the one-act play which he entitled *The Saloon*. It was drawn from a short story called *Owen Wingrave*, later destined to be transformed into an opera by Benjamin Britten. I published in this book the correspondence between James and Shaw. I also described James's friendship with Harley Granville-Barker, who esteemed James's dramatic skills and was to have produced *The Outcry*, which was ultimately turned by James into his last novel, published in 1910. There was also the play *Summersoft*, written for Ellen Terry but never staged by her, and there were the novelist's friendships with his compatriot Elizabeth Robins of Kentucky, the famous Ibsen interpreter, and the Forbes-Robertsons, who staged a late James play, *The High Bid*. The

1

history of James's play-writing had its startling climax in 1895 when his ill-conceived but tender little drama *Guy Domville* was booed by a London audience in the presence of three critics belonging to the new generation of writers: Shaw, H. G. Wells and Arnold Bennett.

These are some of the ingredients that went into the present volume, which I researched before the Second World War and brought out in 1949. The history of *Guy Domville* described the watershed of the novelist's life: he vowed he would never again be led into such "traps, abysses and heart break," or into such a "defeat"—a word he used alongside the word "failure."

The strange side of this book's history resides in the fact that the issues with which it dealt remained alive even after James died. Indeed, the "compensations and solutions" continue to accrue to this day, and probably beyond. As the Victorian and Edwardian theatres gave way to modernity and the curtain and proscenium yielded their dominance to the newer media represented by radio and television, James's dramatic fictions blossomed. His novels became not only plays but films; his short stories were used as the basis for radio plays; television began to appreciate his enormous sense of the value of scenarios. By mid-century, his oeuvre became not only visual and aural—sight and sound—but evolved into various forms of the "electronic" and the operatic.

In the light of James's posthumous success in the "performing arts," it becomes apparent that the *Complete Plays* has acquired a new relevance. It can now be read in relation to a great irony that has played itself out—that of the would-be dramatist who could not make his peace with the practicalities of the stage, and whose works have been metamorphosed into new media. Other less gifted hands have achieved the translation of James's subtle fiction into the audio-visual realm.

It is exactly one hundred years since James entered his "dramatic years." He pleaded for a "second chance" at the time in one of his tales about a dying novelist, *The Middle Years.* Fate has bestowed it on him posthumously. We must now ask ourselves what was the deeper magic James possessed that fulfilled his ambition so long after his theatrical failure. Let us examine these mysteries a bit further.

I

Half a dozen years after Henry James's death, J. C. Squire, a London editor, and John L. Balderston, a man of the theatre who was originally a journalist, seized on James's unfinished novel *The Sense of the Past*, recognizing its dramatic possibilities. It was about an American who, like Mark Twain's Connecticut Yankee, enters into the past when he inherits his ancestral home in London. They made a charming play of this called *Berkeley Square*. It proved a perfect vehicle for the popular actor Leslie Howard, who knew how to project across the footlights an air of meditation and philosophical repose. It played for weeks in London, then moved to Broadway and eventually became a film.

Bit by bit other adaptations based on James's works followed. By the time my edition of the *Complete Plays* appeared in print, James's little novella of the 1870s, *Washington Square*, was destined to become *The Heiress* both on stage and screen, and *The Turn of the Screw* became a play, two films, a distinguished opera by Benjamin Britten, and ultimately a series of television scripts. Britten would later turn James's short story *Owen Wingrave* (published in this volume in James's one-act version as *The Saloon*) into another opera; James's correspondence with Shaw concerning the play, which I unearthed long ago, may be found in my foreword to it. James's late novel *The Wings of the Dove* became both a play and an opera, and in England video viewers were able to see James Clellan Jones's sensitive version of *The Portrait of a Lady*. He also directed James's final and most complex novel, *The Golden Bowl*, for the "Masterpiece Theater" television series, in which the adapter introduced a narrator to overcome the complications of the plot. "The Aspern Papers," turned into a play by Michael Redgrave after existing as a Grade B movie, has recently been entirely rewritten and transformed into an opera by Dominick Argento.

If we seek a touchstone for what the camera can do at its best, even supremely, for James's oeuvre, we find it in François Truffaut's film version of *The Altar of the Dead*, a tale much beloved by Jamesian readers for its delicate pieties and its embodiment of universal grief. The hero, one of James's characteristic middle-aged "poor, sensitive gentlemen," believes the world is too forgetful, that the dead are shunted not only out of sight but out of mind. He has kept a spiritual shrine for the woman he loved; we follow him as he lights imaginary candles until he fixes in his memory the image of a blazing altar. His is, however, a restrictive piety: one candle remains unlit; he refuses this charity to a man who had hurt him; he cannot forgive.

A moment comes when the poor, sensitive gentleman translates his fantasy into reality. He decides to erect a real altar, choosing a church "of the old persuasion." However, he now must deal with actuality: first the ecclesiastics and then the bishop himself, who proves in the matter "delightfully human"; he is "almost amused." He cannot turn his back on religious and spiritual emotion, especially when accompanied by the material evidence of the gentleman's zeal. The real altar has real tapers, and all the gentleman's friends—save one—are memorialized. We are reminded of Marianne Moore's real frogs in imaginary gardens. The sensitive gentleman's final shock occurs when he discovers that a sympathetic woman is lighting candles at this very shrine for the man he excluded. Intruding reality defeats the beauty of fantasy.

James wrote this story in his finest spun prose and its grandest organ tones. Truffaut sensitively picked up all the reverberations: the candles fluttering in the drafty old chapel; the tender feelings for the absent dead; the drama of the conflicting worshippers. He called his film *The Green Room—La Chambre verte*—using a hint from James, who has the grieving woman in the story create a "red room"—doubtless symbolizing passion—filled with memorabilia of the man she loved. The change refers to the theatricality the story acquires: the "green room" was the classical actors' reception room in French theatres.

With the camera returning again and again to the shimmering beauty of the candle-lit altar and the mysticism with which we endow the rituals of death and our religious feelings, Truffaut subtly creates a heart of brightness as against a heart of darkness. The French actor-director did not hesitate to graft onto this film bits from other James stories. Had they not sprung from the same creative imagination? *La Chambre verte* is a recreated work, with an amplified story, which retains the strong emotional mood of the original. Truffaut's own touches seem very Jamesian. Take, for example, his making the man who creates the altar a writer of obituaries. Above all, he conveys our feelings for the dead, the ways in which we try to keep faith with them, and struggle with the pain of our own transience. The film captures the ritualism of grief and the meaning of mourning and melancholy, the subject of Freud's famous essay.

I believe the retention of the Jamesian emotion, the use of image and symbol within the free adaptations, has yielded the best and most vivid renderings. These are instances of artistic rethinking, reshaping, retouching—the transmuted continuity of the creative imagination. We must ask ourselves, however, what there was in James's cry of "dramatize! dramatize!" that proved so attractive to modern producers, directors, cineastes, playwrights, and composers—so alluring even to have given us a Broadway musical derived from James's most structurally complex novel, *The Ambassadors*. The musical was a flop—it wasn't even a good try—but we mustn't discount the possibility of such a musical. George Cukor, creator of high-flown, sentimental films, once talked soulfully to me of his desire to do *Daisy Miller* with Judy Garland in the title role. One can see how the Hollywood mind works: Lambert Strether could become a kind of Wizard of Oz!

What kind of drama—what qualities, techniques and values—exists in James's dramatic novels to result in the transformation of twelve of his twenty novels into new forms? One can trace this right down to the recent Merchant-Ivory film of *The Europeans*, a Jamesian comedy that was treated too solemnly, and their more successful version of *The Bostonians*. Or one can point to a play once drawn from *The Reverberator*, James's amusing comedy of the abuse of privacy by the American press.

II

The appeal of Henry James's works for the theatrical and operatic stages, as well as for the cameras and video of our time, derives from three elements in his artistry: the modernity of his comic subjects, the depth and psychology of his realism, and his extraordinary visual sense. His observations were always acute and they were psychological. He had a sense of picture and scene, a belief that all the arts are one, and that the artist should never hesitate to experiment.

Let us look first at his subjects, the comedy rising out of his contrasts of American and European manners. James was, as we know, the original fictional historian of the American girl in all her innocence, her ignorance and her independence. Later he would portray the American woman in his most famous work, *The Portrait of a Lady,* almost a century before modern feminism. Trollope had used American girls in some of his stories after his trip to the United States, but he had never explored their thematic possibilities and their national character. James's Daisies and Delias, his Isabels and Pandoras were well dressed but rather unsophisticated. Their outlooks were provincial. They had a singular unawareness of the world's evil. They had an eagerness for life but little tolerance for its disappointments. Some of his American girls, like Daisy, made a career of flirting, with no awareness that flirting had sexual meanings over and above the obvious need for catching a husband. They had expensive tastes that were indulged by their affluent parents. They were a novelty on the European continent, where young girls in those days were reared, until their marriage, in a confined atmosphere intended to guard their virginity. In his early years James treated his American–European legend as comedy pure and simple. But when he came to write *The Portrait of a Lady* he was serious. Handicapped by her Emersonian self-reliance, Isabel Archer has no grounded self to meet the assaults of the world. James understood her sufferings. His other tales often deal with "the chase for the husband," and here he predicted, in his pictures of American girls seeking peers, and peers American girls, the American divorcée who toppled a king, or the actress who figured in a Monaco romance. These are all suitable film subjects, and are even capable of being turned into television miniseries. I have always marvelled that Hollywood never unearthed Christopher Newman for Gary Cooper.

Within this international scene James particularly contrasted American and European education—not book learning but the ways in which manners and morals are acquired and how children are unprepared for life in American society. Even when our presidents, at this late date, attend European summits, they seem in some ways reincarnations of Christopher Newman in their mix of self-confidence, geniality, folksiness, but also in their sense of economic supremacy and their feeling that they are moving among treacherous and canny Europeans. Peter Bogdanovich's film version of *Daisy Miller* displayed a distinct awareness of these themes. Although the actress, Cybill Shepherd, was hardly the slip of a girl one imagined Daisy to be, she conveyed the spirit of the invincible American girl and her bewilderment. James's play version of his celebrated tale introduced new characters and elements derived from French farce. Many years later Daniel Frohman, the Broadway producer, told me why he had turned it down: "Too much talk and not enough action."

The second element in the appeal of James's fiction to other media is to be found in his anticipations of modern psychology, so much of which is based on analytical observation of human behavior. The friendly gesture that harbors aggression, the euphoria that betrays depression, the hidden barbs in cultivated language, the slips of the tongue, the self-exaltation derived by ridiculing others—James understood these manifestations of the human personality. He knew his way within the unconscious of suppressed emotions and the emotional blocks resulting from permissive rearing. Above all, he was a master of personal relations in ways that are endlessly appealing to the stage. *The Portrait of a Lady, The Bostonians, The Wings of the Dove, The Ambassadors,* novels supremely devoted to personal relations, have been dramatized or turned into films. James translated his understanding of human anxiety into ghost stories, and we have seen the way in which *The Turn of the Screw* assumed diverse shapes. The psychological tensions between fathers and daughters or mothers and sons, the struggles between brothers—all these and kindred subjects were an innate and essential part of the modern theatre.

Most important in stimulating the adaptations of James's works to the performing arts is the novelist's visual sense. We see through his eyes the Venice of *The Aspern Papers:* its architecture; its distinctive waterway life; the worldly old palaces; the subterranean society; the constant play of the romantic Venetian past and the limited, small-town existence Juliana and her niece made of their life among the Venetians. James's eyes were camera lenses. He turned himself into a mobile camera long before that instrument's potential had been realized. And we are all aware of his technical innovations, his attempts to remove himself from storytelling by making his characters offer us their "point of view," that is, their way of seeing, their particular camera angle of vision. The novel, he told us, is a house with many windows, with each novelist posted at a different window, representing his personal observation of a particular scene. In *The Ambassadors,* Strether's cry of "live all you can" is later translated to mean "see all you can."

In this novel, James's methods still constitute a difficulty for readers accustomed to being told a story by an omniscient author. We are made to see Maria Gostrey as she scans Lambert Strether's countenance; we watch Strether observing Maria's visage. These are novelistic close-ups very much like those in contemporary film. After that, we move back for a long shot and see the two together in the hotel garden. Flaubert tried the effects of sound and picture in his celebrated fair scene in *Madame Bovary,* but it was James who consistently utilized the "movie camera" approach throughout this entire novel, which was written in 1900, when movies were in their infancy. I have always regarded *The Ambassadors* as the first avant-garde novel of the twentieth century, given its consistent "camera eye."

A very brief passage will illustrate James's use of the camera technique. We know how in film or in television a camera can move in on a painting and almost engulf us in it. In Book Eleventh of *The Ambassadors* this is exactly what Lambert Strether does. He goes in search of a suburban landscape, near Paris, that he had once glimpsed in a Lambinet painting hanging in a Boston art dealer's shop. And he finds himself inside its frame:

The oblong gilt frame disposed its enclosing lines; the poplars and willows, the reeds and river—a river of which he didn't know, and didn't want to know, the name—fell into a composition, full of felicity, within them; the sky was silver and turquoise and varnish; the village on the left was white and the church on the right was grey; it was all there in short—it was what he wanted; it was Tremont Street, it was France, it was Lambinet. Moreover he was freely walking about in it.

Passages such as this suggest why James catches the imagination of film-makers and television producers who seek a more elevated form of storytelling than the hackneyed routines offered up to our national television audience of "couch potatoes," the constant explosion of gunfire and aggression.

One likes to imagine James, in his last days, when his acolytes called him "Master," sitting in front of a television set and rubbing his eyes at the wonder of its possibilities—possibilities as yet untried. Cinema was then but a jerky series of movements captured on film by a static camera. James would also rub his eyes, as a tried professional, at the prices he would now be able to command for his work. "I am that queer monster, the artist," he said to Henry Adams, "an obstinate finality, an inexhaustible sensibility." Perhaps the greatest irony of all may be that this master of language and style, this weaver of verbal beauty, should appear to some of his new audience essentially in pictures or music rather than in words. That is perhaps even a greater irony than James's being a dramatist who couldn't write plays.

Honolulu   **L.E.**
May 1990

FOREWORD

"Theatre-stuff . . . Drama-stuff"

In this volume there appear, collected for the first time, the complete plays of Henry James, together with the unfinished scenario for an unwritten play and sundry prefaces and notes relating to his play-writing. So far as we know, the novelist completed twelve plays. Five were published during his lifetime; the remaining seven never before appeared in public print. Four of the unpublished plays were produced on the London stage, three with moderate success and one under circumstances, fully described in this book, which proved disastrous for the novelist's career in the theatre.

It will be asked why James himself never published all his plays upon which he lavished, over many years, the resources of his literary maturity. He lived in an era when, in the Anglo-American world, publication of plays was not as common as it is today; and even today only the highly successful play usually is able to make its way into print. James, on more than one occasion, deplored the failure of the English-speaking audience to demand the text of a play with the same insistence as did the Continental audience. "A comedy or a tragedy," he wrote in the preface to his novel *The Awkward Age,* "may run for a thousand nights without prompting twenty persons in London or in New York to desire that view of its text which is so desired in Paris, as soon as a play begins to loom at all large, that the number of copies of the printed piece in circulation far exceeds at last the number of performances. But as with the printed piece our own public, infatuated as it may be with the theatre, refuses all commerce. . . ." And in that sprightly imaginary conversation on the shortcomings of the British theatre, *After the Play,* published by him at the moment when he was settling down to five years of play-writing, he put into the mouth of one of his personages this same complaint: "There's no text. . . . One can't put one's hand upon it; one doesn't know what one is discussing . . . nothing is ever published." And again: "A play isn't fully produced until it is in a form in which you can refer to it."

He published his dramatization of *Daisy Miller* in America (but not in England) on the strength of its success in the story form, after it had been rejected by both New York and London managers; and in 1894–95 he published in England and in America his two series of *Theatricals,* apologizing in his prefaces for offering to the public plays which had never justified their existence by being performed. *Theatricals* received a poor press and had a negligible sale. Thereafter Henry James never again published his plays.

He did, however, devise a way of getting some of them into the hands of a wider public than they might have reached in their original form. In 1898, in preparing *The Turn of the Screw* for publication, he found that it made too slim a volume by itself; having at hand the one-act *Summersoft*, written for Ellen Terry but never produced by her, he turned it into the story *Covering End*, and it appeared as a companion piece to his now-celebrated ghostly tale, in the volume entitled *The Two Magics*. In a letter to H. G. Wells of December 9, 1898, he explained how he made the transition from play to story: "For three mortal years had the actress for whom it was written (utterly to try to *fit*) persistently failed to produce it, and I couldn't wholly waste my labor. The B[ritish] P[ublic] won't read a play with the mere names of the speakers—so I simply paraphrased these and added such indications as might be the equivalent of decent acting—a history and an evolution that seem to me moreover explicatively and sufficiently smeared all over the thing. The moral is of course Don't write one-act plays."

It is amply clear, thus, that Henry James would long ago have published his plays had conditions been favorable. To a request made in 1913 that he give a critic access to his plays for the writing of an article about them, he replied emphatically:

> While they were being played they of course came in for whatever attention the Press was paying to the actual and current theatre. They were inevitably then Theatre-stuff, and as such took their chance; but they are now, enjoying complete immunity from performance as they do, Drama-stuff—which is quite a different matter. It is only as Drama-stuff that I recognize their exposure to any public remark that doesn't consist simply of the critic's personal remembrance of them as played things. . . . When my Plays, such as they have been, *are* published, then of course the gentleman you mention will enjoy all aid to his examination. I am sorry I can not now oblige you further than by promising you a copy of such volume or volumes on that occasion. . . .

The occasion never came. Henry James died three years after writing this letter and the manuscripts of the unpublished plays were placed in a large chest, together with his notebooks and other papers, and sent to America. There they remained and were examined by the editor of this volume some years before 1942, when the novelist's nephew, the late Henry James of New York, who was his literary executor, presented them to the Houghton Library at Harvard. The text of the one-act *Summersoft* was not among these manuscripts, since the novelist had presented his sole copy to the actress Elizabeth Robins. Copies of the four produced plays—*The American, Guy Domville, The High Bid* and *The Saloon*—also were to be found in the Lord Chamberlain's Office in London, where they were deposited in conformity with British regulations for the censorship and licensing of plays, and their texts, together with other extant texts described elsewhere in this volume, have been carefully collated for the purposes of this edition. This censorship was abolished in recent years.

It is doubtful whether the format in which the plays appear here would have met with the unqualified approval of Henry James, even though his *Daisy Miller* play appeared in just such a form in the pages of the *Atlantic Monthly*. He was, in this respect, a devout and uncompromising follower of the French, and when *Daisy Miller* was to be published in book form he wrote to his American publisher, J. R. Osgood: "I should only make the condition that it be printed in the manner of French comedies—that is, with the names of the characters above the speeches, and not on a line with them." His *Theatricals* were put forth in this form, with much white space around each speech. The considerable bulk of his collected dramatic works makes it impossible, in these days of complex book production, to do the same for them, but in every other way his manuscripts have been faithfully reproduced; such editorial changes as have been made have been largely in the interest of consistency within the given play and are fully explained in the note on the texts.

The editor has, in arranging the volume, taken his cue from Henry James, who remarked, when he was seeking to justify his publication of the two series of *Theatricals*, that if more rejected plays were published "with some history of their adventures" they "would end by constituting in themselves a suggestive, almost a legitimate literature. . . ." In an attempt to meet the conditions which James envisaged, the history of each "adventure" has been set down here as fully as possible.

The appearance of the plays now, after the publication of the two unfinished novels and, more recently, of the *Notebooks,* completes—with a few minor exceptions—the publication of all the posthumous papers of Henry James which were in Lamb House at the time of his death. It should now be possible to evaluate the place these plays occupy in the large body of Henry James's work and, still more important, to estimate, as Allan Wade put it many years ago, "the loss sustained by the refusal of the 19th century theatre to encourage Henry James's attempts to write for it."

NOTES AND
ACKNOWLEDGMENTS

Rereading my Foreword and Introductory Essay, as well as the individual editor's forewords, to *The Complete Plays of Henry James,* written more than forty years ago, I find that little needs to be added to the essential story of the novelist's "dramatic years." The two or three batches of letters that have surfaced since that time offer a few new facts and one or two footnotes. What I cannot convey to the end-of-the-century reader is the chagrin I experience as a literary historian when I think of the avenues of research that this delayed information might have opened up. They are now closed forever: there were individuals still alive in 1949 whom I might have consulted and who might have contributed some sidelights, some wider sense of detail, answered some of the questions that remained unanswered when I sent my manuscript to the publisher. However, when I have such thoughts I remind myself that no story is ever complete, no research final. Historians must work with what they have, and this I did to the full.

My best source of new information about *Guy Domville,* already heavily documented in my editor's foreword (pp. 465–83), were some letters among a batch of forty-five written by James to the actor-manager Edward Compton and his wife, the former American actress Virginia Bateman. These treat of their production of *The American,* the new act for it (see pp. 243–52), and of *Guy Domville,* which James first offered to Compton. I had sought these letters from Compton Mackenzie, the British novelist, during the 1930's. He was the eldest son of the Comptons. The family name had always been Mackenzie, but his grandfather had taken the name Compton for his stage career. The novelist thus combined the nomenclature of the two branches. Compton Mackenzie's brother, Francis, and his three sisters were all on the stage. The novelist wrote me a friendly letter (March 10, 1937) saying he couldn't find any James letters, but he sent me to his mother, then advanced in age and blind. She lived in Soho, in the Theatre Girls' Club which she had founded, and while she had many memories of the Southport and London premieres of *The American,* she sent me back to her son for the letters. These emerged in the 1960's, long after this book was published, when Compton Mackenzie decided, on his eightieth birthday, to write a volume for each of his decades, which he entitled *My Life and Times* (he called the series his Octet). In the second and third volumes he

13

used some of the James letters in an appendix and some in the text. He had by that time committed his papers to the University of Texas at Austin, but he made available some microfilm which enabled me to establish an uncorrupted text: he himself had difficulties with James's handwriting and what he published is filled with misreadings.

From these letters I learned that James worked on the first act of *Guy Domville* in Paris in 1893, which he then sent to his "little Hampstead copyist," Miss Gregory, to be typed. He sent the typescript and the scenario for the remaining two acts to Edward Compton, asking the latter to give him a frank and candid verdict. Compton obliged by telling James that the first act was charming but that the unhappy ending envisioned for the play would doom it for a British public. This is perhaps the most important fact missing from my account. James was thus warned of the fatal defect in his play, which ultimately resulted in its being booed when George Alexander produced it. Having yielded to a happy ending for the dramatized *American,* he was defiant this time. His hero's renunciation and return to the monastery had to stand; it was the only thing that made sense (for James) and "the only ending I have ever dreamed of giving . . . it *is* the play." He argued that it would be ugly and displeasing to an audience to marry off someone who had one foot in the monastery. The Comptons argued that, given the romantic character of the play, it would gratify the audiences to have the marriage take place. James replied stiffly that "my subject is my subject to take or to leave." The Comptons were not prepared to take it.

James had second thoughts. Could the Comptons be right? In the same letter he asked them: "Do I mean something that your audience can't understand? It is a complete surprise to me to suppose so, for I have been going on with a great sense of security." He had been in the same position with William Dean Howells earlier, when his novel *The American* was being serialized in *The Atlantic Monthly.* Howells urged that Christopher Newman marry Madame de Cintré, whom James was sending to a nunnery. James had replied with similar *hauteur:* "They would have been an impossible couple. . . . I should have felt as if I were throwing a rather vulgar sop to readers who don't really know the world."

In reality, it was James who did not *then* know the world. He was following traditional old novels in which females escaped to nunneries and marriages were arranged with considerable intrigue; he was confusing, as he admitted in his old age, "the real and the romantic." Too late he recognized that this was an affront to the readers' or theatregoers' "verisimilitude."

What the Comptons couldn't convey to James was that the artistic discomfort he felt was his own and would not be that of his audience. In the play Guy Domville is destined for the priesthood but inherits a fortune. As the last of his line, he is urged to marry so as not to be "the last of the Domvilles." He has had a close friendship with Mrs. Peverel, whose son he tutored, and once he decides to leave the monastery she feels free to show (if not express) her love for him. Marion Terry, who played the part, revealed this to the audience; but it wasn't apparent to Domville, so long accustomed to the idea that he was destined for celibacy. In the play (as in many of his novels, from *Roderick Hudson* to *The Ambassadors*), James was showing how profound was his own bachelor state, his inability to achieve any intimacy with marriageable women. A supreme example may be found in the aloof Winterbourne, in *Daisy Miller*. In his play, James could not conceive that Guy, troubled by having to leave the Church (and thus abandon his celibate state) might be capable of falling in love. That was the deeper difficulty of his ill-fated comedy. There is a sentence in one of James's letters to Compton which vividly expresses his blindness: "I have a general strong impression of my constitutional inability to (even in spite of intense and really abject effort) realise the sort of simplicity that the promiscuous British public finds its interest in—much more, after this indispensable realization, to *achieve* it. Even when I think I am dropping most diplomatically to the very rudiments and stooping, with a vengeance, to conquer, I am as much 'out of it' as ever, and far above their unimaginable heads."

The rest of the story of *Guy Domville* follows, after these preliminaries, as I have previously related it. James completed the play at Ramsgate that summer, and Alexander accepted it. The Compton letters show that James did try to come up with a different comedy for the Compton Comedy Company that spring in Paris. In the same letter cited earlier there is an allusion to the mysterious "Monte-Carlo play" (see pp. 54 and 457), the idea for which is mentioned—"the man suspected of theft, the girl who believes in him, etc."— but of which we hear no more. And he seems to have tried to convince the Comptons that he could make a comedy out of his tale *The Chaperon* (suggested to him by the playwright Arthur Wing Pinero; see pp. 457–62). He writes to Compton, again in the same letter, that "the way to write comedy is not to take a serious subject and try to make it droll—but to take a droll subject and try to keep it droll."

A bit of additional light can be thrown on the correspondence between James and Bernard Shaw concerning *The Saloon* (see pp. 641–49). This is derived from Stanley Weintraub's edition of Shaw's shorthand diaries, which was published in two volumes in 1986. The diaries reveal that on October 29, 1885, Shaw attended a meeting of the Society for Psychical Research, to which he belonged, and was urged to join a ghost watch that night in a haunted house identified by Weintraub as Ivy House, Grove Road, St. Anne's Hill, Wandsworth. Shaw's shorthand note in his diary reads "Slept there. Terrific nightmare." And *The Pall Mall Gazette*, for which he had apparently agreed to write about the experience, published a note on November 6, 1885, saying that the ghost hunter (Shaw was not named but Weintraub has confirmed that it was he who was being quoted) reported that he "woke up in a corner of the room howling and struggling with imaginary powers of darkness."

This throws a ray of light on the intensity with which Shaw wrote to James when he criticized *The Saloon*. The play was derived from an 1892 short story about a young pacifist named Owen Wingrave, who sleeps in a haunted room in his family's old mansion and is killed that night by the ghost of an ancestor for his defiance of the family's dedication to militarism. In his play version James unknowingly gave partial form to Shaw's old experience as a ghost hunter. Unfortunately Shaw never left a record of his nightmare.

In my search for the correspondence between Shaw and James, published in this book, I spent an amusing half hour with him in November 1929, during which he characterized the nineteenth-century theatre, as "disreputable," praised James as a dramatist and criticized his "inhumanly literary" dialogue. He also acted out for me the drinking scene in *Guy Domville*. Concerning the ghost play, he clearly remembered that he urged James to have young Owen Wingrave kill the ghost and not be killed by it. However, he told me nothing of his own ghostly adventure a quarter of a century before he read James's play.

With the Robert H. Taylor collection of manuscripts and letters, Princeton University acquired fourteen letters to Harley Granville-Barker from James, written during the period when Granville-Barker was preparing *The Outcry* for the repertory season at the Duke of York's Theatre. These letters—written between December 1909 and the beginning of August 1910, when James suffered what he called a "nervous" illness that amounted to a debilitating depression—deal with the period when he was asked by Granville-Barker to make large cuts in the rather overblown play. I described this in my Editor's Foreword (see pp. 761-65) as Granville-Barker told it to me, and these letters add little further information save James's way of expressing his unease and his anxieties. He worked very hard to meet Granville-Barker's demands and his anger emerges in the final words of the last letter (August, 1910), when—the repertory season having been cancelled owing to the death of Edward VII—he asks to have the manuscript back, including the cuts. The language is sufficiently vivid. He wants to

> rescue the cut copy of my ill-starred comedy . . . from the limbo of the vague. Those cuts were the result of an heroic effort. . . . I have only now to think ruefully and gloomily, what other use I shall—or can—make of it. I wish you, for yourself, some prompter inspiration than I strike myself as likely to find. But my first course must be to get the cuts—by which I mean the ensanguined corpse—washed and laid out clean.

He sailed for America a week after writing this letter. In Cambridge, while staying at his brother's house, he turned *The Outcry* into a novel, which had a modest success. I remember Granville-Barker insisting, when we talked in the 1930's, that James's mannered dialogue was quite manageable—in this he differed from Bernard Shaw—and he remarked that "we were able to solve the problems of playing Chekhov—and we could have done so for James as well, I'm sure. The greatest difficulty I had was to find actors capable of speaking the lines."

Specific acknowledgment of my debt to various persons—a goodly number deceased in recent decades—and institutions is made in my notes at the end of the book (see pp. 825–26), but I want to restate my gratitude to certain individuals: Theodora Bosanquet; Harley Granville-Barker; George Bernard Shaw; Percy Lubbock; Edith Wharton; Urbain Mengin; Jocelyn Persse; Elizabeth Gertrude Elliott; Mrs. Edward Compton, Compton Mackenzie; Sir Rupert Hart-Davis; Simon Nowell-Smith; S. Gorly Putt, Allan Wade, and Morton Fullerton.

I did my research in the British Museum (now the British Library), the Brotherton Library in Leeds, the Lord Chamberlain's Office in St. James's Palace, the Bibliothèque Nationale in Paris, the Theater Collection of the New York Public Library, the Firestone Library of Princeton University, and the Victoria and Albert Museum in London.

My principal debt was to the late Henry James, the novelist's nephew, who gave me permission to publish the plays, and to the Guggenheim Foundation for a 1936 fellowship. I found the variant texts of the plays in an old sea chest which James's nephew deposited in the basement of the Widener Library for safekeeping and later presented to Harvard University. I worked on the James papers in the Houghton Library and am indebted to its director, the late William A. Jackson, and his successor, W. H. H. Bond, as well as to Carolyn Jakeman, the then librarian at Harvard's Houghton. I also wish to express thanks to Leonard Woolf and Dr. Wilberforce for help with the Elizabeth Robins papers now at New York University; to Stanley Weintraub for help with Bernard Shaw's mysterious nightmare, and to Alexander D. Wainwright, librarian at the Princeton Library, for help with the Granville-Barker letters.

Abbreviations

ASB .... *A Small Boy and Others,* London and New York, 1913
NSB .... *Notes of a Son and Brother,* London and New York, 1914
N .... *The Notebooks of Henry James,* London and New York, 1947
(U) .... Unpublished document
T&F .... *Theatre and Friendship,* London and New York, 1932
HJ .... Henry James
WJ .... William James
AJ .... Alice James
AJJ .... *Alice James, Her Brothers, Her Journal,* New York, 1934
L .... *The Letters of Henry James,* London and New York, 1920
Ed .... The editor of this volume

Henry James:
The Dramatic Years

An Introductory Essay by Leon Edel

It is of course for my reader to say whether or no what I have done *has* meant defeat; yet even if this should be his judgment I fall back on the interest, at the worst, of certain sorts of failure.——*Henry James*

HENRY JAMES:

THE DRAMATIC YEARS

POINT OF DEPARTURE

In the hours before dawn of January 4, 1910, Henry James—he was then sixty-seven—sat at his work table in Lamb House, Rye, Sussex, scrawling notes for a new novel in a rapid, half-illegible script across large loose sheets, a deluge of words pouring from an image-crowded mind and hurriedly transcribed by a tired old hand. As the balanced sentences formed themselves, exploring the plot, casting about for structural elements, gathering up moments of memory, a sense of exhilaration swept over the novelist—the joy of remembering, assembling, creating. The manuscript pages, with their pencilled scribble, tell the story: the sense of creative strength, the gratitude, mystical and semi-religious, for the guidance of his "blest Genius," the surge of passion, the expression of tender feeling for the Muse—the hidden "powers and forces and divinities" at the source of his art. The passage he wrote has all the quality of a fervent prayer:

> I come back yet again and again, to my only seeing it in the dramatic way—as I can only see everything and anything now. . . . Momentary sidewinds—things of no real authority—break in every now and then to put their inferior little questions to me; but I come back, I come back, as I say, I all throbbingly and yearningly and passionately, oh *mon bon,* come back to this way that is clearly the only one in which I can do anything now, and that will open out to me more and more, and that has overwhelming reasons pleading all beautifully in its breast.

Why was the "dramatic way" the only way? That is our point of departure.

A SMALL BOY AT THE THEATRE

Henry James was taken to the theatre at an early age, probably during his eighth year, and thereafter, for sixty years, he was a consistent (and consistently critical) playgoer. He was a stage-struck boy, a stage-enamored young student, a serious-minded drama critic during his early manhood, and in middle life an anxious, over-eager playwright. The theatre never lost its fairy-tale spell for him. He might grumble at the poorness of the play, sitting deep in his stall, his eyes taking in every detail on the stage; he was seldom satisfied with the actors, save those of the Théâtre Français; he tended to speak of "theatre" as an institution created to "murder" dramatic literature; yet, when the new play opened, at the hushed moment before the curtain's rise, he was there in box or stall, ready to renew the experience, ready to sit glowing with momentary satisfaction or moaning and muttering to himself, or, so it has been reported, rising half-way through a play with an audible "I can't bear it any longer," and stalking from the theatre.

There were times when his attitude was less overtly belligerent. Going to the theatre in the company of actresses—the great Fanny Kemble, Mary Anderson, Elizabeth Robins—provided ears for his running commentary and opportunities for the exercise of wit. Miss Robins has testified that it required courage to accompany the novelist to the play: "One never grew wholly acclimatized to the nipping airs that now and then would blow about the startled stalls. Mr. James's all too audible remarks, conveyed in terms always 'chosen,' often singularly picturesque, sometimes diabolic, as though he revelled in mercilessness—would send cold shivers down his companion's spine." Mary Anderson's testimony sheds further light. "He sat by me and whispered his criticisms. 'You see that fat, rubicund old Colonel on the stage now; well, shortly he is bound to say "Damn it, sir," and the audience will be delighted. Oh, they love trifles and vulgar trifles very often.' He had hardly finished speaking when the fat old Colonel said, 'Damn it, sir,' and the audience laughed long and loud. . . ."

If the middle-aged playgoer thus brought a personal bias and an intricate and highly individual critical apparatus into the theatre, it was because in mid-nineteenth century a small New York boy had been taken to the theatre by his parents with uncommon regularity, and because those nights in the theatres of Broadway, Chambers Street and Park Place provided that familiarity with the "scenic art" which is a pre-requisite to critical theatregoing. Memories of these imaginative, artistic childhood adventures crowd the 436 pages of Henry James's autobiographical *A Small Boy and Others*, a volume which covers only the first fourteen years of his life. Fully one-eighth of the book is filled with the names of plays and actors, what they wore and how they strutted, their very grimaces, as well as of the lamplit and gaslit old theatres—all recounted and pictured with an evident delight at seventy, although six decades separated the old James from the little New York playgoer.

He remembered how he used to wander down lower Fifth Avenue spelling out the names of plays and players on the yellow and white billboards, pasted in those days on large screens and sociably disposed against trees and fences; and he remembered how he used to trudge up Broadway, his hoarded pennies in his pocket, walking the distance to save the fare, averting his eyes as he passed the doughnut stands, in order to attend the matinees at Barnum's "Lecture Room" to which little boys were drawn by the same magic that draws little boys of our era to the movie palace and the "western." Here the dramatic art was embodied for him in the person of such actresses as the red-faced Emily Mestayer, with damp ringlets and a "vast protuberance of bosom" playing in J. Sheridan Knowles's *Love or The Countess and the Serf,* shouting at the top of her lungs that a purse of gold "would be the fair guerdon of the minion" who should start on the spot to do her bidding. He remembered her also as Eliza in *Uncle Tom's Cabin,* "her swelling bust encased in a neat cotton gown" and her flight across the ice blocks "intrepidly and gracefully performed."

The theatre was assigned this role in young Henry's life by the senior Henry James. The book, the literary periodical, the concert stage and the art gallery, all held places of importance in the lives of the four James boys and their sister; but books could be read quietly at home, and pictures studied in picture-books or in a casual stroll through a gallery, whereas going to the theatre involved a trip in a carriage, an encounter, over flickering footlights, with strange and fantastic characters, and after the performance, recapitulation and critical discussion. Henry's parents, he tells us, had a simple theory. They liked the theatre, such as it was in those early American days of lurid melodrama and elaborate farces, Shakespearian productions that would seem heavy-handed to us, and burlesque Dickens characters. They reasoned that if the plays were good enough for them they were good enough for the children.

But first, before he had reached the age considered ripe for theatregoing, there were the allied pleasures: the pantomime, the concert hall, and, inevitably, the circus. Theatres came later. He remembered hearing the infant Adelina Patti, poised in an armchair at the edge of the footlights, warbling precocious notes; visits to Niblo's Gardens to see the Ravels in their pantomime of *Jocko or The Brazilian Ape* and *Zaoul or The Magic Star* (it emerges in James's recollections as *Raoul or The Night Owl*) and to Franconi's "monumental" Hippodrome, which rang with Roman chariot races. There was a visit to the New York version of the Crystal Palace, sprawled over half a dozen acres in the far reaches of "uptown" Forty-second Street; it seemed to Henry James years later that he got the first taste of a voyage to Europe here, in the light of the Palace's Old World origins, so that the return in the autumn dusk on the new Sixth Avenue cars was a "relapse into soothing flatness, a return to the Fourteenth Street horizon from a far journey."

He never forgot that his older brother William was taken to the theatre first. He has left us a record in two places of the incident. In *A Small Boy* the novelist identifies Charlotte Cushman with "a positive sense of having, in the first place, but languished at home when my betters admired Miss Cushman." "My betters" included William, who was a year older than himself. Ten years before this allusion, he had set down a fuller account in a biography of the American sculptor, William Wetmore Story, where a reference to the actress set him off on a digression that concerned his own boyhood rather than the life of Story. He and his brother, one winter's evening in their Fourteenth Street home, were doing their lessons for the next day; the parents were at the theatre seeing

Miss Cushman in Shakespeare's *Henry VIII*. Suddenly the father reappeared; he had driven home from the theatre in haste at the end of the scene or act, impressed with the play's interest for the older of the small boys. William was snatched up from his homework and taken off to see Shakespeare. And the Henry James of 1900, looking back at the small Henry of 1850, is filled with pity and resentment.

> . . . The scene, that evening, at which, through my being inadequately estimated, I did not assist, is one of the most ineffaceable in my tolerably rich experience of the theatre. I recall it as a vivid vigil in which the poor lonely lamplight became that of the glittering stage in which I saw wondrous figures and listened to thrilling tones, in which I knew "Shakespeare acted" as I was never to know him again, in which, above all, I nursed my view of paternal discrimination.

Miss Cushman played in *Henry VIII* in September 1849, again in January 1850 and in June 1851 (always at the Broadway Theatre and not at the Park, as Henry recalled) and at Brougham's Lyceum in 1852. By 1852, however, Henry had been taken to the play and consequently the 1850 date—a winter's night—would seem the most plausible. He was then seven—old enough to sense keenly the "paternal discrimination" in favor of an older brother who would then have been eight.

He has set down in great detail his recollection of the first night of his own theatregoing. He believed the play was *A Comedy of Errors,* produced by William Burton in his small theatre in Chambers Street. The Shakespearian production Henry James describes in his memoirs, however, could not have been his first experience as a playgoer. Burton produced *A Comedy of Errors* during 1853 and again in 1855, and by that time the small boy had already seen many plays. The production he describes fits completely Burton's of April 18, 1855, when Henry was twelve. The novelist recalled that "a celebrated actor, whose name I inconsistently forget, had arrived to match Mr. Burton as the other of the Dromios." Burton was twinned on this occasion by the Dromio of Harry Hall, "an actor of good repute" newly-arrived from London. The novelist remembers also Mrs. Holman as playing Adriana in this production; she was, indeed, in the cast, but in the role of Luciana. The only other productions of the play during this time were at Barnum's "Lecture Hall" in January 1851 and at the Bowery Theatre in March of that year. 1851 could have been that of Henry James's coming-of-age as a theatregoer. He was eight and we have seen that this was the age at which William was judged by his father to be old enough to see Shakespeare. We can speculate therefore that James may have seen the earlier production of *A Comedy of Errors* and telescoped it with the more elaborate Burton production of 1855.

He remembered that the play had been read to him during the day of his theatregoing debut; he recalled the "sacred thrill" once inside the theatre in Chambers Street before the green curtain that refused to go up: "One's eyes bored into it in vain, and yet one knew it *would* rise at the named hour, the only question being if one could exist till then."

We can picture the James family arriving at the theatres of old New York with their two older sons, during the early 1850's: the long-bearded senior Henry, descending from the inevitable carriage—he had lost a leg in an early accident and ever afterwards relied on this means of transport—accompanied by his quiet, soft-spoken wife and two bright-eyed boys, probably attired in brass-buttoned jacket such as Henry wears in a daguerreotype of the period, buttoned right up to the neck, with only an edge of white shirt showing. Young Henry was taken to all the leading New York theatres of the mid-century—Burton's, the Broadway and the National, Wallack's Lyceum, Niblo's Gardens and Barnum's "Lecture Room" attached to the Great American Museum. It was the era when many theatres, in the lingering Puritanism, still masqueraded as gardens, lecture rooms, lyceums—anything in name but what they really were.

At Burton's he saw such familiar farces of the time as *The Toodles* and *The Serious Family;* at the Broadway the super-spectacle of *The Cataract of the Ganges or The Rajah's Daughter* and the popular *Green Bushes;* at Wallack's the clever comedies of Dion Boucicault (James rightly recalls that it was then written Bourcicault), *London Assurance* and *Love in a Maze*. And always there is the vivid recollection of the actors: William Burton, the Aminadab Sleek, Mr. Toodles or Paul Pry, "his huge person, his huge fat face and his vast slightly pendulous cheek, surmounted by a sort of elephantine wink, to which I impute a remarkable baseness"; Madame Ponisi, the Oberon of *A Midsummer Night's Dream* "as representing all characters alike with a broad brown face framed in bands or crowns or other heavy headgear out of which cropped a row of very small tight black curls"; Madame Céline Celeste, "straight out of London" in *Green Bushes* (J. B. Buckston's play which James wrongly attributes to Boucicault), "whose admired walk up the stage as Miami the huntress, a wonderful majestic and yet voluptuous stride enhanced by a short kilt, black velvet leggings and a gun haughtily borne on the shoulder is vividly before me. . . ." Miss Julia Bennett "fresh from triumphs at the Haymarket . . . in a very becoming white bonnet, either as a brilliant adventuress or as the innocent victim of licentious design, I forget which, though with a sense somehow that the white bonnet, when of true elegance, was the note of that period of the adventuress." We can multiply examples of these crowded recollections, sometimes accurate in all details, sometimes mistaken, as when he assures us he saw Fanny Wallack in *London Assurance* "as Lady Gay Spanker, flushed and vociferous, first in a riding habit with a tail yards long and afterwards in yellow satin with scarce a tail at all." Fanny Wallack's last appearance in America was in June 1852 and *London Assurance* wasn't produced at Wallack's until 1854 with Rosa Bennett as Lady Gay. Henry may have been thinking of Miss Bennett as the lady with the long—and later abbreviated—train.

Dickens, next to Shakespeare, probably was the author who figured most frequently in Henry James's boyhood playgoing, although it is a question whether he figured more for him on the stage than in the book. The familiar characters were emerging freshly from magazine and volume and they were thrown hastily upon the stage by play tinkers seeking to give bodily form to the Micawbers and Scrooges, Pickwicks and Copperfields, Oliver Twists and Paul Dombeys, whose very names assured a full house. To Burton, Henry James was indebted for the Captain Cuttle of *Dombey and Son,* and he recalled him as a "monstrous Micawber . . . with the entire baldness of a huge easter egg and collar-points like the sails of Mediterranean feluccas." He must have seen him in that role, if not in 1850 when Burton gave *David Copperfield* at his theatre, then in the revivals of 1853 and 1855. At Burton's too he saw *Nicholas Nickleby* with Lizzie Weston as Smike "all tearful melodrama." In face of his recollection of these productions, the aged Henry mused, "who shall deny the immense authority of the theatre, or that the stage is the mightiest of modern engines? Such at least was to be the force of the Dickens imprint, however applied, in the soft clay of our generation; it was to resist so serenely the wash of the waves of time."

He saw one important drama that was to remain a landmark in the American theatre for successive generations. The Barnum version of *Uncle Tom's Cabin,* in which he had admired Emily Mestayer, was the third to reach the New York stage. Henry did not see the first, which had an abbreviated run at the National in 1852, and which the New York *Herald* reviewed indignantly with the question: "What will our southern friends think of all our professions of respect for their delicate social institution of slavery?" This production, without St. Clare, with no little Eva and no Topsy, and with a spurious happy ending, went to its deserved closing after two weeks. Eleven months later a full version by George L. Aiken, in six long acts, was brought out at the same theatre, eight tableaux and thirty scenes, embracing the whole of Mrs. Stowe's novel. It ran for three hundred performances (colored folk were allowed in the parquet for twenty-five cents through a special entrance). Impressed by this success Barnum produced the third version by H. J. Conway, with a happy ending. Undisturbed by competition, confident in his audiences, and particularly in the patronage of the small boys at the matinees, he mounted it in November 1853 and here Henry saw it for the first time. In due course he saw the full-length production too, an evening particularly remembered, because it happened to be the occasion of his first theatre party and because he could be a critic: he could compare the two versions. He was certain the second Eliza was less dramatic than Miss Mestayer; but the ice floes at the National did seem more genuine than the more obvious carpentry at Barnum's. And Henry James, writing of this evening when he was seventy, hints that it was all the richer for him in that its humor and pathos were collectively shared. He was absorbed as much by the junior audience as by the play. The little sophisticates had gone to *Uncle Tom* with some detachment, but found themselves swept along by the play's strong currents. It was initiation into social as well as aesthetic adventure.

~~~~~~~~~~~~~~~~

On June 27, 1855 Henry Senior sailed for Europe with his wife and children to give the young ones "a better sensuous education than they were likely to get here. . . ." (Years later Henry, seeking to justify his long expatriation, carefully misquoted this remark, contained in a letter to Ralph Waldo Emerson, making it read ". . . such a sensuous education as they can't get here.")

The initiation of the James boys into the European theatre was somewhat slower and less extensive than might have been expected of such devoted young playgoers. Europe provided, Henry recalled, a drama richer than anything that could be found in the theatre, "life in general, all round us, was perceptibly more theatrical." There were other factors; the simple one of distance, for example. In New York the theatres had been within easy reach of Union Square. In London the distances to be traversed to the playhouses from St. John's Wood made theatregoing an elaborate and calculated ceremony. Henry James remembered "two throbbing and heaving cabs" travelling across vast, foggy tracts of the town and then depositing the playgoers, after many twists and turns, before the ancient theatres whose interiors seemed as labyrinthine as the trip to the West End. In Paris there was an additional limiting factor that had nothing to do with distance or the French language, which the boys had studied from an early age. The plays in the French capital were, as James put it, "out of relation to our time of life . . . our cultivated innocence." The plays in Manhattan had been directly addressed to such innocence in the adult audience and so were suited to children as well. This was, to a considerable degree, true also of London. The theatres of London offered in effect the same type of entertainment as those of New York—lurid melodrama and sprawling farce, sentimental drama and ranting eloquence, translations and bowdlerizations from the French. The acting was sometimes more finished; the diction may have been purer, but for the most part the plays of London were foreign counterparts of those seen in their native city.

London offered the excitement of the Christmas pantomime; it offered also Charles Mathews, Frederick Robson, Alfred Wigan and Charles Kean and the small boy saw them all. We have Henry's word for it that the "momentous" event in their London playgoing was Kean's production of *Henry VIII*. (It may have been momentous since it was the play William had been taken to see while he "languished" at home.) Kean played Wolsey, but the children were less conscious of the acting than of the elaborate spectacle, and notably Queen Katharine's dream-vision of beckoning and consoling angels which for weeks afterwards they tried to depict in water colors. "The spectacle had seemed to us prodigious—as it was doubtless at its time the last word of costly scenic science." (He was to see Kean again ten years later in Boston as Macbeth "without a rag of scenic reinforcement" and was struck by the fact that "no actor so little graced by nature probably ever went so far toward repairing it by a kind of cold rage of endeavor.")

Henry saw the stunted Robson, heard his hoarse voice, his grotesque delivery; Robson snarled and leered, he used to grind his teeth and roll his eyes, but he created vivid comedy and painful intensity. At the Olympic he saw Tom Taylor's *Still Waters Run Deep* with Wigan as John Mildmay; he saw Mathews in *The Critic* and a comedy "botched" from the French, *Married for Money*. He remembered the nights at the Olympic in Wych Street, approached through the squalid slums—an "incredibly brutal and barbarous" avenue to an evening of theatrical joy.

They lingered a while in Paris. Here the staunch little playgoers were reduced to the level of circuses—the perpetual Cirque d'Été and the Cirque d'Hiver as well as the Théâtre du Cirque; nevertheless they relished the profusion of clowns and acrobats and the elaborate ballet-pantomime. Only two French plays remained with the old Henry as having been seen at this time, minor dramas whose stars, Rose Chéri and Anaïs Fargueil lingered in his memory. It seemed to him, in retrospect, that his boyhood stay in Paris was one of missed opportunities. It was the golden age of French acting—Rachel was dying, but her name was on everyone's lips. He did not see her; neither did he see Déjazet, Mélingue, Samson; the memory of Mademoiselle Mars lingered; Mademoiselle Georges "a massive, a monstrous antique" had returned for a season. He missed her, as he missed the others.

He has recorded one missed opportunity in particular. "There emerges in my memory from the night of time the image of a small boy walking in the Palais-Royal with innocent American girls who were his cousins and wistfully hearing them relate how many times . . . they had seen Madame Doche in *La Dame aux Camélias* and what floods of tears she had made them weep." Charlotte Doche created the role of the unhappy Marguerite in 1852 and played it five hundred times; and for Henry James the name of Dumas *fils* forever after evoked distant memories: his wonder at the role his cousins gave the pocket handkerchief in the theatre, the manner in which his ears responded to the strange beauty of the title, the complete unawareness of the little girls, and Henry himself, of the social position of the lady of the expensive flowers.

The time was to come, however, when he would make amends for these missed opportunities and when, from the experience of countless evenings in the theatres of five countries, he would evolve his theories of acting and the drama which exercised so significant an influence upon him when he came to write his own plays.

PICTURE AND SCENE

The small boy, an inveterate theatregoer, inevitably developed stage ambitions: he would be an actor; more important still, he would be a dramatist.

His early experiences in stage production were confined, he recalled, to watching his older brother take charge of attic theatricals in which Albany cousins and playmates of the Fourteenth Street neighborhood participated. There was much more preparation than performance, "so much more conversation and costume than active rehearsal." William was in the thick of it all "throwing off into space conceptions that I could stare at across the interval but couldn't appropriate." William was producer, playwright and director rolled into one, while the passive Henry stood in the "wings" bereft of garments, waiting for a costume, "unclad and impatient both as to our persons and to our aims, waiting alike for ideas and breeches. . . ."

There has survived, out of this time, a letter in its original rectangular envelope, postmarked Paris, but without legible date, addressed to "Master E. Van Winkle, 14 st. N. York" which attests to Henry's continued interest in neighborhood theatricals after the James family had taken up residence abroad. We can imagine the small boy, by then twelve or thirteen, sitting down in one of the hotels of the rue de la Paix, in those early days of the Second Empire, to address this missive to far-away New York. The recipient was Edgar Van Winkle, who lived two doors away from the Jameses and for whom Henry had a deep respect ("Edgar walked in a maze of culture," Henry wrote decades later). It is the earliest letter of Henry James's to have survived. "Dear Eddy," it runs, with a brevity the novelist was seldom to achieve in his later correspondence, "As I heard you were going to try to turn the club into a Theatre. And as I was asked w'ether I wanted to belong here is my answer. I would like very much to belong. Yours Truly H James."

His experiments in boyhood "play-writing" were closely related to his brother's activities. William James, at an early age, revealed a talent for drawing and devoted his young manhood to the study of art. Henry, in emulation, also drew, and he evokes for us a picture of his older brother in New York, sitting in the evening under the lamplight sketching, with himself a few feet away plying the pencil, or rather the pen, since in his case he wrote as well as illustrated. "I was so often engaged at that period . . . in literary—or to be more precise in dramatic, accompanied by pictorial composition . . . how could I have doubted . . . with our large theatrical experience, of the nature, and of my understanding of the dramatic form?" Is he trying not only to imitate William, in brotherly rivalry, but to surpass him? William, he explained, "drew because he could, while I did so in the main only because he did."

At any rate he had evolved a ritual for these illustrated dramas: quarto sheets were purchased in a shop on Sixth Avenue, three sheets ruled, the fourth unruled. The drama filled the ruled pages. The blank page provided the space for the illustration. "I thought, I lisped, at any rate I composed in scenes," he tells us in describing what he set down on his quarto sheets. Every scene had its explanatory picture and he strained toward the picture "which had . . . something of the interest of the dramatist's casting of his *personae,* and must have helped me to believe in the validity of my subject."

Picture and Scene. The words were to figure again and again in his critical writings. They became part of the special lexicon of critical terms he created to define the arts of fiction and of the drama as he practised them. We are confronted in this instance, as in others, with the question: how much of his later art, his finished practice, did he read back into his childhood? The later novelist boasted that to the laying of a scene and the launching of a drama he had always been faithful; and it would be entirely understandable that in the circumstances he would think of himself as having lisped and composed scenes at an early age. We do know that during adolescence Henry was "an immense writer of novels and dramas," for his father so described him in a letter from Boulogne in which he spoke of his second son as not as fond of study "properly so-called, as of reading," and as a "devourer of libraries." He added, in this letter, written to Henry's grandmother, "He has considerable talent as a writer, but I am at a loss to know whether he will ever accomplish much."

The "plays" written during this period by the fourteen-year-old Henry perished long ago. However, a family anecdote throws light on their nature. Henry had drawn a picture of a mother and child clinging to a rock in the midst of a stormy ocean and had written underneath it: "The thunder roared and the lightning followed." William James pounced upon the illustration. It is not in the nature of older brothers to correct the mistakes of their juniors with tact and indulgence. That Henry should put thunder before lightning was a meteorological blunder that invited high derision from the scientifically-minded William. He tormented the sensitive young writer with such acerbity that Henry promptly enacted part of his story. He ran for maternal protection and invoked—and received—it for his quarto-sheet manuscript.

Out of this childhood he remembered one particular incident which, more than any other, he used to illustrate his sense of the Scene as well as of the Picture. His father had taken him in the summer of 1854—when he was eleven—on one of their rare visits to an uncle's home, Linwood, at Rhinebeck on the Hudson. It was a broad, roomy estate. He remembered roses, grapes, peaches, currant clusters, the hum of insects, a wide view of the river with "great bright harmonies of air and space." One evening the eleven-year-old boy wandered to the eminence overlooking the Hudson accompanied by his little cousin, Marie. She was of his age, small, brown, with shining black eyes, and, he had been told, "spoiled." That made her especially interesting, since the James boys had never been "spoiled." It gave her a romantic status to young Henry who only half understood the meaning of the term. His uncle, Augustus James, who was sitting near by, remarked with some emphasis that it was Marie's bedtime. The words must have fallen with some weight; by implication it was probably Henry's bedtime too. What he retained, however, as he wrote of the incident half a century later, was Marie's objection, a somewhat emphatic rejoinder from Uncle Augustus, and Marie rushing into her mother's arms "as if to a court of appeal." From the aunt came these simple words that appear to have fallen with a sharp ring in the ears of the small boy: "Come now, my dear; don't make a scene—I *insist* on your not making a scene!"

"That was all the witchcraft the occasion used," wrote Henry, "but the note was none the less epoch-making. The expression, so vivid, so portentous, was one I had never heard—it had never been addressed to us at home; and who should say now what a world one mightn't at once read into it? It seemed freighted to sail so far; it told me so much about life. Life at these intensities clearly became 'scenes'; but the great thing, the immense illumination, was that we could make them or not as we chose."

It matters little the extent to which Henry James read back into his reminiscent pages the subtle implications of the incident in the light of his devotion to Picture and Scene. What is important is that he brought the incident out of the distant days of his childhood, and told it with a vividness that revealed it to have been a significant event in the development of his artist's consciousness. He had in all his fiction seen himself as both a painter and as a dramatist. In the very first novel he reviewed, when he was twenty-two, he had written that "there is no essential difference between the painting of a picture and the writing of a novel," and in the same breath he had held up Balzac as a writer who "lays his stage, sets his scene. . . ."

Who can say how many doors of his mind little Marie James and her mother threw open unwittingly that evening at Linwood? It suffices that Henry James himself considered it a landmark in the history of his imagination.

SCHOOL OF THE DRAMATIST

The father had sought a better "sensuous" education than he believed his sons could find in America. During their early European travels—between Henry's twelfth and seventeenth years including a trip to America and a speedy return to Europe—the small boy was exposed to the rich panorama of the Old World: the London of Dickens and Thackeray, the Paris of the restored monarchy, the pensions and hotels of Switzerland, the provincial seaside life of Boulogne, and a brief glimpse of the stolid Germanic life of Bonn. The future novelist-dramatist was educated neither for the novel nor the drama; but he absorbed the materials for both in his reading of current literature, his nights at the play, his visits to art galleries, and his constant inspection of European architecture and landscape. The young Henry James who came back in 1859 to rediscover America from the placid perspective of Newport in Rhode Island on the eve of the Civil War had developed a sharpened vision of life and art, an international sense, an acute appreciation of Anglo-American culture and a good-humored understanding of the American abroad. He had become a cosmopolitan even before he had had an opportunity to be a provincial.

If this background contributed first and foremost to the creation of a great psychological novelist, it contained also those elements which contributed to his prolonged flirtation with the stage and the writing of his plays. We can disengage them as we follow his development, finding, as he begins his career as a writer, that he turns first to fiction, but never without sidelong—and loving —glances at the drama. In *A Small Boy* he injects the "note" of theatre recurrently: the memory of receiving Lamb's *Tales from Shakespeare* from a long-legged Scotsman who was his tutor in London and who later tutored Robert Louis Stevenson; schooldays at Boulogne with the pastry-cook's son, B. C. Coquelin, whom he was later to admire on the stage of the Théâtre Français; the recollection of the way in which Monsieur Toeppfer, in Geneva, taught him Racine, describing Rachel's playing of Phèdre—her entrance "borne down, in her languorous passion, by the weight of her royal robes—*Que ces vains ornemens, que ces voiles me pèsent!*—the long lapse of time before she spoke"; the memory of a night at the play in Bonn with his father (who in a letter has left us a record of his impression of Adelaide Ristori's portrayal on this occasion of *Maria Stuart* ". . . the vulture counterfeiting Jenny Wren. Every little while the hoarse, exulting voice, the sanguinary beak, the lurid bloated eye of menace, and the relentless talons, looked forth from the feathery mass and sickened you with disgust"). And the recollection of Frau Stromberg at Bonn, at whose home William stayed, and who combined the art of making *Pfannkuchen* with dramaturgy, reading her five-act tragedy of *Cleopatra* to William and her other pensioners. He remembered the neat little volume and the fine print of the text which William borrowed for Henry to read. (Fifteen years later, in his story *Eugene Pickering*, Henry attributed to his Germanic Madame Blumenthal the authorship of an *Historisches Trauerspiel* in fine print entitled *Cleopatra* in five acts.)

Elsewhere he has recorded a never-forgotten image of Fanny Kemble (first glimpsed near New York when he was a little boy and she a celebrity riding on horseback) giving her readings from Shakespeare in assembly rooms in St. John's Wood, the great human thunder roll of the Kemble voice in *Lear*,

Howl, howl, howl, howl.

He remembered how she carried herself, the black velvet she wore on this occasion, the white satin in which she attired herself for a reading of *A Midsummer Night's Dream* and her "formidable splendor." The time was to come when Henry James would escort this formidable creature to the theatre and spend Christmas with her at Stratford-on-Avon.

He was seventeen and at Newport, walking along the moss-clad shore and over sand-starved grass to the Paradise Rocks, talking endlessly to John LaFarge and Thomas Sergeant Perry, reading Balzac and Merimée and the salmon-covered issues of the *Revue des Deux Mondes*, translating Alfred de Musset's *Lorenzaccio* into which, Perry has told us, "he introduced some scenes of his own." Henry James was to write tenderly of the Newport days and particularly of the hours spent with the young LaFarge, who encouraged him in his literary undertakings and introduced him to the poetry of Browning as well as the French writers. It was essentially a period of initiation and discovery, of intensive reading, quiet cogitation and observation, tranquil literary labor.

The young man who turned up at the Harvard Law School at nineteen, during the second year of the Civil War, felt himself somewhat outside the society in which he lived. He was about as much interested in law as he had been in scientific studies attempted earlier at Geneva. William James had preceded him to Harvard and Henry, as in the past, gravitated in the same direction. The picture of the Harvard months, sketched in *Notes of a Son and Brother,* shows us a young man very much in search of himself. He went through the motions of trying for a legal "career," but he moved to one of his own choosing.

Of an evening he would journey into Boston by horse-car to see a play at the Howard Athenaeum. He found that the "half-buried Puritan curse" still lingered. Boston audiences had more guilt feelings about the theatre as a frivolous institution than New York audiences; he felt in the Bostonian attitude "that intimation more than anything else of the underhand snicker. . . ." He tells us that he went to the theatre as often as possible despite the "implication of the provincial in the theatric air and of the rustic in the provincial." At seventy he pictured his student self—always with a touch of benign irony—as a critical and quite elevated young theatregoer, but he was little more sophisticated about the plays while an undergraduate than when the small boy was frequenting Barnum's. He went to see Kate Bateman (who thirty years later was to appear in one of his own plays) and he saw, and never forgot, the celebrated Maggie Mitchell in *Fanchon the Cricket,* translated from a German play by Augustus Wauldaur which in turn was derived from George Sand's *La Petite Fadette.* Miss Mitchell had played the one part up and down the United States ("she twanged that one string and none other, every night of her theatric life"). Yet there was nothing stale about the charm she exercised upon her youthful admirer. Henry returned entranced to his rooms in Winthrop Square and wrote her a letter "from which the admired Miss Maggie should gather the full force of my impression." This she seems to have done, for she reciprocated by autographing for him a printed "acting edition" of the play. The old man amusedly fancied his Harvard self as a dashing young Pendennis with Miss Mitchell as his Miss Fotheringay.

He recalled in particular, however, that the impression of the play and Miss Mitchell's acting prompted him to write an appreciation of the production and of the actress. "I first sat down beside my view of the Brighton hills to enrol myself in the bright band of the fondly hoping and fearfully doubting who count the days after the despatch of manuscripts." He adds coyly that "nothing would induce me now to name the periodical on whose protracted silence I had thus begun to hang. . . ." So far as we can determine James's dramatic criticism never saw the light of print. But it is significant that the first bit of original writing he sent to a publication should have been devoted to a play and to an actress.

We have these anecdotes and incidents, the scattered clues to his reading, theatregoing, gallery-visiting, and yet little to explain the extraordinary maturity, sureness, poise of his writing from the moment that he blossomed out at twenty-one in the pages of the *North American Review* and a few months later in the *Atlantic Monthly*, the newly-founded *Nation* and the *Galaxy*. Youthful the writing is, in its desire to be clever, to score points, to toss off neat epigrams, and in its dogmatism; yet as regards the fundamentals of art it possesses a distinct point of view, an individual terminology, a theory of fiction, of art, of drama that is vigorous and often original. One wonders where the school of the novelist and of the dramatist had been. How could so desultory an education have produced so balanced and coherent a practitioner of the art of writing? Henry James was to develop during the next half century a much more complex aesthetic; he was to develop a style, a manner, an elaborate doctrine relating to fiction and the scenic art: yet from the first he knew what he wanted to do, and how to go about doing it. So much *savoir-faire* in one so young could only be explained in the facts that James himself adduced in his autobiographies: his was the history and growth of an imagination, a curious, observing, retaining and disciplined mind, stimulated and sharpened in the family circle, and flourishing in spite of repeated attempts to regiment it within the framework of "education." The anonymous reviewer in the *Nation* who accorded an extended article to James's first volume of short stories on June 24, 1875, when the novelist was thirty-two, had a valid, if elaborate, explanation: "He has seen more cities and manners of man than was possible in the slower days of Ulysses, and if with less gain of worldly wisdom, yet with an enlargement of his artistic apprehensiveness and scope that is of far greater value to him." His *artistic apprehensiveness*—there perhaps is our answer. And as regards the drama the *apprehensiveness* had only to play over the world of the theatre to make it one of the most important schools he ever attended.

During the first ten years of his creative life, James established himself as a literary critic, a writer of travel pieces, a master of the short story and, at the end of the decade, as a novelist. From 1865, when his critical articles began to appear in ever-increasing numbers, to the end of 1875, the year in which he took up permanent residence abroad, he wrote 26 short stories, 132 book reviews, 43 travel articles, 10 papers devoted to art criticism, seven articles on the drama, three dramatic sketches or comediettas and two novels in serial form. Much of the material for this work was the fruit of his absorption of American life in Boston and New York; most of it stemmed from two trips abroad during 1869–70 and 1872–74; all of it went back to roots buried deeply during the years of his "sensuous" education.

If at the end of this crowded decade of travel, discovery, creation, Henry James

". . . divine principle of the Scenario . . ."
The notebook entry of February 14, 1895

emerged as a full-fledged novelist, he emerged also with a full-fledged theory of the drama. It might be observed that he developed as well his critical notation of painting and that painters and paintings loomed much larger in the work of these years than did the theatre. These were the years of his discovery of Italy and the glories of its art; his enthusiasm for art and architecture overflowed into his travel sketches and from these into his stories. He had always been fascinated by painting, and the painter attracted him as a fictional subject. But the fascination of the drama was something deeper. Play-writing was a craft allied to fiction. Henry James never tried to paint pictures, once he discarded the drawing pencil and brush at Newport. But he *did* write plays. The dramatist was there behind the novelist: both might look upon art with an appraising and critical eye—but each had a separate creative task to perform.

Dramatic interest. He held this essential to good novel-writing. Give me "dramatic compactness" he lectured George Eliot, in his review of *Felix Holt,* criticizing her for creating "intense" characters without showing them in action. Miss Alcott's *Moods,* to take a novelist writing on a completely different level, provoked him to suggest that she was insufficiently acquainted with people "to handle great dramatic passions." As a consequence, he observed, discussing the novel as if it were a drama, "her play is not a real play, nor her actors real actors." Reviewing Miss Braddon's *Aurora Floyd* he speaks of play-writing as "an arduous profession"—as if at twenty-two he had already tried his hand at it and found the going difficult.

Reviewing Swinburne's poetic drama *Chastelard* in the *Nation* (January 18, 1866) when he was twenty-three he remarks with the assurance of his years "it is comparatively easy to write energetic poetry, but . . . it is very difficult to write a good play." He tells Swinburne: "You have to have more than a pretty idea to carry a play." He tells him again: "A dramatic work without design is a monstrosity." He offers him advice: "Chastelard descants in twenty different passages of very florid and eloquent verse upon the intoxicating beauties of his mistress; but meanwhile the play stands still . . . let him talk as much as he pleases, and let him deal out poetry by the handful, the more the better. But meanwhile let not the play languish, let not the story halt."

He had, thus, a decidedly "fixed" view of what drama, action, scene, the "art of representation" should be, and during the ten years that followed his first appearance in print he was to develop a firm and consistent—and quite dogmatic—conception of what acting and production should be in the theatre itself. The young writer who left Cambridge in 1869 at twenty-six on his first adult journey abroad was to spend many nights in the playhouses of Europe. In strange cities, with long evenings before him, he gravitated toward the theatre, arguing that there he would find a reflection of the civilization he was visiting, that a country's culture could be studied at first hand in the plays it mounts and in the audiences that come to see them. He watched the audiences; he strolled through foyers listening to their remarks; and he sat before the plays an enthralled and studious spectator.

Henry James paid his first visits to the Théâtre Français and the theatres of the Paris boulevards during 1870, regretting that he could not tarry longer, asserting emphatically in due course that the French national theatre constituted a school of taste "not elsewhere to be found in the world." During 1872–73 we can follow him from France into Italy. He pauses for a week at Perugia and goes to the theatre nightly, paying twenty-two soldi for an orchestra seat, seeing such plays as *Amore Senza Stima, Severità e Debolezza, La Società Equivoca*, feeling that his study of the audiences brings him close to the people of the Italian town. We catch him in Rome at the Teatro Valle listening to Goldoni's *I Quattro Rustighi* done in the Venetian dialect which he can only half follow: the acting not as fine as the French, but "in some of the women— ugly, with red hands and shabby dresses—an extraordinary gift of natural utterance, of seeming to invent joyously as they go." And we find him that same month in a box at the Apollo, in Rome, surveying Italian princesses in neighboring boxes and watching a violent Othello played by Ernesto Rossi. Othello seized Iago, whacked his head "half a dozen times on the floor" and then flung him "twenty yards away." Wonderfully done, observed the young American, but "in the doing of it, and in the evident relish for it in the house there was I scarce know what force of easy and thereby rather cheap expression."

Early in 1875, while Henry James's first long novel was appearing in the *Atlantic Monthly,* he went to New York for a few months and served as a casual critic for the *Nation,* reviewing art shows and plays. He saw Ristori and Rignold, *The Two Orphans* and a play entitled *Women of the Day* which he described as an "unqualifiable mess of vulgarity . . . ghastly, monstrous, a positive nightmare. . . ." He had little good to say of the New York season, and before the year was out he had decided to take up permanent residence in Europe. Before sailing he gave fullest expression to his theory of the drama, not in any formalized manner, but in a long review of Tennyson's *Queen Mary* written for the *Galaxy,* and published in September 1875. He was to repeat and amplify these views, even as he had forecast them in his dramatic criticism, but he was never to formulate them with greater compactness.

"The dramatic form," he wrote in the review, "seems to me of all literary forms the noblest," and he added promptly this personal note: "I have so extreme a relish for it that I am half afraid to trust myself to praise it, lest I should seem to be merely rhapsodizing. But to be really noble it must be quite itself. . . ." And he goes on:

> The fine thing in a real drama, generally speaking, is that, more than any other work of literary art, it needs a masterly structure. It needs to be shaped and fashioned and laid together, and this process makes a demand upon an artist's rarest gifts. He must combine and arrange, interpolate and eliminate, play the joiner with the most attentive skill; and yet at the end effectually bury

his tools and his sawdust, and invest his elaborate skeleton with the smoothest and most polished integument. The five-act drama—serious or humorous, poetic or prosaic—is like a box of fixed dimensions and inelastic material, into which a mass of precious things are to be packed away. It is a problem in ingenuity and a problem of the most interesting kind. The precious things in question seem out of all proportion to the compass of the receptacle; but the artist has an assurance that with patience and skill a place may be made for each, and that nothing need be clipped or crumpled, squeezed or damaged. The false dramatist either knocks out the sides of his box, or plays the deuce with the contents; the real one gets down on his knees, disposes of his goods tentatively, this, that, and the other way, loses his temper but keeps his ideal, and at last rises in triumph, having packed his coffer in the one way that is mathematically right. It closes perfectly, and the lock turns with a click; between one object and another you cannot insert the point of a penknife.

To work successfully beneath a few grave, rigid laws, is always a strong man's highest ideal of success. . . . In a play, certainly, the subject is of more importance than in any other work of art. Infelicity, triviality, vagueness of subject, may be outweighed in a poem, a novel, or a picture, by charm of manner, by ingenuity of execution; but in a drama the subject is of the essence of the work—it *is* the work. If it is feeble, the work can have no force; if it is shapeless, the work must be amorphous.

An important subject, moulded by "a few grave, rigid laws"—this, then, was Henry James's recipe for a good play, and few persons can quarrel with such a formulation. He is asking for the classical perfection of form and content and a goodly measure of each, harmoniously wedded. What stands out, however, is this concept of the "grave and rigid" laws. We may find it difficult, in the light of the greater scenic fluidity of our theatre and the influence of the cinema, to accept so chaste a definition. For James, in his time, confronted with the anarchy of the Anglo-American stage and the neatness and precision of the French— and given his fastidious personality and his delight in a disciplined and ordered art—there could be no choice. He accepted the "laws" of the theatre of which Francisque Sarcey in Paris was the principal critical exponent: a play had to be "well-made" and its technical structure was all-important. He upheld the French classical theory of the drama, but applied it to the melodramatic, manipulated dramas of Scribe and Sardou. When Henry James, making his start as a playwright, exclaimed, *"À moi, Scribe, à moi, Sardou, à moi, Dennery!"* he was invoking the dramatists who were the special gods of Francisque Sarcey. A brilliant and documented critic, Sarcey nevertheless had one set of laws for all times and all dramatists; he was a man of integrity, but he was also inflexible. For James he was the "inimitable and incorruptible." James saw him as one who believed in the theatre as if it were a religion and loved it with an abiding passion. For Sarcey all France revolved around its stage. Its actors and playwrights were a cultural force, practitioners of an art—no, more, of an exact science. From Sarcey's writings James derived much of his knowledge of the French stage of the time and of its immediate past, and a great deal of theory to match his own observations of the Maison de Molière in the rue de Richelieu, hard by the Louvre.

In fiction Henry James made his own laws; on the stage he bowed to a whole series of laws other playwrights ignored—a minuteness of exposition, a constant fear that the audience would not understand him and therefore the need to explain every detail, an elaborate to-do attending entrances and exits, the traditional fuss of the *ficelle* play. He bowed to them, accepted them as an inevitable "straitjacket," and thus attired—but complaining all the while— he attempted to write plays.

The thirty-odd pieces of dramatic criticism written by James over a quarter of a century or more, collected by Allan Wade in the volume entitled *The Scenic Art,* constitute a plea for substance as well as form in the theatre, and, under the influence of Sarcey, place very considerable emphasis on the form. Their merit, as Mr. Wade has observed, over and above the value of their balanced judgments and the charm of the writing, is in their plea for *standards* of creation and criticism in the theatre. Henry James's own plays were conceived with a general observance of the theatrical doctrines he propounded and a general conformity to standards accepted from the French. Unfortunately the rigid laws of the drama, as he formulated them or derived them, pinned him down. James once complained to Logan Pearsall Smith that he never sat down to write a play without feeling that a thousand devils were besetting him from all sides. His plays became the prisoners of his theories.

NIGHTS IN THE RUE DE RICHELIEU

When Hyacinth Robinson, in *The Princess Casamassima,* took Millicent Henning to a London theatre to see a play called *The Pearl of Paraguay,* "his imagination projected itself lovingly across the footlights, gilded and colored the shabby canvas and battered accessories, losing itself so effectually in the fictive world that the end of the piece, however long or however short, brought with it something of the alarm of a stoppage of his personal life. It was impossible to be more friendly to the dramatic illusion."

In attributing what he also called the "dear old playhouse spell" to his hero, Henry James endowed him with his own deeply subjective attitude toward the stage. For James, to whom fantasy was a form of reality, could not but identify himself with the stage's "fictive world," and the end of a play for him would indeed be the stoppage of his personal life. Henry James has told us how in going to the Théâtre Français he found "an ideal and exemplary world" on its boards, a "world that has managed to attain all the felicities that the world we live in misses."

What were these felicities and what was this world? Henry James describes it: it is smooth, harmonious, artistic. Great attention is paid to detail. The people do the things "that we should like to do; they are gifted as we should like to be; they have mastered the accomplishments that we have had to give up." The women are not all beautiful but they are graceful, agreeable, sympathetic, "ladylike," perfectly dressed, possessed of the best manners, charming, with musical voices. They speak with "irreproachable purity and sweetness." They walk with elegant grace. In short, they are the idealized heroines of James's fiction, the Milly Theales, Isabel Archers, Mme. de Cintrés and Maggie Ververs.

And the men? They were not handsome either (except Mounet-Sully who was an "Adonis of the first magnitude") but they looked whatever part they played; they were as well-mannered and as agreeably spoken as the ladies. "They represent gentlemen, and they produce the illusion." Emotion and passion were controlled, partitioned, into scenes and acts, attaining appropriate well-timed climaxes. For the "observer" Henry James, the "individual so capable as I am of the uncanniest self-effacement in the active exercise of the passion of observation" as he described himself, here was a way to look at life re-created and acted while maintaining a state of sublime passivity. Henry James could sit quietly and drink it in, as his official observers and commentators did in his fiction. This was perfection indeed: an ordered world played out on a large and beautiful stage and with an art as consummate as that which he lavished on his own work.

The Théâtre Français was steeped in the past; it had traditions and standards, rituals and observances. No dinner could be too hastily swallowed in order to get to the seven o'clock raising of the great curtain, to see such actresses as Madame Nathalie in Feuillet's *Le Village;* no uncomfortable stall could diminish the dazzling qualities of the acting of Favart and Croizette, Brohan and Bressant, Regnier and Got, Mounet-Sully and Coquelin; no "pestilential" atmosphere— meaning quite simply the theatre's poor ventilation—could spoil the magic sense that in the air of the building, in the dim reaches of the great dome, there slept the echoes of Rachel's voice, the sense that these footlights had il-luminated the tragedienne's finest moments. Herr Toeppfer had described it all during the novelist's student days at Geneva; now Henry James could discover it for himself.

He saw his first performance in the rue de Richelieu on the eve of the Franco-Prussian war—Augier's *Lions et Renards* with Coquelin or *L'Aventurière,* we cannot be sure which of the two it was. He was in the capital again two years later in the wake of the Commune, visiting the barricades, sensing still the smell of blood and gunpowder in the air, going "every night— or almost" to the Théâtre Français. On Sunday evenings he would dine with James Russell Lowell at his hotel on the Left Bank in the Faubourg St. Germain near the Chamber of Deputies, and he wrote later, "I never cross the Seine amid the wet flare of the myriad lamps, never note the varnished rush of the river or the way the Louvre grows superb in the darkness without a recurrent consciousness of the old sociable errand, the sense of dipping into a still denser Paris with the *Temps* and M. Sarcey in my pocket." Lowell and Sarcey were James's mentors during this Parisian stay in which the Théâtre Français as-sumed an importance in his mind never to be erased.

There were two nights which stood out in memory, both of a later date, the autumn of 1877. On one of these he saw Dumas the Younger's *Le Demi-Monde* which inspired his *The Siege of London;* on the other he saw a play by Charles Lomon, *Jean Dacier,* with Coquelin. In both cases he later described how he left the theatre "agitated" with what he had seen, pacing the streets far into the night, wanting to write plays for such actors, carried away by the spell exercised by the players. He quarreled with the plot of *Le Demi-Monde,* he thought *Jean Dacier* weak as a play, but he was nevertheless stimulated and inspired by the art with which they had been done. "Far away and unspeakably regretted the days, alas, or, more exactly the nights, on which one could walk away from the Français under the spell of such fond convictions and such deep and agitating problems," he wrote thirty years after that Paris autumn.

To Benoît Constant Coquelin Henry James's most vivid impressions of the French stage attached themselves: "the rich, the rare, the admirable and inimitable" Coquelin, the "most joyous and exuberant of pure comedians." They had been to school together as boys at the Collège Communal in Boulogne, and to these memories of childhood was now added the excitement of seeing the mature and accomplished artist. He remembered how, on leaving the theatre after *Jean Dacier,* "I walked about a long time under the influence not so much of the piece as of Coquelin's acting of it, which had made the thing so human, so brilliant, so valuable. I was agitated with what it said to me that I might do—what I ought to attempt."

This was nothing compared to "the state I was thrown into by meeting Coquelin." He met him at Andrew Lang's in 1879 when the Comédie Française came to London. Henry wrote that "it stirred me to the depths. . . . It excited me powerfully," the way in which Coquelin's personality overflowed into his talk. "All day, and for days afterward, I remained under the impression." In his journal he referred to the two Coquelin episodes (one of which he embodied later in a long essay on Coquelin published in 1887 and revised just before his death) as "landmarks" in the history of his theatrical ambitions.

These constituted the final steps in Henry James's education for the theatre. He had assimilated French dramatic theory and he found himself on terms of growing intimacy with some of the players. Coquelin came to lunch, and later wrote to him encouragingly from Paris urging him on in his dramatic ambitions. When are you being acted? Coquelin queried, and he added that James had only to give him a signal and he would come to see him played.

James devoted nine essays and reviews to the French stage. His best-known is the urbane essay he contributed to the *Galaxy* (and included in *French Poets and Novelists*) which summed up his impressions of the Théâtre Français. Shortly after settling in London, in 1877, he did the same for the London theatres. He found British audiences less Bohemian, less blasé, more naïf, "well dressed, tranquil, motionless" suggesting domestic virtue and comfortable homes. The British audience looked to him as if it had come to the play in its own carriage, after a dinner of beef and pudding. The ladies "are mild, fresh-colored English mothers. . . . There are many rosy young girls, with dull eyes and quiet cheeks—an element wholly absent from Paris audiences. The men are handsome and honorable-looking. . . . Altogether they are much more the sort of people to spend a quiet evening with than the clever, cynical, democratic multitude that surges nightly out of the brilliant Boulevards into those temples in which MM. Dumas *fils* and Sardou are the high priests. But," added James, "you might spend your evening with them better almost anywhere than at the theatre."

He was to live the rest of his life among the people he thus described and he was to attempt to write plays for them. "The art of writing a play has apparently. become a lost one with the English race," he wrote, and set about planning to revive this art. "There can be no serious school of acting unless there is a dramatic literature to feed it," and he believed himself capable of creating such a literature. He was unsparing in his criticism of British plays and British acting. For him the French theatre remained the one theatre worthy of emulation. "The French esteem the theatre too much to take rash liberties with it," he wrote, attacking the British theatre for its meagreness, its scenic excesses, its "barbarism." One of these liberties was the way in which it adapted plays from the French: "An English arrangement of a French piece is a pretty woman with her back turned."

The nights in the rue de Richelieu colored his view of the London stage and they were the "light by which one must work" for the theatre. To his journal, in 1881, the novelist confided: "The French stage I have mastered; I say that without hesitation. I have it in my pocket. . . . I have laid up treasures of wisdom. . . ." To William James he had written four years earlier: "My inspection of the French theatre will fructify. I have thoroughly mastered Dumas, Augier and Sardou . . . and I know all they know and a great deal more besides." He is writing here in a light and consciously boastful vein, but with an awareness of the resources he has accumulated.

What did Henry James mean when he boasted that he had the French theatre "in my pocket"? He had studied it with all the earnestness and solemnity of a college student, methodically reading texts and going to see them acted. He had read the critics. He had, moreover, watched the actors. If he wrote of the plays as a literary critic, and complained that French playwrights contrived only endless variations in their well-made plays on the theme of adultery, he wrote of the actors as if he were a professional man of the theatre, a stage director, a producer. In the history of dramatic criticism there are few writers who described scenery and costumes as closely and who dwelt in such detail on the histrionic technique. Like Sarcey, James cultivated the theatrical eye. The manner in which an actor walks is important to him; he pays close attention to his diction; he observes that the trivial act of taking a letter from a servant or placing a hat upon a chair can be made suggestive and interesting. He talks as one who had attended the *Conservatoire*. He not only had advice for the players; he considered himself qualified to go beyond Prince Hamlet, step upon the stage and coach them—which is what he ultimately did.

The extent to which he had steeped himself in the practical side of production is revealed to us in his long novel of the stage, *The Tragic Muse*, which he completed just before beginning his play-writing, seeking to purge himself in it of all his conflicts over the dramatic art. In those portions of the novel which are devoted to the career of Miriam Rooth—a fictional English counterpart to Rachel or Sarah Bernhardt—he not only echoes the lessons of the rue de Richelieu and his dramatic theory (as well as his sense that actors, self-absorbed and exhibitionistic, can have their life only on the stage), but reveals in the process intimate knowledge of the Théâtre Français backstage as well as front. One of the great scenes in the novel, inspired by a visit James paid to the *loge* of Julia Bartet when she was appearing in *L'École des Maris* in January 1889, describes the green room, the actors behind scenes, the corridors, the portraits, and the personality of a French actress such as Bartet.

His feelings about the Théâtre Français are echoed from page to page in the novel. One character ventures to suggest that it is a greater institution than the House of Commons; Madame Carré, the retired French actress, who might have been drawn out of Fanny Kemble and Pauline Viardot, observes, with the delightful French insularity which James understood, *"Je ne connais qu'une scène—la nôtre,"* a view James held to be the truth; and Gabriel Nash, the character in the novel who speaks for—and even resembles physically—the novelist himself, says, "The theatre in our country is puerile and barbarous." When Mrs. Rooth, Miriam's mother, observes that she wouldn't want her daughter to play a bad woman, Madame Carré rejoins: "Ah, in England then, and in your theatre, everyone's immaculately good? Your plays must be even more ingenious than I supposed!" And Gabriel Nash-James comes in, a solemn chorus: "We haven't any plays." Miriam says she wants to play Shakespeare, and Madame Carré wryly observes this is fortunate "as in English you haven't anyone else to play."

~~~~~~~~~~

Thus the nights in the rue de Richelieu overflowed into his writings. His saturation with the theatre was reflected at many points in his fiction, so that he set great scenes in his novels in theatres. He went playgoing with all his London friends, and thought of himself constantly as a playwright-in-the-making. "To be read 200 years after your death," he wrote, "is something, but to be acted is better."

And yet the years passed and he did not write plays.

APOLOGIES FOR THE THEATRE

The years passed but he wrote no plays. His theatrical ship had taken aboard a cargo of experience; its hold bulged with elaborate, heavily-documented dramatic theory, enough playgoing to crowd a lifetime, the memory of performances and performers in many playhouses in many lands. And still the ship did not set sail. At thirty-three he had written to William James: "I know the Théâtre Français by heart." At thirty-five he wrote to him: "It has long been my most earnest and definite intention to commence at play-writing as soon as I can. . . ." And again during the same year: "I am very impatient to get at work writing for the stage—a project I have long had. I am . . . certain I should succeed and it would be an open gate to money-making." And now he was approaching forty—and still the ship had not set sail.

For a man "impatient" to get at play-writing, he was procrastinating to an extraordinary degree. He had written three little closet dramas, chamber plays or comediettas, one when he was twenty-six, and two at twenty-nine, brief experiments in dialogue, but these were not serious efforts, certainly not intended for the theatre. Between his thirtieth and fortieth years he had published three major novels and many short stories; innumerable critical and travel articles. He had a fast-moving pen, and a stream of work left his desk wherever he might be—in England, France or Italy. Yet something was keeping him back from the drama, and one day the question rose to the surface of his mind and crept out of the tip of the pen into the pages of his journal.

It was on December 26, 1881. He had returned to America after an absence of six years. He was in Cambridge and he was taking a sheet of paper into his confidence. He had talked with the owners of the new Madison Square Theatre in New York, the brothers Mallory, one a clergyman, and their manager, Daniel Frohman. They had invited him to dramatize his highly-successful short story, *Daisy Miller*. He wrote in his journal: "After long years of waiting, of obstruction, I find myself able to put into execution the most cherished of all my projects—that of beginning to work for the stage. It was one of my earliest—I had it from the first. None has given me brighter hopes—none has given me sweeter emotions." And then, in a moment of self-questioning, he adds: "It is strange nevertheless that I should never have done anything—and to a certain extent it is ominous. I wonder at times that the dream should not have faded away."

It was strange and it was ominous. What follows in his journal is an illuminating passage of self-examination on the one hand and heavy rationalization on the other. He told himself that there were good reasons for his failure to write plays—because of the "little work at any time that I could do," because he had needed "money on the spot" and this his fiction had provided; because of his "inability to do two things at once," and the "absence of opportunities, of openings." He could afford to wait, he told himself, since the drama was the ripest of the arts and "while I was waiting I was studying. . . ." James wrote that he was reminding himself of these "obstacles" to "justify my innumerable postponements."

Yet he had not quite convinced himself. He went on to hammer home these arguments, underscoring words as he wrote: ". . . it seems to me simply deplorable that I should not have got at work before. *But it was impossible at the time,* and I knew my chance would come. . . ." This need for self-justification can be understood readily. Not one of the arguments he gave himself was completely valid.

He complained of the little work he could do at any time, and indeed he made that complaint often; yet judged by any standards of literary productivity he had accomplished a lifetime of work when he wrote these words. During eighteen years of writing he had published fifteen volumes—fiction, travel, short stories; his novels included, by this time, *Roderick Hudson, The American, The Portrait of a Lady, Washington Square* and such diverse tales as *The Madonna of the Future* and *Daisy Miller*. He had written articles and reviews in the *North American Review*, the *Galaxy*, the *Atlantic Monthly;* he had been correspondent of the New York *Tribune* and the *Nation*. It was true that he always felt that he could have produced more; but it was equally true that so active a pen could have written the plays Henry James kept saying he wanted to write.

The need for "money on the spot"? He lived on a modest scale in some rooms in Piccadilly; he could have maintained them on his income alone, the rents that arrived regularly from Albany and Syracuse properties of the Jameses. His literary earnings only made life more comfortable, provided a broader margin of security. As a matter of fact, when he wrote of his need for money at this particular time, he was receiving substantial pay from two sources for the simultaneous serialization of *The Portrait of a Lady* in *Macmillan's* in England and the *Atlantic* in the United States—not to speak of additional earnings from the occasional pieces he was constantly writing. This does not alter the fact of his sense of insecurity which remained with him throughout his lifetime so that even larger earnings would have seemed to him to be insufficient.

"Inability to do two things at once"? He was doing just that constantly: delivering his monthly instalment of his current novel and at the same time producing short stories and articles. As index of his capacity to juggle a number of literary commitments simultaneously we may cite his work for 1879, the year of his greatest success which attended publication of his tale, *Daisy Miller;* he saw the tale through the press in book form, and published also his study of *Hawthorne*, a two-volume collection of short stories, carefully revised in their transference from magazine to book (*The Madonna of the Future and Other Tales*), all this while feeding his serial *Confidence* to *Scribner's*, and writing three short stories, nine articles in the *Nation*, one for *Lippincott's* and one in the *North American Review*. Nevertheless on this score we must remember that play-writing has more often than not been considered an effort alien to a novelist; James might have been capable of writing several stories at once and would still consider the writing of a play at the same time the doing of "two things at once."

"Absence of opportunities"? In the very journal entry in which he speaks of this, he mentions that John Hare, one of London's leading actor-managers, had asked him to write a play and "offered me his services in the event of my doing so." James knew very well that a playwright need not wait for opportunities to market his work any more than a writer of fiction. He submitted his articles and short stories to editors; he could have submitted his plays just as well to managers. He had, however, been singularly fortunate in his literary opportunities; Charles Eliot Norton, William Dean Howells and James Russell Lowell had opened doors for him, recognizing at once his extraordinary talents. For one of his passive nature, however, the thought of having to push doors open himself in the theatre would be considered an "absence of opportunity."

Deeper reasons than those he gave must have kept him from writing the plays he wanted to write: the fear of turning aside from the already familiar outlets he had found for his work; the hesitation to embark on the practical hazards he felt inherent in the theatre. The contempt he expressed so often for these hazards was alone a symptom of this. Publishers sought out Henry James during those years—theatre managers and actors merely evinced an interest in a possibly "useable" script. In his study he could write as he wished, follow the high demands of "art" in accordance with his own standards and principles and the public could take him—or leave him. "One must go one's way and know what one's about and have a general plan and a private religion—in short have made up one's mind as to *ce qui en est* with a public the draggling after which simply leads one in the gutter. One has always a 'public' enough if one has an audible vibration—even if it should only come from one's self." He put it thus to his brother on the eve of his dramatic years. To venture into the theatre was to forsake this private religion; it involved obtaining approval of one's creations from men with a greater concern for the pocketbook than for "audible vibration" —except as the vibration meant box office returns; of actors interested in the work largely as a vehicle for exhibiting their own talents; and finally it involved a search for the approval of a heterogeneous public for which one had to dot one's i's as with pumpkins—an image he used later in describing the simplicity of statement to which he felt the drama reduced him. The reticent, secretive, aloof literary alchemist of Bolton Street and De Vere Gardens, a feted London "lion" moving in the world as a conscious observer and recorder, rebelled at the very things which are the life of the stage. If he could have become a dramatist as he had become a man of letters he would have long before turned to play-writing. As it was, he found himself in a state of conflict that became increasingly acute with the passage of the years.

He was attracted to the theatre and at the same time was repelled by it. He wanted its successes and rewards and yet was afraid to chance its pitfalls. A work of fiction might receive adverse reviews and fall flat in the market and still remain an honorable performance; it did not involve the public *exposure* that went with a play. When a magazine rejected a story—this was a private matter between editor and writer. But when a play was announced, publicized, promised to the public, and then not produced, or failed in production, the author was, in the process, publicly rejected. This was what Henry James feared more than anything else.

He was not alone in his creative problem. A long line of literary men had sought, long before him, to be playwrights, with varying conflicts and varying success. In his own century Byron had faced the drama with a loathing akin to Henry James's. Tennyson had ventured into it late in life, carried by the tide of his poetic and public stature; Meredith had secretly attempted to write a play, but it had never left his desk; Thomas Hardy dramatized one of his tales, and later wrote *The Dynasts* without regard for the "laws" of the drama; George Moore joined his fellow writers of Ireland in their serious flirtation with the stage; Swinburne had written long poetic dramas which the younger James had tartly reviewed. Henry James's Continental models, Balzac and Turgenev, had written plays without notable success. There was ample precedent for James among the men of literature, so that he might have faced his own attempts with equanimity. For him, however, the theatre became the focus of anxiety, fear, insecurity, conflicting emotions that caused him to approach it with faltering footsteps.

His dramatization of *Daisy Miller* in 1882 was turned down by the Madison Square Theatre and, promptly discouraged, Henry James returned to the writing of fiction. During the next six years he wrote his three major novels of the 1880's—*The Bostonians, The Princess Casamassima* and *The Tragic Muse.* He published the play version of *Daisy* in 1883 and the following year turned down a proposal that he dramatize *The Portrait of a Lady,* writing to the actor Lawrence Barrett, who suggested it, that he could not see a play in that novel. Nevertheless he told him "I should be glad to try something next year. . . . I should probably be prepared to write you a play, to take or to leave, as you should like it or not, on the chance that if you *should* like it, it would open the door to my acquiring a goodish sum of money."

He was not, however, free for a sustained dramatic effort. His big novels, all serialized, kept him constantly at his desk. In 1886 he told one correspondent (Julian R. Sturgis) that he was not interested in trying to write plays because of "the whole general disillusionment that has come over me. . . . When I was younger that was really a very dear dream with me—but it has faded away with the mere increase of observation—observation I mean, of the deadly vulgarity and illiteracy of the world one enters, practically, in knocking at a manager's door. Besides I think, I confess, less highly of the drama, as a form, a vehicle, than I did—compared with the novel which can do and say so much more."

Three years later he was expressing the opposite view; and for one claiming a waning interest in the drama he applied himself to its problems assiduously even if he wrote no plays. When he wrote this letter he was already planning his long novel of the stage, *The Tragic Muse.*

~~~~~~~~~~~~~~~~

At forty Henry James had sought to convince himself that he should write some plays. At the threshold of fifty he turned to the theatre in desperation. "My books don't sell, and it looks as if my plays might." This was the rueful confession he made to Robert Louis Stevenson in 1891.

For the Henry James of the impressive beard and the calm eye found himself, in the late Victorian London, in the anomalous position of being a literary lion whose works were unread. He had caught the public fancy with his "international" tales, and notably *Daisy Miller,* but the success had been short-lived. Within a decade James had found a public and lost it. Or had the public lost him? Publishers still brought him out, because it continued to be an honor to have him on their lists and because he sold modestly and had a limited following. The pages of the *Atlantic* continued to be wide open to him, and now and again one of his shorter pieces created a mild flurry. The golden moment of "success," nevertheless, seemed to have come and gone forever. "I have entered upon evil days," James wrote to Howells, who had been his mentor and companion in the early Cambridge time and to whom he turned constantly for practical advice about the marketing of his work. "I am still staggering a good deal under the mysterious and (to me) inexplicable injury wrought—apparently—upon my situation by my last two novels, the *Bostonians* and the *Princess*. They have reduced the desire, and the demand, for my productions, to zero."

What had happened was that Henry James had turned his back on the "international" novel and had given the public something it did not expect from him. *The Bostonians* was strictly about America; *The Princess Casamassima* was about a young Anglo-French bookbinder in London. James's public had come to expect from him stories about Americans in Europe, or Europeans in America. Moreover, his method and manner in these novels of the middle period had grown increasingly intricate; his continued and ever-deeper exploration of the consciousness made for complexity, and complexity made for public confusion and indifference. This was the price the artist paid for his curiosity, his love of experiment, his desire to reach farther and deeper into life. There is nothing a public resents more than a brusque change in the personality and work of an artist, and the two novels James mentioned to Howells, long, analytical, crowded with observation of the life of Boston and London, attracted few readers, although today they speak eloquently to us.

Why did Henry James turn to new subjects after his fortieth year? What had caused him to turn away from the field he had made his own and to which Howells and his brother William urged him to return? We can only collate the circumstantial evidence, for we touch here the inner life of a complex mind. His last and most important "international" novel, *The Portrait of a*

Lady, was published in 1881 and in the autumn of that year he revisited America after an absence of six years. In January 1882 his mother died. He had barely returned to England when he was recalled to Boston to the death bed of his father. He then returned to Europe and remained away from the United States for more than twenty years.

The change in his artistic production coincided thus with the loss of his parents. He had been a "passionate pilgrim" in Europe, writing brightly and cheerfully about his own and other pilgrimages with objectivity, sympathy, insight. He was conscious that "home" was in the United States even though he resided abroad and that his was an American mind playing over Europe and reflecting the Continent to his American readers as well as his Americanism to his British readers. Now "home" had suddenly ceased to exist. The maternal and paternal ties were severed—the mother, for whom he had always retained a child-like attachment, the awe-inspiring father, whom he could not follow in his re-creations of heavens and hells in his religious thinking—both were gone. His first artistic reaction amounted to an attempt to recover "home." He felt an overwhelming compulsion at this moment—it is recorded in his journal— "to show that I *can* write an American story"; he underscored the word *can.* Few had seriously questioned his ability to do so. He had given ample proof of his capacity to write American stories many times before, and as recently as 1880, in *Washington Square.* Yet in 1883 he felt this need, and he began *The Bostonians.* It is an unusual work for Henry James, a bitter, ironic and derisive attack on the budding suffragette movement, on female reformers, on cults, in the provincial atmosphere of post-Civil War Boston. The hero, Basil Ransom, is a Southerner, hence an "outsider" like the expatriate New Yorker Henry James. He is also a lawyer, practising the profession Henry James forsook for a career in letters. We need not go into the complexities of the plot, save to note that Ransom sets out to wean the gifted and oratorical Verena Tarrant from her suffragette friends and her family and to make her his wife. "The city of Boston be damned!" says the hero in the final phase of the book. Henry James had started out to make peace with "home." He ended by damning it.

The Princess Casamassima (1886) carries the conflict to London. It too deals with characters in revolt—only here, James, writing during the depression of the 1880's, found anarchists instead of suffragettes, French émigrés instead of Boston cultists. The hero, Hyacinth Robinson, born in the slums, belongs to the masses—and yet recoils from them. He too cannot make his peace with himself or with "home." His solution is drastic. Unwilling to destroy a world he is ready to accept, unable to live out his revolt, he destroys himself.

These were the two novels which, despite the richness and brilliancy of their writing and the mature art of their creator, provoked no ripple to speak of in the literature of their time. The next novel, *The Tragic Muse* (1889) brought James's conflict to the surface since it carried it into James's world of art. In it the novelist treated two parallel artistic problems, both akin to his own. A young politician wants to forsake Parliament for the palette; a young actress, "a creature of the stage," is asked to forsake her art and marry, as Verena was asked in *The Bostonians.*

We have in the expression of these varied conflicts a recurring pattern which haunts a score of James's tales as well as his novels. They reflect James's revolt against America and his deeply-rooted belief that an artist must make a choice between art and "the world." A choice between Boston (home, art, the study) and Europe (the world) had imposed itself and he had made it, although in reality without resolution of the inner conflict. So his original choice of letters (home, the study) instead of law (the world). Thus Nick Dormer's conflict, Parliament (the world), the palette (art) and Miriam Rooth's—the art of the stage (world), and marriage (home). In two stories Henry James actually split the conflicting personality of his artist; one sat in the study and wrote while the other moved in society (*The Private Life*); one lived in a flat with an ornate room looking down on the public square, and here wore a rich raiment and received his friends; the other looked upon a quiet garden from his rear bedroom, and wore rusty raiment as he wrote his poems (*Benvolio*). James had always been attracted by the legend of Balzac returning late in the evening from his worldly encounters to don a monkish robe and write through the night.

He believed he had resolved his conflict of law versus letters at Dane Hall when he was nineteen. But now with literary failure—rejection by his public—staring him in the face, it was revived. Revived also were the rejections he had felt in childhood, which he tells us about in *A Small Boy* and *Notes of a Son and Brother,* the sense of rivalry and inferiority to brother and father. Where was the mother he could turn to, now? And here a fortunate circumstance occurred. His sister Alice, ailing, had come to England, and "home" in a sense was reconstructed around her. He could start anew. And he did. He turned to the theatre. He would try once again to venture into the world—Drama (literature) was what he wrote in his study, which he conceived as some monastic "great good place." He would see whether he could make a go of Theatre (the world)—where the Drama comes to competitive life.

He was in Paris in December 1888, freshly come from a stay in Geneva, and a trip to the Riviera, when the offer came: a suggestion by Edward Compton, a young actor-manager, whose company's activities were confined to the British provinces, to dramatize *The American.* Compton's wife, the American actress Virginia Bateman, had read an article in a theatrical publication suggesting that James's 1877 novel was a good subject for a play. Compton's proposal came at a good moment; this was the year during which James was complaining of his waning literary fortunes. It found him also at work on *The Tragic Muse* which he had begun that summer. In a journal note of May 12, 1889, when he was completing the *Muse,* he takes up again the self-examination, on the subject of the drama, of eight years earlier:

I had practically given up my old, valued, long cherished dream of doing something for the stage, for fame's sake, and art's, and fortune's: overcome by the vulgarity, the brutality, the baseness of the condition of the English-speaking theatre today. But after an interval, a long one, the vision has revived, on a new and a very much humbler basis, and especially under the lash of necessity. Of art or fame *il est maintenant fort peu question:* I simply *must* try, and try seriously, to produce half a dozen—a dozen, five dozen—plays for the sake of my pocket, my material future. Of how little money the novel makes for me I needn't discourse here. The theatre has sought me out—in the person of the good, the yet unseen, Compton. I have listened and considered and reflected, and the matter is transposed to a minor key. To accept the circumstances, in their extreme humility, and do the best I can *in* them: this is the moral of my present situation. . . .

He had made up his mind, but he was still in conflict. Compton had written at a propitious moment. Nevertheless almost a year elapsed before James could write his play version of *The American*. During that time he poured into *The Tragic Muse* the pros and cons of play-writing, his contempt for the practical conditions of the stage, his delight in the dramatic form. When Gabriel Nash, in a long outburst in the fourth chapter, describes the problems of writing for the Victorian stage—and it applies to the contemporary as well—he is speaking (and with what vehemence!) for Henry James:

. . . the *omnium gatherum* of the population of a big commercial city at the hour of the day when their taste is at its lowest, flocking out of hideous hotels and restaurants, gorged with food, stultified with buying and selling and with all the other sordid preoccupations of the age, squeezed together in a sweltering mass, disappointed in their seats, timing the author, timing the actor, wishing to get their money back on the spot—all before eleven o'clock. Fancy putting the exquisite before such a tribunal as that! There's not even a question of it. The dramatist wouldn't if he could, and in nine cases out of ten he couldn't if he would. He has to make the basest concessions. One of his principal canons is that he must enable his spectators to catch the suburban trains, which stop at 11.30. What would you think of any other artist—the painter or the novelist—whose governing forces should be the dinner and the suburban trains? The old dramatists didn't defer to them—not so much at least—and that's why they're less and less actable. If they're touched—the large loose men —it's only to be mutilated and trivialised. Besides, they had a simpler civilisation to represent—societies in which the life of man was in action, in passion, in immediate and violent expression. Those things could be put upon the playhouse boards with comparatively little sacrifice of their completeness and their truth. To-day we're so infinitely more reflective and complicated and diffuse that it makes all the difference. What can you do with a character, with an idea, with a feeling, between dinner and the suburban trains? You can give a gross rough sketch of them, but how little you touch them, how bald you leave them! What crudity compared with what the novelist does!

A would-be dramatist approaching his art with so acute a sense of its shortcomings and material difficulties was hardly in a frame of mind to attack it bravely. This passage suggests that James had climbed into the dramatic "straitjacket" even before the actors and managers attempted to force him into it. He set about his play-writing with cheerful alacrity; yet his letters during these early months of what was to prove to be a five-year siege of the theatre betray hesitations, uncertainties, misgivings, anxieties—a continuation of the conflict revealed in his journal entries and his novels. He strikes the same notes in all his letters: he is venturing into the theatre for "exclusively mercenary" reasons; he wants his play-writing to be kept a secret until the play is produced; the dramatic form is admirable, the conditions of the British theatre are vulgar and odious. He is secretive to the point of coyness; he sends his script to his sister Alice and solemnly enjoins her not to write to William about it, or at any rate to "give a sign that he must bury what you tell him in tenfold mystery." To which he adds, half-seriously ". . . but I doubt if even this would be secure—it would be in the *Transcript* the next week." To William he writes that "for all sorts of reasons I desire to be extremely secret, silent and mysterious" about the theatrical enterprises. He explains that this was to be an attempt of the "most resolute and scientific character." He writes: "It is ridiculous at my age, to make only *one* bid for theatrical profit ('one murder makes a villain—millions a hero':) therefore I mean to make—as soon as *may* be—eight or ten."

As Henry continued to be mysterious and secretive about the details of his dramatic work, William in characteristic fashion teased him, saying he assumed the "mysterious fortune-making plans" were probably the "formation of an international 'trust' to produce the plays simultaneously in all the capitals of the earth, or something of the kind." He added: "You ought to know enough critically about the qualities that the stage requires, if you can only cold-bloodedly throw in enough action to please the people. . . ." Later, when William knew the details, Henry was still cautioning him "please breathe no word of these confidences, as publicity blows on such matters in an injurious and deflowering way. And interests too great to be hurt are at stake."

His need for secrecy was explained by him in a letter to his brother many months later, after the failure of one of his projects: "What is heart-breaking is the having to *tell* them and talk about them and answer people's questions (I don't say this for *you!*) mostly indiscreet and idle. *That,* only, is the real giving one's self away. There is *no* answer to be given, or information to be supplied, in relation to any situation one is in with a theatre or manager. *Silence,* till production takes place, if it is ever to, is the only thing that meets the dangers and covers the abysses. Please *know* nothing if anyone asks you about my affairs. I say nothing myself whatever. I only do my business and go my way."

Outside his family, Robert Louis Stevenson was one of a few friends who received his theatrical confidences, and yet always in general terms. To Stevenson he was invariably apologetic: "Don't be hard on me, simplifying and chastening necessity has laid its brutal hand on me and I have had to try and make somehow or other the money I don't make by literature." In the same letter he refers to *The American* as his "tribute to the vulgarest of the muses" and speaks of a "base theatrical errand"—meaning a rehearsal he is about to attend. He writes to Stevenson: "My zeal in the affair is only matched by my indifference . . ." yet in the same letter he says "I find the *form* opens out before me as if it were a kingdom to conquer. . . ." And then, as if he had spoken too kind a word for the theatre, he promptly adds "a kingdom forsooth of ignorant brutes of managers and dense cabotins of actors." And immediately after this there is again an expression of delight: "All the same, I feel as if I had at last *found* my form—my real one—that for which pale fiction is an ineffectual substitute." Again, lest Stevenson take this for genuine enthusiasm, he once more qualifies: "God grant this unholy truth may not abide with me more than two or three years—time to dig out eight or ten rounded masterpieces and make withal enough money to enable me to retire in peace and plenty for the unmolested business of a *little* supreme writing, as distinct from gouging—which is the Form above-mentioned."

To William he had written without qualification a few days earlier: "I feel at last as if I had found my *real* form, which I am capable of carrying far, and for which the pale little art of fiction, as I have practised it, has been, for me, but a limited and restricted substitute. The strange thing is that I always, universally, knew *this* was my more characteristic form—but was kept away from it by a half-modest, half-exaggerated sense of the difficulty (that is, I mean the practical odiousness) of the conditions. But now that I have accepted them and met them, I see that one isn't at all, needfully, their victim, but is, from the moment one *is* anything, one's self, worth speaking of, their *master;* and may use them, command them, squeeze them, lift them up and better them. As for the form *itself,* its honor and inspiration are (*à défaut d'autres*) in its difficulty. If it were easy to write a good play I couldn't and wouldn't think of it; but it is in fact damnably hard (to this truth the paucity of the article— in the English-speaking world—testifies,) and that constitutes a solid respectability—guarantees one's *intellectual* self-respect."

These passages from letters written to brother and to friend during the period of the production of *The American* illustrate strikingly Henry James's waiverings and his terrible need to justify the venture into the theatre as if it were some abnormal undertaking, requiring explanation and apology. Allowing for his habitual tone of banter in his correspondence with Stevenson and his addiction to elaborate euphemism, it is clear, nevertheless, that the reiterated apologies for the theatre sprang from needs other than to amuse and entertain his friends. The tone of the letters might be light, carefree, contradictory, devil-may-care; the inner content was serious, and derived from the deeply-grounded need to put up a good "front" dramatically speaking. He had made a decision; he was not at all sure of himself; he felt he was straying from the dignified path of a man of letters and he wanted to be sure his friends would not think the less of him for it. The late Victorian theatre was an impoverished institution, lacking the artistic richness and freedom of fiction. Henry James recognized the challenge to improve it. But he was afraid. The best justification he could find was his need to earn money. It was true that the dwindling sales of his books created a greater sense of financial need than actually existed. At this time, as in 1881, his earnings were adequate. The *Atlantic* paid him $15 a page for *The Tragic Muse* (a yield of $300 a month) and income from other writings and other sources continued to give him a safe margin of security.

There was, however, another reason now for his emphasis on pecuniary returns. He had reached his "middle years" beset by feelings of literary inadequacy (in the marketplace) and the thought of the years to come, with the prospect of diminishing returns, deeply disturbed him. Therefore one of the reasons he gave was the desire to "provide for one's old age."

And his emphasis on money must be seen in the light of a new friendship he formed at the outset of the dramatic years with a young American, Wolcott Balestier, a friend of Howells's, who had arrived in London shortly before the dramatization of *The American* to represent a New York publisher. Intense, energetic, himself a writer of short stories and novels (he later collaborated with Kipling in the writing of *The Naulahka*), young Balestier undertook to guide James in his financial arrangements for the plays. With a whole-hearted admiration for the middle-aged novelist, and a characteristic enthusiasm that endeared him to London's literary world, Balestier fired James's imagination with stories of fortunes to be derived from dramatic production. "Dear Suzerain of the Drama," he addressed his letters to James with a flamboyance and flattery that delighted the novelist; and presently James was building great castles in the air based on hypothetical royalties he would derive from his plays in England plus those which would pour in from the American rights and even, he fondly daydreamed in a letter to William, from the Australian!

The thought of fabulous fortunes, coupled with an awareness of the large incomes of playwrights such as Arthur Pinero, Henry Arthur Jones and later Oscar Wilde, made Henry James acutely aware of the smallness of his literary income; and it was small indeed, judged by a dramatist's earnings during the successful run of a play. What James overlooked, in his constant reference to the royalties received by his contemporaries in the theatre, was that a playwright too has his ups and downs and that between plays his income can fall to zero.

James's emphasis on money, on secrecy, on the vulgarities and baseness of the British stage, betrayed again and again his ambivalent attitude toward the theatre. For the first time in his life he was seeking to vend his wares in a competitive market. Perhaps one of the elements in his conflict was the strong American impulse that he no doubt possessed—had his Albany grandfather not demonstrated its truth?—that to be worth one's salt in the world one had to elbow one's way to achievement by solid worldly enterprise! He was launched in the theatre; he had abandoned the novel for the time being. Henceforth he kept telling himself, he would write only plays and short stories. He would, like Balzac, seek to leave a multitude of pictures of his time. But it was no accident that most of the stories written while he was wooing the Muse of the Drama are either stories of "unsuccessful" writers, or ghostly tales expressing nightmare terror, anxiety, frustration.

"A MOST UNHOLY TRADE"

He threw himself into his play-writing as one possessed. In all the fifty years of his authorship he was never to create at a pitch of greater or more feverish intensity. He wrote as if he were a soldier engaged in battle and his life depended on the outcome. The words "siege" and "war" recur constantly in his letters. He imaged the world of the theatre as a battleground. He pictured the stage as an "abyss" and by implication placed himself on its brink. He rewrote, he elaborated parts to suit actors and actresses; he contrived happy endings he would never have dreamed of in his novels; he caricatured his fellow countrymen to win laughter from English audiences; he struggled with the "barbarous, the ignorant, the sickening race of managers"; he bowed before "the foul fiend Excision"—speaking of his plays as bloodied, amputated, butchered children. ("Oh, the mutilated, brutally simplified, massacred little play!") Behind the half-exaggerated and elaborate irony and mockery of his pronouncements lay a deep and serious purpose, that of meeting the stage on its terms, and communicating to the audiences. "Forget not," he exploded one day to his publisher, William Heinemann, "that you write for the stupid— that is, that your maximum of refinement must meet the minimum of intelligence of the audience—the intelligence, in other words, of the biggest ass it may conceivably contain." And he added: "It is a most unholy trade!"

Scenario succeeded upon scenario—we shall never know exactly how many— and were circulated among the London managers. At rehearsals James mounted the stage to demonstrate to the actors how parts should be played, drawing upon his memory of bits of "business" seen on the stage of the Théâtre Français: "I spent upwards of five hours yesterday on the deadly cold stage of the Portsmouth Theatre (the 'ladies' had *such* red noses!) going at them tooth and nail, without pause, and then two more with my *grand premier rôle* at his lodgings, coaching him with truly psychological intensity; acting, intonating everything *for* him and showing him simply *how!* The authorship (in any sense worthy of the name) of a play only *begins* when it is written, and I see that one's creation of it doesn't terminate till one has gone with it every inch of the way to the rise of the curtain on the first night. . . ." During his five dramatic years, however, he had only two productions upon which to lavish such effort; the majority of his plays remained unproduced.

He was in a constant state of nervous tension: accustomed to the freedom of fiction, he found himself in a theatre wedged between the backdrop and the proscenium, reaching beyond the footlights to an audience that asked to be entertained and pleased "on the spot." At first he relished the flare of the gaslight, the painted faces, the rituals and superstitions of the stage, the high hopes, the realities backstage and the make-believe on-stage. The reactions of the audience stirred and excited him; the modest, unobtrusive "observer" that was Henry James enjoyed hearing his work applauded, and humanly delighted in the call of "Author, author" that brought him before the people he had sought to entertain. He felt the challenge of the dramatic art, and was stimulated by his contact with creatures of flesh and blood, he who had lived in the fantasied world of his novelist's study. Yet disillusion set in rapidly; inner nightmares plagued him; his anxieties overflowed to disturb and confuse his relations with actors and managers. At fifty, and a famous man of letters, he was impatient over the characteristic delays of the theatre: "The great stumbling block in the whole business is the question of Time—the slowness, the waiting, the delays which are a large part of the very essence of managerial production. They talk of years as we talk of months and I am handicapped by having begun too late and being too old: I ought to have come to it ten years ago. But I shall vanquish all the same."

Recognizing this, he was, nevertheless, unprepared for the theatrical rebuffs which are the common lot of actor and playwright. The children of his brain, upon which he lavished so much ingenuity during the long mornings in De Vere Gardens, lingered ignored in the managerial offices. James was artist enough—and human enough—to feel deep anguish at their treatment. He pleaded, he argued, he worked, he revised, he compromised, and in the end, with the jeers of an audience ringing in his ears, he fled back to his study, to the sanctuary and great good place that had been waiting for him all the time of his struggle in the outer world, exclaiming, as he had many times before: "I may have been meant for the Drama—God Knows!—but I certainly wasn't meant for the Theatre."

We can plot the chart of Henry James's fitful dramatic fever from the casual allusions, hints, veiled vague references to his theatrical enterprises in his letters—information grudgingly vouchsafed to an inquiring older brother, or on occasions to intimate friends close to his efforts in London. *The American,* written early in 1890, was an open secret since it went into production that autumn, but other plays are identified often by numbers in his letters and we are never certain in what order they were written since he only named three of them. Between November and December 1890 he wrote *Tenants,* first known as *Mrs. Vibert,* for John Hare; in mid-December he began Play #3 intended for Compton, who had produced *The American,* and this was completed by January 10, 1891. It was either *The Reprobate* or *The Album*—the two works he described later as designed to be played in country towns and which he ultimately admitted to Edmund Gosse he had intended for the Compton Comedy Company. On February 6, 1891, he wrote to William that he was attacking "my fourth" but we have no way of knowing what this play was and whether he completed it. In the autumn of 1891 he discussed a play for Augustin Daly, the American manager who was planning a London season, and in December of that year he was writing a "three-act contemporary comedy" again for Edward Compton—this again either *Reprobate* or *Album.*

He had completed the play for Daly by the summer of 1892 for he read

Mrs. Jasper, later re-titled *Disengaged,* to Ada Rehan during August of that year, and in November he was planning a second play for her which, however, ultimately became the one-act play he wrote for Ellen Terry. In May of 1893 he sketched the scenario for a "three-act comedy pure and simple" which later that year he offered to George Alexander, the matinee idol and enterprising manager of the St. James's. He spoke at this time also of a play tentatively titled *Monte Carlo.* In May or June of 1893 he set down his first note for the dramatization of *The Chaperon* following a suggestion made to him by Arthur Pinero that his short story of that name had in it all the ingredients of a high comedy.

That summer, at Ramsgate, he wrote *Guy Domville* for Alexander. In November 1893, while negotiating with Daly for the production of *Disengaged,* which he revised, and with Alexander for the production of *Domville,* he had "almost finished . . . another three act play" for Comyns Carr, the London art critic who had leased the Comedy Theatre for a fling at dramatic production. Carr was waiting to decide after seeing the third act. From an allusion to the *Monte Carlo* play in his notebooks at this time we may speculate that this work may have been intended for Carr, but there is no way at present of knowing. By this time Henry James's desk was clearly piled high with scenarios and half-written plays. On December 7, 1893, he slips into a letter to Elizabeth Robins a final exclamatory sentence: "I have begun another play!" and three weeks later, before his Christmas fire, he is dreaming up still another play for Compton, tentatively named *The Promise.* In 1894 he sets down the scenario for this play, and lays it aside when Compton shows no interest in it. (Two years later he turned it into the novel, *The Other House,* and a dozen years after that he turned the novel into a play.) During this year he made the first note of the theme that was to flower into *The Wings of the Dove,* conceiving it first also as a play.

How many of these numerous projects were completed? how many absorbed into his fiction? how many scrapped? We know little more today than James's correspondents did when they received his chary confidences. The two plays which saw production during the 1890's never saw publication. Four comedies written during this period which never reached the stage were issued in book form (the two series of *Theatricals*); a one-act play was converted into a short story; a scenario was converted into a novel; and much later a three-act comedy into a novel. It is quite likely that the novelist did not scrap any of his completed plays, since we know that he did not like work to go to waste. Many of the "plays" written during these crowded months existed only as extended scenarios and these he seems to have destroyed. Perhaps some day some portions of plays and scenarios may turn up among the papers of the late Victorian actor-managers. Yet even here there is little likelihood since James usually reclaimed his scripts. We may surmise that he made copious notes for his plays in those notebooks which he destroyed; the few pages of the first note for *The Chaperon* which survive (because he had hopes of writing this play) were torn from a scribbler such as he used for his notebooks and break off in the middle of a tantalizing sentence. A few words more and we might have learned something about *Monte Carlo*. Searches instituted some years ago by the editor of this volume among the papers of Sir John Hare and J. Comyns Carr yielded neither scenarios nor letters.

The four comedies which Henry James published as a "melancholy subterfuge," seeking to console himself with "the performance imaginary," are conventional and contrived in the tradition of French comedy of manners. James resorts freely to melodrama to untangle his plots; he is prodigal, after the manner of the time, in his use of asides and employs the catch-phrase unhesitatingly as a humorous resource. His characters belong to the stock company of theatrical tradition—"strong" women, double dealers, doting mothers, flirts and philanderers, deep-dyed villains and virtuous, bumbling protagonists. An adventuress seeks to "place" her illegitimate son in the social hierarchy; there is an intrigue to deprive a rightful heir of his fortune; a practical joke results in a man's engagement to a woman, in spite of himself, and there is an intrigue to "disengage" him; a young man, considered a reprobate, develops into a self-asserting individual. There are echoes of Dumas *fils* and Augier in these plays; there is the *coup de théâtre* in the manner of Sardou; the *ficelle* is strained to the breaking point.

Henry James was seeking to write crisp, witty, epigrammatic comedy at the same time as Oscar Wilde, and these comedies inevitably invite comparison with those of his contemporary. James's plays have more substance, weightier machinery, much plot, considerable drollery, less wit, but much sharper caricature. Wilde's plays are tinsel and pasteboard; his people are mouthpieces for his cleverness. There is less gloss in James's comedies, but at every turn one is conscious of the hand of an experienced artist engaged in characterizing people and setting them within the scenic frame. The fundamental difference between Henry James and Oscar Wilde (James called Oscar the "unspeakable one") so far as the failure of one and the success of the other in the theatre is concerned, resides in their approach to the public. Wilde remained true to the figure of himself he had long before projected—that of a cool, arrogant coiner of witty phrases and epigrams, utterly indifferent to his public. James described to a friend how he attended the first night of *Lady Windermere's Fan* in 1892 and Oscar "with a metallic blue carnation in his buttonhole and a cigarette in his fingers" made a curtain speech. "The speech, which, alas, was stupid, was only to say that he judged the audience felt the play to be merely as charming as he did." The audience accepted his condescension because it could laugh at it. James could not be indifferent to his public. He was trying too hard to please it. The public, or the managers who read his plays, sensed this strain, and could neither laugh at him, as at Wilde, nor sympathize with him. The result was fatal for James.

This feeling of anxiety and tension in James is reflected in the prefaces to the two volumes of *Theatricals.* Beneath the polished surface of their prose one can sense the heartbreak. Gallantly James observes that the publication of unproduced plays is in a sense an admission of defeat; he is giving expression at once to a kind of self-pity and exasperation. Stripped of their urbane exteriors the prefaces are a moan of fear mingled with a grunt of anger. In arraying the difficulties faced by the dramatist James also expresses the apprehension surrounding his play-writing—fear of being supersubtle, fear, coupled with a very natural resentment, of the mutilation of his plays by managers, fear of the limitations imposed upon him by the clock. It is no wonder that the shrewd reviewer of the *Daily Chronicle,* discussing *Theatricals,* saw in James's "exaggerated respect and exaggerated contempt" for the stage the frustrating ambivalence arising out of conflict that foredoomed his theatrical undertakings.

"He is fascinated by the very difficulty," wrote the perspicacious reviewer, "yet in his heart he despises himself for yielding to the fascination." The theatrical tight rope, the abyss, the straitjacket, existed in James's own mind. If Henry James could have approached the theatre in a more relaxed fashion— in the manner in which he wrote his fiction—we should probably be telling a different story today.

ONE YEAR MORE . . .

He had thought of himself as a double personality, a monk writing in his cell, a man of the world moving about in society, observing, noting, recording. Now this fantasy reasserted itself. Henry James, the dramatist, walked abroad in the London daylight, was strong, vigorous, masculine, a soldier laying siege to the citadel of the theatre, a champion of Ibsen, a gallant defender of the dramatic art. The other Henry James, the literary man, sat in his Kensington study, contriving scenarios and plays, cursing managers and writing—always writing. He wrote a story about such a double personality in *The Private Life* during the second of his dramatic years, attaching it to the figure of Robert Browning, whom he envisaged as possessing an *alter ego,* a writer who created his poetry for him in private while an unpoetic, a more prosaic, figure moved through the London drawing-rooms. Henry James worried at the "dramatic, the unspeakably theatric form," but he dipped his pen also into the "other ink—the sacred fluid of fiction." Nothing was more soothing, he journalized in 1893, than "to remember that literature sits patient at my door, and that I have only to lift the latch to let in the exquisite little form that is, after all, nearest my heart." (Thus far had he come since his outburst to William James two years earlier about the "pale little art of fiction" and his enthusiastic assertion that the drama was "my more characteristic form.")

For he continued to practise the fictional form and "pale" is the last word most critics would apply to the stories written during the dramatic years. He had forsworn the novel; he confined himself only to the short story (*à la*

Maupassant, he told himself) and with an ardor all the more intense, since his story-writing provided an escape from the frustrations of the theatre. Between the production of *The American* in 1890 and *Guy Domville* in the first days of 1895, he wrote nineteen tales including such masterpieces as *The Real Thing, The Altar of the Dead, Sir Edmund Orme, The Chaperon, The Marriages, The Death of the Lion, The Coxon Fund* and thirteen articles ranging from memorials to his lately dead friends, James Russell Lowell, Fanny Kemble, and Robert Browning, to critical discussions of Ibsen and Flaubert. He saw six volumes of tales and essays through the press during the dramatic years; his output continued to be large, but his determination to write no more long fiction for serialization in the magazines reduced his literary earnings considerably. Writing unproduced plays was proving a costly process.

Into the tales written during these troubled years there flowed very little of his actual theatrical experience. Only one of the nineteen stories dealt directly with a theatrical subject; this was *Nona Vincent,* written immediately after the production of *The American* and reflecting in every detail James's adventures on the road and in London with the Compton Comedy Company. Allan Wayworth, the young, fastidious, nervous playwright, clinging to the safely-married and all-wise Mrs. Alsager, was the Henry James who had read his plays to his friends Mrs. John L. Gardner and Mrs. Hugh Bell. Henry James's boast to his brother: "I feel at last as if I had found my *real* form" was Wayworth's "mastery of the scenic idea"; Henry James's view that the theatre was an "abyss of vulgarity and platitude" was Wayworth's "managerial abyss." Henry James's remark in the preface to the second series of *Theatricals* that a playwright must seek economy by the "periodical throwing overboard of the cargo to save the ship" parallels Wayworth's "You were perpetually throwing over the cargo to save the ship. . . ."

If the overt material did not go into his other stories, the emotions arising from his play-writing did. A reader examining the stories, unaware of James's activities during these years, would discover in them evidence of his personal fears and anxieties, and an ever-deepening sense of frustration. He had written only four ghostly tales between his twenty-second and forty-seventh years; now the supernatural element appears in a series of tales—the daylight ghost of *Sir Edmund Orme,* the overwhelming night-time spirit of the Family in *Owen Wingrave,* the supernatural-fantastic of *The Private Life,* the operation of clairvoyance or telepathy and benign supernaturalism of *Sir Dominick Ferrand* and *Nona Vincent* reflecting James's uneasy state of mind. He wrote twelve such tales during the nineties including the celebrated *Turn of the Screw,* his ultimate record of nightmare set down in the aftermath of dramatic defeat. At the same time there came from his pen tales of writers unappreciated and ignored, public failures, private "successes," triumphant in their art. These are almost completely autobiographical since, in each case, Henry James identified himself with the writer he portrayed. The stories were derived (as James cautiously said in a preface a dozen years later) "in each case, from some noted adventure, some felt embarrassment, some extreme predicament, of the artist enamored of perfection. . . ." *Some felt embarrassment.* We do not have to seek far to discover the person who *felt* the embarrassment. He published a volume after his dramatic years containing four stories, two dealing with unsuccessful writers, and called it *Embarrassments.* In 1893, the year of his fiftieth birthday, James published only one short story. He called it *The Middle Years.* It is the story of a writer who, in middle life, feels that it has taken him too long to learn his craft. "His development had been abnormally slow, almost grotesquely gradual. He had been hindered and retarded by experience. . . . It had taken too much of life to produce too little of his art. At such a rate a first existence was too short. . . ."

Poor Dencombe, the writer, pleads in vain for a second existence in which to write the great works he has in his mind and dies realizing that he has accomplished all he has been capable of doing. The dying Dencombe whispers to the admiring young doctor at his side: "It's frustration that doesn't count."

And the admiring young doctor philosophically replies: "Frustration's only life."

Frustration was only life. At the end of the year in which he wrote these words, Henry James withdrew his comedy, *Disengaged,* from Augustin Daly, after a difference with the producer, gritted his teeth and wrote to William: ". . . *à la guerre comme à la guerre.* I mean to wage this war ferociously one year more—1894—and then (unless the victory and the spoils have not by that [time] become more proportionate than hitherto to the humiliations and vulgarities and disgusts, all the dishonour and chronic insult incurred) to 'chuck' the whole intolerable experiment and return to the more elevated and more independent courses."

And he added: "The whole odiousness of the thing lies in the connection between the drama and the theatre. The one is admirable in its interest and difficulty, the other loathesome in its conditions."

One year more—1894. Henry James's notes during this year are crowded with fantasies of death. Entry after entry betrays his deep sense of frustration, brooding despair that accompanied his sense of time irretrievably lost, the feeling that had grown in the five years since his last novel that he was a figure unwanted in the artistic life of his time. The record of frustration can be read in his letters and stories; the fantasies have been set down for us in his notebook. At the beginning of the year he wrote "The idea of *death* both checked and caught me . . ." and it became the *leitmotif* of the successive notebook entries: ideas for stories of men living a kind of death-in-life, of men who have died emotionally or who have bartered passion for material opportunities and live on in a mockery of life. During this year he set down his fantasy of the literary "lion" discovered late in his career and smothered by uncritical adulation, finally dying of it. During this year he set down the first fantasy of "some young creature . . . who, at 20, on the threshold of a life that has seemed boundless, is suddenly condemned to death" which eight years later became *The Wings of the Dove*. And during this year he wrote his lament for the neglected dead which grew in his hands into *The Altar of the Dead*—the story of the great blazing altar on which George Stransom set his candles, symbols of the tomb, in the knowledge that a candle one day would be lit for him. During 1894 James published only three tales and two of them have Death in their titles—*The Death of the Lion* and *The Altar of the Dead*. To the volume in which he assembled these stories, together with *The Coxon Fund*, written during a sad summer in Italy that year, a story of death-in-life, of a writer who fritters away his talent in talk, and *The Middle Years*, the story of the author seeking a second chance, he gave the lugubrious title of *Terminations*.

1894 was a year of terminations and Henry James knew it. *One year more.* *Guy Domville* was to be the final test and all his hopes and dreams of the past five years went into that play. Rehearsals began during December of 1894, and for a few days Henry James re-experienced all the high elation—and sharp conflict—of the dramatist he had painted in *Nona Vincent*. The year of gloom came to a gloomy end with word of the death of his old friend Robert Louis Stevenson in Samoa; and the new year was but five days old when Henry James walked out on the stage of the St. James's theatre to face the ultimate rejection from the public he had tried to please. In a few stormy seconds, recounted in detail elsewhere in this volume, he lived through the terminal episode of his dramatic years.

"DIVINE PRINCIPLE OF THE SCENARIO"

In *Guy Domville* Henry James had told the story of a young man destined for the priesthood who, on becoming the last of his line, is prevailed upon to forego the monastery and assume the obligations due his family name—to take charge of his estates and to marry. He ventures from the threshold of the cloister into the world only to discover that it is filled with evil. He is surrounded by conniving people, dishonesty, betrayal. He tries to accept this world but to no avail, and finally, shocked and disillusioned by a supreme betrayal, he returns to the embrace of Mother Church.

The situation in the play, which was written at the height of Henry James's struggle in the theatre, clearly parallels the novelist's experience. He could identify himself with his hero to the full. He had always thought of himself as dedicated to the priesthood or fraternity of letters; he had strayed from what he deemed to be his true vocation into a world filled with conniving actors and managers, dishonesty, betrayal. Like Guy he had sought to adjust himself to it. The very play which dramatized his problems had, by a supreme irony, been the instrument of his disillusion and defeat. Like Guy he would now "turn away his face" from that non-literary world which had treated him with such cruelty. He would re-enter his monastic cell of letters.

From Henry James's notebook, January 23, 1895:

> I take up my own old pen again—the pen of all my old unforgettable efforts and sacred struggles. To myself—today—I need say no more. Large and full and high the future still opens. It is now indeed that I may do the work of my life. And I will.
>
> x x x x x
>
> I have only to *face* my problems.
>
> x x x x x
>
> But all that is of the ineffable—too deep and pure for any utterance. Shrouded in sacred silence let it rest.

He had written to William James at the outset of his dramatic years, "I am going to attack, renewedly and repeatedly, the almost impregnable fortress of the theatre." No one had repulsed his attacks. The fortress had remained (for him) quite simply impregnable. Now, at fifty-two, he could return to silence, devotion, contemplation—to the observation post of the mind he had occupied during all the long years that preceded his play-writing. Here no one could challenge him: no manager could reject his dreams and fantasies or apply the brutal axe of Excision to his manuscripts; no actor could dictate his characters for him. He was the undisputed master, the omniscient observer. He could speculate, analyze, lose himself in his fancies—make these the realities of his life to replace the other realities that lay outside and beyond his literary monastery.

And so, immediately after *Guy Domville,* we find him dreaming self-consolatory stories, seeking "compensations and solutions." *His works were not popular?* This was because they were "too good" for the public whose "huge, flat foot" he had sought to measure. Thus he wrote a short story, *The Next Time,* about an author who seeks to create pot-boilers, but is capable of producing only unread masterpieces. *His works were not understood?* This was because their form, their pattern, their texture was not perceived by the mole-like critics. Thus he wrote a short story, *The Figure in the Carpet,* to plead for a criticism that might understand the artist's intentions.

While he thus sought and found reassurance for himself, on a conscious level, in stories that might be termed "rationalizations," he was nevertheless stating truths that the critics of today can readily accept. He was too discriminating for the taste of his time; his art, complex, and conforming to high standards of perfection, eluded critics who should have known him better. And there was indeed a pattern in his work which still seems to elude them, a subtle autobiographical pattern, the manner in which he wrote his life

into his work. In the *order*, the *form*, the *texture*, the very names of his people
and the names he gave to his books, there lay the *figure in the carpet* for those
who wished to find it.

On another level of the mind—and here we skirt more speculative areas—he
was now plunged into a nightmare of fear and insecurity. To have been rejected
brutally by his public amounted to artistic death, and he fought against this
with all the force of his manhood. Three days after *Guy Domville*, he visited
the Archbishop of Canterbury, at his country seat of Addington, near London,
and there, in conversation with members of his family, he described himself as
a man who had "hitherto . . . seemed to himself to have been struggling
in some dim water-world, bewildered and hampered by the crystal medium, and
that he had suddenly got his head above the surface, with a new perspective
and an unimpeded vision." Henry James thus imaged himself as one who had
been drowning and who only now could begin to breathe again. A striking
image for him to have used at this time, and we can watch him, through the
weeks that followed, struggling against the waves that threatened to swallow
him up, groping for a foothold against oblivion. Here was the death-in-life of his
fantasies of the year before. The jeering audience in St. James's had reduced
him to the helplessness of an unappreciated child; it had cut at the heart of
his creativity. It is perhaps no coincidence that the first note he set down after
Guy Domville was that of a tale of horror, a nightmare story, told him by the
Archbishop at Addington, which became *The Turn of the Screw*. He had written
a few years earlier two short stories about ill-starred children; now he moved
into a world of childish fear and terror; the bogey of non-success now merged
with the infantile Bogeyman. Two novels and a novelette are set down in rapid
succession picturing fragile innocents, bright, precocious, blooming, worldly-
wise, pushed and fenced by adult hands, some doomed to early blight.

For the children of the stories he wrote at fifty-five there was no happy
childhood. A child is murdered (*The Other House*); childhood is a special
hell created by adults (*What Maisie Knew*); adults plague children with
phantoms (*The Turn of the Screw*). The Henry James who had retreated from
his older brother rather than compete with him; the celibate Henry, whose life
would never be shared with his own children (whose author in *The Lesson of
the Master* describes children as contributing to "damnation, artistically speaking"), dreamed tales of children assaulted by great forces of aggression. And
since these dreams sprang full-blown from his mind at this climactic moment in
his literary career, we must accept them as evidence of the inner disturbance
provoked by his theatrical failures. He moved from his disturbed present into a
disturbed childish past. It is no wonder that James described the ghostly tale as
the finest form of the fairy tale. In saying this he linked the fear and wonder
of his ghosts with his childhood. There had been too many preceptors and
governesses, too many pushing hands in his own childhood—and apparently
too many little rivals and rejections.

On February 14, 1895, little more than a month after *Guy Domville,* Henry James sat down at his desk to work out the details of a story he had noted the previous year. "I have my head, thank God, full of visions. One has never too many—one has never enough. Ah, just to let one's self go—at last. . . ." He glances at the theme which was to become *The Wings of the Dove,* he goes on to glance at the note that foreshadowed *The Golden Bowl.* He expresses some worry about the "adulterine" element in this theme; it would be difficult to sell such a story to the highly sensitive American "family" magazines. The solution would lie in the handling of the subject. . . . He muses, *"Voyons, voyons* may I not instantly sit down to a little close, clear full scenario of it?" Suddenly at the mention of the word *scenario* he does "let one's self go. . . ."

> As I ask myself the question, *with* the very asking of it, and the utterance of that word [scenario] so charged with memories and pains, something seems to open out before me, and at the same time to press upon me with an extraordinary tenderness of embrace. Compensations and solutions seem to stand there with open arms for me—and something of the 'meaning' to come to me of past bitterness, of recent bitterness that otherwise has seemed a mere sickening, unflavoured draught.

He asks himself a still more important question:

> Has a *part* of all this wasted passion and squandered time (of the last 5 years) been simply the precious lesson, taught me in that roundabout and devious, that cruelly expensive, way, *of the singular value for a narrative plan too* of the (I don't know *what* adequately to call it) divine principle of the Scenario?

If this was the case, he almost blessed the "pangs and the pains and the miseries" of the "whole tragic experience."

> IF there has lurked in the central core of it this exquisite truth—I almost hold my breath with suspense as I try to formulate it; so *much,* hangs radiantly there as depending on it—this exquisite truth that what I call the divine principle in question is a key that, working in the same *general* way fits the complicated chambers of *both* the dramatic and the narrative lock: IF, I say, I have crept round through long apparent barrenness, through suffering and sadness intolerable to that rare perception—why my infinite little loss is converted into an almost infinite little gain. The long figuring out, the patient, passionate little *cahier,* becomes the *mot de l'énigme,* the thing to live by. Let me commemorate here, in this manner, such a portentous little discovery, the discovery, probably, of a truth of real value even if I exaggerate, as I daresay I do, its *portée,* its magicality.

Divine principle of the Scenario. He did not exaggerate its importance, for he was to come back to it again and again in the notebook entries of the remaining years. He called it also "mastery of fundamental statement," and as the months passed he grew increasingly attached to this simple device, derived from his work methods of his dramatic years: that of setting down a full outline of each project, a rough statement, a scenario, even when a trivial short story was involved. He had, in earlier days, communed with himself in his notebooks, never to any extended length. Now there appears in his scribblers full-length scenarios for his novels; this explains the detailed working out of *The Spoils of Poynton* and *What Maisie Knew* and the elaborate "Project for *The Ambassadors*." "Projects" or scenarios or "rough statements" existed for all his later novels; however, after he started dictating directly to the typewriter he did not include these in his notebooks, and most of them were destroyed by him in the flames to which he consigned the bulk of his papers a few years before his death. Henry James now brought to fiction the very mechanics he had invoked for the writing of his plays. He talks of his fiction as if it were drama. "What then is it," he asks himself at one point in working out the *Spoils*, "that the rest of my second little act, as I call it . . . must do?" And he goes on: "What I feel more and more that I must arrive at, with these things, is the adequate and regular practice of some such economy of clear summarization as will *give* me from point to point, each of my steps, stages, tints, shades, every main joint and hinge, in its place, of my subject—give me, in a word, my clear order and expressed sequence. I can then *take* from the table, successively, each fitted or fitting piece of my little mosaic."

This is the carpenter-dramatist at work (as James envisioned him years before) on his knees, disposing of his goods this that and the other way, packing his coffer in the "one way that is mathematically right"; it is not the old-time novelist spinning a discursive narrative, chatting, pausing to describe, taking his reader on diverse journeys, letting his pen run cheerfully away with him; it is the novel given a form as calculated as a fugue or a sonata, the boundaries defined and within them the work built step by step in accordance with its particular substance and logic. In his note for *The Spoils of Poynton* from which we have quoted above, Henry James went on to write:

> When I ask myself what there may have been to show for my long tribulation, my wasted years and patiences and pangs, of theatrical experiment, the answer, as I have already noted here, comes up as just possibly *this:* what I have gathered from it will perhaps have been exactly some such mastery of fundamental statement—of the art and secret of it, of expression, of the sacred mystery of structure. Oh yes—the weary, woeful time has done something for me, has had in the depths of all its wasted piety and passion, an intense little lesson and direction. What that resultant is I must now actively show. . . .

He actively showed it from then on: he attached the utmost importance to his "subject-noting," the "working-out" sessions, the "thinking out . . . pen in hand." In one of his short stories (*The Death of the Lion*) he described an author's scenario as "loose liberal confident, it might have passed for a great gossiping eloquent letter—the overflow into talk of an artist's amorous plan." The survival of the unfinished scenario for *The Chaperon* now published here— the sole play-scenario extant so far as we know—gives us a picture of the way in which James liked to "fumble out" his subject. It belongs with the notes which survived for his unfinished novels, *The Sense of the Past* and *The Ivory Tower* which Percy Lubbock edited after his death.

He thus practised to the full the application to the narrative plan of his "divine principle of the Scenario"; his "patient, passionate little *cahier*" became indeed the key to his work, the *mot de l'énigme,* the figure in the carpet, "the thing to live by." He rejoiced in the elaborate mechanics of his writing—the process of fitting the scenario key, as he had put it, into the "complicated chambers of both the dramatic and narrative lock." In the process, he was equating drama and fiction, the same door and the same lock led him to both. The effect of this method on his later work was extraordinary, for in applying his drama-working methods to the novel he gave to his fiction the qualities of the play. His protagonists would be shown at the crucial moments in their lives, face to face with their conflicts and decisions and in scenes as carefully set as if they were the work of the stage designer and the property man. The theatre had taught him rigid economy and how to allow a situation to unfold without the intervention of the narrator; how to obtain intensity from a given situation by extracting all the elements of drama it contained.

Henry James had arrived at the ultimate integration, in his work, of Picture and Scene. ("I realize—none too soon—that the *scenic* method is my absolute, my imperative, my *only* salvation.") The series of experiments Henry James embarked upon led him from a group of three short, play-like novels, to the final major novels of his career which combine his qualities of analyst and painter with those of the artist of the scene, the dramatist. On the surface these later novels appear the reverse of dramatic; the situation seems to be static while we are in the minds of the Jamesian characters and observers, following them through their analyses and their problems. Each passage of analysis, however, leads invariably to a sharply-defined scene so planned as to advance and resolve the given situation—the whole arranged in a symmetrical and highly logical pattern. The work possesses an organic architectural design. Background is reduced to essentials, as on the stage. The novel is stripped of all trimmings and accessories.

His first novel after the dramatic years was *The Spoils of Poynton,* his second the adaption into fiction of his scenario of *The Other House.* In accomplishing this work, in which, for the first time, he consciously used a scenario designed for a play as the basis for a novel, he carried out what he had adumbrated in his notebooks. A dozen years later, in one of his outbursts of emotion in his notes, he spoke of *The Other House* as "a precedent, a support, a divine little light to walk by." He went on to write *What Maisie Knew, The Turn of the Screw, In the Cage* with an ever more rigorous application of the scenario principle and the scenic structure resulting therefrom, until in *The Awkward Age* (1899) he set down an entire novel in dialogue—one scene for each of his personages and each scene illuminating the central situation. He described it as "all dramatic and scenic" and explained it as "presented episodes, architecturally combined and each making a piece of the building, with no going behind, no *telling about* the figures save by their own appearance and action. . . ." The image James used in his preface to this work was that of a series of lamps disposed around a central subject "the function of each of which would be to light with all due intensity one of its aspects."

Readers of Henry James's prefaces will recall how often he describes the manner in which a subject appealed to him, and how in each case he heard the inner voice say, "Dramatize, dramatize!" It is true that he had "dramatized" long before the dramatic years. But it was only after these years that he applied the scenic method with complete and conscious consistency. In the preface to *What Maisie Knew* he acknowledges the "inveterate instinct" with which his stories "keep conforming to the 'scenic' law" and he adds, "Going over the pages here placed together has been for me . . . quite to watch the scenic system at play. The treatment by 'scene' regularly, quite rhythmically recurs. . . ." He speaks elsewhere of the "charm of the scenic consistency," of "those scenic conditions which are as near an approach to the dramatic as the novel may permit itself," of "the blest operation . . . of my Dramatic principle, my law of successive Aspects. . . ."

Time and time again, seeking to reassure himself, he wondered whether the dramatic effort had really been worthwhile. With the passage of years the conviction grew that it had been his salvation. One day in 1895, when the hurt was still great, he wrote: "Is the beauty of all that effort—of all those unutterable hours—lost forever? Lost, lost, lost? It will take a greater patience than the others to see!" A moment before he had written, "How a click of perception . . . brings back to me all the strange sacred time of my thinking-out, this way, pen in hand, of the stuff of my little theatrical trials. The old patiences and intensities—the working of the old passion. The old problems and dimnesses— the old solutions and little findings of light. . . ."

Six years later, when he was launched in the writing of his three final novels, he set down in his notebook the germ for a story (May 23, 1901) and added: "How, after a long intermission, the charm of this little subject-noting . . . glimmers out to me again—lighting up for me something of the old divine light, rekindling the little old sacred possibilities, renewing the little link with the old sacred days. Oh, sacred days that are still somehow *there*—that it would be the golden gift and miracle, today, still to find *not* wasted!"

Eight years later he comes back to this again:

> A sense with me, divine and beautiful, of hooking on again to the 'sacred years' of the old D[e] V[ere] Gardens time, the years of the whole theatric dream and the 'working out' sessions, all ineffable and uneffaceable, that went with that, and that still live again, somehow (indeed I *know* how!) in their ashes. . . .

In retrospect the aches and pains and harsh struggles of the dramatic years slipped away and what remained was the beneficent memory of the positive good acquired in writing scenarios for his plays and working out, step by step, scene, character, action. For Henry James, the years devoted to the plays were always to be—since he now applied to the full the knowledge and method they gave him—the "strange sacred time" that had yielded the secret of "the sacred mystery of structure," the "old sacred days"—and finally "the sacred years."

THE "TRADE" RESUMED

The later—the final—phase of Henry James's dramatic work occurred toward the end of his life and was a much less disturbing episode than the struggle of the 1890's. It had none of the earlier desperation; there was now no fluttering rise and fall of hope, no sense of being engaged in a life-and-death conflict. This time he was neither besieging the theatre nor besieged by it. He was older, less sanguine of success. Opportunity came his way to write some plays. He embraced it.

Nevertheless, the circumstances which caused him to take this last fling at a form he had so firmly renounced were not unlike those which originally contributed to his dramatic years. Panic had seized him then, when he discovered his literary fortunes were waning, and a compulsive need to assert himself in the world had pushed him into his theatrical adventures. Now the pattern recurred. After the turn of the century, Henry James had revisited the United States following a twenty-year absence. He had been feted, interviewed, lionized; he lectured on Balzac and the American Speech to large audiences; the sales of his books increased. With such circumstances to aid, self-confidence, induced by the universal respect and appreciation he commanded, mounted, and James signed a contract with Scribner's for the publication of an edition of his collected novels and tales. Since an all-inclusive edition would have run to more than forty volumes, it was decided that James should define the limits of his work, selecting only such fiction as he considered to possess "definitive" value. It was agreed that the edition would run to twenty-three volumes—perhaps because Balzac's *Édition Définitive* had that number—but it overflowed into a twenty-fourth. James grouped his tales after the manner of Balzac, according to theme and subject, and wrote a series of analytical and autobiographical prefaces. He revised large segments of his early work and rewrote passages in others, determined to have the edition speak for the mature artist rather than his younger self. It was as if he were rewriting his life. He labored for three years over his edition and, when it had been completed and was appearing volume after volume, he learned that it was having an extremely limited sale. He had offered the world his lifetime of work, or what he deemed to be the quintessential portion of it, only to discover once again, and for the last time, that he remained unread. The "trauma" of *Guy Domville* was repeated here, in attenuated form.

He was in a mood, therefore, to be receptive to the overtures now made to him by the theatre. In 1907, at the request of Johnston Forbes-Robertson, Henry James converted *Covering End*—originally the one-act *Summersoft*—into the three-act *High Bid*. The play was given for a series of matinees and received warm praise in the press. The British theatre, now seeing in the novelist a potential playwright, came knocking at his door. Sir James Barrie urged Charles Frohman to include a James play in a repertory season Frohman was planning at the Duke of York's Theatre and the novelist was, in due course, asked (along with Shaw and Galsworthy) to contribute a work. There came also to Henry James the Anglo-Irish poet-scholar, Herbert Trench, asking for a play for his new repertory theatre at the Haymarket. It took very little to persuade James that perhaps this time the British theatre was ready for him.

There was every reason for thinking so. The dozen years that had elapsed since *Guy Domville* had witnessed a series of far-reaching changes: Ibsen had blown away the cobwebs of the Victorian stage, his cause by now had been fought and won. Oscar Wilde had brought wit back to the stage and Bernard Shaw had added ideas to the wit. Audiences which had formerly come to the theatre to be entertained now came to be stimulated intellectually as well. Arthur Pinero and Henry Arthur Jones had demonstrated that the British public was willing to see "serious" drama and Harley Granville-Barker had shown as actor, playwright, producer and manager that the stage could advantageously embrace both art and scholarship and attract a wide public. The British theatre still lacked many things and was far from satisfying the fastidious Henry James, but an encouraging trend had set in. The novelist, despite his prolonged absences from London, had maintained a constant interest in the theatre. On his occasional trips to the city from his Sussex retreat, he invariably took in a play or two, often, in later years with a dashing young man-about-town, a handsome relative of Lady Gregory, Jocelyn Persse, who was very much in the social world from which James had withdrawn. His letters to Persse between 1905 and 1909 discuss dates to see such plays as *Man and Superman, Major Barbara, The Doctor's Dilemma, Lady Windermere's Fan,* Granville-Barker's *The Voysey Inheritance* and others.

James settled down through 1908 and 1909 to write plays again even while he was dictating his final prefaces and correcting final proof for the Definitive Edition. He had begun to dictate his work during 1896 and by now was addicted to his "remingtonese." His plays, however, were drafted by hand, and dictated from the draft. What is striking in this second phase is his choice of subject when compared with the themes of the dramatic years. With the exception of *The American,* which had been a novel, and *Guy Domville,* which treated a psychological conflict, he had sought largely to be entertaining on a superficial level. The plays of the second phase are impregnated with the spirit of the new drama; they are topical, touched lightly at moments with what we would now call "social consciousness," as if James were making a bid for the audiences of Shaw, Galsworthy and Granville-Barker. There is substance in the comedy of *The High Bid* with its young reforming "passionate, pledged Radical" hero, and this is true of the "highly contemporaneous" *Outcry* written for Frohman. His one-act *The Saloon* dramatizes the problems of a young conscientious objector, a thoroughly Shavian theme (which led to a pointed exchange of letters with Shaw, now published for the first time).

The Other House, the drama written for Trench, is a psychological "shocker" that at the same time has in it all the qualities of an Ibsen play and a heroine derived from *Hedda Gabler* or *Rosmersholm.* He also resumed work on his abandoned plan for the dramatization of his short story *The Chaperon,* which, had he completed it, would have yielded an ironic social satire. Thus it can be said that in the second dramatic phase James approached the theatre with a larger sense of its realities and with a genuine desire to treat material he deemed pertinent to the times.

Of the plays written during these two years only *The High Bid* and *The Saloon* were produced and the worries over the plays, combined with the shock over the failure of the Definitive Edition, together with a growing morbid fear that he was suffering from a heart ailment—of which his doctor in Harley Street could find no sign—brought on a nervous illness and deep depression. In the 1890's he had escaped physical illness by writing out his fears and anxieties in a series of play-like novels, ghostly tales and autobiographical stories. Now, however, he was old and tired, unable to meet the challenge of public neglect. Only the rude shock of the much more serious illness of his older brother diverted attention from his own troubled state of mind. He journeyed with William James to Bad Nauheim for the "cure," and then crossed the Atlantic with him to Chocorua in New Hampshire. His play-production plans collapsed abruptly before his departure from England; he had no heart for them now in any event. William's death in August 1910 plunged him into deep mourning, but at the same time shattered the spell of self-absorption, and opened avenues for memory of family history that set him to the writing of reminiscences during the next four years. After that was to come the greatest shock of all—1914.

TERMINATIONS

And thus it was that in the early morning hours of January 4, 1910, in scrawling the notes that ultimately shaped themselves into *The Ivory Tower,* Henry James set down those words which were our point of departure and which also constitute our termination . . .

> I come back yet again and again, to my only seeing it in the dramatic way
> —as I can only see everything and anything now. . . .

The closer he got to his "dramatic way" he told himself—by which he meant the method of the scenario and the application of the scenic method—"the closer I get to the problem of the application of it in any particular case, the more I get *into* that application, so the more doubts and torments fall away from me, the more I know where I am, the more everything spreads and shines and draws me on and I'm justified of my logic and my passion. . . ."

> *Causons, causons, mon bon*—oh celestial, soothing, sanctifying process, with all the high sane forces of the sacred time fighting, through it, on my side! Let me fumble it gently and patiently out—with fever and fidget laid to rest—

as in all the old enchanted months! It only looms, it only shines and shimmers, *too* beautiful and too interesting; it only hangs there too rich and too full and with too much to give and to pay; it only presents itself too admirably and too vividly, too straight and square and vivid, as a little organic and effective Action.

Celestial, soothing, sanctifying process! The dramatic years—the sacred years —had yielded their full harvest, and not so much in the plays (although twelve plays was as substantial a number as any playwright might produce in a lifetime) as in the consequences for his fiction arising from their creation. It would be inaccurate to dismiss the plays themselves as having served only as a school of experience for the final works, the so-called "major phase." So qualified an authority as Bernard Shaw has described the earlier plays as stageworthy, while rejecting the later works as cast in a dialogue "inhumanly literary"; while, on the other hand, the equally authoritative Granville-Barker considered the later works, particularly *The Outcry*, to be as manageable as a Restoration play or a play of Chekhov's. *Guy Domville,* during its brief existence, was praised alike for its cadenced dialogue and for the human situation it dramatized. Most critics have recognized the high dramatic qualities residing in the plays, as indeed in all the work, of James.

These plays are thus more than literary curiosities. They must be read in the light of the theatre for which they were written and the audience for which they were intended, as well as in the context of Henry James's creative life. They can be read—some of them—for intrinsic merit, for some of their scenes of high comedy, for the drollery or depth of the characterizations, for the intensity of the drama. They represent, in especial for students of the dramatic form, a picture of a highly-cultivated mind at grips with the problem of reproducing life within the proscenium-frame and, as James so often put it, in a civilization in which stage plays must be produced between dinner and the suburban trains. Above all they are part of a very human and a very touching story—that of a writer stumbling and searching, with obstinate passion, to win success on the stage and then, after a series of painful defeats due in large measure to an inability to face the realities of the theatre, wresting from his failures a final and a major victory, finding in the scenic method the salvation that enabled him to pursue his art and arrive at those discoveries which mark him out as one of the great architects of the modern novel.

LEON EDEL

Pyramus and Thisbe
1869

EDITOR'S FOREWORD

Henry James had been writing criticism and short stories for five years when *Pyramus and Thisbe*—his first dramatic composition to be printed—appeared in the April 1869 issue of the *Galaxy*. The future novelist was twenty-six and had left the United States a few weeks earlier on his first adult voyage to Europe. When the piece appeared he was in London, in Half Moon Street, engaged in the "alluring and beguiling" rediscovery of England he was later to record in his autobiographical fragment, *The Middle Years*. A letter from Cambridge, from his brother William, told him: *"Galaxy* got yesterday, and your thing reads very well. Better than when you read it to me. Father says, 'Harry has decidedly got a gift.'"

Aside from Henry James's long-standing interest in the drama and his determination to write plays some day, we have no way of knowing what prompted him to produce this little dialogue at this particular time. He has spoken of the year which immediately preceded his departure for Europe as containing "agitations, explorations, initiations," and *Pyramus and Thisbe* may well be characterized as an exploration.

He had spent the greater part of his early writing years in Cambridge and shortly before sailing had complained that he was bored by the lack of distraction and social life. His brother William had been abroad and he was eager himself to quit the parental roof and venture forth into the world. The boarding house picture evoked in this playlet is one we find elsewhere in his work. He was himself a veteran of the European *pension* and when he set his hero of *The Bostonians*, Basil Ransom, in New York it was in a similar house with the pleasant and distracting company of a fellow boarder, a variety actress. The title, *Pyramus and Thisbe,* fairly obviously, was derived not from James's reading of the classics but from the play within a play in *A Midsummer Night's Dream*. He had seen it many times and he was to draw upon it on other occasions.

PERSONS

STEPHEN YOUNG (thirty-three), *journalist*
CATHERINE WEST (twenty-six), *teacher of music*

PYRAMUS AND THISBE

MISS WEST'S *apartment; plainly but comfortably furnished; a few prints and photographs on the walls; a sofa, a piano. Enter* CATHERINE, *in walking-dress, with a roll of music in her hand.*

CATHERINE. Dear me! this dreadful smell of tobacco again! When it doesn't come in one way, it comes another; when it isn't the door it's the window. There he sits at his own window, puffing his great pipe. I saw him as I crossed the street. And the wind always our way. I'm always to windward of that pipe. What's a poor girl to do? (*Shuts her window with a loud crash.*) There! perhaps he'll hear that! What *am* I to do? I can't go to my lessons smelling like a bar-room; and certainly I can't ask my little girls to come and take their lessons in this blinding cloud of smoke. Pshaw! it's worse with the window shut than with it open. If I'm doomed to suffocate, I might as well do it comfortably. (*Raises the window violently.*) Of course he'll hear that, too. (*Taking off her bonnet at the mirror.*) Heigho! what a dreadful humor I'm in! And on my birthday, too! Well, why shouldn't one be out of sorts on one's birthday as well as at any other time? Is it such a mighty privilege to have been born? Is life so easy and pleasant that I must make it a courtesy whenever I meet it with its grim old stare on the threshold of another year? Another year! another year added to twenty-five makes—makes—upon my word it might as well make thirty at once—when you're so tired, tired, tired! That, by the way, is for not having gone to sleep till four o'clock in the morning—for having a neighbor who turns night into day, talks for the benefit of the whole town, and has a dozen intimate friends against whom he'll nightly measure his lungs on any topic in the range of human ken. It was actually as much as I could do to help throwing my slipper in good earnest against the wall. That would have been scandal, I suppose. But to lie tossing, and sighing, and listening to Mr. Young's interminable sentences—it was all one sentence, I declare, from nine o'clock until three—and to wake up on your birthday with a headache, and a pale face, and hollow eyes—that, of course, is perfect propriety. (*Still at the glass.*) Dear me! I've actually fretted and fumed a real bit of color into my face. (*Looking at her image in silence.*) Nay, I'm not thirty, after all! I've four good years of youth yet! And my hair is certainly very pretty, and life—life, on this soft spring evening—well, life, I do make you my very best courtesy, and if you'll promise to be very good I'll give you a little music. (*Seats herself at the piano and plays with violence. While she is playing the door opens and* STEPHEN YOUNG *looks in. Seeing* MISS WEST, *he advances a few steps—leaving the door ajar—and stops a moment looking at her and listening. He carries a small bouquet in his hand. Finally he speaks.*)

STEPHEN. Bravo! bravo!

CATHERINE. (*Starting up.*) You, Mr. Young!

STEPHEN. Excuse me. If it wasn't for my flowers I'd clap you.

CATHERINE. If it wasn't for your flowers, I'm afraid I should ask you to walk out. Pray, who let you in?

STEPHEN. I let myself in. I knocked three times, but you were playing with such extraordinary fury—

CATHERINE. (*Archly.*) Oh, you can make

yourself heard when you wish, Mr. Young!

STEPHEN. Now I verily believe that's a reproach.

CATHERINE. Of course it is.

STEPHEN. Ah, my dear Miss West, two can play at that game. In the way of noise there's not much, I fancy, to choose between us; there's six of one and—

CATHERINE. I'll admit that there are six of one, but certainly a dozen of the other—especially when there are two of you.

STEPHEN. Bless my stars! It's no more than fair. You have your piano—I have my friend.

CATHERINE. Your bass-drum, you might call him.

STEPHEN. I assure you, he's a very nice fellow.

CATHERINE. I hope, for your sake, he is—so long as he stays till three o'clock in the morning.

STEPHEN. Ah, poor Ellis! Do you mean you actually heard us?

CATHERINE. Distinctly. I came near throwing something at the wall.

STEPHEN. I doubt that we should have heard it, any more than you heard me just now.

CATHERINE. Happily for you, it never would have occurred to me to walk in in person.

STEPHEN. You would surely have been excusable if you had come on so harmless an errand as this of mine. (*Holds up his flowers.*)

CATHERINE. Your flowers are very pretty.

STEPHEN. They are none of mine. When I came in, a couple of hours ago, I found them in my room, on my table. You see they've lost their first freshness. Here is a little card affixed, denoting their proper destination, which the messenger seems, through some extraordinary inadvertence, to have overlooked; as if any one would send me flowers!

CATHERINE. (*Taking the bouquet and reading the card.*) "Miss West, with affectionate good wishes. A. T." I'm much obliged to you for repairing the error.

STEPHEN. I confess there *is* some virtue in it. To give a young lady a bouquet of your own making, or your own buying, is assuredly its own reward. But to serve as a mere bald go-between; to present a bunch of lilies and roses on the part of another—a mysterious unknown—to act, as it were, as the senseless clod of earth in which they're wrapped for transportation, and not as their thrilling, teeming, conscious parent soil, this, Miss West, I assure you, is to make a terrible sacrifice to vanity.

CATHERINE. I appreciate the sacrifice, and I repeat my thanks.

STEPHEN. I might have kept them, you know.

CATHERINE. (*Placing the flowers in water.*) Nay, it would have been a pity to spoil them.

STEPHEN. Spoil them? What do you mean?

CATHERINE. (*Taking the bouquet out of the water and presenting it to his nose.*) What should you call the prevailing odor?

STEPHEN. Geranium—heliotrope—jasmine, I should say.

CATHERINE. I see your sense is completely blunted.

STEPHEN. Why, what should you call it?

CATHERINE. (*Replacing the flowers.*) Tobacco, Mr. Young. Flowers are like women; they don't like you to smoke in their faces.

STEPHEN. Dear me! Do you really object to smoke?

CATHERINE. Object to it? I *hate* it!

STEPHEN. And do you ever perceive my pipe?

CATHERINE. Constantly, Mr. Young.

STEPHEN. Alas! what a terrible neighbor I am! I'm extremely sorry; but what can I do? I strongly suspect that I can't give up talking, and I'm profoundly convinced that I can't give up smoking.

CATHERINE. Don't for a moment suppose that I suggest any such abnegation. If I'm uncomfortable there's an easy remedy.

STEPHEN. Exactly. Patience, my dear Miss West, comes just short, in a woman's life, of being a transcendent virtue, only because, as you so truly say, it's so easy.

CATHERINE. You perfectly express my own sentiments. I regard patience as quite a secondary virtue. There's another that I prize infinitely higher.

STEPHEN. Oh, you go too far.

CATHERINE. I mean action, Mr. Young.

STEPHEN. The deuce! You mean to seek a

remedy in action?

CATHERINE. Oh, don't be frightened. I mean nothing very terrible. I mean that I can move away and take another lodging.

STEPHEN. Oh, that would never do. We must bear and forbear, Miss West. Without a few mutual concessions we shall find but little comfort in life.

CATHERINE. That's doubtless very true, Mr. Young; but, really, are you quite the person to say it?

STEPHEN. Why, if it's the truth, I certainly can't afford to let it pass.

CATHERINE. Well, if it's not impertinent, I should like to know to whom your own concessions are made.

STEPHEN. Oh, to every one.

CATHERINE. They say that every one is no one.

STEPHEN. By no means. It includes, to begin with, my very next neighbor—yourself.

CATHERINE. (*Laughing.*) Truly? I'm actually the object of your generosity? Your charity, I might call it, since it begins so near home. I confess I never suspected it.

STEPHEN. Well, Miss West, the fact is—

CATHERINE. Alas! what *can* the fact be?

STEPHEN. I hate music.

CATHERINE. You hate music! (*Laughing violently.*)

STEPHEN. (*Provoked.*) I absolutely detest it.

CATHERINE. Poor Mr. Young! Well—I pity you.

STEPHEN. You would pity me if you knew what I have suffered.

CATHERINE. From my piano?

STEPHEN. From your piano.

CATHERINE. (*After a pause.*) Decidedly, one of us must move.

STEPHEN. One of us? Good; here comes a chance for concession.

CATHERINE. I said just now that I should go.

STEPHEN. That was à *propos* of your own sufferings.

CATHERINE. Well, in spite of yours, I still think I had better go.

STEPHEN. I oughtn't to consent to it.

CATHERINE. (*Laughing.*) So you detest music, Mr. Young? I don't know why I should laugh; I feel much more like cry-

ing. It's too provoking. I protest I don't understand it. I don't see what such people are made of.

STEPHEN. Of good flesh and blood, Miss West—

CATHERINE. Yes, and not much else.

STEPHEN. In that case, then, they have no tempers to lose. But what call under heaven have I to enjoy the strumming of a piano? I make my bread, you know, by scribbling for the newspapers. Every morning, as I sit down to my table you sit down to that tuneful battery. The very first rattle of the keys is like a scathing fusillade, under which my poor old ideas —maimed and tattered veterans—fall prostrate to the ground. I pick them up and dress their wounds, and coax them once more to the front. The battle rages generally some three or four hours. I deem myself very lucky if, at the end of that time, a small fraction of my little army have escaped with their lives. Once in awhile, in the afternoon, when the fire has subsided, one of the missing turns up, and comes limping back to camp. But, I confess, the whole temper of the service is so utterly demoralized that, instead of being shot for an arrant deserter, the rascal is welcomed like a prodigal son, and the calf that was being so tenderly fatted for the whole regiment is sacrificed to this poor makeshift of a hero.

CATHERINE. The meaning of all this is that you can't write except in absolute silence.

STEPHEN. Why, there's something between absolute silence and—absolute sound.

CATHERINE. I should like to see some of your writing.

STEPHEN. It's very kind of you to say so, after my attack on your music.

CATHERINE. Oh, you make it out to be so bad that I speak from curiosity.

STEPHEN. At any rate it would not be very pleasant for you to reflect that it's your own fault that it's no better.

CATHERINE. Whose fault is it, Mr. Young, that you're no wiser?

STEPHEN. Well, I'm as heaven made me; we're all of us that; and heaven made me, as I say, to hate a piano.

CATHERINE. (*Out of patience.*) Oh, it's my opinion that heaven didn't make you at all! Upon my word, you deserve that I should sit here forever and thump out music from morning till night.

STEPHEN. Is that a threat?

CATHERINE. Take it as you please.

STEPHEN. I take it as a declaration of war; of course in that case I shall choose my own arms. I shall forthwith lay siege to your comfort.

CATHERINE. Oh, my comfort's gone in advance. What comfort shall I have in playing for your annoyance, when I think that I might be playing for my own pleasure? But my revenge will remain.

STEPHEN. Heaven help us, it will be a hard fight.

CATHERINE. Another Waterloo, I assure you. Within a fortnight I shall look for your retreat.

STEPHEN. Oh, I shan't give you more than a week.

CATHERINE. I must make the most of time, then! Quick, to your own lines. I mean to open fire. (*She runs to the piano, seats herself, and begins to play furiously. STEPHEN claps his hands to his ears and hurries out. CATHERINE continues to play for several moments, and then in the midst of a movement suddenly stops short.*) I wonder whether my playing really disturbs him, or whether he invented it all in return for my complaint of his talking and smoking—surely it wasn't the best taste in the world for me to mention those foolish little troubles. If they are a real annoyance, all I have to do is to hold my tongue and change my quarters. I certainly have no right to ask favors of Mr. Young, and I should be very sorry to find myself in his debt. (*Leaving the piano.*) I'll just quietly move away; I can easily find a better room. This one has a dozen inconveniences; it's out of the way, and it's up too high. And yet I'm attached to the old place. When you've occupied a room for five years you seem to have made over a portion of your innermost self to its keeping. It knows you so well; it has all your secrets, and there's no getting them back either; if you go away you leave them for others. I feel as if I had grown up between these four walls.

Here I came after my mother died; here I've learned to know myself, and, thinking over my day's adventures every evening, to know, as far as I do know it, the world; here I've tasted both the bitterness and the sweetness of solitude—all the more reason, by the way, for my not resenting poor Mr. Young's proximity. What on earth has got into me? I came in from the street with my senses thrilling with the whispery and perfumes of spring; I cross the threshold and happen to catch a whiff of my neighbor's cigar—a puff of harmless incense to the season—and straightway I fall into a passion. Decidedly, I've made a fool of myself, and to save my dignity I must decamp. As for this dingy old chamber, I hate it. I shall go and begin life afresh somewhere else. I wonder what Mr. Young means to do? What *can* he do? I'm curious to see. If he really suffers from my piano, I have the advantage. It's not his fault, after all, if he objects to music. But it's such an odd turn of mind. It's really pleasanter though, under the circumstances, than if he happened to have a passion for it. When I play, I feel, I think, I talk, I express my moods, my fancies, my regrets, my desires. I can imagine nothing more disagreeable than to know that some totally superfluous little gentleman may be sitting behind that partition, deciphering my notes and very possibly enjoying them—that I am treating his worship, in short, to a perpetual serenade! I'm spared that annoyance, at any rate! And yet—and yet—and yet I confess that there would be a harmless sweetness in having, once in a while, some other auditor than Susie, and Jennie, and Josie. But what's this? (*Going to the table.*) How came it here? (*Takes up a small parcel.*) "Stephen Young, Esq." He can't have left it here; he brought in nothing but the flowers. Pah! it's his everlasting tobacco. I must get rid of it without loss of time. (*Goes to her door and calls into the entry.*) Mr. Young. (*A pause.*) Mr. Young!

STEPHEN. (*Without.*) At your service, madam! (*CATHERINE returns and replaces the package on the table; STEPHEN reappears with an open letter in his hand.*) No proposals for a compromise, I hope!

CATHERINE. (*Pointing to the package.*) Be so good as to possess yourself of your own property. How it came here I'm at loss to say.

STEPHEN. Why, it's evident; your flowers and my tobacco arrived together. The young woman who brought them up committed the pardonable error of giving you my parcel, and me yours.

CATHERINE. Pardonable! It's easy for you to say.

STEPHEN. Perfectly so, inasmuch as it has given me a pretext for another visit.

CATHERINE. You're reading a letter. I'm sorry to have interrupted you.

STEPHEN. The interruption is most *à propos*. The letter concerns us both. It's like King and Emperor in the middle ages. They prepare with a great flourish and rumpus to knock each other's heads off, when up comes the Pope and knocks off their crowns, without which, of course, their heads are worthless. This letter is the Pope's bull.

CATHERINE. What on earth do you mean?

STEPHEN. Our good landlord is the Pope. May I request your attention for five minutes? This morning, as I went out, I deposited below the amount of my monthly bill, which had been some days due. This answer has just been put into my hands. (*Reads.*) "My dear Mr. Young, I return your bill receipted, with thanks. I take this occasion to make a communication which I have been for some time contemplating, and which it is important you should receive without further delay. I have just sold my house to a party who proposes to convert the ground-floor into a store, and the upper portion into offices, and who will therefore be unable to retain any of my present lodgers. As I have granted immediate occupation I shall be able to allow them to continue or to renew their present leases only to three weeks from this date; namely, to the fifth of May. I have little doubt but that in this interval, my rooms all being let singly, they will find other quarters. I shall immediately advise them to this effect. Yours, etc." What do you think of that?

CATHERINE. Think, Mr. Young? Why, it's horrible, monstrous!

STEPHEN. Man proposes, but landlords dispose. I'm very much afraid we shall have to make peace, in spite of ourselves.

CATHERINE. Peace? Oh, I shall know nothing of peace until I find another resting place. It's very hard to have to leave this old room.

STEPHEN. I had no idea you were so fond of it.

CATHERINE. I beg you to believe that I am fond of it. It's very unreasonable, but when was there any reason in fondness? The room is intensely disagreeable, but, nevertheless, I like it, and I don't choose to be swept out like old rubbish in a house-cleaning.

STEPHEN. The room in itself, or rather, perhaps, in something that isn't exactly itself, is charming. If you were only to see mine!

CATHERINE. For a man, it's different. You have only to stuff a few clothes into a valise and to take it in your hand and march off in search of fortune.

STEPHEN. You put it rather strong, perhaps—the independence of men. Nevertheless, I confess that, compared with you, I can transplant myself with but little trouble. I have no piano, no sofa, no pictures, no curtains, no little work-tables, or other gimcracks.

CATHERINE. I declare, I could sit down and cry. (*Seats herself.*)

STEPHEN. Oh, come, don't say that, or I shall begin to entertain feelings with regard to our wronger which, if they insist upon being expressed, may subject me to the penalties of the law. Perhaps I'd better not have read you the letter.

CATHERINE. It was as well to hear it from you as from that—that wretch!

STEPHEN. To-morrow, probably, he'll give you warning.

CATHERINE. I shall have gained a day, at any rate, or lost one; I hardly know which.

STEPHEN. How, lost one?

CATHERINE. Well, if you wish particularly to know, to-day is my birthday.

STEPHEN. Ah, yes. Well?

CATHERINE. Well, that's all.

STEPHEN. Ah, I see, and I've spoiled it by that detestable piece of news.

CATHERINE. Oh, there was little enough

to spoil, after all.

STEPHEN. (*After a pause.*) Ah, so to-day's your birthday!

CATHERINE. Dear me, it's a nice time to talk about birthdays.

STEPHEN. That accounts, of course, for those flowers.

CATHERINE. Exactly; if there is any need to account for them.

STEPHEN. I might have guessed at something of the sort.

CATHERINE. Something of the sort! You're not very polite. How many anniversaries do you think I keep?

STEPHEN. Upon my word, if I had known this was your birthday I wouldn't have read you that letter.

CATHERINE. The letter was better than nothing. Besides, it is a rule that my birthdays should be the grimmest possible reminders of mortality. Last year I was laid up with a sick headache; the year before I lost my best pupil, who dismissed me in a polite little note; the year before my chimney caught fire—this very chimney. It was a late cold spring, you remember; we had fires into June; I was sitting here alone; I heaped on the coal, for company's sake. In half an hour, I assure you, I had company enough—the landlord, all the lodgers, a dozen firemen, and three or four policemen. That was before you came.

STEPHEN. Why, you've been through everything in this little room. What was it the year before that?

CATHERINE. That year I had no birthday. My mother died. After that, I came here.

STEPHEN. That was three [1] years ago. You must have been lonely.

CATHERINE. At first I was lonely, indeed. Then I began to get lessons, and I had no time. Only sometimes in the evening I missed a few old associations; and now I have got used to it.

STEPHEN. There's nothing you miss, then?

CATHERINE. Nothing—nothing, at least, that I have ever had.

---

[1] In an apparent slip of memory James here changes Catherine's period of residence in this room from five years to three. (*See* page 78 above "When you've occupied a room for five years . . . ")

STEPHEN. You're contented, then. I'll be hanged if I am! O happy woman!

CATHERINE. O stupid man! There's a difference between missing the past and longing for the future. We get used to being without the things that have passed away; we never get used to being without the things that have not yet come; we end by ceasing to think of those; we never cease to think of these; and, as regards them at least, we are never contented.

STEPHEN. Why, you're quite a philosopher! (*Hesitates a moment and then seats himself.*)

CATHERINE. (*Rising.*) You'll admit that I need to be a philosopher with such a landlord! (*Moves out a small table, takes a cloth from the drawer and lays it.*)

STEPHEN. What are you going to do now?

CATHERINE. I'm going, by your leave, to have my tea.

STEPHEN. Ah, yes, by all means; even a philosopher must eat. Do you actually make your tea this way every evening?

CATHERINE. (*Smiling.*) Actually. Tea isn't a thing one has by fits and starts.

STEPHEN. It's something I never have at all. I dine at six, at an eating-house, where I take a cup of very bad coffee. But I haven't really sat down to tea since—since I was young.

CATHERINE. I dine at half-past two, at a school where I give lessons. After running about all the afternoon, of course by this hour I'm quite ready for this little ceremony. It's very pleasant to be able at last to have tea by daylight.

STEPHEN. So I suppose; just as it's disagreeable not to be able to dine by lamp-light.

CATHERINE. Ah, me! to dine by lamp-light is the dream of my life; but I suppose I shall never do it till I'm old and rich.

STEPHEN. As the days grow longer I put off my dinner. In fact, I haven't dined yet.

CATHERINE. (*Laughing.*) Good heaven! what a life! (*During the above, she has been passing to and fro between the cupboard and the table, setting out the articles necessary for tea. Among other things, she has placed a small kettle, and kindled the lamp beneath it.*)

STEPHEN. It's certain that at my eating-house they don't give me a tablecloth like that.

CATHERINE. I suppose they make it up by other things. Ah, there's a little hole in the middle!

STEPHEN. The great Goethe has wisely remarked that man loves freedom and woman order.

CATHERINE. I'll cover it up with my bouquet. (*Places the vase of flowers.*) What do you say about Goethe?

STEPHEN. I knew you were going to do something with those flowers.

CATHERINE. It was knowledge easily gained. Don't look at the kettle, now, or it won't boil.

STEPHEN. Of course I'll not look at the kettle when I can look at you. What are you going to have for tea?

CATHERINE. Nothing to speak of; bread and butter. There's at least an hour of daylight left; if you are very hungry, you are welcome to share of my loaf, *en attendant* your dinner.

STEPHEN. Oh, I'm terribly hungry.

CATHERINE. Dear me, if it's as bad as that you'd better go at once to your eating-house. Stay; do you like sardines?

STEPHEN. Particularly.

CATHERINE. And guava jelly?

STEPHEN. Extravagantly.

CATHERINE. Well, then, perhaps we can blunt the edge of your voracity. (*Returns to the cupboard and takes out a box of sardines and a pot of guava jelly.*)

STEPHEN. Ah, the kettle boils.

CATHERINE. (*Setting down the above.*) Be so good, then, as to move your chair up to the table. Luckily, I have things for two. (*Lays cup and saucer, plate, etc.*)

STEPHEN. I suppose that once in a while you have a visitor.

CATHERINE. (*Seated.*) No one but the cat. You must excuse it, but that's the cat's saucer. Frequently, in the evening, she comes up to drink tea with me. I make her a dish of it just as I do for myself, and she sips it up like a perfect lady. When I move I must have a cat of my own. I shall feel so much more complete.

STEPHEN. Good heaven! if that's all you need to feel complete—

CATHERINE. How do you like your tea?

STEPHEN. Strong, please—as strong as Samson unshorn.

CATHERINE. You mean by that, I suppose, that you want neither cream nor sugar?

STEPHEN. Cream and sugar are the wiles of Delilah.

CATHERINE. I must say, then, that Delilah is a much-abused person.

STEPHEN. It's no more than natural that you should stand up for her. You yourself, Miss West—

CATHERINE. Very well—I myself— (*Laughing.*) I declare I believe you want me to compare you to Samson. But, I assure you, my respect for the sacred legends of Scripture forbids me to do it.

STEPHEN. Don't laugh at me now, or I shall pull down the roof on your head.

CATHERINE. *À propos* of pulling down roofs, our charming landlord is the man to claim the title. Oh, to think of it!

STEPHEN. I protest; I stick to my idea. Delilah was, of course, a very charming woman. To begin with, you and she have that in common.

CATHERINE. Granted. Pursue your argument.

STEPHEN. Well, the long and short of it is that you, being, as I say, a charming woman, here I sit breaking your bread and drinking your tea, as if we were the best friends in the world.

CATHERINE. I must say that you're a very weak Samson. I've treated you with no more than common decency. I couldn't do less than ask you to have a cup of tea.

STEPHEN. No, thank heaven, that you couldn't; but, you know, we had so fiercely resolved, in our future intercourse, to violate the commonest civilities; and then I hated you so!

CATHERINE. From the moment that a term was so suddenly set to our acquaintance, it seemed a great relief to throw those troublesome resolutions overboard. I call them troublesome, for I assure you I felt none of the inspiration of hatred.

STEPHEN. Really, then, I hardly know whether your implacable attitude was the more or the less to your credit.

CATHERINE. Implacable? You use hard words; not that I admit, however, that I was not quite right.

STEPHEN. Oh, it was very becoming. Of course you felt no sordid human passion. You figured simply your divine protectress—the canonized Muse—outraged, insulted, discredited; but cold, relentless and dispassionate. I confess that I felt a good earthly spite.

CATHERINE. I forgive you. Your cause needed it. After all, this new turn of events has saved us some confusion.

STEPHEN. One of us, certainly.

CATHERINE. Well, one of us, if you will. There could have been no graceful termination to our quarrel. And so farewell to the whole business.

STEPHEN. Farewell! You pronounce the word with singular unction.

CATHERINE. I know but one way of pronouncing it.

STEPHEN. Well, I wish you a better neighbor next time; some unappreciated Mozart, some undeveloped Rossini.

CATHERINE. I'm much obliged to you for your wishes, but my own are very different. I had rather have no neighbor at all. It's much simpler.

STEPHEN. I'm quite of your mind. So long as contiguity subsists the parties are bitter enemies, and when they come to part they find suddenly that they are great friends. If I could afford it, I should go and take a house and occupy it alone. Failing that, I don't know what's left for me but to perch like St. Simeon on the summit of some lonely column.

CATHERINE. I shall go to work to-morrow, and if I don't find a lodging before the sun goes down, I shall consent to pass for a very silly creature. I shall not stay here a moment longer than I can help.

STEPHEN. I applaud your spirit. I shall do as much. We can perhaps be of some assistance to each other. I shall doubtless see a number of apartments that are far too nice for such as me. I will note them down and hand you the list. You, on the other hand, will see a great many that you could never think of occupying; you can give me a hint of their whereabouts.

CATHERINE. I had no idea there was that vast difference in our needs.

STEPHEN. Ah, nothing is too nice for you, Miss West.

CATHERINE. Come, you're extravagant.

STEPHEN. And nothing too rough, too dingy, too common for me.

CATHERINE. Oh, do favor me with a reason for this wild antithesis!

STEPHEN. Why, you see, during this half hour that I've been spending in your room, I've gradually become penetrated with the spirit of the place—the simple elegance, the unerring good taste that lurks in the disposition of every little ornament, in every fold of drapery. There isn't a thing—down to the very piano—that I don't profoundly respect.

CATHERINE. Upon my word, Mr. Young, you have a brilliant imagination.

STEPHEN. You wouldn't say so if you were to see the musty, dusty, absolutely naked little hole on the other side of that wall, in which I spend my days and nights. In the middle, a rickety table, with a book under one foot to keep it steady, littered with the direst confusion of dust-covered books and papers, and literally constellated with an infinite diversity of ink blots. A row of bookshelves, with the books thrust in any way but the right way; a cane-seated armchair, a stuffed ditto, a stove, a bed, a washstand, a trunk, a window, four walls, a ceiling and a floor. There you have a complete inventory; that is, it would be complete if I could represent, by any form of words, the lonely, grimy, dingy, late-of-a-November-afternoon expression of the whole place!

CATHERINE. You have what you need, I suppose. Men's and women's requirements are different. Women, even the most inveterate gad-a-bouts, are essentially stay-at-home creatures. Even wretched, shiftless peripatetics like myself cherish a secret ideal of domesticity. I may tramp about half the day, from house to house, but I like to think that I have a little sanctuary at home where I may hang up a few votive knick-knacks to the household gods. This little room is the home of my fancy; it wants no wider field; it calls its guests sometimes from a distance, but it never goes beyond the threshold to meet them. With you it's quite another matter. A man living alone, as you do, can't make a home; he can't live in his shell; he has only one foot at his fireside, the other is in the world.

STEPHEN. One foot here—one foot a mile off! You'll admit that it's a deucedly uncomfortable position.

CATHERINE. (Laughing.) I don't pretend to deny it. Nevertheless, I declare I mortally despise a man whose conversation is forever stretched, as they say, on four pins; who has all his little properties neatly brushed and ticketed and classified. There's nothing I admire so much as a certain generous disorder!

STEPHEN. Heavenly power! If you only knew me how much you would admire me! It's a very happy arrangement, by the way, this exquisite human faculty of admiration. How it amplifies the soul!—how it doubles one's existence! Personally, as you say—as I see for myself—you're the very patron saint of neatness and elegance; you make cleanliness picturesque; you make symmetry natural. And yet, seated in the midst of your native paradise, you bestow an approving smile on the dreary chaos of my unblessed existence. And so, on my side, from the depths of that chaos, I gaze in wonder and worship on the unforced harmony, the tranquil comfort which you shed upon your pathway, and which encircles you with a gentle radiance like that of some wholesome daylight saint.

CATHERINE. It's very strange that precisely those qualities which are most natural to us, and which from long usage have lost every vestige of mystery and charm, and have become as flat and cold as the muffins of this morning's breakfast, should be the very points of attraction to the minds of others, and appear to them as bright and blooming as untrodden islands. Ah, Mr. Young, I'm dismally prosaic, if you only knew me.

STEPHEN. I have a passion for good prose. I've swallowed in my time an amount of indifferent verse!

CATHERINE. I declare I'm quite tired of myself and my lonely, fussy little virtues. Do knock over something and break it, Mr. Young!

STEPHEN. Willingly; if on my side I could only bespeak the touch of those helping, healing hands!

CATHERINE. (Rising.) By the way, it's one of my virtues not to leave my table standing a moment after I've had my tea. If you'll be so good as to rise.

STEPHEN. (Rising.) Give me that vase of flowers and I'll break it.

CATHERINE. Gladly, it's very ugly. (Takes out the bouquet and offers the vase.)

STEPHEN. Oh, I mean the flowers themselves.

CATHERINE. Ah, barbarian! is that the way you understand me?

STEPHEN. Now don't tell me I've made a great mistake.

CATHERINE. It certainly is a mistake to suppose that a woman will ever submit to see flowers wantonly destroyed—unless when, for some good reason, she destroys them herself.

STEPHEN. There's an excellent reason why you should do me a favor.

CATHERINE. What is the favor, pray?

STEPHEN. Throw that bouquet out of the window.

CATHERINE. Dear me! is that all? And what is the reason?

STEPHEN. That I particularly desire it.

CATHERINE. They are quite worthy of each other. The favor must be less, Mr. Young, or the reason greater.

STEPHEN. Tell me, then, who sent you the bouquet?

CATHERINE. The request is peremptory, but I'll satisfy you! Hem! a very dear young friend.

STEPHEN. Do you call that satisfying me?

CATHERINE. Upon my word, you're very exacting.

STEPHEN. And you, Miss West, are very exasperating!

CATHERINE. Good, so our quarrel is open again!

STEPHEN. (Very serious.) I assure you, as far as I'm concerned, it has never been closed.

CATHERINE. Just as you please. I have no time for such trifles now. I have a heavy care on my mind and a long day's work on my hands.

STEPHEN. (With energy.) By Heaven! I could positively howl when I hear you talk so.

CATHERINE. My talk, it seems to me, is

quite as reasonable as yours.

STEPHEN. Doubtless, and your feelings even more so.

CATHERINE. Farewell, Mr. Young.

STEPHEN. (*After a pause, looking at her.*) You said just now that there is but one way of pronouncing that word. I confess I don't know it.

CATHERINE. Very well, I excuse you.

STEPHEN. The best way is not to try it; I'm sure I should break down. In the name of pity, don't you understand me?

CATHERINE. Not in the least. In one word, are we friends or enemies?

STEPHEN. I wish to heaven I could say we were neither.

CATHERINE. Come, Mr. Young, you're foolish.

STEPHEN. Desperately so, I'm a lover.

CATHERINE. Oh, oh!

STEPHEN. Of course, you don't believe it.

CATHERINE. Of course? (*A pause.*) Excuse me, you're no lover.

STEPHEN. Of course you do, then.

CATHERINE. Worse and worse.

STEPHEN. Confound it! Perhaps you do, perhaps you don't!

CATHERINE. (*After a pause.*) Perhaps I do. You'll excuse me if I'm not perfectly sure. The events of the last hour—

STEPHEN. The events of the last hour, believe me, are proof conclusive of my passion. I've known for the last month that it *is* a passion, but only this evening have I read it aright. The sunlight of your presence has cleared up my misty doubts, my dusky illusions. Now, that there is a menace in the air of my losing you, I see that that troubling, tuneful presence, which I took to be the torment of my life, was, in truth, its motive and its delight. I assure you I thought of you far more than your music warranted. We need some other explanation. Do accept this one—that I love you with all my soul.

CATHERINE. (*Smiling.*) It's very true that, considering that that's a good stout wall, we have been singularly conscious of each other's—idiosyncracies.

STEPHEN. Divinely conscious!

CATHERINE. I must say, however, that it's a pity you have such an aversion to a piano.

STEPHEN. My dear Catherine, the secret of the matter was that I couldn't turn your leaves. By the way, you'll perhaps get used to my smoking.

CATHERINE. You best of men! I promise to light your cigar.

STEPHEN. Ah, life will be too sweet. But now that I've stepped into authority, I demand as a right that you tell me the history of that nosegay.

CATHERINE. Why, like that of Viola's love, in "Twelfth Night," it's well nigh "a blank, my lord!" It was sent me as a birthday token by a pupil, a very good little girl of ten.

STEPHEN. Bless her kind little heart! Well, my dear, you may keep it as a farewell.

Still Waters
1871

EDITOR'S FOREWORD

Early in 1870 Henry James visited Paris and paid his first visit to the Théâtre Français. "I saw Molière done—more delicately and deliciously than words can say," he wrote to his mother, expressing regret that he could not have spent more time in the French capital. "I should have learned *bien des choses* at the Théâtre Français. . . ." He returned to Cambridge later that year, and early in 1871 reported to Charles Eliot Norton that he was busy "scribbling some little tales."

That spring a group of Boston ladies decided to stage an elaborate fair in aid of the destitute people of France, victims of the Franco-Prussian war. Susan Hale, sister of Edward Everett Hale, assumed the editorship of a little sheet which was to appear daily during the fair and invited contributions from the literary great of Boston and Concord. Henry James, whose sympathies for the French were keen, contributed *Still Waters* and it appeared in the second of the six numbers of the *Balloon Post,* on April 12, 1871.

The plot of this sketch—that of a passive hero, worshipping the heroine in silence, ready to abdicate in another's favor—resembles that of such early tales as *The Story of a Year* and *A Most Extraordinary Case* and foreshadows many later situations including that of *Guy Domville*. The triangle indeed is not unlike that of the later play and the renunciatory hero has much in common with Guy. His last words, "Farewell. Be happy—be very happy," have the same ring as the speech James was to write for Guy thirty years later. "Be kind to him. Be good to her. Be good to her."

The title of *Still Waters* suggests that of Tom Taylor's play *Still Waters Run Deep* which James saw as a boy; there is no other similarity save in the names of the heroines—James's is Emma, Taylor's was Emily.

The text here published is taken from the Library of Congress copy of the *Balloon Post*.

CHARACTERS

EMMA (twenty)
HORACE (twenty-nine)
FELIX (thirty-two)

STILL WATERS

By the seaside; the piazza of a cottage overlooking the water; an awning, a hammock, chairs, a divan, books; a beautiful view.—A Sunday afternoon, last of August. FELIX seated with a portfolio, sketching the prospect.

FELIX. (*Gaping formidably.*) A long Sunday afternoon! What is a man to do? Poor Mrs. Meredith shut up with a dreadful headache; croquet of course forbidden; the poor little surveyor as timid and about as conversational as a squirrel; and Miss Emma—I suppose—taking care of her sister. No great loss, either, at that. Who was it told me she was pretty? Upon my word, I don't see it. A nice little face enough, if one were to take a magnifying glass to it. She'll never fairly look at you. I haven't to this hour the smallest idea of the color of her eyes. And then the way she blushes when you speak to her! What does she think I want to say? (*Yawning again.*) Heigh ho! This sort of thing can't last forever. Haven't they any neighbors? Where does the pretty girl live who called last evening in the phaeton? "If you are going to stay, we shall be very glad to see you." Those were the pretty girl's identical words. What does she do on Sunday afternoons? Does she take a nap, or read Robertson's Sermons? Perhaps at that house they *do* play croquet.—Decidedly, my sketch is a failure. My rocks on the bosom of the deep look like cows ruminating in a field. I think I might put in a tree, rising straight from the waters, with perfect *vraisemblance*.—Hallo! who is the young person wandering so pensively on the shore? She has a little girl by the hand. Not a nursery-maid evidently, or she'd have a parasol. Nay, by Jove! the young lady of the phaeton. Is she coming up here? No,

she sits; she leans her cheek upon her hand and gazes at the horizon. Surely, I may venture to approach her. I'll stick my pencil in my ear, and pretend I've come down to ascertain, for my sketch, the texture of that pudding-stone. (*He lays down his portfolio.*)

(*Enter* HORACE *from the parlor window.*)

HORACE. Oh! Don't let me disturb you. I thought I should find Miss Emma.

FELIX. No, my dear sir, not where I am. Miss Emma is not so fond of my society.

HORACE. Oh, indeed!—You know poor Mrs. Meredith has a dreadful headache, and Miss Emma—

FELIX. No! it dates, I regret to say, from before the headache. But perhaps our talking here disturbs the headache. She's capital company. It's a great bore having her laid up.

HORACE. I'm in hopes she's asleep. I've just been down to the druggist's, in the village, to get this prescription. (*Takes out a little phial wrapped up.*)

FELIX. Ah, you've walked to the village! Isn't it extremely hot?

HORACE. (*Wiping his brow.*) A little warmish. But I took an umbrella.

FELIX. Oh, you took an umbrella! (*Aside.*) Confound him! My young lady is moving away.

HORACE. You've been sketching, I see.

FELIX. A man must do something, you know, of a Sunday afternoon. (*Eagerly.*) By the way—you're an engineer, you sketch yourself,—wouldn't you like to turn over my drawings? (*Thrusts the portfolio at him.*)

HORACE. Oh, you're very kind.

FELIX. Dear me! Who is the young lady there on the rocks? Really, I think it's Miss

—what's-her-name?—who was here last evening. Isn't it rather unsafe down there, wandering about at haphazard? There's a hole there—you come upon it suddenly! Excuse me, I'll go down and tell her about that hole. (*Disappears in the direction of the shore.*)

HORACE. (*Holding the portfolio and looking after him.*) Happy man!—happy, stupid, clever man! (*Turning over the drawings.*) More stupid than clever, in the matter of drawing. If I were to make such a sketch as that, people would laugh at me. I'm little and modest and ugly! But *he!* he's six feet high, with enormous whiskers and a still more enormous impudence,—and so, with all his enormities, people swallow him whole. I'm a gnat and he's a camel! Emma, poor girl, she has swallowed him whole; but she finds him hard fare. (*Looking a while at* FELIX's *sketch.*) Come; is she in love with the man who has drawn those rocks like parlor settees and that shimmering ocean like parlor carpet? She's in love with some one, that's very plain; and not with me, that's plainer still. With whom then, but with Mr. Felix?—Mr. Felicissimus! And he, under the circumstances—the dromedary!—he can think of nothing more to the point than to go down under her very nose to pick up a flirtation on the rocks. Oh, sensibility! She avoids him, forsooth! Hasn't the man half an eye? Wait till you're in love, Mr. Felix! You may be a little crazy, but you'll not be so idiotic. (*Laying down the portfolio, he sees on the bench a little book, which he takes up.*) Adelaide Proctor's poems. Dear me! Miss Emma's own, and with marginal notes and elucidations, in her own sweet, sloping hand. Lovely womanish scratches and dashes! Happy Miss Adelaide Proctor! I should like immensely to puzzle out her notes. I wonder whether she would miss it. She'll think it's Felix, and that will make her happy,—half-happy, half-miserable, as people are when they're in love—even when the loved object is absolutely indifferent, or, what is worse, partial to another! Poor girl, I ought to feel for her! As she is, I am; shadows chasing shadows. I'll borrow the book for an hour and take it down to the rocks and read these divine hieroglyphics. (*Just as he has put the volume into his pocket,* EMMA *appears.*)

EMMA. (*Entering eagerly, but stopping with an air of impatience.*) O Horace, here you are! We didn't know what had become of you.

HORACE. It was a little hot, Miss Emma. I was unable to walk as fast as I should have liked to do. But I've got the medicine. I hope Mrs. Meredith is better.

EMMA. Better! my dear Horace, headaches don't go off like that! She's trying to sleep. (*Looking round her.*) I thought Mr. Felix was here.

HORACE. (*Aside.*) I've no doubt she did. Behold the pure essence of love! Runs away when he comes and runs after him when he goes. He was here, a few moments ago, but he went down to the rocks. He seems a little—a little bored, if I may say so.

EMMA. Poor fellow! You ought to try and amuse him, Horace.

HORACE. I never amused any one.

EMMA. Yes, you're very odd, sometimes. Oh, I see him from here, and a lady too! What lady is that?

HORACE. The young lady, I believe, who was here last evening. So said Mr. Felix.

EMMA. He must have very good eyes, to recognize her from here.

HORACE. He has an eye for distant objects.

EMMA. (*Aside.*) Yes, rather than for near ones. What does he find to say to Miss Walsingham all this while? He hardly knows her.

HORACE. He is warning her against that hole.

EMMA. What hole, pray?

HORACE. The great hole in the rocks, which one may so easily fall into.

EMMA. My poor Horace, what *are* you talking about? There is no hole within a mile. Ah! whose sketch is that?

HORACE. Not mine, I assure you.

EMMA. (*Taking it up.*) Of course not,—how interesting!

HORACE. There is a lot more in the portfolio. Look them over; I know you want to.

EMMA. (*Coloring.*) You know I want to! Pray, sir, what do you mean?

HORACE. (*Aside.*) Ah, that blush! Could

any one make her blush so for me? Here comes the great painter, himself. You can tell him how much you like it. (FELIX, *crossing the lawn, reappears on the piazza.*)

EMMA. I can't stay: I must be off with my medicine. (*She lingers, however, and, to give herself a pretext, unwraps the little bottle which* HORACE *has given her.*)

FELIX. (*Strolling forward.*) It wasn't Miss Walsingham, after all. But I saw a very pretty face for my trouble.

HORACE. I've been seeing a prettier one, with no trouble at all.

FELIX. (*Staring, aside.*) Compliments! What is the man up to?

EMMA. (*After a silence, turning away, to herself.*) Has he nothing to say to that? But I'm not pretty, after all. (*She has unwrapped her bottle, with a little cry.*) Why, Horace!

HORACE. Dear me! have I erred?

EMMA. Altogether. I told you *essence,* a dozen times—essence, essence, essence; and you've brought me tincture.

FELIX. My dear fellow, how could you?

HORACE. Dear me! can't she take that?

EMMA. Why, they have directly opposite effects.

FELIX. One's a sedative—the other's a stimulant.

HORACE. Why, I thought you said tincture, you know! I went along repeating to myself—tincture, tincture, tincture!

EMMA. I'm sorry. I would send Michael, but unfortunately, Sunday afternoons—

FELIX. He goes in search of a certain tincture on his own account!

HORACE. Oh, I've made the mistake! I shall be happy to repair it.

EMMA. That's a good fellow.

HORACE. (*Aside.*) A good fellow! Blessed mistake!—I shall be back in no time.

EMMA. Don't hurry; you know it's hot. *Essence,* remember.

HORACE. Quintessence, I promise you!

FELIX. (*Aside.*) The squirrel hath a wit! By the way, since you're going into the village again, perhaps you wouldn't mind doing me a favor. Do get me a state-room on to-night's boat. A good one, you know, away from the engine.

EMMA. (*Starting.*) Ah! Mr. Felix, you're going?

FELIX. I'm afraid I must be off.

EMMA. (*After a pause.*) My sister will be sorry.

HORACE. (*Aside.*) Her sister! Divine mendacity!

FELIX. I've just remembered an engagement.

HORACE. (*Aside.*) An engagement. O thou dull Moor! I'll get him the very next state-room to the engine. It takes an engine to affect him!

FELIX. Please disburse for me and I'll repay you.

EMMA. (*Aside.*) Perhaps, so late as this, there are no state-rooms. Horace, you'll find me here.

HORACE. (*Aside.*) This last hour she seizes! (*Looking at her.*) Since you'll kindly allow me, I'll walk slowly. (*He goes away through the house.* EMMA, *slightly embarrassed, strolls to the end of the piazza.* FELIX, *not at all embarrassed, proceeds to collect his drawing materials.*)

EMMA. (*Softly.*) He's going because he's bored. What can I do? I wish I were only a little brighter! He thinks me a common creature! This last hour! I may never see him again. I could do something *wild!* Surely, he's not going to march off to his room. I saw, as I was passing, an uncut novel on his table. Is he going up to read it? Ah, *my* poor little novel, he'll not cut *you!* Oh, stupid, smiling sea! I could cry— I could cry! (*Turning suddenly.*) My sister will scold me dreadfully for letting you go.

FELIX. Pray tell her to keep her scoldings for me. I'm extremely sorry she's under the weather.

EMMA. She's sure to have a headache whenever anything—anything pleasant occurs.

FELIX. It's enough to make one regret one is pleasant.

EMMA. (*Aside.*) How nicely he turns things! (*A pause.* FELIX *continues to arrange his portfolio.*) I should like immensely to have one of his drawings. If I were to ask for one? Indelicate! But it would be delicate to have it, and to keep it in a locked drawer.—I have been looking at your sketch; I hope you don't mind.

FELIX. Not in the least.

EMMA. (*Aside.*) If he would only offer it to me!

FELIX. By the way, I'm stealing off without seeing your sister; suppose you give her this sketch, with my compliments, as a peace-offering. (EMMA *takes the sketch and looks at it in silence.*) I hope you like it.

EMMA. (*After an interval.*) To tell the truth,—I don't.

FELIX. (*Staring but smiling.*) Brava! There's nothing I like so much as a little criticism.

EMMA. I am no critic; but I don't like it. I hate it.

FELIX. (*Laughing.*) Nay, that's not criticism; it's passion.

EMMA. Passion? Well, then, passion! Look at that superb blue sea, Mr. Felix; was there ever such a blue?

FELIX. Never, never, never! (*Aside.*) Her eyes, at last! Blue as well. I don't know about the sea, after all.

EMMA. I can't draw or paint of course; but if I could, it seeems to me I would sketch that sea and sky and the rocks and the surge *almost* as I did then; the blue flashing dark, and the white surf flashing bright, and the sky above clear and vast—

FELIX. And you think my clumsy pencilling a very poor substitute for all that! I quite agree with you. It was the work of a stupid, disconsolate man.

EMMA. You've had a very dull visit.

FELIX. No. I've been a very dull visitor. You'll be glad to get rid of me.

EMMA. (*After a silence.*) I shall not particularly miss you.

FELIX. (*Aside.*) Upon my word, she's coming out. In point of fact, you haven't felt an overwhelming obligation to entertain me.

EMMA. It seems to me, it was rather your place to entertain me.

FELIX. (*Laughing.*) Oh, I beg your pardon. I came down here—

EMMA. Oh, but not by my invitation!

FELIX. Dear me! if you stand on the letter of the law!

EMMA. (*Blushing deeply, but smiling.*) Mr. Felix, have I been rude? (*Aside.*) If he could only think so!

FELIX. (*Smiling back.*) Rude! Rude's a strong word!

EMMA. I needn't say I haven't meant it. My sister said to me an hour ago, "Do try, and do something for that poor man!" I went and sat down in my room, and thought it over.—What *can* I do? what *can* I do? It was too hot, to propose to you to walk—and, besides, would it have been proper?

FELIX. Just improper enough to have made me assent, in spite of the heat!

EMMA. I don't play, I don't sing, I could have offered you no music. Besides, it's Sunday. I don't mind croquet, but if people had heard our balls—

FELIX. We should have been lost! I would gladly have shared perdition with you. But in fact, my dear young lady, you were shooting quite beyond the mark. Croquet and music and a formal walk! I can be happy with less machinery. Your mere presence—

EMMA. My mere presence! Would you really have observed it?

FELIX. Most attentively!

EMMA. (*After a silence.*) I've been unjust. I beg a thousand pardons.

FELIX. I forgive you, but the next time I come don't treat me as a monster, to be fed at the end of a long pole.

EMMA. Will you come again?

FELIX. Do you invite me?

EMMA. Do you accept?

FELIX. Not till I'm invited.—What a jolly sunset!

EMMA. You had better sketch it.

FELIX. Come, that's rough! I must be off.

EMMA. How the crimson deepens as you look at it!

FELIX. Like a pretty girl, blushing as you stare! I feel as if it were impolite. I must go in and put up my things.

EMMA. You're more polite to your pretty girl than to me.

FELIX. (*Looking at her while he hesitates.*) Her eyes are not light blue either—they are dark blue.—If you like, I'll bring down my valise and my duds and pack them up here. Pack them up I must!

EMMA. (*Turning away a moment, to herself.*) Does he wish to force me to ask him to stay? Is there, in men, such a thing as coquetry? We have missed the sweet afternoon,—but the evening here will be sweet!—You insist on my formally inviting you. It's simpler to do so while you're in sight and in mind; simpler, too, for you to stay than to go and come again.

FELIX. You have really a genius for simplification. I wish I could solve the problem of existence as I used, as a boy, to do my algebra on the blackboard, by striking a chalk mark over the bothersome quantities. If I were to stay, you see, it would be easy ciphering; but I shouldn't get my sum total!

EMMA. Oh, if it's a matter of mathematics!

FELIX. It will be a matter of mathematics for a poor man to cover the void in his finances left by the five dollars our friend Horace has been expending on my state-room. I'm a poor man!

EMMA. (Hesitating a moment; then, half-bitter, half-arch.) You'll have to pay five dollars, you know, to come again.

FELIX. (Aside.) Is she laughing at me? Confound her! Must I stay to be civil to her? Bah! I've rather put my foot in it; but consistency is dignity! Perhaps, by that time, I may have sold a picture!

EMMA. (With the same tone.) Dear me, if you wait till then!

FELIX. You may be gentle! Excuse me. I shall see you, of course, for farewell. (EMMA makes him a grave courtesy and he enters the house. She looks after him for a moment and then drops on the divan, with her hands to her face.)

EMMA. "Gentle"! Possibly! I shall be wretched, and wretchedness makes one gentle! Then I shall play no part. Does he wish me to go down on my knees to him! Ah, sir, thank Heaven you're going; it's time. Thank Heaven you're utterly insensate and cruel! A little gleam,—a hint, a word, a smile; that would be enough. Where is he going? where away on the wings of that fierce indifference? Heaven bless him! Heaven help me! (She bursts into tears.) Oh, folly! Have I come to this,—to sit crying out my silliness before the solemn sea, which murmurs nothing to his ear? You've seen it all, now, gray glass of ocean! Now let him come! Am I to bid him farewell with red eyes? Where is my precious Adelaide? (Looking.) Gone?

Surely it was here I left it. Can he have taken it—with all my scribblings? It must have been he. I can't imagine Horace with Adelaide Proctor! Ah, my poor little notes and crosses! Am I to endure every humiliation? Ah, Horace! (HORACE comes out from the parlor window.) I wonder if he has got him a state-room.

HORACE. (Giving her the phial.) This time, I believe it's right. (Aside.) Tears? At last! Poor wounded heart—can I touch it?

EMMA. Thank you for your trouble. (Aside.) How he looked at me! Does he notice? Not he, thank Heaven! (With forced gayety.) Are you tired? Did you see the sunset? I hope you found a good state-room.

HORACE. The best that was left. I met on the way Mrs. Jay: she bade me tell you that she expected you to come this evening. Her son is at home: they are to have some sacred music.

EMMA. Her son—some sacred music! Much obliged.

HORACE. About eight o'clock.

EMMA. About eight o'clock. You'd better go.

HORACE. Oh, you know I don't go to parties.

EMMA. No more do I. I've given it up. If you were a girl, I'd make you a present of my finery.

HORACE. Since when have you given up finery?

EMMA. Never mind; you must go. It will be stupid here. I shall be upstairs.

HORACE. (Aside.) Upstairs, crying again! If I could only speak to her—or speak for her! Now that her heart is wounded and tender, might I say a word for myself? It's hard lines to be able neither to console her nor to help her,—to see it and be powerless! Friend Felix! I wish I had a little more of your superb stolidity.—(With great softness.) Emma!

EMMA. (Unwrapping the phial.) What is this stuff? Is it laudanum? I think I'll take some.

HORACE. Are you crazy?

EMMA. I believe I am.

HORACE. (Snatching at the phial.) Give it to me!

EMMA. Do you think I'm serious? Simpleton! (*She passes rapidly into the house.*)

HORACE. (*Sits down on the divan and folds his arms.*) "Simpleton"! That's the best she can say to me! Poor bewildered little mind! She has given it all up! she has given up gayety, and joy, and happiness—and all for *him*—or rather for the thankless, senseless memory of him! That such a blossom as that maiden's heart of hers should sit trembling on its stem, unnoticed, unplucked! What possesses the man? Is it simple dulness of vision or is it cruel hardness of heart? If I might say a word! Assuredly, in the name of my own poor throttled passion, I have a right to speak. Anything rather than see her lose her color, her smile, her prettiness! What, after all, do I risk? Would waiting twenty years serve my own cause? That's lost in advance. My love was born a cripple, to sit on a stool in a dark corner—hers with the wings of Ariel to flutter and frolic in the light. And the poor wings are ruffled and bound and bleeding! If it weren't Sunday, I should like to swear a bit! (FELIX, *at this moment, comes out from the house.*)

FELIX. Our young lady is gone! I want to bid her farewell. You got me a stateroom, I suppose? (*Taking the ticket which* HORACE *silently offers him and presenting a bank-note.*) Permit me to reimburse you. I'm extremely obliged to you.

HORACE. Do you know how you can express your obligation?—By allowing me to remark—(*Pausing a moment.*)

FELIX. Anything you please!

HORACE. That you're an absolute fool!

FELIX. Upon my word—you exact good measure!

HORACE. Wait a moment and you'll agree that I put it mildly. You wish to bid Emma good-by, eh?

FELIX. I certainly can't go away without—

HORACE. You'll just go up to her, and say,—"Ah, Miss Emma, good-by!" and march off! You *are* an absolute fool! Were you ever in love?

FELIX. If, as you so graciously affirm, I am an absolute fool, need you ask the question.

HORACE. You know then, that the wind bloweth where it listeth.

FELIX. Like your wit, my friend. What are you driving at?

HORACE. Do you think that young girl pretty?

FELIX. Pretty enough. I confess I only noticed just now the remarkable shade of her eyes—a lovely liquid blue.

HORACE. Liquid indeed! especially when they are streaming with tears.

FELIX. With tears? what do you mean?

HORACE. I mean that something has been going on here, fit to make angels groan! I mean that the sweetest of girls has been crying her eyes out for the dullest of brutes! I mean that love has kindled its altar fires beneath your very nose, and that the pale vestal has scattered her ambrosial incense upon the very air you breathe. Isn't the air faint and sweet with its violet fumes? Isn't the evening breeze scented with a maiden's sighs? Don't the breaking waves murmur of a breaking heart? Doesn't your cheek turn crimson at my words? Where are your wits, your senses, your manhood? I confess I can stand it no longer. Common pity cries out! No words of mine can make you over, or turn a log into a lover. I don't speak for your sake, but for hers. Either, when she appears, go down on your knees to her, or vanish this instant without speaking to her, without seeing her, without forcing upon her again a sense of your colossal ingratitude!

FELIX. Tears, sighs, incense, perfumes! Emma in love! Are you sure?

HORACE. You may believe I wouldn't speak without a fair certainty.

FELIX. (*Tapping his forehead, with a smile not untinged with fatuity.*) With me—with me!

HORACE. With you, incredible as it may seem.

FELIX. Now I think, I assure you it's not the least incredible. Admirable girl! Of course she is! By the way, my boy, to give me the news you needn't have put on the air of the angel Gabriel. In the angel Gabriel himself your tone would have been a bit pompous. But I forgive you. I wondered what the deuce was the matter with her; avoiding me; blushing at nothing, at everything; flitting to and fro; now effacing herself altogether and then speaking up as clear as crystal and breaking into that agony of modesty,—that divine impertinence! Ah, the *ewig Weibliche!* You're a passive feminine creature, Horace; you have a fellow-feeling for lovelorn maidens. Seriously, I'm extremely obliged to you. This is real friendship. I fancied you were rather afraid of me; I shouldn't have expected you to muster courage.

HORACE. Why, at heart, we're all in love with you. Happy man!

FELIX. Let me tell you, I haven't been so insensible as I seemed. I felt something; a yearning; a burning! I thought it was Miss Walsingham. You'll see what I *can* do! I've packed up my valise, but I shan't go. See the moon just above the ocean!

HORACE. (*Aside.*) Heavens! I can't stand this. I shall pack up *my* valise. You mean to stay?

FELIX. My dear fellow, do you take me for a brute?

HORACE. Give me your ticket, then. I believe I'll use it. And here is your money again.

FELIX. (*Laughing.*) Let me beg of you to keep it. You've earned as much!

HORACE. Oh, I've earned a little more! But I don't insist. Excuse me, I have only time to tie up my bundle. (*Enters the house.*)

FELIX. Yes, there was something the matter with me. Why was I so bored? I don't generally find myself such poor company. It was that she was at hand—was and yet wasn't. And then I wanted to make her ask me to stay; I wanted, for my heart's pleasure, to hear her say the very words. But she was proud and I was modest! How the light flashes back into it all! I'll give her a touch of audacity! Here she comes through the parlor. The pale vestal—that's a pretty notion of his! But now for the blushes! (EMMA *steps upon the piazza and, going up to the young man, offers him her hand.*)

EMMA. I hope I've not kept you waiting. I believe you have still time.

FELIX. (*Aside.*) How shall I say it?—Plenty of time. I'm not going.

EMMA. Ah, you've thought better of it?

FELIX. I never meant really to go.

EMMA. (*Aside.*) What has happened?—Your valise nevertheless is standing packed at your door.

FELIX. (*Aside.*) I can't say I love her outright *à propos* of a valise. Dear young lady, I have been reading my heart. (*Aside.*) How her blue eyes expand!—Emma, you're terribly pretty.

EMMA. Dear me, it's very sudden!

FELIX. It's very sudden you're looking as pretty as you do. Paleness becomes you.

EMMA. That's a consolation.

FELIX. Nay, now you blush, it's even more becoming!

EMMA. Spare me, sir, or I shall blush quite too red for good looks. It's a great honor to have you noticing my complexion.

FELIX. For these three days I have done nothing else; your complexion, your movements, the sound of your voice, everything that makes you the charming girl you are.

EMMA. (*Aside.*) Gentle Heaven! do I dream?—You're hard to understand.

FELIX. Let me be plain. I love you!

EMMA. Felix!—Weigh your words. I have a heart. Have a conscience!

FELIX. I love you, I love you; on my conscience, I love you! (*Falls on his knees.*)

EMMA. But you don't know me. You've hardly exchanged a hundred words with me.

FELIX. I have studied you in silence. Not a glance, not a movement, has escaped me. I held my tongue; I wished to be sure. I'm not wrong, Emma? You *do* care for me?

EMMA. (*After a silence.*) A little.

FELIX. (*Rising, to himself.*) She doesn't quite fall into my arms! There are women for you. Neglect them and they adore you; adore them—and they are not so sure! I've been brutal, haven't I? But if you knew what it cost me! Don't look at me so solemnly, with your unfathomable eyes. Tell me you love me.

EMMA. I suppose I'm very happy; happiness stupefies a little. And what did you think of me, all the while? I must have seemed a gracious, winning creature.

FELIX. Your very reticence and reserve were charming. I wouldn't have had you running after me.

EMMA. No, indeed, I hope not! I have a

proper pride.

FELIX. It's not yet quite melted away. Come, flatter a man a bit. Confess you don't quite hate me.

EMMA. Ah, the voracious vanity of men! Nay, I kept my secret well; I grew almost fond of it. It's even hard to part with it at such short notice. Felix, you'd better know it; I've a passion for dignity.

FELIX. Dignity as a passion has a ravishing effect. It gives one the brightest little peeps and glimpses of the mysterious background of the heart.

EMMA. If I thought any one had had a glimpse of *my* heart!

FELIX. I have had, my dear—far off in the blue distance. I saw it lying in the shadow, but being a modest man, I hesitated to assume that the shadow was my shadow. Fortunately fate sent me a little telescope.

EMMA. A little telescope? My dear Felix, what are you talking about?

FELIX. Why, Horace just whispered to me,—It is yours; proceed.

EMMA. Horace? Pray what did Horace know about it, and what call had he to be whispering about my heart?

FELIX. Oh, I assure you, Horace is quite a knowing fellow.

EMMA. (*After a silence.*) Horace—of all people! When we're engaged I shall scold him.

FELIX. Not too hard. But for him, I might be rattling down to the boat.

EMMA. Ah!—By the way, I ordered the carriage for you. I must go and countermand it.

FELIX. You'd better let Horace take it. He is going off himself. I gave him my state-room.

EMMA. Indeed! I saw him half an hour ago and he said nothing about it. What has happened to him?

FELIX. You can ask him; here he comes. (HORACE *comes out prepared for departure.*) I say, give an account of yourself. Emma thinks you're a bit uncivil.

HORACE. (*Aside.*) He has spoken. Damnation! (*To* EMMA.) He has perhaps told you I'm going.

EMMA. (*Sotto voce.*) What's the matter with him? He's as grave as an undertaker.—

Have you had bad news?

HORACE. No, but I've suddenly remembered—I've written a line for your sister, —(*With force.*) I can't stay!

EMMA. (*Aside.*) What an odd tone, and how strangely he looks at me!—Perhaps you'll come back.

HORACE. I doubt it. I think of going to Europe.

FELIX. Bully for you! There's energy! I say, Emma, we must go to Europe. (EMMA *is looking at* HORACE *askance, without answering. The latter stands for a moment hesitating and embarrassed.*)

HORACE. (*Aside.*) So! Things have gone fast.—I wish before I go to make a little request. I have here a little book of yours. (*Draws out the volume of Miss Proctor.*)

EMMA. Ah! my Adelaide Proctor! *You* had it. Horace, you're a singular being.

HORACE. Let me claim the privilege of a singular being, then, and ask your permission to keep the volume.

EMMA. Why, it's all defaced with my scribblings.

HORACE. That's nothing. (*He replaces the book in his pocket.*) Emma, it's everything.

FELIX. (*Looking at his watch.*) My boy, you'll be late for the boat.

HORACE. Farewell. Be happy—be very happy! (*She lets him take her hand; he holds it a moment, looking at her, then raising it to his lips springs away through the house. When he has gone she stands silent and musing.*)

FELIX. He might at least have bade me good-night! By Jove, how the moon's coming up! We must go down on the rocks.

EMMA. (*Still musing.*) Poor Horace!

FELIX. You don't mind my lighting a cigar?

EMMA. I'm curious; I'm very curious. How did he know—how did he know?

FELIX. Know what, my dear?

EMMA. What you told me!

FELIX. He guessed, he divined, he perceived. It don't matter how at this time of day. Say he was in love with you, himself! I beseech you to come down on the rocks.

EMMA. *In love with me himself?* And yet he told you?—Horace—little Horace! How strange!

FELIX. Just look at that moonlit spray! Must I carry you? (*Goes towards her.*)

EMMA. (*Sits down.*) Don't touch me, Felix. I'd rather not go to the rocks. I prefer to stay here. (*Still pensive.*) *His* love —*his* sacrifice! Dear, dear!

FELIX. "Don't, don't! I won't, I won't!" Must I already resort to a cigar for consolation?

A Change of Heart
1872

EDITOR'S FOREWORD

The third and last of Henry James's early dramatic experiments extant was published in the January 1872 *Atlantic Monthly* shortly before the novelist sailed aboard the S.S. *Algeric* for his second trip to Europe. Where the comediettas preceding *A Change of Heart* were simple two-character and three-character conversation pieces, this playlet is an attempt in small compass to create a play in the French fashion—each entrance and exit marking the occasion for a scenic division after the form in which French plays were cast. As a result this dramatic trifle boasts no less than fifteen scenes. It has more intrigue than its predecessors; nevertheless there is no evidence to show that James, in writing it, intended it for any stage. Its brevity alone would mark it as distinctly experimental.

With the publication of this piece, James seems to have turned away from all thought of play-writing for the time; he was already at work on the first chapters of his first major novel, *Roderick Hudson,* and for the next decade was to devote himself assiduously to the writing of fiction.

CHARACTERS

Robert Staveley (thirty-seven)
Charles Pepperel (thirty-six)
Margaret (twenty-one)
Martha (twenty-three)

A CHANGE OF HEART

Drawing-room of a house in the country. Glass doors at back into the piazza and garden; doors right and left into the house. Late afternoon. Middle of August.

(*Scene First:* MARTHA, *coming forward, pale and agitated, followed by* PEPPEREL.)

PEPPEREL. What is it to be,—peace or war? I knew you were here, and yet I came. You may imagine whether I like it. I saw you at the window as I came through the garden. I confess that, for an instant, I was on the point of turning away. But when a man has come a-wooing, he has a use for all his gallantry. I should have vastly preferred to respect your seclusion. Do me justice! I'm not so bad as you think. You know it's said that unless we're saints we hate those whom we've wronged. Of course if we're saints, we've not wronged any one. Now I don't in the least hate you. I don't say I pity you,— that would be insulting.

MARTHA. Yes, don't be insulting!

PEPPEREL. I esteem you—there! I esteem you more than any woman in the world. Under the circumstances I call that handsome. Meet me, if not as a friend, at least not as an enemy, and justify my good opinion by your tact.

MARTHA. (*After a silence.*) Is it really you that I hear? Am I really standing face to face with you and listening to you? calmly, after all!

PEPPEREL. It's very odd, certainly. Life leads us a dance, if we happen to have an ear for the tune! But everything's odd, or nothing's odd, according as you look at things. The grand point is not to stand staring, like rustics at a fair. Will you forgive me?

MARTHA. I don't understand you. I only feel that every word you utter *must* be an injury.

PEPPEREL. The deuce! Well, I can't stand and argue the matter. I must play my part and do my work. Of course, at best, I can't expect you to think well of me; but I'm determined you sha'n't think so ill as you'd like to do. I shall therefore be perfectly frank. You know, I suppose, what has brought me here?

MARTHA. I wish to know nothing.

PEPPEREL. You must know everything. I'm engaged—I'm on the way to be engaged—it's the same thing—to Miss Thorne. Time is precious in such a case. If Miss Thorne chooses to come dutifully to spend a month with her aunt (though I'm told the poor lady's ailments don't increase the charm of her conversation), I can hardly be expected to wait till the month is up to make my offer, or to break off my wooing in the middle because you happen to be established here. You see we're just at that point when an offer is *à propos* at any moment. And, really, I'm extremely happy to find you so comfortably settled. You'll not pretend you were better off in that dismal little house of your mother's. Of course, if I could have arranged matters ideally, I shouldn't have chosen to come and make my offer under your very nose. But let me assure you that I shall remember what is due to you as far as I can without forgetting what is due to Miss Thorne.

MARTHA. (*Who has stood silent, with her eyes on the ground, raises them and looks at him.*) Even your very face is altered!

PEPPEREL. I've let my beard grow. You'll forgive me yet.

MARTHA. Don't ask too much. (*Turns to go.*)

PEPPEREL. Yes, you'll forgive me. Allow me five minutes more. I'll prove what I say.

MARTHA. Mr. Pepperel, spare me, I beseech you.

PEPPEREL. You know our account's not squared. I'm your debtor. I seem as offensive as if I were a creditor. But you'll get used to me. An hour or two hence, I shall beg for five minutes. It's a little complicated!—Miss Thorne, I was told, is in the garden. We shall be having her jealous! (*Goes out by the piazza.*)

(*Scene Second:* MARTHA *alone, then* STAVELEY.)

MARTHA. (*Sinks into a chair and remains for some moments plunged in thought.*) I was prepared for much, but I was not prepared for this! Life, you're hard. Six months ago I fancied it the last humiliation to become a paid servant,—for what am I more? But it's the greatest humiliation of all, I verily believe, simply to be a woman; that includes the others: to listen and believe and trust as a woman! Well, the world tells us that it's a great privilege to suffer as a woman. It's a pity I shouldn't at least enjoy that! (*Brushes away her tears; then suddenly rises.*) A voice on the piazza? Yes, it's Mr. Staveley. Nay, there are true men in the world, as well as false, and the woman *he* should address would not have to suffer for it.

STAVELEY. (*Comes in from the piazza with a travelling-bag, which he places on a chair.*) Miss Noel! Your humble servant. You're not at home alone, I suppose.

MARTHA. They're all on the lawn and in the garden,—a party of them. You know it's Miss Thorne's birthday; they're having tea on the grass.

STAVELEY. Yes, I come with my birthday wishes,—such as they are! And why have you run away?

MARTHA. I'm not expected to have any wishes, Mr. Staveley.

STAVELEY. You're morbid; that's what's the matter with you. You're expected to know how you're valued. My aunt looks upon you as a—as a niece!

MARTHA. Not yet! But I'm a very silly girl! Your aunt's not there; she's been unable, as usual, to leave her room. I remain here to be within summons.

STAVELEY. When next she sends for you, pray ask her if she can receive me. There's no hurry. Who are they all, out there?

MARTHA. A dozen. Mrs. Seymour and her daughters, Mrs. Lewis, the two Miss Jessops and their brother, Mr. Hamilton, Mr. Jones, half a dozen gentlemen.

STAVELEY. Including Mr. Pepperel.

MARTHA. (*With a slight effort.*) Mr. Pepperel has just come. Won't you join them?

STAVELEY. Not just yet. *À propos* of Mr. Pepperel, I wish, Miss Noel, to ask you three questions. (*As* MARTHA *turns away, aside.*) Mr. Pepperel's name makes her blush; Mr. Pepperel's presence, if I'm not mistaken, has made her cry. Can this poor girl have been one of his victims? He was crossing the lawn there with the strut of the conquering hero! If she will, she can help me. (*Aloud, as* MARTHA *comes down again.*) I have a particular desire to learn the position of things between Mr. Pepperel and my cousin.

MARTHA. I can hardly tell you. Mr. Pepperel has just come.

STAVELEY. O, but you don't mean to say that you've not guessed! You've had half the evidence; what more does a woman need? Margaret has been here a week, I believe. Has she told you nothing? You and she are of course friends.

MARTHA. Miss Thorne is not communicative, and I'm not inquisitive. Mr. Pepperel's name has never been mentioned between us.

STAVELEY. Ah, there it is! She's in love. Is it an engagement?

MARTHA. (*After a pause.*) You've come to congratulate her?

STAVELEY. I've come to remonstrate with her—if you can believe it. I disapprove of the match—I abominate Pepperel. It's a matter, Miss Noel, in which you can perhaps assist me; unless indeed, like most women, you're silly enough to believe in the fellow.

MARTHA. I thank you for the sex.

STAVELEY. The sex ought really to be obliged to me. But if I can save Margaret, the others may look out for themselves. I'm not a man who is fond of meddling in other people's business; but this time, I confess, I couldn't sit still. Of course it will be a siege. She'll not drop him for my asking her. I fancy, Miss Noel, that you're an observer. You know this terrible Margaret of ours. She's pretty, she's clever, and, when she will, she's charming. She's not charming when she won't! She's positive, I can tell you! In plain English, she's obstinate. If I may allow myself the expression, she's hard! I say all this to you; of course I should never dare to say it to her.

MARTHA. I hope not, I'm sure.

STAVELEY. O, you should hear the sweet things she says to me! Well, this time I mean to brave them! I never carried my point yet, but I've never had one so well worth carrying. My courage has risen with the occasion. Friendship, as well as love, Miss Noel, can make a fool of a man. I've been, first and last, of a hundred minds about my cousin. Sometimes I've been sure for six weeks together that I don't care two straws for her,—that her smiles and her frowns are all the same to me! I've declared that she's cold, heartless, wilful beyond the limits of grace. Then for another six weeks it has seemed to me that her smile is the handsomest thing in the world, and that even her frown is very fine, —as frowns go! It's not that I've been in love with her. Worse than that,—the pains without the pleasures! I've undertaken to befriend her for charity; I've wanted to be her good genius. A wilful woman, sooner or later, is sure to need one. Margaret's too proud, poor girl; she'll make no sacrifice to the unknown gods. If the gods will only not come knocking some fine day at her door, to demand arrears! I've always been absurdly considerate; I've never contradicted her; I've left her to the gods to deal with. She thinks, of course, I haven't the pluck to say boh! to a goose, and I'm in hopes she'll rather like me if I tell her to her face she's a fool. Unfortunately, to like that sort of thing demands a fund of sense! How has *he* done it, what has *he* told her, to bring her to this pass? Miss Noel, the gods *do* avenge

themselves! They don't come nowadays in thunder and pestilence; they don't blast our crops nor slay our children; they quietly punish us through our own passions. Here's the proudest girl in the world infatuated with a man whose arm, if she really knew him, she would refuse to take for five minutes at a ball. (*Observing her.*) But you don't believe me, Miss Noel. How can I hope she will?

MARTHA. It's no affair of mine, save that I admire your zeal.

STAVELEY. O, that's what Mr. Wigmore, my cousin's lawyer, said to me this morning. He's an old friend of her father's, and since my uncle's death, ten years ago, he has been her guardian. I take the alarm, I rush to him and unfold the tale. "Margaret is about to bestow her hand upon Charles Pepperel, of whom you've heard, a man a woman can't marry,—a rank adventurer! I know him, he knows me! To the rescue!" For all answer, he takes out his watch. "At ten o'clock this morning pretty Margaret became her own mistress. Twenty-one years ago to an hour she entered upon her minority. At ten o'clock this morning she issued from it, and my term of office expired. It's now twenty minutes past. I haven't the least desire to overleap my authority. I've had ten years' bother; I've broken off three engagements already,—one before she was out of frocks; I've fought a dozen pitched battles. For heaven's sake, let me rest on my laurels. The gentleman may be no gentleman; nothing is more likely. Let this go for his punishment!" That's all very well, but I'd rather not anticipate Providence. I walked about three hours and thought of it; I worked myself into a rage of benevolence. I packed my bag and jumped into the train, and here I am! Now tell me, Miss Noel, whether, after all, I'm simply a meddlesome fool.

MARTHA. Your intention is surely excellent. But when a woman is deceived— (*She pauses.*)

STAVELEY. (*Attentive.*) No man can undeceive her?

MARTHA. (*Abruptly.*) Try, Mr. Staveley! I'll pray for you.

STAVELEY. I fancy you might help me

better than by your prayers. You don't say much, but I imagine you're very wise.

MARTHA. (*Smiling.*) May I never speak again!

(PEPPEREL *has entered from the garden during the last words; he advances.*)

PEPPEREL. (*With gallantry.*) O, I protest against that!

MARTHA. (*Starts and falters; then collects herself.*) Excuse me; I'm called. (*Exit hastily.*)

(*Scene Third:* STAVELEY, PEPPEREL. *The two men exchange a fixed glance and stand for a moment uncertain.*)

PEPPEREL. (*Suddenly assumes an air of friendly recognition.*) Mr. Staveley! For a moment I was at a loss to place you.

STAVELEY. (*Aside.*) Good heavens! Before such impudence, where's *my* chance?

PEPPEREL. Just here I hardly expected to meet you! But when a man has, like you, the happy pretext of cousinship, where else should one look for him? (*Aside.*) Confound the cousinship! Still Margaret has always made light of it. As one of the "family," I must speak him fair.

STAVELEY. I hadn't the least doubt as to who you were. My only doubt was as to whether I'd speak to you.

PEPPEREL. (*Smiling.*) Admit, then, that I cut a troublesome knot! Miss Thorne just now begged me to outstay her little party; but she didn't mention you as one of the attractions.

STAVELEY. I've only just arrived.

PEPPEREL. I'm just arrived myself. We must have been fellow-travellers; unless indeed you took the train. I always take the boat. It's not so much longer; I've had time to go to the hotel and dress. And then there's nothing I like so much as a summer evening on the water.

STAVELEY. You have simpler tastes than when we last met!

PEPPEREL. O, that was in the—dark ages! We met in some queer places, eh? (*Aside.*) What the deuce is he coming to? I'll meet him half-way, but only half-way! (*Aloud.*) Of course you know this is Miss Thorne's birthday. I've taken the liberty of bring-

ing her a little present. (*Tapping his waistcoat-pocket.*) A ring, with a really uncommon diamond! She has such things in plenty, of course, but I shall beg her to accept this as a token of an altogether peculiar sentiment. She promised to follow me in here and give me my opportunity. I wish all those good people were ten miles away!

STAVELEY. I should indeed fancy a dozen good people might make you very uncomfortable.

PEPPEREL. You seem inclined to try what *one* can do. (*After a pause.*) Evidently, you mean war.

STAVELEY. I mean victory. It will be war only if you choose to adhere to a hopeless cause.

PEPPEREL. My dear sir, you're unforgiving.

STAVELEY. It's not a matter of forgiveness. I can't forget! I might have forgiven you a dozen times any mere wrong of my own, and yet not be able to stand silent and see a woman whom I respect and esteem think of you as a man she can decently marry.

PEPPEREL. You mean, then, I take it, to oppose my marriage?

STAVELEY. I mean to do what I can.

PEPPEREL. I wonder whether you appreciate the difficulties of the undertaking.

STAVELEY. I've given them my best consideration. Have you anything to suggest?

PEPPEREL. Miss Thorne is a woman of a very high spirit.

STAVELEY. Imagine her sensations, then, on finding herself married to you!

PEPPEREL. For a man who doesn't mean war, you hit hard.

STAVELEY. Give it up, and I'll never strike another blow.

PEPPEREL. You're very generous. After all, what do your blows amount to? You can prove nothing.

STAVELEY. It depends upon what you call proof.

PEPPEREL. You can't find chapter and verse, without a vast deal of trouble. Meanwhile, I shall gain time.

STAVELEY. I can tell a plain tale in ten minutes.

PEPPEREL. Your plain tale has a highly

ornamental *dénouement*. The heroine's married! It's a fact! I doubt whether her husband would care to have her come into court. Without that, it's simply your word.

STAVELEY. I have ground to suppose that, with my cousin, my word carries some weight.

PEPPEREL. Why, then, it's just man to man!

STAVELEY. That sounds portentous. Still, I shall do my best. Here she comes. (MARGARET *comes in from the piazza*.)

(*Scene Fourth: The Same,* MARGARET.)

PEPPEREL. (*Meeting her*.) I'm like Louis XIV.,—I almost waited! But I've had good company.

MARGARET. Why, Robert, when did you get here? (*Giving him her hand*.)

STAVELEY. Half an hour ago. I haven't shown myself, because I've my toilet to make.

MARGARET. Go and attend to it, and come and make yourself agreeable.

PEPPEREL. (*Sotto voce to* STAVELEY.) I think, on the whole, I'll defy you.

STAVELEY. Agreeable? O, I don't promise to be that. As to my dressing,—after all, need I? Your friends must be going.

MARGARET. Go and dress for me, then. Where's your gallantry?

STAVELEY. It's not in my coat, Margaret. I'll show you! (*Takes his bag and exit*.)

(*Scene Fifth:* PEPPEREL, MARGARET.)

PEPPEREL. I came here, Miss Thorne, with a design for which my letter, three days since, must have prepared you. But even if my intention had been less definite, the five minutes' talk I have just had with your cousin would have given it instant shape.

MARGARET. Your letter was explicit, certainly. I didn't answer it because, after it, the least you could do was to come. And pray what has my cousin to do with the matter?

PEPPEREL. Margaret, I love you!

MARGARET. (*After a silence*.) I believe you're honest. And what is this about Mr. Staveley?

PEPPEREL. To-day, you once told me, is your birthday. I've not forgotten it. It falls in the nick of time. I have ventured to bring you a ring (*taking it from his waistcoat-pocket*)—such a ring as I've seen women wear of whom it was whispered that they were engaged. (*Takes her hand, which she slowly surrenders. He is about to pass the ring upon her finger, when she withdraws her hand, crosses her arms, and looks at him gravely*.)

MARGARET. Your ring is beautiful, but you must give me time.

PEPPEREL. I've given you three days.

MARGARET. I have your letter here in my pocket; I've been carrying it about with me. But the same words, spoken, sound new and strange.

PEPPEREL. I love you,—I love you,—I love you! Are you used to them now? But you're right to ponder the matter! There's the opinion of the world. Mr. Staveley, for one, altogether disapproves.

MARGARET. Mr. Staveley? What do you mean?

PEPPEREL. He has come down to forbid the banns.

MARGARET. Pray who has asked his opinion?

PEPPEREL. O, you'll not have to ask it to hear it. You're to hear it *gratis*. In three words, Margaret, he owes me a grudge, and he's determined to prevent my marriage. He considers, naturally, that there can be no harsher vengeance.

MARGARET. This is something new. From to-day I'm my own mistress; it shall not be for nothing. I owe it to you to assure you that my decision shall rest on grounds of my own, and not of my cousin's.

PEPPEREL. (*Aside*.) Victory, victory! (*Aloud*.) Do you mean to listen to him?

MARGARET. I take it you're not afraid to have me.

PEPPEREL. I'm not ashamed to say I'm afraid of losing you. He'll surprise you.

MARGARET. It's surprise enough to find him meddling in my affairs.

PEPPEREL. You know your cousin, Margaret. He's one of those men who go about measuring all mankind with the little inch measure of their own imaginations and multiplying their blunders by their prejudices. I've incurred his distinguished displeasure. It's an old story. He has raked up a heap of scandal, with which, apparently, he means to regale your maidenly ears. I frankly confess that I'm a man about whom stories can be told; and I have the fatuity to believe that you'll not care for me the less on that account. You don't suppose that you've taken me out of the nursery; and you'll not complain of having fixed the affections and renewed the youth of a man who had begun to fear that he had no heart and the world no charm. Concerning your cousin, to the best of my knowledge, History is absolutely silent! I doubt that any one will ever come and startle you with "revelations" about Mr. Staveley. It's no revelation, of course, to hear that he's a narrow-minded, rancorous prig. However, there's no smoke without fire, and I've no doubt he has a dozen tales at his fingers' ends, proving, damningly, that I've been idle, reckless, extravagant, selfishly fond of pleasure. I can trust you to believe that they prove nothing worse. I know but one pleasure now, Margaret; and if to cling to that is selfish, I'm a monster of egotism! He has one little anecdote, I believe, which he considers his *cheval de bataille*. He threw out monstrous hints, but I can't imagine to what he alludes. I shall be curious to hear your report. I fancy it's the tragical history of a certain young person whom he had taken it into his head to consider a model of all the virtues. I proved, irrefutably, that the list was incomplete, and he has never forgiven me this impeachment of his taste.

MARGARET. You needn't mind details. (*After a silence.*) Do you know I'm inclined to thank Mr. Staveley? His interference has made us more intimate.

PEPPEREL. You can thank him outright! (STAVELEY *returns.*)

STAVELEY. Am I presentable? I put up my things in such a fever that I find I've forgotten half of them.

MARGARET. Mr. Pepperel, go and amuse those poor people on the lawn. I don't know what they think of their hostess. But when a girl has this sort of thing on her hands—

PEPPEREL. I'll represent you! (*Aside.*) I

fancy I've fixed it, unless Martha speaks! But, Martha's an angel. (*Exit, by piazza.*)

(*Scene Sixth:* MARGARET, STAVELEY.)

MARGARET. For the pretty things you have to say to me, you can hardly be dressed enough. Mr. Pepperel tells me that you don't approve of our acquaintance.

STAVELEY. You must admit that, considering the deep and affectionate interest I have always taken in your affairs, you have never had reason to complain of my zeal, and that I have managed to temper it with a great deal of deference.

MARGARET. You've never had a decent pretext for interference. I know you've been itching to make one.

STAVELEY. I didn't come to blow my own trumpet. I came to beseech you not to throw yourself away. The man whom you have honored with your favor is signally unworthy of it.

MARGARET. There's a beginning!

STAVELEY. You'll excuse me if I lose no time. Those who know him best respect him least. He has neither heart nor conscience. His notions of what is honorable in conduct are absolutely grotesque. He's a cool impostor. I know what I say. I can't stand still and see you sacrifice yourself to a pitiful delusion. Pause and reflect; reconsider your impressions, and question your heart. I speak to you, Margaret, in the name of the tender good-will I have always borne you, in that of your young happiness and freedom, in that of the very pride and temper which make you resent my words.

MARGARET. In the name of my pride and my temper, then, I beg you to know that your words are an insufferable injury. Am I a flighty school-girl? I know him and I love him.

STAVELEY. You're not the first to love him. You'll not be the first to repent. He's incapable of really caring for a woman. He doesn't love you, he loves your money.

MARGARET. My dear cousin, I'm vastly obliged to you. You've shaken me into position. *Do* I love him? I had been asking myself. You've made me say yes!

STAVELEY. You love your own will better; and my impression is that in this matter you're defending him far less than that.

MARGARET. Charming! While you're about it, put an end to us both.

STAVELEY. Are you actually engaged?

MARGARET. Considering the key in which you've pitched the conversation, you'll not think me rude if I tell you it's none of your business.

STAVELEY. Give me a week, and I'll prove what I say. I'll put you into communication with persons who will satisfy you.

MARGARET. Meanwhile, I'll say to Mr. Pepperel: *"À propos,* they tell me you're a monster of vice. I don't know what to say to it, but I think it's very possible. Invitations are out for an inquest; next Monday we shall hear witnesses. My cousin has kindly consented to conduct the proceedings. If you pass muster, I'll have you."

STAVELEY. And your lover, if he's an honest man, will fold his arms and smile serenely.

MARGARET. My lover, if he's the man I take him for, will calmly await the issue; and then, when you and your witnesses have made proper fools of yourselves and —heaven forgive me!—of me, he'll make me his bow: "I had looked for a wife, madam, and not for a judge in petticoats!"

STAVELEY. O, I've no doubt he'll treat you to a pretty piece of impudence!

MARGARET. Really, I'm glad to love a man who has enemies. It's a proof of a strong nature.

STAVELEY. If that's all you want, why don't you take your husband out of the Penitentiary?

MARGARET. Come, don't talk to me again about my temper. I'll go back to my guests; they're not amusing, but they're decently polite.

STAVELEY. You don't suppose I'm afraid to offend you. I came prepared for that. I'll not ask you to wait a week; give me an hour. I promise you in an hour to change your opinion.

MARGARET. Do you know you're amusing? I'm really tempted to consent. Of course, after this everything's at an end

between us, and I want a good round pretext for despising you.

STAVELEY. Ah, my terrible cousin, that's if I don't succeed! But if I do—

MARGARET. I shall hate you. An hour, to a minute, mind! (*Exit, to the garden.*)

(*Scene Seventh:* STAVELEY, *alone.*)

STAVELEY. A pretty pair of alternatives! Well, madam, I don't think I shall love you, at this rate. The trouble of dealing with really superior scoundrels is, that they have a way of wrapping themselves in their dishonor with as many classic folds as a Roman in his virtue. She likes a man who has enemies! O romance, you're no better than an old-clothes man! If I could only make him out the coward he really is! show her the dingy dishabille of his iniquity! For that I must have facts and figures —and with only an hour to collect them. It would be awkward if I were to be wrong, after all, about this poor little Miss Noel. No, I always felt she had a little mystery of grief, and her tears just now, when Pepperel had left her, and her flight when he reappeared, fitted the key to the lock. Ten words from her, emphasized by that charming wise face and those sad gray eyes, ought to go far. The point is, to get a modest girl to speak such words. She'll not do it for revenge, but she may for charity. If she will, she's a trump! And to save me time, here she comes!

(*Enter* MARTHA, *from the house.*)

(*Scene Eighth:* STAVELEY, MARTHA.)

MARTHA. I've seen your aunt. She'll receive you at seven.

STAVELEY. I wish she had called it eight. For the coming hour I have my hands full. Margaret has given me an hour to prove my case.

MARTHA. Poor Mr. Staveley! You see what it is to try and help people in spite of themselves.

STAVELEY. Do you think we ought to shrug our shoulders and let them pass?

MARTHA. Our own troubles make us sceptical. We say it's a weary world, at best, and a little more or a little less—

STAVELEY. O, this will never do! I want you to believe.

MARTHA. I confess, a very little happiness may restore our faith.

STAVELEY. Yours, Miss Noel, has been tried.

MARTHA. I never supposed I should tell you so.

STAVELEY. I don't ask you idly. The fact is relevant. You have suffered, I fancy, as Margaret may suffer, when, having believed her lover an honest man, she finds he's a knave.

MARTHA. How have you guessed all this?

STAVELEY. I've guessed, because I've observed you, if you'll excuse the liberty. And I've observed you, because I admire you.

MARTHA. At that, I must excuse it!

STAVELEY. If I have observed to good purpose, you and Charles Pepperel have not met to-day for the first time.

MARTHA. For the last.

STAVELEY. (Aside.) How under heaven is a man to ask it? (Aloud.) You know him well.

MARTHA. I thought so till one hour ago. I find I've but half known him.

STAVELEY. Poor girl! He has added insult to injury.

MARTHA. He has done me good. Here I am talking to you of him as of a stranger.

STAVELEY. It's a good beginning. Speak of him to Margaret; tell her your story.

MARTHA. I would rather it should end with you, Mr. Staveley.

STAVELEY. Tell me all, then. (As she remains silent, aside.) There's a request!

MARTHA. We were engaged. My mother was dead; I was altogether alone; fair words had a double price. For three days, I believe, he was sincere; in three days I was convinced. I believed—my excuse is that I believed everything. I placed my slender patrimony in his hands, to reinvest to better advantage. We were to be married in a month. It was then, I suppose, that he met Miss Thorne,—richer, prettier, more attractive than I, and apparently as credulous. Poor girl! But she has a cousin! From that moment till an hour ago I've not seen his face. O, he bade me farewell—in a note of three lines, enclosing the titles of a scattered remnant of my property. As this was an insufficient support, I was obliged to earn my living. I found this situation as companion to your aunt, and I consider that I've been fortunate.

STAVELEY. Good heaven!

MARTHA. I don't complain, Mr. Staveley. I'm very happy.

STAVELEY. O, allow me to doubt it.

MARTHA. Your aunt's eccentric, but she's kind.

STAVELEY. My aunt's a fretful old shrew!

MARTHA. (Smiling.) Of course it takes less to content me than it would you. I have no generous dreams of helping and enlightening my fellow-mortals.

STAVELEY. (Looking at her a moment in silence.) Miss Noel, you think I'm a gross idiot!

MARTHA. I place my confessions at your service.

STAVELEY. (Aside.) Ah, the brave girl! (Aloud.) Have you still in your possession that note of three lines?

MARTHA. I've kept it. If you were a woman, you'd know why. I am waiting for a moment in my own room to burn it up.

STAVELEY. Keep it an hour longer. Give it to me. It's for that you've kept it.

MARTHA. Do you really think so?

STAVELEY. (After a pause.) Do you know, Miss Noel, this high and mighty cousin of mine ought to be desperately obliged to us?

MARTHA. She'll not forgive me, that I know.

STAVELEY. We shall be in the same box. I'll not waste my logic upon her. Pepperel will apprehend it better. He shall convince her! If I have ten minutes' talk with him, you'll not object to my mentioning your letter.

MARTHA. To what purpose?

STAVELEY. To bid him repent, by Jove! under pain of exposure. To bid him disgorge! You're too patient by half!

MARTHA. You're Miss Thorne's knight, not mine, Mr. Staveley. It is her interests that are in question. As I can easily keep them distinct from my own, I had better see Mr. Pepperel. Yes, in fact, it's better. An hour ago he asked me for an interview, which I then felt no inclination to grant. But, on reflection, I've changed my mind. I wish to be just. He spoke of our "account." I don't know what he means, but I fancy he has some proposal for the restoration of my property. I shall bid him keep it and give up Miss Thorne.

STAVELEY. Merciful powers! Is that your notion of justice? Let *me* deal with him.

MARTHA. Thank you; it's my own affair.

STAVELEY. I detest the idea of your meeting him again.

MARTHA. I'm very calm. And now while we're talking, your aunt is waiting for you.

STAVELEY. (*Slowly turning to go; at the door.*) This is too much; I give up my cause!

MARTHA. Already! I've almost espoused it.

STAVELEY. I'm sick of it. Miss Margaret, I offer you my compliments. (*Exit.*)

MARTHA. (*Alone.*) I offer you mine, Miss Thorne! (*Enter* MARGARET *from the garden.*)

(*Scene Ninth:* MARTHA, MARGARET.)

MARGARET. They've gone at last; but it's no thanks to you, Miss Noel.

MARTHA. (*Smiling.*) Do you mean that, if I had been present, they would have gone earlier? I have to be within sound of your aunt's bell.

MARGARET. I wish, by the way, you'd bring in from the grass the shawls and cushions she lent us. It's not for my aunt, but for my aunt's nephew, that you've been lingering here, I believe. I hope you found him more civil than I. He treated me to half an hour's abuse of a friend so intimate that it amounted to telling me outright that I had low tastes.

MARTHA. (*After a silence.*) Are you engaged, Miss Thorne?

MARGARET. If you feel disposed to congratulate me, you needn't wait.

MARTHA. I can't in conscience congratulate you.

MARGARET. Really, this is the Palace of Truth! My cousin hasn't wasted his time.

MARTHA. I know Mr. Pepperel, not by your cousin, but by himself. (*Aside.*) I could tell him, but I really can't tell her. (*Aloud.*)

I once did Mr. Pepperel more than justice.

MARGARET. Ah, you are perhaps the young lady he told me of, in whom Mr. Staveley took such an interest and about whom he had his quarrel with Mr. Pepperel! *Hinc illæ lachrymæ;* do you know Latin? Tell me your story.

MARTHA. I know nothing of Mr. Staveley's quarrel, nor its cause. As for my story, your ear has evidently been gained in advance.

MARGARET. Well, whatever it may have been, you've got a respectable situation.

MARTHA. (*Aside.*) O, you poor creature! (*Aloud.*) Excuse me; I think you'll be enlightened yet.

MARGARET. What on earth is going to happen? One would think that, between you, you'd been brewing a thunderbolt! For heaven's sake, let it come! Do you know my private, my very private, opinion? Jealousy! My cousin's in love with me; he wishes to marry me himself; of course, he detests poor Pepperel.

MARTHA. I wonder whether, after all, you're not to be congratulated. You'll not be unhappy; you evidently don't know true coin from false.

MARGARET. Jealousy, jealousy! You, on your side, are in love with Mr. Pepperel, and it will serve *your* turn, of course, to have me give him up. You'll console him. After the kind things you've said of him, he'll vastly need it!

MARTHA. Yes, decidedly, I congratulate you! You have the happy gift of fitting facts to your fancies. Excuse me; I must fetch your aunt's shawls. (*Exit to the garden.*)

(*Scene Tenth:* MARGARET, *alone.*)

MARGARET. Upon my word it's a conspiracy; I've got the clew! One would think I was a child of ten, to be frightened by long faces and big words. With all her demureness, that girl's an *intrigante*. I feel for all the world like the heroine of a novel,—a victim of the Inquisition! (*Enter* STAVELEY.) Your machinery works to a charm! You ought to have been here just now, to hear little Miss Noel rattle off her lesson.

(*Scene Eleventh:* MARGARET, STAVELEY.)

STAVELEY. Ah, she has told you—

MARGARET. She told me that Mr. Pepperel was the blackest of villains,—as plump as you'd say good morning. I confess that I want something more than the word of a spiteful little governess, bursting with jealousy!

STAVELEY. Margaret, you're cruel.

MARGARET. Very likely; I'm hard pushed. But if this is your great stroke, you've lost the game! Remember, your time is nearly gone! Twenty minutes hence, I'm at your service. (*Exit.*)

(*Scene Twelfth:* STAVELEY, *alone.*)

STAVELEY. She has spoken, then, poor girl—with small success. Martha jealous, Martha spiteful,—she the angel of forgiveness, the soul of generosity! Aunt Jane, at least, does her justice. I wonder what on earth Aunt Jane thinks of *my* talk. Three questions about herself, her aches and her pains and her pills, and twenty about Miss Noel! "She's a good girl,—a good girl!" For Aunt Jane, that's great praise. I doubt whether she has ever said it of any other young woman of the present corrupt generation! Of Margaret and of Margaret's choice, she altogether disapproves. *À propos* of which I began to tell her of my scheme for the enemy's confusion, when suddenly a certain gleam in those keen black eyes of hers—the frank stare of a wise old woman—seemed to say to me, "Robert Staveley, you're making a mess!" And truly, Robert Staveley, where's your delicacy? Is Miss Noel's trouble really fit for nothing but to paint a moral and adorn a tale, for Margaret's edification? Is it the part of perfect gallantry to send the poor girl groping back into her dark past for a bugaboo to frighten Margaret? O, Margaret's not afraid! Do I really care so very, very much for my gentle cousin, and so very, very little for Miss Noel, that I'm willing to fold my arms and let Miss Noel fight the battle of my transcendental philanthropy? Miss Noel would have me believe, perhaps, that she has a battle of her own to fight. Confound it, *I'll* fight Miss Noel's battles. Nay, she declines my services! Well, she sha'n't fight mine, at all events! And while I'm pottering here, where is she? Has she seen him? She's seeing him now, I suppose! They're talking it over. They're in the library there, with the door closed. He's pleading, flattering, swaggering; she's listening, blushing, remembering! Ten to one, he's insulting her! Worse than that, he's offering her twenty per cent on her stolen property! Damn her property! Let him keep it! Really, that's very well for me to say! One would think I was jealous. Upon my soul, I *am* jealous. This raking up of her past altogether offends me! Good heavens, where are they? (*As he turns hastily to go out* MARTHA *enters from the garden, carrying several shawls and a couple of cushions.*) Miss Noel, I was going in search of you. You're laden down like a packhorse.

(*Scene Twelfth:* STAVELEY, MARTHA.)

MARTHA. I've been in the garden picking up the relics of the feast. Here's one of them,—a dreadful claret stain on this silk cushion. Do you know what's good for claret stains?

STAVELEY. Turn that side against the wall. Have you seen him?

MARTHA. I've seen Miss Thorne.

STAVELEY. I know what that means. Accept my humble apologies for inducing you to expose yourself to such misinterpretation.

MARTHA. Miss Thorne is the offended one. There was a time when I would have given advice as cold a welcome.

STAVELEY. I wish you'd forget that time, Miss Noel!

MARTHA. You've done something, you know, to remind me of it.

STAVELEY. To my ineffable regret! Have you seen him?

MARTHA. (*Listening.*) I know his step. I hear it on the piazza.

STAVELEY. For heaven's sake, forget that! Do me a favor. Forego this interview.

MARTHA. I can't consent to your seeing him. I prefer to keep my grievance to myself.

STAVELEY. Keep it then and welcome. I

only wish to forget it—to forget him!

MARTHA. You have forgotten apparently your pledge to your cousin.

STAVELEY. My cousin must shift for herself; I've need of my wits for my own cause. Let the gods interfere, Miss Noel; they haven't human hearts! And, after all, do you know I half pity Pepperel? (PEPPEREL, *coming in from the garden, has heard these last words.*)

(*Scene Thirteenth: The Same,* PEPPEREL.)

PEPPEREL. (*Aside.*) He pities me, eh? Does that mean he has made out his case? I've *my* card to play too. If Martha speaks, I'll never believe in a woman again. (*Aloud.*) I'm sorry to interrupt a *tête-à-tête* so intimate! But if Miss Noel will grant me the favor of ten minutes' conversation—

STAVELEY. Miss Noel is engaged.

MARTHA. Five minutes, I think, will be enough. I will join you in the library.

STAVELEY. (*With vehemence.*) Martha, I entreat you—

MARTHA. (*Looking at him for a moment.*) I seem destined to-day to do as you choose.

PEPPEREL. Miss Noel will, as the advertisements say, hear of something to her advantage.

STAVELEY. (*To* MARTHA.) Let there be nothing more between you, for better or worse! He means to offer you your money. Decline it!

MARTHA. O philosopher!

PEPPEREL. To her immediate and substantial advantage.

STAVELEY. You've saved your conscience, sir. You're excused.

PEPPEREL. Madam, to you I speak.

MARTHA. (*After a moment.*) You're answered!

PEPPEREL. (*Stares from one to the other and then turns away with a shrug. Aside.*) Excused, answered! There's a graceful unanimity! Really, I think I'm more frightened than hurt. Jupiter Tonans has forgotten his thunder to flirt with—with Hebe! If I were only an old pagan, I'd spend the money in vows! Truly, I *am* pagan enough for that! But what the deuce then does he pity me for? (*Aloud.*) Your humble servant. (*Makes them a bow in silence, and turns toward the door, where he meets* MARGARET, *with whom he stands a moment in talk, watching* MARTHA *and* STAVELEY.)

STAVELEY. I answered for you, Martha, and you accepted my answer. It is my bold hope that you may allow me to answer for you forevermore.

MARTHA. All this is very strange. You came here for a disinterested purpose. . . . Forgive me. I can't accuse you of having remained for an altogether selfish one.

STAVELEY. You'll join *me* in the library!

MARTHA. You must not desert your cousin.

STAVELEY. I know my cousin better than I did an hour ago. I think I can leave her to consolidate her own prosperity. She'll get full weight, in one way or another. Poor Mr. Wigmore! (MARGARET *comes forward with* PEPPEREL.)

(*Scene Last: The Same,* MARGARET.)

MARGARET. Cousin, I believe we have an appointment. (*Looking at her watch.*) You're overdue.

PEPPEREL. Mr. Staveley has been so busy.

MARGARET. In an hour, you know.

STAVELEY. Really, I'm afraid you must despise me!

MARGARET. (*After a pause.*) No, I feel good-natured. (*To* PEPPEREL.) I give you notice, I'm not always so.

PEPPEREL. Let me take advantage of it to beg you once more to accept my ring.

STAVELEY. (*To* MARTHA, *as she turns away.*) Where are you going?

MARTHA. To the library!

Daisy Miller

A Comedy in Three Acts

1882

EDITOR'S FOREWORD

Henry James was thirty-eight when he returned to the United States in the autumn of 1881 after an absence of six years. He had gone abroad at thirty-two a "promising" novelist. He returned with a substantial literary reputation. The stay abroad had been fruitful. He had written in succession *The American, The Europeans, An International Episode, Daisy Miller, Confidence, Washington Square, The Portrait of a Lady,* assembled several volumes of tales, published *French Poets and Novelists* and his study of Hawthorne, in addition to many fugitive pieces for the magazines.

Daisy Miller, first published in the *Cornhill Magazine,* had been, as James wrote his mother, "a really quite extraordinary hit" and was the story to which his name remained attached, in the public mind, even long after he had done much more important work. A slender little tale, its interest centered in the personality of his heroine and the frosty expatriate appropriately named Winterbourne. The story aroused controversy: had James maligned the American girl in creating the portrait of an innocent little flirt, a fresh daisy in a European garden filled with jaded blooms? James himself said that the "whole idea of the story is the little tragedy of a light, thin, natural, unsuspecting creature being sacrificed as it were to a social rumpus that went on quite over her head and to which she stood in no measurable relation."

The story was not dramatic in the sense of the theatre; but there was a drama latent in it. We do not know whether the idea of dramatization originated with James or the management of the Madison Square Theatre. The theatre, the most modern in New York, had been rebuilt in 1879 by Steele Mackaye backed by the Mallory brothers, one a clergyman, with an interest in the stage and with adequate means to cultivate it. The manager of the theatre, for the Mallorys, was Daniel Frohman, who recalled that James, "a medium-sized man with a beard" who looked like "an ordinary business man," brought him the play. He said he rejected it because, although it was "beautifully written," it was "too literary. It had too much talk and not enough action." James, however, must have also carried on negotiations with the Mallory brothers themselves, since he speaks in his journal of the proprietors who "behaved like asses and sharpers combined," adding "this episode, by itself, would make a brilliant chapter in a realistic novel." There is an allusion to the episode in a letter from William Dean Howells to James who, in describing his own troubled relations with the Madison Square Theatre, said, "When we meet, I will tell you how those gifted brothers led me on protesting over the same path you trod to the same flowery pitfall, with another play. I really begin to admire them; they are masters of no common skill."

Whatever the details of the transaction, it is clear that the entire affair left a deep impression on James. In a letter to Charles Brookfield, the actor, he said only that "the manager and I fell out . . . and I returned to England with my comedy in my pocket," and to Mrs. John L. Gardner he put it: "I had a fundamental disagreement with the manager and got it back just before sailing." But this fundamental disagreement is described in his journal some months later as inspiring "deep and unspeakable disgust"; James wrote that "what it has brought [me] to know, both in New York and in London about the manners and ideas of managers and actors and about the conditions of productions on our unhappy stage, is almost fatally disgusting and discouraging. I have learned very vividly that if one attempts to work for it one must be prepared for *disgust*. . . ."

It is unfortunate that the details are lost to us, for they might indicate, more clearly than the later experiences, what the original set-back and rejection were which so conditioned his attitude of anger and defiance toward the theatre. Allowance must be made for the possibility, however, that the managers quite simply took an option on the play and then lost interest in it, as so often happens in the theatre; and that James, unaccustomed to the "tough" realities of "show business," reacted sharply.

His memory of the writing of the play was somewhat pleasanter, and he looked back upon this period with "a kind of religious veneration." He wrote it in Boston during the three months that followed the death of his mother in January 1882. He lived in bare, ugly rooms in Mount Vernon Street which he nevertheless found comfortable and pleasant. He would walk across the Common in the morning and take his breakfast at Parker's. Then he would return to his lodgings and write until late afternoon, after which he would walk out to Cambridge, four or five days in the week, to the Quincy Street residence of the James family, there to dine with his father and sister. In the evening, under the winter stars and past the colored lamps, he would walk back along the dark and vacant roads listening to the jingle of the horse-cars. His thoughts dwelt constantly on his mother.

When he had completed the play he read it to the Boston socialite, Mrs. John L. Gardner. With the elaborate irony which characterizes all his letters to her, Henry James wrote on June 5, 1882: "I think with extraordinary tenderness of those two pretty little evenings when I read you my play. They make a charming picture—a perfect picture—in my mind, and the memory of them appeals to all that is most *raffiné* in my constitution. Drop a tear—a diminutive tear (as *your* tears must be—small but beautifully-shaped pearls) upon the fact that my drama is not after all to be brought out in New York (at least for the present). . . . It is possible it may see the light here. I am to read it to the people of the St. James's Theatre next week. *Please don't speak of this.*"

We know that he tried to enlist the interest of Charles Brookfield and had hopes that the Bancrofts would do the play at the Haymarket, but nothing came of this. In the autumn of the year he had the play privately printed in order to circulate it more easily among the London managers. The following spring he published it in the *Atlantic Monthly*—in the issues of April, May and June— and later that year it appeared in book form under the imprint of James R. Osgood, after it had been rejected by Houghton and Mifflin. James made some minor revisions in the play between its private printing and its publication.

The play rewrites the original story considerably. Eugenio, the courier of the tale, becomes the villain of the piece and the shadowy lady in Geneva, briefly alluded to in the story as the friend of Winterbourne, becomes the all-important Madame de Katkoff of the play. In the tale Daisy dies of malaria and is buried in the Protestant Cemetery of Rome. In the play we are left with the promise of an early marriage between Daisy and Winterbourne. In transferring the tale to the dramatic form its freshness is lost and a rather artificial comedy is substituted which, for all its defects, reveals its author's skill in dialogue and characterization, but as yet considerable amateurishness in the manipulation of his personages and the handling of stage business. The New York *Tribune* devoted two columns to the book, dismissing it as a "highly impossible comedy" and adding, "we cannot repress some surprise—and regret—that such an accomplished writer and acute critic should not have perceived the full extent of the failure which he has now put permanently on record."

DRAMATIS PERSONAE

FREDERICK WINTERBOURNE   MRS. COSTELLO
CHARLES REVERDY   MADAME DE KATKOFF
GIACOMO GIOVANELLI   ALICE DURANT
EUGENIO   MRS. WALKER
RANDOLPH MILLER   DAISY MILLER

A WAITER

DAISY MILLER

ACT FIRST

Garden and terrace of an hotel on the Lake of Geneva. The portico of the hotel to the left, with steps leading up to it. In the background a low parapet dividing the garden from the lake, and divided itself by a small gate opening upon a flight of steps which are supposed to descend to a pier. Beyond this a distant view of mountains and of the lake, with the Château de Chillon. Orange-trees in green tubs, benches, a few small tables and chairs.

(*Scene First:* MADAME DE KATKOFF, EUGENIO.)

MME. DE KATKOFF. (*Coming in as if a little startled, with a French book in a pink cover under her arm.*) I believe he means to speak to me! He is capable of any impertinence.

EUGENIO. (*Following slowly, handsomely dressed, with a large watchguard, and a courier's satchel over his shoulder. He takes off his hat and bows obsequiously, but with a certain mock respect.*) Madame does me the honor to recognize me, I think.

MME. DE KATKOFF. Certainly I recognize you. I never forget my servants, especially (*with a little laugh*) the faithful ones!

EUGENIO. Madame's memory is perhaps slightly at fault in leading her to speak of me as a servant

MME. DE KATKOFF. What were you, then? A friend, possibly?

EUGENIO. May I not say that I was, at least on a certain occasion, an adviser?

MME. DE KATKOFF. In the way of occasions, I remember only the one on which I turned you out of the house.

EUGENIO. You remember it with a little regret, I hope.

MME. DE KATKOFF. An immense deal—

that I hadn't dismissed you six months sooner!

EUGENIO. I comprehend the regret of Madame. It was in those six months that an incident occurred— (*He pauses.*)

MME. DE KATKOFF. An incident?

EUGENIO. An incident which it is natural that Madame should not have desired to come to the knowledge of persons occupying a position, however humble, near Madame.

MME. DE KATKOFF. (*Aside.*) He is more than impertinent—he is dangerous. (*Aloud.*) You are very audacious. You took away a great deal of money.

EUGENIO. Madame appears to have an abundance.

MME. DE KATKOFF. (*Looking at him a moment.*) Yes, I have enough.

EUGENIO. (*Smiling.*) Madame is to be congratulated! I have never ceased to take an interest in Madame. I have followed her—at a distance.

MME. DE KATKOFF. The greater the distance, the better!

EUGENIO. (*Significantly.*) Yes, I remember that Madame was very fond of her privacy. But I intrude as little as possible. I have duties at present which give me plenty of occupation. Not so much, indeed, as when I was in the employment of Monsieur de Katkoff: that was the busiest part of my life. The Russians are very exacting—the Americans are very easy!

MME. DE KATKOFF. You are with Americans now?

EUGENIO. Madame sees that she *is* willing to talk! I am travelling with a family from New York—a family of three persons.

MME. DE KATKOFF. You have no excuse, then, for detaining me; you know where to find conversation.

EUGENIO. Their conversation is not so agreeable as that of Madame! (*With a slight change of tone.*) I know more about you than you perhaps suspect.

MME. DE KATKOFF. I know what you know.

EUGENIO. Oh, I don't allude to Madame's secrets. I should never be so indiscreet! It is not a secret to-day that Madame has a charming villa on this lovely lake, about three miles from Geneva.

MME. DE KATKOFF. No, that is not a secret.

EUGENIO. And that though she leads a life of elegant seclusion, suited to the mourning which she has never laid aside—though she has lightened it a little—since she became a widow, Madame does not entirely shut her doors. She receives a few privileged persons.

MME. DE KATKOFF. (*Aside.*) What on earth is he coming to? (*Aloud.*) Do you aspire to be one of them?

EUGENIO. I should count upon it the day I should have something particular to say to Madame. But that day may never come.

MME. DE KATKOFF. Let us hope so!

EUGENIO. Let us hope so! Meanwhile Madame is in a position to know as well as myself that—as I said just now—the Americans are very easy.

MME. DE KATKOFF. The Americans?

EUGENIO. Perhaps, after all, Madame doesn't find them so? Her most privileged visitor is of that nationality! Has he discovered—like me—that the Russians are very exacting?

MME. DE KATKOFF. (*Looking at him a moment, then quickly, though with an effort.*) The Russians, when their antagonists go too far, can be as dangerous as anyone else! I forget *your* nationality.

EUGENIO. I am not sure that Madame ever knew it. I'm an Italian Swiss, a native of the beautiful city of Lugano. Is Madame acquainted with Lugano? If she should go that way, I recommend the Hôtel Washington: always our Americans, you see! The Russians? They are the most dangerous people I know, and we gentlemen who take charge of families know everything.

MME. DE KATKOFF. You had better add frankly that you traffic in your knowledge.

EUGENIO. What could be more just? It costs us a good deal to get it.

MME. DE KATKOFF. (*To herself, after a pause.*) It is best to know the worst, and have done with it. (*Aloud.*) How much do you want?

EUGENIO. How much do I want for what? For keeping quiet about Mr. Winterbourne, so that his family shan't think he's wasting his time, and come out from America to bring him home? You see I know even his name! He's supposed to be at Geneva for purposes of study.

MME. DE KATKOFF. How much do you want to go away and never let me see you again? Be merciful. Remember that I'm not rich.

EUGENIO. I know exactly the fortune of Madame! She is not rich, for very good reasons—she was exceedingly extravagant in her youth! On the other hand, she is by no means in misery. She is not rich, like the American lady—the amiable Mrs. Miller—whom I have at present the honor to serve; but she is able to indulge herself with the usual luxuries.

MME. DE KATKOFF. It would be a luxury to get rid of you!

EUGENIO. Ah, I'm not sure that Madame can afford that; that would come under the head of extras! Moreover, I'm not in want of money. The amiable Mrs. Miller—

MME. DE KATKOFF. (*Interrupting.*) The amiable Mrs. Miller is as great a fool as I?

EUGENIO. I should never think of comparing her with Madame! Madame has much more the appearance of one who is born to command. It is for this reason that I approached her with the utmost deliberation. I recognized her three days ago, the evening she arrived at the hotel, and I pointed her out to Mrs. Miller as a Russian lady of great distinction, whose husband I had formerly the honor to serve in a very confidential position. Mrs. Miller has a daughter even more amiable than herself, and this young lady was profoundly impressed with the distinguished appearance of Madame.

MME. DE KATKOFF. Her good opinion is doubtless of great value; but I suppose it's hardly to assure me of that—

EUGENIO. I may add that I didn't permit myself to make any further remarks.

MME. DE KATKOFF. And your discretion's an example of what you are capable of doing? I should be happy to believe it, and if you have not come to claim your reward—

EUGENIO. My reward? My reward shall be this: that we leave the account open between us! (*Changing his tone entirely.*) Let me speak to you very frankly. Some eight years ago, when you were thirty years old, you were living at Dresden.

MME. DE KATKOFF. I was living at Dresden, but I was not thirty years old.

EUGENIO. The age doesn't matter—we will call it twenty, if you like—that makes me younger, too. At that time I was under your roof; I was the confidential servant, on a very exceptional footing, of M. de Katkoff. He had a great deal of business— a great deal of diplomatic business; and as he employed me very often to write for him—do you remember my beautiful hand? —I was not so much a servant as a secretary. At any rate, I was in a position to observe that you had a quarrel with your husband.

MME. DE KATKOFF. In a position? I should think you were! He paid you to spy upon me.

EUGENIO. To spy upon you?

MME. DE KATKOFF. To watch me—to follow me—to calumniate me.

EUGENIO. (*Smiling.*) That's just the way you used to talk! You were always violent, and that gave one an advantage.

MME. DE KATKOFF. All this is insupportable. Please to spare me your reminiscences, and come to the point.

EUGENIO. The point is this—that I got the advantage of you then, and that I have never lost it! Though you didn't care for your husband, you cared for someone else; and M. de Katkoff—with my assistance, if you will—discovered the object of your preference. Need I remind you of what followed, the day this discovery became known to you? Your surprise was great, because you thought yourself safe; but your anger was even greater. You found me for a moment in your path, and you

imagined—for that moment—that I was a Russian serf. The mistake had serious consequences. You called me by the vilest of names—and I have never forgotten it!

MME. DE KATKOFF. I thank you for reminding me of my contempt. It was extremely sweet.

EUGENIO. It made you very reckless. I got possession of two letters, addressed to the person I speak of, and singularly rash compositions. They bear your signature in full.

MME. DE KATKOFF. Can there be any better proof that I have nothing to be ashamed of?

EUGENIO. You were not ashamed then, because, as I have already remarked, you were reckless. But to-day you are wise.

MME. DE KATKOFF. (*Proudly.*) Whatever I have said—I have always signed!

EUGENIO. It's a habit I appreciate. One of those letters I gave to M. de Katkoff; the other—the best—I kept for myself.

MME. DE KATKOFF. What do you mean by the best?

EUGENIO. I mean—the worst!

MME. DE KATKOFF. It can't be very bad.

EUGENIO. (*Smiling.*) Should you like me to submit it to a few of your friends?

MME. DE KATKOFF. (*Aside.*) Horrible man! (*Aloud.*) That's the point, then: you wish to sell it.

EUGENIO. No; I only wish you to know I have it.

MME. DE KATKOFF. I knew that already. What good does it do you?

EUGENIO. You suspected it, but you didn't know it. The good it does me is this—that when, as sometimes happens to us poor members of a despised and laborious class, I take stock of my prospects and reckon up the little advantages I may happen to possess, I like to feel that particular one among them.

MME. DE KATKOFF. I see—you regard it as a part of your capital. But you draw no income.

EUGENIO. Ah, the income, Madame, is accumulating!

MME. DE KATKOFF. If you are trying to frighten me, you don't—very much!

EUGENIO. Very much—no! But enough is as good as a feast. There is no telling what

may happen. We couriers have our ups
and downs, and some day I may be in distress. Then, and only then, if I feel a
pinch, I shall call on Madame. For the
present—

MME. DE KATKOFF. For the present, you
only wish to insult me!

EUGENIO. Madame does injustice to my
manners: they are usually much appreciated. For the rest of the time that we
remain under the same roof—so to speak—
I shall not again disturb your meditations.

MME. DE KATKOFF. Be so good as to leave
me.

EUGENIO. I wish Madame a very good
morning! (*He goes into the hotel.*)

MME. DE KATKOFF. (*Stands a moment,
thinking.*) That's what it is to have been
a fool—for a single moment! That moment
reëchoes through eternity. He has shaken
my nerves, and in this wretched garden
one is always observed. (*Exit into the
hotel.*)

(*Scene Second:* MRS. COSTELLO,
MISS DURANT, CHARLES REVERDY.
They come out of the hotel as MME.
DE KATKOFF *passes into it, looking
at her attentively.*)

REVERDY. (*Who carries a camp-stool.*)
That's the biggest swell in the house—a
Russian princess!

MRS. COSTELLO. A Russian princess is
nothing very great. We have found one
at every hotel.

REVERDY. Well, this is the best of them
all. You would notice her anywhere.

MRS. COSTELLO. The best bred people
are the people you notice least.

REVERDY. She's very quiet, any way. She
speaks to no one.

MRS. COSTELLO. You mean by that that
no one speaks to her.

REVERDY. (*Aside.*) The old lady's snap-
pish this morning: hanged if I'll stand it!
(*Aloud.*) No one speaks to her, because no
one ventures to.

MISS DURANT. You ventured to, I think,
and she didn't answer you. That's what
you mean by her being quiet!

REVERDY. She dropped her fan, and I
picked it up and gave it to her. She thanked
me with a smile that was a poem in itself:

she didn't need to speak!

MRS. COSTELLO. You needn't mind waiting on Russian princesses. Your business
is to attend to us—till my nephew comes.

REVERDY. (*Looking at his watch.*) As I
understand you, he's already due.

MRS. COSTELLO. He's a quarter an hour
late. We are waiting breakfast.

MISS DURANT. I'm afraid the delay will
bring on one of your headaches.

MRS. COSTELLO. I have one already, so it
doesn't matter!

REVERDY. (*Aside.*) Very convenient, those
headaches! (*Aloud.*) Won't you sit down,
at least? (*Offering camp-stool.*) You know
I don't come out for three minutes without our little implement.

MRS. COSTELLO. I don't care for that;
I'll sit on a bench.

REVERDY. (*Aside.*) She insists on my
bringing it, and yet she won't use it! (*The
ladies seat themselves, and he places himself between them, astride the camp-stool.
He continues, aloud.*) If Mr. Winterbourne
is already due, my holiday has legally begun.

MISS DURANT. You won't lose anything
by waiting. After he comes you will be at
perfect liberty.

REVERDY. Oh yes, after that you won't
look at me, I suppose! Miss Durant is
counting very much on Mr. Winterbourne.

MRS. COSTELLO. And I am counting very
much on Miss Durant. You are to be very
nice to him, you know.

MISS DURANT. That will depend on how
I like him.

MRS. COSTELLO. That's not what I
brought you to Europe for—to make conditions. Besides, Frederick's a perfect gentleman.

MISS DURANT. You seem to wish me to
promise to marry him. I must wait till he
asks me, you know.

REVERDY. He will ask you if Mrs. Costello
bids him. He is evidently in excellent training.

MRS. COSTELLO. I haven't seen him for
ten years: at that time he was a model
nephew.

REVERDY. I shouldn't wonder if he were
to turn out a regular "hard" one. That
would be a jolly lark!

MRS. COSTELLO. That's not his reputation. Moreover, he has been brought up in Geneva, the most moral city in Europe.

REVERDY. You can't tell anything from that. Here am I, brought up in New York —and we all know what New York is. Yet where can you find a more immaculate young man? I haven't a fault—I'm ashamed of myself!

MISS DURANT. If Mr. Winterbourne is a little wild, I shan't like him any the less. Some faults are very charming.

REVERDY. Tell me what they are, and I'll try and acquire them.

MRS. COSTELLO. My dear Alice, I'm startled by your sentiments. I have tried to form your taste . . .

MISS DURANT. Yes, but you have only cultivated my dislikes. Those are a few of my preferences.

REVERDY. Tell us a few more of them— they sound awfully spicy!

MISS DURANT. I'm very fond of a certain indifference. I like men who are not always running after you with a camp-stool, and who don't seem to care whether you like them or not.

MRS. COSTELLO. If you like rude men, they are very easily found. If I didn't know you were a very nice girl, I should take you for—I don't know what!

REVERDY. Miss Durant's remarks are addressed to me, and between you two ladies it's hard to know what to do. You want me to be always at your elbow, and you make a great point of the camp-stool. Will you have it a little, for a change? (*Getting up and offering it.* MRS. COSTELLO *refuses with a gesture.*) I don't offer it to Miss Alice; we have heard what *she* think of it!

MISS DURANT. I didn't speak of that piece of furniture: I spoke of the person who carries it.

REVERDY. The person who carries the camp-stool? Is that what I've come to be known by? Look here, my dear friends, you ought to engage a courier.

MRS. COSTELLO. To cheat us out of our eyes? Thank you very much!

REVERDY. A courier with a gorgeous satchel, and a feather in his hat—like those ladies from Schenectady!

MRS. COSTELLO. So that he might smoke in our faces, as he does in theirs, and have his coffee with us after dinner, as he does with them? They have ruined a good servant.

MISS DURANT. They treat him as an equal; they make him their companion.

REVERDY. But they give him handsome wages—which is more than you do me!

MISS DURANT. I have no doubt they give him little tokens of affection, and locks of their hair. But that makes them only the more dreadful!

MRS. COSTELLO. I'm glad to see, my dear, that your taste is coming back to you!

REVERDY. Oh, if taste consists in demolishing Miss Daisy Miller, she can take the prize.

MISS DURANT. Demolishing her? I should be sorry to take that trouble. I think her very vulgar: that's all!

MRS. COSTELLO. Miss Daisy Miller? Is that her distinguished name?

REVERDY. (*Aside.*) Ah, we can't all be named Costello!

MRS. COSTELLO. They are the sort of Americans that one does one's duty by not accepting.

REVERDY. Ah, you don't accept her?

MRS. COSTELLO. I would if I could—but I can't. One should let Europeans know—

REVERDY. One should let them know?

MRS. COSTELLO. That we are not all like that.

REVERDY. They can see it for themselves: she's charmingly pretty.

MISS DURANT. You are extremely impertinent.

REVERDY. (*Aside.*) I put in one that time. (*Aloud.*) I can't help it; she's lovely.

MRS. COSTELLO. And is the mamma lovely, too? Has any one ever seen the mamma?

REVERDY. She's sick in bed—she's always sick.

MISS DURANT. The courier sits with her, and gives her her medicine.

REVERDY. I hope you call that devoted, then?

MRS. COSTELLO. It doesn't matter, because the head of the family is the little boy. He orders the dinner; he has the best seat in the carriage.

REVERDY. He's the most amusing little

specimen. He has the heart of a patriot in the body of a— (*Hesitates for a word.*)

MISS DURANT. In the body of a grasshopper!

REVERDY. He hops a good deal, or, rather, I should say, he flies; for there is a good deal of the spread-eagle about him.

MISS DURANT. He leaves his toys all over the hotel; I suppose you would say his plumes.

REVERDY. Well, he's a dauntless American infant; a child of nature and of freedom.

MRS. COSTELLO. Oh, nature and freedom! We have heard too much of *them*.

REVERDY. Wait till you are stopped at the New York custom-house! The youthful Miller and I have struck up a friendship: he introduced me to his sister.

MRS. COSTELLO. You don't mean to say you spoke to her!

REVERDY. Spoke to her? Yes, indeed—and she answered me.

MISS DURANT. She was not like the Russian princess!

REVERDY. No, she's as little as possible like the Russian princess; but she's very charming in another style. As soon as Mr. Winterbourne arrives (and you must excuse me for saying that he takes a deuce of a time about it), I shall console myself for the loss of your society by plunging into that of the Millers.

MRS. COSTELLO. You won't lose us, Mr. Reverdy: you can console yourself with me.

REVERDY. Oh, thank you!

MRS. COSTELLO. Frederick will devote himself to Alice.

MISS DURANT. We had better wait till he comes! I have no patience with his delay.

MRS. COSTELLO. Neither have I, my dear; but I may as well take the opportunity of remarking that a young lady shouldn't seem too eager . . .

MISS DURANT. Too eager?

MRS. COSTELLO. For the arrival of a gentleman.

MISS DURANT. I see what you mean—more reserve. But simply before you . . .

REVERDY. And before me, please. Am I nobody?

MISS DURANT. Nobody at all!

REVERDY. Well, I don't care, for I descry

in the distance the adorable Miss Miller!

MISS DURANT. I'm glad she's in the distance.

REVERDY. Ah, but she's coming this way.

MISS DURANT. (*Quickly.*) I forbid you to speak to her.

REVERDY. (*Aside.*) Ah, then I *am* somebody? (*Aloud.*) I can't cut the poor girl, you know.

MISS DURANT. You needn't see her. You can look at me.

MRS. COSTELLO. She's always wandering about the garden—the image of idleness and inanity.

REVERDY. She's not as serious as we, nor as well occupied, certainly; but she's bored to death. She has got no one to flirt with.

MISS DURANT. She shall not flirt with you, at any rate!

REVERDY. Do you wish me to hide behind a tree?

MISS DURANT. No, you can sit down here (*indicating the bench beside her*), and take my parasol—so!—and hold it before your face, as if you were shading your eyes.

REVERDY. (*With the parasol.*) From Miss Daisy Miller? It's true she's very dazzling! (DAISY *enters from the right, strolling slowly, as if she has nothing to do, and passes across the stage in front of the others, who sit silent, watching her,* REVERDY *peeping for a moment from behind his parasol.* "*She was dressed in white muslin, with a hundred frills and flounces, and knots of pale-colored ribbon. She was bare-headed; but she balanced in her hand a large parasol, with a deep border of embroidery; and she was strikingly, admirably pretty.*" [1] *She looks at the others as she passes them, and goes out on the left—not into the hotel.* REVERDY *continues.*) Now, then, may I look out?

MISS DURANT. (*Taking back her parasol.*) She saw you, I'm happy to say.

REVERDY. Oh yes, I gave her a wink!

MRS. COSTELLO. That's the way she roams about—

MISS DURANT. Seeking whom she may devour!

REVERDY. Poor little creature! I'm the only tolerably good-looking young man in the hotel.

---

[1] From the story. [Henry James's footnote]

MRS. COSTELLO. Mercy on us! I hope she won't get hold of Frederick!

REVERDY. Not if I can help it, dear Madam. I have never seen Frederick—but I mistrust Frederick.

MRS. COSTELLO. He's not at all in your style. He's had a foreign education. He speaks a dozen languages.

REVERDY. (*Aside.*) An awful prig—I can see that.

MRS. COSTELLO. Let us hope that, thanks to his foreign education, he will be out of danger. Such people as that can only disgust him.

REVERDY. I know the style of fellow you mean—a very high collar and a very stiff spine! He speaks a dozen languages—but he doesn't speak the language of Schenectady. He won't understand an American girl—he had better leave her alone.

MISS DURANT. I am very much obliged to you—for me!

(*Enter a* WAITER *from the hotel.*)

REVERDY. Oh, you are not an American; you're an angel!

THE WAITER. (*Approaching with a bow.*) The breakfast that Madame ordered is served.

MRS. COSTELLO. (*To her companions.*) It's just twelve o'clock; we certainly can't wait any longer.

MISS DURANT. I don't believe he's coming at all!

MRS. COSTELLO. Ah, if I've only brought on a headache for nothing!

REVERDY. (*Aside.*) Won't he catch it when he arrives? (*They pass into the hotel, the* WAITER *leading the way.*)

(*Scene Third:* EUGENIO, *then* WINTERBOURNE *and the* WAITER. EUGENIO *comes out of the hotel, then looks about him and begins to call. He is without his hat and satchel.*)

EUGENIO. Meester Randolph! Meester Randolph! Confound that infernal child—it's the fifth time this morning that I've chased him round the garden! (*Stands calling again.*) Meester Randolph! Meester Randolph! He is always there when he's not wanted and never when he is, and when I find him I haven't even the right to pinch his ear! He begins to kick like a little mule, and he has nails in his boots—for the mountains. Meester Randolph! Meester Randolph! Drat the little wretch —I'm a courier, not a nurse! (*Exit to the right, while* WINTERBOURNE *comes down from the hotel, followed by a* WAITER, *the same who has just appeared, carrying a little tray with a service of black coffee.*)

WINTERBOURNE. I will have my coffee here, it's so close in the hotel. (*The* WAITER *places the tray on a small table, which he draws up to a bench.* WINTERBOURNE *takes out a card, on which, on his pocket-book, he writes a few words.*) And please take that card to the lady whose name I have written there, and ask her when it will be convenient for her to see me.

THE WAITER. (*Looking at the card.*) The Russian lady who arrived three days ago? I will let you know, sir.

WINTERBOURNE. (*Seated at the little table.*) Wait a moment. Do you know whether Mrs. Costello has breakfasted?

THE WAITER. Mrs. Costello? The lady with the young lady, and the gentleman also young?

WINTERBOURNE. I know nothing about her companions. A lady with her hair very high. She is rather—rather—

THE WAITER. Yes, sir, she is rather high altogether! When she gives an order—

WINTERBOURNE. (*Pouring out his coffee.*) I don't ask you to describe her—I ask you if she has breakfasted.

THE WAITER. The party's at table now, sir. I conducted them myself, five minutes ago. I think they waited for you, sir; they expected you to arrive.

WINTERBOURNE. I arrived an hour ago, by the train; but I was dusty, and I had to have a bath. (*Lighting a cigarette.*) Then while I dressed, to save time, I had my breakfast brought to my room. Where do they usually take their coffee?

THE WAITER. They take it in our beautiful garden, sir.

WINTERBOURNE. Very good. I will wait for them here. That's all. (*The* WAITER *re-enters the hotel.* WINTERBOURNE *puffs his cigarette.*) There is no use in being in a hurry. I want to be eager—but I don't want to be too eager. That worthy man is quite right; when Aunt Louisa gives an order, it's a military command. She has ordered me up from Geneva, and I've marched at the word; but I'll rest a little before reporting at headquarters. (*Puffs his cigarette.*) It coincides very happily, for I don't know that, without this pretext, I should have ventured to come. Three days ago, the waiter said? A week ago, at the villa, they told me she had gone. There is always a mystery in that woman's movements. Yes, Aunt Louisa is rather high; but it's not of her I'm afraid! (*Puffs a moment in silence.*)

(*Scene Fourth:* WINTERBOURNE, RANDOLPH, *then* DAISY.)

RANDOLPH. (*He comes in from the back, approaches* WINTERBOURNE, *and stops.* "The child, who was diminutive for his years, had an aged expression of countenance, a pale complexion, and sharp little features. He was dressed in knickerbockers, with red stockings, which displayed his poor little spindleshanks; he also wore a brilliant red cravat. He carried in his hand a long alpenstock, the sharp point of which he thrust into everything that he approached—the flower-beds, the garden-benches. . . . In front of* WINTERBOURNE *he paused, looking at him with a pair of bright, penetrating little eyes."*[1] WINTERBOURNE, *smoking, returns his gaze.*) Will you give me a lump of sugar?

WINTERBOURNE. Yes, you may take one; but I don't think sugar is good for little boys.

RANDOLPH. (*He steps forward and carefully possesses himself of the whole contents of the plate. From these he still more carefully selects the largest lump, depositing the others in his pocket. Biting, with a grimace.*) Oh, blazes! it's hard!

WINTERBOURNE. Take care, young man. You'll hurt your teeth.

RANDOLPH. I haven't got any teeth to hurt; they've all come out. I've only got seven teeth. Mother counted them last night, and one came out afterwards. She said she'd slap me if any more came out. I can't help it—it's this old Europe. It's the climate that makes 'em come out. In

---

[1] From the story. [Henry James's footnote]

America they didn't come out; it's these hotels!

WINTERBOURNE. If you eat all that sugar, your mother will certainly slap you.

RANDOLPH. She's got to give me some candy, then. I can't get any candy here— any American candy. American candy's the best.

WINTERBOURNE. And are American boys the best little boys?

RANDOLPH. I don't know. I'm an American boy!

WINTERBOURNE. I see you are one of the best.

RANDOLPH. That isn't what my mother says, you can bet your life on that!

WINTERBOURNE. Oh, your mother's too modest!

RANDOLPH. (*Astride his alpenstock, looking at* WINTERBOURNE.) She's sick—she's always sick. It's this old Europe! Are you an American man?

WINTERBOURNE. Oh, yes, a fellow-citizen. (*Aside.*) I wonder whether I was once like that!

RANDOLPH. American men are the best.

WINTERBOURNE. So they often say.

RANDOLPH. (*Looking off to the left.*) Here comes my sister. She's an American girl.

WINTERBOURNE. American girls are the best girls.

RANDOLPH. Oh, my sister ain't the best. She's always blowing at me!

WINTERBOURNE. I imagine that's your fault, not hers. (DAISY *comes in from the left in the same manner as on her previous entrance, and on reaching the middle of the stage stops and looks at* WINTERBOURNE *and at* RANDOLPH, *who has converted his alpenstock into a vaulting-pole, and is springing about violently.* WINTERBOURNE *continues, getting up.*) By Jove, how pretty!

DAISY. Well, Randolph, what *are* you doing?

RANDOLPH. I'm going up the Alps. This is the way!

WINTERBOURNE. That's the way they come down.

RANDOLPH. He's all right; he's an American man!

WINTERBOURNE. (*Aside.*) It seems to me

that I have been in a manner presented. (*Approaches* DAISY, *throwing away his cigarette. Aloud, with great civility.*) This little boy and I have made acquaintance.

DAISY. (*She looks at him a moment serenely, and then, as if she had scarcely heard him, addresses* RANDOLPH *again.*) I should like to know where you got that pole!

RANDOLPH. The same way as you get your things. I made Eugenio buy it.

WINTERBOURNE. (*Aside.*) With a little commission!

DAISY. You don't mean to say you're going to take that pole to Italy?

WINTERBOURNE. (*Same manner.*) Are you thinking of going to Italy?

DAISY. (*Looking at him, and then looking away.*) Yes, sir.

WINTERBOURNE. Are you going over the Simplon?

DAISY. I don't know—I suppose it's some mountain. Randolph, what mountain are we going over?

RANDOLPH. Going where?

DAISY. To Italy. (*Arranging her ribbons.*) Don't you know about Italy?

RANDOLPH. No, and I don't want to. I want to go to America!

WINTERBOURNE. Oh, Italy's a beautiful place.

RANDOLPH. Can you get any candy there?

DAISY. I hope not! I guess you have had candy enough, and mother thinks so too.

RANDOLPH. (*Still jumping about.*) I haven't had any for ever so long—for a hundred weeks!

DAISY. Why, Randolph, I don't see how you can tell— (*She pauses a moment.*) Well I don't care! (*Looks down at her dress, and continues to smooth her ribbons.*)

WINTERBOURNE. (*Aside.*) Does she accept my acquaintance or not? It's rather sudden, and it wouldn't do at Geneva. But why else did she come and plant herself in front of me? She is the prettiest of the pretty, and, I declare, I'll risk it! (*After a moment, aloud.*) We are very fortunate in our weather, are we not?

DAISY. Well, yes, we've got nice weather.

WINTERBOURNE. And still more fortunate in our scenery. (*Indicating the view.*)

DAISY. Well, yes, the scenery's lovely. It seems very mountainous.

WINTERBOURNE. Ah, Switzerland *is* mountainous, you know.

DAISY. I don't know much about it. We have only been here a week.

WINTERBOURNE. (*Smiling.*) In a week one can see a good deal.

DAISY. Well, *we* haven't; we have only walked round a little.

WINTERBOURNE. (*Aside.*) What a remarkable type! (*Aloud.*) You must be rather tired: there are plenty of chairs. (*Draws forward two of them.*)

DAISY. (*Looking at them a moment.*) You'll be very clever if you can get Randolph to sit.

WINTERBOURNE. I don't care a fig about Randolph. (DAISY *seats herself. Aside.*) Oh, Geneva, Geneva!

DAISY. (*Smoothing her ribbons.*) Well, he's only nine. We've sat round a good deal, too.

WINTERBOURNE. (*Seated beside her.*) It's very pleasant, these summer days.

DAISY. Well, yes, it's very pleasant. But it's nicer in the evening.

WINTERBOURNE. Ah, much nicer in the evening. It's remarkably nice in the evening. (*Aside.*) What the deuce is she coming to? (*Aloud.*) When you get to Italy you'll find the evenings there! . . .

DAISY. I've heard a good deal about the evenings there.

WINTERBOURNE. In Venice, you know—on the water—with music!

DAISY. I don't know much about it. (*With a little laugh.*) I don't know much about **anything!**

WINTERBOURNE. (*Aside.*) Heaven forgive her, she's charming! I must really ascertain . . . (*To* RANDOLPH, *who has continued to roam about, and who comes back to them with his alpenstock, catching him and drawing him between his knees.*) Tell me your name, my beautiful boy!

RANDOLPH. (*Struggling.*) Well, you drop me first!

DAISY. Why, Randolph, I should think you'd like it!

WINTERBOURNE. (*Aside.*) Jupiter, that is a little strong!

RANDOLPH. (*Liberating himself.*) Try it yourself! My name is Randolph C. Miller.

WINTERBOURNE. (Aside.) Alarming child! But she doesn't seem to be alarmed.

RANDOLPH. (Levelling his alpenstock at DAISY, who averts it with her hand.) And I'll tell you her name.

DAISY. (Leaning back serenely.) You had better wait till you are asked.

WINTERBOURNE. I should like very much to know your name.

RANDOLPH. Her name is Daisy Miller.

WINTERBOURNE. (Expressively.) How very interesting!

DAISY. (Looking at him, aside.) Well, he's a queer specimen! I guess he's laughing.

RANDOLPH. That isn't her real name— that isn't her name on her cards.

DAISY. It's a pity that you haven't got one of my cards!

RANDOLPH. Her name is Annie P. Miller.

WINTERBOURNE. Oh, I see. (Aside.) That doesn't tell me much.

DAISY. (Indicating WINTERBOURNE.) Ask him his name.

RANDOLPH. Ask him yourself! My father's name is Ezra B. Miller. My father ain't in Europe. My father's in a better place than Europe.

WINTERBOURNE. (Uncertain.) Ah, you have had the misfortune . . .

RANDOLPH. My father's in Schenectady. He does a big business. He's rich, you can bet your head!

WINTERBOURNE. (Aside.) Oh, in Schenectady? I thought he meant in Paradise!

DAISY. (To RANDOLPH.) Well, you needn't stick your pole into my eye!

RANDOLPH. (To WINTERBOURNE.) Didn't I tell you she was always blowing? (Scampers away and disappears.)

DAISY. (Looking after him.) He doesn't like Europe; he wants to go back. He hasn't got any boys here. There's one boy here, but he's always going round with a teacher.

WINTERBOURNE. And your brother hasn't any teacher?

DAISY. Mother thought of getting him one, to travel round with us. But Randolph said he didn't want a teacher when school didn't keep; he said he wouldn't have lessons when he was in the cars. And we are in the cars most of the time. There was an English lady we met in the cars; her name was Miss Featherstone—perhaps you

know her. She wanted to know why I didn't give Randolph lessons—give him instruction, she called it. I guess he could give me more instruction than I could give him! He's very smart—he's only nine.

WINTERBOURNE. (Aside.) He might be ninety!

DAISY. Mother's going to get a teacher for him as soon as we get to Italy. Can you get good teachers in Italy?

WINTERBOURNE. Oh, it's the land of art— of science.

DAISY. Well, I guess he doesn't want to study art; but she's going to find some school, if she can. (Pensively.) Randolph ought to learn some more.

WINTERBOURNE. It depends upon what it is!

DAISY. (After a silence, during which her eyes have rested upon him.) I presume you are a German.

WINTERBOURNE. (Rising quickly.) Oh dear, no! I shouldn't have ventured to speak to you, if your brother's mention of my nationality had not seemed a guarantee . . .

DAISY. (Getting up.) I didn't suppose my brother knew. And you do speak queerly, any way!

WINTERBOURNE. I'm a countryman of your own. But I should tell you that I have spent many years in this old Europe, as your brother says.

DAISY. Do you live here—in the mountains?

WINTERBOURNE. (Aside.) Does she think I'm a goatherd? (Aloud.) No, I live just now at Geneva.

DAISY. Well, you are peculiar, anyhow!

WINTERBOURNE. (Aside.) So are you, if you come to that. (Aloud.) I'm afraid I have got rather out of the way— (Pauses for a moment.)

DAISY. Out of the way of what?

WINTERBOURNE. Of making myself agreeable to the young ladies.

DAISY. Haven't they got any over here? I must say I haven't seen any! Of course I haven't looked out much for them.

WINTERBOURNE. You have looked out more for the gentlemen!

DAISY. Well, at Schenectady I didn't have to look out.

WINTERBOURNE. (*Aside.*) Queer place, Schenectady.

DAISY. I had so much society. But over here— (*She hesitates.*)

WINTERBOURNE. Over here?

DAISY. Well, you're the first gentleman that has been at all attentive.

WINTERBOURNE. Ah, you see, they're afraid!

DAISY. (*Continuing.*) And the first I've cared anything about!

WINTERBOURNE. (*Aside.*) And to think that, at the beginning, *I* was afraid. (*Aloud.*) If they knew how kind you are they would be much less timid.

DAISY. I hate gentlemen to be timid. That's only for us.

WINTERBOURNE. (*Aside.*) "For us" is enchanting!

(*Scene Fifth:* DAISY, WINTERBOURNE, EUGENIO, *who comes in hastily from the right, wiping his forehead.*)

EUGENIO. Mademoiselle, I have been looking for an hour for Meester Randolph. He must be drowned in the lake!

DAISY. I guess he's talking to that waiter. (*Serenely.*) He likes to talk to that waiter.

EUGENIO. He shouldn't talk to waiters, Mademoiselle.

WINTERBOURNE. (*Aside.*) Only to couriers —the hierarchy!

DAISY. I want to introduce you to a friend of mine—Mr.—Mr.— (*To* WINTERBOURNE.) I declare, I don't know your name.

WINTERBOURNE. (*Aside.*) To the courier? Excuse me!

EUGENIO. (*Very proper.*) I have the honor of knowing the name of Monsieur.

DAISY. Gracious, you know everything!

EUGENIO. (*Aside.*) The lover of the Katkoff! (*Aloud.*) I found Meester Randolph, but he escaped again.

DAISY. Well, Eugenio, you're a splendid courier, but you can't make much impression on Randolph.

EUGENIO. I do what I can, Mademoiselle. The lunch is waiting, and Madame is at the table. If you will excuse me, I will give up the chase. (*Glancing at* WINTERBOURNE,

aside.) Is he leaving the Katkoff for the child?

DAISY. You needn't be so grand, need he? (*To* WINTERBOURNE.) It's not the first time you've been introduced to a courier!

WINTERBOURNE. (*Stiffly.*) The very first.

EUGENIO. (*Aside.*) He has never kept one. (*Aloud.*) If Mademoiselle will pass into the hotel! (*Aside again.*) The child is not for every one.

DAISY. Tell mother to begin—that I'm talking to a gentleman.

WINTERBOURNE. (*Protesting.*) I shall be very sorry to incommode your mother.

DAISY. (*Smiling.*) I like the way you say such things. (*Familiarly.*) What are you going to do all day?

WINTERBOURNE. (*Embarrassed.*) I hardly know. I've only just arrived.

DAISY. I will come out after lunch.

WINTERBOURNE. (*With extreme respect.*) I shall be here, to take your commands.

DAISY. Well, you *do* say them! About two o'clock.

WINTERBOURNE. I shall not go far.

DAISY. (*Going.*) And I shall learn your name from Eugenio.

EUGENIO. (*Aside.*) And something else as well! He is not for the child. (*Follows* DAISY *into the hotel.*)

(*Scene Sixth:* WINTERBOURNE *alone, then* MADAME DE KATKOFF.)

WINTERBOURNE. She's simply amazing! I have never seen them like that. I have seen them worse—oh, yes!—and I have seen them better; but I've never encountered that particular shade—that familiarity, that facility, that fragility! She's too audacious to be innocent, and too candid to be—the other thing. But her candor itself is a queer affair. Coming up to me and proposing acquaintance, and letting her eyes rest on mine! Planting herself there like a flower to be gathered! Introducing me to her courier, and offering me a rendezvous at the end of twenty minutes! Are they all like that, the little American girls? It's time I should go back and see. (*Seeing* MME. DE KATKOFF.) But I can hardly go while I have this reason for staying!

MME. DE KATKOFF. (*She comes out of the hotel; she has still her book under her arm.*) They brought me your card, but I thought it better I should come and see you here.

WINTERBOURNE. I know why you do that: you think it's less encouraging than to receive me in-doors.

MME. DE KATKOFF. (*Smiling.*) Oh, if I could discourage you a little!

WINTERBOURNE. It's not for want of try-ing. I bore you so much!

MME. DE KATKOFF. No, you don't bore me, but you distress me. I give you so little.

WINTERBOURNE. That's for me to meas-ure. I'm content for the present.

MME. DE KATKOFF. If you had been con-tent, you wouldn't have followed me to this place.

WINTERBOURNE. I didn't follow you, and, to speak perfectly frankly, it's not for you I came.

MME. DE KATKOFF. Is it for that young lady I just saw from my window?

WINTERBOURNE. I never heard of that young lady before. I came for an aunt of mine, who is staying here.

MME. DE KATKOFF. (*Smiling again.*) Ah, if your family could only take an interest in you!

WINTERBOURNE. Don't count on them too much. I haven't seen my aunt yet.

MME. DE KATKOFF. You have asked first for me? You see, then, it *was* for me you came.

WINTERBOURNE. I wish I could believe it pleased you a little to think so.

MME. DE KATKOFF. It does please me—a little; I like you very much.

WINTERBOURNE. You always say that, when you are about to make some par-ticularly disagreeable request. You like me, but you dislike my society. On that prin-ciple, I wish you hated me!

MME. DE KATKOFF. I may come to it yet.

WINTERBOURNE. Before that, then, won't you sit down? (*Indicating a bench.*)

MME. DE KATKOFF. Thank you; I'm not tired.

WINTERBOURNE. That would be too en-couraging! I went to the villa a week ago. You had already left it.

MME. DE KATKOFF. I went first to Lau-sanne. If I had remained there, you wouldn't have found me.

WINTERBOURNE. I'm delighted you didn't remain. But I'm sorry you are altering your house.

MME. DE KATKOFF. Only two rooms. That's why I came away: the workmen made too much noise.

WINTERBOURNE. I hope they are not the rooms I know—in which the happiest hours of my life have been passed!

MME. DE KATKOFF. I see why you wished me to sit down. You want to begin a siege.

WINTERBOURNE. No, I was only going to say that I shall always see with par-ticular vividness your little blue parlor.

MME. DE KATKOFF. They are going to change it to red. (*Aside.*) Perhaps that will cure him! (*Aloud.*) Apropos of your family, have they come to Europe to bring you home?

WINTERBOURNE. As I tell you, I haven't yet ascertained their intentions.

MME. DE KATKOFF. I take a great interest in them. I feel a little responsible for you.

WINTERBOURNE. You don't care a straw for me!

MME. DE KATKOFF. Let me give you a proof. I think it would conduce to your happiness to return for a while to America.

WINTERBOURNE. To *my* happiness? You are confounding it with your own.

MME. DE KATKOFF. It is true that the two things are rather distinct. But you have been in Europe for years—for years and years.

WINTERBOURNE. Oh, I have been here too long. I know that.

MME. DE KATKOFF. You ought to go over and make the acquaintance of your com-patriots.

WINTERBOURNE. Going over isn't neces-sary. I can do it here.

MME. DE KATKOFF. You ought at least to see their institutions—their scenery.

WINTERBOURNE. Don't talk about scen-ery, on the Lake of Geneva! As for Ameri-can institutions, I see them in their fruits.

MME. DE KATKOFF. In their fruits?

WINTERBOURNE. Little nectarines and plums. A very pretty bloom, but decidedly crude. What book are you reading?

MME. DE KATKOFF. I don't know what. The last French novel.

WINTERBOURNE. Are you going to remain in the garden?

MME. DE KATKOFF. (*Looks at him a moment.*) I see what you are coming to: you wish to offer to read to me.

WINTERBOURNE. As I did in the little blue parlor!

MME. DE KATKOFF. You read very well; but we are not there now.

WINTERBOURNE. A quiet corner, under the trees, will do as well.

MME. DE KATKOFF. We neither of us have the time. I recommend you to your aunt. She will be sure to take you in hand.

WINTERBOURNE. I have an idea I shan't fall in love with my aunt.

MME. DE KATKOFF. I am sorry for her. I should like you as a nephew.

WINTERBOURNE. I should like you as a serious woman!

MME. DE KATKOFF. I am intensely serious. Perhaps you will believe it when I tell you that I leave this place to-day.

WINTERBOURNE. I don't call that serious: I call it cruel.

MME. DE KATKOFF. At all events, it's deliberate. Vevey is too hot; I shall go higher up into the mountains.

WINTERBOURNE. You knew it was hot when you came.

MME. DE KATKOFF. (*After a pause, with significance.*) Yes, but it's hotter than I supposed.

WINTERBOURNE. You don't like meeting old friends.

MME. DE KATKOFF. (*Aside.*) No, nor old enemies! (*Aloud.*) I like old friends in the autumn—the melancholy season! I shall count on seeing you then.

WINTERBOURNE. And not before, of course. Say at once you wish to cut me.

MME. DE KATKOFF. (*Smiling.*) Very good: I wish to cut you!

WINTERBOURNE. You give a charm even to that! Where shall you be in the autumn?

MME. DE KATKOFF. I shall be at the villa —if the little blue parlor is altered! In the winter I shall go to Rome.

WINTERBOURNE. A happy journey, then! I shall go to America.

MME. DE KATKOFF. That's capital. Let me give you a word of advice.

WINTERBOURNE. Yes, that's the finishing touch!

MME. DE KATKOFF. The little nectarines and plums: don't mind if they *are* a trifle crude! Pick out a fair one, a sweet one—

WINTERBOURNE. (*Stopping her with a gesture.*) Don't, don't! I shall see you before you go.

MME. DE KATKOFF. (*Aside.*) Not if I can help it! (*Aloud.*) I think this must be your family. (*Goes into the hotel.*)

(*Scene Seventh:* WINTERBOURNE, MRS. COSTELLO, MISS DURANT, REVERDY, *who come out of the hotel, as* MME. DE KATKOFF *enters it.*)

REVERDY. We are always meeting the Russian princess!

MISS DURANT. If you call that meeting her, when she never looks at you!

MRS. COSTELLO. She doesn't look at you, but she sees you. Bless my soul, if here isn't Frederick!

WINTERBOURNE. My dear aunt, I was only waiting till you had breakfasted.

MISS DURANT. (*Aside.*) He was talking with the Russian princess!

MRS. COSTELLO. You might have sat down with us: we waited an hour.

WINTERBOURNE. I breakfasted in my room. I was obliged on my arrival to jump into a bath.

MISS DURANT. (*Aside.*) He's very cold— he's very cold!

WINTERBOURNE. They told me you were at table, and I just sat down here.

MRS. COSTELLO. You were in no hurry to embrace me—after ten years?

WINTERBOURNE. It was just because of those ten years; they seemed to make you so venerable that I was pausing—as at the entrance of a shrine! Besides, I knew you had charming company.

MRS. COSTELLO. You shall discover how charming. This is Alice Durant, who is almost our cousin.

WINTERBOURNE. (*Smiling.*) Almost? I wish it were quite.

MRS. COSTELLO. And that is Mr. Charles Reverdy.

REVERDY. Who is almost their courier!

WINTERBOURNE. I must relieve you of your duties,

REVERDY. (*Aside.*) Oh, thank you, thank you! By George, if I'm relieved I'll look out for Miss Miller. (*Looks about him, and finally steals away.*)

MRS. COSTELLO. My dear Frederick, in all this time you have not changed for the worse.

WINTERBOURNE. How can you tell that—in three minutes?

MISS DURANT. (*Aside.*) Decidedly good-looking, but fearfully distant!

MRS. COSTELLO. Oh, if you are not agreeable, we shall be particularly disappointed. We count on you immensely.

WINTERBOURNE. I shall do my best, dear aunt.

MRS. COSTELLO. Especially for our sweet Alice.

MISS DURANT. Oh, Cousin Louisa, how can you?

MRS. COSTELLO. I thought of you when I invited her to come to Europe.

WINTERBOURNE. It was a very happy thought. I don't mean thinking of me, but inviting Miss Durant.

MISS DURANT. (*To* WINTERBOURNE.) I can't say it was of you I thought when I accepted.

WINTERBOURNE. I should never flatter myself: there are too many other objects of interest.

MRS. COSTELLO. That's precisely what we have been talking of. We are surrounded by objects of interest, and we depend upon you to be our guide.

WINTERBOURNE. My dear aunt, I'm afraid I don't know much about them.

MRS. COSTELLO. You'll have a motive to-day for learning. I have an idea that you have always wanted a motive. In that stupid old Geneva there can't be many.

WINTERBOURNE. Ah, if there's one, it's enough!

MISS DURANT. (*Aside.*) If there's *one?* He's in love with some dreadful Genevese!

MRS. COSTELLO. My young companion has a great desire to ascend a mountain—to examine a glacier.

MISS DURANT. Cousin Louisa, you make me out too bold!

WINTERBOURNE. (*Aside.*) She's not bold, then, this one, like the other? I think I prefer the other. (*Aloud.*) You should go to Zermatt. You're in the midst of the glaciers there.

MRS. COSTELLO. We shall be delighted to go—under your escort. Mr. Reverdy will look after *me!*

MISS DURANT. (*Glancing about for him.*) When he has done with Miss Daisy Miller!

WINTERBOURNE. (*Smiling.*) Even among the glaciers, I flatter myself I can take care of both of you.

MISS DURANT. It will be all the easier, as I never leave your aunt.

MRS. COSTELLO. She doesn't rush about the world alone, like so many American girls. She has been brought up like the young ladies in Geneva. Her education was surrounded with every precaution.

WINTERBOURNE. (*Smiling.*) With too many, perhaps! The best education is seeing the world a little.

MRS. COSTELLO. That's precisely what I wish her to do. When we have finished Zermatt, we wish to come back to Interlaken, and from Interlaken you shall take us to Lucerne.

WINTERBOURNE. (*Gravely.*) Perhaps you'll draw up a little list.

MISS DURANT. (*Aside.*) Perfectly polite, but no enthusiasm! (*Aloud.*) I'm afraid Mr. Winterbourne isn't at liberty; he has *other* friends.

MRS. COSTELLO. He hasn't another aunt, I imagine!

WINTERBOURNE. (*Aside.*) Fortunately not! (*Aloud to* MISS DURANT.) It's very charming of you to think of that.

MISS DURANT. Possibly we are indiscreet, as we just saw you talking to a lady.

WINTERBOURNE. Madame de Katkoff? She leaves this place to-day.

MRS. COSTELLO. You don't mean to follow her, I hope? (*Aside.*) It's best to be firm with him at the start.

WINTERBOURNE. My dear aunt, I don't follow every woman I speak to.

MISS DURANT. (*Aside.*) Ah, that's meant for us! Mr. Reverdy is never so rude. I would thank him to come back.

MRS. COSTELLO. On the 1st of October, you know, you shall take us to Italy.

WINTERBOURNE. Ah! every one is going to Italy.

MISS DURANT. Every one? Madame de

Katkoff, perhaps.

WINTERBOURNE. Madame de Katkoff, precisely; and Mr. Randolph C. Miller and his sister Daisy.

MRS. COSTELLO. Bless my soul! What do you know about that?

WINTERBOURNE. I know what they have told me.

MRS. COSTELLO. Mercy on us! What opportunity?—

WINTERBOURNE. Just now, while I had my coffee.

MISS DURANT. As I say, Mr. Winterbourne has a great many friends.

WINTERBOURNE. He only asks to add you to the number.

MISS DURANT. Side by side with Miss Daisy Miller? Thank you very much.

MRS. COSTELLO. Come, my dear Frederick, that girl is not your friend.

WINTERBOURNE. Upon my word, I don't know what she is, and I should be very glad if you could tell me.

MRS. COSTELLO. That's very easily done: she's a little American flirt.

WINTERBOURNE. Ah! she's a little American flirt!

MISS DURANT. She's a vulgar little chatterbox.

WINTERBOURNE. Ah! she's a vulgar little chatterbox!

MRS. COSTELLO. She's in no sort of society.

WINTERBOURNE. Ah! she's in no sort of society!

MISS DURANT. You would never know her in America.

WINTERBOURNE. If I should never know her in America, it seems to me a reason for seizing the opportunity here.

MRS. COSTELLO. The opportunity appears to have come to you very easily.

WINTERBOURNE. I confess it did, rather. We fell into conversation while I sat there on the bench.

MRS. COSTELLO. Perhaps she sat down beside you?

WINTERBOURNE. I won't deny that she did; she is wonderfully charming.

MISS DURANT. Oh! if that's all that's necessary to be charming—

MRS. COSTELLO. You must give up the attempt—mustn't you, my dear? My poor Frederick, this is very dreadful!

WINTERBOURNE. So it seems; but I don't understand.

MRS. COSTELLO. What should you say at Geneva of a young woman who made such advances?

WINTERBOURNE. Such advances? I don't know that they were advances.

MRS. COSTELLO. Ah! if you wish to wait till she invites you to her room!

WINTERBOURNE. (Laughing.) I shall not have to wait very long.

MISS DURANT. Hadn't I better leave you?

MRS. COSTELLO. Poor child, I understand that you shrink . . . But we must make it clear.

MISS DURANT. Oh, yes, we must make it clear!

WINTERBOURNE. Do make it clear; I want it to be clear.

MRS. COSTELLO. Ask yourself, then, what they would say at Geneva.

WINTERBOURNE. They would say she was rather far gone. But we are not at Geneva.

MRS. COSTELLO. We are only a few miles off. Miss Daisy Miller is very far gone indeed.

WINTERBOURNE. Ah! what a pity! But I thought, now, in New York—

MRS. COSTELLO. (Sternly.) Frederick, don't lift your hand against your mother-country!

WINTERBOURNE. Never in the world. I only repeat what I hear—that over there all this sort of thing—the manners of young persons, the standard of propriety—is quite different.

MISS DURANT. I only know how *I* was brought up!

WINTERBOURNE. (Slightly ironical.) Ah, that settles it.

MRS. COSTELLO. We must take him back with us, to see.

WINTERBOURNE. Not to see, you mean—not to see my dear little friend!

MRS. COSTELLO. In the best society—never.

WINTERBOURNE. Oh, hang the best society, then!

MRS. COSTELLO. (With majesty.) I am exceedingly obliged to you.

WINTERBOURNE. Oh, *you* are the best society! And the little girl with the naughty brother is the worst?

MRS. COSTELLO. The worst *I* have ever seen.

WINTERBOURNE. (*Rather gravely, laying his hand on her arm.*) My dear aunt, the best, then, ought to be awfully good!

MISS DURANT. (*Aside.*) He means that for an epigram! I'll make him go and look for Mr. Reverdy. (*Aloud.*) I wonder what has become of Mr. Reverdy.

MRS. COSTELLO. (*Sharply.*) Never mind Mr. Reverdy; I'll look after him. (*To* WINTERBOURNE.) If you should see a little more of those vulgar people, you would find that they don't stand the test.

WINTERBOURNE. Oh, I shall see a little more of them—in a quarter of an hour. (*Looking at his watch.*) The young lady is coming back at two o'clock.

MRS. COSTELLO. Gracious goodness! Have you made an appointment?

WINTERBOURNE. I don't know whether it's an appointment, but she said she would come back again.

MRS. COSTELLO. (*To* MISS DURANT.) My precious darling, *we* must go in. We can hardly be expected to assist at such a scene.

WINTERBOURNE. My dear aunt, there is plenty of time yet.

MISS DURANT. Ah, no; she'll be before! Would you kindly look for Mr. Reverdy?

WINTERBOURNE. (*Extremely polite.*) With the greatest of pleasure.

MRS. COSTELLO. Later in the afternoon, if this extraordinary interview is over, we should like you to go with us into the town.

WINTERBOURNE. (*In the same tone.*) With the greatest of pleasure. (*Aside.*) They hate her ferociously, and it makes me feel sorry for her.

MRS. COSTELLO. (*To* MISS DURANT.) Quickly, my dear! We must get out of the way.

WINTERBOURNE. Let me at least see you into the house. (*Accompanies them into the hotel.*)

(*Scene Eighth:* CHARLES REVERDY, RANDOLPH, *then* DAISY.)

REVERDY. (*Coming in from behind with the child on his back.*) The horrid little wretch! I'm like Sinbad the Sailor with the Old Man of the Sea! Don't you think you've had about enough?

RANDOLPH. (*Snapping a little whip.*) Oh, no; I haven't had enough. I'll tell you when I've had enough.

REVERDY. Oh, come! I've galloped twenty miles; I've been through all my paces. You must sit still in the saddle a while. (*Pauses in front while* RANDOLPH *bounces up and down.*) I'm playing horse with the brother to be agreeable to the sister; but he's riding me to death!

RANDOLPH. (*Still brandishing his whip.*) I want you to prance about and to kick. Get up, sir; get up!

REVERDY. (*Aside.*) It's the devil's own game—here at the door of the hotel! (*Aloud.*) I'll prance about so that you'll come off.

RANDOLPH. (*Firm in his place.*) If you throw me off, I'll give you a licking! Get up, sir, get up!

REVERDY. (*Aside.*) Damn the little demon! It was a happy thought of mine.

RANDOLPH. (*Kicking.*) These are my spurs. I'll drive in my spurs! Get up, sir, get up!

REVERDY. Oh misery, here goes! (*He begins to imitate the curvetting of a horse, in the hope of throwing* RANDOLPH *off, but, seeing* DAISY *issue from the hotel, suddenly stops.*)

DAISY. (*Staring.*) Well, Randolph, what are you doing up there?

RANDOLPH. I'm riding on a mule!

REVERDY. (*With a groan.*) A mule? Not even the nobler animal! My dear young lady, couldn't you persuade him to dismount?

DAISY. (*Laughing.*) You look so funny when you say that! I'm sure I never persuaded Randolph.

RANDOLPH. He said if I would tell him where you were, he would give me a ride.

REVERDY. And then, when he was up, he refused to tell me!

RANDOLPH. I told you mother wouldn't like it. She wants Daisy and me to be proper.

REVERDY. (*Aside.*) "Me to be proper"! He's really sublime, the little fiend!

DAISY. Well, she does want you to be proper. She's waiting for you at lunch.

RANDOLPH. I don't want any lunch: there's nothing fit to eat.

DAISY. Well, I guess there is, if you'll go and see.

REVERDY. (*Aside.*) It's uncommonly nice for me, while they argue the question!

DAISY. There's a man with candy in the hall; that's where mother wants you to be proper.

RANDOLPH. (*Jumping down.*) A man with candy. Oh, blazes!

REVERDY. (*Aside.*) Adorable creature! She has broken the spell.

RANDOLPH. (*Scampering into the hotel.*) I say, old mule, you can go to grass!

REVERDY. Delightful little nature, your brother.

DAISY. Well, he used to have a pony at home. I guess he misses that pony. Is it true that you asked him that?

REVERDY. To tell me where you were? I confess I wanted very much to know.

DAISY. Well, Randolph couldn't tell you. I was having lunch with mother. I thought you were with those ladies.

REVERDY. Whom you saw me with this morning? Oh, no; they've got another cavalier, just arrived, on purpose.

DAISY. (*Attentive.*) Another cavalier— just arrived? Do you mean that gentleman that speaks so beautifully?

REVERDY. A dozen languages? His English isn't bad—compared with my French!

DAISY. (*Thoughtful.*) Well, he looks like a cavalier. Did he come on purpose for them?

REVERDY. (*Aside.*) What does she know about him? (*Aloud.*) Oh, yes; they sent for him to Geneva.

DAISY. To Geneva? That's the one!

REVERDY. You see, they want him to be always with them; he's for their own particular consumption.

DAISY. (*Disappointed, but very simply.*) Ah, then he won't come out at two o'clock!

REVERDY. I'm sure I don't know. (*The bell of the hotel strikes two.*) There it is. You'll have a chance to see.

(WINTERBOURNE, *on the stroke of the hour, comes out of the hotel.*)

DAISY. (*Joyfully.*) Here he comes! He's too sweet!

REVERDY. (*Aside.*) Oh, I say, she had made an appointment with him while I was doing the mule!

(*Scene Ninth:* REVERDY, *for a moment;* DAISY, WINTERBOURNE.)

WINTERBOURNE. (*To* REVERDY.) I am glad to find you: Miss Durant has a particular desire to see you.

REVERDY. It's very good of you to be her messenger. (*Aside.*) That's what he calls relieving me!

WINTERBOURNE. You will find those ladies in their own sitting-room, on the second floor.

REVERDY. Oh, I know where it is. (*To* DAISY.) I shall be back in five minutes.

DAISY. I'm sure you needn't hurry.

WINTERBOURNE. I have an idea they have a good deal to say to you.

REVERDY. I hope it isn't to complain of you! (*Goes into the hotel.*)

DAISY. (*Looking at* WINTERBOURNE *a moment.*) I was afraid you wouldn't come.

WINTERBOURNE. (*Aside.*) She has a way of looking at you! (*Aloud.*) I don't know what can have given you such an impression.

DAISY. Well, you know, half the time they don't—the gentlemen.

WINTERBOURNE. That's in America, perhaps. But over here they always come.

DAISY. (*Simply.*) Well, I haven't had much experience over here.

WINTERBOURNE. I am glad to hear it. It was very good of your mother to let you leave her again.

DAISY. (*Surprised.*) Oh, mother doesn't care; she has got Eugenio.

WINTERBOURNE. (*Startled.*) Surely, not to sit with her?

DAISY. Well, he doesn't sit with her always, because he likes to go out.

WINTERBOURNE. Oh, he likes to go out!

DAISY. He's got a great many friends, Eugenio; he's awfully popular. And then, you know, poor mother isn't very amusing.

WINTERBOURNE. Ah, she isn't very amusing! (*Aside.*) Aunt Louisa was right: it isn't the best society!

DAISY. But Eugenio stays with her all he can: he says he didn't expect that so much when he came.

WINTERBOURNE. I should think not! I hope at least that it isn't a monopoly, and that I may have the pleasure of making your mother's acquaintance.

DAISY. Well, you *do* speak beautifully! I told Mr. Reverdy.

WINTERBOURNE. It was very good of you to mention it. One speaks as one can.

DAISY. Mother's awfully timid, or else I'd introduce you. She always makes a fuss if I introduce a gentleman. But I do introduce them—the ones I like.

WINTERBOURNE. If it's a sign of your liking, I hope you will introduce me. But you must know my name, which you didn't a while ago.

DAISY. Oh, Eugenio has told me your name, and I think it's very pretty. And he has told me something else.

WINTERBOURNE. I can't imagine what he should tell you about me.

DAISY. About you and someone else—that Russian lady who is leaving the hotel.

WINTERBOURNE. (*Quickly.*) Who is leaving the hotel! How does he know that?

DAISY. (*With a little laugh.*) You see it *is* true: you are very fond of that Russian lady!

WINTERBOURNE. (*Aside.*) She is leaving the hotel—but not till six o'clock. (*Aloud.*) I haven't known you very long, but I should like to give you a piece of advice. Don't gossip with your courier!

DAISY. I see you're offended—and it proves Eugenio was right. He said it was a secret—and you don't like me to know it.

WINTERBOURNE. You may know everything, my dear young lady; only don't get your information from a servant.

DAISY. Do you call Eugenio a servant? He'll be amused if I tell him that!

WINTERBOURNE. He won't be amused—he will be furious; but the particular emotion doesn't matter. It's very good of you to take such an interest.

DAISY. Oh, I don't know what I should do if I didn't take some interest! You do care for her, then?

WINTERBOURNE. (*A little annoyed.*) For the Russian lady? Oh, yes, we are old friends. (*Aside.*) My aunt's right: they don't stand the test!

DAISY. I'm very glad she is going, then. But the others mean to stay?

WINTERBOURNE. The others? What others?

DAISY. The two that Mr. Reverdy told me about, and to whom he's so very devoted.

WINTERBOURNE. It's my aunt and a friend of hers; but you needn't mind them.

DAISY. For all they mind me! But they look stylish.

WINTERBOURNE. Oh, yes, they are very stylish; you can bet your life on that, as your brother says!

DAISY. (*Looking at him a moment.*) Did you come for them, or for the Russian lady?

WINTERBOURNE. (*Aside, more annoyed.*) Ah, too many questions! (*Aloud.*) I came for none of them; I came for myself.

DAISY. (*Serenely.*) Yes, that's the impression you give me: you think a great deal of yourself! But I should like to know your aunt, all the same. She has her hair done like an old picture, and she holds herself so very well; she speaks to no one, and she dines in private. That's the way I should like to be!

WINTERBOURNE. Ah, you would make a bad exchange. My aunt is liable to fearful headaches.

DAISY. I think she is very elegant—headaches and all! I want very much to know her.

WINTERBOURNE. (*Aside.*) Goodness, what a happy thought! (*Aloud.*) She would be enchanted; only the state of her health . . .

DAISY. Oh, yes, she has an excuse; that's part of the elegance! I should like to have an excuse. Anyone can see your aunt would have one.

WINTERBOURNE. Oh, she has five hundred!

DAISY. Well, *we* haven't any, mother and I. I like a lady to be exclusive. I'm dying to be exclusive myself.

WINTERBOURNE. Be just as you are. You wouldn't be half so charming if you were different. (*Aside.*) It's odd how true that is, with all her faults!

DAISY. You don't think me charming: you only think me queer. I can see that by your manner. I should like to know your aunt, anyway.

WINTERBOURNE. It's very good of you, I'm sure; but I am afraid those headaches will interfere.

DAISY. I suppose she doesn't have a headache every day, does she?

WINTERBOURNE. (*Aside.*) What the deuce is a man to say? (*Aloud.*) She assures me she does.

DAISY. (*Turns away a moment, walks to the parapet, and stands there thoughtful.*) She doesn't want to know me! (*Looking at* WINTERBOURNE.) Why don't you say so? You needn't be afraid; I'm not afraid. (*Suddenly, with a little break in her voice.*) Gracious, she *is* exclusive!

WINTERBOURNE. So much the worse for her!

DAISY. You see, you've got to own to it! Well, I don't care. I mean to be like that—when I'm old.

WINTERBOURNE. I can't think you'll ever be old.

DAISY. Oh, you horrid thing! As if I were going to perish in my flower!

WINTERBOURNE. I should be very sorry if I thought that. But you will never have any quarrel with Time: he'll touch you very gently.

DAISY. (*At the parapet, looking over the lake.*) I hope I shall never have any quarrel with any one. I'm very good-natured.

WINTERBOURNE. (*Laughing.*) You certainly disarm criticism—oh, completely!

DAISY. Well, I don't care. Have you ever been to that old castle? (*Pointing to Chillon, in the distance.*)

WINTERBOURNE. The Castle of Chillon? Yes, in former days, more than once. I suppose you have been there, too.

DAISY. Oh, no, we haven't been there. I want to go there awfully. Of course, I mean to go there. I wouldn't go away from here without having seen that old castle!

WINTERBOURNE. It's a very pretty excursion, and very easy to make. You can drive, you know, or you can take the little steamer.

DAISY. Well, we were going last week, but mother gave out. She suffers terribly from dyspepsia. She said she couldn't go. Randolph won't go, either: he doesn't think much of old castles.

WINTERBOURNE. (*Smiling.*) Ah, your brother isn't interested in historical monuments?

DAISY. Well, he's generally disappointed. He wants to stay round here. Mother's afraid to leave him alone, and Eugenio can't be induced to stay with him, so that we haven't been to many places. But it will be too bad if we don't go up to that castle.

WINTERBOURNE. I think it might be arranged. Let me see. Couldn't you get some one to remain for the afternoon with Randolph?

DAISY. (*Suddenly.*) Oh, yes; we could get Mr. Reverdy!

WINTERBOURNE. Mr. Reverdy?

DAISY. He's awfully fond of Randolph; they're always fooling round.

WINTERBOURNE. (*Laughing.*) It isn't a bad idea. Reverdy must lay in a stock of sugar.

DAISY. There's one thing: with you, mother will be afraid to go.

WINTERBOURNE. She carries her timidity too far! We must wait till she has got used to me.

DAISY. I don't want to wait. I want to go right off.

WINTERBOURNE. Ah, you can hardly force her to come, you know.

DAISY. I don't want to force her: I want to leave her!

WINTERBOURNE. To leave her behind? What, then, would you do for an escort?

DAISY. (*Serenely.*) I would take you.

WINTERBOURNE. (*Astounded.*) Me? Me alone?

DAISY. (*Laughing.*) You seem about as timid as mother! Never mind, I'll take care of you.

WINTERBOURNE. (*Still bewildered.*) Off to Chillon—with you alone—right off?

DAISY. (*Eagerly questioning.*) Right off? Could we go now?

WINTERBORNE. (*Aside.*) She takes away my breath! (*Aloud.*) There's a boat just after three.

DAISY. We'll go straight on board!

WINTERBOURNE. (*Aside.*) She has known me for a couple of hours! (*Aloud, rather formally.*) The privilege for me is immense; but I feel as if I ought to urge you to reflect a little.

DAISY. So as to show how stiff you can be? Oh, I know all about that.

WINTERBOURNE. No, just to remind you that your mother will certainly discover . . .

DAISY. (*Staring.*) Will certainly discover?

WINTERBOURNE. Your little escapade. You can't hide it.

DAISY. (*Amazed, and a little touched.*) I don't know what you mean. I have nothing to hide.

WINTERBOURNE. (*Aside.*) Ah, I give it up! (*Seeing* EUGENIO, *who comes out of the hotel.*) And here comes that odious creature, to spoil it!

(*Scene Tenth:* WINTERBOURNE, DAISY, EUGENIO.)

EUGENIO. Mademoiselle, your mother requests that you will come to her.

DAISY. I don't believe a word of it!

EUGENIO. You should not do me the injustice to doubt of my honor! Madame asked me to look for you ten minutes ago; but I was detained by meeting in the hall a lady (*speaking slowly, and looking at* WINTERBOURNE), a Russian lady, whom I once had the honor to serve, and who was leaving the hotel.

WINTERBOURNE. (*Startled, aside.*) Madame de Katkoff—leaving already?

EUGENIO. (*Watching* WINTERBOURNE.) She had so many little bags that she could hardly settle herself in the carriage, and I thought it my duty—I have had so much practice—to show her how to stow them away.

WINTERBOURNE. (*Quickly, to* DAISY.) Will you kindly excuse me a moment?

EUGENIO. (*Obsequious, interposing.*) If it's to overtake the Russian lady, Madame de Katkoff is already far away. (*Aside.*) She had four horses: I frightened her more than a little!

WINTERBOURNE. (*Aside.*) Far away—without another word? She can be hard—when she tries. Very good. Let me see if I can be the same!

DAISY. (*Noticing* WINTERBOURNE, *aside.*) Poor man, he's stiffer than ever! But I'm

glad she has gone. (*Aloud.*) See here, Eugenio, I'm going to that castle.

EUGENIO. (*With a certain impertinence.*) Mademoiselle has made arrangements?

DAISY. Well, if Mr. Winterbourne doesn't back out.

WINTERBOURNE. Back out? I sha'n't be happy till we are off! (*Aside.*) I'll go anywhere—with any one—*now;* and if the poor girl is injured by it, it isn't my fault!

EUGENIO. I think Mademoiselle will find that Madame is in no state—

DAISY. My dear Eugenio, Madame will stay at home with you.

WINTERBOURNE. (*Wincing, aside.*) If she would only not call him her "dear"!

EUGENIO. I take the liberty of advising Mademoiselle not to go to the castle.

WINTERBOURNE. (*Irritated.*) You had better remember that your place is not to advise, but to look after the little bags!

DAISY. Oh, I hoped you would make a fuss! But I don't want to go now.

WINTERBOURNE. (*Decided.*) I shall make a fuss if you don't go.

DAISY. (*Nervously, with a little laugh.*) That's all I want—a little fuss!

WINTERBOURNE. (*Aside.*) She's not so easy as she would like to appear. She knows it's a risk—but she likes the risk.

EUGENIO. If Mademoiselle will come with me, I will undertake to organize a fuss.

(*A steamboat whistle is heard in the distance.*)

WINTERBOURNE. (*To* DAISY.) The boat's coming up. You have only till three o'clock.

DAISY. (*Suddenly decided.*) Oh, I can be quick when I try! (*Hurries into the hotel.*)

WINTERBOURNE. (*Looking a moment at* EUGENIO.) You had better not interfere with that young lady!

EUGENIO. (*Insolent.*) I suppose you mean that I had better not interfere with you! You had better not defy me to do so! (*Aside.*) It's a pity I sent away the Katkoff! (*Follows* DAISY *into the hotel.*)

WINTERBOURNE. (*Alone.*) That's a singularly offensive beast! And what the mischief does he mean by his having been in *her* service? Thank heaven she has got rid of him! (*Seeing* MRS. COSTELLO, MISS DURANT, *and* CHARLES REVERDY, *who issue from the hotel, the ladies dressed for a walk.*) Oh, confusion, I had forgotten *them!*

(*Scene Eleventh:* MRS. COSTELLO, MISS DURANT, CHARLES REVERDY, WINTERBOURNE, *then* DAISY.)

MRS. COSTELLO. Well, Frederick, we take for granted that your little interview is over, and that you are ready to accompany us into the town.

WINTERBOURNE. Over, dear aunt? Why, it's only just begun. We are going to the Château de Chillon.

MRS. COSTELLO. You and that little girl? You will hardly get us to believe that!

REVERDY. (*Aside, still with the camp-stool.*) Hang me, why didn't I think of that?

WINTERBOURNE. I am afraid I rather incommode you; but I shall be delighted to go into the town when we come back.

MISS DURANT. You had better never come back. No one will speak to you!

MRS. COSTELLO. My dear Frederick, if you are joking, your joke is in dreadful taste.

WINTERBOURNE. I am not joking, in the least. The young lady is to be here at three.

MRS. COSTELLO. She herself is joking, then. She won't be so crazy as to come.

REVERDY. (*Who has gone to the parapet and looked off to right, coming back, taking out his watch.*) It's close upon three, and the boat's at the wharf.

WINTERBOURNE. (*Watch in hand.*) Not quite yet. Give her a moment's grace.

MRS. COSTELLO. It won't be for us to give her grace: it will be for society.

WINTERBOURNE. Ah, but you *are* society, you know. She wants immensely to know you.

MRS. COSTELLO. Is that why she is flinging herself at *you?*

WINTERBOURNE. (*Very gravely.*) Listen to me seriously, please. The poor little girl

has given me a great mark—a very touching mark—of confidence. I wish to present her to you, because I wish someone to answer for my honor.

MRS. COSTELLO. And pray, who is to answer for hers?

WINTERBOURNE. Oh, I say, you're cruel!

MRS. COSTELLO. I am an old woman, Frederick; but I thank my stars I am not too old to be horrified!

(*The bell of the steamboat is heard to ring in the distance.*)

REVERDY. There's your boat, sir. I'm afraid you'll miss it!

WINTERBOURNE. (*Watch still in hand, aside.*) Three o'clock. Damn that courier!

MRS. COSTELLO. If she doesn't come, you may present her.

MISS DURANT. She won't come. We must do her justice.

DAISY. (*Hurrying out of the hotel.*) I say, Mr. Winterbourne, I'm as punctual as you! (*She wears a charming travelling-dress, and is buttoning her glove.* EUGENIO *appears in the porch of the hotel, and stands there, with his hands in his pockets, and with a baffled but vindictive air, watching the rest of the scene.*)

REVERDY. Alas, the presentation's gone!

DAISY. (*Half aloud.*) Gracious, how they glare at me!

WINTERBOURNE. (*Hurriedly.*) Take my arm. The boat's at the wharf. (*She takes his arm, and they hasten away, passing through the little gate of the parapet, where they descend and disappear. The bell of the steamer continues to ring.* MRS. COSTELLO *and her companions have watched them; as they vanish, she and* MISS DURANT *each drop into a chair.*)

MRS. COSTELLO. They will *never* come back!

MISS DURANT. (*Eagerly.*) Isn't it your duty to go after them?

REVERDY. (*Between the two.*) They will be lovely company for the rest of the day!

ACT SECOND

A beautiful afternoon in the gardens of the Pincian Hill in Rome. A view of St. Peter's in the distance.

(*Scene First:* WINTERBOURNE, MADAME DE KATKOFF, *meeting from opposite sides. He stands before her a moment, and kisses her hand.*)

WINTERBOURNE. When, at your hotel just now, they told me you had gone out, I was pretty sure you had come here.

MME. DE KATKOFF. I always come here as soon as I arrive in Rome, for the sake of that view. It's an old friend of mine.

WINTERBOURNE. Have you no old friends but that, and wasn't it also—a little—for the sake of meeting one or two of them? We all come here, you know.

MME. DE KATKOFF. One or two of them? You don't mean two—you mean one! I knew you all come here, and that's why I have arrived early, before the crowd and the music.

WINTERBOURNE. That's what I was counting on. I know your tastes. I wanted to find you alone.

MME. DE KATKOFF. Being alone with you isn't one of my tastes! If I had known I should meet you, I think I shouldn't have left my carriage.

WINTERBOURNE. If it's there, at hand, you might invite me to get into it.

MME. DE KATKOFF. I have sent it away for half an hour, while I stretch myself a little. I have been sitting down for a week—in railway-trains.

WINTERBOURNE. You can't escape from me, then!

MME. DE KATKOFF. Don't begin that way, or you'll disappoint me. You speak as if you had received none of my letters.

WINTERBOURNE. And you speak as if you had written me a dozen! I received three little notes.

MME. DE KATKOFF. They were short, but they were clear.

WINTERBOURNE. Oh, very clear indeed! "You're an awful nuisance, and I wish never to hear of you again." That was about the gist of them.

MME. DE KATKOFF. "Unless you promise not to persecute me, I won't come to Rome." That's more how I should express it. And you did promise.

WINTERBOURNE. I promised to try and hate you, for that seemed to be what you wished to bring me to! And I have been waiting for you these three weeks, as a man waits for his worst enemy.

MME. DE KATKOFF. I should be your worst enemy indeed, if I listened to you— if I allowed you to mingle your fresh, independent life with my own embarrassed and disillusioned one. If you have been here three weeks, you ought to have found some profitable occupation.

WINTERBOURNE. You speak as if I were looking out for a job! My principal occupation has been waiting for you.

MME. DE KATKOFF. It must have made you pleasant company to your friends.

WINTERBOURNE. My friends are only my aunt and the young lady who is with her— a very good girl, but painfully prim. I have been devoted to them, because I said to myself that after you came—

MME. DE KATKOFF. You wouldn't have possession of your senses? So it appears. On the same principle, I hope you have shown some attention to the little girl who was at Vevey, whom I saw you in such a fair way to be intimate with.

WINTERBOURNE. (*After a silence.*) What do you know about her?

MME. DE KATKOFF. Nothing but that we are again at the same hotel. A former servant of mine, a very unprincipled fellow, is now in her mother's employ, and he was the first person I met as I left my rooms to-day. I imagine from this that the young lady is not far off.

WINTERBOURNE. Not far off from *him*. I wish she were farther!

MME. DE KATKOFF. She struck me last summer as remarkably attractive.

WINTERBOURNE. She's exactly what she was last summer—only more so!

MME. DE KATKOFF. She must be quite enchanting, then.

WINTERBOURNE. Do you wish me to fall in love with her?

MME. DE KATKOFF. It would give me particular pleasure. I would go so far as to be the confidant of your passion.

WINTERBOURNE. I have no passion to confide. She's a little American flirt.

MME. DE KATKOFF. (*Aside.*) It seems to me there is a certain passion in that!

WINTERBOURNE. She's foolish, frivolous, futile. She is making herself terribly talked about.

MME. DE KATKOFF. She looked to me very

innocent—with those eyes!

WINTERBOURNE. Oh, yes, I made a great deal of those eyes—they have the most charming lashes. But they look at too many people.

MME. DE KATKOFF. Should you like them to fix themselves on you? You're rather difficult to please. The young lady with your aunt is too grave, and this poor little person is too gay! You had better find someone who's between the two.

WINTERBOURNE. You are between the two, and you won't listen to me.

MME. DE KATKOFF. I think I understand your country-people better than you do. I have learned a good deal about them from my observation of yourself.

WINTERBOURNE. That must have made you very fond of them!

MME. DE KATKOFF. It has made me feel very kindly toward them, as you see from my interest in those young ladies. Don't judge them by what they seem. They are probably just the opposite, for that is precisely the case with yourself. Most people think you very cold, but I have discovered the truth. You are like one of those tall German stoves, which present to the eye a surface of smooth white porcelain, without the slightest symptom of fuel or of flame. Nothing at first could seem less glowing; but after you have been in the room with it for half an hour you feel that the temperature is rising—and you want to open a window!

WINTERBOURNE. A tall German stove—that's a very graceful comparison.

MME. DE KATKOFF. I am sure your grave young lady is very gay.

WINTERBOURNE. It doesn't matter; she has got a young man of her own.

MME. DE KATKOFF. The young man who was always with them? If you are going to be put off by a rival, I have nothing to say.

WINTERBOURNE. He's not a rival of mine; he's only a rival of my aunt's. She wants me to marry Miss Durant, but Miss Durant prefers the gallant Reverdy.

MME. DE KATKOFF. That simplifies it.

WINTERBOURNE. Not so very much; because the gallant Reverdy shows a predilection for Miss Daisy Miller.

MME. DE KATKOFF. Ah, then he *is* your rival!

WINTERBOURNE. There are so many others that he doesn't count. She has at least a dozen admirers, and she knocks about Rome with all of them. She once told me that she was very fond of gentlemen's society; but unfortunately they are not all gentlemen.

MME. DE KATKOFF. So much the better chance for you.

WINTERBOURNE. She doesn't know, she can't distinguish. She is incredibly light.

MME. DE KATKOFF. It seems to me that you express yourself with a certain bitterness.

WINTERBOURNE. I am not in the least in love with her, if that's what you mean. But simply as an outsider, as a spectator, as an American, I can't bear to see a nice girl—if she *is* a nice girl—expose herself to the most odious misconception. That is, if she *is* a nice girl!

MME. DE KATKOFF. By my little system, she ought to be very nice. If she seems very wild, depend upon it she is very tame.

WINTERBOURNE. She has produced a fearful amount of scandal.

MME. DE KATKOFF. That proves she has nothing to hide. The wicked ones are not found out!

WINTERBOURNE. She has nothing to hide but her mother, whom she conceals so effectually that no mortal eye has beheld her. Miss Daisy goes to parties alone! When I say alone, I mean that she is usually accompanied by a foreigner with a waxed moustache and a great deal of manner. She is too nice for a foreigner!

MME. DE KATKOFF. (*Smiling.*) As a Russian, I am greatly obliged to you!

WINTERBOURNE. This isn't a Russian. He's a Roman—the Cavaliere Giovanelli.

MME. DE KATKOFF. You spoke of a dozen, and now you have settled down to one.

WINTERBOURNE. There were a dozen at first, but she picked them over and selected. She has made a mistake, because the man she has chosen is an adventurer.

MME. DE KATKOFF. An adventurer?

WINTERBOURNE. Oh, a very plausible one. He is very good-looking, very polite; he sings little songs at parties. He comes of a respectable family, but he has squandered his small patrimony, and he has no means of subsistence but his personal charms, which he has been hoping for the last ten years will endear him to some susceptible American heiress—whom he flatters himself he has found at last!

MME. DE KATKOFF. You ought to advise her—to put her on her guard.

WINTERBOURNE. Oh, she's not serious; she is only amusing herself.

MME. DE KATKOFF. Try and make her serious. That's a mission for an honest man!

WINTERBOURNE. (*After a moment.*) It's so odd to hear you defending her! It only puzzles me the more.

MME. DE KATKOFF. You ought to understand your countrywomen better.

WINTERBOURNE. My countrywomen?

MME. DE KATKOFF. I don't mean me: I mean Miss Daisy Miller.

WINTERBOURNE. It seems very stupid, I confess; but I have lived so long in foreign parts, among people of different manners. I mean, however, to settle the question to-day and to make up my mind. I shall meet Miss Daisy at four o'clock. I have promised to go to Mrs. Walker's.

MME. DE KATKOFF. And pray who is Mrs. Walker?

WINTERBOURNE. The wife of the American consul—a very good-natured woman, who has a passion for afternoon-tea. She took up Miss Daisy when they came; she used to call her the little Flower of the West. But now she's holding the little flower in her fingertips, at arm's length, trying to decide to let it drop.

MME. DE KATKOFF. Poor little flower! It must be four o'clock now.

WINTERBOURNE. (*Looking at his watch.*) You're in a great hurry to get rid of me! Mrs. Walker's is close at hand, just beyond the Spanish Steps. I shall have time to stroll round the Pincian with you.

MME. DE KATKOFF. I have had strolling enough. I shall wait for my carriage.

WINTERBOURNE. Let me at least come and see you this evening.

MME. DE KATKOFF. I should be delighted, but I am going to the opera.

WINTERBOURNE. Already? The first night you are here?

MME. DE KATKOFF. It's not the first; it's the second. I am very fond of music.

WINTERBOURNE. It's always bad in Italy.

MME. DE KATKOFF. I have made provision against that in the person of the Russian ambassador, whom I have asked to come into my box.

WINTERBOURNE. Ah, with ambassadors I stand no chance.

MME. DE KATKOFF. (*Smiling.*) You are the greatest diplomatist of all! Good-by for the present. (*She turns away.* WINTERBOURNE *looks after her a moment.*)

WINTERBOURNE. You decide more easily than Mrs. Walker: you *have* dropped me!

MME. DE KATKOFF. Ah, but you're not a flower! (WINTERBOURNE *looks at her an instant longer; then, with a little passionate switch of his stick, he walks off. Just as he disappears,* EUGENIO *comes in at the back.*) And now I shall have a quiet evening with a book!

(*Scene Second:* MADAME DE KATKOFF, EUGENIO, *who enters hat in hand, with a bow.*)

EUGENIO. It's the second time to-day that I have had the pleasure of meeting Madame.

MME. DE KATKOFF. I should like very much to believe it would be the last!

EUGENIO. (*Twirling his hat.*) That, perhaps, is more than I can promise. We will call it the last but one; for my purpose in approaching Madame is to demand an interview—a serious interview! Seeing Madame, at a distance, in conversation with a gentleman, I waited till the gentleman had retired; for I must do Madame the justice to admit that, with Madame, the gentlemen do usually, at last, retire!

MME. DE KATKOFF. It's a misfortune to me, since they leave me exposed!

EUGENIO. Madame is not exposed; Madame is protected. So long as I have an eye on Madame, I can answer for it that she will suffer no injury.

MME. DE KATKOFF. You protect me as the butcher protects the lamb! I suppose you have come to name your price.

EUGENIO. Madame goes straight to the point! I have come to name my price, but not to ask for money.

MME. DE KATKOFF. It's very kind of you to recognize that I have not money enough.

EUGENIO. Madame has money enough, but the talents of Madame are still greater than her wealth. It is with the aid of these talents that I shall invite Madame to render me a service—a difficult, delicate service, but so valuable that it will release Madame from further obligations.

MME. DE KATKOFF. (*Ironical.*) It's delightful to think of being released! I suppose the service is to recommend you as a domestic. That would be difficult, certainly.

EUGENIO. Too difficult—for Madame! No; it is simply, as I say, to grant me an interview, when I can explain. Be so good as to name an hour when I can wait upon you.

MME. DE KATKOFF. In my apartments? I would rather not see you there. Explain to me here.

EUGENIO. It's a little delicate for a public place. Besides, I have another appointment here.

MME. DE KATKOFF. You do a great business! If you mean that I am to wait upon *you*, we may as well drop negotiations.

EUGENIO. Let us compromise. My appointment will end in a quarter of an hour. If at that time Madame is still on the Pincian—

MME. DE KATKOFF. You would like me to sit upon a bench till you are ready to attend to me?

EUGENIO. It would have the merit of settling the matter at once, without more suspense for Madame.

MME. DE KATKOFF. (*Thoughtfully, aside.*) That would be a merit, certainly; and I am curious about the exercise he wishes to offer my talents! (*Aloud.*) I shall stroll about here till my carriage comes; if you wish to take advantage of that—

EUGENIO. To take advantage is exactly what I wish! And as this particular spot is exceptionally quiet I shall look for Madame here.

MME. DE KATKOFF. (*As she strolls away.*) How unspeakably odious!

EUGENIO. (*Alone a moment, looking after her.*) She shall bend till she breaks! The delay will have the merit, too, of making me sure of Giovanelli—if he only keeps the tryst! I mustn't throw away a card on *her* before I've won the game of him. But he's such a deuced fine gentleman that there's no playing fair! (*Seeing* GIOVANELLI, *who comes in at the left.*) He is up to time, though. (*Bowing.*) Signor Cavaliere!

(*Scene Third:* EUGENIO, GIOVANELLI.)

GIOVANELLI. (*Very elegant, with flowers in his buttonhole; cautious, looking round him.*) You might have proposed meeting in some less conspicuous spot!

EUGENIO. In the Coliseum, at midnight? My dear sir, we should be much more compromised if we were discovered there!

GIOVANELLI. Oh, if you count upon our being discovered! . . .

EUGENIO. There is nothing so unnatural in our having a little conversation. One should never be ashamed of an accomplice!

GIOVANELLI. (*With a grimace, disgusted.*) Don't speak of accomplices: as if we were concocting a crime!

EUGENIO. What makes it a work of merit is my conviction that you are a perfect gentleman. If it hadn't been for that, I never should have presented you to my family.

GIOVANELLI. Your family? You speak as if, in marrying the girl, I should become your brother-in-law.

EUGENIO. We shall certainly be united by a very peculiar tie!

GIOVANELLI. United—united? I don't know about that! After my marriage, I shall travel without a courier. (*Smiling.*) It will be less expensive!

EUGENIO. In the event you speak of, I myself hardly expect to remain in the ranks. I have seen too many campaigns: I shall retire on my pension. You look as if you did not understand me.

GIOVANELLI. Perfectly. You expect the good Mrs. Miller to make you comfortable for the rest of your days.

EUGENIO. What I expect of the good Mrs. Miller is one thing; what I expect of you is another: and on that point we had better be perfectly clear. It was to insure perfect clearness that I proposed this little conference, which you refused to allow to take place either in your own lodgings or in some comfortable café. Oh, I know you had your reasons! You don't exhibit your little interior; and though I know a good deal about you, I don't know where you live. It doesn't matter, I don't want to know: it's enough for me that I can always find you here, amid the music and the flowers. But I can't exactly make out why you wouldn't meet me at a café. I would gladly have paid for a glass of beer.

GIOVANELLI. It was just your beer I was afraid of! I never touch the beastly stuff.

EUGENIO. Ah, if you drink nothing but champagne, no wonder you are looking for an heiress! But before I help you to one, let me give you a word of advice. Make the best of me, if you wish me to make the best of you. I was determined to do that when I presented you to the two most amiable women in the world.

GIOVANELLI. I must protest against your theory that you presented me. I met Mrs. Miller at a party, as any gentleman might have done.

EUGENIO. You met her at a party, precisely; but unless I wish it, Mrs. Miller doesn't go to a party! I let you know she was to be there, and I advised you how to proceed. For the last three weeks I have done nothing but arrange little accidents, little surprises, little occasions, of which I will do you the justice to say that you have taken excellent advantage. But the time has come when I must remind you that I have not done all this from mere admiration of your distinguished appearance. I wish your success to be *my* success!

GIOVANELLI. (*Pleased, with a certain simplicity.*) I am glad to hear you talk about my success!

EUGENIO. Oh, there's a good deal to be said about it! Have you ever been to the circus?

GIOVANELLI. I don't see what that has to do with it!

EUGENIO. You've seen the bareback rider turn a somersault through the paper hoops? It's a very pretty feat, and it brings him great applause; but half the effect depends upon the poor devil—whom no one notices —who is perched upon the edge of the ring. If he didn't hold the hoop with a great deal of skill, the bareback rider would simply come down on his nose. You turn your little somersaults, Signor Cavaliere, and my young lady claps her hands; but all the while *I'm* holding the hoop!

GIOVANELLI. If I'm not mistaken, that office, at the circus, is usually performed by the clown.

EUGENIO. Take very good care, or you'll have a fall!

GIOVANELLI. I suppose you want to be paid for your trouble.

EUGENIO. The point isn't that I want to be paid: that goes without saying! But I want to be paid handsomely.

GIOVANELLI. What do you call handsomely?

EUGENIO. A commission proportionate to the fortune of the young lady. I know something about that. I have in my pocket (*slapping his side*) the letter of credit of the Signora. She lets me carry it—for safety's sake!

GIOVANELLI. Poor Signora! It's a strange game we are playing!

EUGENIO. (*Looking at him a moment.*) Oh, if you doubt of the purity of your motives, you have only to say so. You swore to me that you adored my young lady.

GIOVANELLI. She's an angel, and I worship the ground she treads on. That makes me wonder whether I couldn't get on without you.

EUGENIO. (*Dryly.*) Try it and see. I have only to say the word, and Mrs. Miller will start to-morrow for the north.

GIOVANELLI. And if you don't say the word, that's another thing you want to be paid for! It mounts up very fast.

EUGENIO. It mounts up to fifty thousand francs, to be handed to me six months after you are married.

GIOVANELLI. Fifty thousand francs?

EUGENIO. The family exchequer will never miss them. Besides, I give you six months. You sign a little note, "for value received."

GIOVANELLI. And if the marriage—if the marriage—

EUGENIO. If the marriage comes to grief, I burn up the note.

GIOVANELLI. How can I be sure of that?

EUGENIO. By having already perceived

that I'm not an idiot. If you don't marry, you can't pay: I need no one to tell me that. But I intend you *shall* marry.

GIOVANELLI. (*Satirical.*) It's uncommonly good of you! After all, I haven't a squint!

EUGENIO. I picked you out for your good looks; and you're so tremendously fascinating that even when I lose patience with your want of everything else I can't afford to sacrifice you. Your prospects are now very good. The estimable mother—

GIOVANELLI. The estimable mother believes me to be already engaged to her daughter. It shows how much she knows about it!

EUGENIO. No, you are not engaged, but you will be, next week. You have rather too many flowers there, by the way: you overdo it a little. (*Pointing to* GIOVANELLI's *buttonhole.*)

GIOVANELLI. So long as you pay for them, the more the better! How far will it carry me to be engaged? Mr. Miller can hardly be such a fool as his wife.

EUGENIO. (*Stroking his moustache.*) Mr. Miller?

GIOVANELLI. The mysterious father, in that unpronounceable town! He must be a man of energy, to have made such a fortune, and the idea of his energy haunts me!

EUGENIO. That's because you've got none yourself.

GIOVANELLI. I don't pretend to that; I only pretend to—a—

EUGENIO. To be fascinating, I know! But you're afraid the papa won't see it.

GIOVANELLI. I don't exactly see why he should set his heart on a Roman son-in-law.

EUGENIO. It's your business to produce that miracle!

GIOVANELLI. By making the girl talked about? My respect for her is in proportion to the confidence she shows me. That confidence is unlimited.

EUGENIO. Oh, unlimited! I have never seen anything like that confidence; and if out of such a piece of cloth as that you can't cut a coat—

GIOVANELLI. I never pretended to be a tailor! And you must not forget that I have a rival.

EUGENIO. Forget it? I regard it as a particularly gratifying fact. If you didn't have a rival I should have very small hopes of you.

GIOVANELLI. I confess I don't follow you. The young lady's confidence in Mr. Winterbourne is at least equal to her confidence in me.

EUGENIO. Ah, but *his* confidence in the young lady? That's another affair! He thinks she goes too far. He's an American, like herself; but there are Americans and Americans, and when they take it into their heads to open their eyes they open them very wide.

GIOVANELLI. If you mean that this American's a donkey, I see no reason to differ with you.

EUGENIO. Leave him to me. I've got a stick to beat him with!

GIOVANELLI. You make me shiver a little! Do you mean to put him out of the way?

EUGENIO. I mean to put him out of the way. Ah, you can trust me! I don't carry a stiletto, and if you'll excuse me I won't describe my little plan. You'll tell me what you think of it when you have seen the results. The great feature is simply that Miss Daisy, seeing herself abandoned—

GIOVANELLI. Will look about her for a consoler? Ah, consolation is a specialty of mine, and if you give me a chance to console I think I shall be safe.

EUGENIO. I shall go to work on the spot! (*Takes out his pocket-book, from which he extracts a small folded paper, holding it up a moment before* GIOVANELLI.) Put your name to that, and send it back to me by post.

GIOVANELLI. (*Reading the paper with a little grimace.*) Fifty thousand! Fifty thousand is steep.

EUGENIO. Signor Cavaliere, the letter of credit is for half a million!

GIOVANELLI. (*Pocketing the paper.*) Well, give me a chance to console—give me a chance to console! (*Goes off at the back, while, at the same moment,* MME. DE KATKOFF *reappears.*)

(*Scene Fourth:* EUGENIO, MADAME DE KATKOFF.)

EUGENIO. (*Perceiving her, aside.*) The Katkoff—up to time! If my second little paper works as well as my first, I have nothing to fear. (*Aloud.*) I am quite at the service of Madame.

MME. DE KATKOFF. My carriage has not come back; it was to pick up a friend at St. Peter's.

EUGENIO. I am greatly indebted to Madame's friends. I have my little proposition ready.

MME. DE KATKOFF. Be so good as to let me hear it.

EUGENIO. In three words it is this: Do me the favor to captivate Mr. Winterbourne! Madame starts a little. She will pretend, perhaps, that Mr. Winterbourne is already captivated.

MME. DE KATKOFF. You have an odd idea of my pretensions! I would rather pay you a sum of money than listen to this sort of thing.

EUGENIO. I was afraid you would be a little shocked—at first. But the proposal I make has the greatest recommendations.

MME. DE KATKOFF. For Mr. Winterbourne, certainly!

EUGENIO. For Mr. Winterbourne, very plainly; but also for Madame, if she would only reflect upon the facility—

MME. DE KATKOFF. What do you know about facility? Your proposal is odious!

EUGENIO. The worst is already done. Mr. Winterbourne is deeply interested in Madame.

MME. DE KATKOFF. His name has no place in our discussion. Be so good as not to mention it again.

EUGENIO. It will be easy not to mention it: Madame will understand without that. She will remember, perhaps, that when I had the honor of meeting her last summer, I was in the service of a distinguished family.

MME. DE KATKOFF. The amiable Mrs. Miller? That name has stuck in my mind!

EUGENIO. Permit me to regard it as a happy omen! The amiable Mrs. Miller, as I then informed Madame, has a daughter as amiable as herself. It is of the greatest importance that this young lady should be detached from the gentleman whose name I am not allowed to mention.

MME. DE KATKOFF. Should be detached?

EUGENIO. If he is interested in Madame, he is also a little interested in the Signorina. You know what men are, Madame!

MME. DE KATKOFF. If the Signorina is as amiable as you say, I can imagine no happier circumstance.

EUGENIO. From the point of view of Madame, who is a little tired of the gentleman; but not from my own, who wish the young lady to make another marriage.

MME. DE KATKOFF. Excuse me from entering into your points of view and your marriages!

EUGENIO. (*Abruptly.*) Ah, if you choose to terminate the discussion, it wasn't worth while to wait. (*A pause.*)

MME. DE KATKOFF. (*Aside.*) It was worth while to wait—to learn what a coward I am! (*Aloud, after a moment.*) Is Miss Miller in love with Mr. Winterbourne?

EUGENIO. (*Smiling.*) I thought Madame would come to the name! (*Aside.*) It was the idea that fetched her! (*Aloud.*) Miss Miller is not, perhaps, exactly in love with Mr. Winterbourne, but she has a great appreciation of his society. What I ask of you is to undertake that for the next two months she shall have as little of it as possible.

MME. DE KATKOFF. By taking as much of it myself? You ask me to play a very pretty part.

EUGENIO. Madame would play it to perfection!

MME. DE KATKOFF. To break a young girl's heart—to act an abominable comedy?

EUGENIO. You won't break any one's heart, unless it be Mr. Winterbourne's—which will serve him right for being so tiresome. As for the comedy, remember that the best actresses receive the highest salary.

MME. DE KATKOFF. If I had been a good actress, you never would have got me into your power. What do you propose to do with your little American?

EUGENIO. To marry her to a Roman gentleman. All I ask of you is to use a power you already have. I know that of late it has suited your pleasure not to use it: you have tried to keep Mr. Winterbourne at a distance. But call him a little nearer, and you will see that he will come!

MME. DE KATKOFF. So that the girl may see it too? Your ingenuity does you great honor. I don't believe in your Roman gentleman.

EUGENIO. It is not necessary that you should believe. Believe only that on the day the Signorina becomes engaged to the irreproachable person I have selected, I will place in your hands the document which I hold at your disposition.

MME. DE KATKOFF. How am I to be sure of that?

EUGENIO. (Aside.) They all want to be sure! (Aloud.) Nothing venture, nothing have!

MME. DE KATKOFF. And if she never becomes engaged?

EUGENIO. Ah, then, I confess, I must still hold the document. (Aside.) That will make her work for it! (Aloud.) Why should you trouble yourself with irrelevant questions? Your task is perfectly definite. Occupy Mr. Winterbourne, and leave the rest to me.

MME. DE KATKOFF. I must tell you—disagreeable as it may be to me to do so—that I shall have to make a very sudden turn.

EUGENIO. It will be all the more effective. (Complacently.) Sudden turns are the essence of fascination!

MME. DE KATKOFF. (Aside.) It's insufferable to discuss with him! But if there's a hope—if there's a hope . . . (Aloud.) I told Mr. Winterbourne, not an hour ago, that I wished never to see him again.

EUGENIO. I can imagine no more agreeable surprise to him, then, than to be told, half an hour hence, that you can't live without him! You know the things the ladies say! Don't be afraid of being sudden: he'll think it the more romantic. For you these things are easy, Madame (bowing low); for you those things are easy. I leave the matter to your consideration. (Aside, as he goes off.) She'll do it! (Exit.)

MME. DE KATKOFF. (Alone a moment.) Those things are easy—those things are easy? They are easier, perhaps, than paying out half one's fortune. (Stands a moment thoughtful, then gives a little nervous gesture, as of decision.) If I give him

leave to come to the opera, I must go myself—to Italian music! But an hour or two of Donizetti, for the sake of one's comfort! . . . He said he would come back —from the wife of the consul. (Looking about her, she goes out.)

(Scene Fifth: DAISY, then GIOVANELLI.)

DAISY. (Coming in with a certain haste, and glancing behind her.) It's a pity you can't walk in Rome without everyone staring so! And now he's not here—he's not where he said he would be. I don't care. He's very nice, but I certainly shan't go and look for him. I'll just wait a little. Perhaps, if I don't walk round, they won't stare at me so much. I didn't say good-by to Mrs. Walker, because she was talking to Mr. Winterbourne, and I shan't go near Mr. Winterbourne again till he comes near me. Half an hour in the room, and never within ten yards of me! He looks so pleasant when he talks—even when he talks to other girls. He's always talking to other girls, and not even to girls—to old women, and gentlemen, and foreigners. I've done something he doesn't like, I'm very sure of that. He doesn't like anything—anything that I do. It's hard to know what he does like! He's got such peculiar tastes— from his foreign education; you can't ever tell where you'll find him. Well, I haven't had a foreign education, and I don't see that I'm any the worse for that. If I'd had a foreign education, I might as well give up! I shouldn't be able to breathe, for fear I was breathing wrong. There seem to be so many ways, over here! But I only know one way, and I don't see why I should learn the others when there are people who do like—who do like—what I do. They say they do, at any rate, and they say it so prettily! The English say it very nicely, but the Italians say it best. As for the Americans, they don't say it at all, and Mr. Winterbourne less than any of them! Well, I don't care so much about the Americans: I can make it all right with the Americans when I get home. Mr. Winterbourne isn't an American; I never saw any one like him over there. If I had, perhaps I shouldn't have come away; for over there it would all be different. Well, it isn't different here, and I suppose it never will be. Everything is strange over here; and what is strangest of all is one's liking people that are so peculiar. (*Stands thoughtful a moment, then rouses herself.*) There's Mr. Giovanelli—a mile off. Does he suppose I wish to communicate with him by signs?

(GIOVANELLI *comes in, hat in hand, with much eagerness.*)

GIOVANELLI. I have looked for you everywhere!

DAISY. Well, I wasn't everywhere; I was here.

GIOVANELLI. Standing all alone, without a protector!

DAISY. I wasn't more alone than I was at Mrs. Walker's.

GIOVANELLI. (*Smiling, slightly fatuous.*) Because *I* was not there?

DAISY. Oh, it wasn't the people who were *not* there! (*Aside.*) If they had known I was coming, I suppose there wouldn't have been anyone!

GIOVANELLI. (*In an attitude of the most respectful admiration.*) How can I sufficiently thank you for granting me this supreme satisfaction?

DAISY. That's a very fine name to give to a walk on the Pincian. You had better put on your hat.

GIOVANELLI. You wish to escape notice? Perhaps you are right. That was why I didn't come to Mrs. Walker's, whose parties are so charming! I thought that if we slipped away together it might attract attention.

DAISY. Do you mean they would have thought it improper? They would have thought it still more improper to see me leaving alone; so I didn't say a word to any one—only mother.

GIOVANELLI. Ah, you told your admirable parent? She is with us, then, in spirit!

DAISY. She wanted to get away herself, if that's what you mean; but she didn't feel as if she could leave till Eugenio came for her. And Eugenio seems to have so much to do to-day.

GIOVANELLI. It is doubtless in your interest. He is a very faithful servant.

DAISY. Well, he told mother she must stay there an hour: he had some business of importance.

GIOVANELLI. Let us hope that his business is done, and that the patient Mrs. Miller is released.

DAISY. She was patient enough when I told her I shouldn't come to dinner.

GIOVANELLI. (*Starting, with an air of renewed devotion.*) Am I to understand that you have consented to my little fantasy?

DAISY. Of dining at that old tavern, where the artists go?

GIOVANELLI. The renowned and delightful *Falcone*, in the heart of ancient Rome! You are a person of delicious surprises! The other day, you wouldn't listen to it.

DAISY. I don't remember the other day: all I know is, I'll go now. (*Aside.*) The other day Mr. Winterbourne spoke to me!

GIOVANELLI. My dear young lady, you make me very happy!

DAISY. By going to eat macaroni with you?

GIOVANELLI. It isn't the macaroni; it's the sentiment!

DAISY. The sentiment is yours, not mine. I haven't any: it's all gone!

GIOVANELLI. Well, I shan't complain if I find myself at table with you in a dusky corner of that picturesque little cook-shop, where the ceiling is black, and the walls are brown, and the floor is red!

DAISY. (*Watching him as he describes it.*) Oh dear! it must be very lovely.

GIOVANELLI. And the old wine-flasks, covered with plaited straw, are as big round—are much bigger round—than your waist!

DAISY. That's just what I want to see. Let's go there at once!

GIOVANELLI. (*Consulting his watch.*) Half-past four. Isn't that rather soon to dine?

DAISY. We can go on foot through the old streets. I'm dying to see them on foot.

GIOVANELLI. (*Aside.*) That will be cheaper than a cab! (*Aloud.*) We should get there at five—a little early still. Mightn't we first take a few turns round this place?

DAISY. (*After a pause.*) Oh, yes, if you like.

GIOVANELLI. (*Aside.*) I should like my

creditors to see! (*Aloud.*) Perhaps it doesn't suit you: you are a little afraid.

DAISY. What should I be afraid of?

GIOVANELLI. (*Smiling.*) Not of meeting your mother, I know!

DAISY. If I had been afraid, I shouldn't have come.

GIOVANELLI. That is perfect. But let me say one thing: you have a way of taking the meaning from the favors you bestow.

DAISY. The meaning? They haven't got any meaning!

GIOVANELLI. (*Vaguely.*) Ah!

(MRS. COSTELLO, MISS DURANT, *and* CHARLES REVERDY *appear.*)

DAISY. (*Looking at* MRS. COSTELLO *and* MISS DURANT.) Unless it be to make those dreadful women glower. How d'ye do, Mr. Reverdy?

GIOVANELLI. (*Smiling.*) I see you are not afraid! (*He goes out with her.*)

(*Scene Sixth:* MRS. COSTELLO, MISS DURANT, CHARLES REVERDY.)

MISS DURANT. She has grown to look very hard.

MRS. COSTELLO. The gentleman looks soft, and that makes up for it.

MISS DURANT. Do you call him a gentleman?

MRS. COSTELLO. Ah, compared with the courier! She has a different one every time.

REVERDY. (*With the camp-stool, aside.*) A different one every time, but never, alas, *this* one!

MRS. COSTELLO. There's one comfort in it all: she has given up Frederick.

MISS DURANT. Ah, she goes too far even for him!

REVERDY. Too far with other men: that's the trouble! With him she went as far as the Castle of Chillon.

MRS. COSTELLO. Don't recall that episode. Heaven only knows what happened there.

REVERDY. I know what happened: he was awfully sold. That's why he let you carry him off.

MRS. COSTELLO. Much good it did us! I'm very much disappointed in Frederick.

MISS DURANT. I can't imagine what you expected of him.

MRS. COSTELLO. I expected him to fall in love with you—or to marry you, at any rate.

MISS DURANT. You would have been still more disappointed, then, if I had refused him.

MRS. COSTELLO. (*Dryly.*) I should have been surprised.

REVERDY. (*Sentimentally.*) Would you have refused him, Miss Durant?

MISS DURANT. Yes, on purpose to spite you. You don't understand? It takes a man to be stupid! If Mr. Winterbourne were to marry some one else, it would leave Miss Daisy Miller free.

REVERDY. Free to walk about with the native population? She seems to be free enough already. Mrs. Costello, the camp-stool is at your service.

MRS. COSTELLO. Give it to me, and I will go and sit in the shade. Excuse me, I would rather carry it myself. (*Taking the camp-stool, aside to* MISS DURANT.) If he proposes, mind you accept him.

MISS DURANT. If who proposes?

MRS. COSTELLO. Our young companion! He is manœuvring to get rid of me. He has nothing but his expectations, but his expectations are of the best. (*She marches away with her camp-stool, and seats herself at a distance, where, with her eyeglass raised, she appears to look at what goes on in another part of the garden.*)

MISS DURANT. (*Aside.*) Am *I* one of his expectations? Fortunately, I don't need to marry for money. (*Aloud.*) Cousin Louisa is furious with me for not being more encouraging to Mr. Winterbourne. I don't know what she would have liked me to do!

REVERDY. You have been very proper, very dignified.

MISS DURANT. That's the way I was brought up. I never liked him, from the first.

REVERDY. Oh, he's a stupid stick!

MISS DURANT. I don't say he's stupid—and he's very good-looking.

REVERDY. As good-looking as a man can be in whom one feature—the most expressive—has been entirely omitted. He has got no eyes in his head.

MISS DURANT. No eyes?

REVERDY. To see that that poor little creature is in love with him.

MISS DURANT. She has a queer way of showing it.

REVERDY. Ah, they always have queer ways!

MISS DURANT. He sees it, but he doesn't care.

REVERDY. That's still worse,—the omission not of a feature, but of an organ (*tapping his heart and smiling*), the seat of our purest and highest joys!

MISS DURANT. (*Aside.*) Cousin Louisa was right! (*Aloud.*) Do you mean that he has no heart?

REVERDY. If he had as big a one as the rosette on your shoe, would he leave me here to do all the work?

MISS DURANT. (*Looking at her foot.*) The rosette on my shoe is rather big.

REVERDY. (*Looking as well.*) It isn't so much the size of the rosette as the smallness of the shoe!

MISS DURANT. (*Aside.*) Cousin Louisa is certainly right! (*Aloud, smiling.*) Yours, I suppose, is bigger than that.

REVERDY. My shoe? I should think so—rather!

MISS DURANT. Dear, no! I mean your heart. Though I don't think it's at all nice in you to complain of being left with us.

REVERDY. When I am left with you, I don't complain; but when I am left with *her!* (*Indicating* MRS. COSTELLO.)

MISS DURANT. Well, you are not with her now.

REVERDY. Ah, now it's very pleasant. Only she has got the camp-stool.

MISS DURANT. Do you want it for yourself?

REVERDY. Yes; I have been carrying it for the last six months, and I feel rather awkward without it. It gives one confidence to have something in one's hand.

MISS DURANT. Good heavens! What do you want to do?

REVERDY. I want to make you a little speech.

MISS DURANT. You will do very well as you are.

REVERDY. I'll try it. (*In an attitude.*) Six months ago I had moments of rebellion, but to-day I have come to love my chains! Accordingly— (MRS. COSTELLO *starts up and hurries forward, the camp-stool in her*

hand.) By Jove! if she hears me, she'll rivet them faster.

MRS. COSTELLO. (*Seizing* MISS DURANT's *arm.*) My poor, dear child, whom do you think I've seen?

REVERDY. By your expression, the ghost of Julius Cæsar!

MRS. COSTELLO. The Russian woman—the princess—whom we saw last summer.

MISS DURANT. Well, my dear cousin, she won't eat us up!

MRS. COSTELLO. No, but she'll eat Frederick!

REVERDY. On the contrary, her appetite for Frederick is small. Don't you remember that, last summer, she left the hotel as soon as he arrived?

MRS. COSTELLO. That was only a feint, to put us off the scent. He has been in secret correspondence with her, and their meeting here is prearranged.

MISS DURANT. I don't know why you call their correspondence secret, when he was always going to the post-office!

MRS. COSTELLO. Ah, but you can't tell what he did there! Frederick is very deep.

REVERDY. There's nothing secret, at any rate, about her arrival here. She alighted yesterday at our own hotel, in the most public manner, with the landlord and all the waiters drawn up to receive her. It didn't occur to me to mention it.

MRS. COSTELLO. I don't really know what you are with us for!

MISS DURANT. Oh, Cousin Louisa, he is meant for better things than that!

MRS. COSTELLO. (*To* MISS DURANT, *aside.*) Do you mean that he has proposed?

MISS DURANT. No, but he was just going to.

MRS. COSTELLO. (*Disappointed.*) Ah, you have told me that before!

MISS DURANT. Because you never give him time.

MRS. COSTELLO. Does he want three hours?

MISS DURANT. No, but he wants three minutes!

REVERDY. (*Who has strolled away, observing them, aside.*) Happy thought, to make them fight about me! Mutual destruction would ensue, and I should be master of the situation. (*Aloud.*) I am only a man, dear Madam; I am not a newspaper.

MRS. COSTELLO. If you only were, we could stop our subscription! And, as a proof of what I say, here comes Frederick, to look after his Russian.

(WINTERBOURNE *comes in, with* MRS. WALKER.)

REVERDY. With the wife of the consul, to look after him!

(*Scene Seventh:* MRS. COSTELLO, MISS DURANT, REVERDY, WINTERBOURNE, MRS. WALKER.)

MRS. WALKER. Oh, you dreadful people, what are you doing here, when you ought to be at my reception?

MRS. COSTELLO. We were just thinking of going; it's so very near.

MRS. WALKER. Only round the corner! But there are better reasons than that.

MISS DURANT. There can hardly be a very good one, when you yourself have come away!

MRS. WALKER. You would never imagine what has brought me! I have come in pursuit of little Daisy Miller.

MRS. COSTELLO. And you have brought my nephew to help you!

WINTERBOURNE. A walk in such charming company is a privilege not to be lost. Perhaps, dear aunt, you can give us news.

MRS. COSTELLO. Of that audacious and desperate person? Dear me, yes. We met her just now, on the arm of a dreadful man.

MRS. WALKER. Oh, we are too late then. She is lost!

MRS. COSTELLO. It seems to me she was lost long ago, and (*significantly, at* WINTERBOURNE) that this is not the first rendez-vous she has taken.

WINTERBOURNE. (*Smiling.*) If it does her no more harm than the others, Mrs. Walker had better go back to her teapot!

REVERDY. (*To* MISS DURANT.) That's an allusion to the way he was sold!

MRS. WALKER. She left my house, half an hour ago, without a word to anyone but her idiot of a mother, who thought it all right that she should walk off to the Pincian to meet the handsome Giovanelli. I only discovered her flight just now, by a lady who was coming in at the moment

that Miss Daisy, shaking out her little flounces and tossing up her little head, tripped away from my door, to fall into the arms of a cavalier!

MISS DURANT. Into his arms? Ah, Mrs. Walker!

MRS. WALKER. My dear young lady, with these unscrupulous foreigners one can never be sure. You know as well as I what becomes of the reputation of a girl who shows herself in this place, at this hour, with all the rank and fashion of Rome about her, with no more responsible escort than a gentleman renowned for his successes!

REVERDY. (*To* MISS DURANT.) It's as if you were here with me, you know!

MRS. WALKER. This idea came over me with a kind of horror, and I determined to save her if I could.

MRS. COSTELLO. There is nothing left of her to save!

MRS. WALKER. There is always something left, and my representative position makes it a duty. My rooms were filled with guests —a hundred and fifty people—but I put on my bonnet and seized Mr. Winterbourne's arm.

WINTERBOURNE. You can testify that I didn't wince! I quite agree with you as to the importance of looking her up. Foreigners never understand.

REVERDY. (*Aside.*) My dear fellow, if they understand no better than you! . . .

MRS. WALKER. What I want of you dear people is to go and entertain my visitors. Console them for my absence, and tell them I shall be back in five minutes.

MISS DURANT. It will be very nice to give a reception without any trouble.

MRS. COSTELLO. Without any trouble— scarcely! But there is nothing we wouldn't do—

MRS. WALKER. For the representative of one's country! Be charming, then, as you can so well. (*Seeing* DAISY *and* GIOVANELLI *come in.*) I shall not be long, for by the mercy of Heaven the child is guided to this spot!

REVERDY. If you think you have only to pick her up, we won't wait for you! (*He goes out with* MRS. COSTELLO *and* MISS DURANT.)

(Scene Eighth: MRS. WALKER, WINTERBOURNE, DAISY, GIOVANELLI.)

WINTERBOURNE. (*As the two others slowly come in together, not at first seeing him.*) We shall have a siege: she won't give him up for the asking.

MRS. WALKER. We must divide our forces, then. You will deal with Daisy.

WINTERBOURNE. I would rather attack the gentleman.

MRS. WALKER. No, no; there'll be trouble. Mr. Giovanelli, I should like a little conversation with you.

GIOVANELLI. (*Starting, and coming forward; very polite.*) You do me great honor, Madame!

MRS. WALKER. I wish to scold you for not coming to me to-day; but to spare your blushes, it must be in private. (*Strolls away with him, out of sight.*)

DAISY. (*Aside.*) They have come to take me away. Ah, they are very cruel!

WINTERBOURNE. I had no chance to speak to you at Mrs. Walker's, and I have come to make up for my loss.

DAISY. (*Looking at him a moment.*) What is Mrs. Walker doing here! Why doesn't she stay with her guests?

WINTERBOURNE. I brought her away—to do just what she has done.

DAISY. To take away Mr. Giovanelli? I don't understand you.

WINTERBOURNE. A great many people think that you understand, but that you don't care.

DAISY. I don't care what people think. I have done no harm.

WINTERBOURNE. That's exactly what I say—you don't care. But I wish you would care a little, for your friends are very much frightened. When Mrs. Walker ascertained that you had left her house alone, and had come to meet a gentleman here—here, where all Rome assembles at this hour to amuse itself, and where you would be watched and criticised and calumniated—when Mrs. Walker made this discovery, she said but three words—"To the rescue!" But she took her plunge, as if you had been drowning.

DAISY. And you jumped overboard, too!

WINTERBOURNE. Oh dear, no; I'm standing on the brink. I only interpret her sentiments. I don't express my own.

DAISY. They would interest me more than Mrs. Walker's; but I don't see what either of you have to do with me.

WINTERBOURNE. We admire you very much, and we hate to see you misjudged.

DAISY. I don't know what you mean, and I don't know what you think I want to do.

WINTERBOURNE. I haven't the least idea about that. All I mean is that if you could see, as I see it, how little it's the custom here to do what you do, and how badly it looks to fly in the face of the custom, you would be a little more on your guard.

DAISY. I know nothing about the custom. I'm an American; I'm not one of these people.

WINTERBOURNE. In that case, you would behave differently. Your being an American is just the point. You are a very conspicuous American, thanks to your attractions, to your charms, to the publicity of your life. Such people, with the best intentions in the world, are often very indiscreet; and it's to save the reputation of her compatriots that the fairest and brightest of American girls should sacrifice a little of her independence.

DAISY. Look here, Mr. Winterbourne, you make too much fuss: that's what's the matter with you!

WINTERBOURNE. If I make enough to persuade you to go home with Mrs. Walker, my highest ambition will be gratified.

DAISY. I think you are trying to mystify me: I can tell that by your language. One would never think you were the same person who went with me to that castle.

WINTERBOURNE. I am not quite the same, but I have a good deal in common with him. Now, Mr. Giovanelli doesn't resemble that person at all.

DAISY. (*Coldly.*) I don't know why you speak to me about Mr. Giovanelli.

WINTERBOURNE. Because—because Mrs. Walker asked me to.

DAISY. It would be better if she should do it herself.

WINTERBOURNE. That's exactly what I told her; but she had an odd fancy that I have a kind of influence with you.

DAISY. (*With expression.*) Poor Mrs. Walker!

WINTERBOURNE. Poor Mrs. Walker! She doesn't know that no one has any influence with you—that you do nothing in the world but what pleases yourself.

DAISY. Whom, then, am I to please? The people that think such dreadful things of me? I don't even understand what they think! What do you mean, about my reputation? I haven't got any reputation! If people are so cruel and wicked, I am sure I would rather not know it. In America they let me alone, and no one ran after me, like Mrs. Walker. It's natural I should like the people who seem to like me, and who will take the trouble to go round with me. The others may say what they like. I can't understand Italian, and I should never hear of it if you didn't come and translate.

WINTERBOURNE. It's not only the Italians —it's the Americans.

DAISY. Do you mean your aunt and your cousin? I don't know why I should make myself miserable for *them!*

WINTERBOURNE. I mean everyone who has ever had the very questionable advantage of making your acquaintance—only to be subjected to the torment of being unable either to believe in you or to doubt of you.

DAISY. To doubt of me? You are very strange!

WINTERBOURNE. You are stranger still. But I didn't come here to reason with you: that would be vain, for we speak a different language, and we shouldn't understand each other. I only came to say to you, in the most respectful manner, that if you should consult your best interests you would go home with Mrs. Walker.

DAISY. Do you think I had such a lovely time there, half an hour ago, when you didn't so much as look at me?

WINTERBOURNE. If I had spoken to you, would you have stayed?

DAISY. After I had an engagement here? (*With a little laugh.*) I must say, you expect a great deal!

WINTERBOURNE. (*Looking at her a moment.*) What they say is true—you are a thorough-going coquette!

(MRS. WALKER *reappears, with* GIOVANELLI.)

DAISY. You speak too much of what they say. To escape from you, I'll go anywhere!

MRS. WALKER. (*To* WINTERBOURNE, *while* GIOVANELLI *speaks to* DAISY.) He's very accommodating, when you tell him that if Mrs. Miller gets frightened she will start off for America.

WINTERBOURNE. It's more than I can say of Miss Daisy!

MRS. WALKER. Have you had no success?

WINTERBOURNE. I have had my ears boxed!

MRS. WALKER. (*To* DAISY.) My precious child, you escaped from my drawing-room before I had half the talk we wanted.

DAISY. Are they all waiting there to see me brought back?

MRS. WALKER. Oh dear, no; they have plenty to think about—with Mrs. Costello and Miss Durant.

DAISY. Ah, those ladies are there? Then I certainly shan't go back.

MRS. WALKER. (*Alarmed.*) Hush! They're relations of Mr. Winterbourne.

DAISY. All the more reason for my hating them!

MRS. WALKER. (*To* WINTERBOURNE.) You must excuse her; she is very wicked to-day! (*To* DAISY.) If you won't go home, then I'll stay with you here. Mr. Giovanelli, you promised me you would go to my house.

GIOVANELLI. I am at the orders of Mademoiselle.

DAISY. You may do what you please till dinner-time.

WINTERBOURNE. (*Aside.*) Gracious heavens! is she going to dine with him? (*Aloud, to* DAISY.) We were interrupted, but I have a great deal more to say.

DAISY. More of the same sort? It will be a pleasure to hear that!

WINTERBOURNE. What's coming is a great deal better.—Do you dine at your table d'hôte?

DAISY. Oh, yes. Randolph likes the table d'hôte.

WINTERBOURNE. I will ask for a place there this evening, and, with your permission, it shall be next to yours.

DAISY. I am very sorry, but I am not sure of this evening.

WINTERBOURNE. (*Gravely.*) That's a great disappointment to me. (*A short silence.*)

MRS. WALKER. (*To* GIOVANELLI.) You promised me you would go to my house!

GIOVANELLI. As a man of honor, then, I must go. But I assure you, Mademoiselle (*to* DAISY) that I soon return.

DAISY. As soon as you like! (GIOVANELLI *walks away. To* WINTERBOURNE.) Can't you come some other night?

WINTERBOURNE. Oh, yes, by waiting a little. But with the uncertainty of your stay in Rome, this would be always something gained.

DAISY. What will you do after dinner?

WINTERBOURNE. With your kind permission, I will adjourn with you to your mother's sitting-room.

DAISY. You are very devoted, all of a sudden!

WINTERBOURNE. Better late than never!

DAISY. You are just as you were at that castle!

WINTERBOURNE. So are you—at this moment. We can dream we are in that happy place!

DAISY. (*Aside.*) He can do with me what he will. (*Aloud, quickly.*) I'll tell them to keep you a seat!

WINTERBOURNE. I shall be indebted to you forever!

DAISY. Oh, if I don't see about it, they'll put you at the other end.

WINTERBOURNE. Next you—that's the point.

DAISY. Between me and Randolph! At half past six!

WINTERBOURNE. At half past six.

MRS. WALKER. (*To* WINTERBOURNE.) You can go about your business. I have something to say to her alone.

DAISY. Don't forget half past six!

WINTERBOURNE. Never in the world. At half past six! (*Walks away.*)

MRS. WALKER. (*Alone with* DAISY.) And now may I be permitted to inquire whether you had arranged to dine with that Italian?

DAISY. (*Smiling.*) In the heart of ancient Rome! But don't tell Mr. Winterbourne what I gave up!

MRS. WALKER. (*Aside.*) I'll get you out of Rome to-morrow! (*Aloud.*) I must show you to the crowd—with *me.* (*Goes out leading* DAISY.)

(*Scene Ninth:* REVERDY, RANDOLPH.)

REVERDY. (*Coming in just as the others pass out, and completing* MRS. WALKER'S *phrase.*) The wife of the American consul! The American consul is all very well, but I'll be hanged if I'll carry on the business! It's quite enough to do odd jobs for Mrs. Costello, without taking service at the consulate. Fifty carriages before the door, and five hundred people up-stairs. My companions may get up if they can! It's the first time to-day I've had a moment for a quiet smoke. (*Lights a cigar, and while he is doing so* RANDOLPH *comes in.*) O Lord, the Old Man of the Sea!

RANDOLPH. (*Planted before* REVERDY.) I say, Mr. Reverdy, suppose you offer me a cigar.

REVERDY. My poor child, my cigars are as big as yourself!

RANDOLPH. There's nothing fit to smoke over here. You can't get 'em as you can in America.

REVERDY. Yes, they're better in America (*smoking*); but they cost a good deal more.

RANDOLPH. I don't care what I pay. I've got all the money I want.

REVERDY. Don't spend it; keep it till you grow up.

RANDOLPH. Oh, I ain't going to grow up. I've been this way for ever so long. Mother brought me over to see if I wouldn't start, but I haven't started an inch. You can't start in this old country.

REVERDY. The Romans were rather tall.

RANDOLPH. I don't care for the Romans. A child's as good as a man.

REVERDY. The future of democracy! You remind me of the infant Hannibal.

RANDOLPH. There's one good thing: so long as I'm little, my mother can't see me. She's looking all round.

REVERDY. I was going to ask you if she allowed you to mingle in this human maze.

RANDOLPH. Mother's in the carriage, but I jumped out.

REVERDY. Imprudent little man! At the risk of breaking your neck?

RANDOLPH. Oh, we were crawling along

—we haven't American trotters. I saw you walking about, and when mother wasn't looking I just dropped. As soon as she missed me, she began to howl!

REVERDY. I am sorry to be the occasion of a family broil.

RANDOLPH. She thinks I am run over; she has begun to collect a crowd.

REVERDY. You wicked little person! I must take you straight back to her.

RANDOLPH. I thought you might like to know where my sister is.

REVERDY. At the present moment my anxiety is about your mother.

RANDOLPH. Daisy's gone on a bender. If you'll give me a cigar, I'll put you up to it.

REVERDY. You're a vulgar little boy. Take me instantly to your mother.

RANDOLPH. (Very sarcastic.) Wouldn't you like to carry me on your back?

REVERDY. If you don't come, I'll take you under my arm. (Starts to seize him.)

RANDOLPH. (Dodging.) I won't come, then!

REVERDY. Damn the little wretch! I must relieve his mother. (Makes another attempt to capture RANDOLPH, who escapes, while REVERDY gives chase, and they disappear.)

(Scene Tenth: WINTERBOURNE, then MADAME DE KATKOFF.)

WINTERBOURNE. (Coming in alone.) Remarkable family, the Millers! Mrs. Miller, standing up in her carriage, in the centre of a crowd of Italians, and chattering to them in her native tongue. She falls upon my neck when she sees me, and announces that the gifted Randolph is no more. He has tumbled out of the vehicle, and been trampled to death! We institute a search for his remains, and as it proves fruitless she begs me to come and look for him here. (Looking round him.) I don't perceive any remains! He has mingled in the giddy throng, and the giddy throng may bring him back! It's the business of that ruffian of a courier! (Seeing MADAME DE KATKOFF, aside.) Is she still here? (Aloud.) To meet you again is better fortune than I hoped.

MME. DE KATKOFF. (Strolling in slowly, with an air of deliberation, and standing a moment thoughtful.) Will you do me the favor to dine with me to-night?

WINTERBOURNE. (Startled.) To dine with you to-night?

MME. DE KATKOFF. You stare as if I were a ghost! It's very simple: to dine with me to-night, at seven o'clock, at the Hôtel de Paris?

WINTERBOURNE. (Aside.) It's a little awkward. (Aloud.) Do you dine at the table d'hôte?

MME. DE KATKOFF. At the table d'hôte, with that rabble of tourists? I dine in my own apartments.

WINTERBOURNE. I supposed you had left the Pincian; I had no idea you were lingering.

MME. DE KATKOFF. Apparently I had a purpose, which you seem quite unable to appreciate. You are very slow in accepting!

WINTERBOURNE. To tell you the honest truth, I have made an engagement.

MME. DE KATKOFF. An engagement? A moment ago you were dying to spend the evening with me.

WINTERBOURNE. A moment ago you wouldn't listen to me.

MME. DE KATKOFF. (After a pause.) My dear friend, you are very stupid. A woman doesn't confess the truth at the first summons!

WINTERBOURNE. You are very strange. I accepted an invitation just after we parted.

MME. DE KATKOFF. Send word you can't come.

WINTERBOURNE. It was from the young lady you recommended me so strongly to turn my attention to.

MME. DE KATKOFF. Ah, she gives invitations?

WINTERBOURNE. I confess I asked for this one. They are also at the Hôtel de Paris, and they dine at the table d'hôte.

MME. DE KATKOFF. A charming place to carry on a courtship!

WINTERBOURNE. It's not a courtship— however much I may have wished to please you.

MME. DE KATKOFF. Your wish to please me has suddenly diminished. Apparently, I am to understand that you refuse!

WINTERBOURNE. Even when you are kind, there's something cruel in it!—I will dine with you with pleasure.

MME. DE KATKOFF. Send word, then, to

your little American.

WINTERBOURNE. Yes, I will send word. (*Aside.*) That's uncommonly rough! (*Aloud.*) After dinner, I suppose, you will go to the opera.

MME. DE KATKOFF. I don't know about the opera. (*Looking at him a moment.*) It will be a splendid night. How should you like a moonlight drive?

WINTERBOURNE. A moonlight drive—with you? It seems to me you mock me!

MME. DE KATKOFF. (*In the same tone.*) To wander through the old streets, when everything is still; to see the solemn monuments wrapped up in their shadows; to watch the great fountains turn to silver in the moonshine—that has always been a dream of mine! We will try it to-night.

WINTERBOURNE. (*Affected by her tone.*) We will see the great square of St. Peter's; we will dip our hands in the Fountain of Trevi! You must be strangely beautiful in the moonlight.

MME. DE KATKOFF. I don't know. You shall see.

WINTERBOURNE. What will you do with the Russian ambassador?

MME. DE KATKOFF. Send him about his business.

WINTERBOURNE. An ambassador! For me?

MME. DE KATKOFF. Don't force me to say it; I shall make you too vain.

WINTERBOURNE. I am not used to being treated so, and I can't help feeling that it may be only a refinement of cruelty.

MME. DE KATKOFF. If I have been cruel before, it was in self-defence. I have been sorely troubled, and I don't pretend to be consistent. Women are never so—especially women who love!

WINTERBOURNE. I ask no questions; I only thank you.

MME. DE KATKOFF. At seven o'clock, then.

WINTERBOURNE. You are very strange; but you are only the more adorable. At seven o'clock!

MME. DE KATKOFF. You are not to come with me; my carriage is there. (*Aside, as she leaves him.*) Ingenuous young man!

WINTERBOURNE. (*Alone, standing a moment in thought.*) "Women are never consistent—especially women who love!" I

have waited three years, but it was worth waiting for!

(MRS. WALKER *comes in with* DAISY, *without his seeing them.*)

(*Scene Eleventh:* WINTERBOURNE, MRS. WALKER, DAISY, *then* EUGENIO *and* GIOVANELLI.)

DAISY. Well, Mr. Winterbourne, is that the way you look for my brother? You had better not come to dinner unless you find him.

WINTERBOURNE. I was just wondering which way I had better go.

MRS. WALKER. Mrs. Miller has pressed us into the service, and she wants everyone to go in a different direction. But I prefer (*significantly*) that Daisy and I should stick together.

DAISY. (*Happily.*) Oh, I don't care now. You may take me anywhere!

WINTERBOURNE. (*Aside.*) Poor little thing! And I have got to disappoint her! (*Aloud.*) I suppose I had better separate from you, then.

EUGENIO. (*Arriving hastily.*) Mr. Randolph has been found—by Mr. Reverdy! (*To* DAISY.) If I leave your mother a moment, a misfortune is sure to arrive.

MRS. WALKER. (*Aside.*) The misfortune, indeed, is his being found! (*To* DAISY.) If you will join your mother, I will go back to my guests (*seeing* GIOVANELLI)—whom Mr. Giovanelli has already deserted.

GIOVANELLI. (*Coming in.*) Your guests have deserted me, Madame. They have left your house in a caravan, unable to support your absence.

MRS. WALKER. (*To* DAISY.) I have offended all my friends for you, my dear. You ought to be grateful.

DAISY. The reason they left was not because you came away, but because you didn't bring me back. They wanted to glare at me.

GIOVANELLI. (*With a little laugh.*) They glared at me a good deal!

MRS. WALKER. I will admit that they don't like you. (*To* DAISY.) Let me place you in your mother's hands.

EUGENIO. (*With importance.*) I will take charge of my young lady, Madame.

WINTERBOURNE. (*To* DAISY.) Before you

go, just let me say a word.

DAISY. As many as you please—only you frighten me!

WINTERBOURNE. I am rather frightened myself. I am very much afraid I shall not be able to dine to-night.

DAISY. Not be able—after your promise?

WINTERBOURNE. It's very true I promised, and I am greatly ashamed. But a most unexpected obstacle has sprung up. I am obliged to take back my word—I am exceedingly sorry.

MRS. WALKER. (*In a low voice to* WINTERBOURNE.) Ah, my dear sir, you're making a mess!

DAISY. Your obstacle must have come very quickly.

WINTERBOURNE. Only five minutes ago.

EUGENIO. (*Aside.*) The Katkoff's as good as her word!

DAISY. (*Much agitated.*) Well, Mr. Winterbourne, I can only say I too am very sorry.

WINTERBOURNE. I will come the very first evening I am free.

DAISY. I didn't want the first evening; I wanted this one.

WINTERBOURNE. I beg you to forgive me. My own loss is greater than yours.

GIOVANELLI. (*Aside.*) My friend the courier is a clever man!

DAISY. (*Thoughtful a moment.*) Well it's no matter.

MRS. WALKER. (*To* EUGENIO.) Please take her to her mother.

EUGENIO. I must act at my, convenience, Madame!

DAISY. I'm not going to my mother. Mr. Giovanelli!

GIOVANELLI. (*With alacrity.*) Signorina?

DAISY. Please to give me your arm. We'll go on with our walk.

MRS. WALKER. (*Coming between the two.*) Now don't do anything dreadful!

DAISY. (*To* GIOVANELLI.) Give me your arm. (GIOVANELLI *passes behind* MRS. WALKER *and gives* DAISY *his arm on the other side. She continues, with a sudden outbreak of passion.*) I see nothing dreadful but your cruel accusations! If you all attack me, I have a friend to defend me.

GIOVANELLI. I will defend you always, Signorina!

MRS. WALKER. Are you going to take her to that drinking-shop?

DAISY. That's our own affair. Come away, come away!

WINTERBOURNE. I have done you a greater injury than I supposed.

DAISY. The injury was done when you spoke to me that way!

WINTERBOURNE. When I spoke to you? I don't understand.

DAISY. Half an hour ago, when you said I was so bad!

GIOVANELLI. If people insult you, they will answer to *me*.

WINTERBOURNE. (*To* GIOVANELLI.) Don't be rash, sir! You will need all your caution.

MRS. WALKER. High words between gentlemen, to crown the horrors! (*To* EUGENIO.) Go straight and ask Mrs. Miller if she consents.

EUGENIO. (*Smiling.*) Mrs. Miller consents to everything that I approve.

DAISY. Come away, Mr. Giovanelli!

GIOVANELLI. (*Aside.*) I shall have to take a cab! (*They walk up the stage.*)

MRS. WALKER. Mercy on us! She is lost!

WINTERBOURNE. (*Sternly.*) Leave her alone. She only wants a pretext!

DAISY. (*Who has heard him, turning as she reaches the top of the stage, and looking back a moment.*) Thank you, Mr. Winterbourne! (*She goes out with* GIOVANELLI.)

MRS. WALKER. (*To* WINTERBOURNE.) Yes, my dear sir, you have done a pretty piece of work.

EUGENIO. (*With his hands in his pockets, as at the end of the first act, watching the scene complacently.*) My little revenge on the journey to the castle!

WINTERBOURNE. (*Looking at his watch, to himself.*) Well, *I* shall have that moonlight drive!

ACT THIRD

Rome. Public parlors at the Hôtel de Paris; evening. Wide windows at the back, overlooking the Corso, open upon a balcony, which must be apparent, behind light curtains, to the audience. The Carnival is going on outside, and the flare of torches, the sound of voices and of music, the uproar of a popular festival, come into the room, rising and falling at intervals during the whole act.

(*Scene First:* Mrs. Costello, Miss Durant, Charles Reverdy. *He comes in first at the left, holding the door open for the others to follow.*)

Reverdy. You can see very well from this balcony, if you won't go down into the street.

Mrs. Costello. Down into the street—to be trampled to death? I have no desire to be butchered to make a Roman holiday.

Reverdy. (*Aside.*) They would find you a tough old morsel! (*Aloud.*) It's the last night of the Carnival, and a peculiar license prevails.

Mrs. Costello. I'm happy to hear it's the last night. Their tooting and piping and fiddling hasn't stopped for a week, and my poor old head has been racked with pain.

Miss Durant. Is it very bad now? You had better go to our own quiet sitting-room, which looks out on the back.

Mrs. Costello. And leave you here with this youth?

Miss Durant. After all—in the Carnival!

Mrs. Costello. A season of peculiar license—as he himself confesses. I wonder you don't propose at once to mingle with the populace—in a fancy dress!

Miss Durant. I should like to very much! I'm tired of being cooped up in a balcony. If this is the last night, it's my only chance.

Mrs. Costello. (*Severely.*) Alice Durant, I don't recognize you! The Carnival has affected you—insidiously. You're as bad as Daisy Miller.

Reverdy. Poor little butterfly! Don't speak harshly of *her:* she is lying ill with Roman fever.

Mrs. Costello. Since her visit to the Coliseum, in the cool of the evening, with the inveterate Giovanelli?

Miss Durant. I suppose he'll marry her when she recovers—if she does recover!

Reverdy. It was certainly idiotic, from the point of view of salubrity, to go to enjoy the moonlight in that particularly mouldy ruin, and the inveterate Giovanelli, who is old enough to know better, ought to have a thrashing. The poor girl may never recover. The little Flower of the West, as Mrs. Walker says, is withering on the stem. Fancy dying to the music of the Carnival!

Mrs. Costello. That's the way I shall die, unless you come now and take your last look, so that we may go away and have done with it. (*Goes to the window.*) Good heavens, what a rabble! (*Passes out on the balcony.*)

Reverdy. (*To* Miss Durant, *remaining behind.*) Will you give her the slip, and come out with me?

Miss Durant. (*Looking at him, and listening to the music.*) In a fancy dress?

Reverdy. Oh, no; simply in a mask. I've got one in my pocket. (*Takes out a grotesque mask and holds it to his face a moment, shaking his head at her.*) How d'ye do, lovely woman?

Miss Durant. Dear me, how very hideous!

Reverdy. If *you* put it on, I shall be as handsome as ever.

Miss Durant. (*Aside.*) If he should propose out there, it would hide my blushes!

Mrs. Costello. (*From the balcony.*) Young people, what are you doing? Come out here this minute!

Reverdy. There she is again! (*Aloud.*) Are you afraid they will pelt you with flowers?

Mrs. Costello. A gentleman has already kissed his hand to me!

Reverdy. A season of peculiar license! (*To* Miss Durant.) We can't escape from her now, but it won't be long!

(*They rejoin* MRS. COSTELLO *on the balcony,* REVERDY *holding the mask behind him. While they remain there, apparently absorbed in the spectacle in the street,* EUGENIO *and* GIOVANELLI *come in.*)

(*Scene Second:* EUGENIO, GIOVANELLI; *then* REVERDY, MISS DURANT.)

EUGENIO. You must come in here; we can't talk in the hall.

GIOVANELLI. (*With a bouquet of flowers.*) I have come for news of the dear young lady. I'm terribly nervous.

EUGENIO. You think you may lose her? It would serve you right!

GIOVANELLI. If I lose her I shall never try again. I am passionately in love with her.

EUGENIO. I hope so, indeed! That was part of our agreement.

GIOVANELLI. If you begin to joke, I see she's better.

EUGENIO. If I begin to joke? I'm as serious as you. If she's better it's no thanks to you—doing your best to kill her on my hands.

GIOVANELLI. It was no fault of mine. She had her own way.

EUGENIO. The Coliseum by moonlight—that was a lovely invention! Why didn't you jump into the Tiber at once?

GIOVANELLI. We are not the first who have been there. It's a very common excursion.

EUGENIO. By daylight, of course; but not when the miasma rises.

GIOVANELLI. Excuse me: it is recommended in the guide-books.

EUGENIO. Do you make love according to Murray?—or, perhaps, according to Baedeker? I myself have conducted families there, to admire the general effect; but not to spend the evening.

GIOVANELLI. I was afraid for myself, Heaven knows!

EUGENIO. "Afraid for yourself" is good—with an American heiress beside you!

GIOVANELLI. I couldn't induce her to come away, the moon was so bright and beautiful! And then you wanted her to be talked about.

EUGENIO. Yes: but I wanted you to take her alive. She's talked about enough to-day. It was only a week ago, but the whole town knows it.

GIOVANELLI. *Per Bacco!* That solemn fool of a Winterbourne has spread the story.

EUGENIO. The further the better! But I thought I had given him something else to do.

GIOVANELLI. I don't know what you had given him to do; but, as luck would have it, he turned up at the Coliseum. He came upon us suddenly, and stood there staring. Then he took off his hat to my companion, and made her the lowest of bows.

EUGENIO. Without a word?

GIOVANELLI. Without a word. He turned his back and walked off.

EUGENIO. Stupid ass! But it is all right: he has given her up.

GIOVANELLI. He gave her up that day on the Pincian; he has not been near her since.

EUGENIO. (*Aside.*) The Katkoff is really perfect!—though he comes to ask about her every day. (*Aloud.*) Yes, but he wanted a reason: now he has got his reason.

GIOVANELLI. (*Pretentiously.*) I shall give him a better one than that!

EUGENIO. He's perfectly content with this one; and it must be admitted it would suit most people. We must hope it will suit Mr. Miller.

GIOVANELLI. (*Gloomily.*) Ah, Mr. Miller? I seemed to see him there, too, in the moonlight!

EUGENIO. You're afraid of him, and your fear makes images. What did Miss Daisy do?

GIOVANELLI. After the American had left us? She held her tongue till we got home.

EUGENIO. She said nothing about him?

GIOVANELLI. Never a word, thank goodness!

EUGENIO. (*Thoughtful a moment.*) Cavaliere, you are very limited.

GIOVANELLI. I verily believe I am, to stand here and answer your questions. All this time you have told me nothing about my adored!

EUGENIO. She is doing very well; it has been a light attack. She has sat up these three days, and the doctor says she needs only to be careful. But being careful doesn't suit her; she's in despair at missing the Carnival.

GIOVANELLI. (*Tenderly.*) Enchanting young person! Be so good as to give her these flowers. Be careful of them, you know!

EUGENIO. I should think so—when I pay for them myself.

GIOVANELLI. And ask if I may come up and see her.

EUGENIO. (*Looking at the bouquet.*) You get 'em handsome, I must say.—I don't know what the doctor would say to that.

GIOVANELLI. (*Smiling.*) Let me be the doctor. You'll see!

EUGENIO. You're certainly dangerous enough for one. But you must wait till we go out—the mother and the brother and I.

GIOVANELLI. Where are you going, at this hour?

EUGENIO. To show that peevish little brat the illumination.

GIOVANELLI. Mrs. Miller leaves her daughter—at such a time?

EUGENIO. Master Randolph is the head of the family.

GIOVANELLI. I must get *his* consent to the marriage, then?

EUGENIO. You can get it with a pound of sugar plums.

GIOVANELLI. I'll buy him a dozen to-morrow.

EUGENIO. And charge them to me, of course.

GIOVANELLI. (*Stiffly.*) Please to open the door. I'll wait in the hall till you go out. (EUGENIO *opens the door, looks at him, and then passes out first.* GIOVANELLI *follows. When they have left the room,* REVERDY *and* MISS DURANT *come in from the balcony.*)

REVERDY. (*His finger on his lips.*) Hush, hush! She's looking for the gentleman who kissed his hand.

MISS DURANT. When she kissed hers back, she frightened him away!

REVERDY. I can't stand that balcony business! I want to dance and sing, in the midst of it, with a charming creature on my arm!

MISS DURANT. I forbid you to touch any of your creatures!

REVERDY. In the Carnival one may touch any one. All common laws are suspended.

MISS DURANT. Cousin Louisa won't listen to that.

REVERDY. She's a great deal worse than we herself—having an intrigue with a perfect stranger! Now's our chance to escape; before she misses us, we shall be a mile away.

MISS DURANT. A mile away is very far! You make me feel dreadfully like Daisy Miller.

REVERDY. To be perfect, all you want is to be a little like her.

MISS DURANT. Oh, you wretch—I never!

REVERDY. There, now, you are just like her!

MISS DURANT. I certainly am not used to being a wall-flower.

REVERDY. A plant in a balcony is even worse. Come, come! here's the mask.

MISS DURANT. It's very dreadful. I can't bear to look so ugly!

REVERDY. Don't I know how pretty you are?

MISS DURANT. (*Taking his arm, aside.*) He can do anything with me he wants!

(*Exeunt. Enter* DAISY *on the opposite side.*)

(*Scene Third:* DAISY *alone; then* WINTERBOURNE, *a* WAITER; MRS. COSTELLO.)

DAISY. (*She wears a light dressing-gown, like an invalid, and it must be apparent that she has been ill, though this appearance must not be exaggerated. She wanders slowly into the room, and pauses in the middle.*) Ah, from here the music is very distinct—and the voices of the crowd, and all the sound of the fête. Upstairs, in our rooms, you can hear it just dimly. That's the way it seemed to me—just faint and far—as I lay there with darkened windows. It's hard to be sick when there's so much pleasure going on, especially when you're so fond of pleasure as poor silly me! Perhaps I'm too fond; that's one of the things I thought of as I lay there. I thought of so many—and some of them so sad—as I listened to the far-away Carnival. I think it was this that helped me to get better. I was afraid I had been bad, and I wanted to live to be good again. I was afraid I should die, and I didn't want to die. But I'm better now, and I can walk and do everything I want. (*Listening again.*) Every now and then it grows louder, as if the people were so happy! It reminds me of that poetry I used to learn at school, "There was a sound of revelry by night." That's a sound I always wanted to hear. This is the last night; and when mother and Randolph went out, I couldn't stay there alone. I waited a little; I was afraid of meeting someone on the stairs. But everyone is in the streets, and they have gone out to see the illumination. I thought of that balcony: just to look out a little is better than nothing. (*Listens again a moment.*) Every now and then it increases. (*Goes to the window, but seeing* MRS. COSTELLO *outside comes back.*) Ah, there someone there; and with this old wrapper . . . (*Looking at her dressing-gown.*) Perhaps the night air isn't good for me; the doctor forbids the night air. Ah, what a pity it's the last evening! (*Goes to the window again, and while she stands there a* WAITER *throws open the door and ushers in* WINTERBOURNE, *who at first does not see her.*)

THE WAITER. The ladies are here, sir. (*Surprised not to find them.*) Excuse me. I saw them come in with Mr. Reverdy, but they have gone out again.

WINTERBOURNE. It's not those ladies I want. Please to ask Madame de Katkoff if she can see me.

THE WAITER. Won't you go up to her sitting-room? She has a great many guests.

WINTERBOURNE. (*Annoyed.*) A great many guests?

THE WAITER. A party of friends, who have come to see the fête from one of her windows. Her parlor is in the Square, and the view is even finer than from here.

WINTERBOURNE. I know all about her parlor. (*Aside.*) It's hateful to see her with a lot of others! (*Aloud.*) Ask her if she will kindly speak to me here.

THE WAITER. Ah, you lose a great deal, sir! (*Exit.*)

WINTERBOURNE. The servants in this place are impossible; the young Randolph has demoralized them all! That's the same

fellow who, last summer, wanted to give me a definition of my aunt. (*Seeing* DAISY.) Ah, that poor creature! (*Aloud.*) I am afraid I am intruding on you here.

DAISY. (*Coming forward.*) You have as good a right here as I. I don't think I have any.

WINTERBOURNE. You mean as an invalid? I am very happy to see you better.

DAISY. Thank you. I'm very well.

WINTERBOURNE. I asked about you every day.

DAISY. They never told me.

WINTERBOURNE. That was your faithful courier!

DAISY. He was so frightened at my illness that he couldn't remember anything.

WINTERBOURNE. Oh, yes, he was terribly afraid he should lose you. For a couple of days it was very serious.

DAISY. How do you know that?

WINTERBOURNE. I asked the doctor.

DAISY. (*Aside.*) He's very strange. Why should he care?

WINTERBOURNE. He said you had done what might kill you.

DAISY. At the Coliseum?

WINTERBOURNE. At the Coliseum.

DAISY. Why didn't you tell me that, when you saw me there?

WINTERBOURNE. Because you had an adviser in whom you have much more faith.

DAISY. Mr. Giovanelli? Oh, it's not his fault. He begged me to come away.

WINTERBOURNE. If you didn't mind him, you wouldn't have minded me.

DAISY. I didn't care what happened. But I noticed, all the same, that you didn't speak to me.

WINTERBOURNE. I had nothing to say.

DAISY. You only bowed, very low.

WINTERBOURNE. That was to express my great respect.

DAISY. I had never had such a bow before.

WINTERBOURNE. You had never been so worthy of it!

DAISY. (*Aside.*) He despises me! Well, I don't care! (*Aloud.*) It was lovely there in the moonlight.

WINTERBOURNE. I was sure you found it so. That was another reason I didn't wish to interrupt you.

DAISY. (*Playing indifference.*) What were you doing there, all alone?

WINTERBOURNE. I had been dining at a villa in that part of Rome, and I simply stopped, as I walked home, to take a look at the splendid ruin.

DAISY. (*After a pause, in the same manner.*) I shouldn't think you'd go round alone.

WINTERBOURNE. I have to go as I can; I haven't your resources.

DAISY. Don't you know any ladies?

WINTERBOURNE. Yes; but they don't expose themselves . . .

DAISY. (*With quick emotion.*) Expose themselves to be treated as you treated me!

WINTERBOURNE. You are rather difficult to please. (*Re-enter the* WAITER.)

THE WAITER. Madame de Katkoff will come in about ten minutes, sir.

WINTERBOURNE. Very good.

THE WAITER. She's just pouring out tea for the company.

WINTERBOURNE. That will do.

THE WAITER. (*Smiling.*) You know the Russians must have their tea, sir.

WINTERBOURNE. You talk too much.

THE WAITER. (*Going out.*) He's very sharp to-night! (*Exit* WAITER.)

DAISY. (*Who has turned away a moment, coming down.*) If you are expecting some one, I'll go away.

WINTERBOURNE. There's another public room. I'll see my friend there.

DAISY. I have nothing to do here. (*Goes toward the door, but stops half-way, looking at him.*) You see a great deal of Madame de Katkoff. Doesn't *she* expose herself?

WINTERBOURNE. (*Smiling.*) To dangerous consequences? Never!

DAISY. (*She comes down again, as if unable to decide to leave him. Aside.*) I'm determined to know what he thinks. (*Aloud, in a different tone.*) I was going out on the balcony, to see what's going on.

WINTERBOURNE. Are you not afraid of the night air?

DAISY. I'm not afraid of anything!

WINTERBOURNE. Are you going to begin again?

DAISY. Ah, I'm too late! It's nearly over. (*At the moment she speaks,* MRS. COS-

TELLO *appears in the window, from the balcony. Re-enter* MRS. COSTELLO.)

MRS. COSTELLO. (*To* WINTERBOURNE.) Merciful powers! I thought you were Mr. Reverdy! (*Looking at* DAISY.) And that this young lady was my Alice!

DAISY. Something very different, you see! Now I can have the balcony. (*She passes out of the window.*)

MRS. COSTELLO. What are you doing with that girl? I thought you had dropped her.

WINTERBOURNE. I was asking about her health. She has been down with the fever.

MRS. COSTELLO. It will do her good—make her reflect on her sins. But what have you done with my young companions?

WINTERBOURNE. Nothing in the world. The last I saw of them they were frolicking in the Corso.

MRS. COSTELLO. Frolicking in the Corso? Alice and Mr. Reverdy?

WINTERBOURNE. I met them as I was coming from my lodgings to the hotel. He was blowing a tin trumpet, and she was hiding behind a mask.

MRS. COSTELLO. A tin trumpet and a mask! Have they gone to perdition?

WINTERBOURNE. They are only taking advantage of the Carnival.

MRS. COSTELLO. Taking advantage of my back; I had turned it for three minutes! They were on the balcony with me, looking at this vulgar riot, and they slipped away to come in here.

WINTERBOURNE. You never give them a chance: they hunger and thirst!

MRS. COSTELLO. A chance to masquerade? Think of her education!

WINTERBOURNE. I am thinking of it now. You see the results.

MRS. COSTELLO. I said to myself that I was perhaps too vigilant, and I left them here a moment to talk things over. I saw through the window a young lady and a gentleman, and I took it for granted it was they.

WINTERBOURNE. Ingenuous aunt! They were already a mile away!

MRS. COSTELLO. It's too horrible to believe. You must immediately bring them back.

WINTERBOURNE. Impossible just now. I

have an engagement here.

MRS. COSTELLO. I'll go and look for them myself!

WINTERBOURNE. (*Laying his hand on her arm.*) Don't, don't! Let them have a little fun!

MRS. COSTELLO. I never heard of anything so cynical!

WINTERBOURNE. Don't you want them to marry?

MRS. COSTELLO. To marry, yes; but not to elope!

WINTERBOURNE. Let them do it in their own way.

MRS. COSTELLO. With a mask and a tin trumpet? A girl I've watched like that!

WINTERBOURNE. You have watched too much. They'll come home engaged.

MRS. COSTELLO. Ah, bring them, then, quickly!

WINTERBOURNE. I will go down into the street and look; and if I see them, I will tell them what's expected of them.

MRS. COSTELLO. I will go to my room; I feel a headache coming on. (*Before she goes out, to herself, as if a thought has struck her.*) Had they bribed that monster to kiss his hand?

(*Exeunt.*)

(*Scene Fourth:* GIOVANELLI, DAISY. *He enters the room, and she comes in from the balcony at the same moment. He advances with a radiant smile, takes both of her hands, holds them for a moment devotedly, then kisses each of them.*)

GIOVANELLI. *Carissima signorina!* When I see you restored to health, I begin to live myself!

DAISY. Poor old Giovanelli! I believe you *do* care for me!

GIOVANELLI. Care for you? When I heard you were ill, I neither ate nor slept. I thought I, too, should have to have the doctor.

DAISY. (*Laughing.*) I should have sent you mine if I had known it. You must eat a good supper to-night, for I am all right now.

GIOVANELLI. You look still a little pale.

DAISY. I look like a fright, of course, in this dreadful dress; but I'm only a con-valescent. If I had known you were coming, I would have worn something better.

GIOVANELLI. You look like an angel, always. You might have been sure I would come, after so many days. I was always at your door, asking for news. But now, I think, we shall never again be separated.

DAISY. Never again? Oh, don't talk about the future! What were you doing there in the street?

GIOVANELLI. When I looked up and saw you on the balcony, bending over like a little saint in her shrine? It was that vision that made me come up again.

DAISY. You had gone out to enjoy the Carnival?

GIOVANELLI. I had come here to see you; but I learned from your excellent Eugenio that your mother and your brother were going out in a carriage. They appeared at that moment, and I went down with them to the door, to wish them a happy drive. Little Randolph was greatly excited.

DAISY. He insisted on mother's going; she'll do anything for Randolph. But she didn't want to leave me.

GIOVANELLI. (*Smiling.*) She has left you to me!

DAISY. Did Eugenio go with them?

GIOVANELLI. Oh, yes; he got into the carriage. (*Aside.*) The cheek of that man!

DAISY. They have left me alone, then.

GIOVANELLI. I am almost of the family, dear Miss!

DAISY. (*Apparently not hearing him, listening to the sounds from without.*) They oughtn't to have left me alone—when I'm sick, when I'm weak.

GIOVANELLI. (*Anxiously.*) You are not so well, then, as you say?

DAISY. (*Looking at him a moment, with a little laugh.*) You look so scared at the idea of losing me! Poor old Giovanelli! What should you do if you were to lose me?

GIOVANELLI. Don't speak of it—it's horrible! If you are not well, you should go to your room.

DAISY. Oh, I'm all right. I only wanted to frighten you.

GIOVANELLI. It isn't kind—when you know how I love you!

DAISY. I don't know it, and I don't want

to know it, as I have told you often. I forbid you to speak of that.

GIOVANELLI. You will never let me mention the future.

DAISY. I hate the future; I care only for the present!

GIOVANELLI. The future is the present, when one sees it as we see it.

DAISY. I don't see it at all, and I don't want to see it. I saw it for a moment, when I was sick, and that was enough.

GIOVANELLI. You have suffered much; but it was not my fault.

DAISY. I don't blame you, Giovanelli. You are very kind. Where are they going, mother and Randolph?

GIOVANELLI. Up and down the Corso; wherever there is something to see. They have an open carriage, with lots of flowers.

DAISY. It must be charming. Have you been going round?

GIOVANELLI. I have strolled about a little.

DAISY. Is it very, *very* amusing?

GIOVANELLI. Ah, you know, I'm an old Roman; I have seen it many times. The illumination is better than usual, and the music is lively enough.

DAISY. Listen to the music—listen to it!

GIOVANELLI. (*Smiling.*) You mustn't let it go to your head. (DAISY *goes to the window, and stands there a moment.*) She has never been so lovely as to-night!

DAISY. (*Coming back, with decision.*) Giovanelli, you must get me a carriage.

GIOVANELLI. (*Startled.*) A carriage, signorina?

DAISY. I must go out—I *must!*

GIOVANELLI. There is not a carriage to be had at this hour. Everything is taken for the fête.

DAISY. Then I'll go on foot. You must take me.

GIOVANELLI. Into the air of the night, and the crowded streets? It's enough to kill you!

DAISY. It's a lovely night, as mild as June; and it's only for five minutes.

GIOVANELLI. The softer the night, the greater the danger of the bad air. Five minutes, in your condition, would bring back the fever.

DAISY. I shall have the fever if I stay here listening, longing, fidgeting! You said I was pale; but it's only the delicacy of my complexion.

GIOVANELLI. You are not pale now; you have a little spot in either cheek. Your mother will not be happy.

DAISY. She shouldn't have left me alone, then.

GIOVANELLI. You are not alone when you are with me.

DAISY. Of what use are you, except to take me out?

GIOVANELLI. It's impossible to contradict you. For five minutes, then, remember!

DAISY. For five minutes, then; or for ten! I'll go and get ready. Don't mind about the carriage: we'll do it better on foot.

GIOVANELLI. (*At the door.*) It's at your own risk, you know. I'll try for a cab.

DAISY. My own risk! I'm not afraid.

GIOVANELLI. (*Kissing his hand to her.*) You are awfully beautiful! (*Exit* GIOVANELLI.)

DAISY. (*Alone.*) I'm not afraid—I don't care! I don't like him to-night; he's too serious. I would rather be out-of-doors with him than shut up here. Poor Giovanelli; if he thinks I love him, after all I've said to the contrary . . . I can dress in three minutes. (*She is going to the door opposite to the one through which* GIOVANELLI *has made his exit when* MADAME DE KATKOFF *comes in, meeting her.*)

(*Scene Fifth:* DAISY, MADAME DE KATKOFF. *They stand a moment, looking at each other.*)

MME. DE KATKOFF. (*Very kindly.*) I have not the pleasure of knowing you, though we have spent half the winter in the same hotel; but I have heard of your illness, and you must let me tell you how glad I am to see you better.

DAISY. (*Aside.*) Why does she speak to me? I don't like her, nor want to know her. (*Aloud.*) Thank you, I'm better. I'm going out.

MME. DE KATKOFF. You must be better, indeed; but (*with interest*) you look a little flushed.

DAISY. It's talking with a stranger. I think I must go.

MME. DE KATKOFF. Perhaps you can tell me something first. A gentleman sent me his name, and I was told I should find him here. May I ask you whether you have seen such a person?

DAISY. If you mean Mr. Winterbourne, he was here just now; but he went away with his aunt.

MME. DE KATKOFF. I suppose he'll come back, then. But he oughtn't to keep me waiting.

DAISY. (*Very coldly.*) I haven't the least idea what he ought to do. I know nothing whatever of his movements.

MME. DE KATKOFF. (*Aside.*) Poor little thing, she hates me! But she doesn't hate *him.* (*Aloud.*) I'm a stranger as you say; but I should be very glad to become a little less of one.

DAISY. Why should you want to know me? I'm not of your age.

MME. DE KATKOFF. (*Aside, smiling.*) She hates me indeed! (*Aloud.*) I should be tempted to say that we might know each other a little as mother and daughter—if I hadn't heard that you are already the devoted daughter of a devoted mother.

DAISY. She's good enough for me—and I'm good enough for her.

MME. DE KATKOFF. (*More and more gracious.*) I envy you both, and I am happy to have the opportunity of saying so. One doesn't know how pretty you are till one talks to you.

DAISY. If you are laughing at my dress, I am just going to change it.

MME. DE KATKOFF. Laughing at your dress? It has always been my admiration.

DAISY. (*Aside.*) What does she mean by that? It's not as good as hers. (*Aloud.*) I can't stay with you. I'm going to the Carnival.

MME. DE KATKOFF. It will last all night; you have plenty of time. I have heard Mr. Winterbourne speak of you.

DAISY. I didn't suppose he ever did that.

MME. DE KATKOFF. Oh! very often. That's why I want to know you.

DAISY. It's a strange reason. He must have told you pretty things of me.

MME. DE KATKOFF. He has told me you're a charming young girl.

DAISY. (*Aside.*) Oh, what an awful story!

(*Aloud.*) I don't understand what you want of me.

MME. DE KATKOFF. (*Aside.*) I can hardly tell her that I want to make up to her for the harm I have done her, for I can't do that unless I give up everything. (*Aloud, as if struck by an idea.*) I want to be kind to you. I want to keep you from going out.

DAISY. (*Smiling.*) I don't think you can do that.

MME. DE KATKOFF. You are barely convalescent: you mustn't expose yourself.

DAISY. It won't hurt anyone but me.

MME. DE KATKOFF. We all take a great interest in you. We should be in despair if you were to have a relapse.

DAISY. You all despise me and think me dreadful; that's what you all do!

MME. DE KATKOFF. Where did you learn that remarkable fact?

DAISY. Mr. Winterbourne told me—since you speak of Mr. Winterbourne.

MME. DE KATKOFF. I don't think you understood him. Mr. Winterbourne is a perfect gentleman.

DAISY. Have you come here to praise him to me? That's strange—for you!

MME. DE KATKOFF. You know at least that I consider him an excellent friend.

DAISY. I know nothing whatever about it. (*Aside.*) She wants to torture me—to triumph!

MME. DE KATKOFF. (*Aside.*) She's as proud as she is pretty! (*Aloud.*) Are you going out alone?

DAISY. No, indeed, I have a friend.

MME. DE KATKOFF. (*Aside.*) A friend as well as I. (*Aloud.*) My dear child, I am very sorry for you. You have too many wrong ideas.

DAISY. That's exactly what they say!

MME. DE KATKOFF. I don't mean it as other people may have meant it. You make a great many mistakes.

DAISY. As many as I possibly can! In America I was always right.

MME. DE KATKOFF. Try and believe you are in America now. I'm not an American, but I want to be your friend.

DAISY. I'm much obliged to you, but I don't trust you.

MME. DE KATKOFF. You trust the wrong people. With whom are you going out?

DAISY. I don't think I'm obliged to tell you.

MME. DE KATKOFF. (*Gently.*) I ask for a very good motive.

DAISY. (*Aside.*) She may be better than I think. (*Aloud.*) With Mr. Giovanelli.

MME. DE KATKOFF. (*Smiling.*) A mysterious Italian—introduced by your courier!

DAISY. (*With simplicity.*) Oh, no; Eugenio got someone else!

MME. DE KATKOFF. (*Aside.*) Adorable innocence! (*Aloud.*) That's all I wanted to know.

DAISY. I hope you have nothing to say against him.

MME. DE KATKOFF. Nothing but this: he's not a gentleman.

DAISY. Not a gentleman? Poor old Giovanelli!

MME. DE KATKOFF. (*Aside.*) "Poor old Giovanelli?" Good! (*Aloud.*) If he were a gentleman, he wouldn't ask you to do what you tell me you are on the point of doing.

DAISY. He never asked me. He does what I wish!

MME. DE KATKOFF. (*Aside.*) She doesn't care a fig for him—and I should like to exasperate the courier. (*Aloud.*) It's none of my business; but why do you wish, in your condition, to go out?

DAISY. Because it's the last night of the Carnival, and I have no one else to take me.

MME. DE KATKOFF. Excuse me; but where is your mother?

DAISY. Gone out with my brother.

MME. DE KATKOFF. (*Aside.*) Extraordinary family! (*Aloud.*) Let me make you an offer: I will order out my carriage, and take you myself.

DAISY. (*Staring.*) Take me yourself? (*Then abruptly, ironically.*) Pray, what would become of Mr. Winterbourne?

MME. DE KATKOFF. (*Aside.*) She adores him! (*Aloud.*) Ah, you don't care for Giovanelli!

DAISY. Whether I care for him or not, I mustn't keep him waiting. (*Exit* DAISY, *hastily.*)

MME. DE KATKOFF. (*Alone.*) She's trembling with agitation, and her poor little heart is full. She thought I wished to torment her. My position is odiously false!

And to think I hold her happiness in my hands! (WINTERBOURNE *comes in.*) His, too, poor fellow! Ah, I can't hold it any longer!

(*Scene Sixth:* MADAME DE KATKOFF, WINTERBOURNE.)

WINTERBOURNE. I am afraid I have kept you waiting. I was carried away by my aunt.

MME. DE KATKOFF. Is she keeping the Carnival, your aunt?

WINTERBOURNE. No, but her companions are. They are masquerading in the Corso, and she's in despair. She sent me to hunt them up, but they are lost in the crowd.

MME. DE KATKOFF. Do you mean the young lady whom you described as so prim? If that's a specimen of her primness, I was right in my little theory.

WINTERBOURNE. Your little theory?

MME. DE KATKOFF. That the grave ones are the gay ones.

WINTERBOURNE. Poor Miss Durant isn't gay: she's simply desperate. My aunt keeps such watch at the door that she has been obliged to jump out of the window.—Have you waited very long?

MME. DE KATKOFF. I hardly know. I have had company—Miss Daisy Miller!

WINTERBOURNE. That must have made the time fly!

MME. DE KATKOFF. She is very touching.

WINTERBOURNE. Very, indeed. She has gone to pieces.

MME. DE KATKOFF. Gone to pieces?

WINTERBOURNE. She's quite impossible. You oughtn't to talk to her.

MME. DE KATKOFF. (*Aside.*) Ah, what a fool I have made of him! (*Aloud.*) You think she will corrupt my innocence?

WINTERBOURNE. (*After a moment.*) I don't like you to speak of her. Please don't.

MME. DE KATKOFF. She completes my little theory—that the gay ones are the grave ones.

WINTERBOURNE. If she's grave, she well may be: her situation is intensely grave. As for her native solemnity, you used to insist upon that when, for reasons best known to yourself, you conceived the remarkable design of inducing me to make love to her. You dropped the idea as suddenly as you took it up; but I am very sorry to see any symptoms of your taking it up again. It seems to me it's hardly the moment.

MME. DE KATKOFF. (*Aside.*) It's more the moment than you think.

WINTERBOURNE. (*Rather harshly.*) I was very sorry to learn, on coming here, that you have your rooms full of people.

MME. DE KATKOFF. They have come to look out of my windows. It is not my fault that I have such a view of the Corso.

WINTERBOURNE. You had given me to understand that we should be alone.

MME. DE KATKOFF. I didn't ask them; they came themselves.

WINTERBOURNE. (*Impatiently.*) I wish to heaven they had stayed at home!

MME. DE KATKOFF. Should you like me to turn them out?

WINTERBOURNE. I should like it particularly.

MME. DE KATKOFF. The ambassador and all?

WINTERBOURNE. You told me a month ago that where I was concerned you didn't care a straw for the ambassador.

MME. DE KATKOFF. (*After a moment.*) A month ago—yes!

WINTERBOURNE. If you intended to change so soon, you ought to have notified me at the moment.

MME. DE KATKOFF. The ambassador is very considerate. When I have a few visitors, he helps me to entertain them.

WINTERBOURNE. That proves how little you have need of me.

MME. DE KATKOFF. I have left my guests in his charge, with perfect confidence.

WINTERBOURNE. Oh, if you mean you are at liberty, that's just what I want.

MME. DE KATKOFF. What does it occur to you to propose?

WINTERBOURNE. That you should drive out with me, to see the illumination.

MME. DE KATKOFF. I have seen fifty illuminations! I am sick of the Carnival.

WINTERBOURNE. It isn't the Carnival; it's the drive. I have a carriage at the door.

MME. DE KATKOFF. I have no doubt it would be charming; but I am not at liberty in that sense. I can't leave a roomful of people planted there! I really don't see why they should make you so savage.

WINTERBOURNE. I am not savage, but I am disappointed. I counted on this evening: it's a week since we have been alone.

MME. DE KATKOFF. Do I appear to so little advantage in company? Are you ashamed of me when others are present? I do the best I can.

WINTERBOURNE. You were always strange —and you always will be! Sometimes I think you have taken a vow to torment me.

MME. DE KATKOFF. I have taken a vow— that's very true; and I admit I am strange. We Russians are, you know: you had warning of that!

WINTERBOURNE. Yes; but you abuse the national privilege. I am never safe with you—never sure of you. You turn from one thing to the other.

MME. DE KATKOFF. (*Aside.*) Poor fellow, he's bewildered! (*Aloud.*) Will you do me a favor?

WINTERBOURNE. I am sure it's something horrible!

MME. DE KATKOFF. You say you have a carriage at the door. Take it, and go after that poor girl.

WINTERBOURNE. Oh, are you coming back to *her*? You try my patience!

MME. DE KATKOFF. She has just risen from an attack of fever, and it strikes her as a knowing thing to finish her evening in the streets!

WINTERBOURNE. (*Starting a little.*) She has gone out—looking that way?

MME. DE KATKOFF. (*Aside.*) That will touch him! (*Aloud.*) She won't come home alive.

WINTERBOURNE. (*Attentive.*) Do you believe that?

MME. DE KATKOFF. (*Aside.*) It *has* touched him! (*Aloud.*) I think it's madness. Her only safety was to have left Rome the moment she could be moved.

WINTERBOURNE. (*After a pause.*) I am not sure the best thing that can happen to her is not to die! She ought to perish in her flower, as she once said to me!

MME. DE KATKOFF. That's a convenient theory, to save you the trouble of a drive!

WINTERBOURNE. You are remarkably pressing, but you had better spare your sarcasm. I have no further interest in the fate of Miss Daisy Miller, and no commission whatever to interfere with her movements. She has a mother—in disguise—and she has other protectors. I don't suppose she has gone out alone.

MME. DE KATKOFF. She has gone with her Italian.

WINTERBOURNE. Giovanelli? Ah, the scoundrel!

MME. DE KATKOFF. (*Smiling, aside.*) My dear friend, you are all right. (*Aloud.*) Gently, gently! It's not *his* fault.

WINTERBOURNE. That she is infatuated. Perhaps not.

MME. DE KATKOFF. Infatuated? She doesn't care a straw for him!

WINTERBOURNE. And to prove her indifference, she lets him take her on this devil's drive? I don't quite see it.

MME. DE KATKOFF. He's her convenience—her little pretext—her poor old Giovanelli. He fetches and carries, and she finds him very useful; but that's the end of it. She takes him to drive: he doesn't take her.

WINTERBOURNE. Did she kindly inform you of these interesting facts?

MME. DE KATKOFF. I had a long talk with her. One woman understands another!

WINTERBOURNE. I hope she understands you. It's more than I do.

MME. DE KATKOFF. She has gone out because she's unhappy. She doesn't care what becomes of her.

WINTERBOURNE. I never suspected her of such tragic propensities. Pray, what is she unhappy about?

MME. DE KATKOFF. About the hard things people say of her.

WINTERBOURNE. She has only to behave like other girls, then.

MME. DE KATKOFF. Like your friend, Miss Durant? A pretty model, this evening! You say you hope poor Daisy understands me; but she doesn't—and that's part of the misery. She can't make out what I have made of you!

WINTERBOURNE. A creature as miserable as herself! You might have explained: you had the opportunity.

MME. DE KATKOFF. She left me abruptly—and I lost it forever!

WINTERBOURNE. All this is nothing to *us*. When will your friends leave you?

MME. DE KATKOFF. (*After a pause.*) No, it's nothing to us.—I haven't asked my friends how long they mean to stay.

WINTERBOURNE. Till eleven o'clock—till twelve?

MME. DE KATKOFF. Till one in the morning, perhaps—or till two. They will see the Carnival out. (*Smiling.*) You had much better join us!

WINTERBOURNE. (*Passionately.*) Unfathomable woman! In pity's name, what did you mean by raising my hopes to such a point, a month ago, only to dash them to the ground?

MME. DE KATKOFF. I tried to make you happy—but I didn't succeed.

WINTERBOURNE. You tried? Are you trying now?

MME. DE KATKOFF. No, I have given it up: it's a waste of time!

WINTERBOURNE. Have you forgotten the day on the Pincian, after your arrival, and what you suddenly offered me—what you promised me—there? You had kept me at arm's length for three years, and suddenly the barrier dropped. The angel of justice has kept the record of my gratitude and eagerness—as well as of my surprise; and if my tenderness and respect were not greater than ever, it is because you had already had the best of them! Have you forgotten our moonlight drive through the streets of Rome, with its rich confusion of ancient memories and new-born hopes? You were perfect that evening, and for many days afterwards. But suddenly you began to change—to be absent, to be silent, to be cold, to go back to your old attitude. To-night it's as if you were trying to make me angry! Do you wish to throw me over, and leave me lying in the dust? Are you only the most audacious of coquettes?

MME. DE KATKOFF. It's not I who have changed; it's you! Of course I remember our moonlight drive, and how glad you were to take it. You were happy for an hour—you were happy for three days. There were novelty and excitement in finding that, after all, I had a heart in my bosom; and for a moment the discovery amused you. But only for a moment! So long as I refused to listen to you, you cared for me. From the day I yielded, I became a bore!

WINTERBOURNE. If you want to get rid of me, don't put it off on *me!*

MME. DE KATKOFF. You don't really care for me; your heart is somewhere else. You are too proud to confess it, but your love for me is an elaborate deception.

WINTERBOURNE. The deception is yours, then—not mine!

MME. DE KATKOFF. You are restless, discontented, unhappy. You are sore and sick at heart, and you have tried to forget it in persuading yourself that *I* can cure your pain. I *can* cure it; but not by encouraging your illusion!

WINTERBOURNE. If you thought it an illusion, why did you turn there and smile on me?

MME. DE KATKOFF. Because I was vile and wicked—because I have played a part and worn a mask, like those idiots in the Carnival—because I am a most unhappy woman!

WINTERBOURNE. (*Looking at her, surprised.*) I assure you, I understand you less and less!

MME. DE KATKOFF. I had an end to gain, and I thought it precious; but I have suddenly begun to loathe it! When I met that poor girl just now, and looked into her face, I was filled with compassion and shame. She is dying, I say, and between us we are killing her! Dying because she loves you, and because she thinks you despise her! Dying because you have turned away from her, and she has tried to stifle the pang! Dying because I have held you here—under compulsion of a scoundrel—and she thinks she has lost you forever! I read it all in her eyes—the purest I ever saw. I am sick of the ghastly comedy, and I must tell the miserable truth. If you will believe me, it's not too late!

WINTERBOURNE. (*Amazed and bewildered.*) Under compulsion—of a scoundrel?

MME. DE KATKOFF. I have the misfortune to be in the clutches of one, and so has our little friend. You know that her mother's horrible courier was once in my husband's service. Thanks to that accident, he has some papers of mine which I wish

to buy back. To make me pay for them, he has forced me to play his game.

WINTERBOURNE. His game? What has he to do with a game?

MME. DE KATKOFF. I don't defend him: I explain. He has selected a husband for his young lady, and your superior attractions had somehow to be muffled up. You were to be kept out of the way.

WINTERBOURNE. (*Frowning.*) Because I love her? (*Correcting himself.*) I mean, because he thinks so.

MME. DE KATKOFF. (*Smiling.*) You see I am right! Because *she* loves you: he has discovered that! So he had the happy thought of saying to me, "Keep Mr. Winterbourne employed, and if the young lady marries my candidate you shall have your letter."

WINTERBOURNE. Your letter? What letter?

MME. DE KATKOFF. A very silly—but very innocent—one that I wrote some ten years ago.

WINTERBOURNE. Why didn't you ask me to get it?

MME. DE KATKOFF. Because I didn't want it enough for that; and now I don't want it at all.

WINTERBOURNE. You shall have it—I promise you that.

MME. DE KATKOFF. You are very generous, after the trick I have played you.

WINTERBOURNE. The trick? Was it *all* a trick?

MME. DE KATKOFF. An infamous, pitiless trick! I was frightened, I was tempted, I was demoralized; he had me in his power. To be cruel to you was bad enough: to be cruel to her was a crime I shall try to expiate!

WINTERBOURNE. (*Seated, his head in his hands.*) You will excuse me if I feel rather stunned.

MME. DE KATKOFF. (*Sinking on her knees.*) I ask your forgiveness! I have been living in a bad dream.

WINTERBOURNE. Ah, you have hurt me—more than I can say!

MME. DE KATKOFF. (*Rising to her feet.*) Don't think of yourself—think of her! If I had only met her before, how much sooner *I* should have done that! We will go and find her together; we will bring her back; we will nurse her and comfort her, and make her understand!

WINTERBOURNE. It's all so extraordinary —and I have only your word for it.

MME. DE KATKOFF. See if she contradicts me when you tell her you love her! You don't venture to deny that.

WINTERBOURNE. I have denied it to myself: why shouldn't I deny it to you?

MME. DE KATKOFF. You have denied it to yourself? Who, then, had charged you with it?

WINTERBOURNE. You are not consistent, but you are perhaps more consistent than I. And you are very deep!

MME. DE KATKOFF. I am deep enough to be very sure that from this moment forward I shall be nothing to you. If I have cured you of a baseless passion, that at least is a good work. Venture to say that for these three weeks I have satisfied you.

WINTERBOURNE. (Turning away.) You are pitiless—you are terrible!

MME. DE KATKOFF. (Looking at him a moment.) My vanity bleeds: be that my penance! Don't lose time. Go to her now.

WINTERBOURNE. (In thought, gloomily.) Dying?—Dying?—Dying?

MME. DE KATKOFF. That was a little for the sake of argument. She will live again— for you!

WINTERBOURNE. (In the same tone.) Gone out with that man? Always with him!

MME. DE KATKOFF. My dear friend, she has her little pride, as well as you. She pretends to flirt with Giovanelli because her poor, swollen heart whispers to her to be brave!

WINTERBOURNE. (Uncertain.) Pretends— only pretends?

MME. DE KATKOFF. (Impatient.) Oh, you have been stupid; but be clever now!

WINTERBOURNE. (After a pause.) How am I to know that this is not another trick?

MME. DE KATKOFF. (Clasping her hands, but smiling.) Have mercy on me! Those words are my punishment!

WINTERBOURNE. I have been an idiot— I have been a brute—I have been a butcher!

MME. DE KATKOFF. Perhaps she has come back. For God's sake, go and see!

WINTERBOURNE. And if she is still out there? I can't talk of these things in the street.

MME. DE KATKOFF. Bring her home, bring her home! Every moment's a danger. I offered to go with you; but you would rather go alone.

WINTERBOURNE. (Takes up his hat.) Yes, I would rather go alone. You have hurt me very much; but you shall have your letter.

MME. DE KATKOFF. I don't care for my letter now. There's such a weight off my heart that I don't feel that one. (She leaves the room by the right, and WINTERBOURNE is on the point of quitting it on the other side, when MRS. WALKER, MISS DURANT, and CHARLES REVERDY come in, meeting him.)

(Scene Seventh: WINTERBOURNE, MRS. WALKER, MISS DURANT, REVERDY.)

MRS. WALKER. Pray, where is your aunt, Mr. Winterbourne? I have brought her back her truants.

WINTERBOURNE. She has retired to her room, to nurse a headache produced by the sudden collapse of her illusions.

MISS DURANT. I thought she would be rather shocked; but Mr. Reverdy assured me that in the Carnival all common laws are suspended.

REVERDY. So we thought the law that governs Mrs. Costello's headaches might conform to the others.

WINTERBOURNE. What did you think about the law that governs her temper?

REVERDY. Nothing at all, because, so far as I have ascertained, there isn't any!

MRS. WALKER. (To WINTERBOURNE.) They were jostling along, arm in arm, in the midst of the excited populace. I saw them from my carriage, and, having the Consul with me, I immediately over- hauled them. The young lady had a won- derful disguise, but I recognized her from Mr. Reverdy's manner.

MISS DURANT. There, sir, I told you you had too much!

REVERDY. (Aside.) One needs a good deal, when one's about to make an offer of one's heart. (Aloud.) It takes a vast deal of manner to carry off a tin trumpet!

(WINTERBOURNE *has listened to this absently; he appears restless and preoccupied; walks up, and goes out upon the balcony.*)

MRS. WALKER. (*Noticing* WINTERBOURNE.) What's the matter with him?—All I can say is that in my representative position I thought I must interfere.

REVERDY. (*Aside.*) The wife of the Consul again? Our consuls ought to be bachelors!

MRS. WALKER. You were dragging her along, with your arm placed as if you were waltzing.

REVERDY. That's very true; we were just trying a few rounds.

MRS. WALKER. In that dense mass of people, where you were packed like sardines?

REVERDY. We were all turning together; it was all one waltz!

MRS. WALKER. (*To* MISS DURANT.) Mrs. Costello, my dear, will make you dance in earnest!

MISS DURANT. I don't care for Mrs. Costello now!

REVERDY. Let me thank you for those noble words. (*Aside.*) You understood, then?

MISS DURANT. (*Ingenuous.*) Understood what?

REVERDY. What I was saying when she came down on us.

MISS DURANT. Oh yes, as far as you had gone!

REVERDY. I must go a little farther.

MRS. WALKER. (*Who has gone up to* WINTERBOURNE, *and comes down with him.*) You may be interested to hear that I saw our little friend in the crowd.

WINTERBOURNE. Our little friend?

MRS. WALKER. Whom we tried to save from drowning. I didn't try this time.

WINTERBOURNE. In the crowd, on foot?

MRS. WALKER. In the thickest and roughest part of it, on Giovanelli's arm. The crush was so dense, it was enough to kill her.

MISS DURANT. They are very good-natured, but you *do* suffocate!

MRS. WALKER. She'll suffocate easily, in her weak state.

WINTERBOURNE. Oh, I can't stand this!

Excuse me. (*Exit* WINTERBOURNE.)

MRS. WALKER. What's the matter with him, I should like to know?

MISS DURANT. He has been like that these three weeks, rushing in and out—always in a fidget.

REVERDY. (*To* MRS. WALKER.) He's in love with Miss Durant, and he can't stand the spectacle of our mutual attachment.

MISS DURANT. (*Gayly.*) You horrid vain creature! If that's all that troubles him!

REVERDY. (*Aside.*) She'll accept me! (*Aloud.*) Courage—the old lady!

(*Enter* MRS. COSTELLO.)

(*Scene Eighth:* MRS. WALKER, MISS DURANT, REVERDY, MRS. COSTELLO; *then* DAISY, WINTERBOURNE, GIOVANELLI, MADAME DE KATKOFF.)

MRS. COSTELLO. (*She stops a moment, looking sternly from* MISS DURANT *to* REVERDY.) Alice Durant, have you forgotten your education?

MISS DURANT. Dear Cousin Louisa, my education made no provision for the Carnival!

REVERDY. That's not in the regular course; it's one of the extras.

MISS DURANT. I was just going to your room, to tell you we had come back.

MRS. COSTELLO. I have passed an hour there, in horrible torture. I could stand it no longer: I came to see if, for very shame, you hadn't reappeared.

MRS. WALKER. The Consul and I picked them up, and made them get into our carriage. So you see it was not for shame!

REVERDY. It wasn't for ours, at least; it was for yours.

MRS. COSTELLO. (*With majesty, to* MISS DURANT.) We shall start for America to-morrow.

MISS DURANT. I am delighted to hear it. There, at least, we can walk about.

MRS. COSTELLO. Ah, but you will find no Carnival!

REVERDY. My dear Madam, we shall make our own.

MRS. COSTELLO. (*Aside to* MISS DURANT.) This time, it's to be hoped, he has done it?

MISS DURANT. (*Blushing and looking down.*) He was on the very point, when Mrs. Walker interrupted.

MRS. COSTELLO. I declare, it's beyond a joke—to take you back just as I brought you.

MISS DURANT. It's very tiresome; but it's not my fault.

REVERDY. (*Who has been talking to* MRS. WALKER.) Miss Alice, shall we try the balcony again?

MRS. COSTELLO. It's past midnight, if you please; time for us all to retire.

REVERDY. That's just what I propose: to retire to the balcony!

MISS DURANT. (*To* MRS. COSTELLO.) Just occupy Mrs. Walker!

REVERDY. (*To* MRS. WALKER.) Just keep hold of Mrs. Costello! (*Offers his arm to* MISS DURANT, *and leads her to the balcony.*)

MRS. WALKER. (*Looking after them.*) I must wait till the Consul comes. My dear friend, I hope those young people are engaged.

MRS. COSTELLO. (*With asperity.*) They might be, if it hadn't been for you!

MRS. WALKER. (*Surprised.*) Pray, how have I prevented? . . .

MRS. COSTELLO. You interrupted Mr. Reverdy, just now, in the very middle . . .

MRS. WALKER. The middle of a declaration? I thought it was a jig! (*As the door of the room is flung open.*) Bless my soul! what's this?

(*Enter rapidly* WINTERBOURNE, *carrying* DAISY, *in a swoon, in his arms, and followed by* GIOVANELLI, *who looks both extremely alarmed and extremely indignant. At the same moment* MME. DE KATKOFF *enters from the opposite side.*)

MME. DE KATKOFF. (*With a cry.*) Ah, it's all over! She is gone!

WINTERBOURNE. A chair! A chair! Heaven forgive us, she is dying!

(GIOVANELLI *has quickly pushed forward a large arm-chair, in which* WINTERBOURNE *places* DAISY *with great tenderness. She lies there motionless and unconscious. The others gather round.* MISS DURANT *and* REVERDY *come in from the balcony.*)

MRS. COSTELLO. (*Seeing the two last.*) Ah, they're interrupted again!

MRS. WALKER. This time, she's really drowned!

GIOVANELLI. (*Much agitated, but smiling to* MRS. COSTELLO *and* MRS. WALKER.) It will pass in a moment. It is only the effect of the crowd—the pressure of the mob!

WINTERBOURNE. (*Beside* DAISY, *with passionate tenderness.*) It will pass—because *she's* passing! Dead—dead—in my arms.

MRS. COSTELLO. (*Harshly*). A pretty place for her to be! She'll come to life again: they don't die like that.

MRS. WALKER. (*Indignant, to* GIOVANELLI.) The pressure of the mob? A proper pressure—for a little Flower!

GIOVANELLI. (*Bewildered and apologetic.*) She was so lovely that they all made way; but just near the hotel we encountered one of those enormous cars, laden with musicians and maskers. The crowd was driven back, and we were hustled and smothered. She gave a little cry, and before I knew it she had fainted. The next moment this gentleman—by I know not what warrant—had taken her in his arms.

WINTERBOURNE. By the warrant of being her countryman! Instead of entertaining those ladies, you had better go for a doctor.

GIOVANELLI. They have sent from the hotel. Half a dozen messengers started.

REVERDY. Half a dozen is no one at all! I will go and bring one myself—in five minutes.

MISS DURANT. Go, go, my dear! I give you leave. (REVERDY *hurries out.*)

MRS. COSTELLO. (*To* MISS DURANT.) "My dear, my dear"? Has he done it, then?

MISS DURANT. Oh yes, we just managed it. (*Looking at* DAISY.) Poor little thing!

MRS. COSTELLO. Ah, *she* hasn't a husband!

WINTERBOURNE. (*Angry, desperate, to the others.*) Can't you do something? Can't you speak to her?—can't you help her?

MRS. WALKER. I will do anything in the world! I will go for the Consul. (*She hurries away on the right.*)

MRS. COSTELLO. I have something in my room—a precious elixir, that I use for my headaches. (*To* MISS DURANT.) But I'll not leave *you!*

MISS DURANT. Not even now?

MRS. COSTELLO. Not till you are married! (*They depart on the left.*)

WINTERBOURNE. (*Holding* DAISY'S *hands*

and looking into her face.) Daisy!—Daisy!
—*Daisy!*

MME. DE KATKOFF. (*Who all this time
has been kneeling on the other side of
her, her face buried on the arm of the
chair, in the attitude of a person weeping.*)
If she can hear that, my friend, she's saved!
(*To* DAISY, *appealing.*) My child, my child,
we have wronged you, but we love you!

WINTERBOURNE. (*In the same manner.*)
Daisy, my dearest, my darling! Wake a
moment, if only to forgive me!

MME. DE KATKOFF. She moves a little!
(*Aside, rising to her feet.*) He never spoke
so to me!

GIOVANELLI. (*A little apart, looking
round him.*) Where is he, where is he—
that ruffian Eugenio?

WINTERBOURNE. In the name of pity,
has no one gone for her mother? (*To* GIO-
VANELLI.) Don't stand there, sir! Go for
her mother!

GIOVANELLI. (*Angrily.*) Give your commands to someone else! It is not for me
to do your errands.

MME. DE KATKOFF. (*Going to him pleadingly.*) Haven't you common compassion?
Do you want to see the child die?

GIOVANELLI. (*Folding his arms.*) I would
rather see her die than live to be his!

WINTERBOURNE. There is little hope of
her being mine. I have insulted—I have
defamed—her innocence!

GIOVANELLI. Ay, speak of her innocence!
Her innocence was divine!

DAISY. (*Stirring and murmuring.*)
Mother! Mother!

WINTERBOURNE. She lives, she lives, and
she shall choose between us!

GIOVANELLI. Ah, when I hear *her* voice,
I obey! (*Exit.*)

DAISY. (*Slowly opening her eyes.*) Where
am I? Where have I been?

MME. DE KATKOFF. She's saved! She's
saved!

WINTERBOURNE. You are with me, little
Daisy. With me forever!

MME. DE KATKOFF. Ah, decidedly I had
better leave you! (*Goes out to the balcony.*)

DAISY. (*Looking at* WINTERBOURNE.)
With you? With *you?* What has happened?

WINTERBOURNE. (*Still on his knees beside her.*) Something very blessed. I under-

stand you—I love you!

DAISY. (*Gazing at him a moment.*) Oh,
I'm very happy! (*Sinks back again, closing
her eyes.*)

WINTERBOURNE. We shall be happy together when you have told me you forgive
me. Let me hear you say it—only three
words! (*He waits. She remains silent.*) Ah,
she sinks away again! Daisy, won't you live
—won't you live for *me?*

DAISY. (*Murmuring.*) It was all for you—
it was all for you!

WINTERBOURNE. (*Burying his head in her
lap.*) Vile idiot! Impenetrable fool!

DAISY. (*With her eyes still closed.*) I
shall be better—but you mustn't leave me.

WINTERBOURNE. Never again, Daisy—
never again!

(*At this moment* EUGENIO *strides
into the room by the door opposite
to the one through which* GIOVA-
NELLI *has gone out.*)

(*Scene Ninth:* WINTERBOURNE,
DAISY, EUGENIO, MADAME DE KAT-
KOFF; *then* RANDOLPH, *and all the
others.*)

EUGENIO. (*Looking amazed at* DAISY *and*
WINTERBOURNE.) What does this mean?
What horrible thing has happened?

WINTERBOURNE. (*On his feet.*) You will
learn what has happened quite soon
enough to please you! But in the meanwhile, it is decent that this young lady
should see her mother. (*While he speaks,*
MME. DE KATKOFF *comes back and takes
her place at* DAISY'S *side, where she stands
with her eyes fixed upon* EUGENIO.)

EUGENIO. Her mother is not important:
Miss Miller is in my care. *Cara signorina,*
do you suffer?

DAISY. (*Vaguely.*) Poor mother, poor
mother! She has gone to the Carnival.

EUGENIO. She came home half an hour
ago. She has gone to bed.

MME. DE KATKOFF. Don't you think
there would be a certain propriety in your
requesting her to get up? (RANDOLPH *comes
in at this moment, hearing* MME. DE KAT-
KOFF's *words.*)

RANDOLPH. She *is* getting up, you can bet
your life! She's going to give it to Daisy.

MME. DE KATKOFF. Come and speak to

your sister. She has been very ill. (*She draws* RANDOLPH *towards her, and keeps him near her.*)

DAISY. (*Smiling languidly at her brother.*) You are up very late—very late.

RANDOLPH. I can't sleep—over here! I've been talking to that waiter.

EUGENIO. (*Anxious.*) I don't see the Cavaliere. Where is he gone?

RANDOLPH. He came up to tell mother, and I came back ahead of him. (*To* GIOVANELLI, *who at this moment returns.*) Hallo, Cavaliere!

GIOVANELLI. (*Solemnly, coming in.*) Mrs. Miller is dressing. She will presently arrive.

MME. DE KATKOFF. (*To* RANDOLPH.) Go and help your mother, and tell her your sister is better.

RANDOLPH. I'll tell her through the door—or she'll put me to bed! (*Marches away.*)

GIOVANELLI. (*Approaching* EUGENIO, *aside.*) I shall never have the girl!

EUGENIO. You had better have killed her! (*Aside.*) He shall pay me for his flowers! (*Re-enter* REVERDY.)

REVERDY. The doctor will be here in five minutes.

MME. DE KATKOFF. He will not be necessary now; nor even (*seeing* MRS. COSTELLO *come back with a little bottle, and accompanied by* MISS DURANT) this lady's precious elixir!

MRS. COSTELLO. (*Approaching* DAISY, *rather stiffly.*) Perhaps you would like to hold it to your nose.

DAISY. (*Takes the phial, looking at* MRS. COSTELLO *with a little smile.*) Well, I was bound you should speak to me!

REVERDY. And without a presentation, after all!

WINTERBOURNE. Oh yes, I must present. (*To his aunt.*) I present you my wife!

GIOVANELLI. (*Starting; then recovering himself and folding his arms.*) I congratulate you, Mademoiselle, on your taste for the unexpected.

DAISY. Well, it *is* unexpected. But I never deceived you!

GIOVANELLI. Oh, no, you haven't deceived me: you have only ruined me!

DAISY. Poor old Giovanelli! Well, you've had a good time.

MRS. COSTELLO. (*Impressively, to* WINTERBOURNE.) Your wife?

WINTERBOURNE. My dear aunt, she *has* stood the test!

EUGENIO. (*Who has walked round to* MME. DE KATKOFF, *in a low tone.*) You haven't kept the terms of our bargain.

MME. DE KATKOFF. I am sick of your bargain—and of you!

EUGENIO. (*He eyes her a moment; then, vindictively.*) I shall give your letter to Mr. Winterbourne.

MME. DE KATKOFF. Coward! (*Aside, joyously.*) And Mr. Winterbourne will give it to me.

GIOVANELLI. (*Beside* EUGENIO.) You must find me another heiress.

EUGENIO. I thought you said you had had enough.

GIOVANELLI. I have been thinking over my debts.

EUGENIO. We will see, then, with my next family. On the same terms, eh?

GIOVANELLI. Ah, no; I don't want a rival!

(*Re-enter* MRS. WALKER.)

MRS. WALKER. (*To* DAISY.) I can't find the Consul; but as you're better it doesn't matter.

DAISY. I don't want the Consul: I want my mother.

MRS. WALKER. I went to her room as well. Randolph had told her you were better, and so—and so— (*Pausing, a little embarrassed, and looking round the circle.*)

DAISY. She isn't coming?

MRS. WALKER. She has gone back to bed!

MRS. COSTELLO. They *are* queer people, all the same!

MISS DURANT. (*To* MRS. COSTELLO.) Shall we start for America now?

REVERDY. Of couse we shall—to be married!

WINTERBOURNE. (*Laying his hand on* REVERDY's *shoulder.*) We shall be married the same day. (*To* DAISY.) Shall we not, Daisy—in America?

DAISY. (*Who has risen to her feet, leaning on his arm.*) Oh, yes; you ought to go home!

The American

In Four Acts

1890

EDITOR'S FOREWORD

Southport, January 3, 1891.

On a Sunday morning in May 1889, Henry James recorded in his notebook that he had agreed to do a play for Edward Compton of the Compton Comedy Company, a theatrical troupe which for the past decade had toured the British Isles playing the old classical comedies and "costume pieces." Compton had his eye on London; with an original play by a distinguished writer he felt he would be able to set himself up in a West End theatre and join the ranks of the capital's actor-managers whose acknowledged peer was Henry Irving. Compton proposed that James dramatize *The American* and the novelist noted that he would have to "extract the simplest, strongest, baldest, most rudimentary, at once most humorous and most touching play" from his twelve-year-old novel. ("Oh how it must not be too good and how very bad it must be!") He first gave the play the name of *The Californian,* but later returned to his original title. A note indicates that in February 1890 he completed and sent off to Compton the second act of the play. In April he was confiding to his old friend in Paris, Henrietta Reubell, "I have . . . written a big (and awfully good) four-act play, by which I hope to make my fortune . . . now that I have begun, I mean to follow it up with others."

He went that summer to Italy; before leaving he gave his sister a typescript of the play and when she wrote an enthusiastic note to him he poured out an excited twenty-five page letter of gratitude. He felt he had met "exactly the immediate, actual, intense British conditions, both subjective and objective"; the play would run, to the minute, two and three-quarter hours; the writing of the piece had been an education; superior acting would help but "mediocrity of handling (which is all, at the best, I am pretty sure, that it will get) won't and can't kill it." Wolcott Balestier, who had agreed to act as his agent, had settled with Compton that James would receive ten per cent of the gross and the novelist received a £250 advance on royalties. And James day-dreamed in his letter to his sister of receiving $400 a week during the provincial run and $1,500 a month during the London run, of road companies in England, in America, of tours elsewhere in the British Empire. "These Castles in Spain are at least exhilarating. . . ."

He was back in London late in the summer to begin preparations for the provincial production. He submitted grudgingly to the first managerial cuts and alterations and dashed into the provinces through the rain, damp and fog of the autumn to attend rehearsals wherever the touring company might be. Gradually he found himself coaching the actors and participating in the direction of the play. Most important of all was to teach the tall and handsome Edward Compton how to act like a rich American from California, and what is more, how to talk like one. The typescript sent to the Lord Chamberlain's Office for the licensing of the play seems to have been Compton's; in it, in James's hand, are written the pronunciations of key words for Compton's guidance. The basic principle seems to have been incorporated in a stage direction which instructs Christopher Newman, the American, to speak "a little from the nose."

Southport, near Liverpool, was selected for the first performance of the play. The choice of this resort seems to have been dictated largely by the presence of a large winter population. Compton may have also had a sentimental reason for the choice. Here, in the Winter Gardens Theatre, the Compton Comedy Company had made its start ten years earlier on a bitingly cold winter night, the night of the "great snowstorm." He was returning now to the scene of that snowy debut.

Henry James arrived at Southport on New Year's Day 1891 in a state of feverish excitement. He took rooms at the Prince of Wales Hotel where Compton and his wife, the American actress Virginia Bateman, were staying. The dramatist set himself to the task of reviewing the final rehearsals. The last, a "suprème, complete, exhaustive rehearsal" was held on January 2. The playwright sat alone in the stalls listening and watching, and it seemed to him that someone else had written *The American*. It was an old-fashioned but roomy theatre; the settings were meagre, but he felt a "kind of mystic confidence in the ultimate life of the piece." It would owe nothing to the way it was acted. The actors had all been conditioned to traditional roles in British classical comedy and drama. Now they found themselves playing the life of the Faubourg St. Germain (which Compton was carefully instructed to pronounce "Saint-Germane") into which the Californian intrudes. The play's strength lay, James felt, in its intrinsic vitality. He placed all his hope on this. Such, at least, was the impression James set down after the last rehearsal as he watched Christopher Newman, in a florid chocolate-colored coat with saucer-like buttons, and similarly extravagant costumes, first win, then lose, then win again the beautiful Madame de Cintré, played by Mrs. Compton. James had substituted a happy ending for the unhappy one of the novel. In 1877, when the novel appeared, he had written to Elizabeth Boott, who wanted a happy ending, that he deemed his denouement "the only possible one. What would you have had? Come, now, they couldn't have married. . . ." Other endings were possible, however, in the theatre; here he could give his hero the victory he had denied him in his fiction.

The final rehearsal over, the company, which had been playing in classic repertory in Southport since Christmas night, was given twenty-four hours of rest. Henry set himself to ticking off the nervous hours until the rise of the curtain. It seemed like an eternity. In the short story *Nona Vincent* James published the following year, dealing with the trials of a dramatist, James's hero was "unable to eat or sleep, or sit still, at times almost in terror. He kept quiet by keeping, as usual, in motion; he tried to walk away from his nervousness . . ." but always the path led back to theatre or hotel, to the members of the cast.

Wolcott Balestier arrived full of confidence and enthusiasm. Balestier had been in England for the past two years as representative of a New York publishing house and the friendship between him and James had grown. James later wrote of Balestier's "complete incapacity to recognize difficulties." Two weeks before the Southport first night the young man wrote to William Dean Howells, "My friendship with James is the most precious thing in my 'London life.' We see much of each other and I feel his place a kind of nest or refuge." Balestier was the first of a whole group of younger men who from the 1890's on gathered around James and gave him the admiration and appreciation he craved. "My dear Suzerain of the Drama," he had written to the novelist: "If you will still let me 'assist' at the first performance of the first play of our first dramatist this is to intimate that nothing short of legal proceedings to restrain my liberty can prevent my being present." James couldn't resist this flattery.

The novelist had also received a letter from William Archer, the translator of Ibsen and one of London's leading drama critics. Archer also wanted to come to Southport. He held James in high esteem. James's little dialogue, *After the Play*, published in June 1889, in which he had complained at the absence of good plays in England, had provoked Archer to reply that the theatre needed the active collaboration of writers such as Henry James. The novelist put up a show of trying to dissuade him from coming: "I won't deny that I should be glad to know that the piece was seen by a serious critic, and by yourself in particular, but I shrink from *every* responsibility in the way of recommending such a critic to attempt so heroic a feat. The place is far, the season inclement, the interpretation *extremely* limited, different enough, as you may suppose, from what I should count on for representation in London. The circumstances *may* be definitely uncomfortable . . . my hope is greater than my confidence." William Archer arrived on the evening of the production.

January 3 dawned wet, windy, cold. The Southport papers formally announced that *The American* would be "played this night for the first time on any stage." The scale of admission ran from sixpence to four shillings. Henry James sat at his writing table trying to write away his anxiety and terror. He wrote to his brother William, "I *am* at present in a state of abject, lonely fear. . . . I am too nervous to write more—and yet it's only 3 o'clock and I've got to wait till 8. . . ." He wrote to a French friend, Urbain Mengin, inviting his prayers, as he did those of all of his friends and relatives, with an elaborate flourish. *"Je fais du théâtre—je suis tombé bien bas—priez pour moi. . . ."* To the ever-busy man of letters, Edmund Gosse, he wrote, "After 11 o'clock tonight I *may* be the world's—and I may be the undertaker's. I count upon you . . . to spend this evening in fasting, silence and supplication. . . . I am so nervous that I miswrite and misspell. . . ."

All Southport seemed to be at the theatre that night. In the flare of the gas-light a long string of carriages reminded one of the local reporters of an Italian opera night or of a fancy dress or political ball. The audience was "select as well as numerous." All of the 1,500 seats were filled, including those affording so bad a view of the stage that they were seldom sold.

Alice James reported that her brother told her he became "as calm as a clock" just before the curtain went up. Compton allowed his author to come back-stage, giving him a seat in a corner of the right wing, beside the curtain, and from this point of vantage the novelist saw his first publicly-performed play. The portrait that Henry James drew of Christopher Newman was a very broad caricature of the Christopher Newman of his novel. He did not hesitate to "play" him for every possible laugh at the expense of his countrymen—but always in an easy, good-natured fashion. He is the same American as in the novel, but where, in the work of fiction, he engages our affection throughout by his directness, simplicity, moral integrity, he at first antagonizes in the play. "I want to have a regular good time," he announces early in the first act. "I've been whistling Yankee Doodle all my life and now I should like to try another tune." And yet for all this, he remains one of nature's noblemen, warm-hearted, generous, a figure of stature and authority. The voice of Newman ends by being the voice of a democratic American bringing a gust of fresh air into the Faubourg St. Germain.

There were no first night accidents. The cast was somewhat nervous, but nervousness bred caution and caution aided perfection. The players, long rehearsed, were letter-perfect in their parts, even though some of them later admitted they didn't fully understand them.

The curtain that fell after the first act on a hushed and gratified house which had followed the play with close interest, applauding at moments, laughing in all the right places, brought the author out from his "cubby" where he described himself as having clung to a rail as if he were before an altar (suggesting that he too had been offering prayers). He wrote to a friend later:

"I flung myself upon Compton after the first act: 'In heaven's name, is it going?' ' "Going"?—Rather! You could hear a pin drop!' "

In the story *Nona Vincent* James's young dramatist lives through the same experience:

"Has it gone?—*has* it gone?" he gasped to the people around him; and he heard them say "Rather—rather" . . . he felt it to be long before he could back away, before he could, in his turn, seize the manager by the arm and cry huskily—"Has it really gone—really?"

For the first time in his already long career as an artist Henry James heard his work applauded. The play ended and the storm of provincial applause that mounted was sweet music to the nervous novelist. From beyond the gas-light came the shout of "Author, author." Again we find in *Nona Vincent* . . .

There was by this time a crowd in the wing, all with strange grimacing painted faces . . . he stood for an instant in the glare of the footlights, looking blindly at the great vaguely-peopled horseshoe and greeted with plaudits which now seemed to him at once louder than he deserved and feebler than he desired. . . .

At the third bow and round of applause, Compton turned and seized Henry James's hands and wrung them. With genuine relish the novelist described the scene in a letter to his friend Mrs. Hugh Bell: ". . . at the end of all, one (after a decent and discreet delay) simpered and gave oneself up to *courbettes* before the curtain, while the applausive house emitted agreeable sounds from a kind of gas-flaring indistinguishable dimness and the gratified Compton publicly pressed one's hand and one felt that, really, as far as Southport could testify to the circumstance, the stake was won. Of course it's only Southport—but I have larger hopes. . . ."

A month later he was writing to his brother: "You can form no idea . . . of how a provincial success is confined to the provinces."

William Archer called on James at the hotel where the novelist was waiting in his rooms to entertain the Comptons and Balestier at a late supper. With a want of tact that was all the more disturbing since he was speaking to a dramatist in whose ears applause was still ringing, Archer told him (and it was entirely true), "I think it's a play that would be much more likely to have success in the provinces than in London." He proceeded then and there, taking his critical role with the high seriousness he had always attached to it, to give the author an oral review of the play. After James described the incident to his sister, a few days later, she wrote in her journal: "To H. of course, heated with his triumph these uncalled for amenities . . . seemed highly grotesque. . . . H. was able to receive it with perfect urbanity and the Comptons etc. coming in to supper before long, he bowed Archer out, and served him up as a delectable dish of roast prig done to a turn."

Supper after the play, with the author as host to his principal actors, was accepted by James as an inflexible tradition of the theatre. His guests on this occasion were limited to the Comptons and Balestier. It was a dinner he wrote later, "half-histrionic and wholly confident." The battle, the first major engagement, was over and James felt his hero and heroine "were really as radiant as if we were carousing among the slain. They seem indeed wondrous content." And wondrous content they all were. Balestier was in his characteristically buoyant spirits—Balestier who was to die of typhoid in Germany before the year was out—and James seems to have been in an equally exultant mood. Mrs. Compton, who had recently been ill, said she felt "cured right up." Amid popping corks, and over a gaily bedecked table, the little party was prolonged from 11 o'clock until 1:45 a.m. when the guests retired and the weary and happy dramatist went to bed.

Henry James rose early the following morning. The first thing he did was to dispatch a promised wire to his sister: "Unqualified triumphant magnificent success universal congratulations great ovation for author great future for play Comptons radiant and his acting admirable writing Henry."

Alice received the telegram at her South Kensington hotel and promptly cabled it to William James as had been arranged. In far-off Cambridge, William sat down and wrote to his brother: "Dear Old Harry, A telegraph from Alice this a.m. announces 'unqualified triumph—great future author—ovation.' I am almost as glad as you are, and hope that it is only the beginning of a sort of Sardou or Dumas career. It will of course inspire you with the nine or 90 other plays which you have in mind." William in turn sent the cable on to James Russell Lowell who wrote to Henry James on January 11: "I please myself with fancying how long your piece will run and how much you will get for each performance."

After sending off the telegrams Henry James returned to his rooms and wrote a long letter to his sister. He described the performance, the calls for the author, the general enthusiasm, the gay supper, Compton's acting. He promised "a droll anecdote of William Archer's behaviour and attitude" and reiterated his confidence in the future of the piece. At noon he added the following postscript: "Compton has just come in to tell me that he has already seen a number of people present last night who were *unanimous* about the success of the piece, the great hit he has made it and ergo—the large fortune that opens to it. His own high spirits indeed tell everything."

James and Balestier accompanied the players when they left Southport that afternoon. In the memoir of Balestier that the novelist wrote a year later, he recalled the afternoon as "our sociable amused participation in a collective theatrical fitting, effected in pottering Sunday trains, besprinkled with refreshment room impressions and terminating in all but inaccessible Birmingham, in independent repose and relaxed criticism." James spent the night in Birmingham and went on to Cheltenham the following morning to pay a visit. He was back in London Tuesday evening, January 6, recounting the whole adventure to Alice, and on Wednesday, January 7, she recorded the "Dear Being's" account in her journal. "The great family event . . . has come off . . . it was delightful to hear and see him [Harry] flushed with the triumph of his first ovation. . . . The 'first nights' to come, we shall be less quivering about."

The World, with William Archer's account, came out on the morning of Henry James's return to London. It was a good notice. The critic, in a brief paragraph dated Southport, spoke of finding in James a real "theatrical talent." He wrote:

"As the first theatrical essay of a distinguished man of letters is not, to me, an inconsiderable event I determined . . . to be present on the occasion . . . and here I am, mightily pleased with my adventure." He added that the play was "full of alert and telling dialogue and incidents which show a keen eye for stage effect." The first act he pronounced to be a little masterpiece of exposition. But he withheld any further judgment, until the London production.

This was high praise from London's most advanced critic. The provincial scribes who had more space in which to discuss the play, did not ignore its faults. All felt it required pruning. Some found the literary flavor too pronounced. The critic of the *Southport Guardian* remarked that James made his British Lord Deepmere like a fire-eating Frenchman, while the French Valentin was too like a cheery Englishman. The *Southport Visiter*, discussing Compton's accent, said: "He was quite consistent in the maintenance of the Yankee tone—we shall not say twang nor nasal drawl—in the purely colloquial portions of the dialogue and though in some of the more lengthened declamatory passages he sometimes relapsed into an Englishman the occurrence was so rare as not to be noteworthy. . . ." The *Southport Standard*, however, felt that the accent would be more effective "when he shall have learnt to retain it in the more impassioned portions of his dialogue." The *Southport Visiter* observed that "the author has taken a recognized place in the ranks of British dramatists, for the judgment of Southport audiences is never reversed."

That, however, remained to be seen.

London, September 26, 1891

Two weeks after the Southport first night Balestier wrote to Howells: "The most delightful feature of the success of the piece is its effect on James. He is like a runner ready to run a race. He has the air of one just setting out—a youngster with an oldster's grip and mastery: surely the most enviable of situations." William sensed this change in Henry, writing to him: "It is an extreme delight to see you in your old and sedate age going in for experiences as keen and uproarious as this, and I do most devoutly hope, now that you've made your plunge, that you'll keep at it and become a Dumas *fils*."

Henry James was keeping at it. By this time he had completed two more plays and was filled with plans for the London production of *The American*. Compton decided to keep the play in his repertory throughout the spring in a tour that took him to Scotland and Ireland as well as over his usual circuit in England, and to open the play in London in the autumn. The Compton Comedy Company usually made one-week stands, changing its bill every night, and *The American* was given on an average once a week. In all it was probably performed about twenty-five times on the road, including performances in Edinburgh, Belfast and Dublin, where it was well received. James caught the play at its second performance at the Theatre Royal, Wolverhampton, and a few days later in the Memorial Theatre at Stratford-on-Avon, where he was noticed in the audience and came forward to take a bow at the end of the evening. He saw it once more at Leamington, on January 16, where he was still rehearsing some of the scenes with the actors. "I show 'em how to do it—and even then they don't know!" he wrote to Henrietta Reubell.

Compton had taken a long lease on the old Opera Comique Theatre in the Strand where the early Gilbert and Sullivan operas had been performed.

He invested a substantial sum in renovation, installing the "latest sanitary arrangements" and adding two new stone staircases. He could not, however, alter the theatre's basic design which included a long subterranean passage leading to the stalls, described as "discouraging to playgoers." James had from the first intimated that the play would need better actors for the London production. He began now a systematic search for some key players, in particular for the women's parts. On January 27, at a matinee of Ibsen's *Doll's House* with Geneviève Ward—it was the first Ibsen performance he attended—he saw for the first time his compatriot, Elizabeth Robins; later that spring he saw her again at the Vaudeville where he was greatly taken with her performance of *Hedda Gabler*. "A young American actress . . . has lately revealed herself, strikingly, here, as Ibsen's Hedda Gabler, and has quite leaped into fame. She is slightly uncanny, but distinguished and individual, and she is to do my heroine, a short part, but a very pretty one . . ." he wrote to Mrs. John L. Gardner. He took Compton to see her perform, and it was settled that she should replace Mrs. Compton as Madame de Cintré.

Miss Robins was "uncanny"—young, striking, intense, quick, intelligent. She had been an actress at the Boston Museum with Edwin Booth; visiting Norway she had fallen under the spell of Ibsen and now, with singular conviction and not a little courage, she was in the vanguard of the Ibsenite forces assaulting the Victorian theatre. That such a woman, bristling with energy, and whose *forte* was the strong-minded women of Ibsen, should have been cast by James in the passive renunciatory role of Madame de Cintré is a little puzzling. Mrs. Compton's older sister, Kate Bateman, came out of retirement to play Madame de Bellegarde and the services of a young and vivacious French actress, Adrienne Dairolles, who had been playing in English in London, were obtained for the role of Noémie Nioche. Louise Moodie, a popular character actress "supposed to be one of the two or three first 'old women' in London," got the part of Mrs. Bread.

The new scenery was completed by the end of the summer; the furniture ordered from Paris was arriving and James, who had insisted on supervising the choice of dresses for the women, threw himself again strenuously into rehearsal. Although there is no record that he had a hand in the men's costumes, we must assign some measure of responsibility to him for the extravagant garb he allowed Newman to wear on the London stage. A. B. Walkley, one of the critics sympathetic to James, said that "why the outer man of Christopher Newman should be clothed in a garment of chocolate faced with sky-blue remains a mystery known only to himself and his tailor." Another critic called it a "Noah-ark coat of yellowish brown, with blue facings and mother of pearl buttons almost as large as cheese plates." Justin McCarthy called it "an amazing costume of brown velveteen coat and buff overcoat, which recalls rather the garb of a travelling showman than the costume of an American millionaire."

Elizabeth Robins has described James at the rehearsals. His experience in the provinces gave him confidence; he seemed at his ease among the actors. He

OPERA COMIQUE THEATRE.

SOLE LESSEE AND MANAGER ... ... Mr. EDWARD COMPTON.

This Evening, at 8.20, a Play in Four Acts (*Founded on his Novel of the same name*)

THE AMERICAN

BY HENRY JAMES.

Christopher Newman ...	Mr. EDWARD COMPTON	Doctor	Mr. FRED. W. PERMAIN
Marquis de Bellegarde... ...	Mr. SYDNEY PAXTON	Servant	Mr. W. G. GUNNINGHAME
Comte Valentin de Bellegarde	Mr. CLARENCE BLAKISTON	Marquise de Bellegarde ...	Miss BATEMAN (Mrs. CROWE)
Lord Deepmere	Mr. C. M. HALLARD	Mrs. Bread	Miss LOUISE MOODIE
	(*By permission of Mr. Beerbohm Tree*).	Noémie Nioche ...	Miss ADRIENNE DAIROLLES
M. de Marignac	Mr. HARRISON HUNTER	A Sister of Charity	Miss C. LINDSAY
Monsieur Nioche	Mr. YOUNG STEWART	Claire, (Comtesse de Cintré)...	Miss ELIZABETH ROBINS

Act I. ... ... A PARISIAN PARLOUR. | Act III. AT CHRISTOPHER NEWMAN'S.
Act II. ... THE HOTEL DE BELLEGARDE. | Act IV. ... ... FLEURIÈRES.

NOTE —The Scene is laid in Paris during the first Three Acts, and at an old house near Poitiers, in the Fourth.

The New Scenery by Mr. Joseph Harker.
The Stage furnished by Messrs. FRANK GILES & Co., Kensington.
The Floral Decorations by DICK RADCLYFFE, Holborn.
The Dresses by Messrs. DEBENHAM & FREEBODY, Madame PATRICK. Miss NIMMO, &c.,

Preceded at **7.45,** by a Domestic Drama, in One Act, by W. A. BRABNER.

A Dead Letter.

Ben Somers ... (A Village Postmaster) ... Mr. LEWIS BALL | FredArmstrong(Polly's Lover) Mr. HARRISON HUNTER
Mr. Chadwick (A City Merchant) Mr. SYDNEY PAXTON | Polly ... (Ben's Daughter) Miss EVELYN McNAY

MATINÉE of THE AMERICAN every Saturday, at 2.30. Doors open at 2.

The Etchings & Engravings in the Foyer and Corridors have been kindly lent by Messrs. DOWDESWELL & DOWDESWELLS, Ltd.,
160, New Bond Street, W.
The Grand Piano in the Orchestra by ASCHERBERG & Co., 46, Berners Street, W.

Doors open at 7.15 Commence at 7.45. Carriages at 11.

NO FEES PRICES OF ADMISSION.—Private Boxes, £1 1s. to £3 3s. Stalls, 10s. 6d. Balcony **NO FEES**
Stalls, 7s. 6d. and 6s. Dress Circle. 5s. Upper Circle. 4s. Pit, 2s. 6d. Gallery, 1s.
Box Office (Miss Niven) open Daily from 10 till 5, and during the performance.

Visitors are informed that the Attendants are **NOT** allowed to accept gratuities.
The Management relies on the co-operation of the Public in this effort to promote their comfort and convenience.
Any Attendant breaking this rule will be liable to instant dismissal.

Musical Director ... ... Mr. W. A. LUTZ | Stage Manager ... ... Mr. LEWIS BALL
Business Manager ... ... Mr. J. H. SAVILE.

was "intensely observant, gravely and happily 'there' to help us. We felt his approach to matters of the Stage to be fresh and exciting. We were flattered when he took trouble with us, more hopeful of ourselves."

He exchanged gallantries in French with Mlle. Dairolles; he showed concern over the long hours of rehearsal and was disturbed at the irregular meal hours of the actors. Presently he was having his cook and butler bring down hampers of delicacies; sandwich in hand he would, during waiting periods, quietly steer the actors toward the hampers. "No other playwright," Miss Robins recalled, "in my tolerably wide experience ever thought of feeding his company."

Alice James was dying. After years of suffering from a nervous illness, a tangible fatal symptom finally had appeared. She had a tumor of the breast. No part of the story of *The American* is more touching than the simple faith and joy with which Alice, from the four walls of her sick room, let her imagination soar to the footlights, following through Henry James the vicissitudes of his play and then dictating her report of its progress for her intermittently-kept journal. Anecdotes turn up every few pages showing that Henry James was putting forward the most cheerful side of the story for the patient. In his letters to William he later spoke of his two invalids, Alice and the play. For his sister, the episode was "so shot through with the golden threads of comedy that we grew fat with laughter." But for her nervous and agitated brother, the laughter masked an acute anxiety over her condition and a host of lesser anxieties surrounding the play. Six days before the opening night in London—which was set for September 26, 1891—William James appeared from America, after a sudden crossing of the Atlantic, to see his sister before the end. He was thus able to attend his brother's first night and to go to the gay supper held in De Vere Gardens at the close of the evening. For the Harvard psychologist-philosopher, basking in the success of his recently published *Principles of Psychology,* this part of his ten-day London visit was "one of my finest exotic memories."

The first night in the refurbished theatre was a dubious artistic, but a great social, success. Robert Lincoln, the American Minister to London attended in a private box and several of the stage journals alluded to the presence of "millionaires" from the other side of the Atlantic. The *Echo* reported that "the majority of the ladies conversed in the tongue of the States, while all wore the prettiest frocks." Decidedly the American colony had been loyal to Henry James. The *Echo* report added that "the audience was one of the most cultured ever brought together in so small a space." It included the painters John Singer Sargent and George Frederick Watts, George du Maurier, editor Frank Harris, novelists W. E. Norris, Mrs. W. K. Clifford, Rhoda Broughton, the playwright Arthur Pinero, the American producer Augustin Daly, the actress Geneviève Ward who had hopes then of appearing in James's next play. George Meredith, seldom seen at a London theatre, came up from Dorking with his daughter. Constance Fenimore Woolson, whose stories of the American South and the Lake country James had admired, and who was then living at Oxford, went to London to attend the première and we can glance at it through her eyes:

> I put on my best, and we looked well enough, but were nothing to the others! Pink satin, blue satin, jewels of all sorts, splendor on all sides of us. The house was packed to the top, and the applause great. . . . All the literary and artistic people were there and many "swells" also. . . . When the performance was ended, and the actors had been called out, there arose loud cries "Author, author." After some delay, Henry James appeared before the curtain and acknowledged the applause. He looked very well—quiet and dignified, yet pleasant; he only stayed a moment. The critics have, since then, written acres about the play. It has been warmly praised; attacked, abused, highly commended, etc.

The critics did write "acres" about the play and to read them today is to get a clear picture of the production; they were generally unanimous that the play was more melodramatic than the novel had warranted; they thought the writing obscure at points; they found Elizabeth Robins's playing of Claire

OUR CAPTIOUS CRITIC.

"THE AMERICAN."

Caricatures of Henry James's characters in *The American.*
From *The Sporting and Dramatic,* October 17, 1891

Elizabeth Robins, the Kentucky-born Ibsen interpreter,
in costume for the role of Madame de Cintré
in *The American*, London, 1891

somewhat hysterical, and they felt Compton's American to be too much of a caricature. "We are as anxious as the critics of the newest school to hail the advent on our stage of literary men," the critic of the theatrical journal *Era* remarked, "but it is on condition that they bring their literature with them."

William Archer found in some passages the "touch of the born playwright" and defended the happy ending as not "a mere concession to cheap popular optimism but human and probable." He spoke of the "neat and charming dialogue which is grateful to the ear even when it does not ring dramatically true" (a remark Bernard Shaw was to use on a number of occasions in later years concerning James's dialogue). A. B. Walkley, in *The Speaker,* marvelled at the quality of scrambled action which James had infused into his play: "What, Mr. James?" he asked, alluding to *The Tragic Muse.* "All this 'between dinner and the suburban trains?' *Allons donc!* as our dear Gabriel Nash would say." A review in the *Star,* by "Spectator," who almost certainly was also Walkley, urged James to write an original comedy, and twitted him for his "stage American, with the local color laid on with a trowel, and strong accent, a fearful and wonderful coat and a recurrent catch-word." Arthur Symons, in *The Academy,* asked, "Is it conceivable that the play satisfied the author of the novel?" Clement Scott suggested that an American rather than English actor—say John Drew —should have been cast as Newman. The reviews in the daily journals, from the august *Times* to the eveningers, were tepid. It was generally agreed that Compton had the accent, but that there was not a great deal else, "except in the first act," observed one paper, "where there is a great deal of ugly overcoat."

It was inevitable that the trans-Atlantic criticism would be sharper. The New York *Times* carried a dispatch on the morning after the first night on its front page; its London correspondent labelled the play "a mass of bold melodrama" and alluded to the portrait of Newman as resembling that of "the advance agent of a circus." The American accent was characterized as an "irritating drawl." It was left however to the *Atlantic Monthly* to give a full evaluation of the play of its distinguished contributor. "American vulgarity," observed the review, "is always a tolerably welcome spectacle upon the London stage and even Mr. Compton's American, in some respects an excellent conception, is made quite vulgar enough to atone for many of his virtues." As for Miss Robins, she imported into the play "the hysterical manners of Ibsen's morbid heroines."

Henry James began a death-watch on his play. It was early in the season; much of the stall-buying public was still out of town; the critics had not been helpful, and the play carried at least four poor actors "too terrible a number for any play to carry." He said, in a letter to William, "We shall probably fight it through this month and then the fates must decide. Unfortunately their decision appears only too clear. . . ."

Before the month was over, assistance came from an unexpected quarter— the British Royal Family. The Prince of Wales, the future Edward VII, decided to see *The American.* Here was a windfall indeed! Compton on receiving word hastily telegraphed to James to "dress up" a couple of boxes with "smart people," which the *mondain* American had no difficulty in doing. Calling on his sister that day, Henry James ruefully told her, "I'd do anything for the good Compton, but it will make me charitable to the end of my days." The Royal visit, however, had the desired effect. It gave the play a "lift." Booking for seats improved and the advertisements now read: *"The American* (An unmistakeable success.)"

"I am ashamed," wrote Henry to William on October 21, "to say that the P. of W. on Saturday last, gave it a lift by coming and manifesting an intense absorption. It is humiliating to be so beholden—but it isn't all the Prince." Presently the play had run almost fifty nights, and on the fiftieth, Compton and James did a curious thing. James had by that time made a number of revisions, writing a new love scene into the third act between Newman and Claire, bringing Valentin on-stage to die and taming the Bellegardes somewhat. For the fiftieth night the critics were again invited to see the play in what some of them described as its "second edition." They found this flattering and they announced with pleasure that their strictures had been taken seriously. "The third act," wrote Walkley, "has been reconstructed, simplified and greatly improved . . . and there is less of the hypnotised 'subject' or somnambulist in Miss Robins's Claire. But Mr. Edward Compton has not been persuaded to doff his atrocious garment of chocolate and sky-blue and he still sprinkles his gag 'That's what I want t'see' over the dialogue. . . ."

James was cheered; whatever the outcome, the play had now had an "honorable" run. "Whatever *shall* happen, I am utterly launched in the drama, resolutely committed to it, and shall go at it tooth and nail. *The American* has distinctly done me good," he wrote to his brother.

It closed after its seventieth performance, on December 3, 1871. "Honor is saved," wrote Henry James, "but I grieve to say nothing else, for the piece made no money. . . ." Ten days later, hastily summoned to Dresden, Henry James stood at the graveside of his young friend, Wolcott Balestier, dead at twenty-eight of typhoid. He had rendered James valuable services and the novelist was deeply attached to him. Gloom settled on him as he recrossed the Channel to London. In her journal Alice wrote: "The young Balestier, the effective and the indispensable, is dead!—swept away like a cobweb, of which gossamer substance he seems to have been himself composed; of simply spirit and energy, with the slightest fleshly wrapping." Alice James was writing a tribute of the dying to the dead. Three months later, on March 6, 1892, Henry James stood beside his sister's bed, on a bright, soundless Sunday, and felt her flickering pulse. He described the scene minutely to William: "The pulse . . . came and went, ceased and revived a little again. . . . Her face then seemed in a strange, dim, touching way to become clearer. I went to the window to let in a little more of the afternoon light upon it . . . and when I came back to the bed she had drawn the last breath. . . ." After writing this he crossed out the word *last* and wrote, "the breath that was not succeeded by another."

On March 9, Alice James was cremated at Golder's Green. And Henry James wrote to William: "It is the last—the last forever."

CHARACTERS

Christopher Newman
Valentin de Bellegarde
Marquis de Bellegarde
Lord Deepmere
M. Nioche
M. de Marignac
The Doctor
Madame de Bellegarde
Madame de Cintré
Noémie Nioche
Mrs. Bread
A Sister of Charity
A Servant

THE AMERICAN

ACT FIRST

A shabby sitting-room on a small Parisian quatrième, *with double doors at the back, opening into another room where a table is laid for luncheon; a door on right and on left opening respectively upon the vestibule and staircase, and upon* NOÉMIE's *room. In front, on left, a small easel with a picture in a frame, turned away from the spectator. Enter* NOÉMIE NIOCHE *and* LORD DEEPMERE, *rapidly down from centre; she has on an apron and carries in her hand a palette and brushes.*

NOÉMIE. *(Left.)* I declare that if you touch me I'll paint you all over.

DEEPMERE. *(Left centre.)* You'll convert me into a masterpiece.

NOÉMIE. You're a masterpiece of impertinence. *(Crosses to right and sits on chair.)* Nothing would induce me to sell you a picture.

DEEPMERE. My dear young lady, I'm a great collector.

NOÉMIE. A collector of dear young ladies, yes! You had no right whatever to come here.

DEEPMERE. What could I do? I waited an hour in that accursed gallery.

NOÉMIE. Is that the way you speak of the Salon Carré of the Louvre? If you're as fond of the arts as you pretend to be, you would have been thankful for the opportunity.

DEEPMERE. The art I'm fondest of is that of making up to charming girls. *(Crossing to her and leaning over her: on which she rises.)* Your not being at the Louvre, after giving me so definite a hope, seemed to me simply an opportunity to come here.

NOÉMIE. You're very horrid. *(Goes below table to window.)* How did you find out where I live?

DEEPMERE. It was not *your* fault, certainly. Your discretion is perfect—you never looked behind.

NOÉMIE. You followed me yesterday? Dreadful man, good-bye! *(She goes up toward the back room;* DEEPMERE *following.)*

DEEPMERE. Where are you going?

NOÉMIE. To prepare our midday meal.

DEEPMERE. *(Drawing her to ottoman, on right of doors, where they sit.)* You have plenty of time for that. As I approached the house *(with his hand passed into her arm)* I met your venerable father leaving it. He had a little basket on his arm. I'm sure he was going out to buy a tender chicken.

NOÉMIE. We don't live on tender chickens.

DEEPMERE. *(Stealing his arm round her waist.)* You might easily, if you would!

NOÉMIE. *(Rising.)* I must take refuge from your abominations in my work— there is nothing like that. *(Begins to paint at the easel;* DEEPMERE *follows her, going behind her to left.)*

DEEPMERE. *(Watching her a moment.)* What are you doing there?

NOÉMIE. I'm copying—from memory!

DEEPMERE. And for whom are you performing such a *tour de force?* The inspiration must be great, and you're expecting precisely, now, the person who's the source of it. *(Action—*NOÉMIE *retouches, rubs and stands off from picture.)* That's why you're so feverishly eager to get rid of me! You're afraid of the person's jealousy. It's a person—I won't be more specific! (*There comes a sharp, short ring at the outer door on which* NOÉMIE *puts down her implements on stool and goes to centre.*) That's a person, too! I suppose it's your father's ring; it *sounds* like a meek little octogenarian!

NOÉMIE. (*Moving to right, aside.*) It sounds like the American—punctual to the minute. (*Returning to centre, aloud.*) You will leave this place as soon as I have let my father in. I will close these doors (*indicating those at back*)—and he will come into that room. As soon as he has done so, the vestibule (*pointing right*) will be clear, and you will pass out by *that* door (*indicating door on right*). Don't move till you hear us come out of the vestibule.

DEEPMERE. Where does your father buy his chickens? I didn't notice there was a poulterer so near. (*Another sharp, short ring; on which* NOÉMIE *goes to centre.*) The person is losing his temper!

NOÉMIE. (*On the threshold between the two rooms.*) If you don't obey me to the letter, I'll never speak to you again. (*Exit, centre, closing doors.*)

DEEPMERE. (*Alone.*) That means, I suppose, that if I do obey her, I may enjoy the sweet spontaneity of her conversation. (*Goes up by the fireplace to centre.*) It's a refuge for hours of discouragement, when I feel the vanity of higher and sweeter hopes. If I were happy I should never look at her. But hang it, I ain't happy, and it may worry Bellegarde! (*Goes nearer to the back room—listens a moment.*) It's very odd—her father has the voice of some young fellow I know. (*Coming down, left centre.*) Whose is it? I can't make it out!

(*Re-enter* NOÉMIE, *centre.*)

NOÉMIE. (*Coming back quickly, closing the doors behind her, and opening the door on the right.*) Now, sir, as the coast is clear, you'll please to step out!

DEEPMERE. Let me congratulate you first on your wealth of paternity (*pointing to centre and going to her*)—you seem to have two papas! *I* haven't even one, to-day; that's why I can do what I like.

NOÉMIE. What you like?

DEEPMERE. I should like to leave you a little memento. (*Making, while he seizes her hands, as if to kiss her.*)

NOÉMIE. (*Escaping by crossing him,* DEEPMERE *retaining her hands.*) You may come back in an hour—not before. Then I'll scold you properly.

DEEPMERE. In an hour to the minute, lovely being. Let me at least have something to be scolded for! (*Successfully snatches a kiss, and exit, right.*)

NOÉMIE. (*Seated on ottoman, reflectively.*) His father's dead: then he must be a Peer of the Realm! I remember that phrase when we were in England—I used to think it so fine! But he's not in earnest, any more than the Count. No one's in earnest—unless, perhaps, the American! (*Commences to put things in order at table, right; then goes on to chair, left, dusting it, and so on to fireplace, finishing at easel.*) It's only our friendly, foolish Count; it's not the unsophisticated Yankee. Yankees are never Counts, I suppose: that's why they're unsophisticated and order pictures. (*Daubs a little, to touch it up, at picture on easel.*) Do what he likes, did his lordship say? So can the American, evidently, and *he* may like something better. (*Calls.*) Now you can come in—everything is straight! (*Looks at the picture on the easel, while she daubs at it.*) Everything is crooked—more's the pity! (*Calling again.*) Come in, Count, come in! (*Enter, from back,* VALENTIN DE BELLEGARDE.) I've dusted a chair for you to sit on, and I've put out the little Greuze.

VALENTIN. (*On right of* NOÉMIE *before the picture.*) I shall miss this very much when I go to the Musée.

NOÉMIE. The original will always be there.

VALENTIN. I know your copy better—it's the more original of the two.

NOÉMIE. You're laughing at me, but I don't care, for I have found someone to take my work seriously. (VALENTIN *shrugs shoulders, laughs, goes down to fireplace and puts hat on chest of drawers at left.*) I brought it home yesterday to give it the finishing touches, and when you rang at the door I thought it was the purchaser, who had promised to come this morning and approve.

VALENTIN. You *must* have been disappointed! But I approve! I always approve.

you know.

NOÉMIE. It's more than I do, when you come at the wrong time.

VALENTIN. There's no wrong time for seeing *you*. And you would understand my coming if you knew the good people I live with at home, my cosy family circle, as sociable as a pyramid and as cheerful as your tailor's bill! (*Yawning.*) Ah, they make me like Bohemia! (*Comes down, right centre, above easel.*)

NOÉMIE. (*Who has crossed to left centre.*) Bohemia? I'm much obliged to you! (*Curtsies.*)

VALENTIN. It's a charming country, and when I'm with you I feel as if I were in the capital! Who is this happy explorer of the delightful region whom you are expecting alone? (*Sits on table.*)

NOÉMIE. He's very different from you— *he* respects my innocence.

VALENTIN. Let us all respect his!

NOÉMIE. (*Coming to him severely.*) I'm not to see him alone—papa is to be here. He's a pupil of papa's. (*Leans on back of chair to talk to* VALENTIN.)

VALENTIN. Ah, no wonder he's innocent!

NOÉMIE. *You* needn't stay—*you'll* be of no particular use.

VALENTIN. My right's as good as his— I'm a pupil of *yours*. (*He kisses her hand; she pretends to be offended.*) What does your father teach him?

NOÉMIE. He gives him lessons in French; he's an ambitious, inquiring American.

VALENTIN. Hadn't he better give him lessons in English?

NOÉMIE. I like the way he speaks—it's so distinct.

VALENTIN. Distinct, but not distinguished. I shall certainly stay to see him.

NOÉMIE. You may see him any time at the Grand Hotel. He sits smoking in the court.

VALENTIN. Is that where you found him?

NOÉMIE. Do you suppose I go to such places? Don't you know how Papa's employed there, as commissioner and interpreter?

VALENTIN. Oh yes; he interprets his daughter!

NOÉMIE. As a copyist of the old masters, yes; he brought Mr. Newman to see me at the Louvre. Mr. Newman wants to see more of my copies; he wants to buy some, and that's why he is coming this morning. (*Returns to easel, and resumes work.*)

VALENTIN. Your father has taught him very well. (*Rises and comes to centre.*)

NOÉMIE. Ah, but he won't speak French —though he engaged papa on purpose to practice. Papa's English is so good.

VALENTIN. It isn't so good as yours. You haven't a trace of an accent.

NOÉMIE. We were in London, you know, for years, when I was a child.

VALENTIN. Yes, I have never been able to make out what you did there.

NOÉMIE. Ah, there it was just the contrary; papa was the interpreter for *French* tourists. (*A timid tinkle at the outer bell.*) There's Papa. You had better go. (*Indicating door on right.*)

VALENTIN. Oh, *I'm* a French tourist. I'm all in your father's line. (*Goes, in front, to fireplace.*)

NOÉMIE. Well, he *doesn't* mind you, and a Count, in the house, looks well! Americans like them. (*Exit* NOÉMIE *centre.*)

VALENTIN. Poor Mr. Newman—I'm glad he's going to like me; I take already such a charitable interest in his fate!

(*Re-enter, centre,* NOÉMIE, *and enter* NIOCHE, *who carries a small basket and a parcel done up in a cotton pocket-handkerchief, both of which his daughter takes from him, going with them to table on right.* NIOCHE *is a little old man, dressed with studied, though slightly seedy, gentility, in black. He has a wig, gloves and spectacles, and a habit of folding and unfolding his handkerchief. His hat is on at first.*)

NIOCHE. (*Centre.*) Bonjour, M. le Comte. I salute you very low.

VALENTIN. M. Nioche is always saluting low. You'd salute the executioner if he were going to break you on the wheel.

NOÉMIE. (*Looking into the basket while* NIOCHE *polishes his hat with his handkerchief.*) Well, you won't be tortured for stealing, at any rate. Three unhappy little cutlets! If the Count stays there won't even be one apiece.

VALENTIN. The Count will certainly stay.

NIOCHE. (*Putting on his hat again.*) Then I'll go and get another cutlet. (*Goes to door, right.*)

NOÉMIE. It doesn't matter (*picking up basket and contents and going up centre*) we've got half a cold pie. Mr. Newman knows the difficulties of our life.

VALENTIN. Assuredly, since he comes to relieve them. (*The bell rings again, pretty loud and sharp.*) There he is, the ministering angel.

NOÉMIE. Coming! (*Exit, centre, with the basket and parcel.*)

NIOCHE. He *is* a philanthropist, M. le Comte. (*Fumbles out snuffbox.*)

VALENTIN. And what am I then?

NIOCHE. (*Taking snuff.*) You're the purest relic of our old noblesse.

VALENTIN. Rather an object for philanthropy!

(*Re-enter* NOÉMIE, *centre; enter, behind her,* CHRISTOPHER NEWMAN, *with hat and stick.*)

NOÉMIE. This way, Mr. Newman! (*Pointing to the picture on the easel.*) There's the little thing you took such a fancy to.

NEWMAN. (*Looking at picture.*) That's just what I want[1] to see! (*Stands before picture.*)

NOÉMIE. I think I've improved it.

NEWMAN. Well, yes, I suppose you've improved it; but I don't know but I liked it better before it was quite so *good!* However, I guess I'll take it. (*Goes to right.*)

NOÉMIE. (*Advancing, centre.*) There are plenty more in the other room. (*Pointing centre.*) The light's better there.

NIOCHE. (*Obsequiously, to* NEWMAN, *dusting and giving him chair, right centre.*) I feel it a great honour to receive my munificent patron in my humble home.

---

[1] From this point on in the manuscript preserved at the Lord Chamberlain's Office Henry James inserted in parentheses phonetic aids to the American pronunciation of certain key words as a guide to Edward Compton. This permits the presumption that the copy filed at the Lord Chamberlain's Office was the one used for the provincial production, and in all probability was Compton's. In this instance James indicated that the word "want" was to be pronounced "wauhnt." All subsequent insertions—they are all in James's hand in the manuscript—are given here in footnotes.

NEWMAN. (*Seating himself.*) Oh, I was very glad to come round. When I come to a new country I like to see the *private* life.

NOÉMIE. Oh, sir, we haven't always had it so rough as this!

NEWMAN. Do you call this rough? I've seen it rougher, in my time. I've lived on the beaten earth, between the bare logs.

NOÉMIE. Ah, but you're making that up—at the Grand Hotel!

NEWMAN. My dear young lady, ten years ago, when I was your age, my hotel was grander still—it was sometimes the vault of heaven—the starry night!

NIOCHE. But did you ever lose a fortune, sir, from one day to the other?

NEWMAN. Lose a fortune? Why, I've lost about a hundred! (*Rises.*)

NOÉMIE. Ah, but how many have you made? (*Going up, centre.*) You must come and look at my copies before you lose another.

NEWMAN. Oh, I guess I'm safe now! (*Exit, centre; exit* NOÉMIE, *centre, preceding.*)

VALENTIN. (*To* NIOCHE.) I like your American, and his ideas of private life! (*Comes down, centre.*)

NIOCHE. We're more than private, sir—we're obscure! But he's a grand man.

VALENTIN. Do you mean a Grand Hotel man?

NIOCHE. You remember the capacity in which I'm attached to that establishment? He had just arrived in Paris and he wanted me to point him out the most remarkable objects.

VALENTIN. (*Pointing with his thumb to back.*) So you're pointing out your daughter!

NIOCHE. It was to the museum of the Louvre that I took him first, M. le Comte; I was thoroughly conscientious.

VALENTIN. Certainly; you knew he would find your daughter *there.*

NIOCHE. We came upon her, in fact, copying a beautiful picture with her usual devotion.

VALENTIN. Yes, *I* know; that's the way *I* came upon her—last year!

NIOCHE. I remember the visit with which you honoured us here in consequence.

You gained our confidence—you enjoy it still.

VALENTIN. I enjoy it very much, M. Nioche; it's my principal enjoyment.

NIOCHE. I esteem you for not having abused it.

VALENTIN. That certainly, in Paris, makes me one of the remarkable objects you just spoke of. (*Goes down, left. Re-enter* NOÉMIE *and* NEWMAN, *the latter without hat and stick.*) You should point me out to Mr. Newman.

NEWMAN. (*Left centre, to* NIOCHE.) Well, sir, they seem to me first-rate, and you may put me down for the lot! (*Takes out note-book, in which he makes note.*)

NOÉMIE. (*Right, aside to* NIOCHE.) Three thousand francs!

NIOCHE. (*Right centre, aside.*) My precious child! (*Aloud to* NEWMAN.) Allow me, sir, to introduce you to our noble friend, the Count Valentin de Bellegarde. (*Goes up to centre.*)

NEWMAN. (*Shaking hands.*) Happy to make your acquaintance, Count Valentine.

VALENTIN. (*Left.*) I'm afraid you've lost *another* fortune.

NEWMAN. Perhaps you can help me to get it back! (*They go together to fireplace.*)

NOÉMIE. Oh yes, he'll help you, if it's to play *me* a trick! But while you talk that over, Papa and I'll look after lunch.

NIOCHE. I'll put on the cutlets. (*Exit centre.*)

NOÉMIE. (*Raising the lid of ottoman and taking out knifeboard and knives,* VALENTIN *assisting in the whole movement.*) We must help ourselves!

NEWMAN. (*Coming a little to centre.*) Can't *I* help you?

NOÉMIE. (*Graciously.*) You have already. But M. de Bellegarde has done nothing, so he can clean these knives. (*Exit centre.*)

VALENTIN. (*At chair right of table, right, cleaning a knife.*) Used you to do this when your life was so rough under the vault of heaven?

NEWMAN. (*Half seated on back of chair, left.*) I guess we didn't polish them! And they were sometimes of another kind.

VALENTIN. Bowie-knives—a foot long? Oh, I should like to hear your adventures.

NEWMAN. This is my principal adventure, sir—visiting your beautiful city.

VALENTIN. I'm glad you like our city, and I hope your adventure will turn out well. If I can help *that*, it will give me great pleasure.

NEWMAN. You're very kind! It *would* be rather a comfort to have a pleasant, bright companion to show me around. Someone who's really *acquainted!*

VALENTIN. You seem to me to have made a good beginning.

NEWMAN. Well, I've begun the study of French! I asked for a teacher at the hotel, and they trotted out the old gentleman there. He came in as quick as if he had been behind the door.

VALENTIN. It's where he was, I suppose!

NEWMAN. Well, he seems a regular patriarch—one of the old school.

VALENTIN. Oh, the old school—*I* could show you the old school!

NEWMAN. That's just what I want [2] to see! (*Comes centre; foot on seat of chair left of table.*) I want to see something that will strike me with awe. Only, it's a pity—if I want to learn the language—that you seem all to speak such fine old English.

VALENTIN. I wouldn't, if I could help it; but I can't. My dear mother is English; she has always, from our infancy, addressed us in that tongue.

NEWMAN. Well, if I had had a dear mother—from my infancy—to address me in a tongue—

VALENTIN. You would have learnt it, you may be sure, if she had been anything like mine!

NEWMAN. (*Seated on chair, left, his head on the hand of which the arm is on back of chair.*) Well, I'm afraid I'm rather ignorant—I haven't a relation in the world.

VALENTIN. One certainly learns many things from one's relations.

NEWMAN. I haven't worked round to the *English* yet. I'll see them later.

VALENTIN. Oh, the English'll keep—they won't run away.

NEWMAN. I don't know as they'll keep *me*. I sailed straight for a *French* port—I wanted to see Paris worst of all.

VALENTIN. That shows you're a good

2 wauhnt

American.

NEWMAN. Because the proverb says they come here when they die? Oh, I ain't dead yet; at least, I *think* I ain't—that's just what I want to see! *I* want to have a regular good time. I've been whistling "Yankee-Doodle" all my life, and now I should like to try another tune. (*Rising.*) I want a little change. (*Goes over to table, right.*) As you were so good as to say just now that you're ready to help me, do you know how you can do it? Help me to a little change! (*Sits left of table, right.*)

VALENTIN. (*Finishing his knives.*) I'm afraid I haven't got change for several millions; but I will do what I can for you. Will you have a cigarette? (*Offers case.*)

NEWMAN. Do you think we can smoke here?

VALENTIN. *I* always do. (*Lights up.*)

NEWMAN. Won't the young lady [3] object? (*Takes cigarette and gets light from* VALENTIN.)

VALENTIN. My dear fellow, she smokes herself! But you can ask her.

(*Re-enter* NOÉMIE, *centre.*)

NOÉMIE. (*To* VALENTIN.) You *are* lazy! Is that the way you clean my knives? (*Taking the knives up, between the two men.*)

VALENTIN. They're as bright as your eyes and as sharp as your tongue!

NEWMAN. This gentleman assures me we may smoke; may I, therefore, offer you a cigarette—one of mine?

NOÉMIE. (*Smiling and taking the cigarette, which* NEWMAN *lights for her.*) Anything of *yours!* (*Action with cigarette.*) The cutlets are almost done. (*Exit, centre, with knifeboard.*)

VALENTIN. I might be jealous of you—if I didn't want to like you. I daresay you've got a bowie-knife somewhere?

NEWMAN. Yes, somewhere in a cupboard, in California. If you want to like me I'll show you how, as far as I know. But I don't see what you have [4] to *envy* me—judging from the familiarity with which she treats you.

VALENTIN. Don't say familiarity—say

contempt! I'm the cold dish on the sideboard; who wants it when there's a charming *entrée?*

NEWMAN. What do you mean by that foreign expression?

VALENTIN. I mean *you*—for instance!

NEWMAN. Oh, I shan't show *her* how to like me!

VALENTIN. Aren't you paying a good deal for pure aversion?

NEWMAN. A good deal? Why, I thought the whole thing so cheap!

(*Re-enter* NOÉMIE, *and goes to the chest, left, where she pulls out a drawer.*)

NOÉMIE. There's a clean napkin somewhere for Mr. Newman.

VALENTIN. Ah, if she throws in a clean napkin!

NOÉMIE. The cutlets are almost done—papa is opening the wine. (*Exit, centre, with the napkin.*)

VALENTIN. A fresh bottle! My dear fellow, she *is* throwing you the handkerchief.

NEWMAN. You mean the napkin! Oh, that's no use! (*Snaps fingers, takes knee in hand.*) I want to get *married.*

VALENTIN. I don't see how you escape!

NEWMAN. Oh, the dangers are too small. I want a big one. I've got a sort of preconceived theory of the finest woman on earth.

VALENTIN. And to realise that theory you have left your own country, where I'm told the women are so charming?

NEWMAN. So they are, but they've all come over here. I want [5] a *first-class* woman, and I don't care what she is, so long as she's only perfect: beautiful, amiable, clever, good, the product of a long [6] civilization and a great cultivation! I shall expect her to have everything the world can give—except a fortune. I don't care a fig for that—I've enough for two. (*Rises and goes above chair. Left hand out.*)

VALENTIN. (*Looking at* NEWMAN *from head to foot with a smile of mingled impudence and urbanity.*) My dear sir, don't misunderstand me if I say you've enough for a dozen—I mean enough confidence. And also if I ask you what are your titles to

---

[3] James here pencilled in the direction that this be spoken "A little from the nose."
[4] y'have

[5] wauhnt
[6] lawng

the hand of so exalted a being?

NEWMAN. My titles? Oh, I'll show them to *her!* Meanwhile, I stick to my idea that she must be the rarest flower that grows. I've had a hard life, I've had a rough life, I've had rather an ugly life, and I've had, if I may say so, as regards the inner comfort of the thing, a very lonely life. I've come out all right, but it wasn't all roses and cakes. In that roaring big country of mine everything is big, even to the difficulties and disappointments, the temptations and defeats. But I have come out, thank God,[7] without leaving behind too much of my youth, or too many of my illusions. I've had a long [8] working-day, and *(stretching himself)* now I want a big treat. *(Goes to easel.)*

VALENTIN. Might I venture to intimate sympathetically that you yourself are a big treat?

NEWMAN. *(At easel.)* What else have I toiled and struggled for all these years? I've succeeded, and now what am I to do with my success? To make it a big one, some woman I shall love and admire must be perched on the pile like a statue of marble on a pedestal of gold.

VALENTIN. A very becoming position for the woman you love and admire! *(Rises and comes to NEWMAN.)* May I ask if you have yet come across the lady who would serve for your statue?

NEWMAN. No, hang it—have you?

VALENTIN. *(Putting his hand, with cigarette in it, on NEWMAN's sleeve, as if to speak; then withdrawing it and smoking with hands in his pockets.)* I'll tell you when I know you better!

NEWMAN. Well, I mean to look round.

VALENTIN. Why shouldn't we look round together?

NEWMAN. Oh, I'm afraid the lady'll like *you* best!

VALENTIN. She'll like me for liking you.

NEWMAN. Then you *know* one of the kind I mean? *(Takes out note-book.)*

VALENTIN. Oh, thank heaven, I know some charming women.

NEWMAN. *(With his memoranda.)* Will you just give me their addresses?

VALENTIN. *(Laughing.)* I'll take you to see them! *(Goes to right while NEWMAN goes to chair, left, and sits astride.)* Here comes M. Nioche to announce the feast.

(Re-enter NIOCHE, with a bottle and a corkscrew.)

NIOCHE. In a moment, M. le Comte! My daughter begs you will do her the honour to go and make her an omelette.[9]

VALENTIN. Certainly, if I may break enough eggs! *(Exit VALENTIN, centre, going round up.)*

NIOCHE. *(Struggling unsuccessfully with the cork of his bottle.)* It's a great pleasure to me to observe, sir, that you have established relations of sociability with our distinguished visitor.

NEWMAN. Is he very distinguished?

NIOCHE. One of the purest relics of our old noblesse—brought up in all the traditions.

NEWMAN. The traditions? That's just what I want to see! But your daughter seems to treat him as the family cook.

NIOCHE. He's the only one we have, sir. The traditions of cookery have always been cherished by the French aristocracy. His family is illustrious and historical.

NEWMAN. That's just what I want to see! See here—ask [10] him to show me his family.[11]

NIOCHE. I should think he would do it sir. *(Aside.)* That will go down in my bill: "Introduction to the Faubourg Saint-Germain, five thousand francs." *(Struggling still with his cork.)*

NEWMAN. I'm afraid it sticks. *(He throws away cigarette into fireplace.)* Let *me* have a try.

NIOCHE. It's not work for your honoured hands, sir.

NEWMAN. Oh, if you'd seen some of the work my honoured hands have done! Does our friend there *live* in Paris?

NIOCHE. In the Faubourg Saint-Germain, in the grand old family mansion. It dates from hundreds of years back.

NEWMAN. Hundreds of years? That's just

---

[7] Gawd
[8] lawng

[9] The next four speeches are crossed out in Henry James's copy of the play.
[10] a-ask
[11] The next four speeches are crossed out in Henry James's copy of the play.

what I want to see! Been there yourself?

NIOCHE. Respected sir, I've been everywhere, and I know everything!

NEWMAN. I see (*sits on table, right*); that's why they have you at the Grand Hotel.

NIOCHE. My profession is to answer questions, and it's to my honour that none has ever been asked me to which I haven't instantly produced a reply. For instance I can go straight through the great house of Bellegarde. (*Puts bottle down by fire.*)

NEWMAN. The great house of Bellegarde?

NIOCHE. The relations of my noble guest. It's true there are very few left today— that makes it easy. Only his mother, his elder brother, and his beautiful sister!

NEWMAN. (*Who has been looking at a book on table, right, here turns quickly, leg up on chair.*) Has he got a beautiful sister?

NIOCHE. As beautiful as an old picture— some delicate pastel—and a saint into the bargain.

NEWMAN. That's just what I want to see! (*Quickly taking out again his memorandum-book.*) Her name, please?

NIOCHE. (*Importantly.*) Madame la Comtesse Claire de Cintré.

NEWMAN. Damn it then—she's *married?*

NIOCHE. She was, sir; but that's all over. She's now an elegant young widow.

NEWMAN. (*Jotting down.*) That's just what I want to see! (*He sits in chair, right, and, with his legs stretched well out, takes notes as* NIOCHE *speaks.*)

NIOCHE. Her mother arranged for her, in her tender youth and terribly against her inclination, a marriage that was expected to be brilliant, but that turned out like a lamp that won't burn—all smoke and bad smell. Fortunately, after three or four years, the Comte de Cintré died— died of his disorders and vices. (*Lowering his voice and giving half a dozen backward nods of the head.*) I believe they were something awful, sir.

NEWMAN. Lord, how mean! How could she do it?

NIOCHE. *She* didn't do it, sir—her mother did it.

NEWMAN. And her father—had *he* nothing to say?

NIOCHE. I believe he had a great deal to say, but the old lady shut him up.

NEWMAN. Shut him up—in a lunatic asylum?

NIOCHE. No, no; in his own private room—in his own curtained bed. The poor gentleman turned sick and died there, just when he wanted most to be afoot—and his high and mighty wife could do what she liked.[12]

NEWMAN. She must have curious likings. Was there no one to step right in?

NIOCHE. Two sons, sir, of whom we have the honour of receiving the younger, our accomplished guest; he was only a boy of twenty, and he was got out of the way— he was sent to England for a year. The present Marquis (the eldest son) is simply second fiddle to his mamma.

NEWMAN. Well, between them they seem to play pretty airs! (*Putting away notebook.*) I've seen rough things in my country, but I haven't met that style.

NIOCHE. Oh, they're very remarkable— in the Faubourg Saint-Germain!

NEWMAN. (*Rising.*) See here—I want to go there!

NIOCHE. (*Shrugging his shoulders and pressing his finger-tips together.*) It's very difficult to get the *entrée*. (*Takes up bottle.*)

NEWMAN. Yes; but with our friend who's making the omelette—

NIOCHE. Oh, sir, if you're agreeable to *him!* (*Looking at his watch.*) He takes an extraordinary time to make it.

NEWMAN. I'll get round him—I'll crack up his omelette.

NIOCHE. (*After another vain tussle with his cork.*) I'm ashamed, sir; but we're so dilapidated that my corkscrew doesn't act. We have an accommodating neighbor—I'll borrow a better one. (*Going to door, right.*)

NEWMAN. Just tell me first if she's all right now.

NIOCHE. (*Staring.*) Our accommodating neighbor? I'm afraid she's behind with her rent.

NEWMAN. No, no; I mean the widowed young Countess—in the grand old house.

---

[12] The next three speeches, up to the end of the stage direction in which Newman puts away his notebook, are crossed out in Henry James's copy.

NIOCHE. Oh, she just lives on there—in great seclusion. She has never married again.

NEWMAN. Do you suppose she *would?*

NIOCHE. (*Staring a moment, then aside.*) *Ciel!*—what could we get for that? (*Aloud.*) I'm afraid that's a question you must put to the lady herself.

NEWMAN. Then I've invented the first you can't answer.

NIOCHE. At the Grand Hotel, sir, it isn't matrimony!

NEWMAN. I've done with the Grand Hotel! I shall take a house. (*Goes down to chair, left, and sits.*)

NIOCHE. (*Eagerly.*) I shall be very glad to help you find one.

NEWMAN. Please look out, then, for a fine big, bright one, a regular old *palace.* Try in the Faubourg Saint-Germain.[13]

NIOCHE. As near it as possible. (*Aside.*) Mercy on us, there *is* a chance! (*Aloud, glancing at the other room, of which the doors are closed.*) [14] I can't fancy what they're doing there—an omelette's so quick!

NEWMAN. Ain't it rather slow when there are two? (*Rising and crossing to window and looking out; then in another tone.*) What do you suppose made her go back?

NIOCHE. My little daughter, sir?

NEWMAN. No, no—the young Countess. Why did she return to the old woman if the old woman sits on her?

NIOCHE. Those are the traditions, sir. She couldn't live alone, and when they can't live alone they have to live with each other—there's no one else grand enough.

NEWMAN. (*Aside.*) I wonder if *I* should be grand enough! (*Aloud.*) Why couldn't she live alone?

NIOCHE. I fear there was very little money, sir: there isn't much, in some of those stately homes.

NEWMAN. Won't that make it easier for you to scare me up one?

NIOCHE. (*Considering a moment.*) It will make them put on their price, sir!

NEWMAN. Oh, give them their price.

(*Crosses to fireplace, below table.*) Wasn't he at least rich, then—the old scallawag?

NIOCHE. The Comtesse's husband? Ah, that was Madame de Bellegarde's fond calculation. But he had run through everything—he left nothing but debts. That's how she was punished. (*Takes up hat from floor.*)

NEWMAN. I should like to punish her a little more!

(*Re-enter* VALENTIN, *centre.*)

VALENTIN. The omelette has fallen on its feet, and Monsieur Nioche is served!

NIOCHE. Served by a son of the crusaders! I'll be with you in a moment. (*Exit with his bottle, right.*)

NEWMAN. (*As he goes.*) Don't forget the house!

VALENTIN. Are you going to take a house?

NEWMAN. With the help of that good old man.[15]

VALENTIN. That's capital news if it means that you're to stay with us.

NEWMAN. I'll stay as long [16] as you make it attractive.

VALENTIN. I'll make it as attractive as I can. (*Sits on the table, back to audience.*) To me, here, you know, it's all rather stuffy—and you're so ventilating!

NEWMAN. (*Looking at him a moment and laying a hand on his shoulder.*) Why shouldn't we strike a bargain, you and I—to give and take? If I've got something you want, perhaps you've got something I want.

VALENTIN. The bargain would be very unequal—I've got so very little! But perhaps I can help you to find a house—or help your deputy there.

NEWMAN. Oh, don't go round with him —go round with me! You must come and see me. (*Puts out his hand.*)

VALENTIN. (*Taking* NEWMAN's *hand.*) Delighted, and you must return my visit. (*Shakes* NEWMAN's *hand and looks out of window.*)

NEWMAN. (*Aside, going to left and round to back.*) Good—perhaps I shall see the old pastel. That treatment sticks in my crop! (*Aloud.*) Oh yes, you must show me Paris.

---

[13] Saint-Germane.
[14] The rest of this speech and the next two speeches are crossed out in Henry James's copy.

[15] mehn
[16] lawng

VALENTIN. (*At the window.*) If I do, I shall show you some queer things.

NEWMAN. (*Going to the easel.*) Oh, I want [17] to see only the best.

VALENTIN. The best are the queerest! (*As* NEWMAN *stands before* NOÉMIE'S *picture.*) Well, what do you think of that?

NEWMAN. I was thinking of something else. But isn't *this* a little queer?

VALENTIN. (*Going left and laughing.*) Decidedly, though it's not the best! (*Re-enter* NOÉMIE, *briskly, centre.*) Mr. Newman can't take his eyes off that gem.

NOÉMIE. You may well say gem, since he has given it a golden setting! Everything is ready—please go in. I only want to put on a ribbon, in honour of my munificent patron. (*Exit, left.* VALENTIN *comes centre, right of* NEWMAN, *above easel.*)

NEWMAN. I'm much obliged to her, but I wasn't thinking either of her gem or of its setting. I was thinking of something the old man has just told me. (*Going to* VALENTIN.)

VALENTIN. Oh, I know he deals in wonders.

NEWMAN. He told me about your home.

VALENTIN. Ah, that *is* a wonder! But you must see it for yourself.

NEWMAN. He says you keep it boarded up.

VALENTIN. That's just the reason for you to come in—it wants ventilation!

NEWMAN. Oh, I'll create a draught! (*Takes* VALENTIN'S *arm and they go up. Exeunt, centre,* VALENTIN *and* NEWMAN. *While they are turning away, re-enter* NOÉMIE, *left, with a ribbon in her hand, and quickly closes the central doors be-behind them as soon as they have gone out.*)

NOÉMIE. (*Putting on her ribbon, using powder-puff and arranging her dress before the glass over mantel.*) I'm dreadfully nervous lest the Peer of the Realm should come back before the coast is clear; and yet I don't want to lose him—he's too good for that! He's better than the American, if the American is going to be whirled away by the Frenchman. Papa considers he's so clever to have introduced Mr. Newman to the Count—he can make him a charge

for it. It would have been cleverer to keep him for ourselves—we could make him a charge for that too. Well, whatever happens, we'll make him a charge! (*Pulls down back of her dress.*) I don't know what he thought of me, shut up so long there with a young man distinguished for gallantry! The Count chattered and chattered; but I made him chatter to some profit, since I drew him, cunningly, on the subject of Lord Deepmere, who wants—the double-faced wretch!—to make up to the Count's grand sister. The Count, however, doesn't favour him as a brother-in-law. Well, it serves him right! I didn't let on to the Count that I know him and that *I* do favour him a little; that's just what I want to keep dark. It won't be easy, either, if he comes flaming in. (*Re-enter* LORD DEEP-MERE, *slowly and cautiously, right, peeping in at the door.*) Here he is—flaming enough!

DEEPMERE. Charming creature, isn't my time up?

NOÉMIE. Do you call this an hour? How did you get in?

DEEPMERE. The door on the landing is gaping open.

NOÉMIE. (*Aside.*) Idiotic papa—foraging for his cockscrew! (*Aloud.*) Then it's just right for you to pass out again.

DEEPMERE. (*Coming in.*) Not till you confess that you tricked me just now, turning me out for fear of your stern parent. I heard the voice, I was sure I knew it, and it has come back to me who the person is. He's neither a parent nor stern.

NOÉMIE. (*Coming centre.*) I don't know what you're talking about, and I've no more time to give you.

DEEPMERE. That only clinches my conviction that Count Valentin is on the premises.

NOÉMIE. Count Valentin? How do you know that I know him? He can't have told you!

DEEPMERE. (*Struck.*) Then you know he knows me? He has told you that! (*Goes up to central doors.*)

NOÉMIE. (*Aside.*) Crac! (*Aloud, majestically.*) Considering the extreme shortness of our acquaintance you are wonderfully wise about my affairs.

---

[17] wauhnt

DEEPMERE. (*Listening to sounds from back.*) Do you still pretend that's your father's voice? (*Goes toward the doors—movement from* NOÉMIE, *barring the way.*)

NOÉMIE. You'll please to keep away from there—your suspicions are insulting. My father has a pupil—taking a lesson.

DEEPMERE. A lesson in sword-practice? Count Valentin may need it!

NOÉMIE. (*As if struck with this.*) Why on earth do you dislike him so?

DEEPMERE. Why on earth does he dislike me?

NOÉMIE. It's absurd—he doesn't.

DEEPMERE. Does he say so? Then you *have* seen him! Open the doors yourself, and prove to me that he's not there. I deny the existence of your preposterous pupil—produce him!

NOÉMIE. (*Embarrassed and impatient, going back, left, to her glass.*) I can't be bothered with you any longer. Good-bye!

DEEPMERE. (*Rather mock-sentimental.*) You choose to lose me then forever? Don't think that if I go now I shall ever come back! (*Goes to chair, right.*)

NOÉMIE. (*Aside.*) Perhaps he won't! It's a bore, because I like to keep my interests *separate.* (*Aloud, coming to centre.*) I don't care whether you come back or not; but I won't be falsely accused and I *will* produce the pupil. (*Goes back, opens partly one of the leaves of the door and looks in.*) Mr. Newman, will you be so good as to speak to me a moment? (*To* DEEPMERE.) Now you'll see your folly. (*Re-enter* NEWMAN, *from back,* NOÉMIE *closing the door behind him. Coming down, left centre, to* NEWMAN.) Will you do me a great favour? Will you let this gentleman look at you?

NEWMAN. If it gives him any comfort. (*The two men stand, centre, face to face a moment.*) I hope he'll know me again.

DEEPMERE. I shall certainly know you again. I'm much obliged to you (*and to* NOÉMIE) and to *you.* Good day! (*As if confessing his error, he goes quickly to the door on the right; but before leaving the room he stops and exchanges another look with* NEWMAN. *Exit* LORD DEEPMERE, *right. Action from* NOÉMIE.)

NEWMAN. (*As the Curtain falls.*) I *wasn't* what he wanted to see!

ACT SECOND

One of the smaller salons at the Hôtel de Bellegarde, arranged and lighted for a reception. Half way to each side, right and left, across the obtuse angles of the room, a double door opening into other and different lighted apartments. In the middle, against the wall, between the two open doors, a buffet, with a white cloth, with refreshments, &c. Enter MRS. BREAD, *left upper entrance, followed by a* SERVANT *carrying a tray.*

MRS. BREAD. (*Pointing to the buffet.*) Put the things there. I'll come back, as Madame la Marquise wishes, and serve the tea in case it's wanted. And please bring another lamp for *that* table (*indicating table, left*) it always seems to me there never can be light *enough* in this dark house.

SERVANT. I'm sure it's blazing to-night—with twenty people at dinner and five hun-dred more expected! (*Exit, to come back presently and place a lamp on the table, left, indicated by* MRS. BREAD, *who is going off left, when enter* VALENTIN, *right.*)

VALENTIN. Wait a moment, my dear old friend—you're the very person I want. I never have a moment's talk with you now. (*They stand at back at buffet, she giving him a cup of tea.*)

MRS. BREAD. You do me great honour, to choose a moment when the house is full of grand people. (*Re-enter* SERVANT *with lamp, and places it left.*)

VALENTIN. There's no one in it so grand as you, Catty—especially when you want to snub a fellow!

MRS. BREAD. (*Looking at him affectionately.*) When did I ever snub the creature in the world I love best and have known the longest?

VALENTIN. Since the hour I was born, stern superintendent of my childhood!

MRS. BREAD. And since the hour your sweet sister was born—Heaven help her, poor lady!

VALENTIN. Heaven *is* helping her, by one of it's messengers; it looks very much like it.

MRS. BREAD. Do you mean that your showy American friend is a messenger from Heaven?

VALENTIN. I mean, my dear Catty, that the more I've seen of Mr. Christopher Newman, the more I've liked him, and that I want you to like him as I do. (*Brings her down stage.*)

MRS. BREAD. You want *me*, my dear child? You mean you want the Countess! I'll confide to you that I think she's ready to oblige you.

VALENTIN. Is she ready to oblige *him?*—that's the question.

MRS. BREAD. Let him try—let him try. She doesn't turn her back.

VALENTIN. (*Walking about while* MRS. BREAD *arranges tables.*) She would be perverse if she did, for from the hour I brought him here, five weeks ago, he seemed to fling open the windows of this temple of staleness and stagnation—he laid the irrepressible ghost.

MRS. BREAD. (*Looking round.*) Hush!—don't talk of the ghost!

VALENTIN. There's nobody to hear. (*He forces her to sit right of table, and places himself on arm of her chair.*) The men are still smoking, and the ladies, in the drawing-room, are counting the cost of each other's gowns.

MRS. BREAD. And trying to guess what your mother means this unparalleled entertainment for.

VALENTIN. What can she mean it for but as a sign to Mr. Newman that, like a good American, he may go ahead? She has beaten the drum for our friends and our enemies, as if to say to him: "There they are! Ain't they grand? You may enter the magic circle!"

MRS. BREAD. But what does she say to *them?*

VALENTIN. Only three words: "He has ever so many millions!"

MRS. BREAD. And what does she say to Lord Deepmere?

VALENTIN. There has been no need to say anything—he has gone back to England.

MRS. BREAD. But won't he turn up again?

VALENTIN. A day after the fair.

MRS. BREAD. He won't like being too late, for I've an idea he has received a bit of encouragement.

VALENTIN. From the heads of the family? (*Rises.*) Oh, they've been awfully civil, and if they've hung back a little, it's only because the figure of his income, though high, isn't quite up to their standard. Everything's low compared to *that!*

MRS. BREAD. (*Rising.*) So that if they throw him over now—?

VALENTIN. He'll have a perfect right not to enjoy it!

MRS. BREAD. Oh, if my lady and the Marquis have given him their word—

VALENTIN. Trust them to take it back!

MRS. BREAD. Gracious, I'm glad he's gone—and I oughtn't to give you a chance to utter such horrors! (*Exit* MRS. BREAD, *left.*)

VALENTIN. (*Looking after her.*) Poor old Catty, you have helped us before (*enter* CHRISTOPHER NEWMAN), you shall help us again.

NEWMAN. (*Laying his hand on* VALENTIN's *shoulder.*) You're not just what I want to see; but you're the next best thing. (*Takes* VALENTIN's *arm and brings him over to right.*)

VALENTIN. To appreciate that tribute, I must know whom you *are* looking for.

NEWMAN. (*With his back to fireplace.*) For whom but Madame de Cintré? I want particularly to speak to her. I could scarcely break away from some of your folks.

VALENTIN. (*Seated on the ottoman.*) My dear fellow, you're a great success; but you don't know—you can never know—what a new departure, for *us*, this is to-night!

NEWMAN. Oh, I guess I've guessed!

VALENTIN. You're in a situation in which your national faculty will find plenty of application. But don't shout till you're out of the wood.

NEWMAN. Why ain't I out of it, if Madame de Cintré thinks me a *gentle* savage, as you've told me she does?

VALENTIN. What I've told you is that you've given a good turn to her life.

NEWMAN. Well, one good turn deserves

another! (*Crosses up right above ottoman, and over to left centre.*) That's what I want [1] to remind her of, if I can find her, in this labyrinth of rooms. (*Going to door on right, as if to continue his search.*)

VALENTIN. (*Who has risen, stops him, centre, at back.*) Stay here, *out* of the labyrinth. I want to speak to Claire myself, and I'll bring her this way.

NEWMAN. Oh, Count, if you want to speak to her, speak to her of *me!* [2]

VALENTIN. I never do anything else! (*Exit* VALENTIN, *right, and at the same moment enter, by the other door, left,* LORD DEEPMERE.)

NEWMAN. (*Aside.*) Hallo! Is *he* one of the guests?

DEEPMERE. (*Who has stopped short on seeing* NEWMAN, *so that the two men stand a moment face to face.*) Excuse my recognising you—we met in such a very odd way.

NEWMAN. I should scarcely forget your *not* recognising me, considering that on that occasion I was produced expressly for your benefit.

DEEPMERE. Let me thank you again!

NEWMAN. Having conjured me up, I'm afraid you must bear with me. (*Comes down and sits on ottoman.*) I don't bite!

DEEPMERE. I certainly shall not shirk any of the consequences of my rashness. (*Leaning on chair, right of table.*) I should have been sooner in a position to learn what they may be, if I had not been called over to England for a couple of months. I came back only a few hours ago.

NEWMAN. Let me congratulate you on returning to so pleasant a place—and on having lost so little time in finding out the pleasantest corner in it.

DEEPMERE. My dear sir, I found out the Hôtel de Bellegarde long before I found out—some other things!

NEWMAN. (*Good-humouredly.*) Oh, well, if you're an old friend, we're all jolly old friends together.

(*Re-enter* VALENTIN, *right, hearing the last words.*)

VALENTIN. (*Centre, aside.*) Deepmere back? Oh, bother! (*Aloud.*) Ah, you're jolly old friends?

NEWMAN. Oh yes, that goes away back, but I believe I didn't mention it at the time.

VALENTIN. Good evening, *milord:* welcome again to Paris. (*To* NEWMAN.) Do you know the little blue room? My sister's there, and I daresay she'll be free to see you.

NEWMAN. (*Jumping up.*) I'll free her, if she ain't! (*Exit* NEWMAN, *right centre.*)

DEEPMERE. (*To* VALENTIN.) Madame de Cintré is just the person I was hoping to come across.

VALENTIN. (*Stopping him.*) Please don't go to her now—I'm sure she's engaged.

DEEPMERE. (*Aside.*) Engaged—with *that* customer? (*Aloud.*) I've seen your mother and your brother, but I had no idea I was to fall on such a brilliant *fête*. I hope I'm not indiscreet if I inquire if there's any extraordinary reason—

VALENTIN. For our lighting so many candles? Yes, at last we have something to show. (*Goes to fireplace and stands with his back to* DEEPMERE, *who is at the ottoman, kneeling on it.*)

DEEPMERE. Do you mean a very surprising guest?

VALENTIN. Mr. Newman *is* surprising—to us scions of effete aristocracies!

DEEPMERE. I congratulate you on his want of resemblance to *other* gentlemen, when he's locked up with young ladies you're interested in!

VALENTIN. (*Turning round.*) Locked up—with young ladies? (*Staring.*) Bless my soul, was it *you* that day, when we were at breakfast with a charming person who suddenly called him out?

DEEPMERE. (*Staring in turn.*) Were *you* at breakfast too? (*Rises and goes left centre.*) Then I *was* humbugged!

VALENTIN. (*Moving to centre.*) Did you think Mr. Newman was alone with her?

DEEPMERE. I thought *you* were alone with her! That was why I insisted on seeing the individual—her father's "pupil."

VALENTIN. It was very good of you to insist!

DEEPMERE. I believed *you* were the pupil; and indeed, among you, you seem to form a promising little class!

VALENTIN. I don't recognise your war-

---

[1] wawnt
[2] me-*ee*

rant for interrupting our lesson.

DEEPMERE. My warrant, Monsieur de Bellegarde, is simply that, wherever I find you, you stand, and you have the evident intention of standing, in my way! (*Movement.*)

VALENTIN. (*Seeing* MME. DE CINTRÉ, *left.*) See, after all, then, how little I succeed, and how fortune *favours* you! (*Enter* MADAME DE CINTRÉ, *right; greets* LORD DEEPMERE, *and moves to centre. To* MME. DE CINTRÉ.) I just told a friend of ours that you were in the blue room. I hope he hasn't missed you.

CLAIRE. Do you mean Mr. Newman? I think he never misses anything. He must have been waylaid and captured by lovely ladies—he's having immense success.

VALENTIN. He's the success of the evening.

DEEPMERE. To say that to *you*, Madam—!

CLAIRE. Oh, I have my eye on a very different sort of triumph. I came this way, by my mother's request, to make sure there are enough teacups and spoons. (*Goes to table, centre, or buffet.*)

DEEPMERE. Let me help you count them. There are about five hundred!

VALENTIN. Be ready, then. I'll send you all the thirsty people. (*Exit* VALENTIN.)

DEEPMERE. (*At back, with* MME. DE CINTRÉ.) Your brother knows what I want, and he hopes to interfere with it. So before any one comes, let me tell you frankly what I have returned to Paris for.

CLAIRE. (*Abstractedly.*) Have you been away? (*Counting teaspoons.*)

DEEPMERE. (*Looking at her a moment.*) Haven't you observed it? I went back to England, for a few weeks, in consequence of a conversation I had with your mother. I promised her I would make a thorough examination of the state of my property, with which Madame de Bellegarde was unfortunately but half satisfied. She wanted me to dot my *i*'s.

CLAIRE. What had my mother to do with it? (*Crosses to table, left.*)

DEEPMERE. What is there, in this house, that your mother has not to do with?

CLAIRE. (*Crossing to top of card-table, left.*) Dear Lord Deepmere, your property is not in this house.

DEEPMERE. The thing I value most in the world is! There are, however, other things—many other things—in England. I have spent more than a month going into everything, riding over everything, turning everything inside out. I've had up all my people, and I've kicked out more than half of them. Madame de Bellegarde ought to be satisfied with *that*!

CLAIRE. (*Turning over cards.*) Poor people, I'm sorry for them.

DEEPMERE. It serves them right. They were cheating me.

CLAIRE. (*Putting down cards going down left.*) Ah, take care you're not worse cheated!

DEEPMERE. (*Following her.*) What do you mean?

CLAIRE. (*Moving from him.*) I mean that what you tell me is very interesting, but that I have no desire whatever to elicit a report from you. (*Waltz music, pianissimo, off right; musicians on stage.*)

DEEPMERE. Oh, but listen, and see if you don't like my report! (*His hand is on the back of a chair; he moves it a little to one side.*) Everything is now in the best hands—every mortgage is paid off. I don't want to swagger, but I've got half a dozen places. I don't want to bore you, but I'll tell you my income like a shot, if you care to hear it.

CLAIRE. (*Moving up centre,* DEEPMERE *following her.*) I congratulate you with all my heart on your prosperity, but I can't aspire to contribute to it.

DEEPMERE. (*Pleading; trying to take her hands.*) You won't care for me—never, never?

CLAIRE. It's utterly impossible!

DEEPMERE. And will you give me no reason?

CLAIRE. I thank you humbly. Please excuse me and let me leave you.

(*Re-enter* NEWMAN, *right, as* MME. DE CINTRÉ *is turning quickly away. They meet and talk.*)

NEWMAN. You're just what I wanted to see!

DEEPMERE. (*Aside.*) Can that barbarian be her reason? It's inconceivable! The old lady and her prig of an elder son shall tell me! (*Exit* LORD DEEPMERE, *left.*)

CLAIRE. Have you come for a cup of tea?

NEWMAN. No, I've come for something much stronger! [3] The Count told me you were here, and it's a joy to be face to face with you at last.[4] (CLAIRE *goes to bottom of ottoman.*) It's as if there had been a conspiracy to baffle me to-night—we have been kept asunder from the moment I arrived.

CLAIRE. (*Seating herself on the ottoman.*) It's your universal success that has kept us asunder.

NEWMAN. (*With his knee on the ottoman.*) It will be time to call my success universal when you have given me the supreme proof of it. (CLAIRE *rising, he makes her sink down again.*) Let me talk to you about that—quietly, tenderly, reasonably—on your own terms. Listen to me, trust me—*I'll* check you through! I know you've seen me, as yet, comparatively little—so little that there may even be, to your mind, a kind of failure of respect, or at least of ceremony, in my breaking out this way. That's my misfortune; for I could almost have done so the first time I saw you. The fact is, there was no first time. I had seen you before—I had seen you always, in imagination, in secret ambitions; you seemed an old friend! I felt like that dear old boy Columbus (you know I'm named after [5] him: it's a good omen!) when the ascertained fact bore out his general conclusions and he sighted the New World. Like him I had exercised our national genius (he must have bequeathed it to us!)—I had *calculated.* (*Stands.*)

CLAIRE. (*Laughing.*) Your national genius is very great!

NEWMAN. Of course it is. Otherwise I'm perfectly aware, I shouldn't stand where I do. I had, like Columbus, a theory that *my* new world was here (*bends over* CLAIRE; *she rises*); so that as soon as you rose, pale and lovely, above my horizon, I said to myself: "Old man,[6] I told you so!" You were the very woman I had figured out—except that you were a far bigger result. (*Movement from* CLAIRE.) You hold your head just as that tantalising creature has always held *hers.* You say just the things that I have listened to on *her* lips. (CLAIRE *moves to centre.*) You walk about the room as I've seen *her* walk. (*She stops.*) You stop as I have seen *her* stop—you wear exactly the garments I have seen *her* wear! In short, you come up to the mark, and (*taking her hand*) I tell you, my mark was high!

CLAIRE. (*Smiling.*) I'm glad I come up to the mark!

NEWMAN. I don't *express* it well; but you know what I mean.

CLAIRE. Not a bit, I assure you, when you talk of your secret ambitions. What ambition can *I* possibly gratify?

NEWMAN. Every one I possess—the wildest I ever entertained. No doubt you'll have to renounce your own; but I'll make that up to you.

CLAIRE. I haven't an ambition left (*takes away her hand and seats herself by table, left*)—not the dimmest ghost of one—unless it be to pass *unnoticed!*

NEWMAN. (*Laughing.*) Well, if it will help my case to promise it, I'll lock you up in my safe—I'll keep you back awhile. There's nothing to keep back about *me,* you know—the whole thing can come out. I'm all here, and wherever I am, I'm all there! I've no hidden vices nor nasty tricks. I'm kind (*his hand on her left shoulder*)—kind—(*takes her hand*)—kind. (*Carries her hand to his breast.*)

CLAIRE. (*Slowly, after remaining silent a moment.*) It's strange, Mr. Newman—you don't know how strange it is!

NEWMAN. That I should be in love with you? It would be a queer show if I wasn't!

CLAIRE. (*Rising.*) I don't mean that—I mean that I should trust you as I do.

NEWMAN. You *do* trust me? (*Putting both hands out—taking both her hands.*) That's just what I wanted to see!

CLAIRE. (*Going to fireplace.*) There are not many people I trust.

NEWMAN. You have had unhappy days—you have had unhappy years; I know that! But what on earth have you to do with them now? Turn your back on them forever!

CLAIRE. (*With her head on the mantel-*

---

[3] Strawnger
[4] la-ast.
[5] a-after
[6] mahn

shelf.) I'm *afraid* of happiness—that's what I trust least.

NEWMAN. It will return you good for evil! Is it the cruel failure that met you on the very threshold of life that has made you sceptical?—the fact that, ten years ago, you put your spare cash into a concern that turned out a swindle?

CLAIRE. I was only seventeen. But let that horrible time alone!

NEWMAN. I speak of it only to remind you that it's a reason the more for your having a better time now. The joys we've missed in youth are like back numbers and lost [7] umbrellas; we mustn't spend the rest of life wondering where they are! (*The music ceases.* CLAIRE *turns.*) Ah, Claire! (*Movement to embrace her.*)

CLAIRE. (*Stopping him with both hands up.*) Don't ask me why I say it, but please simply believe that I can't listen to you further till you have spoken to those whom I make it my law not to defy. (*Goes up, centre.*)

NEWMAN. (*At the fireplace.*) Do you mean Madame de Bellegarde and the Marquis?

CLAIRE. (*At the ottoman, her hands upon it.*) They are the heads of the family. Speak to *them* first—obtain *their* sanction.

NEWMAN. (*Following her up.*) I'll do anything in life to please you or to win you. (*With his hands on hers, on the ottoman.*) But doesn't it strike you that you and I together make the only "family" we need think of? You have only to say a word to become the head of mine!

CLAIRE. You must leave me my superstitions—they are all I have!

NEWMAN. *All?*—no sympathy with mine?

CLAIRE. (*At the table, left.*) That too would be a superstition!

NEWMAN. Forgive my profanity, but has your family got *two* heads—like some curious animal in a side-show?

CLAIRE. (*Abruptly, passionately.*) Yes—to make up for having no heart! (*Crosses to ottoman.*)

NEWMAN. You're more profane than I! Isn't this wonderful occasion in itself a practical sanction?

CLAIRE. (*Going round ottoman up to right centre.*) I advise you to get something more explicit.

NEWMAN. All right—I'll go and get it now.

CLAIRE. Don't do that—those crowded rooms are not the place to broach the subject. Are you in a great hurry?

NEWMAN. Did you ever see an American who wasn't?

CLAIRE. (*Going right.*) I'll find Urbain—I'll tell him that he'll oblige me by letting you speak to him.

NEWMAN. Oblige *you?* (CLAIRE *turns and smiles.*) Thank you for that! (*Exit* CLAIRE, *right. At fireplace.*) But how in creation comes it that the thought of her family scares her like a bad dream? What have they done to make her tread the world on tiptoe, as if she were passing and repassing a death-chamber? (*Re-enter* MRS. BREAD, *left. Seeing her.*) I wonder if I could get it out of this deep old lady!

MRS. BREAD. (*Who has gone straight to the buffet, accompanied by the same* FOOTMAN *who has come in with her before and who again carries a tray, to take cream and sugar from her, with which he immediately goes off.*) May I take the liberty of offering you a cup of tea, sir?

NEWMAN. I'll have one with pleasure. (MRS. BREAD *brings him a cup of tea, and he continues, sociably.*) Won't you take one yourself?

MRS. BREAD. (*Curtseying.*) Thank you, sir—not here!

NEWMAN. I'm so glad you speak English—it rests my muscles.

MRS. BREAD. I don't speak anything else. I'm a plain Wiltshire woman, sir.

NEWMAN. (*Laughing.*) Oh, plain. I've seen plainer! (*Drinking his tea, which he keeps in his hand during this dialogue.*) And what do you think of Paris?

MRS. BREAD. Oh I don't think of Paris, sir. I've been here more than forty years. I came over with Lady Emmeline. When others began to come—a year or two after —I was promoted to the supervision of the nurseries. I brought up the young people.

NEWMAN. The children? I wish you'd bring up mine! [8]

[7] lawst

[8] Maihne (drawn out)

MRS. BREAD. (*Staring.*) Yours, sir?

NEWMAN. I'll tell you later what I mean —you're such a venerable domestic presence!

MRS. BREAD. Oh, I keep my eye on most things, sir.

NEWMAN. I guess you've kept it on me, then!

MRS. BREAD. I've taken the liberty of observing you, sir.

NEWMAN. Well, I hope you're on my side. (*Giving back his cup.*)

MRS. BREAD. (*Taking cup.*) I think we're all on your side, sir. Even the Marquis must be—he's not often on any one's side!— for here he comes, apparently looking for you. He mustn't find me mixing with the company! (*Exit hastily, left, with teacup, while the* MARQUIS *comes in at the other door, right, crossing to left and bowing slightly to* NEWMAN.)

MARQUIS. As my sister tells me that you do me the honour to desire some conversation with me, we had better remain on this spot. I have mentioned the circumstance to my mother, who must have the predominant voice in our conference. She will join us here in a moment.

NEWMAN. My time is *all* at your service; but a moment is enough for what I have to say. (*Seats himself on ottoman.*) I have made a proposal of marriage to Madame de Cintré, and Madame de Cintré has told me she can give me no reply till I have received from your mother and yourself a declaration that won't put a spoke in our wheel. Hadn't we better get ahead? Hadn't you better *give* me that declaration on the spot? Now that you've *seen* my scheme, the great hospitality you have already shown me—especially this evening—leads me to hope *very* much, you'll put down your name.

MARQUIS. Such a name as ours is a good deal to put down! Of course I must mention that the idea that my sister should receive the attentions of a gentleman in trade has been something of a novelty.

NEWMAN. My dear sir, I'm no *longer* [9] in trade. If I were I shouldn't be fooling round here!

MARQUIS. But isn't the origin of your—a

—fortune commercial, industrial?

NEWMAN. Isn't the origin of all fortunes commercial, industrial? I have heard of people's losing money in all sorts of ways, but there's only one in which I ever heard of their making it.

MARQUIS. (*Smiling.*) I don't know—we have never made any.

NEWMAN. (*Rising, and with humorous eagerness.*) Do you want [10] to? I'll put you into any damned thing you like!

MARQUIS. You're most refreshing. It may be that the time has come when we should make some judicious concession to the age. (*Re-enter* VALENTIN, *right.*)

VALENTIN. What's that? My brother's making a judicious concession? That's a great historical event! My mother follows me, but she bids me inform you that nothing is to be concluded till she is on the ·field.

NEWMAN. Oh, I guess the battle's won!

VALENTIN. It can only be won according to the rules. You'll see them in a moment. (*Enter* MME. DE BELLEGARDE, *right, whom the* MARQUIS *rises to meet, offering her an armchair, left, in which she sits.*) Here they are: you can see they're pretty straight! (*Goes round to fireplace.*)

NEWMAN. (*Right centre.*) Dear Madam, we just received your commands [11] not to settle anything till you should be able to attend. But I guess we've got ahead of you, and that everything *is* settled. Ain't it, Marquis?

MARQUIS. (*Seating himself.*) My mother has the predominant voice.

MME. DE BELLEGARDE. (*To* MARQUIS.) Have you arranged with Mr. Newman that his man of business shall meet *our* man of business?

NEWMAN. Why, Marquise, what do you mean? I'm my *own* man [12] of business.

MME. DE BELLEGARDE. Then our solicitor will wait upon you.

NEWMAN. Your solicitor? What has he got to do with it?

VALENTIN. (*With his back to the fire.*) Everything, my candid Californian! I see you'll never divine, unless I drop it gently

---

9 lawnger

10 wauhnt

11 comma-a-nds.

12 mahn

into your ear, that they want to know what you're prepared to *do*.

NEWMAN. (*Staring.*) To "do"?

VALENTIN. For your portionless bride, as I may say!

NEWMAN. Why, I'm prepared to—*worship* her!

MME. DE BELLEGARDE. (*Smiling coldly.*) There are many ways of worshipping. We should be glad if, without prejudice to the others, you could make one of them consist of an adequate settlement.

NEWMAN. Do you mean put her into possession of my pile? With all my heart: as I told the Count, a month ago, she shall perch on top of it!

MME. DE BELLEGARDE. Excuse me if I remind you that we are without any definite information as to what your "pile" consists of.

NEWMAN. Why, of the principal precious metals, and a lot of other things. Come round and see me, and I'll tell you all about it!

MARQUIS. We shall have the honour of paying you a visit.

NEWMAN. That's all right. (*Seated on ottoman.*) When will you come?

MME. DE BELLEGARDE. The sooner the better—we'll come to-morrow.

NEWMAN. Won't you come round to *lunch?* I'll show you my new place. I've left that hotel—I've taken a big house.

MME. DE BELLEGARDE. A big house?

NEWMAN. A big house, with a big garden. There's another garden, too, in the rear of it, that I've made arrangements to add on.

MARQUIS. You'll have a great territory.

NEWMAN. Certainly I shall: a kind of virgin forest—the finest, greenest, airiest thing in Paris, with lots of margin and elbow-room.

MME. DE BELLEGARDE. Your margin must remind you of California.

NEWMAN. That's just why I bought it!

MARQUIS. You've *bought* it?

NEWMAN. For Madame de Cintré!

VALENTIN. (*Aside.*) They thought he had only hired it. Oh, he'll do!

NEWMAN. I'm having the whole place rearranged and furnished and decorated. You must tell me, and above all Madame de Cintré must tell me, how I had better have it fixed.

MME. DE BELLEGARDE. My daughter will accompany us.

NEWMAN. (*Turning to* VALENTIN.) That's just what I wanted to see! I'm fixing up the gardens too, and—just for the first ideas, in the whole thing—some clever *artistic* friends are helping me.

VALENTIN. (*Startled, aside.*) Artistic friends? Papa Nioche and Noémie, I'll be hanged!

NEWMAN. (*To* VALENTIN.) Of course you'll come too?

VALENTIN. Rather, my dear boy. (*Aside.*) Fancy Noémie let loose in California! I must go, if only to get her out of the way!

MME. DE BELLEGARDE. (*To* NEWMAN.) You may expect us early.

VALENTIN. The early bird takes the worm!

MME. DE BELLEGARDE. (*To* VALENTIN.) You're incorrigibly profane. Go away this moment and tell your sister to come to me here. (*Exit* VALENTIN, *right, while* MME. DE BELLEGARDE *continues, to* NEWMAN.) It's only fair I should warn you that I'm very proud—that I hold my head very high. Don't flatter yourself that my daughter isn't proud. The form is different, but the feeling is the same. Even Valentin is proud, if you touch the right spot—or the wrong one. Urbain, there, is proud; that you can see for yourself.

NEWMAN. (*Looking at the* MARQUIS.) Oh yes, I see! Well, put your pride in keeping your word to me, and you may all be a set of little Lucifers!

MARQUIS. (*Rising.*) Keep yours to *us,* sir.
(*Re-enter* MME. DE CINTRÉ, *right, and comes right centre.*)

NEWMAN. (*Rising.*) *My* word is to Madame de Cintré. I'll repeat it to her before you.

CLAIRE. (*To* MME. DE BELLEGARDE.) Valentin tells me you want me, mother.

MME. DE BELLEGARDE. Yes, so that we may hear what Mr. Newman promises.

NEWMAN. (*Taking* MME. DE CINTRÉ'S *hand.*) To make you as rich as I possibly can, and to make you far happier than you're rich. (MME. DE BELLEGARDE *rises; she and the* MARQUIS *go up left centre.*)

Edward Compton as Christopher Newman in *The American,* wearing the much-criticized outlandish overcoat

Edward Compton as Christopher Newman and Elizabeth Robins as Madame de Cintré in *The American,* 1891 Newman: "Do you know there is something I should like to form; it's formed with the lips."

Characters from Henry James's *The American*
From *Illustrated London News,* October 10, 1891

CLAIRE. (*After she has held his hand and looked at him gravely and in silence.*) What a pity Valentin couldn't have come back with me to hear you say that!

NEWMAN. What's the matter with him?

CLAIRE. Lord Deepmere pounced on him and walked him away.

MME. DE BELLEGARDE. Poor Lord Deepmere!

MARQUIS. He's *very* unreasonable! (*Exeunt, left,* MARQUIS *and* MME. DE BELLEGARDE.)

NEWMAN. (*Jubilant.*) It's all right—they've caught on! (*Going round the ottoman, he seats himself on it with* CLAIRE.) They're coming to see me to-morrow, to arrange some technicalities.

CLAIRE. Don't speak to me of your technicalities—I care nothing about them.

NEWMAN. They're not *mine*—they're *theirs!* Won't you give me a foretaste of happiness by coming too?

CLAIRE. I should like to see your house. I'll look at that.

NEWMAN. That ain't mine either—it's already yours.

CLAIRE. Shall you, then, insist on our living in Paris?

NEWMAN. Oh, yes—*insisting* will be quite in my line! The world's all before us—we'll go where you like.

CLAIRE. What then, will you do with the house?

NEWMAN. We'll give it to Valentine.

CLAIRE. I should like to see your great country.

NEWMAN. The land of gold—the blue Pacific? We'll start as soon as we're married.[13]

CLAIRE. You take my breath away.

NEWMAN. Didn't you take mine—the first time I ever saw you?

CLAIRE. You live too fast.

NEWMAN. It's you that make me—I've had to catch up! But after we're once off we shall go slower—to make it last!

CLAIRE. (*As if with vague uneasiness.*) Do you think it *will* last?

NEWMAN. Will the fish last in the sea?—will the stars last in the sky? Don't you feel safe?

CLAIRE. I shall (*hesitating a moment and smiling dimly*) in the blue Pacific!

NEWMAN. (*Laughing.*) You speak as if you were going to the bottom! (*With both her hands in his, drawing her closer.*) My own darling—we're going to the top!

CLAIRE. (*Closing her eyes an instant.*) You'll make me dizzy!

NEWMAN. You can be as dizzy as you like, with *my* arm round you! We're going up into the light and the sweet, high air, into the fields of flowers and the great places of love, where we shall look down with pity at the desert in which we didn't know each other.

CLAIRE. Ah, we're out of *that*—we *do* know each other!

NEWMAN. We shall have more to learn, but the more we do learn the more we shall like it. I shall find new things and bigger things to do, but it will be all for *you* I shall do them!

CLAIRE. You've done the newest—and (*smiling*) I think I may say the biggest!—in winning your victory to-night.

NEWMAN. Oh, I sha'n't rest on my laurels—there are always new worlds to conquer. We'll explore them and annex them together, and find at every turn some use that we can *be,* some good that we can *do.* The good that *you'll* do, dearest—

CLAIRE. (*Longingly, as he pauses from the fulness of his emotion.*) Ah! if you'll show me *that!*

NEWMAN. (*With ardent responsiveness.*) I'll show it to the whole *earth!* [14]

CLAIRE. (*Laying her hand upon his, with a deliberate movement of his [her?] own, the only one of this particular kind that she makes during the play.*) I'll follow you, I'll help you, I'll cherish you. But (*withdrawing her hand, and in another tone, half melancholy, half gay*) I may mention to you that, when I used to think, as a girl, of what I would do if I were to marry freely and by my own choice, I thought of a man different from you.

NEWMAN. That's nothing against me—your taste wasn't formed.[15]

---

[13] The conversation which follows between Newman and Claire was inserted by Henry James for the London production.

[14] The inserted conversation ends at this point.

[15] faawmed

CLAIRE. Have *you* formed it?

NEWMAN. (*Looking at her a moment.*) Do you know there's something I *should* like to form? It's formed with the lips!

CLAIRE. (*Rising.*) Not now—not here!

NEWMAN. (*Rising.*) To-morrow, then, when you *come?*

CLAIRE. (*Smiling.*) In that case I'm not so sure I shall come!

NEWMAN. (*Delighted with her.*) You *are* what I wanted to see! (*Kisses her hand.*)
(*Re-enter* VALENTIN, *right, and goes slowly left at once.*)

VALENTIN. If you've got so far as that, you had better go a little further! Just walk through the rooms together—show yourselves all over the place.

NEWMAN. (*Humorously, to* CLAIRE.) Didn't you tell me awhile ago that you wanted to pass unnoticed?

CLAIRE. (*Proudly.*) What I want is to show *you!*

VALENTIN. You've no time to lose, then.
(*Re-enter* MRS. BREAD, *left.*)

NEWMAN. We'll begin with Mrs. Bread. Mrs. Bread, give us your blessing.

MRS. BREAD. (*To* MME. DE CINTRÉ, *who comes to her and kisses her.*) I gave you them all, my sweet lady, when you needed them more! (MME. DE CINTRÉ *remains with her during the next words spoken by* NEWMAN *and* VALENTIN.)

NEWMAN. (*At back of armchair.*) What's the hitch?

VALENTIN. It will be a good precaution against hitches for you to go and bid everyone good night and tell as many people as you can. (NEWMAN *goes up.*)

NEWMAN. (*To* MME. DE CINTRÉ.) Please accept my arm. I'll tell every man and woman in the house. (*Mazurka music, pianissimo, off right.* MME. DE CINTRÉ *takes his arm. Exeunt* NEWMAN *and* MME. DE CINTRÉ, *right.*)

MRS. BREAD. (*Coming down and looking a moment at* VALENTIN, *who has thrown himself into armchair.*) I don't like my boy's looks. You're flushed and excited.

VALENTIN. Give me something cool to drink—I'm all right!

MRS. BREAD. A little iced lemonade, made by my own hands. (*She goes to the buffet, and comes back with a glass,* VALEN-TIN *meanwhile sitting in thought.*)

VALENTIN. (*After he has drunk the lemonade and given her back the glass.*) Dear old Catty, keep the heads of the family—or rather its feet—in the straight and narrow path!

MRS. BREAD. There's something you don't tell me.

VALENTIN. It's merely that our noble friend Deepmere is raging over the place like a young vindictive archangel, with a crush hat and a white waistcoat; he has cornered them there 'and is giving them a piece of his mind. But don't let me detain you—you must be wanted in the cloakroom.

MRS. BREAD. (*Looking round her.*) It doesn't matter; almost everyone's gone.

VALENTIN. Go and blow out the candles then.

MRS. BREAD. I'm afraid to leave you. Something's in the air—you're waiting for Lord Deepmere. Don't, don't have words with him. (*Exit, left.*)

VALENTIN. Not a word too much!
(*Re-enter* LORD DEEPMERE, *right.*)

DEEPMERE. You referred me to the responsible parties, and I have seen the responsible parties. You told me I should find you here—

VALENTIN. And you find me here!

DEEPMERE. I congratulate myself, because it gives me an opportunity to tell you that I have had the satisfaction of convicting Madame de Bellegarde and your brother of gross and shameless duplicity. They've deceived me, they've outraged me, and I think they won't soon forget the five minutes I've just had the honour of spending with them!

VALENTIN. (*Rising.*) *I* certainly sha'n't, milord! [16]

DEEPMERE. But I've not done with them yet—I've still my reparation to demand.

VALENTIN. (*After an instant.*) May I consider that you demand it of *me?*

DEEPMERE. My complaint's of your brother—it's from *him* the apology should come.

VALENTIN. I'm afraid we don't make apologies. But we embrace each other's

---

[16] The next six speeches were inserted for the London production.

quarrels.

DEEPMERE. Oh, the Marquis doesn't quarrel—he gets out of the way!

VALENTIN. You see *I* don't, *milord.*

DEEPMERE. Oh, I don't accuse *you* of double dealing! If you've tried to trip me up from the first, you've done it frankly—you've done it consistently, you've done it elsewhere as well as here!

VALENTIN. The less you say about elsewhere the better. *Here* will do.

DEEPMERE. (*After a moment.*) It will do very well, then—to choose another place.

VALENTIN. A couple of our friends will do it for us. Mine will be instantly ready to meet any gentlemen you may designate.

DEEPMERE. The earlier the better. I shall go straight home. Good night.

VALENTIN. (*Right centre.*) Good night! (*As* LORD DEEPMERE *is going at back to left.*) I may just mention the circumstance that it would be a convenience to me not to go far.

DEEPMERE. The nearer the better.

VALENTIN. There are quiet places in Paris—with a little ingenuity.

DEEPMERE. The quieter the better. Any friends of yours will be sure to be ingenious. Good night.

VALENTIN. Good night. (*They formally bow to each other. Exit* LORD DEEPMERE, *left, after which* VALENTIN, *alone, remains a moment in thought.*) No, no; I mustn't be out of it. (*Goes to the fireplace.*) Who was it was talking of a big disused garden—a tract of country in the midst of old Louis Quatorze mansions? By Jove, it was Newman himself—the convenience that man is! (*Looking at his watch.*) Hallo—it's nearly to-morrow now. I must put my hand on a couple of the right ones—all the men have gone. It's not a nice thing to have to tell them; for there's no doubt Deepmere has been trifled with. Bah! I'll tell them something else. One has to stand up for one's nearest and dearest, even when one knows what they are! (*The music ceases. As* VALENTIN *is going off he is met by the* MARQUIS, *who re-enters hastily, right.*)

MARQUIS. (*Breathless.*) Have you seen Lord Deepmere?—do you know where he is?

VALENTIN. (*Aside.*) That's the sort of thing they're up to! Do they want a little more? (*Aloud.*) I haven't the least idea of his lordship's whereabouts.

MARQUIS. Your mother wishes to speak to him—I hope he hasn't gone! (*Exit* MARQUIS, *rapidly, left.*)

VALENTIN. (*Alone.*) My mother wishes—? God forgive me, if he's not, they want to catch him again before he has time to cool! He has poured forth rent-rolls and vouchers like scalding water, and, seeing that they dropped him too soon, they want to pick him up again! Poor Newman! (*Goes right, and as he is going off meets* NEWMAN *coming in. Re-enter* NEWMAN, *right. They come down,* NEWMAN, *left;* VALENTIN, *right.*)

NEWMAN. Well, we made the grand tour—everyone seemed to like it. (*Seats himself in armchair.*)

VALENTIN. I don't see how they can get out of that. What have you done with Claire?

NEWMAN. Your mother called her off—she must have sent her to bed.

VALENTIN. That's where we all ought to be.

NEWMAN. I want to sit up *all night*—such a grand night as this!

VALENTIN. How much you're in love! You ought to get home to your dreams.

NEWMAN. To my dreams?

VALENTIN. Make the most of them!

NEWMAN. (*Rising and looking at* VALENTIN.) What's the matter with *you?* (*Movement from* VALENTIN.) I'll go as soon as I've seen Claire again—she hasn't bidden me good night. (*Looking about and going up and round to right.*)

VALENTIN. How can she, if she has been sent to bed?

NEWMAN. She ain't a little girl of six! She won't *go* to bed—or else she'll get up again.

VALENTIN. She's in love too, then!

NEWMAN. (*Still looking.*) She'll make me doubt it if she doesn't come back a moment.

VALENTIN. Well, I must go to bed at any rate. (*Goes up to left.*)

NEWMAN. Good night, then. Take care of yourself.

VALENTIN. (*About to go, left, coming down again.*) Do you know I've got an idea? I should like to come in when my mother and brother are with you to-morrow —rather on the quiet.

NEWMAN. I'd rather you came with a band of music! [17]

VALENTIN. No; I should like to appear at the crisis—unexpectedly, dramatically!

NEWMAN. Hide under the table, then, and suddenly pop out.

VALENTIN. I've thought of something better—since you've got a garden.

NEWMAN. A garden?

VALENTIN. The "virgin forest," you know —the big place you swaggered about. I'll come in that way—

NEWMAN. You may come down the chimney if you like!

VALENTIN. Is there room there to hide?

NEWMAN. (*Staring.*) In the chimney?

VALENTIN. No, no; in the virgin forest! How do you get in?

NEWMAN. Why, by the gates on the three back streets. I'll send you the keys. (*Moves to centre.*)

VALENTIN. (*Aside.*) Bravo! (*Aloud.*) I'm going to play a little game.

NEWMAN. Oh, I know your little games!

VALENTIN. So you'll send me the keys early?

NEWMAN. With the peep of dawn.

VALENTIN. God bless you! (*They shake hands.*) Good night. (*Goes up.*) Good night! (*Exit* VALENTIN, *left.*)

NEWMAN. (*Alone, looking after him a moment.*) What in creation's his little game?—what's his elaborate plan? (*Re-enter* MME. DE BELLEGARDE, *right.*) They are elaborate, over here! (*Moves to right.*)

MME. DE BELLEGARDE. Mr. Newman? (*Coldly.*) I had an impression you had taken leave of us.

NEWMAN. Not yet, Madam! I've not yet taken leave of your daughter.

MME. DE BELLEGARDE. Is that ceremony indispensable?

NEWMAN. (*After a moment's look at her.*) I think that in this house *every* ceremony is! Will you be so good as to tell me where you *left* Madame de Cintré?

MME. DE BELLEGARDE. You must find her yourself!

NEWMAN. I'll try! (*Exit* NEWMAN, *right.*)

MME. DE BELLEGARDE. (*Alone.*) Find her if you can! (*Seats herself on ottoman.*)
(*Re-enter the* MARQUIS, *left upper entrance.*)

MARQUIS. Deepmere has left the house. (*Crossing at back.*) Damn his manners! (*Goes to fireplace.*)

MME. DE BELLEGARDE. Do you think his manners would have been better if he had *stayed*, after that scene? Where's Valentin? [18]

MARQUIS. He has also gone out.

MME. DE BELLEGARDE. At this hour?

MARQUIS. You know his habits! I saw him cross the court with two gentlemen.

MME. DE BELLEGARDE. To begin the evening, I suppose. A merry party!

MARQUIS. Frankly speaking, they must be merrier than we.

MME. DE BELLEGARDE. It was a bad quarter of an hour; but I'm not in despair. Lord Deepmere will come back.

MARQUIS. Very likely—if you send for him. But haven't you had enough?

MME. DE BELLEGARDE. One can never have enough of hearing about such a magnificent property. The whole thing cleared —a beautiful fresh start. Four English seats and a house in Park Lane.

MARQUIS. He's better, after all, than Newman!

MME. DE BELLEGARDE. Yes, and he's a gentleman.

MARQUIS. You felt he was a gentleman when he let you have it? You sent him away, a month ago, to dot his *i*'s, and I hope you felt he was dotting them!

MME. DE BELLEGARDE. He has dotted them with great gold pieces! He has taken the bad taste of your American out of my mouth.

MARQUIS. Ah, we took a bigger bite of the poor American than we *can* swallow! But Mr. Newman, to do him justice, has never insulted us.

MME. DE BELLEGARDE. He will—he will! Give him time.

MARQUIS. Definitely, then, even after to-

[17] James suggests in a pencilled note that this be spoken "A little in the nose."

[18] The next six speeches were inserted for the London production.

night you mean to throw him over?

MME. DE BELLEGARDE. How could I do it before I knew what we have missed? But we haven't missed it yet!

MARQUIS. I've known you long, mother; but there are still moments when you frighten me. What do you mean to do?

MME. DE BELLEGARDE. (*Rising.*) I must think it over. I'll tell you to-morrow.

MARQUIS. But to-morrow we go to the American's.

MME. DE BELLEGARDE. That will be just our opportunity—it's providential.

MARQUIS. The day after our promise? And on what pretext?

MME. DE BELLEGARDE. I'll find a pretext! (*After a pause.*) We made no promise to Mr. Newman that didn't strictly depend on his conditions.

MARQUIS. He'll make any conditions we like.

MME. DE BELLEGARDE. I defy him to make any *I* like! (*Re-enter* MRS. BREAD, *right. As she sees* MRS. BREAD.) Hold your tongue and give me your arm to my room. (*To* MRS. BREAD, *crossing her.*) Everything is upside down, but we shall recover ourselves to-morrow.

MRS. BREAD. Yes, my lady: after such an affair!

MME. DE BELLEGARDE. We shall have a grand putting to rights. Is Mr. Newman gone?

MRS. BREAD. I believe he has just left the house.

MME. DE BELLEGARDE. Then see that the lights are out and that everything is closed. (*Exeunt* MME. DE BELLEGARDE *and* MARQUIS, *left.*)

MRS. BREAD. (*Alone.*) I'm afraid nothing will ever be open again! (*Re-enter* NEWMAN, *right. To* NEWMAN.) I just told a fib for you, sir—I knew you weren't gone.

NEWMAN. I want no fibs—I only want Madame de Cintré. (*Goes to right.*)

MRS. BREAD. She's coming—she took refuge with *me*.

NEWMAN. Refuge? (*Re-enter* MME. DE CINTRÉ, *right.* NEWMAN *opens his arms to her.*) Be so good as to understand that your only refuge is in my arms! (MME. DE CINTRÉ *throws herself into them as the Curtain falls.*)

ACT THIRD

A large deep saloon in the fine old house into which NEWMAN *has just moved. The whole place handsome, but rather bare; slight disorder, signs of recent arrival. It must be sufficiently visible that the rooms belong to a set of apartments on the ground floor. The main entrance from outside, is to the left, considerably down to the front. Further up, between left and middle, a wide, high window, opening into the great court of the hôtel. In the middle a door, draped in old tapestry, opening on a passage which leads to a bedroom. To the right of this, balancing with the window, a large open door, leading to staircase and rooms above. Quite at the right, near the front, the entrance of a conservatory which communicates with the grounds.* NOÉMIE, *expensively and showily dressed, as if with the money extracted from* NEWMAN, *and divested of her jacket and gloves, though wearing a* very smart hat, discovered just after she has hung up, in a florid gilt frame, one of her garish "copies."

NOÉMIE. (*On a step-ladder.*) With all the rest upstairs, this makes the seventeenth; I am working them off! (*Enter, left, hat in hand,* VALENTIN DE BELLEGARDE.) Good morning; you get up early!

VALENTIN. So do you, if you come to that!

NOÉMIE. Oh, we've been here an hour—hanging pictures! Papa has gone to get more cord.

VALENTIN. (*Who has looked first on table, left, and then looked, in a different manner, out of window.*) You seem indeed to have the place to yourself. I haven't met a soul.

NOÉMIE. The establishment is still very small.

VALENTIN. Does it consist entirely of *you*?

NOÉMIE. I'm not a member of it—I'm only forming it. We want none but the best people, and they're not so easy to meet.

VALENTIN. (*Looking on piano.*) One of the best people was rather easy to meet when you met the master of this house! May I inquire if he's still in bed?

NOÉMIE. For what do you take him? He dashed out half an hour ago.

VALENTIN. (*Aside.*) Confound him! What then shall I do for my keys? (*Looking vaguely about him.*)

NOÉMIE. (*Coming down from her ladder.*) Is there anything particular you want of him?

VALENTIN. (*Moving toward sofa.*) He promised to do something for me—very early; but he hasn't done it. It doesn't matter; I daresay I can get on. (*He continues to look, covertly, for the keys, and suddenly spies them in a silver bowl on the table, left. Aside.*) Bravo!—there they are. If I could only pick them up!

NOÉMIE. (*Who has seated herself at piano, suddenly turns round on stool.*) You must excuse Mr. Newman if he has forgotten—he's so awfully full of something else. Has he told you about his necklace?—the finest pearls that can be found in Paris—half a dozen rows! He has gone out to buy them, but he'll be back to receive his visitors. (*Suddenly arranging her hat and her hair.*) Do I look very badly?

VALENTIN. Charmingly ill! Are *you* going to help to receive them? See for yourself if you're not in the best form to make an impression.

NOÉMIE. For a wonder, there isn't a mirror in the room; but there are fifty upstairs. Excuse me a moment. (*Exit NOÉMIE, right upper entrance.*)

VALENTIN. *Vanitas vanitatum*—now for my keys! (*Snatches them, at the table, out of the silver bowl.*) These must be right—yes, they're labelled. With those good fellows waiting for me at the back gates I must pass through the grounds and admit them from the inside. The very absurdity of such a place is our protection! If we've only not kept the others waiting! (*Just as he has thrust the keys into his pocket and is hurrying off, he finds himself face to face with* NIOCHE. *Enter* NIOCHE, *left with big roll of red cord.*)

NIOCHE. Our noble friend all alone?

VALENTIN. Your daughter left me this moment. I won't wait to see her again, but please tell her I left these words for her: "Good-bye—be a good girl!" (*Exit* VALENTIN, *rapidly, through the conservatory.*)

NIOCHE. (*Alone, putting cord down on table, right, and staring after him a moment.*) What's the matter with him? She's good enough for *me*!

(*Enter* NEWMAN, *left.*)

NEWMAN. You're just what I want to see.

NIOCHE. Comte Valentin has this moment gone out, but you won't have met him—he went *that* way.

NEWMAN. (*Who carries a small box, reminded, snapping his fingers.*) Ah, poor dear fellow, he must have come for his keys—why couldn't I remember? But it's all right (*looking into the silver bowl*); you gave them to him.

NIOCHE. Begging your pardon, sir—I gave him nothing.

NEWMAN. Then whom else did he see?

NIOCHE. He appeared to have seen my daughter.

NEWMAN. Oh then, *she* gave them. If he has got them, for some fantastic purpose—some "little *game*"—it doesn't matter how he came by them. (*Opening the flat jewelcase which he carries in his hand and exhibiting its contents to* NIOCHE.) I could think of nothing but *this* (*re-enter* NOÉMIE *without her hat*) till I had scrambled out and got hold of it. (*As* NIOCHE, *clasping his hands, gives signs of wonder and admiration.*) Do you think she'll *like* it?

NIOCHE. Your beautiful bride, sir? Just try her!

NEWMAN. (*Left centre to* NOÉMIE, *who comes down.*) I'll try *you*, Miss Noémie. (*Showing her the pearls.*) Do you think they're fine?

NOÉMIE. (*Taking the case from him, with an emotion that breaks out as soon as she looks at it.*) Oh, the lovely darlings! It's *you* that are fine, Mr. Newman!

NEWMAN. I shall be finer when I've put on some clothes. (*Crosses her, going up right.*) Look at it well, and tell me if there's anything the matter with it. (*Exit* NEW-

MAN, *right upper entrance.*)

NOÉMIE. (*Gazes at the jewels for some minutes; after which she raises her eyes in silence to her father's.*) To think we're going to lose such a man.

NIOCHE. (*Going to sit at top of table.*) It's very dreadful—but there are others besides. I found a letter for you at home. (*Carefully extracting the missive from an ancient pocket-book.*) A letter with a coronet on the paper.

NOÉMIE. (*Taking the letter, after having deposited the jewel-case reverently on table, right.*) Yes, there are others besides. It's from Lord Deepmere, about a copy he wants me to do. I shall have to write three lines of answer—just wait for me. (*Goes up to door, right.*)

NIOCHE. (*Crossing to sofa.*) I should tell you Comte Valentin left a message for you —a solemn injunction to be a good girl.

NOÉMIE. I'll be too good for *him!* (*Exit NOÉMIE, right.*)

NIOCHE. (*Alone, goes to the table, and carefully lifting the pearl necklace out of its case, holds it to the light and looks at it, examines it like an old Jew.*) Does he want me to see if there's anything the matter with it? The only thing that's the matter with it is that it isn't *ours!* (*Enter MME. DE BELLEGARDE, left, and stands on the threshold a moment with her glass up, watching him before he sees her. As soon as he does so he quickly puts down the necklace, rubbing his hands, and bowing and backing as she advances.*)

MME. DE BELLEGARDE. (*Aside.*) What an extraordinary person—an old pedlar with jewels! (*Aloud.*) If you're a servant, you had better have been at your post. For want of some one to announce me, I've made my way in alone. My son, who accompanies me, is wandering off into the court in quest of assistance.

NIOCHE. (*Obsequiously, apologetically.*) The staff is only half sketched out!

MME. DE BELLEGARDE. Is that the way you sketch it? (*Re-enter NOÉMIE, right upper entrance.*) Announce Madame de Bellegarde.

NOÉMIE. (*Aside.*) Madame de Bellegarde? I *do* help to receive them! (*Advances and curtsies low to MME. DE BELLEGARDE.*) Mad-

ame! (MME. DE BELLEGARDE *goes up, left, looking about her.* NOÉMIE *gives her father a note.*) Here are two words, in answer to the note—to be taken immediately.

NIOCHE. (*With the note.*) I must first let Mr. Newman know—

NOÉMIE. Never mind that—*I'll* let Mr. Newman know.

NIOCHE. (*Crossing to left.*) Just as you direct. (*About to retire, bowing and retreating before MME. DE BELLEGARDE.*) Madame!

MME. DE BELLEGARDE. (*Having, on NOÉMIE's appearance, gazed at her in amazement, without acknowledging in any manner her salutation, aside.*) A bold young woman—dressed like a mountebank and quite at home! (*Aloud to NIOCHE.*) Look for Monsieur le Marquis, and tell him where I am.

NIOCHE. (*Left down, obsequious, as before.*) Madame! (*Exit NIOCHE, left down, with note, while MME. DE BELLEGARDE scans NOÉMIE from head to foot.*)

NOÉMIE. (*Aside.*) Mercy, how she glowers! (*Aloud, as if going.*) Shall I have the honour of announcing Madame la Marquise?

MME. DE BELLEGARDE. Wait till I've been rejoined by my son. (*Aside, seating herself on sofa.*) I'll go into this. (*Aloud, after another stern survey of NOÉMIE.*) May I inquire if *you're* a member of the staff?

NOÉMIE. (*Mystified.*) Of the staff?

MME. DE BELLEGARDE. Perhaps you attend to the correspondence.

NOÉMIE. (*With spirit, conscious of MME. DE BELLEGARDE's increasing irony.*) I attend to everything that Mr. Newman asks of me—in the way of friendship.

MME. DE BELLEGARDE. (*Aside.*) Friendship? (*Remembering.*) Ah yes, the clever artistic friends; this is one, and the old pedlar with the pearls is another. (*After another look at NOÉMIE.*) I think I can guess what *she* peddles! (*Aloud.*) Mr. Newman is to be congratulated on your valuable services.

NOÉMIE. (*Not at all disconcerted.*) To render such services to Mr. Newman is a great happiness.

MME. DE BELLEGARDE. You certainly look quite peculiarly happy!

NOÉMIE. (*Understanding and stung.*) It's more than I can say of you, Madame!

MME. DE BELLEGARDE. (*Aside.*) The brazen creature! (*Aloud.*) I didn't come here at this hour of the morning (*enter, on the left, the* MARQUIS DE BELLEGARDE) to encounter impudence and vice!

NOÉMIE. (*Smarting, outraged.*) Quelle horreur! (*She checks herself on seeing the* MARQUIS; *then aside.*) Gracious, he's not much like the Count. (*Aloud, with high superiority, while the* MARQUIS *moves round to back.*) I'll tell Mr. Newman you're here, Madame, but I shall describe you in my own terms! (*On the threshold she stops and curtsies exclusively to the* MARQUIS.) Monsieur! (*Exit* NOÉMIE *by the stairs, right.*)

MARQUIS. (*Up right centre, looking round him after he has put his hat and stick on piano.*) What a wonderful place and what wonderful people! to say nothing (*at table, right*) of wonderful jewels tossed about with wonderful cigars!

MME. DE BELLEGARDE. Be firm—he'll try to corrupt us. The pearls are of course a present for Claire.

MARQUIS. (*Taking a cigar out of the box and sniffing it appreciatively.*) Perhaps the cigars are a present for *me!*

MME. DE BELLEGARDE. Be firm—be firm!

MARQUIS. (*Sniffing still at his cigar.*) I'll be a rock!

MME. DE BELLEGARDE. I told you I would find a pretext. Very well, I *have* found a pretext.

MARQUIS. (*Vague, with his cigar.*) And pray what may it be?

(*Re-enter* CHRISTOPHER NEWMAN, *right, very freshly and handsomely dressed, as if to meet his intended; with white flowers in his buttonhole, quite like a bridegroom.*)

MME. DE BELLEGARDE. (*Becoming aware of* NEWMAN, *who, on the threshold, looks at them a moment, while her son quickly drops his cigar back into the box.*) See for yourself!

NEWMAN. You're just what I wanted to see! (*Coming down.*) Make yourselves at home! Claire has gone [1] straight into the grounds?

MME. DE BELLEGARDE. (*After a short silence, during which she exchanges a look with the* MARQUIS.) My daughter has not come with us.

NEWMAN. (*Centre.*) Not come with you? But you promised, and *she* promised!

MARQUIS. (*Seating himself at chair, left of table right.*) My sister's promises are her own affair!

NEWMAN. But yours, Marquis, are mine! I'm greatly disappointed.

MME. DE BELLEGARDE. I'm afraid we've more disappointments than that for you!

NEWMAN. (*Looking from one to the other.*) Look here, my good friends, you don't mean to say you're going to back out!

MME. DE BELLEGARDE. Remember what a very little way we've come in. Fortunately—after what we've just seen!

NEWMAN. (*Staring.*) What you've just seen?

MME. DE BELLEGARDE. A flaunting young woman, on a footing of familiarity—of authority.

NEWMAN. Little Noémie? [2] Do you object to little Noémie? [3] (*Perplexed.*) Ah yes, she told me you were rather rough with her!

MME. DE BELLEGARDE. Rough with her? Do you expect me to bow down to your (*she stops a moment, checked a little by* NEWMAN's *look; then in a' slightly different tone*)—your intimate female friends?

MARQUIS. (*Aside, as his mother's tactics dawn upon him.*) I see—magnificent mother!

NEWMAN. I don't know what you're talking about! That young lady's a charming artist [4]—she does odd *jobs* for me.

MARQUIS. (*Aside.*) That's exactly what we suppose!

MME. DE BELLEGARDE. Your defence of her is compromising! It's even more fortunate than I could suspect that Mme. de Cintré remained at home. I don't mean to say for a moment that we could have apprehended such an encounter. She stayed simply as an unmistakable sign to you that she withdraws from her engagement. (*She*

---

[1] gawne

[2] eee
[3] eee
[4] artust

rises; the MARQUIS *rises.*)

NEWMAN. (*Falling back to chair up right centre.*) An unmistakable sign? Do you expect me to *take* that?

MME. DE BELLEGARDE. You can take it or leave it. It's what we came to tell you. (*Moves over to her son.*)

MARQUIS. We said we would come, and we *have* come! (*Goes to the top of table.*)

NEWMAN. (*Going to table right, and mechanically offering* MME. DE BELLEGARDE *a seat.*) She sends me no message (*raising his hand to his head*)—no explanation?

MME. DE BELLEGARDE. (*Seated on chair left of table right.*) She gave us no fine phrases to bring with us; she trusted *us* to explain!

NEWMAN. To explain that she throws me over—without pity, without remorse?

MME. DE BELLEGARDE. She recognises to the full that it took but a few hours to let daylight into her delusion, and that the matter has gone such a very short distance as to leave us at liberty to request that it shall go no further.

NEWMAN. No *further?* After [5] we blazed through the rooms and announced our engagement to five hundred people?

MME. DE BELLEGARDE. You made too much noise—you must pay for your advertisement!

NEWMAN. And must *she* pay too? She told me she wanted every one to know.

MME. DE BELLEGARDE. Now she wants them to know something else.

NEWMAN. Something else indeed! That you're incapable of keeping common faith, of being honest for twenty-four hours!

MME. DE BELLEGARDE. (*To her son.*) Didn't I tell you he would insult us? (*To* NEWMAN, *rising and coming centre, while the* MARQUIS *steps below table.*) It's now that we're honest, quite as honest as you, even if we're a good deal less rude! We're honest in telling you thus frankly and promptly that, after all's said and done, we *can't* make you harmonise with our traditions, our associations, our ideals, with our prejudices, if you choose to call them so! Call them even narrow, call them bigoted, if you will—they are, after all,

_____
[5] A-a-fter

our religion, our faith, the faith of our ancestors. It has come over us, with the wholesome morning light, which restores the true proportions of things and the true perspective of honour, that we shrink from an intensely new responsibility.

MARQUIS. (*His hand in his waistcoat.*) That of breaking the long chain of an inveterate, a sacred observance. The daughters of our house have, for ages, never contracted alliances but with those of our own species.

NEWMAN. (*Left centre.*) Your species, Marquis? (*With his hands behind his back.*) Ain't that rather hard to find?

MME. DE BELLEGARDE. (*Passing her hands into her son's arm.*) We're quite conscious that we're not like all the world; those who cling to lost causes are certainly less in fashion than the representatives of trade! Let me add, before we retire, that we made no promise to you that didn't explicitly depend on your meeting our conditions.

NEWMAN. And what conditions have I failed to meet? You haven't even mentioned one of them.

MME. DE BELLEGARDE. I'll mention one now. Your having a decent house!

NEWMAN. You go back to *that* folly? It's too *monstrous!* What do you want me to do with the poor girl?

MME. DE BELLEGARDE. Anything in the world you like!

MARQUIS. (*Looking at the stitching of his glove.*) Only wait till we get out of the house! (*He gives his mother his arm to leave the place as they have come in.*)

NEWMAN. I refuse to accept your statement that Madame de Cintré has given her assent to this hideous proceeding. She's not a child—she's not a slave. She's a woman grown—she's her own mistress. What have you done to her—what have you done *with* her?

MME. DE BELLEGARDE. (*Going toward table, right, with* MARQUIS.) My happy power is in the grateful submission of my family. Filial obedience is the oldest tradition of our race. (*She leaves the* MARQUIS's *arm.*)

NEWMAN. Filial obedience be— (*Pulls up short, then with an abrupt change of tone, a visible, successful effort to be heroically reasonable and conciliatory.*) Let me then do all possible justice to your traditions. I understand [6] you've got peculiar ideas—I've noticed that before. I beg your pardon if I've offended you with wild and extravagant words. A man can't smile and bow when you pluck up the fairest flower that ever took root in his life! (*Goes left, and round to centre.*)

MME. DE BELLEGARDE. He can't smile and bow, but when he's face to face with a dead wall he can have the intelligence to see it and turn round. He can be clever enough for that.

MARQUIS. (*Fatuously, repeating.*) He can be clever enough for that!

NEWMAN. He must try and be as clever as *you*, Marquis. (*Goes up towards right upper entrance.*) You can't expect me to let you go without a protest, without a supplication. Pity me enough to think it over once more—not to turn your backs on me yet—to stay a little longer. Be generous, Madame de Bellegarde—just wait ten minutes!

MME. DE BELLEGARDE. What are we to wait for?

NEWMAN. For that clever boy Valentine. He'll be on my side, and the discussion will therefore be fairer. It's past [7] the hour —he'll turn up any minute; and I ask [8] of you but the common charity of this little delay. (*The MARQUIS goes up. Aside, anxiously looking at his watch.*) Why in creation doesn't his little game come off? [9] (*Takes MME. DE BELLEGARDE's hand and leads her up.*) You said you would look at my house, and you haven't looked at anything, for this is the meanest part. Go through it all, take your time, [10] think the whole thing over!

MME. DE BELLEGARDE. (*Smiling.*) Don't say we don't make concessions. [11]

NEWMAN. Ah, make them to Valentine!

-----

[6] sta-and
[7] pahst
[8] ahsk
[9] awf
[10] taihme (drawn out)
[11] This speech and the next were altered by Henry James in his copy from:
MME. DE BELLEGARDE. (*Moving to right upper entrance.*) We're willing to stretch a point —for five minutes.

(*Escorting them.*) That leads to all sorts of fine places, and to the big rooms above. (*Exeunt* MME. DE BELLEGARDE *and* MARQUIS, *right upper entrance.* NEWMAN *looks after them a moment.*) Why, they're regular old serpents! (*Snapping his fingers.*) Ah! (*Seeing* NIOCHE, *who re-enters, left down.*) You're just what I want to see!

NIOCHE. A lady, in a cab, to speak to you, sir!

NEWMAN. A lady—in a cab? Thank God, [12] it's Claire! (*Enter* MRS. BREAD, *ushered by* NIOCHE, *who goes round to right of* NEWMAN.) Ah no, but some better news! Delighted to see you, Mrs. Bread. (*To* NIOCHE.) Do me this service, quickly: go straight up there and join a lady and a gentleman who have just left me and are going through the house. Show them the whole place—spare them *nothing*—keep them as long as you *can!* (*Banging down his hand on piano.*)

NIOCHE. (*Going.*) Oh, I know how, sir— I'll put them through! (*Exit* NIOCHE, *right upper entrance.*)

NEWMAN. (*To* MRS. BREAD, *who is dressed for travelling.*) Where's Madame de Cintré?

MRS. BREAD. She sent me to tell you, sir—to *beg* you to forgive her.

NEWMAN. Forgive her? Then she *has* broken faith?

MRS. BREAD. She has broken her heart— that's what she has broken! We're going to Fleurières. (*After a look from* NEWMAN.) The grey, grim château of the Bellegardes, far from Paris. We take the midday train.

NEWMAN. Then she flies from me— without an explanation, without a look?

MRS. BREAD. She flies from her mother, sir—my lady has come down on us. My lady *can* come down!

NEWMAN. I know she can. She's down here!

MRS. BREAD. There has been an awful scene at home.

NEWMAN. And the Countess *has* yielded? —she has given me up?

NEWMAN. Valentin will be here *before* that (*Escorting,* etc.)
[12] Gawd

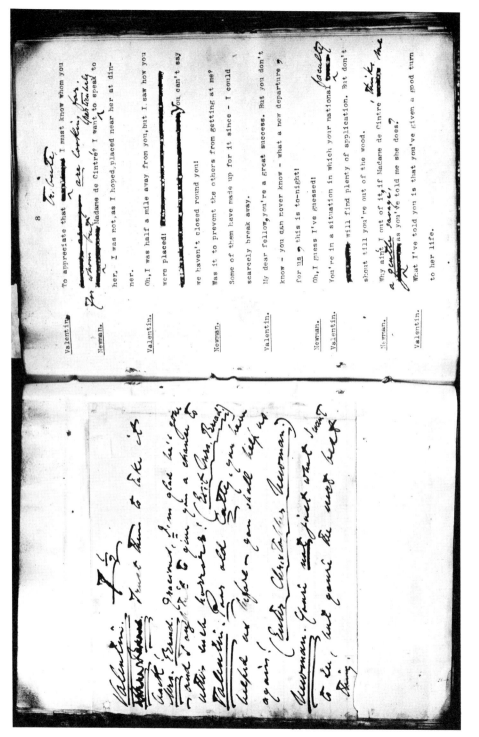

James's revisions of the original manuscript of *The American* (Act II), pp. 7 and 8

Mme.de B.	What are we to wait for?
Newman.	For that ~~dear~~ *clever* boy Valentine. He promised me he ~~would~~ come, *and he's a man of resources.*
Mme.de ~~B.~~	~~Admirbut good~~
Newman.	He'll be on my side, and the discussion will there- fore be fairer. He'll back me up, he'll help me to talk to you, to be eloquent, to be irresistible. It's *pahst* past his hour - he'll turn up any minute; and I *ahsk* ~~ask~~ of you but the common charity of this little delay. (Aside, anxiously looking at his watch:) Why, in crea- tion doesn't his little game come off? *awf*?
Marquis.	~~He's not to be counted on~~ @ Your side, as you call ~~it, abandons you~~
Newman.	You said you ~~would~~ look at my house, and you haven't *meanest* looked at anything, for this is the ~~poorest~~ part. Go through it all and tell me if there are any little *like - or you* ~~things you don't like.~~ Amuse yourselves, take your *tachme (drawn out,)* time, think the whole thing over!
Mme.de B.	Really, if you wish to dazzle ~~me~~ *us* you have already seen that we can stare at the sun. *mea on!*
Newman.	~~Since at the moon there~~ *Well, now you* can *stare at the moon.* *=1 re*
Mme.de B.	We ~~are~~ willing to stretch a point - for five minutes. ⊙

The American accent as spelled out by Henry James for Edward
Compton in the Southport text of *The American* (Act III)

MRS. BREAD. She'll write and tell you—as soon as she can turn round.

NEWMAN. (*Bitterly.*) Oh, don't let her turn round any more—she has turned round enough!

MRS. BREAD. She'll explain everything—she'll write you a beautiful letter.

NEWMAN. Does she expect a beautiful letter to satisfy me? I can't marry [13] a beautiful letter!

MRS. BREAD. No more you can, sir! Only that was my message—and I must go!

NEWMAN. (*Pleading.*) Let me go *with* you—let me see her again!

MRS. BREAD. There isn't a minute, and it would only be a difficulty where there are more than enough already. Be patient! (NEWMAN *goes right.*) The future's dark; but I'll try to help you.

NEWMAN. I shall hold you to that! But (*smiting his forehead*) I'm too *distracted!* (*Drops into chair, right.*) Have you seen Count Valentine?

MRS. BREAD. That's just what I wanted to ask *you.* I'm afraid something's in the wind: his valet spoke to me an hour ago—he has noticed things and he's worried.

NEWMAN. What is he worried about?

MRS. BREAD. The danger of a bloody meeting.

NEWMAN. A bloody meeting? Do you mean a duel? (*Rising.*) With *whom?*

MRS. BREAD. With poor Lord Deepmere—God forgive him!

NEWMAN. The young man [14] with a grievance? [15] And what should they fight about?

MRS. BREAD. The honour of the house of Bellegarde.

NEWMAN. O—oh, that's not worth it!

MRS. BREAD. Tell them so, then—prevent it: before the Countess has an idea!

NEWMAN. She shall have *no* idea—if I can stamp it out!

MRS. BREAD. God keep them, then! God keep *you*—God keep us all! (*Exit* MRS. BREAD *rapidly, left down.*)

NEWMAN. (*Alone, wondering, thinking.*) His valet's worried—he has noticed things? If it comes to that, I've noticed things too! the keys, the grounds, the "virgin forest," his little game! Is *that* damned foolery his little game? (*Strides to conservatory, as if to look out, but turns away quickly.*) Of course they're ever so far away—out of sight and sound! (*Goes to left.*)

(*Re-enter* NIOCHE, *right upper entrance.*)

NIOCHE. They're coming back, sir—they made a short job.

NEWMAN. There's another business now—and a job that may be longer! Go straight into the grounds, and look for Count Valentine. There's some blasted thing on. [16]

NIOCHE. (*Startled.*) What blasted thing?

NEWMAN. That's just what I want to *see!* Go *that* way, and go fast! [17] (*Re-enter, right upper entrance, the* MARQUIS *and* MME. DE BELLEGARDE. NEWMAN *pushes* NIOCHE *out by the conservatory. Exit* NIOCHE, *right,* NEWMAN *remains right, while the others cross to left.*) I'd search myself if I didn't want to have another go at *them!* (*To* MME. DE BELLEGARDE.) Well, have you thought it all over?

MME. DE BELLEGARDE. (*Left centre.*) Do you think we spin round like tops?

NEWMAN. Oh, tops only spin when they're whipped—and that's not your case.

MARQUIS. (*Left, aside.*) Isn't it, though? We were whipped last night!

NEWMAN. Well, all the same, let me make you a supreme appeal. Why should you object to me so?—what's the matter with me, anyhow? I can't [18] hurt you if I would! A representative of trade? Who told you that? I ain't a representative of anything but the passion I feel and the performance I undertake. At any rate, whatever I represent, I don't *mis*represent, and this is the first thing I've taken up for ever so long. [19] Think what such a humiliation as this must be to a woman like *her!* I'll take her right off [20] to the other side of the globe, and you shall never see me nor hear of me again! I'll stay over there the rest of my life—I'll sign a paper that I'll never come back! (*The* MARQUIS *goes down to left.*)

MME. DE BELLEGARDE. Don't say that! We shall be delighted to see you in France

---

[13] ca-ant mahrry
[14] mahn
[15] grievunce

[16] awn
[17] fa-a-hst
[18] ca-ant
[19] lawng
[20] awff

the day you accept your fate. (*She crosses to left down, the* MARQUIS *giving her his arm. Exeunt, left down,* MME. DE BELLE-GARDE *and* MARQUIS.)

NEWMAN. (*Alone, his hand on the back of sofa.*) My fate?—with *you* for my Providence? Accept an empty frame as my picture? Accept an empty glass as my wine? (*Re-enter* NOÉMIE, *right upper entrance.*) Come in! That old swindler's gone! [21] What did the Count say to you when he was here?

NOÉMIE. He said nothing in particular—I don't know why he came.

NEWMAN. If he helped himself to the keys without speaking of them, that adds a symptom.

NOÉMIE. A symptom of what?

NEWMAN. Of his fighting a donkey's duel —with Lord Deepmere.

NOÉMIE. With Lord Deepmere? What about?

NEWMAN. (*Crossing to table, right.*) Perhaps about *you!*

NOÉMIE. (*Crossing at back, aside, joyfully, irrepressibly.*) Oh, that'll give me a lift! (*Aloud.*) Bless me, there's another symptom: his queer words to my father—to tell me particularly to be a good girl. And the worst symptom of all—this letter from Lord Deepmere! (*Pulling out of her pocket and handing to* NEWMAN, *open, the note brought her by her father.*) Read that!

NEWMAN. (*Running his eyes over the note.*) "I may never see you again—yet there's half [22] a chance [23] of it. If I don't, you mustn't forget me. If I do, I won't forget you!" (*Characteristically.*) Why,[24] it's quite a love-letter!

NOÉMIE. (*Clasping her hands.*) I do hope he won't be killed! [25]

DOCTOR.		(*Outside.*) Take care—take care!
MARIGNAC.	(*Together.*)	(*Outside.*) Here we are at last!
NIOCHE.		(*Outside.*) Ah, the poor young man!

[21] gawne
[22] hahlf
[23] chahnce
[24] wh-a-y (drawn out)
[25] The next passage up to the point at which the doctor administers brandy was inserted for the London production.

DOCTOR. (*Outside.*) Gently—gently!

NEWMAN. (*Turning quickly, at the sound of voices, as* VALENTIN *is borne in.*) Much worse than that—damned if he hasn't killed Valentine! (*Moves sofa with* NOÉMIE, *while re-enter by the conservatory* VALENTIN, *pale and wounded, supported, or as far as possible carried, by* NIOCHE *and* M. DE MARIGNAC *and preceded by the* DOCTOR.)

VALENTIN. (*Who has heard* NEWMAN's *words.*) I'm afraid he has, old boy: it was the best thing he could do with me!

DOCTOR. Easy—easy! (*Nodding at sofa.*) This is the thing! (NEWMAN *and* NOÉMIE *quickly wheel sofa still further left, to front.* NEWMAN *then helps thc others to lower* VALENTIN *into it.* VALENTIN, *sinking back with weakness, lies awhile with closed eyes.*) He must have another drop of brandy! (*Administers it from flask and adjusted cup taken from pocket.* NEWMAN *and* NIOCHE *are at back of sofa, the* DOCTOR *in front of it, and* MARIGNAC *at top, having gone round at once.*)

NIOCHE. (*To* NEWMAN.) I met them coming—in the gardens—it was none too soon! (*Goes and kneels with* DOCTOR, *but at bottom of sofa.*)

NEWMAN. (*To the* DOCTOR.) Are *you* one of his bottle-holders?

DOCTOR. No, I'm only the doctor—I'm an Englishman, and I came with Lord Deepmere, who has now less need of me.

NOÉMIE. (*Left, aside.*) Oh, that's good!

NEWMAN. Do you mean he's dead?

DOCTOR. Oh no, he's wounded, but he'll do well enough. His two friends drove him off—he insisted on my attending to the Count. I begged one of the Count's friends to go for his family physician. This is the other, Monsieur de Marignac.

NEWMAN. (*To* MARIGNAC, *a man of a certain age, grave and decorous, but rather a "masher," who salutes him with formal courtesy.*) Happy to see you, sir; or rather —hanged if I am! (*Indicating* VALENTIN.) Is he sinking?—is he very bad? [26]

MARIGNAC. (*With his hand to his left side.*) A bad place—very deep—just in here!

[26] ba-ad

DOCTOR. I stanched the wound, as far as I could, on the ground; but I can answer for nothing till I get him on a bed.

NEWMAN. (*To* NOÉMIE.) A bed—a bed, quickly! Have everything got ready in *there!* (*Points centre, exit* NOÉMIE, *centre.*)

DOCTOR. I'm glad there are no stairs. I was afraid of them, as I was afraid of the movement of a carriage. That's why we judged it best, with your kind permission, to bring him in here.

VALENTIN. (*Beside whom* NIOCHE *has been kneeling, to* NEWMAN, *opening his eyes.*) My dear fellow, I wanted not to be out of the way, but I'm afraid I've put myself a good deal too much *in* it!

NEWMAN. I'll give it to you when you're better! But I'll fix you up first!

VALENTIN. Oh, Deepmere has given it to me—*he* has fixed me up! He was perfect—he made me take the doctor—he didn't think a moment of himself.

MARIGNAC. Yes, *milord* was perfect. A Frenchman couldn't have been better.

VALENTIN. A Frenchman mustn't be worse! (*To* NIOCHE.) My venerable friend, do go to his place, with my compliments, and find out how he is.

NIOCHE. (*To* VALENTIN.) I would rather stay with *you*, M. le Comte; but anything for the honour of France! (*Exit* NIOCHE, *left down.* MARIGNAC *goes round at back and takes* NIOCHE's *place.*)

NEWMAN. (*To the* DOCTOR, *pointing in the direction of the bedroom.*) Will you go and help the young lady? I'm afraid there is a great deal to do. (*The* DOCTOR, *assenting eagerly, goes out by the tapestried door.*)

VALENTIN. Don't move me—don't move me, Newman. I want to talk to you.

NEWMAN. And I want[27] to talk to *you*[28] —depend on it![29]

VALENTIN. Have the heads of the family been to see you?

NEWMAN. (*Cheerfully.*) Oh yes, Madame de Bellegarde and the Marquis paid me quite a solemn visit. *That's* all right!

VALENTIN. (*Lying and looking at him open-eyed.*) And did my sister come with

them?

NEWMAN. Well no, Madame de Cintré; to my disappointment, didn't come round.

VALENTIN. Then it's *not* all right! (*To* MARIGNAC.) Marignac, will you go for my sister? Will you tell her I want her?

NEWMAN. (*Aside.*) Thank God,[30] then, *I* shall see her! (*To* MARIGNAC, *looking at his watch.*) You may just catch her—she's leaving Paris, going to Fleurières—by the midday train.

VALENTIN. (*Repeating.*) Then it *isn't* all right! (*To* MARIGNAC, *beseechingly.*) Stop her—catch her! (*Re-enter* DOCTOR, *centre.*) Bring her to me!

MARIGNAC. (*Picking up his hat, hastily.*) I'll do my very best! (*Just as he is going he is stopped by the* DOCTOR, *while* NEWMAN *brings chair from piano and sits, behind sofa, beside* VALENTIN.)

DOCTOR. (*At left down, to* MARIGNAC, *aside.*) If you're going out, it's indispensable you should send in a nurse from one of the convents.

MARIGNAC. I'll make for the nearest— you shall have one of the nuns. (*Exit* MARIGNAC, *left down, at a run.*)

DOCTOR. (*To* NEWMAN.) They're putting up a bed; but it takes time!

NEWMAN. Yes,[31] curse it; but my *own* room's upstairs—if he'll go there?

VALENTIN. Ah, no stairs! Don't move me yet—don't move me!

DOCTOR. I'll hurry them, then; it's too important. (*Exit* DOCTOR, *centre.*)

VALENTIN. (*To* NEWMAN, *who is seated close to him.*) Have they backed out? Did they come to tell you that?

NEWMAN. I'll tell you all about it. But what's the hurry now?

VALENTIN. Why, if Claire is going to Fleurières, and I'm going to—another place, there's no time to lose! (*In a different tone after looking at* NEWMAN *a moment.*) Tell me the truth before I die?

NEWMAN. (*Gets up a moment and walks away, hesitating, in distress.*) If I don't tell him, *she* will. (*Aloud, coming back.*) You won't die—you'll live to avenge me! They've no use for me, they can't work me in!

---

[27] wauhnt
[28] long
[29] short

[30] Gawd
[31] Ye-es

VALENTIN. Shame, shame! I'm glad to go! But you must avenge *yourself*. Don't give her up!

NEWMAN. She has given *me* up! Why does she change, when she was so firm, so fair—when she gave me her perfect faith?

VALENTIN. She doesn't change—she'll never change! She's only gaining time. Her spirit was broken—long ago! My *mother* has had that malignant magic—that damnable art. She isn't used to her liberty—to the liberty *you* have brought her. She's surrounded by the spectres, by the horrors, of the past. But she'll come to me now. (*Raising himself.*) Marignac will bring her. I'll clear up her fears—I'll give her back to you. I'll join your hands together here—(*sinking back again*) you'll go away together. Only (*with a sudden gasp of pain*) she must be quick!

NEWMAN. Dear old boy; easy—easy! We've lots of time—we've the whole future. If you give her back to me she'll nurse you, she'll heal you, she'll save you; she'll give *you* back to me!

VALENTIN. She'll be too late—I'm sinking. It tortures me to lie ebbing away when *you're* in trouble. But I'll tell you who *can* help you—Mrs. Bread can help you. She knows something about my mother.

NEWMAN. About your mother?

VALENTIN. About my father.

NEWMAN. About your father?

VALENTIN. About my brother.

NEWMAN. About your brother?

VALENTIN. She has a secret—she knows what was done when my father died—when Claire was forced. There was some foul play—something took place. Get it out of Mrs. Bread! It was so base that if I mention it now, it's only because I'm going.

NEWMAN. (*Wondering, calculating.*) It was so *base*?

VALENTIN. Oh, now I've spoken I shall *have* to go.

NEWMAN. (*Pleading.*) Stay, stay, my boy, and I'll never, never think of it again!

VALENTIN. Think of it till you find it out. I'll go to give you a chance—because it will bring them down. They'll come down if they know you know it.

NEWMAN. But my knowledge—what difference will *that* make?

VALENTIN. It will shame them—it will shame them. As it shames *me* now! (*Sinks back exhausted, with closed eyes.*)

(*Re-enter, left down,* M. DE MARIGNAC; *and at the same moment* NOÉMIE, *centre.*)

MARIGNAC. The Countess is coming—she's just behind me! (*Then to* NOÉMIE, *whom he approaches.*) And a trained nurse—a quiet nun, to relieve *you*, when you're tired.

NOÉMIE. (*Who has resumed her hat and jacket, aside.*) Countesses and quiet nuns? I'm not much in *their* line!

(*Re-enter* NIOCHE, *left down, while* NEWMAN *and* MARIGNAC *are on either side of* VALENTIN.)

NIOCHE. (*At back of sofa, to* VALENTIN.) I saw *milord*, and he's not at all bad—he's only bad about his gallant adversary.

NOÉMIE. (*Aside, to her father.*) Has he read my note?

NIOCHE. (*Aside.*) He said it was so graceful! (*Goes to window.*)

NOÉMIE. (*Aside.*) It would be more graceful still of me to go to him! (*Moves to conservatory. Re-enter* DOCTOR, *centre.*)

DOCTOR. (*To* NEWMAN *and* MARIGNAC.) You must help me now—we *must* get him in! (*Goes to front.*)

NEWMAN. (*To* MARIGNAC.) But where *is* Madame de Cintré?

MARIGNAC. I overtook her at the station—she was to follow in a moment. She bade me come on to tell him. (*Goes to* VALENTIN, *and lifts him.*)

NIOCHE. (*At the window.*) There's a carriage in the court—she's here! (*Comes to* NEWMAN.)

NOÉMIE. (*Who has flitted round on tiptoe to the door of the conservatory, and stopped a moment listening, aside.*) I'm off—this way! (*Exit* NOÉMIE, *right.*)

NEWMAN. (*To* NIOCHE.) Help the *Count*, old man. I must meet the *Countess*! (*The* DOCTOR, MARIGNAC *and* NIOCHE *raise and sustain* VALENTIN, *who, at* NEWMAN's *last words, opens his eyes with an "A-ah!" a gasp of sharp pain.*)

VALENTIN. (*To* NEWMAN.) Thank you—I am past all help. But find it out—find it out! (*He is carried away, centre, by* MARI-GNAC, *the* DOCTOR *and* NIOCHE. NEWMAN, *left alone, comes down to table right, and, as if dazed with what* VALENTIN *has said to him, falls into a chair and remains a moment with his head in his hands. Hearing a sound, he turns round, springing up: it is* M. DE MARIGNAC, *who has re-entered, centre. At the same instant enter* MME. DE CINTRÉ, *left down, and* M. DE MARIGNAC, *who is nearest to her, goes to meet her, stands answering mutely, with a slow headshake, the appeal of her eyes, and then discreetly and quickly exit left down.* NEW-MAN, *on the right, stands looking at them—then* MME. DE CINTRÉ *and he are left face to face.*)

CLAIRE. (*Seizing* NEWMAN's *hands.*) How is he? Where is he? Can't I see him?

NEWMAN. They've just moved him to a better place than this; they're arranging him—the doctor'll call you.

CLAIRE. Is he dying? Tell me the truth! What does it all mean?

NEWMAN. He's badly wounded, but we shall see. What *does* it all mean? That's what I ask myself!

CLAIRE. Forgive me—forgive me! you will when you understand!

NEWMAN. Ah, but when shall I *understand?* It's terrible cruel.

CLAIRE. It's crueller for me than for you. We must pity each other.

NEWMAN. I pity *you*—for that dear fellow—too much to utter *now* the reproach that burns my tongue!

CLAIRE. Yes, spare me, in this dreadful hour—spare me and save *him!* He was all I had! (*Giving way, weeping prostrate.*)

NEWMAN. You have *me*—you have *me*—and you won't take me!

CLAIRE. I told you last night that I was *afraid* of happiness. See how right I was, and what a single hour of it has brought! (*Sinks on sofa, with head on back.*)

NEWMAN. Ain't you afraid of something else?—of turning joy to bitterness?—of broken pledges and blighted hopes? Ain't you afraid to go away, as I find you in the inexorable act of doing, and leave me gnashing my teeth and cursing my fate? (*As she makes no answer but to burst into tears he goes on, abruptly, in another tone.*)

Where is Mrs. Bread? Has she stayed behind?

CLAIRE. (*Rising.*) I took the carriage, but she follows. Once away, when I can breathe, when I can think, you shall hear from me.

NEWMAN. When you can *think?* Do you mean when you can repent?

CLAIRE. My repentance will be all my future! But I'm *sick* with this delay—am I not to see my brother?

NEWMAN. Come to him now—let me show you! (*He goes with* MME. DE CINTRÉ *quickly to centre door, where the* DOCTOR *meets them very gravely, bows* MME. DE CINTRÉ *in and follows. Exit* MME. DE CINTRÉ, *centre door. While this takes place, re-enter* MRS. BREAD, *left down, whom* NEWMAN *comes down and meets.*) Have patience—I *see* what you ask [32] me. He's in danger—he must see but one person at a time.

MRS. BREAD. Ah, the fatal folly, that I didn't prevent it last night, when I felt it in the air!

NEWMAN. I didn't feel it, God knows! But you can help us all yet. You know something. (*Movement of* MRS. BREAD.) Something that happened at Fleurières—ten years ago. Something secret—something shameful!

MRS. BREAD. Ah, did the Count tell you? If he told you, God forgive him—he's going! (NEWMAN *goes round to left. Re-enter* MME. DE CINTRÉ, *centre.*)

CLAIRE. (*In the deepest agitation and anguish.*) He's gone—he's gone! (*Falls on piano, right.*)

MRS. BREAD. (*With a loud wail.*) Oh, my boy—my boy! (*Exit, centre, with a rush.*)

NEWMAN. (*Left of* MME. DE CINTRÉ, *stopping her as she hurries left, to go out.*) Gone—gone? [33]

CLAIRE. For ever and ever! (*With quick, sombre passion.*) So shall I go too!

NEWMAN. (*Pleading as she struggles to leave him.*) Claire—Claire! Listen to me—stay with me!

CLAIRE. (*Breaking successfully away.*) Don't oppose me!—don't, in pity, or you'll kill me! (*Exit* MME. DE CINTRÉ, *left down.*)

NEWMAN. (*Alone.*) What in the name

---

[32] ahsk
[33] Gawne—gawne?

of misery does she mean? What strange things does she threaten? (*Re-enter* MRS. BREAD, *centre, in blank despair.* NEWMAN *goes up and comes down right of her, seizing her by the wrist.*) She's gone [34] as well as he, and now you *must* help me, for I'm desperate!

MRS. BREAD. Don't keep me—I must follow her!

NEWMAN. What does she want to do? Where does she want to go? *How* does she want to "repent forever"?

MRS. BREAD. Oh, remember that she's a good Catholic! When they're hard pressed they have a refuge.

NEWMAN. A refuge. Do you mean the convent? A convent for *her*—for *that* woman—for my promised wife?

MRS. BREAD. It's too hideous—you must help me to prevent it!

NEWMAN. Trust me—if you'll show me how!

MRS. BREAD. Come then to Fleurières—come to Fleurières!

NEWMAN. (*Eagerly.*) Will you *tell* me, there?

MRS. BREAD. Will I tell you what?

NEWMAN. The great secret—the great shame!

MRS. BREAD. Come quickly, and I'll see! But come before it's too late! (*Exit* MRS. BREAD, *left down and re-enter* NIOCHE *centre;* NEWMAN *goes right.*)

NIOCHE. (*Gazing mournfully at* NEW-

---
[34] gawne

MAN.) Lord, sir, what a sad inauguration of your beautiful house!

NEWMAN. My beautiful house be hanged —I've done with my beautiful house! (*Crosses to left.*)

NIOCHE. Done with it? And what's to become of it?

NEWMAN. (*Going up, left.*) I don't care a rap! Keep it for yourself!

NIOCHE. (*Staring.*) For myself? With all the valuable objects?

NEWMAN. (*At back.*) Damn the valuable objects!

NIOCHE. (*At the table on which the pearl necklace, which he lifts up, is still lying.*) The most valuable of all—the priceless pearls.

NEWMAN. Give 'em to your daughter! (*Comes down, right, while* NIOCHE *goes centre.*) And I shall want some baggage, some clothes—I leave Paris to-night!

NIOCHE. (*Overwhelmed.*) You shall be obeyed to the letter, sir! (*At this moment his eyes rest on the* SISTER OF CHARITY, *summoned by* MARIGNAC, *who has entered left down, and stands silently just within the threshold. He bows to her solemnly.*) You come too late to nurse, good Sister— but not too late to pray!

NEWMAN. (*Becoming aware of her.*) Good Sister, pray for me! (*Action from* SISTER.) Ah, Valentine, Valentine! (*Flings himself down on the sofa and buries his face on the arm while the Curtain falls.*) Selfish brute that I am!

ACT FOURTH

At the old Château de Fleurières; the closing hours of an early spring day. A high, paneled, central drawing-room, with "subjects," little oval or circular pictures, above the doors, let into the white boiserie, and very tall French windows, with small square panes and long, straight, flowered, faded curtains. Nothing but sparse last century furniture, refined and very much worn. On the left, near the front, a door leading to MME. DE CINTRÉ's *apartments or "wing"; another on the same side, higher up, quite at back, communicating with the general entrance. On the right,* *at back, balancing with this principal entrance, a large window, opening, down to the ground, upon the visible, melancholy, moated terrace of the château. Further down, on the same side, the door of the special apartments, or "wing," of* MME. DE BELLEGARDE *and the* MARQUIS. *During the act the dusk slowly gathers, and at a given moment a pair of candles are lighted. Enter, left upper entrance, a* SERVANT, *the same who has appeared in the second act, but who is now in a mourning livery, preceding* M. DE MARIGNAC. *Enter* M. DE MARIGNAC, *in a high hat with a crape band, carrying in his hand a large bunch of early violets.*

MARIGNAC. (*Crossing* SERVANT, *and taking a card from his pocket.*) I have written a word on this card. (*The* SERVANT *takes the card on salver and exit left, while* MARIGNAC, *alone a moment, has taken off his hat and put it down on table right, looking about the place with a certain wonder.*) It fairly smells of the past—I like my violets better! (*Goes right, sniffing them, while re-enter* SERVANT, *left, holding the door open for* MME. DE CINTRÉ. *Enter* MME. DE CINTRÉ, *left, in the deepest mourning. Exit* SERVANT *left upper entrance, and* MARIGNAC, *advancing to* MME. DE CINTRÉ *with an expression of the greatest sympathy and consideration, takes her hand and, bowing over it, raises it to his lips.*) It's so like your gracious goodness to make an exception in *my* favour.

CLAIRE. It's only for once; I shall never see you again.

MARIGNAC. Do you mean as the penalty of my participation? We couldn't do less for him, and we couldn't do more. He died like a Bellegarde of old, with his hand on his sword.

CLAIRE. Yes, thank God; he was a Bellegarde of old, not one of to-day. (*Crosses to right,* MARIGNAC *goes left.*) But I don't mean anything vindictive; it would become me strangely little at this hour. I accept the fact, I almost rejoice in it, that my brother has done forever with the troubles of this world. (*Leans on window, resting on her arm.*) For the troubles of this world are too heavy to be borne.

MARIGNAC. You speak as if *you* were going to leave it! There's something in your face that I guess the intention of, and it makes my heart sink.

CLAIRE. (*Turning to him.*) Envy me, envy me! (*Turning back to window.*) Farewell!

MARIGNAC. Is there no comfort I can give you? Is there no service I can render you?

CLAIRE. Think of me as more at peace than you have ever known me; take no more trouble for me than that.

MARIGNAC. I took a very small trouble half an hour ago. I gathered these violets for you (CLAIRE *comes down to him*), al-most the very first of the spring, in the sweet old churchyard on the side of the hill, where we laid him to rest this morning.

CLAIRE. (*Taking the flowers and kissing them.*) Thank you, thank you. Good-bye. (*Crosses to left, and is going.*)

MARIGNAC. A moment more. Your brother, the last hour of his life, charged me to give *this* to you (*taking from his waistcoat-pocket a small packet*): he usually wore it; he took it off before this lamentable affair.

CLAIRE. (*Taking the little packet; after a look.*) It's a blessed relic; a little cross that belonged to my father, he wore it round his neck. (*Falls into chair, at table, left, and kisses it as she has kissed the violets.*) I'm going where they renounce—renounce,[1] but I shall carry *this*—beneath!

MARIGNAC. Beneath the rigid folds of the nun? Heaven help me—I should like to prevent that!

CLAIRE. You *can't* prevent it, Monsieur de Marignac.

MARIGNAC. Upon my honour, I can try!

CLAIRE. You can do nothing.

MARIGNAC. I shall see what I can do. Excuse me if I say I warn you.

CLAIRE. Do you mean that you'll communicate (*rising and nodding across the stage to right down.*) with *them?*

MARIGNAC. Your mother and the Marquis? Don't they know it?

CLAIRE. They don't dream of it. It's my own affair, and I appeal to your honour not to betray me. (*Goes to left down.*) Farewell!

MARIGNAC. Oh, I shall see you again!

CLAIRE. Never—never! (*Exit* MME. DE CINTRÉ, *left down.*)

MARIGNAC. If I don't, may charming women never smile at me more! (*Goes right and up to back.*)

(*Re-enter the* SERVANT, *left upper entrance, introducing* NEWMAN, *as he has introduced* MARIGNAC. *Enter* NEWMAN, *left upper entrance.*)

NEWMAN. (*To the* SERVANT.) All right, I'll wait here while you tell her. Mind you

---

[1] The reading of this speech in the printed prompt-book was "I'm going where they have done with gewgaws, but I shall carry *this* beneath." James amended the text in his copy.

tell her it's *me!*

SERVANT. Oh, she'll come to *you*, sir. (*Exit* SERVANT, *left upper entrance,* MARIGNAC *comes down.*)

NEWMAN. (*To* MARIGNAC.) You're just what I want to see! There's a sickly satisfaction in putting my hand on *you*. (*With his hand on* MARIGNAC's *shoulder.*) I'm going to want [2] *you*. (*They go up to fireplace;* MARIGNAC *sits on couch.* NEWMAN *leans on mantelshelf, after putting his hat on table by fireplace.*)

MARIGNAC. Oh, I want to be wanted—if it's for the right thing!

NEWMAN. It's for the right thing *this* time—you may bet your life on that! I saw you this morning [3]—across the churchyard —at those dismal dreadful proceedings; but I was afraid you would have returned to Paris. At what time is your train?

MARIGNAC. I'll take the train that suits *you*. I'll do anything in fact that suits you— as a friend of the friend we buried to-day.

NEWMAN. We were both the friends of that friend—but there he lies, in spite of us. (*Looking at his watch.*) Ah, if Mrs. Bread would only come! I've an appointment with her.

MARIGNAC. I'm waiting for her too, to put into her hand a little supreme remembrance (*taking out another little packet*) that poor Bellegarde committed to me.

NEWMAN. If you don't want to wait, and will give me the object, I'll answer for her receiving it safely.

MARIGNAC. You'll oblige me very much— I'll put the parcel here. (*Coming down and depositing it on table.*) If you've an appointment, it's naturally for a private end, and I give you up the field.

NEWMAN. It's for two private ends, but I don't mind telling you what one of them is. (MARIGNAC *comes back to left.*) It's to ask her to obtain for *me* an interview with Madame de Cintré.

MARIGNAC. (*With his hand on* NEWMAN's *arm.*) The other night—at the Hôtel de Bellegarde—that didn't seem to depend on Mrs. Bread!

NEWMAN. It depended on more than you know—or than I know, either! I won't

pretend to conceal from you—sore and sombre as I am!—that I'm a man with a grievance, and with more than one.

MARIGNAC. I think I've just learned *one*, at least, from Madame de Cintré's lips.

NEWMAN. (*Eagerly.*) You saw her? She was here, and I missed her? Curse my luck! (*Goes to cabinet and round at back.*)

MARIGNAC. Courage, courage; your luck may come back to you.

NEWMAN. That's just what I want to see! What then did you learn from her lips?

MARIGNAC. (*Looking at him a moment in silence.*) Don't you know? Don't you guess? It's more your business than mine!

NEWMAN. Do you mean that atrocity of the convent? (*Comes to centre.*) Yes, that's my business—that's why I'm here!

MARIGNAC. You're none too soon! But I myself let her know that, meddler as I might seem to her to be, I was capable of attempting to make such a step impossible.

NEWMAN. Well, *that* was good.

MARIGNAC. Yes, but she asked me what I could do.

NEWMAN. And what did you say to *that?*

MARIGNAC. I said I would see. But unfortunately I don't see!

NEWMAN. Then I'll show you! (*Taking him sharply by the arm, and pointing to the long window.*) Go out of that window —go out on that terrace—go out into those grounds—stand there till I call you. Be patient.[4] Do you understand?

MARIGNAC. Not a bit!

NEWMAN. Then you won't do it for me?

MARIGNAC. I'll do anything for you! (*They shake hands.*)

NEWMAN. Be quick, then, here comes Mrs. Bread! (MARIGNAC, *pushed by* NEWMAN, *who opens it for him, passes out of the window to the terrace.* NEWMAN *closes the window and turns to meet* MRS. BREAD, *who has entered left down.*) I've kept my tryst—I suppose you saw me this morning.

MRS. BREAD. (*In deep mourning, with reddened eyes, shakes her head tragically.*) Oh, this morning, I couldn't see! Nor can I make out what now you're doing at that

---

2 wauhnt
3 mauhning

4 The words "Be patient" are in the original typescript; are eliminated in the printed version, and are pencilled in in Henry James's copy.

window.

NEWMAN. I've a confederate.

MRS. BREAD. M. de Marignac?

NEWMAN. He has brought you a sacred offering,[5] which lies there on the table, something the Count gave him for you on that abominable morning.

MRS. BREAD. (*Crossing and taking the little packet, which consists of a small case that she opens; she seats herself with it at table, right.*) The rare old ring that he used to wear on his blessed, beautiful hand! Oh, and he thought of *me?* (*Bursts into tears.*) My boy, my boy!

NEWMAN. (*Who has gone to the fireplace, where he stands, with his back to the audience, waiting an instant, in respectful silence, while she sobs.*) Now you know how *I* feel, and how I want to see *her!*

MRS. BREAD. (*Drying her eyes.*) I've been with her, that's what has kept me. (NEWMAN *turns round.* MRS. BREAD *rises.*) She bids me tell you she'll come to you. But you'll find it a sorry joy!

NEWMAN. I'll take the worst part of the sorrow out of it, or I'll know the reason why!

MRS. BREAD. You know it already. The reason why is a horrible big house, twenty miles from here, with high grey walls and little cold cells, full of wasting women who are for ever, on the hard stones, on their knees.

NEWMAN. Well, if it's twenty miles from here it ain't here yet. She has got to get there first!

MRS. BREAD. She expects to get there about midnight, to make it more cheerful!

NEWMAN. (*Coming down right centre to table, aghast.*) Do you mean she leaves to-night?

MRS. BREAD. In less than an hour. (*Goes to left centre.*) She has plotted it all, she's going to drive.

NEWMAN. (*Dryly.*) She'll have to drive over me!

MRS. BREAD. Oh, you'll feel the wheels— you'll feel the hoofs!

NEWMAN. I'll stop the horses—I'll knock the coachman down. Do the heads of the family know?

MRS. BREAD. They haven't an idea. She

has arranged it, in secret, successfully, and now that the moment of her flight is near she's in a fever lest they should find her out. (*As the door on right opens.*) Here she comes! (*Comes down side of stage, left. Re-enter* MME. DE CINTRÉ, *left. Exit* MRS. BREAD, *left.* CLAIRE *stands looking at* NEWMAN, *he having given a shocked start at the sight of her rigid black dress, as if taking it at first for the Carmelite garb.*)

CLAIRE. Don't suffer—you're too good to suffer.

NEWMAN. I think it's only those who are too good who do suffer!

CLAIRE. (*Coming to him.*) There are some whose suffering is expiation. I know I've deceived and injured you—I know I've been cowardly and cruel. I see it as vividly as you, and anything you may have said of me in your angriest passion is nothing to what I've said of myself.

NEWMAN. My angriest passion has spared you—it has clung to you as closely as my tenderest. But there are others whom it hasn't spared—and whom it doesn't mean to spare now!

CLAIRE. Ah, let others go—I'm beyond all others!

NEWMAN. (*Bitterly.*) You seem far away indeed—but you're not in heaven quite yet! Even if you were, however, I should ask you to come down to earth, a moment, to give me a reason, a decent reason, the faintest blush of a reason!

CLAIRE. My reason is all the past—the inseparable, irreparable past. It calls for me (*raising her hands to her head*)—it closes round me! [6]

NEWMAN. It calls for *me*, too—and do you know what it says to me? That you're the victim of some unimaginable rigour, some coercion so unnatural that you're trying to hide it. You *can't* hide it—you're mere plate-glass! It's not by the dead you're haunted; you're haunted by the living!

CLAIRE. (*Looking at him a moment and crossing him round to right.*) Have it then that I'm haunted—if that will do for a reason! They won't haunt me *there!* (*Pointing to the window.*)

---

[5] awferring.

[6] Elizabeth Robins noted in her prompt book that she was to speak this: "half-mystical with a hush in the voice."

NEWMAN. In your living tomb?—you stick to that? You can speak of it with your own mild lips?

CLAIRE. I go to-night—I go in an hour. Farewell!

NEWMAN. (*Passing quickly between her and the lower door on left.*) Answer me a question first, and answer it in common pity. I've read somewhere that in the old times there was a thing called the Papal interdict—the strongest argument of the old domineering Church. (CLAIRE, *arrested by his words, moves right.*) The old Popes used to screw it down, like a big iron roof, over the crowns of the old kings, till all their sky was darkened. The thistles grew in their courts, the terror grew in their hearts, and it was not till the interdict was raised that they were restored to light and reason. That's *your* case to-day: (CLAIRE *drops into chair, right*) the interdict hangs over *you!* The iron roof is on *your* head, the thistles are in *your* court, the dread is in *your* heart! If I sweep these things utterly away, will you listen to me *then?* Will you come back to me?

CLAIRE. (*Moved, her head bowed.*) What are you going to do?

NEWMAN. I'm going to raise the interdict!

CLAIRE. (*Rising.*) You can't—you won't! Don't touch sacred things!

NEWMAN. Have they made you believe they're sacred? They don't play fair! It seems to me you practically acknowledge everything I want!

CLAIRE. I acknowledge nothing—for I *know* nothing. (*Her eyes down, her hands over her ears.*)

NEWMAN. You bandage your eyes, you stuff your ears, for fear of knowing! (*Moves a little left.*) That makes me sure!

CLAIRE. Let me pass—let me pass!

NEWMAN. And *this* makes me strong! (*Catching her in his arms as she tries to pass to left, he holds her for an instant in a close embrace. She breaks away—exit rapidly, left. Enter the MARQUIS from right.*) The Marquis? *Here's* a nuisance!

MARQUIS. (*Stopping short on seeing NEWMAN.*) *You* here, sir? I hadn't the pleasure of knowing it.

NEWMAN. As my visit is exclusively to Madame de Cintré, I judged it superfluous to ask for you, or for Madame de Bellegarde, considering the terms on which we last parted.

MARQUIS. Permit me to express a doubt as to whether my sister will see you.

NEWMAN. Your sister *has* seen me, and I'm not without the hope that she will graciously see me again.

MARQUIS. (*Staggered a little, but recovering himself.*) Ah! (*Then, swinging his eyeglass.*) You've gained an advantage of us—prostrate as you find us with our dreadful bereavement; but I'm afraid you're in *precarious* possession.[7] I emerged from the appropriate seclusion of my mother's apartments only because I thought I should find M. de Marignac, who seems to have vanished.

NEWMAN. He's on the premises—in case *I* want him.[8] (*Taking his hat from table up at fireplace.*) I'll bring him right in.

MARQUIS. (*Aside, coming down while NEWMAN goes up again.*) What's there between them—between Marignac and him? (*Moving to left.[9] Turns round at table, left, and aloud, in a tone he has not yet used.*) Don't put yourself out—allow me the pleasure of sending a servant for M. de Marignac.

NEWMAN. (*Struck by his tone and staring a moment.*) You're too polite. I've a

---

[7] This speech reads in the printed text: "As you've gained an advantage of us, prostrate as you find us with our dreadful bereavement, you can make yourself quite at home! (*Aside, coming down, while NEWMAN, bowing in recognition of this ironical invitation, walks up to the window with an air of keeping an eye on MARIGNAC.*) Why not, perhaps, after all? Valentin's removal has modified many things; some of them—I cheerfully recognize!—for the better. The thing it has modified most is our delicate relations with the sanguinary Deepmere—it has modified *them* out of existence. What a pity Deepmere didn't only wound him—very badly! (*Aloud, leaning on chair, to NEWMAN, who comes down.*) I leave you in possibly precarious possession. I emerged etc." HJ's copy deletes this and emends it as above.

[8] The printed text reads ". . . in that case *I* want him" but the *that* is inked out in Henry James's copy.

[9] At this point Henry James has inked out the words: "I'll tell my mother, and I'll make bold to suggest to her that as for Mr. Newman, after all, *now*—with the modifications!"

word to say to him myself. (*Aside.*) I want to tell him our prospect brightens! (*Exit* NEWMAN, *rapidly, by the window, which he opens.*)

MARQUIS. (*Alone.*) Why should they hang about together? They're as thick as thieves!

(*Enter* MME. DE BELLEGARDE, *right.*)

MME. DE BELLEGARDE. (*Going up a little, then coming right centre.*) Ah, if he's not here, I might have spared myself the effort to meet him.

MARQUIS. He *is* here—very much here! (*Confidentially.*) I may mention to you that he strikes me as a trifle less objectionable than last week.

MME. DE BELLEGARDE. When did we ever find Gaston de Marignac objectionable?

MARQUIS. Pardon my confusion—I thought you meant Christopher Newman!

MME. DE BELLEGARDE. Is Christopher Newman here? (*Grandly, seating herself at head of table, right.*) He presumes on our desolation!

MARQUIS. So he does; but mightn't we, perhaps (*hesitating, stammering a little and swinging his eyeglass, while he seats himself on sofa*)—mightn't we, perhaps, presume upon it a little even ourselves? (*Watching the effect of these words on his mother.*) Remember the modifications!

MME. DE BELLEGARDE. The modifications?

MARQUIS. Everything has been modified but Christopher Newman's millions. (*Suggestively.*) *They* haven't, you know!

MME. DE BELLEGARDE. And the fact that we loathe him and despise him—has that been modified? (*The* MARQUIS *rises and comes down left centre; makes a prompt movement of deprecation and retraction.*) The fact that he's a base-born vulgar shopkeeper and that we were on the point of stooping to him, and to his abysses, and have picked ourselves up in time—has *that* been modified? (*Rises, while the* MARQUIS *repeats the gestures expressing that he humbly backs down. With culminating passion.*) Let us at least hold our heads higher than ever, to make up for having bowed them for an hour! (*Goes up.*)

MARQUIS. (*Aside.*) I see—*that's* settled! Well, it's a comfort to settle it—it's the shifting that tells on me!

(*Re-enter* MARIGNAC *and* NEWMAN *by the window, a portion of which has remained open.*)

MARIGNAC. (*Right centre.*) Good evening, Madame. I arrived an hour ago, to give two persons two mementoes which your lamented son put into my hand for them in the last hour of his life. One of these touching remembrances was for your daughter, to whom I've delivered it; the other was for Mrs. Bread—

NEWMAN. (*Right, interrupting.*) To whom *I've* delivered it!

MARQUIS. (*To* NEWMAN.) You've made good use of your time!

NEWMAN. I hope to make still better! (*Goes up.*)

MARQUIS. (*Left, to* MARIGNAC.) And my brother handed you (*hesitating*) no touching remembrance for *me?*

MARIGNAC. (*Dryly.*) Nothing.

MARQUIS. And none for his mother?

MARIGNAC. (*Putting his hat on table, right.*) Nothing.

MME. DE BELLEGARDE. (*Aside to* MARQUIS.) Idiot!

MARQUIS. (*Uncertain, aside, to* MME. DE BELLEGARDE.) Do you mean Valentin?

MME. DE BELLEGARDE. (*Aside.*) I mean *you!* (MARQUIS *goes up and round to centre. Aloud, to* MARIGNAC.) If your extraordinary association with Mr. Newman permits you to give her a moment, a deeply afflicted mother would be glad to ask you a few questions.

NEWMAN. (*Aside, to* MARIGNAC, *coming right of* MARQUIS.) Look out, she wants to square you! (*Aloud.*) I would offer to retire, Madame, and leave you free to see Monsieur de Marignac on this spot, were it not that just on this spot I presently have a *very* particular appointment. (*Goes up.*)

MARQUIS. (*To* MME. DE BELLEGARDE.) He indulges the hope of another interview with Claire! (*Goes round to door, right.*)

MME. DE BELLEGARDE. Another? Monsiur de Marignac, will you please to pass into my boudoir? (NEWMAN *comes down centre.* MARIGNAC *bows somewhat inexpressively, takes up hat and exit right, the* MARQUIS *holding open the door.* MME. DE

BELLEGARDE *crosses to right, then con-tinues, to* NEWMAN.) You've seen her then?

NEWMAN. Yes, and I'm waiting to see her again.

MME. DE BELLEGARDE. (*After an instant.*) I think you'll wait long! (*Exit* MME. DE BELLEGARDE, *right.*)

MARQUIS. (*To* NEWMAN, *looking at his watch.*) We can't allow you all night, you know!

NEWMAN. (*Looking at his own.*) Allow me a quarter of an hour! (*Exit* MARQUIS, *right. Alone.*) I told Marignac to work them up, and (*as the door of* MME. DE CINTRÉ'S *apartment opens*) here's Mrs. Bread at last, at *last,* to work *me* up!

(*Re-enter* MRS. BREAD, *left down.*)

MRS. BREAD. The poor child's [10] terri-bly nervous; she has but one idea in her head—that her flight may be hindered.

NEWMAN. So it will be, thank God! [11]

MRS. BREAD. Ah, but I've told you their ignorance.

NEWMAN. Their ignorance ain't bliss; they feel there's something in the air.

MRS. BREAD. There's always something in the air now. To-night I can scarcely breathe.

NEWMAN. I can't breathe either—I seem to pant in the void.[12] *What* are you going to give me?

MRS. BREAD. I shall give [13] you strange things, sir, and after I've spoken, this house will be no place for me. I shall have to leave it on the instant.

NEWMAN. That's perfect—you'll come right down to me at the inn. You'll stay right on with me now.

MRS. BREAD. I know a decent woman in the village, and I've just sent my clothes there, and some of the Countess's, in case we stop her.

NEWMAN. Oh, we'll stop her!

MRS. BREAD. Then she'll find her refuge

ready—at my end of the village; while at the other, at the inn, *you* wait for dawn. And when the blessed dawn comes—

NEWMAN. (*Interrupting.*) Praise be to the Highest—she'll marry me!

MRS. BREAD. It will take longer than that! One sees you're an American.

NEWMAN. One sees *you* ain't! It won't take longer than *you* take, I guess!

MRS. BREAD. Well, then! (*On the point of speaking she stops again and looks round her. She rises, then goes right, and stands listening a moment at the door.*)

NEWMAN. (*Impatient.*) Oh, they're all right—Marignac's looking after them!

MRS. BREAD. (*On the same spot, stands for an instant with her eyes on him. Then, while a visible change suddenly takes place in her face and manner, she comes back to him.*) They're murderers—they're mur-derers!

NEWMAN. (*Excited, with a kind of joy, as if it is even better than he has hoped; while they sink together on sofa.*) MUR-DERERS!

MRS. BREAD. My lady put an end to her husband. I have the precious proof—his own declaration, on his deathbed, when, the hour before he passed away in misery, he accused and denounced them.[14] He wrote it down—he signed it!

NEWMAN. (*Incredulous.*) When he was dying?

MRS. BREAD. I held him up on the pil-low, and the God of justice gave him strength.[15] The Comte de Cintré had *loved* my lady—he was her lover still. My lady,

---

[10] The printed text reads "The poor thing's terribly nervous." Henry James's pencilled emendation substitutes the word "child."

[11] Gawd

[12] The printed text reads: "Therefore let's have it! What in creation *did* they do?" Henry James altered this as above.

[13] Henry James altered the printed "I shall tell you . . ." to this reading.

[14] Emended from ". . . he accused them and denounced them and branded them . . ." in the printed text.

[15] The printed text reads:
MRS. BREAD. I held him up on the pillow, and the God of Justice gave him strength. I believed it, because I knew so much. (*They both rise and come down.*) I knew the reason my lady wanted to marry her innocent child to the man her husband hated. (*Listening again a moment.*) I warned you I should tax your faith.
NEWMAN. Well, tax it!
MRS. BREAD. (*Coming closer to him.*) The Comte de Cintré had loved her.
NEWMAN. That *does* tax it!
MRS. BREAD. He had been her lover—he was her lover still. My lady, in her day, went far; and her day was very long!

in her day, went far, and her day was very long.

NEWMAN. Lord, the old hypocrite (*aside*) being shocked at poor little Noémie!

MRS. BREAD. That's how he [16] held her—that's how he made her go! (*Coming closer still.*) He knew things of her [17]—more even than I know! She had had money from him, and to the best of her ability she had made it up to him in money's worth! But he taught her that her debt would hang over her head till she had given him her helpless child.

NEWMAN. (*Attentive, horrified.*) Ah, the infamous scoundrels! No wonder Madame de Cintré takes life hard!

MRS. BREAD. Her father tried to save her, but he was beaten—he was ill. My lady spent half a night in his room—a bitter winter's night.[18]

NEWMAN. And what did she do there?

MRS. BREAD. She stood over him and mocked [19] and threatened him, while the Marquis, in the passage, kept the door. She calculated exactly what would do for him and never leave a mark. The particular potion that the doctor had left to soothe him, to save him, to stop his suffering, which without it was unbearable: do you know what she did with the blessed beneficent drug? She poured it away before his eyes, into the cold ashes of the hearth, and she told him, cruelly, why she did so!

NEWMAN. It sounds like some creepy legend!

MRS. BREAD. I found the traces when she left him [20]—I found the empty phial. She

[16] Printed text: "That's how the Comte de Cintré . . ."
[17] Printed text: "He knew things of my lady . . ."
[18] Printed text:
MRS. BREAD. It would have broken your heart to see her—as it broke the heart of her poor father. He couldn't abide the Comte de Cintré—he declared that sooner than take such a husband as that, Mademoiselle Claire should take none at all. He went to bed, one day, in sharp pain, but he never got up—my lady took care of that! She spent half a night in his room—a bitter winter's night.
[19] Printed text:
MRS. BREAD. She stood over him and mocked him and threatened him . . .
[20] Printed text:
MRS. BREAD. I found the traces afterwards,

had done her work well—but I did mine. My pity warmed him into life an instant—he flickered up into a kind of supernatural flame, and in the very arms of death he was capable of the miracle of writing twenty words. He was like the angel of judgment! (*Sinks back to chair, right, falls into it.*)

NEWMAN. (*Who has followed her closely, critically, and yet with a conviction and a horror that at last completely and visibly hold him.*) And those twenty words, where are they? Ain't I to see them?

MRS. BREAD. As soon as I'm out of the house.

NEWMAN. That makes me want you to go, though unfortunately I'm obliged to recognise that in the eye of the law your wonderful document isn't worth *that!* (*Snapping his fingers.*)

MRS. BREAD. The eye that would look through my lady, in the light of that grim paper, would be a very different one. The eye of a certain society!

NEWMAN. *What* society?

MRS. BREAD. The grand particular world that surrounds her—for which she keeps up appearances.

NEWMAN. The grand particular world to which, last week, she made such a grand particular fool of me?

MRS. BREAD. The only world she recognises or considers or fears!

NEWMAN. Do you mean it suspects her—that you spoke at the time?

MRS. BREAD. Never, never; I held my tongue for the younger children's sake. The doctors wondered immensely, but my lady brazened them down—there was no blood and no poison. But the wonder has never really died out. You could wake it up again!

NEWMAN. (*Silent a moment, as if sifting and settling the story in his thoughts, so that he accepts it.*) Well, I guess I'll wake

and I found the empty phial. Happy in her triumph, she left him in the early dawn, swooning, perishing, within an hour of his end, and when at last I got access to him I found him a dying man. But he flickered up into a kind of supernatural flame, and face to face with death he was capable of the miracle of writing twenty words. He was like the angel of *judgment*.

it up! You say you spared the younger children; but the Count's charge to me shows they've known something.

MRS. BREAD. They've heard the echo—they've hovered on the edge of the truth.[21]

NEWMAN. The edge?—Tonight Claire has *crossed* it! [22]

MRS. BREAD. Then [23] the great blow has fallen, the blow by the fear of which my lady has always held her—the constant menace of her own version, the revelation that the late Marquis was secretly abominable, that, for instance, he could stoop to an intrigue with such a one as *me!* (NEWMAN, *with his hands in his pockets, more and more stirred by all he has listened to, walks restlessly up and stands looking a moment out of the window to the terrace, where thick dusk has now gathered.*) She feels *that's* false—she has guessed what's true.[24]

NEWMAN. (*As he comes quickly down.*) Your paper, your paper, your paper! (*At centre.*) You call it precious, and it has the value of being exactly a test. If they're innocent, it won't have the force of *one* of the heart-beats it has given me to hear about it. But if they're guilty, it will make them perspire! (*Re-enter, right,* M. DE MARIGNAC, *who catches these last words.*)

MARIGNAC. If your talking of our friends in there, they're perspiring pretty freely already. I seem to have administered a Turkish bath!

NEWMAN. Exactly, you're the eye of so-

ciety! (*To* MRS. BREAD, *explaining.*) He's the old lady's grand particular world. She recognises and considers and fears *him,* and she has been keeping up appearances! (*To* MARIGNAC *again.*) Do you remember all those fine people I was laid out for the other night?

MARIGNAC. Remember them? They're mostly my cousins!

NEWMAN. Then you're all the five hundred in one. (MRS. BREAD *lights candles on table, left, with matches that are on table.*) That's why I wanted you.

MARIGNAC. That, perhaps, is also why they've been abusing you to me at such a rate.

NEWMAN. Glory—glory! They're afraid!

MARIGNAC. I took the liberty of defending you, but you'll have them back on top of you—they're coming to turn you out.

NEWMAN. (*To* MRS. BREAD.) My card, my trump card, if I'm going to win the game!

MRS. BREAD. Come with me, M. de Marignac. (MARIGNAC *goes up to left upper entrance with her.*) There's a great service you can render us.

MARIGNAC. (*To* NEWMAN.) Shall I leave you alone, then? Sha'n't I stay to help you?

NEWMAN. You'll help me best by doing exactly what this lovely old lady asks of you. (*Exeunt left upper entrance,* MRS. BREAD *and* MARIGNAC, *and at the same moment, before they disappear, re-enter* MME. DE BELLEGARDE, *right.* NEWMAN, *who has gone up urgently with the others and who, at their exit, has pressed* MRS. BREAD'S *hand jubilantly, as if for a temporary parting, meets her as he comes down, immediately saying.*) Let me anticipate your just curiosity as to the reasons of my continued intrusion by telling you that I'm *still* waiting to see your daughter!

MME. DE BELLEGARDE. Waiting in remarkable company: that of the menial who answers my bell, and of the pretended man of the world who bargained away the safety of my son!

NEWMAN. (*Aside.*) Lord, she *is* pretty bad! (*Aloud, with his hands in his pockets.*) To me they're delightful people—for they've given me a certain confidence.

MME. DE BELLEGARDE. A certain impudence, I judge!

---

[21] Printed text:
    MRS. BREAD. They've heard the echo—the far-off voice (like the dim wail of a ghost!) of their father's wrong and anguish. The Countess, at least, has never understood it—she has only understood it as a vague sound of distress. And she has always stayed still to listen to it; afraid, for pity, to understand more, yet ashamed, for the very same pity, to turn her back.

[22] NEWMAN. Perhaps she has understood tonight.

[23] The original typescript reads as here. The printed version reads: "In that case the great blow has fallen" etc. Henry James restored the original reading in his copy.

[24] Printed text:
    . . . has now gathered.) That, and far worse than that, is what she has held over the poor child's head, and rather than face it, the Countess, who adored her father, has submitted to everything you know!

NEWMAN. Madame de Bellegarde, set your daughter this moment at liberty.

MME. DE BELLEGARDE. (*Looking at him a moment, then, as if altering the intention of her tone before she speaks.*) My daughter's at perfect liberty!

NEWMAN. At liberty to let you grind her to powder! I fully recognise the blight you've cast upon her, but I also recognise that you are perfectly able to dissipate it—that you can do so by saying to her in my presence that you repent of the odious way you've used us, and that you utterly renounce and retract all opposition to our marriage.

MME. DE BELLEGARDE. I shall never utter such words.

NEWMAN. I think I can persuade you to utter them—that I hold in my hand the means. Don't wonder too long what they are. (*Goes close to her.*) Simply remember the night your husband died!

MME. DE BELLEGARDE. I'm not likely to forget it!

NEWMAN. There are other people who haven't forgotten it; but even if they had, a reminder exists.

MME. DE BELLEGARDE. A reminder?

NEWMAN. Written by the hand and signed with the name of the dying man, and denouncing you as his torturer and his murderess. (MME. DE BELLEGARDE *staggers back, catching at chair.*) Your face tells me it isn't waste paper!

MME. DE BELLEGARDE. It's the stupidest of forgeries.

NEWMAN. Oh, not the stupidest! Reflect upon this, that your reputation, however much draped and arranged, can hardly bear a sudden, strong light. If I open a shutter from within, the others will be opened from without!

MME. DE BELLEGARDE. (*Falling back to the door of her apartments.*) Insulter—calumniator—liar!

NEWMAN. The shutter I speak of is still practically closed, but I have my hand upon the bolt. Call back here this instant the woman you've wrenched out of my arms, recant your incantations and reverse your spells, and your congruous darkness may close round you again, never again to be disturbed.

MME. DE BELLEGARDE. (*With her back to her door and her hand upon its latch, immensely affected but still immensely defiant.*) I'll send my son to drive you from the house and hurl your outrage after you!

NEWMAN. Your son ought to have faced me first, but after all you're the tigress, *he's* only the cub! (*Goes centre, while re-enter rapidly, left upper entrance,* M. DE MARIGNAC; *the sight of whom, bearing in his hand a letter with a visible black seal, arrests* MME. DE BELLEGARDE *a moment longer on her threshold.*) You're just what I want to see! (NEWMAN *quickly takes the letter from* MARIGNAC, *and goes on addressing her.*) Send the Marquis to listen to *this!*

MME. DE BELLEGARDE. Is Catherine Bread the forger? (*To* MARIGNAC.) She was my husband's mistress—she was always a monster of deceit.

MARIGNAC. She has left your house, Madame—she has left it forever.

MME. DE BELLEGARDE. Happy for *her!* (*Exit* MME. DE BELLEGARDE, *right.*)

NEWMAN. (*To* MARIGNAC.) I'm getting on beautifully, but the Marquis is coming, and we mustn't be two to one.

MARIGNAC. Then I'll go and wait for you at the inn.

NEWMAN. You've been first-rate (*taking* MARIGNAC's *hand*); and if you want to oblige me further you might order supper.

MARIGNAC. (*With his hand in* NEWMAN's, *smiling.*) For how many?

NEWMAN. Well, I guess you had better say four! (*Exit* MARIGNAC, *left upper entrance, and the moment he has done so re-enter* MME. DE CINTRÉ *left in a long black mantle, with its hood thrown back, adding to her perceptibly nun-like appearance, as if just prepared for her flight.*)

CLAIRE. What are you doing, Mr. Newman—and what have you already done?

NEWMAN. (*With his letter unopened in his hand.*) How do you know I've done anything?

CLAIRE. Mrs. Bread has just been to me, in intense excitement; she tells me she's leaving us forever.

NEWMAN. Oh, you'll see her again!

CLAIRE. When I asked her what had happened she told me you were still here, and that I must come to you and learn it from *your* lips.

NEWMAN. She never gave you happier advice!

CLAIRE. Why then has she gone?

NEWMAN. Because she's a woman of tact. But she has left behind her (*holding up the letter*) something that's almost as good as herself.

CLAIRE. What is it? What *is* it?

NEWMAN. A little scrap of paper that frightens your mother.

CLAIRE. And what are you doing with it?

NEWMAN. I'm raising the interdict!

CLAIRE. I don't understand—you torment me!

NEWMAN. I torment your mother—that's more to the purpose. She'll come back here in a moment and entreat you to forgive the life she has always led you and the injury she has tried to do *me*.

CLAIRE. That won't help you, Mr. Newman—for I'm utterly irrecoverable now! I shall never see her again—the carriage that's to take me away is at the door.

NEWMAN. Well, why don't you go down to it?

CLAIRE. (*Looking at him a moment in silence; then suddenly, passionately.*) Mr. Newman—don't be hard! Be merciful if you're strong! [25]

NEWMAN. *You* plead for mercy for them? —But I *knew* you are an angel!

CLAIRE. (*In the same way.*) You say you torment them. *Don't* torment them!

NEWMAN. What mercy have they had on *you?*

CLAIRE. Me? Oh, I'm safe forever!

NEWMAN. And am *I* safe, please? What mercy have they had on me?

CLAIRE. It's too terrible—and I don't understand. Give me your paper!

NEWMAN. (*Heedless of her request, going somewhat nearer to the door on the right and listening.*) I'm expecting your brother from one moment to another, so that if you wish to escape you have no time to lose.

CLAIRE. Do you mean that you're capable of telling him where I'm going?

NEWMAN. No, not that; I presume that would be mean!

CLAIRE. That's why I appeal to you—because you're generous, because you're loyal! I appeal to you to give me your letter!

NEWMAN. (*With a kind of grim groan, putting the letter behind him.*) Ah, don't ask me that—don't ask me that!

CLAIRE. You speak as if it gave you a power—but *what* power does it give you?

NEWMAN. God forbid I should denounce a mother to her child—however wronged the child may have been, and however iniquitous the mother. I can't tell you what power it gives me, unless I know how much *you* know.

CLAIRE. (*With a wild movement of denial, waving everything away.*) I know nothing—I know nothing!

NEWMAN. Well, *I* know everything, and now they know that I know!

CLAIRE. Isn't that enough, then? Give me your letter—give me your letter!

NEWMAN. To destroy it, to *spare* them, to *save* them, to deprive me of my immense advantage? You say I'm generous, but don't put my generosity on the rack!

CLAIRE. Don't put my terrors and my sorrows—whatever survives of any piety!

NEWMAN. If I keep my advantage we're free, we're strong, we're happy! You're liberated by your mother's hand, you're reprieved from the death you're bent on! The world's all before us again, and we go forth into it again together! Listen to that—*think* of that—and ask for the sacrifice!

CLAIRE. I can't listen and I can't think! You torture me! Only give it to me? (*She presses upon him, round to left and to right, with clasped hands of entreaty.*) Give it to me—give it to me!

NEWMAN. (*Receding before her and holding the letter out of her reach.*) Be mine—be mine—be mine!

CLAIRE. Pity me—how can I choose?

NEWMAN. If I give you this thing, I give up everything forever!

CLAIRE. I hear them coming, and if you keep me till they come you betray me!

NEWMAN. Why, if I don't speak of your intention?

CLAIRE. They'll see me dressed to go—they'll stop the carriage!

NEWMAN. Go, go, then—if you like that better!

CLAIRE. And leave you to destroy them? I can't—it's too horrible! (*Re-enter the* MARQUIS, *right, whom* CLAIRE *sees, giving a cry.*) Urbain, don't come in!

NEWMAN. (*To* CLAIRE, *while the* MARQUIS, *perceptibly pale, stands looking from one of them to the other.*) Now do you see what I mean by my frightening them? But they've frightened each other even more!

MARQUIS. (*Looking from head to foot at* NEWMAN, *who still has the letter behind him, and then turning to* MME. DE CINTRÉ.) Why are you dressed to go out?

CLAIRE. (*Bewildered a moment.*) Mrs. Bread has gone away—I'm going to overtake her! (*Then, hurriedly, feverishly.*) Mr. Newman has something in his hand—I'm trying to get it from him!

NEWMAN. (*To* MME. DE CINTRÉ.) I'll give it to you if you'll promise me on your sacred honour to give it back to *me* and not to another creature.

CLAIRE. (*With her hand out.*) I promise —I promise!

NEWMAN. Then *take* it! (*He holds it out to her, at the sight of which, before she can take it, the* MARQUIS *makes an unexpected desperate spring for it.* NEWMAN *recovers it and, moving to centre, jerks it behind him, smiling. To* MME. DE CINTRÉ.) You see how badly they want it! (*To the* MARQUIS.) It *is* a loaded pistol, Marquis— and dangerous to play with! You can easily understand I don't want to waste the charge!

CLAIRE. (*To the* MARQUIS, *imploringly.*) Let *me* take it—I beseech you! (*To* NEWMAN.) Give it to me now—he'll let you. *Give* it to me!

MARQUIS. (*To* NEWMAN.) I forbid you— don't, don't!

NEWMAN. (*Compassionately.*) How foolish you are! Do you think she'll read it? (*To* MME. DE CINTRÉ.) How little they know you, after all!

CLAIRE. Give it to *him*, then—give it to him! You've offered me innumerable services—so how can you refuse the only one I ever asked you? (*Falls on her knees before him.*)

NEWMAN. (*Struggling hard—passing his hand over his face.*) Refuse it? (*Taking her hands and raising her.*) I *love* it too much! —Hang it all, Monsieur de Bellegarde, I let you off! [26] I let your mother off.[27] (*Looking at* MME. DE CINTRÉ.) I let every one off.[28]

CLAIRE. (*With her hand to her heart and a long exhalation of relief.*) A-ah! (NEWMAN *hands the letter to the* MARQUIS, *who takes it now with a studied absence of eagerness, and* MME. DE CINTRÉ *continues, to* NEWMAN.) Oh, you're perfect!

MARQUIS. (*To* MME. DE CINTRÉ, *while, with affected indifference, he puts the letter, without looking at it, into his breast-pocket.*) That's more than can be said of you, Madame! (*Moving to door, right.*) Your mother will say a word to you, first, on the subject of your overtaking Mrs. Bread. (*Exit* MARQUIS, *right.*)

NEWMAN. (*To* MME. DE CINTRÉ.) He's gone to tell her—on the other side of the door he'll skip! That shows they feel saved from death! (*He goes to take up his hat.*)

CLAIRE. Their satisfaction will last but an instant.

NEWMAN. That's better than to have none—like me!

CLAIRE. (*Right centre, watching him.*) I was right, I was right—you're magnanimous!

NEWMAN. (*With a flicker of returning hope.*) Ah, Claire—don't say such things *now!*

CLAIRE. Now is just the time—as the carriage is there!

NEWMAN. (*Eagerly.*) The carriage? (*Re-enter the* MARQUIS, *right.*)

MARQUIS. (*To* NEWMAN.) You had really better leave the family to itself. My mother's coming.

CLAIRE. (*Giving her left hand to* NEWMAN.) Tell her when she comes that I shall marry Mr. Newman.

NEWMAN. Ah, my beloved! (*Kisses her hand.*)

---

[26] awff
[27] awff
[28] awff

CLAIRE. You've done it—you've brought me back—you've vanquished me!

NEWMAN. That's just what I wanted to see! (*He has caught her with one arm, and gives her a long kiss. He hurries up with her—exeunt rapidly left upper entrance. At the same moment re-enter* MME. DE BELLEGARDE, *right, breaking in with the letter that* NEWMAN *has given the* MARQUIS, *open in her hand.*)

MARQUIS. He's gone—but she's gone with him!

MME. DE BELLEGARDE. (*Crossing swiftly to one of the lighted candles that stand on a table at left and thrusting her paper straight into the flame.*) May they never come back—may they never come back!

MARQUIS. (*On the other side of the stage, watching the paper burn while the Curtain falls.*) Any more than that thing, eh?

Fragment of New Fourth Act

for

The American

1892

EDITOR'S FOREWORD

The "honorable" run of *The American* was not of sufficient duration to establish Edward Compton as a London manager. He gave up the Opera Comique and returned to the provinces, and for two decades he continued to be a part of the British tributary theatre, keeping alive a repertory of half a hundred plays and presenting them in all corners of the United Kingdom. He retained *The American* in this repertory but complained to James that the last act, one of unmitigated gloom—Valentin dead, Claire bound for a convent—was out of harmony with the rest of the play. "He has now played it every Friday for several months and had time to feel country audiences," Henry James wrote to William almost a year after the end of the London run. The audiences were *"very* friendly indeed up to the end of the 3rd" but they drooped over the fourth.

During the autumn of 1892 James wrote a new fourth act "in a comedy-sense—heaven forgive me" and took it to Bath on November 14, where the Compton Comedy Company was playing. "So the 4th is now *another* 4th," he announced to William, "which will basely gratify their artless instincts and British thick-wittedness and thanks to it the poor old play will completely save one's honor (which is all I care for) as a permanent and regular thing. It will be much for it to 'keep the stage.' The Comptons are delighted with the new Act (a feat of unspeakable difficulty) and it is played for the first time at Bristol next week (without of course the smallest reference to any change. Please never *make* any.)"

Apparently the Comptons were not as secretive. The *Bristol Times and Mirror* for November 26, 1892 announced that the new act had won a "distinctly favorable" verdict of a large and enthusiatic audience." The review went on:

> . . . the curtain falls on a fine climax in the third act and Mr. James is to be congratulated on a decided hit. In the fourth act, which he has entirely rewritten, he has strengthened his play considerably. He makes the pretty flirt, Noémie bring about a reconciliation between Lord Deepmere and his antagonist Comte Valentin; and this in the most natural way possible. Though why on earth he should introduce Mrs. Bread to tell again the story of the skeleton in the Bellegarde cupboard it is difficult to imagine. Everyone knows all about it, and a valuable ten minutes of theatrical lifetime might be well spared both to actors and audience.

One advantage of the new act not noted in the press was that there was no scenic change now from Act III to Act IV—a considerable aid to production on the road.

A typescript of the new fourth act—here printed for the first time—with some of the pages missing, was found among James's papers. It is impossible to say whether this was the definitive form of the act or a draft for the version James gave to Compton.

FRAGMENT OF NEW FOURTH ACT

FOR

THE AMERICAN

Same scene as Act Third. On the rise of the Curtain enter rapidly, busily, the Doc-TOR, centre. Feeling in his pocket for a pencil, and looking about for paper, he goes, right, to the table, on which he sees a portfolio and on which his hat has already been placed. He takes a bit of paper from the portfolio and, standing and bending over, hastily writes. Enter Noémie, in her hat and jacket, left, with several unopened letters in her hand.

Doctor. (*Folding the small paper and giving it to* Noémie.) Something to be *sent* for—for the *nurse*.

Noémie. (*Who has laid down her letters, anxious.*) Isn't the Count *better?*

Doctor. (*Taking his hat.*) I can't *say!*

Noémie. (*Disappointed.*) But I thought this morning was to *show!*

Doctor. I promised nothing, Mademoiselle. It was a necessary experiment.

Noémie. But surely it has *succeeded!*

Doctor. It *may* succeed. It's too soon to judge.

Noémie. (*At right, persistent.*) When can you judge?

Doctor. (*At left, hesitating, looking at his watch.*) He's *quiet*—I shall come back at one. (*Exit* Doctor, *left.*)

Noémie. (*At centre, unfolding the small paper he has given her; with, while she looks at it, uplifted eyebrows and a slight grimace of anxiety.*) I must send. (*Then gathering up the letters she has laid down and reading from the postmarks on the envelopes.*) New York, Boston, Chicago, London, Rome, Bombay! (*While she speaks the last word enter* Newman, *centre: perceptibly altered, paler, worn and worried.*

She turns eagerly as she hears him.) Is he quiet?

Newman. (*With a manner different from hitherto—rather curt, preoccupied and impatient.*) As quiet as if he'd *money* on it! Are those my *letters?*

Noémie. (*Giving him the letters.*) I just brought them *in.*

Newman. (*Looking rapidly at the successive envelopes, then, with impatient disappointment, chucking them toward the table, so that they fall and lie scattered on the floor.*) You might as well have brought a row of pins!—They ain't what I *want!*

Noémie. (*After an instant, reassuringly.*) What you want will *come*, Mr. Newman. (*Then with intenser decision.*) I *know* it will come!

Newman. You talk, Miss Noémie, as if you had a private *wire!*

Noémie. (*Precipitately.*) Well, I *have!* (*Then catching herself up.*) I know more than you *think.*

Newman. (*Turning away, on his side, restlessly, with irritation, an eclipse of his old geniality.*) "Think"?—I've ceased to think. I've ceased almost to *feel.*

Noémie. (*Taking the risk, as he goes nervously, vaguely up, as if wandering and looking about him for something that hasn't come to pass, that still doesn't appear.*) You may be sure that *she* hasn't! She'll take pity on you *yet!*

Newman. (*Struck, then facing her abruptly.*) Whom are you *talking* about?

Noémie. (*Slightly disconcerted by his manner and explaining.*) I thought you alluded—to a certain lady!

Newman. (*With strong emphasis.*) I

243

never allude—to a certain lady!

NOÉMIE. (*Apologetic.*) I was misled by your eagerness for (*vague*) some communication.

NEWMAN. The communication I'm eager for is a communication—"answer paid"!

NOÉMIE. There's a quarter, no doubt, from which you're *not* expecting news. But (*after an instant,*) I daresay you'll have some, all the *same!*

NEWMAN. I won't have any if I can *help* it! I've had about enough to *last* me!

NOÉMIE. Of course I'm thinking of some *better* news!

NEWMAN. (*With a certain irritation.*) You think too much, Miss Noémie. (*Knocking over, with his restless motion, and with some violence, a jar, or some object on the table.*) You had better imitate my *repose!*

NOÉMIE. (*Laughing.*) Your repose is bad for the furniture.

NEWMAN. Oh, if I should *really* lie down I guess you'd have to *renew* it! (*Then with a quick revulsion, penitent, with his hand out.*) Forgíve my cussedness! There are moments when I don't know what to *do* with myself!

NOÉMIE. (*With sympathy, taking his hand.*) You're awfully *worried!*

NEWMAN. (*Admitting, explaining.*) About the results of the Count's operation. We hoped for an unmistakeable effect.

NOÉMIE. Which doesn't take *place?*

NEWMAN. It's a bad moment to *pass.* I can see the surgeon's *uneasy.*

NOÉMIE. And the *others*—who were *present?*

NEWMAN. If we're not reassured by this afternoon, they're to meet *again.*

NOÉMIE. And if the operation's a *failure*—

NEWMAN. (*Interrupting, sombre, raising his arms and letting them fall.*) The *worst* may happen!

NOÉMIE. (*With feeling, with resolution.*) The worst shan't happen! His natural strength's immense!

NEWMAN. (*Considering, agreeing.*) Yes, greater, even now, than *mine! I* can't recuperate!

NOÉMIE. (*Smiling at him, soothingly.*) You want a *nurse!*

NEWMAN. I want about *fifty!*

NOÉMIE. If the effect you speak of, for the Count, *does* take place—

NEWMAN. (*Interrupting.*) He'll come up in an hour!

NOÉMIE. (*With surprise.*) In an *hour?*

NEWMAN. (*Confident.*) In a *minute*—in a *day,* in a *week!* (*With a bitter smile.*) Oh, faster than *I!*

NOÉMIE. (*With recurring intention and significance.*) Oh *you,* Mr. Newman—!

NEWMAN. (*Impatient, weary, interrupting.*) Don't speak of *me*—I ain't sure I'm *alive!*

NOÉMIE. (*With spirit.*) Well, some other people are, thank heaven, and *while* there's life, in any quarter, I've always heard there's *hope!* (*Then, as* NEWMAN, *fidgetty, moves away again with a gesture of nervous pessimism.*) We must *pray* for the Count!

NEWMAN. You *can't* pray. (*Then, in a more explanatory tone, as he turns back to* NOÉMIE *again.*) I've a *double* anxiety, and a deadly *impatience.* The letter I'm looking for is a letter from *Mrs. Bread.*

NOÉMIE. (*Struck.*) Their English housekeeper?

NEWMAN. The plain Wiltshire woman! I wrote to her three days ago—I begged her to *come* to me.

NOÉMIE. (*Thinking, suggesting.*) Perhaps your letter never *reached* her.

NEWMAN. To their country home. That's where they've *gone.*

NOÉMIE. (*Wondering again.*) You asked her to come up to Paris?

NEWMAN. To render me a service.

NOÉMIE. (*After an instant.*) What service can *she* render you?

NEWMAN. (*At the centre door.*) That's just what I want to *see!* (*Exit* NEWMAN, *centre.*)

NOÉMIE. (*Alone, picking up the fallen letters and putting them into her pocket while she repeats his words.*) "A double anxiety—a deadly impatience"? And what are *mine,* I should like to know? (*Eagerly, seeing* NIOCHE *at the left. Enter* NIOCHE, *left.*) Who *is* it?

NIOCHE. (*Announcing.*) Milord Deepmere! (*Enter* LORD DEEPMERE, *with his arm in a sling, left.*)

NOÉMIE. (*With relief, as he takes her

hand and raises it respectfully to his lips.) At *last!*

NIOCHE. (*To* NOÉMIE.) Shall I inform Mr. Newman?

NOÉMIE. (*Giving him the little folded paper left by the* DOCTOR *and which she has kept in her hand during the scene with* NEWMAN.) No—you'll go out for *this.* (*Exit* NIOCHE, *who has taken the paper obediently, left; on which* NOÉMIE *goes on, warningly, to* DEEPMERE.) Be very *quiet*— we've reached the *crisis.*

DEEPMERE. (*Disappointed, anxious.*) Isn't he *better?*

NOÉMIE. We shall know at noon. (*Then pressingly.*) Have you been to the *Convent?*

DEEPMERE. I've just *left* it. She'll *come!*

NOÉMIE. *A la bonne heure!* You followed my *instructions?*

DEEPMERE. To the *letter!* I left your note yesterday, with my own card, on which I wrote a few words. This morning I had a gracious line from her asking to see me at an early hour.

NOÉMIE. And she *did* see you?

DEEPMERE. In the parlour, for five minutes. She's free, a *pensionnaire,* she can receive.

NOÉMIE. She has taken no vow?

DEEPMERE. Not so *soon*—in three *weeks!* She has only taken *refuge*—she has only been *waiting.*

NOÉMIE. For Mr. Newman to try *again?*

DEEPMERE. For her brother to come back to *life!* She has a passionate desire to *see* him.

NOÉMIE. Then why hasn't she come before?

DEEPMERE. How could she enter the house of the man she feels she has terribly *injured?*

NOÉMIE. I hope that if she's coming now it isn't because she has *ceased* to feel it.

DEEPMERE. It's because you've appealed to her for poor Bellegarde, from whom it's only her dread of *meeting* Mr. Newman that has separated her.

NOÉMIE. (*Thinking.*) Does she count on me, by chance, to arrange that she shall *not* meet Mr. Newman?

DEEPMERE. She didn't tell me so, but she rather let me see it.

NOÉMIE. (*With decision.*) Then she let you see a great piece of *nonsense!* I've a perfect little plan that the poor things *shall* meet!

DEEPMERE. Your little plans are no business of mine. I performed your errand to render you the service you required, and you may imagine the *courage*—you must do justice to the *heroism,* I needed, to present myself before her while (*with an expression of strong feeling, of repentant bitterness, and a significant nod toward the other room*) her brother lies there in such a state!

NOÉMIE. I rendered *you* a service, rather, by putting it in your power to entreat her to *forgive* you!

DEEPMERE. How *will* she forgive me—if Bellegarde doesn't pull through?

NOÉMIE. (*After an instant.*) I don't know how *she* will, Milord—but I know very well that *I* won't!

DEEPMERE. (*Nervously, gloomily.*) I worry myself half to *death,* I'm sick and sore with *suspense!*

NOÉMIE. You have your *alleviations,* Milord—your frequent visits to this house.

DEEPMERE. I come to *ask*—I come to *watch;* but it's *not* an alleviation—for you only torment me *more!*

NOÉMIE. Mr. Newman makes it *up* to you—he makes everything up to *everyone!*

DEEPMERE. He's as kind as he's *queer*— I never did him justice. But what comfort is there in a man who's in still worse spirits than myself?

NOÉMIE. He *is,* to-day, I admit. Therefore you had better not *see* him.

DEEPMERE. I don't *want* to see him. When there's a bad report of Bellegarde I don't want to look any one in the *face!*

NOÉMIE. (*Minimising.*) There isn't exactly a *bad* report.

DEEPMERE. (*Objecting.*) But if there isn't exactly a *good* one—? The only good one will be to see him standing *there!*

NOÉMIE. (*After another instant.*) Well, Milord—you *shall* see him!

DEEPMERE. (*Incredulous, with a backward nod of his head.*) If you could only have a little plan for *that!*

NOÉMIE. I *have* a little plan! I'm wiser than the doctors. *Leave* it to me!

DEEPMERE. I don't know what you mean,

but I'm ready to say *this* to you—that if he gets *well*— (*Pausing, hesitating.*)

Noémie. (*Waiting.*) If he gets well?

Deepmere. (*Continuing.*) By any intervention of *yours*, there's nothing on *earth* you may ask of me that I won't gladly *give* you!

Noémie. Thank you, Milord. As a general thing I don't *have* to "ask"!

Deepmere. Don't you sometimes have to *choose?*

Noémie. (*After a moment.*) Do I understand that in the event you speak of I *may?*

Deepmere. (*Emphatically.*) Anything that's mine!

Noémie. (*After another instant, looking at him.*) I'll *choose!*—Now leave me to receive the Countess! (*Seeing* Nioche, *left.*) My father will show you out.

(*Re-enter* Nioche, *left with a small packet.*)

Nioche. (*With the packet, to* Noémie.) I give it to the nurse?

Deepmere. (*To* Nioche, *on a motion of assent from* Noémie.) Don't mind me! (Nioche *bows and exit with packet at centre, and* Deepmere *goes up, to* Noémie.) You must really let me come *back!*

Noémie. (*Looking at him an instant.*) Did you *mean* what you said just now?

Deepmere. Did you mean what *you* said?

Noémie. (*With a nod of decision.*) I *meant* it!

Deepmere. Well—*I* meant it!

Noémie. Then shake hands—*à l'anglaise!* (*He gives her his hand and she gives it a vigorous "British" shake, up and down.*) Come back at *one.*

Deepmere. At one! (*Exit* Lord Deepmere, *left. Re-enter* Nioche, *centre.*)

Noémie. What does she say?

Nioche. (*With his finger to his lips.*) Shshsh!

Noémie. (*Imitating him.*) "Shshsh" indeed! We've got hold of the *Countess!*

Nioche. (*Astonished.*) Got *hold* of her?

Noémie. She's coming at any moment.

Nioche. (*Bewildered.*) Then what shall we do with Mr. Newman?

Noémie. Get hold of *him!*

Nioche. (*Alarmed.*) But think of the possible consequences of their meeting!

Noémie. They're just what I *have*

thought of! I shall bring them together, and you must *help* me.

Nioche. What shall I *do?*

Noémie. See that she comes straight in *here.*

Nioche. (*Troubled, incredulous.*) If he knows she's in here he'll go *out!*

Noémie. I'll keep him at home! (*Seeing* Newman, *centre.*) Here he *is*—watch for *her!*

(*Re-enter* Newman, *centre. Exit* Nioche, *left.*)

[Four pages of the manuscript are missing at this point.]

. . . *his hand into* Newman's *arm—exeunt* Newman *and* Doctor, *centre. Re-enter* Nioche, *left.*)

Nioche. (*Announcing.*) Madame la Comtesse de Cintré.

Noémie. (*To herself, with happy emotion.*) Ah!

(*Enter, left,* Madame de Cintré. *Exit* Nioche, *discreetly, left.*)

Noémie. (*Curtseying very respectfully.*) Madame!

Claire. (*Graciously, but very gravely.*) Mademoiselle.—Let me acknowledge instantly my great obligation to you; but let me also say that I have presumed to find in your intervention a pledge that the step I am taking in response to it shall be attended with inconvenience—to *no* one.— May I see my brother *instantly?*

Noémie. You must allow me to prepare him for your visit.

Claire. (*Surprised.*) He doesn't *expect* me?

Noémie. (*Smiling.*) We don't let him expect!

Claire. (*Anxious.*) He's very *weak*, then —he's *worse?*

Noémie. He'll be better when he has seen you!

Claire. (*Nervous.*) I shall be very brief.

Noémie. So shall I, Madame. (*Then, indicating a chair.*) Be so good, meanwhile, as to be seated.

Claire. (*Uneasy, standing, looking round the room and recognising it.*) Is there no place in the house in which my intrusion will be less apparent than *here?*

NOÉMIE. (*Smiling.*) Trust me, Madame, to have measured your risk and to have your interests at *heart!*

CLAIRE. It's only because I trust you that I'm here. Shall I see you again before I leave the house?

NOÉMIE. That will depend, Madame, on your own inclination.

CLAIRE. Let me make sure, at any rate, of this opportunity of thanking you for the kindness Lord Deepmere informs me you have shown my brother. (*Hesitating, then with suppressed emotion, a kind of painful effort.*) And if there have been *other* ministrations—and *other* charities— (*Hesitating again with her emotion, pausing.*)

NOÉMIE. (*At right, seeing* NEWMAN, *centre.*) I've done what I *could*, Madame!

(*Re-enter* NEWMAN, *centre.*)

CLAIRE. (*At left, violently struck, to herself.*) Ah! (*Exit* NOÉMIE, *rapidly, discreetly, by the staircase. Arrested, at centre, violently, on his side, a moment, by the sight of* MADAME DE CINTRÉ, *then controlling himself with a strong effort,* NEWMAN *comes down on right. They stand an instant on opposite sides of the stage, not looking at each other. At last, sadly, coldly, but without anger,* CLAIRE *exclaims.*) The work of that young lady!

NEWMAN. (*After an instant, looking straight before him.*) That young lady *means* well!

CLAIRE. I hesitated half the night—but I've *come!*

NEWMAN. I know what it's for. It must have seemed to you hard you *shouldn't!*

CLAIRE. It seemed *impossible!* But I never *dreamed*—of disturbing *you.* (*NEWMAN looks at her, at this, and there is another silence between them while she stands, motionless and expressionless, with her eyes on the ground.*) Mayn't I go to him?

NEWMAN. I must say a word to him *first.*

CLAIRE. (*After an instant, as* NEWMAN *doesn't move.*) I hoped he might *know.*

NEWMAN. I haven't told him.

CLAIRE. (*Struck, vague.*) You *knew* then I was coming?

NEWMAN. I learned it five minutes ago. If I had done so sooner I would have kept out of your way.

CLAIRE. (*As impersonally as possible.*) Let me get out of yours. (*Then, after another instant, as he still doesn't move.*) But before I do so, let me express in one word— (*Pausing, faltering in her effort to efface all emotion, to be utterly passionless.*)

NEWMAN. (*With a sudden faint hope.*) In one word?

CLAIRE. (*As if to say all she means, but at the same time to check him by her manner—to make any outbreak impossible.*) The intensity of my gratitude.

NEWMAN. (*After standing an instant with his eyes on the ground suddenly shaken by irresistible feeling and breaking out into a single abrupt cry of passionate appeal.*) Claire!

CLAIRE. (*Straightening herself and speaking with rapid and colourless formality.*) Be so very good as to *tell* him! (*NEWMAN, who has instantly, at the sight of her manner, controlled himself again, stands one instant more and gives her one long, fixed and intensely searching look. Then, as if satisfied afresh that he has indeed lost her forever and that nothing more can pass between them, he decides, gives a gesture in which he seems to dash away the last shadow of his hope, and goes out rapidly at centre.* MME. DE CINTRÉ, *left alone, sinks slowly, and as if with the sense of momentary liberation from the worst distress, into the nearest chair, where she sits an instant staring, with infinite sadness, before her. Then slowly, dolorously, hopelessly.*) Ah, miserable *me!*

(*Re-enter, left,* NIOCHE, *at the sound of whose entrance* MME. DE CINTRÉ *quickly springs up.*)

NIOCHE. (*Announcing.*) Mrs. Bread!

(*Enter* MRS. BREAD, *while* NIOCHE, *always on tiptoe, retires. Exit* NIOCHE, *left.*)

CLAIRE. (*Startled at the sight of* MRS. BREAD.) *You?*

MRS. BREAD. (*Equally startled on her own side.*) Have you come *back* to him?

CLAIRE. (*With a sharp, clear gesture of negation, then, as if to explain everything.*) Valentin's very *ill!*

MRS. BREAD. (*Surprised.*) He told me he was *better!*

CLAIRE. (*Vague.*) *Who* told you?

MRS. BREAD. Mr. Newman—he *wrote* to me.

CLAIRE. (*Still more surprised, wondering.*) To come to Valentin?

MRS. BREAD. To come to *him.*

CLAIRE. (*Struck, wondering.*) To *him?* For what purpose?

MRS. BREAD. To answer some questions.

CLAIRE. (*After an instant, mystified, with dawning anxiety.*) What questions?

MRS. BREAD. That's what I came up to find out. (MME. DE CINTRÉ *stands looking at her an instant, then, as if with an idea, an alarm, goes up nervously to centre, where, as if listening, she remains another instant.* MRS. BREAD, *who has passed to right, goes on.*) Is the Count *worse?*

CLAIRE. (*Coming quickly and abruptly down to her.*) Catty—what does Mr. Newman *want* of you?

MRS. BREAD. (*Impenetrable.*) Have you seen Mr. Newman?

CLAIRE. For a moment. He's coming back!

MRS. BREAD. Then can't you take pity on him?

CLAIRE. (*Alarmed, listening.*) Hush!

MRS. BREAD. (*Persisting, pleading.*) Everything's not over?

CLAIRE. Everything! (*Then, with abrupt decision.*) Catty—you must leave the house with me.

MRS. BREAD. (*Reluctant, vague.*) Now?

CLAIRE. When I've seen my brother.

MRS. BREAD. And before *I've* seen Mr. Newman?

CLAIRE. (*With the climax of her uneasiness and her appeal, repeating her question of a moment before.*) Catty—what does he *want* of you?

MRS. BREAD. (*Seeing* NEWMAN, *centre.*) *Ask* him!

(*Re-enter* NEWMAN, *centre.*)

NEWMAN. (*After stopping an instant, moved, at the sight of* MRS. BREAD, *says to her formally.*) You shall *see* him. (*Then to* CLAIRE.) Please go in *first.*

CLAIRE. (*Who has given him a long, fixed, searching look, exactly like the one he has given her before his last exit, and who has then transferred her eyes to* MRS. BREAD *with the same effect until* MRS.

BREAD *uneasily turns away and* NEWMAN *passes up to hold back the drapery of the door at centre.*) With the understanding, please, that her visit terminates with *mine.*

NEWMAN. (*Surprised.*) That you take her *away?*

CLAIRE. (*Down at the left, after looking again from* NEWMAN *at centre to* MRS. BREAD *at right.*) In a very few minutes. (*Exit* CLAIRE *rapidly, centre.*)

NEWMAN. (*Sombre, still holding the curtain and looking after her.*) She's lost—she's lost! (*Then dropping the curtain, almost dashing it from him with a gesture of sudden anguish; coming down to* MRS. BREAD *and speaking in a different tone.*) Are you going *away* with her?

MRS. BREAD. She told me she *wishes* it!

NEWMAN. (*Struck, thinking.*) *Why* does she wish it?

MRS. BREAD. My arrival upsets her.

NEWMAN. (*Catching at every ray of hope.*) Upsets her?

MRS. BREAD. Just as my departure upsets her mother.

NEWMAN. (*Struck, cheered.*) The Marquise tried to prevent it?

MRS. BREAD. (*Smiling.*) Almost by force!

NEWMAN. (*Smiling.*) That's just what I want to *see!*

MRS. BREAD. (*More gravely.*) It has cost me my *home.*

NEWMAN. I'll give you another. You've made a great sacrifice for me.

MRS. BREAD. Wasn't that what you *asked* for?

NEWMAN. It was *indeed*, Mrs. Bread! But no one knows better than I that we don't always *get* what we ask for!

MRS. BREAD. Sometimes we get more! (*After an instant.*) The *Marquis* has also come.

NEWMAN. (*Struck.*) He's *here?*

MRS. BREAD. He's in *Paris.* He must have arrived last night.

NEWMAN. (*Greatly interested.*) Will he come to this *house?*

MRS. BREAD. (*After an instant.*) He never was particularly *shy!*

NEWMAN. (*Encouraged, considering.*) Well, I think that's *good.*

MRS. BREAD. What do you think it's good *for?*

NEWMAN. I'll tell you in a moment, but there's something I want you to tell me first. (*She gives a sign of willingness, and he goes on.*) From what you know of the state of my account should you suppose I had about *one cent* in the bank?

MRS. BREAD. (*Vague.*) In the bank?

NEWMAN. The *Countess*, Mrs. Bread, is the bank—a splendid but deadly institution. Should you say she had been touched for one *instant* by the miserable spectacle I present?

MRS. BREAD. I was struck just now by the way she *looked* at you.

NEWMAN. The way she looked at me (*thinking, piecing it together*) seemed to me to show that she's *afraid* of something; and if she's afraid of anything—she ain't indifferent.

MRS. BREAD. I owe you the truth, Mr. Newman. Whatever she may be afraid of she's not afraid of relenting!

NEWMAN. How can you answer for *that?*

MRS. BREAD. I *begged* her, before you came *in*, to relent.

NEWMAN. And what did she say?

MRS. BREAD. She says it's too *late*.

NEWMAN. (*Struck, smitten, with his last hope dashed, and giving a gesture of despair which definitely indicates this.*) Well then—if it's too late for *her*, it's not too late for *me!* I stand before you, Mrs. Bread, as a man with a damnable grievance, and I call upon you to help me to prove that I can give back blow for blow.

MRS. BREAD. (*After an instant, impressed, very gravely.*) *Now* I understand, sir, why you've *sent* for me.

NEWMAN. I can't blow my head, and I can't break my spirit! It may be very rude, it may be a trifle barbarous of him, but the injured man, the *natural* man, in me, cries *out*. He cries to you, Mrs. Bread, and I'm glad you've guessed the *reason!*

MRS. BREAD. You'll make a tremendous *demand* of me.

NEWMAN. (*Anxious.*) You don't mean to say you'll *reject* it?

MRS. BREAD. I can't help thinking a little of the consequences.

NEWMAN. They're just what I want to *see!*

MRS. BREAD. But if I satisfy you—too

late (*hesitating*)—where's the use—

NEWMAN. (*Interrupting.*) It's never too late to feel better, and there's *always* some use in being satisfied!

MRS. BREAD. (*After considering an instant and composing herself.*) Permit me then to ask what it is you already *know.*

NEWMAN. I already know that in that abominable hour, ten years ago, when two French gentlemen lost their lives— (*Pausing.*)

MRS. BREAD. Yes, Mr. Newman.

NEWMAN. The late Marquis, instructed by his daughter, *did* find on the spot a person—suspected, individually or *unsuspected*—who was keeping an appointment with his son-in-law.

MRS. BREAD. And that person—?

NEWMAN. That person, Mrs. Bread— that person, I have been able to ascertain, was M. de Bellegarde's own wife, the mother of his children, the mother of her *lover's* wife! (MRS. BREAD *sinks into a chair and sits an instant with her face covered with her hands, while* NEWMAN, *pausing with the effect of his words, stands looking at her.*) So that in the miracle of her successful disappearance and the consequent security of her abominable secret, her audacious reproach to her daughter of having, without justice and without mercy, sent a father and a husband to their death—

MRS. BREAD. (*Interrupting, rising, completing, with a different manner.*) Has made the darkness of that daughter's life, has made her seeming ignorance a ground on which the Marquise has always triumphantly appealed.

NEWMAN. Therefore if such an ignorance is turned to knowledge and such a ground is knocked away—

MRS. BREAD. (*Interrupting again, with decision.*) The Countess will only plunge deeper into her convent!

NEWMAN. (*Struck with the painful and plausible force of this, but resolutely throwing it off.*) Then I shan't be worse off than I *am!*

MRS. BREAD. But if you know the truth what more do you *want?*

NEWMAN. I want the evidence.

MRS. BREAD. (*Thinking, with a sad and*

ominous but affirmative nod.) Ah, the evidence—!

NEWMAN. The evidence *exists?*

MRS. BREAD. It exists.

NEWMAN. And in your *hands!*

MRS. BREAD. In my hands.

NEWMAN. Then *give* it to me.

MRS. BREAD. I'll give it to you. But you must give me my *time.*

NEWMAN. Certainly—that's why I want you to *stay* with me.

MRS. BREAD. If I stay with you I can't go with the Countess.

NEWMAN. (*With decision.*) Of *course* you can't go with the Countess!

MRS. BREAD. (*After another instant.*) I'll *stay* with you!—But (*looking round her*) *where* shall I stay?

NEWMAN. (*Seeing* NOÉMIE *at the foot of the stairs, and with a gesture that indicates and introduces her to* MRS. BREAD.) This young lady'll *show* you.

(*Re-enter, at the moment* MRS. BREAD *speaks and so as to encounter* NEWMAN's *presentation,* NOÉMIE *from the staircase. She inclines herself graciously to* MRS. BREAD, *but before she can speak the* DOCTOR *breaks joyously in from the centre. Re-enter the* DOCTOR, *centre.*)

DOCTOR. (*Coming down, in high jubilation.*) Great news—great news! He's *better!*

THE THREE OTHERS. (*Eagerly at once.*) Better!

[One page of the manuscript is missing at this point.]

. . . *instant; then, uncontrollably, she breaks out.*) Mr. Newman, what do you *want* of her?

NEWMAN. (*After an instant.*) I want her to talk about *you!*

CLAIRE. (*Passionately.*) *Don't* talk about *me!* I can't *leave* her to you.

NEWMAN. (*Bitterly.*) It's little enough indeed you *leave* to me!

CLAIRE. (*After an instant during which she has stood with her eyes on the ground and then raised them, speaking gently, pleadingly.*) Don't I leave you *my brother?*

NEWMAN. (*With a slow headshake.*) He's *my* brother, *now.*

CLAIRE. Then act as if you were *his!* He'll take *care* of you—as you have taken care of *him.*

NEWMAN. (*Struck, thinking.*) He'll take *care* of me!

CLAIRE. (*Pressingly.*) Then *call* her to me!

NEWMAN. (*After an instant.*) What you ask of me is a terrible *sacrifice.*

CLAIRE. I ask it because you're loyal—because you're generous.

NEWMAN. I want to be generous—but (*after an instant, struggling*)—don't put my generosity on the *rack!*

CLAIRE. Don't put my terrors and my sorrows, and don't refuse the only service I ever *asked* you!

NEWMAN. (*Passing up and round, struggling, thinking, stops short, arrested, close to* VALENTIN's *door; then suddenly, after listening a moment, breaks out to* MME. DE CINTRÉ, *with irresistible cheer and from where he stands.*) I hear his old *laugh!*

CLAIRE. God be praised!

NEWMAN. (*Coming down.*) God be praised!

CLAIRE. (*At right, suppliant.*) Call her to me!

NEWMAN. (*At left, after a moment of intense inward struggle, culminating in a victory, while he again, for an instant, stands looking at her.*) Hanged then if I care! (*With a snap of his fingers and a tone of high decision, giving up, as it were all his own cause.*) I'll *call* her to you! (*Exit* NEWMAN, *rapidly, with all the energy of his renunciation, centre.*)

CLAIRE. (*Alone an instant at right, with the strong emotion of her relief.*) He *is* loyal—he *is* generous!

(*Re-enter* NIOCHE, *left.*)

NIOCHE. (*Announcing.*) Milord Deepmere!

(*Re-enter* DEEPMERE, *left. Exit* NIOCHE, *left.*)

DEEPMERE. (*Eagerly, anxiously, to* CLAIRE.) Is your brother *better?*

CLAIRE. He's *better!* (*Then checking a happy demonstration on* DEEPMERE's *part, as if she too just hears the laugh that has been heard by* NEWMAN.) Shshsh—you can *hear* him!

(*Re-enter* NIOCHE, *left.*)

NIOCHE. (*Announcing.*) Monsieur le Marquis de Bellegarde!

(*Enter, left, the* MARQUIS DE BELLEGARDE. NIOCHE *remains.*)

DEEPMERE. (*Grave, formal, to the* MARQUIS.) Your brother's *better.*

MARQUIS. (*More formal still and very superior.*) It was in the hope of hearing so that I took this unconventional step! (*Then to* MME. DE CINTRÉ, *whom he has made some demonstration of surprise at finding, and with whom he has exchanged a fixed, firm look.*) We were under the impression, Madam, that you had retired to a convent.

CLAIRE. (*With a touch of intensely refined and exquisite comedy.*) Your impression, my dear brother, was an impression I've *hitherto* shared!

DEEPMERE. (*Struck by this, eager, appealing to her.*) Ah, you've come *back—?*

CLAIRE. (*Troubled, struggling with herself and turning away from him.*) Don't *ask* me!

(*Re-enter, rapidly,* MRS. BREAD, *centre.*)

MRS. BREAD. (*Coming down, excited, joyous.*) The Count's on his *feet*—the Count's coming *in!*

NIOCHE. (*Catching up the good news, jubilant also.*) Perhaps we shall see him at luncheon—which I've just been requested to *announce!*

MARQUIS. Luncheon? I've scarcely come to a *meal!*

MRS. BREAD. (*To* MME. DE CINTRÉ.) I'm at your ladyship's service—I'm ready to *go.*

CLAIRE. (*After an instant, abruptly.*) Then *I'm* not!

MRS. BREAD. (*Astonished.*) You're *not?*

CLAIRE. (*Still with her agitation, abruptly again.*) Stay *with* me! (*Then seeing* VALENTIN, *between* NEWMAN *and* NOÉMIE, *at the door.*) Here he *is!*

(*Enter, centre,* VALENTIN, *supported on either side by* NEWMAN *and* NOÉMIE. *In a short silk dressing-jacket and light trousers and slippers, with a bright silk handkerchief round his neck, he is pale and weak but smiling and happy; he has an arm in the arm of each of his companions. They stop with him half*

way down, and he pauses an instant, looking at the others; then he sinks, gently and with relief into the chair which NIOCHE *has gone quickly round to place in a position to receive him.*)

VALENTIN. (*To* CLAIRE.) My sister—you've worked a *miracle.*

NEWMAN. (*Who has looked, surprised, at the* MARQUIS.) A miracle!

NOÉMIE. A miracle!

VALENTIN. (*To* DEEPMERE.) My poor friend, give me your hand. (*He holds out his hand to* DEEPMERE, *who rushes forward and grasps it.* DEEPMERE *then comes down again, following* NOÉMIE, *who when* VALENTIN *sinks into the chair, behind which* NIOCHE *remains standing, has passed to the extreme right.*)

NEWMAN. (*Still at* VALENTIN's *left, after a continued fixed look at the* MARQUIS.) Marquis, I guess you had better give him *yours.*

(*The* MARQUIS *comes forward, more majestically, for this purpose, and he and* MRS. BREAD *address themselves together to* VALENTIN *while* NIOCHE *continues behind his chair and* NEWMAN *moves further to left.* CLAIRE, *on the right, after her brother's words to her, has dropped into the chair at the table and sits there, with her eyes on the ground, in intense concentration.*)

NOÉMIE. (*Triumphant, down in front, to* DEEPMERE.) *Don't* you see him there before you?

DEEPMERE. (*Grateful, ardent.*) Exquisite woman—how did you *do* it?

NOÉMIE. (*Radiant with the success of her machination, and indicating with a nod* MME. DE CINTRÉ, *behind them and at their left.*) I made *her* do it!

DEEPMERE. (*Pressing.*) Couldn't you make her do something *else?*

NOÉMIE. (*After a glance back at her.*) She *will* do it!

DEEPMERE. (*Looking too, embracing the situation and thoroughly satisfied with it.*) Well—what shall I *give* you?

NIOCHE. (*Behind* VALENTIN's *chair, before* NOÉMIE *can answer, to* NEWMAN.) I ought to mention, sir, that I've been requested to announce your *luncheon.*

NEWMAN. (*Speaking gaily to* VALENTIN *and quitting the position from which he has been watching* MME. DE CINTRÉ, *to change places with* NIOCHE, *who passes to the left.*) My dear fellow, what do you say to *luncheon?*

VALENTIN. (*Leaning back in his chair.*) I am afraid I must have it *here* and that I must ask you to *join* me.

NEWMAN. (*Behind* VALENTIN'S *chair, while the* MARQUIS, *quitting* VALENTIN, *comes down on left and* MRS. BREAD *comes down on right, below* MME. DE CINTRÉ *and above* NOÉMIE *and* DEEPMERE.) With pleasure, Valentin. Marquis, won't *you* join him?—Lord Deepmere, won't *you?*—Miss Noémie, won't *you?*

NOÉMIE. (*To* NEWMAN, *while the* MARQUIS, *down at the left, considering, hesitating, solemnly smooths his hat and* NEWMAN *and* VALENTIN *wait and watch for his answer.*) Thank you very much—I must *go!*

DEEPMERE. (*Eagerly, to* NOÉMIE, *while* VALENTIN *and* NEWMAN *continue to watch the* MARQUIS, *and* MRS. BREAD, *on the right, rests her eyes expectantly on* MME. DE CINTRÉ *who, at her table, sits motionless, detached, immersed in repressed agitation.*) Before you go—what shall I *give* you?

NOÉMIE. Give me (*hesitating*)—give me— (*Pausing, smiling.*)

DEEPMERE. (*In the liveliest suspense.*) *What, Mademoiselle?*

NOÉMIE. (*Aloud, so that the others hear her and* NEWMAN's *invitation to* DEEPMERE *is practically answered.*) Give me your arm! (*She takes it while* DEEPMERE, *breathing again, offers it with extravagant alacrity, and they stand together at right.*)

MRS. BREAD. (*To* CLAIRE.) I *am* at your ladyship's service to leave the *house.*

NEWMAN. (*Looking at* CLAIRE, *who, still seated in her agitation, has made no answer.*) Perhaps *you*, Madame de Cintré, will give us the honour of your company?

MARQUIS. (*Down at left, majestically, during the silence that follows on* CLAIRE's *part.*) I regret, Mr. Newman, that I am unable to accept your invitation. (*After an instant.*) I must carry to my mother, without delay, this remarkable news of her son.

CLAIRE. (*Rising rapidly, checking him as he is in the act of going, while, as she moves,* NEWMAN, *quitting* VALENTIN, *comes nearer to her, and* MRS. BREAD, *passing to centre, occupies* NEWMAN's *place behind* VALENTIN's *chair.*) Urbain! (*The* MARQUIS *stops, surprised, as with a challenge, and* CLAIRE *goes on speaking out loud and clear.*) You can carry our mother as well some remarkable news of her *daughter*—the news that I've determined—and (*looking about to the others*) I'm glad you should all *hear* it!—to become Mr. Newman's *wife!*

NEWMAN. (*Springing to her, and as he folds her in his arms.*) That's just what I wanted to *see!*

Theatricals: Two Comedies
Note, 1894
Tenants, 1890
Disengaged, 1892(?)

EDITOR'S FOREWORD

NOTE TO *THEATRICALS: TWO COMEDIES*

The two plays which follow, *Tenants* and *Disengaged,* written at the outset of the dramatic years, were published by Henry James late in 1894. He did this despite the fact that he had once criticized Howells for publishing a play before it was acted. "This," he wrote, "from a Parisian point of view, seems quite monstrous." Nevertheless, there was the precedent of his publication of *Daisy Miller,* and he yielded to the temptation to enshrine his plays in book form, as he explained to Elizabeth Robins, to keep them from " 'dying with all their music in them.' . . . I mean going down into utter silence and darkness." The note which follows prefaced the first of his two "play-books."

NOTE

It is but fair to these two little entertainments, as well as to two others that are to follow, to mention that they were conceived and constructed wholly in the light of possible representation—representation in particular conditions which it was hoped they might successfully meet, but with which in the event they had not the good fortune to consort. They were addressed in each case with extreme, perhaps with extravagant, deference to a theatre, to a company, and especially to the presumable interpreter of the part supposed to be the most actable or the most "sympathetic," and are therefore experiments essentially proportionate and practical. They are also experiments in the line of comedy pure and simple. If it be very naturally and somewhat sternly inquired, accordingly, why, failing of their sole application, they appear in a form which is an humiliating confession of defeat, I am afraid the only answer is that the unacted dramatist has still the consolation—poor enough, alas!—of the performance imaginary. There are degrees of representation, and it breaks his fall and patches up his retreat a little to be correctly printed—which is after all a morsel of the opportunity of the real dramatist. As Labiche and Ibsen would only be partly real to us if we had not their indispensable text, so the baffled aspirant may in offering his text delude or amuse himself with a certain pretension to indispensability. He recommends on this occasion his melancholy subterfuge to his numerous fellow-sufferers, who are surely welcome to such comfort as they can get. The covers of the book may, in a seat that costs nothing, figure the friendly curtain, and the legible "lines" the various voices of the stage; so that if these things manage at all to disclose a picture or to drop a tone into the reader's ear the ghostly ordeal will in a manner have been passed and the dim foot-lights faced. The publication of these simple attempts—so calculated for a "fit" or for a "bid" that they doubtless missed their way through an anxious excess of simplicity—is in a word a faint make-believe.

The situation presented in the first act of the first piece was directly, though long since, suggested by a short tale of the late Commandant Henri Rivière, a tale published some five-and-twenty years ago, if not more, in a single number of *La Revue des Deux Mondes*. The action of the play, which is a free translation of the subject of the story, greatly deviates, it must be admitted, from this original, though remaining distinctly indebted to it again for an incident in the third act. The idea on which *Disengaged* mainly reposes was supplied to the author by a little story of his own.

H. J.

EDITOR'S FOREWORD

TENANTS

In his prefatory note to *Theatricals: Two Comedies* Henry James, with that vagueness with which he liked to shroud literary origins, tells us that *Tenants* was inspired "by a short tale of the late Commandant Henri Rivière, a tale published some five-and-twenty years ago, if not more, in a single number of *La Revue des Deux Mondes.*" An examination of Rivière's stories, frequently published in the *Revue* earlier in the century, points to *Flavien: Scènes de la vie contemporaine,* of November 1, 1874, as the source for *Tenants. Flavien* is the story of a General d'Herbel who retires and devotes himself to his ward, the daughter of his brother. Léonie d'Herbel, like Mildred in *Tenants,* is heir to a substantial fortune and falls in love with the General's son, Emmanuel, a captain of the French forces in Algeria. A former mistress of the General, the Countess Sampara, arrives on the scene with her son Flavien, and his tutor, the Chevalier Griotti. After considerable intrigue the tutor is killed in a duel and the lovers are united.

This was the situation James transposed into an English setting, matching the French story, character for character, and weaving out of it a play with the strong moral tone of Dumas *fils* and Augier. He wrote it in November 1890 during rehearsals for the Southport opening of his play *The American.* On December 9 he wrote to William James: "I have just finished (written in a month, but working tooth and nail) *another* drama, of which I am tomorrow to read the third (and last) act to the interpreters (that is, the two leading ones) who have taken it in hand." This was Play Number 2, tentatively named *Mrs. Vibert* and later renamed *Tenants.* The two leading interpreters were the formidable Geneviève Ward, a native of New York, who had had a long career first on the operatic stage and later in the theatre, and W. H. Vernon, who had been her leading man in a number of productions. The reading James spoke of was announced by him in a letter, written two days before he wrote William, to Mrs. Hugh Bell, herself the author of a number of closet dramas. In his characteristically extravagant manner, James told her that the third act of his play was "a pure *movement,* intensely interesting and suspense-producing, lasting forty minutes, and subtly calculated to captivate the Genevan and Vernonese mind. . . . I have likewise 'cut' my second act as effectually and bloodily as the most barbarous dramatic butcher could desire; and have retouched and amended the first. My III is, I think, absolutely produceable *tel quel*—I learn so fast!"

The day after the reading he wrote to Mrs. Bell that it had been a "high success . . . my auditors 'rose at' me, gave themselves away and were flushed and effusive." Miss Ward agreed to take the play to John Hare, the actor-manager, who as far back as 1879 had asked James for a play. She kept her word, for on January 27, 1891, James told Mrs. Bell he had received a letter from Hare "placing *Mrs. Vibert,* I think, on a very favorable basis for discussion" as soon as the actor-manager should be free of the rehearsals of his new play, Pinero's *Lady Bountiful,* produced at the Garrick March 7, 1891. We get some inkling of the contents of Hare's letter in James's account of it to his brother on February 6, 1891: "No. 2 is in the hands of a high London manager, in conditions as to which I prefer at present to maintain absolute silence—suffice it that he tells me (I quote a letter) that it is 'a masterpiece of dramatic construction' a good phrase for a 'high London manager' to apply to the first production he has read of a beginner." On April 13, James announced to Mrs. Bell that "Hare has definitely accepted both the venerable heroine and her interpreter." A note in Alice James's journal of April 23 carries the history of *Mrs. Vibert* forward a step, and indicates also that Hare was in no hurry to produce James: "H. came in a few days ago, all heated with a most sympathetic interview with John Hare, who not only accepts play number two, *Mrs. Vibert,* which H. wrote before Christmas for Miss Geneviève Ward, but accepts it with enthusiasm and calls it a 'masterpiece of dramatic construction.' His [Hare's] talk was most intelligent and his view of the English public all that can be desired. He talked a great deal about the cast and repeated, 'It is meant for the Français.' *Lady Bountiful,* which he has just brought out, has fortunately fallen, and he apparently would bring out H's play now, but that he wants, for a rest, to revive an old play, and he has promised to bring out another new play next. So H. won't come until autumn or winter, I am afraid."

In the autumn, when rehearsals for the London production of *The American* began, Henry told William that Hare was having difficulty casting *Tenants.* Hare and Miss Ward had their roles, and Vernon presumably was intended for Captain Lurcher. The problem was to find an actor for Claude. Henry wrote to his brother: "The only thing I *do* care to speak of now (and *only* to you) is the drama in three acts, *Mrs. Vibert,* which John Hare is to produce at the Garrick some time this season. But here there are irrepressible delays, produced largely—indeed almost wholly—by the intense difficulties of casting. One tries to write as simple and feasible a thing as possible and still—with the ignoble poverty of the English stage—the people capable of *beginning* to attempt to do it are not findable. There's a career for talent—to act my plays. *Mrs. Vibert* is blocked largely by the difficulty of putting one's hand on a young man who can *touch* an important little part of a boy of 20—who must be a character, a touching one."

Throughout that autumn the theatrical press spoke freely of *Mrs. Vibert,* a comedy "of society," as a play Hare would soon produce. The months passed; then the years. In 1893 the announcement that Oscar Wilde had written *A Woman of No Importance* worried James. He was in Paris and the title suggested a theme similar to his play. He wrote to Elizabeth Robins, ". . . tell

me three words about Oscar W's piece—when it is produced; and if in particular the *subject* seems to discount my poor three-year-older (or almost) that
Hare will neither produce nor part with." To Mrs. Bell, a few days later,
". . . don't neglect Oscar!" To Elizabeth Robins, "I am consumed with
curiosity . . ." To Mrs. Bell, again, ". . . may I have an echo of it?" Apparently the ladies did not assuage his curiosity; but in due course he found out
for himself. The question was of academic importance. Long before James
finally wrenched the comedy free from Hare to publish it, he sought to engage
the interest of Helena Modjeska in a probable American production of the
play. She had been interested in the possibility of doing Madame de Cintré
in *The American*. James, on November 17, 1891, wrote an eighteen page letter
to the Polish-American actress to tell her that *Mrs. Vibert* was much more the
sort of play she should do and offering to send her a script. After reading it
she sent it back saying she had studied the first act but saw the play as essentially
a vehicle for Miss Ward rather than for herself. In his letter to Modjeska James
expressed the view that *Tenants* "would—largely—stand or fall by the degree of
perfection with which a scene—*the* scene—between the mother and son, in the
third act, should be acted; to which degree of perfection it would be *indispensable* that the actor representing the young man should contribute."

Readers of James's tales will recognize the familiar figures of earlier Jamesian
stories in this play—the young ward, the guardian, the continental youth, his
loyal tutor. That he should have been partial to the situation in the Rivière
story of a young man and his preceptor at this time is not surprising, for he had
a few months earlier written *The Pupil* with a somewhat younger protagonist
than Claude and a sympathetic rather than a villainous tutor.

CHARACTERS

SIR FREDERICK BYNG
NORMAN BYNG
CAPTAIN LURCHER
CLAUDE VIBERT
FROST
MRS. VIBERT
MILDRED
MISS DYER

The action takes place at Beechingham Manor, a sequestered old house in Devonshire.

TENANTS

ACT FIRST

The spacious, sociable, old-fashioned hall at Beechingham, panelled in clear colours and used as a place of reunion. It opens, largely, into an ante-room, through the wide window of which the avenue of a small park and a charming horizon are shown, and which conducts on the left to the entrance of the house as well as to various apartments, and on the right to the staircase, to other apartments and to the billard-room. On the right of the hall the door to the drawing-room; on the left the door to the library. The place shows signs of constant and familiar habitation and of studied comfort, but not of conspicuous luxury. Miss Dyer *comes down impatiently from the window of the ante-room.*

Miss Dyer. What a bore to have to wait half the day for your letters! The next position I accept, I shall make an early London post a condition.

(*Enter* Mildred *through the ante-room from the left, with several letters in her hand.*)

Mildred. Here they are: I looked out for the groom in the park.

Miss Dyer. I'm not quite sure you ought!

Mildred. Dear Miss Dyer, you're never quite sure I ought! Here's a letter for you.

Miss Dyer. (*With the letter.*) Only one?

Mildred. Only one.

Miss Dyer. How stupid—from mamma! And are all the others for you?

Mildred. For me? who ever writes to me? Some of them are for Sir Frederick; the others are for Mr. Byng.

Miss Dyer. I suppose those are the ones you looked out for in the park!

Mildred. (*Holding up a letter.*) This is the one. It has a big official seal, which I've taken the liberty to examine.

Miss Dyer. I'm not quite sure you ought!

Mildred. The deed is done, and the horrible thing is from the people in London, to put an end to his leave.

Miss Dyer. I think it high time!

Mildred. After a month—only a little month?

Miss Dyer. A month isn't so little, when one makes such a big use of it.

Mildred. (*Vague.*) What use, pray—?

Miss Dyer. To make love to you!

Mildred. Why shouldn't he, if he likes me?

Miss Dyer. I'm not quite sure he ought!

Mildred. Neither am I. But perhaps he can't help it!

Miss Dyer. I think Sir Frederick will come to his aid. And since we're discussing the subject—

Mildred. Dear Miss Dyer, we're not discussing the subject.

Miss Dyer. Yes—I'm not quite sure we ought!

(*Enter* Norman Byng *through the ante-room from the right.*)

Norman. (*Hearing the last words.*) You certainly oughtn't—if you mean reading my letters.

Mildred. I was just going to carry them to you. (*Then as* Norman *takes the letters.*) There's one with a dreadful seal.

Norman. (*Looking.*) Governmental? My death-knell!

Miss Dyer. Oh, you won't die, Mr. Byng —you'll get better.

Mildred. Certainly, my dear—if *you* nurse him! I must take Sir Frederick his letters.

261

NORMAN. You'll come back, won't you?

MILDRED. (*At the door of the library.*) To hear if you must go?

NORMAN. Oh, I can read that without breaking the envelope!

MILDRED. I'll come back. (*Exit* MILDRED *to the library.*)

MISS DYER. In that case I shall be in the way!

NORMAN. (*Preoccupied, looking over his letters.*) Oh, Miss Dyer—don't say that!

MISS DYER. You know that's what I am here for—to be in the way.

NORMAN. (*Still absent.*) I see—we must do our duty. I've got to do mine.

MISS DYER. (*With much expression.*) Be brave, then, Mr. Byng, and face it at whatever cost!

NORMAN. (*Surprised at her manner.*) It's all in the day's work.

MISS DYER. You won't go without bidding me good-bye?

NORMAN. Oh, dear no! Good-bye now, if you like.

MISS DYER. (*Gazing at him a moment; then with unspeakable reproach.*) Farewell! (*Exit* MISS DYER *to the drawing-room.*)

NORMAN. (*Alone.*) She *is* a "companion" with a vengeance! She was engaged to be Mildred's, but she seems to want to be mine. (*Re-enter* MILDRED *from the library.*) My dear child, the bolt has fallen—the end of these golden days.

MILDRED. (*With a soft sigh of wonder and regret.*) So suddenly—so soon?

NORMAN. Doesn't it seem only yesterday that I came?

MILDRED. (*Musing.*) I don't know what it seems, Norman. It has made such a difference.

NORMAN. Ah, they come quickly, such differences as that!

MILDRED. Isn't it wonderful?—when everything is changed!

NORMAN. Yes, a great new life is born, somehow, in a little instant of time. We've got to take care of it, Mildred—we've got to bring it up!

MILDRED. (*Smiling sadly.*) I hope you don't think it's delicate.

NORMAN. I daresay it will thrive! (*Grave, tender.*) It's "promising"—it will be the support of our old age.

MILDRED. Our old age? Shall we have to wait for that?

NORMAN. I mean it will be the security, the foundation of our future. That's what you've done for me, darling—you've made me a future.

MILDRED. You've made *me* a past—that began a month ago; blessed memories after you're gone!

NORMAN. Ah, think of me—think of me then, dear girl!

MILDRED. I shan't have to "think" of you—I shall see you, I shall hear you, I shall touch you.

NORMAN. We shall be doing just the same thing, in that case, at just the same moment.

MILDRED. We shall be together then, shan't we, after all?

NORMAN. People *are* together when they hate sufficiently the things that keep them apart.

MILDRED. You can trust me to hate them sufficiently!

NORMAN. (*Who has looked off through the wide window.*) This picture of peace and summer, of fragrant, fruitful confidence, of a kind of sacred safety, is the image of what has passed between us. I shall carry it with me, and it will be the world I shall really live in.

MILDRED. But don't take it down yet! Surely they give you time.

NORMAN. Five days. They'll do to break our hearts in!

MILDRED. They'll do to break your father's. He asked me if you were here; so I judge he's coming to you. I must go.

NORMAN. Don't be nervous—wait for him. If our minutes are numbered, let us at least not be cheated.

MILDRED. When you talk of sacredness and safety, what do you do with the wolf in the fold?

NORMAN. My father? He's the sheep-dog biting the lambs! Yes, he's sacred, dear man, but he's not particularly safe.

MILDRED. I'm sure he's going to be dreadful—he has his ideas.

NORMAN. He'd be so wise without them!

MILDRED. (*As the door of the library opens.*) Here he comes.

NORMAN. We *are* cheated!

MILDRED. (*From the ante-room.*) We shall make it up! (*Exit* MILDRED *to the right.*)

(*Enter* SIR FREDERICK BYNG *from the library.*)

SIR FREDERICK. (*Who has seen* MILDRED.) You're not behaving well, Norman—neither is that girl.

NORMAN. You don't know our excuse. (*Handing one of his letters.*) See what I've just received.

SIR FREDERICK. (*With the open letter; glancing over it and handing it back.*) It's a great relief to me. If this summons hadn't arrived I should have been under the painful necessity of asking you to bring your visit to Beechingham to a close.

NORMAN. You'd have turned me out of the house?

SIR FREDERICK. Wouldn't that have been better than turning Mildred?

NORMAN. I may be utterly wanting in acuteness, but I can't for the life of me understand why you should turn either of us.

SIR FREDERICK. You're not in the least wanting in acuteness, but you're remarkably wanting in delicacy.

NORMAN. Do you mean because I'm such a coarse brute as to be in love?

SIR FREDERICK. Be in love as much as you please; but hold your tongue about it!

NORMAN. What good will that do me?

SIR FREDERICK. The good of keeping you a gentleman—so long as Mildred's my charge. She came into this house, as you know, by no inclination or invitation of mine, two years ago; when, the day after my return from India, my oldest friend, the friend of my earliest years, took it into his head to impose on me unexpectedly, on his death-bed as it were, the guardianship of his only daughter—of her unprotected youth, her unspotted honour, and her very considerable fortune.

NORMAN. It *was* a favour to ask of a quiet widower—with so little experience of women!

SIR FREDERICK. (*Dry.*) Stanmore judged of my experience, and I appreciated his. His marriage had been deeply unhappy; it had led him to make some gloomy generalisations, and to wish, perversely if you

like, but intensely, to consign Mildred to hands other than those *he* had fallen into. In a word, he held that the best influence for her would be an honest gentleman as nearly as possible like himself. I accepted his confidence—I hold it sacred. But it has been a great complication.

NORMAN. He overlooked your other incumbrance.

SIR FREDERICK. You were in training for your career—taking your first far-away steps in it. He had scarcely seen you—he didn't focus you.

NORMAN. Why should you assume that if he had done me that honour—

SIR FREDERICK. He would have checked your aspirations? I assume nothing, and that's precisely why I don't assume that he would have wished his daughter—simply because you're my son—to bind herself to you before she has had a glimpse of another fate.

NORMAN. The Rhadamanthus your early friend has made of you, sir, is a thing to make one beware of early friendships!

SIR FREDERICK. (*After a moment.*) Do that indeed—in every sense of the term: make the largest application of the moral! Remember that when you reach my age, if you've had time to have a past you also still have time to suffer from it. Your past is on your back, and at fifty-seven you may have a good way farther to carry it.

NORMAN. I should have thought your age delightful—it certainly makes *you* so! But your description of it sounds indeed alarming.

SIR FREDERICK. The more reason for keeping an eye on it in advance. Reflect on that, and beware of entanglements. I didn't—but that's none of your business.

NORMAN. None whatever, father.

SIR FREDERICK. Don't be impertinent. You *are*, horribly, when you affect to criticize me for not thinking it consistent with the dignity of my office to throw my helpless ward, who has seven thousand a year, into the arms of my ambitious son, who has nothing.

NORMAN. I'm not a beggar, you know.

SIR FREDERICK. You're the next thing to it! You have no prospects to speak of from me. I left India with my pension, but with very little else—save the ruins of my constitution. I'm so little at my ease, at this moment, that I've made up my mind to a tiresome sacrifice.

NORMAN. The sacrifice of what?

SIR FREDERICK. The old lodge at Clere—the dowerhouse of the estate. I've determined to let it.

NORMAN. That will rather be a gain, if you let it to pleasant people.

SIR FREDERICK. Pleasant people are what I hope for. They may make a little company for Mildred.

NORMAN. Especially, I suppose, if there's a sweet young man among them who hasn't the misfortune to be your son.

SIR FREDERICK. He may be as sweet as he likes—he'll have to wait till she's of age.

NORMAN. Which, by the terms of her father's cold-blooded will, is not to be till she's twenty-two.

SIR FREDERICK. That gives you the measure of his circumspection, which I rigidly emulate.

NORMAN. So that as she's only eighteen now—

SIR FREDERICK. The sweet young men will have exactly four years to wait. For yourself, the first on the charming list, you'll be so good as to wait in silence, and to go about your business meanwhile. In a word, you'll postpone all further overtures to Miss Stanmore till she is in a position to reflect, to compare, to choose—to dispose intelligently of her hand and her money.

NORMAN. Your conditions are hard, sir.

SIR FREDERICK. If you rebel against them you give me a pretext for making them harder.

NORMAN. How *can* they be?

SIR FREDERICK. My dear boy, don't force me to request you to go about your business on the instant.

NORMAN. (*After a moment.*) Will you give me the very few days they allow me at headquarters?

SIR FREDERICK. It's lucky for you they're numbered! (*Crosses to the door of the drawing-room.*) But I count on your absolute discretion.

NORMAN. You may count.

SIR FREDERICK. Meanwhile kindly tell me if you've seen Miss Dyer.

NORMAN. She was here a moment ago—she went to the drawing-room.

SIR FRANCIS. (*Ceremoniously.*) Thank you. (*Exit SIR FREDERICK to the drawing-room.*)

NORMAN. (*Alone.*) He wants to tell her to keep an eye on Mildred. Ah, Miss Dyer's eye!

(*Re-enter MILDRED through the ante-room from the right.*)

MILDRED. May I come back?

NORMAN. Yes, but I mayn't speak to you.

MILDRED. (*Coming down.*) And mayn't I speak to you?

NORMAN. What good will it do if I can't answer?

MILDRED. We understand each other without words. Was your father very dreadful?

NORMAN. Quite ghastly! But I've accepted his conditions.

MILDRED. And what are they?

NORMAN. To wait the four years.

MILDRED. (*Dolorous.*) Ah! (*After a moment.*) Well, I accept them.

NORMAN. I can't tell you what I feel when I hear you say that—because I've promised not to. But I may feel it all the same, mayn't I?

(*Re-enter MISS DYER from the drawing-room.*)

MILDRED. (*Pointed.*) I'm not quite sure you ought!

MISS DYER. My dear Mildred, I've opened the new piano for you. I think you'd better go and try it.

NORMAN. (*Privately to MILDRED.*) Miss Dyer's eye!

MILDRED. (*In the same way.*) It's better than Miss Dyer's ear! (*Then aloud.*) What shall I play?

NORMAN. "When we two parted—in silence and tears!"

MILDRED. I know the air. (*Exit MILDRED to the drawing-room.*)

MISS DYER. (*Looking at NORMAN sentimentally, and warbling the rest of the Byronic quotation.*) "Half broken-hearted—to sever for years!"

NORMAN. (*At the door of the library.*) Only for four! (*Exit NORMAN to the library.*)

MISS DYER. (*Alone, plaintive.*) He hates me when I call her away from him. It's hard to be obliged to make him hate me! (*Then seeing* MRS. VIBERT, *who has appeared in the ante-room from the left, and stands there looking at her.*) A lady—a stranger?
(*Enter* MRS. VIBERT, *who slowly comes down.*)

MRS. VIBERT. If I venture to come in unannounced, I'll tell you presently why.

MISS DYER. In these soft September days, in the depths of Devonshire, we leave everything open.

MRS. VIBERT. I like open houses—and open hearts! And I'm not dangerous, though you look at me as if I were a gipsy.

MISS DYER. (*Mystified, fluttered, but responsive; having surveyed her charming appearance and French dress, and taken in her cosmopolitan air.*) Not the kind that tell one's fortune!

MRS. VIBERT. I've walked across your park—your park is lovely.

MISS DYER. It's not mine—I wish it were!

MRS. VIBERT. (*Gay.*) Oh, I know where I am—I know your facts! (*Then as* MISS DYER *slightly starts.*) Don't be frightened: I'm sure you've no secrets.

MISS DYER. (*With superiority.*) A woman who has no secrets must be rather a frump!

MRS. VIBERT. Not so great a frump as the woman who doesn't find them out! What I meant is that I know about Beechingham Manor—I've come to see it.

MISS DYER. Are you under the impression that it's shown?

MRS. VIBERT. Not in general; but (*with a flattering, insinuating smile*) you could be my cicerone.

MISS DYER. I'm not quite sure I ought! I haven't the honour of knowing—

MRS. VIBERT. In the least who I am? *Je vous tombe des nues*, precisely.

MISS DYER. (*Pleased.*) I do know French!

MRS. VIBERT. Let me tell you in plain English that I'm a possible tenant for Clere.

MISS DYER. The dowerhouse?

MRS. VIBERT. At the other end of the park. I heard it was to let, I'm in search of a quiet refuge in the country, I came over this morning from a little watering-place on the Cornish border, I looked at the whole thing and fell in love with it.

MISS DYER. It's a sweet little nest.

MRS. VIBERT. (*Who has looked about her.*) And in the shadow of such pleasant things!

MISS DYER. I do what I can here, but I fear I can't boast of my material.

MRS. VIBERT. Whatever your material, it appeals to me, since I'm to be a neighbour: it may make a great difference to me. So I sent the agent away and just wandered across—to explore and to propose.

MISS DYER. (*With a slight movement.*) To propose?

MRS. VIBERT. (*Laughing.*) Oh not in the sense *you* naturally attach—! But I'm a very frank, direct person—I like to stand up to my landlord.

MISS DYER. It's a pity Sir Frederick's so shy!

MRS. VIBERT. That's perhaps only with you! May I inquire if he's at home?

MISS DYER. He was in the drawing-room a moment ago—he went into the garden.

MRS. VIBERT. Could you kindly cause him to be informed that his tenant would like to see him?

MISS DYER. What name shall I have the honour to give?

MRS. VIBERT. Please simply say a lady—to treat! (*Exit* MISS DYER *through the ante-room, to the right.* MRS. VIBERT, *alone, looks round her.*) It *is* charming, and if I wanted to reconnoitre I've succeeded beyond my hope.
(*Re-enter* MILDRED, *without perceiving her, from the drawing-room.*)

MILDRED. (*Weary, impatient, while* MRS. VIBERT *goes up to look further.*) The new piano's deadly flat—everything, to-day, is deadly flat. (*Seeing* MRS. VIBERT; *to herself.*) Ah no, *she's* not!

MRS. VIBERT. (*Seeing* MILDRED *and coming down again.*) Excuse me, mademoiselle —while I wait for your father.

MILDRED. (*Blank.*) My father? I have no father.

MRS. VIBERT. (*Looking at her with compassion and admiration.*) Forgive my mistake! It's a pity: he would have adored you!

MILDRED. (*Simply, wonderingly, yet with a certain suggestion of mistrust.*) And I have no mother.

MRS. VIBERT. Then you must let *me* be kind to you.

MILDRED. I don't know who you are, madam!

MRS. VIBERT. I'm nobody yet, but to-morrow (*curtseying to her with indulgent jocularity*) I shall be your neighbour! (MILDRED *formally returns her curtsey and passes back to the door of the drawing-room, where she stands looking at her.*) So we shall meet again. (*To herself.*) That will be up-hill!

(*Re-enter* MISS DYER *through the ante-room from the right.*)

MISS DYER. (*To* MRS. VIBERT.) Sir Frederick tells me he'll come to you. (*To* MILDRED, *passing her arm round her.*) And you, my child, you'll come to me. We'll go out!

(*Exeunt* MILDRED *and* MISS DYER *to the drawing-room.*)

MRS. VIBERT. (*Alone.*) Now then, my dear, toe the mark!

(*Re-enter* SIR FREDERICK *through the ante-room, from the right, approaching* MRS. VIBERT *with businesslike civility.*)

SIR FREDERICK. (*Inquiring.*) Madam?

MRS. VIBERT. (*After a moment.*) That's not what you called me of old!

SIR FREDERICK. (*Startled by her voice, staring an instant, then utterly surprised.*) Good God—Eleanor!

MRS. VIBERT. Frederick!

SIR FREDERICK. You rise before me—after all these years—like the ghost of my youth!

MRS. VIBERT. And you stand before me, my friend, like the hope of my future!

SIR FREDERICK. You're not, perhaps, so young; and yet you're somehow—so new!

MRS. VIBERT. I've been revised and improved: I'm the latest edition! Let me reassure you—I'm better reading than I was.

SIR FREDERICK. Ah, don't speak of what you were!

MRS. VIBERT. Why shouldn't I? When I see *you* again, I'm not ashamed of it!

SIR FREDERICK. (*After a moment.*) What has led you to take steps to see me again?

MRS. VIBERT. Everything else that I have seen!

SIR FREDERICK. Eleanor, have you come to put your hand on me?

MRS. VIBERT. To lean on you, do you mean? As your ivy there leans on your wall! The wall can bear it.

SIR FREDERICK. Oh, I'm not stone; and everything is different now.

MRS. VIBERT. Different indeed—that's exactly why I've come. (*After an instant.*) My husband's dead.

SIR FREDERICK. Not lately, I see, for you're not in weeds.

MRS. VIBERT. It doesn't matter when. We had wholly ceased to meet.

SIR FREDERICK. That was the case even before I knew you.

MRS. VIBERT. Have I forgotten my circumstances then? They were almost my exoneration. He was living abroad, but after you and I parted, after you went to India, he came home. Then *I* went abroad—to escape him. But I never really escaped him—till the day he died.

SIR FREDERICK. What a history! What has become of your son?

MRS. VIBERT. My son's alive. Him we *can't* escape.

SIR FREDERICK. (*Takes her hand and, bending over it, raises it to his lips.*) We don't desire to! (*He walks away a few steps and comes back.*) Did your husband ever learn?

MRS. VIBERT. He learnt everything.

SIR FREDERICK. And what did he do?

MRS. VIBERT. He made me pay.

SIR FREDERICK. (*Vague, helpless, compassionate.*) Dearest friend—!

MRS. VIBERT. I'm paying still.

SIR FREDERICK. Yet Claude's now of an age to be something of a compensation: he's—

MRS. VIBERT. (*As he hesitates; with a sad smile.*) I remember! He's twenty.

SIR FREDERICK. And where is he?

MRS. VIBERT. Half an hour ago he was at that charming old house of yours that I want to take.

SIR FREDERICK. Does *he* know?

MRS. VIBERT. He knows nothing.

SIR FREDERICK. (*After an instant.*) My charming old house, I surmise, has only been your pretext.

MRS. VIBERT. It may have been my pretext, but I want it to be my home!

SIR FREDERICK. Close to mine, Eleanor, at this time of day?

MRS. VIBERT. The closer the better; and just because it *is* this time. It wouldn't have done of old.

SIR FREDERICK. Yes, you were all for appearances then.

MRS. VIBERT. So I am still. Only now I want them to correspond with the facts!

SIR FREDERICK. What do you call the facts?

MRS. VIBERT. Isn't the principal one that at last we've found each other?

SIR FREDERICK. I've taken for granted you'd avoid me.

MRS. VIBERT. I should have avoided you twenty years ago! You drew me back to England.

SIR FREDERICK. You had kept away?

MRS. VIBERT. For nineteen years. When I went abroad after you went to India, it was to live expatriated. But when I heard you had come back—

SIR FREDERICK. You came back yourself? I've been at home two years.

MRS. VIBERT. Yes, but you've been buried.

SIR FREDERICK. And you're digging me up!

MRS. VIBERT. By the oddest chance! I came down to Trecothick, which is pretty and quiet—and cheap, and happened to see there, in an agent's window, a photograph of your delightful lodge, which took my fancy so that I made inquiries about it. I learned it belonged to you—a fact that, after my first astonishment, made me like it still better. I came over to see it, and then I came over to see its master. (*Pleadingly.*) He won't close its door to me?

SIR FREDERICK. How your early tone—the one that used to stir me—falls upon my ear!

MRS. VIBERT. Not surely *then* the tone of supplication. I never asked you for anything.

SIR FREDERICK. (*After a silence.*) Never.

MRS. VIBERT. Give me the benefit of that to-day. I'm weary of the dusty roads, of effort and exile and motion; weary of going from pillar to post and of all the beaten tracks and haunted corners of the Continent. For pity's sake, let me sink down to rest in that sheltered nook. Let me take my stand there on the firm ground of your friendship, and I shall find a new interest in life.

SIR FREDERICK. Why should you want a "new" interest, if you've a son of twenty?—assuming, that is, that he's what he ought to be.

MRS. VIBERT. (*After a moment.*) He *is* what he ought to be! But it's exactly for him that I want it! I ask of you nothing for him; I only ask you to know him.

SIR FREDERICK. Since he can't know *me?* Be it so! But how strange it seems for you and him to have been so absent all these years only to be so intensely present now!

MRS. VIBERT. (*Smiling.*) You can't say we've worried you!

SIR FREDERICK. You've spoiled me!

MRS. VIBERT. By letting you suppose us in our graves? Thank you.

SIR FREDERICK. Eleanor, I feel as if *I* had been in my grave! It's *I* who have come to life. But when you propose yourself as a tenant, how can I have a relation of business with you?

MRS. VIBERT. *Les bons comptes font les bons amis!* Your house isn't dear, with your society thrown in.

SIR FREDERICK. I should have to throw in more than my own.

MRS. VIBERT. Ah? (*After a moment.*) Have you married again?

SIR FREDERICK. For what do you take me? I've accepted a more thankless charge.

MRS. VIBERT. *You,* my dear friend? I don't believe it!

SIR FREDERICK. You don't do me justice! I had a friend who did, when, two years ago, in dying, he placed his only daughter in my hands.

MRS. VIBERT. The young lady I saw just now?

SIR FREDERICK. You saw her?

MRS. VIBERT. She was here a moment. She's lovely.

SIR FREDERICK. She's good, clever, considerate; but she makes me less independent.

MRS. VIBERT. You mean that she can't meet such a person as me?

SIR FREDERICK. Dear Eleanor—you're terrible! (*Embarrassed.*) Your grace, your charming forms, are on the contrary just the sort of thing she ought to have near her.

MRS. VIBERT. I see: if they could only be found in some other person! Perhaps they *are* found in the lady who received me.

SIR FREDERICK. Miss Dyer, Mildred's companion? Oh, *that* woman's an idiot!

MRS. VIBERT. So are most women! I can understand that your little inmate should be a great responsibility.

SIR FREDERICK. So great that it's a comfort to gossip to you about it.

MRS. VIBERT. (*Smiling.*) I ought to have come sooner!

SIR FREDERICK. You might have prevented my son from falling in love with her.

MRS. VIBERT. Your children are naturally susceptible! I was waiting for *you* to speak first of this one.

SIR FREDERICK. Thanks for your delicacy.

MRS. VIBERT. I suppose he too can't meet me.

SIR FREDERICK. (*After an instant.*) He can meet, I take it, any one I expect him to meet, and I look to him to consider that he has caused me embarrassment enough without causing me any more.

MRS. VIBERT. (*Irrepressible, sincere.*) Frederick—you're a pearl!

SIR FREDERICK. (*Blank, guarded an instant.*) Eh?

MRS. VIBERT. I'll explain later: I've much to explain! (*Then after a moment.*) Mr. Byng wants to marry—

SIR FREDERICK. His father's ward. So he pretends to have discovered.

MRS. VIBERT. Has the young lady a fortune?

SIR FREDERICK. A very solid fortune—and that's exactly why.

MRS. VIBERT. (*Vague.*) Why he wants to marry her?

SIR FREDERICK. Why I won't hear of it. Luckily he's off to India.

MRS. VIBERT. He's in the service?

SIR FREDERICK. The Civil, and doing well. He has gone in for his father's career, and I expect him to improve on it.

MRS. VIBERT. (*Smiling, deprecating.*) Dear friend, to improve on his father—!

SIR FREDERICK. Oh, Norman's very sharp!

MRS. VIBERT. (*After an instant.*) So I infer. When does he start?

SIR FREDERICK. I wanted to pack him off this evening, but I've given him a respite.

MRS. VIBERT. (*Arch.*) Procrastinator! (*After another instant.*) The young lady's *very* rich?

SIR FREDERICK. Seven thousand a year.

MRS. VIBERT. (*With a suppressed movement.*) My dear man, it's grave. (*Then after a further pause.*) If your son were to go this evening he *wouldn't* meet me.

SIR FREDERICK. When you put it that way you humiliate me.

MRS. VIBERT. Does it humiliate you to be helped? I only want to help you.

SIR FREDERICK. (*After an instant.*) There *ought* to be a clever woman about!

MRS. VIBERT. It has been known to make a difference! If Mr. Byng goes to-night there's another person he won't meet.

SIR FREDERICK. Another person?

MRS. VIBERT. (*After an instant.*) His brother.

SIR FREDERICK. (*Considering.*) That perhaps would be better.

MRS. VIBERT. Does it "humiliate" you?

SIR FREDERICK. You do what you like with me. Where is he, the other person?

MRS. VIBERT. I left him in the park; he walked most of the way with me.

SIR FREDERICK. If I were to go out there should I see him?

MRS. VIBERT. Perfectly—unless they've turned back. But they were fascinated with this house; it's better than Clere.

SIR FREDERICK. "They"? Who's with him?

MRS. VIBERT. (*After an hesitation.*) My dear Frederick, his tutor.

SIR FREDERICK. Has he a "tutor"—at twenty?

MRS. VIBERT. What they call abroad a preceptor—with young princes a governor.

SIR FREDERICK. But Claude isn't a young prince.

MRS. VIBERT. Far enough from it! He has none the less inspired a loyalty, a devotion, on the part of a friend who has stood by us, in strange lands, all these years, who has helped to make a man of him, as a poor mother alone can't do, and to whom he's inevitably much attached.

SIR FREDERICK. I should like to see his devoted friend.

MRS. VIBERT. For God's sake don't be jealous of him! (*Then in another tone.*) You may see Captain Lurcher in the park.

SIR FREDERICK. Captain Lurcher? Is he English?

MRS. VIBERT. He has come back to find out. (*Laughing.*) So have Claude and I. You must pronounce!

SIR FREDERICK. (*Making a short movement toward the ante-room, as if to look; then checking himself and coming down.*) How you've all your old power!

MRS. VIBERT. My old power is simply my old affection.

SIR FREDERICK. (*Passing his hand over his eyes and head.*) Eleanor, you're wonderful! You bewilder me—you've set all my life vibrating! I want to pull myself together—I want to think.

MRS. VIBERT. Think, think: the more you do so the better perhaps for *me!* Leave me a little if you find me so agitating. I too shall be glad to recover myself, for our encounter has ploughed me up.

SIR FREDERICK. I've offered you no hospitality—I'll send you some tea. And Miss Dyer to make it.

MRS. VIBERT. I shall be grateful for tea, but I won't monopolise Miss Dyer. Leave me alone a moment—leave me with my shaken nerves.

SIR FREDERICK. I'm rather afraid to be alone with mine!

MRS. VIBERT. Go and find my companions then. Speak to them, bring them in. And bring me your answer.

SIR FREDERICK. My answer?

MRS. VIBERT. About the lodge.

SIR FREDERICK. (*From the ante-room.*) In five minutes. (*Exit* SIR FREDERICK *to the left.*)

MRS. VIBERT. (*Alone.*) The lodge is mine —and *he's* mine! (*Looking embracingly round her.*) I think it's *all* mine—the dream come true: peace and security, credit and rest, quiet waters and flowery pastures.

Dear old rural, respectable England, take me again to your bosom! (*Enter* FROST *through the ante-room, from the left, with the tea-tray, which he places on a small table, afterwards going out.* MRS. VIBERT *approaches the table and, seated by it, pours herself out a cup.*) The tea's sure to be good. (*Having raised the cup to her lips.*) Excellent! (*Re-enter from the library* NORMAN BYNG, *whom she immediately sees as he stands arrested on perceiving her. To herself.*) Ah, *that* sort! (*To* NORMAN, *graciously.*) Have you come for your tea? Perhaps you'll let me give it to you.

NORMAN. I won't incommode you; and, to my loss, I don't drink tea.

MRS. VIBERT. You don't incommode me if you happen to be Mr. Byng.

NORMAN. I plead guilty to that misfortune.

MRS. VIBERT. I hope I shan't make the case worse by mentioning that I'm your father's tenant.

NORMAN. (*Who has crossed to the door of the drawing-room; with his hand on the knob.*) Not worse for *him*. (*Gives her a still more searching look, which she returns; then goes into the drawing-room.*)

MRS. VIBERT. (*Alone.*) So that's the son, and that's the suitor? He's not a trifle. But neither are seven thousand a year! (*Finishes her tea standing.*) He must go to-night!

(*Re-enter* SIR FREDERICK *through the ante-room from the left.*)

SIR FREDERICK. I don't see your companions.

MRS. VIBERT. It doesn't matter; I'll present them to-morrow. They've returned to the lodge; let them stay there.

SIR FREDERICK. (*Demurring.*) Ah, my dear friend, there are difficulties!

MRS. VIBERT. I know there are. (*After a moment.*) Mr. Byng doesn't like me.

SIR FREDERICK. (*Blank.*) My son? What does he know about you?

MRS. VIBERT. He was here—he saw me. I can't say I please him.

SIR FREDERICK. (*Dry.*) I neither choose my friends nor drop them to please my son.

MRS. VIBERT. (*Philosophic.*) You can't please every one! But trust me to bring him round.

SIR FREDERICK. I don't think you'll have the chance.

MRS. VIBERT. (*Struck.*) In the time?

SIR FREDERICK. (*Hesitating, considering.*) Eleanor—!

MRS. VIBERT. (*As she watches him; abrupt, touching, irresistible.*) Frederick—don't turn me away! (*Goes back to the tea-table and pours him out a cup, handing it to him deftly, gently, without looking at him, as a matter of course; almost as if in her own house. He takes the cup from her in silence, in a kind of charmed mechanical submission, drinks it while she waits and returns it to her, on which she places it back on the tray.*)

SIR FREDERICK. The lodge is yours!

MRS. VIBERT. (*Taking his hand and raising it, holding it to her lips in silent satisfaction; then as she releases it.*) It's better, after all, that they shouldn't meet to-night.

SIR FREDERICK. (*Vague.*) That they shouldn't meet—?

MRS. VIBERT. Your son—and mine!

SIR FREDERICK. What is there gained—if they're to meet to-morrow.

MRS. VIBERT. It's better that they shouldn't meet even to-morrow. (*Smiling.*) We'll hide!

SIR FREDERICK. From what?

MRS. VIBERT. From Mr. Byng's stony stare!

SIR FREDERICK. His stony stare? (*Looking at his watch.*) Mr. Byng's going!

MRS. VIBERT. (*Smiling.*) You *can* act! Well, it *is* better, if you really wish to nip in the bud any projects he may have formed—!

SIR FREDERICK. In regard to Mildred? I hope you don't question the reality of my disapproval.

MRS. VIBERT. Heaven forbid I should question! But the world may—the world's so charitable! The way to be right with the world is to separate the young people on the spot.

SIR FREDERICK. Well, I had only given him five days.

MRS. VIBERT. Do you remember what five days—when we got them—could be for *us?*

SIR FREDERICK. The more I see you the more I remember!

MRS. VIBERT. (*Sententious.*) If we had had more resolution our case to-day would be simpler.

SIR FREDERICK. (*Prompt.*) We must make the best of our case to-day! I'll see Norman immediately.

MRS. VIBERT. I'll leave you to see him. May I take possession?

SIR FREDERICK. (*After kissing her hand exactly as she has kissed his.*) You *have* taken possession! Let me start you on your way.

MRS. VIBERT. I mustn't devour your time —you'll need it for your son.

SIR FREDERICK. I hate to let you go alone.

MRS. VIBERT. Then let me wait till you've parted with Mr. Byng. Don't stand on ceremony—I mean, of course, with *me!*

SIR FREDERICK. (*Laughing.*) Coquette!

MRS. VIBERT. (*Laughing.*) Ah, not now!

SIR FREDERICK. (*Opening the door of the library.*) Please pass in here.

MRS. VIBERT. (*At the door.*) Be mild! (*Exit* MRS. VIBERT.)

SIR FREDERICK. (*Alone.*) Mild? I shall be firm! (*Rings the bell.*) She clears things up—but I daresay I shall have a battle. (*Re-enter* FROST *through the ante-room from the left.*) Please ask Mr. Byng to speak to me.

FROST. He's in the drawing-room, sir. (*Exit* FROST *to the drawing-room.*)

SIR FREDERICK. If it's to be a battle, there's all the more reason! (*Re-enter* FROST, *and holds the door of the drawing-room open for* NORMAN. *Re-enter* NORMAN.) Frost, wait a moment.

NORMAN. I'm at your service, father.

SIR FREDERICK. I must test that statement. (*To* FROST.) Pack a few things for Mr. Byng—for immediate use. (FROST *bows and goes out through the ante-room to the left.* SIR FREDERICK *looks again at his watch.*) There's a fast train to town at 5.45. Can you catch it?

NORMAN. Catch it! Then you *do* turn me out?

SIR FREDERICK. I've considered more fully, and I see my duty clearer. You've half an hour.

NORMAN. It's liberal of you, sir, to give me "half an hour" to start for the other side of the globe—for arduous work, for a detestable climate, for an absence of many years!

SIR FREDERICK. If you'll give me your word of honour that you wish to linger for *me,* I'll withdraw my pressure on the instant!

NORMAN. (*After a moment.*) It's not altogether for you.

SIR FREDERICK. Thank you. Frost is putting up what's most necessary, and the day after to-morrow I'll join you in London with the rest of your luggage and remain with you till you leave England.

NORMAN. (*In the same tone his father has just used.*) Thank you. May I at least take leave of Miss Stanmore?

SIR FREDERICK. Is it extravagant to appeal to you not to?

NORMAN. I don't ask it for myself, however much I may wish it. I ask it for *her.*

SIR FREDERICK. (*With a gesture of irritated acceptance.*) I'll send her to you, and I'll make your arrangements. (*Exit* SIR FREDERICK *through the ante-room to the right.*)

NORMAN. (*Alone.*) Damn my arrangements! What has happened, what has made him wheel round? (*Reflecting; much struck.*) Who was that lady, installed there (*glancing round, as if for a trace of her, at the tea-table*) and with what do I dimly connect her? He was warning me a while ago against early ties. Is *she* an early tie? (*As* MILDRED *reappears.*) Oh, early ties are blest!

(*Re-enter* MILDRED *through the ante-room from the right.*)

MILDRED. Coming in from the garden I meet your father, and he tells me to come and speak to you. What strange thing has happened?

NORMAN. Exactly what I'm wondering! He orders me off the premises, and I'm only waiting for the dogcart.

MILDRED. Then we haven't even our five days?

NORMAN. We have only our five minutes. Dearest, be strong!

MILDRED. Why has he changed? (*Thinking.*) Norman, who was that lady?

NORMAN. Did *you* see her? She told me she was his tenant.

MILDRED. His tenant?

NORMAN. For the lodge. He's letting it.

MILDRED. And who were those men?

NORMAN. What men?

MILDRED. Two gentlemen I met by the lake: a strange young man, younger than you, with another—still stranger!—a good deal older.

NORMAN. "Tenants" too, no doubt! If there are so many, I must go off to make room for them!

MILDRED. I felt it hanging over us. We must have courage.

NORMAN. I have it for myself; but how can I have it for you?

MILDRED. Oh, I'm not a coward! You can trust me.

NORMAN. I do trust you: that's a blessing!

MILDRED. I feel as if the day had darkened!

NORMAN. So do I—and that makes it doubly cruel for me to go.

MILDRED. Never mind—if we've perfect faith!

NORMAN. Do you know how you can show me the perfection of yours? Call for me, *cable* to me, if there's danger.

MILDRED. Danger?

NORMAN. I don't know what it is—I only seem to scent it in the air. At the first hint of it I'll come back to you, at no matter what sacrifice. Do you understand? It's a solemn vow.

MILDRED. I've so much ambition for you that I shall have to be in a very tight place before I put you to such a disadvantage.

NORMAN. Well, you *may* be in a very tight place!

MILDRED. (*After an instant.*) Then I'll cable! (*They separate as* FROST *reappears.*)

(*Re-enter* FROST *through the ante-room from the left.*)

FROST. The dogcart is at the door, sir.

(*Exit* FROST. NORMAN *takes* MILDRED *in his arms and holds her for an instant in a silent, close embrace; then he goes quickly up. Exit* NORMAN *through the ante-room, to the left.*)

MILDRED. (*Alone, looking round her.*) The day *has* darkened!

(*Re-enter* MISS DYER *from the drawing-room.*)

MISS DYER. Where is Mr. Byng?

MILDRED. Gone to India.

MISS DYER. Without bidding *me* good-bye?

MILDRED. So it would seem!

MISS DYER. (*Disconcerted, wounded.*) I'm not quite sure I ought!

MILDRED. Dear Miss Dyer, there are many things we shall not be quite sure of now!

(*Re-enter from the library* MRS. VIBERT, *who stands a moment, looking from* MILDRED *to* MISS DYER.)

MRS. VIBERT. (*Graciously, to* MISS DYER.) Would you kindly let Sir Frederick know I'm ready?

(MISS DYER *bows and goes out through the ante-room to the left, and* MILDRED *is left confronted with* MRS. VIBERT.)

MRS. VIBERT. (*In the same tone.*) You look as if you'd lost something.

MILDRED. (*After an instant.*) I've lost a friend.

MRS. VIBERT. Then we must give you another.

(*Re-enter* SIR FREDERICK *through the ante-room from the left.*)

SIR FREDERICK. I'm quite at your service.

MRS. VIBERT. Then inaugurate me!

(*She takes* SIR FREDERICK'S *arm; they pass up together, and* MILDRED *also goes up a few steps and looks after them. Exeunt* SIR FREDERICK *and* MRS. VIBERT *through the ante-room to the left, while* MILDRED *comes down.*)

MILDRED. (*With confirmed alarm, staring before her and dropping upon a sofa.*) She *is* the danger!

ACT SECOND

The hall at Beechingham on Christmas Eve, with decorations of evergreen and holly. Through the wide window which looks out from the ante-room the wintry landscape glooms through the gathering dusk. Lamplight and firelight within; the Christmas blaze from a tall fireplace on the right, beyond the door of the drawing-room.

CLAUDE VIBERT *stands with his back to the fire and a little toy in his hands, a wooden figure that jerks up its legs and arms when pulled by a string. On the other side of the stage sits* MISS DYER, *beside a table heaped with Christmas packages and trifles, occupied in attaching to small objects the bits or ribbon by which they may be tied to a Christmas tree. Up at the window, with her back presented, stands* MILDRED, *looking out into the cold twilight, but turning away and coming down with a restless, preoccupied air as* CLAUDE *speaks.*)

CLAUDE. If I were in the least like Bluebeard, I should venture to think Miss Stanmore like Sister Anne! She's always looking out of windows.

MISS DYER. I'm not quite sure she ought! Perhaps she's watching for the Captain: it's

time indeed he should turn up.

MILDRED. I didn't even know Captain Lurcher has been away.

MISS DYER. For a whole week in London—on very important business.

MILDRED. I haven't missed him.

MISS DYER. (*Gay.*) Well, *I* have! But I've been in correspondence with him.

CLAUDE. (*With mock reproachfulness.*) I'm not quite sure you ought!

MISS DYER. It's a great secret, but you'll see when he comes.

CLAUDE. (*To* MILDRED.) Doesn't that make you want him to come?

MILDRED. (*Completely detached.*) Not a bit!

MISS DYER. He must be in time for our great occasion—our Christmas tree, after dinner, for the village children; and the old-fashioned dance, after that, for the dear simple people. We've cleared the billiard-room—it has the best floor.

CLAUDE. So that poor Sir Frederick has had to go without his game.

MISS DYER. It hasn't mattered, without Captain Lurcher to play with him.

CLAUDE. Yes, Sir Frederick, at least, has missed the Captain. The Captain always lets himself be beaten.

MISS DYER. He has such tact—I think he

does it on purpose.

MILDRED. He may be beaten once too often to like it.

CLAUDE. Surely not by Sir Frederick!

MILDRED. (*After an instant, turning away.*) No, not by Sir Frederick.

MISS DYER. (*To* CLAUDE; *mysterious, important.*) I don't mind telling *you* my secret. I wrote to him to buy some more toys for our tree!

CLAUDE. (*Laughing.*) What dark machinations! But you were quite right. Too many Christmas cards with quotations from the poets; and, for the dear simple people, as you say, not enough charming objects like this. (*Playing with his toy.*)

MISS DYER. What good are the charming objects if you worry them to death? Go and finish dressing the tree.

CLAUDE. I'll go like a shot if Miss Stanmore will come with me. Miss Stanmore, will you come and help me?

MILDRED. Excuse me, Mr. Vibert—I'm quite out of it.

CLAUDE. (*Flings down his toy and looks at her a moment; then gentle, pleading, persuasive.*) Won't you do it for the poor little children?

MILDRED. (*After an instant.*) Well! for the poor little children!

MISS DYER. (*To* CLAUDE, *rising and giving him a number of her packets of sweets.*) Then please take these. (*To* MILDRED.) And you take these.

CLAUDE. (*With eager courtesy, intercepting the objects offered to* MILDRED.) I'll carry them for Miss Stanmore. (*He bows for* MILDRED *to pass first, and they go up together. Exeunt* MILDRED *and* CLAUDE *through the ante-room to the right.*)

MISS DYER. (*Alone.*) How nice he is, with his little Frenchified jokes and his little foreign ceremonies! But what has got into *her* at this sociable time? She, alas, is *not* sociable! However, if she hasn't confidence in me, how can she have it in any one? (*Then as* CAPTAIN LURCHER *appears.*) Ah, the Captain at last! (*Enter* CAPTAIN LURCHER *through the ante-room from the left.*) Welcome back, you brilliant fraud!

LURCHER. (*In travelling dress, an Inverness cape and gloves; placing on* MISS DYER's *table a considerable parcel.*) Good day, sweet child of nature. Had you given me up?

MISS DYER. I shall never give you up!

LURCHER. I've brought you a museum of curiosities—enough to stock a bazaar. And also (*taking a small paper of bonbons from the pocket of his cape*) a little private parcel for your own consumption.

MISS DYER. (*With the bonbons.*) Chocolate creams? You know the way to a woman's heart!

LURCHER. Not down her throat, surely!

MISS DYER. (*With the larger parcel.*) Mildred and Mr. Claude shall suspend these to the branches.

LURCHER. And where *are* those interesting young people?

MISS DYER. In the billiard-room, dressing the tree.

LURCHER. With no one else?

MISS DYER. With no one else.

LURCHER. (*Gratified.*) Christmas is a great invention!

MISS DYER. It's not appreciated as much as one could wish by Mrs. Vibert. She has not been here to lend a hand.

LURCHER. She doesn't lend—she borrows. Sir Frederick's at Clere; I stopped there on my way from the station.

MISS DYER. Precisely; he lunched there: he went over at eleven o'clock.

LURCHER. (*Laughing.*) Is that the hour he lunches?

MISS DYER. It's the hour he has started—every day of your absence.

LURCHER. (*After an instant.*) And when has he come back?

MISS DYER. Very late for dinner.

LURCHER. (*After another instant.*) Most irregular. But if Claude has made up for it—

MISS DYER. He has regularly lunched here.

LURCHER. Coming also at eleven?

MISS DYER. Coming at ten.

LURCHER. That's quite as it should be. But there's something else that isn't.

MISS DYER. Pray, what's that?

LURCHER. Your deplorable inaction. You disappoint me!

MISS DYER. I always disappoint wickedness! (*Then as if to change the subject.*) Is London as shocking as ever?

LURCHER. London bored me. (*Gallant.*) My personal joys are here.

MISS DYER. You're a mass of corruption! Isn't Mrs. Vibert coming over now?

LURCHER. Very soon, I gather; she's to drive across with Sir Frederick. But why do you worry about *her*? Mrs. Vibert's not our model.

MISS DYER. She's mine—for clothes!

LURCHER. (*Flattering.*) You've not the need of them that she has! (*Then as she flirts away a little.*) Will you listen to me?

MISS DYER. I'm not quite sure I ought!

LURCHER. That will make it all the nicer. We might do so much together! Union is strength.

MISS DYER. Strength for what?

LURCHER. For success! The making of the most charming young couple in the world—which young couple would, by the same token, be the making of *us*.

MISS DYER. Your theories are complicated!

LURCHER. I address them to a fine intelligence. You'll win my eternal gratitude by persuading Miss Stanmore—as you have so rare an opportunity of doing—that the best guarantee of her happiness would be a union with that engaging, brilliant boy —one of the most finished, the most accomplished, the most amiable young men in Europe; a flower of my own assiduous raising, a nature in which art and culture, the highest training and the purest atmosphere, have only added to the bloom of the rarest gifts.

MISS DYER. Mr. Claude is certainly a perfect gentleman; he does the greatest honour to your care. But must I remind you that Mildred already sees what you call the best guarantee of her happiness in a union with somebody else?

LURCHER. Mr. Byng? Dear Miss Dyer, Mr. Byng's out of it.

MISS DYER. Out of what? He's never out of her memory; he's never out of her thoughts.

LURCHER. Then we must turn him out! Everything's against him.

MISS DYER. That's why she loves him.

LURCHER. Yes, you women are so tortuous! I maintain it, Miss Dyer, you're tortuous yourself!

MISS DYER. It's only because I wriggle in your grasp!

LURCHER. You've been quiet enough in *other* hands. (*After an instant.*) Aren't you secretly pledged to Mr. Byng? Aren't you in his interest and, if I may use the expression, in his service? Hasn't he bribed, suborned, corrupted you?

MISS DYER. (*Almost shrieking.*) "Corrupted" me?

LURCHER. It would be a deep regret to me to have to recognise it, for my fondest hope has been that you are free.

MISS DYER. (*With intensity.*) Captain Lurcher, I'm as free as air!

LURCHER. Then, in the name of all that's bracing, don't let us muddle away a prize! We've a clear field, a high stake, a strong side. Mr. Byng's in the torrid zone.

MISS DYER. Yes; and he went there with a frigidity!

LURCHER. Butter packed in ice? Is that the sort of nature you're enslaved to?

MISS DYER. (*As if breaking her chains.*) I'm *not* enslaved!

LURCHER. Then do justice to our opportunity. We should be such common triflers to let it slip that, as a man of the world—for I *am* a man of the world—I should really blush for our form. Why can't we turn Mr. Byng out when we have a first-rate subject to turn in? Our young lady has the plasticity of youth, and we have lots of time—we can work at our leisure.

MISS DYER. (*Participating more and more.*) Yes, we've months—we've years.

LURCHER. Claude's taking, he's brilliant, he's near. Juxtaposition is much.

MISS DYER. (*Quite carried away.*) Juxtaposition is everything!

LURCHER. Last not least, he's in love.

MISS DYER. That smooths the way.

LURCHER. And *I* can do something, can't I?

MISS DYER. Certainly! You're taking too; you're brilliant too—and you're "near."

LURCHER. (*Coming closer.*) Very near, Miss Dyer! And I'm also in love! (*Passes his arm round her waist.*)

MISS DYER. (*Disengaging herself with a nervous laugh.*) Ah, but you're not twenty!

LURCHER. Not yet, but I *shall* be! (*Plead-*

ing.) You won't help me?

MISS DYER. Yes, if you'll help *me.* (*Placing in his hands the parcel that he has deposited on the table.*) Take all this, to be hung on the tree. (*As he takes the parcel from her he gets hold of one of her hands, hastily kissing it, and goes up. Exit* CAPTAIN LURCHER *through the ante-room to the right.* MISS DYER *looks at her hand.*) He *is* a man of the world; and Mr. Byng didn't behave like one! (*Re-enter* MILDRED *through the ante-room from the right.*) The Captain just went to you.

MILDRED. That's precisely why I came out. (*Then abruptly.*) Miss Dyer—he's on his way!

MISS DYER. (*Blank; then startled.*) Mr. Byng—coming back? (*Quite aghast.*) When —why?

MILDRED. I can't tell you when—probably from one day to the other. But I can tell you why. Because I cabled to him.

MISS DYER. "Cabled"?

MILDRED. Six weeks ago.

MISS DYER. And why did you do that?

MILDRED. (*As* SIR FREDERICK *and* MRS. VIBERT *appear together.*) See for yourself!

(*Enter* SIR FREDERICK *and* MRS. VIBERT *through the ante-room from the left;* MRS. VIBERT *dressed for the evening.* MILDRED *passes up as they come down.*)

SIR FREDERICK. May I take the liberty of asking where you're going?

MILDRED. To my room.

SIR FREDERICK. And may I take the further liberty of asking for a few words of conversation with you?

MILDRED. In my room?

SIR FREDERICK. No—here. (*Looking at his watch.*) Say in a quarter of an hour.

MILDRED. (*Curtseying.*) In a quarter of an hour. (*Exit* MILDRED *through the ante-room to the left.*)

SIR FREDERICK. (*To* MISS DYER.) Our charming young friend isn't very easy to get hold of. One has to make appointments with her.

MISS DYER. (*Agitated and obsequious.*) I'll speak to her about it, Sir Frederick. (*Exit* MISS DYER *through the ante-room to the left.*)

MRS. VIBERT. Your charming young friend hates your charming *old* friend— that's the explanation!

SIR FREDERICK. That's just why I want to see her.

MRS. VIBERT. Make allowances for her. I can understand it.

SIR FREDERICK. (*Taking off* MRS. VIBERT's *cloak.*) That's more than *I* can!

(*Re-enter* CAPTAIN LURCHER *through the ante-room from the right.*)

LURCHER. I'm not much use with toys and little candles; my strength is in other directions.

SIR FREDERICK. Oh, Captain, I know your strength!

LURCHER. You know my weakness, Sir Frederick. But, fortunately, it won't be exposed so long as the billiard-room is given up to these revels.

SIR FREDERICK. (*Surprised.*) Given up?

LURCHER. Go and see!

SIR FREDERICK. (*Going half-way; then to* MRS. VIBERT.) Won't you come too?

MRS. VIBERT. Captain Lurcher will say we're inseparable.

LURCHER. (*Laughing.*) Oh, I must separate you! (*To* SIR FREDERICK.) May I ask leave to detain Mrs. Vibert a moment?

MRS. VIBERT. (*Who has crossed to the fire, smiling at* SIR FREDERICK.) I've to report on Claude.

LURCHER. (*To* SIR FREDERICK.) Tell him we're overhauling him!

SIR FREDERICK. (*Nodding to the left; alert.*) He's there? Be fair to him! (*Exit* SIR FREDERICK *through the ante-room to the right.*)

LURCHER. (*While* MRS. VIBERT, *with her back to him and one hand on the chimney-piece, stands warming her foot at the fire.*) Sir Frederick favours him.

MRS. VIBERT. (*looking down at the fire.*) Sir Frederick likes him.

LURCHER. (*Imperious, abrupt.*) Then where's that girl? (*As* MRS. VIBERT *makes no answer.*) Where's Miss Stanmore?

MRS. VIBERT. I'm not Miss Stanmore's keeper.

LURCHER. She went out of the billiard-room as soon as I came in.

MRS. VIBERT. Yes, and she went out of this room as soon as *I* came in.

LURCHER. She's an invidious little wretch!

MRS. VIBERT. She makes comparisons. She's not an easy conquest.

LURCHER. (*Impatient.*) Not even with her guardian to help us? (*Then while she again remains silent, still looking down at the fire, he throws off with irritation, a little with the movement of stripping for a "row," his Inverness cape, which he flings upon a sofa; beginning in the same manner to pull off his gloves, which he has worn during the scene with* MISS DYER.) You'll permit me to remark that you strike me, during this interesting crisis, as having retired prematurely to your tent.

MRS. VIBERT. (*Turning round slowly, with visible weariness.*) I'll permit you to remark anything you like, if in return you'll permit *me* to remark nothing at all!

LURCHER. On the principle that silence is golden? Common honesty, madam, is more so. You were voluble enough last summer—*then* you had plenty of ideas. Our ship was in port and our cargo disposed of.—If our ship's in port we're forbidden even to land!

MRS. VIBERT. On the contrary, I've brought you ashore. You must do the rest for yourself. Remember that I never was in command.

LURCHER. Which means that you're as much as ever under my orders.

MRS. VIBERT. So you periodically remind me.

LURCHER. Your habit of presuming on my indulgence makes it necessary. I place before you the articles of our association.

MRS. VIBERT. One would think they had been drawn up by a lawyer!

LURCHER. You know who they were drawn up by! I've always allowed you a latitude; but now I fall back on our agreement. I take my stand on our Act of partnership.

MRS. VIBERT. (*With sudden, passionate expression.*) I despise our Act of partnership!

LURCHER. (*After an instant.*) You never did till you came into this house.

MRS. VIBERT. You mean I never *said* I did. There are a great many things I never said!

LURCHER. I see—and at present you can say them! (*Then as* MRS. VIBERT *leaves the fire and, with a movement of extreme oppression, as of a checked longing to escape, passes slowly across or round the room, while he stands watching her.*) You've been deucedly different since you came into this house!

MRS. VIBERT. You've remained the same, and that will do as well!

LURCHER. I accept the imputation, as a tribute to my fidelity and consistency. But now I want to see so much virtue a little rewarded!

MRS. VIBERT. Four months ago your virtue took its chances and reckoned with its risks.

LURCHER. The lovely day you swam ashore and dropped at Sir Frederick's feet? That was because that night, when we were back at the inn at Trecothick—and, as you perfectly remember, we sat up long and late!—you pledged yourself to do your best, to act your part.

MRS. VIBERT. (*With rising impatience.*) And haven't I done my best? Am I not acting my part from morning till night?

LURCHER. You've become unconscious of so many things that it's refreshing to find you don't forget the conference which gave so much more intimate a form to our union. I consider that on that occasion the bond of our joint speculation was immeasurably tightened.

MRS. VIBERT. (*Who has moved away and still away from* LURCHER *during his last two speeches, but whom he has followed round a part of the room; with unspeakable fatigue.*) Merciful powers!

LURCHER. (*Authoritative.*) Come, madam; our comedy is for others, but our arithmetic is for ourselves! It was on speculation we came here—the frankest and the shrewdest; and the brilliant idea was your own. I adopted it, I embraced it, and now I seem really fonder of it than *you* are! Thanks to your disenchantment, we're wasting our time.

MRS. VIBERT. I'm not in the least disenchanted.

LURCHER. You're pacified, I fully recognise, because you're getting your personal returns. But what returns am *I* getting?

MRS. VIBERT. A harvest of glory! Leave

the rest to Claude.

LURCHER. I've left it—for four months. How much longer do you expect?

MRS. VIBERT. As much longer as *he* expects. Time is an element in the question. All things considered, we're remarkably secure; we have a liberal margin, and a single act of precipitation may dash this advantage away.

LURCHER. Perfect—I see. A game of chess on a rainy day, with a nice long nap between the moves! Meanwhile what am I to live on?

MRS. VIBERT. You've too fine a conception of life!

LURCHER. Observe that I've had an example to set: which has signally failed, however, to impress my creditors. Pray, what have you done with yours?

MRS. VIBERT. (*After an instant.*) I have none.

LURCHER. (*Surprised, resentful.*) You've had money, and kept it?

MRS. VIBERT. I haven't kept a penny.

LURCHER. (*Blank, disgusted.*) Then where's your delicacy?

MRS. VIBERT. In my infinite patience!

LURCHER. (*Derisive.*) The refinement of your egotism. If you're out of the draught yourself, you don't care who sneezes!

MRS. VIBERT. I suffer when you sneeze in my face. But you needn't talk of draughts —you've never been less exposed.

LURCHER. I've never been less guaranteed. You suggest that I live in clover; but the clover's over the fence, and I'm confined to the thinnest grass. Miss Stanmore's fortune's the tender herbage, and I haven't had a sniff of that. You trifle with grave realities in affecting to sink, from one day to the other, the memory of the fact that for the last five years I've laboured without a wage.

MRS. VIBERT. But never without an alternative.

LURCHER. (*Vague.*) An alternative?

MRS. VIBERT. That of simply leaving us.

LURCHER. Leave the work of my hands and the mainstay of my age? Sacrifice my investment before I've taken a dividend? Claude's my capital, and I continue to nurse it!

MRS. VIBERT. You were paid with the utmost punctuality the first years you were with us.

LURCHER. Yes, till your funds ran low. But the habit of devotion was formed.

MRS. VIBERT. Without prejudice to the habit of calculation.

LURCHER. Call them together the habit of obedience! I promised your husband on his death-bed that I would cleave to you.

MRS. VIBERT. Don't speak to me to-day of my husband!

LURCHER. Why not, when he was the first to speak to me of you? He made us acquainted.

MRS. VIBERT. He made *me* acquainted— with most of the ill I know.

LURCHER. You had to take what came; you were so little in a position to choose. So when, in the last year of his life, I encountered a reverse of fortune; when my old comrade, my dear Vibert, living apart from you, learned that I was looking for a position and *you* were looking for a preceptor to a certain interesting infant (a first-rate, all-round man), he simply, in his perfect command of the situation, nominated to the post his most tried and trusted friend.

MRS. VIBERT. Trusted, exactly—to poison even my freedom!

LURCHER. Your freedom was only relative, and the "poison" agreed, wonderful to say, with the delicate constitution of the infant.

MRS. VIBERT. It was not for that it was prescribed. Your commission had another stamp.

LURCHER. Sealed orders, to sink the vessel? I spoiled Mr. Vibert's revenge, and spared the precious child. Bettering my instructions, I had the perversity to take a positive fancy to my victim. Your know how Claude adores me.

MRS. VIBERT. I know it from you, but not from him.

LURCHER. (*After an instant.*) Then I advise you to repair that deficiency!

MRS. VIBERT. I should deprive you of your favourite menace.

LURCHER. Let me have then, before I lose it, the supreme pleasure of repeating it! On the day our young companion ceases to appreciate the man who has formed his youth, who has fortified his mind and set him, personally and socially, on his feet—

MRS. VIBERT. (*As he pauses.*) Well?

LURCHER. I shall hold you responsible for the accident.

MRS. VIBERT. You take a great deal for granted.

LURCHER. I take all there is!

MRS. VIBERT. (*After a moment.*) What do you require of me—that isn't too base?

LURCHER. To make a better use of Sir Frederick. I needn't teach you what I mean by that, nor how to meet my views. Bring him up short—show him, so he won't forget it, what we rigidly expect of him.

MRS. VIBERT. What "we" expect? I never speak to him of *you!*

LURCHER. Nothing could prove better how constantly you think of me!

MRS. VIBERT. (*After an instant.*) Sir Frederick is to speak to Miss Stanmore this evening.

LURCHER. (*Dubious.*) When will it come off?

MRS. VIBERT. Immediately—on this spot.

LURCHER. Then I shall expect immediate results. (*Picking up his cape and hat.*) I'm going over to dress. (*Then from the ante-room.*) I'll come back to see them! (*Exit* CAPTAIN LURCHER *to the left.*)

MRS. VIBERT. (*Alone.*) Ah, yes you'll come back—and back, and back, and back: as one's evil genius comes, as one's evil passions come, and one's errors, and one's burdens, and one's shames! (*Then as she sees* SIR FREDERICK: *re-enter* SIR FREDERICK *through the ante-room, from the right.*) Have you been with Claude?

SIR FREDERICK. Helping him, upon my honour, to deck the tree. But as I set it on fire he turned me out.

MRS. VIBERT. (*Smiling and shaking her head slowly and tenderly.*) He *shouldn't* turn you out!

SIR FREDERICK. Oh, I let him play; the poor boy's good for that. (*After an instant.*) Eleanor, I really take to him. He has lots of pluck, even though he hasn't been at a rough English school.

MRS. VIBERT. He has been at the roughest school of all, the school of adversity.

SIR FREDERICK. Adversity? with *you* to curl his hair!

MRS. VIBERT. Curling the hair doesn't do much for a young dishonoured head.

SIR FREDERICK. "Dishonoured," my dear, is extravagant. And you've assured me he doesn't dream—!

MRS. VIBERT. Claude's deep, he's delicate: who knows what a clever boy dreams? But (*after an instant, as if throwing off her fears*) we must never let him dream of *that!* We've done him a great wrong, and to the utmost of our power we must make it up to him. I've shown you the way.

SIR FREDERICK. Yes, I've been trying to learn it. But, somehow, it's hard to my feet!

MRS. VIBERT. With your position, your authority, your extraordinary advantages? Be a little politic!

SIR FREDERICK. I see. You want me to strain a point.

MRS. VIBERT. The virtue of the effort is the virtue of the cause. When one has strained a point to commit a wrong, one can surely do no less to make a reparation. (*Coming down after passing up.*) Mildred's here—I'll wait.

SIR FREDERICK. Wait in the drawing-room.

MRS. VIBERT. (*Smiling, at the drawing-room.*) Be very clever! (*Exit* MRS. VIBERT.)

SIR FREDERICK. (*Alone.*) I shall never be as clever as you!

(*Enter* MILDRED *through the ante-room from the left.*)

MILDRED. You told me you wished to see me.

SIR FREDERICK. Exactly so, Mildred! I've wished to see you for some time past.

MILDRED. There would have been no difficulty about it if you hadn't been surrounded with other people.

SIR FREDERICK. I'm quite aware that you've avoided me in consequence of my interest—so perfectly legitimate—in our charming neighbours; and avoided *them,* more markedly, for the same reason.

MILDRED. I don't avoid anything or any one, Sir Frederick. I quietly go my way and bide my time.

SIR FREDERICK. When Mrs. Vibert proposed herself as a tenant for Clere, my first thought was of the pleasant effect such a delightful person would produce at Beech-ingham.

MILDRED. I've fully perceived the pleasant effect.

SIR FREDERICK. Then you might have done more to thank her for it.

MILDRED. That would have given a false impression.

SIR FREDERICK. A pleasanter impression than you've succeeded in giving!

MILDRED. I'm sorry I don't satisfy you, Sir Frederick, because in your house I've had much to be grateful for. But I've gone as far as I can.

SIR FREDERICK. (Smiling.) On Christmas eve, my dear, one should go a little further! That's why I've taken it as an occasion to speak to you. (A little embarrassed.) It's an occasion, you know, for charitable sentiments, for give and take, and peace on earth, and that sort of thing. You know what I mean—it's a solemn hour!

MILDRED. I assure you I feel its solemnity.

SIR FREDERICK. Just so, but you must also feel its cheer! Therefore I'll mention to you that there's a person in the house whom it would give me joy to see you treat a little more in the spirit of the day.

MILDRED. (Imperturbable.) What person, Sir Frederick?

SIR FREDERICK. A young man—generous, ambitious, accomplished—in whom I take a particular interest.

MILDRED. (After an instant.) Do you insist on my listening to you?

SIR FREDERICK. I "insist" on nothing—not even on your listening to Claude. I only beg you to let him speak for himself.

MILDRED. He deserves a better fortune.

SIR FREDERICK. What fortune, Mildred, could be better—?

MILDRED. (Interrupting.) Than making love to me? He'll tell you when he has had his answer.

SIR FREDERICK. (With a nervous laugh.) You reduce things, my dear, to a simplicity—! But that's, in point of fact, what I want. May he have his answer to-night?

MILDRED. (After an instant.) Yes, to-night will be a good time.

SIR FREDERICK. Then I'll send him to you now. (Seeing MISS DYER reappear: re-enter MISS DYER through the ante-room from the left, dressed for dinner.) Miss Dyer, do me the favour to bestow your company on Mrs. Vibert, who's alone in the drawing-room.

MISS DYER. For all it's worth, Sir Frederick!

SIR FREDERICK. (From the ante-room, genial.) Everything to-night is worth double! (Exit SIR FREDERICK to the right.)

MILDRED. (Who has taken a telegram from her pocket; with decision.) Then this is! (Handing it to MISS DYER.) Read it!

MISS DYER. (With the telegram; agitated.) Mr. Byng—to-night? How romantic!

MILDRED. (Her emotion breaking out.) To-night—to-night (then suddenly, as she drops upon a seat, bursting into the hysterical tears that she has with difficulty repressed during the scene with SIR FREDERICK)—at last!

MISS DYER. (At the door of the drawing-room.) I won't betray you! (Exit MISS DYER.)

MILDRED. (Springing up and brushing away her tears.) I mustn't betray myself!

(Re-enter CLAUDE VIBERT through the ante-room from the right. He comes down quickly and stands for a moment confronted in silence with MILDRED, who has as quickly controlled herself.)

CLAUDE. Sir Frederick tells me I may speak to you, and he knows what I want to say. (MILDRED has turned away from him; he follows her a few steps.) Therefore, perhaps, you've also an idea of it.

MILDRED. I did give him leave to send you to me.

CLAUDE. I thank you for that from the bottom of my heart.

MILDRED. You won't thank me, perhaps, when you know what's at the bottom of mine!

CLAUDE. Let me know it, Miss Stanmore.

MILDRED. A very real compassion for you! You're better than the part you play.

CLAUDE. I play no part, Miss Stanmore, unless it be one to be under the charm—

MILDRED. (Breaking in.) Of my unmistakable indifference? If my studied bad manners have had a charm for you, you must have been easy to please! I don't apologise for them, because they've been my only, and my necessary, defence. But I haven't expected you to admire them!

CLAUDE. You're a strange girl, and what I do admire is strangeness—it amuses me, it appeals to me. I delight in originality and in everything that's not—how do you say it in English?—not *banal*.

MILDRED. What I have to say I shall not say in French, Mr. Vibert, even at the risk of your not understanding it. You were brought here to make love to me, and you've made it very well, considering how little you had to make it of. But you must stop to-night.

CLAUDE. (*Smiling.*) Why to-night?

MILDRED. Because it's your necessary limit.

CLAUDE. Don't say that at the very hour when you're more charming, more lovely than I've ever seen you before!

MILDRED. I say it because you're in danger.

CLAUDE. Danger only inspires—danger only intoxicates me! I don't pretend not to know I've made no great way with you: I have no illusions on that score. But let me serve my time, let me plead my cause; let me submissively, appealingly (*with an insinuating, conciliatory gesture*) come a little nearer to you!

MILDRED. You've a very well-stored mind, and a very well-trained manner, and I do perfect justice to your attitude. But I'm still more struck with that of the people who are behind you—the people who push you on.

CLAUDE. (*Surprised.*) The people? what people? (*Then smiling.*) It's the passion I feel that pushes me on!

MILDRED. Ah, but who pushes on the passion you feel? You're too nice, you know, and too clever, to be a puppet in vulgar hands.

CLAUDE. (*Blank.*) Pray, of what hands do you speak?

MILDRED. Of the hands that meddle—of the hands I've never touched! (*After an instant.*) Your mother can assure you I haven't.

CLAUDE. (*Greatly moved.*) In what an extraordinary connection to refer to my mother! She's the gentlest and noblest of women.

MILDRED. I'll believe as much when she proves it.

CLAUDE. (*Vague.*) "Proves" it?

MILDRED. By taking you away from here. (*Then after she has gone up; from the ante-room.*) Until she does that, Mr. Vibert, you must excuse me if I differ with you, and leave you. (*She makes him a formal curtsey. Exit* MILDRED *to the left.*)

CLAUDE. (*Alone, wonderstruck.*) She makes my face burn—as if she had lashed it! (*Passionately, as* MRS. VIBERT *reappears.*) Mother!

(*Re-enter* MRS. VIBERT *from the drawing-room. She goes to him, holding out her hands; he takes them, she draws him to her, and he stands for a moment in her embrace, burying his head on her neck. Then he turns from her, brushing away a tear with his pocket-handkerchief.*)

MRS. VIBERT. Claude, something has happened to you!

CLAUDE. Yes, mother—something has happened to me!

MRS. VIBERT. You're flesh of my flesh and bone of my bone. I guessed it, there, on the instant—it brought me here. You've spoken!

CLAUDE. Yes, I've spoken; and she has spoken.

MRS. VIBERT. And what did she say?

CLAUDE. (*Sombre, resentful, reflective.*) She said that I'm not a man! (*Breaking out suddenly.*) Mother, who am I? what am I? why am I not independent?

MRS. VIBERT. (*Smiling sadly.*) You would be independent, Claude, if you were to marry Miss Stanmore.

CLAUDE. I should be something (*intently thinking*) that I'm determined she shall know I am—shall confess I am! I can't rest under her scorn.

MRS. VIBERT. The scorn of pretty girls is the spice of courtship! You'll get over that.

CLAUDE. *She* shall get over it—that will be more to the purpose. She says I'm put up to such ideas.

MRS. VIBERT. By me, of course she means.

CLAUDE. By you and by the Captain.

MRS. VIBERT. If we desire what you desire, is that such a crime?

CLAUDE. Mother, I shall force her to

think of you more justly.

MRS. VIBERT. I don't care how she thinks of me!

CLAUDE. Any wife of mine shall first understand this mother of mine!

MRS. VIBERT. If once she is your wife, I shall care less than ever.

CLAUDE. (*After an instant.*) You do want it then, intensely?

MRS. VIBERT. I want it if your own pride, if your own heart is committed to it. But you evidently feel afresh that Miss Stanmore has (*hesitating an instant*) prejudices that will not be easy to surmount.

CLAUDE. That's exactly why I shan't give her up. The way she treats me puts me on my mettle to try to win her more than any other way would do. She's not as other girls are, and, before heaven! I would do anything to make her like me.

MRS. VIBERT. You give me your word of honour on that?

CLAUDE. My word of honour.

MRS. VIBERT. Then let me kiss you.

(*Re-enter* SIR FREDERICK *through the ante-room from the right.*)

SIR FREDERICK. I don't know what your mother's kissing you for, but I congratulate you at a venture.

MRS. VIBERT. (*To* CLAUDE.) Go and dress for dinner, and I'll explain to Sir Frederick.

(*Exit* CLAUDE *through the ante-room to the left.*)

SIR FREDERICK. I told him he must dress here; I've sent for his things.

MRS. VIBERT. It's charming what you do for him. He needs all your kindness now that he has spoken to Miss Stanmore. He's as much in love as you please!

SIR FREDERICK. (*Looking at her a moment.*) The real thing?

MRS. VIBERT. (*Smiling.*) The genuine article!

SIR FREDERICK. (*After another instant.*) Then it's a horrid bore!

MRS. VIBERT. Why, it's all we require to be right.

SIR FREDERICK. When it's a case of squeezing I'd rather be wrong! I can't put Mildred on bread and water.

MRS. VIBERT. You might put her on her good behaviour. She might sweeten your

responsibility, instead of making it bitter. You've twisted your life out of shape to make it fit into hers; you've given up your habits, your traditions, your privacies, your comforts, to carry out a duty you might perfectly have declined. Is she to do nothing in return? to render no homage, to learn no lesson, to make no sacrifice?

SIR FREDERICK. (*Embarrassed.*) You forget, Eleanor, that after all— (*pausing while he looks at his finger-nails.*)

MRS. VIBERT. (*Waiting.*) After all?

SIR FREDERICK. If I sent Norman away I didn't disown him, and that if I challenged him—

MRS. VIBERT. (*As he pauses again.*) Well?

SIR FREDERICK. I'm extremely fond of him!

MRS. VIBERT. Yes, I must remember! He's your happy, lawful, acknowledged son, your fortunate pride and joy! (*Suddenly, with a change of tone.*) Forgive me, Frederick, if I'm jealous, forgive me if I taste to the full the irony of certain differences and contrasts. When I feel what *my* poor boy is, I'm conscious at once of the elevation of his character and of the infirmity of every pretension he may ever make.

SIR FREDERICK. Believe me when I tell you that I too, in much searching of my conscience, have thought these things over; over and over, in particular, since the words that fell from your lips a while ago, the words about wrong and reparation. It's late in the day to repair; but I have my idea, I have my honest wish. It's not too late for me to have felt the advantage, the magic, of your presence here. (MRS. VIBERT *looks at him with quickened attention, the dawn of an expectation, while he goes on.*) Eleanor, if I may call you my wife we shall do something to help our son to call me his father.

MRS. VIBERT. (*Strongly, exquisitely moved, but checking herself.*) Ah, my only friend!

SIR FREDERICK. We're not too young, but we're not too old! Life will spread quietly round us, and affection, and rest, and reason; and something we dreamed of in youth will seem at last to have come to us. It won't change everything now, for too much has gone; but it will improve what remains, it will consecrate, it will harmonise.

MRS. VIBERT. (*Shaking her head with mournful dignity and as if with a sense of hindrances and complications.*) Are you very sure it will harmonise?

SIR FREDERICK. Why not, if it makes us *one?* Then, perhaps, on a basis more convenient, we can do something better for Claude than trying to marry him to girls who love somebody else!

MRS. VIBERT. (*Thoughtful.*) Something better might be something bad!

SIR FREDERICK. (*Blank.*) I don't understand you.

MRS. VIBERT. I mean it might be something strange! (*Then in a different tone.*) You make me deeply happy; yet you make me feel that I need to consider.

SIR FREDERICK. Ah, don't consider too much!

MRS. VIBERT. As you said to me four months ago, there are particular difficulties.

SIR FREDERICK. Why, the beauty of this is that it meets and settles them all!

MRS. VIBERT. (*After an instant.*) Do you mean that, as your stepson, frankly adopted and patronised, Claude may have a better prospect with Miss Stanmore?

SIR FREDERICK. No, honestly; I mean just the contrary: that we needn't think of Miss Stanmore again.

MRS. VIBERT. How can Claude help thinking of her if he happens to adore her?

SIR FREDERICK. He'll happen to get over it!

MRS. VIBERT. I see, I see. (*Considering.*) By marrying Claude's mother you will have rendered him a service that will absolve you from further exertion.

SIR FREDERICK. (*After an hesitation, with slight surprise and just visible irritation.*) You put it crudely, dear lady. I'm disappointed that I should have to struggle with you.

MRS. VIBERT. Don't think me ungrateful; all my heart goes out to you! But, as you said just now, we're not juvenile: let us therefore not be superficial. You attach to your generous offer a kind of condition, of stipulation. The price of my position here will be that I shall do my best to keep Miss Stanmore for Mr. Byng.

SIR FREDERICK. Mr. Byng can do his own keeping; but (*dryly*) I must be just even to him. It's not his fault, after all, if he's my absent and my elder son!

MRS. VIBERT. I thank you immensely for "elder"!

SIR FREDERICK. (*Still colder.*) I can account for your apparently very qualified interest in my proposal only by the supposition that you have hindrances that I am ignorant of. (*Studying her face a moment; then breaking down, more tenderly.*) Eleanor, you've some trouble you don't tell me!

MRS. VIBERT. I'll tell you some other time. Meanwhile, if I seem odious, I throw myself on your mercy.

SIR FREDERICK. I'll show you every mercy if you'll accept me!

MRS. VIBERT. (*Oppressed, nervous, with increasing emotion.*) Give me time; I must indeed think! Go and pray for me, and go and dress.

SIR FREDERICK. (*Laughing.*) We're agreed that we're not juvenile, but I shall show you that I can dress in five minutes. (*Exit* SIR FREDERICK *through the ante-room to the right.*)

MRS. VIBERT. (*Alone, dropping again in despair upon a sofa.*) Ah, when at last it comes, to be only afraid of it!

(*Re-enter* LURCHER, *in evening dress, through the ante-room from the left.*)

LURCHER. Has Sir Frederick spoken?

MRS. VIBERT. (*Rising quickly.*) Sir Frederick has spoken.

LURCHER. And what assurance can he give us?

MRS. VIBERT. He can give us no assurance!

LURCHER. In spite of your eloquent pressure?

MRS. VIBERT. You had better try your own!

LURCHER. (*Startled, indignant.*) You've given up the case?

MRS. VIBERT. (*After a silence and with an effort.*) I've given up the case.

LURCHER. Well then, you've had my warning.

MRS. VIBERT. (*After another silence.*) I

don't care for your warning now!

LURCHER. (*Staring and insolent.*) "Now"? You're not dead yet! (*Then as if divining.*) *Santo Dio,* you've been squared? (*Seeming surer and coming closer.*) You've got your price? (*Eagerly.*) How much?

MRS. VIBERT. (*Turning for an instant, in vague distress, this way and that; then facing him in desperation.*) How much, Captain Lurcher, is yours?

LURCHER. I've told you before. Seven thousand a year! (*As* MRS. VIBERT *turns away with the same blind oppression.*) If you've really sold me, we've an account indeed!

MRS. VIBERT. (*Seeing* MISS DYER.) We'll settle our account in private.

LURCHER. Excuse me: it's the publicity that *makes* the settlement!

(*Re-enter* MISS DYER *from the drawing-room.*)

MISS DYER. Isn't our little party gathered?

MRS. VIBERT. (*At the door of the library.*) I shall be here when I'm wanted. (*Exit* MRS. VIBERT.)

LURCHER. (*With a complete change of face and manner.*) Well, Miss Dyer, I hope you've been able to give me a lift!

MISS DYER. (*Very vague.*) A lift, Captain Lurcher?

LURCHER. As you promised an hour ago.

MISS DYER. (*Now completely detached.*) I'm afraid it's out of the question.

LURCHER. You don't care then for my approval?

MISS DYER. I'm not quite sure I ought!

LURCHER. You might have found that out before!

MISS DYER. Ah, *then* I didn't know!

LURCHER. (*Blank.*) Didn't know what?

MISS DYER. (*Seeing* MILDRED.) Ask Miss Stanmore!

(*Re-enter* MILDRED *through the ante-room from the left, brilliantly dressed for the evening.*)

LURCHER. (*To* MISS DYER.) Why, her very dress is a promise! (*Passes up with a salutation not acknowledged by* MILDRED, *who comes down to the fire.*)

MISS DYER. (*Meeting* MILDRED *at the fire.*) I'm in such a flutter, darling!

MILDRED. (*Surprised.*) You?

MISS DYER. (*Arch, accusing.*) And you too, little trembler!

MILDRED. (*After an instant.*) My trembling's over!

(*Re-enter through the ante-room from the right* CLAUDE VIBERT, *in evening dress.*)

LURCHER (*To* CLAUDE.) I've a word to say to you.

CLAUDE. (*Preoccupied, coming down.*) There's no time now.

LURCHER. (*Following him.*) There'll be time to-morrow, then! We'll *keep* Christmas!

(*Re-enter through the ante-room from the right* SIR FREDERICK, *in evening dress.*)

SIR FREDERICK. Where's Mrs. Vibert?

MISS DYER. I'll call her. (*Exit* MISS DYER *to the library.*)

SIR FREDERICK. (*To* LURCHER.) What a pity, Captain, that our game can't come off!

LURCHER. Ah, Sir Frederick, our game *will* come off!

(SIR FREDERICK *turns and walks up, passing his hand over his eyes and head and visibly preoccupied; and* LURCHER *passes to the left, where he watches* CLAUDE, *who has crossed to* MILDRED, *before the fire.*)

CLAUDE. (*To* MILDRED.) May I say three words to you?

MILDRED. I don't recommend it!

CLAUDE. I love. I hope. I wait.

MILDRED. You'll not have to wait long!

(*She turns away as* MISS DYER *and* MRS. VIBERT *reappear; and* CLAUDE *goes up to the left.* LURCHER *catches his hand as he passes him, and gives it a surreptitious shake of approbation. Re-enter from the library* MISS DYER *and* MRS. VIBERT.)

SIR FREDERICK. (*Looking round him.*) Well then, are we all here?

(*Re-enter, as he speaks,* NORMAN BYNG *through the ante-room from the left, in travelling dress.*)

NORMAN. (*Loud.*) Yes, father, we're all here!

SIR FREDERICK. (*Astounded.*) You, Norman, back from India!

NORMAN. This minute, father, to spend

my Christmas.

, SIR FREDERICK. (*Recovering, with a violent effort from his shock; smiling and gallant.*) Well then, you're exactly in time to hear what I was on the point of announcing. (*Taking Mrs. VIBERT's hand to present her.*) My intended marriage to Mrs. Vibert!

LURCHER. (*To himself, with a gasp.*) Ah, that's her price?

MILDRED. (*To NORMAN, as he rapidly comes to her.*) That's why I called you!

ACT THIRD

The hall at Beechingham as in Act Second; early on the next afternoon. CLAUDE VIBERT *on a sofa, leaning forward with his elbows on his knees and his head in his hands. Enter through the ante-room from the left* CAPTAIN LURCHER, *from church.*

LURCHER. So you're here, my boy? and in spite of your regimentals you didn't turn up at church?

CLAUDE. I went to the door with my mother, but I didn't go in.

LURCHER. And why did you betray so just an expectation?

CLAUDE. I was worried, restless, nervous.

LURCHER. I noticed as much this morning, being early on the scene.

CLAUDE. (*Getting up.*) You're always early on the scene!

LURCHER. That habit's precisely what has brought me here now, before they come back from their devotions. At the end of half an hour I saw you wouldn't turn up, and I slipped out—I was near the door—on the chance of this particular treat. I went home, but you weren't at home: so I said to myself, "When he's not at home—"

CLAUDE. (*Breaking in.*) "He's mooning at the big house!" He *is*, Captain; he's waiting till church is out. But he's almost as ill at ease here as he would have been under a sermon.

LURCHER. You haven't escaped a sermon from your chaplain in ordinary! I've come to do you good. (*Looking round him.*) We've got the big house to ourselves.

CLAUDE. (*Thoughtful.*) The big house and the little house will come to the same thing in the light of my mother's marriage.

LURCHER. (*Disgusted.*) Oh, your mother's marriage—!

CLAUDE. (*Struck.*) Don't you do her the honour to approve of it?

LURCHER. (*As if struck, on his side, with something in* CLAUDE's *tone; then very deliberate.*) It's not your mother we want for the nuptial altar. My dear Claude, it's your mother's son.

CLAUDE. (*Going up; detached, irresponsive.*) Your interest in the family discriminates!

LURCHER. (*Seated on the sofa and watching him.*) Is it your stepbrother who makes you nervous?

CLAUDE. My stepbrother?

LURCHER. Isn't that what your mother's transformation makes of Mr. Byng?

CLAUDE. (*After an instant's thought; coming down again.*) He's no relation to me!

LURCHER. It's a bit complicated, but we must figure it out. His sudden return adds a nasty number to the sum!

CLAUDE. His sudden return's his own affair. I've nothing to do with it!

LURCHER. It's a delicate attention to his father, whose marriage, at this time of day, requires, no doubt, his supervision.

CLAUDE. Is his father afraid of him?

LURCHER. It's a compliment also to your mother, unless, peradventure, it's a criticism.

CLAUDE. Is my mother afraid of him?

LURCHER. I can't answer for her courage! But I see that I can for yours, which, as we used to say, is what was to be demonstrated. I should be ashamed of my creation if my creation broke down!

CLAUDE. There can be but one consequence, for me, of Mr. Byng's return: to do before his face exactly as I would have done behind his back. That's rudimentary.

LURCHER. (*Laughing.*) And we long ago mastered the rudiments!

CLAUDE. There's something due to one's mere dignity.

LURCHER. For mere dignity you're a very prince! Continue to sustain the character.

CLAUDE. If I haven't backed out for *her* attitude—

LURCHER. (*Breaking in.*) You won't back out for his, eh? I should like to see you!

CLAUDE. The sight of them together, last night in our dance, was a torment that only made me take a vow.

LURCHER. To get in ahead? I back you heavily. (*Then after an instant, suggestive.*) He was a danger only by his absence. On the spot he's a common fellow!

CLAUDE. (*After an instant.*) Candidly, where's his distinction?

LURCHER. (*Laughing.*) Some day the young lady will ask you!

CLAUDE. (*Thinking.*) If I can make him think *me* a danger—!

LURCHER. All you've got to do is to *be* one! (*Going up and coming down.*) Here's a chance; they're coming.

CLAUDE. Please go out then.

LURCHER. I'll smoke my cigar on the terrace.

(*Enter* NORMAN BYNG *and* MILDRED *through the ante-room from the left, from church, and come down together with* CLAUDE *on the right of the stage, before the fire, and* LURCHER *on the left.*)

NORMAN. Good morning, Mr. Vibert. (*To* LURCHER.) Good morning.

CLAUDE. (*To* MILDRED.) I'm rather early, but Sir Frederick was so good as to ask me to luncheon.

MILDRED. You're always punctual.

LURCHER. (*To* MILDRED.) I shall be punctual too, Miss Stanmore. Sir Frederick has done me the same honour. (*Exit* LURCHER *through the ante-room to the left.*)

MILDRED. Sir Frederick showers his honours!

NORMAN. Of every kind! But if Captain Lurcher has brought Mr. Vibert over, he must of course be here to take Mr. Vibert back!

CLAUDE. Do you think I'm so easily removed?

NORMAN. I'm told you're handled with a facility—!

MILDRED. (*Privately pleading.*) Norman! (*Turns away and goes up.*)

NORMAN. Where are you going?

MILDRED. To take off my bonnet.

NORMAN. When you've done so, please go to the library: I want to show you some wonderful things I've brought home.

MILDRED. Delighted! (*Exit* MILDRED, *through the ante-room to the left.*)

CLAUDE. You mustn't mind what you've heard of me, Mr. Byng; you must judge for yourself.

NORMAN. That will indeed be wise, as it's exactly what I came back from India for.

CLAUDE. Your return, last night, added greatly to the brilliancy of our little fête.

NORMAN. Your little fête had a lustre unexpectedly dazzling to *me!*

CLAUDE. Yet your expectations must have been high, if you returned on purpose to see us.

NORMAN. They were, I confess; but they've been surpassed. I've been admitted to a view, and I'm delighted to have come in time.

CLAUDE. In time? Why, we're not going away!

NORMAN. You've made your plans to remain, I know. But I seem to see that they're not yet wholly settled, and when plans are going on I'm so pushing—it's very meddlesome—as to like to have a finger in the pie!

CLAUDE. Your taste can easily be gratified. Since your father's to be married, you're on the spot to give him away.

NORMAN. Just as you're there to perform a similar office for your mother.

CLAUDE. There's none that may conduce to her comfort or her credit that I'm not eager to render.

NORMAN. (*After an instant.*) She'll require every service you're capable of.

CLAUDE. (*Smiling.*) Perhaps you exaggerate the dangers to which she's exposed!

NORMAN. Don't say that, Mr. Vibert, till you know what they are.

CLAUDE. When I listen to your threatening accents, Mr. Byng, I feel that I do know what they are!

(*Enter* MISS DYER *through the ante-room from the left, from church.*)

MISS DYER. (*Coming down as* CLAUDE

speaks.) Threatening accents, on Christmas day? (*Then after looking from one of the young men to the other.*) Do you know what's going to happen?

NORMAN. Mr. Vibert has evidently a notion!

MISS DYER. As sure as the world, it's going to snow!

NORMAN. (*To* CLAUDE.) Of course if you're snowed up you'll *have* to stay.

CLAUDE. It will be very snug!

MISS DYER. What a change, Mr. Byng, from the torrid zone, and how you must feel it!

NORMAN. Oh yes, I feel it!

MISS DYER. We're all so delighted to have you back.

NORMAN. So Mr. Vibert was just telling me!

MISS DYER. (*With suspicion and anxiety in her manner.*) Gentlemen shouldn't gossip in corners; they should keep their good things for the ladies. Do you mind if I take my things off here?

CLAUDE. Dear Miss Dyer, we'll even help you!

MISS DYER. (*Engaging.*) Mr. Byng shall help me! (*Presenting the back of her bonnet to* NORMAN.) There's a long pin there: do you think you can get at it?

CLAUDE. (*At the door of the library, to* NORMAN.) While you're divesting Miss Dyer, I'll join Miss Stanmore.

MISS DYER. (*Alert, dissuasive.*) I'm afraid she's writing a letter.

CLAUDE. Perhaps I can suggest to her something to say! (*Exit* CLAUDE *to the library.*)

MISS DYER. (*Taking off her mantle with* NORMAN's *help.*) When I said *we* all rejoice, Mr. Byng, of course I spoke mainly for myself!

NORMAN. I believe in speaking for one's self; that's what *I* mean to do!

MISS DYER. I could see that last evening, when you suddenly burst in. It was quite romantic.

NORMAN. I didn't come back for romance, Miss Dyer; I came back for reality.

MISS DYER. Ah yes, Sir Frederick's marriage. That *is* reality!

NORMAN. We had better wait a little before we say so, especially (*seeing* SIR FRED-

ERICK) as here he comes.

(*Enter* SIR FREDERICK *through the ante-room from the left, from church.*)

SIR FREDERICK. (*To* MISS DYER.) I've left Mrs. Vibert in the greenhouse, selecting the flowers for to-night's dinner, which, under all the circumstances (*looking at* NORMAN) must be exquisite, eh? I wish you'd go and help her. (MISS DYER *inclines herself and goes up, placing her bonnet and mantle on a chair on the right. Exit through the ante-room to the left.*) I've a luxurious confidence in her taste.

NORMAN. Are you speaking of Miss Dyer?

SIR FREDERICK. I'm speaking of Mrs. Vibert.

NORMAN. I'm glad of that, because Mrs. Vibert is exactly a subject on which, if you permit me, I should like to have three words with you.

SIR FREDERICK. Permit me first a subject of my own. If I've waited till this morning to ask you the reason of your unceremonious reappearance—

NORMAN. (*Taking up his words.*) It's not that you don't want to know it? Well, sir, the two subjects are one and the same.

SIR FREDERICK. Do you mean that Mrs. Vibert is the reason? (*Then on a movement of admission from* NORMAN.) What did you know about her?

NORMAN. What I could read between the lines of your letters.

SIR FREDERICK. I see you're as sharp as ever! Why didn't you pay me the compliment of telling me you were coming?

NORMAN. Because I thought you might pay me that of ordering me not to.

SIR FREDERICK. You deemed your presence, then, so urgent?

NORMAN. Extremely urgent, father; and now that I'm on the ground I see everything to confirm that view.

SIR FREDERICK. Very good! I would certainly rather be married with your participation than without it; and I shall now have the advantage of hearing you express it.

NORMAN. I must decline to express anything of the sort. (*The two men face each other a moment.*) Where was *your* "participation" four months ago?

SIR FREDERICK. (*Slightly embarrassed.*) I'm keeping it for four years hence. You shall see it as soon as I can properly let you.

NORMAN. Let it be a bargain then! You shall see mine on the same occasion.

SIR FREDERICK. Do I understand that you prescribe me the terms on which you consent to my doing as I like?

NORMAN. Haven't I a right to make conditions when I've been wronged by trusting you?

SIR FREDERICK. (*Indignant.*) What language, sir! What trust have I violated?

NORMAN. My just confidence that as soon as you had got me out of the way you wouldn't eagerly promote the overtures that other persons have had the execrable taste to make to Miss Stanmore.

SIR FREDERICK. You do me the grossest injustice. I've taken particular measures that no overtures whatever shall be made to Miss Stanmore.

NORMAN. I can scarcely regard them effective when she is, at the present moment, in the library, a prey to the odious familiarity of your young foreign friend.

SIR FREDERICK. Can I help it if Claude is over head and ears in love with her?

NORMAN. You could help it well enough when *I* was! But of course I labour under the singular disqualification of happening to be your son! (*Movement of* SIR FREDERICK.) If you make so much of your good faith, will you give me a signal proof of it? Will you order that little humbug out of the house.

SIR FREDERICK. (*Greatly moved.*) Your manner of dealing with the question, sir, makes it unworthy of me to meet you. Mr. Vibert—Mr. Vibert— (*Faltering.*)

NORMAN. Well, Mr. Vibert?

SIR FREDERICK. Is the son of the person in the world whom I most cherish and respect.

NORMAN. That's very well for you; but I'm not so heavily handicapped! Since you wash your hands so completely of my interests, I shall simply look after them myself. (*Strides towards the library.*)

SIR FREDERICK. (*Alarmed.*) Where are you going?

NORMAN. To show him the way to the door!

SIR FREDERICK. (*Passing quickly before him to the entrance of the library and defending it.*) Don't touch him, at your cost! (*As* MRS. VIBERT *appears in the ante-room; in a different tone.*) I appeal to you in God's name!

(*Enter through the ante-room from the left* MRS. VIBERT, *from church and from the greenhouse, accompanied by* MISS DYER. *With her hands full of the finest flowers and foliage, as she pauses, as if struck by the mutual attitude of the two men, looking from one of them to the other. Then she deposits her flowers carefully on a table.* MISS DYER, *who also has flowers, does the same.*)

MRS. VIBERT. (*To* MISS DYER.) Would you kindly keep my mantle for me?

(MISS DYER *helps her to take the mantle off, and goes out with it through the ante-room to the left.*)

MRS. VIBERT. (*Who has selected a white rose from the flowers on the table; to* NORMAN, *coming down.*) Will you accept from me, on Christmas day, this modest peace-offering? (NORMAN *takes the flower from her in silence, looks at her a moment; then turning to go up, flings it on a table.* MRS. VIBERT *looks at* SIR FREDERICK, *who extends his clasped hands to her appealingly, deprecatingly, as if to confess that there is grave trouble; on which she says to him.*) May I speak to him alone?

SIR FREDERICK. Do what you can, and come and tell me! (*Exit* SIR FREDERICK *through the ante-room to the right.*)

MRS. VIBERT. (*To* NORMAN, *who is at the drawing-room door.*) Mr. Byng, will you listen to me a moment? (*Then as* NORMAN *assents slightly, in silence, and comes down.*) Your father and I are very old friends.

NORMAN. That, madam, is your own affair.

MRS. VIBERT. (*As if without hearing his remark.*) So that the understanding we have come to in the afternoon of life, which strikes you as abrupt and unexplained, is really only the fulfilment of an early dream.

NORMAN. I've nothing to do with your

early dreams; I've nothing to do with my father's; and I ask you for no explanations.

MRS. VIBERT. I shall do my utmost to make him happy.

NORMAN. And what will you do to make me so?

MRS. VIBERT. (*After an instant.*) Whatever you demand of me.

NORMAN. Then take your son out of the house!

MRS. VIBERT. (*With a moan of distress.*) Ah, Mr. Byng (*Then seeing* CAPTAIN LURCHER.) Don't speak of that now!

(*Re-enter* CAPTAIN LURCHER *through the ante-room from the left, looking hard as he comes down from* MRS. VIBERT *to* NORMAN.)

LURCHER. (*To* MRS. VIBERT.) I saw you come in just now, and as I happen to desire particularly to speak to you, I've taken the liberty to follow you for the purpose.

MRS. VIBERT. It's very good of you to be so eager!

LURCHER. I only waited to finish my cigar.

MRS. VIBERT. (*To* NORMAN.) We're interrupted, Mr. Byng; but I've more to say to you. Will you grant me the precious favour of another moment?

NORMAN. To what purpose?

MRS. VIBERT. (*After an instant; abrupt.*) Mr. Byng, I beseech you!

NORMAN. I'll come back; with Captain Lurcher's gracious leave. (*Exit* NORMAN *through the ante-room to the right.*)

LURCHER. (*Calling after him with cheerful assurance.*) Don't go too far, it's beginning to snow! (*Then to* MRS. VIBERT.) We shall be buried here for the day.

MRS. VIBERT. Charming news, in *your* company! Isn't the nightmare of your perpetual presence enough at home, without the confusion and the shame of it here?

LURCHER. Dear lady, it was precisely to make you taste that bitterness that I asked for this audience. I couldn't administer the draught last night; that's why my present minutes are precious. What do you wish to say to our rude young friend?

MRS. VIBERT. What do you wish to say to me?

LURCHER. That you'll please answer that question. (*Then as she remains silent.*) By

which of the most irresistible of your arts are you winning him over?

MRS. VIBERT. By the exercise of one you never practise—speaking the simple truth.

LURCHER. I never speak it to the wrong person; but Mrs. Vibert should be the first to know that I usually speak it to the right one!

MRS. VIBERT. You explain this aggression by your wish to gain time. Don't you perceive you're already too late?

LURCHER. It's never too late to mend! You favoured me yesterday with an intimation which I confess I didn't wholly understand. But I grasp it better now, for Sir Frederick's brilliant announcement has lighted up the prospect. Your marriage is an exchange of commodities, a neat little commercial transaction. He gives you a home, an income, a future, a position; and you give him—

MRS. VIBERT. (*As he pauses.*) You've not the least idea what!

LURCHER. I beg your pardon—the assurance that you won't worry him any more. You hand him over the contract by which you're indissolubly tied to *me,* and you flatter yourself that he can burn it up. Dear lady, I've looked after that: it's more adapted to quench a flame than to feed one!

MRS. VIBERT. With all your intelligence you've stupid moments. Don't you see the difference Mr. Byng's return has made?

LURCHER. What did you know of Mr. Byng's return, when, last evening, before it took place, you basely sacrificed me? —said to yourself, "*I'm* all right; dear Lurcher may go to the devil!"

MRS. VIBERT. You reproduce my soliloquies with a vividness!

LURCHER. Mr. Byng's return *has* made a difference; but it's luckily all to my profit.

MRS. VIBERT. You talk of your profit as a cannibal might talk of his diet! There's no provision for it in polite society.

LURCHER. That fellow suspects you, he sees through you, he despises you.

MRS. VIBERT. Didn't you just declare that I'm winning him over?

LURCHER. I just declared that you're trying to—which is a very different thing. He'll prevent your marriage.

MRS. VIBERT. Let me use your distinction—he'll "try" to!

LURCHER. He'll turn you out of the house.

MRS. VIBERT. My dear man, I've a lease.

LURCHER. Not of this one. Therefore you'll turn him out first.

MRS. VIBERT. Again?

LURCHER. Practice makes perfect: this time you'll do it better. You've a grievance —you'll work it.

MRS. VIBERT. My grievances are taking a rest—I should have to work yours!

LURCHER. Mr. Byng's attitude—his hostility, his defiance, his irresistible itch to insult you, are a precious resource to us. (Looks at his watch.) You'll immediately make these things the basis of a declaration to Sir Frederick that your dignity is concerned in your not being exposed to outrage.

MRS. VIBERT. So that Sir Frederick may request Mr. Byng to depart?

LURCHER. To minimise the danger of your own departure.

MRS. VIBERT. You're ,as clear as a bell!

LURCHER. I know what I want.

MRS. VIBERT. Yes, but do you know why you want it?

LURCHER. When you've made your protest and Sir Frederick has made his concession, when you've protected your position and got rid, between you, of the enemy within the gates, you'll do the generous, you'll do the graceful, you'll reward Sir Frederick's sacrifice by a sacrifice of your own: you'll let him off his engagement.

MRS. VIBERT. Don't put it as if he had met another woman!

LURCHER. You'll decline to hold the poor dear to a profession of preposterous chivalry.

MRS. VIBERT. Don't I perceive that the age of chivalry has come back?

LURCHER. You'll return to the old footing.

MRS. VIBERT. And you'll do the same!

LURCHER. We'll remain at the little house —we'll cancel our surrender—we'll have our hands free again—we'll get Miss Stanmore! Claude shall be sublime.

MRS. VIBERT. (After a silence.) He certainly shan't be ridiculous.

LURCHER. You'll combat his passion, eh?

MRS. VIBERT. What if, between Mr. Byng and me, Sir Frederick prefers to let me retire?

LURCHER. You'll make that quite too hard for him.

MRS. VIBERT. (After another silence.) And the penalty of my not adopting your admirable programme—?

LURCHER. Is that the instant I encounter practical proof that you've departed from it, I will, on this very spot if necessary, make known to Claude the unspeakable truth you've succeeded in keeping from him; announce to him, in the heyday of his spirits and the morning of his pride, that he's a creature of shame, an indubitable, a proveable—bastard!

MRS. VIBERT. (Sinking upon a seat, and seated a moment with her eyes closed.) God have mercy on me!

(Re-enter through the ante-room from the right, MISS DYER, who takes up her bonnet and mantle from the chair on which she has placed them. MRS. VIBERT, who has quickly risen on becoming aware of her entrance, as if, as she comes down on the right, to avoid her, goes up on the left and reaches the window of the ante-room, where during the next short scene she stands absorbed and looking out at the thick-falling snow.)

LURCHER. (With instant urbanity.) Dear Miss Dyer, I've an attack of nerves. I should like to work it off at billiards.

MISS DYER. On such a day as this? I'm not quite sure you ought!

LURCHER. I've been so good: I've been to church!

MISS DYER. For ten minutes—I saw you go out!

LURCHER. It was my nerves, and I hoped you'd follow me. We might have had a quiet walk!

MISS DYER. You're a very wicked man, and I wouldn't have come near you again if I hadn't to get my things.

LURCHER. Must you leave me already?

MISS DYER. I've my hands full of affairs.

LURCHER. My affairs, I hope—our affairs!

MISS DYER. (*Hesitating.*) Isn't that castle in the air blown down?

LURCHER. By Mr. Byng's return? I assure you it's not so shaky!

MISS DYER. (*Thinking.*) I wish I could have your confidence!

LURCHER. You should, if I didn't believe you had already been undermined.

MISS DYER. Undermined?

LURCHER. Hasn't that fellow made up to you again?

MISS DYER. To me? He has other occupation!

LURCHER. Then he's the greater fool! (*After an instant.*) You *have* my confidence.

MISS DYER. I meant your impudence.

LURCHER. (*As* MRS. VIBERT *comes down again.*) Have *hers!*

MRS. VIBERT. (*To* MISS DYER.) Will you kindly tell me what you did with my mantle?

MISS DYER. (*Surprised.*) Are you going out? It's snowing hard!

MRS. VIBERT. I don't care what it's doing —I'm going home.

MISS DYER. You'll find your mantle in the morning-room. (*Exit* MISS DYER *through the ante-room to the left.*)

LURCHER. (*Who has gone up to look.*) It *is* snowing—I shan't budge. You forget that you've an appointment with Mr. Byng.

MRS. VIBERT. I shall not keep it.

LURCHER. (*As* NORMAN *reappears.*) Not when he does? (*Coming down.*) Stir him up —put him through!

(*Re-enter* NORMAN BYNG *through the ante-room from the left. Exit* LURCHER *through the ante-room to the right.* MRS. VIBERT *drops again on the sofa and sits gazing before her.*)

NORMAN. (*Who has watched* LURCHER'S *exit.*) Where has he gone?

MRS. VIBERT. I suppose to the billiard-room.

NORMAN. I've come back at your request.

MRS. VIBERT. (*Rising.*) You've a sense of justice—you're willing to give me a chance.

NORMAN. I may have a sense of justice, but I've also a sense of wrong. Therefore it's useless to flatter me.

MRS. VIBERT. I'm ready to do something that will cost me more than that. (*After an instant.*) I'm ready to send away my son.

NORMAN. For how long?

MRS. VIBERT. Ah, you're not gracious! Can't you trust me?

NORMAN. (*After an instant.*) I can't trust my father.

MRS. VIBERT. I'll advise him loyally.

NORMAN. Excuse me if I remember how you *have* advised him!

MRS. VIBERT. What do you know about it?

NORMAN. Was it not by your loyal advice that, four months ago, I was turned out of the house at five minutes' notice?

MRS. VIBERT. What made you imagine that?

NORMAN. Everything!

MRS. VIBERT. I'll confess to you that I cast my weight into the scale; I deprived you of the few more days at home that you might have enjoyed. But I was moved by a very powerful and a very natural reason. The single moment I had had the honour of spending in your society sufficed to convince me that you disliked and mistrusted me.

NORMAN. (*Simply.*) How *could* I? I didn't know you.

MRS. VIBERT. (*Smiling.*) Perhaps that was exactly why! You had a poor opinion of me.

NORMAN. I certainly had not the opinion that you had come into the house to injure me.

MRS. VIBERT. I didn't! I didn't come for trouble, Mr. Byng—I came for peace!

NORMAN. Do you call *this* peace?

MRS. VIBERT. (*After an instant; abrupt, passionate.*) It *shall* be—if you'll help me!

NORMAN. I don't understand you.

MRS. VIBERT. Listen to me and you will. I'm not a bad woman—I'm only a very unhappy one.

NORMAN. On the eve of your brilliant marriage?

MRS. VIBERT. Ah, don't call it brilliant! (*In another tone.*) My son shall go to-morrow.

NORMAN. Why not to-night?

MRS. VIBERT. Can't you give me a few hours?

NORMAN. How many did you give me?

MRS. VIBERT. (*Struck; then after a moment.*) He shall go this minute.

NORMAN. Thank you. (*Re-enter* MILDRED *from the library.*) Can you inform Mrs. Vibert of the whereabouts of her son?

MILDRED. (*Indicating the library.*) I left him there.

NORMAN. I'll join you.

MILDRED. (*Who has crossed to the drawing-room door.*) Join me here. (*Exit* MILDRED.)

NORMAN. (*At the drawing-room door; standing an instant with his eyes on* MRS. VIBERT.) You know where to find him. (*Exit* NORMAN.)

MRS. VIBERT. (*Alone; after a silence.*) Poor little Claude!

(*Re-enter* MISS DYER *through the ante-room from the left.*)

MISS DYER. I'm collecting the company for luncheon.

MRS. VIBERT. You needn't collect my son —he's going too.

MISS DYER. (*Surprised.*) Mayn't I at least secure the Captain?

MRS. VIBERT. (*At the door of the library.*) I wish to God you would! Farewell. (*Exit* MRS. VIBERT.)

MISS DYER. (*Alone; blank.*) "Farewell"? She takes leave? (*After an instant.*) I'm not quite sure she ought! (*Re-enter* LURCHER *through the ante-room from the right.*) You at least will stay?

LURCHER. Rather! Who fails us?

MISS DYER. Mrs. Vibert and her son.

LURCHER. (*Struck.*) Her son? Why in the world?

MISS DYER. I haven't the least idea. (*Engaging.*) Should you like me to sit next you at luncheon?

LURCHER. (*Disconcerted, preoccupied.*) I don't care where you sit at luncheon!

MISS DYER. (*Mystified and reproachful.*) Do you only like me here?

LURCHER. (*Impatient.*) I don't like you anywhere!

MISS DYER. Monster! (*Exit* MISS DYER *to the drawing-room.*)

LURCHER. (*Alone.*) What has happened, then? Where are they? What base conspiracy—? (*Hesitating, looking about; then considering while his eyes rest a moment on the door of the library.*) Is it hatching there? (*Goes to the door and, with his hand on the knob, stands an instant listening.*)

(*Re-enter* NORMAN BYNG *from the drawing-room.*)

NORMAN. (*Observing* LURCHER *before he is aware.*) Perhaps I can save you that trouble, if it's a question of curiosity!

LURCHER. (*Startled, annoyed.*) Excuse me! (*Then recovering himself.*) I was just proceeding to my young friend.

NORMAN. Proceeding through the keyhole? The place to find your young friend, from this moment, will not be in this house.

LURCHER. (*With returning assurance.*) Do you mean that he has left it?

NORMAN. (*After a moment's hesitation.*) He has left it.

LURCHER. At your request?

NORMAN. That will do for a reason.

LURCHER. (*Protesting.*) Oh, scarcely!

NORMAN. (*Looking at him a moment and then coming nearer.*) Don't you believe, in such a case, in the efficacy of my requests?

LURCHER. (*With sudden briskness, after meeting* NORMAN's *eyes and standing his ground.*) I'll go and bring him back! (*Exit* LURCHER *through the ante-room to the left.*)

NORMAN. (*Alone, laughing and calling after him.*) Don't bring him through the keyhole! (*Re-enter* MRS. VIBERT *from the drawing-room, closing the door behind her quickly as she sees* NORMAN.) Has he gone?

MRS. VIBERT. Ah, Mr. Byng, you're not reasonable!

NORMAN. Do you mean that *he's* not?

MRS. VIBERT. Of course he's not—with the state of his affections. Will you do me a favour? Avoid him before he goes.

NORMAN. Avoid him?

MRS. VIBERT. Don't let him see you.

NORMAN. (*Smiling.*) Do you mean I'm in danger?

MRS. VIBERT. It's absurd, but he's jealous.

NORMAN. Absurd? It's terrific!—I'll be on my guard. But [I] should like a pledge from you first.

MRS. VIBERT. Another? I've given you one already.

NORMAN. You told me he should go, but you didn't tell me he shouldn't come back.

MRS. VIBERT. (*After an instant.*) Haven't *you* come back?

NORMAN. I come to my father's house.

MRS. VIBERT. (*After another instant.*) He'll come to his mother's.

NORMAN. To take the place you'll have kept warm for him till I shall have been once more got out of the way?

MRS. VIBERT. (*Wounded, indignant.*) Ah, you go too far—you insult me!

(*Re-enter, as she speaks,* CLAUDE VIBERT *from the library. He starts with the shock of her last words; then quickly goes to her.*)

CLAUDE. "Insults" you, mother, before *me?*

MRS. VIBERT. (*Alarmed, confused, recovering herself.*) No, my dear boy, not before you! Mr. Byng, will you be so good as to leave us?

CLAUDE. (*Authoritative.*) A moment, sir! Before you go, you'll apologise to my mother for your outrage.

MRS. VIBERT. (*Seizing his arm.*) Claude, don't interfere! You know nothing of what has occurred.

CLAUDE. It's enough for me to be sure, from looking at Mr. Byng and from my observation of his attitude from the moment he arrived, that he has made himself deliberately offensive.

MRS. VIBERT. (*To* NORMAN.) I beseech you to leave us.

NORMAN. (*After he has quietly looked at* CLAUDE *up and down.*) Excuse me, madam, if—in my father's house—I decline to take flight before the preposterous attitude of your son.

CLAUDE. Mr. Byng may stay or go: I shall not lose sight of him till I've given him a lesson in respect.

NORMAN. You ought to be qualified— as you've just had one yourself from Miss Stanmore!

CLAUDE. (*With a movement toward* NORMAN.) Brute!

MRS. VIBERT. (*Interposing, struggling with her son.*) Come away, Claude, I command you!

CLAUDE. Yield an inch before *him?* Not till I know the reason why!

MRS. VIBERT. Let it be enough for you that *I* know it!

NORMAN. Yours won't content him, I think. Please leave me to give him a better.

MRS. VIBERT. God forbid I should leave you! (*Passionately.*) I came here for peace —only for peace!

NORMAN. You had better go away for peace!

CLAUDE. (*Supremely exasperated.*) A threat? to my mother! (*Passing rapidly across* MRS. VIBERT, *with a blow at* NORMAN.) That's the way to treat you!

NORMAN. (*Flashing up his arm to return the blow.*) Ah!

MRS. VIBERT. (*Throwing herself between them and staying his arm.*) Don't strike him —he's your brother!

NORMAN. (*Bewildered, dropping his arm.*) My brother!

CLAUDE. (*Falling back.*) His brother?

MRS. VIBERT. (*To* CLAUDE.) Forgive me, and pity me! (*Looking from one to the other.*) Forgive each other! (*Then to* NORMAN.) Farewell! (*Exit* MRS. VIBERT *rapidly through the ante-room to the left.*)

(NORMAN *and* CLAUDE, *left confronted, stare at each other as if trying to understand, to complete her meaning; after a moment they appear to do so, and the extraordinary truth grows clear to them. As this happens* CLAUDE *turns slowly away from* NORMAN, *looks about him as if dazed, at bay; then sinks down on the sofa, utterly overcome, covering his face with his hands.* NORMAN *stands a moment longer, looking down at* CLAUDE *and seeming to hesitate; after which, as if with a strong determination and at the same time an irresistible impulse, he goes quickly up and out through the ante-room to the left. As soon as he has gone, re-enter* MILDRED *from the library. She hesitates an instant, seeing* CLAUDE; *then, as if struck and surprised by his attitude, comes forward. She perceives still more that something has happened to him, and, looking at him wonderingly in her passage, while he continues absorbed in the shock he has received and unconscious of her, she goes noiselessly up the stage and reaches the ante-room. Here she pauses, considering a moment; then she comes down a few steps toward* CLAUDE.)

MILDRED. Mr. Vibert, if I wounded you a while ago, I'm sorry. (CLAUDE *starts at the sound of her voice and rises—looks at her as if collecting his thoughts.*) You wearied out my patience, but we'll never speak of such things again.

CLAUDE. (*Slowly and with infinite sadness; standing a minute with his eyes on the ground and raising them to* MILDRED'S *face.*) Never again—never again!

MILDRED. Thank you! (*She lingers an instant, mystified; then goes up again. Abruptly, however, she comes down once more and looks at* CLAUDE *as if with a vague sense that his case is bad.*) Shake hands on that; we can at least be friends. (*She puts out her hand to him; with a sudden impulse, passionately and as if in utter farewell, he bends over it, kisses it, drops it and turns away.* MILDRED *goes up and pauses momentarily, looking back at him till* LURCHER *reappears, when she goes out through the ante-room to the right.*)

CLAUDE. (*To himself; lost.*) Does every one know it? does *she* know it? (*Re-enter* LURCHER *through the ante-room from the left.*) Does *he?* (*Then vehemently.*) Where's my mother? what has become of her?

LURCHER. Never mind your mother; you must learn to manage for yourself! I found it a gross fabrication that you had gone.

CLAUDE. (*To himself; haunted, wondering, turning away.*) Does he know? *does* he?

LURCHER. (*Nodding to the right.*) Why *should* you go, indeed, from that sweet, kind face? Don't tell me the maiden's cruel!

CLAUDE. (*Abrupt, startling.*) I've a request to make of you, Captain. Never speak to me of Miss Stanmore again!

LURCHER. (*Dismayed.*) Why, it's what I'm here for!

CLAUDE. Then it's not what *I* am!

LURCHER. (*Aghast.*) You've renounced the prize?

CLAUDE. For ever and ever!

LURCHER. You've given way?

CLAUDE. I've given way.

LURCHER. To that mediocrity?

CLAUDE. Don't speak to me of Mr. Byng!

LURCHER. (*Still more mystified.*) Will you be so good as to mention a person or two I *may* speak to you of? (*Then definitely apprehensive.*) Has some one scared you?

CLAUDE. Almost to death! In God's name, Captain, what does it mean? What do you know? To what misery have I waked up?

LURCHER. (*Staring, staggered.*) Your mother has had the gross indelicacy—?

CLAUDE. (*Precipitately.*) You know it— you've always known it—and you never told me?

LURCHER. (*After an instant.*) "Told" you? Of what use would you have been then?

CLAUDE. I wouldn't have had the folly, I wouldn't have had the front—! (*Checks himself as* MILDRED *reappears.*)

(*Re-enter* MILDRED *through the ante-room from the right.*)

MILDRED. Mr. Vibert, Sir Frederick has asked me to say that he would like to speak to you.

CLAUDE. (*To himself, with a start.*) My father? (*To* MILDRED.) Thank you! (*Exit* CLAUDE *through the ante-room to the right.*)

LURCHER. Can you tell me what has become of Mrs. Vibert?

MILDRED. Mrs. Vibert? (*Seeing* NORMAN: *re-enter* NORMAN *through the ante-room from the left.*) Where *is* Mrs. Vibert?

NORMAN. She's here (*to* LURCHER—) to say a word to *you!*

(*Re-enter* MRS. VIBERT *through the ante-room from the left, in her mantle, while* NORMAN *opens the door of the library and signs to* MILDRED *to pass out. Exeunt* MILDRED *and* NORMAN *to the library.* MRS. VIBERT *comes down and stands an instant face to face with* LURCHER.)

LURCHER. I should have thought the most convenient thing would have been for you to take to your heels!

MRS. VIBERT. Mr. Byng followed me to the door—he stopped me. But I've only come back to take leave.

LURCHER. Of *me*, madam? Very pretty of you!

MRS. VIBERT. Of you, Captain Lurcher, for ever and ever.

LURCHER. That's as I shall determine.

MRS. VIBERT. Claude shall determine now.

LURCHER. Your sentence—among other things?

MRS. VIBERT. I've accepted my sentence.

LURCHER. From Mr. Byng?

MRS. VIBERT. (After an instant.) Mr. Byng's a gentleman.

LURCHER. (As CLAUDE reappears.) And Mr. Vibert, alas, isn't!

(Re-enter CLAUDE through the ante-room from the right.)

CLAUDE. (Holding out his arms.) Mother!

LURCHER. (With ineffable disgust, while MRS. VIBERT swiftly throws herself into them.) Oh, gratitude! It's a noble service she has rendered you!

MRS. VIBERT. (To CLAUDE.) I escaped from my long bondage—I answered his eternal threat.

CLAUDE. (Vague.) His eternal threat?

MRS. VIBERT. To open your eyes, as they are open now. The secret of my strange patience—the misery of my hidden life!

CLAUDE. (With unspeakable compassion.) Mother—mother!

MRS. VIBERT. Judge of the rest when I tell you that this is almost bliss.

LURCHER. You can judge of the bliss by the quality she has conferred on you!

CLAUDE. (Silent a moment, as if bewildered with revelations; but pulling himself together.) I think I shall be happier, Captain Lurcher, when you and I are severed.

LURCHER. You too turn against me—the very creature I've fashioned?

CLAUDE. Your work's complete; I can go alone!

(Re-enter SIR FREDERICK through the ante-room from the right.)

SIR FREDERICK. (Who stands a moment looking from MRS. VIBERT to CLAUDE.) Captain Lurcher, I've a service to ask of you. Will you kindly pass into the drawing-room?

LURCHER. (After an instant.) Sir Frederick, I've ceased to believe in drawing-rooms! Permit me a remoter refuge. (Then from the ante-room, with a sarcastic flourish of his hat.) I wish you all a merry Christmas and a very intimate New Year! (Exit LURCHER to the left.)

SIR FREDERICK. (Who has accepted his withdrawal with a gesture of mystified resignation.) Eleanor, you told me on our way from church that you would fix the day for our marriage. I'm deeply impatient it should be settled.

MRS. VIBERT. I'm in Claude's hands—let Claude settle it.

CLAUDE. (To SIR FREDERICK.) I'm much obliged to you; but my mother is mine now—only mine!

SIR FREDERICK. Ours, my dear boy; more than ever ours!

CLAUDE. Too late, too late—after too many years! Come, mother.

SIR FREDERICK. (Greatly moved.) You're going?—you're leaving me alone?

MRS. VIBERT. No, not alone.

CLAUDE. I've been ignorant all my life: that kept me a child. Now that I know, I've become a man. I'll take care of my mother.

SIR FREDERICK. (Plaintively, desperately.) And who'll take care of me?

MRS. VIBERT. I'll tell you! (To CLAUDE.) Mr. Byng and Miss Stanmore are in the library—please call them. (CLAUDE opens the door of the library; on which re-enter NORMAN and MILDRED.) Grant me a last favour—consent to their marriage.

SIR FREDERICK. It shall be early in the new year.

MRS. VIBERT. They'll take care of you.

CLAUDE. (To NORMAN.) I raised my hand against you—forgive me. (NORMAN takes his hand and holds it while they stand looking at each other.)

SIR FREDERICK. (With a supreme appeal.) Eleanor!

MRS. VIBERT. She'll take care of you. (Then to MILDRED, pleadingly, touchingly.) You will be devoted?

MILDRED. (Looking an instant, with intensity, from MRS. VIBERT to NORMAN and from NORMAN to SIR FREDERICK.) We'll all be devoted!

MRS. VIBERT. (With mingled deprecation and relief.) All?

MILDRED. (Resolutely, gratefully, while she throws herself into MRS. VIBERT's arms.) All!

EDITOR'S FOREWORD

DISENGAGED

"The idea on which *Disengaged* mainly reposes was supplied the author by a little story of his own," Henry James wrote in his prefatory note to the first series of *Theatricals.* The story was *The Solution,* published by him in three issues of the *New Review* (December 1889, January and February 1890) and republished in *The Lesson of the Master and Other Tales,* 1892. The tale had been inspired by an anecdote told James some years earlier by Fanny Kemble concerning a young and wealthy member of the diplomatic corps in Rome who was talked by some mischievous companions into believing that he had compromised a young girl and thereupon proposed to her and in due course was married to her. James developed this into a situation in which one of the companions, conscious-stricken, solicits the good offices of a woman he loves to "disengage" the couple. She not only performs the disengagement but falls in love with the young man and marries him herself.

In the play, which he described as his first attempt at a *"comedy,* pure and simple," James moved the setting to England, and altered the names of the characters from those of the story, seeking to evoke the spirit and humor—if not the morality—of a Restoration comedy. He wrote it either late in 1891 or early in 1892. According to his own account, he met Ada Rehan, the American actress and star of Augustin Daly's company, at the home of some friends during the autumn of 1891; she gave him a message from Daly asking him to do a play for the company in which Miss Rehan would have a leading role. In August of 1892 he read to the actress the first draft of a comedy tentatively entitled *Mrs. Jasper,* and she took the manuscript to Daly. The American manager wrote James that the play pleased him but did not completely satisfy him. James replied that he was far from satisfied with it himself. "Its fault is probably fundamental and consists in the slenderness of the main motive—which I have tried to prop up with details that don't really support it." James conceded there was a lack of action "vainly dissimulated by a superabundance (especially in the last act) of movement."

After an interview with Daly he revised *Mrs. Jasper* and sent the text late in October of 1892 to him in New York. Daly accepted the play and it was agreed that James would be paid a flat fee of $25 a night. Daly was to have exclusive performance rights for five years. Settlement of these details led James to believe the play would be promptly produced in New York. Late in November 1892, however, Daly requested further revisions. He wanted the part of Mrs. Jasper built up for Miss Rehan; he objected to having the first act curtain fall with the actress not on the stage. He wondered whether Henry James could supply rhymed couplets at the end of the play for Miss Rehan, Restoration style. James replied this was "an idea that fills me with confusion and dismay."

The novelist, however, made most of the revisions. He brought Mrs. Jasper on-stage at the end of Act I. He cut a scene in Act II between Mrs. Jasper and Coverley. He kept Coverley out of the climax of Act II in order to render Act III more dramatic. He rewrote a scene between Mrs. Jasper and Trafford. And he wrote a final speech for Mrs. Jasper which, however, does not seem to have been retained in the printed version since James described it to Daly as "a pretty, genial, graceful final speech—neither too short nor too long. It has—in intention at least—a kind of slight doubleness of meaning. . . . Though it's pure prose, too, I have endeavored to make it in a manner rhythmic. . . ."

Daly came to England in the spring, opened up his new theatre in Leicester Square, and publicly announced James's play as the only novelty he planned for his first season there. In August 1893 James went over the models of the sets with the stage designer, Joseph Harker. The account books for the season show that Daly paid Harker £11 during the week of October 23–28 "for models"— presumably those intended for *Mrs. Jasper*. The summer passed and James came up a number of times from Ramsgate to confer with Daly about the production. Meanwhile Daly's season ran into serious difficulties. The manager discovered that the London public was attached to specific playhouses; that when his productions had been given in established theatres they attracted the audiences of those theatres, so that now he had to win an audience for his new playhouse by slow stages. "Daly has been having a very bad season," James wrote to his brother, "owing to the losses of his company and the blunders of his repertory—so that I see myself *en perspective* converted from a creature propped (by his *prestige*—which I supposed I was,) into a creature *propping*. My play, inconceivable as it appears, is the only 'novelty' with which he seems to have armed himself for his campaign in his new and beautiful theatre. . . . If I 'save' him it will be so much wind in my sails—and if I don't, the explanation will be, largely, not dishonorable to me. But I long for the reality, the ingenuity and the combined amusement and disgust of rehearsals. . . ."

The time for rehearsal drew near. Late in October Daly re-read the play apparently with misgivings (especially in the light of his continued waning fortunes) and asked for some cuts and revisions. "I will go over the copy . . . carefully," James replied, "and be as heroic as I can." Six days later James reported "utter failure." The play seemed to him so tightly written that little could come out of it. Parallel to this came demands from Daly for a more telling title. James had first proposed *Disengaged*, as a substitute for *Mrs. Jasper*. Daly did not like it. James then sent him, in what must have been either a burst of carefully-dissimulated anger or annoyance, or of elaborate irony, no less than sixty-four alternate titles. Daly rejected them all. Not one had the Ada Rehan role in it and Daly had sought to shape the play for her. James then responded with a dozen more titles, and *Mrs. Jasper's Way* was selected by Daly, although James did not care for it.

Alternate titles for *Disengaged* submitted by Henry James to
Augustin Daly

Daly had his own methods of work and his own traditions, and James, who
had followed the production of *The American* step by step, felt himself now
held at an arm's length from his play. This may have been intentional, but
we have no way of knowing what state of feeling now existed between the over-
eager playwright and the harassed manager. One or two readings of the play
took place privately at Daly's and the first James heard of these was a letter from
Daly on December 3, 1893 informing him that the play seemed to lack "story."
Since James had long ago conceded this point it seemed late in the day to be
bringing it up again. "I am very sorry, not a little alarmed," James replied,
and it was settled he would attend a reading on December 6. To Elizabeth
Robins he confided "they have begun, or are just beginning, I believe, some
intensely private preliminaries at Daly's—which make me very uneasy."

What happened at the rehearsal we shall never completely know. We have
only James's account of it and it is charged with considerable anger. Certain
facts are clear: the actors and Daly had no confidence in the play. They read it
in a manner that could only fill an author with rage. "To Ada Rehan (white,
haggard, ill-looking almost in *anguish*) I couldn't bring myself to *speak*. . . .
I was not given a simple second's opportunity of having the least contact

or word with any other member of the company: who began and stammeringly read their parts the instant I came in, and vanished the instant the third act ended."

The next morning James wrote to Daly, "I cannot for a moment profess that the scene I witnessed on your stage yesterday threw any light on the character of the play. . . ." He told Daly he should have appreciated being notified sooner that the play was unsuitable and added, "Your few words of Saturday so definitely express, in spite of their brevity, or perhaps indeed by reason of the same, the sudden collapse of your own interest in it, that I withdraw it from your theatre without delay. . . ." In a letter to William James, Henry bitterly suggested that Daly had stage-managed the rehearsal so as to induce him to back out. "He is an utter cad," he wrote, "and Ada Rehan is the same. They simply kicked me between them (and all in one 'rehearsal') out of the theatre. How can one rehearse with people who are dying to get rid of you . . . ?"

A close reading of the correspondence between James and Daly does not substantiate James's charge that Daly deliberately staged the rehearsal as a device to get rid of his playwright. Daly replied to James that the readings of the play "however crude they may have seemed to you"—convinced him that the lack of a "situation" and dramatic climax could not be overcome by the actor's art. As instance of his own good faith he reminded James of scenery under construction and of costumes ordered in Paris by Miss Rehan. James's reply was a long, bitter recapitulation of the entire history of the negotiations. He complained that he had never had an opportunity to discuss the role of Mrs. Jasper with Miss Rehan and that Daly had not demonstrated to him the inadequacies of the play. He took a parting shot at both Daly's unsuccessful season and Miss Rehan by expressing "the regret that the actress who has been willing to act the parts I have, for the most part, seen her act this winter, should not have been moved even to *study* that of the heroine of my comedy."

There is no doubt that the play and the possibility of production loomed much larger in Henry James's life than in that of Daly and there is little doubt that the "rehearsal" or reading would have more meaning for an experienced producer such as Daly than for the relatively inexperienced and, at this juncture, highly nervous James. The keenness of James's disappointment undoubtedly contributed to the network of motivation he wove around what amounted to a typical and frequent situation in the theatre—that of a producer losing interest in a play. It was not likely that in the circumstances the actors would have been inspired to provide a brilliant reading.

James was justified in placing high hopes in Ada Rehan's capacity to make the most of the part he had written for her. W. Graham Robertson felt that "Miss Rehan's brilliant artificial comedy would have lent itself marvellously to James's dialogue," and Bernard Shaw believed her to possess an "unrivalled charm of poetic speech."

The play was given an amateur production in New York in 1902 by the

American Academy of Dramatic Arts and the Empire Theatre Dramatic School, and in 1909 it had one professional performance, at the Hudson Theatre, in aid of a hospital. William Dean Howells attended both productions and reported on them enthusiastically to James. "The dear young ingenuous benighted things," James replied on the occasion of the amateur production, "I could kiss them all with tears." The critics on both occasions referred to what they termed the unemotional, heartless, unsympathetic qualities of the play: "nerveless, heartless, soulless," said the *Sun*. And the *Times* called it "fantastic nonsense."

CHARACTERS

Sir Montagu Brisket, Bart., M.P.
Captain Prime
Percy Trafford
Charles Coverley
Mrs. Jasper
Lady Brisket
Mrs. Wigmore
Blandina
A Parlour-maid

*The first two Acts within the domain of Brisket Place;
the third in London.*

DISENGAGED

ACT FIRST

An old-fashioned lawn or small pleasance, in a slightly neglected or deserted condition, on a height or a slope, commanding, in the distance, across a valley, a little winding, shining river, with a rustic bridge which leads over to an extensive park, a part of the same property. A bright, warm day, early in the autumn, with bright October tints, the gleam of the river in the valley, the spire of a country church on the opposite uplands; the whole making a particularly beautiful, peaceful English view. At the back, obliquely, to the right, the old grey front of a small but highly picturesque manorhouse, once of some distinction, but now more humbly tenanted, with a porch or approach of three broad semicircular stone steps. Further to the right, a good way down, a piece of garden wall, with a small wooden gate. At the back, all across the stage, from the house to the left, the low, red, mossy wall or parapet of the garden, interrupted in the centre by a charming old gate, surmounted by an arch of fanciful rusty ironwork, outlined against the sky and partly muffled in red Virginia creeper. On the hither side of the wall, on the left, a good way down and facing the wooden gate, an old stone garden bench with a highish back, mossy and picturesque, at the base of a weather-stained statue or image which is set in a high clump of shrubbery and which, with its screen of verdure, forms one side, the side nearest the audience, of a passage or exit, the short cut to the neighbouring ruins of an old abbey.

Sir Montagu Brisket *seated on the stone bench with a newspaper in his hand, to which he gives a vague, bored, yawning attention, and several other newspapers beside him. There are three or four garden chairs about.* Mrs. Wigmore *comes out of the house, carrying or propelling before her with difficulty a light wicker bench or settee, with a back, capable of holding two persons, and proceeds with a business-like air to get it into place, well up at the right, near the garden-wall, between the house and the centre.*

Sir Montagu. (*Looking up.*) Bless my soul, Flora, is there no one to help you?

Mrs. Wigmore. (*Going back for a cushion and a bright-coloured travelling rug which have been deposited on the steps of the house.*) No one but your keeper's wife —she's busy preparing tea.

Sir Montagu. (*Going on with his paper.*) Do you mean to say we're going to have tea?

Mrs. Wigmore. After our lunch on that precipitous slope? (*Arranging the cushion, with little pats, on the settee, and the rug, tentatively, in combination with it.*) I mean to say that *I* am!

Sir Montagu. (*Looking up again, mystified afresh by what she is doing.*) And what has that to do with it?

Mrs. Wigmore. (*Trying the settee and then getting up.*) It's a place to sit.

Sir Montagu. There are plenty of places to sit!

Mrs. Wigmore. (*Disposing the rug in another manner.*) You've got the best!

Sir Montagu. It's a bad best, my dear.

Mrs. Wigmore. That's your own fault— letting this dear old place tumble to pieces.

Sir Montagu. (*Goodhumouredly, once more going to his paper.*) Well, the pieces serve our purpose!

Mrs. Wigmore. Your wife's purpose, yes!

301

SIR MONTAGU. That of coming over, with a few friends, to spend a happy day.

MRS. WIGMORE. Do you find such days so happy?

SIR MONTAGU. (*Looking at his watch.*) They're apt to drag a little, perhaps, about this hour.

MRS. WIGMORE. When you're left alone with *me?* Thank you!

SIR MONTAGU. My dear sister, I haven't your resources. (*Watching her an instant again, while she continues her odd proceedings with the settee.*) I'm amazed at the extent of them now.

MRS. WIGMORE. I want to make my poor child comfortable.

SIR MONTAGU. Is all that for Blandina?

MRS. WIGMORE. Isn't everything I do for Blandina?

SIR MONTAGU. You do too much, you work her too hard.

MRS. WIGMORE. My dear brother, if you were a parent you'd perhaps have parental instincts, and if you had any instincts at all you'd perhaps open your eyes. I'm not ashamed· to keep mine fixed on certain manifestations, and it's a pity you on your side are so blind to certain others.

SIR MONTAGU. (*Trying to follow.*) Do you allude to the manifestations of my political opponents?

MRS. WIGMORE. Bother your political opponents!

SIR MONTAGU. That's exactly what I try to do! I see in this morning's *Times*—

MRS. WIGMORE. (*Breaking in.*) What I want you to see is something you won't see in the *Times!* You have opponents who are not political—though they're profound enough, no doubt.

SIR MONTAGU. Are they as profound as you? You're unfathomable!

MRS. WIGMORE. (*As a light laugh is heard to the left, a short distance off.*) Here they come! Take me somewhere—to the ruins.

SIR MONTAGU. The formidable persons you describe? Let me face them at least!

MRS. WIGMORE. I mean Blandina and her worshipper.

SIR MONTAGU. Have you succeeded in making her the object of a cult?

MRS. WIGMORE. Captain Prime's devotion has assumed a character not for a moment to be mistaken.

SIR MONTAGU. Since when? I haven't seen him at Brisket.

MRS. WIGMORE. You'll see him there tomorrow!

SIR MONTAGU. Having provided him with an idol, you expect him to go to the expense of a shrine?

MRS. WIGMORE. He leads a blameless life, though he *is* in the Guards; and he has a decent income, though he *is* a younger son.

SIR MONTAGU. Oh, I know; property from his mother.

MRS. WIGMORE. With country neighbours—it's such a blessing—one does know. (*Disappointed, seeing* LADY BRISKET *accompanied by* PERCY TRAFFORD.) But it's not my pair, it's your pair!

SIR MONTAGU. Well, then, come to the ruins.

MRS. WIGMORE. You needn't take me—the ruins are here.

SIR MONTAGU. (*Blank.*) Here?

MRS. WIGMORE. The ruins of your domestic security!

(*Enter from the left, from the ruins,* LADY BRISKET *and* PERCY TRAFFORD, *he carrying a photographic camera and certain accessories, with which he is considerably encumbered and embarrassed, while she, very pretty and elegant, in light gloves, with her lace-fringed parasol up, nurses in its case a prepared plate, ready to be inserted into the instrument.*)

LADY BRISKET. This is the place; this charming view and the dear old keeper's house. And we can take in Montagu.

MRS. WIGMORE. Oh yes, you can take in Montagu!

LADY BRISKET. Dear Flora, can't we take *you* in?

MRS. WIGMORE. Never in the world!

LADY BRISKET. (*To her husband.*) I'm having immense fun with Mr. Trafford—I'm giving him lessons!

SIR MONTAGU. (*Watching* TRAFFORD, *who is rather awkwardly setting up the camera on its tall supports.*) Is photography a branch now required in the diplomatic service?

TRAFFORD. (*Gay.*) Dear Sir Montagu, there's a standing rule in the diplomatic service: learn everything you can from the ladies!

LADY BRISKET. I must have an assistant, and I'm bound to say Mr. Trafford's a very good one.

TRAFFORD. (*Coming down.*) It seems, on Lady Brisket's part, a veritable mania.

SIR MONTAGU. The infatuation of an hour! She'll have a new one to-morrow.

TRAFFORD. A new infatuation perhaps, but (*smiling devotedly at* LADY BRISKET) not, I hope, a new assistant!

LADY BRISKET. (*After acknowledging this remark with a gracious bow.*) Montagu, you must sit for us—say on the pretty bench (*indicating the settee*) that seems to have been arranged on purpose; you and Flora (*smiling candidly at* MRS. WIGMORE), side by side.

MRS. WIGMORE. (*To herself, struck; seeing at the right* CAPTAIN PRIME *and* BLANDINA.) "Side by side"? That'll do for *them!* (*Enter from the right by the wooden gate* CAPTAIN PRIME *and* BLANDINA, *while* MRS. WIGMORE *continues eagerly to* LADY BRISKET.) I don't think I'm in your style of art. But you shall do my charming child.

TRAFFORD. (*Very responsive.*) We shall be delighted. Miss Wigmore is particularly charming.

MRS. WIGMORE. (*Sharp.*) Then why are you dangling after married women?

TRAFFORD. (*Startled, but recovering himself and highly complimentary.*) Dear madam, are *you* unconscious of their attraction?

LADY BRISKET. (*With her prepared plate, to* TRAFFORD.) Here's the plate; make everything ready.

SIR MONTAGU. (*To his wife, while* TRAFFORD, *who has taken the plate, goes and gets under the voluminous cloth which covers the camera.*) And then the results are called yours?

LADY BRISKET. We'll call these ours!

SIR MONTAGU. (*Looking at her a moment, then turning his back; dry.*) Thank you; I'm out of it! (*He meets* CAPTAIN PRIME, *with whom he stands talking.*)

MRS. WIGMORE. (*Down on the left.*) Blandina, come here!

BLANDINA. (*Instantly coming.*) Yes, mamma.

MRS. WIGMORE. Try not to look dreadful.

BLANDINA. Yes, mamma.

MRS. WIGMORE. Stick .in that hairpin; you're going to be taken.

BLANDINA. (*With her hands at her hair.*) Yes, mamma.

MRS. WIGMORE. Keep down your hands.

BLANDINA. Yes, mamma.

MRS. WIGMORE. You'll be taken with Captain Prime.

BLANDINA. Oh, mamma, must I *ask* him?

MRS. WIGMORE. (*After consideration.*) No, you mustn't ask him.

BLANDINA. Then what must I do?

MRS. WIGMORE. You must make him. Where were you going with him?

BLANDINA. (*Dropping her eyes.*) To the ruins.

MRS. WIGMORE. You'll go to the ruins afterwards.

BLANDINA. Yes, mamma.

MRS. WIGMORE. Visit them thoroughly. Do you remember their history?

BLANDINA. No, mamma.

MRS. WIGMORE. One of the most celebrated sanctuaries of the Middle Ages; begun in the eleventh century, terminated in the fourteenth.

BLANDINA. Yes, mamma.

MRS. WIGMORE. Favourite burial-place of the Norman queens.

BLANDINA. Yes, mamma.

MRS. WIGMORE. Injured by fire under Henry the Seventh; despoiled of its treasures under Henry the Eighth.

BLANDINA. Yes, mamma.

MRS. WIGMORE. But take your little attitude first.

BLANDINA. Yes, mamma.

(BLANDINA *goes straight up to the settee, while* SIR MONTAGU *approaches* MRS. WIGMORE *and* CAPTAIN PRIME *wanders to the stone bench and dejectedly takes up a newspaper left there by* SIR MONTAGU.)

SIR MONTAGU. (*To* MRS. WIGMORE.) Will you come to the ruins now?

MRS. WIGMORE. Oh no, not now: we'll go to the dairy.

SIR MONTAGU. What did you mean about Amy?

MRS. WIGMORE. (*Down on the right.*) And her "assistant"? (*Very sarcastic.*) It's a new name!

SIR MONTAGU. (*After an instant.*) A new name for what?

MRS. WIGMORE. (*Passing out of the wooden gate.*) I'll tell you at the dairy.

SIR MONTAGU. (*With an uncomfortable laugh, following her.*) I believe you'll sour the milk! (*Exeunt SIR MONTAGU and MRS. WIGMORE.*)

TRAFFORD. (*With the camera, to BLANDINA, who has disposed herself as attractively as possible on the settee.*) I think we can do something with you, Miss Wigmore, if you'll assume a cheerful expression of face.

BLANDINA. (*Smiling seductively.*) Captain Prime!

PRIME. (*His face to the stone bench, with his newspaper, without turning round.*) Miss Wigmore?

BLANDINA. Have *you* ever been taken?

PRIME. Taken? I've been pursued, but I've never been captured.

TRAFFORD. (*Busy with the apparatus.*) Oh, we'll capture you now—I warn you we never miss! Miss Wigmore, keep extraordinarily still.

BLANDINA. (*Agitating herself.*) Then Captain Prime must keep still too—he fidgets me so!

TRAFFORD. (*Reproachful.*) My dear Captain, *don't* fidget Miss Wigmore.

PRIME. (*In the same position.*) I'm not dreaming of Miss Wigmore; I'm half a mile away.

LADY BRISKET. (*To BLANDINA.*) *I'*ll keep him quiet, my dear. (*To CAPTAIN PRIME, passing to the left.*) You've been quite lost to us; you disappeared directly after luncheon.

PRIME. Miss Wigmore took me away.

LADY BRISKET. (*Encouraging.*) And where did Miss Wigmore take you?

PRIME. (*Casual, vague.*) Oh, I don't know —all over the place.

LADY BRISKET. And did you come across Mrs. Jasper?

PRIME. No, I wish we had. (*Expressively, invidiously.*) Mrs. Jasper's attractive!

LADY BRISKET. (*After an instant.*) So all you gentlemen seem to think.

PRIME. She's so enviable, in her freedom.

LADY BRISKET. Her freedom is the freedom of a woman who has lost her husband early.

PRIME. (*Laughing.*) Better late than never!

LADY BRISKET. There are always the husbands of others. Mine is particularly devoted to her, and has a convenient theory that she's my best and oldest friend. It's in that capacity that she's now staying at Brisket.

PRIME. Sir Montagu has a rival. We met Charles Coverley.

LADY BRISKET. Of course Charles Coverley was looking for her.

PRIME. He asked eagerly if we'd seen her.

LADY BRISKET. He never does anything else.

PRIME. (*Seeing MRS. JASPER at the centre.*) We're to have that privilege now.

LADY BRISKET. *She's* looking for Montagu. (*Enter MRS. JASPER by the great gate from the right. To MRS. JASPER.*) I must see about tea. Please to control Captain Prime! (*Exit LADY BRISKET to the house.*)

MRS. JASPER. (*To PRIME, smiling and coming down with her finger in a sketchbook that she carries.*) You belong to a species that is usually beyond my control!

PRIME. How do you know, Mrs. Jasper, to what species I belong?

MRS. JASPER. Why, you've the general form, the costume, and some of the distinguishing signs. But now that I look at you more attentively, these features are perhaps only the redeeming ones.

PRIME. It's very kind of you to look at me more attentively!

MRS. JASPER. You see that if I'm to do what Lady Brisket asks, I must exert the power of my eye.

PRIME. You're happy to have so many powers to exert!

MRS. JASPER. Don't begin on that principle, or I shall think you do belong to the species! (*After an instant, explaining.*) I mean the species of Mr. Coverley. (*Looking round her.*) And of Mr. Trafford. (*Then after another moment.*) And even of poor dear Sir Montagu.

PRIME. (*Smiling.*) I know what you mean now! Sir Montagu isn't here.

MRS. JASPER. (*With laughing confidence.*) Oh, he'll be back in a moment!

PRIME. Coverley's on his way, at any rate. He has been making the copses ring with your name.

MRS. JASPER. I heard him, but I lay low. I found such a quiet little nook to sketch.

PRIME. Are you very fond of sketching?

MRS. JASPER. I find it a kind of refuge.

PRIME. (*Wistful.*) I wish *I* had a kind of a refuge!

MRS. JASPER. (*Slightly struck.*) From what, Captain Prime?

PRIME. (*After an instant.*) I'll tell you another day.

MRS. JASPER. I shall particularly remind you!

TRAFFORD. (*Who during this and the foregoing dialogue has been trying with* BLANDINA *different attitudes, different distances and focuses.*) Captain Prime, come and keep Miss Wigmore quiet. Her head goes up and down like a dinner-bell.

PRIME. (*Plaintive.*) To call *me* to dinner! (*With a gesture of desperation he goes up while* TRAFFORD *comes down; but, to keep away from* BLANDINA, *he gets under the cloth of the camera and remains during the next dialogue focussing other objects.*)

TRAFFORD. (*To* MRS. JASPER *at the left.*) I wish awfully we might take *you!*

MRS. JASPER. I like your editorial "we"! You're at the most a contributor.

TRAFFORD. Then won't you be a subscriber?

MRS. JASPER. I don't encourage improper publications!

TRAFFORD. You're always accusing me of something dreadful. The last time I think it was of flirting.

MRS. JASPER. The last time? The first time! I never saw such a case.

TRAFFORD. If you mean that I'm susceptible, I confess it's an infirmity of my nature. But I struggle with it—I assure you I do!

MRS. JASPER. Are you getting Miss Wigmore to help you to struggle? You might leave *her* alone!

TRAFFORD. I do, you see, as soon as another woman appears. I really wish you'd sit!

MRS. JASPER. To figure in the gallery of your conquests?

TRAFFORD. You'd be the gem of the collection—the flower of the family!

MRS. JASPER. Your collection's too large, and your family already, I should think, about as much as you can comfortably maintain.

TRAFFORD. I'd desert it without remorse for you!

MRS. JASPER. (*Plaintive.*) Every one wants to do everything for "me." I wish they'd do a little for somebody else!

TRAFFORD. There's nobody else so inspiring. You inspire us all.

MRS. JASPER. (*After an instant, considering, with a faintly melancholy headshake.*) No. Not "all."

TRAFFORD. I'm glad to hear it—it makes more chances for the rest.

MRS. JASPER. It will never make a chance for Mr. Percy Trafford.

TRAFFORD. Ah, if you turn him off, he won't care what he does!

MRS. JASPER. He's a very dreadful sort of person.

TRAFFORD. I make you responsible! Appreciation's a need of my being—I shall continue to look for it!

MRS. JASPER. (*Looking after him as he goes up, while* SIR MONTAGU *reappears at the right.*) You'll find it, more's the pity—I blush for my sex! (*Re-enter* SIR MONTAGU BRISKET *by the wooden gate; on which* MRS. JASPER *goes on, as she sees him come straight to her.*) Oh, dear—I blush for his!

SIR MONTAGU. There's something I want particularly to say to you.

MRS. JASPER. Again? (*Then having seated herself on the stone bench, where she retouches with a pencil a page of her sketchbook.*) I listen, Sir Montagu.

SIR MONTAGU. (*Seating himself beside her.*) I wish you hadn't so many accomplishments: they're fatal to your friends!

MRS. JASPER. (*With a sigh.*) I'd exchange them all for one I don't possess!

SIR MONTAGU. Ah, which one don't you possess?

MRS. JASPER. The art of passing unperceived.

Sir Montagu. Dear lady, you'll never cease, I think, to "draw."

Mrs. Jasper. (*Continuing to work.*) As I'm not remarkably old, that's a terrible prospect.

Sir Montagu. You're not remarkably old, but you're remarkably wise.

Mrs. Jasper. (*With another sigh.*) Oh, I've been through such a lot!

Sir Montagu. That opens one's eyes indeed. Mine are open now.

Mrs. Jasper. Yours? (*Working her pencil.*) What have you been through?

Sir Montagu. A *tête-a-tête* with my sister. That's precisely why I want—

Mrs. Jasper. (*Interrupting, rising.*) Another with me? (*Laughing.*) Not milk and water after champagne!

Sir Montagu. (*Still seated; having caught her hand, detaining her.*) The milk of human kindness and the water of oblivion! You must help me!

Mrs. Jasper. (*Becoming aware of* Lady Brisket, *who has reappeared on the steps of the house.*) Be quiet—your wife! (*Reenter* Lady Brisket *from the house, stopping short as she sees* Sir Montagu *and* Mrs. Jasper *and notes her husband's marked attitude of appeal; to counteract which* Mrs. Jasper *gaily calls across to her.*) Amy dear, I'm coming in for tea!

Lady Brisket. (*Ironical.*) Pray don't hurry, darling! (*Exit* Lady Brisket *to the house.*)

Sir Montagu. (*Drawing* Mrs. Jasper *down again.*) That's just what I want—that you should speak to her.

Mrs. Jasper. What do you wish me to say?

Sir Montagu. That I justly resent her behaviour.

Mrs. Jasper. (*Vague.*) Her behaviour?

Sir Montagu. Don't pretend, in your good-nature, not to have observed it!

Mrs. Jasper. (*After a moment.*) Amy justly resents yours, Sir Montagu.

Sir Montagu. (*Blank.*) Mine?

Mrs. Jasper. Your propensity to draw me into corners, and (*as he still detains her*) to contend with me there!

Sir Montagu. It's only to discuss with you the situation she herself has created.

Mrs. Jasper. Is your view of this situa-tion the result of your interview with Mrs. Wigmore?

Sir Montagu. Flora deemed it her duty to speak to me—she's jealous of the family honour.

Mrs. Jasper. (*After a pause, during which* Sir Montagu *continues the importunate pressure of the arm by which he has forced her to seat herself again.*) Does the family honour demand (*looking down at her arm*) that you should appropriate so much of my arm? (*He releases her with a promptly apologetic gesture, and she goes on.*) It's very absurd, you know. Mr. Trafford, as you can easily see, is making himself agreeable to Blandina.

Sir Montagu. (*Who has looked round with his eyeglass at the other group—* Blandina *and* Captain Prime *close together on the settee, by the dimensions of which they are much compressed, while* Trafford *has gone for a few moments, on business conspicuously connected with photography, into the house.*) I beg your pardon, it's Captain Prime who is doing that!

Mrs. Jasper. (*Just visibly struck, retouching her sketch again.*) Oh—is it?

Sir Montagu. You can see for yourself!

Mrs. Jasper. (*After an instant.*) I don't want to see!

Sir Montagu. (*Sociable, taking it for granted.*) So you'll remonstrate with Amy, won't you?

Mrs. Jasper. I must be sure of my facts first. These are things that a woman feels a delicacy in mentioning; but Mr. Trafford presents an unmistakable appearance—

Sir Montagu. (*Attentive, as she pauses.*) Yes?

Mrs. Jasper. Of not being indifferent to myself.

Sir Montagu. (*Disconcerted.*) Does he—the rascal?

Mrs. Jasper. You see we must be clear. If he's a rascal for me, he's not a rascal for Amy.

Sir Montagu. (*After an instant.*) He takes you in rotation!

Mrs. Jasper. Everything, I admit, is grist to his mill! (*Then after consideration.*) Should you like me to localise his affection, so that Amy shall be safe?

SIR MONTAGU. (*Embarrassed; then with decision.*) On the contrary—make him universal!

MRS. JASPER. (*Amused.*) I like your provision for morality! (*Rising.*) I'll speak to Amy.

SIR MONTAGU. (*Rising but reluctant; still keeping her.*) Now, do you mean?

MRS. JASPER. This very moment.

SIR MONTAGU. (*Pleading.*) But you'll come back to tell me what she says?

MRS. JASPER. Why is that necessary?

SIR MONTAGU. Surely we must talk it over.

MRS. JASPER. (*After looking at him an instant.*) Does the "family honour" require it? (*As he gives an embarrassed shrug she waves him off to the right.*) Go and ask Mrs. Wigmore!

(*Exit* SIR MONTAGU *by the wooden gate.* MRS. JASPER *goes up to the house, but as she approaches it, putting her sketch-book to rights, she drops a loose page, which* CAPTAIN PRIME *instantly perceives. He quits* BLANDINA *with alacrity, picks it up and hands it to her; she receives it with a gracious acknowledgment which makes a momentary passage between them, and goes into the house.* PRIME, *liberated from* BLANDINA *by this movement and by* TRAFFORD'S *return from the house simultaneously with* SIR MONTAGU'S *exit and before* MRS. JASPER'S, *comes down to the left with an expression of extreme relief.*)

BLANDINA. (*Still fast to her settee.*) Don't forget, Captain Prime, that we're going to the ruins.

TRAFFORD. (*Who has come down to the right.*) Ah, you must do them; they're uncommonly fine!

BLANDINA. (*Rising, advancing and taking her stand as if to recite a lesson.*) One of the most celebrated sanctuaries of the Middle Ages; begun in the eleventh century, terminated in the fourteenth.

PRIME. (*Down on the left; amazed.*) I say!

BLANDINA. Favourite burial-place of the Norman queens.

TRAFFORD. (*Down on the right; to* PRIME.) She's wonderful!

(*Re-enter* LADY BRISKET *from the house, with a cup of tea in her hand.*)

BLANDINA. Injured by fire under Henry the Seventh; despoiled of its treasures under Henry the Eighth. (*She returns to the settee.*)

LADY BRISKET. (*Who has stopped on the steps of the house to listen.*) That deserves a cup of tea! (*Coming away with her cup.*) Captain Prime, please hand this to Miss Wigmore. (PRIME, *at the left, hesitates an instant; then, with a sigh of desperate docility, comes and takes the cup from* LADY BRISKET *and carries it up to* BLANDINA. TRAFFORD, *hereupon, at an expressive look from* LADY BRISKET, *bounds from the right to her side; while, down at the centre, she breaks out to him, with intensity.*) Take them together, it's important!

TRAFFORD. (*Ardent.*) Anything in life to gratify you.

LADY BRISKET. It's not to gratify me, it's to gratify Flora. (*Agitated.*) She suspects something.

TRAFFORD. What does she suspect?

LADY BRISKET. (*Dropping her eyes.*) The intimacy of our friendship.

TRAFFORD. (*With energy, plausibility.*) She exaggerates it!

LADY BRISKET. She exaggerates it! We must keep her occupied with Blandina's marriage.

TRAFFORD. To that simple soldier?

LADY BRISKET. Flora's frantic to make him propose. If she knows we're working for her—

TRAFFORD. (*Seizing her idea.*) She'll leave us alone? (*With intensity.*) We'll work for her!

LADY BRISKET. You're an angel! I'll send you out some tea.

TRAFFORD. I don't want any tea, I want your society! Let me walk home with you.

LADY BRISKET. I ordered the wagonette.

TRAFFORD. So much the better: it will take the others. But I'll make him propose first.

LADY BRISKET. In so many words?

TRAFFORD. As many as you like!

LADY BRISKET. (*Hesitating, then yielding.*) Well, Montagu has *his* friends!

TRAFFORD. They won't look at any one else.

LADY BRISKET. (*Struck.*) Won't they? (*With decision.*) Then I'll walk.

TRAFFORD. Adorable woman!

LADY BRISKET. (*Seeing* MRS. WIGMORE.) Be careful!

(*Re-enter* MRS. WIGMORE *by the wooden gate, and stops a moment while she looks very hard at* LADY BRISKET *and* PERCY TRAFFORD *and at* BLANDINA *and* CAPTAIN PRIME; *the last of whom, at* BLANDINA's *command, has again seated himself dejectedly beside her.* LADY BRISKET *rapidly returns to the house.* TRAFFORD *hurries back to his camera, and* PRIME, *at the sight of* MRS. WIGMORE, *springs up and comes down again on the left.*)

TRAFFORD. (*At the camera, under the cloth of which he has hastily thrust his head.*) Come, come, Captain—into position!

MRS. WIGMORE. (*Crossing to the left and thereby causing* PRIME *to fly to the right.*) Captain, into position!

TRAFFORD. My dear fellow, we're waiting!

MRS. WIGMORE. (*On the stone bench, to* PRIME.) My dear fellow, they're waiting!

TRAFFORD. (*Who has come down to the right and taken possession of* PRIME, *carried him up and forced him down on the settee, close beside* BLANDINA, *where he settles him and poses him.*) There now, the shoulder a little more presented.

MRS. WIGMORE. (*While she looks over the newspaper which she has taken up from beside her.*) The shoulder a little more presented, Captain Prime.

TRAFFORD. The cheek a little more inclined, Miss Wigmore.

MRS. WIGMORE. The cheek a little more inclined, love.

TRAFFORD. If Captain Prime could only wear a little happier expression!

MRS. WIGMORE. Captain Prime, wear a little happier expression.

PRIME. (*With a perfunctory simper.*) This way?

TRAFFORD. That way! (*Watch in hand.*) Now keep perfectly still.

MRS. WIGMORE. Keep perfectly still!

(*A short silence, during which enter* CHARLES COVERLEY *by the wooden gate, stopping with surprise at the scene, startled at the conjunction of* CAPTAIN PRIME *and* BLANDINA. *As this attitude and the silence are prolonged,* PERCY TRAFFORD, *very expressively, with the cover of the lens in one hand and his watch in the other, warns* COVERLEY *to be quiet. On this* COVERLEY *comes round on tiptoe to* MRS. WIGMORE.)

COVERLEY. (*In a loud whisper.*) Have you seen Mrs. Jasper?

MRS. WIGMORE. Keep perfectly still.

COVERLEY. (*In the same way to* TRAFFORD, *who has his back still turned to the sitters.*) Have you seen Mrs. Jasper?

TRAFFORD. Keep perfectly still. (*Another instant elapses, after which* TRAFFORD, *facing round again to* PRIME *and* BLANDINA, *claps the cover on the lens.*) Now you may move—I'll go and develop it. (*Exit* TRAFFORD *with the slide to the house.*)

COVERLEY. (*To* PRIME, *who, having sprung up from the settee, comes rapidly down with a fresh movement of relief.*) Have you seen Mrs. Jasper?

PRIME. (*Thinking an instant, as if bewildered and irritated with his ordeal.*) You ask that too often!

COVERLEY. (*Arresting* BLANDINA, *who comes down on the heels of* PRIME.) Have you seen Mrs. Jasper?

BLANDINA. She's in the house.

COVERLEY. Thank you—I want to speak to her. (*Going up.*)

MRS. WIGMORE. (*Who has risen when* PRIME *and* BLANDINA *rise.*) Mr. Coverley, please stay here; Mrs. Jasper's occupied.

COVERLEY. (*Sitting down on the steps of the house.*) I'll wait till she's free.

MRS. WIGMORE. (*Privately to* BLANDINA.) Have you taken him to the ruins?

BLANDINA. No, mamma.

MRS. WIGMORE. Then take him immediately.

BLANDINA. I want to see it developed.

MRS. WIGMORE. *I'll* see it developed!

BLANDINA. (*To* PRIME; *seductive.*) I think it's time for the ruins.

MRS. WIGMORE. It's time for the ruins.

PRIME. (*To himself, dolorous.*) Ill-omened name! (*He surrenders his arm to* BLANDINA. *Exeunt* PRIME *and* BLANDINA *to the left.*)

MRS. WIGMORE. (*To* COVERLEY, *looking after them.*) He has got what he wants!

COVERLEY. Well, *I* haven't! May I go to Mrs. Jasper now?

MRS. WIGMORE. Here she comes. (*Re-enter* MRS. JASPER *from the house with a cup of tea.*) For whom is that cup of tea?

MRS. JASPER. (*Smiling.*) Not for you!

MRS. WIGMORE. (*With resentment.*) I'll have some! (*Exit* MRS. WIGMORE *to the house.*)

COVERLEY. Is it for me?

MRS. JASPER. It's for Captain Prime.

COVERLEY. (*Summarily; taking the tea from her.*) He has got what he wants. (*After drinking.*) Where on earth have you been hiding?

MRS. JASPER. (*Holding up her sketch-book.*) Between the leaves of this.

COVERLEY. (*Who has put down his cup on the stone bench.*) Mayn't I see your work?

MRS. JASPER. (*Surrendering the sketch-book.*) I only came away for some tea: I'm going back to finish it.

COVERLEY. Leaving me all alone?

MRS. JASPER. (*As* SIR MONTAGU *reappears*). You'll not be alone—here's Sir Montagu.
> (*Re-enter* SIR MONTAGU *by the wooden gate.*)

SIR MONTAGU. (*To* MRS. JASPER.) Have you come across Amy?

MRS. JASPER. I just left her in the house.

SIR MONTAGU. With Mr. Trafford?

MRS. JASPER. (*Reassuring, smiling.*) Mr. Trafford's in the panelled room, developing.

SIR MONTAGU. (*Startled.*) Further?

MRS. JASPER. I mean his plate!

SIR MONTAGU. Then I can take her home.

MRS. JASPER. Leave her; she's happy enough.

SIR MONTAGU. I'm not "happy enough," Mrs. Jasper! (*Possessing himself of her hand, which she puts out to him protestingly at this.*) But thank heaven, *you're* a good woman! (*Raises her hand to his lips and kisses it. Exit* SIR MONTAGU *to the house.*)

COVERLEY. You never told me he makes love to you!

MRS. JASPER. I don't betray you to each other.

COVERLEY. What's the matter with him?

MRS. JASPER. His wife worries him.

COVERLEY. More than you worry me?

MRS. JASPER. Naturally: I'm not your wife.

COVERLEY. It's strange you should refuse to accept the position when you think of the opportunities it would give you.

MRS. JASPER. I don't think of them, Mr. Coverley; I've other things to think of. Give me my sketch-book.

COVERLEY. (*Still retaining it.*) Mayn't I carry it for you?

MRS. JASPER. No, you'll worry *me*, though you're not my husband.

COVERLEY. Consider that if I were I shouldn't wish to render you these services. Marry me therefore to get rid of me.

MRS. JASPER. It's a great temptation; but I don't quite want to kill you.

COVERLEY. I'd willingly die for you. Haven't I behaved beautifully—not going to stay at Brisket?

MRS. JASPER. How could you, when Amy didn't invite you?

COVERLEY. She was just going to when you prevented her.

MRS. JASPER. Much good it did me, with a rustic inn at the gates! I ought to have taken all the rooms.

COVERLEY. Then where would poor Trafford have put up?

MRS. JASPER. Instead of pairing with you there, he might have joined us at Brisket, where—though he's not scrupulous, I admit—a sense of what he owed to hospitality might have kept him straight. Will you do me a great favour, Mr. Coverley?

COVERLEY. (*Considering.*) What will you give me for a great favour?

MRS. JASPER. You have influence with Mr. Trafford; persuade him therefore to leave this place. Persuade him to return to his post.

COVERLEY. His post's at Copenhagen.

MRS. JASPER. So much the better!

COVERLEY. Very good; I'll talk to him to-night.

MRS. JASPER. Talk to him on the spot—there's no time to lose. Do me this service; I'm very much in earnest.

COVERLEY. And how will you reward me?

MRS. JASPER. (*After an instant; laughing.*) By letting you live! (*Takes her sketchbook and goes out by the great gate to the right.*)

COVERLEY. (*Alone, with a discouraged sigh, looking after her.*) Ah, what's the use of life?

(*Re-enter* SIR MONTAGU *from the house.*)

SIR MONTAGU. (*To* COVERLEY.) I have the honour to bid you good-bye.

COVERLEY. You're going off?

SIR MONTAGU. I'm going home.

COVERLEY. Good-bye, Sir Montagu. (*Exit* SIR MONTAGU *by the great gate to the left.*) From which I infer that her ladyship declines to budge! I must really speak to Percy Trafford, if it will do any good. (*After an instant.*) Do *me* any good!

(*Re-enter* MRS. WIGMORE *from the house.*

MRS. WIGMORE. Which way did my brother go?

COVERLEY. He said he was going home.

MRS. WIGMORE. I happen to have other views!

COVERLEY. (*As she hastily passes out of the great gate.*) She'll drag him back! (*Exit* MRS. WIGMORE *to the left. Re-enter* PERCY TRAFFORD *from the house and goes to take up from the ground a box of photographic plates which on his first entrance he has deposited near the camera.*) What are you doing?

TRAFFORD. (*With his box, coming down.*) Getting these for Lady Brisket.

COVERLEY. And what is Lady Brisket doing?

TRAFFORD. She's developing.

COVERLEY. Let her develop alone. I want to talk to you!

TRAFFORD. About Prime, you mean?—the way he's compromising that girl?

COVERLEY. *Is* he compromising her?

TRAFFORD. Horribly—unless he has intentions. (*Going up.*) Bye-bye!

COVERLEY. As much as you're compromising Lady Brisket?

TRAFFORD. (*Arrested, blank.*) Who put such stuff into your head?

COVERLEY. I see what I see.

TRAFFORD. I don't then! (*Coming down again.*) I've simply repaid courtesy with sympathy, and hospitality with—

COVERLEY. (*As he hesitates.*) Photography? I shall take you to the station to-morrow, but I should like to know first what you mean about the Captain.

TRAFFORD. I simply mean that the Captain must offer marriage to Miss Wigmore. If you want to know why, go and look at that plate.

COVERLEY. What's the matter with it?

TRAFFORD. The matter with it is that it's coming out beautifully! When a gentleman presents himself to the recording angel, as I may call it, with a young lady's head on his bosom, he creates expectations that must be definitely met! He gives a pledge. The Captain evidently recognises that: he's following the pledge up!

COVERLEY. (*Rather impressed, but reflecting.*) Following it up?

TRAFFORD. At the ruins. (*Looking at his watch.*) They're not staying there for nothing.

COVERLEY. Oh, they'll soon come back!

TRAFFORD. Unless they're ashamed of the comment they've excited!

COVERLEY. You ought to destroy the plate.

TRAFFORD. Not for the world! I shall obtain a fine clear impression of it, on the exhibition of which the Captain will face the music.

COVERLEY. Do you mean he'll propose?

TRAFFORD. Certainly—he'll redeem his pledge.

COVERLEY. He must believe in his pledge first.

TRAFFORD. He can be made to believe in it.

COVERLEY. Who's to make him? You?

TRAFFORD. (*After an instant.*) You, my dear fellow.

COVERLEY. Thank you! Why should I play him such a trick?

TRAFFORD. Because he knows you—he looks up to you—he'll mind what you say.

COVERLEY. All the more reason I

shouldn't say what I oughtn't! *You* mind what I say—that'll do! (*Going up.*)

TRAFFORD. (*Ironical.*) Have you seen Mrs. Jasper?

COVERLEY. (*Stopping short.*) Is that your way of insinuating that she asked me to speak to you?

TRAFFORD. I'm much obliged to her for her interest!

COVERLEY. Mrs. Jasper's interest is in Lady Brisket.

TRAFFORD. I see! And yours is in Mrs. Jasper. That's the vicious circle!

COVERLEY. Exactly; and it's why I should be delighted if I could get you to leave Lady Brisket alone.

TRAFFORD. (*After an instant.*) I'll accommodate you in that way if you'll accommodate me in another—in the way I spoke of just now. (*Then as* COVERLEY *appears not to follow.*) If you'll give Miss Wigmore a lift!

COVERLEY. What profit will you derive from Miss Wigmore's elevation?

TRAFFORD. It will make Lady Brisket happy!

COVERLEY. (*Laughing.*) Ah, your particular conception of Lady Brisket's happiness is just what we don't want!

TRAFFORD. What conception, particular or general, could be more innocent? If Mrs. Jasper takes an interest in Lady Brisket, Lady Brisket takes an interest in her niece. The girl's a martyr, with her terrible mother, and Lady Brisket would give everything to see her relieved. Prime's the man to relieve her, if it can only be made to come home to him. I say, Coverley, *make* it, and I'll let you lecture me by the hour!

COVERLEY. "Make" it is easily said! You talk as if I were one of the fellows who make rabbits come out of their neckties.

TRAFFORD. You've got such a light hand! Try a few hynotic passes—an appeal to his higher feelings.

COVERLEY. Questionable practices! What shall I gain by them?

TRAFFORD. Calculate and see! You'll gain by them that Blandina will gain, that Lady Brisket will gain by Blandina's gain, and that Mrs. Jasper, whom you want to gratify, will gain by Lady Brisket's. You'll be able

immediately to say to Mrs. Jasper—

COVERLEY. (*Interrupting.*) "That archhumbug says he'll listen to me"? But what if you don't listen?

TRAFFORD. I give you my honour I will! (*Coaxingly.*) My dear boy, I *am* listening—I *have* listened! If you'll put it into my power to demonstrate to Lady Brisket that I persuaded you to throw your weight into the scale, I'll (*thinking a moment*) take myself off on the spot. The words I mention will constitute on my part a disinterested, an exemplary farewell. Lady Brisket's not in danger, but since Mrs. Jasper does me the honour to think so, Mrs. Jasper will rejoice in my departure, and it will all be a good note for yourself.

COVERLEY. (*As if half persuaded.*) When will you go?

TRAFFORD. (*Scratching his head an instant.*) When will the Captain do *his* part?

COVERLEY. Well—say it comes off to-night.

TRAFFORD. Then I'll go to-morrow.

COVERLEY. (*Still sceptical.*) Why should I believe you?

TRAFFORD. Because I've never deceived you.

COVERLEY. Diplomatist! But it *won't* come off to-night.

TRAFFORD. (*With resolution.*) Then I won't go to-morrow! (*As* LADY BRISKET *reappears; with intention and calculation.*) So much the better; she's too good to lose!

(*Re-enter* LADY BRISKET *from the house.*)

LADY BRISKET. (*Between them.*) Where's Captain Prime? I want to show him our result.

TRAFFORD. Still at the ruins, pressing his suit.

LADY BRISKET. Mr. Coverley, it's in the panelled room. Pronounce upon it!

COVERLEY. Your result? (*Having gone up to the house; from the steps.*) I can at least pronounce on your process!

LADY BRISKET. (*Preoccupied, resentful.*) Montagu *hates* me—my life's a burden!

TRAFFORD. (*With ardent sympathy.*) Let me help you to carry the load!

(*Re-enter* MRS. JASPER *by the great gate from the right.*)

MRS. JASPER. (*To herself, as she hears*

him.) They're a Mutual Aid Society! (*To the others*.) I've spoiled my picture—I'm sick of life!

LADY BRISKET. So am I!

TRAFFORD. (*To* MRS. JASPER.) It's not because she has spoiled *her* picture! Do go and see how it has come out.

MRS. JASPER. Can't you bring it to me?

TRAFFORD. It won't bear daylight.

MRS. JASPER. (*Looking round her at the fading light and the slow moonrise*.) Daylight's going. How shall I find it in the dark?

> (*From this moment a clear autumn twilight, which has been just perceptibly gathering, slowly settles upon the scene, deepening toward the close of the act into the dusk, with the glow of lights in the windows of the house*.)

LADY BRISKET. Mr. Coverley will show you—in the panelled room.

MRS. JASPER. (*As* COVERLEY *reappears*.) No, he won't—he has had his turn!

> (*Re-enter* COVERLEY *from the house*.)

COVERLEY. (*Privately to* TRAFFORD.) It's pretty serious!

TRAFFORD. (*Looking at his watch*.) So is their protracted absence!

LADY BRISKET. Is it time to go home?

MRS. JASPER. Don't you hear the wagonette?

TRAFFORD. (*Privately to* LADY BRISKET.) Not for *us*!

MRS. JASPER. (*To* LADY BRISKET.) My dear child, is there anyone you can send for my traps?

COVERLEY. (*Ardent*.) Send *me*!

MRS. JASPER. You won't find the way.

COVERLEY. Come and show me.

MRS. JASPER. I'll start you.

> (MRS. JASPER *and* COVERLEY *go up together to the great gate and stand there a moment talking. Then exit* COVERLEY *to the right*.)

LADY BRISKET. What became of Montagu?

TRAFFORD. I suppose he walked home.

LADY BRISKET. And what became of Flora?

TRAFFORD. Let us hope she did the same.

LADY BRISKET. (*As* SIR MONTAGU *and* MRS. WIGMORE *reappear*.) No such luck!

> (*Re-enter* SIR MONTAGU *and* MRS. WIGMORE *by the great gate from the right, joining* MRS. JASPER *and coming down with her*.)

MRS. WIGMORE. (*To* LADY BRISKET.) Your husband was going home, but I overtook him and brought him back.

SIR MONTAGU. We've been taking it easy.

MRS. JASPER. (*At the steps of the house; gay*.) The only way to take it! Mr. Coverley wants me to examine the group. (*Exit* MRS. JASPER.)

MRS. WIGMORE. Amy, the wagonette's there.

LADY BRISKET. The wagonette can wait! Blandina's still at the ruins.

MRS. WIGMORE. (*Complacent*.) In that case the wagonette must indeed wait!

SIR MONTAGU. (*Looking at his watch, to* MRS. WIGMORE.) You ought to go for them.

MRS. WIGMORE. (*Horrified*.) "Go" for the sweet things? Barbarian! (*Then to* TRAFFORD.) Am I the only one who is not to examine the group? (*To* LADY BRISKET.) The least you can do, under the peculiar circumstances, is to place such a memento in my hands.

LADY BRISKET. (*Gracious*.) Dear Flora, you're welcome to our humble effort. (*Privately to* TRAFFORD.) Take her away!.

TRAFFORD. (*To* MRS. WIGMORE, *gallant*.) Kindly accept my arm. (*Exeunt* TRAFFORD *and* MRS. WIGMORE *to the house*.)

SIR MONTAGU. (*After going up nervously and vaguely, looking about him and then coming down, while he again refers to his watch*.) Amy, you had better go and sit in the carriage.

LADY BRISKET. (*On the stone bench*.) Why should I do anything so uncomfortable?

SIR MONTAGU. So as to be all ready to start.

LADY BRISKET. I'm not in the least eager to start!

SIR MONTAGU. We shall be shockingly late for dinner.

LADY BRISKET. I ordered it for nine o'clock.

SIR MONTAGU. Remember we've company.

LADY BRISKET. The Stoners and the

Spicers? They know the hour.

SIR MONTAGU. How do you propose to occupy yourself till nine o'clock?

LADY BRISKET. (*After an instant.*) I propose to walk home.

SIR MONTAGU. With your "assistant"?

LADY BRISKET. (*With a nervous laugh.*) To help me over the stiles!

SIR MONTAGU. My dear child, you'll do nothing of the sort. Your assistant has doubtless been useful, but from this hour we'll dispense with his services. You'll give him notice.

LADY BRISKET. After so much zeal?

SIR MONTAGU. To prevent any more.

LADY BRISKET. (*Seeing* COVERLEY.) Be careful!

(*Re-enter* CHARLES COVERLEY *by the great gate from the right, with* MRS. JASPER'S *small easel, paint-box and camp-stool, which he puts down by the gate.*)

COVERLEY. The young couple are still absent?

SIR MONTAGU. (*Looking once more at his watch.*) Mr. Coverley, will you do me a particular favour? Will you go and fetch them?

COVERLEY. (*Demurring.*) Would it be discreet, Sir Montagu?

SIR MONTAGU. Hang it then, I'll go myself!

(*Re-enter from the house* MRS. WIGMORE *and* PERCY TRAFFORD.)

MRS. WIGMORE. (*On the steps, sharp.*) Montagu, where are you going?

SIR MONTAGU. To recover Blandina.

MRS. WIGMORE. (*Coming down energetically and getting between him and the way to the ruins.*) Over my prostrate form!

SIR MONTAGU. Then what shall we do?

MRS. WIGMORE. We'll simply wait.

LADY BRISKET. It's only fair!

COVERLEY. It's only decent!

TRAFFORD. We must put ourselves in their place!

(*Re-enter* MRS. JASPER *from the house.*)

MRS. JASPER. Do you wait, Sir Montagu?

SIR MONTAGU. I do exactly what you do.

MRS. JASPER. You must do exactly the contrary. Don't look at me! (SIR MONTAGU, *with one of his vague shrugs of reluctant resignation, goes up restlessly to the great gate and stands there with his back turned, looking across the darkening valley.* MRS. WIGMORE *seats herself beside* LADY BRISKET *on the stone bench.* COVERLEY *goes for* MRS. JASPER'S *camp-stool, on which she sits after he has placed it in the middle of the stage.* TRAFFORD *places himself on the steps of the house.* COVERLEY *brings one of the chairs and sits by* MRS. JASPER, *who, on her camp-stool, goes on addressing him.*) You're a faithful servant!

COVERLEY. (*Gratified.*) Try me again!

MRS. JASPER. If I had my way I'd send you for the truants.

MRS. WIGMORE. (*To* MRS. JASPER.) Respect their thoroughness. I've taught Blandina not to be superficial.

MRS. JASPER. She profits by your instructions.

MRS. WIGMORE. I've shown her how to study the monuments of our ancient national life.

MRS. JASPER. And she's handing on the lesson to Captain Prime.

MRS. WIGMORE. They're exploring an endless subject.

LADY BRISKET. Poring over a delightful book.

TRAFFORD. (*Smiling, approving.*) With their heads, no doubt, very close together!

MRS. JASPER. It's terrible to think of all they'll know!

TRAFFORD. One of the most celebrated sanctuaries of the Middle Ages; begun in the eleventh century, terminated in the fourteenth.

MRS. WIGMORE. (*Starting, recognizing.*) What's that?

TRAFFORD. Favourite burial-place of the Norman queens.

MRS. WIGMORE. (*Still more surprised.*) How do *you* know?

TRAFFORD. Injured by fire under Henry the Seventh—

MRS. WIGMORE. (*Mystified and suspicious, interrupting and rising.*) You've got it all wrong!

SIR MONTAGU. (*Coming down to* MRS. JASPER.) Will *you* give me your company home? The wagonette can come back.

MRS. JASPER. (*Rising, to* LADY BRISKET.) Amy, won't you give us your society?

LADY BRISKET. (*Rising.*) I shouldn't dream of intruding on your privacy!

MRS. JASPER. Our "privacy"? Dear Amy, I shall sit with the coachman.

SIR MONTAGU. (*To* MRS. JASPER.) I shall be the coachman, you know.

MRS. JASPER. Then I'll sit inside. Won't you join us, Amy?

LADY BRISKET. (*Turning away.*) Montagu would manage to spill me.

SIR MONTAGU. (*To* MRS. JASPER.) I won't spill *you.* Leave her to her wicked ways!

MRS. JASPER. (*Privately to* COVERLEY.) Keep hold of Mr. Trafford.

COVERLEY. (*Privately to* TRAFFORD.) I'm watching you, my boy!

TRAFFORD. Certainly you must stay—to put the Captain through.

COVERLEY. (*As he sees* PRIME *and* BLANDINA *reappear.*) Well—for the woman I love!

(*Re-enter from the left* BLANDINA *and* CAPTAIN PRIME.)

SIR MONTAGU. (*Impatient.*) At last, young people—at last!

MRS. WIGMORE. (*Significant and suggestive.*) Well, I must say, Captain Prime—!

MRS. JASPER. (*Gay, to* PRIME.) I've been hearing about your studies.

PRIME. (*Blank.*) My studies?

MRS. JASPER. (*Smiling.*) The Norman queens. We must talk them over.

PRIME. (*With alacrity.*) Now, Mrs. Jasper?

MRS. WIGMORE. No, not now. Another time.

MRS. JASPER. (*Still smiling at* PRIME.) Another time.

PRIME. Another time.

BLANDINA. (*Conscious, looking round at the company.*) Have we been dreadfully long?

MRS. JASPER. Not if you've seen everything.

SIR MONTAGU. (*To* MRS. JASPER, *impatient.*) Never mind what she has seen!

MRS. WIGMORE. Excuse me. It's a case in which her mother wants to hear.

SIR MONTAGU. (*Privately.*) Then look after Amy. (*To* MRS. JASPER.) Please take my arm.

MRS. JASPER. (*To* LADY BRISKET.) Amy, wait for the return of the carriage. (*Then coming down to* COVERLEY.) Can I trust you to put her into it?

COVERLEY. By force, if necessary. But I hate you to go.

MRS. JASPER. (*Hesitating, looking round at* LADY BRISKET; *then as if still insufficiently satisfied.*) I'll only go as far as the carriage—I'll come back.

(*She rejoins* SIR MONTAGU *and takes his arm, lingering while she does so for an instant during which she exchanges a fixed look with* LADY BRISKET. SIR MONTAGU *consciously avoids meeting his wife's eyes, and* LADY BRISKET *watches him while, at the great gate, he goes out to the left with* MRS. JASPER. LADY BRISKET *then makes, in reference to them, a nervous, sarcastic gesture to* TRAFFORD.)

MRS. WIGMORE. (*To* BLANDINA, *while* LADY BRISKET, TRAFFORD, *and* COVERLEY *surround* CAPTAIN PRIME.) Has he done it?

BLANDINA. No, mamma.

MRS. WIGMORE. Then you *are* a donkey!

BLANDINA. Yes, mamma.

MRS. WIGMORE. (*Imperious.*) Have it out on the spot!

BLANDINA. (*Vague.*) On what spot?

MRS. WIGMORE. (*Looking about; then indicating the house.*) Find one in there!

BLANDINA. Yes, mamma.

MRS. WIGMORE. Confront him with the picture.

BLANDINA. Yes, mamma. (*Exit* BLANDINA *to the house.*)

LADY BRISKET. (*To* MRS. WIGMORE, *while* COVERLEY *and* TRAFFORD *remain with* PRIME.) You had better be away.

MRS. WIGMORE. (*Mistrustful.*) And leave you to frisk?

LADY BRISKET. Dear Flora, I'll go with you.

MRS. WIGMORE. (*Indicating* PRIME.) And what will become of that person?

LADY BRISKET. They'll send him into the house. (*To the others.*) Excuse us, gentlemen; we're going to the old garden.

MRS. WIGMORE. To gather some lavender. (*Exeunt* MRS. WIGMORE *and* LADY BRISKET *by the wooden gate, which* TRAFFORD *opens for them.*)

TRAFFORD. (*Coming back to* PRIME, *who*

is at the right while COVERLEY is at the left.) My dear fellow, you *have* roused the tigress!

PRIME. (*Startled.*) The tigress?

COVERLEY. Didn't you see how she packed her charming cub into the cage? She dissimulates for the moment, so as not to make the matter worse by a public scene.

TRAFFORD. That's why Lady Brisket has dragged her off.

COVERLEY. For fear she should break out!

TRAFFORD. Sir Montagu and Mrs. Jasper fled before the storm.

COVERLEY. Poor Miss Wigmore bowed her head.

PRIME. (*More and more blank, looking from one of his companions to the other.*) Bowed it?

TRAFFORD. To the maternal thunder.

COVERLEY. You'll hear from her to-morrow.

PRIME. From Miss Wigmore?

COVERLEY. From Miss Wigmore's mamma. Jupiter tonans!

TRAFFORD. It was a bad quarter of an hour.

COVERLEY. The minutes were little blushing ages!

PRIME. (*Bewildered.*) The minutes? What minutes?

TRAFFORD. Those of your abandonment.

PRIME. Abandonment to what?

COVERLEY. (*Laughing.*) Would it be discreet of us to specify?

PRIME. (*With growing distress.*) Tell me at least what you mean!

TRAFFORD. Do you pretend it doesn't come home to you?

PRIME. Home? I don't understand!

COVERLEY. Isn't the situation plain?

PRIME. (*Stupefied.*) Plain?

COVERLEY. Would you rather call it coloured?

TRAFFORD. A scandal's always a scandal!

PRIME. (*Aghast.*) A scandal? Such as they talk about at the clubs?

TRAFFORD. Or publish in the papers. From the moment you were so carried away by your feelings—

PRIME. (*Distracted, indignant.*) Feelings? I *have* no feelings!

COVERLEY. (*Reproachful, edifying.*)

Doesn't it occur to you that that poor girl may have?

TRAFFORD. She'll have a few when she finds she's compromised!

PRIME. (*To COVERLEY, appalled, appealing.*) You don't mean to say she's *that?*

COVERLEY. (*For TRAFFORD; after looking at him a moment and then turning away and tossing down nervously a cigarette.*) Hang it—it's beyond me!

TRAFFORD. (*To PRIME, more soothing.*) Fortunately there's an easy way out.

PRIME. An "easy" way?

TRAFFORD. Easy for your honour. When you've excited expectations—

PRIME. (*Breathless, as he pauses.*) Yes, when I have?

TRAFFORD. Why, you must meet them.

PRIME. (*Blank.*) And how in the world shall I meet them?

TRAFFORD. By marrying your victim.

PRIME. (*With a despairing wail.*) Mercy of heaven! (*Grasping the arm of COVERLEY, who, recalled by this exclamation, comes down from the detachment in which, during the previous moments, he has stood.*) Must I, on my honour; *must* I?

COVERLEY. (*Faltering, hanging fire.*) Must you what?

PRIME. (*Desperately, while TRAFFORD passes round to COVERLEY's right and BLANDINA reappears.*) Must I make her my wife?

(*Re-enter BLANDINA from the house.*)

BLANDINA. (*On the steps.*) Captain Prime!

PRIME. (*With a jump.*) There she *is!* (*Recovering himself.*) Miss Wigmore?

BLANDINA. Our picture looks so odd!

PRIME. (*Between COVERLEY and TRAFFORD, and after looking in supreme anguish from one impenetrable face to the other.*) I'll do what I can about it! But (*to COVERLEY, suppliant*) must I make her *that?*

TRAFFORD. (*Privately, on COVERLEY's right.*) Nail him, and I'm off!

COVERLEY. (*After an instant.*) Your wife, my dear fellow? You can't very well make her anything else!

BLANDINA. (*Still on the steps.*) Llewellyn!

PRIME. Blandina!

(*Exit BLANDINA to the house.*

PRIME, *smiting his forehead, makes a wild dash for it and follows her in.*)

TRAFFORD. (*While* COVERLEY, *who has gone up uneasily, stands listening near the house.*) Now of course I'll go!

COVERLEY. (*With a reaction, already remorseful.*) Go or stay—I wash my hands of it!

TRAFFORD. Too late, my boy—they're imbrued!

COVERLEY. (*Uneasily laughing.*) With human gore? He won't come to the point.

TRAFFORD. He's coming now!

COVERLEY. (*Irritated.*) Ah, but it isn't fair!

TRAFFORD. My dear fellow, she's a charming girl.

COVERLEY. Then marry her yourself!

TRAFFORD. (*With elation and as* LADY BRISKET *and* MRS. WIGMORE *reappear.*) Too late—too late!

(*Re-enter by the wooden gate* LADY BRISKET *and* MRS. WIGMORE.)

MRS. WIGMORE. (*With a big bunch of lavender.*) Where's Captain Prime?

COVERLEY. In the house.

MRS. WIGMORE. (*Passing anxiously up.*) What's he doing?

TRAFFORD. Coming to the point!

MRS. WIGMORE. (*Starting, as a loud, droll shriek proceeds from the house.*) Mercy on us!

TRAFFORD. (*Laughing.*) That's the "point"!

MRS. WIGMORE. My precious child! (*Makes a rush for the house, which she precipitately enters.*)

TRAFFORD. (*To* COVERLEY.) Blandina has accepted! (*To* LADY BRISKET, *as* COVERLEY, *with quickened alarm, turns away.*) Now we can go!

LADY BRISKET. (*After an instant.*) Well—if Flora's squared!

(TRAFFORD *gives her his arm while* COVERLEY, *with his back turned, listens again, intently, on the steps of the house; and they hurry out of the great gate to the right.*)

COVERLEY. (*Alone, staring, convinced, coming down and across to the left.*) Tremendous smacks? They're *kissing!*

(*Re-enter* MRS. JASPER *through*

the great gate from the left.*)

MRS. JASPER. (*Surprised.*) Where are Lady Brisket and Mr. Trafford?

COVERLEY. (*Startled, looking round, going up as she comes down.*) Bless me—they've escaped!

MRS. JASPER. (*Down at the left, disappointed, vexed.*) You don't keep faith! (*Re-enter, as she speaks,* MRS. WIGMORE *from the house. Agitated, calling across to her.*) They've escaped!

MRS. WIGMORE. (*Radiant, jubilant, descending the steps.*) No, they haven't! (*With a gesture of happy majesty, indicating* BLANDINA *and* CAPTAIN PRIME *as they reappear.*) Behold them! (*Re-enter* CAPTAIN PRIME *and* BLANDINA *from the house;* PRIME, *pale and breathless, coming instantly down to the left of* MRS. JASPER, *and* BLANDINA, *as he does so, arriving at the right of* COVERLEY. MRS. WIGMORE, *between the two couples, looks with significant satisfaction from* PRIME *to* BLANDINA *and from* COVERLEY *to* MRS. JASPER; *then with a kind of official grandeur she goes on.*) I have the honour to announce to you a piece of news in which you'll both rejoice—my daughter's engagement to Captain Prime!

COVERLEY. (*Overwhelmed.*) Immortal gods! (*Then agitatedly seizing* MRS. WIGMORE's *wrist.*) Is it true, Mrs. Wigmore?

MRS. WIGMORE. (*Staring at him a moment in resentful surprise; then sarcastically to* BLANDINA.) Is it "true," love?

BLANDINA. Yes, mamma.

COVERLEY. (*Passing with emotion to* BLANDINA's *right, while she, coming to* MRS. WIGMORE, *throws herself into her arms; then to himself, smiting his forehead with extravagant compunction and despair.*) What have I done—what have I done? (*Dashes confusedly, to conceal his discomposure, into the house.*)

PRIME. (*Dazed, bewildered, with smothered anguish, at the extreme left, to* MRS. JASPER *while* MRS. WIGMORE *presses* BLANDINA *to her bosom.*) Is it true, Mrs. Jasper?

MRS. JASPER. (*Who on* MRS. WIGMORE's *announcement has given the same shocked start as* COVERLEY *and an ejaculation inarticulate and, while she carries her hand a moment to her heart, instantly checked,* looks at him smiling intensely and with recovered self-control. Then with the lightest, gayest sarcasm.) You can't believe in your happiness? (Looks at him another instant; after which, laughing and with a mocking, ironical, extravagantly ceremonious curtsey.) Let it receive from me, the first, a hearty congratulation!

ACT SECOND

The hall at Brisket Place, soon after breakfast; large, light and bright, wainscoted and panelled in white, in the style of the last century. Last-century portraits and other features. At the back, facing the audience, a wide window, with the small panes of the period, looking into the court. On a line with it, to the left, a double door leading through a vestibule to the court. High up to the right a double door leading to the staircase and other parts of the house. Lower down, on the left, a door leading into the so-called Red Room. Down on the right, corresponding with this, the door to the library. Down toward the left, with its back presented to the audience, a writing-table completely appointed.

BLANDINA comes out of the library, meeting CHARLES COVERLEY, who bursts in from the Red Room.

COVERLEY. (Eager, feverish.) Have you seen Mrs. Jasper?

BLANDINA. (Surprised.) Why, where have you come from?

COVERLEY. I've been rushing about—I came in by the glass doors. Have you seen Mrs. Jasper?

BLANDINA. Not since breakfast.

COVERLEY. (Disappointed.) You should keep her in sight! (Seeing TRAFFORD—enter PERCY TRAFFORD from the court.) Have you seen Mrs. Jasper?

TRAFFORD. By the river, sketching. (Complacently.) She put me into it!

COVERLEY. (Irritated.) Into the river, I hope!

TRAFFORD. Into the sketch.

BLANDINA. That's a great compliment.

TRAFFORD. (Smiling.) Oh, yes, to the sketch!

COVERLEY. (With rueful confidence.) Art's her only love! (Hurries off to the court.)

TRAFFORD. He must want to see her—he left our little inn while I was still in bed.

BLANDINA. (Dropping her eyes.) When people are in love they get up early.

TRAFFORD. (Laughing.) Is that why Miss Wigmore's afoot?

BLANDINA. (Demure.) I rose at six.

TRAFFORD. I rose at seven! But there must be some exception to the rule, if Captain Prime isn't here.

BLANDINA. Is Captain Prime in love?

TRAFFORD. I supposed he was, or I shouldn't have come over at this hour to congratulate both of you on your engagement.

BLANDINA. (Raising her eyes to him.) That's not what you came over for—at this hour!

TRAFFORD. (Surprised.) There's more in you, Miss Wigmore, than meets the eye. Why then did I come?

BLANDINA. To see my aunt.

TRAFFORD. (Smiling.) Your acuteness, I confess, surprises me. But it's a matter of course to ask Lady Brisket how she finds herself after her walk.

(Enter, as he speaks, MRS. WIGMORE from the stairs.)

MRS. WIGMORE. Spare at least the innocence of a young woman scarce affianced! (To BLANDINA.) Captain Prime hasn't come?

BLANDINA. No, mamma.

MRS. WIGMORE. Is the Red Room empty?

BLANDINA. Yes, mamma.

MRS. WIGMORE. Then go there to receive him.

BLANDINA. Yes, mamma. (Exit BLANDINA to the Red Room.)

TRAFFORD. (All urbanity.) As I was eager to congratulate Miss Wigmore, so I'm eager to congratulate you!

MRS. WIGMORE. (After an instant; incorruptible.) Stuff and nonsense!

TRAFFORD. (Disconcerted but conciliatory.) I should think your impressions would reach you through the medium of your happiness.

MRS. WIGMORE. Great as it is, it doesn't deprive me of my senses.

TRAFFORD. The more senses, Mrs. Wigmore, the more sympathies.

MRS. WIGMORE. And the more sympathies, I suppose, the more scandals. You must have been sympathetic last night!

TRAFFORD. (Blank.) Last night?

MRS. WIGMORE. While we were waiting for you—blushing for you.

TRAFFORD. Blushing?

MRS. WIGMORE. Keeping the dinner till ten o'clock, with the Stoners and the Spicers looking at each other.

TRAFFORD. (With hopeless gaiety and gallantry.) I should have thought they'd been looking at you! We were indeed a little late: we found our walk so beguiling.

MRS. WIGMORE. That was Amy's remarkable expression.

TRAFFORD. Dear Mrs. Wigmore, you're not grateful.

MRS. WIGMORE. Grateful for what?

TRAFFORD. For your extraordinary windfall. I mean you're not indulgent.

MRS. WIGMORE. To criminal frivolity, to public indecorum? Why should I be?

TRAFFORD. You exaggerate awfully.

MRS. WIGMORE. As the fireman exaggerates when he plays the hose!

TRAFFORD. (With futile mirth.) Oh, I shall not resist a stream of water! I shall go next month.

MRS. WIGMORE. Why not next year? Every hour that you stay she'll pay for.

TRAFFORD. (Pleading.) Ah, don't say that!

MRS. WIGMORE. She'll pay for this.

TRAFFORD. (Vague.) This?

MRS. WIGMORE. Your being here now.

TRAFFORD. (With a change of tone, seeing LADY BRISKET.) She'll pay me; here she comes to do it!

(Enter LADY BRISKET from the Red Room.)

LADY BRISKET. (While she nods to TRAFFORD.) Flora, darling, you'll be pleased to know that Captain Prime has turned up.

TRAFFORD. (Warningly.) Oh, Mrs. Wigmore takes her pleasure sadly!

MRS. WIGMORE. I take it as some others

would be the better for taking theirs—modestly! (Then to LADY BRISKET, indicating the Red Room with her thumb.) Is he in there?

LADY BRISKET. I met him at the door and showed him in myself.

MRS. WIGMORE. Then I won't intrude.

LADY BRISKET. Don't miss him—he may show himself out.

MRS. WIGMORE. (At the door of the Red Room, listening; then quickly opening it.) Captain! (Exit rapidly MRS. WIGMORE.)

TRAFFORD. That's no use—she's awful.

LADY BRISKET. Awful enough to him. But I shall worry her with him, and it will make a diversion till you get off.

TRAFFORD. Dear friend, do you banish me?

LADY BRISKET. Montagu insists on it. We had a fearful battle.

TRAFFORD. Last night, when you came back?

LADY BRISKET. On this spot, after every one had gone. He says the Stoners and the Spicers will do for me.

TRAFFORD. (Blank.) Do what for you?

LADY BRISKET. Bruit it abroad—our belated, our beautiful walk.

TRAFFORD. What matters, since it was beautiful? We must have another.

LADY BRISKET. Not at present. You must leave the place.

TRAFFORD. (Insisting.) If I go up to London we'll have one there.

LADY BRISKET. (Vague.) In Oxford Street?

TRAFFORD. In Kensington Gardens, in Battersea Park. (Suggestive.) You'll join me for a day.

LADY BRISKET. Not for a minute.

TRAFFORD. (Pleading.) It will be our good-bye.

LADY BRISKET. This is our good-bye.

TRAFFORD. So inadequate, so brief?

LADY BRISKET. Make it briefer: catch the train!

TRAFFORD. I'll go back to the inn to see to my things. But I'll return for another word.

LADY BRISKET. You won't get it.

TRAFFORD. For another look, then—an hour hence.

LADY BRISKET. Montagu's coming—go, go! (She hurries him to the door to the *court, urging him off. He snatches one of her hands, to kiss it; then exit quickly to the court.* LADY BRISKET *comes down as her husband appears at the door of the library.*)

> (*Enter* SIR MONTAGU *from the library, dressed for a ride; with his hat on and pulling on his gloves.*)

SIR MONTAGU. Before I go out, there's another point I should like to make clear.

LADY BRISKET. Another? That will make about the fiftieth!

SIR MONTAGU. To match the number of your indiscretions! What I want to say is that I shall not be satisfied with a merely general assurance that Mr. Trafford will absent himself from our neighbourhood.

LADY BRISKET. Should you like a witnessed paper?

SIR MONTAGU. I should like a distinct pledge that during the next few days he will have placed the breadth of Europe between us.

LADY BRISKET. Between you and me?

SIR MONTAGU. Between himself and our distracted home! As many miles as it may be to Copenhagen.

LADY BRISKET. (*After a silence.*) If I'm to go into these refinements, it will be necessary for me to meet Mr. Trafford.

SIR MONTAGU. You can acquit yourself perfectly by a note—you have plenty of servants to carry one.

LADY BRISKET. If I may not transact the business with decent courtesy I decline to transact it at all.

SIR MONTAGU. (*Buttoning his glove.*) There are many things more decent than your courtesy!

LADY BRISKET. Your language, for instance?

SIR MONTAGU. Amy—I don't trust you.

LADY BRISKET. I know whom you trust! (*She goes up, meeting* CHARLES COVERLEY, *who re-enters on the rush from the court.*)

COVERLEY. (*Panting.*) Have you seen Mrs. Jasper?

LADY BRISKET. Ask my husband!

COVERLEY. (*To* SIR MONTAGU.) Have *you* seen Mrs. Jasper?

SIR MONTAGU. Unfortunately not.

COVERLEY. (*Indicating suggestively the Red Room.*) Would she be in there?

LADY BRISKET. By no means.

COVERLEY. (*Indicating suggestively the library.*) Would she be in there?

SIR MONTAGU. She wasn't just now.

COVERLEY. (*Embarrassed.*) She has such a talent for hiding!

LADY BRISKET. You haven't Sir Montagu's talent for finding her!

SIR MONTAGU. (*Indicating the library.*) She may have passed in since.

COVERLEY. (*At the door of the library.*) I'll just look.

SIR MONTAGU. There's a suite of rooms beyond—look further.

COVERLEY. Thank you, Sir Montagu. (*Exit* COVERLEY *to the library.*)

SIR MONTAGU. He runs in and out of the house as if it were a railway station.

LADY BRISKET. He's always missing the train!

SIR MONTAGU. (*In thought a moment longer, with his eyes on his wife, while he finishes button his glove.*) Write to that fellow austerely. Do you understand? (*Exit* SIR MONTAGU *to the court.*)

LADY BRISKET. (*Alone.*) I understand! I'll write to him, but *I'll* deliver the letter!

> (*Enter from the Red Room* MRS. JASPER, *with several letters in her hand.*)

MRS. JASPER. I came in that way, but I'm not wanted!

LADY BRISKET. Is Flora there?

MRS. JASPER. Marching up and down outside.

LADY BRISKET. So as to leave Blandina free?

MRS. JASPER. To make eyes at Captain Prime!

LADY BRISKET. And whom are *you* going to make eyes at?

MRS. JASPER. (*Smiling, goodhumoured, holding up her letters.*) My correspondents! But don't tell me I'm not a woman of order when I've dragged myself home to catch the midday post.

LADY BRISKET. I'll leave it to your correspondents to praise you. You seem to have enough!

MRS. JASPER. (*Counting her letters.*) One, two, three, four, *nine!* But they won't all "praise" me, I can assure you,

LADY BRISKET. Are you going to be very severe?

MRS. JASPER. Inordinately!

LADY BRISKET. You keep your severity for your letters.

MRS. JASPER. (*After an instant, smiling.*) Try to do the same, my dear, with yours!

LADY BRISKET. I *have* something odious to write. I'll do it in the library.

MRS. JASPER. Then may I write here?

LADY BRISKET. Certainly. (*After an instant.*) It's a good place for your other friends to find you.

MRS. JASPER. (*With a little comical wail.*) Ah, don't tell me they're looking for me!

LADY BRISKET. (*At the door of the library.*) There's one of them here that I'll send you. (*Exit* LADY BRISKET.)

MRS. JASPER. (*Alone.*) "One of them"? Sir Montagu?—I'll send him straight back to her! (*At the writing-table, seeing* COVERLEY: *re-enter* CHARLES COVERLEY *from the library.*) I'm sorry to see you, but you might be worse!

COVERLEY. (*Breathless.*) Do you fully realise what has happened to the Captain?

MRS. JASPER. (*Vague.*) The Captain?

COVERLEY. The unfortunate, the miserable Prime!

MRS. JASPER. Oh, his engagement! (*After an instant.*) "Fully realise" it? Mrs. Wigmore would box my ears if I didn't!

COVERLEY. Box hers! It's too awful!

MRS. JASPER. (*Occupying herself at the writing-table.*) Awful for whom?

COVERLEY. Why for me!

MRS. JASPER. Do you want Blandina for yourself?

COVERLEY. You know whom I want for myself!

MRS. JASPER. (*Getting settled at her letters.*) Ah, don't make love to me!

COVERLEY. You're clever, you're ingenious, you're sympathetic, you're benevolent.

MRS. JASPER. Don't—I beseech you!

COVERLEY. Therefore you must interfere.

MRS. JASPER. Do you call that benevolent?

COVERLEY. It would be to me.

MRS. JASPER. What have you to do with it?

COVERLEY. Everything!

MRS. JASPER. (*Blank, writing.*) Everything?

COVERLEY. More than enough for remorse. I drove him to it, I made him believe it was his duty.

MRS. JASPER. (*Gay.*) Well, perhaps it was!

COVERLEY. I'll be hanged if it was!

MRS. JASPER. Then why did you tell him so?

COVERLEY. To please *you*—to make you like me.

MRS. JASPER. It does nothing of the sort!

COVERLEY. Of course it doesn't—it can't! (*Desperately.*) Therefore you must just undo my work.

MRS. JASPER. Thank you—I must do my own!

COVERLEY. You must invent something; you must help me.

MRS. JASPER. (*After an instant.*) I must simply understand you—first!

COVERLEY. It happened last evening, after you and Sir Montagu went home. Trafford and I were there with the deluded being, and we convinced him that by their long dawdle at the ruins, after dark, you know, he had fatally compromised that girl.

MRS. JASPER. (*Astonished, amused.*) Compromised Blandina? What a funny idea!

COVERLEY. So it seemed to me then; but in this morning's light—the cold, hard light of reality—it's simply dreadful. You told me to talk to Trafford, to get him to go away. I obeyed your commands, and he promised me he'd go if I would help him to pacify Mrs. Wigmore, who, as you know, has more than suspected his flirtation with her sister-in-law. The way to pacify her was to bribe her, and the way to bribe her was to make the poor Captain propose to her daughter. Trafford gave me his word he would go if I would bring on this event. I had only your wishes in mind; so, in spite of the difficulty, which was immense, I did bring it on.

MRS. JASPER. But Mr. Trafford hasn't gone.

COVERLEY. That's *his* look-out! I exerted myself.

MRS. JASPER. To what purpose, pray, since, within the hour, he was to expose poor Amy to such comments?

COVERLEY. The comments are your affair, if you helped to make them. I only went too far for you.

MRS. JASPER. Yes (*impatiently, looking over her papers*) how could you be such a noodle?

COVERLEY. An opprobrious name is all my thanks?

MRS. JASPER. You must look for your thanks to Blandina.

COVERLEY. Blandina be dashed! In a moment of criminal aberration I've sacrificed my innocent friend.

MRS. JASPER. How could *he* be such a noodle?

COVERLEY. He isn't a noodle, he's a snow-white lamb. You should have seen him when he fixed his blue eyes on me and bleated: "For my honour, for hers, must I?"

MRS. JASPER. The honour of a lamb—it's too lovely!

COVERLEY. I feel as if I'd sent him to the butcher.

MRS. JASPER. Your comparison is rude to Blandina. She's an estimable girl.

COVERLEY. She isn't a girl, she's a parrot. The Captain loathes her.

MRS. JASPER. Then how could he attach her for life?

COVERLEY. Because he's a hero.

MRS. JASPER. To be eaten with mint-sauce? He should be kept at least for mutton!

COVERLEY. We must save him, we must get him off. And *you* must find a way.

MRS. JASPER. (*Taking up her pen again.*) I've no time; I've my letters to write.

COVERLEY. Yesterday you asked me a favour; to-day I ask *you* one.

MRS. JASPER. Ah, they're not equal!

COVERLEY. This one's the easiest. You wanted me to interfere for Lady Brisket, who's a silly woman. I want you to interfere for Llewellyn Prime, who's a brave man.

MRS. JASPER. (*After an instant.*) If he's so awfully brave why don't you leave him to his fate?

COVERLEY. Because his fate's horrid and his character noble.

MRS. JASPER. (*Rising after an instant; then by degrees quitting the table.*) Is he so extraordinarily nice?

COVERLEY. You've seen him yourself.

MRS. JASPER. Only a few times.

COVERLEY. Then don't you like him?

MRS. JASPER. (*After an instant.*) Yes, he lets me alone! (*After another moment.*) He must be quite original.

COVERLEY. To let you alone? I should think so!

MRS. JASPER. No, I mean with his fastidious sense of honour. Most men have none at all.

COVERLEY. He's different from most men; he's a *preux chevalier,* a knight of romance.

MRS. JASPER. I see, he's a type. I'm rather interested in types. (*After an instant.*) Why don't you go to him and tell him frankly you made a fool of him?

COVERLEY. That would only commit me the more to save him.

MRS. JASPER. Let alone that he might knock you down! Then go to Blandina.

COVERLEY. Who in that case would save *me?*

MRS. JASPER. Go to Mrs. Wigmore.

COVERLEY. (*Seeing* MRS. WIGMORE.) I needn't.

(*Re-enter* MRS. WIGMORE *for the Red Room.*)

MRS. WIGMORE. (*Who has paused a moment, sternly and suspiciously, at the sight of the others, and then advanced majestically, passing in front of them and looking at them up and down.*) Excuse me.

MRS. JASPER. (*Gay, going back to her table.*) Don't mention it!

MRS. WIGMORE. I left Lady Brisket here, and I left Mr. Trafford.

COVERLEY. (*Irritated at the interruption; as* MRS. WIGMORE *looks round.*) They're not under the sofa!

MRS. WIGMORE. May I presume to inquire what has become of them?

MRS. JASPER. I happen to know that Amy's in the library.

MRS. WIGMORE. Alone?

MRS. JASPER. Alone. (*Then, as* MRS. WIGMORE *stands looking at her searchingly, as if to challenge this statement.*) If you don't believe me, you can go and see.

MRS. WIGMORE. (*Back at the door of the Red Room.*) I never impose an unappreciated presence. (*Exit* MRS. WIGMORE.)

MRS. JASPER. (*Laughing.*) Delicacy! (*Coming down again.*) Poor Captain Prime —I do pity him.

COVERLEY. Then for pity's sake be suggestive, be inspired! Find some way to get him off.

MRS. JASPER. (*Abrupt; after a moment's thought.*) Where's Mr. Trafford?

COVERLEY. (*Disconcerted, impatient.*) What has *he* got to do with it?

MRS. JASPER. You promised you'd take him away.

COVERLEY. Oh yes, I'll take him! Give me time.

MRS. JASPER. That policeman in petticoats will pull down the house.

COVERLEY. I'll take him to-morrow.

MRS. JASPER. You must take him to-day.

COVERLEY. To-day I must save the Captain.

MRS. JASPER. (*Abrupt again; after another moment's quick, intense meditation.*) Mr. Coverley, I'll tell you what I'll do. If you'll save Amy, *I*'ll save the Captain!

COVERLEY. (*Vague.*) How can *I* save Amy?

MRS. JASPER. Take Mr. Trafford back to his post.

COVERLEY. "Take" him—all the way?

MRS. JASPER. Put him on the ship.

COVERLEY. You don't go to Copenhagen on a ship.

MRS. JASPER. Well, whatever you do go on! And book his luggage through.

COVERLEY. Very good—to-night.

MRS. JASPER. Don't wait till to-night; do it to-day. Do it this morning; do it this minute. Lay hands on him; push him off!

COVERLEY. (*Encouraged but bargaining.*) And if I do, you'll rescue my victim?

MRS. JASPER. I'm not a shepherdess, but I'll do what I can for the blue-eyed lamb.

COVERLEY. Ah, don't laugh at him!

MRS. JASPER. I mean for the knight of romance.

COVERLEY. I shall love you still better.

MRS. JASPER. That's a circumstance that rather takes it out of me.

COVERLEY. Oh, I shall be quiet! But how will you operate?

MRS. JASPER. I must think it over; I shall find a way.

COVERLEY. (*Participating.*) Yes, why else

should you be so clever? It will be my right to worship you, as it will be my occupation to reward.—I'll go to the inn; I'll catch hold of Trafford.

MRS. JASPER. Go quickly!

COVERLEY. I'll pack him off, and I'll come back and tell you.

MRS. JASPER. You needn't come back.

COVERLEY. (*Going up.*) How else shall I see how you're getting on?

MRS. JASPER. Before you go, at any rate, tell me this. Is he absolutely (*after a pause*) all you say?

COVERLEY. He's only too much of a gentleman. That's why he put himself out.

MRS. JASPER. But he must be strangely simple.

COVERLEY. He's not too simple to suffer.

MRS. JASPER. (*After an instant.*) He mustn't suffer!

COVERLEY. (*At the door to the court.*) He mustn't, exactly! If he wasn't such a good sort I shouldn't care. (*Exit* COVERLEY *to the court.*)

MRS. JASPER. (*Alone.*) Neither should I! (*Going to the table, shuffling her letters together and putting them into her pocket.*) My correspondence is nipped in the bud. (*Coming down, uncertain, and continuing to turn over* COVERLEY's *appeal in her mind.*) He must indeed be a knight of romance; he must indeed be a gentleman. And if he's simple, I like simple people. Well, if I'm to find a way, where shall I find it? Oughtn't I to converse with him first, to sound him, to observe him? Yes, that's the right beginning. But how can I converse with him under Mrs. Wigmore's guns?

(*Re-enter* LADY BRISKET *from the library, with a sealed and directed letter.*)

LADY BRISKET. I've written my letter, and it may relieve your solicitude to know that it's to Mr. Trafford.

MRS. JASPER. Has he already gone away?

LADY BRISKET. No, but he's going.

MRS. JASPER. You're taking time by the forelock.

LADY BRISKET. Montagu ordered me to write.

MRS. JASPER. You've just missed an opportunity to send your letter; Mr. Coverley would have taken it.

LADY BRISKET. It doesn't matter; I mean to give it myself.

MRS. JASPER. You'll surely not see Mr. Trafford again?

LADY BRISKET. He's coming to bid me good-bye.

MRS. JASPER. I beseech you not to permit it!

LADY BRISKET. Not when he's going so far?

MRS. JASPER. How far?

LADY BRISKET. (*After an hesitation.*) To Copenhagen.

MRS. JASPER. Direct?

LADY BRISKET. You must get the details from Mr. Trafford.

MRS. JASPER. Let me *have* your letter then; I'll give it to him.

LADY BRISKET. After you've shown it to Montagu for approval?

MRS. JASPER. (*After an instant.*) My poor dear, you're in a bad way!

LADY BRISKET. Do you mean that you'll tell him of our meeting? (*As* MRS. JASPER *hesitates a moment.*) You'll have plenty of opportunities.

MRS. JASPER. I don't think you know what you say.

LADY BRISKET. I know, for the most part, what *you* say; and that will do as well.

MRS. JASPER. It will do best of all, I think, that I should bring my visit to a close.

LADY BRISKET. So that I shall appear to have been rude to you?

MRS. JASPER. You wouldn't be if you understood me a little better.

LADY BRISKET. You make me feel then that in losing your company—

MRS. JASPER. You lose that opportunity? We'll wait for a better one and I'll go as soon as possible.

LADY BRISKET. Are you sure Montagu will consent?

MRS. JASPER. (*Up at the window.*) Here he comes. (*Smiling, coming down.*) I can ask him!

LADY BRISKET. (*At the door to the stairs.*) Remind him that he can follow you! (*Exit* LADY BRISKET *to the stairs.*)

MRS. JASPER. (*Alone, struck.*) He *may* follow me; it's an awful thought. (*Think-ing.*) But it's the smaller risk; I'll fly. (*Then suddenly checked, thinking again.*) Dear me, if I fly, what will become of the snow-white lamb? Shall I forsake him? (*After another pause.*) No, I won't forsake him; I'll first see him. (*Re-enter* SIR MONTAGU *from the court.*) Have you been to ride?

SIR MONTAGU. Only a mile. I didn't enjoy it; I came back to see you.

MRS. JASPER. If you had been good enough to go another mile I might have got away.

SIR MONTAGU. (*Vague.*) Away where?

MRS. JASPER. I'm bringing my visit to a close.

SIR MONTAGU. (*Indignant.*) What folly! When?

MRS. JASPER. As soon as I've made my preparations.

SIR MONTAGU. Your principal preparation will be to reconcile your host to the idea, and that will take at least a week.

MRS. JASPER. I've stayed a week too long. You know my reason.

SIR MONTAGU. Your reason for having stayed, of course!

MRS. JASPER. My reason for going now.

SIR MONTAGU. (*Horrified.*) This morning?

MRS. JASPER. In an hour or two. You've your own behaviour to thank.

SIR MONTAGU. (*Pleading.*) Remain to abuse it—if you'll only remain!

MRS. JASPER. I've much more interesting work in hand, and the foolish advantage you try to find in my presence only gives Amy an excuse more foolish still.

SIR MONTAGU. (*Suspicious, scandalised.*) Has Amy been capable of a failure of courtesy?

MRS. JASPER. Amy's failures don't signify, but there might be much to say about some of yours. You take exactly the wrong way with her.

SIR MONTAGU. Stay to show me the right one!

MRS. JASPER. You should be the first to be faultless.

SIR MONTAGU. Let me study you as a model for that!

MRS. JASPER. Study me at a distance. It's forty miles, thank heaven, to London!

SIR MONTAGU. Are you going home?

(After an instant, with decision.) I'll come up for your advice!

MRS. JASPER. *(Weary, sad.)* I've no more to give you. You've worn out your pretext!

SIR MONTAGU. It has not *been* a pretext, Mrs. Jasper. *(After an instant.)* I swear that I love my wife!

MRS. JASPER. Do you think I would have staid here three days if I didn't know it? She loves you too, and that's why you so ingeniously torment each other. But you must do so without my help, and *(gently, but very firmly)* this conversation, please, must end.

SIR MONTAGU. Won't you see me before you go?

MRS. JASPER. *(After an instant.)* Yes, if you'll do me a service. *(Indicating the Red Room.)* Go and take Blandina out.

SIR MONTAGU. *(Vague.)* Out where?

MRS. JASPER. Into the garden—for a little talk.

SIR MONTAGU. *(Blank.)* Can Blandina talk?

MRS. JASPER. No, but you know *you* can!

SIR MONTAGU. What about?

MRS. JASPER. Your favourite subject, the duties of a wife. You might change it to-day for the duties of a husband!

SIR MONTAGU. *(At the door of the Red Room.)* I shall not at least neglect the duties of a host! *(Exit SIR MONTAGU.)*

MRS. JASPER. *(Alone.)* You exaggerate them! *(Then thoughtful.)* Cruel to dash the cup from Blandina's lips! But I won't let her die of thirst. *(With an irrepressible start, as PRIME reappears.)* Heavens! *(Enter CAPTAIN PRIME from the Red Room.)* Are you ill?

PRIME. *(Pale, constrained, agitated.)* I'm not particularly well.

MRS. JASPER. *(With genuine concern.)* You look quite emaciated!

PRIME. I daresay I *have* lost weight.

MRS. JASPER. Since yesterday? You must get it back!

PRIME. I don't miss it—I feel heavy enough.

MRS. JASPER. I promised Mr. Coverley I would speak to you.

PRIME. Your voice will be a blessed change.

MRS. JASPER. *(Smiling.)* Are you already tired of matrimony?

PRIME. I feel as if I had been married ten years!

MRS. JASPER. Then I'm a little late to congratulate you. It was for that I asked to see you.

PRIME. Don't you remember that you congratulated me yesterday?

MRS. JASPER. *(Remembering.)* So I did! You see I keep at it.

PRIME. Do keep at it, Mrs. Jasper—it prevents any one else. *(Then as if uneasily hearing a sound from the Red Room.)* There *is* some one.

MRS. JASPER. *(Listening.)* Blandina?

PRIME. *(Comforted.)* No—*she's* gone out.

MRS. JASPER. She'll be back in time.

PRIME. For the day? It isn't fixed. *(Then with another start of anxiety.)* Won't Mrs. Wigmore come?

MRS. JASPER. To fix it? If she does I'll protect you!

PRIME. *(Rueful.)* You should have protected me yesterday.

MRS. JASPER. Alas, I was taken up!

PRIME. Of course you're in high demand.

MRS. JASPER. Yes—people seem to want me.

PRIME. I hope no one will want you now.

MRS. JASPER. *(After an instant.)* I shan't care if they do! *(After another instant.)* I can deal with them!

PRIME. Oh, yes—you have your resources!

MRS. JASPER. *(Laughing.)* The resources of the hunted animal!

PRIME. *(With eager sympathy.)* Are *you* hunted too?

MRS. JASPER. All the year round!

PRIME. But you told me about your refuge.

MRS. JASPER. My sketching? Oh, I've a better refuge than that!

PRIME. *(With intense curiosity.)* What is it?

MRS. JASPER. My indifference!

PRIME. Ah, I've tried indifference; but it isn't enough!

MRS. JASPER. *(Thinking, conceding.)* No, it isn't exactly a regular occupation. It isn't, after all, absorbing.

PRIME. I want to be absorbed—I want something to take hold of!

MRS. JASPER. Take hold *(vaguely)* take

hold—! (*Suddenly checking herself.*)
PRIME. (*All attention.*) Yes?
MRS. JASPER. (*To herself, turning away.*)
I really can't tell him to take hold of *me!*—
Isn't your profession an occupation?
PRIME. Only in the sense of being an
exposure!
MRS. JASPER. (*Reflecting.*) Well, we must
find something. Something very safe.
PRIME. There can be nothing so safe as
a quiet corner and a box of water-col-
ours.
MRS. JASPER. (*Thoughtful.*) Yes, they're
a kind of burrow!
PRIME. A burrow is what I require.
MRS. JASPER. I see. (*Then after an in-
stant.*) You must come down into mine!
PRIME. (*Earnest.*) Is there room in it for
two?
MRS. JASPER. (*Smiling.*) With mutual ac-
commodation! I'll give you lessons.
PRIME. (*Delighted, eager.*) Will you give
me one now?
MRS. JASPER. (*Suddenly embarrassed.*)
Now?
PRIME. It's the time of all times!
MRS. JASPER. (*Disconcerted.*) The time
I'm going away?
PRIME. (*Alarmed.*) Away? (*Then with de-
cision.*) All you've got to do is to wait!
MRS. JASPER. (*After a moment.*) I *will*
wait—just to begin. We must therefore
begin immediately. If you'll excuse me,
I'll go and get our materials.
PRIME. Don't be long!
MRS. JASPER. (*Gay, at the door to the
stairs.*) Don't run away! (*Exit MRS. JASPER.*)
PRIME. (*Alone.*) Never from *you!* (*Then
as MRS. WIGMORE reappears.*) Caught!
          (*Re-enter MRS. WIGMORE from the
          Red Room.*)
MRS. WIGMORE. (*Struck, staring.*) Pray,
where's Blandina?
PRIME. Sir Montagu took her out.
MRS. WIGMORE. Out where?
PRIME. I haven't the least idea.
MRS. WIGMORE. It's a point on which, in
your position, you ought to be perfectly
clear.
PRIME. I've a general confidence in un-
cles.
MRS. WIGMORE. I haven't any confidence
in anybody!

          (*Re-enter CHARLES COVERLEY
          from the court.*)
COVERLEY. (*To MRS. WIGMORE.*) Have
you seen Mrs. Jasper?
MRS. WIGMORE. I'm not her keeper!
COVERLEY. (*Reaching PRIME.*) Have *you*
seen Mrs. Jasper?
PRIME. Here she is!
          (*Re-enter from the stairs MRS.
          JASPER, with a box of water-colour
          paints and a sketching-block.*)
COVERLEY. (*Rushing to her while MRS.
WIGMORE confines her observation to
PRIME, who assumes an attitude of extreme
innocence and detachment.*) Have you
found the way?
MRS. JASPER. I'm looking for it.
COVERLEY. Trafford's packing—he'll
catch the 1.20.
MRS. JASPER. Hurry him then—precipi-
tate him!
COVERLEY. I will. But if I could only
precipitate *you!*
MRS. JASPER. You can do so by leaving
me alone.
COVERLEY. I'll come back. The 1.20!
(*Exit COVERLEY with all speed, saluting the
other two, to the court.*)
MRS. WIGMORE. (*To MRS. JASPER.*) Do
you happen to know the occasion of my
daughter's incongruous absence?
MRS. JASPER. A lecture from her uncle.
MRS. WIGMORE. (*Blank.*) Hasn't she a
mother to lecture her?
MRS. JASPER. She's taking a course! (*To
PRIME.*) I think we shall do best in the
library.
PRIME. Let *me* carry your things!
(*Springs forward, but is arrested by the
instant interposition of MRS. WIGMORE,
who challenges him with a stony stare, so
that he falls back abashed and even
alarmed.*)
MRS. WIGMORE. (*To MRS. JASPER.*) What
are you doing with that young man?
MRS. JASPER. Giving him a lesson in
sketching.
MRS. WIGMORE. And what is your pretext for so extraordinary a proceeding?
MRS. JASPER. (*After an instant.*) To keep
him from running away! (*Exit MRS. JASPER
to the library, while PRIME hurries after
her, running the gauntlet of MRS. WIG-*

MORE'S *continued reprobation.*)

(*Re-enter* LADY BRISKET *from the stairs.*)

MRS. WIGMORE. What is she doing with him?

LADY BRISKET. (*Who has seen the others go out; reckless.*) Making love to him!

MRS. WIGMORE. (*Aghast.*) And who's making love to Blandina?

LADY BRISKET. (*After an instant.*) Nobody!

MRS. WIGMORE. (*With indignant energy.*) I'll bring her back! (*Exit* MRS. WIGMORE *to the court.*)

LADY BRISKET. (*Alone.*) Our subservience was a false calculation—I've ceased to grovel! (*Seeing* TRAFFORD.) Oh, you impossible man!

(*Re-enter* PERCY TRAFFORD *from the Red Room, looking in cautiously first, then closing the door noiselessly behind him.*)

TRAFFORD. I came in by the glass doors—Coverley's at my heels.

LADY BRISKET. (*Vague.*) What does he want of you?

TRAFFORD. To take me to the station.

LADY BRISKET. What concern is it of his?

TRAFFORD. To please Mrs. Jasper.

LADY BRISKET. What concern is it of hers?

TRAFFORD. She disapproves of our friendship.

LADY BRISKET. So she has done me the honour to tell me!

TRAFFORD. She interferes too much!

LADY BRISKET. Much too much! She has grabbed the Captain.

TRAFFORD. (*Surprised.*) Grabbed him?

LADY BRISKET. (*Nodding at the library.*) In there. She knows we favour his marriage.

TRAFFORD. We do—for all the good it does us!

LADY BRISKET. Little enough—so she needn't try to make it less.

TRAFFORD. Dear lady, in what difficulties I leave you!

LADY BRISKET. They may subside—Mrs. Jasper goes.

TRAFFORD. (*Struck.*) Goes! (*With irrepressible curiosity.*) By my train?

LADY BRISKET. Which is your train?

TRAFFORD. The next—the 1.20.

LADY BRISKET. She has just set her maid to pack; she may catch it.

TRAFFORD. (*Appreciative, inadvertent.*) Oh, that'll be— (*Then in a suddenly changed tone, with a feigned grimace, seeing that he has excited* LADY BRISKET'S *attention.*) That'll be a horrid bore!

LADY BRISKET. You'll not be under the least obligation to talk to her. (*Producing her letter.*) You can confine your attention to this.

TRAFFORD. (*With the letter.*) What is it?

LADY BRISKET. A few pages of farewell.

TRAFFORD. (*Putting the letter with decision into his pocket.*) I'll not read them.

LADY BRISKET. (*Mistrustful.*) You'll prefer then Mrs. Jasper's conversation?

TRAFFORD. (*With energy.*) Never! I'll get into another carriage, and think only of the day you'll come up.

LADY BRISKET. That day shall not dawn. When she has gone I shall feel less aggravated.

TRAFFORD. Why *should* she go, if she's making up to Prime?

LADY BRISKET. I shan't care, if she stays for that.

TRAFFORD. Won't your husband care? (*Then as* LADY BRISKET *seems struck.*) That'll stir up Sir Montagu!

LADY BRISKET. Perhaps that's why she does it!

TRAFFORD. Then he'll keep her on.

LADY BRISKET. (*Still more impressed.*) If he keeps her on— (*Hesitating.*)

TRAFFORD. (*Pressing, expectant.*) You'll come up?

LADY BRISKET. (*After an instant.*) I'll come up! (*Then up at the window, alarmed.*) Here's Flora! (*Coming down.*) Go *that* way! (*Pushes him hurriedly to the door of the Red Room, thrusts him out and closes the door.*)

(*Re-enter from the court, the moment she has done so,* MRS. WIGMORE *and* BLANDINA. MRS. WIGMORE *marches down to the right, followed submissively by* BLANDINA, *who wears her garden hat, and majestically opens the door of the library.*)

MRS. WIGMORE. (*Commanding.*) Go in there!

BLANDINA. (*As her mother gives her a smart push.*) Yes, mamma. (*Exit* BLANDINA *to the library.*)

MRS. WIGMORE. (*Triumphantly facing about.*) There!

LADY BRISKET. You may be interested to know that Mr. Trafford has taken leave of us; he's starting for Copenhagen.

MRS. WIGMORE. In charge of whom?

LADY BRISKET. (*Seeing* COVERLEY.) Of Mr. Coverley.

> (*Re-enter* CHARLES COVERLEY *from the court.*)

COVERLEY. (*Still breathless, coming down to* LADY BRISKET.) Have you seen Mrs. Jasper?

LADY BRISKET. She's leaving the house. (*Exit* LADY BRISKET *to the stairs.*)

MRS. WIGMORE. She hasn't left it yet. (*Indicating the library.*) She's in there.

COVERLEY. (*Anxious.*) Is she going?

MRS. WIGMORE. She *has* to! (*Then with exultation, as* MRS. JASPER *reappears.*) See? (*Re-enter* MRS. JASPER *from the library. Derisive.*) May I inquire how the sketching comes on?

MRS. JASPER. (*Gay.*) Beautifully. He's copying hard.

MRS. WIGMORE. (*Disconcerted.*) Copying?

MRS. JASPER. A little thing of mine.

MRS. WIGMORE. (*Blank.*) And what's Blandina doing?

MRS. JASPER. (*Laughing.*) Go and see! (*Exit* MRS. WIGMORE *quickly to the library.*)

COVERLEY. You don't mean to say you're going?

MRS. JASPER. Yes, Mr. Coverley, I'm going.

COVERLEY. Then have you found the way?

MRS. JASPER. (*After an instant.*) Patience!

COVERLEY. Preach that to Prime! You surely won't go till you've thrown him a rope.

MRS. JASPER. Ropes are tangled things, and unfortunately my hour has struck.

COVERLEY. Ah, but you must save him first!

MRS. JASPER. (*Thoughtful, conceding.*) Yes, I must save him first. (*After an instant.*) You see it's awfully hard.

COVERLEY. That's just why I asked you.

If it wasn't I could do it myself!

MRS. JASPER. (*Still thoughtful.*) I daresay it will come to me.

COVERLEY. (*Urgent.*) And you'll wait till it does come?

MRS. JASPER. (*After an instant.*) I'll wait! (*In a different tone, with movement.*) But don't *you* wait. You've to catch the 1.20.

COVERLEY. With Trafford, yes. But he has given me the slip.

MRS. JASPER. (*Impatient.*) Look for him, then.

COVERLEY. (*Vague, helpless.*) I am looking!

MRS. JASPER. (*Waving him off.*) Don't look here; look somewhere else. (*Then as* COVERLEY *reaches the door.*) Don't stop half-way!

COVERLEY. (*At the door to the court; imperative.*) Don't *you*! (*Exit* COVERLEY.)

MRS. JASPER. (*Alone.*) How can I? (*As* PRIME *reappears.*) He has recovered flesh!

> (*Re-enter* CAPTAIN PRIME *from the library, with a sketching-block covered with a water-colour drawing.*)

PRIME. (*At the right, smiling at* MRS. JASPER *and holding the drawing, rather shyly and awkwardly, with its face against his breast.*) I came to show you my copy.

MRS. JASPER. (*With concern.*) Ah, don't smudge it! (*Meeting him and taking the drawing from him.*) Why, it's charming!

PRIME. It's consoling.

MRS. JASPER. (*Looking at his work with her head inclined.*) You've a serious talent.

PRIME. It *is* a refuge!

MRS. JASPER. You see there's room for two.

PRIME. I don't incommode you?

MRS. JASPER. I can turn round! The sky only wants a little lighting up.

PRIME. (*Eager, taking back his drawing.*) I'll light it up. (*Exit* PRIME *to the library.*)

MRS. JASPER. (*Alone.*) What a gift!

> (*Re-enter* SIR MONTAGU *from the court.*)

SIR MONTAGU. I purchased the right to see you again by taking Blandina out.

MRS. JASPER. Then I suppose I may take advantage of it to tell you that Mr. Trafford's fairly off. Mr. Coverley's dragging him.

SIR MONTAGU. And who's dragging Mr. Coverley? (*As she hesitates, embarrassed for an answer.*) You see it isn't so simple. What has become of Amy?

MRS. JASPER. (*Seeing* LADY BRISKET.) Here she is—leave us.
  (*Re-enter* LADY BRISKET *from the stairs.*)

SIR MONTAGU. (*To his wife.*) I'm trying to induce Mrs. Jasper to reconsider her departure. Please add your voice. (*Exit* SIR MONTAGU *by the vestibule.*)

MRS. JASPER. Don't take that trouble. Any extension I may be guilty of shall be studiously short.

LADY BRISKET. You really mustn't speak as if I were turning you out of the house! I came back here to tell you that I'm sorry I forgot myself.

MRS. JASPER. (*Gay, goodhumoured.*) We mustn't be sorry for anything whatever; we must only rejoice.

LADY BRISKET. (*Cold.*) I confess I don't see what there is to rejoice at!

MRS. JASPER. Why, everything is turning out so well! (*Disconcerted, as* LADY BRISKET *has stared, puzzled and suspicious, and she herself sees* TRAFFORD *at the door of the Red Room; then to herself.*) Ah, no, it isn't; here he is again! (*Re-enter* TRAFFORD *from the Red Room. Severely.*) Mr. Trafford, Mr. Coverley's looking for you.

TRAFFORD. I've been in and out that way (*indicating the Red Room*) looking for Mr. Coverley.

LADY BRISKET. (*Seeing* COVERLEY.) Here he is!
  (*Re-enter* CHARLES COVERLEY *from the court.*)

MRS. JASPER. (*Privately to* COVERLEY.) Now seize him!

TRAFFORD. (*Having eluded* COVERLEY'S *attempt; to* MRS. JASPER.) I only looked in to see if I'm not to have the pleasure of your company.

MRS. JASPER. Thank you—I'm waiting over.

COVERLEY. (*To* MRS. JASPER, *anxious.*) It hasn't come to you?

MRS. JASPER. Be careful! (*Goes up with him, quieting him, while* TRAFFORD *hurries to* LADY BRISKET.)

TRAFFORD. That's what I came back to hear.

LADY BRISKET. It's for Montagu!

TRAFFORD. It's for Montagu. So you'll come up?

LADY BRISKET. (*With resolution.*) I'll come up. (*Exit* LADY BRISKET *to the stairs.*)

MRS. JASPER. (*Coming down.*) To Copenhagen, Mr. Trafford!

TRAFFORD. To Copenhagen!

COVERLEY. (*With enthusiasm, seizing* TRAFFORD *by the arm.*) To Copenhagen! (*Exeunt* COVERLEY *and* TRAFFORD *arm in arm to the court.*)
  (*Re-enter* CAPTAIN PRIME *from the library.*)

PRIME. (*With his copy.*) Is that a little better?

MRS. JASPER. (*Taking it.*) Ever so much —you're making strides.

PRIME. You're a wonderful teacher.

MRS. JASPER. You're a delightful pupil.

PRIME. (*Taking back his drawing.*) May I have another lesson to-morrow?

MRS. JASPER. Here, do you mean?

PRIME. I must come here, you know: I'm engaged.

MRS. JASPER. Oh, yes; I forgot you're engaged!

PRIME. So did I, but I am!

MRS. JASPER. (*Thoughtful before she commits herself.*) Oh, yes, you are!

PRIME. (*Abruptly, after a moment during which he has gazed at her fondly.*) Mrs. Jasper, I should come back even if I wasn't!

MRS. JASPER. (*Smiling.*) For more instruction?

PRIME. I should like to learn *all* you can teach me.

MRS. JASPER. You exaggerate my acquirements.

PRIME. It's not only your acquirements; it's your natural gifts!

MRS. JASPER. Your extravagant faith in me makes me feel rather a humbug.

PRIME. (*Pleading.*) Ah, don't be *that*— be straight with me!

MRS. JASPER. (*To herself, enthusiastic.*) He *is* a lamb!

PRIME. (*Sadly shaking his head.*) There's no glory in trying things on me: it's too easy!

MRS. JASPER. You're candid, you're generous.

PRIME. (*With touching simplicity.*) I take people at their word.

MRS. JASPER. (*After an instant.*) You're splendidly simple.

PRIME. (*Attenuating with another sad headshake.*) Oh, "splendidly"!

MRS. JASPER. That's the sort of nature I like.

PRIME. I'm certainly not brilliant, and *I* like brilliancy.

MRS. JASPER. (*After another instant.*) You'll find it in Miss Wigmore.

PRIME. (*Abrupt.*) Mrs. Jasper, I don't require Miss Wigmore.

MRS. JASPER. (*Laughing.*) You speak as if she were a doctor—or a cab!

PRIME. May I be very frank with you?

MRS. JASPER. Surely, when in half-an-hour we've become such friends.

PRIME. The best half-hour of my life. Misfortune draws people together.

MRS. JASPER. (*Smiling.*) I'm not conscious of misfortune!

PRIME. Heaven forgive me, *I* am! (*Seizing her arm.*) Hush!

MRS. JASPER. What's the matter?

PRIME. (*Looking toward the library.*) Are they coming?

MRS. JASPER. (*As he listens nearer the door.*) I think not.

PRIME. (*Coming back.*) I think not. Mrs. Jasper, I don't want Miss Wigmore. (*Intensely confidential.*) I don't love Miss Wigmore.

MRS. JASPER. (*Demurring.*) Not just a little?

PRIME. (*Making a clean breast of it.*) Mrs. Jasper, I hate Miss Wigmore!

MRS. JASPER. Then how do you come to be engaged to her?

PRIME. Why, she said she'd marry me.

MRS. JASPER. But you asked her, at least!

PRIME. Oh, yes—they told me I *had* to.

MRS. JASPER. Who told you?

PRIME. Two men of the world—Coverley and Trafford.

MRS. JASPER. Coverley and Trafford are busy-bodies!

PRIME. Then I needn't, I mustn't? (*Grasping her arm once more.*) Must I, Mrs. Jasper—*must* I?

MRS. JASPER. Do you mean if there's any way out of it?

PRIME. *Is* there? Can you discover one?

MRS. JASPER. I'll try, if you like.

PRIME. You restore me to life. Let me try *with* you!

MRS. JASPER. You must give me time!

PRIME. Do you mean till to-morrow?

MRS. JASPER. To-morrow's too soon—I mean it's too late!

PRIME. (*Frightened.*) Too late?

MRS. JASPER. (*Confused, agitated.*) I don't know *what* I mean!

PRIME. It will be all right if we try together.

MRS. JASPER. We mustn't try together—we must try apart! So now you must leave me.

PRIME. (*Reluctant.*) Give you up?

MRS. JASPER. Leave the house—leave me to think!

PRIME. Think—think hard. But let me come back for my lesson.

MRS. JASPER. To-morrow? The difficulty is that I'm (*after an instant*) going away.

PRIME. (*Aghast.*) And giving me up?

MRS. JASPER. (*Embarrassed.*) I must give you up some time!

PRIME. Grant me a day, at least!

MRS. JASPER. (*After an instant.*) Well—a day! (*Then with a smile, giving him her hand.*) But only for your lesson!

PRIME. (*Holding her hand.*) You've made me want doubly to be free! (*As she quickly withdraws her hand, turning away from him.*) Because now I know what I should do with my freedom!

MRS. JASPER. (*Going up and round.*) Go, go—I want to be alone!

PRIME. (*Taking up his hat and gloves.*) I shall come early to-morrow.

MRS. JASPER. But you must say good-bye to Miss Wigmore.

PRIME. (*Disconcerted.*) *Must* I do that?

MRS. JASPER. Oh, yes, you must do that! (PRIME *smites his forehead in the same way as when dashing into the house at the end of Act First. Exit* PRIME *to the library.*) He's not a child—he's a man! I admire him; I like him; I—a-ah! (*Checks herself with an ejaculation which is half a burst of mirth, half a gasp of dismay, and, sinking into the nearest chair, covers her face with her hands.*)

(*Re-enter* CHARLES COVERLEY *from the court.*)

COVERLEY. (*In suspense.*) Has it arrived?

MRS. JASPER. (*Startled, jumping up.*) It's on its way! You didn't go with Mr. Trafford?

COVERLEY. I put him in the fly.

MRS. JASPER. Then I don't want you any more.

COVERLEY. Just when I want *you* most?

MRS. JASPER. (*Nervous, irritated, moving away from him.*) What do you want of me?

COVERLEY. To thank you for all you're doing for me.

MRS. JASPER. Don't thank me yet!

COVERLEY. I see—you're in the fever of invention.

MRS. JASPER. I'm in the fever of invention.

COVERLEY. And where's the Captain?

MRS. JASPER. (*Indicating the library.*) In there—but he's coming back: you mustn't meet him.

COVERLEY. Mustn't meet him?

MRS. JASPER. He suffers so!

COVERLEY. (*Rueful.*) Oh, if he suffers so—!

MRS. JASPER. He's going in a moment. (*As the door of the library opens.*) Here he comes—pass in there! (*She pushes* COVERLEY *toward the Red Room, opens the door, thrusts him in and closes it; then turns to meet* CAPTAIN PRIME, *who has come out of the library.*)

PRIME. (*Agitated, rebellious, distracted.*) I can't keep it up, you know, Mrs. Jasper; I really can't!

MRS. JASPER. You must, a few days—to gain time!

PRIME. To lose it, you mean! Why go so far?

MRS. JASPER. (*Her own emotion increasing.*) Why indeed did you? You've gone too far!

PRIME. That's just what I feel!

MRS. JASPER. Too far to retreat, I mean. Therefore you must advance!

PRIME. (*Pleading.*) To my destruction?

MRS. JASPER. We'll avert your destruction! Trust to your star; something will turn up!

PRIME. That's the difficulty—that *you're* my star! Something *has* turned up.

MRS. JASPER. (*Ardently.*) It has—it has: it will turn up again!

PRIME. The more it turns up the less I can advance! How can I be "engaged" when I love another woman?

MRS. JASPER. (*Startled and embarrassed by this new complication.*) Do you love another woman?

PRIME. (*Breaking out.*) Mrs. Jasper—I love *you!*

MRS. JASPER. (*With alarm.*) Don't utter it! (*Waving him away.*) Go—fly!

PRIME. (*Following her as she flies before him.*) Mrs. Jasper, I adore you!

MRS. JASPER. (*Holding him in check.*) You *can't*—not yet!

PRIME. When *can* I then? Tell me when!

MRS. JASPER. I must look about me—I must see!

PRIME. You'll tell me to-morrow?

MRS. JASPER. To-morrow.

PRIME. You won't put me off?

MRS. JASPER. (*At the end of her patience, driving him up to the left.*) Not if you'll go!

PRIME. (*Resisting.*) Do you like me?

MRS. JASPER. (*To get him off.*) I like you!

PRIME. (*Holding his ground.*) Would you marry me?

MRS. JASPER. (*Continuing to push him off.*) I'll tell you to-morrow!

PRIME. Early?

MRS. JASPER. About this time!

PRIME. Noon? (*At the door to the vestibule, with exultation, possessing himself of her hand.*) Angel!

MRS. JASPER. (*Laughing in spite of her dread of* COVERLEY's *return, snatching back her hand, which he has managed to carry to his lips, and finally getting rid of him.*) Lamb!

ACT THIRD

MRS. JASPER'S *drawing-room; modest and elegant. Entrance at the centre from the hall and staircase; entrance at the right from another room.*

MRS. JASPER seated, lost in thought, on a small Louis Quinze sofa; which, with a table beside it of the same period, are down at the left. A book is in her lap, which she has begun to cut, but is not reading. Enter the PARLOUR-MAID from the hall.

PARLOUR-MAID. A telegram, ma'am.

MRS. JASPER. (*Who has taken the telegram, opened it and glanced at it; with a gesture of impatience and disappointment.*) Sir Montagu! No answer. (*Exit the PARLOUR-MAID. MRS. JASPER rises, reads aloud.*) "In town to-day; will come to lunch." (*Thinking; then with decision.*) I'll lunch out!

(*Re-enter the PARLOUR-MAID.*)

PARLOUR-MAID. Captain Prime!

MRS. JASPER. (*Struck.*) No, I won't: I'll lunch at home!

(*Enter CAPTAIN PRIME from the hall. Exit the PARLOUR-MAID.*)

PRIME. (*As MRS. JASPER lets him, with extreme devotion, take and keep her hand.*) You told me at Brisket you were coming home for courage. (*Anxiously.*) I hope you've found it.

MRS. JASPER. I've hunted it up and down London. I'm resting a moment.

PRIME. I'm not; they're too close behind me!

MRS. JASPER. (*Startled.*) They're coming here?

PRIME. Not yet; we've time.

MRS. JASPER. That's all I want—time!

PRIME. We've only an hour; they'll arrive. They've fixed the day.

MRS. JASPER. (*Alarmed.*) To-morrow?

PRIME. The twenty-fifth. There I am!

MRS. JASPER. I see; you had to consent.

PRIME. I had to consent, but I also had to fly.

MRS. JASPER. When did you come away?

PRIME. This morning, at the peep of dawn. (*Then nervous, pleading; with a sudden fear.*) You won't give me back to

them—you won't?

MRS. JASPER. (*Smiling.*) Not without a struggle. But mercy on us, how far we've come!

PRIME. For the time it has taken, yes. But we surely can't stop where we are.

MRS. JASPER. Dear Captain Prime, where *are* we, you know? That's what I ask myself.

PRIME. Well, I don't care where, so long as we're together.

MRS. JASPER. If we advance together it must be step by step, and armed to the teeth. Remember that we're in the enemy's country.

PRIME. That was the case at Brisket; it's not the case here.

MRS. JASPER. Here we shall have the enemy in ours; it comes to the same thing. (*After an instant.*) There's a difference, however; for now I've a better conscience.

PRIME. Mine was perfect from the first!

MRS. JASPER. Oh, mine required clearing up: I've been busy setting it in order! Our pace on that wonderful occasion was so rapid; it made the situation so false. It was as if I had dreamed a dream or drunk a potion. I had to recover my reason; I had to return to reality. (*Giving him her hand again.*) I think this *is* reality.

PRIME. (*Rueful.*) I think so too, Mrs. Jasper, with my position so much worse.

MRS. JASPER. Ah no, not worse. Essentially better!

PRIME. How in the world is it better, dearest, since we've been able to do nothing?

MRS. JASPER. We've been able to do everything. We've learned to know each other, to be sure of ourselves. It was that second day at Brisket, before my own flight, that made us sure. It signed and sealed the treaty.

PRIME. Well then, if the treaty's signed and sealed we can act on it.

MRS. JASPER. (*After an instant, dubious.*) Act on it—yes.

PRIME. I mean we can take the shortest cut.

MRS. JASPER. What do you call the shortest cut?

PRIME. Why, simply announce that we're engaged!

MRS. JASPER. Dear Captain Prime, wouldn't that make you guilty of a sort of sketchy bigamy? Before we simply announce that we're engaged (*after a pause*) we must simply become so!

PRIME. That only depends on you—this very instant.

MRS. JASPER. This very instant is premature.

PRIME. Why so, if we're sure of ourselves?

MRS. JASPER. We must be sure of some other people!

PRIME. You told me at Brisket that you wanted to "save" me. The only way to save me is to lead me to a different altar.

MRS. JASPER. I must find a different one for Blandina! (*After another short, intense reverie.*) Perhaps it might be possible to make Mr. Coverley take her. (*Then catching herself up, discouraged.*) Oh, I forgot—he's in love with *me!*

PRIME. Yes, fancy the wretch!

MRS. JASPER. You ought to be able to fancy him!

PRIME. (*Good-humouredly, after an instant during which, in rejoinder to her last speech, he has playfully kissed her hand.*) Oh, I'll forgive him everything; for without him where should we be?

MRS. JASPER. He was what they call a blessing in disguise.

PRIME. And so was that brute of a Trafford.

MRS. JASPER. (*With an idea, suddenly seizing his arm.*) Make *him* take her! (*Then relapsing in the same way as before.*) Oh, I forgot, he's in love with me too!

PRIME. (*Blank.*) Is every one in love with you?

MRS. JASPER. Yes, it makes every one, now that you are. I ought to let you know it.

PRIME. Thank you. (*After an instant.*) Well, it can't be helped! I thought Mr. Trafford was in love with Lady Brisket.

MRS. JASPER. He's differently affected; he's in love with every one.

PRIME. With every one, alas! but Blandina.

MRS. JASPER. He's capable even of that.

PRIME. (*Eager.*) *Is* he? Then there's an issue!

MRS. JASPER. (*Struck.*) It might be, if Amy didn't bar it.

PRIME. Lady Brisket? (*Then gravely, as if with apprehension.*) She doesn't reciprocate his passion?

MRS. JASPER. You're shocked, you dear; very properly. But it isn't shocking. Poor Amy's in love with no one but her husband, and only made foolish by his own folly. (*Giving a specimen.*) He's coming to lunch with me!

PRIME. (*Surprised.*) Is he in town?

MRS. JASPER. Just arrived; he has wired. *He's* made foolish by his wife's folly.

PRIME. (*Quick, with an inspiration.*) So that if each could be got straight—?

MRS. JASPER. (*Catching his idea.*) Mr. Trafford would be sent about his business! (*Plausible, convincing.*) His business is to marry Blandina. (*Then with immense decision.*) We'll *get* them straight!

PRIME. Then the thing is to catch Trafford.

MRS. JASPER. (*Arrested, disconcerted.*) Oh, I forgot—he has left the country!

PRIME. We must bring him back.

MRS. JASPER. (*With a happy thought.*) I'll send Mr. Coverley after him!

PRIME. Without delay, then: every minute counts. Remember that I'm sinking into the sand.

MRS. JASPER. (*With elation.*) I don't care for the sand—I'm the Sphinx!

PRIME. Ah, but I'm not one of the Pyramids!

MRS. JASPER. No, indeed, you're a pilgrim in the desert; you're a breathing, struggling man. Therefore Sir Montagu mustn't find you here.

PRIME. Why not? He knows you like me.

MRS. JASPER. Then we've no occasion to remind him!

PRIME. Appeal to him, on the contrary; tell him the simple facts.

MRS. JASPER. The less I tell him the better! (*Going for PRIME's hat and stick, which he has put down on coming in.*) I can manage him only if you go.

PRIME. (*Regretful, reluctant, taking his things.*) Where in the world *shall* I go?

MRS. JASPER. Can't you run round to your club?

PRIME. Dear lady, think of the Wigmores!

MRS. JASPER. (*Thinking of them.*) Would they enter the building?

PRIME. Enter it? They'd occupy it! (*Supplicating.*) Let me remain at least on the premises.

MRS. JASPER. While you're still Blandina's?

PRIME. All the more reason! (*Nodding toward the other room.*) I'll stay in there.

MRS. JASPER. It's my dear old "den"—it's full of my things.

PRIME. They're just what I want to see!

MRS. JASPER. (*Struck by a sound.*) Hush, he's coming! (*Waving him into the other room.*) Then hide!

(*Exit* PRIME *rapidly into the other room. Re-enter the* PARLOUR-MAID.)

PARLOUR-MAID. Mr. Trafford.

(*Enter* PERCY TRAFFORD *from the hall. Exit the* PARLOUR-MAID.)

MRS. JASPER. (*Surprised, struck, relieved, recognising with a joy she can scarcely conceal, though she endeavours to hide it with an air of disapproval, the opportunity indicated in the preceding scene.*) Oh, you?

TRAFFORD. No, I've not got off; I anticipate your displeasure. (*Then puzzled, mystified, as* MRS. JASPER, *with her eyes fixed on him, slowly and mysteriously circles round him as it were, in silence, while, not unwilling to bewilder him, she asks herself how she had best proceed with him.*) Are you too displeased to speak to me? (*She still remains silent, retracing her steps and revolving in the opposite sense, so that at last quite bewildered he goes on with a droll suppliant uneasiness.*) Are you trying to hypnotise me?

MRS. JASPER. (*Stopping, but still with her eyes on him.*) Pray, what has prevented your getting off?

TRAFFORD. (*Breaking out, to conciliate her.*) The desire to see *you* once more!

MRS. JASPER. How did you know I was in town?

TRAFFORD. I just came on the chance—to ask.

MRS. JASPER. At this extraordinary hour?

TRAFFORD. It's the eve of my departure and the fault of my impatience. I feel already an exile.

MRS. JASPER. (*Visibly debating within herself an instant; then, as if in consequence of the definite determination to assume with him a certain attitude and take a certain line, after she has seated herself again on her sofa with her book and her paper-cutter.*) So that you've come to me for consolation?

TRAFFORD. (*Reassured, led on by her tone.*) You've said it, Mrs. Jasper. Be kind to me this once.

MRS. JASPER. (*Considering, while she cuts her book, then raising her eyes to him with strange expressiveness.*) Well, this once. (*Still looking at him in the same way, while she points to a seat.*) Sit down.

TRAFFORD. (*Who has eagerly seated himself.*) My motive for a step of this boldness has been the wish not to start without bidding you good-bye.

MRS. JASPER. (*Smiling.*) Good-bye is soon said, Mr. Trafford, when it has to be! I tried to say it with all possible distinctness at Brisket.

TRAFFORD. (*Smiling as she smiles, and drawing his seat a little nearer.*) So did I, Mrs. Jasper, but I couldn't utter the sound! I felt therefore to-day the yearning to address you a last word.

MRS. JASPER. (*Very busy with the leaves of her book.*) You prolong the agony, don't you see, Mr. Trafford?

TRAFFORD. (*Insinuating.*) I prolong the agony, as you justly remark, Mrs. Jasper; but I also shorten a little—don't *you* see?—the separation!

MRS. JASPER. Our separation is surely too fundamental to be affected by a visit, on your part, the more or the less. Don't you remember that I was obliged to tell you at Brisket there never would be anything in the nature of a chance for you?

TRAFFORD. (*Arguing with increased confidence.*) Yes, but your manner just now seemed to promise—it seems to promise, Mrs. Jasper, even while I speak!—a certain relaxation of your rigour; and since you refer to what passed between us at Brisket, I may remind you, on *my* side, that I expressed to you there how deeply I long for sympathy.

MRS. JASPER. You seemed to me not to long for it in vain!

TRAFFORD. So I ventured to believe at moments, and yet I have asked myself, these last days, what has happened to deprive me, in the connection to which you so indulgently allude, of any further symbol of it.

MRS. JASPER. (*To herself.*) He takes us in rotation! (*Then looking at him a moment.*) Do I correctly infer that you have come to me for news of Lady Brisket?

TRAFFORD. (*Smiling, slightly embarrassed.*) I've said enough to show you that that was not *all* my errand! But if you have any news of Lady Brisket to communicate, I won't deny that I shall be properly grateful for it.

MRS. JASPER. I left her at Brisket, from which she gave no indication at all of an intention to stir.

TRAFFORD. (*Betraying inadvertently a slight surprise.*) No symptom at all?

MRS. JASPER. (*Struck; then ironical.*) Have you been expecting her to travel up and pay you a visit?

TRAFFORD. I've been simply hoping that I might, before I go, have a last word from her.

MRS. JASPER. You're very fond of last words! This miracle of her silence, then, you've come to *me* to explain?

TRAFFORD. (*Alarmed by her tone and extenuating.*) I was restless, I was disappointed—

MRS. JASPER. (*Interrupting him, insisting on her advantage and following it up.*) And you thought *I* might amuse you—in the absence of anything better? (*Closing her book and rising sharply.*) I seemed a woman you might come to—to talk of another woman?

TRAFFORD. (*Springing up, startled, mystified; then, after staring a moment, falling into the trap and almost plaintively explaining.*) Dear Mrs. Jasper, there are so few subjects that your great severity allows! Only let me feel that I'm at liberty, and there's one on which I shall be eloquent

enough!

MRS. JASPER. (*After an instant, more gently.*) Don't be eloquent, Mr. Trafford. Leave the country in silence.

TRAFFORD. (*Ardent.*) I can't leave it till I've explained my position.

MRS. JASPER. If you explain it you'll spoil it. It's so fine as it is!

TRAFFORD. (*Infatuated, beguiled.*) You mean my conscientious retreat—to spare Lady Brisket any shadow of annoyance? Let me prove to you its reality by telling you that I've made my arrangements to leave England (*after an hesitation; bringing it out*) to-day.

MRS. JASPER. (*As if suppressing a shock.*) To-day?

TRAFFORD. I take the club-train. But, Mrs. Jasper—

MRS. JASPER. (*As if waiting in averted suspense, while he nervously hangs fire.*) Yes, Mr. Trafford?

TRAFFORD. I take the club-train because I gave my word, at Brisket, not to linger too long. But my leave of absence isn't really at an end, and though prompt departure has been prescribed to me in an amiable quarter, I should be delighted to make a later start if it should be even so much as hinted at in another!

MRS. JASPER. (*After an instant, facing round to him with a kindled countenance and a complete change of manner.*) Your assurance, Mr. Trafford, ought to carry you very far in your profession! (*As, taken aback by her unexpectedness, he makes a vague gesture of protest.*) You produce in that unhappy house as pretty a domestic muddle as one could wish to see, and then, at the very moment you've a chance to retrieve it by an act of common decorum, you throw yourself with all your levity into a declaration which is neither more nor less than an impertinence to two women at once!

TRAFFORD. (*Staggered a little, but recovering himself.*) Can I help it if the charm you exercise—?

MRS. JASPER. (*Breaking in.*) Is it too much to hope that the charm I exercise may make you ashamed of yourself?

TRAFFORD. (*After a bewildered silence.*) I'll take the club-train.

MRS. JASPER. (*Abrupt, imperative.*) You'll do nothing of the sort!

TRAFFORD. (*Blank.*) What then *am* I to wait for?

MRS. JASPER. Your punishment!

TRAFFORD. (*Rueful.*) Dear lady, I feel as if I had had it!

MRS. JASPER. You'll feel so still more before I've done with you!

TRAFFORD. Will you be so good as to tell me what it's to consist of?

MRS. JASPER. (*After an instant.*) I should like first to know the hour.

TRAFFORD. (*Looking at his watch.*) It's getting on to one.

MRS. JASPER. (*Arranging the bosom of her dress.*) Then I haven't time—I'm expecting Sir Montagu.

TRAFFORD. (*Startled.*) Is he in town?

MRS. JASPER. He has just come up—to see if you've gone.

TRAFFORD. (*Putting on his gloves and still more uneasy.*) If I haven't then, it will be your fault!

MRS. JASPER. I'll take the responsibility, for I have the satisfaction! But he mustn't find you yet.

TRAFFORD. (*Alert, but not exactly in a panic, inasmuch as he must, so far as possible, indicate that if he wishes to avoid* SIR MONTAGU *it is not so much for the sake of his own skin as because he owes it to* LADY BRISKET.) Good-bye, then.

MRS. JASPER. (*Listening, catching his arm.*) Wait—a ring at the door!

TRAFFORD. (*Listening.*) Is it he?

MRS. JASPER. I daresay!

TRAFFORD. (*Anxious.*) Which way shall I go?

MRS. JASPER. (*With vivacity, as, to take a different door from the one he has come in by, he goes up to the centre.*) Not there!

(*Re-enter the* PARLOUR-MAID.)

PARLOUR-MAID. Mr. Coverley!

(*Enter* CHARLES COVERLEY *from the hall. Exit the* PARLOUR-MAID.)

MRS. JASPER. You arrive in the nick of time—I commit Mr. Trafford to your keeping.

COVERLEY. (*Astonished at finding* TRAFFORD.) Again?

MRS. JASPER. Please shut him up till he's wanted.

TRAFFORD. (*Seizing his chance to get off.*) Coverley will know where to find me! (*Exit* TRAFFORD *briskly to the hall.*)

MRS. JASPER. (*Anxious.*) Shall you know where to find him?

COVERLEY. He has always the same hotel. But I thought he had gone.

MRS. JASPER. So did I! (*Then pressing* COVERLEY.) Don't lose him—follow him!

COVERLEY. (*Evading her and coming round, vague, on the other side.*) To see him off?

MRS. JASPER. To keep him on! (*With extreme urgency.*) Do look out, or he'll go.

COVERLEY. (*Bewildered.*) I thought that was what you clamoured for.

MRS. JASPER. I did, but I've changed. At present you must help.

COVERLEY. That's exactly what I've come for. I returned to town as soon as I knew you had left Brisket.

MRS. JASPER. Make yourself useful then; secure Mr. Trafford.

COVERLEY. (*Uneasy, refusing to be hustled off.*) I want to secure *you!* I want, moreover, an account of your proceedings.

MRS. JASPER. (*With affected blankness.*) What proceedings?

COVERLEY. The Captain is still in his chains. An hour after I first appealed to you, you told me you had found a way to get him off. I was delighted with your promptitude, and that evening I asked you what the way might be. You requested me to wait to see.

MRS. JASPER. Well, wait a little longer.

COVERLEY. I've already waited an eternity.

MRS. JASPER. Wait till to-morrow.

COVERLEY. That's what you said at Brisket.

MRS. JASPER. Wait till to-night.

COVERLEY. Why the deuce is it such a mystery?

MRS. JASPER. It's difficult; it's delicate; it's complicated.

COVERLEY. Upon my honour, it *must* be! Incantations and mystic spells!

MRS. JASPER. I know what I'm about. When I consented to oblige you, I made it clear to you that you must give me a free hand; you must trust me. If you don't trust me it's all over.

COVERLEY. (*Yielding, throwing up his objections.*) How can I help trusting you when I adore you?

MRS. JASPER. Adore me a little less, and trust me a little more.

COVERLEY. Ah, but it isn't only me. It's the victim of my wretched rashness. Can the Captain trust you?

MRS. JASPER. (*After an instant.*) I think he does. (*Then after another instant.*) I'll tell you my idea. (*Laying her hand on his arm and, while he waits, hopeful, looking at him.*) It's to give her to your accomplice. Make Trafford take her.

COVERLEY. (*Astonished.*) Blandina? *Will* Trafford take her?

MRS. JASPER. He'll simply have to!

COVERLEY. Why will he have to?

MRS. JASPER. That's my secret.

COVERLEY. How can I "help" if I don't know it?

MRS. JASPER. By not letting him escape.

COVERLEY. (*Alert, seizing his hat.*) I'll bring him back.

MRS. JASPER. (*With her hand on his arm.*) Wait a moment! (*Then after an instant during which, in her mind, she visibly and anxiously tries to harmonise her difficulties.*) What time is it now?

COVERLEY. (*Looking at his watch.*) It's one.

MRS. JASPER. Then bring him at two.

COVERLEY. (*With eager assent, going inadvertently, in his headlong haste, up to centre.*) At two!

MRS. JASPER. Not there! (*Explaining.*) My den.

COVERLEY. (*At the door to the hall.*) I wish I were Daniel! (*Exit COVERLEY.*)

(*Re-enter PRIME from the other room.*)

PRIME. Has he gone?

MRS. JASPER. It wasn't Sir Montagu. But take care!

PRIME. That room there is like a fortress. My gratitude overflows.

MRS. JASPER. It can overflow later.

PRIME. I must live in the moment. To be there among your possessions—your books, your sketches, your flowers—gives me a sense of strength.

MRS. JASPER. (*Fortified also an instant and rejoicing without reserve.*) In a word you feel at home!

PRIME. As I've never felt anywhere. Yet at the same time, do you know? I've a wild desire to go off with you.

MRS. JASPER. Why should we go off?

PRIME. To break with everything; to insist on our freedom.

MRS. JASPER. (*After an instant.*) Dear Captain Prime, you showed, on a momentous occasion, a delicacy the vision of which won my heart. We must keep at that beautiful height; we mustn't fall below it.

PRIME. There would be nothing so delicate or so beautiful as to forget all these people *with* you. And we should come back in the fulness of time only the more united.

MRS. JASPER. You must *wait* for the fulness of time. Otherwise you'll be terribly judged.

PRIME. Oh, I don't care how I'm judged!

(*Re-enter, without their perceiving it, the PARLOUR-MAID.*)

MRS. JASPER. Do you care how *I* am?

(*Enter SIR MONTAGU BRISKET from the hall.*)

PRIME. (*Passionate.*) You? You're an angel!

PARLOUR-MAID. Sir Montagu Brisket. (*Exit the PARLOUR-MAID.*)

SIR MONTAGU. (*As MRS. JASPER and PRIME precipitately separate.*) I appear to have interrupted a scene of considerable intimacy!

MRS. JASPER. (*At the right to PRIME at the left.*) We must accept the interruption, Captain Prime.

PRIME. Does that mean that I must leave you?

MRS. JASPER. If you'll be so very good.

(*PRIME, who is without his hat and stick, which he has taken out with him on his former exit, passes up to the centre. SIR MONTAGU comes down to the left. PRIME pauses, looks at him an instant, without defiance but with visible deliberation, and then goes into the other room.*)

SIR MONTAGU. (*Surprised.*) Where is he gone?

MRS. JASPER. To my boudoir.

SIR MONTAGU. Do you give him the run of your house?

MRS. JASPER. He comes to call.

SIR MONTAGU. What does Blandina say to that?

MRS. JASPER. It's a question you must put to Blandina.

SIR MONTAGU. (*After an instant.*) Shall I tell her he thinks you an angel?

MRS. JASPER. She'll not be surprised, for she knows you do.

SIR MONTAGU. (*Nettled.*) An angel, dear lady, with somewhat drooping wings! Did you get my telegram?

MRS. JASPER. It made me deplore your precipitation.

SIR MONTAGU. My reception is even more frigid than I feared.

MRS. JASPER. Your wife will take an unfortunate view of a visit to London which so quickly follows my return.

SIR MONTAGU. My conscience is clear about my visit to London. I came up to make sure that fellow has gone.

MRS. JASPER. Mr. Trafford? (*After an instant.*) Why should you suppose *I* can inform you?

SIR MONTAGU. I take you by the way; I ask you to feed my hunger.

MRS. JASPER. Will that be fair to Amy?

SIR MONTAGU. Does she want even to starve me?

MRS. JASPER. You know my attitude; I've made it plain. I wish to be without reproach.

SIR MONTAGU. (*After an instant, with attention.*) And without observers?

MRS. JASPER. I don't understand.

SIR MONTAGU. Let me be sure then that *I* do. You won't give me luncheon?

MRS. JASPER. No, Sir Montagu, it's impossible.

SIR MONTAGU. (*After looking into his hat a moment.*) You say you wish to be without reproach. Excuse me if I reply that you take a singular way to become so. (*As she makes a movement of impatience and indifference.*) Has anything occurred to free Captain Prime from his pledge to my niece?

MRS. JASPER. Nothing.

SIR MONTAGU. Then you must permit me to observe that his proper place is not in your boudoir.

MRS. JASPER. He must judge for himself of his proper place.

SIR MONTAGU. May I inquire if *he's* to remain to luncheon?

MRS. JASPER. I daresay he will if *I* invite him.

SIR MONTAGU. If you wish to be fair to Amy, why be grossly the opposite to Blandina?

MRS. JASPER. You'll see that I shall not be.

SIR MONTAGU. (*After an instant.*) You mean you'll let her have her lover on condition that you don't lose your own?

MRS. JASPER. (*Starting, wounded, indignant, her hand on her heart.*) Ah, Sir Montagu—!

SIR MONTAGU. (*Supremely satiric, at the door to the hall.*) I'll acquaint her with your extraordinary terms! (*Exit* SIR MONTAGU.)

MRS. JASPER. (*Alone with her emotion.*) It's to *that* I expose myself? Ah, it's too hard! (*Sinks into a chair and, overwhelmed, upset, bursts into tears. The bang of the house-door, downstairs, is heard.*)

(*Re-enter* CAPTAIN PRIME *from the other room.*)

PRIME. He has gone; I hear him. (*Then following* MRS. JASPER, *who at his entrance has very quickly sprung up and moved away from him; his suspicions aroused by his first glance at her.*) But what on earth did he say to you?

MRS. JASPER. (*Who has quickly brushed away her agitation, disguising it with her bravery.*) It doesn't signify what he said.

PRIME. It signifies to me when people insult you!

MRS. JASPER. You're not in a position to defend me.

PRIME. Not in a position, when I worship you?

MRS. JASPER. To worship me now is to dishonour me.

PRIME. (*Discouraged.*) Heavens—you too?

MRS. JASPER. I think perhaps it's I who dishonour *you*. I expose you more than I guard you.

PRIME. (*In despair.*) You do turn me away then?

MRS. JASPER. I must—till we're free.

PRIME. For people to come and outrage you?

MRS. JASPER. They won't if we're separate.

PRIME. (Struck.) Ah, how I make you suffer!

MRS. JASPER. I'm willing to suffer—for *you*. If I wish you to go, it's for yourself.

PRIME. To feel that I desert you, and leave you all the burden? I'll only go if you come *with* me!

MRS. JASPER. (Discouraged, faltering an instant.) Give me up rather; I'm not worth your trouble. Go off and escape: a man can! Take wings and forget us all.

PRIME. No, I have my answer to your visitors. This is the very place for me to give it.

MRS. JASPER. You shall never give your answer before I've given mine!

PRIME. Then you'll have to be quick.

(Re-enter the PARLOUR-MAID.)

PARLOUR-MAID. Lady Brisket.

MRS. JASPER. (Startled; then, with confidence.) . I *shall* be quick! (Enter LADY BRISKET from the hall. Exit the PARLOUR-MAID. To LADY BRISKET.) I'm the more surprised to see you as Sir Montagu didn't mention that you had come up with him.

LADY BRISKET. (Who has stopped short, astonished, between them, looking from PRIME to MRS. JASPER.) Has he been here then?

MRS. JASPER. He has just left me. (Gay.) Perhaps you didn't come up with him?

LADY BRISKET. He took the ten.

MRS. JASPER. And you took the eleven?

LADY BRISKET. (Looking at PRIME.) The Wigmores were to take the twelve.

MRS. JASPER. (To PRIME.) Be in the other room to receive them.

(PRIME inclines himself gravely to both ladies and goes out again.)

LADY BRISKET. You're right in supposing they'll come here. They suspect you.

MRS. JASPER. Every one suspects me, dear Amy. You yourself most of all.

LADY BRISKET. Well, you've just admitted that Montagu has been here.

MRS. JASPER. That was so little my fault that I allowed him to stay but five minutes.

LADY BRISKET. (After an instant.) You

sacrificed him to Captain Prime?

MRS. JASPER. The sacrifice cost me nothing, for I saw that my own attractions had had little to do with his adventure. (After a moment.) His visit was for Mr. Trafford.

LADY BRISKET. (Sceptical, mocking.) Did he expect to find him *here*?

MRS. JASPER. He missed him by only ten minutes.

LADY BRISKET. Mr. Trafford's still in London?

MRS. JASPER. Didn't you know it? (As LADY BRISKET turns away in silence.) Let me express my regret that you've come up.

LADY BRISKET. I came up to watch my husband.

MRS. JASPER. Well, he came up to watch his wife.

LADY BRISKET. How, since he left her at Brisket?

MRS. JASPER. Believing that Mr. Trafford was still on the scene, he had his reasons for suspecting that she would presently arrive. You see that, finding a fortunate colour in Sir Montagu's own movements, she *has* arrived.

LADY BRISKET. Mr. Trafford has had nothing to do with it.

MRS. JASPER. (With a sad, discouraged shrug.) You and your husband watch each other too much!

LADY BRISKET. (After a moment.) Then Montagu doesn't know—

MRS. JASPER. That Mr. Trafford hasn't gone? No, I didn't betray to him that very objectionable fact. But I think it right that you should be informed—

LADY BRISKET. (As MRS. JASPER hesitates.) Of what?

MRS. JASPER. That Mr. Trafford came here to make love to me.

LADY BRISKET. (Blank.) To *you*?

MRS. JASPER. Not for the first time!

LADY BRISKET. Are you telling me the real truth?

MRS. JASPER. Yes, and only a fraction of that.

LADY BRISKET. (After a moment; with irritation.) When *does* Mr. Trafford go?

MRS. JASPER. (Smiling.) Whenever I like!

LADY BRISKET. (With growing resentment.) He's very obliging.

MRS. JASPER. (Gay.) To a degree that

would surprise you!

LADY BRISKET. I've more surprises than one. (*After an instant.*) What are you doing with Captain Prime?

MRS. JASPER. Do you want very much to know?

LADY BRISKET. (*Relenting, more confiding.*) So much so that, to tell you the perfect truth, that has been the reason of my coming.

MRS. JASPER. There surely was never anything in the world for which there were so many reasons!

LADY BRISKET. When we learned at Brisket this morning that Captain Prime had vanished, it set us women thinking.

MRS. JASPER. Let me help you women to think. (*After an instant.*) Captain Prime has confided to me his trouble.

LADY BRISKET. (*With an embarrassed, somewhat rigid contrition.*) His trouble has been partly *my* fault.

MRS. JASPER. A very happy fault for me!

LADY BRISKET. (*Seizing* MRS. JASPER'S *arm.*) You care for him then?

MRS. JASPER. (*Looking at her a moment fixedly; then, with a droll smile which is half a grimace of pain, looking down at her arm, which* LADY BRISKET *continues to clutch.*) Do you know you have your nails in my flesh?

LADY BRISKET. (*Withdrawing her hand and pleading.*) Do care for him; *do*, to oblige me!

MRS. JASPER. My dear child, I never cared for any one in my life!

LADY BRISKET. (*Wondering, earnest.*) Not even, really, for Montagu?

MRS. JASPER. Some day he'll tell you how I've treated him.

LADY BRISKET. I'll make him!

MRS. JASPER. When he does, you'll find it hard to forgive me.

LADY BRISKET. I'll forgive you if you'll marry Captain Prime!

MRS. JASPER. You mean by that that you'll believe me. (*After an instant.*) Well, I want to be believed!

LADY BRISKET. (*Intensely insistent.*) Marry him! (*Then with a kind of suppliant triumph over her fears, a joy in seeing the way to prove to herself that she is safe.*) I'll dance at your wedding!

MRS. JASPER. You forget, my dear that he's engaged to Blandina.

LADY BRISKET. (*After a moment.*) We'll break that off.

MRS. JASPER. What then will become of Miss Wigmore?

LADY BRISKET. (*Thinking an instant; then with an impatient gesture disposing of the question as if it is of very secondary importance.*) She'll find another husband.

MRS. JASPER. She must. But where will she find him?

LADY BRISKET. (*Vague, perplexed, indifferent; casting about her with rapid motion.*) I don't know; I'll think of one.

MRS. JASPER. (*Urgent.*) Think of him as hard as you can. While you're thinking I'll give an order for luncheon.

LADY BRISKET. (*Pleased, reconciled.*) Do you wish me to stay to it?

MRS. JASPER. (*At the door of the other room.*) Rather, my dear! And to dinner! (*Exit* MRS. JASPER.)

LADY BRISKET. (*Alone, at a loss.*) Think of one, yes! But whom *can* I think of?

(*Re-enter the* PARLOUR-MAID.)

PARLOUR-MAID. Mr. Coverley!

(*Re-enter* COVERLEY. *Exit the* PARLOUR-MAID.)

COVERLEY. Have you seen Mrs. Jasper?

LADY BRISKET. (*Struck, impatient.*) Never mind Mrs. Jasper. Will you take Blandina?

COVERLEY. (*Blank.*) Take her where?

LADY BRISKET. To your home; to your heart. Will you marry her?

COVERLEY. (*Bewildered but decided.*) No, Lady Brisket; I can't go so far as that.

LADY BRISKET. (*Resentful.*) It seems to me that in your position you ought to do something!

COVERLEY. (*Plaintive.*) Why, Lady Brisket, it seems to myself that I do everything. I've been rushing round again after Trafford.

LADY BRISKET. (*Struck, curious.*) After Trafford?

COVERLEY. I've brought him back; he's downstairs.

LADY BRISKET. (*Still more struck; quite feverish.*) Then send him up to me.

COVERLEY. I'll send him up to you. (*At the door to the hall.*) Alone?

LADY BRISKET. (*Impressive.*) Alone.

COVERLEY. (*Compliant.*) Alone. (*Exit* COVERLEY.)

LADY BRISKET. He has been making love to *her?* I'll give him some one to make love to!

(*Re-enter* PERCY TRAFFORD *from the hall.*)

TRAFFORD. (*Bounding toward her with irrepressible assurance.*) So you've come to me at last?

LADY BRISKET. (*Distant, chilling.*) You take too much for granted, Mr. Trafford. I've not come to *you!*

TRAFFORD. (*Disconcerted.*) It's the less to your credit, then, after your solemn promise.

LADY BRISKET. My promise was made in ignorance of your extraordinary manner of understanding our friendship.

TRAFFORD. I cease to understand it indeed when you address me in such a tone.

LADY BRISKET. My tone is doubtless a contrast to that in which you address Mrs. Jasper!

TRAFFORD. (*Affecting blankness.*) Mrs. Jasper?

LADY BRISKET. I know everything; she has told me all!

TRAFFORD. (*After an instant.*) Mrs. Jasper misrepresents me.

LADY BRISKET. One thing is very certain, that you don't make the faintest impression on her!

TRAFFORD. (*After another instant; irritated, with intention.*) Ah, you told me at Brisket who does make an impression on her!

LADY BRISKET. Well, it was all a mistake. He doesn't!

TRAFFORD. You get over your mistakes with a rapidity—!

LADY BRISKET. I've been cured of that delusion by the evidence. (*Then after an instant.*) Mrs. Jasper's in love with Captain Prime.

TRAFFORD. (*Startled, scandalised.*) With a person who's all but married?

LADY BRISKET. (*Smiling and tranquil.*) Don't be shocked! He's not married yet.

TRAFFORD. Pray, who's to prevent it?

LADY BRISKET. All of us together. It's out of the question.

TRAFFORD. Have you forgotten that last week you were crazy about it?

LADY BRISKET. Last week I was crazy about several things. I've recovered my reason.

TRAFFORD. What then does that valuable organ suggest to you to do with Miss Wigmore?

LADY BRISKET. (*After an instant; with resolution.*) To make *you* take her.

TRAFFORD. (*Blank.*) Take her where?

LADY BRISKET. To Copenhagen, as your wife. It's your duty.

TRAFFORD. (*Aghast.*) My duty?

LADY BRISKET. You sacrificed Captain Prime; you must save him.

TRAFFORD. (*Indignant.*) And did *you* do nothing? You put it into my head.

LADY BRISKET. I did wrong. I'm bound to repair my fault.

TRAFFORD. By sacrificing me?

LADY BRISKET. No more than you've sacrificed me!

TRAFFORD. (*Staring.*) You? How?

LADY BRISKET. On this spot, an hour ago. You're convicted. Besides, you said Blandina was charming.

TRAFFORD. (*Recalling, overwhelmed.*) Well, she is!

LADY BRISKET. Then if you think so, she's yours. No one will dispute your title!

(*Re-enter* MRS. JASPER *from the other room.*)

MRS. JASPER. (*To* TRAFFORD, *startled, genuinely alarmed at seeing him with* LADY BRISKET, *but assuming on the instant, in addition to this, an appearance of concern amounting almost to terror.*) You here, with Sir Montagu at the door? (*To* LADY BRISKET, *explaining.*) I've seen him from the window; he's paying his cab. What if he finds you together?

LADY BRISKET. (*Instantly impressed and throwing herself with equal rapidity into the same agitation as* MRS. JASPER.) What shall I do? where shall I go?

MRS. JASPER. (*Catching* LADY BRISKET *as she casts about, ready to rush.*) Don't stir, or you'll encounter him. (*With resolution.*) There's only *one* course!

TRAFFORD. (*Affected by their excitement; in suspense.*) What's that, Mrs. Jasper?

MRS. JASPER. Face him where you stand.

TRAFFORD. (*After an instant, pulling himself together.*) Very good; I'll face him.

LADY BRISKET. (*Quick as a flash, to* TRAFFORD.) And what good will that do *me?*

MRS. JASPER. (*To* TRAFFORD, *very gravely and ominously.*) It's not enough to protect yourself, Mr. Trafford. You ought to take an attitude that will protect this lady.

TRAFFORD. (*Quick, nervous, at a loss; falling at haphazard into a droll, wild position of defence.*) I'll take any attitude you like!

MRS. JASPER. (*As if with pity for his simplicity.*) I don't mean that of physical violence, Mr. Trafford. You must find some plausible pretext, some other explanation of your presence.

TRAFFORD. (*Thinking, heated.*) Some "other"? That's all very well. (*With helpless anguish.*) What other?

LADY BRISKET. (*With growing agitation.*) Think of one, for pity's sake; think of one quickly!

TRAFFORD. (*Desperate, to* LADY BRISKET, *who has turned her back in her own despair.*) Well then, I came for Mrs. Jasper. I came for her alone!

LADY BRISKET. (*Flashing round indignantly.*) You proclaim it, then; you glory in it?

MRS. JASPER. (*With high and terrible reproach.*) You should be more considerate, Mr. Trafford, of a woman you've sorely embarrassed, a woman you've grievously (*hesitating an instant, then bringing, with immense expression, the word out*) compromised!

LADY BRISKET. (*Dropping out of it; sinking into a chair with her face in her hands.*) Oh heaven!

TRAFFORD. (*Looking from one to the other, then at* MRS. JASPER *and appealing to her in dismay.*) You don't mean to say I've done that?

MRS. JASPER. You may not have done it for *me,* Mr. Trafford, but it's sufficient if you've done it for her husband.

TRAFFORD. (*Impatient, incredulous; with a movement of rebellion.*) Oh, damn her husband!

MRS. JASPER. (*Quick.*) Isn't it enough to have damned *her?* (LADY BRISKET *springs up in her distress, and* TRAFFORD *as quickly*

sinks into another chair and into the overwhelmed posture she has just quitted. LADY BRISKET *crosses swiftly to* MRS. JASPER *and throws herself into her arms.* MRS. JASPER, *holding* LADY BRISKET *in her arms, looks a moment fixedly at* TRAFFORD, *who then rises slowly, returning, in blank despair and confessed humiliation, her look.* LADY BRISKET *on this quits* MRS. JASPER *and goes up, and* MRS. JASPER *continues to* TRAFFORD.) There's *one* way to avert suspicion that's comparatively easy.

TRAFFORD. Easy?

MRS. JASPER. Easy for your honour.

TRAFFORD. (*Breathless.*) What is it?

(*Re-enter the* PARLOUR-MAID.)

PARLOUR-MAID. Sir Montagu Brisket!

MRS. JASPER. (*To* TRAFFORD.) You'll see what it is. (*Re-enter* SIR MONTAGU. *Exit the* PARLOUR-MAID. MRS. JASPER *continues, meeting* SIR MONTAGU's *eyes before, in his sudden astonishment at the sight of his wife and of* TRAFFORD, *he can speak, and addressing him with bright assurance.*) Mr. Trafford is still in England; but for whom do you suppose he has stayed?

SIR MONTAGU. (*Undecided, but looking at* TRAFFORD *coldly and sternly, in a manner to place upon him the burden of proof and to justify* MRS. JASPER's *picture of the gravity of the situation and the degree of an aggravated husband's displeasure.*) I shall be glad to learn from Mr. Trafford himself.

TRAFFORD. (*To* SIR MONTAGU, *with an heroic effort and after a moment's supreme hesitation, but bringing it out at last with a gallantry calculated to redeem his character.*) For Miss Wigmore!

SIR MONTAGU. (*A little staggered, but catching at the reassurance and addressing* MRS. JASPER.) What will Captain Prime say to that?

MRS. JASPER. We shall hear in a moment.

SIR MONTAGU. And what will Mrs. Wigmore say?

MRS. JASPER. "You must take what you can get."

SIR MONTAGU. And what will Blandina?

MRS. JASPER. (*Very sweetly.*) "Yes, mamma."

(*Re-enter the* PARLOUR-MAID.)

PARLOUR-MAID. Mrs. and Miss Wigmore!

MRS. JASPER. You see if they don't!

(*Enter* MRS. WIGMORE *and* BLAN-
DINA. *Exit the* PARLOUR-MAID.)

MRS. WIGMORE. (*Majestical, to* MRS.
JASPER, *recovering herself after the shock
immediately produced by the presence of*
TRAFFORD.) We have tracked Captain
Prime to this retreat.

MRS. JASPER. (*Gay, as* PRIME *reappears.*)
Here he is, Mrs. Wigmore, peeping out!

(*Re-enter* CAPTAIN PRIME *from
the other room.*)

PRIME. I just saw you alight.

MRS. WIGMORE. (*With formidable significance, to* PRIME.) We came in a four-
wheeler. It waits!

PRIME. (*Good-humoured.*) Be easy, Mrs.
Wigmore; I'll pay it.

MRS. JASPER. (*To* TRAFFORD.) Mr. Trafford, those are privileges that another
ought now to claim.

MRS. WIGMORE. I can scarcely express
my amazement at meeting Mr. Trafford
again.

TRAFFORD. (*Who has accepted the situation and tries to make the best of it.*) I'm
sure *I'm* delighted to meet Miss Wigmore!

MRS. WIGMORE. (*Staring.*) Miss Wigmore?

MRS. JASPER. (*To* MRS. WIGMORE.) Your
daughter's the innocent cause of Mr. Trafford's procrastination. He will be obliged
to me for revealing to you that he has
conceived a respectful passion for Blandina.

MRS. WIGMORE. (*Stupefied.*) Since when?

MRS. JASPER. Since the first day he beheld
her. (*Then after an instant.*) He made dear
Amy his confidant.

LADY BRISKET. (*Emulating* MRS. JASPER'S
assurance.) Perpetually!

SIR MONTAGU. (*Also rather stupefied, but
at the same time both reassured and
amused.*) I say, dear Amy!

LADY BRISKET. You needn't say anything.

MRS. WIGMORE. (*Who, after looking in
her astonishment from one person to the
other, rests her eyes on* CAPTAIN PRIME.)
And what does Blandina's affianced husband say to the respectful passion of another?

PRIME. He says, dear madam, that he
resigns that high position. Miss Wigmore,
I restore you to liberty.

MRS. JASPER. (*To* MRS. WIGMORE.) I have
the honour then—in my own house and
on Mr. Trafford's behalf—to ask you for
your daughter's hand.

TRAFFORD. (*Who has been gazing at*
BLANDINA *a moment, now crossing to her.*)
Miss Wigmore, you *are* charming!

MRS. WIGMORE. (*To* TRAFFORD, *struck,
recalling.*) I remember you told me you
thought so. (*Then in another tone.*) Blandina! (*She pauses, considering and looking
round at the others an instant, during
which* BLANDINA *is submissively silent.*) You
must take what you can get.

BLANDINA. (*After a moment.*) Yes,
mamma.

MRS. WIGMORE. (*Majestically and, as it
were, officially, to the company.*) I have
therefore a still greater honour: that of
announcing to you my daughter's engagement to Mr. Trafford.

SIR MONTAGU. (*Smiling, to* LADY BRISKET,
while TRAFFORD *kisses* BLANDINA'S *fingers
and* COVERLEY *reappears.*) I rejoice in that!

(*Re-enter* CHARLES COVERLEY
from the hall.)

PRIME. (*To the company.*) I have the
greatest honour of all, that of announcing
my engagement to Mrs. Jasper.

LADY BRISKET. (*To* SIR MONTAGU.) I rejoice in *that!*

SIR MONTAGU. (*Pleading, to* MRS. JASPER.)
Forget my blind words; I came back only
to be forgiven.

LADY BRISKET. (*To* MRS. JASPER.) Forgive mine, dear friend; I won't stir from
here till you do.

MRS. JASPER. I'll forgive you both if
you'll forgive each other.

SIR MONTAGU. It's done!

MRS. JASPER. And understand each other.

LADY BRISKET. I think we're beginning.

COVERLEY. (*Amazed, appalled; reaching*
MRS. JASPER'S *left while* PRIME *is on her
right and after he has, on hearing* PRIME'S
*last speech and during her momentary
dialogue with the* BRISKETS, *passed questioning, or almost reeled, in his incredulity
and dismay, successively to* TRAFFORD, *to*

BLANDINA, *to* MRS. WIGMORE *and to* PRIME.) Are you really going to *marry* him?

MRS. JASPER. (*Looking at him an instant with a compassionate, confessing smile in which, before she speaks, he already reads his doom and from which he turns with a movement of extravagant despair, while she transfers her happy eyes and gives her right hand to* CAPTAIN PRIME.) I'm really going to marry him!

Theatricals: Second Series
Note, 1895
The Album, 1891
The Reprobate, 1891

EDITOR'S FOREWORD

NOTE TO *THEATRICALS: SECOND SERIES*

Theatricals: Two Comedies was followed early in 1895 by *Theatricals: Second Series* containing the two plays which follow, *The Album* and *The Reprobate*. For this volume James wrote a somewhat more extended prefatory note which, to be fully appreciated, should be read together with his *After the Play* (in *Picture and Text,* Harper, 1893) and the passages in *The Tragic Muse* in which the writer Gabriel Nash discusses the theatre. The two series of plays came out in uniform binding on both sides of the Atlantic. The second series was being reviewed at the time of the failure of *Guy Domville* and had a colder press than the first. Both volumes—pioneer volumes so far as the printing of modern plays was concerned—had an inconsequential sale and aroused little interest. William Archer, analyzing the preface to the second series in the *Daily Chronicle,* observed that "Mr. James has never taken up a natural and unconstrained attitude towards the stage. . . . If he will only clear his mind of critical cant . . . and write solely for the ideal audience within his own breast, he will certainly produce works of art, and not improbably successful plays." The *Pall Mall Gazette,* which had once invited Henry James to be its dramatic critic, said, ". . . we wish very much that Mr. James would write some farces to please himself, and not to please the stage." *Theatricals: Second Series* was prefaced by the "Note" which follows.

NOTE
‿‿‿‿‿‿‿‿

One may have a lively general mistrust of the preface to a work of fiction and the explanation of a work of art, and yet recognise that an unacted play stands in a certain need of introduction. A play is normally introduced the night it is performed, and if it has not been performed at all the conditions there was a question of its meeting remain inconveniently obscure. These conditions have been those very personal factors a manager and his company. Of a published play, however, it cannot exactly be said that it has not been performed at all; for the disconcerted author at least—if, as he has wrought, the thing has arrived at adequate vividness—the printed book itself grows mildly theatrical, the frustrated effort approximately positive. Anything he may make use of his margin to superadd becomes therefore simply a substitute for the representation originally aimed at, the particular representation which, in its meagreness or its merit, would, for better or worse, have spoken for itself. In just the degree indeed in which his confidence had been qualified by that prospect, in just that degree may the naked text of the piece, dragged ashore only to stand shivering, appear to him to plead for some argued equivalent of the merciful curtain that was never either to rise or to fall.

Of both of these little experiments in theatrical brevity it is as true as of a pair of others lately preceding them [1] that if they had not been conceived in a given emergency they would never have been conceived at all. Their brevity was what the occasion demanded, and there were pressing reasons why the author should fix his eyes on lively simplicity and deadly directness. If it was an hour for doing anything at all it was an hour for doing something elaborately plain. Again, of course, as with the other pieces to which I have alluded, the question, in the face of overestimated chances, ultimately came up of whether the dread of supersubtlety had not weighed too much. It is a question that matters little now, but let none of the more, or even of the less, initiated blame him for this fine scruple, or rather for this overmastering terror, in any case in which such a censor may not personally have learnt the lesson of that bitter humiliation, that unrecorded anguish of the novice, the inexorable, the managerial "cut." Into the soul of this particular novice, nourished in the faith that brevity is intelligible only when organic, that iron had entered deep, and the consequent desire to make in advance, in a new hazard, every sacrifice that might propitiate the god was naturally not a stranger to this anxious cultivation of limits. The greater danger is really doubtless that when one is under such a discipline one may, in one's trepidation, transport the cultivation of limits too much to the plane of subject. To treat a "big" subject in the intensely sum-

---

[1] *Theatricals: Two Comedies.* 1894.

marised fashion demanded by an evening's traffic of the stage when the evening, freely clipped at each end, is reduced to two hours and a half, is a feat of which the difficulty looms large to a writer accustomed to tell his story in another form. The only writer who can regard, and can treat, such a difficulty as small is the writer whose early practice as well as his later has been in the theatrical strait-jacket.

Let me not indeed speak of the difficulty of meeting the requirements of the stage as if for a writer, of whatever antecedents, having any business at all *dans cette galère* it could be anything less than a fascination. I know not whether for the effective playwright the fascination be less than for the perverted man of letters freshly trying his hand at an art of which, in opposition to his familiar art, every rule is an infraction, every luxury a privation and every privilege a forfeiture, so that he has if possible even more to unlearn than to learn: certain it is such a desperate adventurer promptly perceives that if the job were easy it would not be worth undertaking. It has need at every step of the dignity of its difficulty, and its difficulty, at every step, is of a sort that the innumerable un-dismayed are destined complacently never to discover. One's first practical demonstrations of this attachment have inevitably something of the quality of the "exercise," a statement particularly exact when they have not been happy to the end, that end, I mean, of which the beginning is the tuning of the fiddles. On the one hand, doubtless, one should not publish one's exercises; yet on the other it is the very fact of publication that is required so to label them. If the unacted play, in England, be not quite hopelessly unacted till it is printed, so this sealing of its doom constitutes precisely the ground for an obituary notice.

Any composition, for that matter, is an exercise when there has been in connection with it a meek and lowly review of the right ways to keep on the right side of a body of people collected together at a particular hour and having paid money—really a good round sum—to be amused. This speculative study of what the public, as the phrase is, may in the good-humour of that ferocious love of a bargain by which it is so healthily animated possibly "like," gives the taint of the perfunctory even to the cleverest play—and still more of course to any that is not the cleverest. The author's tact goes above all to feeling for the particular pound of flesh that the Shylock of the box-office may happen for the hour to pronounce best weight; considerations coloured equally by the circumstances imposed, the circumstances in which the author exerts himself. Those under which both the entertainments comprised in this volume were projected, and under which the first was partly and the second fully elucidated, carried with them a particular economy of production. This is indeed more or less the prospect which every dramatist has to face; the situation differs, however, with the rigour of the economy—a term I am far from applying in any invidious sense. In other words the question immediately comes up of the amount of interpretation a piece may depend on receiving, a question the answer to which can hardly fail to regulate the experiment from the germ. These things—the formula prescribed, the adjustments required, the direction imposed, the quantity of acting supplied—are, taken together, the star under which it is born.

It may help at any rate to account for what would otherwise be inexplicable in *The Album* and *The Reprobate* to say that the act of propitiation on their behalf seemed most securely to lie in the uttermost regions of dramatic amiability, the bland air of the little domestic fairy-tale, a species of which we had recently enough welcomed, with wonderment and envy, sundry successful specimens. It became perforce a part of that fascination of which I spoke just now (in connection with the question of difficulty) to try and

> see with eye serene
> The very pulse of the machine,

discover in other words the secret, master the specific type. The different fairies had to be summoned to the cradle, from the fairy Genial to the fairy Coincidence, and one was not to feel the omens propitious till the scheme bristled with as many of these old friends as a nursery-tale. And yet the nursery-tale had to be rigorously a comedy—unless it should have the good fortune to prove rigorously a farce. If indeed it should find itself striking for freedom in that quarter it would encounter on the path, with warning finger raised, the incorruptible fairy Sentiment. The fairy Sentiment in turn had to mind what she was about under the eye of the foul fiend Excision, "the blind Fury with th' abhorred shears," from under whose feet every inch of ground was if possible to be cut in advance. Then the mixture was to be stirred to the tune of perpetual motion and served, under pain of being rejected with disgust, with the time-honoured bread-sauce of the happy ending. Perpetual motion would be the tide floating the boat off the sands of the superficial, and the happy ending, staring out of the funny round eyes of the type itself, was as much designated as a necessity as it was supposedly little foreseen as a result. Add to this that, as a door must be either open or shut and a play be either one thing or the other, conformity to the tone of the particular variety had to be kept well in view.

Authors, I fancy, differ on the point greatly from managers, but it is difficult to enter into the ethics of an author who is not clear about the duty resting on a drama, large or small, to make up its mind about itself and decide definitely what it shall pretend to pass for. A comedy only, and nothing else but a comedy, *is* a comedy; likewise, as it can only arrive at its distinguishing form if the idea at its root be a comedy-idea, so the possession of this idea commits it from the first to the responsibility of congruity. It must be pitched in the key of its nature—for its nature has a key. If it forfeits its harmony with its type it forfeits everything. But that is all rudimentary. Last not least these compositions were to have met the pressure of easy and early production. In the case of *The Reprobate* this requirement was particularly operative, and the whole experiment was intensely submissive to it. I hasten to parenthesise, in connection with the title of the piece, which recalls so nearly that of a conspicuous contemporary drama, that I have ventured to retain it because it is worn in the first place by a thing of mere drollery—so far as the miscarried intention goes, and in the second by a thing unacted. If the play had been performed it would certainly have been performed under a name less usurped. The author of *The Profligate*,[2] as the case stands, will view with indulgence an usurpation of so little practical import. The convenience the piece had to square with was the idea of a short comedy, the broader the better, thoroughly simple, intensely "pleasant," affording a liberal chance to a young sympathetic comedian, calling for as little acting as possible besides, skirting the fairy-tale, straining any and every point for that agreeable falsity, entailing no expense in mounting, and supremely susceptible of being played to audiences unaccustomed to beat about the bush for their amusement—audiences, to be perfectly honest, in country towns. This last condition was rigorous for both pieces, and the one the author took most into account.

But his calculation to this particular end, as well as to others, proved wide of the mark; which means accordingly that—like their predecessors and like every other dramatic bid made by the neophyte and not taken up—they do, in an intenser degree, practically confess themselves exercises. (It is impossible to doubt, by the way, that if more such rejected addresses were only given to the light, with some history of their adventures, they would end by constituting in themselves a suggestive, almost a legitimate, literature and adding greatly to the lively interest taken, in our day, in the concerns of the English theatre.) There would be nothing more to say about this volume were it not that the fascination I mentioned above clings almost as much to the theory of the matter as to the practice; so that in regard to any given collapse it may never be quite idle to glance at the influence that has made the exercise irretrievably hollow. Shall it have been mainly that terror of excision to which I have alluded and which engenders precautions that vitiate a scheme by making it abound, so to speak, in the sense of its meagreness? The hard meagreness inherent in the theatrical form, committed to think after all so much more of the clock than of the subject—the subject which runs so breathless, so fearfully flogged a race with the galloping dial-hands—this danger of death by starvation tends too much to undermine the faith of the neophyte, tends to make him give up, as lost in advance to his idea, the advantage of development. From such a renunciation to choosing the ideas that require least to be developed is, one must fear, but a short and specious step. The most important ideas, he reflects, are those that require most looking after—the least important are those that require least. "You can't feed a big stomach," he says to himself, "on a gobble between trains"; and the solution accordingly seems to lie in the region of small receptacles. "Give me an hour more, just an hour," he pleads; "Dumas and Augier never lacked it, and it makes all the difference; and with its aid I shan't fear to tackle the infinite." He does not get his hour, and he will probably begin by missing his subject. He takes, in his dread of complication, a minor one, and it's heavy odds that the minor one, with the habit of small natures, will prove thankless.

---

[2] Arthur Pinero

The only beauty of this consummation lurks probably in the private generalisation it leads our gentleman to make. Heaven forbid we should too rashly drop in upon his private generalisations: those that have gathered about the kindled fire of our hypothetical inquirer will surely constitute a family party whose secrets it were best not to overhear. They are not prepared for company, they are not dressed to go out, and some of them will certainly startle us in their abandonment of the manners of society. We must give him, however, all the benefit of the presumption that they swarm about his hearth. These are the associations that attach him to the insufferable little art with which he is so justly infatuated: ties of infinite reflection and irritation, relations of lively intimacy and of endless discovery. The consistent pursuit of it comprehends, I think, more private generalisations, more stores of technical experience, than any other æsthetic errand; and these secret hoards may not unreasonably be expected to supply sooner or later, in most cases, the ringing metal with which the adventurer shall pay his way. It is an expensive journey—it costs ever so much a mile. But the nature of the infatuation, as I have called it, enlivens, if it does not shorten, the road. The man who pretends to the drama has more to learn, in fine, than any other pretender, and his dog's-eared grammar comes at last to have the remarkable peculiarity of seeming a revelation he himself shall have made.

The lesson consists for the most part, as the author of these remarks has somewhere else [3] ventured to express the matter, in the periodical throwing overboard of the cargo to save the ship. The ship is always in danger—the most successful play has come within an ace of sinking, and the peril recurs every night; so that universal sacrifice is always in the air. The freight, the fittings, the ballast, the passengers, the provisions, the luggage, the crew, the whole thing must inexorably "go," and the vessel is not in proper trim till she is despoiled of everything that might have appeared to make her worth saving; till the last survivor in the last rag of the rigging has been consigned to the fishes, uttering that shriek of despair which lives on in the playwright's ear and becomes eventually the sweetest music he knows. The scientific name of this ferocious salvage is selection—selection made perfect, so that effect, the final residuum, shall become intense—intense with that sole intensity which the theatre can produce and for the sake of which much perhaps will be forgiven it. There is no room in a play for the play itself until everything (including the play, the distracted neophyte pantingly ascertains) has been completely eliminated. Then the fun, as the vulgar phrase is, begins. That it will be found to have begun in the present very simplified studies is much more than shall be here predicted; but the moral of my observations is that, if there have been many occasions when it was recognised as fast and furious, these have been conspicuously occasions when the dramatist himself has alone known (as he has doubtless alone cared) why. His privilege, his duty rather, is to cultivate that mystery. His still more distinguishing function, I hasten to add, is of course to bring it about.

---

[3] In his short story *Nona Vincent*.

EDITOR'S FOREWORD

THE ALBUM

We know little concerning the origin of *The Album* save that James wrote the play for Edward Compton. In the foregoing note to *Theatricals: Second Series* he describes it as one of two comedies designed on broad lines "calling for as little acting as possible" but "affording a liberal chance to a young sympathetic comedian . . . entailing no expense in mounting, and supremely susceptible of being played to audiences unaccustomed to beat about the bush for their amusement—audiences, to be perfectly honest, in country towns." He added: "This last condition was rigorous for both pieces, and the one the author took most into account."

This was only a half-truth; James did, indeed, suit the play to the limited capacities of the Compton Comedy Company, but he had London audiences in mind as well as those of the country towns. A letter to Edmund Gosse of late 1894, when he was bringing out *Theatricals: Second Series* describes *The Album* and its companion piece as both of "inferior origin." They were written, said James, "to bolster up poor Edward Compton three years ago, when after withdrawing my other play [*The American*], he found himself (asininically) with a theatre on his hands and nothing successful to produce; and they were addressed much to the actual vulgar compass of his and his company's little powers. Then he would have none of 'em."

The Album may have been "Play Number 3" which James wrote that he was completing in 1891 or the "three-act contemporaneous comedy" he was doing for Compton in December of that year, although either allusion could apply to *The Reprobate* as well. The word "contemporaneous" furnishes a slight clue, since in the play itself the all-important album bears the date September 1891. On the other hand, the names of the characters are contained in notebook lists of late 1892. This does not necessarily invalidate the theory that the play is of 1891; the names could always have been altered. James's remark to Gosse in December 1894 that the two comedies were written "three years ago" is perhaps our most accurate means of dating them. The novelist was unusually accurate in measuring time; his slips of memory in respect to dates are rare.

CHARACTERS

Sir Ralph Damant, Bart.
Mark Bernal
Teddy Ashdown
The Vicar
The Footman
Grace Jesmond
Lady Basset
Maud Vanneck

THE ALBUM

ACT FIRST

The convenient, inhabited hall of a handsome modern country-house, which exhibits several signs of confusion and disarray, as if something has happened to interrupt the regular routine. Up toward the left the passage to the outer hall, the entrance to the house, and also to some of the apartments. Up toward the right the passage to other apartments. Half-way down, to the right, a large French window, open to the garden and park. Corresponding to it, to the left, the door to the library, constituting another entrance to the house. LADY BASSET enters briskly from the outer hall, in her hat and mantle, dressed for a journey, carrying with her a dressing-bag substantially stuffed. She places it on one of the tables; then hunting about a moment finds a book in another part of the room and, bringing it over, proceeds to pack it into her bag. While she is so engaged TEDDY ASHDOWN enters from the outer hall, in his hat and Inverness cape, likewise carrying a dressing-bag. In his other hand he carries a note in an enclosed envelope. He stops short an instant, watching LADY BASSET.

TEDDY. Is that the second volume?

LADY BASSET. (*Serenely packing.*) Dear Maud has it. This is the third. You had better take the first.

TEDDY. (*Coming down, putting his bag on another table.*) Oh, I've read it!

LADY BASSET. That doesn't matter—it completes the set.

TEDDY. But it deprives the house—!

LADY BASSET. (*Her bag in her hand; now all ready to go.*) The house can afford it, and in this upheaval it's an advantage there should be fewer things to lie about.

TEDDY. (*Artless.*) To "lie" about?

LADY BASSET. When confusion reigns I take a line. There's not a creature anywhere—I carry my own luggage.

TEDDY. (*Taking his bag again.*) So do I!

LADY BASSET. (*Perceiving the note in his hand.*) You also carry the letters?

TEDDY. (*Reading again the superscription.*) Till I find the Vicar. (*Then handing her the note, quoting.*) "Very urgent"!

LADY BASSET. (*Who has taken the note from him.*) Then why *don't* you find the Vicar?

TEDDY. (*Putting down his bag again; very vague.*) I'm looking!

LADY BASSET. (*Preoccupied with the note, which she retains.*) Dear Maud has him.

TEDDY. (*Startled, decided.*) Then I must find dear Maud.

LADY BASSET. You won't—one never does. (*Turning the note over and round.*) From Mr. Lamb?

TEDDY. (*Assenting.*) The solicitor: to be particularly attended to.

LADY BASSET. (*With unfaltering decision.*) I'll attend to it.

TEDDY. (*Surprised.*) You'll read it?

LADY BASSET. When confusion reigns I take a line. (*Then having resolutely opened and reading the note.*) "Sir Ralph wires arrival—please see that he's met at Junction." (*Struck, thinking.*) Sir Ralph Damant?

TEDDY. The next of kin—they've sent for him.

LADY BASSET. (*Thoughtful; refolding the note.*) The next of kin? I know—unmarried. I'll see that he's met! (*Then deter-*

mined.) I'll meet him!

TEDDY. (*Still more surprised.*) But you go by the other station.

LADY BASSET. I don't go. I stay.

TEDDY. (*In suspense.*) And dear Maud?

LADY BASSET. You'll take her off.

TEDDY. (*Eager.*) In a moment—if she'll come.

LADY BASSET. But you'll first take my bag.

TEDDY. (*With the bag she has again placed on the table.*) Take it—?

LADY BASSET. Back to my room.

TEDDY. And tell Miss Jesmond?

LADY BASSET. Miss Jesmond's out. She's heartless.

TEDDY. (*Blank.*) Heartless?

LADY BASSET. With her protector, her patron, dying!

TEDDY. (*Still more blank.*) Dying?

LADY BASSET. If the nearest of kin is sent for.

TEDDY. (*Struck; rueful.*) What a pity *we're* not near!

LADY BASSET. One is—when one's on the spot. I've been in houses before when the head has been taken ill and the guests have scattered like frightened sheep. But I hold that guests have duties, and I've always remained at my post. (*Seeing* MAUD VANNECK: *enter* MAUD VENNECK *from the outer hall, dressed also for travelling.*) Mr. Bedford's dying!

MAUD. (*In a waistcoat, with an eye-glass.*) Already?

LADY BASSET. Before one can turn round. It has taken only a summer night to empty the house.

MAUD. It seems to me *we* fill it a good deal! But I've sent the Vicar for my bag.

LADY BASSET. You go with Mr. Ashdown.

MAUD. (*After an instant.*) And whom do *you* go with?

TEDDY. She doesn't go. You and I go together!

LADY BASSET. I remain—to act.

TEDDY. (*To* MAUD; *explaining.*) For poor Mr. Bedford—to receive the heir.

MAUD. (*Struck.*) Is there an heir?

TEDDY. (*Taking his note with quick compunction back from* LADY BASSET.) By the way, he must be met!

MAUD. (*Surprised, ironic.*) By her lady-ship?

LADY BASSET. For common decency. There's no one else!

MAUD. Isn't there Miss Jesmond?

LADY BASSET. Miss Jesmond doesn't count. A person in her position—a dependent.

TEDDY. Besides, she's out.

MAUD. Only at the station—hurrying people off.

LADY BASSET. (*Struck.*) The station? (*Catching* MAUD's *arm and in the inadvertence of her discomposure precipitately betraying herself.*) Then she'll see him first!

MAUD. (*With reproachful superiority.*) Is it your kind calculation that *I* shall see him last?

TEDDY. Don't see him at all! Travel with *me!* (*Then as the* VICAR *appears.*) Here's your bag!

(*Enter the* VICAR *from the outer hall wearing his hat and carrying a lady's dressing-bag.*)

MAUD. Take it back! (*Seating herself with resolution.*) I remain.

TEDDY. (*Seating himself in the same manner.*) Then *I* remain.

LADY BASSET. (*To the Vicar; abrupt, imperative.*) Take me to the Junction—it's your duty.

THE VICAR. (*Youngish, bland, blond, flustered.*) There isn't a conveyance—everything's out!

MAUD. (*To* LADY BASSET.) If you go there, my dear, *I* go!

TEDDY. (*To* MAUD.) And if you go, I go! (*Then to the* VICAR, *as* LADY BASSET *turns away with a disconcerted shrug.*) You must go—to meet the heir!

THE VICAR. Sir Ralph? he's coming?

TEDDY. This moment. (*To get rid of him.*) Go quick!

LADY BASSET. Receive him with all the honours.

MAUD. (*Laughing.*) Don't mind that—leave the reception to us!

THE VICAR. (*At a loss, with his bag.*) But how shall I get there?

TEDDY. Catch a pony—ride!

THE VICAR. (*With a happy thought.*) I'll run! (*Exit the* VICAR *with the bag to the outer hall.*)

TEDDY. (*To* MAUD, *amused.*) He has sneaked your bag!

MAUD. Recover it—take it back to my room.

LADY BASSET. Do nothing of the sort—take mine.

TEDDY. (*With* LADY BASSET's *bag.*) I'll take both! (*Exit* TEDDY *to the outer hall.*)

MAUD. (*With dignity and resentment.*) That's not the sort of girl I am!

LADY BASSET. What sort do you mean?

MAUD. The sort that goes up to London with unscrupulous young men. You interpret strangely your pledge to my absent mother.

LADY BASSET. You talk as if your absent mother were in paradise!

MAUD. She's only at Zanzibar, I know—on her tour round the globe. But I'm none the less entitled to your conscientious care.

LADY BASSET. Why then are you so nasty when I endeavour to dispose of you properly?

MAUD. Do you call it disposing of me properly to dispose of me to Mr. Ashdown?

LADY BASSET. He's the only person I've met who takes any notice of you!

MAUD. You don't meet many people, I know, for every one runs away from you!

LADY BASSET. My mother never did, my dear, as yours has done from you!

MAUD. She'll come back as soon as she receives the account I've written her of your selfishness.

LADY BASSET. It doesn't compare with hers, I think; for I accepted, when I rashly consented to take you out, the problem she unnaturally shirked!

MAUD. You took me from cold calculation—you knew I would prove attractive.

LADY BASSET. (*Protesting, derisive.*) Attractive?

MAUD. To single gentlemen—and others. And then let *you* get hold of them! (*After an instant, with triumphant emphasis.*) That's not the sort of girl I am!

LADY BASSET. If I had been aware of the sort you are I never would have looked at you! I cable to Zanzibar that I throw you up.

MAUD. You leave me unprotected? Very well: I can face the usual dangers!

LADY BASSET. You seem highly familiar with them! (*Then, after a moment, in a different tone, as if with a new, supersed-ing thought.*) Can you face Miss Jesmond?

MAUD. (*Blank.*) What danger does *she* present?

LADY BASSET. That of producing an early impression on Sir Ralph Damant.

MAUD. The gentleman about to arrive?

LADY BASSET. The nearest of kin, the heir to this lovely Courtlands.

MAUD. How are you sure he's the heir?

LADY BASSET. Mr. Bedford's to make a new will. Mr. Lamb, his solicitor, is with him.

MAUD. To make it in favour of Sir Ralph?

LADY BASSET. Naturally—if he has called him to his bedside.

MAUD. (*Thoughtful.*) Yes; he wouldn't bring him from London only to cut him off! But aren't there other relatives?

LADY BASSET. Far-away kindred—people with means of their own. I used to hear of them from my husband.

MAUD. In the improvident days when you *had* a husband! Has no one else expectations?

LADY BASSET. Miss Jesmond has plenty, I suppose!

MAUD. (*Blank.*) Do you mean he'll do *more* for her? Hasn't she lived on him for years?

LADY BASSET. For the last four or five. She has enjoyed every luxury, in return for promiscuous services rendered as an "amanuensis"—functions mysterious and elastic! But as the daughter of an old friend—the clergyman who was this one's predecessor and who died without leaving a farthing—he may think her a deserving object.

MAUD. (*After an instant.*) Do you mean she'll lie in wait for Sir Ralph?

LADY BASSET. She's just that kind of person. It's the way she's dangerous. Therefore keep an eye on her.

MAUD. (*After another instant.*) Do you set me to watch her so that you may be free to look after Sir Ralph?

LADY BASSET. I give you my reasons for thinking that he may be of interest to her.

MAUD. But why should she be of interest to him?

LADY BASSET. Because she's so pretty and so clever.

MAUD. Has she had the Higher Education? No? Then she's not a trained intelligence!

LADY BASSET. I believe it *is* an intellectual gymnastic to cope with the coldness of Sir Ralph!

MAUD. Is he so exempt from the weaknesses of his sex?

LADY BASSET. I've never seen him, but I've heard of his peculiar attitude—the dread of the dizziness of great heights. He has a terror of eminent women—the fascination of the abyss. It's a fixed idea with him that if he neglects his defences he may some day take the jump.

MAUD. Find himself practically engaged?

LADY BASSET. Find himself legally married.

MAUD. Are there such a lot of things to marry him for?

LADY BASSET. Figure them up! A good old title—a creation of Elizabeth. A quiet mind about other women. A very good fortune, and (*with a gesture for the whole place about them*) a very fine prospect!

MAUD. If .he has money enough to go in fear, why does poor Mr. Bedford leave him more?

LADY BASSET. To increase his terror—a harmless joke of the dear man!

MAUD. Do you mean because Mr. Bedford himself has a passion for us?

LADY BASSET. Uncontrolled—but platonic! Beside, there's no other cousin.

MAUD. None at all?

LADY BASSET. There *was* one, I believe, but he's lost to sight.

MAUD. Trust him to turn up!

LADY BASSET. They have trusted him, but always in vain. He was wild, he was worthless—good for nothing but America, to which he went.

MAUD. If he went he can come back.

LADY BASSET. Not, luckily, from the grave—luckily, I mean, for Sir Ralph. Mr. Bedford·has knowledge of his death.

MAUD. And have you knowledge of his name?

LADY BASSET. His name? Mark Bernal.

MAUD. (*After an instant, rising.*) I thank you for your solid facts. Very nice of you!

LADY BASSET. Haven't I justified my warning about Miss Jesmond?

MAUD. Perfectly. (*After another instant, in the tone of one who has won a diplomatic victory.*) Make her your charge!

LADY BASSET. (*Blank; then disconcerted, indignant, rising.*) You're ungrateful—and you're sly!

(*Enter* MARK BERNAL *from the outer hall.*)

MAUD. (*Seeing him first; privately.*) Not a bit—see how frank I shall be with Sir Ralph!

LADY BASSET. (*To herself, startled, turning; taking in* MARK BERNAL *with emotion and surprise.*) Sir Ralph?

BERNAL. (*A man of some three-and-thirty; very good-looking, but of unconventional aspect; with a long fair moustache, a mixed, informal suit, composed of articles that don't match; a soft hat, a light overcoat over one arm and a painter's album, a sketch-book of moderate size—new and covered with brown linen—carried in the other: stopping short as he sees the two women, looking vaguely from one of them to the other; then, eagerly, as he comes down.*) My cousin's ill? I heard in the village how grave it is.

LADY BASSET. (*Solemnly sympathetic, but intensely gracious and reassuring.*) The dear man suffers, but I'm watching!

MAUD. (*With the same effusion of condolence; very ingratiating.*) The party broke up; but it seemed to me (*smiling significantly at* BERNAL) quite *not* the moment to turn one's back!

LADY BASSET. At the door there was no one to receive you?

BERNAL. It stood wide open, and, as I rang in vain, I ventured at last to walk in.

MAUD. (*Seductive.*) You needn't have been afraid, with the place as good as your own!

LADY BASSET. (*Irresistible.*) You must let me share your authority till the servants are again at their posts.

BERNAL. (*Who has looked, as they alternately address him, in bewilderment and mystification from one of the women to the other.*) My "authority," madam, is small, and my title to possession *nil!*

LADY BASSET. You speak from your characteristic reserve!

MAUD. You'll find your essential strength when you've seen Mr. Bedford.

BERNAL. (*More and more confounded, but also dawningly amused.*) My essential strength?

LADY BASSET. (*Arch.*) You can't evade your fate!

BERNAL. (*Blank.*) My fate?

LADY BASSET. The way to learn it is to let me take you to our honoured friend.

MAUD. (*Eagerly interposing.*) Permit me to recommend your waiting, while this lady goes to ask leave.

BERNAL. (*Hesitating afresh, thinking, looking still, in his guarded wonderment, from one of them to the other.*) Is his present state very critical?

LADY BASSET. Dear Maud will oblige you by ascertaining. He's shut up at present with his solicitor.

MAUD. Inevitably, alas, at such a moment, with the future of such possessions at stake!

LADY BASSET. Their commanding extent demands the presence of the family.

BERNAL. (*Dazed, echoing.*) The family?

LADY BASSET. Reduced to *you*, happy man, though you pretend you don't appreciate it!

BERNAL. You accuse me of pretending, madam; but I won't pretend I understand you! (*After an instant.*) Give me time to turn round—I'm painfully affected. (*Indicating the long window.*) I'll go out a moment.

MAUD. (*Almost pouncing on him.*) Into the air? I'll take you!

LADY BASSET. (*Baffled by MAUD's alertness, looking round her quickly and spying BERNAL's album, which he has placed on a table and of which she possesses herself.*) I'll take your charming companion!

BERNAL. (*Anxious, ingenuous, demurring.*) Then who'll be near my cousin?

LADY BASSET. The vicar, the lawyer, the doctor, the nurse.

MAUD. (*With a sarcastic inflection.*) And also Miss Grace Jesmond!

BERNAL. (*Vague.*) Miss Grace Jesmond?

LADY BASSET. A person employed.

MAUD. One of the fixtures.

BERNAL. (*Innocent.*) She goes with the house?

LADY BASSET. Scarcely to enhance its value!

MAUD. She has value enough to be paid!

BERNAL. (*Vague.*) Paid?

LADY BASSET. Wages. She writes for the dear man, she reads for him, and I daresay she ciphers!

MAUD. (*Who has possessed herself, officiously, to carry it, of BERNAL's light overcoat in the same way that LADY BASSET has appropriated the sketch-book.*) But she hasn't had the Higher Education!

BERNAL. (*Laughing and trying to take his coat back from MAUD.*) I haven't had it myself! (*Then as she whisks away the coat, escaping to the right.*) Take care—there are things in the pockets!

MAUD. (*Victorious, challenging; in the long window with the coat.*) Then come and get them! (*Flirts out to the park.*)

LADY BASSET. (*Nursing the sketch-book; sociably, while BERNAL, at the window, appearing to hesitate, looks at her an instant.*) Which of us do you prefer?

BERNAL. (*Clapping the empty pockets of his waistcoat and jacket, as if with alarm, successively and quickly.*) I prefer my cigarettes! (*Exit BERNAL by the window.*)

LADY BASSET. (*Disconcerted, considering.*) Shall I follow—with this? (*Opening the album; turning a page or two.*) Real art?—my passion! (*Then to herself, as she sees GRACE JESMOND at the left—enter GRACE JESMOND from the library—dropping the book on a table as if to disconnect herself from every sign of the visitor's passage.*) Ah!

GRACE. (*Back from the station, in her hat and jacket; stopping short, surprised at still finding LADY BASSET, and speaking impulsively.*) You're not gone?

LADY BASSET. (*Uncompromising.*) And not going!

GRACE. (*Struck, eager.*) Then Mr. Bedford's better?

LADY BASSET. (*At the window; vicious.*) Mr. Bedford's worse! (*Exit LADY BASSET to the park.*)

GRACE. (*Alone, dolorous, interrogative.*) "Worse"?

(*Enter a FOOTMAN from the outer hall.*)

FOOTMAN. Sir Ralph Damant!

(*Enter* Sir Ralph Damant. *Exit* Footman.)

GRACE. (*Instantly, sadly.*) Mr. Bedford's worse!

SIR RALPH. (*Stopping short with the force of his contained emotion.*) Ah? (*Then, after an instant, while he has stood with lowered eyes.*) How much worse?

GRACE. Even a little (*thinking, discouraged*) may be more than enough!

SIR RALPH. How lately have you seen him?

GRACE. Not this morning. I've been at the station—seeing people off.

SIR RALPH. He has had "people" again?

GRACE. A large party.

SIR RALPH. Women, as usual?

GRACE. Several ladies.

SIR RALPH. They've all gone?

GRACE. Not quite all.

SIR RALPH. All but you?

GRACE. I don't go (*after an instant, with the note of quiet irony*) quite yet. And two others remain.

SIR RALPH. (*With a slight start and a glance round him.*) Two others? Where *are* they?

GRACE. (*Nodding toward the window.*) I think in the park.

SIR RALPH. (*Peremptory.*) Then send them off!

GRACE. (*Cold.*) I'll leave you to do that.

SIR RALPH. I've more immediate duties—I've been sent for.

GRACE. So I heard—before going out.

SIR RALPH. You range the country—with poor Mr. Bedford dying?

GRACE. (*After an instant.*) I've not said that he's dying.

SIR RALPH. (*Perceptibly pulled up.*) Then, pray, why was I dragged here?

GRACE. I had nothing to do with dragging you. His doctor's with him—and his clergyman. And Mr. Lamb, his lawyer.

SIR RALPH. (*After a moment.*) For testamentary purposes?

GRACE. Very likely. It was Mr. Lamb's idea to wire to you.

SIR RALPH. What does he want me to do?

GRACE. I haven't the least idea.

SIR RALPH. He shouldn't trifle (*hesitating*) with my habits! I've not been here for years.

GRACE. Just five. Your last visit was the year I came.

SIR RALPH. There have always been too many women.

GRACE. I've had the misfortune to be one of them.

SIR RALPH. "One" is quite enough. In some cases, indeed, too much. I recognise—in general—your inevitable character, but I hate to be the subject of manœuvres.

GRACE. It must be very odious. It has never been my fate.

SIR RALPH. I can easily believe it. Keep out of them!

GRACE. We can each—for ourselves—abstain from them!

SIR RALPH. (*Looking at her hard an instant.*) That's exactly what I do! I neither practise nor permit them. (*Then after another instant, during which* GRACE *gives a silent, decorous, but inexpressive movement of assent.*) Have other relations been summoned?

GRACE. Others? I think there *are* no others.

SIR RALPH. (*Gratified, complacent.*) Only me? There are persons remotely connected, but I appreciate the discrimination.

GRACE. Mr. Lamb, last night, asked me a question.

SIR RALPH. In regard to your personal pretensions?

GRACE. (*Surprised.*) Mine? (*With genuine melancholy dignity.*) What pretensions have *I*, Sir Ralph?

SIR RALPH. You're the sort of person who usually has extraordinary ones!

GRACE. How do you know what sort of person I am?

SIR RALPH. I admit that I've been reduced to speculate. (*After an instant, somewhat tentatively.*) I've wondered, for instance, if you're paid.

GRACE. For my work?

SIR RALPH. Or have only your bed and board.

GRACE. And my washing? Let me relieve you. I've had a salary.

SIR RALPH. (*Relieved.*) Ah, that settles the question!

GRACE. (*Vague.*) What question?

SIR RALPH. That of your expectations. You took them out in his life.

GRACE. You speak as if his life were over!

SIR RALPH. An inadvertence. But from the moment the lawyers take the field—!

GRACE. It was to ask me about Mark Bernal.

SIR RALPH. (*Struck; vague an instant.*) Mark Bernal?

GRACE. Who was mentioned in an earlier will.

SIR RALPH. (*Thinking.*) Little Mark, shabby little Mark—whom I knew as a boy, a small boy when I was a big one: my cousin's cousin and my own cousin? (*With extreme emphasis and decision.*) Why, all the world knows he's dead.

GRACE. Mr. Lamb's aware of that rumour.

SIR RALPH. It ain't a rumour—it's a fact!

GRACE. Requiring proof. There are four thousand a year—

SIR RALPH. (*Breaking in.*) Four thousand a year?

GRACE. For somebody!

SIR RALPH. (*After an instant.*) Not for shabby little Mark!

GRACE. So it would appear. Mr. Bedford, last night, was not to be disturbed; so that Mr. Lamb's question was as to whether, during the five years I've lived here, I had heard of any communication from Mr. Bernal.

SIR RALPH. (*Complacently affirmative.*) And you've heard of none!

GRACE. None whatever.

SIR RALPH. Then that's the proof required. Mark's mother was a cousin of our cousin—that's the degree.

GRACE. The same degree as your degree.

SIR RALPH. (*After an instant, as if reluctant to admit it.*) The same degree as mine. (*Then with much more alacrity.*) But a connection—undesirable. They were people of no position.

GRACE. (*Ironically dubious, surprised.*) Cousins of *yours?*

SIR RALPH. (*Totally unconscious of her irony: candidly confidential.*) I never ran after them. The mother died, the father died, and Mark, who used to come here for his holidays, made a sad mess of his prospects.

GRACE. Prospects? What prospects?

SIR RALPH. A presumptive interest in the four thousand. He took to low courses; I believe he took to painting portraits. He wore queer clothes and knew queer people. He was wild—I'm convinced he was wicked. His tastes were vulgar; his abilities mean. He went to the bottom—he went to America.

GRACE. Where—in the far west—he died, in a brawl, unappreciated.

SIR RALPH. But not uncommemorated. (*After an instant.*) The papers mentioned it.

GRACE. And if they hadn't?

SIR RALPH. (*Pointing judiciously the moral.*) Why, he might have come in for something!

GRACE. (*Turning away with a vague general sigh.*) It makes one hate them! (*Then seeing the* VICAR, *and addressing him, introducing* SIR RALPH. *Re-enter the* VICAR *from the outer hall, heated and breathless, still with* MAUD VANNECK's *bag.*) Sir Ralph Damant.

THE VICAR. I missed you by crossing the fields!

SIR RALPH. (*Distant, sarcastic, superior.*) I'm never to be found in the "fields"!

GRACE. Will you kindly inform Mr. Lamb?

THE VICAR. And what shall I do with the bag?

GRACE. (*Amused, indicating indulgently a place to put it down.*) Part with it—there!

THE VICAR. (*Depositing the bag with scrupulous care and extreme relief.*) There! (*Then up at the right.*) I'll announce Sir Ralph. (*Exit the* VICAR *to the right.*)

(*Re-enter from the outer hall* TEDDY ASHDOWN.)

TEDDY. (*Seeing the bag.*) He's back with it? (*Confidingly, familiarly, to both the others.*) Such a chase!

SIR RALPH. (*Struck with the elation of his tone and regarding the bag—conspicuously and showily a lady's—with cold suspicion.*) Pray, sir, is it yours?

GRACE. It belongs to Miss Vanneck.

SIR RALPH. And who on earth's Miss Vanneck?

GRACE. (*Up at the door to the outer hall, to* TEDDY.) Your friends are in the park. Instruct Sir Ralph while I see about his room. (*Exit* GRACE JESMOND.)

TEDDY. (*Artless, guileless; producing his effects on* SIR RALPH *without intention*.) Fearfully clever girl, Miss Vanneck; she's had the Higher Education.

SIR RALPH. Mercy!

TEDDY. A trained intelligence. She came with Lady Basset.

SIR RALPH. And who on earth's Lady Basset?

TEDDY. Awfully sharp too. She's waiting for you.

SIR RALPH. (*Dismayed*.) Waiting for me?

TEDDY. She was going; but she stayed.

SIR RALPH. (*Echoing*.) Stayed?

TEDDY. On purpose to meet you. She knows you're the Heir!

SIR RALPH. Good God, I'm *not* the Heir!

TEDDY. (*Surprised*.) You're not?

SIR RALPH. I *am;* but it's none of her business!

TEDDY. (*Innocently disconcerted*.) Mayn't I tell her, then?

SIR RALPH. Don't dream of it! Be so good as to remain with me.

TEDDY. (*Who has gone to the long window*.) I was thinking of joining "dear Maud"!

SIR RALPH. The trained intelligence? (*As if with a hopeful thought*.) Are you in love with it?

TEDDY. I suppose that's what's the matter with me!

SIR RALPH. Then marry the creature!

TEDDY. She won't look at me; she wants a decent fortune.

SIR RALPH. (*After an instant*.) What does she call a decent fortune?

TEDDY. Four thousand a year.

SIR RALPH. (*Dismayed again*.) Four thousand?

TEDDY. She has fixed that figure. Of course I'm stone broke. My governor has stopped payment.

SIR RALPH. Then make an effort—find something to do.

TEDDY. That's exactly what I'm looking for!

SIR RALPH. Continue to look—look hard! (*Then, as* TEDDY *seems restless*.) And whatever you do, stay here! (*Encouraging, reassuring*.) Sit down—amuse yourself! (*Looking round, nervously, for pretexts for detaining, beguiling him,* SIR RALPH'S *eye falls on* MARK BERNAL'S *album, which* LADY BASSET *has placed on one of the tables and which he takes up*.) I see you sketch.

TEDDY. (*Seated*.) Oh yes; I've the artistic nature.

SIR RALPH. Fall back on it!

TEDDY. I *am* falling! I feel I've a little gift that only requires direction.

SIR RALPH. Then direct it! (*Turning over two or three pages of the album; patronisingly, commendingly*.) I like the steam-roller!

TEDDY. (*Vague*.) What steam-roller?

SIR RALPH. (*Passing him the open book*.) That one.

TEDDY. (*With the album*.) It's not mine. (*Looking at the cover*.) It's awfully *like* mine! (*Then on his feet again*.) It belongs (*turning to the flyleaf and reading*) to "Mark Bernal."

SIR RALPH. (*Immensely startled*.) Mark Bernal?

TEDDY. (*Unconscious of his start, continuing to read from the page*.) "Mark Bernal, Vandyke Lodge, Chelsea; September '91." (*Then glancing again at the outside of the album*.) A jolly new book.

SIR RALPH. (*Taking it back from* TEDDY'S *hand and repeating, in his guarded amazement, interrogatively, but mechanically*.) A jolly new book?

TEDDY. Dated last month. Who *is* Mark Bernal?

SIR RALPH. (*Who has stared hard a moment at the name on the flyleaf, and then, looking up, presented a pale, alarmed, conjectural face*.) I haven't the least idea!

TEDDY. (*To whom, recovering himself with a great effort, and as if it doesn't matter or mean anything to him, he has surrendered the album again*.) Somebody has left it. (*Then reverting to the drawing of which* SIR RALPH *has spoken*.) By Jove, I'll copy the steam-roller!

SIR RALPH. (*Uneasy, as* TEDDY, *with the album under his arm, goes to the long window*.) Where are you going?

TEDDY. To join the ladies! (*Exit* TEDDY ASHDOWN, *with the album, to the park*.)

SIR RALPH. (*Alone, deeply agitated, wonderstruck*.) Mark Bernal—last month? Here, and nobody knows? (*Then, to him-*

self, seeing the VICAR *reappear: re-enter the* VICAR *from the right.*) Will *he* know? (*To the* VICAR, *eager.*) My cousin's worse?

THE VICAR. (*With a memorandum in his hand.*) He keeps up—for Mr. Lamb—but the doctor deprecates his seeing you. Therefore I'm desired by Mr. Lamb to put you an important question.

SIR RALPH. (*Nervous, anxious.*) An important question?

THE VICAR. (*Highly responsible and a little embarrassed.*) Confided to my discretion—on the subject of a relative.

SIR RALPH. (*More guarded.*) A relative?

THE VICAR. (*Who has again consulted his memorandum; looking at* SIR RALPH, *while his pencil taps his chin, over his glasses.*) Mr. Mark Moorsom Bernal.

SIR RALPH. (*Silent, motionless a moment; then, with intensely studied collectedness, while he sees* GRACE JESMOND *reappear.*) What of Mr. Mark Moorsom Bernal?

(*Re-enter, as he speaks,* GRACE JESMOND *from the outer hall, with several open letters in her hand.*)

THE VICAR. He's believed not to be living.

SIR RALPH. (*While* GRACE, *who on recognising the manner in which they are engaged, has first stopped short and then, on reflection, come down discreetly on the side of the stage opposite* SIR RALPH's *and remained there effacing herself and waiting; only looking over her letters.*) Believed—universally!

THE VICAR. (*Referring again to his paper.*) Mr. Bedford has taken it for granted! But it has occurred to him, for his completer satisfaction, to cause it to be inquired of you, while he has still power to inquire, if any intimation to the contrary—(*Pausing scrupulously an instant, smiling blandly, explanatorily at* GRACE.)

SIR RALPH. If any intimation to the contrary—?

THE VICAR. Has lately reached your ears.

SIR RALPH. (*After a moment, during which his eyes have met* GRACE's, *raised from her letters fixedly to his own in consequence of the* VICAR's *invitation to her.*) No intimation to the contrary has ever reached my ears.

THE VICAR. (*Appreciative, satisfied, fold-* *ing up his paper.*) Most definite; thank you. (*Then to* GRACE, *sentimentally, professionally.*) Awfully sad!

GRACE. (*Grave.*) Awfully! (*Then to* SIR RALPH.) I came back to tell you that your apartment is ready for you—the King's Room, as we call it. As I've pressing letters to answer (*indicating the library*) perhaps the Vicar will kindly take you to it.

SIR RALPH. (*Reluctant to leave the room and with an uneasy movement looking covertly about him as if still preoccupied with the rapid disappearance, the whereabouts, of the album.*) I won't trouble the Vicar. I remember the King's Room.

THE VICAR. (*Up at the right, obliging, punctilious.*) Off the main gallery—three steps! (*Exit the* VICAR *to the right.*)

(*Re-enter* LADY BASSET *by the long window.*)

GRACE. (*At the door of the library.*) I leave you then to Lady Basset! (*Exit* GRACE *to the library.*)

LADY BASSET. (*Breathless.*) Mr. Ashdown has just told me it's *you* who are Sir Ralph!

SIR RALPH. (*Staring, unapproachable.*) Pray who else should it be?

LADY BASSET. (*As if with relief and rapture.*) I like you the better of the two!

SIR RALPH. (*Blank.*) Of which two?

LADY BASSET. Why, there's a gentleman passing for you!

SIR RALPH. (*Aghast.*) Passing for me?

LADY BASSET. Passing for the Heir—it's the same thing!

SIR RALPH. (*After an instant.*) Possibly! (*After another instant.*) Where is this gentleman?

LADY BASSET. You must ask Miss Vanneck; she has designs on him.

SIR RALPH. Designs?

LADY BASSET. Matrimonial. Fancy her crudity!

SIR RALPH. I can easily fancy it! But if he isn't me, who may this person be?

LADY BASSET. Ask the man! It's enough for *me* that *you* are you!

SIR RALPH. It's enough for you, madam; but it's sometimes too much for myself! Your news is not agreeable to me, and I beg you to permit me to retire.

LADY BASSET. You're going to your room? Allow me to show you the way!

SIR RALPH. I know the way. (*Then to settle the matter—keep her quiet.*) Off the main gallery—three steps.

LADY BASSET. (*Delighted.*) Three steps? So is mine! I'm going to mine.

SIR RALPH. (*After an instant.*) Then I remain. When did this scoundrel arrive?

LADY BASSET. But a moment, I judge, before yourself.

SIR RALPH. And who else has seen him?

LADY BASSET. No one but Miss Vanneck.

SIR RALPH. Not Miss Jesmond?

LADY BASSET. Not Miss Jesmond. She's remiss!

SIR RALPH. (*Looking at his watch.*) What's his appearance?

LADY BASSET. Very fine, I'm bound to confess. (*Then significantly.*) But you can hold your own, Sir Ralph!

SIR RALPH. I pass my life, madam, in trying to! Is this interloper plausible—artful?

LADY BASSET. (*After an instant.*) Artful—in a sense. He cultivates art!

SIR RALPH. (*Struck.*) He draws—he paints?

LADY BASSET. In a style of his own. He had an album. (*Looking about her.*) It was here.

SIR RALPH. (*Precipitate.*) I haven't seen it! (*Then after a moment's intense and troubled thought; breaking out frankly and abruptly.*) Will you grant me a favour, madam?

LADY BASSET. (*Radiant.*) Every favour a woman can!

SIR RALPH. One is enough. Simply not to mention that I've asked you these questions.

LADY BASSET. (*Struck, diplomatic, considering.*) Not to "mention" it?

SIR RALPH. To forget our conversation.

LADY BASSET. That will surely be difficult! (*Then after reflection.*) What do you offer me for this failure of memory?

SIR RALPH. "Offer" you? My gratitude, madam—my enlightened esteem.

LADY BASSET. "Esteem," Sir Ralph, is rather cold. The price of discretion is always high. (*Then, smiling, as he appears to demur.*) A woman's silence, you know, comes dear!

SIR RALPH. There's nothing in life so

expensive. Therefore I don't haggle with you. I extend to you my personal regard.

LADY BASSET. (*Arch.*) How "personal" are you prepared to make it?

SIR RALPH. (*After a moment.*) My opportunities shall show you.

LADY BASSET. I await the demonstration!

SIR RALPH. On the distinct understanding—?

LADY BASSET. It's for *you* to treat it as one!

SIR RALPH. (*At the door to the outer hall as that of the library opens.*) Then I begin. Silence to *her!* (*Exit SIR RALPH rapidly.*)
(*Re-enter GRACE JESMOND from the library.*)

LADY BASSET. (*Disconcerted, blank.*) Does he call that "beginning"? (*Then in a totally different tone to GRACE, who has two sealed and stamped letters which she takes straight up to the big letter-box of the house.*) Sir Ralph's adorable!

GRACE. (*After an instant, as she posts her letters.*) Adorable!

LADY BASSET. And Mr. Bedford?

GRACE. (*Coming down.*) He keeps up.

LADY BASSET. (*With a shade of disappointment.*) No alteration?

GRACE. None whatever.

LADY BASSET. (*After an instant.*) When it comes, please let me know. (*Exit LADY BASSET to the outer hall.*)
(*Re-enter TEDDY ASHDOWN, with the album, by the long window.*)

GRACE. (*Kind, as she sees the album.*) Have you been sketching?

TEDDY. (*Discouraged.*) I've been looking for "dear Maud"!

GRACE. All in vain?

TEDDY. High and low. I've no heart for the steam-roller!

GRACE. (*Vague.*) The steam-roller?

TEDDY. (*Holding out the album, which GRACE takes.*) There's one in there. You should send it after him.

GRACE. After whom?

TEDDY. Mark Bernal.

GRACE. (*Blank.*) Mark Bernal?

TEDDY. There's his address. (*Then as he perceives her surprise.*) He hasn't been here?

GRACE. (*Who has opened the book and turned to the flyleaf; staring, astounded, at *the inscription.*) Been here? He's dead!

TEDDY. (*Bewildered.*) "Dead"?

GRACE. (*With all her mystification, but a dawning relief and pleasure almost a cry of exultation.*) He's alive! (*Then as she rapidly turns the book over.*) Where did you *get* this?

TEDDY. From Sir Ralph Damant.

GRACE. (*Struck.*) Sir Ralph Damant?

TEDDY. (*Increasingly surprised at her emotion, at the importance she appears to attach to the circumstance.*) He gave it to me. (*Indicating the table.*) He picked it up there.

GRACE. (*Staring.*) There? How did it come there?

TEDDY. Blessed if I know! No more did he.

GRACE. Did he see this name?

TEDDY. I read it out—I showed it to him.

GRACE. And what did he say?

TEDDY. He said he didn't know the person.

GRACE. (*After a moment.*) How long ago was this?

TEDDY. (*Looking at his watch.*) Before I went out—half an hour.

GRACE. Are you certain?

TEDDY. Certain! I noticed the clock.

GRACE. (*Who has stood a moment intensely wondering and thinking, then has gone up impulsively to the right with the album and, checking herself, come down again.*) Can you keep the secret?

TEDDY. Is it a secret?

GRACE. Make it one! Tell no one you've seen this.

TEDDY. But Sir Ralph knows I have.

GRACE. And you know *he* has. That's why I want you to be dumb.

TEDDY. (*Staring.*) But if he speaks?

GRACE. He won't speak!

TEDDY. Then *I* won't!

GRACE. Thank you! (*Then, while* MARK BERNAL, *unseen by either, reappears: re-enter* MARK BERNAL *by the long window.*) Now go to Miss Vanneck!

BERNAL. (*Smiling, coming down.*) You'll find her beyond the village, sketching the old mill! (*Then while the others, startled, stare at him interrogatively, he goes on, after an inclination to* GRACE, *soothingly and sociably.*) I posted her there with a block and a pencil.

TEDDY. (*Precipitate.*) Then I'll join her! (*Exit* TEDDY *by the long window.*)

BERNAL. (*Frankly, amicably.*) I see *you* have my album; but I had fortunately in my overcoat pocket another string to my bow!

GRACE. (*After a moment, breathless, amazed.*) Are you Mark Moorsom Bernal?

BERNAL. (*Assenting, smiling.*) Are *you* Grace Jesmond?

GRACE. (*Surprised, touched.*) What do you know of Grace Jesmond, Mr. Bernal?

BERNAL. What those ladies, what my brilliant pupil out there, have been so good as to tell me.

GRACE. You've seen them—you've had time to talk with them?

BERNAL. They received me when I came.

GRACE. And when on earth did you come—and whence?

BERNAL. From London—an hour ago. To find a troubled house!

GRACE. Mr. Bedford's very ill—and unaware of your presence.

BERNAL. I've been taken for some one else!

GRACE. Sir Ralph Damant? He has just arrived.

BERNAL. Will he see me?

GRACE. (*After an instant.*) It would surprise him to do so! He thinks you're dead.

BERNAL. (*Struck, smiling, penitent.*) That's one for my bad manners!

GRACE. (*Kind, impulsive.*) Your manners seem good enough! (*Then after an instant.*) But you must save your inheritance.

BERNAL. (*Vague.*) My inheritance?

GRACE. Mr. Bedford's making his will, and you've a primary title to figure in it.

BERNAL. (*Surprised, slightly disconcerted.*) Ah, Miss Jesmond, I didn't come to life for *that!*

GRACE. Didn't you know of your chance?

BERNAL. Know of it? I don't even understand it!

GRACE. Surely you're aware of the fewness of your relatives.

BERNAL. I've been conscious mainly of a different order of privation!

GRACE. The only person interested, as they say, is Sir Ralph.

BERNAL. And you, Miss Jesmond—are *you* not interested?

GRACE. (*Surprised.*) I, Mr. Bernal? (*Then after an instant.*) I'm a servant!

BERNAL. A servant?

GRACE. I mean that I've done my work and had my wage. And in that useful capacity, by your leave, I should announce your arrival to Mr. Bedford.

BERNAL. (*Demurring.*) Let him learn it, please, at his convenience.

GRACE. Do you think nothing of your own?

BERNAL. (*Vague.*) My own?

GRACE. With his weakness—time presses.

BERNAL. If he's so weak, why worry him? I've neglected him too long to have rights.

GRACE. I happen to know that he has had your rights in mind.

BERNAL. Then he'll leave me something!

GRACE. Unfortunately he supposes that they've lapsed. But from the moment that lapse is repaired—

BERNAL. (*Breaking in.*) He'll "remember" me, as they say? I don't want to be remembered as a beggar!

GRACE. You're no more a beggar than others!

BERNAL. (*Vague.*) What others?

GRACE. There are people who are not here for sentiment.

BERNAL. You take a kind view of me, Miss Jesmond.

GRACE. (*After an instant; frank.*) I want you not to be sacrificed.

BERNAL. It would convey a startling suggestion of my being good for something! I smoke pretty much everywhere, but I've never smoked on the altar!

GRACE. If you're not serious now, I'm afraid you'll never be!

BERNAL. (*Sympathetic, emphatic.*) Yes— on the day I can do something to contribute to your interests! Please believe that I'm deeply touched by the attention you give to mine.

GRACE. (*After an instant, taking again from a table the album which at the beginning of the scene she has laid on it.*) Do you know how to acknowledge it? (*Then as he stares while she holds up the book.*) By giving me this.

BERNAL. (*Blank.*) "Giving" it to you?

GRACE. Letting me keep it.

BERNAL. (*Assenting with mystified amusement.*) For all it's worth!

GRACE. We'll see what it's worth. (*Then moving to go.*) But every moment counts.

BERNAL. Because he's failing?

GRACE. He *shan't* fail!

BERNAL. If the shock may hurt him, I decline the responsibility.

GRACE. (*At the door to the right.*) Then I'll take it! (*Exit* GRACE *with the album.*)

BERNAL. (*Alone.*) What an interesting crisis—and what an attractive woman!

(*Re-enter* SIR RALPH DAMANT *from the outer hall, precipitate, headlong in his discomposure.*)

SIR RALPH. (*With an agitated grievance that breaks out, beyond any other preoccupation, to the first person he sees.*) Is there no place in the house that's safe from her?

BERNAL. (*Vague.*) From Miss Jesmond?

SIR RALPH. From Lady Basset! (*Then startled, with a wild stare.*) Heavens! are *you* Mark Bernal?

BERNAL. (*Smiling.*) Did you know I was here?

SIR RALPH. Never in the world! But your face comes back to me.

BERNAL. I thought you thought I was dead.

SIR RALPH. You played the part so well!

BERNAL. I indeed forgot the "house"! But I now feel as if I were making my bow to it—though I'm not wholly sure I've had a call! (*Then after another look at* SIR RALPH.) You don't look, cousin, as if the call had come from *you*!

SIR RALPH. I'm not fond of theatricals: I go in for the real thing. Why have we been elaborately deceived?

BERNAL. Because that was the scale of your credulity! I did engage, at Portland, Oregon, in a silly row, from an honourable motive, a motive with a funny accent, but with lovely appealing eyes. I interfered, in other words, in a domestic discussion, in the settlement of which I was left for dead on the field.

SIR RALPH. It served you right; you interfered on the wrong side!

BERNAL. That was the opinion of the lively local press, which, in huge headlines, pointed the moral of my error. It therefore remained silent when I at last picked myself up, for my recovery was a different reading of the lesson.

SIR RALPH. You might have given us a sign!

BERNAL. A sign of what? That I was an ass? You had let me suspect you knew it already!

SIR RALPH. Yet you've faced us to-day.

BERNAL. It has taken me a month—since my return—to make up my mind to it!

SIR RALPH. You brought back a fortune?

BERNAL. Of exactly five pounds!

SIR RALPH. Don't you practise your trade?

BERNAL. Of which of my trades do you speak? I've tried too many—I've wasted my time!

SIR RALPH. You've been dissolute?

BERNAL. I've been universal!

SIR RALPH. Then you're not a painter?

BERNAL. The critics say so; but I can't afford to believe them. I've returned to my early faith!

SIR RALPH. Taking portraits?

BERNAL. (*Amused.*) At so much a head!

SIR RALPH. *How* much?

BERNAL. (*Looking at him an instant; then jocular.*) A thousand pounds! (SIR RALPH *gives a gesture of solemn dismay, and at the same moment* BERNAL *sees* MAUD VANNECK. *Re-enter* MAUD VANNECK *by the long window; on which* BERNAL *continues, indicating her sociably.*) My portraits are dear, but Miss Vanneck can tell you for how little I give lessons!

MAUD. (*To* BERNAL, *coming down eagerly.*) Introduce me!

SIR RALPH. (*Still more peremptory.*) Don't!

BERNAL. (*With a humorous want of mercy and the gesture of presenting.*) Sir Ralph Damant—my favourite pupil!

MAUD. (*Arch and engaging, to* SIR RALPH.) If he's nothing but a drawing-master, you must forgive my mistaking him at first for *you!*

BERNAL. Now that your error is righted, I expect to be completely neglected!

SIR RALPH. (*Much disconcerted and disgusted, turning his back on* MAUD.) You should keep your favourites in hand!

(*Then seeing* LADY BASSET: *re-enter* LADY BASSET *from the outer hall.*) Ain't *she* a favourite too? For God's sake keep *her!*

LADY BASSET. (*Who has removed her hat and exchanged her travelling-dress for something very smart and advantageous; smiling significantly at* SIR RALPH.) You see I've taken off my things!

MAUD. (*Presenting, with an undiscouraged smile, the sleeve of her jacket to* SIR RALPH.) Sir Ralph himself will kindly take off mine!

(SIR RALPH *makes a gesture of incorruptible austerity, and* TEDDY ASHDOWN, *at the moment* MAUD *speaks, re-enters by the long window.*)

TEDDY. (*Rushing forward, assisting* MAUD.) I say—that's *my* privilege!

MAUD. (*Provoked at* SIR RALPH *and in her petulance thrusting at* TEDDY *a long pin taken from her dress.*) Then keep this pin!

TEDDY. (*Wounded by the pin and giving a start, a sharp cry while* GRACE JESMOND *reappears.*) Aie!

(*Re-enter* GRACE JESMOND *from the right.*)

GRACE. (*On one side of the stage while* BERNAL *is on the other.*) I've been with the Doctor, Mr. Bernal. (*Then, after an instant, grave, as the* VICAR *reappears: re-enter the* VICAR *from the right.*) He sends the Vicar with a request.

THE VICAR. (*Flurried and formal as before, addressing them all.*) I request your indulgence for my errand. The Doctor considers that a high standard of tranquillity has not been successfully maintained.

BERNAL. (*Solicitous, precipitate.*) Of course we're an awful nuisance—do tell him I'll go this moment!

GRACE. (*Promptly interposing.*) Mr. Bernal—please remain!

THE VICAR. We must part—reluctantly! —with those who've so conscientiously—

GRACE. (*Helping him out.*) Misconceived their duty. Lady Basset and Miss Vanneck will find a carriage at the door.

LADY BASSET. (*Deeply disconcerted and disgusted, looks resentfully from* GRACE JESMOND *to the* VICAR; *then with the move-*

ment of accepting under compulsion an odious necessity, turns expressively to SIR RALPH.) We're separated by violence—but I return to take leave of you! (*Exit* LADY BASSET *to the outer hall.*)

MAUD. (*Playfully, to* SIR RALPH.) Not even violence, if a single word—

SIR RALPH. A single word? Farewell!

MAUD. (*In the same way.*) Ah, that *is* violence!

TEDDY. (*With frank alacrity, to* GRACE.) I'll also go in the carriage.

GRACE. A moment, Mr. Ashdown. (*Then after an instant.*) Sir Ralph, can we part with Mr. Ashdown?

SIR RALPH. (*Struck and surprised, mystified and alarmed by her tone; but presently replying with an impenetrable face.*) If I may answer for myself—without a pang!

GRACE. (*Kind, to* TEDDY.) See to your things then, and come back and take leave of us!

TEDDY. (*Who has been admiring* MAUD'S *sketching-block, looking sociably at* BERNAL.) I hate to take leave of Mr. Bernal, because I want him to give me a lesson.

BERNAL. (*Vague, good-humoured.*) A lesson?

TEDDY. In Miss Vanneck's class!

BERNAL. (*Assenting amicably; amused.*) Look me up in town.

TEDDY. (*Highly pleased.*) In town! (*Exit* TEDDY *to the outer hall with the sketching-block.*)

THE VICAR. The Doctor consents that Sir Ralph and Mr. Bernal shall each see his patient.

SIR RALPH. (*Taking instant precedence.*) Then I go!

GRACE. (*Arresting him.*) A moment, Sir Ralph! (*To* BERNAL.) Mr. Bernal, you go first. (*Then as* BERNAL *hesitates, indicating* SIR RALPH's *prior right.*) I've something to say to Sir Ralph.

THE VICAR. (*To* BERNAL *at the door to the right.*) This way!

BERNAL. (*To* GRACE, *grave, hesitating.*) Will he know me?

GRACE. Try!

BERNAL. (*At the door to the right; his eyes on her with the same seriousness.*) I'll try! (*Exeunt* MARK BERNAL *and the* VICAR.)

GRACE. (*After an instant.*) The will's made!

SIR RALPH. (*Staring.*) Then what's the use of Mark's going?

GRACE. It's not too late to make another.

SIR RALPH. He'll hold out?

GRACE. The Doctor hopes so—with the sight of Mr. Bernal.

SIR RALPH. Sufficiently to make the effort—?

GRACE. After a rest—to-morrow.

SIR RALPH. (*Stupefied; artless.*) He'll live till to-morrow?

GRACE. Possibly much longer—with care. There must of course be no drawback.

SIR RALPH. Won't it be a drawback to see Mark?

GRACE. It will be a great joy. The drawback will be the sense of his mistake.

SIR RALPH. (*As if vague.*) His mistake?

GRACE. His failure—an hour ago—to be aware that, at the very moment he consented to accept as certified the death of a possible legatee, that legatee, by the most extraordinary of chances, had passed through his house and might, but for a fatality, have stood beside his bed!

SIR RALPH. A fatality?

GRACE. That of his having escaped observation.

SIR RALPH. (*Conscious, but very emphatic.*) Completely!

GRACE. And left no sign of his presence.

SIR RALPH. (*With the same serene assurance.*) None at all! (GRACE, *with an irrepressible nervous movement, turns away at this, and he goes on.*) So that our poor friend *did* accept my cousin's death as certified?

GRACE. With your attestation to sustain him, how could he do less?

SIR RALPH. (*Complacent.*) My attestation was unconscious of its fallacy!

GRACE. Just as poor Mr. Bernal was unconscious of your attestation!

SIR RALPH. A fellow shouldn't really do such things!

GRACE. Return so unexpectedly?

SIR RALPH. After having vanished so finally.

GRACE. There's no doubt he has behaved very ill; so that if Mr. Bedford does hold out, he'll come off better than he deserves!

SIR RALPH. And if Mr. Bedford passes away—?

GRACE. Don't the actual dispositions take effect?

SIR RALPH. (*Thinking an instant; then just a shade rueful.*) Unless Mark fights.

GRACE. Oh, he may fight!

SIR RALPH. (*Prompt.*) Do you think he will?

GRACE. That would depend on his suspicion of how narrowly he had missed his luck!

SIR RALPH. (*Considering, as if objecting to the expression.*) How "narrowly"?

GRACE. He might guess that it had hung by a hair.

SIR RALPH. What do you call a hair?

GRACE. Why, your fatal answer to the Vicar.

SIR RALPH. If it was fatal, madam, it was at least perfectly natural.

GRACE. (*After an instant.*) So is Mr. Bernal's disappointment!

SIR RALPH. (*As if with forced and resentful resignation to her objectionableness.*) Which it's in your power, doubtless, to exacerbate!

GRACE. (*Quiet.*) I don't know what's in my power, Sir Ralph! We never know till we try.

SIR RALPH. Your threats are in shocking taste, if Mr. Bedford's to make another will!

GRACE. Let us take that quite for granted! (*At the door of the library.*) And now I must go back to my letters.

SIR RALPH. Before you do so you'll perhaps let me know the motive of this extraordinary aggression. (*Then more defiant as, with her hand on the door of the library,* GRACE *only stands looking fixedly at him.*) What the mischief do you mean by it?

GRACE. (*After a moment more of the same significant and expressive attitude.*) Can't you guess? (*Exit* GRACE JESMOND.)

SIR RALPH. (*Alone, staring, wondering; then as if with a sudden vision of the truth.*) By all that's portentous, I can guess! She wants to make me propose! (*Then eager, as he sees* MARK BERNAL: *re-enter* MARK BERNAL *from the right.*) Did he know you?

BERNAL. The Doctor thought so. He stared for a long moment, dear man— then he closed his kind eyes.

SIR RALPH. (*In suspense.*) Is he much weaker?

BERNAL. About the same.

SIR RALPH. Then he'll go on?

BERNAL. (*Confident.*) If all goes well.

SIR RALPH. (*Considering; then after an instant.*) And I'm to go up now?

BERNAL. (*Looking at his watch.*) At one, please. (*Looking round him.*) Where's Miss Jesmond?

SIR RALPH. She has left me, thank God!

BERNAL. (*Surprised.*) Why abnormal gratitude?

SIR RALPH. For miraculous relief. She wants to marry me. She's like the others.

BERNAL. The others?

SIR RALPH. The old woman and the girl. They've marked me, you know. But Miss Jesmond has marked me biggest.

BERNAL. (*Amused.*) In bright red chalk?

SIR RALPH. (*With a nervous wriggle.*) I feel it between the shoulders! She's an *intrigante*—of a peculiarly dangerous type.

BERNAL. Why, I thought her so charming!

SIR RALPH. She has made up to *you* too?

BERNAL. (*Smiling.*) Like the others!

SIR RALPH. She's a hungry adventuress.

BERNAL. With me it doesn't matter; I'm not worth their powder.

SIR RALPH. Because you're poor?

BERNAL. Because I'm nobody.

SIR RALPH. Be duly grateful. It protects you.

BERNAL. My dear man, I like danger!

SIR RALPH. You don't *know* it! To know it, you must be exposed.

BERNAL. I see—even as you are.

SIR RALPH. My position is one of the highest peril.

BERNAL. You're a match, a catch, a swell: you pay for it!

SIR RALPH. I pay too much and too often. I pay with my comfort, my health, my nerves! My nerves are gone to pieces—I live in a state of siege!

BERNAL. But you seem to hold out.

SIR RALPH. There are very serious breaches. It's the modern methods of attack—they've reduced it to a science.

BERNAL. Lady Basset's a kind of Moltke? [1]

SIR RALPH. And Miss Jesmond's a kind of Armstrong! [2] I vow I'm doomed to fall!

BERNAL. My dear fellow, don't you desire to fall?

SIR RALPH. At my own time, in my own place—not in the din of battle, amid the yells of victory.

BERNAL. I enjoy the din of battle; and the yells of victory have only to come from pretty lips—!

SIR RALPH. Do you mean you actually *like* women?

BERNAL. It sounds dreadful, but I should be a brute if I didn't. They've been my consolation.

SIR RALPH. They're the luxury of the poor! You can afford natural pleasures. You ought to recognise the fact that your limitations are your liberty.

BERNAL. The liberty to love? May I never lose it!

SIR RALPH. I shall be glad to assist you to retain it. Remain exactly as you are, and you will.

BERNAL. I'm afraid there's very little doubt that I shall remain exactly as I am. I always *have* remained exactly as I am! You make me feel indeed a sort of eternal *tableau vivant,* and inspire me to positively decline to rise. But while I luxuriate in my limitations, as you so happily describe them, what on earth will become of *you?*

SIR RALPH. I shall probably succumb to the mockery of my advantages and the ferocity of my pursuers.

BERNAL. The real way to escape, my dear man, is to marry.

SIR RALPH. (*With a start.*) Marry whom?

BERNAL. (*Diverted, staring.*) Any one you like!

SIR RALPH. (*With his hand to his heart.*) I thought you meant Miss Jesmond! (*Giv-ing him his hand.*) See how my pulse throbs!

BERNAL. (*Feeling the hand while* SIR RALPH *pants.*) You're indeed a wreck!

SIR RALPH. (*Instinctively, unconsciously wiping his hand with his pocket-handkerchief and going on argumentatively.*) You say "any one I like." But I don't like any one! I hate them all, and yet they're always *with* me!

BERNAL. (*After looking at him an instant with amused compassion.*) Let me help you!

SIR RALPH. Upon my soul, I think you ought! You've the happy lot—the ideal life: you owe something to others!

BERNAL. But what can I do?

SIR RALPH. Draw the assailants off—keep them at bay!

BERNAL. (*Considering, responding, entering into it.*) While you gain time—get away? Happy thought! I'll do what I can: I'll cover your retreat.

SIR RALPH. I count upon you! And your profit, your reward—

BERNAL. (*Taking the words out of his mouth, gaily expressing the idea.*) Will be in the very nature of the task—the exercise of my essential freedom!

SIR RALPH. (*Pleased, patronising.*) The exercise, say, of your characteristic genius! (*Then after an instant.*) In return for this relief I should be willing to entertain the idea of (*hesitating a moment*) a formal acknowledgment.

BERNAL. (*Vague.*) A formal acknowledgment?

SIR RALPH. Pecuniary! (*Complacent.*) You may paint my portrait.

BERNAL. Delighted. You're a great subject!

SIR RALPH. But not for a thousand.

BERNAL. (*Smiling.*) For how much?

SIR RALPH. (*Debating an instant; then with the same complacency.*) For a hundred.

BERNAL. (*With the same good-humour.*) For a hundred. (*Then while* GRACE JESMOND *reappears.*) When will you sit?

(*Re-enter* GRACE JESMOND *from the library, with more addressed and stamped letters.*)

SIR RALPH. (*Privately, with intensity, to*

---

[1] Helmuth Carl Bernhard von Moltke (1800–1891), considered the greatest military strategist of the late nineteenth century.

[2] Apparently an allusion to William George, Baron Armstrong (1810–1900) who perfected the wire-wound breech loading gun and revolutionized gun-making. The merits of the gun were widely debated during the late nineteenth century.

BERNAL.) "Sit"? I can only run! Cover my retreat! (*Exit* SIR RALPH *hastily to the right.*)

GRACE. (*Eager; keeping her letters.*) Did Mr. Bedford know you?

BERNAL. (*Smiling, kind.*) I think I was mysterious to him—very much as you are to *me!* (*Then after an instant.*) Are you greatly attached to him?

GRACE. He has been good to me. I've been of use to him, and this beautiful place has been my home.

BERNAL. Shall you leave it—after this?

GRACE. Naturally I shall leave it. With regret!

BERNAL. And where shall you go?

GRACE. I don't know, Mr. Bernal, where I shall go.

BERNAL. Have you no friends?

GRACE. We don't know what friends we have till we test them.

BERNAL. And have you none of yours whom you've tested?

GRACE. (*Smiling.*) I give people the benefit of doubts!

BERNAL. Don't be too fond of doubts. Try a little confidence!

GRACE. I daresay I shall have to from this time. You must set me the example!

BERNAL. Is there anything I can do for you—offer you?

GRACE. (*As if much touched, but smiling, and with a certain gentle mockery.*) You speak as if you were powerful!

BERNAL. You do right to take me up on it. My situation is preposterous—there's indeed no service I can render.

GRACE. Your situation will change—and then you'll become conscious of your power.

BERNAL. Even if I do, I don't think I shall believe in it. The only thing I've ever believed in is my freedom!

GRACE. (*After an instant.*) Is freedom very sweet?

BERNAL. Have you never known it?

GRACE. Perhaps I shall know it now.

BERNAL. If I lose mine, I shall take a tremendous interest in yours.

GRACE. You're very kind—but you'll lose nothing. The best freedom is to be rich!

BERNAL. Why are you so bent, Miss Jesmond, on my being "rich"?

GRACE. (*With genuine intensity.*) Because it costs me too much, here, to-day, to believe you're too late!

BERNAL. (*Gallant.*) Never too late when in time to see *you!* (*Then as* LADY BASSET *reappears.*) And the rest of this wonderful company!

(*Re-enter* LADY BASSET *from the outer hall, again fully equipped for departure.*)

LADY BASSET. (*Eager.*) Sir Ralph's not here?

BERNAL. He's with our cousin.

LADY BASSET. (*In the same manner.*) The will's made?

GRACE. The will's made.

LADY BASSET. And what does he get?

GRACE. (*After an instant.*) He gets everything!

(*Re-enter* MAUD VANNECK *from the outer hall.*)

LADY BASSET. (*In the excitement and effusion of the news; inadvertent, to* MAUD.) He gets everything!

(*Re-enter* TEDDY ASHDOWN, *dressed to go, with the two bags.*)

MAUD. (*Excited.*) Everything? (*Then passing on the news to* TEDDY.) He gets everything!

TEDDY. (*Staring.*) Everything?

MAUD. (*Enthusiastic.*) Everything!

LADY BASSET. (*Re-echoing, jubilant.*) Everything!

(*Re-enter from the right, as she speaks,* SIR RALPH DAMANT, *pale and grave, who pauses in the doorway at the sight and sound of these demonstrations, with outstretched, warning, commanding hands.*)

SIR RALPH. (*With stern authority.*) Ladies and gentlemen, we're in a house of mourning. Our generous host and kinsman has passed away!

ACT SECOND

MARK BERNAL'S *studio, Vandyke Lodge, Chelsea; a bare, impecunious, but more or less shabbily-picturesque room, furnished with odds and ends and with various signs of a roving past, hand-to-mouth, picnicking habits and a Bohemian manner of life: not vulgar, however; only unconventional and casual. The right side is occupied by the high glazed studio north-light. At the centre, toward the right, the door to the so-called parlour. At the centre, toward the left, the door to street, opening first into a small vestibule. Down on the left the door to the kitchen and the pantry. Under the big window an old faded, battered Chippendale sofa. Down on the left an old-fashioned but dilapidated "property" chair with a small table beside it. Up at the centre, between the two doors, a bare chimney-piece with an unframed picture above it and a table covered with an ancient, damaged piece of brocade in·front. Half-way down on the right, with its face to the light, a large easel with a big new canvas set up on it, and a stand beside it with a colour-box and implements. Down on the left a smaller easel with a smaller canvas. Watercolour sketches and charcoal drawings are tacked on the walls; several old and new canvases are stacked together on the floor. On stools, chairs and promiscuous pieces of furniture are scattered in confusion various articles of apparel and homely domestic utensils. The air of the whole place disgarnished and makeshift. The stage is unoccupied till the bell from the street-door, suspended within sight, tinkles on its old relaxed spring. At the sound of the bell* TEDDY ASHDOWN *hurries out of the parlour, carrying the· retarded breakfast-things on an extemporised tray.*

TEDDY. (*Flurried, in extreme dishabille, only his shirt and trousers, without a necktie.*) A sitter? Sir Ralph, by Jove! (*Scuttling down to the kitchen with the tray.*) And nothing washed up! (*Disappears momentarily into the kitchen, where the crash of crockery hurriedly set down is heard while the bell again, in the studio, more sharply tinkles.* TEDDY *emerging, more excited, looks about among the scattered garments for something more to put on.*) I'm scarce "washed-up" myself, and (*while he catches up a pair of braces and fastens them behind*) certainly not dressed-up! (*While the bell sounds a third time he reaches and opens the street-door. Then surprised as* LADY BASSET *is disclosed.*) Lady Basset!

(*Enter* LADY BASSET.)

LADY BASSET. (*Equally surprised.*) I find you in possession?

TEDDY. (*His braces dangling behind.*) Sadly uncontested—unless you've come for your portrait!

LADY BASSET. (*While she looks anxiously round her.*) I've come for Sir Ralph Damant's—knowing his intention to sit.

TEDDY. He hasn't sat, worse luck! We're waiting.

LADY BASSET. You too? What have you to do with it?

TEDDY. I'm employed by Mr. Bernal.

LADY BASSET. (*Looking at him up and down with extreme disapproval.*) Employed—as a model?

TEDDY. (*Vague; then amusedly taking the hint.*) You mean for the—undraped? No, I don't pose—except to our creditors!

LADY BASSET. (*With visible rigour.*) Have they left you nothing to put on?

TEDDY. (*Feverishly looking.*) Plenty—if I can only find it! (*Then when, after buttoning his braces, he has laid his hands on a waistcoat, a jacket, and a necktie.*) Reduced by a parent's rigour to a mere miscellaneous wardrobe, I've fallen back on my artistic nature.

LADY BASSET. (*Struck, emphatic.*) Just what *I've* fallen back on!

TEDDY. Mr. Bernal had been so kind to me in those agitated hours at Courtlands that I ventured to come to see him. I feel I've a little gift that only requires direction.

LADY BASSET. (*Encouraged.*) Exactly what *I* feel! (*Resolute.*) He shall also direct mine!—He's out?

TEDDY. He'll be back in a moment. He kindly puts me up.

LADY BASSET. (*Struck; then eager.*) Does he *board* his pupils?

TEDDY. On the lowest terms!

LADY BASSET. I shall discuss them with him.

TEDDY. (*Surprised.*) Do you wish him to put *you* up?

LADY BASSET. In order to be present at the sittings.

TEDDY. (*Vague.*) The sittings?

LADY BASSET. That Sir Ralph has promised to give. To watch the painter's method.

TEDDY. (*After an instant.*) Ain't you afraid he may watch yours?

LADY BASSET. I have none. I'm a creature of inspiration.

TEDDY. But while you're abandoned to your inspiration what will become of dear Maud?

LADY BASSET. I've thrown her up. (*After an instant.*) Dear Maud's at large!

TEDDY. (*Alert.*) Then I may enjoy her?

LADY BASSET. When did I ever prevent you?

TEDDY. (*Recollecting, conceding.*) You did give a fellow a chance!

LADY BASSET. (*With abrupt and winning familiarity.*) Then let a fellow give *me* one! (*Appealing sociably.*) Back me up! (*Then after an instant.*) I've come to stay! (*Eager, as the street-door opens.*) Here he is! (*Then disconcerted, disappointed, as* MARK BERNAL *appears: enter* MARK BERNAL *from the street.*) Oh!

TEDDY. (*To* BERNAL.) She's come to stay!

BERNAL. (*In informal but recognisable mourning; coming down, gay, gallant, to* LADY BASSET.) That's a note of defiance. We *never* release the fair!

TEDDY. She wants to study your method.

BERNAL. (*To* LADY BASSET.) Of dealing with the fair?

LADY BASSET. (*Flattered, arch.*) That I know too well! (*After an instant.*) Of dealing with the timid!

BERNAL. (*Sociable, encouraging, moving a chair.*) I begin with asking them to be seated.

LADY BASSET. (*Taking the seat.*) I'm not speaking of myself—I'm speaking of Sir Ralph.

BERNAL. (*Eager.*) You've brought him *with* you?

LADY BASSET. (*Alarmed.*) Brought him? Won't he come of himself?

BERNAL. (*Unscrupulously amiable.*) He would if he knew you were here! (*Then, as with a happy thought, to* TEDDY.) I say— go and tell him!

TEDDY. (*Vague.*) This moment?

BERNAL. At his noble mansion in Portland Place.

LADY BASSET. (*Staring.*) Has he moved to Portland Place?

BERNAL. With his great new wealth!

LADY BASSET. (*Rueful.*) While I've been writing to his chambers!

BERNAL. (*Prompt, plausible.*) That's why you've had no answer! He has now set up a palace.

LADY BASSET. (*Much impressed.*) A palace?

BERNAL. (*Laughing.*) Perhaps I should say a fortress!

LADY BASSET. (*Considering, politic, to* TEDDY.) Don't go—I'll wait!

BERNAL. He must go for the beer. (*Very friendly, to* LADY BASSET.) If you consent to share our fortunes, you'll perhaps share our refreshment!

LADY BASSET. (*Looking at him tenderly significant.*) I'll pretend so—to be alone with you!

BERNAL. (*Responsive, smiling.*) I delight to be alone with *you!* (*To* TEDDY.) Have you any money?

TEDDY. No; have you?

BERNAL. Look in the teacup. (*To* LADY BASSET, *while* TEDDY *goes up to the chimney-piece.*) The teacup's our bank—a bank that's always breaking!

TEDDY. (*Accidentally, as he reaches up for the cup, knocking it over and smashing it.*) It's broke now!

BERNAL. (*As he looks at the fragments; good-humoured.*) Naturally—with nothing *in* it! Won't they trust me?

LADY BASSET. (*With renewed archness.*) They're wiser than *I*, Mr. Bernal! (*Then to* TEDDY, *with her hand in her pocket.*) But here's a shilling—to get rid of you! (*To* BERNAL, *as* TEDDY *accepts the shilling and he protests with a gesture.*) I'll take it out in lessons.

TEDDY. (*Who has picked up his hat; at the street door, to* BERNAL.) I told her your terms were low! (*Exit* TEDDY *to the street.*)

BERNAL. (*Struck, as if with a happy thought.*) Do you desire a course of instruction?

LADY BASSET. (*Simpering.*) I feel I've a little gift that only requires direction.

BERNAL. (*Amused, encouraging.*) Your little gifts are profuse! (*Then as he picks up the morsels of the teacup.*) If I form a school (*cheerful, hopeful*) I can go in for a little jug with a slit! (*Having put away the pieces.*) You're a messenger from heaven—we're living on hopes!

LADY BASSET. (*Vague.*) Hopes of what?

BERNAL. Of bread and butter. Of my cousin's arrival, and his splendid pose. (*With the vivid artistic vision—a flourish of his hand before his eyes.*) I see his pose already!

LADY BASSET. (*With the same flourish.*) So do I!

BERNAL. (*With sudden ruefulness.*) But what I don't see yet is the "honorarium"!

LADY BASSET. Is it to be so heavy?

BERNAL. A hundred pounds—the Millennium. (*Sad.*) The Millennium never comes!

LADY BASSET. (*Reassuring.*) *I'm* not the Golden Age, no doubt; but I'll pay every week.

BERNAL. (*Gallant.*) Dear lady, you pay every minute! (*Then jovial, making his preparations for her lesson, drawing out the smaller easel.*) Oh, I shall get on—Teddy saves me a butler.

LADY BASSET. (*As she draws off her gloves, smiling at him engagingly.*) What shall *I* save you?

BERNAL. (*After an instant; rising to the occasion.*) The pursuit of lovely woman—if I may worship her at home!

LADY BASSET. (*Warningly, with arch-prudery.*) You must speak to me only of Art—for in Art there is no Impropriety!

BERNAL. (*Gay.*) I quite understand that if there were, you'd never have entered (*indicating with amused irony his shabby surroundings*) this dedicated temple! (*Reassuring.*) It's a ground on which we may meet with perfect delicacy! (*Then after placing a drawing-board on the smaller easel.*) What's the nature of your talent?

LADY BASSET. (*Rising.*) The nature? (*Thinking, while he helps her off with her jacket; then with effusion.*) Sincere!

BERNAL. (*Giving her a charcoal study of his own.*) Then copy that head—it's nice and fresh!

LADY BASSET. (*With the head, examining it.*) I must do it, you know, as I *feel* it!

BERNAL. (*Anxious.*) Don't "feel" it too much—it may come off! (*Then, as she has put the sketch on a rest near the easel and seated herself.*) Do you mind if I change my coat?

LADY BASSET. (*Seated at the easel, beginning her work from the sketch.*) Don't we agree that in Art there is no Impropriety?

BERNAL. (*Amused, while he puts on an old black velveteen jacket taken down from a nail on which he has suspended his other coat.*) I don't change it for "Art"—I change it for economy. Do you mind if I smoke a pipe?

LADY BASSET. (*Very vivacious, while she works.*) Do you mind if *I* do?

BERNAL. Alas, we've only two, and Teddy has the other! (*Then behind her, overlooking her start, while he stuffs and lights his pipe.*) Haven't you got the head awfully in the corner?

LADY BASSET. (*Leaning back, with her own head very much on one side.*) That's how I feel it!

BERNAL. (*Amused, resigned, going over to his own easel.*) You feel it in a funny place!

LADY BASSET. (*Working.*) My talent's intensely personal.

BERNAL. Forgive me if my remarks are!

LADY BASSET. Absorbed in my inspiration, I become a monster of indifference. (*Then after a fit of rubbing her work and falling back, while* BERNAL *lifts the big blank canvas off his easel, stands it against the wall and prepares something he can go on with.*) What on earth *does* keep him?

BERNAL. (*Preoccupied, standing at his easel.*) Teddy, with that blessed beer?

LADY BASSET. (*In attitudes.*) Sir Ralph—the false, the faithless!

BERNAL. (*Painting.*) He's paralysed by his prudence.

LADY BASSET. He may indeed have been prudent with *me,* but I can't pretend he has been paralysed. I've had startling glimpses of his passion!

BERNAL. Don't build on his passion—it's hollow.

LADY BASSET. (*Uneasy, getting up.*) Hollow?

BERNAL. (*Seating himself at his easel as she leaves her place.*) Inane—insane. Fate has marked him to stand alone!

LADY BASSET. (*Alarmed, protesting.*) Alone?

BERNAL. (*With great sincerity, as he works.*) He's so rich, so brilliant, so gifted, that he's condemned to a splendid solitude. He sees all men as sordid—he sees all women as venal. A cruel doom has forbidden him to believe in human affection.

LADY BASSET. And do *you* believe in it?

BERNAL. (*Leaving his easel, smiling.*) I think it's my only faith! And I've one thing that he hasn't—the freedom to cultivate it!

LADY BASSET. You've cultivated it in vain, since—like him!—you stand alone.

BERNAL. Alone? Not a bit—with *you* here!

LADY BASSET. You're evidently afraid to marry.

BERNAL. You're quite mistaken. Try me!

LADY BASSET. (*Startled, vague.*) "Try" you?

BERNAL. (*Cheerful, encouraging.*) Propose—and you'll see! (*Then laughing, as she gives a shocked gesture.*) They do to Ralph!

LADY BASSET. (*Struck, assenting.*) Dear Maud has done it, I know! (*Then after an instant.*) And I strongly suspect Miss Jesmond.

BERNAL. (*Wondering.*) Miss Jesmond?

LADY BASSET. I know she has proposed to others!

BERNAL. (*After an instant.*) Well—she has been refused all round!

LADY BASSET. (*Struck again, alarmed, seizing his arm.*) Do you suppose she has got him now?

BERNAL. (*Vague, just wondering again.*) Now?

LADY BASSET. (*With a sudden vision of the truth, while* TEDDY ASHDOWN *reap-*

pears: re-enter TEDDY ASHDOWN *precipitately, with his tankard of beer, from the street, leaving the door open behind him.*) That creature keeps him away!

TEDDY. (*As he comes down with his beer and* LADY BASSET *turns back to her work; privately and excitedly to* BERNAL.) He's come! he's come: his footman's looking for the house!

BERNAL. (*Startled; then, as if abruptly confessing, with great urgency and plausibility, to* LADY BASSET.) Teddy announces a model!

LADY BASSET. (*Agitated.*) A female?

TEDDY. The sort of thing you thought *I* was!

LADY BASSET. (*Hesitating.*) For the figure?

BERNAL. (*Assenting, smiling.*) But not a female. (*Then, on a gesture of* LADY BASSET'S; *as if out of consideration for her delicacy.*) Will you retire to the parlour?

LADY BASSET. (*Considering, as if to measure the full bearings of the situation; then majestically catching up her jacket; to protect her purity.*) I'll retire! (*At the door of the parlour, which* TEDDY *has opened for her; resolute.*) I've come to stay! (*Exit* LADY BASSET.)

BERNAL. (*Urgent, to* TEDDY.) Stay *with* her! (*Exit* TEDDY ASHDOWN *to the parlour, while* BERNAL *eagerly meets* SIR RALPH, *who appears in the open doorway. Enter* SIR RALPH DAMANT *from the street.*) You've come to sit?

SIR RALPH. (*In deep, distinguished mourning; visibly and unfavourably impressed by his cousin's Bohemian accessories.*) Do you consider there's anything to sit on?

BERNAL. (*Laughing.*) Some of the chairs have legs, and some have backs—

SIR RALPH. (*As he looks critically round.*) But none have both! (*Then checking* BERNAL *gravely in the movement to provide him with a seat.*) There are preliminaries—conditions.

BERNAL. (*Arrested but amused.*) Why, I thought we had settled them at Courtlands!

SIR RALPH. (*After an instant.*) Do you mean the sum to be paid?

BERNAL. Paid, my dear Ralph (*hesitat-*

ing, smiling) as soon as you're so very good as to pay it!

SIR RALPH. *(Surprised and as if resenting his avidity.)* How can I pay it before I judge of the likeness?

BERNAL. How can you judge of the likeness before I've a chance to catch it? *(Laughing.)* "First catch your hare!"

SIR RALPH. Your images make me shudder!—all the more that (thanks to the rigour of my mourning!) I've enjoyed for a while a period of exemption from the chase. Now that I've quitted my retreat—

BERNAL. It's only to remind me of that charming feature of our contract—

SIR RALPH. Your guarantee of safety—!

BERNAL. *(Interrupting again in turn; good-humoured.) And* resemblance! So that it's not till I hand you these commodities—

SIR RALPH. Over the counter, as it were, that I hand *you* a hundred pounds!

BERNAL. *(Disappointed, but trying to be cheerful; about to lay his hands gaily on* SIR RALPH, *as if to put him in position.)* The attitude's found—I'll do you in the act!

SIR RALPH. *(Struck, approving.)* And call the picture "The Patron of Art," or "The Friend in Need"? Before I can throw myself into that character with the requisite calm, I've a deep anxiety to allay.

BERNAL. *(Impatient.)* Another?

SIR RALPH. There's *always* another! How have you disposed of Miss Jesmond?

BERNAL. *(Blank.)* Disposed of her? Not at all!

SIR RALPH. *(Displeased.)* Then you *don't* carry out our bargain?

BERNAL. Such a bargain as that? It takes three to make it! I haven't seen the tip of her nose.

SIR RALPH. *(Wondering, grave.)* She's lying low?

BERNAL. *(Raising and dropping his arms; irresponsible.)* She has vanished from my ken!

SIR RALPH. *(Reflecting.)* She's laying a train.

BERNAL. Then it's a very long one! You remember when she quitted Courtlands?

SIR RALPH. *(Assenting.)* The day of her patron's death.

BERNAL. *(With a certain veiled, sarcastic bitterness.)* His patronage had limits —as appeared by his will!

SIR RALPH. *(After an instant.)* Do you allude to his overlooking you?

BERNAL. To his overlooking *her.*

SIR RALPH. She had five years of pickings.

BERNAL. Do you mean that she still has resources?

SIR RALPH. *(With the same serenity.)* Her character—which is unmistakable— supplies them in abundance.

BERNAL. *(After an instant; as if thinking this over.)* If you haven't seen her, how should I?

SIR RALPH. You were so grossly indiscreet as to boast to her of my order.

BERNAL. *(Smiling.)* Forgive my natural pride! But if she has found no pretext for approaching you—

SIR RALPH. *(Interrupting.)* I tremble at every ring! *(Then with a violent start, as the bell of the street-door sounds out.)* There she is! *(To himself, seeing* TEDDY *burst out of the parlour to answer the bell: re-enter* TEDDY ASHDOWN *from the parlour.)* And there *he* is! *(Then to* BERNAL, *while* TEDDY *passes to the street-door; quickly moving to the parlour.)* Let me escape!

BERNAL. *(Alarmed, catching, intercepting him, while* TEDDY *opens the street-door and* MAUD VANNECK' *appears.)* Not there!

(Enter MAUD VANNECK *from the street.)*

TEDDY. *(Welcoming* MAUD; *delighted.)* So jolly of you to look a fellow up!

SIR RALPH. *(Relieved, but still highly disgusted.)* Permit me to dissent from that!

TEDDY. *(Explaining her to the others.)* Lady Basset chucks her.

MAUD. *(Cheerful.)* But I can face the usual dangers!

SIR RALPH. That's more, madam, than *I* can do! *(Then aside to* BERNAL, *while* MAUD *allows* TEDDY *joyfully to divest her of her jacket and feather boa.)* I leave the house!

BERNAL. *(Genuinely distressed.)* Where'll you go?

SIR RALPH. *(Thinking; with dignity.)* I'll drive on the Embankment.

BERNAL. (*Urgent.*) And you'll come back—?

SIR RALPH. (*At the street-door.*) When you've worked her off! (*Exit* SIR RALPH.)

MAUD. (*Disconcerted; with compunction.*) I've driven Sir Ralph away!

TEDDY. What do you want of Sir Ralph when you've got a fellow like me?

BERNAL. (*Impatient.*) She has got nothing of the sort, Teddy. You'll please to return to your studies.

TEDDY. (*Resenting this decree, with injured dignity.*) If you didn't take me, Mr. Bernal, for nothing—

BERNAL. (*Good-humoured, gay.*) I should take you for a dangerous rival! And on the mere chance I banish you!

TEDDY. (*At the door to the parlour.*) When I can I'll pay you! (*Exit* TEDDY ASH-DOWN.)

BERNAL. (*To* MAUD.) To what do I owe the honour of your visit?

MAUD. Abandoned by my natural protectors, I've fallen back on my artistic nature. I feel I've a little gift that only requires direction.

BERNAL. (*Eager.*) You enter my school?

MAUD. (*Reluctant, indicating the parlour.*) Do you mean *that* place?

BERNAL. It's there that I hold my class!

MAUD. But where do you paint Sir Ralph?

BERNAL. (*Disconcerted.*) Did I tell you too I was to paint him?

MAUD. Miss Jesmond told me—at Courtlands. You know we came away together.

BERNAL. (*Alert.*) Where did Miss Jesmond go?

MAUD. She came to London.

BERNAL. And where is she now?

MAUD. (*With asperity.*) I haven't the least idea! (*Then more persuasive.*) You must let me see you at work.

BERNAL. At work on Sir Ralph? You mustn't let me see *you!*

MAUD. (*After an instant; arch.*) Do you fear him too as a rival?

BERNAL. (*Blank.*) A rival?

MAUD. Isn't that what you call Mr. Ashdown?

BERNAL. As a manner of speaking! If I fear my cousin as a rival, it's as a rival to Teddy. (*After an instant, coaxing.*) I

should like much better to see you at work on *him!* He's a fine little chap, is Teddy.

MAUD. (*Impatient.*) Dear Mr. Bernal, I don't want a fine little chap. I want a man of the world—and a man of means. I want social distinction. I want (*thinking; then with vain emphasis*) oh, I want a lot of things!

BERNAL. Yes; you all want a lot of things. I should think it would be enough to want a little thing called happiness!

MAUD. But happiness depends on such a lot!

BERNAL. Does yours depend on your bringing down Sir Ralph?

MAUD. (*After an instant.*) You're awfully vulgar, you know! (*Then after another instant.*) Do you believe I *can?*

BERNAL. I believe almost any woman can experiment successfully on almost any man.

MAUD. (*Eager.*) Make him love her?

BERNAL. Yes—and make him hate her for doing it! You're young, you're pretty, you're clever—

MAUD. (*Interrupting, complacent.*) And I've had the Higher Education!

BERNAL. (*Smiling.*) The Higher, but not the Highest! (*Then more gravely, but very kindly.*) The education of unselfish affection! (*Pleading, sociably, tenderly.*) Think a little more of that, and a little less of baubles and baronets! Don't misapply your gifts; don't pervert your youth; don't harden your heart. (*After an instant.*) Don't try to get on without love!

MAUD. (*As if struck, incipiently charmed, by his appeal.*) Have *you* tried?

BERNAL. Not for a single hour! I've loved, though I've lost! So, bare as you see me here, I dispense with a lot of things. I'm rich in faith.

MAUD. Faith in what?

BERNAL. In the present woman—whoever she is!

MAUD. And what do you do about the absent?

BERNAL. (*Laughing.*) I don't recognise the absent. She's always the loser!

MAUD. (*After an instant.*) If I were to marry you I think I'd look after you!

BERNAL. I want some one awfully to look after me.

MAUD. With such a person, and (looking rather compassionately round her) such a home, you'd enter upon a union—?

BERNAL. (Prompt.) In a moment—in Teddy's place!

MAUD. (Disconcerted, called back to reality while the bell of the street-door rings.) Oh, Teddy's—!

(Re-enter TEDDY ASHDOWN precipitately from the parlour.)

BERNAL. Teddy's place is to answer the bell.

MAUD. (Eager, while TEDDY goes to the door.) Sir Ralph back?

TEDDY. (Opening the street-door, announcing, exclaiming.) Dear old Miss Jesmond!

(Enter GRACE JESMOND.)

BERNAL. (With astonishment and alacrity, meeting her.) Miss Jesmond!

GRACE. (Who has paused an instant, as if, at the sight of MAUD, with a last irrepressible hesitation.) I had your address.

BERNAL. (Rejoicing.) How jolly—it was in that book!

TEDDY. (Sociable, ingenuous.) Oh yes, in that book!

GRACE. (Pale, tired, appreciably altered; in simple, economical mourning; addressing TEDDY very kindly, but markedly as if to check him.) I'm glad to find you, Mr. Ashdown.

MAUD. (Who on GRACE's entrance has passed in visible displeasure to the sofa under the window, where she has seated herself; hearing this.) Mr. Ashdown! (TEDDY hurries over to her and talks with her.)

BERNAL. (To GRACE, in frank wonderment and appreciation.) You've put on mourning—when he left you nothing?

GRACE. (At the left, gravely indicating his own garb while she sinks upon the other sofa.) What did he leave you? (Then as BERNAL, with a motion as of cheerful, resigned dismissal of the subject, places himself beside her.) I've come to see you (after an instant) on account of your profession.

BERNAL. (Struck, amused.) You too have a little gift—?

GRACE. (Vague.) A little gift?

BERNAL. (Laughing.) That only requires direction!

GRACE. (Smiling sadly.) I'm afraid I've no gift at all—that's exactly why I've come. (After an instant.) I must find employment.

BERNAL. (Vague.) As an amanuensis?

GRACE. I've tried for that—in vain.

BERNAL. (Sympathetic.) Nobody wants one?

GRACE. (With the same sad smile; discouraged, resigned.) Everybody has one!

BERNAL. (Smiling.) I haven't, Miss Jesmond; but on the other hand—

GRACE. (As he pauses.) You've so little correspondence?

BERNAL. I fear it's of a sort (after an instant, laughing) not to be deputed to another.

GRACE. It's not with that idea that I've ventured to approach you. (Then after a supreme hesitation.) You're the only artist I happen to know—and I've come to suggest myself as a model.

BERNAL. (Wonderstruck.) A model?

MAUD. (Overhearing, rising; to TEDDY.) A model? (Then as she seizes the idea; with emphatic compunction.) That's what I ought to have done!

TEDDY. (On his feet, equally struck, delighted.) It's not too late—will you sit to me? (Then eager, to BERNAL, indicating MAUD.) May she sit to me?

BERNAL. (Rising, struck, thinking an instant; then happy to adopt the suggestion.) Certainly—in the parlour!

TEDDY. (Disconcerted, objecting.) With Lady Basset?

MAUD. (Astonished.) Lady Basset?

TEDDY. (Explaining.) She's the Second Pupil.

BERNAL. (Insistent.) The Second Pupil must have the same advantages as the First! Therefore (settling the matter, to MAUD) you must sit to both of them!

MAUD. (Majestic and sarcastic, looking at GRACE.) While Miss Jesmond sits to you?

BERNAL. (After an instant, gay.) Miss Jesmond's professional!

(MAUD, at this, gives a shocked gesture and, as if retiring to avoid some indecorous exhibition, goes up with TEDDY, who ushers and follows *her into the parlour while* BERNAL *returns to* GRACE.)

GRACE. (*Who during this discussion has sat motionless, only with her eyes attentively wandering over the tell-tale indications of the place.*) Not yet—but I really want to be!

BERNAL. (*On the sofa again.*) You're quite without resources?

GRACE. (*Very simple.*) Quite without resources.

BERNAL. You've never been able to save?

GRACE. I've a sister (*after an instant*) whom I help. Her husband's dying—she has children—she has troubles. So you see I must do something—and do it soon. There are people I've seen, in past years, at Courtlands—it's to those people I've been. It was at Courtlands I saw *you*—and it's to you I come last. (*After a moment.*) I've been to shops, first. I've been told to come again—and I've gone again. But it's the same everywhere—there's nothing to be had. It occurred to me at last that I had heard of girls who earn money—however little!—by sitting to painters; sitting for the head, the hair, the hands, for—what do you call it?—the "type": in storybook attitudes, in short-waisted frocks, in old faded Kate Greenaway dresses. So I thought there might be a demand (*smiling again*) and that I might—with a little patience!—do something to meet it. I'm perhaps not clumsier—nor uglier!—than some. I'm willing to try hard, to do my best; and if it's only a question of keeping still—oh, I can do that: so still—*so* still! (*Then after an instant, brave, simple.*) Anything to boil the pot!

BERNAL. (*Who has listened intently.*) Your idea's ingenious—but is there nothing else you can do?

GRACE. I've hunted up and down for a month. And the only definite thing I've found is how many others are hunting—a thousand partners in the chase!

BERNAL. (*Laughing.*) Diana and all her nymphs! So you've kindly come to me—?

GRACE. In my ignorance of the next best step.

BERNAL. (*Very kind.*) It's a cruel change —from your life at Courtlands.

GRACE. Do you remember you told me at Courtlands that freedom is sweet? (*After an instant.*) I'm tasting its sweetness!

BERNAL. (*After a moment.*) I wish I could assist you!

GRACE. (*With extreme but suppressed apprehension.*) I'm *not* the "type"? I've not the appearance—?

BERNAL. (*Abrupt.*) You've the appearance, Miss Jesmond, of an angel!

GRACE. (*Rising quickly; concluding.*) But you've simply no present use for me!

BERNAL. (*Rising; then with the artist's gesture of evocation.*) I see you perfectly— I place you—I catch you. But (*with a sad smile and a slow head-shake*) I lose you again!

GRACE. (*Looking vaguely about.*) Of course you've plenty of people. (*Then after an instant.*) Do you happen to know some painter—?

BERNAL. (*Falling in, thinking.*) Who would be ready for such a sitter? There isn't a fellow in London who wouldn't rejoice in the chance! (*Then feeling his pockets for a notebook; looking round for something to write on.*) I'll give you the best addresses.

GRACE. (*As he comes down again, finding nothing.*) You're looking for notepaper?

BERNAL. (*Embarrassed, ashamed; still looking.*) We had a sheet—last week! (*Then blushing, conscious, smiling, while he confesses his destitution.*) You're not in a land of plenty!

GRACE. (*Looking at him an instant, then abruptly drawing the sketch-book of Act First from under her mantle.*) Write in that.

BERNAL. (*Recognising gaily his book.*) My album—you've brought it back?

GRACE. I've brought it back. (*After an instant.*) I thought you might need it.

BERNAL. (*Laughing, scribbling addresses on a leaf of the album.*) You see I do!

GRACE. (*Looking about the place again while he writes.*) It's your only one?

BERNAL. (*Writing, preoccupied, smiling.*) My one ewe-lamb!

GRACE. It was good of you to give it to me.

BERNAL. (*Still writing.*) Don't praise me —when I take it back!

GRACE. (*Smiling.*) I put you to special expenses!

BERNAL. (*Tearing out of the album the leaf on which he has written; folding and giving it to her.*) You see I stagger beneath them!

GRACE. (*With the paper, which she slowly puts into her portemonnaie.*) But I also see you have pupils.

BERNAL. (*Smiling.*) I take them for nothing.

GRACE. You're too generous. (*Then after a moment.*) But you've had orders.

BERNAL. For portraits? I've had one, thank heaven!

GRACE. (*After another moment.*) From Sir Ralph Damant?

BERNAL. (*Struck.*) You knew it?

GRACE. You told me at Courtlands. (*Then as he gives a lively gesture of recollection.*) You've had no other?

BERNAL. (*Philosophic.*) No other.

GRACE. Is Sir Ralph finished?

BERNAL. He's not begun. He begins to-day.

GRACE. (*As if definitely influenced by this; thinking.*) To-day?

BERNAL. (*Noticing her interest in the question; attentive.*) He comes to sit—you may meet him.

GRACE. (*Considering, assenting.*) I see—I may meet him.

BERNAL. (*Laughing.*) He may meet *you!*

GRACE. (*Who has moved away an instant, and once more has turned her eyes over the room; speaking at last, as she faces him again, abruptly.*) Mr. Bernal—are you very poor?

BERNAL. Do you suppose if I were not I would decline your splendid offer? The stupid, sordid truth, Miss Jesmond, is that I can't *afford* a model!

GRACE. (*Grave.*) I see. (*Then with infinite gentleness.*) I'm very sorry.

BERNAL. You can't be sorrier than I! It was awfully nice of you to come; but you've brought your empty pitcher to a thirsty land!

GRACE. (*After an instant.*) You're as poor as I am?

BERNAL. You make me feel much poorer! And it's the first time my condition has seemed to me (*bringing out the word with expression, resentment*) ugly!

GRACE. It's the first time mine has seemed to me endurable! (*Then as she visibly lingers, delays to go, takes another survey of the studio.*) Do you live without—comfort?

BERNAL. (*Laughing.*) With such comfort as you behold!

GRACE. (*Taking out again the paper he has given her.*) And these artists are rich?

BERNAL. They're richer. Do try them!

GRACE. (*Looking at the list.*) I'll try them. (*Then still stationary, with the list in her hand.*) It's your cousin's hour?

BERNAL. It's my cousin's hour.

GRACE. Then I suppose I ought to go.

BERNAL. (*After a moment.*) Your time of course is limited.

GRACE. (*Continuing to twist her paper nervously, without any movement of departure.*) My necessity indeed presses. (*Then after an instant.*) From the moment my business is over—

BERNAL. (*Smiling, as she vaguely pauses.*) You've no reason to stay?

GRACE. None I can conveniently express. (*Smiling.*) I'm not, like Miss Vanneck, a pupil.

BERNAL. (*Laughing.*) Nor like my Lady Basset! (*After an instant.*) *They* can express their reason!

GRACE. (*As if thinking what this can be; then bringing it out.*) Sir Ralph Damant?

BERNAL. They want to corner him!

GRACE. (*Looking down while she speaks.*) To "corner" him?

BERNAL. To marry him!

GRACE. (*After an instant.*) Both?

BERNAL. (*Laughing.*) Both!

GRACE. And they're waiting for him?

BERNAL. They're waiting for him!

GRACE. (*After an instant, smiling, but as if thinking.*) I won't, then.

BERNAL. (*Pretendingly jocular.*) You'll call on him at home?

GRACE. (*With her eyes on him a moment in silence.*) Where does he live?

BERNAL. Portland Place, 130.

GRACE. Thank you. (*Then looking again at her list.*) If these gentlemen employ me—

BERNAL. (*Emphatical but sad, as she pauses.*) You'll be so taken up that I shall never see you again!

GRACE. (*Who has finally, wearily put away her paper and gathered her mantle round her.*) Good-bye, Mr. Bernal.

BERNAL. (*After an instant.*) Good-bye, Miss Jesmond.

GRACE. (*Turns away from him as if to move to the door, taking as she does so a supreme look round. Then suddenly, in this act, she falters, totters slightly, raises her hand to her head, as if faint or giddy, with an ejaculation of distress.*) Ah!

BERNAL. (*Moving, anxious, quick, to her assistance.*) You're ill?

GRACE. (*Reaching out to support herself.*) I'm faint!

BERNAL. (*Catching, sustaining her.*) You're exhausted—you're quite done!

GRACE. (*Panting, trying to recover herself, while* LADY BASSET *reappears.*) Walking over London—since breakfast!

(*Re-enter* LADY BASSET *from the parlour.*)

LADY BASSET. (*Stopping short, arrested, scandalised by the sight of* BERNAL *closely holding, apparently embracing,* GRACE.) Mr. Bernal, what on earth are you doing?

BERNAL. (*Startled, while he quickly separates from* GRACE; *embarrassed, but smiling and plausibly explaining.*) Setting up my model!

LADY BASSET. Your model? (*Then struck, inspired, looking from one of them to the other.*) I've come in to tell you that my little gift requires more direction than you seem to have time for. So, with leisure on my hands, why shouldn't *I* perform that function?

BERNAL. Sit for me—in character? (*Gay.*) You'd come expensive.

LADY BASSET. (*Who is divested of her hat and is now essentially arranged to "stay"; prompt.*) Let it not be a question of money. I'll do it for love!

GRACE. (*Gathering herself together again with a wan smile for* BERNAL.) Profit by such a chance. Good-bye!

BERNAL. (*Doubly reluctant now to let her go; seizing a pretext for detaining and refreshing her.*) You've had nothing since breakfast? Models have appetites! (*Bethinking himself, casting about.*) They particularly depend on their tea.

LADY BASSET. I particularly depend on mine!

BERNAL. I think there *is* some—somewhere or other.

GRACE. (*Pulling herself together.*) Then I won't refuse it.

BERNAL. (*To* LADY BASSET, *invitingly, after he has quickly opened the door of the kitchen.*) I daresay it's in there. There's something in the nature of a kettle—!

LADY BASSET. (*Aloof, mindful only of her dignity and her clothes.*) Shall I call Mr. Ashdown to make it boil?

GRACE. (*Suddenly reviving, interposing, catching at the occasion to remain.*) Let *me* make it boil! (*With a brightened smile.*) I'm all right as soon as I work!

BERNAL. (*Unwilling, protesting, while she eagerly unfastens her mantle.*) Work? Not in your condition!

GRACE. (*Quite gay.*) Isn't it exactly what my condition wants? (*Then while he has helped her off with her cloak and taken it from her.*) I'll take off my hat! (*Removing and giving it to him to put with the cloak.*) And pin up the skirt of my only frock! (*Turning up her dress till it shows half her petticoat, and passing* BERNAL *a pin.*) Will you do it?

LADY BASSET. (*Watching her with discomfiture as* BERNAL *fastens the skirt behind; to herself.*) Why didn't I think of that?

BERNAL. (*Vague, hopeful, to* GRACE, *who has reached the door of the kitchen.*) There *are* things—if you can make them out.

GRACE. (*Who has taken her hat and jacket back from him; at the door.*) I'll make them out! (*Exit* GRACE JESMOND.)

LADY BASSET. Is there bread and butter?

BERNAL. I've an earnest trust!

LADY BASSET. (*While* GRACE *reopens the door of the kitchen.*) And any little extra?

GRACE. Mr. Bernal!

BERNAL. (*While he hurries to* GRACE *and* TEDDY ASHDOWN *reappears; addressing* LADY BASSET *from the door of the kitchen.*) I'll ascertain!

(*Exit* MARK BERNAL. *Re-enter* TEDDY ASHDOWN *from the parlour.*)

TEDDY. (*Disconcerted, coming down.*) Dear Maud won't sit!

LADY BASSET. (*Preoccupied with her tea.*)

Is there any little extra?

TEDDY. (*Vague.*) In the course of instruction?

LADY BASSET. In the course of recreation. (*Indicating the kitchen.*) They're making tea.

TEDDY. Oh, we don't *have* little extras!

LADY BASSET. I introduce a new system.

TEDDY. (*Blank.*) How in the world?

LADY BASSET. What have you done with my change?

TEDDY. From the beer? (*Pulling out a few coppers and looking at them in deprecation.*) It ain't enough!

(*Re-enter* MAUD VANNECK *from the parlour.*)

LADY BASSET. Miss Vanneck—contribute!

TEDDY. (*Explaining, coaxing.*) To the purchase of some little extra. (*Then as* MAUD, *staring, gives a gesture of depressed destitution and the bell of the street-door sounds.*) It's Sir Ralph!

MAUD. (*While* TEDDY *hurries to the door.*) Get the money from *him!*

(*Re-enter* SIR RALPH *by the door that* TEDDY *opens; then stops in dismay at the sight of the two women.*)

LADY BASSET. (*Instantly advancing upon him.*) Will you give us half-a-crown?

MAUD. (*Engaging.*) To buy some innocent relish.

SIR RALPH. (*Bewildered, shocked.*) Half-a-crown—for an innocent relish? (*Then as if considering.*) It's a monstrous price!

LADY BASSET. (*Persuasive.*) For a treat to Mr. Bernal?

TEDDY. He has nothing for tea!

SIR RALPH. Nothing? (*As if reflecting, calculating, while he takes out his purse.*) Then I'll advance—two shillings.

(*Re-enter* MARK BERNAL *from the kitchen.*)

TEDDY. (*To* MAUD, *taking the money.*) I'll be back in a moment! (*Exit* TEDDY ASHDOWN *to the street.*)

SIR RALPH. (*To* BERNAL.) There are two shillings to deduct.

BERNAL. (*Amused.*) I'll deduct them! Shall I also deduct the ladies?

LADY BASSET. Never—till we've had our tea!

MAUD. (*Seeing* GRACE *reappear.*) Here it comes now!

(*Re-enter* GRACE JESMOND *with a tea-tray, teapot, cups and saucers.*)

SIR RALPH. (*To himself; still more discomfited and more aghast.*) Miss Jesmond! (*Then, down on the right, resentful, to* BERNAL, *while* GRACE *sets the tray on the table before the chimney and the other ladies clear a place for it.*) Where's your honour?

BERNAL. (*Vague.*) My honour?

SIR RALPH. (*Indicating the women.*) Your engagement.

BERNAL. To absorb them?

SIR RALPH. To prevent their absorbing *me!*

BERNAL. I *have* prevented it. They're making love to me!

SIR RALPH. (*Dubious.*) Miss Jesmond?

BERNAL. (*After an instant, thinking.*) I'm not so sure of Miss Jesmond.

SIR RALPH. (*Peremptory.*) Then what's she here for? (*As* BERNAL *hesitates.*) She's here to make love to *me!*

BERNAL. (*After another instant.*) I think you're hard on her.

SIR RALPH. Didn't she know I was coming?

BERNAL. I admit she did.

SIR RALPH. (*Triumphant.*) Then it's proved!

BERNAL. (*Affected by what* SIR RALPH *has said, worried and discomposed; watching* GRACE *an instant at the table with the other ladies; then with a nervous laugh.*) Yes—it's "proved"! (*He goes uneasily up while* LADY BASSET, *carrying a cup of tea, comes down to* SIR RALPH.)

LADY BASSET. A cup of tea, dear friend?

SIR RALPH. (*Taking the cup from her as if under uncanny coercion; looking at her in deep mistrust.*) What have you put in it?

LADY BASSET. (*Beaming.*) My gratitude, Sir Ralph!

SIR RALPH. (*Guarded, blank.*) Gratitude for what?

LADY BASSET. (*Secure.*) The devotion you promised.

SIR RALPH. (*Impatient.*) Oh, damn the devotion!

LADY BASSET. (*Resentful.*) You withhold it?

SIR RALPH. (*Looking at her hard a moment; then politic, accommodating.*) To your very good health! (*He drains down the cup, under her eye, with submission, then hands it summarily back to her; after which she goes up to put it down and* MAUD *descends on the other side with a plate of bread and butter.*) She has drugged it! (*Then very sarcastic, as* MAUD *offers him her bread and butter.*) What have I promised *you?*

MAUD. (*Sad, sentimental.*) Nothing, alas!

SIR RALPH. (*Turning unceremoniously away from her.*) Then I decline your poison!

(*He crosses to the other side of the stage, as if to break with her for ever, and she, checked in her overture, discouraged, goes up again with her plate.* TEDDY ASHDOWN *meanwhile has re-entered from the street with his purchase, which he lays down on table before the others; coming down immediately after to* SIR RALPH.)

TEDDY. (*Giving* SIR RALPH *a sixpence and coppers.*) The change.

SIR RALPH. (*Looking at the money.*) Elevenpence?

TEDDY. Tenpence!

(*He goes up while* SIR RALPH *pockets the money, and as he rejoins the others* GRACE JESMOND, *who has drunk her tea and turned away from the table, stands looking an instant at* SIR RALPH. *Then she comes down to him while* BERNAL, *who has noticed her movement, continues to observe her.*)

GRACE. (*With veiled irony, to* SIR RALPH.) Immensely graceful of you to sit!

SIR RALPH. (*With decision.*) I shall *not* sit!—I object to the conditions!

GRACE. (*With repressed emotion.*) You'll not keep faith?

SIR RALPH. It's *he* who has broken it!

GRACE. I beg you to accept the conditions.

SIR RALPH. Accept *you* as one of them?

GRACE. (*Feeling the impertinence, the insult of this; then quickly controlling herself; with a smile.*) Am I one of the worst, Sir Ralph?

SIR RALPH. The worst for his job!

GRACE. (*Considering.*) I should be very

sorry to injure Mr. Bernal.

SIR RALPH. You do awfully, you know, by your conduct.

GRACE. (*Still wondering.*) In what manner can I modify it?

SIR RALPH. By ceasing to spring up in my path!

GRACE. (*Smiling.*) I only spring up to check your retreat!

SIR RALPH. (*Demurring to the term.*) My "retreat"?

GRACE. From your agreement to assist Mr. Bernal. (*After an instant.*) Mr. Bernal needs assistance.

SIR RALPH. (*Curt, impatient.*) Why on earth should he?

GRACE. (*Indicating the whole place.*) Look about you and see!

SIR RALPH. (*After a glance.*) I see a lot of women!—Mark *likes* 'em! (*Then after an instant.*) I'll sit if he'll clear the place.

GRACE. He will—of those ladies.

SIR RALPH. (*Sharp.*) But not of you?

GRACE. If he turns me out he'll separate me— (*Pausing, significantly hesitating.*)

SIR RALPH. Separate you—?

GRACE. (*Smiling.*) From you, Sir Ralph!

SIR RALPH. That's exactly what I demand! (*Turning away from her, he crosses to the other side of the stage.*) I say, Mark! (*Then on* BERNAL's *coming down as* GRACE *goes up.*) You'll have to take that girl by the shoulders! (*On* BERNAL's *blankness.*) To put her out.

BERNAL. (*Thinking, demurring, while he looks at* SIR RALPH.) I'm more and more struck with her charm!

SIR RALPH. (*As if scandalised.*) Her charm?

BERNAL. Her spirit, her cleverness, her character! The more you've reason to dread her the more she needs my eye!

SIR RALPH. Your eye can rest a bit. I let you off.

BERNAL. It's a joy as well as a duty!

SIR RALPH. Your joy should be to paint my portrait, and to clear the place for the purpose.

BERNAL. (*Prompt.*) I'll clear it! (*Then to the others.*) As I must get to work with Sir Ralph I beg my pupils to retire!

LADY BASSET. (*Resentful.*) Without seeing your method?

BERNAL. (*Bending over her hand, kissing it in farewell.*) This, dear lady, is my method! (*Then urging her up to the parlour with* MAUD.) Put on your lovely things! (*Indicating all the tea-things.*) Teddy, remove!

LADY BASSET. (*At door of the parlour; to* BERNAL.) Begin—while I dress! (*Exit* LADY BASSET.)

MAUD. (*To* SIR RALPH, *at the door of parlour.*) That takes her an hour!

(*Exit* MAUD VANNECK, *while* TEDDY ASHDOWN, *gathering up the tea-things, goes out with them to the kitchen and* SIR RALPH, *with bare patience, sits rigidly detached on the sofa under the window.*)

GRACE. (*To* BERNAL.) Do you begin immediately?

SIR RALPH. (*Resolute.*) We don't begin till you've gone.

GRACE. (*To* BERNAL.) Before I go I should like to speak to Sir Ralph.

SIR RALPH. (*Rising in dismay.*) Again, Madam?

GRACE. (*To* BERNAL.) If you'll give me the fortunate chance.

BERNAL. Do you mean alone?

GRACE. (*Smiling.*) I mean alone!

BERNAL. (*Who has looked at her hard an instant; mystified, perplexed, tormented by everything that appears to give colour to* SIR RALPH's *account of her.*) Shall I leave you, Ralph?

SIR RALPH. (*Falling back helpless and hopeless on the sofa.*) I meet my doom!

BERNAL. (*At the street-door, having taken up his hat and holding up an empty tube of oilcolour.*) There's a chap next door—I'll borrow some blue! (*Exit* MARK BERNAL.)

GRACE. (*Who has taken up from the table where* BERNAL *has placed it after tearing out the leaf the album of Act First.*) Allow me to ask (*after an instant, while she looks at the book*) if you've ever seen this.

SIR RALPH. (*From the sofa, with his glass.*) That?

GRACE. (*Holding out the album.*) This sketchbook.

SIR RALPH. (*Struck, then slowly rising.*) Seen it?—Where?

GRACE. At Courtlands—the hour you arrived.

SIR RALPH. How can I remember what I saw the hour I arrived?

GRACE. Mr. Ashdown can remember. He told me.

SIR RALPH. (*Startled, staring.*) Told you?

GRACE. Half an hour later. That you had seen Mr. Bernal's name.

SIR RALPH. His name—where?

GRACE. (*Handing him the album.*) On that page—with that date.

SIR RALPH. (*With the album; looking hard an instant at the page; then hard an instant at* GRACE.) I believe I have. What then?

GRACE. You denied it—in my own presence. (*Then after an instant.*) You denied it to the Vicar.

SIR RALPH. (*After looking at the book again, chucking it away as if with indignant impatience.*) What the devil are you talking about?

GRACE. About the great wrong you were guilty of. You deceived a dying man—you robbed a living.

SIR RALPH. Living? I didn't *dream* he was living!

GRACE. It seems to me that book might have made you dream!

SIR RALPH. It would if I had seen it in time.

GRACE. You did see it in time—in time to show it to Mr. Ashdown.

SIR RALPH. (*Staring, as if recalling.*) That was after the Vicar—

GRACE. (*As he just hesitates.*) Had put you that solemn question? No, Sir Ralph, Mr. Ashdown has satisfied me that it was before.

SIR RALPH. Satisfied you? How?

GRACE. By his comparison of notes with me, and by his positive declaration.

SIR RALPH. His positive declaration's a lie.

GRACE. (*After an instant.*) Will you say that to *him*?

SIR RALPH. With all the pleasure in life!

GRACE. (*Passing to the kitchen.*) Then I'll call him to hear it!

SIR RALPH. (*As she reaches the door.*) A moment, madam. (*Then after an instant abrupt, as she stops with her hand on the latch.*) What is it you want?

GRACE. (*Vague an instant.*) Want?

SIR RALPH. To let me alone. (*As she leaves the door.*) I asked you that, you know, at Courtlands.

GRACE. Yes, and I told you to guess.

SIR RALPH. (*After an instant.*) I couldn't guess so soon.

GRACE. Can you guess at present?

SIR RALPH. (*After consideration.*) Fifty pounds?

GRACE. (*Echoing, stupefied.*) Fifty pounds?

SIR RALPH. Not enough? A hundred? (*Then at a loss; as she only stands looking at him.*) It's not money? (*As if with a fuller vision of the real question and his inevitable fate.*) It's the *other* thing?

GRACE. (*Back at the kitchen, while* MARK BERNAL *reappears.*) It's the other thing! (*Exit* GRACE JESMOND.)

SIR RALPH. (*Aghast, fatalistic, to himself, as* BERNAL *comes in.*) Marriage!

(*Re-enter* MARK BERNAL *from the street.*)

BERNAL. (*Struck, arrested by* SIR RALPH'S *appearance and discomposure; speaking with the note of real anxiety.*) She has proposed?

SIR RALPH. (*Throwing up his arms from his sides and letting them fall.*) She has proposed!

BERNAL. (*Dismayed, credulous.*) And you've accepted?

SIR RALPH. I've asked for a minute!

BERNAL. (*Wonderstruck, turning it over.*) A minute?

SIR RALPH. To decide—to think!

BERNAL. (*Uneasy, painfully mystified; throwing himself quickly, in the interest of delay, of diversion, into the question of the portrait; shifting his easel.*) That's it— you'll decide at your ease; you'll think while you sit!

SIR RALPH. I'll be hanged if I'll sit! (*Then after an instant, while* BERNAL *stares with dismay.*) At any rate not here. (*As* TEDDY *reappears: re-enter* TEDDY ASHDOWN *from the kitchen.*) I'll sit at home.

TEDDY. (*Surprised, ejaculating.*) At home?

SIR RALPH. (*Looking very hard at* TEDDY.) At home.

TEDDY. (*Mystified, bewildered by the way* SIR RALPH *glares at him, fascinatedly returns his stare; then to* BERNAL.) May I go out?

SIR RALPH. (*Precipitately interposing.*) Go out? Never!

BERNAL. (*Surprised, pleading.*) Dear Ralph, it's his day!

SIR RALPH. (*In alarm.*) His "day"? (*Then, while the two ladies reappear; as if everything is overwhelmingly against him.*) Mercy on us!

(*Re-enter* LADY BASSET *and* MAUD VANNECK *from the parlour, dressed for departure.*)

TEDDY. (*Delighted.*) I'll go with *them!* (*Then to the ladies, indicating* SIR RALPH.) He'll sit at home!

LADY BASSET. At home? (*Coming down to* SIR RALPH, *who, on the right, has collapsed upon the sofa.*) I shall *be* there! (*Exit* LADY BASSET *to the street, the door to which* BERNAL *holds open.*)

MAUD. (*Coming down to* SIR RALPH; *disgusted.*) I shall *not!*

(*She goes up as* BERNAL *comes down, and is received by* TEDDY, *who offers her his arm. Exeunt* TEDDY ASHDOWN *and* MAUD VANNECK *to the street.*)

SIR RALPH. (*Who has sat engulfed in reflections, wholly heedless of what the two women have said to him, rises grave and pale; then to* BERNAL.) I've decided!

BERNAL. (*Eager.*) You refuse?

SIR RALPH. (*Fatalistic.*) I accept!

BERNAL. (*Dismayed.*) On the spot?

SIR RALPH. It's to come! (*Lifting and dropping his arms to his sides as before.*) Let it come! (*Then as* GRACE *reappears: re-enter* GRACE JESMOND *from the kitchen, dressed to go.*) Miss Jesmond!

BERNAL. (*Still more alert, anticipating, interposing.*) Miss Jesmond!

SIR RALPH. (*While* GRACE, *surprised, arrested by the intensity of* BERNAL'S *tone, stands looking from one of the men to the other.*) I've something to say to you.

BERNAL. (*Strenuous, insistent, with a gravity and anxiety altogether new, like his whole aspect and manner in what follows.*) I've something to say first!

GRACE. (*Uncertain.*) To me, Mr. Bernal?

BERNAL. (*Indicating* RALPH.) To him! (*Then very urgent.*) While I say it will you kindly wait?

GRACE. (*Still more vague.*) Wait?

BERNAL. (*Who has opened the door of the parlour.*) In there! (GRACE *hesitates an instant, looking in the same wondering perplexity from one of the men to the other. Then, after resting her eyes intensely on* BERNAL'S, *she abruptly decides and goes quickly into the parlour.* BERNAL *closes the door on her and, with his eyes on* SIR RALPH, *stands a moment holding the handle. Then coming down with decision, and with the rising passion of all his doubt in the question.*) That girl—after your fortune?

SIR RALPH. After my fortune—and (*hesitating an instant, as if in resentment at that's being thought his only attraction, while he smartly taps his breast*) after me!

BERNAL. (*Worried, frowning, challenging, incredulous.*) You say she proposed?

SIR RALPH. (*Very definite.*) She made me an offer!

BERNAL. But of what?

SIR RALPH. Why, of her hand—and her person.

BERNAL. (*Amazed.*) You didn't understand her!

SIR RALPH. It was painfully clear.

BERNAL. (*After an instant.*) My dear Ralph—I don't believe it!

SIR RALPH. (*After another instant.*) You impute to me—misrepresentation?

BERNAL. I impute to you—aberration! (*Then as if he can't get over it.*) You intend to *marry* her?

SIR RALPH. (*Fully determined; as if with the resignation of the highest wisdom and enlightenment.*) It will keep her quiet!

BERNAL. (*Dissuasive, ironic.*) An *intrigante*—of a dangerous type?

SIR RALPH. (*Demonstrating his cleverness.*) I conjure the danger away!

BERNAL. (*Almost derisive.*) A hungry adventuress?

SIR RALPH. I thought you contested that! (*Then as* BERNAL, *in his agitation, moves nervously away.*) She has beauty—and mind!

BERNAL. (*Echoing, realising.*) Beauty and mind! (*Then in a different tone, with high decision.*) My dear fellow, you mustn't *do* it!

SIR RALPH. (*Irritated at his opposition.*) To oblige *you*?

BERNAL. (*After an instant.*) To oblige me!

SIR RALPH. Pray, are you in love with her?

BERNAL. (*Evasive.*) If I am, it's your fault. (*As if it settles the matter.*) You told me to be!

SIR RALPH. (*Positive.*) I told you to pull up!

BERNAL. It was too late to pull up—and it's too late now.

SIR RALPH. (*More uneasy, suspicious, wondering.*) Now?

BERNAL. (*Smiling.*) I want to keep on!

SIR RALPH. (*In still deeper disapproval and alarm.*) Paying your court?

BERNAL. Paying my court!

SIR RALPH. To make her your wife?

BERNAL. To make her (*in deep uncertainty, agitation, distraction, faltering*) I'll be hanged if I know what!

SIR RALPH. (*As if following up an advantage and looking about him in reprobation.*) The partner of your misery?

BERNAL. (*In despair, troubled, impatient compunction.*) Yes—I'm too deadly poor! (*Then after an instant, with returning clearness and resolution.*) But I do know what I want. I want to prevent *you*!

SIR RALPH. (*Wound up, taking up the challenge.*) You shan't prevent me! (*Then at the door of the parlour, which he has quickly opened.*) Miss Jesmond!

BERNAL. (*As quickly opening the door to the street, while* GRACE *reappears.*) Miss Jesmond!

(*Re-enter* GRACE JESMOND.)

SIR RALPH. (*Pressing.*) Will you do me a favour?

BERNAL. (*Forestalling her answer; passionate.*) Will you do *me* one first?

GRACE. (*Still more mystified by their heated aspect; looking from one to the other and then addressing* BERNAL.) Anything—for *you*!

BERNAL. Then walk out of the house!

GRACE. (*Startled, pained, for the moment, by the manner of the request.*) Out of the house—?

BERNAL. (*Feverishly peremptory; point- to the open door.*) This moment!

GRACE. (*Looking once more from one* of the men to the other as they stand on either side of the stage; then, with a visible effort, deciding and sadly, supremely addressing BERNAL.*) Good-bye! (*Exit* GRACE JESMOND, *while the two men stand defiantly confronted.*)

ACT THIRD

SIR RALPH DAMANT'S *drawing-room in Portland Place; handsome, cold, conventional and characteristic. A door at the centre from the hall and staircase; doors right and left from other reception rooms.* GRACE JESMOND *is seated in her hat and cape; not the same garments as in Act Second, but, as to mourning, perceptibly modified and brightened. The* FOOTMAN *who has appeared in Act First enters from the hall.*

FOOTMAN. I find Sir Ralph is *not* at home, Miss; but he gave orders that if you should call you were to be particularly asked to wait.

GRACE. Till he comes in?

FOOTMAN. He may be expected at any moment.

GRACE. (*After an instant.*) When were these orders given?

FOOTMAN. On Thursday, Miss, on our return from Vandyke Lodge. (*Then expansive, as if glad of an opportunity to converse.*) I was there with the carriage— and I joined in the chase.

GRACE. (*Struck.*) The chase?

FOOTMAN. For you, Miss. Sir Ralph drove hard—to catch up with you.

GRACE. (*After an instant; quiet.*) He didn't catch up.

FOOTMAN. (*Smiling.*) We had wasted precious moments.

GRACE. You mustn't waste them now.

FOOTMAN. He remarked that you'd turn up!

GRACE. (*After reflection.*) Since I'm expected, I'll wait.

FOOTMAN. (*Increasingly sociable.*) We've another party in another room.

GRACE. (*Rising, wondering.*) Another party?

FOOTMAN. From Vandyke Lodge.

GRACE. (*Startled, changing her mind.*) I believe, after all, I won't wait!

FOOTMAN. (*As* TEDDY *appears.*) Here's the other party.

(*Enter* TEDDY ASHDOWN *from the right.*)

GRACE. (*Dropping into her chair again with relief.*) Oh!

TEDDY. (*Much pleased.*) You're just the person I want!

FOOTMAN. (*Privately; ironical.*) *All* of 'em? Gracious! (*Exit the* FOOTMAN *to the hall.*)

GRACE. (*Rising again; anxious.*) Is Mr. Bernal here?

TEDDY. He'd be if he suspected *you* are! I'm looking for him, and he's looking for Miss Jesmond.

GRACE. He's coming for the portrait?

TEDDY. By appointment. They've patched it up.

GRACE. (*Vague.*) The portrait?

TEDDY. Oh no—their quarrel!

GRACE. (*Still vague.*) Their quarrel?

TEDDY. About you! I know what happened.

GRACE. (*Smiling.*) That's more than I do, Mr. Ashdown!

TEDDY. Then I'll tell you.

GRACE. (*Postponing.*) When does Mr. Bernal come?

TEDDY. (*Looking at his watch.*) Not till twelve. He put me on a 'bus with the traps—they're all in there. (*Indicating the adjoining room.*) He's walking to save the fare.

GRACE. Then he'll take some time?

TEDDY. He crawls along—because he looks out for you in the streets. He peeps under every bonnet! He has sent me to all those fellows for news of you.

GRACE. The artists? I've been to none

of them.

TEDDY. He said you'd require to go.

GRACE. I do "require"! (*Then after an instant.*) But I don't go.

TEDDY. (*After a moment.*) You come here instead.

GRACE. I come here instead.

TEDDY. But not, I fear, for Mark.

GRACE. Not for Mr Bernal. For Sir Ralph Damant.

TEDDY. (*After another moment.*) Was it for Sir Ralph you came to *us?*

GRACE. It was for myself.

TEDDY. That was what their row was about—when Mark was so rude.

GRACE. How rude was Mr. Bernal?

TEDDY. Rude enough to repent! He has repented fearfully of what he did to you.

GRACE. (*After an instant.*) He asked me to leave his house.

TEDDY. Oh, he has told me; he talks of nothing else!

GRACE. I've talked of it—to no one.

TEDDY. (*Alert.*) Then you've forgiven him?

GRACE. (*With the same smile.*) I've forgiven him.

TEDDY. (*With the same eagerness.*) May I tell him, when he comes?

GRACE. (*After an instant.*) I've asked you before to keep a secret.

TEDDY. About that sketch-book? (*With emphatic satisfaction.*) I've kept it!

GRACE. Beautifully. Then keep this one.

TEDDY. (*Vague.*) Your forgiving him?

GRACE. My being in this place. I wish not to see him.

TEDDY. (*Perceptibly mystified.*) And yet you remain?

GRACE. Only for one reason,—that if I go now I shall not have courage to return.

TEDDY. "Courage"?

GRACE. It was not easy!

TEDDY. To face Sir Ralph? Why, *I* have to!

GRACE. (*After a moment.*) Yes—you have to.

TEDDY. I do it for Mark!

GRACE. (*After an instant; with her tired smile.*) And *I* do it for "Mark"! To render him a service.

TEDDY. (*Eager.*) Then you like him?

GRACE. (*Hesitating, but still smiling.*) You ask too many questions!

TEDDY. I asked that one because he likes you.

GRACE. I guessed so when he turned me out.

TEDDY. Did you? He has been afraid you wouldn't!

GRACE. I didn't at first. But then I thought about it.

TEDDY. (*Sympathetically interested.*) And then it came to you?

GRACE. Little by little. (*After a moment.*) It came to me last night.

TEDDY. And that brought you here?

GRACE. Early, as you see. To acknowledge his favour!

TEDDY. But how—if you don't meet him?

GRACE. I shall meet Sir Ralph.

TEDDY. (*Alert.*) Meet him and refuse him?

GRACE. (*Consciously blank.*) "Refuse" him?

TEDDY. (*Surprised at her blankness.*) Doesn't he want to marry you?

GRACE. (*Grave.*) Quite the contrary!

TEDDY. And *you* don't want it?

GRACE. (*With controlled emotion; after an instant.*) Has he asserted that?

TEDDY. To Mark—on Thursday. You made him an offer.

GRACE. (*Rising quickly.*) Which he saw reason to accept—precisely!

TEDDY. It was why Mark banished you. To separate the parties—to avert the danger!

GRACE. To prevent Sir Ralph's accepting?

TEDDY. To choke him right off!

GRACE. (*Eager.*) Mr. Bernal believed it?

TEDDY. (*Vague.*) That Sir Ralph would?

GRACE. No—that I had done such a thing.

TEDDY. (*After an instant's reflection.*) It didn't prevent him from wanting you—

GRACE. (*As he modestly pauses.*) "Wanting" me?

TEDDY. For his own use!

GRACE. (*Dropping into a seat again; sitting there an instant in thought; then rising and with frankness and courage, as well as with a forced gaiety intended to dissimulate her sadness and make her discussion of such a matter with* TEDDY *pass.*)

Mr. Bernal may "want" me, Mr. Ashdown; but Mr. Bernal can't have me!

TEDDY. (*Vague, disappointed.*) Can't have you?

GRACE. It ties my hands.

TEDDY. (*Blank.*) I don't understand!

GRACE. I do—at last! I had thought it all out—but you greatly help me.

TEDDY. (*Kind, simple, loyal.*) I *want* to greatly help you.

GRACE. You did so, you know, at Courtlands.

TEDDY. By holding my tongue? It was hard!

GRACE. I shall set you to-day an easier task. You will be so good as to speak.

TEDDY. (*Alert.*) Tell Mr. Bernal—?

GRACE. (*Interrupting.*) That I'm in the house.

TEDDY. But where shall you be?

GRACE. (*At a momentary loss; looking round her, then pointing to the door on the left.*) In there.

TEDDY. Why not in here?

GRACE. So you may prepare him.

TEDDY. (*Blank.*) "Prepare" him?

GRACE. Give him his choice—of seeing me or not.

TEDDY. (*Laughing.*) He'll take it! (*Then more gravely.*) And if I speak for you, will you speak for me?

GRACE. (*Vague.*) To whom?

TEDDY. To "dear Maud." I want her—for *my* own use!

GRACE. (*Smiling.*) I'll approach her—if I've a chance.

TEDDY. (*With resolution.*) I'll make you one!

(*Re-enter the* FOOTMAN *from the hall.*)

FOOTMAN. (*To* GRACE.) Mr. Bernal.

GRACE. (*Startled.*) Coming up?

FOOTMAN. (*Who has crossed to the door on the left, which he has opened.*) If you'll pass in there.

TEDDY. (*Anxious, while* GRACE *reaches the other room.*) Can I trust you?

GRACE. (*At the door, with a smile.*) If you can trust *her!* (*Exit* GRACE JESMOND *to the left.*)

FOOTMAN. (*Explaining, after closing the door on her.*) Sir Ralph's orders.

TEDDY. (*Vague.*) His orders?

FOOTMAN. If Mr. Bernal should come.

TEDDY. (*Disconcerted.*) He's not to see her?

FOOTMAN. (*Self-complacent, responsible.*) For fear of complications!

TEDDY. (*Disgusted; thinking.*) Why, what does Sir Ralph call *that?* (*Then seeing* BERNAL.) Silence!

(*Enter* MARK BERNAL *from the hall. Exit the* FOOTMAN *to the hall.*)

BERNAL. Ralph's not here?

TEDDY. I've been waiting.

BERNAL. With everything ready?

TEDDY. (*Embarrassed, at fault.*) Not yet; I thought—

BERNAL. (*Breaking in; with kindly impatience.*) You think too much—you always *did!* (*Then indicating the door on the right.*) Be quick!

TEDDY. (*Demurring, hesitating.*) Before I go—

BERNAL. (*As he pauses.*) Before you go?

TEDDY. Miss Jesmond's in the house!

BERNAL. (*Amazed.*) Here?—now?

TEDDY. She told me to tell you.

BERNAL. (*Eager.*) Then I can see her?

TEDDY. You can see her.

BERNAL. (*Struck, in the midst ·of his relief; mistrustful, wondering.*) But what's she doing?

TEDDY. (*Vague.*) Doing?

BERNAL. For what purpose has she come?

TEDDY. For the purpose of helping you.

BERNAL. (*Blank.*) But how in the world—?

TEDDY. I give it up!

BERNAL. (*Uneasy, peremptory; suddenly nervous and discomposed; passing his hand over his head.*) Make ready!

(*Re-enter, as he speaks, the* FOOTMAN *from the hall.*)

SERVANT. (*Announcing.*) Lady Basset!

BERNAL. (*Starting, as if struck with a quick idea, then still more imperative, to* TEDDY, *who has lingered, looking at him, with a hand on the door at the right.*) Leave us!

(*Exit* TEDDY ASHDOWN *to the right. Enter* LADY BASSET *from the hall. Exit the* FOOTMAN.)

BERNAL. (*As if amused.*) How did you get in?

LADY BASSET. The butler passed me up.

(*Jubilant, exultant.*) I'm invited!

BERNAL. By Sir Ralph?

LADY BASSET. By Sir Ralph. (*Triumphant.*) He wants me!

BERNAL. (*Surprised.*) For what?

LADY BASSET. (*With lively confidence.*) You'll see when he comes!

BERNAL. But he doesn't come! (*Looking at his watch.*) You must help me to bear it.

LADY BASSET. (*Self-complacent, coquettish.*) I helped you, you know, to bear it the other day!

BERNAL. (*Preoccupied with the idea of* GRACE's *presence.*) Indeed you did—immensely!

LADY BASSET. We had recourse to my artistic nature.

BERNAL. (*Vague.*) Do you wish to have recourse to it again?

LADY BASSET. (*After serious reflection.*) Not to the same extent. (*Then with serenity and lucidity.*) If I was present the other day as an artist, I'm present to-day as a woman.

BERNAL. (*With the same vagueness as before.*) Is it in that capacity he has sent for you?

LADY BASSET. (*Blank.*) In what other capacity, pray—? (*After an instant.*) The very servants recognise it!

BERNAL. (*Not following.*) Recognise it—?

LADY BASSET. By their eagerness to usher me in!

BERNAL. (*Suddenly struck; with a light.*) In here—to *me*?

LADY BASSET. (*Vague, surprised at the point he makes of this.*) They mentioned I should find you!

BERNAL. (*As the fuller light breaks upon him; with amused elation; seizing her arm.*) That's what he wanted of you!

LADY BASSET. (*Blank, disconcerted.*) To amuse you?

BERNAL. To captivate me—as he wants me to captivate you!

LADY BASSET. (*Candid, jovial.*) You do, my dear man!

BERNAL. (*Laughing.*) And so do you!

LADY BASSET. But why does Sir Ralph desire it?

BERNAL. To protect himself. He fears you.

LADY BASSET. (*Exultant.*) I feel that he does!

BERNAL. (*Amused and relieved by his discovery.*) I see it all!

LADY BASSET. All what?

BERNAL. Why, he means you to draw me off!

LADY BASSET. (*Vague.*) Off somebody else?

BERNAL. (*Smiling.*) A person he wants for himself!

LADY BASSET. (*Struck, alarmed.*) For himself? (*Then with quick dismay.*) Maud Vanneck?

BERNAL. (*Amused.*) No, not Maud Vanneck.

LADY BASSET. (*Thinking; then with eager intensity.*) Grace Jesmond?

BERNAL. She's in the house!

LADY BASSET. (*Still more alarmed.*) Invited?

BERNAL. No, not invited—he hasn't her address.

LADY BASSET. She has come of herself?

BERNAL. (*After an instant, as if recognising the full gravity of this.*) She has come of herself.

LADY BASSET. (*Stupefied, scandalised.*) What effrontery!

BERNAL. Her reason is doubtless good.

LADY BASSET. (*As if struck with the tone in which he says this.*) You're in love with her?

BERNAL. Ralph thinks so.

LADY BASSET. (*Imperative.*) Then for God's sake marry her!

BERNAL. (*After an instant; troubled, sincere.*) How can I—in my position?

LADY BASSET. (*Coinciding.*) Yes—she's after money. (*Then with decision.*) But she won't get it!

BERNAL. Do you mean that *you* will?

LADY BASSET. (*After an instant.*) Sir Ralph is pledged to me.

BERNAL. (*Uncertain, bewildered, nervous.*) Then why does he want *her*?

LADY BASSET. (*Blank a moment; then with resentment.*) Because he's false!

BERNAL. (*Pleading.*) Ah, no— he's honest! (*After an instant.*) See how he makes us meet!

LADY BASSET. You and me?

BERNAL. For you to swallow me up!

LADY BASSET. (*Impressed with the unsuspected truth.*) And you to swallow *me?*

BERNAL. (*Smiling.*) So that you won't have room for *him!* (*After an instant.*) You admitted just now that there wasn't much!

LADY BASSET. (*With decision.*) You're a very brilliant man, but I reject you.

BERNAL. Ralph has counted on your appreciating me enough— (*Hesitating, pausing, as if with a last scruple; then in a changed tone.*) Hang it—I can tell you *now!*

LADY BASSET. (*Eager.*) To let Sir Ralph off?

BERNAL. To be merciful.

LADY BASSET. For the benefit of that creature? Never!

BERNAL. You really hold out?

LADY BASSET. Against you? I loathe you!

BERNAL. And you permit me to loathe back?

LADY BASSET. If you love another woman!

BERNAL. I haven't told you I do!

LADY BASSET. That's because you're such a flirt. You won't part with one victim—

BERNAL. (*Laughing, interrupting.*) Before I make sure of another? (*Then again preoccupied.*) Yes, I must make sure. (*After an instant.*) And while I'm making sure—

LADY BASSET. *I* shall be doing the same!

BERNAL. (*Amused.*) You'll be all there?

LADY BASSET. (*With clear resolution.*) All here!

BERNAL. (*After a moment's intense reflection; going up to the bell, which he rings.*) I must see my way!

LADY BASSET. (*Vague.*) What are you doing?

BERNAL. I'm making sure! (*Re-enter the* FOOTMAN *from the hall. To the* FOOTMAN.) Am I correct in believing that Miss Jesmond's in the house?

FOOTMAN. (*Embarrassed.*) Did the young gentleman tell you, sir?

BERNAL. Of course the young gentleman told me.

FOOTMAN. Would it do for me, then, to deny it?

BERNAL. (*Staring.*) Deny it? Why should you deny it?

FOOTMAN. Because Sir Ralph said she wasn't to see you.

BERNAL. (*Struck; then with high decision.*) Then he should be at home to prevent it!

FOOTMAN. He may be at any moment, sir.

BERNAL. Then I must see her quickly!

FOOTMAN. I'll inform her. (*Exit the* FOOTMAN *to the left, leaving the door open.*)

LADY BASSET. She can scarcely be said to shrink!

BERNAL. (*Amused.*) If you compare it with *your* shrinkage!

LADY BASSET. Mine, such as it is, forbids me to witness your encounter!

BERNAL. (*Indicating the room on the right.*) Then kindly pass in there.

LADY BASSET. (*Vaguely demurring.*) In there?

BERNAL. Where Sir Ralph's to sit.

LADY BASSET. (*At the door, alert.*) I'll wait for him! (*Exit* LADY BASSET *to the right.*)

(*Re-enter* GRACE JESMOND *from the left.*)

GRACE. (*Pausing where she enters.*) I asked Mr. Ashdown to tell you of my presence—strange as it must inevitably appear to you.

BERNAL. As your presence must appear?

GRACE. No—as my request to him must.

BERNAL. In the light of the extraordinary leave I last asked you to take of me! It's to explain that monstrous proceeding that I have begged for these words with you. I've hunted for you hard, but in vain—to make you hear them.

GRACE. There is a word I myself should like to speak. (*After an instant.*) The simple request to you to believe—

BERNAL. (*Waiting, as she pauses.*) To believe?

GRACE. Nothing Sir Ralph Damant may say of me.

BERNAL. You're aware then of what he has in fact said?

GRACE. It's because I think I divine it that I've come here.

BERNAL. (*After an instant.*) Not, I suppose, at his request.

GRACE. He couldn't request me—in ignorance of where to find me.

BERNAL. The ignorance you've *me* to

thank for!

GRACE. As I do thank you, Mr. Bernal.

BERNAL. You thank me for showing you the door, for turning you out of my house? —turning you without mercy into the great city you had scoured in vain, and in which I myself soon enough cursed the folly that had deprived me of a possible clue to you?

GRACE. We meet again in spite of that folly.

BERNAL. We meet again in spite of it. (*Then after an instant.*) But we meet again in a manner to which it would take but little more of my perplexity to make me prefer our separation.

GRACE. (*After an hesitation.*) Is that because you do believe Sir Ralph?

BERNAL. If he has told me a strange story of you, why do you, on your side, take a step which gives a detestable colour to it?

GRACE. This step of coming to see him? Because it's the only way to say to him— something that I *have* to say.

BERNAL. I've no right whatever to ask you what that may be.

GRACE. I've a limited power, none the less, to tell you. He has misunderstood me; and it is important to me that he should be informed that he has.

BERNAL. Important? (*Then after an instant, half-impatient, half-pleading.*) Ah, *why* is it important?

GRACE. (*Hesitating, momentarily embarrassed.*) I'm afraid I can only say to you— because I hold it to be!

BERNAL. (*With an apologetic, penitent gesture.*) I insult you with my curiosity when I only wanted to convince you of my regret. It was my respect for you the other day, that made me use a freedom!

GRACE. The sense of that respect consoles me!

BERNAL. I'm delighted to hear it; but what's to console *me*?

GRACE. (*After an instant.*) For what, Mr. Bernal?

BERNAL. For seeing Sir Ralph Damant again stand between us!

GRACE. (*After another instant.*) Excuse me if I don't perceive how it should matter to you where Sir Ralph Damant stands.

BERNAL. You saw how it mattered the other day!

GRACE. (*Quiet.*) I saw the fact, but not the reason. (*Then with a sad smile.*) You ask me, I think, for more explanations than you give!

BERNAL. (*Admitting this; speaking very kindly.*) You must be generous with me, for I'm much troubled.

GRACE. It's because you're much troubled that I'm here. (*Then while he stares; explaining.*) I saw your poor home the other day, and I heard your confession.

BERNAL. (*Struck, alert.*) Of want of means?

GRACE. (*Tender, indulgent.*) My intrusion, my appeal brought it out.

BERNAL. So that you're here for money?

GRACE. (*After an instant.*) I'm here for money!

BERNAL. (*Wondering, amazed.*) For my relief?

GRACE. (*After another pause.*) Are you too proud to accept relief?

BERNAL. If I'm proud at all, Miss Jesmond, I'm proud of having inspired—by such an accident—such a sympathy! (*After an instant.*) Your charity is (*hesitating for his word; then bringing it out with an extravagance of warmth in which there is just a shade of the irony of his imperfect credulity, his sense of strangeness*) magnificent!

GRACE. (*Gentle.*) Such as it is, it's all my motive!

BERNAL. (*Going on.*) Still more magnificent is your belief in my cousin's sensibility.

GRACE. You mean it's extravagant? (*After an instant.*) It would be—if I hadn't grounds for it.

BERNAL. (*Struck.*) Grounds? (*Then after reflection.*) Shall I strike you as the most graceless of men if I venture to ask what they are?

GRACE. I can't tell you, Mr. Bernal, what they are!

BERNAL. And yet you said just now that you give more explanations—

GRACE. (*As he hesitates.*) Than *you* do? (*After an instant.*) I was wrong. (*With pathetic dignity.*) I feel that I don't give enough!

BERNAL. (*Worried, agitated, almost feverish.*) You give enough to enchant me, but not enough to satisfy! Why should you wish to remedy my preposterous predicament?

GRACE. Because I regret it!

BERNAL. (*With the same troubled spirit as before.*) Your "regret" is more mystifying than the steps for which it accounts, and your good faith only ministers, somehow, to the impulse that makes me challenge you!

GRACE. My ambiguity is my misfortune.

BERNAL. Say rather it's mine! If I appealed to you just now kindly to see me, it was to make my own behaviour clear. How *can* I make it clear—

GRACE. (*Interrupting.*) If I don't make mine?—You can't!

(*Enter* SIR RALPH DAMANT *from the hall. Re-enter at the same moment* LADY BASSET *from the right.*)

BERNAL. (*To* SIR RALPH, *who has his latchkey visible and has stopped short, deeply disconcerted, on finding him with* GRACE.) I asked to see Miss Jesmond.

GRACE. (*To* SIR RALPH.) I arrived before Mr. Bernal.

LADY BASSET. (*On the right.*) I arrived after!

SIR RALPH. And I've arrived last of all! (*Controlling with an effort, as he comes down, his discomfiture at* MARK'S *meeting with* GRACE, *and taking now the line of a smoothly astute and diplomatic manner of dealing with his difficulties.*) I've been detained, but I'm all the more pleased to find you gathered!

GRACE. (*Grave.*) I've not presumed you'd care to find *me.*

SIR RALPH. (*Urbane, engaging, gay.*) Then I must teach you presumption! I bid you welcome to Portland Place.

LADY BASSET. (*Impatient but majestic.*) And have you no welcome for another friend?

SIR RALPH. The warmest, dear lady. I summoned you to be present at the sittings.

LADY BASSET. (*Disappointed at the inadequacy of this explanation.*) I should still have been if you hadn't!

SIR RALPH. (*Imperturbable; indicating the room on the right.*) They take place there. (*Then motioning her to pass out*

again.) Be so good as to await me.

LADY BASSET. While you dally with Miss Jesmond?

SIR RALPH. (*Answering the question but addressing* GRACE.) To make up for the occasion of which Mark so cruelly deprived me!

BERNAL. (*Gay.*) I've made up a little, on my side, for the loss I equally suffered!

SIR RALPH. I take my revenge in kind! (*Opening the door on the right and pointing the way out to* BERNAL.) Be so good as to leave the room.

BERNAL. (*Troubled, demurring.*) This moment?

SIR RALPH. This moment!

BERNAL. (*At the door; looking at* GRACE; *after an instant.*) Good-bye! (*Exit* MARK BERNAL *to the right.*)

SIR RALPH. (*To* LADY BASSET, *while* GRACE, *with emotion, nervous, restless, wanders up to a window on the left.*) Won't you join him? (*Then as her attitude appears a refusal; insinuating.*) He admires you!

LADY BASSET. (*Staring; as if stupefied.*) Do you mean by that that *you* don't?

SIR RALPH. (*Conciliatory, heroic.*) My admiration's of a different strain!

LADY BASSET. Such as it is, I'm here for you to show it.

SIR RALPH. I do show it—I *am* showing it. (*Then as he indicates the open door and other room again.*) By this privilege!

LADY BASSET. That of Mr. Bernal's company?

SIR RALPH. (*Pleadingly argumentative.*) Doesn't he tell you what he thinks of you?

LADY BASSET. Every one does that!

SIR RALPH. (*Still pleading.*) *I* will—in three minutes!

LADY BASSET. (*At the door; having looked at her watch.*) I shall time you! (*Exit* LADY BASSET *to the right.*)

SIR RALPH. (*Having closed the door and remaining an instant at the right, while* GRACE *is up at the left.*) I followed you in vain, and it was sweet of you to come!

GRACE. (*Coming down.*) It may have been "sweet," Sir Ralph, but it has not been easy!

SIR RALPH. It gives me the chance to say what I wanted so much to say!

GRACE. (*Seating herself.*) And it gives me the chance to hear it!

SIR RALPH. What I wanted to say is that I accept your proposition.

GRACE. Are you very sure, first, that you understand it?

SIR RALPH. (*Surprised at her question.*) There was surely little room to blink it! (*Then after an instant.*) And I've taken my time to consider.

GRACE. (*Very quiet.*) I gather then the fruit of my exertions.

SIR RALPH. If your exertions were extraordinary, you must admit that the fruit is splendid!

GRACE. There's nothing so splendid as the triumph of justice.

SIR RALPH. (*Struck, demurring.*) Do you call it by that name?

GRACE. By what name do *you* call it?

SIR RALPH. Generosity—extravagant! But we won't quarrel about the description!

GRACE. We won't quarrel about anything, in the presence of the accomplished fact.

SIR RALPH. (*Wincing, momentarily failing.*) *That's* a description that, I confess, does give me a start! (*Reflecting with intense gravity.*) It brings my position home to me.

GRACE. Exactly where it *should* be brought.

SIR RALPH. I'm a bit of a fatalist; it's the finger of doom! My line of argument has been that sooner or later I should feel the knife at my throat—*have* to make the sacrifice; and that it constitutes after all the purchase of my freedom.

GRACE. When you have paid the price your freedom will be perfect!

SIR RALPH. (*Struck, eager.*) I may do as I like—I may go my way?

GRACE. My dear Sir Ralph, I'll never speak to you!

SIR RALPH. (*Following up the conception of this advantage; thinking.*) And of course, on that footing, nobody else will! (*More confident.*) Nobody else *can!*

GRACE. (*Confirmatory.*) There'll be nothing left to say!

SIR RALPH. Precisely, no *locus standi.* (*Ingenuous.*) That's the one thing that reconciles me.

GRACE. (*After an instant.*) The one thing? (*Then as he stares, struck, incipiently alarmed by her intonation.*) No sentiment —no emotion?

SIR RALPH. (*Still staring; plainly surprised.*) Since you press me, Madam, none whatever!

GRACE. The mere bald concession?

SIR RALPH. (*More markedly surprised, even scandalised at her qualification of his sacrifice.*) Do you consider it such a trifle to "concede" my existence?

GRACE. (*Blank.*) Your existence?

SIR RALPH. Even with what I reserve! My fortune, my position, my name!

GRACE. Your name? What have I to do with that?

SIR RALPH. (*Bewildered.*) You don't propose to bear it?

GRACE. (*Rising.*) Heaven forbid, Sir Ralph! (*Then lightly and quietly, as he stares, stupefied.*) You make me an offer?

SIR RALPH. (*With precipitate and indignant eagerness.*) Never in the world!

GRACE. Then what are you talking about?

SIR RALPH. Your horrible ultimatum!

GRACE. (*After an instant.*) It's your impression that I've made *you* an offer?

SIR RALPH. Twice over, in so many words!

GRACE. Which you've done me the honour to accept?

SIR RALPH. For the advantage I've named!

GRACE. (*Amused, smiling in spite of her disgust and dismay.*) Your view of the "advantage" touches me! I did not make you an offer, Sir Ralph, but it was only the offer of a chance.

SIR RALPH. (*Vague, anxious.*) A chance?

GRACE. To make a restitution—to divide your inheritance.

SIR RALPH. (*Staring; with his assurance flickering back.*) Divide it with *you?*

GRACE. With Mr. Bernal. That was my "ultimatum"!

SIR RALPH. (*Dropping, overwhelmed, into the seat from which* GRACE *has risen.*) That?

GRACE. I appealed to you to give him his share—the share he would clearly have enjoyed if your kinsman had lived another day.

SIR RALPH. (*With the same amazed ruefulness.*) Make him a present of a fortune?

GRACE. (*Simple.*) Two thousand a year.

SIR RALPH. (*After an instant during which he has risen.*) So that you may offer to marry *him?*

GRACE. You exaggerate my impatience to marry.

SIR RALPH. You exaggerate mine to indulge in preposterous gifts!

GRACE. (*After an instant.*) You don't accept your chance?

SIR RALPH. You must permit me to view it in the light of reason!

GRACE. That's exactly what I appeal to you to do. You treated me just now to the argument of security. Let me treat you to the same! Your security is your honour.

SIR RALPH. (*After an instant.*) And my honour, you seem to imply, is your sport?

GRACE. I daresay I could have a game with it!

SIR RALPH. (*After another instant.*) With that little ass to help you?

GRACE. Mr. Ashdown? He's in the other room.

SIR RALPH. (*With excited derision.*) Quite the Chamber of Horrors!

GRACE. I should apply that title to this one.

SIR RALPH. (*As she moves to go.*) You leave me, Miss Jesmond?

GRACE. (*At the door to the hall.*) I've corrected your mistake.

SIR RALPH. (*Still with his nervous and ironic laughter.*) Won't you give me your address?

GRACE. (*Blank.*) For what purpose?

SIR RALPH. I may have a word to say to you!

GRACE. (*After an instant's hesitation.*) If you have a word to say, say it to Mr. Bernal!

SIR RALPH. (*Smiling.*) It may not do— for Mr. Bernal!

GRACE. (*Turning to the door again.*) Then it won't do for me!

SIR RALPH. (*As she has her hand on the door; with a sudden complete, quite violent change of manner and accent.*) Miss Jesmond, listen to me! (*Then as GRACE,*

struck, arrested by this transformation, stops short, looking at him.*) You say you've corrected my mistake; but I confess I've made more than one! (GRACE, *as if, after a momentary hesitation, under the influence of a puzzled hope that his oddly altered tone may denote his readiness to do the justice she has demanded, comes slowly a few steps down, while he goes on.*) I told you a while ago that if I stood ready to marry you it was without sentiment, without emotion. But those words were a wrong to you—they were a greater wrong to myself. (*She continues to rest her wondering, expectant eyes on him, and he proceeds with gathered assurance.*) The emotion, charming woman, has come—the sentiment insists on a voice. (*Then, under the permission of her silence, producing his confident climax.*) I make you, Miss Jesmond, the proposal that I regret you didn't make *me!*

GRACE. (*After a moment of intensely controlled disappointment and horror; with the cold irony of her stupefaction.*) Your mistakes are sufficiently strange; but I think your corrections are stranger!

SIR RALPH. (*Insistent, persistent.*) You say that you offer me a chance; but what is it compared to the chance I offer *you?* What you ask of me for another, I press on you for yourself! (*Then with an exasperation rising from the vision of the incorruptibility with which she stands there.*) Do you measure what I mean and what I possess? Can you reflect on it and refuse? I've guessed your poverty; I've sounded your depths. Without a home, without protection in this cruel city, consider in what a refuge you stand! (*Then as she simply turns from him with a movement that expresses all her sickened inaccessibility, and he has got between her and the door to the hall, more and more urgent and imperative, half-pleading, half-resentful and altogether passionate.*) You really refuse?

GRACE. To be bought off? (*With an almost wild motion of clearing him from her path, while the door opens from the hall and the* FOOTMAN *reappears: re-enter the* FOOTMAN *from the hall.*) Let me go!

FOOTMAN. (*Announcing.*) Miss Vanneck!

(*Enter* MAUD VANNECK *from the hall.*)

SIR RALPH. (*Disconcerted, overwhelmed, furious, to the* FOOTMAN.) Who let her in?

MAUD. (*Serene.*) The butler, Sir Ralph; I asked for Lady Basset!

FOOTMAN. Your things are put out, sir.

SIR RALPH. Things? What things?

FOOTMAN. To sit for your picture, sir—the costoom.

SIR RALPH. Damn the costoom!

(*Exit* SIR RALPH *rapidly to the hall, while the* FOOTMAN *holds open the door. Exit the* FOOTMAN.)

GRACE. (*To* MAUD.) You asked for Lady Basset?

MAUD. To take me out again. (*After an instant.*) I find I can't face them!

GRACE. Face what?

MAUD. The usual dangers.

GRACE. (*With a sad, sincere smile and headshake.*) They're horrible! Don't try. (*Then after a moment.*) Don't trouble Lady Basset. I'll take you out.

MAUD. (*Surprised.*) You, Miss Jesmond? Where?

GRACE. Out of this house, to begin with. It's not a very nice place!

MAUD. (*Struck with her tone and air; then kind.*) I see it has been horrid somehow for *you*—and yet you have ideas for others.

GRACE. I've ideas for Mr. Ashdown! He asked me to speak for him.

MAUD. Is he here?

GRACE. (*Turning away as she sees* BERNAL.) Ask Mr. Bernal.

(*Re-enter* MARK BERNAL *from the right.*)

MAUD. (*Joyous, spontaneous, to* BERNAL, *who has stopped short on finding* GRACE *still in the room.*) Why, Miss Jesmond's charming!

GRACE. (*Facing about again quickly.*) She says so because I spoke to her of Mr. Ashdown.

BERNAL. (*Behind whom the door of the other room has closed; to* MAUD.) He's in there with Lady Basset.

MAUD. And what's Lady Basset doing?

BERNAL. Waiting for Sir Ralph.

MAUD. (*With striking ingenuousness.*) How very vulgar!

GRACE. (*To* BERNAL, *smiling.*) Miss Vanneck's not here for *that!*

BERNAL. (*To* MAUD.) It wouldn't help you if you were!

GRACE. (*To* BERNAL, *urgent.*) You must appeal for your friend.

BERNAL. (*To* GRACE.) Your friend too, Miss Jesmond. He simply adores you.

MAUD. (*Struck.*) Does he indeed?

GRACE. (*Amused.*) Because I intercede!

BERNAL. I've interceded too! (*To* MAUD.) Didn't I struggle hard for him?

MAUD. At Vandyke Lodge? (*After an instant.*) I've not forgotten it!

GRACE. (*To* MAUD.) Let him struggle for himself!

BERNAL. (*To* MAUD.) Shall I call him in?

MAUD. (*At the open door on the left; hesitating; then to* GRACE.) What's beyond that room?

GRACE. (*Smiling.*) A conservatory.

MAUD. (*To* BERNAL.) Please call him! (*Exit* MAUD VANNECK *to the left.*)

(BERNAL *opens door on the right, and on his summons re-enter* TEDDY ASHDOWN.)

GRACE. (*To* TEDDY.) I've spoken for you!

TEDDY. (*Eager.*) To dear Maud?

BERNAL. (*Indicating the left.*) She's in the conservatory.

TEDDY. (*At the door on the left, in suspense, his hand to his heart.*) Will she have me?

BERNAL. Go and see!

TEDDY. (*Ardently, to* GRACE.) Benefactress!

GRACE. (*Grave, sad.*) Ah, don't call me *that!*

TEDDY. Then angel!

BERNAL. (*Laughing.*) Keep that for Miss Vanneck!

TEDDY. (*Indicating* GRACE.) Then *you* thank her! (*Exit* TEDDY *to the left.*)

GRACE. (*Smiling sadly.*) You shouldn't, for they haven't a penny!

BERNAL. What of that? No more have we!

GRACE. (*Vague.*) "We"?

BERNAL. (*Seeing* SIR RALPH.) It doesn't matter!

(*Re-enter* SIR RALPH DAMANT *picturesquely dressed to sit for his portrait; a costume carefully selected and studied.*)

SIR RALPH. (*Stopping short, in high displeasure, on seeing* BERNAL *reunited to* GRACE.) You've come back?

BERNAL. (*With a gesture of abdication, of frank, final confession.*) My necessity forced me—I expected to find you. (*After an instant.*) I throw up my charge.

SIR RALPH. (*Aghast, indicating the room to the right.*) That woman?

BERNAL. That avalanche! I can't arrest its course!

SIR RALPH. (*Dismayed, indignant.*) You don't appreciate her?

BERNAL. I can't handle her, and I judged it right to notify you.

SIR RALPH. (*Thinking intently, in his alarm.*) She's not amenable—?

BERNAL. To any argument I can use!

SIR RALPH. But she has plenty of her own!

BERNAL. I perceive them, but somehow I resist them!

SIR RALPH. (*Contending, protesting, insisting.*) Such brilliant points?

BERNAL. She doesn't see mine!

SIR RALPH. You told me she did!

BERNAL. It was what she first told *me!* But now she takes it all back.

SIR RALPH. (*In deeper dismay the more he thinks.*) Back?

BERNAL. She objects to me!

SIR RALPH. And you object to *her?*

BERNAL. I'm not so rude as to tell her so—but I do!

SIR RALPH. (*In the tone of indignant injury; scandalised.*) Do you call such an objection loyal?

BERNAL. (*Blank.*) "Loyal"?

SIR RALPH. After all I have done for you!

BERNAL. Pray what have you done?

SIR RALPH. (*Pulled up, embarrassed an instant, by the question; then indicating, with angry fatuity, the nobleness of his appearance.*) Dressed myself—as you see!

BERNAL. (*Taking him in, up and down.*) For your portrait?

SIR RALPH. (*Exhibiting himself.*) As the "Patron of Art"!

BERNAL. My dear Ralph, *my* art must go unpatronised! (*With the note of rueful melancholy, but smiling.*) No song no supper!

SIR RALPH. (*Outraged.*) You won't paint me?

BERNAL. Wasn't I to paint you only if I saved you?

SIR RALPH. (*With a wail of despair.*) So I'm lost?

BERNAL. (*Seeing* LADY BASSET.) Ask her ladyship!

(*Re-enter* LADY BASSET *from the right.*)

LADY BASSET. (*Pausing at the door and glaring with majestic reproach and displeasure at* SIR RALPH.) I've come for you!

SIR RALPH. (*In mortal anguish.*) Come for me?

LADY BASSET. I gave you three minutes.

SIR RALPH. (*Looking at his watch, confessing in despair his transgression.*) And I've taken thirty!

BERNAL. (*To* LADY BASSET, *indulgently extenuating, explaining.*) You see, there's to be no portrait!

SIR RALPH. (*Eagerly, in the same way.*) I'm not to sit to him.

LADY BASSET. (*Staring an instant; then formidably indicating the open door.*) Then you're to sit to *me!*

SIR RALPH. (*Demoralised, tragic, looking blankly at the open door while she points the way out; and then, with the climax of despair, appealing supremely to* MARK BERNAL.) Help me!

BERNAL. (*Hesitating, thinking an instant; then indicating* GRACE *as, after having wandered up the stage in impatient suspense during his dialogue with* SIR RALPH, *she now comes down again.*) Help *me!*

SIR RALPH. (*As if with the last terrified lucidity of reflection, the sudden dawn of a new idea, which he leaps at, making up his mind, while his eyes move an instant from* GRACE *to* BERNAL *and while* LADY BASSET *still stands in control of the open door.*) Wait for me! (*Exit* SIR RALPH *to the right.*)

LADY BASSET. (*To the others, smiling triumphantly.*) He'll not be long! (*Exit* LADY BASSET *to the right.*)

BERNAL. (*To* GRACE.) I bade you goodbye; but, thank heaven, you were kept for me!

GRACE. I was kept by my occupations.

BERNAL. The first of your occupations

now (*tender, ardent*) must be to forgive me!

GRACE. For believing a story so monstrous?

BERNAL. I didn't believe it, but it puzzled me; it puzzled me because I cared—I mean because I loved you! (*Then, as she starts at this, turning away.*) I hadn't the right to tell you so, any more than I have it now; and that made me wild, it made me mad, it made things crooked and dark to me.

GRACE. (*Very sad.*) And still they're not straight, not clear! I've tried to serve you, but I haven't served you yet.

BERNAL. (*Passionate.*) You serve me at this moment by letting me tell you that I trust you!

GRACE. What if you trust me to little profit?

BERNAL. The "profit" is the joy of confidence! The confidence was there though I was troubled; it was there though I was mystified. I want no proof that you're precious, for the only thing I ask of you is to let me deserve your charity!

GRACE. You make me almost want to have failed—in order to have the right to listen to you. You must never be able to say of me that my effort was half for myself.

BERNAL. Give up your "effort"—give up what exposes and divides us! How can I possibly desire any boon that has made you cruelly suffer for me?

GRACE. (*After quick, intense reflection.*) I haven't cruelly suffered "for" you; but (*with another pause of hesitation*) I believe I could suffer *with* you!

BERNAL. You shan't, if you'll take me; I declare you shall only enjoy! You'll teach me a better way to live; you'll teach me a finer way to work! (*Taking up his hat, which he has put down on coming in.*) Let us go forth as we *are*—together!

GRACE. (*Thinking, yielding, but hesitating.*) And forego the advantage—

BERNAL. (*As she pauses.*) The advantage?

GRACE. Of further communion with Sir Ralph!

BERNAL. Has that communion been so sweet? (*With a decisive, comprehensive motion as of final and total rupture.*) Goodbye to it!

GRACE. (*With a last perfunctory scruple.*) You don't really want to know—?

BERNAL. (*Energetically breaking in.*) I don't want to know anything! (*Laughing.*) I revel in my ignorance and in the prospect of your society! (*Then as if to vanquish her last lingering hesitation.*) It was not for you to help *me*, dearest—it is for me to help *you*!

GRACE. (*Thinking, assenting, but looking about her with a faint, vague sigh of regret for what she gives up.*) So fate may have decreed! (*Then as she surrenders her hand, surrenders herself wholly.*) And I like it as well!

BERNAL. (*With a joyous laugh, drawing, pressing her to his bosom.*) I like it much better!

(*Re-enter* TEDDY ASHDOWN.)

TEDDY. (*Arrested an instant; then as they quickly separate; radiant.*) Dear Maud has accepted me!

BERNAL. (*In the same manner.*) And Miss Jesmond has accepted *me*!

(*Re-enter* MAUD VANNECK *from the left.*)

MAUD. (*After a moment's modest pause in the doorway; demurely to* GRACE.) Mr. Ashdown will take me out!

GRACE. (*Smiling at her and accepting* BERNAL'S *arm as if to represent the immediate application of the words.*) And Mr. Bernal will take *me*!

BERNAL. (*Seeing* SIR RALPH.) Though Sir Ralph looks dangerous!

(*Re-enter* SIR RALPH *from the right.*)

SIR RALPH. (*White, haggard, almost ravaged.*) I've accepted Lady Basset!

BERNAL. (*Smiling, as* LADY BASSET, *radiant, reappears.*) We all do the same!

(*Re-enter* LADY BASSET *from the right.*)

SIR RALPH. (*Looking with concentrated and agitated significance at* LADY BASSET *and speaking with intense and calculated deliberation.*) You'll do so with double relish when you see with what zeal she joins me—

LADY BASSET. (*Vague, as he invitingly pauses; as if made uneasy by his look and tone.*) Joins you—?

SIR RALPH. (*Encouraged and sustained by her alarm.*) In an act of enlightened justice.

GRACE. (*With irrepressible joy.*) Justice?

LADY BASSET. (*Growing darker.*) Sir Ralph, what madness—?

SIR RALPH. (*Hopefully exalted.*) The madness, my lady, of making over to Mark the inheritance I've held in trust for him!

LADY BASSET. (*Aghast, astounded.*) Four thousand a year?

SIR RALPH. Four thousand a year! (*To* BERNAL.) You *would* have had it!

BERNAL. (*Amazed, bewildered.*) The whole property? I might have had a little!

SIR RALPH. (*Uplifted by the assurance of his success, while he looks at* LADY BASSET.) You shall have all! You have nothing of your own, and I have enough.

LADY BASSET. (*Almost shrieking in her derision and dismay.*) Enough?

SIR RALPH. My dear, in having *you!*

LADY BASSET. (*Overwhelmed, indignant, with a gesture of outraged retractation.*) You *haven't* "me"! (*With the violent motion of clearing her path, throwing up the whole thing, she goes rapidly up. Then at the door to the hall, with concentrated repudiation.*) Betrayer! (*Exit* LADY BASSET *to the hall.*)

BERNAL. My dear Ralph, you're too splendid!

GRACE. (*to* BERNAL.) Wait till you get it!

MAUD. (*On* TEDDY's *arm; demurely, to* SIR RALPH.) You'll never see her again!

SIR RALPH. (*Relieved, restored, reassured; measuring, satisfied.*) It's cheap!

EDITOR'S FOREWORD

THE REPROBATE

Most of what has been said concerning *The Album* applies to *The Reprobate,* a play designed for production at the Opera Comique in London after the run of *The American,* as well as for use on tour. In his letter to Gosse of December 1894 James described *The Reprobate* as "much the better" of the two comedies. Its subject was noted October 23, 1891, during the London run of *The American,* a reminiscence of James family history: "Surely it would be possible to make another and a less literal application of the idea of poor H.W. and the queer tragedy of his relation with Cousin H. I might make a little tale of it in which the motive would really be an idea, and a pretty and touching one— the idea of the *hypnotization* of a weaker character by a stronger, by a stronger will, so that the former accepts a certain absolute view of itself, takes itself from the point of view of another mind, etc. and then, by the death of the dominant person, finds itself confronted with the strange problem of liberty."

This reads like a variant of the *Trilby* theme; and the words "to make another and a less literal application" suggests an application already made. It may be that this "application" was *The Reprobate,* which could have been written by October 1891. The entry in the notebook leads us to the basic elements upon which the comedy was written. H.W. and Cousin H. are Henry Wykoff and his wife Cousin Helen. James's account of them in *A Small Boy and Others* reads like a sketch for *The Reprobate.* Henry Wykoff passed "for a slave of his passions from the moment he was allowed the wherewithal in the least to indulge them. . . . It was in truth an extraordinary situation and would have offered a splendid subject, as we used to say, to the painter of character, the novelist or the dramatist, with the hand to treat it." Cousin Henry "was suffered to indulge his passions but on ten cents a day . . ." although he was heir to a substantial fortune. James went on to describe how later, his cousin "at large and supplied with funds was exactly as harmless and blameless as poor Henry stinted and captive. . . . Not his heart, but his imagination, in the long years, had been starved. . . ."

In a letter to Dr. C. E. Wheeler of the Incorporated Stage Society, who had written to James asking him about this play, the novelist wrote on June 26, 1908: "Coming back to him after fifteen years I do find him light and neat and quick and ironic and amusing—yes, quick and *clear,* I think, and in short (such as he is) really in the line of Comedy. All those things! But you will try for yourself. Paul Doubleday's part absolutely strikes me as a pretty, a charming one, and worthy to solicit any intelligent and ambitious young *Comedian.* Only, alas, where *are* such?" On July 7 he again wrote to Wheeler: "I do think of it as pleasantly do-able by a handful of players capable of understanding their little artistic problem—capable above all of not heavily and portentously dragging it. Done lightly, quickly, and yet carefully, it seems to me it *might* quite justify itself—and done with the *Saloon*—ah me, what an amusing little bill it would be for me to think of!"

His words "lightly, quickly, and yet carefully" forecast the way in which Allan Wade produced this play after the First World War (three years after the novelist's death) in London for the Incorporated Stage Society. Mr. Wade had known James's work for many years; he insisted upon fidelity to text and assembled for the production a group of competent actors, some of whom made their reputation by their performance of this farce. Athene Seyler played Mrs. Freshville and scored a personal triumph; the cast included Lawrence Hanray as Pitt Brunt, M.P., Brember Wills in the role of Mr. Bonsor and Meggie Albanesi as Blanche Amber.

"I had only to alter *one* of James's stage directions," Mr. Wade wrote of the production. "The play had a brilliant cast who entered into the fun of the thing with spirit, and I have rarely heard so great a spontaneous burst of laughter as that which greeted Mr. Bonsor's last entrance, in boating costume. The play was, of course, given in the costumes of the period."

The critical opinions provoked by the play ran from high praise to sharp dislike. (William Archer, upon first reading the play, had found that "its extravagant farcical theme verges on the nauseous.") Bernard Shaw, who attended one of the two performances—the play was given December 14 and 15, 1919—pronounced it "quite successful." Arnold Bennett, on the other hand, while admitting it contained "some agreeable bits," found that "the spectacle it provided of an unusually able and gifted man trying to do something for which his talents were utterly unfitted was painful; it was humiliating."

The differences of opinion were exemplified particularly in the reviews of the *Times* and the *Daily Telegraph*. The *Times* critic, whose review was captioned "A New Side of Henry James," spoke of the "snip-snap of the dialogue throughout." The play revealed, he wrote, "an unusual, unexpected, almost incredible side of Henry James. . . . No psychological supersubtleties, no intricate involutions and convolutions of style, not a mark of the Henry James we all know and some of us love 'on this side idolatry'; just a plain tale in plain language, an action all bustle and snap, characters all the broadest, drollest caricatures."

The *Daily Telegraph* critic began by being complimentary. "No one but Henry James could have written *The Reprobate;* style, characterization, epigrammatic brilliancy, all proclaim the fact . . ." but he immediately added, "not more emphatically than the writer's constant lack of lucidity, one of the most unpardonable sins which can be laid to the charge of a playwright."

It was quite clear from Mr. Wade's experiment that acting and production were all-important for Jamesian comedy. The same play, produced in Boston at the Copley Theatre during the week of March 12, 1923, with little rehearsal and a mediocre cast, prompted the critic of the *Transcript* to describe it as "Blither in a Void." He observed that London had undoubtedly seen a different conception of the play. "There was no action," he wrote of the American performance "only an incessant bustling on and off the stage."

CHARACTERS

Mr. Bonsor
Paul Doubleday
Captain Chanter
Pitt Brunt, M.P.
Cubit
Mrs. Doubleday
Mrs. Freshville
Blanche Amber

THE REPROBATE

ACT FIRST

Whitsuntide. The drawing-room at MR. BONSOR'S *villa at Hampton Court. Wide double doors, across the upper angle on the right, open from the hall and other parts of the house. Half-way down on the right a door to the adjacent rooms. On the left, far up, at the other angle, a wide French window, open to the lawn. Further down on the left the door to the library. A table with drawers and several objects upon it somewhat to the left, near the front. More to the right a table for a tea-tray. To the right, below the lower door, a tall cabinet. The room old-fashioned but cheerful, comfortable but slightly severe. Plenty of chintz and mahogany; wall-paper, hung with steel-engravings, of 1850. An old bachelor's house; the whole aspect ugly. Enter* CUBIT *and* MRS. FRESHVILLE *from the hall, he backing down a little before her as if she may be forcing her way.* MRS. FRESHVILLE *smart and showy, with hair conspicuously "golden."*

CUBIT. Certainly, ma'am, you may come in; but Captain Chanter's positively not in the house.

MRS. FRESHVILLE. Where then *is* Captain Chanter?

CUBIT. He may have gone up to town.

MRS. FRESHVILLE. For what purpose?

CUBIT. I haven't the least idea.

MRS. FRESHVILLE. Is there any one in the house who *has* an idea?

CUBIT. Oh yes—lots of them!

MRS. FRESHVILLE. (*Looking at him a moment.*) They must be rubbish. Any women?

CUBIT. (*Vague and slightly shocked.*) Women, ma'am?

MRS. FRESHVILLE. Petticoats. All men?

CUBIT. (*Clearer.*) Two men and a boy.

MRS. FRESHVILLE. (*Looking round her, taking everything in.*) What sort of a boy?

CUBIT. In buttons—to do the knives.

MRS. FRESHVILLE. Oh *that* sort! They're a fraud! (*Seeing* PITT BRUNT *at the open window, through which* BRUNT *steps in from the lawn.*) Who's *this* person?

(*Enter* PITT BRUNT.)

CUBIT. (*Announcing.*) Mr. Pitt Brunt!

PITT BRUNT. (*Coming down; privately to* CUBIT, *while* MRS. FRESHVILLE *seats herself at the right of the table on the left.*) Who's that person?

CUBIT. No idea, sir! (*Exit* CUBIT *to the hall.*)

MRS. FRESHVILLE. I'm waiting—I'm awfully tired.

PITT BRUNT. (*In a modified boating-suit, with a double eyeglass, very neat and deliberate, and slightly hesitant and puzzled.*) A—tired of waiting?

MRS. FRESHVILLE. Not yet—in your company! Been on the river?

PITT BRUNT. I put in an hour each day.

MRS. FRESHVILLE. *I* used to put in hours —the dear old river!

PITT BRUNT. It's hygienic—if you're moderate.

MRS. FRESHVILLE. I *ain't* moderate! I never was!

PITT BRUNT. It's best, you know, to be safe.

MRS. FRESHVILLE. (*Looking at him an instant, while he smiles complacently; then rising suddenly.*) Do you think you are?

PITT BRUNT. (*Startled a little, retreating a step, then smiling at her again.*) I'm not very sure!

MRS. FRESHVILLE. (*Laughing.*) If you were, I'd do for you! Are you staying in the house?

PITT BRUNT. No—are you?

MRS. FRESHVILLE. Till I've done what I've come for. (*Then abrupt, familiar.*) What have *you* come for?

PITT BRUNT. I put in an hour each day.

MRS. FRESHVILLE. Here too? Why, you must have a time-table!

PITT BRUNT. My life is thoroughly organised.

MRS. FRESHVILLE. Mine is deliciously irregular.

PITT BRUNT. Ah, but you're not in the House!

MRS. FRESHVILLE. (*Vague.*) What house?

PITT BRUNT. The House of Commons!

MRS. FRESHVILLE. Do you mean *you* are?

PITT BRUNT. I sit for Blackport.

MRS. FRESHVILLE. At your ridiculous age?

PITT BRUNT. (*With dignity.*) My constituents have never inquired it.

MRS. FRESHVILLE. That's the sort of people I' like! Where are such ducks to be found?

PITT BRUNT. On the banks of the Smutt, in the extreme north. I meet them there, I address them, in a day or two; but in the meantime I'm spending the Whitsuntide recess at Teddington.

MRS. FRESHVILLE. And what are you doing at Teddington?

PITT BRUNT. I'm reading.

MRS. FRESHVILLE. Reading what?

PITT BRUNT. (*After an hesitation.*) Everything!

(*Re-enter* CUBIT *from the hall.*)

CUBIT. Mr. Bonsor has come in, sir.

PITT BRUNT. And Miss Amber?

CUBIT. Not arrived.

MRS. FRESHVILLE. (*To* CUBIT, *as he waits.*) You may go. (*Exit* CUBIT *to the hall. To* PITT BRUNT, *as he takes up his hat to follow him.*) You may not! (*Then as* BRUNT *puts down his hat.*) Who in the world's Miss Amber?

PITT BRUNT. Mr. Bonsor's niece.

MRS. FRESHVILLE. And who in the world's Mr. Bonsor?

PITT BRUNT. (*Surprised at the question.*) The master of this house. One of my strongest supporters. He has interests at Blackport—I look after them. I have interests here—

MRS. FRESHVILLE. (*Interrupting.*) And *he* looks after them! Tit for tat! Is he married?

PITT BRUNT. Not yet.

MRS. FRESHVILLE. There's always time! What's his age?

PITT BRUNT. (*Hesitating.*) He's getting on!

MRS. FRESHVILLE. And are *you?*

PITT BRUNT. Remarkably well!

MRS. FRESHVILLE. Remarkably well married?

PITT BRUNT. Not married at all! I mean I'm getting on.

MRS. FRESHVILLE. I'm glad to hear it. Is she good-looking?

PITT BRUNT. Who, madam?

MRS. FRESHVILLE. Mr. Bonsor's niece.

PITT BRUNT. I should use a still stronger expression.

MRS. FRESHVILLE. Always use the strongest there is! Is she one of your interests here?

PITT BRUNT. (*Smiling.*) The greatest!

MRS. FRESHVILLE. And Mr. Bonsor looks after it?

PITT BRUNT. He desires our union.

MRS. FRESHVILLE. "Union" is tame. Where is she to arrive from?

PITT BRUNT. From the' continent, where she has spent most of her life, and where —in Germany, six months ago—I was so fortunate as to make her acquaintance.

MRS. FRESHVILLE. (*To herself.*) Germany? Then it's not *she!* (*To* BRUNT.) Isn't there another woman?

PITT BRUNT. (*With simpering ardour.*) There's *no* other woman!

MRS. FRESHVILLE. For you—I see! But for him?

PITT BRUNT. For whom?

MRS. FRESHVILLE. (*Checking herself, reconsidering.*) Never mind whom! (*As she looks about her she suddenly spies, on the table on right, a roll of unfinished embroidery, on which she pounces. Holding it up.*) Whose untidiness is that?

PITT BRUNT. (*Looking at it with his glasses.*) That embroidery? Perhaps it's Mrs. Doubleday's.

MRS. FRESHVILLE. And who on earth is

Mrs. Doubleday?

PITT BRUNT. A lady in the house.

MRS. FRESHVILLE. (*With a little vindictive shake of the embroidery, which she clutches.*) Then I've got her! Rich?

PITT BRUNT. Five thousand a year.

MRS. FRESHVILLE. Good-looking?

PITT BRUNT. (*After an instant.*) I should use a still weaker expression.

MRS. FRESHVILLE. (*Promptly suggestive.*) Hideous?

PITT BRUNT. (*Hesitating again.*) Fat.

MRS. FRESHVILLE. And old—horribly old? (*Pressing.*) *How* old?

PITT BRUNT. (*Thinking.*) She's getting on.

MRS. FRESHVILLE. She ought to be ashamed of herself! Where's her husband?

PITT BRUNT. (*Grave.*) Beneath the sod.

MRS. FRESHVILLE. (*Gay.*) Like mine! What then is she doing here?

PITT BRUNT. Spending a month.

MRS. FRESHVILLE. With a bachelor?

PITT BRUNT. They have a common object.

MRS. FRESHVILLE. What sort of object?

PITT BRUNT. A child.

MRS. FRESHVILLE. Hers?

PITT BRUNT. His!

MRS. FRESHVILLE. Mr. Bonsor's?

PITT BRUNT. (*With a somewhat scandalised movement of repudiation.*) Mr. Doubleday's—the son of his first marriage. This lady, the stepmother, is one of the joint guardians. As Mr. Bonsor is the other, they have often to meet.

MRS. FRESHVILLE. How old is the child?

PITT BRUNT. He's getting on.

MRS. FRESHVILLE. You seem *all* to be getting on!

PITT BRUNT. He's about thirty.

MRS. FRESHVILLE. Then why the deuce guardians?

PITT BRUNT. It's a peculiar case—he's vicious.

MRS. FRESHVILLE. Stuff—I don't believe it!

PITT BRUNT. There *are* such men.

MRS. FRESHVILLE. You should give them their head!

PITT BRUNT. Doubleday can't be trusted. He requires the iron hand—and he knows it!

MRS. FRESHVILLE. I see—like *my* young man!

PITT BRUNT. (*Vague.*) Yours?

MRS. FRESHVILLE. *He* requires it—and *he* knows it. But I forgot—*you* don't!

PITT BRUNT. Permit me then to retire.

MRS. FRESHVILLE. Send me the butler! (*Exit* PITT BRUNT *to the hall. Unfolding the embroidery, she looks at it a moment.*) Hideous! the work of an ugly woman. Never mind, it's evidence! (*Rolling the embroidery up with decision, she thrusts it into her pocket.*) I see my way. No warning—a pounce! (*Seeing* CUBIT, *she extracts her purse from a small smart reticule which she carries on her arm, and takes a gold coin from it. Re-enter* CUBIT *from the hall. Having put the reticule upon the table on the left and the purse into her pocket, she hands the coin to* CUBIT.) Can you change me that?

CUBIT. (*With the sovereign, mystified.*) I've only sixpence.

MRS. FRESHVILLE. (*Taking the sixpence which* CUBIT *has produced.*) Sixpence will do.

CUBIT. (*Still more mystified.*) And the rest?

MRS. FRESHVILLE. (*Significant, with something very like a wink.*) Enjoy the rest!

CUBIT. (*To himself, gleefully, while he promptly pockets the sovereign.*) Nineteen-and-six? What a rum tip!

MRS. FRESHVILLE. I'm awfully thirsty. Is there any place near?

CUBIT. *I* could give you something— for the money!

MRS. FRESHVILLE. The money's for something else—the money's to hold your tongue.

CUBIT. Hold it to the Captain?

MRS. FRESHVILLE. Don't mention me— see?

CUBIT. I see. But who'll hold Mr. Brunt's?

MRS. FRESHVILLE. I'm already his secret: I *feel* I am! Good-bye.

CUBIT. I *could* throw in a glass of sherry.

MRS. FRESHVILLE. I loathe sherry. I'm coming back.

CUBIT. Let me show you the place.

MRS. FRESHVILLE. (*Motioning him back.*) I always find the place! Don't attract attention! (*Exit* MRS. FRESHVILLE *to the hall.*)

CUBIT. (*Alone, looking after her.*) It'll be a near thing if *you* don't! I'd remark her anywhere! (*Perceiving her reticule on the table.*) Hullo! has she left me *another* souvenir? (*Taking up the reticule and hesitating while he looks at it.*) Shall I go after her? No—I'll give it to her when she comes back back. (*Sniffing at it.*) My favourite scent—what-do-you-call-'em! (*Startled, seeing* MR. BONSOR, *and immediately dropping the reticule on the table.*) Oh!

(*Enter* MR. BONSOR *by the lower door on the right.*)

MR. BONSOR. (*Who has seen his movement.*) To whom does that article belong?

CUBIT. I was just wondering, sir.

MR. BONSOR. Is your nose your organ of wonder? I seem myself to become aware of the recent presence of a female.

CUBIT. A lady who has just gone, sir.

MR. BONSOR. Gone where?

CUBIT. No idea, sir.

MR. BONSOR. What did she want?

CUBIT. She didn't seem to know!

MR. BONSOR. To whom was her visit presumably addressed?

CUBIT. Couldn't make out, sir! (*To himself.*) Nineteen-and-six! What'll *he* go?

MR. BONSOR. (*To himself, struck.*) To Paul? (*To* CUBIT.) Did she make no observation?

CUBIT. She observed that she'd come back.

MR. BONSOR. (*To himself.*) Is he at it *again?* (*To* CUBIT.) When may we expect her?

CUBIT. Really can't say, sir; but when she comes—

MR. BONSOR. Let me instantly know. (*Looking for a moment, with his glasses, without approaching it, at the reticule which* CUBIT *has restored to its place on the table on the left.*) Let me examine that object. (CUBIT *presents him with the reticule, which, while* CUBIT *holds it, he continues, without touching it, to look*

at in the same way.) Ruby velvet? Ostentatious.

CUBIT. Slightly scented, sir. Shall I remove it?

MR. BONSOR. Not offensive. You may leave it. (*After* CUBIT *has again placed the reticule on the table.*) Where is Mrs. Doubleday?

CUBIT. Visiting the palace, sir.

MR. BONSOR. Again? She visited the palace yesterday.

CUBIT. Great historical interest, sir. Often spend an hour there myself.

MR. BONSOR. (*In his reflections.*) Not alone, I suppose.

CUBIT. (*Hesitating an instant, smiling.*) Usually with a companion, sir.

MR. BONSOR. (*Aloof.*) I'm not interested in your companions. I allude to Mrs. Doubleday.

CUBIT. Beg your pardon, sir. *Her* companion would probably be the Captain.

MR. BONSOR. I thought Captain Chanter was to go to London.

CUBIT. (*Smiling.*) I didn't, sir. He was out with her yesterday.

MR. BONSOR. (*Struck, prompt.*) *Was* he? (*Then dry.*) I didn't ask you to watch their movements. Is Mr. Paul with them?

CUBIT. They don't take him, sir. *He* might watch their movements!

MR. BONSOR. (*To himself.*) It's the time to watch his! (*To* CUBIT.) Where *is* Mr. Paul?

CUBIT. In the library, sir.

MR. BONSOR. Then call him immediately.

CUBIT. (*Without moving.*) I might call him all day, sir—he would never be able to come.

MR. BONSOR. What's the matter with him?

CUBIT. He's locked in. Mrs. Doubleday has the key.

MR. BONSOR. Oh yes, I forgot! (*Feeling in his pocket.*) I carry duplicates. (*Producing a key and giving it to* CUBIT.) Let him out.

CUBIT. (*To himself.*) One would think he was a domestic animal! (*Exit* CUBIT, *with the key, to the library.*)

MR. BONSOR. (*Alone, taking up the reticule.*) A mysterious female, with a meretricious appendage? Why not state her business? I hate anything underhand. (*Trying to open the bag.*) Confound the catch! (*Opening it.*) A photograph? (*Taking one out of the bag.*) Merciful powers —it's Paul! What fresh connection has he formed, with all our safeguards? And what's this written on the back? "Dudley —to his Nina!" She's his Nina, of course, but why is he her Dudley? Has he an *alias*—like a burglar? What dreadful revelations! Shall I confront him with this? No, I'll conceal it—I'll confer with my associate. (*Slips the photograph into his breast-pocket; thrusts the reticle into the cabinet on the right. Enter* PAUL DOUBLEDAY, *from the library, with a book in his hand. To himself, seeing him.*) Dudley!

PAUL. Oh, Mr. Bonsor, is *this* a book I may read?

MR. BONSOR. (*With the book.*) *The Experience of Life?* Decidedly not—it doesn't sound safe!

PAUL. Shall I put it back?

MR. BONSOR. By no means. (*Looking at him strangely.*) *I'll* put it back! Have you perused any portion of it?

PAUL. Not a word—I waited to ask you.

MR. BONSOR. Then how have you been occupied?

PAUL. (*Melancholy.*) I haven't been occupied!

MR. BONSOR. (*Significant.*) We must occupy you!

PAUL. Do, Mr. Bonsor—I so want to fill the hours!

MR. BONSOR. (*Suspicious.*) You say that in a tone—

PAUL. (*Conciliatory, explanatory.*) The tone of conviction, Mr. Bonsor! I've tried to speak of it to Mamma, but Mamma *is* occupied.

MR. BONSOR. The occupation we shall propose for you is not the same as that which now engrosses your mamma.

PAUL. Oh, yes—I don't mean *that!*

MR. BONSOR. It's comparatively legitimate—for Mrs. Doubleday.

PAUL. Yes, and it must be so jolly! (*Then on a movement of* MR. BONSOR's, *quick.*) When it *is* legitimate!

MR. BONSOR. When it is we may perhaps concede that! But there are cases

in which it isn't. I needn't remind you that you've forfeited—

PAUL. (*With a sigh.*) Oh, I know what I've forfeited!

MR. BONSOR. I needn't remind you that our confidence in you isn't all that we could wish.

PAUL. (*Genuinely meek.*) You do remind me, Mr. Bonsor.

MR. BONSOR. Occasionally, perhaps—for it's indispensable.

PAUL. Yes—it's indispensable!

MR. BONSOR. Such an occasion has now presented itself. If I just sent for you, it's to call your attention to the propriety of another sacrifice.

PAUL. (*Pleading.*) Another, Mr. Bonsor?

MR. BONSOR. I count upon you to make it.

PAUL. (*Pulling himself together.*) Well —I'll make it!

MR. BONSOR. You know our system— your mother's and mine. (*Complacent.*) The more sacrifices you make, the easier it is to make 'em!

PAUL. They come very easy now, Mr. Bonsor.

MR. BONSOR. The present occasion will perhaps be something of a test.

PAUL. There's no test, Mr. Bonsor, that I shrink from!

MR. BONSOR. (*Still more complacent.*) You perceive then the success of our system!

PAUL. (*Virtuous, like a prize pupil.*) It works, Mr. Bonsor—in perfection!

MR. BONSOR. There's a young lady about to arrive here.

PAUL. Yes, Mr. Bonsor.

MR. BONSOR. My niece, Miss Amber, who has been living abroad. She has come to spend three months with me— I've very particular views for her. What I want you to understand is that I look to you not to interfere with them.

PAUL. Tell me what they are, Mr. Bonsor, and I will regulate myself accordingly.

MR. BONSOR. I don't see my way to describe them to you correctly as anything but matrimonial.

PAUL. (*With continued docility.*) You wish me to marry her?

MR. BONSOR. (*Shocked.*) Not for worlds! I wish you to do the very opposite.

PAUL. (*Vague.*) The very opposite? Make up to her without intentions?

MR. BONSOR. Not make up to her at all! She's guileless—she's fresh—she's pure. Let her remain so!

PAUL. You mean that I'm not to speak to her?

MR. BONSOR. (*Stern.*) Never—till she speaks to *you.* (*To himself.*) I'll take care she doesn't!

PAUL. (*Following closely.*) Then I may answer her?

MR. BONSOR. With extreme reserve.

PAUL. (*As if learning his lesson.*) With extreme reserve. Is she possessed of—a—personal attractions?

MR. BONSOR. Unfortunately.

PAUL. (*With intense assent.*) Unfortunately!

MR. BONSOR. Fortunately you are not!

PAUL. (*With intenser assent.*) Fortunately!—And is her future husband?

MR. BONSOR. Her future husband is that rising young star of his party, Mr. Pitt Brunt.

PAUL. (*Precipitate.*) Oh, *he's* not beautiful!

MR. BONSOR. (*Pointed.*) No, but he's good!

PAUL. (*Checked, humiliated.*) Yes—that's everything!

MR. BONSOR. I've sent him to the station to meet Blanche.

PAUL. (*Alert, in spite of himself.*) Is her name Blanche?

MR. BONSOR. (*Severe.*) You'll have no occasion to pronounce it! (*Looking at his watch.*) I'm also expecting your mother's return.

PAUL. (*Somewhat rueful.*) So am *I,* Mr. Bonsor!

MR. BONSOR. (*Significant.*) She forgets herself!

PAUL. (*Reassuring, yet ominous.*) Oh, she'll remember *me!*

MR. BONSOR. I hope so! You constitute, in her absence, a responsibility of which I feel the weight! (*Deliberating.*) I don't quite know what to do with you.

PAUL. (*Passive.*) Whatever you like, Mr. Bonsor!

MR. BONSOR. (*Significant.*) There are many things to consider.

PAUL. Shall I return to the library?

MR. BONSOR. (*Dubious, taking up the book given him by* PAUL *and turning over a page or two.*) Not till I've weeded it out! (*Tosses down the book as if with a sense of contamination.*)

PAUL. (*Suggestive.*) Mamma sometimes keeps me in her room.

MR. BONSOR. (*Considering.*) I'm afraid that ground is forbidden me. (*Austere.*) I never enter your mother's apartment.

PAUL. Mightn't you put me in yours?

MR. BONSOR. That ground would be forbidden *her,* should she have occasion to visit you.

PAUL. She sometimes confines me in my own little room.

MR. BONSOR. Your own little room's the best place for you. I'll ring for Cubit to convey you there.

PAUL. (*Angelic.*) Let *me* ring! (*Rings.*) May I come down to tea?

MR. BONSOR. I don't know that to-day it will be advisable.

PAUL. (*Venturing to plead.*) I'm uncommonly thirsty, Mr. Bonsor.

MR. BONSOR. We're acquainted with some of the aberrations of your thirst—which it is one of the leading features of our system to keep under control.

PAUL. Dear Mr. Bonsor, tea isn't an aberration! (*Seeing* CUBIT.) Here it is!

(*Re-enter* CUBIT *at the lower door on the right, followed by a footman with a tea-tray.*)

CUBIT. (*To* MR. BONSOR.) Tea, sir.

MR. BONSOR. Put it down. (*The footman deposits the tray and retires. While he is doing so* BLANCHE AMBER *appears, unperceived by the others, at the open window, on the lawn.*) And take Mr. Paul to his room.

(*Enter* BLANCHE AMBER.)

BLANCHE. (*Precipitate, to* CUBIT.) Oh, I say—please don't!

MR. BONSOR. (*Startled, meeting and embracing her.*) Dearest child! Where's Pitt Brunt?

BLANCHE. I left him behind—I came across the lawn. We walked from the station—my maid has my things.

CUBIT. (*Announcing, as* PITT BRUNT *appears at the window.*) Mr. Pitt Brunt!

(*Re-enter* PITT BRUNT, *from the lawn.*)

PITT BRUNT. (*Slightly dignified and injured, to* BLANCHE.) I should have been glad to pursue my explanation.

BLANCHE. (*Laughing.*) Pursue it—but don't pursue *me!*

MR. BONSOR. (*To* BRUNT.) You can pursue everything here.

BLANCHE. (*Who has been looking at* PAUL.) Oh, not all at once, please!

MR. BONSOR. (*Cheerful.*) There'll be plenty of time!

PITT BRUNT. (*Hopeful.*) Plenty of time!

MR. BONSOR. Delighted to welcome you at last, Blanche.

BLANCHE. So happy to arrive, at last, dear uncle, and to be already (*looking round her*) so charmed with your surroundings!

CUBIT. (*To* MR. BONSOR.) Beg your pardon, sir—am I to remove Mr. Paul?

BLANCHE. (*Smiling, to* MR. BONSOR.) Won't you let me plead for him?

PITT BRUNT. (*To* PAUL.) Oh, how d'ye do, Doubleday? I didn't notice you!

PAUL. (*Ingenuously delighted, privately to* PITT BRUNT.) Miss Amber does!

BLANCHE. (*Privately to* MR. BONSOR.) Forgive my rash interference—Mr. Brunt has told me all about him.

MR. BONSOR. It was to warn you in time. (*To* CUBIT.) Mr. Paul will first have his tea.

BLANCHE. (*Approaching the tea-tray.*) And mayn't I have mine?

MR. BONSOR. Won't you have, after your journey, something more invigorating—a glass of wine?

CUBIT. I've brought wine, sir. (MR. BONSOR *signifies to* CUBIT *that nothing more is wanted, on which* CUBIT *goes out by lower door on the right.*)

BLANCHE. (*To* PAUL, *seeing him approach the tea-table.*) Will *you* give me a glass of wine?

(PAUL, *at this darts in silence to the decanter and, filling a glass, hands it to* BLANCHE. *While he is in the act of doing so enter* MRS. DOUBLEDAY *from the hall, perceiv-*

ing with visible horror what is tak-·ing place.*)

MRS. DOUBLEDAY. (*With loud abruptness.*) Paul!

PAUL. (*With a startled jump, letting his wine-glass fall.*) Mamma?

MRS. DOUBLEDAY. (*To herself, coming down.*) Drinking—with a woman!

MR. BONSOR. (*To* MRS. DOUBLEDAY.) My niece has arrived from Germany. (*To* BLANCHE.) My amiable friend Mrs. Doubleday. (MRS. DOUBLEDAY, *without shaking hands, greets* BLANCHE *with a distant and majestic curtsey.*)

BLANCHE. (*After returning her salutation very much in the same way, to* PITT BRUNT, *who, having seized from the agitated* PAUL *the decanter and another glass, approaches her obsequiously.*) Amiable? I don't believe it!

PITT BRUNT. (*Pouring out wine.*) An exemplary woman.

BLANCHE. I detest exemplary women!

PITT BRUNT. (*Reprehensive.*) Oh, Miss Amber!

BLANCHE. And also examplary men!

PITT BRUNT. You *are* paradoxical! Let *me* give you a glass of wine!

BLANCHE. Thank you—I've changed my mind. (*Seeing that* PAUL, *after his accident with the wine-glass, has poured out a cup of tea.*) But I'll have a cup of tea.

(PAUL, *taking the invitation, darts to her with the cup. Enter at the same instant from the hall* CAPTAIN CHANTER.)

MRS. DOUBLEDAY. Paul!

PAUL. (*Startled, jumping as before, and all but letting the cup drop.*) Mamma?

CHANTER. (*Rushing forward and catching the cup.*) Saved!

MRS. DOUBLEDAY. (*Seated down on the left.*) Then bring it to *me!* (CHANTER *brings her the tea.*)

MR. BONSOR. (*Introducing.*) Captain Chanter—Miss Amber!

BLANCHE. (*After nodding gaily at* CHANTER, *who has bowed to her.*) I seem dangerous to the glass and china!

CHANTER. (*Gallant, with his hand on his heart.*) Not only, I take it, to such fragile objects!

MRS. DOUBLEDAY. Captain!

(CHANTER *veers round and talks to her.* PITT BRUNT *meantime has gone back to the tea-table and exchanged his decanter and glass for a cup of tea, with which he returns to* BLANCHE. MR. BONSOR, *going up, has poured out a cup of tea and administered it, as it were, to* PAUL, *who stands helpless and rueful.*)

PITT BRUNT. (*With the cup, to* BLANCHE.) Let *me* serve you.

BLANCHE. Don't think me very capricious if I change my mind again. (*To* MR. BONSOR.) I think what I really and truly want is to go to my room.

MR. BONSOR. Let me instantly conduct you.

PITT BRUNT. (*To* BLANCHE.) Let *me* wait for you here.

MR. BONSOR. (*To* PITT BRUNT.) You're to stay to dinner, you know.

PITT BRUNT. I've brought my things.

MR. BONSOR. Cubit will show you where to dress.

PITT BRUNT. (*At the door to the hall to* BLANCHE, *whose back is turned.*) Auf Widersehen! (*Exit* PITT BRUNT.)

MR. BONSOR. (*To* MRS. DOUBLEDAY.) Shall I find you here in ten minutes?

MRS. DOUBLEDAY. (*Appealing to* CAPTAIN CHANTER.) In ten minutes?

CHANTER. (*Looking at his watch and smiling; to* MR. BONSOR.) Say a quarter of an hour!

MR. BONSOR. A quarter of an hour. (*He opens the lower door on the right for* BLANCHE, *who, during the appeal to* MRS. DOUBLEDAY, *has passed round and paused an instant before* PAUL, *whom she looks at sympathetically and a trifle strangely; a movement, a passage between them, observed by* MRS. DOUBLEDAY.)

BLANCHE. (*At the door, to* MRS. DOUBLEDAY, *smiling.*) Excuse me!

MRS. DOUBLEDAY. Don't mention it! (*Exeunt* BLANCHE *and* MR. BONSOR.) Paul!

PAUL. (*Who has his eyes fixed musingly on the door; startled.*) Yes, Mamma!

MRS. DOUBLEDAY. Go to *your* room.

PAUL. Mayn't I come down to dinner?

MRS. DOUBLEDAY. (*After consideration.*) On the understanding that you sit by *me.*

CHANTER. (*Protesting tenderly.*) Then, dear lady, whom shall *I* sit by?

MRS. DOUBLEDAY. (*Privately, warning.*) Hush—before *him!* (*To* PAUL.) Go!

PAUL. Yes, Mamma. (*Exit* PAUL, *submissive, to the hall.*)

MRS. DOUBLEDAY. (*Looking on the table.*) Where in the world's my embroidery?

CHANTER. (*Helping her to look.*) Your embroidery?

MRS. DOUBLEDAY. It was here—it's gone.

CHANTER. (*Gallant.*) If I had seen it I should doubtless have purloined it—treasure-trove! But I really haven't seen it.

MRS. DOUBLEDAY. (*Glancing about.*) I should prefer you to see it.

CHANTER. (*Pleading.*) Not just now, you know—I want *all* your attention.

MRS. DOUBLEDAY. You've had it these three hours.

CHANTER. Three hours were not enough—for all I had to say!

MRS. DOUBLEDAY. Yet you spoke with eloquence.

CHANTER. Say indeed with passion—with all the ardour of a sentiment long repressed, bursting forth in a flood!

MRS. DOUBLEDAY. And I followed you with natural embarrassment.

CHANTER. With nothing more natural than embarrassment? With no indulgence for my faults, with no encouragement for my hopes?

MRS. DOUBLEDAY. I must consider—I must consult.

CHANTER. Consult with *me!* It's just for that I offer myself! Didn't you tell me, moreover, that you would answer me in this place?

MRS. DOUBLEDAY. I've immense responsibilities.

CHANTER. It's for the way you discharge them that I revere you.

MRS. DOUBLEDAY. They've quite worn me out. What's left is—what you see.

CHANTER. What I see is the most charming creature in England—a woman the picture of whose rich maturity is but the voluminous record of her extraordinary virtue.

MRS. DOUBLEDAY. I believe I've done my duty—but the burden has been heavy indeed.

CHANTER. Let me take it on *my* shoulders!

MRS. DOUBLEDAY. Wait till you know what it has been in the past, to judge what it may be in the future.

CHANTER. (*Smiling.*) In the future we shall be two.

MRS. DOUBLEDAY. Say, alas, we shall be three!

CHANTER. Oh, if you count that way we shall be four. We mustn't forget dear Bonsor.

MRS. DOUBLEDAY. Never—he has been everything to me.

CHANTER. (*Dubious.*) Everything?

MRS. DOUBLEDAY. In my interminable martyrdom.

CHANTER. He'll always be at his post. There's no fear of *his* ever marrying!

MRS. DOUBLEDAY. There never was. He's impervious to female charms.

CHANTER. (*Smiling.*) That makes one more comfortable.

MRS. DOUBLEDAY. Oh, I haven't thought of conquest—I've thought only of my daily round. Mr. Bonsor will accuse me of deserting him.

CHANTER. (*Argumentative, cogent.*) You reinforce him!

MRS. DOUBLEDAY. I certainly shouldn't look at you unless I thought you were good.

CHANTER. (*Self-complacent.*) I do try to be good. The best of us can only try.

MRS. DOUBLEDAY. And not all who try succeed. You do.

CHANTER. (*Simpering.*) Very kind of you to have noticed it.

MRS. DOUBLEDAY. That's why I shrink from telling you everything.

CHANTER. To the pure all things are pure!

MRS. DOUBLEDAY. So I've had often to say to myself—in the atmosphere of Paul's propensities.

CHANTER. It has left you unspotted.

MRS. DOUBLEDAY. (*Anxious.*) Will it leave *you* so? That's the question that haunts me now.

CHANTER. Just try me and see!

MRS. DOUBLEDAY. You know, then, in a general way, the task I accepted on the lamented death of Mr. Doubleday.

CHANTER. To watch over the product of his earlier union. You may be said to have watched.

MRS. DOUBLEDAY. Night and day—it was a sacred trust. His earlier union had been a blunder.

CHANTER. He didn't know *you.*

MRS. DOUBLEDAY. He couldn't. I was scarcely born.

CHANTER. If you *had* been you'd have been saved—

MRS. DOUBLEDAY. This crushing legacy? It's not improbable. But I came too late.

CHANTER. Not too late to save Paul.

MRS. DOUBLEDAY. *Have* I saved him? That remains to be seen! His mother, alas, was—indelicate!

CHANTER. There *are* such women!

MRS. DOUBLEDAY. She was a person of some appearance; but she was bold.

CHANTER. Yet not unattractive!

MRS. DOUBLEDAY. There were persons who thought so; but don't ask for details.

CHANTER. I know you well enough to know it would be useless. But even without them I can judge of the blood that flows in Paul's veins.

MRS. DOUBLEDAY. Heredity, heredity! My husband's favourite expression. He saw it bear dreadful fruit.

CHANTER. From the child's earliest years?

MRS. DOUBLEDAY. Almost in the cradle. Fortunately he was on the lookout.

CHANTER. (*Impulsive.*) Poor old chap! (*Then prompt.*) I mean Paul!

MRS. DOUBLEDAY. It's indeed his misfortune even more than his fault. But it was to the advantage of every one when the fatal fountain of such dangers at last ceased to flow. My predecessor succumbed —to the last penalties of impropriety; and Mr. Doubleday, after a considerable interval, did what he could to repair his original error.

CHANTER. He married a faultless being.

MRS. DOUBLEDAY. That's what he was so good as to pronounce me. Unhappily his compensation was not so complete as I could have wished. I presented him with a second son, who, alas, didn't live.

CHANTER. If he had, he too would have been faultless.

MRS. DOUBLEDAY. Heredity again! It was

then that we looked in the face—that we sadly but heroically accepted—our responsibilities to our little incumbrance: not with the vain hope of making him what his brother would have been, but with that of repressing his inclinations.

CHANTER. And in some degree you succeeded?

MRS. DOUBLEDAY. Till his twentieth year. Then they burst forth.

CHANTER. (*Pressing.*) What did he do?

MRS. DOUBLEDAY. (*Hesitating, scrupulous.*) Can I safely tell you?

CHANTER. To the pure all things are pure!

MRS. DOUBLEDAY. Suppose I should communicate a taint?

CHANTER. I must get accustomed to my danger.

MRS. DOUBLEDAY. One does. Paul disappeared.

CHANTER. How did he manage it?

MRS. DOUBLEDAY. By the assistance of another person.

CHANTER. What description of person?

MRS. DOUBLEDAY. The lowest description. A singer, from the "Waterloo."

CHANTER. The Waterloo?

MRS. DOUBLEDAY. The name of a popular music-hall. *You* don't know such things —but I've had to learn them! *Her* name was Nina.

CHANTER. (*Startled.*) Nina?

MRS. DOUBLEDAY. Did you ever see her?

CHANTER. Dear me, no! (*To himself.*) Nina?

MRS. DOUBLEDAY. They went to Paris.

CHANTER. (*Impulsive, inadvertent.*) That's the best place!

MRS. DOUBLEDAY. (*Surprised.*) What do you know about it?

CHANTER. (*On his guard.*) One can't help hearing.

MRS. DOUBLEDAY. *I* can't, but *you* should! We pursued him, we had a hunt! and, after unspeakable anxieties and incredible efforts, we finally ran him to earth.

CHANTER. (*With increasing interest.*) Where *was* he?

MRS. DOUBLEDAY. In sumptuous apartments—steeped to the lips in vice. He had given the rein to his passions.

CHANTER. (*Breathless.*) All of them?

MRS. DOUBLEDAY. Without exception. He had changed his name, he had waxed his moustache, he had overdrawn his account.

CHANTER. Then you arrived just in time.

MRS. DOUBLEDAY. To take him home. We took him.

CHANTER. Did he kick?

MRS. DOUBLEDAY. He was prostrate, he couldn't deny it.

CHANTER. No, poor fellow, he does own up!

MRS. DOUBLEDAY. Our only mercy. He sees himself as he is. Well he may, when he killed his father.

CHANTER. (*Startled.*) Do you really mean—?

MRS. DOUBLEDAY. I mean that my husband died of the scandal. But in his last hours he cut me out my work.

CHANTER. To keep hold of Paul?

MRS. DOUBLEDAY. To prevent a recurrence.

CHANTER. And you've prevented it!

MRS. DOUBLEDAY. With the help of Mr. Bonsor, whom, as my husband's oldest and dearest friend, he appointed, as it were, my joint-supervisor. A childless widow with an ample provision, I had command of my time, and an equally childless bachelor with an equally adequate fortune, Mr. Bonsor had command of his. We've given it all to our work, we've had no other life.

CHANTER. It's time to have another now.

MRS. DOUBLEDAY. Sometimes—when I falter—I think so.

CHANTER. You've done so much.

MRS. DOUBLEDAY. We've reduced it to a science. To *act* on the slightest symptom.

CHANTER. To cry "Fire!" on the first puff of smoke!

MRS. DOUBLEDAY. If we so much as sniff it, we turn on the hose. We flood the whole place.

CHANTER. So that Paul lives, as it were, under water.

MRS. DOUBLEDAY. It has taught him to swim, it has made him amphibious. We organise his hours; we regulate his thoughts; we control his imagination. We're intensely particular, for instance, about his reading. Nothing that treats of the passions.

CHANTER. That cuts it down!

MRS. DOUBLEDAY. We cut it down. We cut everything down. We allow him no pocket-money.

CHANTER. None at all?

MRS. DOUBLEDAY. Sixpence a day.

CHANTER. You can't be very bad on that!

MRS. DOUBLEDAY. You can be very good! He gives it to the poor. We allow him no tobacco, no wine, and no female acquaintance.

CHANTER. What then *do* you allow him?

MRS. DOUBLEDAY. Nothing. To such a nature everything's an opportunity. He reports himself at fixed hours, and, as you know, I rarely leave his side.

CHANTER. Yes, I had a job to get you off.

MRS. DOUBLEDAY. I locked him up.

CHANTER. But he got out.

MRS. DOUBLEDAY. Mr. Bonsor must have taken the responsibility. Four times a year we spend a month here—for Mr. Bonsor to do his part.

CHANTER. He seems to do it very well.

MRS. DOUBLEDAY. (*Dubious.*) Mr. Bonsor requires to be kept up. He shouldn't have invited that girl.

CHANTER. Oh, I'll look after *her!*

MRS. DOUBLEDAY. Don't take the trouble, *I'll* look after her! Now you see my life.

CHANTER. To see it is to admire it; but there's one thing I don't understand! Paul's healthy, hearty, independent—

MRS. DOUBLEDAY. He's still an infant.

CHANTER. An infant of thirty?

MRS. DOUBLEDAY. By the terms of his father's will. He doesn't come of age till he's forty; unless before that, in the exercise of our discretion, if it seems to us finally safe, we anticipate a little, we put him in possession.

CHANTER. He could break such a will in an hour!

MRS. DOUBLEDAY. It would never occur to him—he takes *our* view.

CHANTER. Very obliging of him!

MRS. DOUBLEDAY. I do him justice—he repents. He's afraid of his passions.

CHANTER. (*As if with the deliberate resolve to face, courageously, considerable exposure.*) Well, I ain't!

MRS. DOUBLEDAY. (*Anxious, ominous.*) Are you sure they're not contagious?

CHANTER. I'll set him the example of mine.

MRS. DOUBLEDAY. Yours?

CHANTER. I've only one—it's for *you!*

MRS. DOUBLEDAY. You're almost irresistible—but think it well over! (*Seeing MR. BONSOR.*) Here's Mr. Bonsor, for one of our regular councils, which we never postpone. (*Re-enter MR. BONSOR from the lower door on the right. Waving CAPTAIN CHANTER toward the library.*) Think it over and over!

CHANTER. (*At the door of the library.*) Coquette! (*Exit CAPTAIN CHANTER.*)

MR. BONSOR. On what are you inviting him so peculiarly to brood?

MRS. DOUBLEDAY. My peculiar position.

MR. BONSOR. What has he got to do with it?

MRS. DOUBLEDAY. (*Modest.*) That he must confide to you himself.

MR. BONSOR. Mrs. Doubleday, you've a bad conscience!

MRS. DOUBLEDAY. (*With spirit.*) Not worse than *you* ought to have!

MR. BONSOR. I'm not straying into languid by-paths—I'm not thinking of a sacrifice to Hymen.

MRS. DOUBLEDAY. Of marriage? You think of nothing else but that girl's!

MR. BONSOR. Well, if I'm a victim of duty, I'm also Blanche's uncle.

MRS. DOUBLEDAY. And if *I'm* a victim of duty, I'm also— (*Checking herself as if from delicacy.*)

MR. BONSOR. Not the Captain's aunt— though you might be!

MRS. DOUBLEDAY. There's something *you* might be, Mr. Bonsor: a little more correct in your figures!

MR. BONSOR. This is not a time to recriminate—it's a time for harmonious action. (*Taking the photograph from his pocket.*) Look at that!

MRS. DOUBLEDAY. (*With the photograph.*) Paul!

MR. BONSOR. Dudley!

MRS. DOUBLEDAY. (*Looking at the back.*) Nina!

MR. BONSOR. She's here!

MRS. DOUBLEDAY. (*Horrified.*) Here?

MR. BONSOR. Come back for him!

MRS. DOUBLEDAY. After all these years?

MR. BONSOR. They've been wasted! She was here an hour ago—she may return at any moment.

MRS. DOUBLEDAY. Prevent her—head her off!

MR. BONSOR. Shall I see her alone?

MRS. DOUBLEDAY. (*Dubious.*) No, that won't do! *I'll* see her!

MR. BONSOR. Such a person? It's indecorous. *I'll* see her! (*Exit* MR. BONSOR *rapidly to the hall.*)

MRS. DOUBLEDAY. (*With the photograph in her hand.*) He's too proper by half; he needn't accuse *me!* (*Tosses the photograph on the table and goes quickly to the door of the library, where she calls.*) Captain! (*Then as* CHANTER *reappears: reenter* CAPTAIN CHANTER.) She's come back!

CHANTER. Who's come back?

MRS. DOUBLEDAY. Nina!

CHANTER. (*Bounding in.*) Nina?

MRS. DOUBLEDAY. We must double the guard!

CHANTER. (*To himself, excited, alarmed.*) Heavens! if it's *my* Nina? (*To* MRS. DOUBLEDAY.) Where *is* she?

MRS. DOUBLEDAY. Mr. Bonsor's gone to look.

CHANTER. (*Nervous, starting to go up.*) I'll go to look!

MRS. DOUBLEDAY. (*Commanding.*) Captain! (*As* CHANTER *comes down again.*) You'll stay here. (*Indicating the table.*) There's his photograph.

CHANTER. (*Taking the photograph.*) And where's hers? (*Tosses the photograph back.*)

MRS. DOUBLEDAY. (*Struck.*) Why should you want it?

CHANTER. (*Rueful.*) True—when we have the reality!

MRS. DOUBLEDAY. I'll turn the key in Paul's door!

CHANTER. (*Looking at his watch.*) You must dress for dinner.

MRS. DOUBLEDAY. His room is next to mine. (*Then with sudden seductiveness.*) *Now* do you want me?

CHANTER. (*Ardent.*) More than ever, beloved!

MRS. DOUBLEDAY. (*Giving him her hand to kiss.*) Then take me!

(CHANTER *seizes it and kisses it with an air of rapture, on which* MRS. DOUBLEDAY *snatches it away and goes out hastily to the hall. Reenter* CUBIT *by the lower door on the right.*)

CUBIT. I've put out the embroidered waistcoat, sir.

CHANTER. (*To himself, agitated.*) Embroidered by Nina's hand! (*Exit* CAPTAIN CHANTER *by the lower door on the right.*)

CUBIT. (*Alone.*) Does he know she was here? has he seen what she left? Where *is* that elegant object? (*Seeing* BLANCHE AMBER *at the window.*) Here's an elegant object! (*Re-enter* BLANCHE, *dressed for dinner, from the lawn.*) Quite comfortable in your room, Miss?

BLANCHE. Perfectly, thank you!

CUBIT. (*Looking at his watch.*) Dinner in ten minutes.

BLANCHE. I'm quite ready. (*Exit* CUBIT *to the hall.*) What sociable servants! (*At the table on the left.*) But what dreary books! (*Taking up one.*) The Experience of Life? (*Turning it over.*) Improving! (*Flinging it down.*) I hate improvement! The usual photographs? (*Taking up the photograph of* PAUL.) Ah, no, not quite! Poor Mr. Paul—in all his impropriety! What a history! He *is* handsome! (*Turning over the photograph.*) But why "Dudley"? Some wild pet name! How romantic! And who's "Nina"? (*Musing while she looks again at* PAUL's *image.*) Some great lady, perhaps, whose head he has turned—her pet name! Is *she* handsome? (*With her eyes for a moment on the picture.*) I hope not! (*Seeing* PAUL, *who has appeared at the window, she is so startled that, as he comes in and down, she slips the photograph, to prevent his seeing it, precipitately, instinctively into her pocket. Enter* PAUL DOUBLEDAY *from the lawn; shyly, hesitatingly, tentatively, as if his pretext has suddenly failed him. He is not dressed for dinner. He comes down, however, with a visible mixture of impetuosity and caution, which gives him an odd air that makes* BLANCHE *appear to wonder, with sudden amusement, what is the matter with him.*) Are you looking for anything?

PAUL. (*Panting a little.*) No, thank you!

—I mean I *am!*

BLANCHE. Anything that was on that table?

PAUL. (*Looking vaguely and as if a little surprised.*) Nothing that was on that table. (*Seeing* "The Experience of Life.") Not that book—I mayn't touch it.

BLANCHE. *The Experience of Life?* Don't —it's dreadfully slow!

PAUL. (*Surprised.*) It's too fast for *me!* Have *you* any books?

BLANCHE. (*Thinking.*) Any books?

PAUL. Any safe ones. They're all impossible here.

BLANCHE. Impossibly dull?

PAUL. Impossibly lively! They excite a train of thought.

BLANCHE. In *this* good house—my uncle's?

PAUL. I mean for *me.* But I'm not like others—I'm so easily upset!

BLANCHE. (*Looking at him an instant with compassionate assent and interest.*) Ah, yes—I know!

PAUL. (*Struck.*) You know already?

BLANCHE. My uncle has mentioned it.

PAUL. (*With a sigh of resignation.*) Yes, he always mentions it!

BLANCHE. And Mr. Pitt Brunt had hinted—

PAUL. (*With a flash of spirit.*) Mr. Pitt Brunt? I'd thank him *not* to hint!

BLANCHE. He spoke of it kindly—he's sorry for you. I've a charming book upstairs—a railway novel.

PAUL. (*With a sigh of renunciation.*) Ah, railway novels won't do! Quite forbidden!

BLANCHE. (*With the same compassion.*) They do keep you short!

PAUL. (*Making every concession.*) They *have* to, you see. (*After an instant.*) My propensities, you know.

BLANCHE. (*Grave, impressed.*) Are they so awfully marked?

PAUL. With big black numbers—one, two, three!

BLANCHE. (*Wondering.*) Three?

PAUL. Oh, there are more than that! But don't ask me to count.

BLANCHE. Not for the world. (*Then after an instant, smiling.*) *I'll* count!

PAUL. As you see them appear? You'll get tired!

BLANCHE. They don't appear—it seems to me—in your appearance!

PAUL. Ah, the very worst of them is my duplicity! But if you know I'm not naturally good, you must also know that I at least struggle to be.

BLANCHE. Why, I do that myself!

PAUL. Yes, but you don't fall. I invariably do. I did just now, at my window.

BLANCHE. (*Laughing.*) You don't mean you fell out of it!

PAUL. That would have hurt me less. No. I looked at you—I looked at you in the garden.

BLANCHE. Oh yes, I went down there— I had finished dressing.

PAUL. *I* hadn't—but I unblushingly gazed at you.

BLANCHE. I didn't see you—I was admiring the garden. It's very lovely.

PAUL. (*Explosive.*) Never so lovely as with *you* in it!

BLANCHE. Oh, Mr. Doubleday!

PAUL. See how bad I am! After I had stared a few moments I came straight down —I followed you in here.

BLANCHE. But how does that "hurt" you?

PAUL. It excites a train of thought.

BLANCHE. (*Laughing.*) Like the railway novels? Thank you!

PAUL. Mr. Bonsor gave me a tremendous caution.

BLANCHE. So he did me!

PAUL. And I gave him a tremendous pledge.

BLANCHE. Well, I didn't!

PAUL. Oh, you're free—because you're good!

BLANCHE. It's better to have passions and control them.

PAUL. That's just what I didn't do— when I came down here!

BLANCHE. (*After an instant.*) Was it a passion that brought you?

PAUL. I don't know what to call it, Miss Amber. It was an emotion not to *be* controlled! See, I'm getting worse!

BLANCHE. (*Smiling.*) You must pull up —you must recover yourself!

PAUL. I shall try to do so presently; but, before I begin, let me say this one thing, which was really, I think, the idea that made me break my vow! I want you to understand my reserve.

BLANCHE. (*Smiling.*) I don't *see* your reserve, Mr. Doubleday!

PAUL. (*Quickly, reassuring.*) You will in a moment! Then please remember this, that if I don't speak to you it's because I'm forbidden, and if I don't look at you, it's because I'm afraid.

BLANCHE. What are you afraid of?

PAUL. I'm afraid of myself!

BLANCHE. (*Impressed, taking it very seriously.*) You live, then, in such terror?

PAUL. Not quite in terror, perhaps, but in very grave anxiety. I never know what I may do next!

BLANCHE. (*Smiling.*) You frighten *me* a little!

PAUL. Oh, now that I've explained, I shall again put on the mask!

BLANCHE. (*Sighing.*) The tragic mask!

PAUL. Not even that: the expressionless!

BLANCHE. Well, if you mayn't express, *I* may!

PAUL. (*A little ironic.*) Mustn't you first ask Pitt Brunt?

BLANCHE. Never! *He* has no passions.

PAUL. Yes, he has an easy life of it.

BLANCHE. He talked to me just now about the Bill of '86. I attach no importance to the Bill of '86!

PAUL. (*Vague.*) You think it didn't go far enough?

BLANCHE. Mr. Brunt says it went too far!

PAUL. He always thinks everything does. That is doubtless the danger!

BLANCHE. (*Sympathetic.*) It's the danger that makes the hero!

PAUL. Oh, *I'm* not a hero! I'm too often beaten!

BLANCHE. (*With pity and curiosity.*) The enemy's so strong?

PAUL. Overwhelming, Miss Amber!

BLANCHE. It makes your problem wonderfully interesting—your situation intensely dramatic. I should like immensely to help you!

PAUL. How *can* you?

BLANCHE. By fighting at your side.

PAUL. In the thick of the fray? You'd be scandalised!

BLANCHE. Ah, not so easily! I can understand temptation—I can allow for it!

PAUL. What do you know about it?

BLANCHE. (*After an instant, quite exalted.*) I've felt it!

PAUL. But always resisted!

BLANCHE. (*After another hesitation, in the same way.*) Not always!

PAUL. (*With vehemence.*) Ah, don't undermine me!

BLANCHE. Not for the world—but I must look the enemy in the face! (*Seeing* PITT BRUNT.) Silence!

(*Re-enter* PITT BRUNT *from the hall and stands looking an instant from* BLANCHE *to* PAUL.)

PITT BRUNT. (*To* PAUL.) You're not dressed for dinner? (*As if with the habit of setting a superior example.*) I am!

PAUL. Oh, *you're* good! But I'll dress now. (*Exit* PAUL *to the hall.*)

BLANCHE. (*With slight irony, to* PITT BRUNT.) Yes—you're faultless!

PITT BRUNT. (*Much gratified.*) Delighted to hear it from *you*, Miss Amber!

BLANCHE. You wouldn't be if you knew— (*Pauses, as she turns away, with a vague shrug.*)

PITT BRUNT. If I knew what?

BLANCHE. That I can enter into—every aberration!

PITT BRUNT. (*Shocked.*) Every one?

BLANCHE. (*Reconsidering.*) Well, most! (*Pointing at the door on the left.*) What's in there?

PITT BRUNT. The library.

BLANCHE. I'll look at the books.

PITT BRUNT. They're perfectly unobjectionable.

BLANCHE. So much the worse! (*Exit* BLANCHE *to the library.*)

PITT BRUNT. Awfully paradoxical, but awfully charming!

(*Re-enter, from the hall,* MRS. FRESHVILLE *accompanied by* CUBIT.)

MRS. FRESHVILLE. (*To* CUBIT.) Don't announce me—go away! (CUBIT *bows obsequiously and exit to the hall. To* BRUNT, *familiarly.*) Dinner-time, eh?

PITT BRUNT. (*Surprised.*) Do you dine with us?

MRS. FRESHVILLE. No, but I suppose *he* does, doesn't he?

PITT BRUNT. (*Freshly mystified.*) Again, madam, I'm in doubt—

MRS. FRESHVILLE. No matter—*I* ain't!

PITT BRUNT. You're very mysterious, but it's attractive! Whoever the gentleman is, he's dressing.

MRS. FRESHVILLE. (*Looking about her for her reticule.*) *I'll* dress him! Where's my bag?

PITT BRUNT. Your bag?

MRS. FRESHVILLE. I forgot it here—it contains treasures. Please produce it.

PITT BRUNT. Dear madam, how shall I produce it?

MRS. FRESHVILLE. By finding it. I must have it. Look for it.

PITT BRUNT. (*Glancing about.*) I am looking; I don't see it!

MRS. FRESHVILLE. Look more. Go and ask the butler.

PITT BRUNT. I usually ring—for a servant.

MRS. FRESHVILLE. *I* don't—I pounce. Try pouncing.

PITT BRUNT. (*Amused.*) I often try it in the House!

MRS. FRESHVILLE. Then "go for him"—there's a dear!

PITT BRUNT. Oh, if you put it *that* way—!

MRS. FRESHVILLE. (*Smiling.*) I'll put it any way you like!

PITT BRUNT. You're more and more mysterious!

MRS. FRESHVILLE. Not when you know me!

PITT BRUNT. (*After an instant.*) I should be glad to make time to know you.

MRS. FRESHVILLE. (*Gay.*) Naughty man! what would the young lady say? (*Then as he protests.*) First see about my bag.

PITT BRUNT. (*Gratified.*) I'll see about it. (*Exit* PITT BRUNT *to the hall.*)

MRS. FRESHVILLE. (*Alone.*) The member for Blackport? There's more in him than meets the eye! (*Then in another tone.*) They assemble here for dinner? Then for my gentleman! (*As she sees* CHANTER.) As large as life—in *my* old waistcoat!

(*Re-enter* CAPTAIN CHANTER *by the lower door on the right; stopping short, transfixed, appalled.*)

CHANTER. Nina? Horrors! (*Then with a quaver of dismay as she simply stands before him unmistakable and imperturba-*

ble.*) What does this *mean?*

MRS. FRESHVILLE. Can't you imagine?

CHANTER. Nothing so awful! Go away!

MRS. FRESHVILLE. Not without *you,* my duck. I've come for you!

CHANTER. (*More and more alarmed.*) You're mad—you're wicked—you're indecent! They'll all *be* here!

MRS. FRESHVILLE. Then you can present me! That's what I've waited for.

CHANTER. You've waited?

MRS. FRESHVILLE. All the afternoon.

CHANTER. And who has seen you?

MRS. FRESHVILLE. Only one or two, as yet; but the rest shall have the treat.

CHANTER. (*Scared, helpless, going up to look out and coming down.*) Nina, do you want to crush me?

MRS. FRESHVILLE. Yes, to small pieces. And to pick them up and keep them.

CHANTER. Keep them in a mortuary urn —you're killing me! How did you get here?

MRS. FRESHVILLE. The same way as you, I suppose. By the aid of my wits.

CHANTER. Your wits are remarkable, but they've sadly misled you. You've taken a fatal step!

MRS. FRESHVILLE. Fatal, no doubt (*whipping out the roll of tapestry she has appropriated in the first scene*) to the perpetrator of this!

CHANTER. *You* took it?

MRS. FRESHVILLE. To convict you. The last link in the chain!

CHANTER. Give it back to me!

MRS. FRESHVILLE. To give back to *her?* Let her give *you* back first. (*Then tossing the tapestry away.*) Faugh!

CHANTER. (*Distracted.*) They're coming! Let me meet you somewhere else!

MRS. FRESHVILLE. (*Austere.*) At the altar, Captain Chanter—to-morrow!

CHANTER. Make an appointment with me—we'll talk it over!

MRS. FRESHVILLE. We'll talk it over now —it'll save time.

CHANTER. I can't—I'm faint!

MRS. FRESHVILLE. I've no doubt you are!

CHANTER. For want of food!

MRS. FRESHVILLE. Doesn't she give you enough—with the fortune you're hunting so hard? Come with *me* and you shall have plenty!

CHANTER. There's no such person as you suppose!

MRS. FRESHVILLE. Then why are you so afraid she'll see me?

CHANTER. There *are* ladies here, but they're innocent—!

MRS. FRESHVILLE. I don't suspect them all—*one* will do!

CHANTER. Who poisoned your mind?

MRS. FRESHVILLE. You, and your flagrant bad faith; your unnatural absences and your still more unnatural explanations. So I sent for the doctor.

CHANTER. You do run up bills!

MRS. FRESHVILLE. I sent for two or three. They had a consultation and found out what was the matter.

CHANTER. I could have told you for nothing!

MRS. FRESHVILLE. They put their finger on the place!

CHANTER. (*Blank.*) What place?

MRS. FRESHVILLE. *This* place! They followed you; they tracked you.

CHANTER. Detectives? (*Reproachful, bantering.*) Oh, bad Nina!

MRS. FRESHVILLE. They showed me the way! I took it.

CHANTER. (*With his hand fumbling in his pocket, going up again and coming down, irresolute, desperate, on pins and needles.*) Then what'll you take *now*?

MRS. FRESHVILLE. Nothing, thanks: I had something at the inn!

CHANTER. What can I *do* for you?

MRS. FRESHVILLE. Redeem your solemn vow—make me your wedded wife!

CHANTER. (*Stands for an instant thinking, covering his face with his hands.*) Meet me then—to-morrow. I'll come up to town.

MRS. FRESHVILLE. With the ring in your hand?

CHANTER. And bells on my toes—all the jewelry you want!

MRS. FRESHVILLE. My wants are limited to a plain gold circle. And you needn't come up to town—I shall be here.

CHANTER. If you don't allow me my freedom of action, how can I square her?

MRS. FRESHVILLE. Allow me mine. *I'll* square her!

CHANTER. Don't you see that if you make a scene—? (*Checks himself, listening.*)

MRS. FRESHVILLE. Well, if I make a scene?

CHANTER. Why, I'm nowhere!

MRS. FRESHVILLE. Well, *I* ain't—so it doesn't matter! But I don't mind giving you an hour now—for I flatter myself I've got you!

CHANTER. (*Frightened, as she is going up.*) Don't go *that* way—wait!

MRS. FRESHVILLE. Wait here?

CHANTER. (*Still more alarmed.*) No, wait *there!* (*Pushing her to the lower door on the right.*) Don't come out till we've gone to dinner!

> (*Exit* MRS. FRESHVILLE, *hustled out; on which* CHANTER *turns, deeply agitated, to meet* MRS. DOUBLEDAY. *Re-enter* MRS. DOUBLEDAY *from the hall, dressed for dinner.*)

MRS. DOUBLEDAY. Where's Mr. Bonsor?

CHANTER. I haven't seen him.

MRS. DOUBLEDAY. Still looking for that woman?

CHANTER. (*Vague, on his guard.*) That woman?

MRS. DOUBLEDAY. Why, Paul's dreadful connection.

CHANTER. Oh yes! (*To himself.*) I wish she *were* Paul's! (*Thinks an instant.*) Perhaps she *is!* (*Then breathless with the happy thought.*) That photograph!—she *must* be! (*Exultant.*) Saved!

> (*Re-enter* MR. BONSOR *from the hall, dressed for dinner.*)

MRS. DOUBLEDAY. (*To* MR. BONSOR.) Did you see her?

MR. BONSOR. No, I hunted—but I had to dress.

MRS. DOUBLEDAY. She'll come back—we'll catch her!

CHANTER. (*Nervous.*) Oh, let's have dinner first!

MR. BONSOR. Where are the young people?

CHANTER. (*Impatient, seeing* BLANCHE.) Here's one of them—that's enough!

> (*Re-enter* BLANCHE AMBER *from the library.*)

MR. BONSOR. And where's Pitt Brunt?

BLANCHE. And where's Mr. Paul?

MRS. DOUBLEDAY. (*Reminded, clapping her hand to her pocket.*) The key's in my other dress—I quietly locked him in.

BLANCHE. (*Smiling.*) He must have escaped—he was here!

MRS. DOUBLEDAY. (*Alarmed.*) Here?

BLANCHE. Ten minutes ago.

MR. BONSOR. (*To MRS. DOUBLEDAY, severe.*) You quietly locked him out!

MRS. DOUBLEDAY. Mercy—where *is* he then?

(*Re-enter CUBIT from the hall.*)

CUBIT. (*To MR. BONSOR.*) Dinner, sir.

CHANTER. (*Pressing, catching MRS. DOUBLEDAY by the arm and hurrying her up to the hall.*) It doesn't matter—come!

(*Exeunt CAPTAIN CHANTER and MRS. DOUBLEDAY, and, hurrying after them, MR. BONSOR and BLANCHE. As CUBIT is about to follow, re-enter PITT BRUNT from the lawn.*)

CUBIT. Dinner, sir.

PITT BRUNT. (*Resentful.*) I've looked for you everywhere.

CUBIT. Doing my 'air, sir.

PITT BRUNT. Where's that lady?

CUBIT. (*Blank, giving it up.*) Showed herself out!

PITT BRUNT. But where's her bag?

CUBIT. No connection with the luggage, sir.

PITT BRUNT. (*Mystified.*) I give it up! (*Exit PITT BRUNT to the hall.*)

CUBIT. (*Alone, glancing about him.*) Where *is* the blessed bag? A liberal reward— (*Pauses as he sees MRS. FRESHVILLE.*)

(*Re-enter MRS. FRESHVILLE by the lower door on the right.*)

MRS. FRESHVILLE. (*Giving CUBIT, in a business-like way, as soon as she sees him, another sovereign with which she has already provided herself.*) Add that!

CUBIT. (*With the sovereign.*) Sixpence back, ma'am?

MRS. FRESHVILLE. No—keep it!

CUBIT. For silence, ma'am?

MRS. FRESHVILLE. For anything you like!

CUBIT. (*To himself.*) Thirty-nine and six!

(*Exit CUBIT to the hall. Re-enter PAUL DOUBLEDAY from the garden.*)

MRS. FRESHVILLE. (*Before seeing PAUL.*) But my reticule—with the dear old photo? (*Then as PAUL appears.*) Gracious powers—the original!

PAUL. (*Staring, amazed, coming down.*) Nina?

MRS. FRESHVILLE. (*With a shriek, throwing herself into his arms.*) Dudley!

ACT SECOND

MR. BONSOR's *drawing-room. MR. BONSOR, at the table on the left, busily hunting for something, lifting up one object after the other. Enter CUBIT from the hall.*

CUBIT. Did you ring, sir?

MR. BONSOR. Yes, I want a photograph—a photograph of Mr. Paul.

CUBIT. Delighted to have him took, sir.

MR. BONSOR. He has *been* "took," unfortunately; and the result, which was placed upon this table yesterday, by Mrs. Doubleday, has been surreptitiously removed.

CUBIT. Never put my hand to anything, sir.

MR. BONSOR. I wish you'd put your head! I want Captain Chanter.

CUBIT. His photograph, sir?

MR. BONSOR. His presence.

CUBIT. Here it is, sir.

(*Enter CAPTAIN CHANTER from the hall; to which exit CUBIT.*)

MR. BONSOR. (*Opening drawers, to CHANTER.*) Did you appropriate that photograph—the one Mrs. Doubleday showed you?

CHANTER. (*Embarrassed.*) Oh, the picture of Paul?

MR. BONSOR. The picture of Dudley! It has irrecoverably vanished.

CHANTER. I put it back on the table. (*To himself.*) Nina recovered it?

MR. BONSOR. Then who can have taken it?

CHANTER. (*Thinking.*) Dudley!

MR. BONSOR. The record of his shame?

CHANTER. (*Prompt.*) To cancel his shame.

MR. BONSOR. (*Severe.*) There must be no cancelling!

CHANTER. To annihilate the proof.

MR. BONSOR. There must be no annihilation. We'll get it back.

CHANTER. *I'll* get it back! Perhaps you've already heard from Mrs. Doubleday that I've accepted onerous functions.

MR. BONSOR. It was precisely on the subject of those functions that I desired to converse with you. Mrs. Doubleday has imparted to me her project of a second union.

CHANTER. I hope you don't regard it as a defection. It doubles the guard!

MR. BONSOR. (*With dignity.*) The guard has hitherto been adequate.

CHANTER. How can you say so in the face of our present alarm?

MR. BONSOR. (*Still with dignity.*) It's very good of you to share it!

CHANTER. I feel strongly that you require relief.

MR. BONSOR. (*Virtuous.*) I've never asked for it!

CHANTER. You're a Stoic—you're a hero! But remember that Mrs. Doubleday's essentially a woman.

MR. BONSOR. It's just what I've endeavoured to forget!

CHANTER. Such endeavours are vain—I never make them. (*Looking at his watch.*) Mrs. Doubleday's late—I'm waiting.

MR. BONSOR. What are you waiting for?

CHANTER. To take Paul over.

MR. BONSOR. (*Blank.*) Over where?

CHANTER. To receive him from her hands. She commits him to me—ceremonially.

MR. BONSOR. They're preparing, then, for the ceremony.

CHANTER. (*Grave.*) I've been preparing too.

MR. BONSOR. In what manner?

CHANTER. By meditation. We hope you'll assist at it.

MR. BONSOR. I'll not refuse to show you that I appreciate your singular zeal. The more so that it's manifested in a critical hour.

CHANTER. It was just the crisis that appealed to me!

MR. BONSOR. Are you ready to meet it?

CHANTER. With your inspiring confidence!

MR. BONSOR. (*After an instant.*) You *have* it! (*They shake hands solemnly; then* MR. BONSOR *looks at his watch.*) She must be decking him for the solemn rite.

CHANTER. With ribbons and garlands?

MR. BONSOR. With sackcloth and ashes.

CHANTER. (*Impatient.*) I want to get *at* him!

MR. BONSOR. It's my individual conviction that he has *been* got at!

CHANTER. You allude to last evening?

MR. BONSOR. While we were at dinner. Just after the member for Blackport had taken his place among us, we were startled by the sound of a remarkable concussion. It seemed to proceed from the drawing-room.

CHANTER. Which we all invaded—to find it didn't.

MR. BONSOR. All except Blanche. One of the parties to the encounter had already vanished, but Paul was on the spot.

CHANTER. Declaring—when examined—that he hadn't laid eyes on any one.

MR. BONSOR. It's the first time, remarkable to say, that he has ever told an untruth.

CHANTER. Are you sure it *is* an untruth?

MR. BONSOR. He was pale, agitated, unnatural.

CHANTER. He didn't wish to compromise the lady!

MR. BONSOR. Hadn't she compromised *him?*

CHANTER. He has no character to lose. But the question shall be probed to the bottom.

MR. BONSOR. Please probe it!

(*Re-enter* CUBIT *from the hall.*)

CUBIT. (*Announcing.*) Mr. Pitt Brunt!

(*Enter* PITT BRUNT *from the hall.*)

MR. BONSOR. Have you brought your luggage?

PITT BRUNT. It consists mainly of my quotations—twenty volumes of Hansard.[1]

_____

[1] The official report of the proceedings of the British Houses of Parliament which for a long period were compiled by Messrs. Hansard. Although the name ceased to be

CHANTER. Your quotations must be singularly copious!

MR. BONSOR. (*To* CHANTER.) He will contribute to those of posterity. (*To* CUBIT.) Arrange the twenty volumes.

PITT BRUNT. (*To* CUBIT.) Chronologically!

(*Exit* CUBIT *to the hall.*)

MR. BONSOR. (*To* CHANTER.) The member for Blackport is to meet his electors.

PITT BRUNT. I'm writing my speech—and trying it on Mr. Bonsor.

CHANTER. I hope it'll be a comfortable fit. I'll not interfere with the process. (*Exit* CAPTAIN CHANTER *by the lower door on the right.*)

MR. BONSOR. (*To* BRUNT.) It will save time to have you in the house. And then there's another reason.

PITT BRUNT. (*As* BLANCHE *appears.*) Here's the other reason! (*Enter* BLANCHE AMBER *from the hall with a railway novel in her hand.*) Good morning. I've come to stay!

BLANCHE. I'm very happy, this morning, to feel that that's just what I've done!

PITT BRUNT. Isn't it a remarkably interesting house?

BLANCHE. Fascinating! (MR. BONSOR *and* PITT BRUNT *look at each other, and* BLANCHE *considers a moment the cover of her railway novel. Then she speaks abruptly.*) Dear uncle! (*Holding out her book.*) Is *that* improper?

MR. BONSOR. (*With the book, looking at the cover with his glasses.*) A lady and gentleman, engaged—

BLANCHE. Oh, they're not engaged!

PITT BRUNT. (*Interested.*) What are they doing?

MR. BONSOR. Embracing! (*Dubious, disapproving, while he still looks.*) If they're not engaged—

PITT BRUNT. They ought to be! (*To* BLANCHE.) Every one who isn't ought to be.

BLANCHE. From a sense of duty? I'm afraid I've no conscience. (*To* MR. BONSOR.) May I lend that book to Mr. Paul?

MR. BONSOR. (*Looking at her severely over his glasses.*) The question exemplifies your deficiency!

PITT BRUNT. You may lend it to *me*.

BLANCHE. (*Taking the book back.*) You wouldn't understand it!

MR. BONSOR. You've got your Hansard. (*Re-enter* CUBIT *from the hall.*)

CUBIT. (*To* BRUNT.) I think I've set them straight, sir.

MR. BONSOR. Chronologically?

CUBIT. (*Blank an instant.*) No, sir, on their sides.

MR. BONSOR. (*To* BRUNT.) Go and see.

PITT BRUNT. (*Smiling to* BLANCHE.) I must make them sit up!

(*Exit* PITT BRUNT *to the hall. Exit* CUBIT.)

MR. BONSOR. He makes the House!

BLANCHE. (*Tossing down her book.*) Isn't he supposed to know *anything*?

MR. BONSOR. (*Who has taken up the book.*) The member for Blackport?

BLANCHE. The prisoner of Chillon!

MR. BONSOR. He's supposed to know too much! The harm's done, but we endeavour to prevent its spreading. (*He goes to the cabinet on the right, opens it and, seeing* MRS. FRESHVILLE'S *reticule, which he has put away there, considers an instant, and then, as if with a happy thought, plumps the book into it. To himself.*) Just do for *her*!

BLANCHE. (*Who has not seen this proceeding; musing, objecting.*) He seems after all to *do* nothing!

MR. BONSOR. (*Triumphant.*) What did he do last night?

BLANCHE. I haven't the least idea. (*Then after an instant.*) But I should like to help you!

MR. BONSOR. (*Suspicious.*) Everyone would like to "help" me!

BLANCHE. You must double the guard!

MR. BONSOR. That's what they *all* say!

BLANCHE. It shows there's something in it!

MR. BONSOR. There may be something in it, but it's not what I sent for you for.

BLANCHE. (*Turning away with a groan.*) Ah, dear uncle, I know what you sent for me for!

MR. BONSOR. The member for Blackport's the Idol of the North!

_____

used on the title page of the reports the year after this play was written, it remains the colloquial term of reference to the official parliamentary record.

BLANCHE. The idol should remain in his temple.

MR. BONSOR. (*Indignant.*) What would the House do without him?

BLANCHE. Perhaps it would wake up!

MR. BONSOR. The House *is* his temple! He's the young man of the hour.

BLANCHE. Do you mean of the dinner-hour?

MR. BONSOR. There's not a question of the day that he has not made his own.

BLANCHE. Well, dear uncle, as *I'm* not the question of the day—

MR. BONSOR. You would none the less have your appointed place. His private life would be worthy of his public.

BLANCHE. But should *I* be worthy of his private?

MR. BONSOR. Let him read you his momentous speech.

BLANCHE. Is it very long?

MR. BONSOR. Not yet; but it will be. It's growing fast.

BLANCHE. (*Smiling.*) Then I'll take it when it's little. (*In another tone.*) But, all the same, I'm interested in Mr. Paul.

MR. BONSOR. (*Disconcerted.*) "Interested"?

BLANCHE. I regard him as an object of charity.

MR. BONSOR. Why so? His wants are provided for!

BLANCHE. There are wants and wants. Why not let him have—

MR. BONSOR. (*As she pauses, thinking.*) Let him have what?

BLANCHE. One's scraps of leisure—one's ideas of life.

MR. BONSOR. He's not a person for you to meet on a social basis.

BLANCHE. Oh, I want to approach him in a missionary spirit.

MR. BONSOR. You won't convert him.

BLANCHE. Perhaps not. (*Smiling.*) But I'll clothe him!

MR. BONSOR. That *is* the first proper step; but have you the material?

BLANCHE. (*Laughing.*) Yards and yards and yards!

(*Re-enter* CAPTAIN CHANTER *from the lower door on the right.*)

CHANTER. Have they come?

MR. BONSOR. They've come.

(*Enter* MRS. DOUBLEDAY *and* PAUL *from the hall while* BLANCHE *and* CHANTER *converse.*)

MRS. DOUBLEDAY. (*Perceiving this.*) Captain! (CHANTER *instantly quits* BLANCHE *and comes to her, a movement which leaves* PAUL *exposed. As* BLANCHE *moves a little nearer to* PAUL MRS. DOUBLEDAY *resumes.*) Paul!

PAUL. (*Startled, coming down to her.*) Mamma?

(*Re-enter from the hall* PITT BRUNT, *with several volumes of* Hansard *under one arm and a portfolio under the other.*)

PITT BRUNT. (*To* MR. BONSOR.) May I work in the library?

MR. BONSOR. (*Assenting.*) My niece will assist you.

PITT BRUNT. Oh, Miss Amber!

MR. BONSOR. She's eager to listen to your speech.

PITT BRUNT. She *shall!* (*Then looking round complacently at the company.*) Perhaps you'd *all* like to listen.

PAUL. (*Very prompt.*) Mamma, would it be safe for *me?*

PITT BRUNT. (*Smiling.*) It wouldn't if you had to reply to me!

MRS. DOUBLEDAY. He's never allowed to reply!

CHANTER. (*To* BRUNT.) An arrangement is pending by which I shall henceforth answer *for* him. But I'm afraid that, for the present, we must occupy ourselves exclusively with this arrangement.

MRS. DOUBLEDAY. Before we enter upon it, I beg Mr. Bonsor to mention—

MR. BONSOR. (*Blank, while she pauses as if from delicacy.*) To mention—?

CHANTER. The nature of the connection about to be formed.

BLANCHE. (*Eager.*) Matrimonial?

PAUL. (*Struck, echoing.*) Matrimonial!

MRS. DOUBLEDAY. (*With reprobation.*) Paul!

BLANCHE. (*Wondering.*) Is that *not* the nature of the connection?

MR. BONSOR. (*With reprobation.*) Blanche!

BLANCHE. (*To* PAUL, *smiling.*) But it must be either one thing or the other, mustn't it?

PAUL. I'm never allowed to reply.

MRS. DOUBLEDAY. You will therefore receive without comment—

MR. BONSOR. (*As she hesitates.*) As *I* have done—

CHANTER. The news of your mother's intended marriage—

BLANCHE. (*As he hesitates.*) To Captain Chanter, I'm sure.

PAUL. (*Struck, precipitate.*) The Captain?—By jingo!

MR. BONSOR. (*Privately, to* MRS. DOUBLEDAY.) He *hadn't* taken it in!

MRS. DOUBLEDAY. We never crossed the line.

MR. BONSOR. It excites a train of thought.

MRS. DOUBLEDAY. That was just our scruple.

MR. BONSOR. He thinks it relieves him.

MRS. DOUBLEDAY. (*Emphatic.*) It doesn't!

PITT BRUNT. (*Gay, to* MRS. DOUBLEDAY.) I'm sorry for Mr. Bonsor! (*To* MR. BONSOR, *summarily presenting the Hansards in a pile.*) Just take these.

MR. BONSOR. (*Vague, but receiving the Hansards.*) What am I to do with them?

PITT BRUNT. (*Prompt.*) Verify.

MR. BONSOR. Can't *you* verify?

PITT BRUNT. I must give my attention to Miss Amber.

MRS. DOUBLEDAY. Miss Amber had better give hers to *us!*

BLANCHE. With pleasure, Mrs. Doubleday.

MRS. DOUBLEDAY. To see Paul committed.

PAUL. (*Alarmed.*) Committed?

MRS. DOUBLEDAY. I'm going to make you over.

PAUL. (*Rueful.*) You've been trying that all my life!

MRS. DOUBLEDAY. This time I shall succeed. I deliver you to the Captain.

CHANTER. (*Passing between* MRS. DOUBLEDAY *and* PAUL.) I beg to acknowledge receipt!

MRS. DOUBLEDAY. (*To* PAUL.) You're to look up to him as you've looked up to *me.*

CHANTER. I become, as it were, your second mother.

MR. BONSOR. As I've been, as it were, your second father!

PAUL. (*Resigned, bewildered.*) I seem to have plenty of relations!

BLANCHE. Shouldn't you like a sister thrown in?

MRS. DOUBLEDAY. The family is quite large enough! (*Privately to* CHANTER.) I wanted her to take it in!

CHANTER. She *shall* take it in!

MRS. DOUBLEDAY. (*Who has extracted a small coin from her portemonnaie.*) Let me hand you this.

CHANTER. (*With the coin, vague.*) Sixpence?

MRS. DOUBLEDAY. His allowance.

CHANTER. It doesn't pass through his hands?

MRS. DOUBLEDAY. We apply it to some benevolent object.

CHANTER. (*Pocketing the sixpence.*) It shall be devoted to a worthy one!

MR. BONSOR. (*To* CHANTER.) You'll find your place no sinecure.

CHANTER. (*Virtuous.*) No—but Mrs. Doubleday will breathe!

MRS. DOUBLEDAY. Not yet—I disseminate the news.

CHANTER. You rush up to London?

MRS. DOUBLEDAY. I rush to my writing-desk. (*Exit* MRS. DOUBLEDAY *to the hall.*)

PITT BRUNT. (*To* MR. BONSOR.) I sent the others to your room.

MR. BONSOR. Most kind of you.

PITT BRUNT. Thirteen volumes—to verify.

MR. BONSOR. (*Going up.*) I'll verify.

PITT BRUNT. You're forgetting these. (*Takes and presents again those he has brought in.*) Twenty in all.

MR. BONSOR. (*Impressive, to* BLANCHE, *as he takes the pile in his two arms.*) The Idol of the North! (*Exit* MR. BONSOR *to the hall with the books.*)

PITT BRUNT. (*Gracious, opening the door of the library to* BLANCHE.) He's ready to mount his pedestal.

BLANCHE. Do you want me to hold it while you get on?

PITT BRUNT. (*Smiling.*) It won't run away!

BLANCHE. I wish *you* would!

PITT BRUNT. (*Arch, at the door of the library.*) For you to run after me? (*Exit* PITT BRUNT.)

CHANTER. (*Looking from* BLANCHE *to* PAUL *a moment, then reflecting, deciding and taking two half-crowns out of his pocket.*) Let me hand you this!

PAUL. (*With the money, surprised.*) Five shillings?

CHANTER. Your allowance.

PAUL. Four and sixpence too much!

CHANTER. I change the system—I increase the sum!

PAUL. (*Helpless, appealing.*) What shall I *do* with it?

CHANTER. (*Gay, cynical.*) Whatever you like!

BLANCHE. (*Looking from* PAUL *to* CHANTER; *then resolutely, as if with a sudden inspiration.*) Captain Chanter, will you leave me a moment with Mr. Paul?

CHANTER. Do you want to rifle him?

BLANCHE. I want to advise him!

CHANTER. As much as you like! (*Exit* CAPTAIN CHANTER *by the lower door on the right.*)

PAUL. (*Amazed, quite scandalised, looking after* CHANTER *while he puts the money in his waistcoat-pocket.*) I can't look up to him!

BLANCHE. (*Laughing.*) He inspires me with positive reverence!

PAUL. Mamma wouldn't have left me with you!

BLANCHE. I wouldn't have asked her!

PAUL. Mr. Bonsor wouldn't have done it either!

BLANCHE. I wouldn't have asked him!

PAUL. You knew your man, eh?

BLANCHE. I divined him!

PAUL. You just took a shot!

BLANCHE. You see it succeeded.

PAUL. Yes, isn't it awful?

BLANCHE. Ah, don't say that when I'm fighting at your side!

PAUL. Thanks—but you do undermine me!

BLANCHE. Why, if I asked him to go it was on purpose to prop you up.

PAUL. It's just when you prop me, you know, that I seem most to come down!

BLANCHE. Don't think of me as a mere young lady; think of me as an invalid's attendant—as a doctor—as a district nurse.

PAUL. A sort of sister of charity, eh?

BLANCHE. Yes, but not in the least of a strict order.

PAUL. Strict orders are issued to me daily!

BLANCHE. Oh, I shall be easy with you, for I know you're in trouble.

PAUL. (*Anxious, looking round.*) Indeed I *am* in trouble!

BLANCHE. Your wild past comes back to you.

PAUL. It came back last night. But it only stayed a minute.

BLANCHE. Such minutes must be wonderful!

PAUL. They do upset one!

BLANCHE. They make you feel you live!

PAUL. Yes, but in the tomb of my reputation.

BLANCHE. Ah, you're not buried; your tomb is open to the sky. You see the sun and the stars; you feel the wind and the weather!

PAUL. The wind and the weather very much, Miss Amber. I shouldn't wonder if I were taking cold!

BLANCHE. What of that? You won't, at least, have vegetated! (*Then as she goes.*) I shall!

PAUL. Where are you going?

BLANCHE. To study to be a cabbage!

PAUL. Well, it's simpler!

BLANCHE. Oh, I shall be simple. I should say the penny kind!

PAUL. Meanwhile I must continue the struggle.

BLANCHE. Yes, till you can fight no more!

PAUL. And *when* I can fight no more?

BLANCHE. (*At the door of the library, considering.*) I'll tell you then what to do! (*Exit* BLANCHE.)

PAUL. (*Alone.*) Yes, I shan't have vegetated! I should have been only yesterday the ornament of a kitchen-garden, but *her* hand has plucked me up! (*Then, as he sees* MRS. FRESHVILLE.) For *hers* to prepare me for the table?

(*Enter* MRS. FRESHVILLE *from the hall.*)

MRS. FRESHVILLE. (*Breathless, hurrying down.*) Dudley!

PAUL. (*Who has receded to the door of the library, looking at her in melancholy contemplation.*) Nina!

MRS. FRESHVILLE. (*Stopping short in the*

middle of the stage.) No hug for Nina?

PAUL. (*Checking her with his finger to his lips.*) When we hug they hear it!

MRS. FRESHVILLE. Did they hear it last night?

PAUL. Distinctly. They rushed in. Fortunately you had rushed out.

MRS. FRESHVILLE. Yes, my boy, you did bundle me!

PAUL. How did you get in now?

MRS. FRESHVILLE. The same way as before. I've bought the butler.

PAUL. Cubit must be rather expensive!

MRS. FRESHVILLE. A pound a visit.

PAUL. It comes pretty high.

MRS. FRESHVILLE. About the same as a high-class doctor. But, my dear child, I consider you worth it! (*Looking at him a moment.*) You do look so fresh!

PAUL. (*Uneasy, distressed.*) Nina, I beg you not to allude to my appearance!

MRS. FRESHVILLE. Why should you be ashamed of it? You look awfully young.

PAUL. I *feel* awfully young!

MRS. FRESHVILLE. Taken care of yourself, eh?

PAUL. I should say, rather, I have been taken care of!

MRS. FRESHVILLE. Well, *I* haven't! How do *I* look?

PAUL. You look like somebody else.

MRS. FRESHVILLE. You think I've a different type?

PAUL. Haven't you got different hair?

MRS. FRESHVILLE. Oh yes; it used to be red.

PAUL. My dear, it used to be black!

MRS. FRESHVILLE. Oh, black, was it? Red the year before. But yours, darling, is the same!

PAUL. My hair may be the same, Nina, but everything else is changed.

MRS. FRESHVILLE. Yes, everything does change, Dudley!

PAUL. One's very name, to begin with. I'm not Dudley now!

MRS. FRESHVILLE. (*Surprised.*) Then what *are* you, pray?

PAUL. A mere anonymous nobody!

MRS. FRESHVILLE. (*In friendly compassion.*) It's all over, eh?

PAUL. It was over long ago!

MRS. FRESHVILLE. Short and sweet, eh?

(*Then as he checks her again, listening, with his finger to his lips.*) What's the matter?

PAUL. I thought they were coming!

MRS. FRESHVILLE. (*Undisturbed.*) But they ain't, eh?

PAUL. I hope not. I'm trying to be good.

MRS. FRESHVILLE. So am I; but I'm not very sure it pays!

PAUL. (*Struck, suppliant.*) Ah, Nina, don't say that!

MRS. FRESHVILLE. Why not, if it's true? You live up to a standard because you think some others do; and after you've had all the worry—

PAUL. (*As she pauses.*) Yes, Nina?

MRS. FRESHVILLE. Why, you find they don't!

PAUL. (*Wondering.*) Don't they really?

MRS. FRESHVILLE. See what an awful sell! You go spinning along the path of virtue, and if at the end of the run you happen to look back, what do you see?

PAUL. I never look back!

MRS. FRESHVILLE. All of them sitting down!

PAUL. I never sit down!

MRS. FRESHVILLE. Partaking freely of refreshment.

PAUL. I never partake!

MRS. FRESHVILLE. No more do I; but I feel the want of it!

PAUL. You have your equivalent: you've acquired the habit of virtue.

MRS. FRESHVILLE. Yes, that's the worst of it: you've got to go on.

PAUL. Let me earnestly entreat you to do so!

MRS. FRESHVILLE. I'm going on; that's what has brought me here!

PAUL. Yes, on the railroad of virtue this is certainly a lively station! But how did you find it out?

MRS. FRESHVILLE. By the aid of the police.

PAUL. (*Alarmed.*) The police? Are *they* after me?

MRS. FRESHVILLE. You, my dear fellow? I didn't come for *you!*

PAUL. (*Blank.*) Who did you come for?

MRS. FRESHVILLE. Ain't there *another* rascal on the premises?

PAUL. (*Amazed.*) Mr. Bonsor?

MRS. FRESHVILLE. Try again!

PAUL. Captain Chanter? (*Then perceiving her assent.*) The police are after *him?*

MRS. FRESHVILLE. Not now—but *I* am! It's better.

PAUL. What do you want of him?

MRS. FRESHVILLE. I want to marry him.

PAUL. Marry him? Why, he's engaged!

MRS. FRESHVILLE. Right you are—to *me*.

PAUL. (*Stupefied.*) You and my mother?

MRS. FRESHVILLE. Is she your mother?

PAUL. My stepmother.

MRS. FRESHVILLE. That monster?

PAUL. Don't abuse her, Nina—she's my guardian!

MRS. FRESHVILLE. Your guardian? (*Struck.*) Are *you* the common object?

PAUL. (*Blank.*) The common object?

MRS. FRESHVILLE. That I heard about yesterday—such a peculiar case.

PAUL. I *am* a peculiar case!

MRS. FRESHVILLE. You're vicious, eh?

PAUL. Fundamentally!

MRS. FRESHVILLE. (*Dubious.*) So bad you require *two* of them?

PAUL. I require three—with the Captain.

MRS. FRESHVILLE. (*Amazed.*) Is *he* one?

PAUL. He looks after my morals.

MRS. FRESHVILLE. And who looks after his?

PAUL. (*Wondering, artless.*) Why, I thought they were perfect!

MRS. FRESHVILLE. So did I. But they ain't!

PAUL. (*Thinking.*) That won't suit Mamma!

MRS. FRESHVILLE. Then let her drop him!

PAUL. That won't suit *him!*

MRS. FRESHVILLE. He's too particular. Leave him to *me*.

PAUL. (*Anxious.*) And what'll you do with him?

MRS. FRESHVILLE. Do with him? (*After an instant, considering.*) See he lets you alone.

PAUL. (*Anxious.*) Then what'll become of me?

MRS. FRESHVILLE. I'll look after you myself!

PAUL. (*Astonished.*) After both of us?

MRS. FRESHVILLE. It will be all one job! (*After looking at him at moment.*) As for you—I don't believe it!

PAUL. Don't believe what?

MRS. FRESHVILLE. Why, that you're a peculiar case.

PAUL. Then look at the evidence!

MRS. FRESHVILLE. Hang the evidence! Try—and see.

PAUL. Try? Try what?

MRS. FRESHVILLE. Try everything!

PAUL. Why, everything's wrong!

MRS. FRESHVILLE. *You* are, my dear, to begin with! Everything's right!

PAUL. (*Bewildered.*) Everything's deuced awkward, at any rate!

MRS. FRESHVILLE. Your dear old face, as you say that, comes back to me!

PAUL. Don't let it, Nina—for heaven's sake send it away!

MRS. FRESHVILLE. With that sweet little waxed moustache. What have you done with the ends?

PAUL. They've followed those of all the candles and cigars!

MRS. FRESHVILLE. The burnt-out fires?— the withered flowers? You always had a lovely buttonhole.

PAUL. I've given up buttonholes—they look too dissolute.

MRS. FRESHVILLE. Dissolute?—the flowers of the field? I never heard of such rot!

PAUL. Neither have I, Nina! But they wouldn't like me to say so.

MRS. FRESHVILLE. "They"? Mamma and the Captain?

PAUL. Perhaps the Captain wouldn't object—

MRS. FRESHVILLE. I should like to see him!

PAUL. But such an expression wouldn't go unrebuked by Mr. Bonsor.

MRS. FRESHVILLE. The old busybody who chased you to Paris?

PAUL. (*Prompt.*) Oh, *he* was my father! (*Then struck.*) Gracious, what have I said?

MRS. FRESHVILLE. The simple truth. They did make a rumpus about nothing!

PAUL. Not exactly nothing!

MRS. FRESHVILLE. Nothing worth speaking of!

PAUL. I don't speak of it!

MRS. FRESHVILLE. But they do still, eh?

PAUL. To every one they see!

MRS. FRESHVILLE. To the Captain, do you suppose?

PAUL. Oh, above all to the Captain!

MRS. FRESHVILLE. (*After consideration.*) Well, that's no matter. He doesn't know it was me.

PAUL. He'll find it out.

MRS. FRESHVILLE. I don't care if he does!

PAUL. Not if he wants to marry you?

MRS. FRESHVILLE. He doesn't!

PAUL. (*Reasoning, perplexed.*) Still—if he's engaged—?

MRS. FRESHVILLE. He's engaged to your mamma. If he can stand your mamma, he can stand me.

PAUL. But how can he marry you both?

MRS. FRESHVILLE. Trust him to manage it—if it's necessary! But it ain't necessary.

PAUL. I'm glad of that!

MRS. FRESHVILLE. He'll chuck your mamma.

PAUL. (*Rueful.*) So that I shall receive her on the rebound?

MRS. FRESHVILLE. (*Struck, compassionate.*) No, that won't do, you poor dear, will it? (*After another instant, sociable.*) We did hit it off, me and you, didn't we, Dud?

PAUL. I confess I was rather afraid of you.

MRS. FRESHVILLE. You've got over that, I hope!

PAUL. I think I'm gaining confidence.

MRS. FRESHVILLE. So am I, though you gave me, last night, a turn.

PAUL. I didn't sleep a wink!

MRS. FRESHVILLE. Nor me, fancy! I thought of the old days—of the way I used to sing to you!

PAUL. (*Beguiled.*) Do you remember your old songs?

MRS. FRESHVILLE. (*Eager.*) Should you like to hear one?

PAUL. (*Suddenly alarmed.*) Heavens, no!

MRS. FRESHVILLE. (*As he goes up, on his guard.*) They're out of fashion now; they've got a new lot!

PAUL. (*Coming down.*) Are you still at the Waterloo?

MRS. FRESHVILLE. Dear, no; bless the old shop!

PAUL. (*After an instant, gentle.*) Your voice was very sweet, Nina.

MRS. FRESHVILLE. So was yours, old chap. Do you still sing?

PAUL. (*Aghast.*) Sing? Why, I scarcely speak!

MRS. FRESHVILLE. I remember how little you thought of your own powers. You only wanted *me* to develop!

PAUL. I'm bound to say you did develop!

MRS. FRESHVILLE. Through the course of instruction you so liberally provided. It was for that we went to Paris.

PAUL. (*Recalling, recognising.*) Yes, it was simply for that!

MRS. FRESHVILLE. Our musical studies. Where was the awful harm?

PAUL. (*Thinking.*) After all, where *was* it?

MRS. FRESHVILLE. We simply went in for a thorough course.

PAUL. We thought it our duty to hear what they were doing.

MRS. FRESHVILLE. (*Reminiscent, wistful.*) Ah, they do such a lot! What was that place? The Alcazar!

PAUL. And that other? The Eldorado!

MRS. FRESHVILLE. And the Valentino!

PAUL. And the Solferino!

MRS. FRESHVILLE. That was where at last they collared us!

PAUL. (*Starting, seeing* CHANTER.) They've collared us again!

(*Re-enter* CAPTAIN CHANTER, *with a yellow-covered French novel and a box of cigars, by the lower door on the right.*)

CHANTER. (*Bland.*) Good morning, Mrs. Freshville.

PAUL. (*Surprised.*) Is that your name now?

MRS. FRESHVILLE. (*Ominous, looking at* CHANTER.) Not the one he generally uses! Didn't I mention that I've been married?

CHANTER. (*Smiling.*) You must have had so much else to say! (*To* PAUL.) She belongs to the category of irresistible widows.

MRS. FRESHVILLE. But not to the most irresistible part of it. (*With intensity, to* CHANTER.) Those with five thousand a year.

PAUL. (*To* CHANTER; *still meek and respectful, but explanatory and lucid.*) I've had the pleasure of some previous acquaintance with Mrs. Freshville.

CHANTER. (*Genial.*) My dear fellow, I know all about it!

PAUL. (*To* MRS. FRESHVILLE, *rueful.*) He knows all about it!

MRS. FRESHVILLE. I don't care a rap what he knows!

CHANTER. (*Frank and gay.*) I shall make you care! (*To* PAUL, *sociable, handing the cigar-box.*) Have a Regalia?

PAUL. (*Looking at the cigars hard an instant, then hard at* CHANTER, *as if to fathom his tortuous ways.*) What will Mamma say?

CHANTER. (*Smiling, tempting.*) I won't tell her! (PAUL, *hesitating, takes a cigar out of the case, turns away with it and stands a moment looking at it.* CHANTER, *meanwhile, selects one for himself.* PAUL, *suddenly, with a nervous movement, jerks away his own cigar, tosses it on a table and goes up, uneasily, nervously.* CHANTER, *lighting a cigar, continues to* MRS. FRESHVILLE.) Shall I offer *you* one?

MRS. FRESHVILLE. (*With her hand on her pocket.*) I've got my cigarettes! (*Feeling.*) No, I haven't; they're in my reticule. (*Looking, with renewed despair, about her.*) Where the dickens *is* it?

CHANTER. (*Cool, without moving.*) Don't mind. I'll find it! (*Then to* PAUL.) I say, here's a book for you.

PAUL. (*Eager, coming down.*) A book?

CHANTER. (*Handing him his yellow-covered volume.*) A little French novel!

PAUL. (*Timid, taking the book.*) Zola?

CHANTER. (*Puffing his cigar.*) Zola!

PAUL. (*Gazing at the cover.*) What will Mamma say?

CHANTER. I won't tell her!

(PAUL *turns away slowly, with his novel, as he has done with his cigar, and looks in the same way at the cover without opening it. Then he tosses it down, as he has tossed his cigar, and goes up, with the same nervous movement, to stand an instant at the window and look out at the lawn.*)

MRS. FRESHVILLE. (*Seated, to* CHANTER.) Ain't you ashamed, you horrid thing?

CHANTER. Ain't you, you designing woman? (*Then as he draws a pack of cards from his pocket and holds it out to* PAUL.) I say, choose a card.

PAUL. (*Alert, coming down.*) A card?

CHANTER. One of these.

PAUL. What will Mamma say?

CHANTER. I won't tell her!

PAUL. (*Looking at the cards, fascinated but hesitating.*) What are you doing?

CHANTER. A little trick. Take any you like. (*As* PAUL *draws out a card.*) What is it?

PAUL. The Queen of Hearts!

MRS. FRESHVILLE. (*Seated.*) Graceful allusion to *me!*

CHANTER. Please keep it till I take it back.

(PAUL *turns away in the same manner as before, stops, looks irresolutely at the card, then gets rid of it as he has done of the cigar and the book.*)

MRS. FRESHVILLE. (*To* CHANTER, *nodding at his pack.*) My old pack?

CHANTER. (*Vague.*) Yours?

MRS. FRESHVILLE. The one we generally use.

CHANTER. I just sent out to buy it. (*Then after he has placed the cards well in evidence on the table.*) Dudley!

PAUL. (*More dryly, coming down.*) Sir?

CHANTER. Will you do me a favour? You'll find on the table in my room—

PAUL. (*Anxious, as* CHANTER *pauses.*) I shall find—?

CHANTER. A flask of brandy.

PAUL. (*Blank.*) What shall I do with it?

CHANTER. Anything you like!

PAUL. (*Horrified.*) Captain, have mercy on me!

CHANTER. Then bring it here to me! (*As* PAUL *looks at him in a silent appeal, he adds.*) Do get it, old fellow!

PAUL. (*Divided, to* MRS. FRESHVILLE.) Shall I get it?

MRS. FRESHVILLE. Oh, *I* don't care what Mamma says!

PAUL. (*After another instant, snapping his fingers.*) No more then do I! (*Exit* PAUL DOUBLEDAY *to the hall.*)

MRS. FRESHVILLE. (*Rising, abrupt.*) Are the invitations out?

CHANTER. I haven't the faintest idea what you mean!

MRS. FRESHVILLE. For your marriage to that old dragon.

CHANTER. I suppose I may keep a secret —after discovering that you've nurtured one for years.

MRS. FRESHVILLE. All the more that *yours* is so horrid! Dudley liked me, and I liked him, and I'm not ashamed of it. I was grateful to him for his interest in my voice.

CHANTER. (*Sarcastic.*) Oh, your voice!

MRS. FRESHVILLE. Don't sniff at it—*you* were glad enough to hear it!

CHANTER. And to which of us, this morning, have you come here to sing?

MRS. FRESHVILLE. You'll understand when I tell you that though last night I had engaged my room at the inn, I went back to town for my music.

CHANTER. Your music?

MRS. FRESHVILLE. Perhaps I ought to say yours! Your notes of hand.

CHANTER. The stuff I wrote you? (*Thinking.*) You can't make a scene with my letters now.

MRS. FRESHVILLE. Why ain't it a happy moment?

CHANTER. Simply because you'll do for Dudley.

MRS. FRESHVILLE. I don't mind that—if I do for you!

CHANTER. Where *are* the few lines I inadvertently traced?

MRS. FRESHVILLE. There are enough of them to stuff out my pocket. (*As he looks at her, up and down, askance.*) You needn't crouch for a spring—I'll fight for them!

CHANTER. (*Nervous, throwing away his cigar.*) You're criminally vulgar!

MRS. FRESHVILLE. I often think it's a comfort! But I feel as if I had a small family in my pocket, and now I should like my reticule.

(CHANTER *goes to the cupboard on the right, in which* MR. BONSOR *has placed the reticule, and takes it out. He brings it to her and she receives it and opens it. She pulls out* BLANCHE'S *railway novel, which* MR. BONSOR *has put into it, and looks at the book with surprise. Then she flings it down on the table.*)

That book's not mine!

CHANTER. (*Taking up the book.*) Who's is it? (*Reading the name on the title-page.*) Blanche Amber?

MRS. FRESHVILLE. (*Who has fumbled in the reticule, in dismay.*) And the photo's gone!

CHANTER. The photo?

MRS. FRESHVILLE. (*Looking about her, vexed.*) Dudley's!

CHANTER. Was it in there?

MRS. FRESHVILLE. I carry it about.

CHANTER. And what do you do with mine?

MRS. FRESHVILLE. Lock it up at home! Where *is* the confounded thing?

CHANTER. (*Still with* BLANCHE'S *book.*) Some one obviously sneaked it.

MRS. FRESHVILLE. (*Vague.*) Who the mischief—?

CHANTER. The person who left this instead.

MRS. FRESHVILLE. That nasty book? Who *is* the brute?

CHANTER. The brute is Miss Blanche Amber.

MRS. FRESHVILLE. (*Recalling.*) The girl who arrived yesterday?

CHANTER. Just in time to grab it!

MRS. FRESHVILLE. The one who's engaged to the public man?

CHANTER. The member for Blackport? They're not engaged quite yet.

MRS. FRESHVILLE. He's awfully spoony.

CHANTER. Well, *she* isn't! (*After a moment.*) I'll get the photograph back from her.

MRS. FRESHVILLE. Very good of you. Get it immediately.

CHANTER. You must give me time—she'll cleave to it!

MRS. FRESHVILLE. Cleave to my property —the horrid little thief?

CHANTER. You must allow for her feelings!

MRS. FRESHVILLE. (*Vague.*) What feelings, pray?

CHANTER. Why, she's in love with him!

MRS. FRESHVILLE. With Dudley? Since when?

CHANTER. (*With assurance.*) Since yesterday! He makes them toe the mark!

MRS. FRESHVILLE. Does he make them steal?

CHANTER. He makes them do anything! (*He goes up rapidly to the win-*

dow as soon as he has spoken; while MRS. FRESHVILLE *sinks slowly again into the chair from which she has risen, and, with her reticule open on her knees, transfers to it mechanically, with an air of intense preoccupation, one by one, a dozen loose letters that she has taken from her pocket. She takes them out successively, looking at the superscriptions.*)

MRS. FRESHVILLE. (*Who has counted the letters and fastened her reticule.*) Thirteen, and five telegrams!

CHANTER. (*Who has stood uneasily at the window, coming down, looking at his watch.*) Give me half an hour, and I'll bring you the photo at the inn!

MRS. FRESHVILLE. (*Rising again, smiling, with the reticule on her arm.*) In exchange for your letters? Too dear!

CHANTER. Oh, bother my letters—do what you like with them! Make any row your bad taste may suggest, but for heaven's sake let it be a row that won't hurt Dudley!

MRS. FRESHVILLE. Hurt him—how?

CHANTER. By showing that you and he are at it again!

MRS. FRESHVILLE. We ain't at it again!

CHANTER. You present an appearance of it that won't improve his situation.

MRS. FRESHVILLE. His situation's a farce!

CHANTER. So it is, but you must sit the farce out.

MRS. FRESHVILLE. And you? Were *you* sitting it out just now?

CHANTER. Oh, I'm in the performance.

MRS. FRESHVILLE. As the leading villain? You corrupt his innocence?

CHANTER. His innocence is a thin veneer. Scratch the Russian and you find the Tartar—scratch Paul and you find Dudley!

MRS. FRESHVILLE. Well, if you scratch him again I'll scratch *you,* I can promise you!

CHANTER. I'm weak with him—I humour him—I spoil him: all that I admit. But that's nothing compared to the mess that you'll make for him by compromising him.

MRS. FRESHVILLE. (*After a moment*). You're a mass of deceit, but I don't see what you'll gain by not bringing me the

photo.

CHANTER. (*Pressing, watchful.*) I swear to you I'll bring it in half an hour. I hear some one coming!

MRS. FRESHVILLE. (*Thinking.*) Poor dear old Dud! (*Then to* CHANTER.) It's a pity you're such a fiend!

CHANTER. (*Pleading, feverish.*) Don't *you* be one—don't sacrifice him!

MRS. FRESHVILLE. (*Looking at her watch.*) In half an hour?

CHANTER. To the minute!

MRS. FRESHVILLE. You're unspeakable—but I've got you *here!* (*She slaps her reticule triumphantly and goes up.*)

CHANTER. (*Who is up before her, listening by the door of the hall and checking her.*) Wait!

MRS. FRESHVILLE. (*Indicating the lower door on the right.*) I won't go in *there* again!

CHANTER. (*Passing quickly to the window.*) *This* way! It's an escape!

MRS. FRESHVILLE. (*As she goes; warning.*) Not for *you!* (*Exit* MRS. FRESHVILLE *to the lawn.*)

CHANTER. (*Alone, exhausted but exultant.*) She has "got" me, eh? Not quite so tight as I've got *her!*

(*Re-enter* PAUL DOUBLEDAY *from the hall with a silver-mounted travelling-flask.*)

PAUL. (*Tossing the flask down.*) There!

CHANTER. (*Taking it up and shaking it as he smiles at* PAUL.) You haven't drunk it up?

PAUL. (*Looking about him after a gesture of disgusted repudiation.*) She's gone?

CHANTER. (*Laying the flask on a table.*) Thank our stars!

PAUL. (*Breaking out.*) I say, you know—what are you up to?

CHANTER. (*With sudden wild gestures.*) I'm in a fever—I'm in a frenzy: my head goes round! (*As* PAUL *stares at him, bewildered.*) I don't know what I say—I don't know what I do!

PAUL. (*After a moment.*) You seem indeed in an extraordinary position!

CHANTER. Dudley, I throw myself on your mercy!

PAUL. If you really want it, don't call me Dudley.

CHANTER. I'll call you anything you like if you'll only help me.

PAUL. How on earth can I help you?

CHANTER. By your generous influence. I was an ass to yield to her!

PAUL. To yield to Mamma?

CHANTER. No, *that* was inevitable.

PAUL. So I've always found it!

CHANTER. I succumbed—originally—to Nina.

PAUL. It wasn't original! Where did you meet her?

CHANTER. (*Waving away inquiries.*) Oh, in society! She has my written vows.

PAUL. (*Struck.*) I wonder if she has mine!

CHANTER. Oh, yours don't matter!

PAUL. Don't they, though!

CHANTER. They *shan't* matter, Paul, if you'll save me!

PAUL. How on earth can I save you?

CHANTER. As I tell you, by squaring her.

PAUL. (*Vague.*) Squaring Mrs. Double-day?

CHANTER. Squaring Mrs. Freshville! (*More agitated the more he thinks.*) It's quite too awful!

PAUL. (*Considering.*) How far have you gone with her?

CHANTER. With Mrs. Freshville? Very far indeed. I once went to Brighton.

PAUL. Oh, *I* went to Paris!

CHANTER. I know you did; so you can feel for me! (*Going up.*) Keep her quiet!

PAUL. Where are you going?

CHANTER. (*With wild gestures.*) Away—away!

PAUL. Who then will keep *me* quiet?

CHANTER. You mustn't *be* quiet; you must act!

PAUL. (*Staring, wondering.*) Act?

CHANTER. Save me! By-bye! (*Exit CHANTER rapidly to the hall.*)

PAUL. (*Alone, still blank.*) That's all very well; but who'll save *me*? (*He moves about during the rest of his soliloquy, looking round him, wonderingly, interrogatively, as he sifts his situation in his mind, taking up successively and laying down again the different objects he mentions.*) I'm in dreadful danger, I suppose! I *must* be, for I'm face to face with everything that, for years, I've been taught to dread— have dreaded. Tobacco, cards, wine, (*then taking up the French novel*) women! Here they are—all in a row! (*Looking round him.*) The real thing—and I'm alone with them! I'm therefore free, ain't I? free as I haven't been since— Ah, when *was* it? It seems only yesterday; yet it seems another life! (*With the different objects again.*) Women, wine, cards, tobacco! (*As he tosses the cigar into the box again.*) Temptation, ain't it? Yes, it *must* be: what else can it be? I'm tempted! The danger's right here at last—the danger of the happy chance! Well, the happy chance is just what I can't resist. (*After a moment.*) Is it, indeed? Pray, *why* can't I? (*Standing off with his hands in his pockets, looking at the different things.*) Because I'm the slave of my passions, and my passions, alas, are awful! (*Taking up the flask of liquor.*) This, for instance—this is one of my passions. (*He has uncorked the flask; he smells it.*) Do I yearn for it? Somehow I don't feel as if I did! Could I even raise it to my lips? (*After an instant.*) What's the matter with me that I can't? (*Still with the flask in his hand.*) I'm wicked—I'm weak —I can't be trusted; and yet my funny fate takes it into her head to trust me! She treats me all of a sudden with flattering confidence. (*Thinking.*) It may be a trap of my funny fate. But if it's a trap, I ain't caught! I *am* resisting; I *have* resisted. (*Following up his induction.*) I ain't so bad, then, now; I must be getting better! (*Still standing with the uncorked flask in his hand, he sees* PITT BRUNT. *Re-enter* PITT BRUNT *from the library; to whom, as the idea last uttered comes over him, he breaks out spontaneously, joyously, artlessly.*) I say, Brunt, I'm getting better!

(PITT BRUNT, *with his pen stuck into his ear, surprised at the image* PAUL *presents with his uncorked flask, approaches him as if supposing him intoxicated. He takes the flask from him and smells it; then, in horror at its contents, replaces it in his hand, looking at him with high superiority.*)

PITT BRUNT. On brandy? (*He crosses to the lower door on the right, where he pauses an instant and gives* PAUL *another look of shocked reprobation.*) Out of the very bottles? (*Exit* PITT BRUNT *by the lower door on the right.*)

PAUL. (*Alone, stares, reflects a moment, then corks and puts down his flask with a sigh of resignation, taking up mechanically the French novel.*) No one will ever believe it!

(*Re-enter* BLANCHE AMBER *from the library.*)

BLANCHE. (*At the door.*) Are you still alone?

PAUL. More alone than ever.

BLANCHE. Then I'll come in.

PAUL. Do; *he* won't mind!

BLANCHE. Do you mean the member for Blackport?

PAUL. Oh no, not *your* keeper. Mine!

BLANCHE. Mine has left me too; gone to my uncle for an idea.

PAUL. Couldn't you give him one?

BLANCHE. I gave him twenty, but he was afraid of them all.

PAUL. (*Smiling.*) I fancy you've some terrible ideas; eh, Miss Amber?

BLANCHE. Not so bad as some of yours, Mr. Paul!

PAUL. Oh, you exaggerate mine!

BLANCHE. Scarcely, when you've confessed to so many!

PAUL. (*Embarrassed.*) Yes, I've made a clean breast!

BLANCHE. Don't dissimulate, then: keep it up!

PAUL. (*Vague.*) Keep it up?

BLANCHE. Your honourable frankness. Your desperate candour.

PAUL. It does win me your sympathy?

BLANCHE. As nothing else could!

PAUL. (*After an instant, resolute.*) Then I *will* keep it up.

BLANCHE. There's plenty of it, whenever you require it.

PAUL. I should like to take it all, and keep it for ever!

BLANCHE. (*Smiling.*) Take it in instalments—a dose every day.

PAUL. Then such a person as me isn't repulsive to you?

BLANCHE. Repulsive—in your lonely grandeur?

PAUL. Oh, Miss Amber, I'm lonely, but I'm not particularly grand! I'm a kind of moral leper, with a warning cowbell round my neck. It's the solitude of misfortune.

BLANCHE. It's better than the rush and crush of vulgar happiness. Do you know what you remind me of?

PAUL. Of any victim of fatality, I suppose—any freak of nature or melancholy monster: the pig-faced lady or the piebald man!

BLANCHE. You remind me of some great wide-winged, wounded bird!

PAUL. Do you feel like the sportsman who has brought him down? Do you want to keep me as a trophy?

BLANCHE. Stuffed—in a glass case? No, I want you living; I want you fluttering; I want you perched on your rock, at least, if you *must* be tied to it!

PAUL. Dear Miss Amber, I'll perch anywhere, if you'll perch near me! I hope you've come here to stay.

BLANCHE. I'll stay as long as you hold out. But I said to you a while ago that I would tell you what to do in case at last you can't.

PAUL. I can scarcely hold out now.

BLANCHE. Then give in!

PAUL. (*Agitated.*) Give in?

BLANCHE. If you *must* slip up—

PAUL. (*As she hesitates.*) If I must?

BLANCHE. Do it immensely! (*Then as for the first time she becomes conscious of the book in his hand.*) But it seems to me you *have* slipped up!

PAUL. (*Who has put the book quickly behind him.*) Immensely!

BLANCHE. Zola?

PAUL. (*Producing the book.*) Zola!

BLANCHE. (*Compassionate.*) Your Mentor failed you—and you fell?

PAUL. To where you find me!

BLANCHE. In an hour?

PAUL. In a minute!

BLANCHE. (*Who has taken the book from him an instant, giving it back.*) Even to that?

PAUL. (*Flinging it down.*) Even to that!

BLANCHE. (*Looking round her and seeing the flask, which she takes up.*) And to this?

PAUL. To that too.

BLANCHE. (*With the pack of cards.*) And to this?

PAUL. Also to that!

BLANCHE. (*With a cigar.*) And to this?

PAUL. To everything!

BLANCHE. (*With exultation.*) There's something magnificent in it!

PAUL. (*Seeing* MRS. DOUBLEDAY, *who has appeared at the entrance from the hall.*) If you could only make Mamma think so!

(*Re-enter* MRS. DOUBLEDAY *with several sealed and directed letters.*)

MRS. DOUBLEDAY. (*Sniffing the air as she comes down.*) Tobacco? (*To* BLANCHE, *as she tosses down her cigar.*) Are you smoking with him?

BLANCHE. (*Deciding and indicating the flask after an instant during which* MRS. DOUBLEDAY *peremptorily rings the bell.*) Yes—and drinking! (*Then indicating each of the other objects.*) And gambling! And reading a dreadful book.

MRS. DOUBLEDAY. (*Seeing the name as* BLANCHE *waves the book.*) Zola?

BLANCHE. Zola!

PAUL. Dear Mamma—it's Miss Amber's German humour. She has but this moment come into the room!

BLANCHE. To take the place of Captain Chanter.

MRS. DOUBLEDAY. (*Looking from one of them to the other.*) Where *is* Captain Chanter?

PAUL. (*Privately to* BLANCHE.) Don't tell her!

BLANCHE. Then *you* tell her!

MRS. DOUBLEDAY. (*To* PAUL; *formidable.*) Does he neglect you?

PAUL. (*Alert.*) Dear no, I shouldn't call it neglect!

MRS. DOUBLEDAY. Then why isn't he here?

(*Re-enter* CUBIT *from the hall.*)

CUBIT. Did you ring, ma'am?

MRS. DOUBLEDAY. Stamp these letters.

PAUL. (*Privately to* BLANCHE, *while* CUBIT *takes the letters from* MRS. DOUBLEDAY.) She'll repudiate him!

BLANCHE. It will serve him right.

PAUL. It will serve *me* wrong! (*To himself.*) I'll save him! (*Then as* MRS. DOUBLEDAY *turns to him again for an answer while* CUBIT *stamps letters at one of the tables.*) I turned the Captain out!

BLANCHE. (*To herself.*) You darling!

PAUL. I got so bad—he fled in horror!

MRS. DOUBLEDAY. He couldn't stand you?

PAUL. He couldn't stand me!

(*Re-enter* MR. BONSOR *by the lower door on the right, while* BLANCHE *goes up in agitation.*)

MRS. DOUBLEDAY. (*Dismayed, to* MR. BONSOR.) He couldn't stand him!

MR. BONSOR. (*Dismayed.*) The Captain?

MRS. DOUBLEDAY. He fled in horror!

PAUL. (*Ecstatic.*) And I've had at last an hour of freedom!

MRS. DOUBLEDAY. (*Showing* MR. BONSOR *all the dreadful signs.*) An hour of freedom!

BLANCHE. (*Coming round and down on the right to* PAUL.) You're simply sublime! (*She goes up again.*)

PAUL. (*To himself.*) I'm saving him!

MRS. DOUBLEDAY. (*To* CUBIT.) Have you seen Captain Chanter?

CUBIT. (*With his letters stamped.*) I think he left the house, ma'am.

MRS. DOUBLEDAY. (*Excited.*) Then pursue him. (*Imperious, as* CUBIT *stands.*) Look for him!

CUBIT. (*At a loss.*) Where, ma'am, shall I look?

MRS. DOUBLEDAY. (*Frantic, hurrying up.*) *I'll* look! (*Exit* MRS. DOUBLEDAY *to the hall.*)

MR. BONSOR. (*To* CUBIT, *who is going.*) Whose letters are those?

CUBIT. Mrs. Doubleday's, sir.

MR. BONSOR. (*Austere.*) Don't post them. They are to announce a marriage which will probably not take place.

PAUL. (*At the left, privately, with decision, to* BLANCHE, *who has come down again on his left.*) It *shall* take place! (*He surreptitiously catches her right hand with his left and gives it a shake which she surreptitiously returns—a movement perceived by* MR. BONSOR.)

MR. BONSOR. (*Going up.*) Blanche!

(*She quickly joins him, and, after a few words, when they have gone up, he appears to dismiss her disapprovingly. Exit* BLANCHE *to the hall.*)

PAUL. (*While this takes place.*) Cubit!

(*Then, as* CUBIT, *with the letters, comes to him.*) Post them!

CUBIT. But Mr. Bonsor—

PAUL. Hang Mr. Bonsor!

CUBIT. (*Astounded; then, with a gesture, smiling and taking another line.*) What'll you give me?

PAUL. For hanging Mr. Bonsor? (*Taking from his waistcoat-pocket the money* CHANTER *has given him.*) This!

CUBIT. (*With the money.*) Five shillings? (*Delighted.*) I'll post them! (*Exit* CUBIT *to the hall.*)

MR. BONSOR. (*Stern, coming down to* PAUL.) Are you intoxicated?

PAUL. (*With an exhilaration, a familiarity, wholly new to* MR. BONSOR.) Dear Mr. Bonsor, I never was so lucid in all the whole course of my existence!

MR. BONSOR. (*Struck, and with his suspicions confirmed by* PAUL's *manner and tone, seeing* PITT BRUNT: *re-enter* PITT BRUNT *by the lower door on the right.*) He's simply·dead drunk!

PITT BRUNT. I'm perfectly aware! I rejoin Miss Amber.

MR. BONSOR. (*Indicating the hall.*) She's in the morning-room.

PITT BRUNT. Shall I apprise her?

MR. BONSOR. (*Complacent.*) She's perfectly aware.

(*Exit* PITT BRUNT *to the hall. Re-enter* CAPTAIN CHANTER *from the lawn.*)

MR. BONSOR. (*Eager, to* CHANTER.) Do you know he's dead drunk?

CHANTER. (*Coming down with his hat on—a little on the back of his head.*) Intimately!

MR. BONSOR. You couldn't stand him?

PAUL. (*At whom* CHANTER *has looked; privately.*) I told them you couldn't!

CHANTER. (*With assurance.*) I couldn't stand him!

MR. BONSOR. (*Heroical.*) Well, *I* can!

CHANTER. But I've pulled myself together again. I can now.

MR. BONSOR. It's a very dreadful sight.

CHANTER. To the pure all things are pure!

MR. BONSOR. Then they're pure to *me!* I'll take him myself.

CHANTER. (*Uneasy, protesting.*) Ah no—

I've my rules to enforce!

MR. BONSOR. You told me I must rest. *You* must.

CHANTER. I *have* rested!

MR. BONSOR. (*Looking at* PAUL *a moment, then reconsidering, deciding.*) I'll take him when he has slept it off! (*Exit* MR. BONSOR *to the hall.*)

CHANTER. (*Eager, hopeful, to* PAUL.) Are you dead drunk?

PAUL. Yes—with the sense of freedom!

CHANTER. That'll do—if you'll save me!

PAUL. I *am* saving you!

CHANTER. Now's your time, then—she's coming back!

PAUL. (*Visibly disconcerted.*) Nina?

CHANTER. I saw her on the bridge—she followed me. (*Seeing* MRS. FRESHVILLE *at the window.*) Here she is! (*Exit* CHANTER *rapidly to the library.*)

(*Re-enter* MRS. FRESHVILLE *from the garden.*)

MRS. FRESHVILLE. Was that the Captain who left you?

PAUL. Yes—do you want him?

MRS. FRESHVILLE. (*With resolution.*) No! (*After an instant.*) That's what I've come back to tell you!

PAUL. (*Civil, but vague.*) Very good of you to come back!

MRS. FRESHVILLE. (*With sudden intensity.*) Dudley—my feelings dragged me! I don't want any one in the world if I can only get *you!*

PAUL. (*Confused.*) Me, Nina?

MRS. FRESHVILLE. My earliest friend—my most generous—and my best!

PAUL. (*Embarrassed.*) My dear Nina, do I understand that you desire to make me your husband?

MRS. FRESHVILLE. That's the description of you that I confess I should find it most convenient to be able to give.

PAUL. But isn't your proposal rather rashly precipitate?

MRS. FRESHVILLE. Precipitate—when for years I've loved you in silence? That silence, when I see you, I naturally break!

PAUL. But I thought the object of your affection was our whimsical friend the Captain.

MRS. FRESHVILLE. So did I, till I perceived that I was fundamentally mistaken.

The Captain, though whimsical, is attractive; but he has no heart. You *have* a heart, Dudley.

PAUL. Ah, but it doesn't make me attractive! Nothing *can!*

MRS. FRESHVILLE. Your situation can—your situation *does*. You suffer.

PAUL. Oh, I can bear it!

MRS. FRESHVILLE. I can't then—when you're a captive!

PAUL. Captivity has changed me—I'm not what I was!

MRS. FRESHVILLE. Never mind what you were—you'll do very well. You're still young—you're still charming—you're still free.

PAUL. Free? Why, you recognise yourself that I'm bound!

MRS. FRESHVILLE. (*Suspicious, seizing his arm.*) "Bound"—to whom?

PAUL. (*After an instant.*) No one—in the way you mean!

MRS. FRESHVILLE. Then come to Paris!

PAUL. (*Moved.*) To Paris?

MRS. FRESHVILLE. To the Alcazar!

PAUL. (*Struck, thinking.*) The Eldorado?

MRS. FRESHVILLE. The Valentino!

PAUL. The Solferino? (*After a moment.*) Too late!

MRS. FRESHVILLE. (*Resentful.*) Too late? It isn't too late for me to chivey your photograph about!

PAUL. (*Vague.*) My photograph?

MRS. FRESHVILLE. (*Indicating her reticule.*) In this thing—wherever I go! (*Abrupt.*) Dudley, *who* stole it?

PAUL. (*Blank.*) I haven't the least idea!

MRS. FRESHVILLE. Then *I* have!

PAUL. Who in the world?

MRS. FRESHVILLE. (*Reconsidering.*) I'll tell you when we're married!

PAUL. Dear Nina, marriage is a serious step—a step to think well over.

MRS. FRESHVILLE. We'll think it well over—together!

PAUL. Give me more time, Nina!

MRS. FRESHVILLE. How much more do you want?

PAUL. (*After an instant.*) Why, say till to-morrow.

MRS. FRESHVILLE. Then to-morrow I'll rush to you.

PAUL. Thank you—I'll rush to *you*.

MRS. FRESHVILLE. At the inn? Will they let you?

PAUL. (*After reflection, with extreme resolution.*) I won't ask them!

MRS. FRESHVILLE. (*Irrepressible, triumphant.*) Ah, I've got you!

PAUL. (*Struck, wondering.*) *Have* you, Nina?

MRS. FRESHVILLE. (*With a laugh.*) Don't look at me as if I had said I'd got the measles! Look at me as if you really remembered—

PAUL. (*As she hesitates.*) Remembered, Nina?

MRS. FRESHVILLE. That I'm a dear good soul.

PAUL. You *are*, Nina.

MRS. FRESHVILLE. And that I give you a radical change.

PAUL. You do, Nina. By-bye.

MRS. FRESHVILLE. By-bye. (*She goes up and then comes down again, while he stands lost in thought.*) Just look here, Dud. (*Then after an instant.*) Why arrangements?

PAUL. (*Vague.*) Arrangements?

MRS. FRESHVILLE. What you call preliminaries. Fly with me without 'em! The preliminaries can follow.

PAUL. (*Vague.*) Do you allude to our luggage?

MRS. FRESHVILLE. (*Laughing.*) You *are* a daisy! Let me pluck you now!

PAUL. (*Rueful, unready.*) This moment?

MRS. FRESHVILLE. You shrink—you desire some regular form?

PAUL. I've been taught in all these years that some regular form is proper.

MRS. FRESHVILLE. Then we'll have one—for *you!* And we'll see about it to-morrow. (*At the window, smiling, bantering.*) Propriety! (*Exit* MRS. FRESHVILLE *to the lawn.*)

PAUL. (*As he sees* CHANTER.) Poor old Nina!

(*Re-enter* CAPTAIN CHANTER *from the library.*)

CHANTER. (*Who has looked in first cautiously and speaks in a loud, eager whisper.*) Well?

PAUL. She wants me to go to Paris!

CHANTER. Then why the deuce *don't* you?

PAUL. Because I don't want to!

CHANTER. (*Blank, vexed.*) Don't "want" to?

PAUL. (*Excited.*) Not the least bit in the world!

CHANTER. Then you *ought* to want to!

PAUL. Isn't that just my difficulty—that I don't do what I ought?

CHANTER. I'm here to make you. You're free!

PAUL. (*Passing his hand over his head.*) That's just where it is!—I'm free! She wants me to fly with her.

CHANTER. Don't stand pottering, then. Fly!

PAUL. I *can't* fly!

CHANTER. (*Trying to push him off.*) You must!

PAUL. (*Disengaging himself with a flare of passion, and coming round and down.*) I won't!

CHANTER. What the devil's the matter with you?

PAUL. I don't know, Captain! I ain't so bad—I ain't tempted!

CHANTER. (*Indignant.*) You *are* tempted!

PAUL. Then I resist!

CHANTER. (*Furious.*) Wretch!

(*Re-enter* CUBIT *from the hall.*)

CUBIT. (*to* CHANTER.) Mrs. Doubleday's quite wild, sir.

CHANTER. I go to her. (*To* PAUL, *privately, with concentrated urgency, as he goes up.*) Nina's a revelation! Try her! (*Exit* CAPTAIN CHANTER *to the hall.*)

CUBIT. (*To* PAUL.) Letters gone, sir!

PAUL. (*With rising spirit.*) Well, I ain't, old man, *am* I?

CUBIT. (*Surprised, gratified.*) No indeed, sir; you seem quite on the spot! (*Exit* CUBIT *to the hall.*)

PAUL. (*Alone, echoing, with the sense of his victory growing stronger, overwhelming him at last.*) "Nina's a revelation"? There are other revelations than Nina! "Try her"? I don't *want* to try her! I don't want to try anybody! (*Looking about him.*) I don't want to do anything! (*Drops into the chair on the right of the table.*) What *is* the matter with me? I *am* free and I ain't bad! Upon my honour (*rising slowly with the force of the revelation and the surprise*) I believe that, after all—it's awfully queer (*pauses a moment, then drops back into the chair*)—upon my honour, I'm *good!*

ACT THIRD

MR. BONSOR'S *drawing-room.* BLANCHE AMBER *comes in from the hall, meeting* PITT BRUNT, *dressed in the same manner as at the beginning of Act First, who comes in from the garden.*

PITT BRUNT. Dear Miss Amber, I'm delighted to put in a few minutes with you—my solitude, since luncheon, has been positively uncanny.

BLANCHE. Haven't you had my uncle to comfort you?

PITT BRUNT. There's no comfort in your uncle, now that Mr. Doubleday has disappeared!

BLANCHE. Isn't there any in Mrs. Doubleday—exhilarated by the triumph of her charms?

PITT BRUNT. She buries her charms at the railway-station—waiting for the fugitive to alight!

BLANCHE. (*Disappointed.*) You don't mean to say he returns so soon!

PITT BRUNT. I don't know, dear Miss Amber, what you call "soon." (*Looking at his watch.*) A debauch of twenty hours!

BLANCHE. Why, he went for at least sixty!

PITT BRUNT. (*Surprised.*) Did he communicate to you his programme?

BLANCHE. It was impossible—yesterday afternoon—to remain ignorant of his condition.

PITT BRUNT. Indeed it was!

BLANCHE. When he was missed—I understood. I know that when such natures fall—

PITT BRUNT. They fall to the very bottom? I've no doubt whatever that he's as far down as you can go. Fortunately Captain Chanter has been let down after him.

BLANCHE. By a rope round the waist—to pull him out? I perfectly know for what purpose he followed Mr. Paul to London.

PITT BRUNT. The engagement he had conscientiously taken left him no alternative, and he surmounted the repugnance he naturally felt. When he brings the culprit back we shall clear up the mystery of where the money came from—the money for Doubleday's fare.

BLANCHE. By the train to town? It was only two shillings.

PITT BRUNT. He had no such amount in his possession. We are reluctantly driven to the belief that he stole the two shillings.

BLANCHE. (Indignant.) Your belief's a false belief! He didn't!

PITT BRUNT. To say nothing of the money for the other excesses that were his objective. You admitted just now that such natures sink to the bottom. Well, the bottom is theft!

BLANCHE. Then he stopped half-way. He borrowed the money.

PITT BRUNT. From whom, pray—since the very servants have been examined? (Then as she remains silent.) Will you accompany me on the river? I put in an hour each day, and my hour has come round.

BLANCHE. Your hour may have come round, Mr. Brunt, but your humble servant hasn't. You don't take the right way to make her!

PITT BRUNT. I'll take it in the boat. (Confident, engaging.) You see if I don't!

BLANCHE. (Impatient.) Ah, your boat's not my boat, and it's impossible for me to embark with you!

PITT BRUNT. (More pressing.) I want you to embark, you know, on the river of life; to float with me down the crystal stream—

BLANCHE. That flows into the Smutt at Blackport? I don't find that a tempting voyage!

PITT BRUNT. (As MR. BONSOR appears.) Only give me a chance to point you out the beauties!

(Enter MR. BONSOR from the hall.)

MR. BONSOR. (Encouraging.) Ah, you're pointing out to Miss Amber the beauties?

PITT BRUNT. Even as you have pointed them out to me!

BLANCHE. (At the door of the library; with a curtsey.) I must leave you to discuss them together! (Exit BLANCHE AMBER.)

PITT BRUNT. She won't come out with me in the boat.

MR. BONSOR. The best place to command her attention, as I instructed you.

PITT BRUNT. I seek in vain, Mr. Bonsor, to command her attention or to carry out your instructions.

MR. BONSOR. They seem indeed, in the light of the present crisis, to have been singularly futile! (Then seeing CUBIT with a telegram.) I tremble at every telegram!

(Enter CUBIT from the hall.)

CUBIT. (As MR. BONSOR takes the telegram from his tray.) The ninth, sir!

MR. BONSOR. (Opening the telegram.) The Captain reports to us from hour to hour his alternations of confidence and despair.

PITT BRUNT. I hope this time it's confidence.

MR. BONSOR. (Who has read.) Despair!

CUBIT. (As MRS. DOUBLEDAY appears; announcing.) Mrs. Doubleday! (Enter MRS. DOUBLEDAY, in her bonnet, from the garden.) Despair, ma'am! (Exit CUBIT to the hall.)

MRS. DOUBLEDAY. (Agitated.) Despair?

MR. BONSOR. (Reading.) "Last hope dashed—evidently sunk to bottom."

PITT BRUNT. Sunk to bottom! That's what Miss Amber says.

MR. BONSOR. (Struck.) She admits it—she expresses it? Then follow that up!

PITT BRUNT. In the library?

MR. BONSOR. In the boat.

PITT BRUNT. But if she won't enter the boat?

MR. BONSOR. (After an instant.) I'll see her on board.

PITT BRUNT. (At the door of the library.) I'll detain her till you're free. (Exit PITT BRUNT.)

MRS. DOUBLEDAY. Do you propose to carry her on board?

MR. BONSOR. It may come to that!

MRS. DOUBLEDAY. (Injured.) You might take a little less interest in Miss Amber's marriage—!

MR. BONSOR. And a little more interest in yours? I consider that you should make a condition.

MRS. DOUBLEDAY. (Vague.) For the retention of my hand?

MR. BONSOR. The success of the Captain's pursuit. He must bring Paul back.

MRS. DOUBLEDAY. But if Paul has sunk lower than any sounding?

MR. BONSOR. The Captain requires the equipment of a diver!

MRS. DOUBLEDAY. (*Decided.*) We'll have no more diving: he must come back without him! Paul will have dropped to his natural level.

MR. BONSOR. You allude to the supposed companion of his orgy? That she *is* his companion is after all but an hypothesis.

MRS. DOUBLEDAY. An hypothesis for which the evidence is crushing. It was the ground for the Captain's action—an action admirably prompt.

MR. BONSOR. Oh yes, when the horse was stolen!

MRS. DOUBLEDAY. If the horse *is* stolen, there are consolations. For really, to receive Paul—

MR. BONSOR. (*As she falters.*) From the arms of such a creature?

MRS. DOUBLEDAY. Would cost me more than I can say!

MR. BONSOR. I would protect you by receiving him first—I would pump him dry.

MRS. DOUBLEDAY. I should feel as if he would never *be* dry!

MR. BONSOR. We should have doubtless more than ever, in our intercourse with him, to make use of the moral mackintosh.

MRS. DOUBLEDAY. I impressed upon Captain Chanter from the first the necessity of such a garment.

MR. BONSOR. However, since he has muffed his catch—

MRS. DOUBLEDAY. (*With asperity.*) Why the dickens doesn't he come back? (*Up at the long window.*) I'll wire that question! (*Exit* MRS. DOUBLEDAY.)

MR. BONSOR. (*Alone, surprised.*) Not, I hope, in those words! (*Then as he sees* BLANCHE: *re-enter* BLANCHE AMBER *from the library.*) Mr. Brunt's gone without you?

BLANCHE. No, dear uncle; he's in there.

MR. BONSOR. And what's he doing?

BLANCHE. When I left him he was making a speech.

MR. BONSOR. (*Struck; at the door of the library.*) On what subject?

BLANCHE. Try to make out!

MR. BONSOR. (*As he listens, with his eyes on* BLANCHE *and an admonitory motion.*) Hear, hear! (*Exit rapidly* MR. BONSOR.)

BLANCHE. (*Joyous, as she sees* PAUL.) Ah, what a blessed change!

(*Enter* PAUL DOUBLEDAY *from the hall; with a complete transformation of appearance, expression, demeanour. He is bright, confident, assured, and dressed in the height of the fashion; with flowers in his buttonhole, his moustache bravely curled, his high hat, of a striking shape, gallantly worn. He carries in his hand a magnificent bouquet, and is followed by* CUBIT, *who bears an armful of parcels.*)

PAUL. (*In high spirits.*) Dispose them on the table, Cubit, and treat them with respect—they're the spoils of a great campaign!

CUBIT. And what shall I give the cabman?

PAUL. Give him my blessing!

CUBIT. I'm afraid he won't go for that, sir.

PAUL. If he won't go he can stay!

CUBIT. (*Scandalised.*) At half-a-crown an hour?

PAUL. *I* stayed for less, Cubit—all those years.

CUBIT. (*Deprecating.*) Oh *you*, Mr. Paul—!

PAUL. Well, I wasn't such a fool as we thought!

BLANCHE. (*Who has produced her portemonnaie; giving* CUBIT *a coin.*) Dismiss the cab.

CUBIT. (*With the money.*) And bring back the change?

BLANCHE. Keep the change.

CUBIT. (*To himself.*) Seven-and-six! (*Exit* CUBIT *to the hall.*)

PAUL. (*Who has dashed at* BLANCHE *to kiss her hand.*) Has my absence excited remark?

BLANCHE. It has been the only subject of our conversation.

PAUL. Have you mentioned, in the course of that conversation, the motive of my little break?

BLANCHE. (*Smiling.*) How can I have mentioned it when I haven't known it?

PAUL. (*Surprised.*) Didn't I make it clear—?

BLANCHE. When I rejoined you in the garden—after your fall?

PAUL. (*Oblivious.*) My fall?

BLANCHE. Why, to the old wild life.

PAUL. (*Prompt, perfunctory.*) Oh yes, the old wild life!

BLANCHE. I don't strike a man when he's down.

PAUL. Certainly, I forgot—I'm down! (*Offering his bouquet; smiling.*) And I gathered on my way down this handful of flowers.

BLANCHE. (*With the bouquet.*) Flowers as wild as yourself?—flowers of folly, flowers of passion? (*Inhaling their odour.*) They're sweet—but ought I to say so?

PAUL. Why not?—I got them in Baker Street. (*Then as* BLANCHE *looks disconcerted.*) A jolly good shop—with an awfully pretty girl.

BLANCHE. (*More reassured; after an instant.*) Perhaps you had better not tell me about people of that sort. I don't wish to draw you out.

PAUL. I see. (*Then after an instant.*) But perhaps you think I'm worse than I am!

BLANCHE. Not worse than you were when you let everything go.

PAUL. When—and where—did I let *anything* go?

BLANCHE. Why, yesterday afternoon, in the garden, as I say, when you finally told me you must get off by yourself.

PAUL. For the first time for such an age?

BLANCHE. You declared you must go up to town.

PAUL. Precisely, for a little change.

BLANCHE. You disguised your necessity under a singular expression.

PAUL. I said I must take a look round?— Well, I took a look.

BLANCHE. (*Prompt.*) Oh, you needn't tell me what you've seen!

PAUL. (*Bringing a parcel from the table.*) I saw some *bonbons* in Bond Street—and brought you a box.

BLANCHE. (*With the box.*) Was there a pretty girl in that shop too?

PAUL. (*Laughing.*) Oh yes, two or three! (*Then showing a small parcel.*) I got something else, you see—as a present to Mamma.

BLANCHE. Well, you've certainly made the money fly!

PAUL. All over the place! Why shouldn't I—hang it!—if I happen to feel flush?

BLANCHE. (*Struck.*) Isn't *that* the old wild tone?

PAUL. I daresay it is, the devil take it!

BLANCHE. (*Alert.*) There it is again!

PAUL. It seems as if it had come to stay, doesn't it?

BLANCHE. We mustn't let it stay any longer than it positively must. Remember that I'm fighting on your side.

PAUL. (*Laughing.*) Dear Miss Amber, you're even more adorable, upon my word, than when you first took service under my flag!

BLANCHE. You mustn't say such things to me till you've recovered.

PAUL. That I've recovered is precisely what's the matter with me!

BLANCHE. (*Vague.*) Do you mean from the effects of yesterday?

PAUL. I mean from the effects of these ten years. (*Reckless.*) My dear girl, confound it, you know, I'm all right!

BLANCHE. (*Disappointed.*) Already?

PAUL. Surely it has taken long enough.

BLANCHE. Not long enough for *me*. (*After an instant.*) I don't care for saints! There's one at me already.

PAUL. The member for Blackport? (*Prompt.*) Oh, I'm not so good as *he!*

BLANCHE. If you were you'd be too awful.

PAUL. But I'm as good as—as good as—

BLANCHE. (*Challenging, while he considers.*) As good as who?

PAUL. Well, as good as most men!

BLANCHE. (*Disgusted.*) That's far *too* good!

PAUL. (*Trying again.*) Then I'm as good as Captain Chanter.

BLANCHE. I don't believe it! Captain Chanter's far too good. (*Then after an instant.*) If you're so tremendously virtuous, and you happen to feel flush, please repay me—

PAUL. The money you so kindly lent me?

It was a return-ticket. I could neither have started nor come back without the pecuniary assistance you were so good as to render my distress; but I'm sorry to say that distress remains very much what it was.

BLANCHE. Then how can you have felt flush?

PAUL. By the purchase of hats and coats and trousers. Ready made—I told them to put them down.

BLANCHE. (*Vague.*) Down to *me?*

PAUL. Down to Mamma. (*Indicating the other objects.*) Put down everything.

BLANCHE. (*Exultant.*) Then you're gloriously in debt! And your mother won't pay.

PAUL. (*Decided.*) She'll have to!

BLANCHE. (*Decided.*) She shan't!

PAUL. (*Blank.*) Then who will?

BLANCHE. (*After an instant.*) What if *I* should?

PAUL. (*Gazing at her with surprise and emotion, then bounding to her, seizing her hand, and raising it again to his lips.*) Angel!

(*Re-enter* MRS. DOUBLEDAY *from the garden.*)

MRS. DOUBLEDAY. (*Arrested, amazed.*) Paul!

PAUL. (*With undisturbed self-possession and good-humour.*) I was saluting Miss Amber in the joy of my return. Permit me, under the influence of the same emotion, to extend to *you,* dear Mamma (*approaching her with open arms*), an embrace more comprehensive.

(*Re-enter* MR. BONSOR *from the library.*)

MR. BONSOR. (*Arrested, amazed, while* MRS. DOUBLEDAY *bewilderedly submits.*) Mrs. Doubleday!

MRS. DOUBLEDAY. (*Confounded, but bridling and indicating* BLANCHE.) I found him kissing *her!*

MR. BONSOR. (*Aghast, as* PITT BRUNT *reappears.*) Her?

(*Re-enter* PITT BRUNT *from the library.*)

PITT BRUNT. (*Echoing, indignant.*) Her?

BLANCHE. (*Exalted, audacious, passing in front of* PITT BRUNT *on her way up left.*) Her *what?* Her finger-tips!

PAUL. (*To* PITT BRUNT, *laughing.*) Aren't

even the finger-tips more than ever *you've* got at?—How d'ye do, Mr. Bonsor? Noticed my little break?—remarked my lucid interval? (*Then as the others exchange expressions of stupefaction.*) Deplored it, then, bewailed it, felt it in the seat of sensibility? Very charming of you all!

MR. BONSOR. If you designate by those extraordinary terms your unaccountable absence, I have only to observe that, though it has been briefer than we apprehended, we've been amply occupied in considering the questions with which we should find ourselves confronted on its coming to an end.

MRS. DOUBLEDAY. If it *should* come to an end!

PAUL. (*Surprised, amused.*) If it *should?* Why, what did you think I was in for?

MRS. DOUBLEDAY. We didn't permit ourselves to name it!

MR. BONSOR. You mean not to each other.

PITT BRUNT. Only to hint it to a third person.

BLANCHE. (*Who has come down smiling, on the right.*) And yet draw the line at a fourth!

MR. BONSOR. That line, Blanche, is not yet effaced.

PAUL. (*To* MRS. DOUBLEDAY.) Did you miss the usual forms of separation? You see I had to pop off. (*Then as they are again visibly startled.*) To catch the 4.40—the particular train I wanted! I *required* those hours in town, don't you know?—there were things I had imperatively to do. But I put on a spurt—I managed to rush them through!

MR. BONSOR. You speak as if they had been odious necessities!

PAUL. There's no doubt, Mr. Bonsor, they were necessities, and distinctly urgent ones; but, urgent as they were, it would indeed be wide of the mark to call them in the least odious. In fact the whole thing was a treat!

MRS. DOUBLEDAY. Paul!

MR. BONSOR. Blanche! Please leave the room. (*To* PITT BRUNT.) He has really reached a point—

PITT BRUNT. That embarrasses even *me.* (*Opening the lower door on the right for*

BLANCHE.) Your retreat.

PAUL. (*Opening for her with a laugh the door of the library.*) Spare my blushes!

BLANCHE. (*Between the doors a moment, then at* PAUL'S, *giving him a brush in the face with her bouquet.*) Reprobate! (*Exit* BLANCHE AMBER *to the library.*)

PAUL. You see it was the first time for years, and there wasn't a single moment of it that hadn't its appreciable quality! (*Then while* MRS. DOUBLEDAY *and* MR. BONSOR *indulge in manifestations of increasing dismay.*) Whatever delights the future may hold for me, I feel I never shall forget the rapture of those hours. Everything, in such a case, conspires to intensify the bliss: it's the sort of thing that, as I may say, don't you know? one makes for ever one's own!

MR. BONSOR. Mrs. Doubleday, shall I face it alone?

PITT BRUNT. (*Springing to the lower door on the right, which he holds open for her.*) While you step in here!

MRS. DOUBLEDAY. I think I shall suffer less if *you* step in there. (*To* MR. BONSOR.) Tell him to leave us.

PITT BRUNT. (*Disconcerted.*) Then I'll mingle my innocence with Miss Amber's.

PAUL. (*Checking him with a gesture as he crosses to the library.*) My dear fellow, I wish to mingle mine!

MRS. DOUBLEDAY. After this extraordinary exhibition of your having none?

PAUL. (*Arrested, chagrined.*) Ah yes—for her! (*To* PITT BRUNT.) What I mean is, don't you know? that I aspire to her myself.

PITT BRUNT. (*To* MR. BONSOR.) I believe he's still drunk!

PAUL. (*At the lower door on the right, which he holds open for* PITT BRUNT.) *In vino veritas*—when I'm drunk I'm pressing!

PITT BRUNT. (*Crossing at last to the door, where he stands again an instant with his eyes on* PAUL.) Reprobate! (*Exit* PITT BRUNT.)

PAUL. And where, all this while, is the dear old Captain?

MRS. DOUBLEDAY. (*With high significance.*) That's what I should like particularly to know!

MR. BONSOR. He has not returned from London.

PAUL. (*Surprised.*) What's he doing in London?

MRS. DOUBLEDAY. I wish you would find out!

MR. BONSOR. He went up to track you.

MRS. DOUBLEDAY. But he has given you up.

MR. BONSOR. Prematurely, we can't but think.

MRS. DOUBLEDAY. He reports that you've disappeared.

MR. BONSOR. For ever—with a female.

MRS. DOUBLEDAY. The same female.

PAUL. The old female—Nina?

MRS. DOUBLEDAY. (*Alert.*) Is she old, Dudley?

PAUL. Dear me, yes—about your age. And she's here.

MR. BONSOR. You brought her back?

PAUL. I didn't take her!

MR. BONSOR. And she didn't take *you?*

PAUL. (*With a gesture of repudiation; almost wounded.*) How *could* she?

MRS. DOUBLEDAY. (*With deepening uneasiness.*) Then what's she here for?

PAUL. (*Bethinking himself.*) Perhaps after all she has gone.

MRS. DOUBLEDAY. Perhaps after all she hasn't! You'll be so good as to find out.

MR. BONSOR. (*Astonished.*) You wish to throw them together?

MRS. DOUBLEDAY. I wish to keep them apart!

PAUL. (*Vague.*) Of whom, Mamma, do you speak?

MRS. DOUBLEDAY. I speak of Captain Chanter!

PAUL. (*After an instant; diplomatic.*) There's plenty of time.—He reports that I've vanished?

MR. BONSOR. He wires that you're practically extinct.

PAUL. Does he take me for a species—or for a volcano? In the latter case I'm in lively eruption!

MRS. DOUBLEDAY. (*Suspicious.*) Why hasn't he mentioned the position of the second crater?

PAUL. The lady to whom we just alluded?—The second crater's temporarily quiet. (*At the table on which he caused his parcels to be deposited.*) Such a pity the Captain's away—I've brought him a charming present: a couple of French novels—the last things out.

MRS. DOUBLEDAY. And pray where have you picked up such insidious productions?

PAUL. In Leicester Square—such a funny little shop.

MR. BONSOR. The contents of which you also appropriated—

MRS. DOUBLEDAY. (*As he hesitates.*) When the proprietor didn't happen to be looking!

PAUL. (*Staring; then laughing.*) You mean I bagged them? (*With two other mementoes from the table.*) Yes, and I prigged something for each of *you!*

MRS. DOUBLEDAY. (*With her present, opening a small case.*) A massive bracelet?

MR. BONSOR. (*Doing the same.*) And an expensive pin?

PAUL. So glad you like them! I had them booked.

MR. BONSOR. And how will you pay for them?

PAUL. Why, as one always pays—out of income.

MRS. DOUBLEDAY. (*Triumphant.*) You haven't *got* any income!

PAUL. I shall have a very good one when we settle.

MR. BONSOR. That will be ten years hence. We don't settle till you're forty.

PAUL. My dear Mr. Bonsor, I *am* forty.

MRS. DOUBLEDAY. Since when? You were thirty last week.

PAUL. So I was. But I've grown.

MR. BONSOR. Ten years—in a week?

PAUL. Ten years in an hour! I'm of age.

MRS. DOUBLEDAY. (*Aghast.*) To cease to be looked after?

PAUL. To begin to look after *you.* I am beginning—I *have* begun. So you'll pay me up.

MRS. DOUBLEDAY. The wages of sin?

PAUL. I really think the only sin is the sin of impertinence! Don't you so much as thank me for the reward of yours?

MR. BONSOR. Your mother will hardly go through such a form for an ornament she is incapable of retaining. She will take it back—

MRS. DOUBLEDAY. (*Who has slipped the bracelet over her arm, where she has complacently regarded it; after a little renunciatory wriggle at the clasp.*) As soon as I succeed in removing it. And Mr. Bonsor will only keep his pin—

PAUL. To stick into *me* when he's vicious? I warn him that I've ceased to be a pin-cushion! (*With an illustrated "society-paper," which he hands, open, to* MR. BONSOR.) There's something—just out! —for the member for Blackport.

MR. BONSOR. (*With the coloured cartoon.*) "The Idol of the North"—!

PAUL. Putting in an hour!

MR. BONSOR. I'll pass it on to Blanche.

PAUL. Don't do that: it's too awfully like! (*Taking from his pocket a small paper.*) That's the figure of what I've spent.

MRS. DOUBLEDAY. (*With the paper, in dismay, to* MR. BONSOR.) Seventy pounds!

PAUL. Nine and sevenpence. I'll trouble you for a cheque.

MR. BONSOR. (*With the paper, after an instant, to* MRS. DOUBLEDAY.) Will you write one?

MRS. DOUBLEDAY. (*Indignant, at the window.*) Never! (*Exit* MRS. DOUBLEDAY *to the garden.*)

PAUL. Will you?

MR. BONSOR. (*At the lower door on the right.*) Never! (*Exit* MR. BONSOR.)

(*Enter* CAPTAIN CHANTER *from the hall.*)

PAUL. Hang it then, will *you?*

CHANTER. (*Aghast.*) You're not off with her, as I instructed you?

PAUL. I'm no more off than she is. I'm to call on her.

CHANTER. (*Frantic.*) Then by all that's desperate, call!

PAUL. There's no hurry, my dear fellow. Nina won't go!

CHANTER. She'll go if *you'll* go. You told me so yourself!

PAUL. Yes, but I won't—that's what I've an appointment to make her understand. (*Then on a wild motion of despair of* CHANTER's.) If you thought we *had* bolted, why did you give chase?

CHANTER. To speed you on your way—to smother your remorse. You promised to save me, and I've been living in the blind confidence that I *was* saved!

PAUL. You shall be if you keep your head—if you'll do exactly what I tell you. In the first place, you must assist me with Miss Amber. You must not let her find out that I ain't what I thought.

CHANTER. Nor what I thought, either! I thought I could trust you!

PAUL. You thought I had every vice. So did I, till I was put to the test. You put me to it yourself—you proved me utterly wanting. But it's the fond belief that I'm a splendid Satan that's the singular source of her interest.

CHANTER. That interest is quenched, then, from the moment you moon about here. The way to impress her is obviously to do something Satanic.

PAUL. A good way to begin, then, will be to keep a devil of an eye on *you*. You're indispensable to my plan.

CHANTER. I operate as a diversion to Mrs. Doubleday!

PAUL. If you'll direct her activity into a different channel—

CHANTER. You'll also find a different one for Nina's? What channel *is* there—

PAUL. But the one from Dover to Calais? I'll *find* one, if I have to dig it! Leave me to do so.

CHANTER. (*Uneasy.*) With Nina all over the place?

PAUL. *I'm* all over the place! Do as I tell you. (*Then as* CHANTER *still stands reluctant; authoritative.*) Go to your room! (*Exit* CAPTAIN CHANTER *with quick docility to the hall. Re-enter* MR. BONSOR *by the lower door on the right.*) Have you come to tell me you *will* write the cheque?

MR. BONSOR. For half the amount—on a condition. That of your withdrawing your opposition—

PAUL. To the Idol of the North as an active rival? (*Thinking, amused.*) For thirty-five pounds?

MR. BONSOR. Four and ninepence ha'penny. Permit him regular access—

PAUL. To the young lady he bores? Not for the money!

MR. BONSOR. (*Disappointed.*) Then on what terms can we arrange it?

PAUL. (*Up at the door to the hall as* BLANCHE *re-appears.*) Ask the young lady herself! (*Exit* PAUL DOUBLEDAY.)

(*Re-enter* BLANCHE AMBER *from the library.*)

BLANCHE. (*With her bouquet.*) I must delay no longer to put my flowers into water.

MR. BONSOR. I beg you to come back then as soon as you've supplied them with a sustenance of which I decline to regard them as deserving. The member for Blackport—

BLANCHE. What on earth does he want now?

MR. BONSOR. What you've never yet frankly given him—the chance to catch your eye.

BLANCHE. Dear uncle, I'm not the Speaker!

MR. BONSOR. He'll make you feel like the House itself. And when the House divides—

BLANCHE. (*Laughing.*) I shall be in the right lobby! (*Then as she sees* PITT BRUNT: *re-enter* PITT BRUNT *by the lower door on the right.*) I'll be back! (*Exit* BLANCHE AMBER *by the lower door on the right.*)

PITT BRUNT. (*Anxious.*) And where'll *he* be?

MR. BONSOR. It will be impossible henceforth to calculate with any exactness. Hitherto we've done it to a second.

PITT BRUNT. (*Aggrieved.*) You should really have taken him in hand!

MR. BONSOR. The way to begin was by taking that woman.

PITT BRUNT. (*After a moment.*) That may possibly be the way to end!

MR. BONSOR. (*Struck.*) It *might* be—all the more that she's somewhere about. (*After an instant.*) I suppose her attractions are pronounced.

PITT BRUNT. (*Prompt.*) Very easily, with a little practice!

MR. BONSOR. (*Surprised.*) Then you've seen her?

PITT BRUNT. (*On his guard.*) Not to know it was she! But if she's somewhere about, her confederate must also be.

MR. BONSOR. (*At the lower door on the right.*) Thank heaven, he can't be in two places at once! (*Exit* MR. BONSOR.)

PITT BRUNT. (*Alone.*) My only comfort! (*Then thinking, bewildered.*) Yet he behaves as if he wanted them both!

(Re-enter Cubit *from the hall.)*

Cubit. *(Announcing.)* Mrs. Freshville!

(Enter Mrs. Freshville. *Exit* Cubit.)*

Mrs. Freshville. *You* here still? How d'ye do to-day?

Pitt Brunt. I never feel quite fit when I haven't put in my hour.

Mrs. Freshville. I've come to put in mine—I'm tired of messing about.

Pitt Brunt. I heard just now you *were* messing—

Mrs. Freshville. *(Amazed.)* The man has the cheek to mention it?

Pitt Brunt. Oh no, he doesn't mention it—but the whole thing's known.

Mrs. Freshville. *(Alert.)* Then how does the woman take it?

Pitt Brunt. *(Deprecating.)* She's scarcely a woman—!

Mrs. Freshville. *(Impatient.)* I know—she's a monster! What does she make of it?

Pitt Brunt. You're severe! But she doesn't make quite so much of it as you might expect. She takes it rather easy. In fact you might suppose she almost likes it!

Mrs. Freshville. *(Astounded.)* Likes his goings on with *me?*

Pitt Brunt. Then they've been as bad as we all suppose?

Mrs. Freshville. They've been beyond everything that ever was! *(With renewed stupefaction.)* She likes his being engaged to another woman?

Pitt Brunt. *(Surprised.)* Do you mean to say he's literally engaged?

Mrs. Freshville. As much as a man ever was in the world. Engaged up to his eyes—engaged down to his boots!

Pitt Brunt. Happily I don't think she knows that!

Mrs. Freshville. Then I shall have the pleasure of telling her!

Pitt Brunt. I daresay it will produce some effect. She doesn't mind anything *except* that.

Mrs. Freshville. Except marriage—or the next thing to it? And she calls herself a respectable woman?

Pitt Brunt. *(Wincing; after an instant.)* I'm bound to say she's very hard to shock.

Mrs. Freshville. Put it stronger. She's a monster of what-do-you-call-it!

Pitt Brunt. *(At a loss.)* Do you call it paradox?

Mrs. Freshville. I call it immorality! But wasn't I jolly right to come!

Pitt Brunt. Do you argue that he'll see you?

Mrs. Freshville. Not if he can help it! But I argue that I'm perfectly visible. Where do you suppose he is?

Pitt Brunt. *(Looking at his watch; melancholy.)* I'm afraid he's somewhere with *her.*

Mrs. Freshville. Don't take it harder than *I* do! *(After an instant.)* Could you bring us together?

Pitt Brunt. *(Vague.)* You and him?

Mrs. Freshville. Me and her.

Pitt Brunt. *(Disconcerted.)* Dear no—not *that!*

Mrs. Freshville. Well, you needn't scratch my eyes out! *(Holding up several of* Chanter's *letters.)* It will do quite as well to hand her these. His letters—nine of 'em—breathing every vow.

Pitt Brunt. *(With the letters; alert.)* Vows of passion—vows of marriage?

Mrs. Freshville. Vows of everything on earth—and every vow a lie. Poke 'em in her face.

Pitt Brunt. *(Intensely eager.)* I'll poke 'em! But how can I ever thank you?

Mrs. Freshville. Thank me for nothing! I didn't do it for *you!* *(Then as* Cubit *reappears: re-enter* Cubit *from the hall.)* That way?

Pitt Brunt. *(Surprised.)* You're going off?

Mrs. Freshville. I'm going on. *(Up at the door to the hall.)* Work her up! *(Exeunt* Mrs. Freshville *and* Cubit *to the hall.)*

Pitt Brunt. *(As* Blanche *reappears.)* I'll work her up!

(Re-enter Blanche Amber *by the lower door on the right.)*

Blanche. My uncle has just told me you wish to catch my eye.

Pitt Brunt. In order to direct it, Miss Amber, to unprecedented documents.

Blanche. *(Smiling.)* Parliamentary papers?

Pitt Brunt. Not exactly Blue Books! *(Giving her* Mrs. Freshville's *letters.)* I place them in your hands.

BLANCHE. (*With the letters, vague.*) You mean I'm to look them through? But they're letters—they're private. (*Then after hastily glancing at a word here and there.*) They're all about love!

PITT BRUNT. They're all about marriage—you'll easily see!

BLANCHE. I don't *want* to see—especially if they're yours?

PITT BRUNT. How can you think they're mine when you know my hand?

BLANCHE. (*With a look at the letters again.*) Yes—it's a better hand than yours! (*Then suddenly tossing them down.*) But I never read such stuff!

PITT BRUNT. They may well bring the blush to your cheek, but I regret to be obliged to deepen it!—You haven't seen that writing?

BLANCHE. (*With a letter that is out of its envelope, trying ineffectually to remember, then suddenly catching sight of something.*) Oh yes, I recall a name!

PITT BRUNT. (*Exultant.*) May I inquire *what* name?

BLANCHE. The name that was on his photograph.

PITT BRUNT. (*Struck.*) He has given you his photograph?

BLANCHE. Oh yes. That is he hasn't!

PITT BRUNT. But you recognize the writer?

BLANCHE. (*Troubled, uncertain.*) Mr. Paul?

PITT BRUNT. (*Triumphant.*) Mr. Paul!

BLANCHE. (*With emotion, thinking.*) "Dudley"!

PITT BRUNT. (*Vague.*) Dudley?

BLANCHE. (*After another glance at the open letters.*) It's the pet name. "To his Nina"!

PITT BRUNT. (*At the door of the library; impressive.*) Say, Madam, to his miserable victim! (*Exit* PITT BRUNT.)

BLANCHE. (*Alone, agitated.*) He *makes* victims—and makes them miserable? (*Hastily gathering the letters together.*) Who should know it better than I?—But what has Mr. Brunt to do with these things—how did he ever get them? He gave them to me as a warning? (*After an instant.*) Miserable as I am, I reject the warning! I'll give them back to the writer! (*Then as she*

sees PAUL *and instinctively puts the letters behind her.*) Oh, Mr. Paul, you're just the man—! (*Re-enter* PAUL DOUBLEDAY *from the hall, in an elaborate change of costume.*)

PAUL. (*Anxious, flurried.*) You're just the woman, Miss Amber, but I'm trying to track the Captain. I've something special to say to him.

(*Re-enter* CAPTAIN CHANTER *from the hall.*)

CHANTER. (*To* PAUL.) I've just seen Cubit—he tells me you want me.

BLANCHE. (*At the lower door on the right, to* PAUL, *smiling.*) Then you don't want *me*! (*Exit* BLANCHE AMBER *with the letters.*)

PAUL. (*Breathless.*) Mamma knows all—she has your letters!

CHANTER. (*Appalled.*) Nina has been here?

PAUL. She *is* here—in my retreat.

CHANTER. (*Astonished.*) You've *got* one?

PAUL. The Chinese room—I've taken it. She arrived—fearfully out of patience—as I was on the very point of going to her, and I thought it best to have her right in. But she had already passed in the letters. She proclaims her vengeance on you as successfully accomplished, and I left her there gloating over it to come and warn you. The fat's on the fire—but I told her I can't oblige her.

CHANTER. (*Rueful, resentful.*) You can't oblige anybody! So what the mischief is she waiting for?

PAUL. For her photograph—I mean for mine. You broke your promise to carry it to her, and she declines to leave the house without it.

CHANTER. How could I carry it to her when I couldn't find it?

PAUL. (*Looking blankly about.*) I'm in exactly the same predicament!

CHANTER. (*Helpless, hopeless.*) So she's here for the rest of our lives?

PAUL. (*As* MRS. DOUBLEDAY *reappears.*) I'm terribly afraid not!

(*Re-enter* MRS. DOUBLEDAY *from the garden. Instantly astonished by the presence of* CHANTER, *she hurries down toward him; then, between the two men, stopping short, looks with sudden wonderment and suspicion from one of them to the other.)*

CHANTER. (*Embarrassed, confused, but trying to meet her.*) Dearest friend!

MRS. DOUBLEDAY. (*Retaining, with resentment and severity, possession of the hand he tries to kiss.*) Your dearest friend has come to get you! (*Then as* CHANTER *exchanges with* PAUL *a look of confirmed dismay.*) You grossly desert your dearest friend!

CHANTER. (*Collapsing, pleading.*) I know that my conduct has been dreadful—!

MRS. DOUBLEDAY. I must clear it up with you. (*Indicating the garden.*) I've been perched there on the lookout.

PAUL. His arrival happened to escape your notice—it has just taken place.

MRS. DOUBLEDAY. Long enough ago for me to remark that his first impulse has not been the impulse to fly to me.

PAUL. He was in the very act of spreading his wings!

MRS. DOUBLEDAY. It has come home to me since your own return that he spread them very wide in town. (*Then to* CHANTER, *while he exchanges with* PAUL *another woeful regard.*) You see the condition in which your pupil has reappeared? Your responsibilities sit very light!

PAUL. He has just been explaining to me that he has every intention to meet them.

MRS. DOUBLEDAY. They have increased tremendously this morning, and he shall presently hear from me on the subject. In the meantime he'll go to my room and ask my maid for a precious packet, conspicuous on the mantel-piece, sealed with large red seals and containing papers of grave importance. (*To* CHANTER, *who stands bewildered while* PAUL *goes up in agitation.*) You'll take them straight to my boudoir, and we'll go through them together. (*With high resolution.*) We'll have it right over!

CHANTER. (*Lingering, paralysed.*) I see what you mean!

PAUL. (*Coming down again, with irrepressible authority.*) Then march!

(*Exit* CHANTER, *startled, with a rush of desperation, to the hall.*)

MRS. DOUBLEDAY. (*Who has massively seated himself.*) What did you remark to him?

PAUL. (*Familiar, gay.*) I remarked, my dear lady, that there's no resisting you; and there evidently isn't, unless a fellow's like *me*. But, you know, I'm adamant, whereas the Captain's all fiddle-strings and moonbeams. (*Then as she stares, astounded at his new tone.*) There's one thing, however, you know—you mustn't, as I may say, *presume,* you mustn't stake everything, on the force—or, as you would perhaps yourself prefer to call it, the charm—of your certainly remarkable personality. You'll tell me it has seen you through often enough to show you how far you can go; and I fully recognise that time has given it those comfortable curves, those generous gradients over which the railroad of social intercourse may be laid at any expense not incompatible with the hope that it will pay. You *can* go a certain length, Mamma, you can achieve certain runs—but you can't make the time you did! A road may be well kept up, but if you go in for heavy traffic you must lay your account with a smash. Don't therefore, as I say, don't magnify small accidents. Don't cry out about a collision when there has only been a casual bump! (*Laughing, flattering.*) *Your* casual bumps, Mamma, certainly oughtn't to bruise!

MRS. DOUBLEDAY. (*Rising in stupefaction.*) You take advantage, sir, of the absence of the few protectors I possess—!

PAUL. (*Good-humoured, imperturbable.*) Only to enjoin upon you not to make too much of such things.

MRS. DOUBLEDAY. (*After an instant.*) Of what things, I beg to know, are you indecent enough to speak?

PAUL. Why, for instance, of those trashy papers.

MRS. DOUBLEDAY. Pray, do you take into account their authorship?

PAUL. It's just their authorship that makes them mere hyperbole!

MRS. DOUBLEDAY. (*After another moment.*) Will you be so good as to tell me what you're talking about?

PAUL. (*Surprised.*) The letters you sent the Captain for.

MRS. DOUBLEDAY. What's your reason for calling them letters?

PAUL. (*Checked, embarrassed.*) I don't insist on the name. Outbursts of momentary ardour.

MRS. DOUBLEDAY. (*Very alert.*) Then *I* insist on the name!—What abyss have you unguardedly opened?

PAUL. (*After an instant.*) What are the papers you are to go over with the Captain?

MRS. DOUBLEDAY. Instructions from the late Mr. Doubleday—drawn up in view of the contingency which has now presented itself.

PAUL. That of your chucking up his son?

MRS. DOUBLEDAY. That of *your* "chucking up" his widow!

PAUL. (*Amused.*) Something seems to tell me the instructions are voluminous!

MRS. DOUBLEDAY. I've every confidence. But it's a mystery I've always respected. The large red seals are intact.

PAUL. And you propose to delegate to the Captain the office of breaking them?

MRS. DOUBLEDAY. After first assuring myself that he is really worthy of it. (*Then after an instant, abrupt, distressfully appealing, with a complete change of tone and manner.*) Paul—is he really worthy?

PAUL. (*Laughing.*) Doesn't it strike you I'm an extraordinary person to ask?

MRS. DOUBLEDAY. You're the person who knows most about such things.

PAUL. Let me inquire in turn what things you're talking about.

MRS. DOUBLEDAY. The horrible things men do. You've betrayed him—and he has betrayed himself.

PAUL. I've never betrayed anybody, and I can promise you I never will! We'll respect the mystery of the late Mr. Doubleday's instructions—we'll keep our hands from the large red seals.

MRS. DOUBLEDAY. You practically proclaim, then, that the Captain's are impure? (*With another outburst of entreaty.*) Paul, who *is* the woman to whom he has been writing? (*Then as PAUL throws up his arms in embarrassed repudiation.*) I'll draw you a cheque for half the amount of your bills.

PAUL. Thirty-five pounds?

MRS. DOUBLEDAY. Four and ninepence ha'penny—if you'll tell me the truth.

PAUL. (*Thinking.*) The real truth?

MRS. DOUBLEDAY. (*Ardent.*) The whole truth!

PAUL. (*After another moment.*) Not for the money!

MRS. DOUBLEDAY. (*Indignant, flouncing off.*) I'll get it from *him!* (*Exit MRS. DOUBLEDAY to the hall.*)

PAUL. (*Alone, disconcerted.*) She'll break with him! (*Then, alarmed, as MR. BONSOR reappears: re-enter MR. BONSOR by the lower door on the right.*) Mr. Bonsor, *will* she break with him?

MR. BONSOR. My ungovernable niece? I'm sorry to have to recognise that she has already practically done so. She has levelled against my young friend an accusation under the effect of which I have fairly staggered from her presence—an accusation of conduct—

PAUL. (*As he can't bring it out.*) Unparliamentary? What has he done?

MR. BONSOR. I am just looking for him to inquire. (*Then as he sees CHANTER: re-enter CAPTAIN CHANTER from the garden.*) Have you seen the member for Blackport?

CHANTER. He's in the garden. (*Agitated, blanched, to PAUL as MR. BONSOR goes up.*) I can't *do* it!

PAUL. She hasn't got them!

(*Re-enter MRS. DOUBLEDAY from the hall.*)

MRS. DOUBLEDAY. (*With a large sealed packet and with energy, as CHANTER moves quickly away from PAUL and she sees MR. BONSOR going.*) Mr. Bonsor! (*Then as he obediently comes down with her.*) Be present! That's more, apparently, than Captain Chanter had courage to be!

PAUL. Dear Mamma, he has come back for you.

MRS. DOUBLEDAY. I've come back for *him!* (*Then having looked hard from one of them to the other; holding out her packet to CHANTER.*) Break those seals! (*To MR. BONSOR.*) The instructions.

MR. BONSOR. A new lot?

MRS. DOUBLEDAY. For the new crisis. The supreme measures.

MR. BONSOR. (*Complacent.*) Our second line of defence!

PAUL. Abandon, Captain, your second line. We'll dispense with the supreme measures. (*Then as* CHANTER *stares.*) Touch the seals at your peril. Give *me* the packet.

CHANTER. (*With his packet; tormented, perplexed, to* MRS. DOUBLEDAY.) What will be the penalty, love, of my surrendering my precious charge?

MRS. DOUBLEDAY. The inevitable inference that you have reasons for grovelling before your pupil. (*After an instant; formidable.*) He has seen the fatal letters.

MR. BONSOR. (*Blank but prompt.*) Where are they to be seen?

MRS. DOUBLEDAY. That's exactly what I want to know! Paul doesn't deny the impeachment.

CHANTER. (*Scandalised, tossing his packet to a table.*) Then I call upon him instantly to do so. (*To* PAUL.) What letters does your mother mean?

PAUL. (*After a moment.*) I let the cat out of the bag! (*Then as* PITT BRUNT *reappears.*) The fatal letters exist!

(*Re-enter* PITT BRUNT *from the garden.*)

PITT BRUNT. (*Struck, coming quickly down as* BLANCHE *reappears.*) The fatal letters exist!

(*Re-enter* BLANCHE AMBER *by the lower door on the right.*)

CHANTER. (*Amazed, to* PITT BRUNT.) How the devil, sir, do *you* know?

PITT BRUNT. (*Arrested, conciliatory.*) I hasten to explain, sir, that I don't attribute them to *you!*

MRS. DOUBLEDAY. (*Astonished.*) Then to whom in the world do you attribute them?

BLANCHE. (*Precipitate, very loud.*) Ahem!.

PAUL. (*While the others stare in surprise at her ambiguous ejaculation.*) I'll save Mr. Brunt the trouble of saying. (*After a moment.*) The fatal letters are mine!

MRS. DOUBLEDAY. (*Blank.*) Then who in the world *has* them?

BLANCHE. (*Passing close to* PITT BRUNT; *privately, with ferocity.*) Say at your peril!

PAUL. (*To* MRS. DOUBLEDAY.) I thought they had come into your hands. (*Then indicating* CHANTER.) Take him away to beg his pardon.

CHANTER. (*To* MRS. DOUBLEDAY, *smiling.*) Naughty doubting dear!

MRS. DOUBLEDAY. (*Breathing again, but severe.*) Naughty frightening man!

PAUL. (*Impatient; motioning them off.*) Oh, make it up somewhere else!

MRS. DOUBLEDAY. (*Startled, giving ground, but hesitating.*) Without the instructions?

PAUL. You evidently require no teaching! (*Then highly authoritative.*) Go!

MRS. DOUBLEDAY. (*Who has hurried up; to* CHANTER, *at the door to the hall.*) Come! (*Exit* MRS. DOUBLEDAY.)

CHANTER. (*Uneasy; privately to* PAUL.) But the letters?

PAUL. I'll find them!

CHANTER. (*Up at the door to the hall; aloud.*) Reprobate! (*Exit* CAPTAIN CHANTER.)

PAUL. (*At the left; peremptory, to* MR. BONSOR *and* PITT BRUNT, *who have been conversing down at the right.*) Leave me alone with Miss Amber!

BLANCHE. I require to be alone with Mr. Paul.

MR. BONSOR. You will neither of you have forgotten that *I* wish to be alone—

PAUL. With the member for Blackport? So do *I!* But I'll take him later.

PITT BRUNT. I shall suffer nothing to blind me to the fact that I have still my hour to put in.

MR. BONSOR. On the water. You can take me out—I'll join you directly in the garden. (*Then to* PAUL, *while* PITT BRUNT, *intensely preoccupied, approaches* BLANCHE.) Reprobate! (*Exit* MR. BONSOR *to the hall.*)

PITT BRUNT. (*To* BLANCHE.) You accept the shocking evidence?

BLANCHE. Of an existing connection?— I accept everything!

PITT BRUNT. (*Up at the window, scandalised.*) I call it immorality! (*Exit* PITT BRUNT *to the garden.*)

BLANCHE. (*To* PAUL.) I daresay it is; but I forgive you.

PAUL. (*Vague.*) For saying such a thing?

BLANCHE. For doing it! *I* have the letters!

PAUL. (*Amazed.*) How in the world—?
BLANCHE. In my room—from Mr. Brunt.
PAUL. (*Bewildered.*) How did Mr. Brunt get them?
BLANCHE. I give it up! But I'm keeping them for you.
PAUL. (*Anxious.*) Don't "keep" them—bring them to me! (*Then checking her as she is going.*) But there's something you can keep for me. (*Placing in her hands the sealed packet.*) Keep this!
BLANCHE. (*With the packet, exalted, at the lower door on the right.*) To the death! (*Exit BLANCHE AMBER.*)
    (*Re-enter MRS. FRESHVILLE from the hall.*)
PAUL. (*Nervous, curt.*) I've been too busy to come back to you—and I'm too busy to converse with you now!
MRS. FRESHVILLE. You're a very superior person, Dud; but you can be awfully nasty when you like. You know I've declined to leave the house without that memento —doubly dear to me now—of our brighter and happier hours. Your precious photo has been appropriated, and after very patiently and very vainly waiting there for you to recover it for me, I demand here the production of my property.
PAUL. Accept as a substitute, my dear Nina, the assurance that I'll be taken again!
MRS. FRESHVILLE. What I desire, Dudley, is the representation of your more juvenile and—since you force me to say so—your more attractive personality.
PAUL. (*Alarmed, as PITT BRUNT reappears.*) Don't bring it up—there's some one there!
    (*Re-enter PITT BRUNT from the garden.*)
MRS. FRESHVILLE. You gave her the letters?
PITT BRUNT. (*Embarrassed.*) She has them in her hands.
MRS. FRESHVILLE. And what does she say about the shocking evidence—
PITT BRUNT. Of an existing connection? She accepts it. She accepts everything!
MRS. FRESHVILLE. (*Stupefied.*) Everything? Then she's a cat!
PITT BRUNT. (*Emphatic.*) She's a cat!

PAUL. (*Smiling.*) No—she's only a woman in love! (*To PITT BRUNT, who stands blank.*) Have you come back for something?
PITT BRUNT. For Mr. Bonsor—to put in my hour.
PAUL. I daresay he's dressing. (*Then with a happy thought; inspired.*) Put it in with Mrs. Freshville!
MRS. FRESHVILLE. (*Struck.*) On the river —the dear old river?
PITT BRUNT. (*Struck.*) I put in an hour each day. (*After an instant, engaging.*) Could you give me as much as that?
MRS. FRESHVILLE. (*Looking from PITT BRUNT to PAUL.*) By-bye?
PAUL. By-bye!
MRS. FRESHVILLE. (*Giving her reticule to PITT BRUNT.*) Stick it in the boat.
PITT BRUNT. (*Alert, with the reticule; up at the window, to PAUL.*) Patch it up with Mr. Bonsor! (*Exit PITT BRUNT to the garden.*)
MRS. FRESHVILLE. (*After a moment; thoughtful.*) Not engaged?
PAUL. I can answer for that!
MRS. FRESHVILLE. Much of a swell?
PAUL. (*Handing her from the table the copy of the "society-paper."*) The papers are full of him.
MRS. FRESHVILLE. (*With the cartoon.*) "The Idol of the North"!
PAUL. The young man of the hour.
MRS. FRESHVILLE. More than ever *you* were! By-bye.
PAUL. By-bye.
MRS. FRESHVILLE. (*With the copy of the paper under her arm; up at the window, contemptuous, sarcastic.*) Perfection! (*Exit MRS. FRESHVILLE to the garden.*)
    (*Re-enter CAPTAIN CHANTER from the hall.*)
CHANTER. (*Anxious.*) Has she gone?
PAUL. (*Coming down from the window, indicating the garden, while CHANTER, interrogative, goes up, and BLANCHE and MR. BONSOR reappear.*) She has found an opening!
    (*Re-enter BLANCHE AMBER by the lower door on the right. Re-enter MR. BONSOR, in boating costume, from the hall.*)

BLANCHE. (*With* MRS. FRESHVILLE's *letters, eager, to* PAUL.) Here are the letters!

CHANTER. (*Struck, turning, bounding down to grab them.*) Mine!

PAUL. (*Smiling, having seized them first.*) Mine!

CHANTER. (*To* BLANCHE, *resentful.*) You should have given them to *me!*

BLANCHE. They belong to the writer.

CHANTER. He's *not* the writer!

BLANCHE. (*Aghast, to* PAUL.) You're not the writer?

PAUL. I blush to confess it—I'm so much less bad than you want me!

CHANTER. He took them on himself to save his friend.

BLANCHE. (*Struck, eager.*) He told a glorious lie?

PAUL. (*Laughing, while he tosses* CHANTER *the packet of letters.*) Don't mention it!

BLANCHE. (*Overjoyed.*) But I don't want you any worse than *that!*

MR. BONSOR. (*To* CHANTER.) Are you very sure his friend is saved?

PAUL. Not if you basely blab, Mr. Bonsor.

CHANTER. (*Confident, complacent.*) Oh, he may basely blab! (*After an instant.*) I'm sure!

MR. BONSOR. (*To* BLANCHE.) But where did *you* get them?

BLANCHE. From the member for Blackport.

MR. BONSOR. (*Blank.*) And where did *he* get them?

PAUL. From the lady to whom they were addressed.

MR. BONSOR. (*Startled.*) Nina—the unspeakable Nina? (*Indignant.*) He never went near her!

PAUL. He's remarkably near her now—he's out on the river with her!

MR. BONSOR. (*Stupefied.*) Then it was for *him* the woman came?

PAUL. She came for a certain photograph!

MR. BONSOR. (*Struck.*) I remember! (*Looking ineffectually round.*) What on earth became of it?

BLANCHE. (*Producing it from her pocket.*) Here it is!

MR. BONSOR. (*To the others, amazed.*) *She* had it all the while?

BLANCHE. (*Embarrassed, hesitating.*) I took it because—because—

PAUL. (*Radiant.*) You must keep the reason for *me!*

BLANCHE. May I tell him, uncle?

MR. BONSOR. Tell him what you like! (*Then looking at her a moment in bewildered abstraction, raising and dropping his arms at his sides in helpless and humiliated renunciation and going up.*) The Idol of the North!

PAUL. (*Ardent, triumphant, with his two hands out.*) Blanche!

BLANCHE. (*Meeting him in happy freedom while he takes both her hands and respectfully kisses them.*) Paul!

(*Re-enter* MRS. DOUBLEDAY *from the hall.*)

MRS. DOUBLEDAY. (*Startled, instinctive, loud, as before.*) Paul!

CHANTER. (*Eager, as the others, absorbed, pay no attention.*) It's all right! (*Then, irresistible, as* MRS. DOUBLEDAY *surrenders herself to his endearment.*) Beloved!

PAUL. (*Suddenly observing, good-naturedly but loudly and ominously warning, while* MRS. DOUBLEDAY *gives a violent start.*) Mamma!

Note for

The Chaperon
1893

EDITOR'S FOREWORD

On May 27, 1893 Henry James, freshly arrived in London from a trip to the Continent, went to the St. James's Theatre to attend the first night of a new play by Arthur Pinero, *The Second Mrs. Tanqueray*. He was sufficiently excited by it to write to Pinero the next morning that the occasion had been "momentous." It is easy to see why. Aside from the strength and honesty of the play itself, in a theatre addicted to the "time-honored bread-sauce of the happy ending," it dealt with a woman "with a past," in highly dramatic terms and was played with remarkable intensity by Mrs. Patrick Campbell. James, who had treated such a woman in *The Siege of London* and in *Tenants,* who had, moreover, been fascinated by the *demi-mondaines* of Dumas *fils,* found much in Paula Tanqueray to interest him. He had just published, in a volume of short stories entitled *The Real Thing*, a social-satirical tale of such a woman and her daughter entitled *The Chaperon*. "You do not need me to tell you," Pinero wrote in reply to James's letter of praise, "that in *The Chaperon* you have the germ of a fine comedy for the theatre."

James immediately asked himself in his notebook "Is there a subject for comedy—for a pretty three-act comedy—latent in *The Chaperon?*" The note which follows was not included in *The Notebooks of Henry James* and is published here for the first time. It was written on pages torn from a scribbler and since it ends in the middle of a sentence it seems quite likely that it came from one of the notebooks James had destroyed. The note owes its preservation to the fact that James intended to write the play, and he did in fact, fourteen years after this original jotting, begin an extended scenario (*see* page 609) which he never completed.

NOTE FOR
THE CHAPERON

[May or June, 1893]
The Chaperon: 3 act Comedy.

Is there a subject for comedy—for a pretty three-act comedy—latent in *The Chaperon?* It seems to shimmer before me that there *is*—but I can't tell till I try. Three questions (exclusive of this matter for E.C.) rise before me in a row, with importunate solicitous faces. One is the question of the play I began so long ago on the subject that, for convenience, I have provisionally labelled *Monte-Carlo;* the other is the question of having something in my hand ready for Daly in the event of there arising between us a question of a second play. The third is this desire to thresh out the *Chaperon* a little and see what's in it. The sense of a margin (absit omen!) makes all the difference. It makes one good-humoured and patient and pliant and impersonal and divinely willing, makes one care only for the process and the prize and not a bit for the subjective accidents. The definitely wise, the concretely practical thing is probably for me to sit down, without delay and before the Monte-Carlo idea; and I hereby declare myself ready (ready?—ah, passionately eager and impatient!) to begin my siege. I should like, however, *en attendant,* to make a note, to make a notch against the question of what may be feasible with the *Chaperon;* to look into it a moment as I pass—have the amusement of having just started my hare! The idea of the play is expressible enough—the idea of a girl who, reversing with courage and compassion, the usual relation, takes out and imposes on society, making sacrifices to do so, her discredited mother. A part of the drama (either of the story or the play) is in the sacrifices in question. In the tale, which is very brief and simple, she stands ready to sacrifice her lover. He doesn't exact it—he comes round to her and she does her work and keeps him as well. But the tale can, essentially, contain only the germ of the play. What presents itself, offhand, as indispensable for the play—without *approfondissement* or more than the results of a mere glance—is an intensification of the element of sacrifice and an intensification of the element of the mother's *milieu,* of the signs and tokens, the associations and appendages, the stamp and colour that are part and parcel of it and offer it to the view. Everything, in a word must be satirically intensified and dramatically pointed. The struggle must be more arduous than in the tale, the renunciation more heroic, the difficulty greater, the personality and situation of the mother more contrasted, the victory more brilliant. The whole thing must be at once more general, more typical, and more special. All sorts of things, as it were, must depend on the daughter's success. There must be *complications* in the mother's life, and yet a picture—very droll, very satiric—of the whole "desolation of propriety," as the story calls it, in which that life is consciously past. There are the people whom the girl's struggle is with, and who must be intensely *selected*, to make it dramatic. There must be something, someone whom the girl must deal with *in* the mother's past as well as the mother herself. How directly, as one approaches it, one begins to see the drama open out; see it give, *give, give* as one presses! It *always* gives—gives something; the question that remains is whether in the particular case it gives *enough*. The charming thing is that even if it doesn't one is when one reaches that question, so far—so much the farther—on the general way. The Maresfield interest becomes, in the play, one of the big wheels of the action. May the added someone or something, in the mother's "past," in the problem that the daughter has to deal with, not perhaps be the old lover, the co-respondent for whom the mother was divorced. I needn't absolutely have a divorce unless I want to. It may have been only a scandalous separation and thereby serve my purpose; especially if it disposes of some questions—why the mother didn't marry her lover etc. etc. Let us assume then, for the moment, that the lover *is* there, to add to the girl's difficulty and danger. Make the machinery to *capture* her, to prevent her, more important; the Maresfield machinery, I mean—the Maresfield bribe. Make the girl's second lover more dramatically active than Guy Mangler. In this way one gets the bribe, somehow, as well as the loss—what she gives up—at home—and what is held out to her elsewhere. Not what is held out to her to make her drop her mother as Bertram Jay wishes to make her drop her: (he's on the family—her own family side)—but what is held out to make her *sacrifice* her, give up trying to put her through and look out only for herself. The way Rose *works* this, in the tale, is of course a thing to be made intensely dramatic and ironic in the play. Mrs. Vaughan-Vesey becomes—can only become—important in the play. On the other hand the family must be reconstituted—the grandmother doesn't seem to me to be what I can find *de mieux*. Aunt Julia—yes, a representative of property etc.—another sister, yes—a representative of the opposite—the proper course (comedy-character—with secret flirtation of her own verging on scandal)—and possibly, conceivably, the *father?* No; I think not—the struggle isn't with him, it's with the world, I mean that from the moment it's not a question of making *him* reaccept her mother, he can only be awkwardly placed in the action. Therefore he's out of it, and one gets by that the benefit of his inheritance for Rose—her means, the thing that makes her valuable. She must sacrifice money—yes; that is her *family* prospect. But she must sacrifice a *lover*—or have the question of sacrificing him above all. I seem to see a pretty part that would make a *third* suitor—and perhaps the successful one: the part of a clever *observant,* sincere fellow (the real "hero") who has had no *parti-pris* about her in advance and who is won to help her by the gallantry of her course. The thing assumed here (D.V.) is an action in which he *may* help her—help her, say, with the lover, who constitutes a difficulty. I seem to see all sorts of things—they swarm upon me. I see Aunt Julia as an *uncle,* a rich, intolerant bachelor, to diminish the number of women (Rose 1, sister 2, Mrs. Tramore 3, Mrs. Vaughan-Vesey 4, Lady Maresfield 5). In the way of men there would seem to be: The Hero, Bertram Jay (2), Guy Mangler (3), the Ex-Lover (4) and the young man whom her sister (Edith) has her flirtation with (5). I must add that Lady Maresfield and Mrs. Vaughan-Vesey may be resolved into one person, and this may also happen to the "hero" and Bertram Jay. (I don't, I confess, just in a glance, at all see *that* duplication.) Nor at the first blush is the role of the lover very apparent to me. Of course at the first blush there is nothing but the germ of the subject: I mean a kind of *faith* in it, enveloped in a mist of confusion. Out of the mist there looms, somehow, a first act in which the various things (and more) are settled that are settled in the first chapter of the tale. I vaguely see a place in which a meeting of the various people is possible: an hotel in Switzerland, at Aix-les-Bains—or at the Italian lakes. The girl here is *introduced* to her mother, made acquainted with her, has the mother's situation revealed to her. She sees her cold-shouldered etc. She is shocked, pained by it—affected, in a word, as also is in the tale, and is moved to take up the position she takes in the tale. What depends upon it—what she loses by it, made clear to her. The Maresfield-Vesey interest must be, here, the cold-shoulderers, and *their* evolution, their transition is that they see, later, how she draws. The "observant" suitor (the added one) plays, practices, ironizes as I may say, on the situation in conjunction with Mrs. V.-V.—or on *her* in conjunction with the situation. *He* believes in the girl, is charmed, has no doubts. By making him so, however, I lose the chance of bringing him over—making him serve her work, as Rose makes Captain Jay in the tale. There may be a way of attaching this personage— in some way—to Mrs. Tramore. I see that the difficulty—one of them, and the main one, in what the story gives at least—is the sufficiently unheroic character of Bertram Jay. He doesn't *do*—as he is—for the hero. And yet his being as he is, is important for the comedy interest. Can't I imagine the other fellow, the inserted personage, making Rose's acquaintance for the *first* time on the very occasion of this crisis of the first act. He's an outsider when the curtain rises— but drawn into the action by the very effect of her behaviour. If I keep the ex-lover, discredited, disreputable now (may there not be a question of his *marrying* her (Mrs. Tramore) now that her husband is dead?—marrying her to satisfy the claims of respectability, the standards of the Philistines) if I keep him, I say, and keep him as an annoyance, a mortification to Mrs. Tramore, I get a kind of *lien* for the new hero, a link of introduction or attachment. I am wondering in other words whether an entrance may not be found for him, and after an entrance a strong and valid part, as a kind of relative, a cousin, of the lover, to whom Mrs. Tramore has applied, to whom she has appealed, to interfere, to relieve her of him, to help her to get rid of him. He is on the spot for that purpose, and his situation gives him his vision of Rose. Two alternatives arise (for *me*): the idea of making Mrs. Tramore's lover a perfect *bore* of fidelity, desiring to *marry* Mrs. T; while she now *doesn't* want that, has outlived the phase of desiring it; and the idea of her wanting it and having sent for New

Hero, his kinsman, to force it on, and then been moved to a different determination by the entrance into her life of her daughter. The idea would be here that the girl conceives the bold and superior design of acting for mother *without* the marriage—putting her through *herself*, independently, without it; on the basis of disliking so the poor ex-lover. Both she *and* his kinsman dislike him: they *meet* on *that*. Ignominy—satiric treatment—of the social view, the social standard, that makes it the condition—*et encore!*

x   x   x

One seems, yes, to see, *à peu près*, a first act, of a good deal of life: but not at an hotel abroad, on second thoughts, no. The two sisters have been living abroad—with their father: partly *on account of* their mother, who is in England and whose presence there has been a reason for their keeping away. They only know—Rose only knows, what this father has *bien voulu* tell them about her. The father dies—they have a prim, rich, fussy bachelor uncle to whom they devolve more or less by this circumstance. He goes for them—or they come back, and the first act takes place in his house in London just after their return. It is abroad—during her last year—that Rose has met Bertram Jay. It is the proper, conventional, worldly uncle who has embraced the idea of Mrs. Tramore's now marrying her former lover—regularising her position. He has, fatuously, busy-bodily *sent* for the lover to express to him, thus opportunely, his views on this subject. The lover, for reasons, has sent his kinsman—a cleverer, more creditable, more distinguished person—to treat, to converse, to see *de quoi il s'agit*, etc. This is *his* introduction to Rose, his first encounter with her. Happy thought—that is it seems to twitch my sleeve as one. Keep the ex-lover personally out of the play altogether—make him present, like Mme Benoîton,[1] only by reference and contention. So the kinsman, the new lover, the Hero, is hereby brought. Mrs. Tramore is brought, in the simplest and most natural way in the world, by her own act. She has meditated, planned her visit as a kind of bold, calculated *coup*—she has had in mind its "*effect*" on her daughter—as a means of capturing her, of making a good impression on her, before a bad one is made by the representations and machinations of others. She is ignorant of Mr. Tramore's (her brother-in-law's,) *ingérence*—and is confronted now for the first time with the machinery set in motion, in the name of the grotesque proprieties, to make her (and *encore* only questionably!) tidy herself up by this tardy union. It is *part* of the ground—this new knowledge, this present pressure, on which she meets her daughter. Mrs. Vaughan-Vesey has come, partly at Mr. Tramore's instance and partly at that of her own speculations—to see what can be done for her brother Guy Maresfield. It is for her, also, perhaps—or doubtless—that Mr. Tramore has sent as a form of feminine support, of chaperonage, to advise about the girls and look in particular after Edith.

x   x   x

[1] In *La Famille Benoîton*, five-act play by Victorien Sardou (1831–1908), Mme Benoîton, mother of the family is alluded to but never appears on stage.

I reflect, however, that it may be a mistake to reduce Lady Maresfield and Mrs. Vaughan-Vesey to a common identity. Don't I sacrifice, thereby, lose something indispensable? The number of women needn't disturb me so much— it's a part of the essence of the subject, which represents, for Rose, a struggle with society. I don't get my "society" if I make my women too few. Lady Maresfield and her daughter perform totally different, perform opposed functions. Mrs. V.V. is the intensely modern woman who is with Rose etc. Let me, therefore, begin with, try to see Lady M. in first act, alone. She needn't even have been "sent for" by Mr. Tramore: she has come, by her own officiousness etc. on speculation. She wants to get Rose for her younger son. Her opposition, her scandalization, when she hears or divines what Rose forfeits. This counts as part of the public opinion that the girl has to face and fight. Then *elle se rabat,* for Guy, on Edith—but with the divided mind of watching to see how it turns out for Rose, and if she (Rose) may not perhaps get, somehow, from her mother, *more* than she forfeits from her uncle. The young Edith, meanwhile, flirtatious and hypocritical, which her sister is not, is meanwhile, carrying on surreptitious commerce with some detrimental—some German music-master, or some such person. Make Bertram Jay by no means military—make the hero military if you like. Bertram Jay becomes political and parliamentary. He becomes the timid, the prudent, the shockable lover as contrasted with the brave. He is another of the "social forces" with which the girl has to count. But in this connection, of course, one sees rise before one the question, the difficulty of the "love-interest" and the marriage-question from the moment the serious side of this matter is taken from the circumspect lover and attached to another man. In the story the girl *uses* Bertram Jay, as it were—and then, later, marries him. To make her marry the Hero *without* using him offers, of course, infirmities. He *must* be an *agent,* in other words; and we shall manage that. Bertram Jay is a *comedy-agent,* and a reluctant and unwilling one; and the Hero is a sentimental agent—an eager and sympathetic, or at least clever, wise, observant and sustaining one. He must find his activity partly in being the showman of the human spectacle. Bertram Jay drops out by being too cautious, *too* anxious, too tactless, too parliamentary. He must fail her on a crucial occasion, when, instead, she finds the Hero there. This occasion must be the climax of an action extremely *corvée,* thoroughly overhauled and solidified. In the simplest expression it consists of the effort of the girl to *place* her mother. The intensity and the interest of this effect depend largely upon the question of *where* she wants to place her. This point, this *where,* must become supremely and admirably concrete in the third act. It must be a great occasion—it must have high importance. It must be something higher than Lady Maresfield—something for which Mrs. V.V. is operative in the spirit she exhibits in the tale. Is it a great party at a Duchess's—is it something more than a party? Is it a charity bazaar?

x   x   x

June 6th, 1893.

I postpone, I drop the above for the hour *pour me recolleter* with the question of the Scenario sketched for Compton, and as to which it is tolerably clear that, as regards complexity of action, it can be considerably improved. It can be improved with patience—it can be improved with resolution and devotion and above all it can be improved with *reflection.* The main little mass of it is there, but something more is wanted—and I must take some quiet creative hour (ah, quiet creative hours—their very name in this general connection is sweet!) to thresh that out. Little by little, D.V., the right thing will come. As I in a primary way rest my eyes on it, I seem to see the required, the augmented interest to the . . . [the manuscript breaks off at this point].

Guy Domville
1893

EDITOR'S FOREWORD

The Author and the Matinee Idol

Guy Domville was written by Henry James during the summer of 1893 at Ramsgate on the Channel for George Alexander, the popular and highly successful young manager of the St. James's Theatre. Alexander's production of *The Second Mrs. Tanqueray* had convinced James that he had at last found a manager for whom he could do a serious play. He actually discussed three play projects with Alexander and promised him scenarios of all of them: the first was a romantic costume play about a young man destined for the priesthood; the second was "a three-act comedy, pure and simple" and the third "a three-act contemporary play, less purely a comedy, but on a subject very beautiful to my sense. . . ." The first subject appealed to James, however, and instead of submitting his three "exhibits" he sent Alexander a completed first act of the play about the priestly candidate and a scenario of the remaining two acts. Alexander seems to have liked it, for they began to discuss terms almost immediately.

The germ of *Guy Domville* had been noted by James a year earlier at Lausanne. He had just spent some days in Venice, after a journey through Italy with Paul Bourget and his wife, and he wrote in his notebook:

> Situation of that once-upon-a-time member of an old Venetian family (I forget which), who had become a monk, and who was taken almost forcibly out of his convent and brought back into the world in order to keep the family from becoming extinct. He was the last *rejeton*—it was absolutely *necessary* for him to marry. Adapt this somehow or other to today.

Immediately below this note, in one of the lists of names James regularly entered in his notebook for use in his tales and plays, occurs the name Domville. The subject of the play touched the novelist's life closely, since it dealt with the conflict of many of his heroes—the worldly life versus the dedicated life, compromise with "success" versus renunciation. *Guy Domville* was a reiteration of the problems presented in *The Tragic Muse*, and it foreshadowed another tale James was to write some years later, *The Great Good Place*, whose hero, George Dane, a writer (with initials similar to Guy Domville's) is translated in a dream from worldly pressures to a monastery-like retreat "some great abode of an Order, some mild Monte Cassino, some Grande Chartreuse . . ." The name Dane figures in the same list as Domville, and we may speculate that in James's mind it may have been associated with Dane Hall at Harvard where James himself made the crucial decision of his life—renunciation of Law for

Letters—which he describes, in an as yet unpublished autobiographical fragment as "the turning point of my life."

Guy Domville (as has already been suggested in the introduction to this
volume) also, on another level, was a projection of James's actual conflict in
the theatre—that is the "world" represented by London "show business" of
the time and the alternative, ever possible for James, of retreat to his literary
study. Many other elements enter into the creation of this play: the novelist's
deep interest in Catholicism as a "refuge" and a retreat, his own sense of
"dedication" to his art expressed in several of his tales of the literary life, and
notably in *The Lesson of the Master,* in which James half-humorously, half-
seriously advocated celibacy for the artist; his fantasy of the artist as a double-
personality, moving in the world, on the one hand, but living, on the other
hand, a separate anchorite life in the privacy of his study (*Benvolio, The Private Life*), his deep sense that the fraternity of letters constituted an "Order" of
the pledged and dedicated, analogous to the priesthood. Students of "sources"
might find also a congruity between *Guy Domville* and the fact that the one
novel of his friend Howells which James reviewed twice in one month was
A Foregone Conclusion—the story of a Venetian priest who falls in love with
an American girl and is unable to resolve his conflict between the spirit and
the flesh.

The partnership of Henry James and George Alexander represented the
linking of a fastidious man of letters with a dapper matinee idol. Henry Irving
had once remarked to Alexander at a rehearsal, "Now Alexander, not quite
so much Piccadilly." The actor-manager *was* "Piccadilly" to his fingertips—a
dandy of the 1890's endowed by nature with straight-cut, handsome features
and an excellent pair of legs that made him partial to costume pieces. When
he was not displaying his legs in breeches of another era or in riding boots, he
wore the most perfectly creased trousers in the West End; in an era when trousers
were worn baggy Alexander's were pressed to perfection. They were the talk of
the clubs and the subject of cartoons in *Punch*. Alexander's trousers were a distinct part of a man variously described as a tailor's dummy and hard-headed
businessman; but for his acting the critics had chary praise. "Mr. Alexander,"
wrote Bernard Shaw of one of his performances, "gave us a finished impersona-
tion of Mr. George Alexander." Nevertheless he had his loyal following, and
many a lady sighed away an afternoon over his handsome dashing manner.

Decidedly Alexander was not a man of large imagination; he compensated
for it by kind of furious efficiency. His theatre was a model of good management. If he lacked the depth and understanding that makes for a great actor,
if he was what the critics tend to describe when they feel charitable as "competent," he was nevertheless pleasant, affable, shrewd. He had taken the measure
of his talents and knew how to make the most of them. He was careful to
surround himself with good actors, but careful, too, that he should not be
eclipsed. In one notable instance he was, and his quarrels with Mrs. Patrick
Campbell, on stage and off—the meeting of a tempestuous and passionate

actress with a cool and calculating man of attitudes—are a part of the theatrical history of the 1890's. Alexander's loyal "fans" would fill his house for a month even if his play were pronounced a failure. And he showed, on the whole, considerable discrimination in his choice of plays—so long as they had good strutting parts for him.

Alexander's terms, as might be expected in the case of such a hard-headed businessman, were stiff. He offered James, as Daly had done, £5 a night, but placed a ceiling of £2,000 on royalties with full rights in the play to go to him after the ceiling was attained. "I should be obliged to you if you can put the case to me more dazzlingly another way," the author wrote to the matinee idol. We do not know how "dazzingly" Alexander finally put it. James brought the completed play to him during the autumn of 1893 in the hope of an early production after the run of *Mrs. Tanqueray*. To his chagrin he now discovered that Alexander was committed to do a play by Henry Arthur Jones ahead of his own. This meant a long wait. James had, at this time, his difference with Augustin Daly over *Disengaged,* and this accumulation of discouragements and delays caused him to write that he would wage the theatrical struggle for "one year more" and then, if no sign of victory were forthcoming, he would return to the independent courses of fiction.

It took exactly another year. Alexander finally started rehearsing the play in December 1894. A few weeks before rehearsals began, the author and the actor-manager went over the script. Alexander asked for the elimination of certain parts and certain changes in his role. This was, Henry wrote to his brother, the "hideous, supreme ordeal," and later he exclaimed of *Guy Domville,* "Oh, the mutilated, brutally simplified, massacred little play!" In October 1894 a few acting copies of the play were printed "in intense secrecy, for use in the theatre." (These have since become valuable collectors' items.) Jones's *The Masqueraders* ended its run in November, and Alexander promptly went down with an attack of German measles, while the novelist fretted through the two more weeks of unexpected delay. The first reading of the play to the assembled cast took place on Friday, December 7, 1894, and Henry James, who had looked forward to this moment, was forced by a sore throat to abdicate in favor of Alexander, and sit by silently while the actor-manager went over the piece, scene by scene and act by act.

His letters of the next month tell the story of the rehearsals and of his mounting agitation, as, day after day and, toward the end, twice a day, he went to the St. James's, sat alone in the dim theatre, watching his work assume shape and proferring criticisms and suggestions. The cast was good. Henry wrote to his brother that the play would be "exquisitely mounted, dressed &c and as well acted as London can act. My only anxiety is as to how Alexander will carry the weight of his own part—which is a very beautiful and interesting one. So awfully much depends on him."

The play had originally been titled *The Hero,* then tentatively *Guy Domville,* and finally this title was kept although Henry wrote to William, "I hate it."

He made the concession to Alexander, however, since "the said Guy Domville is himself." James went on to ask his brother to "unite in family prayer for me on Saturday, January 5 at 8.30 . . . spare a thought to the lone and nervous dramatic artist." On New Year's Day 1895 he wrote to Mrs. Bell that "the dew of agony is already on my brow. . . ." He began to debate whether he should attend his first night. In talk with Edmund Gosse it was suggested that James should remain in a near-by pub and beguile the "tremulous" hours between 8:30 and 11. On January 3, the novelist announced, "I have changed my policy. I recognize that the only way for me to arrive at 10 o'clock with any patience is to *do* something active or at least positive; so I have had the luminous idea of going to see some other play." He added: "I am more or less, already under chloroform."

The Last of the Domvilles

The first in the series of unusual incidents that accompanied the opening night of *Guy Domville* occurred on the afternoon of the climactic day at the Sloane Street post office in Chelsea. Two ladies, whose identity was never established, created a flurry among the postal employes by dispatching an unsigned telegram to George Alexander: "With hearty wishes for a complete failure." Alexander received the message but he was merciful. He did not show it to his nervous and excited author until after the performance.

Henry James had seldom been in such a state of agitation. The tension preceding *The American* seemed trivial by comparison. As on the previous occasion, in the late afternoon, he tried to walk away from his nerves. Finally he returned to his De Vere Gardens flat and dashed off a series of letters to friends and relatives. To William James he mailed one of the *Guy Domville* playbills and wrote to him: "I am counting on some Psychical intervention from you—this is really the time to show your stuff. . . . The omens, Thank God, are decently good. But what are omens? *Domine in manus tuas—!* This is a time when a man wants a religion . . . my hand shakes and I can only write that I am your plucky, but, all the same, lonely and terrified Henry." The letter is, indeed, in a pathetically shaky and almost illegible hand.

James had selected the theatre and the play with which to fill the evening while his own play would be running its course. He would go to the Haymarket to see Oscar Wilde's *An Ideal Husband.* It was an easy walk to Alexander's theatre. He had never been one of Oscar Wilde's admirers, but he had followed his career with a kind of fascinated amazement. Wilde, at the time of *Guy Domville,* was at the height of his fame—and within a few weeks of his tragic trial. At the Haymarket, James found himself sitting in his stall amid a fashionable audience. He listened to the Oscarisms and was increasingly unnerved by the audience's delighted laughter. The epigrams burst like well-timed firecrackers. "Men can be analyzed, women merely adored." "Only dull people are brilliant at breakfast." "Morality is simply the attitude we adopt toward people whom we personally dislike." Henry James's agitation grew rather than diminished. The play did not have the soothing effect he had anticipated. He felt uneasy, lonely, afraid. His anxieties gave way to genuine alarm. It amounted, one might say, to a state of panic.

While the author of *Guy Domville* sat uneasily in his stall at the Haymarket, carriage after carriage was depositing ladies in rich wraps and shimmering gowns and well-groomed, fashionably dressed gentlemen before the St. James's Theatre. The combination of a George Alexander first night and the first original play by the distinguished American who had chosen to make his home in England, had proved irresistible to the London social world. It was an audience of celebrities, one of the most distinguished ever to be assembled in a London theatre.

There was one section which laid no claim to distinction. It had queued up for some hours in the raw, biting cold at the entrances to the pit and gallery, shivering and stamping its feet as it waited for the doors to open. It was doubtful whether many of these theatregoers had ever heard of Henry James. They came in search of an evening's entertainment. They knew they could rely on "Alick." Any play with "Alick" in it was worth seeing.

Inside, the theatre was bright and cheerful. Alexander took pride in an up-to-date house ("the theatre is lighted by electricity," the playbills proudly announced). There was a rustle of silks as the elaborately attired ladies, in glistening jewelry, took their places, and a hither-and-thithering in the aisles and between the boxes. Necks were craned to see the celebrities. There seem to have been only celebrities in the stalls that night.

Looking at this brilliant house, in the bright light of its new electric bulbs, we see the great artists of London there, Sir Edward Burne-Jones, bearded and sedate; the academician Sir Frederick Leighton, whose ponderous personality Henry James had embodied in a short story three years earlier; George Frederick Watts, creator of great, elaborate and much-admired canvasses; George du Maurier, one of James's closest friends, nearing the end of his unusual career first as cartoonist for *Punch* and then as the author of *Peter Ibbetson* and *Trilby;* the fashionable illustrators Frank D. Millet and Alfred Parsons. John Singer Sargent has come to see the work of his countryman, accompanied by the slim and handsome W. Graham Robertson, a gifted artist and writer whose portrait Sargent had painted two years earlier and exhibited with much success.

The author's loyal literary lady friends are there in force: Mrs. W. K. Clifford, novelist and playwright; Mrs. Humphry Ward, whose success in the literary market was a Victorian phenomenon, Mrs. Hugh Bell, who had had a play produced at the Théâtre Français. The walrus-mustached, ubiquitous man of letters, Edmund Gosse, is there almost as excited as James himself; and the novelist's compatriot, F. Marion Crawford; the journalist H. D. Traill and Thomas Anstey Guthrie ("F. Anstey") novelist and a valued contributor to

Punch; William Lestocq, actor, dramatist, manager; Elizabeth Robins, who has come with Mrs. Bell, and Kate and Florence Terry, Ellen's sisters, who will at the rise of the curtain be watching another sister, Marion, in the play. There are other popular actresses in the house as well: Mrs. Bernard Beere and Fanny Brough, and Lily Hanbury, who is Mrs. Alexander's guest, sitting with her in the special box that Mrs. Alexander occupies on all of "Alick's" first nights. It commands a perfect view of the stage—and of her handsome husband.

Most of the members of that audience could have pointed out three of London's first-rank dramatic critics—William Archer of the *World,* A. B. Walkley, then of the *Star* (later of the *Times*) and the irascible Ibsen-hater, Clement Scott of the *Daily Telegraph.* Some would have pointed also to a red-bearded Bernard Shaw, who sat in the stalls in a modest brown jacket suit while most of his critical colleagues wore boiled shirts and black or white ties. He was then better known to the operagoers at Covent Garden as a vigorous and discriminating music critic than as a man of the theatre. Shaw's face was very white and his whiskers very red. He had already offered substantial proof of his creative ability, but his major works were yet to be written. *Widowers' Houses* had been produced by J. T. Grein at the Independent Theatre and *Arms and the Man* at the Avenue. That very week Shaw had ceased to write musical criticism for the *World* and agreed to do dramatic criticism for Frank Harris on the *Saturday Review.* He had entered upon his critical duties four days earlier. *Guy Domville* was the third play he reviewed.

Few would have pointed to young H. G. Wells. Mr. Wells, more conformist than Mr. Shaw, came dressed in a brand-new evening suit, made for him at twenty-four hours' notice three days before when he had discovered that he was to be the *Pall Mall Gazette* drama critic. He had reviewed *An Ideal Husband* two nights before; this was his second play and he was not destined to do many more, for he had already sold *The Time Machine* for £100 and its publication a few weeks later was to start him on the long and famous road in English letters which he subsequently travelled. Wells was never much interested in the theatre; it seemed to him artificial and without significance in a world of scientific realities. He was too stubborn a realist to accept the make-believe that goes on behind the footlights and too rigorous a journalist to care for an "art" whose essence is illusion. Years later he said that the incidents of this night at the St. James's only confirmed his distaste for the theatre. He never seriously tried to write a play. "I was forming a conception of a new sort of human community with an unprecedented way of life and it seemed to me to be a minor detail whether this boxed-up performance of plays, would occur at all in that ampler existence I anticipated." Wells's denial of the fundamental appeal of the scenic art on his utopian grounds (a form of make-believe he *was* willing to indulge in) was not shared, happily, by Shaw. He too wanted new worlds, socialist worlds, but he found he could best preach them within the boxed-up performances that Wells disdained. And great national theatres were included in Bernard Shaw's blueprints for a future world. It was on this night that Wells spoke to Shaw for the first time. They left the theatre together, walking northward to their respective lodgings.

There was still another unknown figure in that audience, almost as obscure as Wells. This was Arnold Bennett, lately come to London and then working for a magazine called *Woman* of which he eventually became editor. Bennett did not sign his name to his theatrical column, which he called "Music and Mummery." The review that he wrote of *Guy Domville* is signed Cécile.

ST. JAMES'S THEATRE.

SOLE LESSEE AND MANAGER   -   -   -   MR. GEORGE ALEXANDER.

Saturday, Jan. 5th, 1895, & Every Evening at 9,

A Play in Three Acts,

By HENRY JAMES,

ENTITLED

"GUY DOMVILLE."

Guy Domville	-	-	- Mr. GEORGE ALEXANDER
Lord Devenish	-	-	- Mr. ELLIOT
Frank Humber	-	-	- Mr. HERBERT WARING
George Round	-	(Lieutenant, R.N.)	- Mr. H. V. ESMOND
Servant	-	-	- Mr. FRANK DYALL
Mrs. Peverel	-	-	- Miss MARION TERRY
Mrs. Domville	-	-	- Mrs. EDWARD SAKER
Mary Brasier	-	-	- Miss EVELYN MILLARD
Fanny	-	-	- Miss IRENE VANBRUGH
Milliners	-	{	Miss BLANCHE WILMOT / Miss VIOLET LYSTER

PERIOD   -   -   1780.

Act I.	- - -	THE GARDEN AT PORCHES
Act II.	-	MRS. DOMVILLE'S RESIDENCE AT RICHMOND
Act III.	- - -	AN INTERIOR AT PORCHES

G.B.S., for so Shaw signed his reviews, was thirty-nine. Wells was twenty-nine, Bennett twenty-eight. They sat unknown to each other among the greater celebrities of the time, waiting for the play to begin.

The orchestra fussed its way through the "Guy Domville Prelude," a special concoction for the occasion by Walter Slaughter, the orchestra's conductor. There was a curtain raiser, *Too Many by Half* by Julian Field, which gave the latecomers some leeway, and which Shaw described as "deftly turned out from old and seasoned materials," and "capital fun for the audience." The evening at least began on a note of laughter.

The curtain rose on one of George Alexander's expensive and elaborately realistic settings which were the pride of his management. The scene was a garden at Porches, the time 1780. Clustering rose bushes and honeysuckle trailed round quaint lattice windows; borders of multi-colored flowers and a close-cut privet hedge set a tone of peaceful rural charm. In this setting the dramatist developed with great simplicity his delicate tale of love and renunciation, of a young man called upon to choose between a career in the Church and his obligation to his family to marry and perpetuate his line—a young man who, unaware of his love for the heroine, and of her love for him, pleads with her to lend an attentive ear to the suit of his best friend. The graceful and rhythmic dialogue of the first act delighted the audience. Marion Terry, as Mrs. Peverel, the object of Frank Humber's and Guy Domville's love, was an appealing figure. She wore a silken gown of pale gray, bordered with tiny frills and caught in to the waist by black velvet bows. She also wore a quaint loosely hanging jacket, with muslin collar and ruched edges; and her Leghorn hat was tied by narrow black velvet strings. Her voice, her manner, her warmth, her feeling—and she seems to have put a great deal of feeling into the part—charmed everyone. To Guy, who is the tutor of her young son, she is a maternal image he does not even dare to admit to himself he loves. Alexander, in sober black raiment, as befits a young churchman, provided a contrasting figure on the brightly lit stage. The actors caught and sustained the romantic mood. The dialogue fell with a pleasing sound on the music critic's ears of Bernard Shaw, who described it "as grateful to my ear as the music of Mozart's *Entführung aus dem Serail* would be after a year of *Ernani* and *Il Trovatore*."

Temptation arrived in the form of Lord Devenish, a designing, evil, Mephistophelian figure played by W. G. Elliot with operatic broadness. A. B. Walkley spoke of his acting as "a prolonged grimace, a caricature, too uniformly in the violent style of Hogarth," while Shaw accused him of "withering all sense and music of Mr. James's lines with a diction which I forbear to describe." The *St. James Gazette* suggested that the part might be rendered a "little less glaringly obnoxious" and *Today* said flatly: "Willie Elliot was hopelessly at sea as a wicked nobleman and looked as if he belonged to a comic ballet and had strayed into the St. James's by mistake." (In his memoirs, years later, Elliot recalled that during rehearsals James had asked him to try to make Lord Devenish appear "as much of a gentleman as is feasible—possible—to you.")

The curtain fell, the lights came on, and a deeply stirred audience rose for the first intermission. The critics were agreed that Henry James had written a beautiful first act. They referred later to its "tender idyllic grace" and the "unforced truthfulness of the dialogue." William Archer found it a "masterly and exquisite piece of emotional comedy"; Arnold Bennett said that it was "studded with gems of dialogue" and A. B. Walkley spoke of it as "one of the most fragrant first acts I know, nimbly and sweetly recommending itself to the senses." The anonymous critic of the *Graphic* wrote: "What may not be hoped for from a dramatist who can take us so far away from the conventionalities of the professional playwright, impress on the spectator with so little apparent effort the relations of his various personages, and awaken our sympathies by means so simple and so legitimate."

Henry James, sitting in the Haymarket, uncomfortably squirming at the Oscarisms, at this moment was unaware of the extent to which he had moved his audience and of the admiration he had evoked. Perhaps it was just as well.

Whatever may have been hoped for from the author of such a first act was not the act that followed.

The plot suddenly thickened. The scene was the dower house of Mrs. Domville, a villa at Richmond. The Guy Domville who faced the audience here was not the devout and noble character of the first act. He was a young man who, during the three months that elapsed between the acts, had been learning the way of the world from Lord Devenish. Clad in the costume of a dandy, full of swagger and talk of cards, the young churchman had been converted with great rapidity into a young blade addicted to the joys of good living, and embroiled now in a situation filled with intrigue.

In forsaking the simplicity of his first act Henry James had yielded to the clap-trap of artificial drama, to the *ficelle* structure of Sardou and the other dramatists he had studied with such assiduity at the Théâtre Français. He had discarded for the entire act two of his best personages, Frank Humber and Mrs. Peverel. And this after arousing such acute interest in his love story. His hero had been brought face to face with a series of ill-motivated and quite irrelevant situations. The mood created by the first act had been utterly destroyed.

It is no wonder that some members of the audience began to fidget; there was some coughing, and coughing in an audience under such circumstances is contagious: an unmistakeable sign that things are not "going." To no one is this clearer than to the actors themselves, who are invariably attuned to every fluctuation in an audience's mood. We must allow for first night nervousness, and such nervousness as existed was aggravated by the tension and it, in turn, increased the restlessness of the audience. The cool matinee idol, George Alexander, gave way to his feelings by the workings of his mouth. John Singer Sargent kept whispering to Graham Robertson: "Why does he open his mouth on one side like that? It makes his face all crooked."

Such tension requires but a single incident to shatter the make-believe of theatre. It came in a curious and unexpected form, as a result of those very costumes that were the pride of the play. Mrs. Edward Saker, in the role of the dowager Mrs. Domville, appeared in what Shaw described as a "falstaffian make-up." She wore an elaborate gown of the period and a tall velvet hat shaped like a muff, towering on her head under nodding plumes. However accurate this costume was historically, it struck an incongrous note of caricature for a pit and gallery whose patience was being sorely tried by an excess of stage business. The critics later said that beauty had been sacrificed to strict accuracy in costume; that, however, was really beside the point. The truth was that part of the audience already had been lost to the play. A pleased audience is always willing to forgive, and is not disturbed for too long by errors in costume. But this audience was ready to titter as well as to cough. From somewhere in the back a voice yielded a line from the popular song, "Where Did You Get That Hat." Very little was required to unnerve Mrs. Saker, who was managing with some difficulty her voluminous skirt of black satin over a *panier* crinoline of huge dimensions. The impression given Graham Robertson, himself a successful costume designer, was that "the dress was particularly fine, but it wanted wearing; the huge hoop, and great black hat perched upon a little frilled undercap should have been carried by one filled with the pride of them and the consciousness of their beauty." Mrs. Saker found it difficult to have either pride or dignity. She tried instead to be self-effacing—a difficult thing with a costume that fills a large area on the stage, and when one's plumes wave with every toss of the head. Titter succeeded upon titter. The pit and gallery became unruly, like a group of children facing an object of derision. The audience was now participating in the play, reaching across the footlights to the actors instead of being reached by them—and with the childish cruelty that mass hostility frequently assumes.

Unfortunately Henry James gave further provocation in his drinking scene. James had written Alexander that this scene could only be judged after the test of rehearsal. It had stood that preliminary test, but in the present circumstances its feeble comedy became a glaring weakness, an excrescence upon the surface of the play. It is easy to see what the dramatist had intended. Years earlier, at the Théâtre Français, he had seen Emile Augier's *L'Aventurière* and relished the drinking scene in the second act in which Fabrice, a clever young soldier, plies Don Annibal with liquor in order to find out from him the true character of Dona Clarinde, an adventuress who is the subject of the play. James's own account of this scene, and his delight in it, shows us precisely what he wanted to do in *Guy Domville*. "The scene was played by Bressant and Regnier, and it has always remained in my mind as one of the most perfect things I have seen on the stage. The gradual action of the wine upon Don Annibal, the delicacy with which his deepening tipsiness was indicated, its intellectual rather than physical manifestations, and, in the midst of it, the fantastic conceit which made him think that he was winding his fellow drinker round his fingers—all this was exquisitely rendered." But James admitted that, on the whole, drunkenness on the stage was "both dreary and disgusting."

With perfectly serious intent Henry James asked of his two characters to attempt to make each other drunk while each was shamming drunkenness. As actually performed there was a great deal of surreptitious disposal of the drinks in flower pots—a scene that Bernard Shaw remembered and recounted many years later. What was more, Alexander played it, in the words of Shaw, "with the sobriety of desperation."

The scene was so roundly condemned in the press that Henry James lost no time in eliminating it from the play. One critic suggested that he might have eliminated the entire act.

The evening was lost for Henry James, but he was still at the Haymarket and spared the torment of this knowledge. A miracle was needed to save it, and the third act, although it recaptured some of the charm of the first, did not possess miraculous qualities. The curtain rose on the interior at Porches. A solemn-looking grandfather clock presided over the room; there were white shelves built of solid wood, with quaintly designed china upon them; the doors were likewise solid, and they had genuine brass knobs. Through an open lattice one could see bright sunshine and be reminded that the charming garden of Act I lay just outside. Alexander invariably insisted upon a maximum of reality. Nothing was left to the imagination. But the actors could no longer restore reality to their lines.

The play ended on a touching and dramatically effective scene of parting. In taking leave, Guy once again commends Mrs. Peverel to the care of Frank Humber. The last lines, with their delicate phrasing and calculated repetitions, spoken by actors less nervous and irritated than were Alexander and his cast on this night, could be extraordinarily moving, in spite of all the confusion that had gone before.

But the audience's sympathies were not with Guy. The audience tended to agree with Devenish that Guy didn't deserve to know of Mrs. Peverel's love. *She* had won the affection of the audience and the hero was rejecting her—however noble his acceptance of the religious alternative. His sense of his vocation had been insufficiently strong when it was a question of family name and a worldly marriage; and yet it became strong when confronted with a deep and devoted love such as Mrs. Peverel's. This seemed to the greater part of the audience the height of perversity. In a James novel all this would have been explained in a way that it could not be on the stage. In the novel Henry James would have taken us into the minds of his characters and revealed to us, in particular, the nature of Guy's deep conflict. On the stage Guy is merely uncertain, lacking in steadfastness, a prey to temptation, easily turned from one course to another so that we begin to doubt whether he should take orders without a deep searching of his religious feelings. To the audience his conduct could seem only capricious and arbitrary.

The most direct expression of the audience's impatience came in the temporarily hushed house when Alexander, with a great show of feeling, delivered himself of the speech:

"I'm the last, my lord, of the Domvilles. . . ."

A voice from the gallery burst into the stillness.

"It's a bloody good thing y'are."

At the Haymarket, Henry James had listened to the last epigrams and to the overwhelming applause from the audience. He came out into the cold night and threaded his way through the line of carriages. He walked down the short street leading into St. James's Square, his heart beating rapidly, anxious, disturbed, overcome with fear. Oscar Wilde's play had struck him as helpless, crude, clumsy, feeble, vulgar. He later threw all these adjectives at it. And yet it had been accepted by the audience, accepted with eagerness, with laughter, with unstinted applause. Its success, it seemed to Henry James, could only be an ill omen for *Guy Domville*.

The thought caused him to stop in the middle of St. James's Square, trans-fixed and paralyzed "by the terror of this probability." He was afraid to go on and learn more.

We can believe him. We can believe him because he had good reason to feel unsure himself in the theatre, because he knew the sort of play he had written, because he was possessed by the anxieties of a man repeatedly rejected by a wider public of readers, repeatedly rejected by his managers—and yet trying his utmost to please—a man afraid and lonely in the cold and dreary London world that closed about him that night and through which the carriages were rolling on all sides as Piccadilly came to life at the after-theatre hour. Henry James, standing in the middle of the Square, suddenly found himself asking, with a sinking heart, as he thought of Oscar's play:

"How *can* my piece do anything with a public with whom *that* is a success?" In his heart he knew the answer.

Henry James entered the St. James's Theatre by the stage door during the last minutes of his play. Out on the stage Alexander had backed toward the exit, somewhat awkwardly saying to Mrs. Peverel, in slowly measured accents, "Be *keynd* to him. . . . Be good to her. . . ." By nature, H. G. Wells was to recall years later, Alexander had a long face, but "at that moment with audible defeat before him, he seemed the longest and dismallest face, all face, that I have ever seen. The slowly-closing door reduced him to a strip, a line, of per-pendicular gloom."

Backstage in those hurried moments no one told Henry James of the mishaps of the second act. The actors were reassuring. The curtain came down and the frightened author faced the troubled manager. There was first a great roar of applause beyond the proscenium. Then there were curtain calls and the actors were applauded. Alexander received the usual ovation to which he was accus-tomed. Then came a brief lull, and voices, from the stalls called, "Au-thor, au-thor." A manager, possessed of a level head, would have known what to do that night. He would not have brought on Henry James. Perhaps Alexander hoped to impress the recalcitrants by introducing the author to them. Perhaps H. G. Wells was right when he speculated that a "spasm of hate for the writer" must have seized Alexander. We shall never know what prompted Alexander to act as he did. He took Henry James by the hand and led him into the bright glare of the footlights.

What followed can be told only in the words of the man who lived through that moment ". . . all the forces of civilization in the house waged a battle of the most gallant, prolonged and sustained applause with the hoots and jeers and catcalls of the roughs, whose roars (like those of a cage of beasts at some infernal 'zoo') were only exacerbated . . . by the conflict. It was a cheering scene, as you may imagine, for a nervous, sensitive, author to face. . . ." And again: "I no sooner found myself in the presence of those yelling barbarians . . . and learned what could be the savagery of their disappointment that one wasn't perfectly the *same* as everything else they had ever seen, than the dream and delusion of my having made a successful appeal to the cosy, childlike, naif, domestic British imagination . . . dropped from me in the twinkling of an eye."

It seemed to some of the spectators that they stood there, the matinee idol and the author, for hours, while sections of the audience acted out the Miltonic lines,

> . . . from innumerable tongues,
> A dismal universal *hiss,* the sound
> Of public scorn.

It was not universal in this case, but the scorn was painfully audible. The last thing that Henry James, a long-rejected, little-read author could face with equanimity, was public scorn. Bernard Shaw, trained in the give-and-take of Hyde Park, could shout back with genial, good humor at the lone individual who hissed *Arms and the Man* amid general applause: "Personally I agree with my friend in the gallery—but what can we two do against so many?" Henry James was too involved in this production, personally, emotionally, to find his tongue at this crucial moment; too eager for the audience's appreciation to be scornful, as Wilde might have been, too bewildered to have done what Charles Lamb did many years before—joined in the hissing of his own play. He stood there thunderstruck. The dark beard framed a half-open mouth, set off the pallor of the cheeks, the shocked stare that some witnesses described as "scornful coolness" and others as displaying such quiet gallantry that for a moment the applause drowned out everything. John Singer Sargent wanted to leap upon the stage to rescue his friend. It must have been a common impulse among those who knew James. Douglas Ainslie, the translator of Croce, and not a close friend of James's, relates in his memoirs a similar impulse.

Then James, in those seconds that seemed like hours, standing there white and tense, made a deprecatory gesture, a movement of the arms, a shrug of the shoulders. Alexander shifted nervously from one position to another. The novelist turned suddenly, and fled, with Alexander close behind him. Two members of the cast, Irene Vanbrugh and Franklyn Dyall, told the editor of this volume years afterwards that they never forgot the expression of agony on James's face as he came into the wings. Dyall said he seemed "green with dismay."

Pandemonium continued. The audience had no desire to leave. Phil Burne-Jones turned in his box and applauded in the direction of those who were booing. The answer was a new storm of hisses and catcalls. It was no longer an attack on Henry James or George Alexander. In these moments it became a war between the intellectual élite, the friends, the well-wishers, and the rowdies to whom the applause was an act of defiance. This was hardly the battle for *Hernani*. There were no Théophile Gautiers in the audience at the St. James's to lead a romantic revolt against the *pérruques*. Nor was Henry James a Victor Hugo or the leader of a literary movement. London audiences are not addicted, by and large, to battles over artistic ideologies such as occur with interesting regularity in Paris theatres. This was a strange and peculiar theatrical brawl, uncharacteristic of London—a sudden flare-up of anger and spite, half-lark, half-serious. It is quite unlikely that Henry James remembered that he himself had once, in an article written twenty years earlier, prescribed hissing for certain plays since "the deceived spectator ought to hold in his hand some instrument of respectful but uncompromising disapproval." Hissing, he had written, ceases to be brutal when it is directed only at the play and not at the performers. It had not occurred to him to discuss the hissing of the authors. On January 5, 1895, Henry James joined a select company of hissed authors—Sheridan, Goldsmith, Fielding, Coleridge, Hugo, Scribe, Sardou, Shaw. He was qualified now for membership in the Parisian club of hissed authors to which his friends Flaubert, Zola and Daudet had belonged. However, Henry James had hardly faced the "respectful disapproval" which he himself had advocated.

And Alexander? He was as unaccustomed to such treatment as Henry James. His few years at the St. James's had been a triumph of management and here, of a sudden, an audience—one of his invariably faithful audiences—had expressed itself with a fierce crudity, an upsurge of hostility, that was a blow to his pride and his self-assurance. "Alick lost his head," said Bernard Shaw. He left Henry James in the wings and came forward to the footlights. Now there was only applause—as if to exempt him. There were cries of "speech, speech." A voice from beyond the footlights shouted: "T'aint your fault, gov'nor, it's a rotten play."

Alexander made his speech. He spoke slowly and with emotion. "Ladies and Gentlemen: In my short career as a manager I have met with so many favors at your hands that these discordant notes tonight have hurt me very much. I can only say that we have done our very best, and if we have failed, we can only try to deserve your kindness by trying to do better in the future."

There was another flurry of applause. The incident was over. The house lights were turned on, the National Anthem was played, and the audience began to disperse. The well-dressed poured into the narrow outer lobby to wait for carriages. The gallery emptied itself into dark cold streets. An unidentified American woman, a friend of Clement Scott, rushed over to him in the lobby and said: "You all ought to be ashamed of yourselves. Won't it give you a misery ever after to have to own up that you're an Englishman."

The drama critic solemnly recorded the remark in his memoirs, without comment.

We know that Henry James walked home to his flat in 34 De Vere Gardens, Kensington, after the *Guy Domville* opening. He was weary and bruised, sickened and disgusted with what the audience had done to him. He used these words to describe his state in letters written during the ensuing days. He had passed, he wrote, "the most horrible hours of my life." Fortunately he had not planned a supper party, but he had invited certain friends to breakfast with him the next morning. These included Edmund Gosse and the Victorian novelist W. E. Norris who had come up from Torquay to see James's play. Gosse later wrote that he found James calm. The novelist remarked to his guests "at all events, I have escaped forever from the foul fiend Excision!"

Post Mortem

The battle that raged in the St. James's Theatre on the night of January 5, 1895, was transferred in the ensuing days to the press. Few papers, however, accepted the verdict of the pit and the gallery; and even when they did, as was the case with the *Times,* it was to reproach George Alexander for his curtain speech. The *Times* called it a "rueful apology." The *Daily Chronicle* called it a "painful exhibition." The Manchester *Guardian* deplored Alexander's lack of courage in apologizing "for a play which, whatever its ultimate fate, is certainly a credit to his theatre and management." But it was left to Bernard Shaw to express in vigorous language, the feelings of many who sat in the *Guy Domville* audience on that first night:

". . . Is it good sense to accuse Mr. Henry James of a want of grip of the realities of life because he gives us a hero who sacrificed his love to a strong and noble vocation for the Church? And yet when some unmannerly playgoer, untouched by either love or religion, chooses to send a derisive howl from the gallery at such a situation, we are to sorrowfully admit, if you please, that Mr. James is no dramatist, on the general ground that 'the drama's laws the drama's patrons give.' Pray, which of its patrons?—the cultivated majority who, like myself and all the ablest of my colleagues, applauded Mr. James on Saturday, or the handful of rowdies who brawled at him? It is the business of the dramatic critic to educate these dunces, not to echo them. . . . Mr. James's dramatic authorship is valid . . . his plays are *du théâtre* when the right people are in the theatre. . . ."

Some of the newspapers questioned Alexander's wisdom in bringing on Henry James when he knew the feelings of the house. Others took an intensely British attitude and decried the poor sportsmanship of the audience, especially since Henry James was a distinguished American who, as they put it, had done Britons the honor of making his home in their midst. Perhaps the most interesting post mortems were those of the *Westminster Gazette* and the periodical *Today,* edited by Jerome K. Jerome, which invited spectators to describe what had happened in the immediate areas in which they had been seated.

The letters written to these journals gave rise to the story that Henry James had in reality been the victim of a cabal directed against Alexander. It was now recalled that two ladies had sent a mysterious and hostile telegram to Alexander just before the production was scheduled to start. A spectator reported there were some twenty men in the gallery and as many in the upper boxes, the "veriest roughs" who could not possibly have paid four shillings for their seats. Each set had a leader who gave signals for the hooting. Drinks seem to have been served freely between acts. They went out and came back a little less sober each time and they were responsible for most of the noise. One rumor had it that these men had been hired by friends of an actress who was said to have been slighted by Alexander. This, however, did not explain the initial applause Alexander had received.

So the stories went. On subsequent nights during *Guy Domville*'s five-week run there was no trouble. Henry James went on the second night, choosing to sit in the gallery. He watched a hushed house give the play a cordial reception. G. W. Smalley, the New York *Tribune*'s London correspondent, who also was in the gallery that night, reported: "There was nothing there or anywhere in the house but the deepest interest and most genuine enthusiasm. . . . After the last act there was a perfect storm of applause. . . ." Alexander received many curtain calls.

One is led to the conclusion that there must have been a multiplicity of causes for the troubles of the first night. There seemed to have been "predetermined mischief," as James put it, in the audience; and the play itself—and first night accidents on stage—only contributed to the restlessness of sections of the audience. There is no evidence to show that the gallery was anti-American, or that Henry James's personality was in question. Nor is it likely that the play could have offended Catholic members of the audience. On the contrary, the Catholic critics were delighted with the piety of the work.

The critics in general were unanimous that the play was ill-motivated and that its hero was perverse and fickle—"with a strong infusion," observed the unfriendly critic of the *Times,* "of what Mr. Henry James's fellow-countrymen would call 'cussedness.'" They agreed that W. G. Elliot's over-acting and the drinking scene, the fuss of the second act and the lack of clarity in the third, as well as the cumbersome and over-elaborate costuming of Mrs. Saker, had contributed to the shipwreck of the play. Yet by and large Henry James had an excellent press. He had the complete sympathy of most of the critics. Strictures were confined to Alexander's obsequious speech and to the defective second act. There was unanimous admiration for the first act. "The man who can write that first act will some day write a play that will live," Clement Scott predicted. James had proved convincingly that he had the stuff of a playwright in him. A brilliant first act, however, is not a whole play, as Henry James himself very well knew; and his sense of failure did not permit him to accomplish what other less discouraged playwrights have achieved despite initial set-backs—write another play that would justify the promise of *Guy Domville*.

Reading the criticisms of the three relatively unknown drama critics who later achieved great success in letters, we can now, after half a century, see how just was their appraisal (and note, at the same time, how distinctly, even then, they wrote in character). Shaw, as we have seen, wrote with his customary verve and acerbity. "There is no reason," he said, "why life as we find it in Mr. James's novels . . . should not be represented on the stage. If it is real to Mr. James it must be real to others." Of the dialogue he said: "Line after line comes with such a delicate turn and fall that I unhesitatingly challenge any of our popular dramatists to write a scene in verse with half the beauty of Mr. James's prose. . . . I am speaking of the delicate inflexions conveyed by the cadences of the line. . . . *Guy Domville* is a story and not a mere situation hung out on a gallows of plot. And it is a story of fine sentiment and delicate manners, with an entirely worthy and touching ending." Of Alexander's role he said: "Mr. Alexander, having been treated little better than a tailor's dummy by Mr. Wilde, Mr. Pinero, and Mr. Henry Arthur Jones successively, found himself treated as an artist by Mr. James. . . ."

H. G. Wells observed that *Guy Domville* was a "play finely conceived and beautifully written," but found the second act "tedious and impossible." "People come and go in the house unchallenged like rabbits in a warren, and it was played with singular lack of spirit." He demolished Alexander in a single sentence: "In the first act Mr. Alexander, as Guy Domville, is a didactic puritan; in the second a fine generous blade; in the third he is that impossible, noble, iron-grey Mr. Alexander that we have seen before."

Arnold Bennett's review was written with the same pedestrian simplicity he cultivated later in his writings for the daily press. He found the "gems of dialogue" of Act I of "too modest and serene a beauty to suit the taste of an audience accustomed to the scintillating gauds of Mr. Oscar Wilde and Mr. Henry Arthur Jones." He found the behaviour of pit and gallery "quite inexplicable. The piece is assuredly not faultless—far from it, but it is so beautifully written, it contains so many exquisite scenes, it is so conscientiously and artistically acted and so lavishly staged, that the *longueurs* of the second act, one would have thought, might have been either forgiven or endured in respectful silence."

It was left to the sensitive and subtle A. B. Walkley to write the most balanced appraisal of all. Attuned to James's quality of mind he saw the irony in the public's acceptance of Wilde and its rejection of James. He wrote:

"Two plays have been produced during the past few days with widely different fortunes at their birth. One, Mr. Oscar Wilde's *Ideal Husband,* at the Haymarket, a strepitous, polychromatic, scintillant affair, dexterous as a conjuror's trick of legerdemain, clever with a cleverness so excessive as to be almost monstrous and uncanny, was received with every token of success. The other, Mr. Henry James's *Guy Domville* . . . laboriously wrought, pitched in a minor key, sometimes fuliginous, at others . . . subfusc, maladroit, teasing to the pitch of exasperation, was so despitefully used by many of the audience that the manager virtually went down on his marrow-bones and sued for pardon. Yet, of these two plays, I have not the slightest hesitation in declaring that the brilliant success is infinitely outweighed by the ostensible failure, not merely in actual achievement, but in significance, in promise for the future. Mr. Wilde's play will not help the drama forward a single inch, nor—though that is a comparatively unimportant matter—will it in the long run, add to Mr. Wilde's reputation. Mr. James's play is a defeat out of which it is possible for many victories to spring; in gathering the enemy's spears into his heart he has made a gap through which his successors will be able to pour in triumph."

Walkley went on to discuss what he considered the essence of the matter: the relations of each of these two dramatists with his "silent collaborator"—his public. The great difference "between Mr. Wilde and Mr. James is that one is on good terms with his collaborator, while the other is not. Mr. Tout-le-Monde confronts every dramatist with his rigorous attitude; be like me—or be damned. Mr. James failing to offer the required resemblance, has been—more or less— damned. Mr. Wilde is practically of the same mind as his audience, and gets his reward." Wilde, Walkley observed, flattered his public, gave it "inverted commonplaces," the things it believed to be true, and ended up in cheapness and in sterility.

"Turn to Mr. Henry James's play and you are in another planet. Here women can be wayward yet delicate, men infirm of purpose yet magnanimous; self-sacrifice and cloistered peace are made loveable to us; minute samples of the 'inner life' are there; and chivalrous ideals of conduct, and a fine old-world courtesy . . . a sort of fastidious, frugal quietism pervades the whole." The play was, wrote Walkley, a "memory to be wrapped in lavender-scented linen."

James received more mail from sympathisers and well-wishers than he had in all his years as a writer. Ellen Terry invited him to come and talk to her about doing a play; Sir George Henschel, the composer and conductor, invited him to write a libretto on a New England theme which he would set to music. James refused to do the libretto ("I am unlyrical, unmusical, unrhythmical, unmanageable") and the story of his negotiations with Ellen Terry constitutes the preface to *Summersoft* in this volume.

William James wrote a characteristically tender and affectionate letter to Henry, proffering, with his expression of sympathy, some cogent elder-brotherly advice, the counsel of a philosopher:

"Beloved Heinrich, We prayed on the bended knees of our souls all day Saturday for the play, but as no telegram with 'invest' on it, or any other kind of telegram, arrived I began to fear on Sunday evening that the success had not been so brilliant. On Monday Mr. Boott called and said the *Advertiser* had con-

tained a cablegram from London saying the play had 'proved a failure'. . . .
If failure it was, of course, many a first night's failure has proved a success later.
But in any case the blow to you will have been a hard one, and a bitter Sunday
you must have passed. I can't quite understand anything like *failure* direct and
palpable in a play of yours, though I can conceive of lack of flagrant success.
After your five years of devotion to this problem, the disappointment must be
tremendous and lasting. I only hope, however, that you won't take it tragically
from the social point of view, if it be a case of bad failure, and conceive yourself to be humiliated in the eyes of public and friends, because public and
friends never do or can look on such things with the dead serious eye. It will
be rather regarded as a larky kind of thing and a joke to have tried your hand
and failed at that sort of job, and I profoundly recommend *je m'en fich-isme* to
you as the only really sane and adequate philosophy for the occasion."

Guy Domville ran its allotted four weeks, the minimum time required to
exhaust Alexander's loyal audience, and lasted an extra week that included
a profitable trip to Brighton. At the end James acknowledged that "what
appears largely to have enabled *Guy Domville* to go even a month is the fact
that almost everyone who has been to see it at all appears to have been three
or four times." And irony of ironies! On January 12 George Alexander announced that he had a new play—by Oscar Wilde. It was called *The Importance
of Being Earnest.* Alexander paid Henry James the equivalent of $1,300 in
royalties earned during the play's forty performances. The actor-manager lost
£1,873, or almost $9,000, chiefly owing to the expensive setting and costuming.

"There is nothing, fortunately, so dead as a dead play—unless it be sometimes a living one," Henry wrote to William on February 22. "Oscar Wilde's
farce which followed *Guy Domville* is, I believe, a great success—and with his
two roaring successes running now at once he must be raking in the profits."

On the night of the closing Henry James said good-bye to the cast. Then he
wrote to Elizabeth Robins: "It has been a great relief to feel that one of the
most detestable incidents of my life has closed."

CHARACTERS

GUY DOMVILLE
LORD DEVENISH
FRANK HUMBER
GEORGE ROUND, *Lieutenant R.N.*
SERVANT
MRS. PEVEREL
MRS. DOMVILLE
MARY BRASIER
FANNY
MILLINERS

Period—1780

GUY DOMVILLE

ACT FIRST

The garden of an old house in the West of England; the portion directly behind the house, away from the public approach. Towards the centre a flat old-fashioned stone slab, on a pedestal, formed like a table and constituting a sun-dial. Close to it a garden-seat. On the right a low wooden gate, leading to another part of the grounds. On the left a high garden wall with a green door. A portion of the house is visible at the back, with a doorway, a porch and a short flight of steps. A waning June afternoon. Enter FRANK HUMBER, *by the wooden gate. Enter* FANNY *from the house.*

FANNY. You're wanted, sir! Excuse me, sir; I thought you were Mr. Domville.

FRANK. Isn't Mr. Domville in the house?

FANNY. No indeed, sir: I came out to look for him.

FRANK. He's not *that* way: I left my horse at the stable, where, I may mention, I had to put him up myself.

FANNY. I'm not afraid of beasts, sir, and if I had been there I would have taken hold of him. Peter's away with my mistress.

FRANK. And where has your mistress gone?

FANNY. Over to Taunton—in the old green gig.

FRANK. A plague on the old green gig! I've ridden five miles to see her.

FANNY. You often do *that*, sir!

FRANK. Not half so often as I want!

FANNY. We all know at Porches what you want, sir! (*Sympathetically.*) She'll come back to you!

FRANK. It was just in that hope I rode over!

FANNY. (*With a laugh.*) Oh, I mean back from Taunton!

FRANK. I trust so—if the gig holds out! And who is it then wants Mr. Domville?

FANNY. It is my mistress that mostly wants him, sir!—she sends me for him to this place and that. But at present he happens to have a different call. This visitor!

(*Enter* LORD DEVENISH *from the house.*)

FRANK. Leave me with him!

FANNY. (*With a curtsey to* LORD DEVENISH.) I'll try the pond—or the river, sir! (*Exit by the green door.*)

LORD DEVENISH. Does she mean to *drag* 'em? I hope he ain't drowned!

FRANK. My friend Mr. Domville has the habit of fishing, sir.

LORD DEVENISH. The most innocent of pleasures—yet perhaps the most absorbing! In Mr. Domville's apparent absence I rejoice to find myself introduced to one of his friends.

FRANK. May I inquire if *you* also enjoy that title?

LORD DEVENISH. I hope to win it, sir! I've travelled for the purpose all the way from London! My business with Mr. Domville is urgent—so urgent that while impatiently waiting, just now, till he should be summoned, I ventured to step out of the house in the hope of meeting him the sooner.

FRANK. Under the impression that he *lives* at Porches?

LORD DEVENISH. That impression has already been corrected. A modest habitation in the village was pointed out to me on my arrival.

FRANK. Mr. Domville's humble lodging —at the baker's.

LORD DEVENISH. I smelt the warm bread a mile off! I had the privilege of an interview with the baker's wife, and it was in consequence of the information she gave me that I knocked without delay at *this* door.

FRANK. Mr. Domville spends most of his time here.

LORD DEVENISH. A charming place—to spend most of one's time!

FRANK. That depends on what one spends it in!

LORD DEVENISH. *Mine* must all go to business—business of marked importance.

FRANK. A matter, evidently, of life and death!

LORD DEVENISH. You may judge, sir, that I haven't posted night and day for a trifle! I learned ·from the baker's wife that Mr. Domville *does* come home to bed: but the nature of my errand forbade me to wait till he should happen to be sleepy. I stand engaged, moreover, not to let Mr. Domville slip.

FRANK. I may let you know, then, that you've arrived in the nick of time! He goes to-morrow.

LORD DEVENISH. (*Startled.*) Goes where?

FRANK. Into retreat, as we Catholics call it.

LORD DEVENISH. (*Raising his hat.*) The true and only Church!

FRANK. (*Gratified.*) You're one of us, sir?

LORD DEVENISH. The blackest sheep in the fold!

FRANK. The fold here is very small. But we're protected by my Lord Edenbrook.

LORD DEVENISH. He provides, I know, for your spiritual nourishment.

FRANK. His private chapel, his worthy chaplain, are precious comforts to us.

LORD DEVENISH. The centre, of course, of your little cluster of the faithful. Why then should Mr. Domville forsake such privileges?

FRANK. For the sake of others that are greater. To enter a religious house.

LORD DEVENISH. As a preparation for holy orders?

FRANK. The time for his ordination has at last come. He starts in the morning for Bristol.

LORD DEVENISH. Thank God, then, I swore at the postboys! He takes ship for France?

FRANK. For Douai and the good Fathers who brought him up, and who tried, heaven reward them! to do the same by *me!*

LORD DEVENISH. The Benedictines? You were both at school with them?

FRANK. A part of the time together. But *I'm* not of the stuff of which churchmen are made!

LORD DEVENISH. And you consider that Mr. Domville *is?*

FRANK. It's not I—it's everyone. He has what they call the vocation.

LORD DEVENISH. Then have I come too late? (*Re-enter* FANNY *from the green door.*) Can't you find him?

FANNY. Not by the water, sir. But the dairy-maid has seen him: he's gone to walk with the little master.

FRANK. The little master's the little pupil.

LORD DEVENISH. Mrs. Peverel's son?

FRANK. Her only one—poor little fatherless imp! Guy Domville, ȑecommended to her by Lord Edenbrook's chaplain, has had for the last year the happiness of being his tutor. Thank you, Fanny. We'll wait.

(*Exit* FANNY *to the house.*)

LORD DEVENISH. Your own preference, sir, is to stay?

FRANK. Assuredly—when I've ridden five miles to take leave of him.

LORD DEVENISH. At so private an interview with so old a friend my presence will perhaps be indiscreet. May I therefore ask you to be so good as to make it clear to him that I await him impatiently at the inn?

FRANK. I shall be able to make it clearer if I'm permitted to mention your name.

LORD DEVENISH. (*Drawing from the breast of his waistcoat a letter without a seal.*) My name is on this letter, which expresses the importance of my mission and which I have been requested to place in his hand. He will receive it, however, with deeper concern from yours.

FRANK. (*With the letter.*) He shall have it as soon as he returns. (*Indicating the wooden gate.*) That's the short way to the village.

LORD DEVENISH. Before I go may I ask you another question? Is Mrs. Peverel of the Sussex Peverels?

FRANK. Her late husband was of that family. She's a niece of my Lord Edenbrook.

LORD DEVENISH. Very good blood! And a widow of some—antiquity?

FRANK. Antiquity? Why she's just *my* age!

LORD DEVENISH. (*Laughing.*) The very flower of youth!—And very charming?

FRANK. Judge for yourself, sir!

(*Enter* MRS. PEVEREL *from the house.* LORD DEVENISH, *removing his hat, remains a moment meeting her eyes while she returns his look. Then he makes a ceremonious bow and goes out by the wooden gate.*)

MRS. PEVEREL. (*Surprised.*) What does the gentleman desire?

FRANK. To have speech of our young divine.

MRS. PEVEREL. Pray, who *is* he?

FRANK. I believe that letter tells.

MRS. PEVEREL. (*With the letter.*) "For Mr. Domville, introducing my Lord Devenish."

FRANK. (*Surprised.*) My Lord Devenish?

MRS. PEVEREL. (*Wondering.*) Isn't that the name—the name—?

FRANK. The name of a nobleman of extraordinary assurance!

MRS. PEVEREL. That's just what I mean —the one who was said to be Mrs. Domville's great adorer.

FRANK. Do you mean the lady's lover? I never knew any Mrs. Domville but the mother of our good friend.

MRS. PEVEREL. I speak of the widow of one of his kinsmen—the one that was the head of the family.

FRANK. (*Smiling.*) He's not the head of *ours*! God bless you for such a letter!

MRS. PEVEREL. (*Turning over* LORD DEVENISH's *letter.*) It's not sealed, you see. (*Absent.*) What does he want of Mr. Domville?

FRANK. I don't mean *that* one—I mean *yours,* that came yesterday. You see it has brought me over.

MRS. PEVEREL. Didn't you come over to see your friend?

FRANK. *You're* my friend, and when I come to your house you're always the person I come for! Especially when you let me know that you desire it.

MRS. PEVEREL. (*Surprised.*) Is that what my letter conveyed?

FRANK. It conveyed that I might ride over if I liked—which comes to the same thing. And it conveyed some other things. Have you already forgotten?

MRS. PEVEREL. I don't remember—I'm miserably sad. We're losing our best company.

FRANK. Dear lady, it's you who are mine, and I haven't lost you yet!

MRS. PEVEREL. You haven't yet gained me, Mr. Humber!

FRANK. What then did your letter mean?

MRS. PEVEREL. I don't know *what* it meant! I'll tell you some other time!

FRANK. Thank you for that. I assure you I look forward to other times.

MRS. PEVEREL. Oh, we shall have leisure! It stretches out like the Great Desert! The cruel loss will be Geordie's. He parts with his comrade—with his idol!

FRANK. The child loves him so?

MRS. PEVEREL. Loves him? He clings to him—he's spending his last hour with him! Such devotion as my boy has enjoyed and such perfect tenderness—such an influence and such an example! And now it all goes!

FRANK. It goes to a greater work!

MRS. PEVEREL. (*Musing, with a vague shrug.*) Yes, yes—a greater work!

FRANK. He'll rise to high honours—be one of the Princes of the Church.

MRS. PEVEREL. I don't know if he'll be one of its "Princes"—but he may very well be one of its Saints.

FRANK. (*Laughing.*) Ah, *that's* more difficult! for that you must give up things!

MRS. PEVEREL. (*With decision.*) Well—

he'll give them up! He's one of those who can!

FRANK. Dear lady, your boy loses one friend, but he keeps another! I don't compare myself—except for the interest I may take—with such a companion, with such a benefactor as Guy. I'm not clever, I'm not learned, I shall never rise to honours, much less to holiness! But I can stand firm—I can keep watch—I can take his little hand in mine. Mrs. Peverel, let *me* be something to him!

MRS. PEVEREL. You can be as good-natured as you like—my house is always open to you. What more do you want?

FRANK. You know what I want—what I've wanted these two years. I've taken you on this side and on that, but you always have some side that's turned away. Haven't I gone all round you *yet?*

MRS. PEVEREL. (*Smiling.*) You talk as if you were buying a horse!

FRANK. I'd buy fifty, if you'd sit behind 'em! Let me stand to-day on the ground we just spoke of! Let your affection and your anxieties be mine. Let your boy be *my* boy!

MRS. PEVEREL. (*As if consentingly, resignedly.*) Well—he has given you a bit of his heart.

FRANK. He's a fine example to his mother!

MRS. PEVEREL. Remain then in his good graces! They ought to be back. He'll be very tired.

FRANK. (*Smiling.*) With *me* he needn't fear that!

MRS. PEVEREL. I'm speaking of Mr. Domville.

FRANK. *I'm* speaking, dear lady, of myself! You haven't admitted me at last only to put me off once more! What did your good words mean if they didn't mean that I should at last have my answer?

MRS. PEVEREL. You shall have it to-morrow.

FRANK. (*Gravely impatient.*) Ah, you don't treat me well!

MRS. PEVEREL. (*As if admitting this, conciliatory.*) You shall have it to-night!

FRANK. Why not now?

MRS. PEVEREL. Give me this last hour! (*Then in a totally different tone and as if forcibly to change the subject, while she draws from her pocket a very small box, from which she removes the cover.*) What do you think of that?

FRANK. (*With the box, pleased, interested.*) A fine gem, an intaglio?

MRS. PEVEREL. A precious antique that belonged to my father. I made the gold-smith at Taunton set it as a seal.

FRANK. And you went over to get it?

MRS. PEVEREL. For a gift at parting.

FRANK. (*Disconcerted.*) At parting?

MRS. PEVEREL. With Mr. Domville.

FRANK. (*Ruefully.*) Oh! (*Gives her back the box and turns away.*) Here he is to receive it!

(*Enter* GUY DOMVILLE *from the house.*)

GUY. We went further than we knew and Geordie's a little lame. It's nothing—I think his shoe wasn't right and that it will pass before morning. But I've sent him to bed and told him I would ask you to go to him.

MRS. PEVEREL. (*Very prompt.*) I'll go to him!

GUY. I'll wait for you here.

(*Exit* MRS. PEVEREL *to the house.*)

FRANK. You can't do that when you're waited for yourself.

GUY. Waited for—by whom?

FRANK. That letter will tell you.

GUY. (*With the letter; vague.*) "My Lord Devenish"?

FRANK. He's cooling his heels at the inn.

GUY. (*Reading.*) "Dear and honoured kinsman: This is to entreat you to give such welcome as is fitting to our noble friend, my trusty messenger, the Lord Devenish, and lend a patient ear to all he will say to you—much better than she herself can—for your loving cousin and humble servant Maria Domville." (*Vaguely recalling.*) She must be the widow of my cousin who died ten years ago.

FRANK. And the reputed mistress of her noble friend?

GUY. (*Disconcerted.*) His reputed mistress?

FRANK. (*Laughing.*) Pardon me, Guy—I forgot your cloth!

GUY. I'm not of the cloth yet!

FRANK. You might be, with your black

clothes and your shy looks: such an air of the cold college—almost of the cold cloister! Will you go to his lordship? He's counting the minutes.

GUY. (*Hesitating, glancing at his letter again.*) "A patient ear"?—I must take leave of Mrs. Peverel first.

FRANK. Can't you do that later?

GUY. Not if my visitor's to command me and the coach is to start at dawn.

FRANK. Then *I* mustn't take your time!

GUY. Be easy, dear Frank. We're old, old friends. You must let me tell you how often I shall think of you and how much happiness I wish you.

FRANK. Do you remember, when you say that, the happiness I most long for?

GUY. I remember it. I desire it.

FRANK. You speak out of your goodness!

GUY. Out of our long affection—yours and mine.

FRANK. I can remember as far back as your mother, and the wonder with which I listened when she told me that you were to be bred up a priest.

GUY. God rest her pure spirit—it was an honest vow! The vow has been fulfilled!

FRANK. You must help me to fulfil mine —I think you can.

GUY. I shall always be glad to help you.

FRANK. I mean now—on the spot—before you're lost to us. You go for years, I suppose; perhaps even forever.

GUY. Yes; perhaps even for ever! I give up my life—I accept my fate.

FRANK. (*Laughing.*) You're not dead yet! But for *us*—it *is* your last hour.

GUY. My last! My *last!* I must therefore do something very good with it. *How* can I help you, Frank?

FRANK. By speaking for me—by telling her to *believe* in me. She thinks all the world of you.

GUY. She's attached to our holy Church.

FRANK. That's just what I mean. Your thoughts are not as other men's thoughts: your words are not as other men's words. It's to a certain extent her duty to act on them, so you're the man of all men to plead my cause.

GUY. (*After a moment.*) Will you be very good to her?

FRANK. I give you my word before heaven.

GUY. Some men—are not gentle. And *she*—she's *all* gentleness!

FRANK. Oh, I know what she is!

GUY. Then you'll be faithful, tender, true?

FRANK. My dear man, I worship the ground she treads on! And I've a good estate and an ancient name.

GUY. (*After a moment.*) I'll plead your cause.

FRANK. Now, then, is your time!
        (*Re-enter* MRS. PEVEREL.)

MRS. PEVEREL. The child's only tired— but he's very wide awake. He wants to hug you again!

GUY. I'll go and be hugged!

MRS. PEVEREL. Not yet—he'll be quieter. (*To* HUMBER.) You've ridden far enough to deserve refreshment. They've put some out in the White Parlour.

FRANK. I'll drink to Domville's preferment! (*Exit to the house.*)

GUY. He worships the ground you tread on, and he swears before heaven he'll be good to you.

MRS. PEVEREL. (*Smiling.*) Did he ask you to tell me so?

GUY. And he has a good estate and an ancient name.

MRS. PEVEREL. Not so ancient as yours, my friend—one of the two or three oldest in the kingdom!

GUY. Oh, I'm giving up my name! I shall take another!

MRS. PEVEREL. You have indeed the vocation, Mr. Domville.

GUY. I have the opportunity. I've lived with my eyes on it, and I'm not afraid. The relinquished ease—the definite duties—the service of the Church—the praise of God: these things seem to wait for me! And then there are people everywhere to help.

MRS. PEVEREL. If you help others as you've helped me, your comfort will indeed be great!

GUY. I *have* my comfort, for under your roof I've found—my only way, my deepest need. I've learned here what I am—I've learned here what I'm not. Just now, as

I went from place to place with the child, certain moments, certain memories came back to me. I took him the round of all our rambles, yours and mine—I talked to him prodigiously of his mother.

MRS. PEVEREL. *I* shall talk to him of his absent tutor.

GUY. Talk of me sometimes with Frank Humber!

MRS. PEVEREL. (*Abrupt, irrelevant, with her eyes on the letter that lies on the stone.*) Who's my Lord Devenish?

GUY. (*Startled.*) I ought to go and learn!

MRS. PEVEREL. Doesn't your letter tell you?

GUY. Read it, and you'll see.

MRS. PEVEREL. I won't read it—thank you!

GUY. He *will* be very good to you.

MRS. PEVEREL. Of whom are you speaking?

GUY. Of Frank Humber. He'll help you —he'll guard you—he'll cherish you. Make him happy.

MRS. PEVEREL. That's easily said!

GUY. Marry him!

MRS. PEVEREL. Why do *you* speak of marriage, Mr. Domville?

GUY. I, the first law of whose profession, the rigid rule of whose life, is to abstain from it? I don't speak of it as a man of the world—I speak of it as a priest. There are cases in which our Mother-Church enjoins it. We must bow to our Mother-Church. (*Exit to the house.*)

MRS. PEVEREL. (*Alone.*) To bow to our Mother-Church? Am I *not* bowing to her— down to the very earth? (*Restless, nervous, she once more turns her eyes to the open letter on the table, and, taking it up with decision, stands reading it.* LORD DEVENISH *meanwhile reappears at the wooden gate and remains unperceived by her, watching her. Re-enter* LORD DEVENISH.) You're impatient, my lord.

LORD DEVENISH. (*Smiling and indicating the letter.*) Not more so than *you,* Madam!

MRS. PEVEREL. With Mr. Domville's permission.

LORD DEVENISH. My license for returning is almost as good—my insurmountable anxiety! That anxiety came into being when, in the act of retiring from this spot, I had the honour to see you face to face. It suggested reflections, and I may as well confess frankly that it forbade my going back to the inn. It keeps me at my post!

MRS. PEVEREL. I don't understand you, my lord.

LORD DEVENISH. You probably will— when Mr. Domville does!

MRS. PEVEREL. I'll send him to you—and give orders for your lordship's entertainment! (*Exit to the house.*)

LORD DEVENISH. There's no such entertainment as the presence of a charming woman! If he gave her the letter she's exactly what I seemed to guess—his confidant, his counsellor. In that case I smell contradiction! (*Enter* GUY DOMVILLE *from the house.*) But *this* fellow is worth a pass or two!

GUY. I was on the point of waiting on your lordship.

LORD DEVENISH. I've come so far to see you, sir, that I made no scruple of a few steps more. My visit has, of course, an explanation.

GUY. I receive indeed so *few*—!

LORD DEVENISH. It only lies with yourself, sir, to be surrounded with the homage of multitudes!

GUY. You're ignorant, probably, how little, my lord, things lie with myself!

LORD DEVENISH. On the contrary, sir— it was just that knowledge that brought me hither in person, and brought me so fast. My credentials, as you've assured yourself, testify to the importance of my errand.

GUY. Mrs. Domville does me unexpected honour.

LORD DEVENISH. Not as much as you'll do *me,* sir, if you'll give me your best attention. Be seated, I pray you. It's my painful duty to begin with announcing to you the death of your nearest kinsman—your only one, the late Mr. Domville of Gaye. His horse has broken his neck for him—he was mostly too drunk to ride!

GUY. I could have wished him a more edifying end!

LORD DEVENISH. You might have wished him a seemlier life—and a little less numerous progeny! He never married.

GUY. (*Surprised.*) Yet he had children?

LORD DEVENISH. They're not worth speaking of!

GUY. Surely they're worth commiserating!

LORD DEVENISH. For losing the estate?

GUY. (*Still more surprised.*) *Do* they lose it?

LORD DEVENISH. It's shrunken, it's burdened, the old domain of Gaye, but it has stood there from the Conquest, sir, and it has never been out of your family.

GUY. But if the late Mr. Domville's children *are* my family—?

LORD DEVENISH. (*Scandalised.*) They— a pack of village bastards?

GUY. (*Bewildered.*) Yet if there's no one else—?

LORD DEVENISH. If there had been no one else, Mr. Domville (*ruefully feeling his loins*), I wouldn't have posted till I ached! You yourself, sir, are your family.

GUY. (*As if roused from a dream.*) I?

LORD DEVENISH. You're the next in succession—you're the master of Gaye.

GUY. (*Stupefied.*) I?

LORD DEVENISH. The heir of your kinsman, the last of your name.

GUY. (*Dazed.*) To *me,* my lord, such things are fables!

LORD DEVENISH. That's exactly why I came to announce them. You mightn't take 'em in from another!

GUY. I've chosen my part, my lord. I go to-morrow to take it.

LORD DEVENISH. The purpose of my visit, sir, is to protest against your going. Your duty is nearer at hand—it's first to the name you bear. Your life, my dear sir, is not your own to give up. It belongs to your position—to your dignity—to your race.

GUY. (*Quietly, firmly.*) I was bred up, my lord, to be a priest.

LORD DEVENISH. You were not bred up, I suppose, not to be a Domville!

GUY. The very Domville that, in our branch, was always given to the Church! As long ago as I remember, the Church had accepted the gift. It's too late to take it back.

LORD DEVENISH. Too late? Not by several hours! Your coldness seems to remind me that to your consecrated character there are images unsuitable, forbidden! Do me the favour, then, to suppose that character a moment discontinued. (*Laughing.*) Do you owe your ferocity to Mrs. Peverel?

GUY. (*Surprised, slightly resentful.*) Mrs. Peverel has been my kindest friend—she approves for me of the religious life.

LORD DEVENISH. And her way of showing her approval has been to hurry you off to Bristol?

GUY. She has not "hurried" me, my lord—she has even, from day to day, detained me.

LORD DEVENISH. (*Struck, dryly.*) Ah!— Thank heaven for that detention!

GUY. For the sake, you know, of my pupil.

LORD DEVENISH. Thank heaven for your pupil!—Have your pupil, and your pupil's mother, sir, never opened your eyes to *another* possible life—the natural, the liberal, the agreeable, the life of the world of men—and of women—in which your name gives you a place? I put you that question for Mrs. Domville.

GUY. Mrs. Domville's inquiries are a wondrous civility to a person she has never seen.

LORD DEVENISH. Let me express to him, without reserve, the extravagance of her wish to see him! When she married into your family, sir, into which she brought a very handsome accession, it was with a great zeal to serve it and to contribute, if might be, to its duration. Your kinsman who died last week succeeded to his nephew, that only son whom, in his early childhood, Mrs. Domville had the bitterness to lose. She has been twice a widow, and she has from her first marriage an amiable daughter, a consolation imperfect indeed, however prized, for the great affliction of her life.

GUY. The death of the boy you speak of?

LORD DEVENISH. The heir to your name, dear sir, the tender hope, as it then seemed, the little opening flower of your race.

GUY. When the flower was gathered the race was doomed!

LORD DEVENISH. Doomed? Not to such easy extinction! Don't you feel the long past in your blood, and the voice of the future in your ears?—You hold in your hand, sir, the generations to come!

GUY. (*Much shaken.*) What is it then, my lord—what is it you want to *do* with me?

LORD DEVENISH. To carry you to-night to your kinswoman. She has paramount things to say to you.

GUY. I ask nothing of this lady but to let me lead my life!

LORD DEVENISH. Exactly what she wants you to do! She only wants to show you *how* and to see you face to face.

GUY. I doubt if you measure, my lord, I doubt if Mrs. Domville measures, so large a sacrifice, to considerations never yet present to me—to everything I've learned to put away.

LORD DEVENISH. If you've learned to put away your proper pride, you've learnt a very ill lesson!

GUY. I know no pride so proper as that of the office I've been appointed to fill.

LORD DEVENISH. The office to which you have been appointed is that of a gallant gentleman, and the place in which to fill it is the brave old house of your fathers! Do as they did in *their* day—make it ring with the voices of children! The more little Domvilles the more good Catholics! Do what you can for *them,* and you'll do quite enough for your Church!

GUY. Break with all the past, and break with it this minute?—turn back from the threshold, take my hand from the plough? —The hour is too troubled, your news too strange, your summons too sudden!

LORD DEVENISH. I reckoned on your great understanding, sir, and the fine effect of your studies! If *before* our meeting, sir, I attached a price to your person, that price has doubled since I've had the honour to converse with you! Your place in the world was in my eye—but at present I see how you'd adorn it!

GUY. I've *no* place in the world!

LORD DEVENISH. I'll take leave of you on the spot, sir, if you'll declare to me, on your honour, that you're dead to the pleasures of life. I shall be happy to introduce you to them all! Can't you figure them, as a gentleman? Remember, for God's sake, that you *are* one! Stand forth like one—one of the first, as you may be, in England! That character's a treasure that you can't throw away at your will! Your kinsman, just dead, dipped it woefully into the mire. Pick it up, and brush it off, and wear it!

GUY. Who *are* you, what *are* you, my lord, that you have come here to trouble me—to tempt me?

LORD DEVENISH. (*Smiling.*) To "tempt" you? Thank you, sir, for that word! The world is wide—and youth is short—and opportunity shorter!

GUY. Those are exactly reasons for my leaving your lordship this instant.

LORD DEVENISH. Life is sweet, and friends are fond, and love—well, love is everything! (*Re-enter* MRS. PEVEREL *from the house. Aside.*) He *has* it here under his nose! You come to rescue Mr. Domville from my clutches?

MRS. PEVEREL. I come to beg your lordship to have patience with my country larder.

LORD DEVENISH. If my appetite is undeniably great, Madam, your hospitality is evidently greater!

MRS. PEVEREL. Its very modest effort awaits you in the White Parlour, with Mr. Humber, whom you have already met, I think, eager to do you the honours.

LORD DEVENISH. (*After looking a moment from* MRS. PEVEREL *to* GUY.) Put your case to Mrs. Peverel, sir. I leave him, Madam, in your hands! (*Exit to the house.*)

GUY. Who *is* he, Madam—*what* is he, that he comes here to draw me off?

MRS. PEVEREL. To draw you off?

GUY. My cousin is dead—there are no other kin—and I'm sole heir to the old estate, to the old honours, to all the duties and charges. I'm lord of the Manor of Gaye!

MRS. PEVEREL. (*With great and joyous emotion.*) What news, my friend—what news! It makes my heart beat high!

GUY. I'm sole of all our line, I'm sole of all our name.

MRS. PEVEREL. It has come to you, this way, in an instant, sought you out and taken you by the hand? Then God be praised for *your* life—since he has taken to himself the others!

GUY. And hasn't he taken *mine*—haven't I given it up to him?

MRS. PEVEREL. (*Embarrassed but for an instant.*) Given it up—yes, partly! But a priest may inherit property!

GUY. He may do good with it—yes. He may devote it to the poor—he may offer it to the Church!

MRS. PEVEREL. (*Smiling.*) He may even, without sin, keep a little of it for himself! Is the property great? shall you be rich?

GUY. God forbid me riches! The domain is shrunken and burdened. But such as it is, what they want of me is to keep everything for myself.

MRS. PEVEREL. What "they" want of you? Who are "they," if they be all dead?

GUY. Mrs. Domville's alive, and she has a plan. She clings to the name—she wants to keep it up. She has sent his lordship with the tidings.

MRS. PEVEREL. I could love his lordship for coming!

GUY. I could hate him—for coming tonight! To-morrow he'd just have missed me.

,MRS. PEVEREL. But sure the lawyers would have caught you. They'd easily have followed you to France.

GUY. It's not the lawyers that trouble me!

MRS. PEVEREL. What is it then, Mr. Domville?

GUY. It's the vision of such a change, the startling voice of such an injunction! That of my forefathers' name—which has lasted from century to century!

MRS. PEVEREL. Ah yes—the command to wear it—to wear it with honour and do great things for it!

GUY. To preserving an old, old name—to giving it to others that they, in their turn, may give it!

MRS. PEVEREL. (*Excitedly.*) They want you to *marry?*

GUY. They want me to marry.

MRS. PEVEREL. (*Eager.*) Not to marry *her?*

GUY. Her?

MRS. PEVEREL. Mrs. Domville—your cousin!

GUY. Why, she's fifty years old!

MRS. PEVEREL. (*Prompt.*), I daresay she's sixty! Then it's their simple duty—to plead for your name.

GUY. I don't care a button for my name!

MRS. PEVEREL. You do, you *do*—you've often told me so! (*In an edifying tone.*) Such a name as yours is a vast obligation!

GUY. Too great—too great for *me* to carry!

MRS. PEVEREL. *Why* too great, when you're young, when you're strong, when you've a boundless life before you?

GUY. The life I have before me is not that life—the life I have before me is simply my greater duty.

MRS. PEVEREL. Your greater duty is to listen to such a call!

GUY. Half-an-hour ago you uttered different words—words that were sweet to me about the office on which I was to enter!

MRS. PEVEREL. I uttered different words because I spoke of different things!—Half-an-hour ago everything wasn't changed!

GUY. How can everything change when my heart remains the same?

MRS. PEVEREL. Are you very sure of your heart?

GUY. No, I'm not sure! Therefore I go to-night to Bristol and Father Murray. I won't wait till the morning.

MRS. PEVEREL. (*Pleading.*) You'll give up —in one minute—so great a tradition? You'll cast away something precious as if it were something mean? Life is good, Mr. Domville: you said so and you know it.

GUY. Then why have you always spoken of renouncement?

MRS. PEVEREL. (*Smiling.*) Because, when I did so, there was nothing to renounce! Now there's too much—ask Mrs. Domville! You'll hear from her, as the lawyers say, of something to your advantage.

GUY. What advantage is like the advantage of keeping faith with one's vows?

MRS. PEVEREL. What vows do you speak of? You've taken no vows.

GUY. Not in form perhaps—I haven't burnt my ships. But the irrevocable words are seated on my lips. What has my life been but a preparation?

MRS. PEVEREL. For this—perhaps: for just this hour! To choose with understanding—to act with knowledge—to live in the world with importance!

GUY. (*Sad and ironical.*) You talk of the "world," my friend; but what do you *know* of the world?

MRS. PEVEREL. Little enough—in this country nook! But I should like to hear of it—from *you!*

GUY. I'll tell you—when I come back—everything that's base and ill of it.

MRS. PEVEREL. (*Catching at this.*) Yes—when you come back!

GUY. Then everything I shall say of it will show you that *we* are safer! (*Then still nervously, restlessly irreconcileable.*) But what will Father Murray say to so black a desertion?

MRS. PEVEREL. He'll say you obeyed a much clearer call. I'll despatch him a quick messenger—I'll make your reasons good to him.

GUY. If they could only be good to *me!* But they're mixed with wild thoughts and desires! Things I can't tell you—words I can't speak!

MRS. PEVEREL. (*Soothing, encouraging.*) Be yourself, be your generous self, and all will be straight and smooth to you!

GUY. "Myself"—the self of yesterday? I seem suddenly to have lost it for ever!

MRS. PEVEREL. Then God be praised! (*Eagerly.*) May I tell him you'll *go* with him?

GUY. (*Breaking and stopping short.*) Mrs. Peverel!—

MRS. PEVEREL. (*Nervously wondering and waiting.*) How can I help you?—what can I say to you?

GUY. How much of your friendship may I ask—how much of your help may I take?

MRS. PEVEREL. You may ask anything—you may take all!

GUY. (*Surprised, agitated.*) All? (*Then as he sees* FRANK.) All that *he* doesn't want!

(*Re-enter* FRANK HUMBER *from the house.*)

FRANK. (*Excited, delighted, ironical.*) Here's a fine pother, you rascal—with your reverence going to Court!

MRS. PEVEREL. (*Affected by the interruption, coldly.*) You've heard it from his lordship?

FRANK. His lordship counts on a fresh start and a long day's run for the Dom-

villes! And I, my dear lad, I pat you on the back! But you look as white as my Yorkshire colt. (*Mystified by* GUY's *look and appealing, as if scandalised, to* MRS. PEVEREL.) You don't mean to say he won't *take* it?

MRS. PEVEREL. Mr. Domville starts for London—to-morrow very early.

FRANK. (*Elated, sympathetic.*) Shall I go and let his lordship know?

GUY. Thank you, Frank, you can leave it to *me!*

FRANK. So much the better—I've something to say to Mrs. Peverel.

MRS. PEVEREL. (*Disconcerted.*) What you have to say had better wait, Mr. Humber.

FRANK. Oh, not *again!* (*Confident, but sarcastic.*) Why not send me home at once?

MRS. PEVEREL. It's much the safest place for you!

FRANK. I call on you to witness, Guy, how cruelly she treats me!

MRS. PEVEREL. She treats you beautifully when she drives four miles for you. (*With her eyes on* GUY; *producing the box.*) To bring you an old gem that I've had set as a seal.

FRANK. (*Delighted.*) Then it *is* for *me?*

MRS. PEVEREL. It's for *you!*

FRANK. (*With the box.*) How can I thank you enough?

MRS. PEVEREL. (*Dryly.*) Don't thank me too much! (*To* GUY.) Won't you relieve his lordship?

GUY. (*Rousing himself, with loud emphasis, from what he has just observed.*) I'll relieve him. I'll accommodate him! (*With a complete transformation and a passionate flourish.*) Long, long live the Domvilles!—Away, away for London! (*Exit to the house.*)

MRS. PEVEREL. (*Surrendering herself to her joy.*) He's free—he's free!

FRANK. (*Disconcerted, detached.*) "Free"? Oh, I see. Well, so am *I*, you know; and there's other news in the air; the good news you promised, an hour ago, on this spot, to give me in your gracious answer.

MRS. PEVEREL. I can't give it now—it's impossible; please don't *ask* me.

FRANK. (*Dismayed.*) Not "ask" you when I've been counting the minutes—not "ask" you when you've given me your word?

Guy: "It is *I* who shall go!"
Guy Domville (Act III). Herbert Waring (Frank Humber),
Marion Terry (Mrs. Peverel), George Alexander (Guy Domville)
and W. G. Elliot (Lord Devenish)

The Hat
Guy Domville (Act II). W. G. Elliot
(Lord Devenish) and Mrs. Edward
Saker (Mrs. Domville)

Round: "Then I'll even drink to my
cruel cousin." The Drinking Scene,
Guy Domville (Act II). H. V. Esmond
(Lieut. Round) and George Alexander
(Guy Domville)

34, DE VERE GARDENS. W.

January 15th 1899

My dear Henschel.

I am touched by the kindness of your letter: — please accept my hearty thanks for it. The theatre is an abyss of vulgarity & platitude & I suppose one ought

"The Theatre is an abyss of vulgarity and platitude."
Henry James's letter to Sir George Henschel

MRS. PEVEREL. I've given you *no* word!—I beseech you to leave me.

FRANK. (*Bewildered, astounded.*) Then my patience that you were to reward, and this present that you've just pressed on me—?

MRS. PEVEREL. (*Impatient, brusque, eager only to get rid of him.*) I'm sorry—but your patience is wasted. I'm sorry—but the present is nothing.—It's a gift at parting.

FRANK. (*Horrified.*) You mean you *refuse* me?

MRS. PEVEREL. Utterly, Mr. Humber! And don't return to the question again!

FRANK. (*Angry.*) *That's* the sweet answer you've kept me waiting for?

MRS. PEVEREL. I couldn't give it before. But it's positive *now!*

FRANK. (*Staring.*) What's the riddle of "now"?

MRS. PEVEREL. It's not a riddle—but it's a different matter. (*Summarily.*) Good-bye!

FRANK. Where on earth's the difference? (*Then divining; overwhelmed.*) By all that's monstrous—you love *him!*

MRS. PEVEREL. (*Vehemently brushing away the charge, waving away his presence.*) Don't speak to me—don't look at me—only *leave* me! (*Almost imperiously.*) Good-bye!

FRANK. (*Pulling himself up short, making a violent effort.*) Good-bye!

(*Re-enter* LORD DEVENISH *from the house. Exit* FRANK *by the wooden gate.*)

LORD DEVENISH. (*Sarcastic.*) I'm sorry you're losing your friend!

MRS. PEVEREL. (*Who has not seen him; startled, confused.*) Mr. Humber?

LORD DEVENISH. (*Amused.*) Mr. Humber as well? You'll be lonely!

MRS. PEVEREL. (*Mystified by his manner, resenting his familiarity.*) My lord—!

LORD DEVENISH. It's Mr. Domville's last minute, and I'm not sure you'll see him henceforth. We've particular need of him, in another place,[1] to lead a young lady to the altar: Mrs. Domville's daughter by her first marriage, the amiable and virtuous Miss Brasier; a bride in a thousand—a Catholic, a beauty, and a fortune. (*Seeing* DOMVILLE.) Long, *long* live the Domvilles!

(*Re-enter* DOMVILLE *from the house.*)

GUY. I leave you to your happiness.

LORD DEVENISH. You couldn't leave a lady at a properer moment.—It's time we *should* leave her. Come, come!

GUY. Long, long live the Domvilles!

Passage between GUY *and* MRS. PEVEREL. *Exit* GUY *and* LORD DEVENISH. MRS. PEVEREL *alone.*

[1] The Huntington Library prompt-book contains an inserted speech here for Mrs. Peverel. She echoes: "Particular need!"

ACT SECOND

MRS. DOMVILLE'S *villa at Richmond.* MRS. DOMVILLE *and* GEORGE ROUND *discovered.*

ROUND. The reason of my "wicked return," ma'am, is simply the respect I owe you, and the respect I owe to my cousin, your too amiable daughter.

MRS. DOMVILLE. Have you forgotten that I informed you six months ago how you could best express that respect?

ROUND. By keeping out of your sight—by permitting you to forget my existence and encouraging you to hope I had forgotten yours? I obeyed your command,

ma'am; I immediately joined my ship. But my ship came back last week.

MRS. DOMVILLE. It didn't come back to Richmond, I suppose. This house is not your port!

ROUND. I think, indeed, rather, it's a rough and unfriendly coast!

MRS. DOMVILLE. Take care, then, what befalls you in attempting to land.

ROUND. What worse can befall me than what befell me six months ago? The life was knocked out of me then, and if I meet your eyes once more it's simply that the mere wreck of my old presumption has been washed ashore at your feet.

MRS. DOMVILLE. I'll warrant you a wreck that will take some time to sink—though indeed you do seem to have parted, in the tempest, with your uniform.

ROUND. On calculation, ma'am. As you appear to despise my profession, or at least my want of advancement in it, I thought it good taste not to fly my poor colours.

MRS. DOMVILLE. The taste of your calculations is better than that of your tailor!

ROUND. A man's tailor doesn't matter, perhaps, when he hasn't come to conquer. I am no longer a suitor for your daughter's hand. But I have a right to remind you—and this, ma'am, has been my errand—that I never promised to forget the tie of blood, the fine freedom of kinship.

MRS. DOMVILLE. The fine freedom of exaggeration! You blow the trumpet too loud over the ridiculous honour of having been poor Mr. Brasier's nephew.

ROUND. Why is it more ridiculous for *me* to have been his nephew than for *her* to have been his daughter?

MRS. DOMVILLE. (*After a moment.*) It ain't!

ROUND. I've come to tell you that I engage to make the best of your conditions.

MRS. DOMVILLE. "Conditions," my dear creature? We offered you none whatever. You were condemned without appeal.

ROUND. Say then that I accept even that. A man is suffered to see his family before he's hanged!

MRS. DOMVILLE. That plea doesn't hold, sir, for my daughter has ceased to belong to your family!

ROUND. (*Blank.*) Pray, then, to what family does she belong?

MRS. DOMVILLE. To mine.

ROUND. Yours?

MRS. DOMVILLE. The ancient house of Domville—of whose history, and whose fidelity to the old persuasion, you needn't affect a barbarous ignorance. My daughter's about to enter it, as her mother—less worthy!—did ten years ago. She's to marry Mr. Domville of Gaye.

ROUND. Almighty Powers!

MRS. DOMVILLE. Kinsman for Kinsman, he's a much finer figure—

ROUND. Than a paltry lieutenant in the King's Navy? For you, I can understand it. But for *her?*—has submission been so easy?

MRS. DOMVILLE. The poor child has submitted to *him!* She's in love, with the most brilliant of men—the talk of the town, the wonder of the day! She's as gay as a lark and as proud as a queen.

ROUND. I shall believe that when I have it from *her!*

(*Enter* LORD DEVENISH.)

LORD DEVENISH. By all that's undesired sir—You!

ROUND. With her hand so splendidly bestowed, at any rate, there can be no longer any hindrance to my seeing her.

LORD DEVENISH. Surely in so changed a case, dear sir, there can no longer be any reason for it!

ROUND. You talk of reasons, my lord, only to remind me that I've been long in discovering that of the authority you appear to enjoy in the private concerns of this house!

MRS. DOMVILLE. Everyone knows his dear lordship is our oldest friend—and our most affable!

ROUND. His affability I'm scarce in a position to enjoy. I'm willing however to beg that you appeal to it to grant me permission to take leave of Miss Brasier face to face.

LORD DEVENISH. Egad, sir, if *my* voice on that matter were sought, I wouldn't give you even a minute to take leave of Mrs. Domville!

MRS. DOMVILLE. (*Gracious.*) After the important event, you can come as often as you like!

ROUND. The important event takes place—?

MRS. DOMVILLE. (*After a moment's hesitation.*) We had given it out for Saturday; but we anticipate.

LORD DEVENISH. (*Emphatically.*) We anticipate. The wedding's *to-night.*

ROUND. (*Aghast.*) To-night?

LORD DEVENISH. And my chaplain ties the knot!

ROUND. (*After an instant, concentrated.*) *Out* on your knot! *Curse* your chaplain! (*Exit.*)

LORD DEVENISH. Curse the beggar's intrusion! Is everything quite in hand?

MRS. DOMVILLE. What does it matter if she doesn't see him?

LORD DEVENISH. Who can say what Mary sees? But everything's quite in hand!

MRS. DOMVILLE. The wedding-gown hasn't come home!

LORD DEVENISH. The bride's? It *will* come! Yours, dear Madam, is at any rate in the house!

MRS. DOMVILLE. You don't remind me, I suppose, that I've two old ones on the shelf. The third takes longer to make!

LORD DEVENISH. Do you presume to convey to me that you cry off our bargain?

MRS. DOMVILLE. You talk as if we were a pair of hucksters in the market!

LORD DEVENISH. Fie on the comparison! Sovereign, treaty-making powers! Need I remind you of the *terms* of our treaty? The day after your daughter, pursuant to my explicit undertaking, becomes Mrs. Domville of Gaye, Mrs. Domville of Richmond, to crown the happy enterprise, becomes Vicountess Devenish.

MRS. DOMVILLE. You make a great flourish of it, but you've your engagement still to perform!

LORD DEVENISH. Ain't I performing, Madam, every hour? Didn't I perform, just now, to that rascal sailor?

MRS. DOMVILLE. That rascal sailor has given me the fidgets! (*As he goes up.*) What are you going to do?

LORD DEVENISH. To say a word to Mary.

MRS. DOMVILLE. And what is that word to be?

LORD DEVENISH. Not, Madam, what I understand you fear: the voice of *nature* —in a tell-tale sigh. I stifle the voice of nature—for *you!*

MRS. DOMVILLE. Not for *me.* For *her;* and as a penance for all your falsity!

LORD DEVENISH. That I was ever false, Madam, was a pleasant fable of your own —to accompany the stern moral of your second marriage.

MRS. DOMVILLE. I would have married you out of hand when my compunction was fresh; but by the time I was free—

LORD DEVENISH. It had lost its early bloom? Fie upon compunction! Marry me

for bravery! And suffer me to proceed. I must satisfy myself again—

MRS. DOMVILLE. That he has really brought her round? Pray if he sensibly hadn't, how could he be so at ease?

LORD DEVENISH. (*Laughing.*) He's mighty fond of "ease"! The fellow's a born man of pleasure.

MRS. DOMVILLE. It's not all such gentry that confer as much of it as they take!

LORD DEVENISH. He only desires to be agreeable to *you,* Madam.

MRS. DOMVILLE. He succeeded from the moment he looked at me.

LORD DEVENISH. That's sufficiently denoted every time you look at *him!* (*Bantering.*) I don't mean to hint that poor Mary has her *mother's* inclination—!

MRS. DOMVILLE. Her mother, my lord, if she were asked, would marry the dear creature on the spot. As it is, she can only bustle about to adorn a younger bride!

LORD DEVENISH. You'll go for the gown yourself?

MRS. DOMVILLE. In the biggest coach in my stables! I want to make everything sure!

LORD DEVENISH. Everything *is* sure! (*Seeing* Guy.) And surest of all, Mr. Domville! It's a gage of his trust to *look* at him!

(*Enter* GUY DOMVILLE.)

GUY. I've been at your lodgings, my lord, to pay you my punctual duty; feeling that I owed you on so great a day an early visit and a close embrace.

LORD DEVENISH. It has been to render you a like attention that I have just presented myself here.

MRS. DOMVILLE. I admire the way you quit your beds to do each other honour; above all when I think of the hour, last night, at which you must have got into them!

GUY. It was an hour, Madam, I admit, that left us no choice of conclusions. The bright star that commands my attendance had long since sunk to obscurity; that luminary, indeed, to find a single fault with it, shines all too fitfully and sets all too soon! When Miss Brasier vanished we went for comfort to my Lady Mohun—but her ladyship's comfort proved singularly cold.—She engaged us deeply at cards.

MRS. DOMVILLE. Surely there's a fine

warmth in cards!

GUY. Only in the warm side of them! I lost, on the spot, to her ladyship almost the clothes that covered me!

LORD DEVENISH. Guy always loses to the ladies!

GUY. I oughtn't in modesty, I suppose, to lose my *garments!* But it's done advisedly, my lord, since by the common saying, that kind of ill-fortune makes another kind of good.

LORD DEVENISH. Good fortune in love. Hark to the fellow!

GUY. Perhaps on your example I ought to aim at both kinds; but what's a man to do at ombre when a lady *corrects* the luck?

LORD DEVENISH. This lady would say you're to take no notice!

MRS. DOMVILLE. What on earth does his lordship mean?

GUY. I won't pretend not to know! I think I always know, now, what his lordship means.

MRS. DOMVILLE. Sometimes it's a doubtful safety.

GUY. (*Laughing.*) Oh, I've had a lifetime of safety, Madam!

LORD DEVENISH. (*Laughing.*) The wretch quite dotes on his danger!

MRS. DOMVILLE. It's such a dear *good* wretch—it needn't fear communications!

GUY. I don't know how good it is, cousin, but I'm learning every day how ignorant.

MRS. DOMVILLE. Your ignorance, love, was a mighty pretty thing!

GUY. It goes down like an ebbing tide! I pick up fresh feelings as you gather pink shells; and when I hold these shells to my ear I find in each the mysterious murmur of the world!

MRS. DOMVILLE. You've a trick of fine speeches that make us women refuse you nothing.

GUY. You women, Madam, are even kinder than I always supposed you. You gave me confidence, you know, and upon my soul, I delight in confidence. I don't know how much I inspire, but I revel in all I feel. On such a day as this, it's universal. It doesn't stop even at my tailor!

LORD DEVENISH. You may trust your tailor when he's *my* tailor!

GUY. Egad, my lord, you've ordered my very garters!

LORD DEVENISH. With an eye to your interesting air! We shall see you in white and gold.

MRS. DOMVILLE. You can see he likes a fine coat!

GUY. I think, Madam, I like a fine anything! I can carry, at any rate, what you put on my back—and I think I can carry my happiness! Let it keep coming—and let me keep trying it! As I said to Mary anon, I enjoy my very gratitude. I meant, Madam, to *you.*

MRS. DOMVILLE. I hope you don't *always* talk to her of *me!*

GUY. When I want to please her most of all.

LORD DEVENISH. Didn't I promise you'd fall into the way of it? Didn't I tell you at Porches that you didn't do justice to your parts?

GUY. You told me at Porches some truths, my lord; and as regards the aptitudes you're so good as to praise, I'm almost frightened—

LORD DEVENISH. ⎱ (*Together.*)   Fright-
MRS. DOMVILLE. ⎰   ened?

GUY. At the way your prophecy's fulfilled. You told me I should find knowledge sweet—and life sweeter—

LORD DEVENISH. And love sweetest of all.

GUY. I had a shrewd notion of that!

LORD DEVENISH. The rascal had tried his hand!

MRS. DOMVILLE. Of course he had turned heads ere now.

LORD DEVENISH. He sees how he has turned all ours!

GUY. It was not to turn heads I came, Madam, but to do my duty to my line.

MRS. DOMVILLE. And to help me, dear Guy, to do mine.

GUY. I think, if I may say so, that you make too much of yours.

MRS. DOMVILLE. (*Grave, sincere.*) You were not at Mr. Domville's deathbed.

LORD DEVENISH. (*As if with the privilege of having assisted at a most edifying scene.*) I *was,* my dear Guy!

MRS. DOMVILLE. And you never knew my boy.

LORD DEVENISH. You're taking the boy's place, you know.

GUY. Peace then to these guardian spirits.

LORD DEVENISH. Precisely. And before we sacrifice to them—

MRS. DOMVILLE. I *must* put my hand on the bride's petticoat. (*To* GUY.) Did she go to her room?

GUY. My only complaint of her is that she's there too much.

MRS. DOMVILLE. I'll send her back to you.

LORD DEVENISH. I'll instruct him that he's to keep her.

MRS. DOMVILLE. (*To* GUY, *significant.*) Till her mother takes her. (*To* LORD DEVENISH.) Make sure of Father White. (*Exit.*)

LORD DEVENISH. She'd like to have it over this minute!

GUY. What in the world is she afraid of?—

LORD DEVENISH. Of your *other* love, my lad; your first!

GUY. (*Blank.*) My first?

LORD DEVENISH. I don't mean Mrs. Peverel!

GUY. (*Very grave.*) You couldn't, my lord—in decency.

LORD DEVENISH. Decency—bless us— looks quite another way; decency points to our Mother-Church! Mrs. Domville is jealous of *that* high mistress.

GUY. I don't know what I could do, that I haven't done, to set such jealousy at rest. There's scarcely a rule I haven't utterly abjured—there's scarcely a trust I haven't rigidly betrayed—there's scarcely a vow I haven't scrupulously broken! What *more* can a man do for conscience?

LORD DEVENISH. What a man does for conscience, Guy, comes back to him for joy!

GUY. Is that why *you're* so happy?

LORD DEVENISH. My happiness is the happiness of others.

GUY. Mine then ought to content you! Never once have I looked behind. I've taken what you've given me—I've gone where you led me—I've done what you've told me.

LORD DEVENISH. You've done it monstrous well!

GUY. And no one is the worse for me?

LORD DEVENISH. As a man of the world that's the only spot on your glory!

GUY. I must be sure that everyone is the *better* for me, for that makes me as right as the proof of a sum!

LORD DEVENISH. (*Smiling.*) You'll be precious sure to-morrow!

GUY. Then let to-morrow come, and many, many to-morrows!

LORD DEVENISH. Egad, we're catching up with them! I shall find Father White at his devotions.

GUY. Then let him *leave* his devotions! Remind him that *I've* left mine!

LORD DEVENISH. (*Attenuating.*) It's not after all to call him to cards! When Miss Brasier comes to you, be so good as to engage her closely.

GUY. (*Surprised.*) Will she grudge me her company?

LORD DEVENISH. Only from agitation. *Dispel* her agitation! (*Exit* LORD DEVENISH.)

GUY. Dispel her agitation? (*Thinking, with emotion.*) Face to face with my fortune I feel much more my own. Truly I've travelled far from all that might have been, and to say the words I must say, I must forget the words I didn't! (*Re-enter* GEORGE ROUND. *Startled.*) Pardon my inattention, sir, I didn't hear you announced.

ROUND. I came, sir, to deliver this packet to Miss Brasier.

GUY. Oh, another wedding-gift?

ROUND. Another wedding-gift.

GUY. From the toyman? A pretty bauble?

ROUND. A gold ring, sir—with a pearl.

GUY. (*Laughing.*) Only *one?* Pearls should come in dozens! But if you'll leave your packet with me, I'll take care Miss Brasier receives it.

ROUND. My errand, sir—my errand—

GUY. (*As he stands embarrassed.*) Was to place it in Miss Brasier's hand?

ROUND. To make sure it reaches her straight.

GUY. It shall reach her on this spot. She's coming to me. (*Then smiling as* ROUND *starts slightly.*) Quite lawfully, sir! I'm the bridegroom.

ROUND. (*After another hesitation.*) Then you can give it.

GUY. Is there anything to say with it?

ROUND. Only that I'll come back to see if it pleases. (*Exit.*)

GUY. To see if it pleases? For a tradesman, the fellow's blunt! (*Enter* MARY BRASIER.) You've just missed the toyman. He brought you a ring—with a pearl. (*Then as she appears blank and startled.*) Won't you look at it?

MARY. Give it to me.

GUY. From whom does it come?

MARY. (*With the box, in suppressed agitation.*) From no one. Where is the person who brought it?

GUY. He'll barely have reached the gate. Shall I call him?

MARY. (*Uneasy, prompt.*) No, no.

GUY. He's coming back to see if it pleases.

MARY. (*Troubled, but turning the matter off.*) It serves its purpose.

GUY. (*Laughing.*) Why, you've not even *tried* it!

MARY. It's a trifle—it's nothing! My mother told me to come to you.

GUY. (*Smiling.*) Your mother doesn't trust me!

MARY. I think she's wrong!

GUY. Do *you*, Mary? *Your* trust will be enough for me.

MARY. You're extraordinarily good to me.

GUY. How can I be good enough, when I think of all you're giving me?

MARY. (*With feeling.*) You ought to have more—than *I* can ever give!

GUY. More than beauty? More than virtue? More than fortune? More than your rising before me and letting me look into your eyes? I came here stammering and stumbling; but when I saw *you* it was as if I had caught the tune of my song!

MARY. Everything had been thoroughly arranged for you.

GUY. As things are arranged in the fairy-tales—only, you know, vastly better! The enchanted castle and the lovely princess, but never a giant nor a dragon.

MARY. (*Grave.*) The lovely princess seemed to *expect* the adventurous prince?

GUY. With all the charity in life! It was as if she too had been touched by the wizard.

MARY. She *had* been touched by the wizard!

GUY. (*With tender significance.*) The wizard whose name—?

MARY. (*Prompt.*) We mustn't *speak* it!

GUY. Because they never do, in fairy-tales, and our romance must conform to the rules. May our rules *all* be as easy! You leave me again?—You won't stay?

MARY. Yes, if I may make a condition. That of your telling me who brought the ring.

GUY. (*As if he had quite forgotten the incident.*) The ring?—from the toyman? Why, a young man with a brown face.

MARY. What sort of a manner?

GUY. No manner at all! You *know* him?

MARY. (*Embarrassed.*) I had better speak to him.

GUY. You easily can—he's coming back.

MARY. But *when*, did he say?

(*Re-enter* GEORGE ROUND.)

GUY. Here he is!

MARY. (*Greatly discomposed, but dissimulating; to* GUY.) Will you allow me five minutes with this gentleman?

GUY. (*Surprised.*) This gentleman?

ROUND. George Porter Round, at your particular service, sir.

MARY. I've something important to say to him.

GUY. (*Vague.*) Alone?

MARY. (*Finding a pretext.*) It's about *you*! And the ring.

GUY. (*Amused.*) Is it *my* finger it's to fit? Talk it over, then and send it back if it's not my quality! (*Exit.*)

MARY. (*With emotion.*) You've come *back*!

ROUND. I sent you back your early pledge as a sign.

MARY. I *have* it. I must give you back yours—that you so trustingly changed for it.

ROUND. Then the hideous story's true—and that's Mr. Domville?

MARY. You know then—you've been told?

ROUND. I was here an hour ago—straight from my ship.

MARY. You saw my mother?

ROUND. And your mother's— (*Catching himself up.*) The Lord Devenish.

MARY. They consented to your return?

ROUND. They opposed it—with all disparagement. But I've come back in spite of everything—for one glimpse of you!

MARY. They've hurried this business from the fear of you.

ROUND. Yet they must have little to fear of *you*—from your conduct!

MARY. Forgive me a little—*you* don't know!

ROUND. It's *I* who do know, Madam—and I think it's you who don't. They drove me off, and I went—in the state you may think. Then I got back my reason, and it came to me that I wanted you to know—to know that *I* know, and something, on my soul, of what I feel! I went to the goldsmith's in the town, and wrenching off that little ring of yours that I've worn so long, made him clap it into a new case. I thought some accident might protect me—that I might pass it in to you as coming from a shop. As fortune does sometimes favour the desperate, I succeeded. The coast was clear and I found myself face to face with *him!*

MARY. But this second time?

ROUND. The porter demurred, but passed me—for I asked for Mr. Domville. Mr. Domville had done me the honour—he still does it, happily—to mistake me for a peddler! But he had taken charge of my token.

MARY. The token of your inevitable scorn!

ROUND. When we parted, I could never have believed it!

MARY. We submitted, didn't we?—We consented to wait.

ROUND. In consenting I cursed your fortune, which made impatience look mercenary. If you had been poor, I would have consented to nothing!

MARY. My fortune is still the same. But some other things are different. The appeal to me pressed hard. And on my life it presses!

ROUND. Do you mean he makes such pretty love?

MARY. I'm speaking of my Lord Devenish. He's the oldest friend we have—he has ever studied to please me.

ROUND. I think *I've* studied harder! I don't know what poison has worked in you, but I can't look on you again without feeling that you're the thing in the world I most desire! By the blessing of heaven we're alone an instant, and all my life is yours! Break with this monstrous betrayal, and commit yourself to my guard. Escape while we *can* escape! I came by the river, and my boat's at the garden-foot.[1]

MARY. In a minute he'd miss me—he'd intercept us; a public dispute? Not that. (*Then in deep distress.*) And there are contentions too ugly!

ROUND. But your mother's not here.

MARY. It would reach her. She's only at the milliner's.

ROUND. And your mother's friend?

MARY. His lordship? He's mustering the company.

ROUND. Then deal with this gentleman as we *can*. Overreach him!

MARY. (*Vague.*) Deceive him?

ROUND. He *is* deceived—make it better. Break it to him that I'm your cousin and that your mother has put an affront on me. Bring us acquainted, and, egad, we'll drink together!

MARY. (*Blank.*) Drink?

ROUND. (*Going up to table.*) Permit me to prove the liquor. (*Pours out a glass and drinks.*) Faith, it'll do. I can carry more than he.

MARY. (*Blank.*) But what do you purpose?

ROUND. To draw him on to it, and lay him on the floor.

MARY. Hush!

(*Re-enter* GUY.)

GUY. (*Surprised and amused before* ROUND *has time to set down his glass.*) Ah, the wine-cup already flows.

ROUND. For a very thirsty messenger!

GUY. (*Smiling and addressing* MARY.) The messenger's perquisite? Then you've settled the great question?

---

[1] The drinking scene which ensues here was deleted by Henry James from the play after the first performance. The reader desiring to obtain an idea of the emended version must skip from Round's speech here to page 504 where, at the point indicated below, the play continued with Round still speaking: "It's *me, love,* you'll marry to-night!"

ROUND. We've agreed on what's to be done. Shall I disclose it, Madam?

MARY. Disclose it.

(*Exit* MARY *upstairs.*)

ROUND. (*Promptly moving back to table.*) I was faintish a moment since—I've had a long walk in the sun.

GUY. Then help yourself, man. (*Then as* ROUND *appears shy about handling the wine.*) You'd rather I should help you?

ROUND. (*While* GUY *pours it for him.*) You're most obliging, but I'd fain take it *with* you, sir.

GUY. (*Surprised.*) "With" me? (*Laughing. Accommodating.*) It's the wedding feast begun!

ROUND. (*With his full glass.*) For the poor folk that are not bidden!

GUY. None shall be poor to-day! You're drinking a royal wine.

ROUND. I shall feel more worthy of it if I *share* it with you.

GUY. (*More surprised, but still amused; humouring him.*) To the complete restoration of your comfort!

ROUND. (*As if still unwell.*) To the speedy establishment of yours! (*Waits for* GUY *to drink; then on* GUY's *smiling and waiting, drains his glass.*) I think another would right me!

GUY. (*Offering his own untouched glass.*) Then take this!

ROUND. (*Reluctant.*) Yours?—*You* take it! (GUY *drinks and fills again for* ROUND, *and then again, on* ROUND *insisting, for himself; and, glass in hand, they look at each other, till* ROUND *breaks out suddenly as if the wine has begun to go to his head.*) I *ain't* the toyman!

GUY. (*Amazed.*) For whom I mistook you?

ROUND. (*Trying it on further.*) No, I ain't a peddler! (*Familiar, sociable.*) 'Pon my soul I ain't a peddler.

GUY. (*Blank, but still amused.*) Then who the devil *are* you?

ROUND. George Porter Round—lieutenant in the King's Navy! Near relation—in fact *poor* relation!—to that virtuous lady!

GUY. (*So mystified that he doesn't believe it.*) Who yet didn't introduce you—to the man she's about to marry?

ROUND. Her mother's liquor, you see, has done that.

GUY. (*Still sceptical and increasingly astonished.*) It shouldn't be left to the liquor, sir—and to the accident of a glass too much!

ROUND. Whose is the glass too much? Not yours, sir—no glass at all! Not mine, sir—glass too little! Leave, on the contrary, *everything* to the liquor! (*With the appearance of growing more fuddled.*) The liquor good enough for anything. The liquor as good as the young lady and much better than the old!

GUY. (*As if the incident is beginning to strike him as more serious.*) Pray in what relation do you stand—?

ROUND. Relation of worm in the dust! I mean to the old one!

GUY. (*With a nervous laugh.*) *I* mean to the young one!

ROUND. Relation of first cousin—nephew of poor Mr. Brasier. Remember poor Mr. Brasier?

GUY. (*After a moment, but still smiling.*) I neither remember Mr. Brasier, sir, nor quite understand Mr. Brasier's nephew!

ROUND. Take me down that and you *will!* (*Then as* GUY, *with growing bewilderment and still glass in hand, hesitates to drink.*) Won't drink, either, with a poor relation?

GUY. (*As if this note touches him.*) I will indeed, if it will give you pleasure. (*Drains his glass.*)

ROUND. Nothing will give me so much!—Fill it again!

GUY. (*Again nervously laughing.*) I'm afraid I haven't quite your head!

ROUND. (*Imitating complete intoxication.*) *I've* no head—worm in the dust! Is a man of your rank afraid?

GUY. Not of you, sir!

ROUND. Then fill it again. (*Insistent, persuasive.*) You should be free on your wedding day.

GUY. (*After a moment.*) I'll be free! (*Drains another glass.*)

ROUND. (*Confidentially.*) The old lady *loves* me—not a bit! That's why the young lady—never mentions me at all! Quite ashamed of me too!—Keep it up!

GUY. (*After he has courteously complied*

by drinking a little.) I should have been glad to hear of you sooner.

ROUND. Never too late to mend! But she has a feeling heart; bless it, I say.

GUY. Miss Brasier? Bless it by all means.

ROUND. I thank you for that, you know. I particularly thank you.

GUY. Why the devil so particularly?

ROUND. Oh, you'll see, sir, if you ain't proud. (*Motioning him to keep it up.*) Come, don't be proud. You are when you don't meet me. (*Going up to table for another decanter.*)

GUY. What trap is he baiting? I'll be caught.

ROUND. (*Foolishly ingratiating.*) Meet me *once* in your life! [2]

―――――――――――

[2] The text of *Guy Domville* reveals clearly, as indicated above, that Henry James expunged the drinking scene from the play after the ill-fated first night. But a scrap of dialogue found among his papers shows that he would have liked to retain at least part of the scene, emending it only to render it more plausible. The dialogue was intended to be inserted as follows, after Round says "Meet me *once* in your life!"

GUY. (*As before.*) I'll meet you!
    (*Re-enter* MARY.)
I was about to *meet* him, Madam.

MARY. (*Troubled.*) I came back to save you―

ROUND. (*Assured, disappointed.*) Save him from *what*? He ain't proud!

GUY. (*To* MARY.) *He* has cured me, I think, of pride!

MARY. May I speak to him again?

GUY. Is it very necessary?

MARY. It's a word or two more―I *must* say it.

GUY. You may say it on a condition: that he give me his hand. Will you give it to me, sir?

MARY. (*As* ROUND *hangs back.*) Won't you give him your hand? Do it for me!

GUY. (*Checking her; very gravely.*) Enough, Madam. I'm answered.

MARY. (*Uneasy, unhappy.*) You should be answered *better!*

GUY. (*At the door.*) It will serve!
    (*Exit* GUY.)

ROUND. (*Impatient, semi-reproachful.*) In a moment I should have *had* him; he thinks I'm tipsy―he was coming on!

MARY. He was *not* coming on―and I couldn't allow it. He saw you were acting― he knows we have a secret!

ROUND. (*Astounded.*) Then why does he leave us with it?

MARY. Because he thinks I've taken part―! It's a crime to practise on him: he's too *good!*
At this point James intended the play to

GUY. (*After a moment, with his suspicion of* ROUND's *design now fairly kindled.*) I'll *meet* you! I know who you are, sir.

ROUND. (*Coming down with decanter and filling for* GUY *who with a changed manner, frankly welcomes it.*) I've filled to your wedding day.

GUY. You've filled, my dear fellow, but I'll be hanged if you've drunk!―Let me set you the example! (*Drinks deep.*)

ROUND. (*Who still doesn't drink.*) What do you think of the wine?

GUY. No judgment till the fifth glass!― Left your ship to come and see us?

ROUND. I left it last week. We had been three months out.

GUY. Three months out (*vaguely computing*) is just what *I've* been out! Devil of a time to be at the mercy of the waves!

ROUND. (*Laughing.*) That's the opinion of a judge who has not been much at sea!

GUY. Why, I'm at sea this blessed moment―never more at sea in all my life! A pack of things may happen in the course of three months―you may make a devil of a run. *I've* made a devil of a run―been off and round the world! Ever been round the world, in a cockle-shell like mine? (*Then laughing as* ROUND *laughs.*) I've trusted my life to a craft―as odd as any afloat. I think it's beginning to blow―do you suppose my boat'll hold? I put out, like you, this summer― but I haven't come into port.

ROUND. (*Hilarious.*) If you haven't come into port, I'll be bound you've come into burgundy. Take care how you sail your ship!

GUY. Got my orders, you know, for a voyage―a voyage of―What-do-you-call-it? You know what I mean to convey― 'spedishun o' 'scovery!

ROUND. (*Looking round the place.*) Blest if you haven't made, then, a monstrous fine coast!

GUY. Mons'ous fine coast. Mons'ous fine house. Mons'ous fine wine. Mons'ous fine women. 'Spedishun o' 'scovery!

ROUND. (*Allowing himself to become soberer as* GUY *appears more tipsy.*) I, on

―――――――――――

proceed, as in the case of the previous deletion, from the speech on page 504 "It's *me, love,* you'll marry to-night!"

my side, have discovered a monstrous fine gentleman in monstrous fine clothes!

GUY. Mons'ous fine clo'se! Clo'se and clo'se and clo'se! *See* me to-night in my clo'se—dance to-night at my what-do-you-call-it? (*Then as if apprehending refusal.*) *Don't* dance in the King's Navy?—*Teach* you, egad, to dance! (*More and more falsely fuddled.*) Fifth glass. Now for judgment! Judgment *good.* (*Hilariously.*) Keep it up, toyman!

ROUND. The moral of my visit, you know, is that I'm postively *not* a toyman!

GUY. Then why the missch'f come with little box?

ROUND. The little box was only a little present for the bride.

GUY. It wasn't for the bridegroom?

ROUND. (*Filling for him in the exhilaration of the success of his own plan.*) The best offering for the bridegroom, sir, is another bumper of wine!

GUY. (*Stupidly submitting.*) Sixth glass —judgment bad.—Why do you drink so much? (*Raising his glass.*) To the health of old friends! (*Holding out his hand in foolish amity.*) No such comfort in trouble as the clasp of the *hand* of old friends. (*Then as* ROUND, *with a stiff, instinctive scruple, holds off from accepting his hand.*) We *ain't* old friends? We ain't poor relations? Come I've drunk enough to cure me o' pride!

ROUND. Then I'll even drink to my cruel cousin!

GUY. (*With his glass raised.*) To the good health of Mrs. Domville?

ROUND. Ah, never—I mean of the girl!

GUY. (*Abruptly, with capricious tipsy irritation.*) Thank you to girl me no "girls" —on such a day as this!

(*Enter* MARY.)

ROUND. (*Good humoured.*) I mean of the sweet young lady!

GUY. (*As abruptly mollified.*) I mean of the sweet young lady. To the health of the sweet young lady. Here she *comes,* the sweet young lady! Your own relation, one of these days *my* relation, *our* relation. Keep it up!

ROUND. Now you see him, Madam, for what he is.

GUY. Eighth glass. Judgment gone!

ROUND. So indecently drunk that his very grossness belies his professions.

GUY. I'll be free, free on my wedding day.

ROUND. Fly with me now.

MARY. I cannot!

ROUND. You do love him, then?

MARY. No, no!

GUY. 'Spedishun of discovery! (*Exit* GUY.)

ROUND. It's *me, love,* you'll marry to-night! [3]

MARY. (*Painfully agitated and divided.*) How *can* I till I've seen my lord again? He put it to me so dreadfully on Sunday that I could save his life. My mother has promised to marry him! Overwhelmed with debt and difficulty, he has *that* one issue. But she becomes his wife only if *I* become Mr. Domville's!

ROUND. You spoke to me often of your mother's great taste for the Domvilles— but you never spoke to me of yours!

MARY. I *have* none. But I felt a private obligation to listen to my lord. I don't know *what* it was touched my heart when he went down on his knees to me! I thought I might tell him I'd please him— and yet escape with my honour. I believed Mr. Domville would guess the truth in time—would set me free. But now I must *face* my lord!

ROUND. Mr. Domville holds fast to your money!

MARY. Don't say that when he's so good to me!

ROUND. If he doesn't, he has only to know the truth to give you up.

MARY. He can only know it if I tell him!

ROUND. Tell him, then—tell him *now.* If you don't, your heart is *false* to me!

MARY. It's not false, but it's cruelly torn. Don't I owe a *duty* to my lord—to repay him for the kindness of years?

ROUND. You owe him *no* duty that's a sacrifice; you're the creature in the world of whom he's least entitled to demand one! (*After a moment of indecision.*) I know to-day what I didn't know when we parted—what it appears that every-

---

[3] Henry James picked up the dialogue at this point after the deletion of the drinking scene.

one else knows, and what I shouldn't have been fool enough to be blind to if I hadn't tasted more of my ship's mess than of the London tea-tables, that the man who is ready to traffic in your innocence with Jews and gamesters—

MARY. (*Crying out with dread.*) Ah, what are you going to tell me?

ROUND. Will you leave this house with me?

MARY. Not till I learn the worst!

ROUND. The Lord Devenish, Madam—is your father.

MARY. (*Horror-stricken.*) My father!

ROUND. (*Seeing* GUY.) Hush!

(*Re-enter* GUY, *as much changed from beginning of Act as between Acts First and Second.*)

GUY. (*With excited sternness.*) Our time is precious. You're attached to this lady!

ROUND. I'm in the very act of begging her to place herself under my honourable protection.

GUY. You're not in danger, Madam—if you're unhappy!

MARY. If you've been deceived, it's not I who first deceived you.

ROUND. Miss Brasier has been acting from the first under compulsion damnable!

MARY. (*To* ROUND.) Will you let *me* tell him?

ROUND. Ah, if you'll be quick!

MARY. (*To* GUY.) Will you guard him —will you preserve him?

GUY. You ask strange things of me! But I'll preserve him the more that I think I've not quite done with him. I'm at your service, sir, in any place.

MARY. (*To* ROUND.) *Leave* me with him!

GUY. Stay, sir—one word! You put on me just now a strange undertaking.

ROUND. And what undertaking had you first put on *me*?

GUY. That's exactly what we shall clear up.

MARY. (*Alarmed.*) My mother's coach— she's back!

ROUND. Do you wish me, sir, to *encounter* Mrs. Domville?

MARY. (*To* GUY.) Will you go and prevent her somehow from coming in?

GUY. (*With high emphasis.*) You love this gentleman?

MARY. I love him.

GUY. Then I'll do better. Will you pass in there?

ROUND. Shall I?

MARY. Mr. Domville's apartment.

GUY. Three fine rooms in a row, which I owe to the bounty of Mrs. Domville.

ROUND. Thank you, sir.

GUY. (*Closes door.*) Thank *you!* sir. (*Exit* ROUND.) [4] To what dire bewilderment am I exposed? I *see*—but I only *half* see; so I've kept you here—that in this dire bewilderment, and before we lose another moment, I may learn the truth.

MARY. Our engagement then has been

---

[4] At this point James had a brief entrance for "Mrs. Domville with two milliner's girls" and the following scene, later eliminated, ensued:

MRS. DOMVILLE. You dear inseparables! I understand your desire to be together; but I'm afraid that for a moment, (*to* MARY) long enough to pass on a petticoat, I must divide you. (*To* GUY.) You'll make it up later!—You *won't* give us ten minutes, to make sure of the set of a tucker?

GUY. As many minutes as you need, Madam. On such an occasion one can't make *too* sure!

MRS. DOMVILLE. You haven't fallen out—at this time of day? Wait till you see her in white satin!

MARY. (*Distressed.*) Mother!

GUY. I should like indeed to see you in white satin!

MRS. DOMVILLE. Then there ain't a moment to lose. May we have for five minutes the convenience of your bower? (*To the* MILLINERS.) Pass in there.

GUY. (*Protecting his door.*) Not in here! Forgive me if I seem ungracious; but my own preparations—

MRS. DOMVILLE. Are going on with such taste? I hope indeed they're splendid!

GUY. With a splendour that will surprise you.

MRS. DOMVILLE. Ah, then we won't spoil it! (*To* MARY.) Come quickly to your room.

GUY. Suffer me to speak to her first.

MRS. DOMVILLE. (*Disconcerted.*) After you've had the whole day?

MARY. It doesn't seem enough for what Mr. Domville has to say!

MRS. DOMVILLE. The rascal has a tongue —even with *me*!

GUY. It's to settle a question of weight!

MRS. DOMVILLE. Settle your question—but look at that shawl!

(*Exit* MRS. DOMVILLE *with the* MILLINERS.)

a bargain between my mother and my lord! My mother was to marry him if you married *me.* My lord's quite ruined—he doesn't know where to turn.

GUY. And your mother's rich—and I was poor?

MARY. You had the great name. She clings to that.

GUY. If his lordship caught me, he was to be paid?

MARY. Paid high! His lordship caught you!

GUY. Like a blind bat in a handkerchief. While I wondered at his love of the chase!

MARY. These things were dark to you— and they've but just grown clear to *me.*

GUY. Dark as deceit! Dark as dishonour! I believed too easily. I was tempted. You were offered to me—pressed upon me. And you were fair. You were given to me with a lie—a bribe! They declared you were free—were happy. Your submission itself misled me, for you suffered when you had only to speak.

MARY. I suffered, but I went on—I thought I was gaining time. Time, I mean, for you to see. But you were too dazzled.

GUY. I was dazzled by life!

MARY. You see what life is.

GUY. Some of it, yes. Why should you have feared to disappoint me, when I was nothing to you?

MARY. It wasn't you—it was my lord.

GUY. *He's* nothing to you.

MARY. He's my father.

GUY. (*Aghast.*) Your father?

MARY. I didn't know it then—I've known it but a moment. It makes strange things clear—the farce of his appeal. That appeal was like a voice that cried to me to make a sacrifice of my affection. I tried, but it was more than I could do.

GUY. You paid for my folly, for my madness—you paid for the vices of others! And now we pay together!

MARY. (*With decision.*) We've paid *enough*—we're free!

GUY. *I* haven't paid—what I've cost you. (*Wondering, harking back.*) He's your father?

MARY. It *had* to come (*indicating* ROUND's *refuge*) from *him!* It makes all the past confused.

GUY. And what does it make your mother?

MARY. *Forgive* my mother!

GUY. God pity us all! How can you forgive me for doing you so great a wrong?

MARY. You're already forgiven!

GUY. Ask *him* to forgive me. He had never harmed me. But I've hurt myself most; for I've been deluded with a delusion that was built upon an injury to others. It was to flaunt it in it here that I was brought. But that's over. Good-bye.

MARY. Good-bye.

GUY. Yet if I go, how can I leave you to *them?*

MARY. Ah. Let me not *look* on them!

GUY. Shall I commit you rather to the man you love?

MARY. *Trust* him!

GUY. Then join him there. Here is a key that opens the door on the river.

MARY. He has a boat, thank God. (DEVENISH *is heard off centre calling,* "Guy-Guy.")

GUY. (*Coming down from the window.*) His lordship—be quick!

MARY. (*Apprehensive.*) But *you?*

GUY. Me? *I'll* look on him! (*With a laugh of bitterness.*) It serves me right!

MARY. (*Carrying his hand to her lips.*) Heaven do as much for *you!* (*Exit* MARY.) (*Re-enter* LORD DEVENISH.)

LORD DEVENISH. My chaplain's robing— but you, dear boy, are *not!*

GUY. I've been here till this moment with Mary—engaging her closely, I promise you!

LORD DEVENISH. (*Laughing.*) I know the way you engage! You shall have guests enough—and noble ones. I put my hand on a score.

GUY. But none so noble as yourself, my lord!

LORD DEVENISH. I'm a neat figure, eh?

GUY. Scented like a duchess! Beams of light in clouds of fragrance!

LORD DEVENISH. Do I dazzle?—I love a fine odour! (*Holding out his gloves.*) Carry *that* to your nose!

GUY. (*Sniffing.*) My nose is regaled! (*Looking at the gloves.*) Something French, you prodigal? To the finger-tips! And every seam silver!

LORD DEVENISH. Straight from Paris. They set one off! Take 'em, my son.

GUY. (*Disconcerted.*) Take 'em?

LORD DEVENISH. Wear 'em to hand the bride. I've given you *nothing*.

GUY. You've given me too much, my lord!

LORD DEVENISH. Well, as you like! But you must be none the less a figure.

GUY. (*With a laugh.*) I've had a notion of my own for that!

LORD DEVENISH. Then quick, man; change!

GUY. I'll change! (*Exit.*)

LORD DEVENISH. He's half a monk still! (*Then laughing.*) But to-morrow—! (*Re-enter* MRS. DOMVILLE *followed by two* MIL-LINERS *carrying boxes.*) Ah, *you* at least are ready!

MRS. DOMVILLE. *Is Mary here?*

LORD DEVENISH. She was here till a moment since.

MRS. DOMVILLE. I've been to her room with these women.

LORD DEVENISH. Guy's dressing—we shall have a company!

MRS. DOMVILLE. We must first have a bride—and at least a footman!

LORD DEVENISH. The footmen are dressing too—making up white favours.

MRS. DOMVILLE. I bade them be brave—but not stone deaf!

LORD DEVENISH. The rascals are all at the barber's!

MRS. DOMVILLE. (*Calling out.*) Mary—Mary!—The hussy!

LORD DEVENISH. (*Calling.*) Mary! Mary!

MRS. DOMVILLE. Is she in there?

LORD DEVENISH. With Guy? Go and see.

(*Exit* MRS. DOMVILLE *to* GUY'S *apartment, where she is heard knocking and calling "Cousin, cousin! Daughter, daughter!"* LORD DEVENISH, *alone. Enter a* FOOTMAN.)

LORD DEVENISH. You've come from above. Is Miss Mary there?

FOOTMAN. I've come across the water, my lord. Miss Brasier's left the house.

LORD DEVENISH. Left it for where?

FOOTMAN. I've taken a guinea, my lord, not to say.

LORD DEVENISH. Then take another, damn you, to do your duty.

FOOTMAN. By my duty then, my lord, she's off in a great boat, a gentleman close beside her and three watermen to pull.

LORD DEVENISH. The boat of a man of war. The ruffian, the serpent!

(*Enter* MRS. DOMVILLE.)

MRS. DOMVILLE. He's locked in. I'll be hanged if he'll answer.

LORD DEVENISH. This knave has sufficiently answered. The hussy's gone with the villain she was leagued with and who reached here in time.

MRS. DOMVILLE. And you saw it, and gave no alarm!

FOOTMAN. I only saw, Madam, what Mr. Domville himself saw. He waved his hat from the terrace.

LORD DEVENISH. Domville, the false wretch, has abetted them.

MRS. DOMVILLE. Pursue them. Start the hue and cry!

LORD DEVENISH. Be off! The horse is stolen and it's all too late. From the moment they met we were dished. Let them go!

MRS. DOMVILLE. (*Horrified.*) Go and be married?

LORD DEVENISH. Go and be damned. We still have Guy! He's as much of a Domville as ever! He can still have heirs.

MRS. DOMVILLE. *He* can—but *I* can't!

LORD DEVENISH. Not of your body—but of your vows. *Mary* he never loved!

MRS. DOMVILLE. More shame to him.

LORD DEVENISH. He's in love with Mrs. Peverel.

MRS. DOMVILLE. (*Highly impatient.*) So are *you*, I believe, from the way you prate of her!

LORD DEVENISH. If I prate of her now, it's because our contract *stands*.

MRS. DOMVILLE. How does it stand, when you've not performed your task?

LORD DEVENISH. My task, Madam, was not to hold Mary—it was to hold *Guy!* We *do* hold him, i'faith—through the blessed lady of Porches. If I don't demonstrate *that* —if I don't please you *still*—

MRS. DOMVILLE. (*Taking the words out of his mouth.*) I may *then* turn you off? God knows I *will!*

LORD DEVENISH. And not, Madam, be-*fore!* We can catch Mrs. Peverel—if we act in time: from this moment forth she's the only woman he'll look at. She'll retrieve our defeat.

MRS. DOMVILLE. (*Breathless.*) Where are you going?

LORD DEVENISH. To Porches again—to see she doesn't marry her neighbour. (*Elated with his idea; confident.*) You'll marry *yours*! (*Exit in hot haste.*)

MRS. DOMVILLE. I believe I *shall*—before he has done with me! (*Then as she sees* GUY.) Mercy on us! (*Re-enter* GUY DOMVILLE *in plain array.*) What on earth, sir, have you done?

GUY. I think, Madam, I've done justice.

I've seen them on their way.

MRS. DOMVILLE. Their way's a fine one!

GUY. It seems to me finer than mine has been. It seems to me finer even than yours!

MRS. DOMVILLE. (*Dismayed.*) Mine?

GUY. Yours.

MRS. DOMVILLE. (*Conscious, faltering.*) Does she—know?

GUY. She knows. She made *me* know. I helped her. Farewell!

MRS. DOMVILLE. (*In anguish, with a supreme appeal.*) Cousin!

GUY. (*Inexorable.*) Farewell!

MRS. DOMVILLE. Where are you going?

GUY. I'm going back! (*Exit.*)

ACT THIRD

The White Parlour at Porches. Door from the hall left; door to the bookroom right. MRS. PEVEREL *is seated by fire. Enter* FANNY *from the hall with a letter on a tray.*

FANNY. A letter, please, ma'am. (*Then as* MRS. PEVEREL, *gazing at fire, doesn't answer.*) Please, ma'am, a *letter*.

MRS. PEVEREL. (*Starting at last; eager.*) A letter? (*On looking at it, disappointed, uninterested, tosses it down unopened.*) Oh!

FANNY. And a whole shilling to pay, ma'am. (*Then, as* MRS. PEVEREL *has dropped again into her reverie.*) He'll take nothing less than a shilling, ma'am.

MRS. PEVEREL. (*Vaguely roused.*) A shilling?

FANNY. (*Picking the letter up.*) It's a deal to pay for a letter to lie on the floor!

MRS. PEVEREL. *Give* him a shilling, child, and hold your tongue!

FANNY. But where am I to *find* the shilling, ma'am?—

MRS. PEVEREL. With my money—where my money is.

FANNY. But *where's* your "money" in these dull days? (*Then perceiving a coin on the dresser.*) Here's a piece, ma'am.

MRS. PEVEREL. Then give it to him!

FANNY. (*Dismayed.*) Give it *all*?

MRS. PEVEREL. (*With an irritated, bored movement, takes the coin from her; then without looking at it.*) Here's your money, man. Go!

FANNY. (*Aghast.*) Why, it was half a crown!

MRS. PEVEREL. I didn't heed!

FANNY. There are few things you *do* "heed," ma'am, just now!

MRS. PEVEREL. There's one thing I *must*! (*Indicating a book lying on a cabinet.*) Is that book Latin?

FANNY. Laws, ma'am, how should *I* know? (*Giving the book as if almost awestruck.*) Are you taking to ,"Latin," ma'am?

MRS. PEVEREL. For my son's lesson. Please tell him to come in and have it.

FANNY. He won't come in for *my* telling, ma'am.

MRS. PEVEREL. (*Flinging the book down disheartenedly.*) And he won't come in for mine!

FANNY. He'd only come in for a gentleman, I think.

MRS. PEVEREL. (*Musing.*) He must feel a stronger hand!

FANNY. Such another as Mr. Domville's!

MRS. PEVEREL. There *isn't* "such another"! Mr. Domville's was so strong—yet Mr. Domville's was so light.

FANNY. (*Glancing down complacently, while she gives it a turn, at the pocket of her apron.*) Mr. Domville was so *free*!

MRS. PEVEREL. (*With latent bitterness.*) Well, it's not "free" now!

FANNY. Do you mean he has lost money?

MRS. PEVEREL. (*Dryly.*) He has gained it. By his marriage.

FANNY. Mercy, ma'am, is he married?

MRS. PEVEREL. By this time—to-day.

FANNY. And he quite the same as a priest!

MRS. PEVEREL. He's *not* quite the same. He never *was!*

FANNY. Well, if he was here he'd pay for a fiddler—to make us all dance for his wedding!

MRS. PEVEREL. He'll never be here again!

FANNY. (*Sad, wistful.*) Nor any other gentleman at all? (*Prompt.*) I mean for the Latin!

MRS. PEVEREL. I'm looking for another. There should certainly *be* one.

FANNY. (*Diplomatic.*) I suppose they're precious hard to come by!

MRS. PEVEREL. (*With a weary sigh.*) Especially if one doesn't look!

FANNY. (*Circumspect, after a silence.*) Mr. Humber, ma'am—does *he* know Latin?

MRS. PEVEREL. I haven't the least idea what Mr. Humber knows!

FANNY. *I* have, ma'am—for *one* thing: he knows Mr. George is mighty fond of him.

MRS. PEVEREL. If Mr. George is mighty fond, Mr. George is mighty fickle! Mr. George shifts his affections!

FANNY. Mr. Humber don't—do he, ma'am?—Mr. Humber, ma'am, is constant.

MRS. PEVEREL. (*With a sudden flare of irritation and peversity.*) Then why hasn't he *been* here for weeks?

FANNY. (*At the window, startled.*) Law, ma'am, he *is* here now! He's at the door in his coach!

MRS. PEVEREL. (*More capriciously still, with decision.*) Then he mustn't get out!

FANNY. He *is* out—he's coming in.

MRS. PEVEREL. I won't see him. (*Dismissing* FANNY, *getting her off.*) Meet him—stop him—send him away! (*Exit* FANNY.) I *won't* see him! (*After an instant.*) I can't! (*After another instant.*) I oughtn't!

(*Re-enter* FANNY, *breathless.*)

FANNY. He's on the stairs—now!

MRS. PEVEREL. Then I must be tidy! (*Exit hastily to the bookroom.*)

(*Enter* FRANK HUMBER.)

FANNY. She's in the bookroom—she'll come.

FRANK. Thank you, Fanny. What's the good news at Porches?

FANNY. There's neither good nor bad at Porches, sir; but there's wonderful news at Richmond. Mr. Domville's married to-day! (*Exit to the hall.*)

FRANK. (*Immediately affected.*) To-day? —Will *that* help me? Nothing will help me! (*Re-enter* MRS. PEVEREL.) You must wonder at the motive of my visit.

MRS. PEVEREL. It was never my wish that you should never come back.

FRANK. It was once mine. It was at least my purpose.

MRS. PEVEREL. (*Kindly.*) I rejoice in your recovery from so desperate a mood.

FRANK. If it was a mood, Madam, it was a mood that has remained. The purpose I speak of has grown.

MRS. PEVEREL. Then your visit is certainly odd!

FRANK. It's worse than "odd"—it's abject! But I've ceased to pretend to make a figure!

MRS. PEVEREL. You place me in the painful position of scarce being able to show you that I'm sorry to see you so altered.

FRANK. I doubt not you're sorry, Madam —and there can be nought but sorrow between us. I'm leaving the country.

MRS. PEVEREL. (*Surprised.*) For where— for what?

FRANK. For the ends of the earth—and for everything!

MRS. PEVEREL. (*Anxious.*) For a long time?

FRANK. For ever!

MRS. PEVEREL. (*Astonished, compassionately remonstrant.*) But your estate? your home?

FRANK. What *use* have I for a "home"— a home empty and barren? We're neighbours, after all, till I go; so I come to take leave of you.

MRS. PEVEREL. You go to travel?

FRANK. I go to wander.

MRS. PEVEREL. And who goes *with* you?

FRANK. I go alone.

MRS. PEVEREL. Alone into strange lands —alone into exile?

FRANK. It's better than alone here: close to you, yet separate!

MRS. PEVEREL. It seems to me then it's *I* who ought to go!

FRANK. (*Startled, flickering up.*) If you do, I'll follow you!

MRS. PEVEREL. Then I'll *stay!* (*Sadly smiling.*) I'll not follow *you!*

FRANK. I wish you a long life—in all this tranquillity!

MRS. PEVEREL. I shall remember you well—I shall miss you much. I'm not a woman of many friends—I've not a life of many diversions. This country will seem an empty place.

FRANK. All the more that I can recall, without a reminder, the loss you lately suffered.

MRS. PEVEREL. As I can allude to it without a scruple. Mr. Domville's a support—withdrawn. Do you know what happens to-day?

FRANK. (*With a glance at the clock.*) It's over?

MRS. PEVEREL. It's over. I wish him all happiness and length of days!

FRANK. I wish him all peace and plenty! Plenty of children, I mean! A numerous and virtuous posterity!

MRS. PEVEREL. (*Abrupt, irrelevant.*) Is your beautiful house to be closed?

FRANK. It will always be open to *you.* It's full of my grandmother's books—old novels in ten volumes. If you lack diversions you can go and take down the "Grand Cyrus"[1] or eat pears[2] in the great garden.

MRS. PEVEREL. (*With a frank smile.*) Along with the child? Do you want to kill him? There are too many pears for him *here!*

FRANK. (*Beguiled, with a laugh.*) Is he perched even now in a tree?

MRS. PEVEREL. We'll go anon together and pull him out!—What strange land do you go to first?

FRANK. (*Impatiently.*) What does it matter, when they're all strange alike?

---

[1] *Artamène, ou le Grand Cyrus*, a French heroic romance by Madeleine de Scudéry (1607–1701) was published in ten volumes between the years 1649–53. The translation was very popular in England.

[2] James originally wrote "plums" then substituted "pears."

MRS. PEVEREL. (*With sudden feeling.*) Mr. Humber—forsake this wild plan! Don't give up your own lands and your own people—don't give up the sweet, safe things you love!

FRANK. (*With a newborn, unexpected tremor of hope and suspense.*) Don't give *you* up—is that what you mean?

MRS. PEVEREL. I mean— (*Faltering.*) I mean—!

(*Re-enter* FANNY.)

FANNY. (*Loudly announcing.*) My Lord Devenish!

(*Enter* LORD DEVENISH.)

LORD DEVENISH. I came in the hope of finding you alone, Madam.

MRS. PEVEREL. Mr. Humber is going to a great distance. He is here to bid me good-bye.

LORD DEVENISH. Well, if that affecting ceremony is over I should like the honour of half-an-hour's conversation with Mrs. Peverel.

FRANK. (*Disconcerted, resentful.*) That affecting ceremony is by no means "over"!

LORD DEVENISH. (*Unperturbed.*) May I none the less, in view of the extreme importance of time in the case, venture to ask Mrs. Peverel for an immediate interview?

MRS. PEVEREL. I've no doubt Mr. Humber will excuse me, since (*smiling at* FRANK) I'm sure his haste is less than yours!

FRANK. (*Significantly.*) My haste, thank God, is less than when I came, Madam!

LORD DEVENISH. That's good news if it refers to Mr. Humber's leaving the country.

MRS. PEVEREL. (*To* FRANK.) If you must go—

FRANK. (*In suspense.*) If I must go?

MRS. PEVEREL. (*Smiling.*) You can first pull Geordie out of the tree!

FRANK. (*Displeased, with decision.*) I'll get into it *with* him! (*Exit.*)

LORD DEVENISH. Mr. Domville, Madam, is *free!* His wonderful marriage is off!

MRS. PEVEREL. (*Astonished.*) And what has occurred to stay it?

LORD DEVENISH. Everything has occurred—and on top of everything my coming down here to tell you so. You may expect Mr. Domville in this place, and I judged it wise to prepare you for his return. To that good end I've got here first.

MRS. PEVEREL. (*Anxious.*) Does he follow anon?

LORD DEVENISH. Oh, not till he has turned round, I conceive—found his feet and recovered his fall from the height of his great match. In honest terms, Madam, he has been misused.

MRS. PEVEREL. (*Startled, with indignation.*) Jilted?—*Such* a man?

LORD DEVENISH. By practices most underhand! The young lady was clandestine!

MRS. PEVEREL. She must have been abominable!

LORD DEVENISH. (*Just visibly wincing.*) She was beguiled, Madam, by a villain!— Mr. Domville has suffered much.

MRS. PEVEREL. I vow I pity him!

LORD DEVENISH. He knows that you *must!*

MRS. PEVEREL. And that's why he's coming? I shall indeed be kind to him!

LORD DEVENISH. Kind, Madam, but firm! Firm with his inclination.

MRS. PEVEREL. (*Struck, apprehensive.*) You mean he'll take up again—

LORD DEVENISH. The cruel profession he forsook? That's the fear that has brought me! Suffer him, Madam, *not* to! You'll find a way when you see him. You'll see a braver gentleman; greater by the greatness I've taught him!

MRS. PEVEREL. (*Much interested.*) He must have a different air!

LORD DEVENISH. Finer, Madam, and nobler! To stifle such an air in a *cassock*—

MRS. PEVEREL. Would be a grievous sin! But why, if he's only dejected, should he come to this dull place?

LORD DEVENISH. (*With great intended effect, as if having waited for just the right moment to make the revelation.*) "Why," Madam? Because he loves you! Because he worships you!

MRS. PEVEREL. (*Astounded, confounded.*) And yet was so ready to wed another woman?

LORD DEVENISH. Overborne by Mrs. Domville! He never *loved* Miss Brasier.

MRS. PEVEREL. (*Catching her breath; stupefied.*) Never loved her?

LORD DEVENISH. He feels the indignity, but not the loss; and he had never dreamed that with *you,* who had only known him

as the tutor of your son and the nursling of the Church, there was the smallest human hope for him. The way to save him is to *give* it to him! *That,* Madam, is the truth I came to utter. Having satisfied my conscience, I retire. To pay another visit in the West. (*Invitingly, persuasively.*) I shall not be too far to hear from you.

MRS. PEVEREL. To hear, I judge you mean, from Mr. Domville.

LORD DEVENISH. I bow to your modesty! But Mr. Domville had better not know—

MRS. PEVEREL. Of your lordship's kind warning?

LORD DEVENISH. Don't advertise my kindness!

MRS. PEVEREL. Your presence will be the talk of the village.

LORD DEVENISH. The village is dumb— my carriage is a mile off.

MRS. PEVEREL. And you walk back to it?

LORD DEVENISH. (*Smiling, urbane, successful, with the movement of complacently swinging a cane.*) Across the quiet fields!

MRS. PEVEREL. But Mr. Humber has seen you.

LORD DEVENISH. Isn't Mr. Humber going?

MRS. PEVEREL. (*After an instant.*) I can't answer for it!

LORD DEVENISH. (*Smiling.*) I should have thought it the thing in the world you could *most* answer for! Ask him to hold his tongue!

MRS. PEVEREL. (*Embarrassed, considering.*) I'm scarce in a position to ask him a service.

LORD DEVENISH. (*As if struck by a new and intenser idea.*) Then send him to *me!*

(*Re-enter FANNY, carrying a tray of refreshments and wine, which she places on a table.*)

MRS. PEVEREL. I'll send him! (*To FANNY.*) What wine have you brought?

FANNY. The best, ma'am—and the other.

MRS. PEVEREL. (*Smiling at LORD DEVENISH.*) Don't give his lordship the "other"! (*Exit.*)

FANNY. (*Pouring out wine.*) Mr. Domville, my lord, used to like it!

LORD DEVENISH. (*After he has tasted the wine.*) Mr. Domville wouldn't like it now!

FANNY. I suppose there's much better in London.

LORD DEVENISH. (*Amused.*) There's nothing much better in London, my dear, than a pretty country lass!

FANNY. (*Curtseying low.*) Oh, my lord!

LORD DEVENISH. (*Quickly.*) Go away!

(*Re-enter* FRANK HUMBER. *Exit* FANNY.)

FRANK. Your lordship desires my company?

LORD DEVENISH. (*Pouring out a second glass.*) To have a glass with you. (*Then after a conscious pretence, on each side, of drinking.*) Mr. Domville's in love with this lady!

FRANK. (*Blank.*) In the very act of marrying another?

LORD DEVENISH. He's *not* in the act. The act's undone; through his coldness at the last. The young lady guessed it—the young lady broke!

FRANK. (*Amazed.*) And he took back his word?

LORD DEVENISH. (*Very ready.*) She took back hers! He retired in silence, conscious of his secret preference.

FRANK. (*After a moment; coldly, stiffly.*) The object of such a preference is surely *most* concerned—!

LORD DEVENISH. That object, sir, he has never addressed!—Do you conceive that Mrs. Peverel would *listen* to him?

FRANK. (*Dryly.*) I know nothing about it. How is it I can serve your lordship?

LORD DEVENISH. (*Consciously rebuffed, but still assured.*) By acting a noble part. It rests with you to rout Father Murray. (*With commanding authority.*) Mr. Domville must *marry!*

FRANK. (*Struck, sombre.*) Marry Mrs. Peverel?

LORD DEVENISH. Understand that he *may!*

FRANK. What *prevents* his understanding?

LORD DEVENISH. (*Very pointedly.*) If *you* know of nothing, sir, the question I wish to ask you is answered!

FRANK. (*Deeply troubled, thinking.*) He *loves* her—Guy?

LORD DEVENISH. Did you never scent it?

FRANK. Why, he spoke to her for *me,* when, never supposing, never *dreaming,* I pushed him to 't!

LORD DEVENISH. (*Decided.*) Then *that,* of course, prevents him!

FRANK. (*Still realizing, remembering.*) For *me*—poor wretch—when he loved her himself!

LORD DEVENISH. Mr. Domville was magnanimous!

FRANK. He was heroic! You call upon *me* to be so, my lord. There's only *one* way! Not to talk of absence, but to practise absence. If I'm gone, he'll know why!

LORD DEVENISH. I'll take care he knows why!

(*Re-enter* MRS. PEVEREL.)

MRS. PEVEREL. (*Breathless.*) Mr. Domville! His carriage has entered the gate.

FRANK. (*Strongly disconcerted.*) And I'm not off!

LORD DEVENISH. (*Deeply dismayed.*) And I still less! (*At left, hurriedly.*) I leave you, Madam.

MRS. PEVEREL. Not that way—you'll meet him!

FRANK. (*Putting out his hand to* MRS. PEVEREL.) Farewell!

MRS. PEVEREL. (*Keeping his hand.*) You won't wait to take leave of him?

LORD DEVENISH. (*Pressing.*) You should do *that* Mr. Humber! (*Then while* FRANK *gives a gesture of pained resignation.*) How *then* am I to go?

MRS. PEVEREL. (*Anxious, at a loss.*) Some other way!

FRANK. (*Surprised.*) Your visit's private?

LORD DEVENISH. (*Angrily.*) Private!

FRANK. (*Amusedly.*) His step's on the stair! Here he comes!

MRS. PEVEREL. (*Quickly, at the door right.*) Pass in!

(*Exit* LORD DEVENISH *on tiptoe.*)

FRANK. The bookroom—with no way out?

MRS. PEVEREL. (*Ruefully.*) None at all! (*Then making the best of it.*) I'll free him! —Silence!

(*Enter* GUY DOMVILLE.)

GUY. (*After having looked hard an instant from* MRS. PEVEREL *to* FRANK.) Forgive the old trick in the old place—I've come up as I used to come up.

MRS. PEVEREL. And you're welcome as

you used to be welcome!

GUY. The abruptness of my return deserves, I fear, less honour.

MRS. PEVEREL. It shall have all we can give it—and that of some instant preparation for your staying.

GUY. Madam, I didn't come to quarter myself—

MRS. PEVEREL. (*Ironic.*) Anywhere but on the baker?

GUY. I sent on my shay to the inn.

MRS. PEVEREL. It shall come back! (*Exit.*)

GUY. (*After precautions; in eager suspense.*) Has she accepted you?

FRANK. She has *not* accepted me!

GUY. Then, since I helped you, spoke for you, did everything I *could* for you, I tell you that she's dearer to me than *life*, that I'm not bound but free, and that I've come back again to tell her so!

FRANK. I know to what tune she's "dear" to you!

GUY. (*Astonished.*) You know it?

FRANK. Take care!

(*Re-enter* MRS. PEVEREL.)

MRS. PEVEREL. I've sent for your shay.

GUY. (*Gratefully resigned.*) Then I'm in your hands! (*Unsuspiciously, to* FRANK.) You're going?

FRANK. (*Impenetrable.*) I'm going!

GUY. But I shall see you again!

FRANK. You'll have to be alert! And only, too, if so soon again this lady will consent to part with you.

MRS. PEVEREL. (*Smiling.*) I think it will be found that the consent most necessary is Geordie's.

GUY. (*Completely genial.*) And how is that victim of the rudiments? Would he come and absolve his tormentor?

MRS. PEVEREL. In a moment, if he knew you were here.

GUY. Then won't you *let* him know?

FRANK. I'll acquaint him!

MRS. PEVEREL. (*Demurring, embarrassed.*) Not yet, please: say nothing! I've a reason for his not romping in!

GUY. (*To* FRANK.) I shall overtake you before you mount.

FRANK. (*In weary self-derision.*) I shall only mount a cushion.

GUY. You drove?

FRANK. Like a helpless fat dowager—

in an old yellow coach.

GUY. (*Concerned.*) Do you mean to say you're ill?

MRS. PEVEREL. (*Significantly.*) He knows the way to get better! (*The more gaily, to* FRANK.) Keep Geordie quiet! (FRANK, *at the door, looks at her fixedly a moment, as if on the point of saying something; then checking himself, exit rapidly.*) I needn't keep you here. We can talk as well—anywhere.

GUY. Shall we go into the garden?

MRS. PEVEREL. (*Demurring.*) We shall have the child!

GUY. (*Suggesting the bookroom.*) Then in there?

MRS. PEVEREL. No—it's encumbered!

GUY. (*Looking about him appreciatively, fondly.*) This old White Parlour has the friendly face to me! I've seen it, since we parted, in visions—I've missed it in grander places. Its pannelled walls close me in—the tick of the clock seems to greet me. It's full of faint echoes and of lost things found again. We sat here o' winter nights.

MRS. PEVEREL. (*Coerced by his tone, wishing not to break the spell.*) Then we can sit here again!

GUY. I think it was for *that* I came back!

MRS. PEVEREL. (*Smiling.*) On the eve of your great marriage?

GUY. That eve has had no morrow!

MRS. PEVEREL. I fear you've been shamefully used!

GUY. Not by the person in whom I liked most to believe. That person was honest. But I think that, save at Porches, there are very few others who are.

MRS. PEVEREL. At Porches—if we're not much else—we're honest!

GUY. That's why my heart turned back to you and why my footsteps ran a race with it!—Do you remember how, at the last, we talked together of the world?

MRS. PEVEREL. You said all manner of ill of it!

GUY. I told you I'd come back to say more. I've seen it—and it doesn't answer!

MRS. PEVEREL. You must describe to me what you've seen.

GUY. Ah, much of it I wish to forget!

MRS. PEVEREL. What you must forget is that you've suffered.

GUY. What I must forget is that I've strayed!—from the happiness that was near to the happiness that was far!

MRS. PEVEREL. But the happiness that was "near" was a life you had put away.

GUY. The happiness that was near was a treasure not mine to touch! I believed that treasure then to be another's.

MRS. PEVEREL. You had too great things to think of—and now I see how they've changed you. You hold yourself in another way.

GUY. (Smiling.) I try to carry my "name"!

MRS. PEVEREL. (Triumphant, to prove how right she has been.) You carry it better than you did!

GUY. People have cried me up for it. But the better the name, the better the man should be.

MRS. PEVEREL. He can't be better than when his duty prevails.

GUY. Sometimes that duty is darkened, and then it shines again! It lighted my way as I came, and it's bright in my eyes at this hour. But the brightness, in truth, is yours—it grows and grows in your presence. Better than anything I sought or found is that purer passion—this calm retreat! (Then on an ironic movement of MRS. PEVEREL's.) Aye, calm, Madam (struck with the sight of LORD DEVENISH's white gloves), save for these! I've seen them before—I've touched them. (Thinking, recalling; then with light breaking.) At Richmond!

MRS. PEVEREL. (Deeply discomposed, at a loss.) My Lord Devenish left them.

GUY. (Astounded.) Was he here?

MRS. PEVEREL. An hour ago.

GUY. And for what?

MRS. PEVEREL. (Seeking a pretext.) To see Mr. Humber.—He was passing to the West—to see a friend—and stopped to pay me his compliments. As Mr. Humber happened to be here, he had no occasion to seek further. He asked me not to put it about.

GUY. (Abrupt, intense.) What does he want of Frank?

MRS. PEVEREL. Ah, that you must ask him!

GUY. (With a start.) His lordship? Not

yet!—I must ask Frank!

MRS. PEVEREL. I meant Mr. Humber.

GUY. (Thinking, sharply demurring. Dismissing this as impossible. Then as he sees FANNY: re-enter FANNY.) Has Mr. Humber gone?

FANNY. Mr. George won't let him!

MRS. PEVEREL. Ask him to please come back! (Exit FANNY.) Can you think of no good motive—?

GUY. For his lordship's presence here?—Have you got one to tell me?

MRS. PEVEREL. (Making a visibly immense, a quite pathetic effort.) He came to let me know—

GUY. (In suspense.) To let you know?

MRS. PEVEREL. (Checking herself, giving it up with a motion of disappointment.) Mr. Humber!

(Re-enter FRANK HUMBER. Exit MRS. PEVEREL.)

GUY. (With excited abruptness.) I know my Lord Devenish is here!

FRANK. (Surprised.) Mrs. Peverel has told you?

GUY. He betrayed himself. (Pointing to the gloves.) For a conspirator, he's careless!

FRANK. (Loyally feigning blankness.) Is he a "conspirator"?

GUY. In what other character can he have stolen such an extraordinary march? (With passionate earnestness.) Frank—what has he come to obtain of you? It was you he came to have speech of?

FRANK. (Grave, impenetrable.) He has had it!

GUY. And to what end, please?

FRANK. To the end that I'm leaving England for ever.

GUY. (Bewildered.) To go where?

FRANK. Anywhere that's far enough!

GUY. (With fresh dismay.) For that man?

FRANK. For myself. For everyone!

GUY. (Peremptory.) For me, Frank?

FRANK. (Still evasive.) For peace—for life!

GUY. But at his strange suit—his instance?

FRANK. He thinks it right!

GUY. (With a bitter laugh.) What he thinks right won't do! He came to undermine you!

FRANK. It didn't matter—I saw my duty.

GUY. Your duty to whom?

FRANK. To myself!

GUY. If it was so clear, why were you at Porches?

FRANK. (*Passing this question by.*) And my duty to *you*. Don't I know you love her?

GUY. (*Quick.*) You didn't know till I told you!

FRANK. On the contrary, you saw I *did!*

GUY. (*Recalling, seeing clear.*) Devenish told you—betrayed me?

FRANK. He rendered you a service!

GUY. His "services" are selfish. His services are base. His offices are curst! (*Explaining to himself now completely, and as if, therefore, to* FRANK.) He got here first to practise on my freedom, on my honour. He guessed my secret, and he used it! He has driven you from home.

FRANK. Not *he,* man! My own discomfort.

GUY. Your own discomfort is his lordship's own plan—the fruit of his visit!

FRANK. The fruit of my miserable failure!

GUY. Is it *your* miserable failure that brings you—without a warrant—to the feet of this lady?

FRANK. I only came to tell her I'm going.

GUY. And let that danger plead for you? (*Triumphantly.*) Frank—you had a hope!

FRANK. (*After an instant, pleading guilty.*) Well, I had one spark!

GUY. Which was quick to be a flame! His lordship quenched it.

FRANK. (*Convicted, confessing.*) His lordship arrived—it went out! He told me you were free again.

GUY. "Free—free"? Free only to undo? My freedom, verily is vast! My freedom, Frank, is wonderful! My freedom's a boon to his lordship! (*Then in a sudden different tone; still sarcastically but ominously.*) He shouldn't touch my freedom! For *me* these things are done, and for me another good man suffers?

FRANK. You did what you could for me three months ago—I'm ready to help you now.

GUY. Help me by considering that I hold you fast! I've known you long, sir: I wish you no manner of ill.

FRANK. (*Moved, perplexed.*) Then what am I to believe?

GUY. Not that I do a damage wherever I turn! I was called into the "world"—but I didn't come for sorrow! I cost no pang, as I *was!*

FRANK. My dear fellow—you don't know!

GUY. (*Struck, wondering.*) Do *you* know, Frank?

FRANK. (*Turning away.*) Ask me not too much! [3]

(*Re-enter* MRS. PEVEREL.)

MRS. PEVEREL. It's a simple case of conscience—I must free his lordship!

FRANK. He's in *there!*

GUY. (*Astonished, then smiling.*) All this while?

MRS. PEVEREL. (*Gravely.*) He has had patience!

GUY. (*Imperatively checking her.*) He'll have to have more! There's something I wish to say to you first. (*To* FRANK.) Will you do me the favour of letting his lordship know that I've arrived and of asking him if I may wait upon him? (*Exit* FRANK *to the bookroom. After an instant, solemnly.*) I'm the last of the Domvilles! Three months ago—in that dear old garden—you spoke to me, with eloquence, for my line. *I* believed what you said to me—and I went forth into the world to test it. That belief has passed away. But the older, the higher abides. I tried to forget it—I did my best. But in this place again (*looking round him as if with the rush of old memories*) it comes back to me, it surrounds me. It looks me in the face, and it looks with reproachful eyes.

---

[3] At this point James wrote the following speech for Guy, later deleting it:

GUY. (*Gazing before him; visionary.*) I only see what I see! Such a counsel—was *no* counsel; such a duty—was none! They offered me "life"! But "life"—for *me*—is evil! It's planted in a sacrifice of others. I put that away yesterday, to meet it again to-day. (*With clear resolution.*) I put it away once more—for a sacrifice that's all my own. The high call I obeyed had a hidden vice, a fatal flaw, which the *other* call has not. It was all a wild error—a wild error from the first; a dark sophistication—and a snare! I bend, Frank, to my lesson!

MRS. PEVEREL. There should be no reproach for *you,* Mr. Domville—because you're heroic.

GUY. We *talked* of heroism here—when we talked of renouncement.

MRS. PEVEREL. But the hour came when *against* renouncement—I lifted my feeble voice.

GUY. Your voice was sweet to me—and it's sweeter than ever now.

MRS. PEVEREL. Yours has a tone, Mr. Domville, that's different—that's strange.

GUY. It sounds strange to myself, believe me, when I ask you—to let me plead again—for Frank. Take pity on him—don't send him forth from his home.

MRS. PEVEREL. You speak for him as if—(*Breaking down with excess of feeling. Reenter* FRANK HUMBER *and* LORD DEVENISH.)

GUY. As if I didn't love you to passion—heaven hear me! And as if—heaven hear me!—I hadn't come down here to *tell* you so!

FRANK. Tell her so—tell her so, Guy. And if "heaven" *doesn't* forgive you I'll set heaven an example.

GUY. As if I spoke without an effort and held my peace without a pang? I grant you freely, Madam, it wasn't for *that,* I came.

FRANK. He came on a mighty different business!

GUY. I came for a good thing, but I shall have found occasion for a better, and I think that in all the future I shall have an equal joy of both! It is *I* who shall go!

LORD DEVENISH. I've consented, sir, to meet you.

GUY. I'm the *last,* my lord, of the Domvilles! (*Then, anticipating* DEVENISH'S *reply and speaking on his quick gesture of impatient despair.*) You've been so good as to take a zealous interest in my future—and in that of my family: for which I owe you, and now ask you to accept, all *thanks.* But I beg you, still more solemnly, to let that prodigious zeal rest, from this moment, for ever! I listened to your accents for a day—I followed you where you led me. I looked at life as you showed it, and then I turned away my face. That's why I stand here again; for (*with intensely controlled emotion*) there are other things—there are partings. (*Then very gently to* MRS. PEVEREL.) Will my conveyance have come back?

MRS. PEVEREL. (*Listening an instant, and as if subjugated by his returning sanctity.*) I think I hear it now.

GUY. Then I start this moment for Bristol. (*Sadly, kindly smiling.*) Father Murray has had patience. I go with him to France, to take up my work in the Church! if the Church will *take* again an erring son!

MRS. PEVEREL. She'll take him.

LORD DEVENISH. And *you* give him?

MRS. PEVEREL. To *her!*

LORD DEVENISH. (*With high sarcasm, to* GUY.) I hope you do justice to this lady's exemplary sacrifice!

GUY. (*Blank.*) Sacrifice?

LORD DEVENISH. That of a sentiment my consideration for her forbids me to name.

FRANK. She loves you, Guy!

LORD DEVENISH. He doesn't deserve to know it. (*Then smiling, gallant to* MRS. PEVEREL.) If it were *me,* Madam! (*From the threshold.*) Pity me!

MRS. PEVEREL. It was a dream, but the dream is past!

GUY. (*Gathering himself slowly from a deep, stupefied commotion.*) The Church takes me! (*To* MRS. PEVEREL.) Be kind to him. (*To* FRANK.) Be good to her. (*At the door.*) Be good to her.

FRANK. Mrs. Peverel—I shall *hope!*

MRS. PEVEREL. Wait!

Summersoft

A Comedy In One Act

1895

EDITOR'S FOREWORD

It has been commonly believed that Henry James turned his back on the theatre of the 1890's with the failure of *Guy Domville*. He did indeed re-enter his novelist's study a chastened dramatist and he ceased to write for the immediate stage or to seek actively to be produced. But even as he was telling his friends that he had washed his hands of the theatre and its "vulgarities and platitudes," that he rejoiced in the *Guy Domville* incident as something that had disengaged him from the stage, he had begun a new flirtation with it.

He still could be tempted—especially when temptation took the seductive—and authoritative—form of Ellen Terry. Henry James had never been a whole-hearted admirer of Miss Terry's acting; but he had always been conscious of her charm. "Miss Terry has charm—remarkable charm," he had once written, adding, however, somewhat sharply ". . . this beguiles people into thinking her an accomplished actress." He considered her wholesome and English and womanly and he added this praise: "Miss Terry has that excellent thing, a quality; she gives one the sense of something fine." In 1895 she was forty-seven and had for years been a force in the theatre. What was more, her soft side, Bernard Shaw has told us, was her "mothering side, her sensitive pity" and, after *Guy Domville,* Henry James must have been open both to sensitive pity and to mothering. We do not know what Miss Terry wrote to James after seeing the ill-fated production in which her sister had played, but, given her personality, we can imagine that she was moved to warm sympathy. It is clear she offered congratulations and condolences. But she also offered hope. Would Henry James come to see her? Would he be interested in doing a one-act or two-act play with a central role for herself which she could produce during her forthcoming American tour?

Guy Domville was but three days in its grave when Henry James paid his call. The following morning, February 6, 1895, he noted as a possible theme for a play for Ellen Terry the idea of a Madame Sans-Gêne in reverse—instead of a woman of the people being called upon to play the role of an exalted lady, he would have an exalted lady called upon to play the role of a woman of the people. As he toyed with this idea he recalled a chance remark of Miss Terry's that she would "have a fancy to do an American woman." The idea appealed to James. The thought of Madame Sans-Gêne in reverse drew him back to an idea he had sketched two years earlier for Ada Rehan when he had hopes of doing a second play for Augustin Daly: that of an American woman who, in given circumstances, turns out to be more British than the British. He had recorded this broad idea in his notebook: that this woman from the United

States should step in to clear up a muddle or predicament in a British household.

He now re-read this note and elaborated it, under the stimulus of his talk with Ellen Terry, arriving at the broad situation of *Summersoft,* "the bright, kind, comic, clever charming creature—in the agitated, convulsed, threatened, somehow troubled and exposed *show* house." From that point on the one-act play seems to have come rapidly into being, despite the fact that James strenuously resumed the writing of fiction and was working consistently during the summer of 1895 at another story about a "show house"—*The Spoils of Poynton.* An unpublished journal entry made nineteen years later, on the eve of the First World War, recalled that the play was posted to Ellen Terry from Torquay toward the end of August 1895.

Among Ellen Terry's papers were found two letters from Henry James, one of August 24, 1895 expressing the novelist's satisfaction that the play had pleased her. "You are indeed the Gentle Reader; you read with imagination and see what one meant and feel what one wanted. But you spoil one for the big, flat, vague, vacant public. . . . I want to write you another (already!) one-act play—yearn after such. There will be time to talk of this—but the very difficulty of the job preoccupies me and fascinates me, and in the one-act form one comes a little nearer being able to make time for it. I hope you find yourself able to gird your loins as it were for that huge American circus—where you have to revolve in a ring 3,000 miles round!"

The second letter, written August 31, acknowledges receipt of £100 in advance of royalties and suggests that James by this time knew the play would not be produced during the American tour ". . . if the Americans are not to have the Gem, do excruciate them with a suspicion of what they lose. . . ." He added, "It will seem a long year—but art *is* long, ah me!" which would suggest that the actress spoke of doing *Summersoft* on her return. But Ellen Terry never produced the play and three years later Henry James reclaimed the script and turned it into a short story. It was published in *The Two Magics* as a tale of "white magic" and companion piece to the "black magic" of *The Turn of the Screw* under the title of *Covering End.*

Henry James named the play *Summersoft* after the name of the country house in his tale *The Lesson of the Master.* We know, from a letter to the Countess of Jersey, that the house which served as model for the story, and therefore presumably for the play, was Osterley House, near Heston, Middlesex, a red-brick mansion set in a park of some 750 acres; the Countess tells us in her memoirs that Henry James first visited Osterley in the company of James Russell Lowell. The novelist is speaking of Osterley when he writes in *The Lesson of the Master* that its great gallery was "a cheerful upholstered avenue into another century," and it is Mrs. Gracedew speaking before her time when he says: "It all went together and spoke in one voice—a rich English voice of the early part of the 18th century. . . ." When he rewrote the one-act play into the short story he changed the name of the house to *Covering End* since he did not want to retain a name he had used in an earlier tale.

If Summersoft and Covering End were Osterley they were also the projection of Henry James's "sense of the past," and Mrs. Gracedew's passionate plea for the preservation of the old and cherished things went back to James's *Passionate Pilgrim,* to Christopher Newman's search for the old values of "Europe," to Caroline Spencer's life-long dream of an Old World she barely glimpses, to his own musings as he sought to draw his "sketches" and "portraits" of places. "At Warwick the past joins hands so stoutly with the present," wrote James in one of his travel sketches, "that you can hardly say where one begins and the other ends. . . ." This is again the voice of Mrs. Gracedew as it could be the voice of Fleda Vetch in *The Spoils of Poyton. Summersoft–Covering End* is, in a sense, a by-product of the *Spoils.* Captain Yule's old house is but a less elaborate, a down-at-the-heels Poynton. Like Poynton, it is the focus of a struggle over property, and the essential theme, that beautiful things should belong to those capable of appreciating them, is also to be found here. Mrs. Gracedew, like Fleda, is an outsider who becomes involved in the struggle. Henry James's account of Fleda, in the preface to the *Spoils* written a decade later, can very easily be applied to Mrs. Gracedew. He observes that "a subject residing in somebody's excited and concentrated feeling about something has more beauty to give out than under any other style of pressure." Mrs. Gracedew's excited and concentrated feeling for the old house is the essence of play and story. She belongs in Henry James's gallery of the American female in Europe. She is a product of what James once called the "age of Mrs. Jack"— Mrs. Jack being Mrs. John L. Gardner who shuttled between America and Europe in search of the "spoils" of the Old World now enshrined in Boston's Fenway Court. That Mrs. Gracedew could be more English than the English was an irony James frequently invoked. He relates in his life of William Wetmore Story that Mr. Justice Story of the Supreme Court, who never went abroad, once surprised a London visitor at Cambridge by identifying an obscure London street of which the traveller himself was ignorant. Judge Story, James observed, "knew his London because even at that then prodigious distance from it, he had a feeling for it." Mrs. Gracedew has an abundance of feeling for Summersoft and its destitute owner, Captain Yule.

Yule too has his antecedents in James. In *The Portrait of a Lady* Isabel Archer, talking to Lord Warburton's sisters, inquires whether it is true that his lordship is "a great radical." They assure her he is "immensely advanced" and Isabel then poses the question whether, as a radical, he would be willing to part with his estates and properties. The bewildered sisters fail to understand such a concept and Isabel observes ". . . if I were he I should wish to be a conservative. I should wish to keep everything." In the New York Edition James revised this speech so that Isabel speaks not for conservatism but for that very past for which Mrs. Gracedew pleaded. He makes her say, ". . . if I were he I should wish to fight to the death: I mean for the heritage of the past. I should hold it tight." The problem thus adumbrated in *The Portrait of a Lady* became subsequently the central theme of *The Princess Casamassima,* and Yule's conflict between his radicalism and the preservation of his property, sketched on a superficial comedy plane, has in it elements of the deeper conflict of young Hyacinth Robinson troubled between the status quo of a world attractive to him and the dynamic revolutionary theories to which he has committed himself. For James, who had stood among the barricades of the Commune in Paris, who had friends among nihilists and anarchists, who had known Prince Kropotkin—the James who had witnessed the social unrest of the 1880's and noted the contrasts of wealth and poverty in his European travels—experienced that conflict himself. Intellectually oriented toward social progress and social reform—the heritage of his socially progressive father—his emotions could accept more readily tradition, conformity, the world as it presented itself to his artist's eyes, than the worlds-in-the-making. He was an historian rather than one who would change the course of history. One wonders, nevertheless, how a writer who had created Nick Dormer and his renunciation of Westminster for the artist's studio could entertain even for a moment Yule's renunciation of idealism for "property," and make him implausibly fickle to the social reform that is his way of life, even under the verbal witchery of Mrs. Gracedew. We are led to the conclusion that for the stage (and particularly in the tightness of the one-act) Henry James was prepared as usual to make concessions. He was prepared to sacrifice verisimilitude in his other characters so long as he could make Mrs. Gracedew consistent. Wasn't she the *raison d'être* of the play? He was happy to create a spell-binding American woman and this counted for him more than anything else. And he counted on Ellen Terry to do the spellbinding.

With the publication of the tale, *Covering End,* Henry James and the theatre of the 1890's finally parted company, except for one mild flurry, a momentary welling up of the old passion. It is recorded in the notebook, in an entry of January 22, 1899: "George Alexander writes me to ask for *Covering End,* for him and Miss Davis to do, and I've just written to him the obstacles and objections. But I've also said I *would* do him a *fresh* one-act thing; and it's strange how this little renewal of contact with the vulgar theatre stirs again, in a manner and moves me. . . ."

In its play form *Summersoft* had found no producer. In its story form it was attracting interest as a possible play. Now Johnston Forbes-Robertson wrote also suggesting that it be dramatized. James finally said "no" to both actor-managers. Alexander pleaded with James. The novelist had given his only copy of the script to Elizabeth Robins and in the late autumn of 1899 he appealed to her to send it back. A few days later he returned it to her. Alexander had read it and changed his mind. "I send you back poor Mrs. Gracedew, (even as she has been returned on *my* hands, after all:) for you to have and to hold, to do what you like with—above all to *produce*, absolutely at your freedom and discretion, when the right occasion rises. Obviously, in the light of the '*story*' in the volume of the *Two Magics* there is much more to be got out of her and put into her; and indeed the tale constitutes for her rather a unique and rich prompt-book."

This was quite true. In the tale James considerably improved on his original one-acter. He elaborated the characterizations, softened the hard lines of the play, put more flesh on his stage puppets and strengthened the motivation. He did not, however, overcome its inherent weakness, the about-face of Yule. Miss Robins submitted the play to the reading committee of the New Century Theatre, a group formed to produce plays artistically worthy but considered a commercial risk. William Archer wrote a three-page single-spaced report on the play which began "I think the enclosed a gem with a single flaw . . ." and ended "on the whole I think the piece a delightful one, which a few quite inessential alterations ought to render (with good acting) genuinely successful and popular." The flaw was, of course, Yule's capitulation. Archer believed it to be utterly implausible, and one that in real life would make a political figure the laughing stock of all England. The New Century decided not to do it and the play remained unproduced until 1907 when it suddenly acquired a new life and a new history, recounted in the preface to *The High Bid* in this volume.

CHARACTERS

CAPTAIN CLEMENT YULE
MR. PRODMORE
CHIVERS
MRS. GRACEDEW
CORA PRODMORE
VISITORS

SUMMERSOFT

The Scene is the hall, the spacious central apartment, of an old English country-house; which has the mark of extreme antiquity and of several very beautiful and curious architectural and decorative features. It shows, definitely, the fallen fortunes—the reduced income—of the people who have, for ages, inhabited it, but still contains some very charming and valuable old objects, domestic treasures, portraits, relics of the past, carefully preserved. It is a Saturday afternoon in August, a hot, still day, and the windows stand open to the old park in one quarter, to the old garden in another. There are four entrances and exits, of which the most striking is a high staircase leading to an upper gallery. Another is the door or passage of the vestibule connected with the main entrance to the house—the way in from the park. Another is the way to the drawingroom, another the way to the garden. CHIVERS *stands at the foot of the staircase, looking up, as if in conversation with someone above, who appears to have been speaking or calling to him from the upper gallery.*

CHIVERS. Oh no, mum, there ain't no one come *yet:* it's all right. (*Coming down.*) If I leave her to range, ain't it just my poor pickings? (*As if hearing a voice from above.*) Lots of lovely—? Lovely *what,* mum? (*Back at the staircase.*) Little ups and downs? As you *say,* mum—as many as in a poor man's *life!* (*Listening hard.*) Dear little crooked *steps?* Please *mind* 'em, mum: they be cruel in the dark corners! (*To himself, with vague pleasure.*) She do fancy the place! (*Then again to the voice above.*) Coming up? Not if you'll indulge me, mum—I must be where I can hear the bell. (*As the bell of the house-door*

rings out.) Mercy—I can hear *that!* (*Shuffles across to the vestibule, in which he disappears, re-entering from it the next moment with* MR. PRODMORE.)

PRODMORE. (*Looking round, disappointed.*) No one here?

CHIVERS. No one has come, sir; but I've had a telegram from Captain Yule.

PRODMORE. (*Apprehensive.*) Not to say he ain't coming?

CHIVERS. He was to take the 2.40 from Paddington: he certainly *should* be here.

PRODMORE. He should have been here this *hour.* And so should my daughter!

CHIVERS. (*Timid, tentative.*) Were they coming—a—*together,* sir?

PRODMORE. (*Shocked, staring.*) Together? —for what do you *take* Miss Prodmore? (*Then with a more conciliatory second thought.*) It *is* in a sense true, however, that their "coming together," as you call it, is exactly what I've made my plans for to-day: my calculation was that we should all punctually converge on this spot. Attended by her trusty maid, Miss Prodmore, who happens to be on a week's visit to her grandmother at Bellborough, was to take the 1.50 from that place. I was to drive over—ten miles—from my most convenient seat. Captain Yule was at last to shake off for a few hours the peculiar occupations that engage him.

CHIVERS. They *must* be peculiar, sir— when a gentleman comes into a property like this and goes three months without so much as a *nateral* curiosity—! I don't speak of anything but what's *nateral,* sir; but there have *been* people here—

PRODMORE. (*Interrupting; complacently.*) There are *always* people here!

CHIVERS. As you say, sir—to be shown over. And the master himself has *never*

525

been shown!

PRODMORE. He *shall* be, from top to bottom—it's precisely what I've *come* for! (*Looking round him.*) He'll be *struck*—though he *has* been up to his eyes in such very different matters.

CHIVERS. (*Timorous, wondering.*) But nothing but what's right, sir—?

PRODMORE. (*With extreme emphasis.*) Everything that's utterly *wrong*! (*As the bell again sounds.*) Here he *is*. (CHIVERS, dismayed, hurries off to the door and disappears in the vestibule. PRODMORE, alone, looks complacently round him.) But if he resists the house— (*breaking off as he hears his daughter's voice in the vestibule*) Cora?—he won't resist the *girl*! (*Re-enter* CHIVERS, ushering in CORA PRODMORE, whom her father addresses severely.) I've *waited*.

CORA. (*Flurried, breathless.*) I'm so *sorry*, Papa!

PRODMORE. (*Suspicious, stern.*) Would you have wished then not to *find* me?—Why are you late?

CORA. (*Agitated, embarrassed.*) I'll *tell* you, Papa. (*Looking vaguely round her, in distress, for relief; then abruptly.*) I feel rather *faint*—could I have some *tea*?

PRODMORE. (*After considering the idea.*) Well, as I shall expect you to put forth your powers—*yes*. (*To* CHIVERS.) Some tea.

CHIVERS. (*Taken aback.*) I don't hardly know what you'll *make* of *my* tea! But you shall have it at least in the drawingroom. (*Exit to the drawingroom.*)

CORA. It was my *train*, Papa—so awfully *behind*! And then I walked up from the station—there's such a lovely footpath across the park.

PRODMORE. You've been roaming the country, then, *alone*?

CORA. (*Conscious.*) Oh dear, no; not alone! There were ever so many people about.

PRODMORE. There are sometimes *too* many!—And where's your trusty maid?

CORA. (*Confused.*) I didn't *bring* her: she seemed so very unwell.

PRODMORE. (*Blank.*) What on earth is the matter with her?

CORA. I don't quite *know*—I think that at Granny's she *eats* too much.

PRODMORE. (*With decision.*) I'll put an end to *that*! You expect then to pursue your adventures into the *night*?—to return to Bellborough as you *came*?

CORA. (*With more confidence.*) Exactly as I came, Papa dear—under the protection of a new friend I've just made, a lady whom I met in the train and who is also going back by the 6.15. Like *me*, she was on her way to this place, and I expected to *find* her here.

PRODMORE. (*Vague.*) What does she want at this place?

CORA. She wants to *see* it.

PRODMORE. (*After an instant.*) *To-day*? To-day won't *do*!

CORA. So I suggested—but she said it would *have* to do!

PRODMORE. (*Resentful.*) Why in the world—?

CORA. Because she's a wild American—she *says* she is: so I wonder why she hasn't arrived.

PRODMORE. I know nothing about her, and I recommend you not to pick up wild Americans, or strange women of any kind, in trains.

CORA. She'll turn up, I'm sure, because she was awfully keen. She *is* a strange woman—but she's awfully nice. I noticed her yesterday at Bellborough.

PRODMORE. What was she doing at Bellborough?

CORA. Staying at the Blue Dragon, to see the old abbey. She says she just loves old abbeys. It seems to be the same feeling that has brought her over to-day to see this old house.

PRODMORE. She "just loves" old houses? Then why the deuce didn't she accompany you, properly, to the *door*?

CORA. Because she went off in a fly to see, first, the old hospital. She just loves old hospitals. She asked me if this isn't a showhouse. I told her I hadn't the least idea.

PRODMORE. It *is*. You're an idiot!

CORA. (*With humility.*) She said, herself, that I evidently ain't a show-girl.

PRODMORE. I wish to goodness you *were*! But she sounds distinctly vulgar.

CORA. Don't judge her till you *see* her. She's tremendously clever—she knows everything about everything.

PRODMORE. And you know nothing about *anything!* You're *not* tremendously clever —so I demand of you your best attention. —I'm expecting Captain Yule.

CORA. The owner of this property?

PRODMORE. He came into it, three months ago, by the death of his great-uncle, who lived to ninety-three, but who having quarrelled mortally with his father, had always refused to receive either of them.

CORA. But *now*, at least, doesn't he *live* here?

PRODMORE. So little that he comes to-day for the first time. I've some business to discuss with him that can best be discussed on this spot; and it's a vital part of that business that you too should take pains to make him welcome.

CORA. (*Staring.*) In his own house?

PRODMORE. It's *not* his own house. Practically speaking, it's *my* house. It's mortgaged, as it stands, for every penny of its value—and I happen to hold the mortgages.

CORA. (*Surprised, thinking.*) To the full extent?

PRODMORE. If I went in at all, it was to come out the other side. It's on the other side that I find the Captain.

CORA. (*With a vague, faint, nervous laugh.*) Poor Captain!—Well, Papa—don't be *hard* with him.

PRODMORE. What do you call being hard with him?

CORA. I don't understand business; but I think I understand *you*, Papa, enough to gather that you've got a fine advantage.

PRODMORE. Fine if I use it finely. What you would like me to do is to give it *up?* Thank you, Miss Prodmore, I *do* mean to use it, and what I have wished to say to you today, just where we stand—for it's here we do stand, and very fast, thank heaven!—is that I look to you to see me through.

CORA. Through what, Papa?

PRODMORE. Through my speculation. I want you to receive an impression, and I want you, even more, to *make* one.

CORA. (*In dawning consternation.*) On Captain Yule? (*Seeing the whole thing.*) To make him *propose?*

PRODMORE. If he does, it will be better for *both* of you! And he *will*—for I shall do *my* part.

CORA. (*Extremely discomposed and alarmed.*) How on earth can I do *mine?* To begin with, I've never *seen* him.

PRODMORE. You'll see him, *now*, (*looking at his watch*) from one moment to the other. He's young, good-looking, clever; he has one of the best and oldest names in England—a name that, in this part of the country, one can do *anything* with. I propose to do everything, and it's accordingly my plan that my daughter shall gracefully bear it.

CORA. And pray is it also Captain Yule's plan?

PRODMORE. (*After an instant.*) His plans have not yet *matured*. But nothing is more natural than that they shall do so on the sunny south wall of Miss Prodmore's best manner.

CORA. You speak as if they were little sour *plums!* You exaggerate, I think, the warmth of Miss Prodmore's temperament. I'm a remarkably cold nature.

PRODMORE. Then you'll be so good as to start a blaze! I've spent twenty years in giving you what your poor mother used to call advantages, and they've cost me hundreds and hundreds of pounds. It's time now I should get my money back. I couldn't help your temper nor your taste, nor even your looks—but I paid it out that you should have, damn you, a good manner. You never show it to me, certainly, but do you mean to tell me that after all—for—a—other persons—you *haven't* got one?

CORA. If you mean by other persons, persons who are *nice* to me—well, Captain Yule may not *be* so, and may not think so.

PRODMORE. If you'll be nice to Captain Yule, Captain Yule will be incapable of gross perversity!

CORA. I remember your saying once— some time ago—that that was just what he had been guilty of in going in for his dreadful ideas—

PRODMORE. (*Taking her up.*) About the "radical programme," the "social revolution," the spoliation of the rich? I shall forgive him the aberration if he renounces it for *you*.

CORA. (*More and more adverse.*) He *mustn't* renounce it! He *shan't!*

PRODMORE. You mean that you'll take him as he *is?*

CORA. (*Determined.*) I won't take him at *all!* (*Then, agitated, as the sound of wheels is heard on the gravel.*) A fly—here he *is!* Surely you don't want me to pounce on him *thus!*

PRODMORE. (*Interrogative, eyeing her up and down.*) Your frock won't *do*—with what it *cost* me?

CORA. It's not my "frock"—it's his thinking I've come here for him to *see* me.

PRODMORE. He *doesn't* think it, and he shan't *know* it.

CORA. But he knows that you want me to *catch* him!

PRODMORE. (*As if with offended delicacy.*) The way to "catch" him will be not to be *vulgar*. He doesn't know that you know anything. (*As the house-bell rings.*) Await us in the drawingroom—and mind you toe the mark!

(*Re-enter, to answer the bell,* CHIVERS, *from the drawingroom, the door of which he leaves open.*)

CORA. (*Really anxious, pleading, passionate.*) Don't *kill* me, father—give me time! (*Exit to the drawingroom, closing the door with a bang.*)

PRODMORE. (*Alone;* CHIVERS *having passed, before* CORA'S *last speech, into the vestibule.*) If she could only look with such eyes at *him!* (*Then, with florid cordiality, as he sees* CAPTAIN YULE, *who enters from the vestibule accompanied by* CHIVERS.) Delighted at last to see you here!

YULE. If I've not come before, Mr. Prodmore, it was—very frankly speaking—from the dread of seeing *you!*

PRODMORE. But surely my presence is not without a *motive*—!

YULE. It's just the motive that makes me *wince* at it! Certainly I've no illusions about the ground of our meeting. Your high financial genius has placed me at your mercy, and you hold me in the hollow of your hand.

PRODMORE. (*Smiling fatuously.*) Well, I won't, on my side, deny that when I went

in so deep, I knew pretty well what I was about!

YULE. So well that, if I've understood you, you can do quite as you like with this preposterous place. Haven't you brought me down to *see* you do it?

PRODMORE. I've certainly brought you down to open your eyes! (*Then, after a moment.*) Of couse you can *clear* the property—you can pay off the mortgages.

YULE. (*Blank.*) Pay them off? What can I pay them off with?

PRODMORE. You can always raise money.

YULE. What can I raise it on?

PRODMORE. (*Laughing.*) On your great political future.

YULE. I've not taken the lucrative line, and I know what you think of *that*.

PRODMORE. I think you keep, in public, very dangerous company; but I hold that you're extravagant only because you've nothing at stake. A man has the right opinions as soon as he has something to lose by having the wrong ones. Haven't I already hinted to you how to straighten yours out? You're a firebrand because you're a bachelor. Marry a nice little heiress!

YULE. (*Smiling ironically, but as if thinking.*) Of course I could do that in a moment!

PRODMORE. That's exactly my danger—that *any* woman would jump at you.

YULE. *My* danger, Mr. Prodmore, is as great, though of a different sort. I've yet to see the woman I'd "jump" at!

PRODMORE. Well, you know, I haven't asked you to risk your neck—I've only asked you to consider.

YULE. I've complied with your request, and one of the strange results is that my eyes have got accustomed to my darkness. I seem to make out in the depressing gloom that at the worst I can let the whole thing go.

PRODMORE. (*Anxious.*) Throw up the property?

YULE. Isn't it the property that throws *me* up? If I can afford neither to redeem it nor to live on it, I can at least let it save its own bacon and pay its own debts. I can say to you: "Take it and be hanged to you!"

PRODMORE. (*Apprehensive, conciliatory.*) You wouldn't be so shockingly rude!

YULE. Why *not,* if I'm a firebrand? Sacrifice for sacrifice, that might very well be the least!

PRODMORE. How do you *know,* if you haven't compared them? It's just to do *that* that you're here to-day. Now that you stretch yourself—for an hour's relaxation —in the cradle of your race, can you seriously entertain the idea of parting with such a venerable family relic?

YULE. (*Looking round the depressed old hall with a sad and skeptical eye.*) The cradle of my race looks to me much more like its tomb! Melancholy—musty— mouldy! Is this its character throughout?

PRODMORE. You must judge for yourself—you must go over the house. It looks a bit run down, but I'll tell you what I'll do—I'll do it up for you—neatly: I'll throw *that* in!

YULE. (*With a sarcastic, melancholy smile.*) Will you put in the electric light?

PRODMORE. (*Taking it seriously.*) Well— if you'll meet me half way!—We're dealing, here, with fancy-values. Don't you feel a kind of *thrill,* as you take it all in?

YULE. Call it a kind of *shudder,* as at something queer and cold, and almost cruel: all the old mortality with which the place is saturated—the old presences—the old absences—the old voices—the old ghosts!

PRODMORE. The old ghosts, Captain Yule, are worth so much a *dozen!* But look about you a little more. (*Encouragingly, patronizingly.*) Make yourself at home.

YULE. Thank you very much, Mr. Prodmore. May I light a cigarette?

PRODMORE. In your own house, Captain?

YULE. That's just the question—it seems less my own than before this grim vision of it! (*Then, as he lights and begins to smoke a cigarette, offering one also to* PRODMORE, *which* PRODMORE *takes.*) As I understand you, you *lump* your two conditions? I mean I must accept both or neither?

PRODMORE. You *will* accept both, for you'll clear the property at a stroke. The way I put it is that if you'll stand for Gossage you'll get returned for Gossage.

YULE. (*Completing.*) And if I get returned for Gossage I shall marry your daughter. Then if I marry your daughter—

PRODMORE. (*Completing.*) I'll put those vile obligations, before your eyes, into the fire; there won't be a penny to pay; and you'll live here in honour and length of days!

YULE. Are you very sure of the "honour," if I turn my political coat?

PRODMORE. You'll only be turning it *back* again—the way it was *always* worn. Gossage will receive you with open arms and press you to a heaving Tory bosom. That bosom has never heaved but to sound Conservative principles. The cradle—or at least the coverlet—of your race, Gossage was the political property, so to speak, of generations of your family. Stand in the good old interest, and you'll stand like a lion.

YULE. I'm afraid you mean that I must first roar like one!

PRODMORE. *I'll* do the roaring—leave that to *me.*

YULE. Then why the deuce don't you stand yourself?

PRODMORE. Because I'm not a handsome young man with the old home and the right name. If I haven't these advantages, my idea has been precisely that my *daughter* shall have them.

YULE. I confess you have not yet made me understand the attraction you discover in so large a pecuniary sacrifice.

PRODMORE. My sacrifices are my own affair, and as I never—on principle—give anything for nothing, I daresay I've, myself, another *name* for 'em. You come high —yes; but I intend you shall be the comfort of my life!

YULE. (*After an instant.*) May I inquire if Miss Prodmore's ideas of comfort are as modest as her father's? Is she a responsible party to this ingenious arrangement?

PRODMORE. Miss Prodmore, Captain Yule, is a sheet of blank paper! No image of any tie but the pure and perfect *filial* has yet, I can answer for it, formed itself on the fair expanse. But for that image to be projected—

YULE. (*Laughing, embarrassed, incredu-*

lous.) I've only to appear—

PRODMORE. And, naturally, to be *kind* to her. Do you remember what you said when I first laid this question before you in London?

YULE. I think I said it struck me I should first take a look at the *corpus delicti.*

PRODMORE. You should first see, in person, what you had really come into. I was not only eager for *that,* but I'm willing to go further; I'm quite ready to hear you say that you think you should also first see the young lady!

YULE. (*Laughing.*) There *is* something in that, then—since you mention it!

PRODMORE. I think you'll find that there's everything. (*Looking at his watch.*) Which will you take first?

YULE. (*Vague.*) First?

PRODMORE. The young lady or the house?

YULE. (*Much taken aback.*) Do you mean your daughter's *here?*

PRODMORE. (*Indicating.*) In the drawingroom.

YULE. (*Apprehensive.*) *Waiting* for me?

PRODMORE. (*Reassuring.*) As long as you *like!*

YULE. (*As if fearing* CORA *may burst in upon him.*) Ah, a few moments, I *beg* you!—Do you mean she *knows*—?

PRODMORE. That she's here on *view?* (*After a moment.*) She knows nothing whatever. She's as unconscious as the rose on its stem!

YULE. (*Relieved.*) That's right—let her *remain* so! (*Drawing a long breath.*) I'll first take the house.

PRODMORE. Shall I go round with you?

YULE. I think, under the circumstances, I would rather go round alone.

(*Re-enter* CHIVERS *from the drawingroom.*)

CHIVERS. (*Timorously, tentatively, to* YULE.) There's *tea* on, sir!

PRODMORE. (*To* YULE.) Then I'll join my daughter. (*At the drawingroom door; expressively.*) The rose on its stem! (*Exit* MR. PRODMORE.)

YULE. (*To* CHIVERS, *musingly, abruptly.*) I say, what *colour* is the rose?

CHIVERS. (*At first bewildered, then catching on.*) A very brilliant red. (*Nod-*

ding out of the open door to the garden.) It's the only one *left*—on the old east wall.

YULE. (*After a laugh.*) My dear fellow, I'm alluding to the young lady in the drawingroom. Is she pretty?

CHIVERS. (*Embarrassed.*) Laws, sir—it's a matter of taste. I fancy 'em myself more merry-like.

YULE. (*Struck, wondering.*) She *isn't* merry-like, poor Miss Prodmore? Well, neither am *I!* But it doesn't signify. What are *you?*

CHIVERS. Well, sir, I'm not *that.* Whatever has there been to *make* me, sir?

YULE. How in the world do *I* know? I mean, to whom do you belong?

CHIVERS. If you could only *tell* me, sir! I do seem to waste away—for someone to take *orders* of!

YULE. (*Amused.*) Who pays your wages?

CHIVERS. No one at all, sir.

YULE. (*Producing a coin.*) Then there's a sovereign. (*As* CHIVERS *accepts it with undisguised satisfaction.*) I haven't many.

CHIVERS. (*With sudden, tender compunction.*) Ah then, let it stay in the family!

YULE. (*Struck; very kindly.*) I think it *does,* old boy.

CHIVERS. (*Much gratified.*) I've served your house, sir.

YULE. How long?

CHIVERS. All my life.

YULE. Then I won't give *you* up!

CHIVERS. Indeed sir, I hope you won't give up anything.

YULE. It remains to be seen! (*Looking round him.*) Is that the garden?

CHIVERS. (*Sadly.*) It *was!* Shall I show you how it *used* to be?

YULE. It's just as it *is,* alas, that I require it! (*At the garden-door.*) Don't come —I want to *think!* (*Exit* CAPTAIN YULE.)

CHIVERS. (*Alone, vague.*) What does he want to think about? (*Then as he hears* MRS. GRACEDEW'S *voice calling from the gallery above, with great animation:* "Housekeeper—Butler—Old Family Servant!") Oh, I should have told him of *her!*

(*Enter* MRS. GRACEDEW *at the top of the stairs.*)

MRS. GRACEDEW. (*As she comes down.*) Did you think I had got snapped down in an old box, like that *girl*—what's her name? the one that was poking round too —in the poem? My dear man, why didn't you *tell* me?

CHIVERS. (*Vague.*) Tell you, mum?

MRS. GRACEDEW. Why that you're so perfectly—*perfect!* You're beyond my wildest dreams! You're beyond my wildest dreams! You're everything in the world you ought to be, and not the shade of a *shade* of anything you *oughtn't!*

CHIVERS. (*Bewildered.*) *Me*, mum?

MRS. GRACEDEW. Yes, you too, you old *picture!* The house is a vision of beauty, and you're worthy of the house. I can't say *more* for you!

CHIVERS. (*Fluttered, pleased.*) I think, mum, you say too much!

MRS. GRACEDEW. So everyone always thinks; but I haven't come here to suffer in silence—to suffer, I mean, from envy and despair! You're so deadly *complete*, you know—every fascinating feature that I had already heard of, and ever so many others that I hadn't!

CHIVERS. I saw as soon as you arrived, mum, that you had heard of a good few more than *I* ever did!

MRS. GRACEDEW. I had got you by heart —from books, from photos; I had you in my pocket when I came: so when you were so good as to let me loose up there I knew my way right through. It's all there, every inch of it, and now at last I can do what I want.

CHIVERS. (*Wondering.*) And pray, mum, what might *that* be?

MRS. GRACEDEW. Why, to take you right *back* with me—to Missourah Top.

CHIVERS. (*Freshly bewildered.*) Do I understand you, mum, that you require to take *me?*

MRS. GRACEDEW. (*Staring a moment, then breaking out into glee.*) Do you mean to say you'd *come?* As the Old Family Servant? Then *do*, you nice, *real* thing: it's just what I'm *dying* for—an Old Family Servant! You're somebody else's, yes—but everything, over here, is somebody else's, and I want a second-hand one, all ready-made. You're the best I've seen yet. I wish I could have you *packed*—put up in paper and bran, as I shall have my old pot there: don't let me forget my crockery!

(*As* CHIVERS *goes and takes up the pot which has been stood aside, on a table.*) It's rare old Chelsea.

CHIVERS. (*With the pot, looking at it and thinking.*) Where is it I've known it this many a year—though not, to say, by name? (*Then as it comes to him.*) In the sexton's front parlour!

MRS. GRACEDEW. No, in his best bedroom—on his chest of drawers. I've got the drawers too, and his brass fender, and the chair his grandmother died in. Not in the *fly*—they're to *follow*.

CHIVERS. (*Handling the pot with agitated zeal.*) You did right to take this out when it went to the stables. Them flymen —they do be *rough*, with anything that's delicate. (*Going to put down the pot again, he makes, in his nervousness, a false movement and lets it fall to the ground, where it breaks to pieces; whereupon, overwhelmed with consternation, he collapses into the nearest chair.*) Mercy *on* us, mum, I've brought shame on my old grey hairs!

MRS. GRACEDEW. (*Who has smothered a shriek of dismay; after she has looked at him an instant.*) Oh, but the way you *take* it!—you're too quaint to *live!* The way you said that, now—it's the very *type!* That's all I want of you—just to *be* the very type. It's what you *are*, you know, poor thing—you can't *help* it, and it's what everything and everyone *else* is, over here. There was a type in the *train* with me—the "awfully nice girl" of all the novels, the "simple maiden in her flower": *she* couldn't help it, either! (*Then suddenly remembering.*) By the way, she was coming here—has she *come?*

CHIVERS. Miss Prodmore is here, mum— she's having her tea.

MRS. GRACEDEW. (*Eagerly.*) Yes, that's exactly it—they're always having their tea!

CHIVERS. With Mr. Prodmore—in the drawingroom. Captain Yule's in the garden.

MRS. GRACEDEW. (*Vague.*) Captain Yule?

CHIVERS. The new master—he has also just arrived.

MRS. GRACEDEW. (*After an instant.*) She didn't tell me about *him*.

CHIVERS. It's such a cur'ous thing to tell,

mum. He had never seen the place.

MRS. GRACEDEW. (*Vague.*) Before to-day? —his very own?—Well, I hope he *likes* it!

CHIVERS. I haven't seen many, mum, that like it as much as *you!*

MRS. GRACEDEW. I should like it still better if it were *my* very own!

CHIVERS. Well, mum, with all respect, I wish indeed it were! But the Captain, mum, is the lawful heir.

MRS. GRACEDEW. That's *another* of your dear old things—I adore your lawful heirs! He has come to take possession?

CHIVERS. He's a-taking of it *now.*

MRS. GRACEDEW. (*Struck, immensely interested.*) What does he *do*—how does he do it? Can't I *see?* (*Then, disappointedly, as* CHIVERS *looks blank.*) There ain't any fuss about it?

CHIVERS. I scarce think him the gentlemen to make any about *anything!*

MRS. GRACEDEW. (*Resignedly, smiling, thinking.*) Well, I like them, *too,* when they *don't!* (*Looking round her, with a wistful, leave-taking, appreciative sigh.*) I also have taken possession!

CHIVERS. (*Smiling.*) It was you, mum, did it *first!*

MRS. GRACEDEW. Ah, but for a poor little *hour!* He's for life!

CHIVERS. For mine, mum, I do hope.

MRS. GRACEDEW. I shall think of you together here. (*After an instant, as if reluctant to recognise that she must presently be going.*) Will he be *kind* to you?

CHIVERS. (*Simply.*) He has already been, mum.

MRS. GRACEDEW. Then be sure to be so to *him.* (*Startled, as the house-bell sounds out.*) Is that his *bell?*

CHIVERS. (*Alert.*) I must see *whose!* (*Exit to the vestibule.*)

MRS. GRACEDEW. (*Alone, looking round her again, wandering about the room and detaching from the wall a small framed plaque of enamel, which she examines lovingly.*) Why it's Limoges!—I wish awfully I were a *bad* woman—then, I hope, I'd just *take* it! (*Re-enter* CAPTAIN YULE *from the garden; on which she immediately greets him, keeping the object familiarly in her hand.*) Oh, Captain Yule, I'm delighted to meet you. It's such a comfort to ask you if I *may!*

YULE. (*Staring, mystified, charmed.*) If you may, Madam—?

MRS. GRACEDEW. Why, just *be* here, and poke round. Don't tell me I *can't* now—because I already *have:* I've been upstairs, and downstairs, and in my lady's chamber! I got round your lovely servant;— if you don't look out, I'll *grab* him! If you don't look out I'll grab everything! That's what I came *over* for—just to lay your country *waste.* Your house is just an old *dream*—and you've got some good things. Oh yes, you *have*—several: don't coyly pretend you haven't! Don't you *know* it? (*Handing him her enamel.*) Just look at that! (*Then as he holds the plaque, bewildered, blank, looking only at herself.*) Don't you know *anything?* It's Limoges!

YULE. (*Amused, interested.*) I don't know my *house*—I've never *seen* it!

MRS. GRACEDEW. (*Eagerly seizing his arm.*) Then do let me *show* it to you!

YULE. I shall be delighted. (*Then as he sees* CHIVERS: *re-enter* CHIVERS *from the vestibule.*) Who's there?

CHIVERS. (*Excited.*) A party!

YULE. (*Vague.*) A party?

CHIVERS. Over from Gossage—to see the house.

MRS. GRACEDEW. (*With redoubled eagerness.*) Yes, let *me* show it! (*Then with a second thought, to* CHIVERS.) Oh, I forgot— you get the tips! But, you dear old creature, *I'll* get them too—and I'll *give* them to you! (*After an instant, looking from* CHIVERS *back to* YULE.) Perhaps they'll be bigger—for *me!*

YULE. (*Laughing.*) I should think they'd be *enormous,* for you! But I should like to go over with you *alone.*

CHIVERS. (*To* YULE.) Shall I show them in?

YULE. By all means—if there's *money* in it!

(*Exit* CHIVERS *to the vestibule.*)

MRS. GRACEDEW. Oh, and I promised to show it to Miss Prodmore—do call her too.

YULE. (*Taken aback.*) "Call" her? Dear lady, I don't *know* her!

MRS. GRACEDEW. You *must*—she's charming. (*Re-enter* CORA PRODMORE *from the drawingroom; on which* MRS. GRACEDEW *goes on, indicating her.*) Just *see* if she ain't! Miss Prodmore, let me present Captain Yule. Captain Yule, Miss Prodmore. Miss Prodmore, Captain Yule.

(*Re-enter, while* YULE *responds stiffly and coldly and* CORA *agitatedly to this introduction,* MR. PRODMORE *from the drawingroom.*)

CORA. (*Promptly, eagerly, on seeing her father.*) Papa, let me "present" you to Mrs. Gracedew. Mrs. Gracedew, Mr. Prodmore. Mr. Prodmore, Mrs. Gracedew.

MRS. GRACEDEW. (*With a little bow, all cordiality, to* MR. PRODMORE.) Mr. Prodmore. So happy to meet your daughter's father. Your daughter's such a lovely girl!

PRODMORE. (*Responding heartily and hurling the words at* YULE.) Ah yes, such a *lovely* girl!

MRS. GRACEDEW. (*Smiling benevolently at* CORA.) So fresh and natural and unexpected!

PRODMORE. (*In the same way as before, to* YULE.) Most fresh—*most* natural—MOST unexpected!

(*Re-enter, during the presentations,* CHIVERS, *from the vestibule, accompanied by four or five tourists, simple, awestruck, provincial folk.*)

CHIVERS. (*As with the habit of years, immediately beginning.*) This, ladies and gentlemen, is the most striking feature of the 'ouse—the old 'istorical, feudal 'all. Bein', from all accounts, the most ancient portion of the edifice, it was erected in the earliest *ages*. Some say in the fifteenth century.

MRS. GRACEDEW. (*Who has followed with active attention; irrepressibly.*) I say in the *fourteenth*—you're robbing us of a hundred years!

CHIVERS. (*Confessing his aberration; abashed.*) I do seem to go astray in them centuries! The Gothic roof is much admired—the west gallery a modern addition.

MRS. GRACEDEW. (*In the eagerness of her interest; laughing.*) What on earth do you call modern? It existed at the time of the visit of James the First, in 1611, and is supposed to have served, in the charming detail of its ornament, as a model for sev-

eral that were constructed in his reign. The great fireplace *is* Jacobean.

CHIVERS. The tapestry on the left is Flemish—the elegant woodwork Italian.

MRS. GRACEDEW. Excuse me if I take you up. The elegant woodwork is Flemish—the tapestry on the left Italian. (*Smiling, pleading, to* CHIVERS.) Do you really mind if *I* just do it? Oh, I know *how*—like the housekeeper, last week, at Castle Gaunt.[1] (*To the party, comprehensively, sociably.*) How do ye do? ain't it thrilling? (*Then as she laughingly does the housekeeper.*) Keep well *together,* please—we're not doing puss in the *corner!* I have my duty to all parties—I can't be partial to *one!* (*To an individual who appears to have asked a question.*) How *many* parties? The party up and the party down. (*Pointing to an escutcheon in a stained-glass window.*) Observe the family arms. (*Then to an old full-length portrait, a long-limbed gentleman in white trunk-hose, relieved against a black background.*) And observe the family legs! Observe the suit of armour worn at Tewksbury—observe the tattered banner carried at Blenheim. (*Then on a graver note, but still with brightness, looking round at them all, in their circle, and taking in particularly* CAPTAIN YULE, *down at right or at left.*) Observe, above all, that you're in one of the most interesting old houses, of its type, in England; for which the ages have been tender and the generations wise; letting it change so slowly that there's always more left than *taken*—living their lives in it, but letting it *shape* their lives!

PRODMORE. (*In high elation.*) A most striking tribute to Summersoft!—You do, Madam, bring it out!

A VISITOR. (*To another.*) Doesn't she, Jane, bring it out.

MRS. GRACEDEW. (*Staring, laughing.*) But who in the world wants to keep it *in?* It ain't a *secret*—or a mean government! (*With a free indication of the fine arch, the noble spring, of the roof.*) Just look at those lovely lines! (*The visitors nudge each other, exclaiming, under their breath,* "Look—look!" *and all heads, save* YULE's,

---

[1] Gaunt House, a moated dwelling of the fifteenth century, near Oxford.

are jerked up, everyone staring at the roof and much impressed. Then pointing successively to the high ancient window and the other objects, to which all turn.) Just look at the tone of that *glass*—and the cutting of that *oak*—and the dear old flags of the very *floor*. To look, in this place, is to *love!*

A VISITOR. (*Sniggling.*) Laws—to love!

ANOTHER. It depends on who you look at!

PRODMORE. (*Exhilarated, arch.*) Do you hear *that,* Captain? You must look at the right person!

MRS. GRACEDEW. (*Who has been watching YULE during this last moment.*) I don't think Captain Yule cares. He doesn't do justice—!

YULE. (*After an instant during which he gives her back a long look.*) To what, Madam?

MRS. GRACEDEW. To the value of your house.

YULE. I like to hear *you* express it!

MRS. GRACEDEW. I *can't* express it. (*After an instant, as if she has tried.*) It's too inexpressible!

PRODMORE. (*Encouraging.*) Have a little try, Madam—it would bring it quite 'ome to us.

MRS. GRACEDEW. Well—the value's a *fancy*-value!

PRODMORE. (*Triumphant, to* YULE.) Exactly what I *told* you!

MRS. GRACEDEW. When a thing's unique, it's unique!

PRODMORE. It's unique!

A VISITOR. (*Very assentingly.*) It's unique!

MRS. GRACEDEW. It's worth anything you like.

PRODMORE. Anything you like!

A VISITOR. (*With increasing boldness.*) Twenty·thousand, now?

MRS. GRACEDEW. I wouldn't *look* at twenty thousand!

PRODMORE. (*Eagerly, to* YULE.) She wouldn't look at twenty thousand!

THE VISITOR. (*Sociable.*) Thirty, then, as it stands?

MRS. GRACEDEW. (*Looking round her, hesitating.*) It would be giving it away!

PRODMORE. (*To* YULE.) It would be giv-

ing it away!

ANOTHER VISITOR. You'd hold out for forty, eh?

MRS. GRACEDEW. (*After another consideration, fixing her eyes, with a smile, on* YULE.) Fifty, Captain Yule, is what I think I should *offer!*

A VISITOR. (*In admiration.*) Fifty thousand pound!

ANOTHER. (*In stupefaction, simultaneously.*) Fifty thousand pound!

PRODMORE. (*Victoriously to* YULE.) Fifty thousand pound! (*Then with gaiety and decision to* MRS. GRACEDEW.) He'll never part with his ancestral 'ome!

MRS. GRACEDEW. (*With equal gaiety.*) Then I'll go over it again while I've a chance! (*To the party, doing again the housekeeper.*) We now pass to the grand staircase!

YULE. (*Who has assisted at this scene without moving, very attentive, but inexpressive and impenetrable; abruptly addressing* MRS. GRACEDEW.) Please let them pass *without* you!

MRS. GRACEDEW. (*Surprised, staring.*) And stay here with *you?*

YULE. If you'll be so *good.* I want to speak to you. (*With perceptible impatience, to* CHIVERS, *hurrying the others off.*) I say—*take* them!

CHIVERS. (*With instant obsequiosity, to the party.*) We now pass to·the grand staircase. (*Exeunt the visitors to the staircase, marshalled and conducted by* CHIVERS.)

CORA. (*Breaking out, uneasily.*) Mrs. Gracedew—may *I* speak to you?

PRODMORE. (*Interposing sharply.*) After Captain Yule, my dear. You must also see the *house.* (*He pushes her off peremptorily—while* YULE *moves nervously away, with his back turned—in the wake of the party. Then he exclaims, quickly and privately, to* MRS. GRACEDEW.) Pile it *on!* (*Exit, by the staircase, rapidly, with* CORA, *whom, though she visibly wishes to communicate again with* MRS. GRACEDEW, *who gaily and unsuspiciously kisses her hand to her, he hurries off.*)

YULE. (*After an instant of embarrassed silence, when he is left alone with* MRS. GRACEDEW.) How do you come to know so much about my house?

MRS. GRACEDEW. (*Laughing.*) How do *you* come to know so *little?*

YULE. (*After an instant.*) A combination of misfortunes has forbidden me, till this hour, to enter it.

MRS. GRACEDEW. (*With the friendliest compassion.*) Why, you poor thing—now that you've got here I hope you'll *stay!* Do make yourself comfortable—don't mind *me!*

YULE. That's exactly what I wanted to say to *you!*

MRS. GRACEDEW. Well, I *haven't* minded you much, have I?

YULE. Oh, it's you who seem in complete possession, and I the vague outsider.

MRS. GRACEDEW. Then you must let me put you up!

YULE. (*After an instant, smiling; more and more charmed.*) Up to *what?*

MRS. GRACEDEW. Up to *everything!*— You were smoking when you came in. (*Looking about her.*) Where's your cigarette?

YULE. (*Producing a fresh cigarette.*) I thought perhaps I *mightn't*—here.

MRS. GRACEDEW. You may *everywhere.*

YULE. (*With docility, receiving instruction.*) Everywhere.

MRS. GRACEDEW. (*Laughing at the way he says it.*) A rule of the house!

YULE. (*Looking round him, pleased.*) What delightful rules!

MRS. GRACEDEW. How could such a house have any *others?* (*After an instant, full of her happy sense of the place.*) I *may* go up again, mayn't I? to the Long Gallery?

YULE. (*Vague.*) The Long Gallery?

MRS. GRACEDEW. I forgot you've never seen it! It's a *glory!* (*Thinking but of seeing it again and showing it.*) Come right up!

YULE. (*Smoking, without moving.*) There's a party up.

MRS. GRACEDEW. (*Laughing, remembering.*) So *you* must be the "party down"? Well, you must give me a chance—that Long Gallery's the principal thing I came over for.

YULE. (*After smoking a moment and staring at her in candid mystification.*) Where, in heaven's name, did you come

over from?

MRS. GRACEDEW. Missourah Top, where I'm *building*—just in this style. I came for my *plans*—I felt I must look at you.

YULE. (*Amazed.*) But what did you know about us?

MRS. GRACEDEW. Everything!

YULE. (*Incredulous.*) At Missourah Top?

MRS. GRACEDEW. Why not? It's a growing place—thirty thousand the last census. My husband *left* it to me.

YULE. (*After an hesitation.*) You're a widow?

MRS. GRACEDEW. (*With quiet assent.*) A very lone woman. (*With a sad smile.*) My loneliness is great enough to require a great receptacle—and my taste is good enough to require a beautiful one. You see, I had your picture.

YULE. (*Bewildered.*) Mine?

MRS. GRACEDEW. (*Smiling.*) A watercolour I chanced on— (*nodding in the direction*) of that divine south front. So I got you up—in the books.

YULE. (*Surprised, artlessly.*) Are we in the books?

MRS. GRACEDEW. (*Equally surprised.*) Did you never discover it? (*After an instant.*) Where, in heaven's name, Captain Yule, have *you* come over from?

YULE. The East End of London.

MRS. GRACEDEW. What were you doing *there?*

YULE. Working. When I left the army— it was too slow—I began to see that, for a fighting man—

MRS. GRACEDEW. There's always somebody to fight?

YULE. The enemy—in all his power. Misery and ignorance and vice—injustice and privilege and wrong! Such as you see me—

MRS. GRACEDEW. You're a rabid reformer? I wish we had you at Missourah Top!

YULE. (*Smiling.*) I fear my work is nearer home. I hope—as a representative of the people—to achieve a part of it in the next House of Commons. My electors have wanted me—

MRS. GRACEDEW. And you've wanted *them*—and that has been why you couldn't come.

YULE. From my childhood up, there was another reason. (*Smiling.*) A family feud!

MRS. GRACEDEW. (*Delighted.*) Oh, I'm so glad—I *hoped* I'd strike a "feud"! That rounds it off, and spices it up, and, for the heartbreak with which I take leave of you, just neatly completes the fracture! (*As if the time for her departure is already there—looking round her for some personal belonging she has laid down.*) Must I really wait—to go up?

YULE. (*After an instant.*) Only till you tell me this: if you literally *meant*—a while ago—that this place is so wonderful.

MRS. GRACEDEW. (*As if in astonishment, almost in compassion, at his density.*) Do you literally require me to *say* it? Can you stand there and not *feel* it? (*Looking round her again; then with a fresh rush of her impression.*) It's a place to Love—

YULE. (*As she hesitates an instant.*) To Love?

MRS. GRACEDEW. Well, as you'd love a *person!* (*With abrupt decision, going up.*) Goodbye!

YULE. (*As she reaches the foot of the stairs.*) I think I feel it—but it's largely you who *make* me. The greater the pity—that I shall have to give it up!

MRS. GRACEDEW. (*Turning, with a sudden stop and stare.*) Give it up? Why in the world—?

YULE. Because I can't afford to keep it.

MRS. GRACEDEW. (*Coming down again, promptly; thinking.*) Can't you *let* it?

YULE. (*Smiling.*) Let it to *you?*

MRS. GRACEDEW. (*With a laugh.*) I'd take it in a minute!

YULE. I shouldn't have the face to charge you a rent that would make it worth one's while, and I think even you, dear lady, wouldn't have the face to offer me one. My lovely inheritance is Dead Sea fruit. It's mortgaged for all it's worth, and I haven't the means to pay the interest. If by a miracle I could scrape the money together, I shouldn't have a penny left to live on. So I see it at last (*looking round the place*)—only to *lose* it!

MRS. GRACEDEW. (*Immensely disconcerted.*) I never heard of anything so dreadful! Surely there's a way of arranging.

YULE. Yes—a way of arranging has been proposed to me.

MRS. GRACEDEW. For heaven's sake, then, *accept* it!

YULE. I've made up my mind in the last quarter of an hour that I *can't*. It's too peculiar.

MRS. GRACEDEW. What's the peculiarity?

YULE. A change in my essential attitude. The mortgages have all found their way, like a flock of silly sheep, into the hands of one person—a devouring wolf, a rich, a powerful capitalist. He holds me in this manner at his mercy. He consents to make things comfortable for me, but he requires that, in return, I shall do something very serious for *him*.

MRS. GRACEDEW. (*Wondering.*) Something wrong?

YULE. (*Decided.*) Yes—exceedingly so.

MRS. GRACEDEW. (*After a moment.*) Anything immoral?

YULE. Yes, I may literally *call* it immoral.

MRS. GRACEDEW. (*After another hesitation.*) Is it too bad to *tell?*

YULE. (*Bringing the thing out, leaving her to judge.*) He wants me to change my opinions!

MRS. GRACEDEW. (*Amazed.*) Your "opinions"? Is that *all?*

YULE. Surely it's quite enough—considering how *many* I have!

MRS. GRACEDEW. Well, I've a neat collection too, but I'd change the whole set for—(*looking about an instant for an equivalent, then pointing to the chimney-piece*) that set of old fire-irons.

YULE. (*With amused compassion.*) I don't think you *understand* me. He wants me to change my *politics.*

MRS. GRACEDEW. (*Undaunted.*) I'd change *them* for the hearthbrush!

YULE. (*Laughing.*) You've not issued a scorching address. You're not a pure, pledged Radical, suddenly invited to present yourself to this neighbouring borough of Gossage as a full-fed Conservative.

MRS. GRACEDEW. Is it Mr. Prodmore who invites you?

YULE. I didn't mean to mention his name; but since *you* have done so—!

MRS. GRACEDEW. It's he who's the devouring wolf—it's he who holds your mortgages? (*Then, after an instant, on* YULE's *assent.*) Why doesn't he stand himself?

YULE. Well, like other devouring wolves, he isn't personally adored.

MRS. GRACEDEW. (*Catching on; seeing clear.*) I see. You would be, you poor lamb, and that's why he *wants* you!

YULE. I'm the bearer of my name, I'm the representative of my family; and to my family—since you've led me to it—this countryside has been for generations indulgently attached.

MRS. GRACEDEW. (*Who has listened with deep interest.*) You do what you *will* with the countryside?

YULE. If we do it as genuine Yules. Now your genuine Yule's a Tory of Tories. It's Mr. Prodmore's view that I should carry Gossage in that character, but that they wouldn't look at me in any other.

MRS. GRACEDEW. And what's the extraordinary interest that he attaches—?

YULE. (*Taking her up.*) To the return of a Tory? Oh, his desire is born of his fear—his terror on behalf of Property. He has got so *much*—and he hasn't got anything *else.*

MRS. GRACEDEW. (*Gaily.*) He has got a very nice daughter!

YULE. (*After an instant.*) I really didn't *look* at her—and moreover she's a *part* of the Property. He thinks things are going too far.

MRS. GRACEDEW. (*With abrupt, high decision.*) Well, they *are!*

YULE. (*Struck, more grave, as if surprised at her tone.*) Aren't you a lover of justice?

MRS. GRACEDEW. A passionate one! (*After an instant.*) Where's the justice in your losing this house? To *keep* it—(*with renewed decision*) you must carry Gossage!

YULE. (*Aghast.*) As a renegade?

MRS. GRACEDEW. As a genuine Yule. What business have you to be anything else? You must close with Mr. Prodmore —you must stand in the Conservative interest. (*After an instant.*) If you will, I'll conduct your canvass!

YULE. (*Laughing.*) That puts the temptation high!

MRS. GRACEDEW. (*Impatient.*) Ah, don't look at me as if *I* were the temptation! Look at this sweet old human home, and

feel all its gathered memories. Do you want to know what they *do* to me?—they speak to me for Mr. Prodmore!

YULE. Well, dear lady, there are other things that speak to me—things for which I've spoken, repeatedly and loudly, to *others.* One's "human home" is all very well, but the rest of one's humanity is better.—I see—you're disgusted with me, and I'm sorry; but one must take one's self as circumstances and experience have made one, and it's not my fault if they've made *me* a very modern man! I see something else in the world than the beauty of old show-houses and the glory of old show-families. There are thousands of people in England who can show no houses *at all,* and I don't feel as if it were utterly shameful to share their poor fate!

MRS. GRACEDEW. We share the poor fate of humanity whatever we do, and we do something to help and console when we've something precious to show. What on earth is more precious than what the ages have slowly wrought? They've trusted you to *keep* it—to do something for *them.* It's such a virtue, in anything, to have *lasted*— it's such an honour, for anything, to have been *spared.* To a struggler from the wreck of time—hold out a pitying hand!

YULE. (*Struck by what she says and the way she says it, but turning it off with a laugh.*) What a plea, dear Mrs. Gracedew, to come from Missourah Top!

MRS. GRACEDEW. We're making a Past at Missourah Top as fast as ever we can— and I should like to see you lay your hand on an hour of the one that we've made! It's a tight fit, as yet—I admit—and that's just why I like, in *yours,* to find room to turn round. You're *in* it, over here, and you can't get out; so just make the best of it and treat it as part of the fun!

YULE. The whole of the fun, to me, is in hearing you defend it! It's like your defending chronic rheumatism—something that I feel aching in every bone of these walls and groaning in every draught that, I'm sure, blows through them.

MRS. GRACEDEW. If there are draughts (*looking about her*)—there *may* be—you're here to stop them up. And do you know what *I'm* here for? If I've come so far and so straight, I've almost wondered myself. I've felt with a kind of *passion*—but now I see *why* I've felt. I'm here for an act of salvation—I'm here to avert a sacrifice!

YULE. (*With great acknowledgment and admiration.*) You're here, I think, Madam —to be a memory for my future!

MRS. GRACEDEW. You'll be one for *mine*, if I can see you by that hearth. Why do you make such a fuss about changing your politics? If you'd come to Missourah Top you'd change them quick enough! What do politics amount to—compared with *religions*. Parties and programmes come and go, but a duty like *this* abides. There's nothing you can break with that would be like breaking *here*. The very *word's* a violence—a sacrilege: your house is a kind of altar! You *must* have beauty in your life—that's the only way to make *sure* of it for the life of others. Keep leaving it to *them*, and heaven knows what they'll *do* with it! Does it take one of *us* to feel that?— to preach you the *truth*? Then it's good we come *over*, to see what you're about! We know what we *haven't* got, and if *you've* luckily got it, you've got it also for *us*. You've got it in *trust*, and oh! we have an *eye* on you. You've had it so for *me*, all these dear days, that, to be grateful, I've wanted to *do* something. (*Pleading.*) Tell me now I shall have *done* it—I shall have kept you at your *post*!

YULE. (*Strongly troubled, rendered nervous and uncertain by her appeal; moving restlessly about.*) You have a strange eloquence! Of course I don't pretend that I don't *care* for Summersoft.

MRS. GRACEDEW. You haven't even *seen* it, yet! I think you're *afraid*.

YULE. (*After an instant.*) Perhaps I *am*! But if I am—it isn't only Summersoft that *makes* me.

MRS. GRACEDEW. (*Vague.*) What *else* is it?

YULE. It doesn't *matter*—you may be *right*. When we talk of the house, your voice seems somehow its very *soul*. I like to *listen*.

MRS. GRACEDEW. (*With joyous relief.*) Then I've done a good day's work!

YULE. Not yet: I must wait—I must think.

MRS. GRACEDEW. When have you to answer Mr. Prodmore?

YULE. (*Thinking, fidgetty.*) He gives me time.

MRS. GRACEDEW. *I* wouldn't! For God's sake, go upstairs!

YULE. (*Reluctant.*) And *meet* Mr. Prodmore?

MRS. GRACEDEW. (*Seeing* CORA *on the stairs.*) He's coming *down*.

          (*Re-enter* CORA PRODMORE *by the staircase.*)

YULE. (*After a straight, distracted stare at* CORA, *hesitating a moment more, then sharply deciding.*) I'll go up! (*Exit rapidly by the staircase.*)

CORA. (*Agitated, eager.*) I've come *back* to you—I've wanted so to *speak* to you! (*With intensity.*) May I *confide* in you?

MRS. GRACEDEW. (*Staring, struck, amused.*) You *too*? It *is* good we come over!

CORA. It is *indeed*! You were so *kind* to me—and I'm alone with my tremendous *news*, which met me at the *door*. (*Bringing it out with all the force of her excitement.*) He wants me to *marry* him!

MRS. GRACEDEW. (*Not following.*) "He" wants you—?

CORA. Papa, of course. He has *settled* it!

MRS. GRACEDEW. (*Blank; thinking.*) That you're to marry *whom*?

CORA. Why, Captain Yule, who just went out.

MRS. GRACEDEW. (*Startled, but still vague.*) Has Captain Yule *asked* you?

CORA. No—but he *will*: to keep the house. It's mortgaged to *Papa*—he buys it *back*.

MRS. GRACEDEW. (*Wonderstruck.*) By "marrying" you?

CORA. (*Lucid.*) Giving me his name and his position. They're the *price*—Papa *wants* them.

MRS. GRACEDEW. (*Bewildered.*) But his name and his position—are his dreadful *politics*!

CORA. You *know* about his dreadful politics? He's to *change* them—to *get* me! And if he gets me—

MRS. GRACEDEW. (*Taking her up with intensity.*) He keeps the *house*?

CORA. I go *with* it—he's to have us *both*. But only if he changes. The question is: *Will* he change?

Mrs. Gracedew. I see. *Will* he change?

Cora. (*Thinking, speculating.*) *Has* he changed?

Mrs. Gracedew. (*With a note of irritation.*) My dear child—how in the world should *I* know?

Cora. He hasn't seemed to care enough for the house. *Does* he care?

Mrs. Gracedew. (*After a moment.*) You had better *ask* him!

Cora. If he does, he'll propose.

Mrs. Gracedew. (*Seeing* Yule *on the stairs; after an instant, convinced, struck.*) He'll propose.

(*Re-enter* Captain Yule *by the staircase.*)

Cora. (*Fluttered, alarmed.*) Then I *fly!*

Yule. (*As* Cora *has moved to the garden-door.*) I drive Miss Prodmore away.

Mrs. Gracedew. (*Very promptly.*) It's all right! (*To* Cora.) I've something to *say* to Captain Yule.

Cora. I've something more to say to *you* —before you *go.*

Mrs. Gracedew. Come *back* then—I'm not *going!*

(*Exit* Cora *to the garden.* Yule *stands there gravely, rigidly, with his eyes fixed to the ground. There is a considerable awkward silence, during which* Mrs. Gracedew *moves vaguely about the room without looking at him.*)

Yule. (*At last.*) It will doubtless give you pleasure to know that I've closed with Mr. Prodmore.

Mrs. Gracedew. (*After another silence.*) I thought you said he gave you *time.*

Yule. (*Still very grave.*) You produced just now so deep an effect on me that I thought best not to *take* any. I came right *upon* him there—and I burnt my ships!

Mrs. Gracedew. (*Without looking at him.*) You do what he requires?

Yule. I do what he requires. I felt the tremendous force of all you said to me.

Mrs. Gracedew. (*After a moment.*) So did *I*—or I shouldn't have *said* it!

Yule. You're perhaps not aware that you wield an influence of which it's not too much to say that it's practically irresistible!

Mrs. Gracedew. (*Graver even than* Yule: *thinking; just faintly ironical.*)

You've given me the most flattering *proof* of my influence that I've ever enjoyed in my *life!*

Yule. (*As if beginning to be struck by her manner; explanatory, attenuating.*) This was inevitable, dear Madam, from the moment you had promptly converted me into the absolute echo of your raptures.

Mrs. Gracedew. (*Vague, as if she has suddenly forgotten them.*) My "raptures"?

Yule. (*Surprised.*) Why, about my home.

Mrs. Gracedew. (*Recalling; with indefinable dryness.*) Oh yes—your home. It's a nice tattered, battered old thing.—It has defects, of course; but it's no use mentioning them *now!*

Yule. (*Uneasy, sad.*) I'm singularly sorry you didn't mention them *before!*

Mrs. Gracedew. (*After a moment.*) If you had gone *over* the house, as I literally besought you to do, you might have discovered some of them yourself.

Yule. I was precisely in the very *act* of it; but the first person I met, above, was Mr. Prodmore; when, feeling that I must *come* to it, sooner or later, I just *yielded* him his point, on the spot—to have it well *over.*

Mrs. Gracedew. Let me then congratulate you on at last knowing what you *want!*

Yule. I only know it so far as *you* know it!—I struck while the iron was hot—or at any rate while the *hammer* was!

Mrs. Gracedew. Of course I recognise that it can rarely have been exposed to such a fire. I blazed up, and I know that when I burn—!

Yule. (*As she pauses, thinking.*) When you burn?

Mrs. Gracedew. I burn as Chicago burns.

Yule. Down to the ground?

Mrs. Gracedew. (*Throwing up her arms.*) Up to the *sky!*—I suppose you've still *formalities* to go through.

Yule. With Mr. Prodmore? Oh, endless, tiresome ones, no doubt!

Mrs. Gracedew. You mean they'll take so very *long?*

Yule. Every hour, every month, that I can possibly make them last!

Mrs. Gracedew. (*After an instant.*) You

mustn't drag them out *too* much—must you? or he'll think that you perhaps want to *retract*.

YULE. (*With abrupt expressiveness.*) I shouldn't be so terribly upset by his mistake if he *did!*

MRS. GRACEDEW. Oh, it would never do to give him any colour whatever for supposing that you have any doubt that, as one may say, you've pledged your honour.

YULE. Of course not—not when I *haven't* any doubt!

MRS. GRACEDEW. How can you *possibly* have any, any more than you can possibly have that one's honour is everything in the world?

YULE. Oh yes—everything in the world.

MRS. GRACEDEW. We *spoke* of honour a while ago—didn't we?—and of the difficulty of keeping it unspotted; so that there's no more to be said except that I leave you to that engrossing occupation. I hope you'll enjoy your cosy little home, and appreciate such a fury of affection.

YULE. (*Wondering, alarmed.*) Do you suppose it will be a "fury"?

MRS. GRACEDEW. (*Representing surprise.*) Why, what do you call the love of twenty thousand? (*Then on his gesture of consternation.*) That's my rough estimate of the population of Gossage. Such a lovely figure!

YULE. (*Struck, off his guard, confused.*) *Who* has a lovely figure—?

MRS. GRACEDEW. (*With a nervous laugh.*) Gossage!—Goodbye.

YULE. (*More and more disconcerted.*) You don't mean to say you're going?

MRS. GRACEDEW. Haven't I done what I told you I had been mysteriously moved to *come* for? (*Looking about; addressing herself to the house.*) You're *saved!*

YULE. (*Troubled, earnest.*) For God's sake don't go till I can come back to *thank* you! I promised to return immediately to Prodmore.

MRS. GRACEDEW. Oh, don't let me stand in Prodmore's way—you must have such lots to talk comfortably over!

YULE. (*Agitated.*) I certainly feel that I must see him again.—Yes, decidedly, I *must!*

MRS. GRACEDEW. (*As if this is highly obvious.*) Then *go* to him!

YULE. (*Pressing.*) Will you *wait* for me?

MRS. GRACEDEW. (*Having first hesitated, then looked round her for a chair, into which she drops.*) Go to him. (YULE goes to the staircase and begins slowly to mount it, looking back at her as she sits there by his—as it were—quiet fireside. Half way up he pauses, hesitates, and then comes down a few steps again, as if to approach her once more and break out into something. His doing this startles her, so as to make her turn round, rising again and looking at him. Hereupon he stops a second time and stands there—still on the staircase—exchanging with her a fixed, silent gaze; after which, taking a sharp decision, he starts off and very rapidly ascends the rest of the steps. Exit* CAPTAIN YULE. MRS. GRACEDEW *then comes down.*) Why didn't he tell me *all?* (*After an instant, taking herself up, repudiating the question.*) It was none of my business! (*Wondering again.*) What does he mean to *do?*— What *should* he do but what he has done? —and what *can* he do when he's so *deeply* committed, when he's practically engaged, when he's just the same as *married?*—The thing for *me* to do is just to *go:* to remove from the scene they encumber the numerous fragments (*seeing* CORA *reappear and spying, on the table on which he has gathered them together, the pieces of the vase* CHIVERS *has smashed—*) of my old Chelsea pot!

(*Re-enter* CORA *from the garden.*)

CORA. Ah, Captain Yule's gone?

MRS. GRACEDEW. Upstairs again—to rejoin your father.

CORA. Papa's not there—he has come down, the other way, to rejoin *me.*

MRS. GRACEDEW. (*After an instant.*) He can do so here—I'm going.

CORA. (*Disconcerted.*) Just when I've come *back* to you (*slightly arch*)—at the risk of again interrupting your conversation with Captain Yule?

MRS. GRACEDEW. I've nothing to say to Captain Yule.

CORA. You had a good deal to say a few minutes ago!

MRS. GRACEDEW. Well, I've *said* it—and it's *over!* (*With great decision.*) I've nothing more to say at all! (*Then, as if to change the subject and involuntarily lingering, in spite of her successive announcements of departure.*) What's become of the "party"?

CORA. Dismissed, through the grounds, by the other door. But they've announced the arrival of a fresh lot.

MRS. GRACEDEW. (*Gaily.*) Well, *you* must take the fresh lot—since the house is now practically *yours!*

CORA. (*Blank.*) Mine?

MRS. GRACEDEW. (*Surprised at her surprise.*) Why, if you're going to marry Captain Yule.

CORA. (*Very resolute.*) I'm *not* going to marry Captain Yule!

MRS. GRACEDEW. (*In stupefaction.*) Why on earth then did you tell me just now you *were?*

CORA. (*Extremely astonished that* MRS. GRACEDEW *has believed this.*) I told you nothing of the sort. I only told you he had been *ordered* me!

MRS. GRACEDEW. (*Amused, wondering.*) Like a dose of medicine or a course of baths?

CORA. As a remedy for the single life. But I won't *take* him!

MRS. GRACEDEW. Ah then, why didn't you *tell* me?

CORA. I was on the very point of it when he came in and interrupted us. It's what I came *back* for.

MRS. GRACEDEW. (*Relieved, smiling.*) Excuse me—I misunderstood. I somehow took for granted—!

CORA. You took for granted I'd jump at him? Well, you see I *don't!*

MRS. GRACEDEW. You prefer the single life?

CORA. No, but I don't prefer *him!*

MRS. GRACEDEW. (*Struck, interested.*) You prefer someone *else?* (*Then as* CORA *turns away from her, nervously faltering a moment; gently, encouragingly.*) He seems remarkably *nice.*

CORA. (*Impatiently.*) Then why don't you marry him *yourself?*

MRS. GRACEDEW. (*Staring; with a laugh.*) Well, I've got *fifty* reasons! I think *one* of them is that he hasn't *asked* me.

CORA. I haven't got "fifty" reasons, but I've got *one!*

MRS. GRACEDEW. (*Struck, then smiling.*) I see. An older friend!

CORA. (*With emotion.*) I've been trying, this *hour*, in my need of advice, to *tell* you about him! After we parted at the station he suddenly turned up there, and I took a little quiet walk with him which gave you time to get here before me and of which my father is in a state of ignorance that I don't know whether to call desirable or dreadful.

MRS. GRACEDEW. (*Who has taken this earnestly in; turning it over.*) You want me then to *inform* your father?

CORA. (*Embarrassed, distressful.*) I really don't know *what* I want! I think I want support.

MRS. GRACEDEW. (*Thinking, then taking a large resolution.*) Then I'll *support* you!

CORA. (*With effusion.*) You *dear* woman! —He's intensely sympathetic.

MRS. GRACEDEW. So are *you*—and he must have a nice nature, to be conscious of an *affinity* with you!

CORA. His affinity is greater than poor Captain Yule's—I could see at a glance that *he* had *none!* Papa has seen him, but we've been so sure Papa would hate it that we've had to be awfully careful. He's the son of the richest man at Bellborough, he's Granny's godson, and he'll inherit his father's business, which is simply immense. He has been away for three days, and if he met me at the station, where, on his way back, he had to *change*, it was quite by the purest *chance*. He's clever, and he's good—and *I know he loves me!*

MRS. GRACEDEW. Then what's the matter with him?

CORA. (*Faltering.*) His name.

MRS. GRACEDEW. What *is* it?

CORA. (*Bringing it out.*) Buddle.

MRS. GRACEDEW. (*Repeating it interrogatively and a trifle dubiously. Then with courageous decision.*) Well—Buddle will *do!*

CORA. Then, for heaven's sake, make my father *think* so!

MRS. GRACEDEW. (*After a moment.*) I'll *make* him—if in return you'll do something for *me.* Give me a clear assurance.

CORA. (*Vague.*) Of *what?*

MRS. GRACEDEW. That if Captain Yule *should* propose to you, you'd unconditionally refuse him.

CORA. With my dying breath!

MRS. GRACEDEW. (*After an instant.*) Will you make it even a promise?

CORA. (*Emphatically.*) A promise.

MRS. GRACEDEW. (*In whose hand* CORA *has placed her own.*) Then let me *kiss* you!

CORA. (*After the embrace, at the door of the vestibule.*) We'll meet at the *station*.

MRS. GRACEDEW. (*Vague.*) Where are you going?

CORA. (*Smiling.*) Can't you *guess*? (*Exit to the vestibule.*)

MRS. GRACEDEW. (*Alone.*) To Mr. Buddle! (*Then, with great decision, as if she herself now knows thoroughly what she's about.*) Thank *goodness* for Mr. Buddle!

(*Re-enter* MR. PRODMORE *from the garden.*)

PRODMORE. My daughter's not here?

MRS. GRACEDEW. Your daughter's not here. But it's a convenience to me, Mr. Prodmore, that *you* are, for I've something very particular to *ask* you.

PRODMORE. (*Who has crossed to the drawingroom.*) I shall be delighted to answer your question, but I must first put my hand on Miss Prodmore. (*Then having checked himself at the door.*) Unless indeed she's occupied in there with Captain Yule.

MRS. GRACEDEW. I don't think she's occupied—anywhere—with Captain Yule.

PRODMORE. (*Uneasy.*) Then where the deuce *is* Captain Yule?

MRS. GRACEDEW. His absence, for which I'm responsible, is just what renders the inquiry I spoke of to you possible.—What will you *take*—for your interest in this property?

PRODMORE. (*Staring, coming down.*) Eh? —You *know* about my interest?

MRS. GRACEDEW. Everything.

PRODMORE. Then you must know it has just ceased to *exist*. I've given it up—for an equivalent.

MRS. GRACEDEW. For a son-in-law?

PRODMORE. That will presently be Captain Yule's proper designation.

MRS. GRACEDEW. Then Miss Prodmore has already accepted him?

PRODMORE. In spite of the doubt which you appear to throw on the idea, it is my intimate conviction that she is accepting him at this moment.

MRS. GRACEDEW. (*After a moment; abruptly.*) Dear Mr. Prodmore, why are you so imprudent as to make your daughter *afraid* of you? You should have taught her to *confide* in you. She has clearly shown me that she *can* confide.

PRODMORE. (*Blankly anxious.*) She confides in *you*?

MRS. GRACEDEW. Completely. Let me suggest that as fortune has thrown us together here, for a moment, you follow her good example.—Tell me, for instance, the ground of your objection to poor Mr. Buddle. I mean Mr. Buddle of Bellborough, the godson of your daughter's grandmother and the associate of his father in their flourishing house—to whom (as he is to *her*) Miss Prodmore is devotedly attached.

PRODMORE. (*Gasping, amazed.*) It has gone as far as *that*?

MRS. GRACEDEW. It has gone so far that you had better let it go the rest of the way!

PRODMORE. (*Astounded, indignant.*) It's too monstrous, to have plotted to keep me in the dark—!

MRS. GRACEDEW. I'm afraid it's only when you're kept in the dark that your daughter's kept in the light! It's at her own earnest request that I plead to you for her liberty of choice. She's an honest girl, and she's not a baby: she has a perfect right to her preference.

PRODMORE. And pray haven't I a perfect right to *mine*?

MRS. GRACEDEW. Not at her expense. You ask her to give up too much.

PRODMORE. And what does she ask *me* to give up? The desire of my heart and the dream of my life! Captain Yule announced to me but a few minutes since his intention to offer her his hand.

MRS. GRACEDEW. I think Captain Yule will find that his hand will be simply *declined*.

PRODMORE. (*Resolutely.*) It *won't* be declined!

MRS. GRACEDEW. (*Still more resolutely.*) It *will*!

PRODMORE. (*Dashing again towards the drawingroom, or better still, to some other door.*) It *shan't!*

MRS. GRACEDEW. (*Springing before him; passionately.*) It *shall!* (*Then after a moment, while he stands arrested, bewildered.*) Now tell me how much!

PRODMORE. How can I tell you anything so preposterous?

MRS. GRACEDEW. Simply by computing the total amount to which, for your benefit, this unhappy estate is burdened.—If I've troubled you by showing you that your speculation is built on the sand, let me atone for it by my eagerness to take off your hands an investment from which you derive so little profit.

PRODMORE. (*Blank, wondering.*) And pray what profit will *you* derive—?

MRS. GRACEDEW. That's my own secret. I want this house!

PRODMORE. So do *I*, damme!—and that's why I've practically *paid* for it!

MRS. GRACEDEW. (*Pleadingly.*) *I'll* practically pay for it, Mr. Prodmore, if you'll only tell me your figure.

PRODMORE. (*As if struck, dimly, with a new light; thinking.*) My figure?

MRS. GRACEDEW. Your figure.

PRODMORE. (*After an instant, dryly; dismissing the question as if vain.*) My figure would be distinctly *high.*

MRS. GRACEDEW. (*Smiling.*) You have all the greater interest in letting me *know* it. As soon as you've done so I cable to Missourah Top to have the money sent right out to you.

PRODMORE. (*Contemptuously amused at her simple notions of business.*) Having the money sent right out to me won't make you owner of this place.

MRS. GRACEDEW. (*Thinking, conceding.*) No—not quite. But I'll settle the rest with Captain Yule.

PRODMORE. (*Self-complacent.*) Captain Yule has nothing to sell.

MRS. GRACEDEW. (*After an instant.*) Then what have you been trying to buy?

PRODMORE. (*Starting, staring.*) Do you mean to say you want to buy *that?* (*Then as she turns away disgusted, protesting, but slightly embarrassed.*) Is your proposal that I should transfer my investment to

you for the mere net *amount* of it your idea of a fair bargain?

MRS. GRACEDEW. (*Vague.*) Pray, what is *yours?*

PRODMORE. Mine would be, not that I should simply get my money back, but that I should get the effective value of the house.

MRS. GRACEDEW. But isn't the effective value of the house just what your money *expresses?*

PRODMORE. (*After an instant; triumphant.*) No, Madam—it's just what *yours* does! It's moreover just what your lips have already expressed so distinctly!

MRS. GRACEDEW. (*Thinking, recalling.*) To those people—when I said it was charming?

PRODMORE. (*Categorical.*) You said it was "unique." You said it was the *perfect* specimen of its class in England. (*With gross elation.*) Oh, you got in *deep!*

MRS. GRACEDEW. (*Realising, wincing, but smiling bravely.*) All that doesn't tell me how deep *you're* in!

PRODMORE. For *you?* (*After a moment.*) I'm in to the tune of fifty thousand!

MRS. GRACEDEW. (*Disconcerted, staggered; after an instant.*) That's a great deal of money.

PRODMORE. (*Imperturbable.*) So I've often had occasion to *say* to myself.

MRS. GRACEDEW. If it's a large sum for you then, it's a still larger one for *me!* (*After an instant, attenuating, debating.*) We women have more modest ideas.

PRODMORE. Is it by that term you describe your extraordinary intrusion—?

MRS. GRACEDEW. I mean I think we measure things often—more *exactly!*

PRODMORE. Then you measured this thing exactly half an hour ago.

MRS. GRACEDEW. (*Blank, oblivious.*) I *raved* about it?

PRODMORE. You said you'd *offer* fifty!

MRS. GRACEDEW. *Did* I say that? (*After an instant.*) It was a figure of *speech!*

PRODMORE. (*Promptly.*) That's the kind of figure we're *talking* about! (*Then sharply, as he sees* CHIVERS: *re-enter* CHIVERS *from the garden.*) Have you seen Miss Prodmore?—If you haven't, *find* her!

MRS. GRACEDEW. (*To* CHIVERS.) You

won't. (*To* PRODMORE.) I happen to know she's gone for a walk.

PRODMORE. (*Blank an instant; then reassured and taking it in.*) What I was *sure* of! With Captain Yule.

MRS. GRACEDEW. (*After an instant.*) No—with Mr. Buddle.

PRODMORE. (*Confounded.*) Buddle has *been* here?

MRS. GRACEDEW. He walked with her from the station.

PRODMORE. (*Stupefied, gasping.*) When she *arrived?* That's why she was so *late?*

MRS. GRACEDEW. Why I got here first. (*Laughing.*) I get *everywhere* first!

PRODMORE. (*Overwhelmed, but pulling himself together.*) In which direction did they *go?*

MRS. GRACEDEW. I think I must let you ascertain for *yourself!*

PRODMORE. (*Catching up his hat; peremptorily to* CHIVERS.) Call my carriage! (*Exit* CHIVERS *to the vestibule.*) You've *protected*, then, Madam, this intrigue?

MRS. GRACEDEW. I think it's this intrigue, as you call it, that has protected *me!* Drive after them, overtake them and forgive them. If you'll do *that*, I'll give you your price!

PRODMORE. (*After a concentrated stare into his hat.*) What do you *call* my price?

MRS. GRACEDEW. Why, the sum you just mentioned—fifty thousand.

PRODMORE. (*Indignantly derisive.*) That's not my price—and it never *was!* Besides—my price is up!

MRS. GRACEDEW. (*With a wail.*) Up?

PRODMORE. *Seventy* thousand.

MRS. GRACEDEW. (*Overwhelmed, prostrate.*) Oh, deary *me!*

PRODMORE. (*Stern, curt.*) It's to take or to leave!

MRS. GRACEDEW. (*Recovering herself with a strong effort and staying him with a gesture as he reaches the door of the vestibule and as he sees* CAPTAIN YULE, *who appears at the top of the stairs: reenter* CAPTAIN YULE, *with whom, before he has come down, she exchanges the same long look as before his last exit.*) Seventy thousand, then!

PRODMORE. (*Closing.*) Seventy thousand! (*Exit with violence to the vestibule.*)

YULE. (*Coming down, wondering.*) He's gone? I've been *looking* for him!

MRS. GRACEDEW. I don't think you *need* him, now.—You must deal with *me.* I've arranged with him that I take it *over.*

YULE. (*Blank.*) Take *what* over?

MRS. GRACEDEW. (*Smiling.*) Your debt!

YULE. (*Bewildered.*) *Can* you—without arranging with *me?*

MRS. GRACEDEW. (*Radiant.*) That's precisely what I *want* to do. Surely you consent.

YULE. (*Thinking.*) If I *do,* how do I perform my engagement—?

MRS. GRACEDEW. To *him.* (*Smiling.*) You *don't* perform it!

YULE. (*Excited.*) He lets me *off?*

MRS. GRACEDEW. He lets you off.

YULE. (*Enchanted, wondering; then with a disconcerted drop.*) Oh—I lose my *house!*

MRS. GRACEDEW. (*Eager.*) Ah no—*that* doesn't follow! (*Faltering an instant.*) You arrange with *me* to keep it.

YULE. But *how* do I arrange?

MRS. GRACEDEW. (*Embarrassed, at a loss, but still plausible, cheering.*) We must think—we must wait—we must *find* some way!

YULE. (*Quite at sea.*) But what way *can* we find?—With Prodmore it was simple enough: I could marry his daughter.

MRS. GRACEDEW. (*Quietly but poignantly, ironically smilingly reproachful.*) *Could* you?

YULE. (*Staring; then after an instant, rapturously.*) *Never*—when it came to the *point!* But I had to—

MRS. GRACEDEW. (*Taking him up, as he pauses; artless, innocent.*) You had to—?

YULE. (*Ruefully.*) Think a lot *about* it! —You didn't *suspect* it?

MRS. GRACEDEW. (*With a nervous laugh, turning away.*) Don't ask me too many questions!

YULE. (*Suddenly, joyfully divining.*) You guessed it—and, heaven *bless* you!—you *saved* me?

MRS. GRACEDEW. What a pity, now, *I* haven't a daughter!

YULE. (*With strong feeling.*) What a much *greater* pity that *I* haven't—

MRS. GRACEDEW. (*As he hesitates.*) That you haven't—?

YULE. Something to offer you in *compensation*. (*Then after an instant, as the light comes to him.*) But I *have* it, of course: *Keep* the house—

MRS. GRACEDEW. (*Taking him up, shocked.*) All to *myself?*

YULE. All to *yourself*—you *like* it so much.

MRS. GRACEDEW. I like it more than *ever;* but in that case you *would* lose it.

YULE. Well, after all, why *shouldn't* I? What have I *done* for it—and what *can* I do? I've done nothing whatever—it's you who have done *all*.

MRS. GRACEDEW. I should have nothing without *you*—you gave me my head.

YULE. (*Laughing.*) You certainly went off at a *pace!*

MRS. GRACEDEW. (*Laughing responsively.*) You mustn't pull me up too *short!* If you're just where you were before, how are you "saved"?

YULE. By my life's being my *own* again—to do what I *want!*

MRS. GRACEDEW. What you "want" is what made you close with Prodmore. What you "want" is these walls and these acres. What you "want" is to take the way I *showed* you.

YULE. (*Perplexed, thinking.*) Why, the way you showed me was to marry *Cora!*

MRS. GRACEDEW. I didn't *know* that *then* —you didn't *tell* me.

YULE. I felt a delicacy!

MRS. GRACEDEW. Cora didn't—Cora told me.

YULE. (*Astonished.*) Then she *knew*—?

MRS. GRACEDEW. She knew *all*—and if her father said she didn't, her father *deceived* you. (*Then on a movement of continued surprise and indignation on* YULE'S *part.*) She was quite *right*—she would have *refused* you.

YULE. (*Struck, and with a slightly disconcerted note.*) Oh! (*Then, with a smile, after an instant.*) Do you call that "quite right"?

MRS. GRACEDEW. (*Smiling.*) For *her*— and for Prodmore.

YULE. (*With strong emphasis.*) For Prodmore—with all my *heart!*

MRS. GRACEDEW. To stay at your *post*— *that* was the way I showed you.

YULE. (*Puzzled, bewildered; then expressing, gently, remonstrantly, almost ironically, with a smile, his sense of the hopelessness of the problem.*) How can I take it, dear lady—if, you see, you only *block* it?

MRS. GRACEDEW. (*After an instant; very grave and gentle.*) I won't block it a moment 'more. (*Finally, decisively ready to go.*) I make perfect *room* for you.

YULE. (*Blank.*) You surrender your *rights?*

MRS. GRACEDEW. Weren't you ready to surrender *yours?*

YULE. I *hadn't* any—I hadn't *paid* for them.

MRS. GRACEDEW. Your ancestors *had*— it's the same thing. You're just in a manner my *tenant*.

YULE. (*Less and less satisfied.*) But on what *terms?*

MRS. GRACEDEW. On *any* terms—the easiest! (*With her belongings all gathered.*) You can *write* to me about them.

YULE. (*Vague.*) To Missourah Top?

MRS. GRACEDEW. I go right back.—Goodbye.

YULE. (*Starting as if the word is a sudden knell to him, rapidly getting between her and the door; then almost commandingly.*) A moment, please.—If you won't tell me your own terms, you must at least tell me Prodmore's.

MRS. GRACEDEW. (*Disconcerted, embarrassed.*) Prodmore's?

YULE. How you *did* it—how you *managed* him. (*Waiting; in suspense.*) You bought him out?

MRS. GRACEDEW. (*After an instant, as if she can, with decent plausibility, give no other account of it.*) I bought him out.

YULE. For how *much?* (*As she doesn't answer.*) I *must* know.

MRS. GRACEDEW. You shall *never* know.

YULE. (*Resolute.*) I'll get it from *him*.

MRS. GRACEDEW. (*Smiling sadly.*) Get it if you *can!*

YULE. (*Much moved, overwhelmed.*) He won't *say*—because he *did* you? (*With deep resentment.*) The scoundrel!

MRS. GRACEDEW. (*Impatient, enthusiastic.*) Why, he's *lovely!* (*Then, in her turn, almost commandingly.*) Let me go!

YULE. (*Excited, inflamed, still barring her way.*) With the barren beauty of your *sacrifice?* You pour out *money,* you move a *mountain,* and to let you "go"—to turn you *out*—is all I do for you? (*Passionately.*) You're the most generous, you're the noblest of women! The wonderful chance that *brought* you here—

MRS. GRACEDEW. (*Interrupting, smiling.*) Brought *you* at the same happy hour! I've done what I *liked*—the only way to thank me is to *believe* it!

YULE. You've done it for a proud, *poor* man. He has nothing—in the light of such a power as yours—either to give or to hope; but you've made him, in an hour, *think* of you—

MRS. GRACEDEW. (*Very kindly, as he falters with the rush of his emotion.*) How have I made him think of me?

YULE. As he has thought of *no* other woman! (*Pressing her, pleading tenderly.*) Mrs. Gracedew, don't *leave* me. (*Taking in the place again.*) If you made me *care*—

MRS. GRACEDEW. (*Laughing.*) It was surely that you had made *me* care!

YULE. Then let me go *on!* When I asked you just now for a possible *arrangement,* as my new creditor, you said we must *wait* —we must *find* the possible arrangement. Haven't I found it on this spot? In finding *you,* I've found the impossible *everything!* I offer you in return the only thing I have to give—I offer you my hand, my *life!*

MRS. GRACEDEW. (*Moving away from him as if to disengage herself from his pressure, to get time to think; and speaking with bright, vague, almost remonstrant kindness.*) Ah, Captain Yule—!

(*Re-enter* CHIVERS *from the vestibule.*)

YULE. (*Irritated at the interruption.*) What *is* it?

CHIVERS. Another party!

MRS. GRACEDEW. (*Laughing, exhilarated.*) The "party up!" (*To* CHIVERS.) Show them in.

(*Exit* CHIVERS.)

YULE. (*Surprised.*) You'll *have* them?

MRS. GRACEDEW. Why, mayn't I be proud of my *house?*

YULE. (*Delighted, breathless.*) Then you *accept*—?

MRS. GRACEDEW. (*Cautious, as she sees* CHIVERS.) Hush!

(*Re-enter* CHIVERS *with party much more numerous than the first, while* MRS. GRACEDEW *and* YULE, *instantly separating, pass to opposite sides of the stage.*)

A VISITOR. (*Looking round; pleased, loud and cheerful.*) Old family portraits?

CHIVERS. (*Pointing to one of the portraits.*) Dame Dorothy Yule—who lived to a hundred and one!

ANOTHER VISITOR. (*Before another portrait, while* YULE *goes nervously, impatiently up, as if to close, through the vestibule, the door of the house, left open by the last of the party.*) Who's this?

MRS. GRACEDEW. (*Speaking joyously out, while* YULE *disappears in the vestibule.*) John Anthony Yule—who passed away, poor duck! in his *flower!*

THE VISITOR. (*Before a portrait of a lady hung over the door of the vestibule, while half the party stare with sheepish but undisguised curiosity at* MRS. GRACEDEW *and the other half gregariously cock up their heads at the picture.*) Who's *that?*

MRS. GRACEDEW. (*As* YULE *reappears, framed in the door of the vestibule.*) That? (*With her eyes, in the direction in which, from a distance, the* VISITOR *points, lighting, with happiness, only on* YULE.) Oh, that's my future *husband!*

The High Bid
1907

EDITOR'S FOREWORD

Sir Johnston Forbes-Robertson has told in his memoirs how one evening, sitting in a provincial hotel after a performance and waiting for an early morning train, he read *Covering End* "which struck me as being admirably suited for the stage." He wrote to James (in 1899) but the novelist then would not consider reconverting the story to its earlier stage form. In 1907 Forbes-Robertson renewed his request and this time James, thirteen years removed from his "siege" of the theatre, consented. On October 9, 1907 he once more asked Miss Robins to send him her copy ("Please believe I shall quite understand if the poor disactualized thing has simply become the dust of time!") and on October 20 in a letter to Mrs. W. K. Clifford he was murmuring "in absolute abysmal confidence and privacy and secrecy" that it appeared virtually settled that the Forbes-Robertsons would produce the "one-act thing I did for the perfidious Ellen Terry long years ago and that has been buried ever since in the printed marginal commentary of the pretended second tale of the volume of *The Two Magics*."

He had assented he said "for the lust of a little possible gold." What appealed to him was Forbes-Robertson's idea "to play *it all*, without one bloody cut (which is bribery and balmery to me,) and as it is very long for that, and, as he thinks, *full*, to treat it as three divisions or Cantos or Stanzas (not Acts)! by two very short curtain-drops without fiddles—in which case I get three-act terms for it." On October 23, with a copy of *The Two Magics* in front of him, he began dictating *Summersoft–Covering End* as a three-act play. He worked rapidly, inserting elaborate stage directions, improving the already-improved dialogue of the story form and further strengthening the characterizations. Within twenty days the completed script had been sent to Forbes-Robertson.

There began then, for James, an episode much like that of *The American*. *The High Bid* was to be produced first in Scotland, and then played on the road, with London as its ultimate destination. This time there was no question of the capacity of the actors. James was doubly fortunate in having not only the great Forbes-Robertson, but his highly skilled actress wife, Gertrude Elliott, a sister of Maxine, for the role intended for Ellen Terry. Forbes-Robertson was temperamentally suited to appreciate the artistry of James as few other actors of the British stage at the time. An intensely artistic nature, a gifted painter, an avid reader, he was far from being the stage-type James usually dismissed as *cabotin*. He could, and did, bring intelligence and sympathy to his part and this was what James had been looking for in the productions of his plays. *The High Bid* was an ideal comedy for a touring company; it required a single set and a handful of actors. The question of American accent for Mrs. Gracedew was not even raised, as it had been for Christopher Newman. Miss Elliott was American-born and seemed admirably suited in every way to her part. The novelist threw himself with renewed excitement into the theatre he had abandoned under such painful circumstances more than a decade earlier.

From notes kept in a diary by Theodora Bosanquet, James's amanuensis, we can follow his work on this play through its various stages. On December 15, after Forbes-Robertson had studied the script, James dictated some changes. During January and February 1908, he went up to London from Rye for conferences with his producer and during the first week in February the play went into daily rehearsal with its author in close attendance. On February 19 and 20, James made further revisions, bringing Cora's "Young Man" on stage at the very outset. He felt the play greatly enhanced by this change, and during rehearsals on the road wired Miss Bosanquet in a burst of enthusiasm, "Omen happiest young man immense."

James joined the company at Manchester March 21, and travelled with it to Edinburgh where he arrived on March 23. Here he was joined in due course by his young friend Jocelyn Persse, whom he had invited to be his guest at the first night, and his agent, J. B. Pinker. Immediately after his arrival he wrote to Edith Wharton, raising again the old familiar cry of his dramatic years *à la guerre comme à la guerre*. . . . He had travelled, he wrote, "by special train for my whole troupe and its impedimenta—I traveling with the animals like the lion-tamer or the serpent-charmer in person and quite enjoying the caravan-quality, the bariole Bohemian or *picaresque* note of the affair." The omens were good "the little play pretty and pleasing and amusing and orthodox and mercenary and *safe (absit omen!)*—cravenly, ignobly *canny*: also clearly to be very decently acted." James told Mrs. Wharton that Gertrude, Elliott was showing "a gallantry, capacity and *vaillance,* on which I had not ventured to build. She is a scrap (personally, physically) where she should be a presence, and handicapped by a face too *small* in size to be a field for the play of expression; but allowing for this she illustrates the fact that intelligence and instinct are *capables de tout*—so that I still hope. And each time they worry through the little 'piggery' it seems to me more firm and more intrinsically without holes and weak spots—in itself I mean and not other in short, than 'consummately' artful."

On March 26, *The High Bid* had its first performance at the Royal Lyceum Theatre in Edinburgh. The evening passed off smoothly. James sat in a box with his friends Persse and Pinker and Lady Pollock and Mrs. W. K. Clifford, who had also come especially to be present on the occasion. He quietly slipped away at the end, when calls for the author were raised, so that Forbes-Robertson had to announce he was not in the house. The Edinburgh press gave the play a tepid reception, grumbling that Forbes-Robertson had accepted a secondary role which, said the *Evening News,* "would have been well enough filled by a fifth-rate actor and probably Mr. Forbes-Robertson was of that mind. . . ." The *Scotsman* observed that he was "far from word perfect" and added that the play did not seem likely to "increase his reputation as an actor."

By a coincidence Ellen Terry was playing in Edinburgh that week (in Shaw's *Captain Brassbound's Conversion*); she read the notices and promptly telegraphed Forbes-Robertson: "You have my play." It developed indeed that she believed she had never surrendered her acting rights when she authorized James to convert *Summersoft* into a short story. There followed flurries and consultations; Forbes-Robertson, embarrassed, asked for immediate clarification; Pinker was present, and a survey of the facts revealed that there had never been any contract between Miss Terry and James. Consequently the rights remained with the novelist and in due course the question was considered amicably straightened out.

James was tremendously pleased over this renewed "tussle with the Black Devil of the Theatre." To his nephew Henry he wrote that *The High Bid* "had a *great* and charming success before a big house in Edinburgh—a real and unmistakeable victory—but what was most brought home thereby is that it should have been discharged straight in the face of London. That will be its real and best function." He had hoped for a London production in May or June but Forbes-Robertson was unable to lease a theatre and production was put over until the autumn. In truth, however, Forbes-Robertson felt that the play had limited appeal; he described it as of "far too delicate a fibre and literary elegance" to be a great success. It was, moreover, essentially a vehicle for Gertrude Elliott and audiences seemed disappointed—as the Edinburgh press had implied—that Forbes-Robertson did not have the centre of the stage.

There was another and more important manifestation in the audience that began to trouble Gertrude Elliott during the performances in the provinces. She discovered that when she delivered her great appeal for the preservation of the past to Captain Yule, and when she pleaded, "Look at this sweet old human home, and feel all its gathered memories," the audience did not feel with her. It received her appeals and perorations in silence. But when Captain Yule, in the fine accents and moving voice of Forbes-Robertson answered her quietly, "I see something else in the world than the beauty of old show-houses and the glory of old show-families. There are thousands of people in England who can show no houses *at all,* and I don't feel it utterly shameful to share their poor fate," great bursts of applause greeted his words.

To an actress who had worked hard over her role nothing could be more disconcerting. She wrote to James: "From the general audience's point of view Mrs. Gracedew's appeal for beauty is not so fine as Yule's point of view that it is his duty to throw in his lot with the needy. . . . I used to be very worried about it because it is the crux of the play and if she is not convincing to the audience at that point, they can't understand why a man of such radical views should renounce them so quickly. Perhaps I did not do it with enough conviction but I tried very hard to and I came to the conclusion that they did not see her point of view." She asked James whether the play could not be modified. He was adamant; to modify the play in this respect would mean writing a new play. "My small comedy treats its subject—and its subject is Mrs. Gracedew's appeal and adventure—on Mrs. Gracedew's grounds and in Mrs. Gracedew's spirit, and any deflection from these and that logic and consistency would send the whole action off into a whirlwind of incoherence. Remember that my little piece was conceived quite primarily for *American* production (it was largely on that delusive ground that it took birth in response to Miss Terry's appeal—and she immediately started for America waving it over her head). That character intensely abides in it, and *can* only intensely do so, and stared out of it from the outset, and had so to be reckoned with."

However, the novelist agreed to see what he could do to strengthen the second act. "It is always interesting to measure and reconsider things in the light of their apparent effect (or non-effect) on audiences—if they [are] not things of the essence." At the end of the year he sent the alterations but by that time a more serious difficulty had arisen. In the interval between the Edinburgh production in the spring and the following autumn the Forbes-Robertsons had read a play by Jerome K. Jerome and, struck by its appeal, had produced it in a small theatre, Terry's. *The Passing of the Third Floor Back* caught on and became the most successful play ever produced by them. Sir Johnston played it in England and America for the next four years. While so long a career for the play could not have been foreseen late in 1908 and early in 1909, it was clear that it was a great hit and that the chances of a full-fledged London production for *The High Bid* had been lost. James was sounded out on the question of a matinee series and replied, "I shall be delighted to see my play acted at *any* hour of the twenty-four." Terry's Theatre, however, proved to be too small to accommodate the large set for the James play.

The actor-manager and his wife then accepted Herbert Beerbohm Tree's invitation to put on the play for a series of matinees at the "Afternoon Theatre" at His Majesty's and there *The High Bid* was given on February 18, 1909 and for four matinees thereafter on a bill with Louis Tiercelin's one-act play *A Soul's Fight* (although James had hoped his own one-acter *The Saloon* would be given instead). It played to good houses and had an excellent press. James had finally achieved a modest success in the theatre, but it was a *succès d'estime*. Max Beerbohm wrote a delighted notice in the *Saturday Review* and A. B. Walkley an enthusiastic one in the *Times*. Beerbohm found that Forbes-Robertson had got at the soul of Henry James's lines: he spoke of the "delight it is to hear Mr. James's dialogue from the lips of Mr. Forbes-Robertson who is not merely Captain Yule but a figure that evokes innumerable cherished memories of Mr. James's books—the very spirit of Jacobeanism." He added that "little though Mr. James can on the stage give us of his great art, even that little has a quality which no other man can give us; an inalienable magic."

Walkley wrote that Gertrude Elliott "can seldom have done anything quite so good as this Mrs. Gracedew of hers; a charming reconciliation of opposite qualities—authority and girlishness, earnestness and raillery, American independence and an accent as English as the old houses and lawns. She does it all with a kind of breathless, half-timid, half-audacious glee." In the *World,* H. Hamilton Fyfe wrote that "the only memory I shall have of *The High Bid* a year hence will be embodied in a tall spare figure, with ascetic features lit up by a rapturous smile, moving dreamily indecisive, through a dreamily beautiful old house."

The *Evening Standard* described the play as "an afternoon of sheer delight" and the *Daily Chronicle* spoke of James as a dramatist "inexpressibly delightful and incorrigibly impossible." James could not complain of the critics this time. The praise only sharpened his regrets, and when the final matinee had been played, he wrote to his brother ". . . the Forbes-Robertsons go forth on their spring tour with their insufferable 'vulgar' play. But he tells me they have had very good audiences—much the best of *any* of the set of plays given in the same 'Afternoon' conditions at the same Theatre; and I feel as if the thing had done definite good to my 'reputation' and position. Also it's hung up, but not abandoned, and it will remain and revive. On the other hand, alas, I shall have made almost no money by it—since the sum 'down' on account of royalties paid me before the Edinburgh production a year ago."

CHARACTERS

Captain Clement Yule
Mr. Prodmore
Chivers
Mrs. Gracedew
Cora Prodmore
Young Man
Visitors, Tourists, etc.

THE HIGH BID

ACT FIRST

The central hall, high and square, brown and grey, flagged beneath and timbered above, of an old English country-house; originally very fine, and still very interesting, but much worn, and not a little decayed, though retaining its principal features and properties: the old oak panelling, reaching high on the walls with faded tapestry above it in some places and dark old portraits in others; and with, besides the great chimney-piece, four important points for entrance and exit. One of these is the fine old stone or oak staircase, descending, in full view of the audience, as from a gallery, above, which connects it with the upper parts of the house; the next, quite at the back and to the right, the door of the vestibule or ante-room forming part of the main approach to the hall from without. Further down, also to the right, so that it is, by the width of the stage, opposite the high old chimney-place, which is to the left, the door to other apartments on the same level. At the back, or wherever it can conveniently and suitably come, to the left, the door to the old garden, which opens, and which stands open at the rising of the curtain, to a quarter visibly different from that of the main entrance, spoken of hereafter as the ingress and egress from and to the Park. The air of a long and beautiful summer afternoon comes in from some high old window or two, where glazed escutcheons and quartering of family arms make a faded colour, and from the glimpse, if possible, of the old garden in the open doorway. Enter CHIVERS, *the old white-haired servant of the house, dilapidated, much darned and repaired, but scrupulously neat, and with a little aged, conciliatory stoop, a perfect manner and tone and a universal gentleness and sadness, comes in from apartments to right and goes restlessly and nervously towards the issue to the Park as if expectant of somebody or something. While he shuffles across, is pulled up by the high gay* VOICE *that comes down from above.*

THE VOICE. (*Clear and bright, but as from far off.*) I hope you don't mind the awful Time I take!

CHIVERS. (*Immediately, as alertly as possible, at foot of stairs and anxiously listening up.*) Oh it's all right, mum—you can please yourself. There ain't nobody come yet!

THE VOICE. I'm roaming round as I *told* you. I like to poke round alone!

CHIVERS. (*Assenting, encouraging, cheerful.*) Oh, mum, I gave you the whole free range!

THE VOICE. (*With a happy laugh.*) Well, I'm *taking* it, anyway—but don't you fear I'll be lost!

CHIVERS. (*Reassuring, cordial.*) Oh, I quite *trust* you, mum!

THE VOICE. (*As if liking to keep up the talk.*) I guess I know my way round!

CHIVERS. (*Quaintly amused.*) Ah, I'll be bound you do!

THE VOICE. (*As enchanted with everything.*) I *must* tell someone—I never saw anything so sweet.

CHIVERS. (*Accommodating, gratified.*) It do indeed, mum, be mainly thought grand! (*Then warning, conscientious.*) Only please, mum, mind the low doors!

THE VOICE. (*Confident, gay, ringing out.*) Oh, I ain't too tall! I'll mind the low doors all right! And the lovely little

Ups and Downs—ever so deliciously many!

CHIVERS. (*In position.*) Many, many—as you *say*, mum! (*With a little quavering old expressive sigh.*) As many as in a poor man's life!

THE VOICE. (*Continuing to rave.*) And the dear little crooked steps—all over the place!

CHIVERS. Ah, *mind* the little crooked steps! (*Kindly, fatherly, quavering out his joke.*) We mustn't ever take too many of *them*, mum—eh? (*Listening still, but losing the answer to this, he catches something else instead, which he repeats.*) "Not coming up too?" (*Apologetic, conciliating.*) Not if you'll kindly *indulge* me, mum—I must be where I can watch the bell! (*After which, as, while he has waited an instant, no further sound comes, he turns away with the resigned explanatory sigh for himself.*) It takes watching as well as hearing! Poor dear old bell, broken down old bell. (*Then as he seems to have his eye up to where. it may tinkle in its dusky corner, the old bell hoarsely but limply sounds, and he starts for the door to the Park as if he has been sleeping at his post.*) Mercy, if I didn't watch—! (*He opens the house-door and* CORA *appears, breathless and anxious, lest she should be too late. She comes in with this fear.*)

CORA. (*Two-and-twenty, high-coloured, unsuccessfully over-dressed, uncontrollably embarrassed, flurried and frightened, but a well-meaning creature and a good "sort."*[1]) My father has he come?

CHIVERS. Mr. Prodmore? Not yet, Miss—but I've had his Orders.

CORA. (*Panting a little.*) So have I, and I'm glad I'm not late. He's to *find* me here—I'll wait.

CHIVERS. Certainly, Miss—at your *ease*; and if there's anything I can *do* for you—!

CORA. Nothing at all, thanks; I'll just stay here.

CHIVERS. (*Moving to the tea-room; encouraging, accommodating.*) Then I shall

---

[1] This description of Cora has been inserted here although it occurs in the ms. at the point when Cora encounters Prodmore—originally Cora's first entrance. When Henry James moved her entrance forward he neglected to move his description of her with it. *See below,* p. 558.

be close at hand. (*Exit* CHIVERS, *right.*)

CORA. (*Left alone, has a look about, but only to start, in an instant, at sight of* YOUNG MAN, *who meets her eyes of a sudden, at left in the open doorway to garden, and from whom she almost recoils. When* CHIVERS *has gone; all sudden alarm and dismay on seeing "Young Man" left.*) Goodness gracious!—you've got here? (*With intense reproach; as if he's utterly in the wrong.*) My dear— My dear— How *could* you?

YOUNG MAN. (*Coming in with every precaution; and breathless with his whole situation.*) After we parted I felt I couldn't *stand* it—couldn't either wait there *alone* or leave you to your *fate;* and as a fellow at work in the Park told me your father hadn't yet passed—in *state!*— I came on and got round quicker, by the shortest cut and three sunk fences: reaching the garden, I'm sure, *unseen.*

CORA. (*All wonder, horror, and despair at his perversity.*) And what good does such folly *do* you?

YOUNG MAN. (*Ardent, insistent.*) The good of letting me stay with you, after all —rather than hang *about*, like a *sneak*, a mile *off!* (*Pressing it upon her; pleading, sincere.*) The good, Cora—won't you please *see?*—of our meeting him *together!*

CORA. (*With undiminished dismay and protest.*) How can you be so *mad?*—when we've had all that *out?* As if, on his great occasions—his field-days, as they call them at home—I can do *anything* but grovel!

YOUNG MAN. (*Impatient, contradictious, rebellious.*) You talk, you know, without a notion of what this occasion *is!*

CORA. (*Holding her ground.*) I never know till I *see* him—I have to *come* to find out: he wires me an order, when I'm away, as he presses a button for a clerk. Whatever it may be I've first to *take* it: so do as we *agreed*, or I shall be ruined by having consented—!

YOUNG MAN. (*Breaking in with spirit.*) What you consented to was my keeping you in view, so long as we might be noticed, at a respectful distance; and I couldn't even do *that*, when we got to the train at Bellborough—with you and that chattering woman in a first-class carriage, and *me* in a beastly Third that was as crowded as a cattle-truck!

CORA. (*Insisting on her policy and more and more anxious.*) I *gave* you at the cost of much danger and delay, the walk to the old grotto by that wild footpath—

YOUNG MAN. (*Taking her up in his impatience.*) And it's to that damp hole I've got to go *back?*

CORA. (*In reprehension and derision of his tone about it.*) You didn't think it so damp when you kept me there so long. (*Then as the house-bell rings; with sharpest anxiety.*) There he *is*—for Heaven's sake *go!*

YOUNG MAN. (*At garden door, but still unwilling and uncertain.*) And let you face him *alone?*

CORA. (*Casting about her in her apprehension and agitation, as if helpless where to turn.*) You've upset me so that I can't yet face him! (*Supplicating with intensity; all this for both of them, rapid and breathless.*) Go away, go, go!

YOUNG MAN. (*In doorway; as for a new understanding.*) Where and what then now—?

CORA. (*Panting, deciding.*) I'll *tell* you there (*as she points to the garden*). But *quick!*

(*On which the* YOUNG MAN *vanishes before* CHIVER'S *re-entrance. Re-enter* CHIVERS *from tea-room.*)

CORA. (*Just barring his way with a flurried, intense appeal, which makes her grab his arm.*) If it's my father, I'm not *here!*

CHIVERS. (*Bewildered.*) Then *where,* Miss—?

CORA. (*Feverish.*) Not here, not here, not here! *Understand?*

CHIVERS. (*All at sea, but as accommodating as ever, while the bell sounds afresh and* CORA *has gained the door to garden.*) You *leave*—?

CORA. (*At door.*) I come *back*—but I've not *arrived!* (*With which she disappears while* CHIVERS *goes up to admit* PRODMORE: *with a dazed word to himself as he does so.*)

CHIVERS. What *does* come over them?

(*Enter* MR. PRODMORE *and comes down, followed in all humility by* CHIVERS *after the latter has closed*

the entrance almost in the manner, or with the gravity, of a warden dropping the drawbridge of an old castle.*)

PRODMORE. (*A massive, important, vulgar man, dressed as for an occasion of weight, and with an air of expecting on all occasions every possible attention. He looks at nothing, but, as having encountered from the very threshold a disappointment, speaks with surprise and disgust.*) No one here even yet?

CHIVERS. (*Still in all humility.*) No, sir; but I've had a telegram from Captain Yule.

PRODMORE. (*Sternly deprecating, as if it would be the old man's fault.*) Not to say he ain't coming?

CHIVERS. (*Reassuringly.*) He was to take the 2.5 from Paddington: he certainly *should* be here!

PRODMORE. (*Absolute.*) He should have been here this hour or more. And so should my fly-away *daughter!*

CHIVERS. (*Respectfully taking the liberty to wonder.*) Would they be—a—coming—a—*together,* sir?

PRODMORE. "Together"?—for what do you take Miss Prodmore? (*Then after the other has deprecated with protesting hands any imputation, he condescendingly explains.*) It *is* in a sense true that their "coming together," as you call it, is exactly what I've made my plans for to-day; my calculation was that we should all punctually converge on this spot. Attended by her trusty maid, Miss Prodmore, who happens to be on a week's visit to her grandmother at Bellborough, was to take the 1.40 from that place. I was to drive over—ten miles—from the most convenient of my seats (*speaking as if he had twenty*). Captain Yule (*this with a climax of complacency*) was finally to shake off for a few hours the peculiar occupations that engage him.

CHIVERS. (*Who has listened all deferentially, but a little blankly; rising to this last vivid image.*) They *must* be peculiar, sir, when a gentleman comes into a property like this and goes three months without so much as a nat'ral curiosity—! (*Hastening to be clear.*) I don't speak of anything but what *is* nat'ral, sir; but there have *been* people here—

PRODMORE. (*Taking him up as with the pride of positive proprietorship; his head much in the air.*) There have repeatedly been people here!

CHIVERS. (*Abounding in his sense.*) As you *say*, sir—to be shown over. (*Then as it so sadly comes over him.*) With the master himself *never* shown!

PRODMORE. (*With high decision.*) He *shall* be—so that nobody shall miss him.

CHIVERS. (*Making good his own sense of it all.*) It will be a mercy indeed to look on him; but I meant that he has not been taken round.

PRODMORE. (*As if requiring no light; least of all from such a source.*) That's what I meant too. *I'll* take him round and round and round: I'll take him till he spins; it's exactly what I've come for! (*With the vision of this intended proceeding he looks with a sweep over the place; concluding with a confidence that fairly makes him sociable.*) He can't fail to be affected, though he *has* been up to his neck in such a different class of thing.

CHIVERS. (*As wondering what class of thing it can be, expresses a timid loyal hope.*) In nothing, I daresay, but what's right, sir—?

PRODMORE. (*Distinct, assured, resonant.*) In everything that's abominably *wrong!* (*Then as the doorbell again sounds in the same manner as before.*) But here he *is!*

(*Chivers, as under the surprise and shock of this last revelation, has been but the more agitatedly launched upon his duty of quickly answering the bell. He reaches the door from the Park while* MR. PROD-MORE, *his large white waistcoat fairly expanding with his increase of presence, continues to pervade the foreground. He is thus important and expectant there a little when the sounds from the back suddenly cause the collapse of his tension. Enter* CORA. *She has appeared at the door opened to her, and, while her father's back is presented to her view, has eagerly, yet as if always a little in fear, surrendered her parasol and extra*

wrap to the old man. Her father meanwhile, adjusting his consciousness to what has happened, proceeds:*)

PRODMORE. Only Cora? (*But then rectifying his thought as she comes down.*) Well, whatever he resists, he shan't at any rate resist *her!* (*He receives the girl, however, as with the habit and on the principle of strict discipline.*) I've *waited.* What do you *mean?*

CORA. Waited, Papa? Oh I'm too *sorry!* [2]

PRODMORE. (*As with the habit of snubbing and confounding her even when she more or less grovels.*) Would you then, if I had *not* had patience for you, have wished not to *find* me? (*Following it up as from enjoyment of the effect of this.*) Would you have preferred me to have cleared *out?* (*Then as she but gasps her protest.*) Why the dickens are you so *late?*

CORA. (*With imperfect presence of mind.*) I'll *tell* you, Papa! (*But as he waits for her definite statement it fails her, almost as for the terror of him; so that, looking about her as for vague help in her trouble, all she can do is to close her eyes to her danger. She catches at her one possible relief from it!*) I feel rather *faint.* Could I have some *tea?*

PRODMORE. (*After considering both the idea and his daughter's substantial shape.*) Well, as I shall expect you to put forth all your powers—yes! (*To* CHIVERS, *who, after admitting the girl, has been vaguely occupied, up, with his general domestic anxieties, and has again, unnoticed by the others, stopped at the foot of the stairs with an interest in some sound of movements above; after which, his ear catching* CORA'S *appeal, he has come down.*) Some tea.

CHIVERS. (*All responsive, and as to be very agreeable to the young lady.*) I did think it might be required! (*Then when he has gained the door of the other apartments.*) I'll lay it out here.

(*Exit* CHIVERS.)

CORA. (*Recovering enough to rise from the chair into which she has sunk on professing faintness.*) It was my train, Papa—

---

[2] This was Cora's original entrance. *See above,* p. 556.

so very awfully behind. I *walked* up, you know, too, from the station—there's such a lovely footpath across the *Park*.

PRODMORE. (*As with the habit of examining almost any statement made him.*) You've been roaming the country then alone?

CORA. (*Precipitate.*) Oh dear, no, not alone! (*She speaks as if she has never heard of such a thing and has really had a train of attendants; yet is able to fill it out only by saying.*) There were *ever* so many people about.

PRODMORE. (*Speaking from the point of view as of his personal convenience; and even from that of a new exclusiveness.*) Nothing is more possible, everywhere, than to find *too* many! But where, among them all, is your trusty *maid*?

CORA. (*Making up in a wild promptitude what she lacks in real assurance.*) I didn't *bring* her—Granny thought—

PRODMORE. Granny shall stop thinking. (*With instant decision.*) You expect then to pursue your adventures quite into the night—to return to Bellborough as you *came*?

CORA. (*Finding her feet a little more.*) Exactly as I came Papa dear—under the protection of a new friend I've just made, a lady who was in my railway-carriage, a wonderful American widow.

PRODMORE. (*Chilling on the spot any such expectations.*) What then does your wonderful American want at this place?

CORA. (*Clearly stronger for her new friend than for herself.*) She wants to see it.

PRODMORE. (*Reflecting on this complication.*) To-day? (*Then as if it's practically presumptuous on the new friend's part.*) To-day won't *do*.

CORA. (*With courage for the odd lady, and as seeing how little she will accept such a sentence.*) Well, when I told her it perhaps wouldn't, she said it would just *have* to.

PRODMORE. (*Amused at such fatuity.*) For *what* then, with such grand airs?

CORA. (*Ready.*) Why, I suppose, for what Americans want.

PRODMORE. (*Who has measured that quantity.*) They want *everything*!

CORA. (*Taking it from him, wishing for*

her *friend.*) Then I wonder she hasn't arrived.

PRODMORE. (*Prepared for this formidable person.*) When she does I'll tackle her; and I shall thank you, in future, not to take up, in trains, with loud—and possibly loose!—women of whom you know nothing.

CORA. (*Glad to controvert this.*) Oh, I did know something—for I saw her yesterday at Bellborough.

PRODMORE. (*As if resenting for her even this experience.*) And what was she doing at Bellborough?

CORA. Staying at the Blue Dragon, to see the old Abbey. She says she just *loves* old abbeys. (*To which the girl adds with rising intelligence.*) It seems to be the same feeling that brought her over, to-day, to see this old house.

PRODMORE. (*Derisive and superior.*) She "just loves" old houses? Then why the deuce didn't she accompany you properly—since she *is* so pushing!—to the door?

CORA. Because she went off in a fly to see first the old Hospital. (*Sympathetically.*) She just loves old hospitals. She asked me if this isn't a show-house. I told her (*with a look at her father, and then as uncertain and anxious to disclaim responsibility*) that I hadn't, really, the least idea.

PRODMORE. (*Almost with ferocity.*) It *is* —if there ever *was* one! (*And then as she stands snubbed.*) I wonder, on such a speech, what she thought of *you*.

CORA. (*Candidly and humbly confessing.*) I know. She *told* me.

PRODMORE. (*Considering his offspring.*) That you're really a hopeless frump?

CORA. (*Appearing, oddly enough, almost to court this description.*) That I'm not, as she rather funnily called it, a *show-girl*.

PRODMORE. (*Ruffled.*) To think of your having to be *reminded*—by the very strangers you pick up—of what my daughter should pre-eminently be! (*Then, however, as making the best of this humiliation.*) Your friend, at any rate, is evidently at high pitch!

CORA. (*With confidence.*) Well, when she comes, you'll hear her distinctly enough! (*Then warming to her plea.*) But don't judge her, Papa, till you do. She's tremendously clever: there seems to be nothing she doesn't know.

PRODMORE. (*Prompt.*) And there seems to be nothing you *do*. You're not tremendously clever, Miss Prodmore; so you'll permit me to demand of you a slight effort of intelligence. Make one as you've *never* made it. (*Then as, having impressed and even alarmed her, he holds her gaping attention a little and sounds the high note.*) I'm expecting Captain Yule.

CORA. (*Taking it rather blinkingly in.*) The owner of this property?

PRODMORE. (*With reservations.*) That's what it depends on you to *make* him.

CORA. (*Gaping and wondering.*) On me—?

PRODMORE. (*Facing the need of lucidly instructing her.*) He came into it three months ago by the death of his great-uncle, who had lived to ninety-three, but who, having quarrelled mortally with his father, had always refused to receive either sire or son.

CORA. (*Vague, scantily enlightened.*) But *now* at least doesn't he live here?

PRODMORE. So little that he comes here to-day for the very first time. I've some business to discuss with him that can best be discussed on this spot; and it's a vital part of that business that you also should take pains to make him welcome.

CORA. (*Struck with the oddity.*) Welcome to his own house?

PRODMORE. (*Emphatic.*) That it's not his own house is just the point I seek to make! The way I look at it is that it's my house. The way I look at it even, my dear (*and in his demonstration of his ways of looking he quite genially expands*) is that it's *our* house. The whole thing is mortgaged, as it stands, for every inch of its value; and I enjoy the high advantage—do you follow me? (*He fairly trumpets it.*)

CORA. (*Fairly bounding, on her side, to a full perception.*) Of holding the mortgages?

PRODMORE. (*Surprised and even gratified at her unprecedented quickness.*) You keep up with me better than I *hoped*. I have Captain Yule in my hands. I hold every scrap of paper, and it's a precious collection.

CORA. (*Making out more in this, and looking, for the first time, with attention, over the impressive place itself.*) Do you mean that you can come down on him?

PRODMORE. (*Triumphant.*) I don't need to "come," my dear—I *am* "down." *This* is "down"! (*He raps, jubilantly, with his stick, the hard pavement of the hall.*) I "came" many weeks ago—commercially and financially speaking—and haven't since budged from the place.

CORA. Well, I don't understand business; but I think I understand *you*, Papa, enough to gather that you've got, indeed, as usual, a striking advantage.

PRODMORE. (*Complacent, but consciously reasonable.*) As usual, I *have* scored; but my advantage won't be "striking" perhaps till I've sent the blow home. (*More blandly, but still firmly.*) What I, as a father, appeal to you at present to do is—well, to nerve my arm! I look to you, Cora, to see me through.

CORA. (*Attentive, cautious.*) Through what, then?

PRODMORE. Through this most *important* transaction. Through the speculation of which you've been the barely-dissimulated subject. (*Letting her have it practically all.*) I've brought you here to receive an impression, and I've brought you, even more, to *make* one.

CORA. (*Pretending by a quick instinct to more vagueness than she feels.*) But on *whom*?

PRODMORE. On *me*, to begin with—by being neither a minx nor a milksop! And then, Miss, on *him*.

CORA. (*Alarmed as she really takes it in.*) On Captain Yule?

PRODMORE. By bringing him to the point.

CORA. But, father, (*quavering in anguish*) to *what*?

PRODMORE. (*Lucid.*) The point where a gentleman *has* to.

CORA. (*Wondering and faltering.*) Go down on his knees?

PRODMORE. (*After debate and demur.*) No—they don't *do* that.

CORA. (*With all her apprehension.*) What *do* they do?

PRODMORE. (*Declining responsibility for details.*) He will know himself.

CORA. (*Distressed and impetuous.*) Oh no indeed he won't! (*Natural.*) They don't ever.

PRODMORE. (*Peremptory.*) Then the sooner they *learn*—whoever teaches 'em— the *better:* the better I mean in particular (*with an intention perceptibly vicious*) for the master of this house. (*As to make her easy about it.*) I'll guarantee that he shall *understand that,* for I shall do my proper part.

CORA. (*More aghast the more she thinks of it.*) But how on earth, sir, can I ever do mine? (*Earnestly impressing it on him.*) To begin with, you know, I've never *seen* him.

PRODMORE. (*Who has taken out his watch and then, having consulted it, puts it back with a gesture that seems to dispose at the same time and in the same manner of the objection.*) You'll see him *now,* and *plenty* of him—from one moment to the other. He's remarkably handsome, remarkably ambitious, remarkably clever. He has one of the best and oldest names in this part of the country; a name that, far and wide here, one could do so much with that I'm simply indignant to see him do so little. I propose, my dear, to do with it all he *hasn't* done, and I further propose, to that end, first to get *hold* of it. (*Then, as presenting her almost graciously with his whole thought.*) It's you, Miss Prodmore, who shall take it, with your fair fingers, out of the fire.

CORA. (*Gaping still at the terrible figures he employs.*) The fire?

PRODMORE. Out of the *mud* then if you prefer! You must pick it up—with a graceful movement—do you see? My plan is, in short (*with the full bright, cheering demonstration*) that when we've brushed it off and rubbed it down a bit, blown away the dust and touched up the rust, as we've all *facility* for doing, my daughter shall worthily *bear* it.

CORA. (*Grave, with the dawn of a deeper resistance.*) You speak of *your* plan, Papa. But does it happen also to be Captain Yule's?

PRODMORE. (*Looking at her hard, as if to warn her off the ground of irony.*) His plans have not yet quite matured. But nothing is more natural than that (*with high significance*) they shall do so on the sunny south wall of Miss Prodmore's best manner. Cora, I've spent twenty years in giving you what your poor mother used to call first-rate advantages—and they've cost me hundreds and hundreds of pounds. What *I* call an advantage you know is a thing that shall be an advantage to *me.* It's now time, therefore, that both as a parent and as a man accustomed to do business, I should have some news of my investment. (*Treating the subject luminously.*) I couldn't help your temper—*that* I recognise; nor your taste, nor even your unmistakeable resemblance to the estimable but far from ornamental woman who brought you forth; but if I laid your education on so thick it was just that you should have, damn you, what we *want* of you to-day. (*Formidable.*) Do you mean to tell me you haven't got it?

CORA. (*Distressed, at a loss.*) Doesn't it depend on what you *do* want?

PRODMORE. (*Highly definite.*) I want what *Captain Yule* will naturally want!

CORA. (*Immensely wondering.*) And Captain Yule—?

PRODMORE. Will want *charm!* Do you mean to say you haven't got any?

CORA. (*Modest, infinitely embarrassed.*) How can I *tell,* Papa? He may not *think!*

PRODMORE. (*Winding up sharp.*) Do your duty, Miss, and never mind what he "thinks"! (*Supremely impatient.*) Don't look at him like a sick cow, and he'll be sure to think *right!*

CORA. (*Wounded, but resisting, clinging to some line of defence.*) I remember your saying once, some time ago, that this was just what he'd be sure *not* to do: I mean when he began to go in for his dreadful ideas—

PRODMORE. (*Taking her again boldly up.*) About the "radical programme," the "social revolution," the spoliation of everyone and the destruction of everything? (*Amused at her simplicity.*) Why, you stupid thing, I've worked round to a complete agreement with him. The taking from those who have by those who haven't, what is it but just to *receive,* from consenting hands, the principal treasure of the rich? *That's* quite the style of opinion I *want* him to have. (*Then while she hangs attentive.*) I regard my daughter—let it flatter her to know—as my largest property and I freely hand her *over*. I shall, in other words, forgive his low opinions if he renounces them for *you*.

CORA. (*As with a glimpse, then, of salvation.*) He *won't* renounce them! (*With brave resolution.*) He *shan't!*

PRODMORE. (*Still glowing, to the point of good-humour, with conscious felicity of statement.*) If you suggest that you're in political sympathy with him, you mean then that you'll take him as he *is?*

CORA. (*Her head very high and quite ringing out.*) I won't take him at all! (*But then, agitated, by the sound of the bell and with her dignity dropping straight.*) It must be *he!* (*She turns right and left for a retreat or an escape, but her father has already caught her by the wrist; which causes her pitifully to pant.*) Surely you don't want me to pounce on him *thus?*

PRODMORE. (*Holding her off by the arm as to judge of the force of this deprecation of her appearance.*) Your fine frock won't do—with what it *cost* me?

CORA. (*Her decent dignity coming back; pleading.*) It's not my frock, Papa—it's his thinking I've come here for him to *look* at me!

PRODMORE. (*Who, as if rather struck by this, and even a little touched, has released her.*) He doesn't think it, and I'll see that he shan't—in any manner to *shock* him—be *aware* of it!

CORA. (*Who has reached, for retreat to right [of] the door of the apartments, and speaks distressfully.*) But he's aware you want me to *hook* him!

PRODMORE. (*Whom the apparent approach of his visitor has already thrown back upon his "manner."*) The way to "hook" him will be not to be hopelessly *vulgar*. (*Then sharply definite.*) He doesn't know that *you* know anything. (PRODMORE *waves the girl off to the apartments.*) Await us there with tea, and mind you have Charm!

(*Exit* CORA, *throwing up her arms as to disclaim everything; while* CHIVERS *has shuffled straight up to*

back to answer the bell, opening the house-door and admitting the visitor. Enter* CLEMENT YULE, *whom* CHIVERS *straightway precedes down the stage as for the eager joy of proclaiming him.* PRODMORE, *who under the impression for an instant of his daughter's final air, for better or for worse, has at once become, none the less, all "attitude" for the reception of* YULE.)

CHIVERS. (*Announcing.*) Captain Yule! (*Exit* CHIVERS, *right.*)

PRODMORE. (*Who has during the previous scene either kept on his hat or put it on at a given moment for emphasis, now removing it.*) Delighted at last to *see* you here!

YULE. (*Of distinguished and refined, but in a high degree manly appearance, dressed in a darkish tweed suit, and with a red necktie in a sailor's knot; has, on entering, taken off, instinctively, as in sudden homage to all the ghosts of all his ancestors, a soft brown hat. He has clearly felt himself at once struck with their collective presence, and with the whole place; but he puts out his hand with responsive simplicity, though also a shade of friendly amusement.*) If I've not come before, Mr. Prodmore, it was—very frankly speaking —from the dread of seeing *you!*

PRODMORE. (*Highly genial, rejoicing in the promise of his aspect.*) Ah, but my presence, sir, is not without its honourable motive!

YULE. (*With a sad, intelligent smile.*) It's just its honourable motive that makes me wince at it! (*Frank, resigned, good-humoured.*) Certainly I've no illusions about the ground of our meeting; though indeed I may not know quite so well what I'm about—in my poor way—as *you* know what *you* are. Your thorough knowledge of what you're about has at any rate placed me at your mercy. You hold me in the hollow of your hand.

PRODMORE. (*Not afraid of any tribute, even if slightly ironic, to his financial subtlety.*) Well, Captain Yule, if an honest man or two, in this old country of ours, didn't take care to know what he's about, where should we *any* of us be? (*After an instant, while he has shone with the force of this homely question; recognising the reality of things.*) I don't deny that when, in general, I go in deep I don't go in for *nothing.* (*Smiling shrewdly.*) I make my plunge pay double!

YULE. (*Quietly amused.*) You make it pay so well—"double" surely doesn't do you justice!—that, if I've understood you, you can do quite as you like with this preposterous, this (*as he looks about him*) prodigious place. Haven't you brought me down just to treat me to the *sight* of your doing it?

PRODMORE. (*Diplomatic.*) I've decidely brought you down to make you open your eyes! (*Then as if more specifically to business.*) Of course, you know, you can always *clear* the property. You can pay off the— a—rather heavy encumbrances.

YULE. (*Always a trifle ironic, and as if taking in constantly, no matter how much in spite of himself, the fine old elements of the place.*) "Pay off," Mr. Prodmore? What can I pay off with?

PRODMORE. (*Deep, yet easy.*) You can always raise money.

YULE. (*Vague to positive blankness.*) What can I raise it on?

PRODMORE. (*Massively gay.*) On your great political future!

YULE. (*With a movement which disposes of the idea.*) Oh, I've not taken—for the short run at least—the lucrative line; and I know what you think of *that.*

PRODMORE. (*Granting then, indulgently, that he does; but as desiring none the less to help his friend through; all benevolently.*) I hold that you keep, in public, very dangerous company; but I also hold that you're extravagant mainly because you've nothing at stake. (*Developing with pleasant confidence.*) A man has the right opinions as soon as he finds he has something to *lose* by having the wrong. Haven't I already hinted to you how to set your political house in order? You're reduced to the lower regions because you keep the best rooms empty. *These* are the best rooms, sir, (*indicating the whole place*)— even of your *political* house. (*Then, as having let him take in, attentive and wondering a little this pregnant image.*) You're

a firebrand, in other words, my dear Captain, simply because you're the most wasted of charming *men,* and the most unnatural of *bachelors. That* ailment's one of the early complaints we all pass through, but it's soon over, and the treatment quite simple. I have your *remedy.*

YULE. (*Detached and "off," perfunctory and sceptical, as through the more important effect on him of the interesting place, though all still in spite of himself.*) One of those sad remedies that are worse than the disease?

PRODMORE. (*Prompt and positive.*) There's nothing worse, that I've ever heard of, than your particular fix. (*With assurance.*) Least of all a heap of gold—!

YULE. (*As he lets the bright image dangle, but still detached.*) A heap of gold—!

PRODMORE. (*With a flourish.*) In the lap of a fine, fresh lass! (*With energy.*) Give pledges to fortune, as somebody says— then we'll talk. You want money—that's what you want. Well, *marry* it!

YULE. (*Never stirring, save that his eyes, which can't close themselves to the place, vaguely stray. He speaks with his rather indifferent smile.*) Of course I could do that in a moment!

PRODMORE. It's even just my own *danger* from you. I perfectly recognise that *any* woman would now jump—

YULE. (*Breaking in a bit drily.*) I don't like jumping women, Mr. Prodmore; though that perhaps is a detail. It's more to the point that I've yet to see the woman whom by an advance of my *own*—

PRODMORE. But I haven't *asked* you, you know, to make a marked advance.

YULE. (*With his detachment.*) You've only asked me to *receive* one?

PRODMORE. (*Just faltering.*) Well, I've asked you—I asked you a month ago—to think it all over.

YULE. (*Without hesitation.*) I *have* thought it all over, and the strange effect seems to be that my eyes have got accustomed to my darkness. I seem to make out, in the gloom of my meditations, that, at the worst, I can let the whole thing slide.

PRODMORE. (*With a scandalised start.*) This great property?

YULE. Isn't it this great property that

positively throws me up? If I can afford neither to live on it, to work it, nor to free it, I can at least let it save its own *bacon* and pay its own *debts*. I can say to you simply: "Take it, my dear sir, and the devil take *you!*"

PRODMORE. (*Still more shocked, but persuasively smiling it off.*) You wouldn't be so recklessly *rude!*

YULE. (*Generally and particularly amused at him.*) Why *not*—if I'm a firebrand and a keeper of low company and a general nuisance? Sacrifice for sacrifice that might very well be the *least!*

PRODMORE. (*Arrested but an instant; still acute and plausible.*) How do you *know*—if you haven't compared them? It's just to make the comparison in all the right conditions—that you're here at this hour. (*He takes, with a large, though vague, exhibitory gesture, a turn or two about.*) Now that you stretch yourself—for an hour's relaxation and rocked, as it were, by my friendly *hand*—in the ancient cradle of your race, can you seriously entertain the idea of *parting* with such a venerable family relic?

YULE. (*Affected a little by this appeal, turns away, moves up, his hands in his pockets, looks about; then stands a moment, his back presented, his face not seen, in a brief concentration of thought. Then as with a certain impatience he faces about.*) The cradle of my race bears, for me, Mr. Prodmore, a striking resemblance to its *tomb.* (*A trifle perversely and profanely.*) Oh dear, dear, dear— (*It ends in a small ambiguous, inscrutable wail—not without tenderness. But he has adopted the profane view.*) Mercy on us, how melancholy!

PRODMORE. (*His lips pursed out, deprecates from a business point of view this depreciation.*) Melancholy? More, you think, than is favourable—?

YULE. (*Who has taken in certain decayed details.*) No, not more than is favourable—to ghosts, to rats, perhaps to other parasites, and certainly to bad *dreams!* (*He repeats the refrain.*) Melancholy, musty, mouldy (*then with a poke either of his toe or of his stick, from the table on which he has laid it, at a gap in the old stuff, with which a low seat has been re-covered*)—

mangy! Is this the character *throughout?*

PRODMORE. (*His practical eyes on the tell-tale tatter, but his assured gesture making light of it.*) You must judge for yourself—you must go *over* the house. (*Disconcerted but for an instant, he sees his right line.*) It does look a bit run down, but I'll *tell* you what I'll do. I'll do it *up* for you—neatly; I'll throw *that* in!

YULE. (*Consistently amused.*) Will you put us on the telephone—? install the electric light?

PRODMORE. (*A little perplexed at this irony, but holding his course.*) Well, damn it, if you'll meet me half *way!* (*He explains, expatiates.*) We're dealing here, if you take me, with *fancy-values*. Don't you feel, as you embrace the scene a sort of something-or-other down your back?

YULE. (*Who again and again loses himself and then abruptly reverts.*) If I should begin to tell you what I "feel," I think I should have to name first a strange stiffening of the spine—as if from the sense of my having instinctively swallowed, on the spot, the whole ramrod of *reaction.*

PRODMORE. Reaction?

YULE. Reaction, I mean, against *these* pretensions. (*Candidly, sincerely.*) The whole face of things is too queer. Too cold. Too cruel.

PRODMORE. (*Quite failing to follow; yet in virtuous protest.*) "Cruel"?

YULE. (*Completing his thought as he moves about.*) Like the face of some stuck-up distant relation who won't speak first. I see in the stare of the old dragon, I smell in the damp of his very breath, all the helpless mortality he has tucked away!

PRODMORE. (*Really at a loss.*) Lord, Captain—you *have* fancies!

YULE. (*Half interested, half irritated, as his fancies multiply.*) I don't know what's the matter—but there *is* more here than meets the eye. (*He tries, as might be, to puzzle it out.*) I miss all the presences. I feel all the absences. I touch old hands. I hear old voices, I see the old ghosts.

PRODMORE. (*His commercial shrewdness reviving.*) The old ghosts, Captain Yule, are worth so much a dozen, and with no reduction, I must remind you—with the rate indeed rather *raised*—for the quantity taken! (*Then as feeling the air cleared by this sally; cheering, patronisingly.*) Look about you, at your ease, a little *more*. Make yourself quite at *home*.

YULE. (*After having looked at him rather hard an instant.*) Thank you very much, Mr. Prodmore. May I light a cigarette?

PRODMORE. (*Bland for the question.*) In your own house, Captain?

YULE. That's just the question: it seems so much less my own house than before I had come into it! (*He offers his friend a cigarette, which that gentleman accepts, also taking a light from him, then he lights his own and begins to smoke.*) As I understand you, you *lump* your two conditions? I mean I must accept both or neither?

PRODMORE. (*As if this is indeed what he wants to talk about.*) You will accept *both*, for, by doing so, you'll clear the property at a stroke. The way I put it is this—see—that if you'll stand for Gossage you'll get returned for Gossage.

YULE. (*Taking it in.*) And if I get returned for Gossage I shall marry your daughter. Accordingly—(*lucid and definite*) if I marry your daughter—

PRODMORE. (*Prompt, loyal.*) I'll burn up before your eyes every scratch of your pen, I'll make such a bonfire of your obligations as the whole country will flock to see. There won't be a penny to *pay*—there'll only be a position to take. You'll take it with peculiar *grace*.

YULE. (*Appearing to consider, but keeping most of his thoughts to himself.*) Peculiar, Mr. Prodmore—*very!*

PRODMORE. (*Completing the picture without heeding his tone.*) You'll settle down here in comfort and honour.

YULE. (*Irritated, but turning away as to turn it off.*) Are you very sure of the "honour"—if I turn my political coat?

PRODMORE. (*Making nothing of this.*) You'll only be turning it back again to the way it was *always* worn! (*Persuasive, convincing.*) Gossage will receive you with open arms and press you to a heaving Tory bosom. That bosom (*he follows himself up*) has never heaved but to sound Conservative principles. The cradle, as I've called it—or at least the rich warm coverlet—of your race, Gossage was the political property, so to speak, of generations of your family. Stand therefore in the good old interest, and you'll stand like a lion.

YULE. (*Amused.*) Ah, I'm afraid you mean that I must first *roar* like one.

PRODMORE. Oh, I'll do the roaring! (*It's as if he shakes his mane.*) Leave that to *me*.

YULE. Then why in the name of political good manners don't you stand yourself?

PRODMORE. (*Ready.*) Because, you see, my good manners aren't *all* political. My *best* ones, Captain Yule, are just those I'm showing you now and here. I don't stand myself because I'm not a remarkably handsome young man with the grand old home and the right old name. Because I'm a different sort of matter altogether. But if I haven't these advantages, you'll do justice to my natural desire that my *daughter* at least shall have them.

YULE. But I confess I don't quite grasp the deep attraction you appear to discover in so large a surrender of your interests.

PRODMORE. (*All at his ease.*) My surrenders are my own affair; and, as for my interests, since I never, on principle, give anything for nothing, I daresay I may be trusted to know 'em when I see 'em. You come high—I don't for a moment deny it; but when I look at you, in this pleasant intimate way, my dear boy—if you'll allow me so to describe things—I recognise one of those cases, unmistakeable when really met, in which one must put down one's money. There's not an article in the whole shop, if you don't mind the comparison, that strikes me as better value. (*With a frank bold burst.*) I intend you shall be, Captain, the true comfort of my life!

YULE. (*Motionless, smoking.*) May I inquire if Miss Prodmore's ideas of comfort are as well defined—and in *her* case, I may add, as touchingly *modest*—as her father's? Is she a responsible party to this ingenious arrangement?

PRODMORE. (*Embarrassed, yet after an instant.*) I appreciate the high character of your scruple. (*Then as after hesitating how best to describe the young lady.*) Miss Prodmore, sir, may perhaps best be described as a large smooth sheet of blank, though gilt-edged paper. No image of any tie but the pure and perfect *filial* has yet, I can answer for it, formed itself on the considerable expanse. But for that image to be projected—!

YULE. (*As trying really to face this possibility; though putting it jocosely.*) I've only in *person* to appear?

PRODMORE. (*Full of sympathetic assent.*) And, naturally, in person, do yourself, as well as the young lady, credit—by which I mean justice! Do you remember what you said when I first, in London, laid the matter before you?

YULE. (*Recalling.*) I think I said it struck me I should first take a look at—what do you call it—the *corpus delicti.*

PRODMORE. You should first see for yourself what you had really come into? I was not only eager for that, but I'm willing to go further. (*Hanging fire an instant, but hopeful.*) I'm quite ready to hear you say you think you should also first see the young *lady!*

YULE. (*Doing justice to this precaution.*) There *is* something in that then—since you mention it!

PRODMORE. I think you'll find that there's everything! (*Looking again at his watch.*) Which will you take first?

YULE. (*A bit vague.*) "First"?

PRODMORE. The young lady or the house?

YULE. (*Astonished.*) You don't mean to say your daughter's *here?*

PRODMORE. (*Taking all the responsibility.*) In the morning-room.

YULE. (*In consternation.*) Waiting for me?

PRODMORE. (*Reassuring.*) Ah, as long, you know, as you *like!*

YULE. (*Really dismayed at his push.*) Oh, longer than *this*, please! (*Then as it comes over him.*) Do you mean she *knows?*

PRODMORE. That she's here on *view?* (*Faltering but an instant; equal to the occasion.*) She knows nothing *whatever.* She's as unconscious as the rose on its stem!

YULE. (*Visibly relieved.*) That's *right* then, please—let her *remain* so! (*Looking also at his watch.*) I'll first take the house.

PRODMORE. (*All ready to oblige.*) Shall I go round *with* you?

YULE. (*More gravely now than by his* tone hitherto, and after briefest reflection.) Thank you—I'd rather—on the whole, go round alone.

(*Re-enter* CHIVERS *from right. He looks from under a bent brow, all uncertain and anxious and with much limpid earnestness, as feeling his own fate at stake, from one of the men to the other, and then with an appeal for sympathy seems to cast himself upon* YULE.)

CHIVERS. (*With gentle, but extreme encouragement, as he passes round the young man.*) There's tea on, sir! (*With which he waits, putting some object straight, or otherwise busying himself, as if, quite yearningly, either to remain with* YULE *or to accompany him.*)

PRODMORE. (*As with discretion and decision.*) Then I'll join my daughter. (*Then as he has gained door on right, with an appropriate smile and a gathering-in of his fingers as to present a flower.*) The *rose,* Captain—on its *stem!* (*Exit to apartments.*)

YULE. (*Left thinking, with his eyes rather absently at first on* CHIVERS, *whom he then seems to focus.*) I say, my friend, what colour is the "rose"?

CHIVERS. (*At a loss, but ready to meet him on anything; staring through a dimness that presently glimmers.*) The rose, sir? (*He turns to the open door of the old garden, and the shining day; they suggest to him the application of the question.*) Rather a kind of brilliant—

YULE. (*Interested, struck.*) Oh, a "brilliant"—

CHIVERS. (*Innocent, earnest.*) Old-fashioned *red*—just tending a little to purple. (*Smiles as with the pride of thus being able to testify: though his smile the next instant drops.*) It's the only one *left*—on the old west wall.

YULE. (*Much amused, but in all kindness.*) My dear man, I'm not alluding to the sole ornament of the garden, but to the young lady at present in the morning-room. Do you happen to have noticed if she's *pretty?*

CHIVERS. (*Who stands queerly rueful.*) Laws, sir!—it's a matter I mostly *do* notice. (*Then deeply, mildly discreet.*) But wouldn't it rather be, sir, on such an occasion as this, sir, a matter—like—of *taste?*

YULE. That's just why I appeal with such confidence to yours.

CHIVERS. (*Facing then, with all his gentleness, his responsibility.*) Well, sir—mine was always a sort of fancy for something more merry-like.

YULE. She isn't merry-like then, poor Miss Prodmore? Ah, if you come to that, neither am I! (*He throws up the subject, however, without further pressure; he drops for the present* MISS PRODMORE.) But it doesn't signify. (*He's really more interested in* CHIVERS *himself.*) What are *you,* my dear man?

CHIVERS. (*As if he really has to think a bit.*) Well, sir, I'm not quite *that.* (*Appealing to his friend's indulgence.*) Whatever in the world has there been to *make* me?

YULE. (*Washing his hands of it.*) I mean to whom do you beautifully *belong?*

CHIVERS. (*Who has really to think it over.*) If you could only just *tell* me, sir! I seem quite to waste *away*—for someone to take an *order* of.

YULE. (*Looking at him in compassion.*) Who pays your *wages?*

CHIVERS. (*Very simply.*) No one at *all,* sir.

YULE. (*Taking from his waistcoat pocket a gold coin, which he places with a little sharp click on a table near at hand.*) Then there's a *sovereign.* (*Then having turned resignedly away.*) And I haven't *many!*

CHIVERS. (*Leaving the money on the table and only watching his friend.*) Ah then, shouldn't it stay in the *family?*

YULE. (*Wheeling round, struck by the figure he makes in this offer; visibly touched and bridging a long transition with a single tone.*) I think it *does,* I think it does.

CHIVERS. (*All his appreciative eyes on him now.*) I've served your house, sir.

YULE. How long?

CHIVERS. All my *life.*

YULE. (*After they have stood a bit face to face; the younger man making things out.*) Then I won't give *you* up!

CHIVERS. Indeed, sir, I hope you won't give up *anything!*

YULE. (*Taking up his hat.*) It remains to be *seen.* (*He looks over the place again; his eyes wander to the open door.*) Is that the *garden?*

CHIVERS. It *was!* (*With a sigh like the creak of the wheel of time.*) Shall I show you how it *used* to be?

YULE. (*Taking an instant for what he sees of it from where he stands.*) It's just as it *is,* alas, that I happen to require it! (*Then at garden door.*) Don't *come.* I want to *think.* (*Exit* YULE *to garden.*)

CHIVERS. (*Left alone, takes up the coin that has remained on the table, and, after a look sufficient fully to identify and appreciate it, puts it in his pocket.*) What does he want, poor dear, to "think" about?

(*His speculation, however, is checked by the high, clear vocal sound that heralds the appearance at the top of the stairs of the wonderful figure of the visiting lady; who, having taken possession of the place above, prepares, with the high pitch of her interest, gaily to descend. Enter* MRS. GRACEDEW *from the gallery, speaking as she comes down.*)

MRS. GRACEDEW. (*On the stairs.*) Housekeeper! Butler! Old Family Servant!

CHIVERS. (*In quick remembrance, half dismayed, half dazzled, of a duty neglected.*) Oh, I should have told him of *her!*

MRS. GRACEDEW. (*With beautiful laughter and rustling garments; as if approaching amid an escort and with music.*) Did you think I had got snapped down in an old box like that poor girl—what's-her-name? the one who was poking round *too* —in the celebrated poem? You dear, delightful man, why didn't you *tell* me?

CHIVERS. (*Under the charm again, but vague.*) "Tell" you, mum—

MRS. GRACEDEW. (*Prompt, happy.*) That you're so perfectly—perfect! (*As if she had almost been swindled.*) You're ever so much better than anyone has ever said. Why, in the name of all that's lovely has nobody ever said *anything?*—as nobody for that matter, with all the fun there is, *does* seem ever to say anything! (*Then, as to tell him all about the place he seems, poor dear, really to understand so little.*) You're everything in the world you *ought* to be, and not the shade of anything you *oughtn't!*

CHIVERS. (*Fluttered, flattered, bewildered.*) Well, mum, I try!

MRS. GRACEDEW. (*Downright.*) Oh no you don't—that's *just* your *charm.* (*She explains with her free benevolence.*) I try—I have to; but you do *nothing.* Here you simply *are.* You can't help it.

CHIVERS. (*Overwhelmed.*) Me, mum?

MRS. GRACEDEW. (*Who has been speaking of the house itself, applies her delight to his image as well.*) Yes, you *too*—you positive old *picture.* (*Perfectly familiar in her appreciation.*) I've seen the old masters—but you're the old master! "The good and faithful *servant*—Rembrandt van Rhyn." With three Baedeker *stars. That's* what you are! (*His humility doesn't check her.*) The house is a vision of beauty, and *you're* just worthy of the house, I can't say *more* for you!

CHIVERS. (*Candidly helpless.*) I find it a bit of a strain, mum, to keep up—fairly to call it—with what you *do* say.

MRS. GRACEDEW. (*Quite happily understanding.*) That's quite what everyone *finds* it! Yet I haven't come here to suffer in *silence,* you know—to suffer, I mean, from envy, or rage, or despair. (*Full of movement, and of sincerity of interest, observing, almost measuring, everything in the place, she takes notes, while she gossips, jots down signs for her own use in a small book of memoranda that she carries.*) You almost kill me—however, I take some killing! (*Then again, to explain herself to his perpetual amaze.*) I mean you're so fatally *right,* and so deadly *complete,* that if I wasn't an angel I could scarcely *bear* it; with every fascinating feature I had already heard of and thought I was *prepared* for, and ever so many others that, strange to say, I *hadn't* and *wasn't,* and that you just spring right *at* me like a series of things going off; a sort of what-do-you-call-it, eh? A royal *salute,* a hundred *guns!*

CHIVERS. (*With a dim vision of what she means.*) I saw as soon as you arrived, mum, that you were looking for more things than ever *I* heerd tell of!

MRS. GRACEDEW. Oh, I had got you by *heart,* from books, prints, photographs; I had you in my pocket when I came; so, you see, as soon as you were so good as to give me my head, and let me loose, I knew my way *about.* You're all here, every inch of you, and now at last (*with decision*) I can do what I *want!*

CHIVERS. (*In dim apprehension.*) And pray, mum, what might *that* be?

MRS. GRACEDEW. Why, take you right *back* with me, to Missoura Top.[3]

CHIVERS. (*Trying, heroically to focus this fate.*) Do I understand, mum, that you require to take *me?*

MRS. GRACEDEW. (*Leaping, delighted at the idea.*) Do you mean to say you'd *come* —as the old Family Servant? Then *do,* you nice real thing; it's just what I'm dying for—an old family servant! You're somebody else's—yes—but everything over here is somebody else's, and I want, too, a second-hand one, in good order; all ready *made,* as you are, but not too much done up. You're the best I've struck yet, and I wish I could have you *packed*—put up in paper and *bran*—as I shall have my old *pot* there. (*She whisks about, remembering, recovering, eager.*) Don't let me *forget* my precious pot! (*Excited, with quick transitions, she appeals all sociably to the old man, who shuffles up sympathetically to where, out of harm, the valuable piece she has originally brought in with her as a trophy, has been placed, to await her departure, on a table.*) Don't you just love old *crockery?* That's awfully sweet old *Chelsea.*

CHIVERS. (*Who has taken the pot up with tenderness, though, in his agitated state, not with all the caution usually at his command, and, struck with something, turns the precious piece round.*) Where is it I've known this *very* bit?—though not to say, as *you* do, by name! (*Then as it suddenly comes to him.*) In the pew-opener's front *parlour!*

MRS. GRACEDEW. No, in the pew-opener's best *bedroom:* on the old chest of drawers, you know—with those ducks of brass handles. I've got the handles *too*—I mean the whole *thing;* and the brass fender (*as she*

---

[3] James altered the spelling from "Missourah" in *Summersoft.*

looks at her notes) and the fire-irons, and the sweet blue pig off the chimney, and the chair her grand-mother *died* in. (*Then as with real regret.*) Not in the *fly*—it's such a bore they have to be *sent!*

CHIVERS. (*With the pot still in his hands, gaping at the list of acquisitions, but approving her prudence as well.*) You did right to take this out, mum, when the fly went round to the stables. Them flymen do be cruel rash—with anything that's *delicate.* (*About to return the vessel to its safe niche, he himself has, however, betrayed by his trembling zeal, a dreadful little disaster; the matter of a few seconds, a false movement, a stumble, a knock, a gasp, a shriek, then an utter little crash. He almost shouts with despair.*) Mercy on us, mum—I've brought shame on my old grey *hairs!*

MRS. GRACEDEW. (*Who has simultaneously shrieked, but has quickly recovered herself, struck more than with anything else by the beauty of* CHIVER'S *compunction.*) The way you *take* it it's too sweet—you're too quaint really to *live!* (*She keeps it up to cheer him.*) The way you *said* that, now—it's just the very *type!* That's all I *want* of you now—to *be* the very type. It's what you *are,* you poor dear thing—for you can't *help* it; and it's what everything and everyone *else* are, over here: so that you had just better all make up your minds to it and not try to *shirk* it. There was a type in the *train* with me, the "awfully nice girl" of all the English novels, the "simple maiden in her flower" of—*who* is it? your great *poet. She* couldn't help it either—in fact I wouldn't have let her! (*With which, starting, she remembers.*) By the way, she was coming right here. *Has she come?*

CHIVERS. (*Who has picked up in dire silence the fragments of the pot, to place them carefully elsewhere, makes no answer till he has returned from these dumb rites of burial.*) Miss Prodmore is here, mum. She's having her tea.

MRS. GRACEDEW. (*Amused, recognising.*) Yes, that's exactly *it*—they're always having their tea!

CHIVERS. With Mr. Prodmore—in the morning-room. (*Then to be exact.*) Captain Yule has not yet joined them.

MRS. GRACEDEW. (*Vague.*) Captain Yule?

CHIVERS. The new master—who's in the garden. He's also just arrived.

MRS. GRACEDEW. (*Still vague.*) Oh? (*Then as if noting it—though not as if it much matters.*) She didn't tell me about him.

CHIVERS. Well, mum, it's a strange sort of *thing* to tell. He had never—like, mum—so much as *seen* the place.

MRS. GRACEDEW. (*Interested, but not amazed.*) Before to-day—so? His very own? (*Then as for the oddity of it.*) Well, I hope he *likes* it!

CHIVERS. (*Moved to boldness.*) I haven't seen many, mum, that like it as much as *you.*

MRS. GRACEDEW. Oh! (*She makes a motion of the head that means more than she can say, and throws up her arms half in a sort of embrace, half in a sort of despair at privation.*) I should like it still better if it were *my* very own!

CHIVERS. Well, mum, if it wasn't against my duty I could wish indeed it *were!* (*Then conscientiously.*) The *Captain,* mum, is the lawful heir.

MRS. GRACEDEW. (*Struck, as if this charms her.*) That's another of your lovely old things—I adore your lawful heirs! (*Then as with growing interest.*) He has come to take possession?

CHIVERS. (*With importance.*) He's a-taking of it now.

MRS. GRACEDEW. (*Her interest immediately clinched.*) What does he do and how does he do it? Can't I *see?* (*Then as he looks blank.*) There's no grand fuss—?

CHIVERS. (*A bit reproving.*) I scarce think him, mum, the gentleman to make any about *anything!*

MRS. GRACEDEW. (*Thinking; a little disappointed, then resigned.*) Well, perhaps I like them better when they *don't!* (*Then always all familiar.*) I daresay you think *I* fuss. For I, you see, (*as she turns about again and lovingly sighs*) have also taken *possession!*

CHIVERS. (*Really rising to her with a smile.*) It was you, mum, took it *first!*

MRS. GRACEDEW. (*Sadly shaking her head.*) Ah, but for a poor little *hour! He's* for *life.*

CHIVERS. (*Discreetly granting that.*) For mine, mum, I do at least *hope!*

MRS. GRACEDEW. (*Who makes again the circuit of the hall and picks up without interest, as a sign of the intention of going, some small object, a rolled up pair of gloves say that she has deposited on her first arrival in some place where the others won't have seen it; or even simply resumes possession of the note-book she has within a few moments put down, sticking the pencil back into its sheath; anything, in short, that will strike in a small way the note of departure.*) I shall *think* of you, you know, here *together.* (*She looks vaguely about as for anything else; then abruptly, with her eyes on him quite tenderly.*) Do you suppose he'll be *kind* to you?

CHIVERS. (*His hand in his trousers-pocket, turning over his sovereign.*) He has already been, mum.

MRS. GRACEDEW. (*With emphasis.*) Then be sure to be so to *him!* (*After which, as the house-bell sounds.*) Is that his bell?

CHIVERS. (*Wondering.*) I must see *whose!* (*He hurries up to back. Exit* CHIVERS, *disappearing in the ante-room of the approach from the Park.*)

MRS. GRACEDEW. (*Alone a moment, with her air in which happy possession is so oddly and charmingly mixed with desperate surrender, and with a last look round as for something she may possibly have missed; a look that carries her eyes straight to some small object, a plaque suspended on one of the walls, say, and on which she pounces with her cry of recognition.*) Why, bless me if it ain't *Limoges!* (*She detaches it, to admire it; she has it in her hands a minute to take it in; then, with a tragi-comic sigh and a violent effort, she hooks it up again, dusting off her fingers as she turns away in renouncement.*) I wish awfully I were a *bad* woman. (*Quite sincerely.*) Then—if I were the right sort—I'd take it and run! (*She stands an instant, thinking of it hard, she turns again for another look at it from where she is; then with a wail of protest.*) What a place for *Limoges!* (*With the thought she goes straight back to it, unhooks it afresh, and, looking at it with*

renewed intelligence, comes down with it in her hands. Startled, however, while she thus holds it, by a sound up at left, she whisks about to become aware of the gentleman who has appeared in the doorway from the garden and has been arrested there at sight of her. But she has all her familiar presence of mind; catches straight on, all gaily, to his identity.*) Oh, Captain Yule, I'm delighted to meet you! It's such a comfort to ask you if I *may!*

(*Re-enter* YULE *from the garden.*)

YULE. (*To whom this has been said as with the whole compass of the stage between them; coming down, surprised, but taking her in and ready for anything in the way of vague courtesy.*) If you "may" Madam—?

MRS. GRACEDEW. Why, just *be* here, don't you know?—and poke round. (*The plaque in her hands, and not now embarrassed by it, she presents such a course as almost vulgarly natural.*) Don't tell me I *can't* now, because I already *have:* I've been upstairs and downstairs and in my lady's chamber! —I'm not even sure I haven't been in my lord's! I got round your lovely *servant*— if you don't look out I'll *grab* him! (*Then as if fairly provoked to the last familiarity by some charm in the very stare with which he meets her amazing serenity.*) If you don't look out, you know, I'll grab everything! (*She gives fair notice, she plays with his frank stupefaction.*) That's what I came *over* for (*she explains*) just to lay your country *waste.* Your house (*she explains further*) is a wild old dream; and besides (*dropping, oddly and quaintly, into real responsible judgment*) you've got some quite good things. Oh yes, you *have* —a number; don't coyly pretend you haven't! (*Her familiarity, her equality, her everything, take these flying leaps and alight before him, as it were, without turning a hair.*) Don't you *know* you have? Just look at *that!* (*She thrusts her plaque before him, but he takes and holds it so blankly, with an attention so merely engaged and dazed by herself, that she breaks out as in pity for his ignorance of his values.*) Don't you know *anything?* Why it's *Limoges!*

YULE. (*Who can only laugh out his*

mystification.) It seems *absurd,* but I'm not in the least acquainted with my *house.* I've never happened to *see* it.

MRS. GRACEDEW. (*Upon him like a flash.*) Then do let me *show* it to you!

YULE. (*Able to say nothing else.*) I shall be *delighted!* (*But he has spoken also as if really wanting nothing better; so that he has a change of tone on seeing* CHIVERS *return breathless from his answering of the bell at back. Re-enter* CHIVERS *from ante-room.*) Who in the world's there?

CHIVERS. (*Coming down, full of it.*) A Party!

YULE. (*Just disconcerted.*) A "Party"—?

CHIVERS. (*Confessing to the worst.*) Over from Gossage—to see the *house.*

MRS. GRACEDEW. (*For whom this "worst" is quite good enough, and who blazes up as at a spark.*) Oh, let *me* show it! (*Then bethinking herself, remembering kindly and ruefully for* CHIVERS.) Dear me, I forgot—*you* get the tips! (*Then with a better light.*) But I'll get them too—see?—and simply hand them *over!* (*And she appeals to* YULE *on it.*) Perhaps they'll be bigger—for *me!*

YULE. (*All amused and interested now.*) I should think they'd be enormous—for *you!* (*Only, with more concentration.*) But I *should* like—I should like extremely, you know—to go over with you *alone.*

MRS. GRACEDEW. (*Struck, smiling at him sweetly.*) Just you and me?

YULE. (*Falling absolutely in.*) Just you and me—as you *did,* you know, kindly propose.

MRS. GRACEDEW. (*Standing reminded, but, as on second thoughts, revising, even pleading, a little, and having her first inconsequence.*) That must be for *after*—!

YULE. (*Urgent.*) Ah, but not too *late.* (*He looks at his watch.*) I go back *to-night.*

CHIVERS. (*With a quaver of disappointment and protest.*) Law-a-*mercy,* sir!

MRS. GRACEDEW. (*Struck by this note, touched by it and addressing herself straight to the old man, while* YULE, *at sound of her question, turns away.*) You want to *keep* him? (*But before* CHIVERS *can answer she takes in something, as from* YULE'S *motion and presented back, that determines her.*) Then I'll help you—

CHIVERS. (*Relieved, ravished, and so far forgetting himself, while the* CAPTAIN *still doesn't see, as to put out his hand all gratefully, which* MRS. GRACEDEW *meets with a small quick amused shake of it that is equivalent to a vow.*) Shall I show them straight *in,* sir?

YULE. (*Responsively and gaily enough, but still a little off and without looking at him.*) By all means—if there's *money* in it!

(*Exit* CHIVERS *to ante-room.*)

MRS. GRACEDEW. (*Who, left with* YULE, *has suddenly bethought herself.*) Oh, and I promised to show it to Miss Prodmore! (*Apparently all happy in this thought, she appeals on the spot to the young man.*) Will you kindly *call* her?

YULE. (*Instantly cold; blank.*) "Call" her? Dear madam, I don't *know* her!

MRS. GRACEDEW. (*Smiling but decided.*) You *must* then—she's wonderful! (*He answers with a sign of impatience, which, zealous for the girl, she doesn't take up because aware the next instant of* CORA'S *having appeared in doorway to right.*) See? She's charming! (*Re-enter* CORA *from the tea-room; pausing but for a glare of recognition, then hurrying across, under* YULE'S *almost equally scared eyes, to seek her friend's protection. This protection* MRS. GRACEDEW *promptly and genially gives, at once addressing her.*) Miss Prodmore, let me present Captain Yule. (*She bridges the great gulf with her quick, free span.*) Captain Yule, Miss Prodmore, Miss Prodmore, Captain Yule.

(*Re-enter* MR. PRODMORE *from tea-room.*)

CORA. (*At sight of her father, clutching at what seems her best resource, and emulating as by instant contagion* MRS. GRACEDEW'S *form.*) Papa, let me "present" you to Mrs. Gracedew, Mrs. Gracedew, Mr. Prodmore, Mr. Prodmore, Mrs. Gracedew.

MRS. GRACEDEW. (*With a free salute, taking in* MR. PRODMORE *as she has taken everything else, and distinctly repeating his name.*) Mr. Prodmore. So happy to meet your daughter's *father.* Your daughter's so perfect a *specimen.*

PRODMORE. (*Who has come down, in his importance, and has been at first left by this ceremony very much at sea, suddenly, like a practical man, feels in it something to his interest.*) So perfect a specimen—*yes!* (*With which he radiates toward* YULE *as if to pass it on.*)

MRS. GRACEDEW. (*As unconscious of this manoeuvre and only lost in appreciation of* CORA, *whom she covers with a gaze that practically keeps her there fixed and exposed, quite on exhibition.*) So fresh, so quaint, so absolutely the real *thing!*

PRODMORE. (*Testifying in his degree also to her influence by the way he irresistibly takes it from her as to his advantage for an effect on* YULE.) So fresh, so quaint, so absolutely the real *thing!*

> (*Its action on* YULE *is to throw him off to his distance, and the whole space of the stage is now between him and* MRS. GRACEDEW, *with what next takes place occupying the large interval. Re-enter* CHIVERS *from the ante-room, leading his train, accompanied and half-surrounded, that is, by the Party visiting the house; simple sight-seers of the half-holiday order, plain provincial folk who are, on the spot, at sight of the ladies and gentlemen, rather awestruck. The old man's effort, is to keep them well together, and as he gets his squad to centre* MRS. GRACEDEW, *all interest, all wonder for his discharge of his function, is nearest them.*)

CHIVERS. (*Mechanical, perfunctory, as with the habit of long years he shows the place off.*) This, ladies and gentlemen, is perhaps the most important feature—the grand old 'istoric baronial 'all. Being, from all accounts, the most ancient portion of the *edifice,* it was erected in the very earliest *ages.* Some do say (*detached, dispassionate*) in the course of the *fifteenth* century.

MRS. GRACEDEW. (*All sympathetic attention, but uncontrolledly breaking in.*) I say in the course of the *fourteenth,* my dear—you're robbing us of a hundred years!

CHIVERS. (*Yielding without a struggle.*) I do seem, in them dark old centuries, sometimes to *trip* a little. (*Rather pathetically put out, while his audience, pressing*

close, stand further expectant, though visibly more interested in the beautiful lady than in anything else and he yet endeavors to address the group with a dignity undiminished.*) The Gothic roof is much *admired,* but the west gallery a modern *addition.*

MRS. GRACEDEW. (*Amused, horrified, protesting.*) What in the name of Methuselah do you call "modern"? (*Then irresistibly, with an immediate benignant authority, she can't help making it right.*) It was here at the visit of James the *First,* in 1611. The great fireplace (*directing their unanimous attention to it*) *is,* however, 14th century.

CHIVERS. (*All gratefully takes it from her; though as, after waiting for her to proceed, not wishing to lay on her the whole of the burden. His companions stand gaping at her while she genially smiles back; whereupon he again takes up his tale; their heads all moving toward each thing he notes.*) The tapestry on the left *Italian*—the elegant wood-work *Flemish.*

MRS. GRACEDEW. (*Who really can't conscientiously let it pass, but who speaks with the sweetest charity.*) Pardon me if I just put that *right.* The elegant *wood-work* Italian—the tapestry on the left Flemish. (*She puts it to him before them all; the fun of it, of having her say about the beautiful place, drives her on; she wants in fine to relieve* CHIVERS.) Do you really mind if *I* just do it? Oh, I know *how:* I can do quite beautifully the Housekeeper at Castle Gaunt.[3] (*As if already intimate with each visitor, she treats them all as if it's a game they must play with her; greeting the two or three nearest, breaking down their awe. Then really to do it and as if to take them everywhere, she imitates the grand manner of the housekeepers in castles.*) Keep well *together,* please—we're not doing puss-in-the-corner. I've my duty to all parties—I can't be partial to *one!*

A VISITOR. (*Spokesman for his group, making bold.*) How many parties, now, can you manage?

MRS. GRACEDEW. (*Perfectly prompt.*) Two. The party up—and the party down.

---

[3] Gaunt House, a moated dwelling of the fifteenth century, near Oxford.

(*Then while poor* CHIVERS *gasps no less at her presence of mind than at the liberty just taken with her, she kisses her hand at him for reassurance and proceeds, in the highest spirits, with her business, pointing to one of the escutcheons in the high hall window.*) The stained glass in the windows is the *record* of the race! Observe in that centre the style of the family *arms*. (*Then carrying all eyes to another quarter and a tall black old picture of a long-limbed worthy in white trunk-hose.*) And observe in that portrait the style of the family *legs!* (*She leaps from point to point; shows her friends what is best for them.*) Observe the suit of armour worn at Tewkesbury. Observe the tattered banner carried at Blenheim. (*Her auditors, hanging on her words, bob their heads wherever she points, but* YULE, PRODMORE *and* CORA, *in their way equally held, visibly have eyes but for herself alone. She observes this on* YULE'S *part and smiles at him in all confidence. This pause, this exchange of a long look between them, seems to determine in her a sort of climax: which she utters really with her eyes on him, as if most of all for his benefit.*) Observe, above all, that you're in one of the most interesting old houses, of its *type,* in *England;* for which the ages have been tender and the generations *wise:* letting it change so slowly that there's always more left than *taken;* living their lives in it, but (*with charming persuasive unction*) letting *it shape* their lives!

PRODMORE. (*Rising to the miraculous effect of this wonderful stranger who, dropped for him from the skies, seems so extraordinarily to play his game.*) A most striking and suitable tribute to a real historical monument! (*All approving and encouraging, and, for that matter, not backward in gallantry.*) You do, Madam, bring the whole thing out!

VISITOR. (*The one who has already with such impunity ventured, has on this a loud renewal of boldness, but for the benefit of a near neighbor, whom he delightedly nudges.*) Doesn't she indeed, Jane, bring it *out?*

MRS. GRACEDEW. (*With a friendly laugh catching the words in their passage.*) But who in the world wants to keep it *in?* It isn't a *secret,* the beautiful *truth!* It isn't a frightened *cat* or a political party! (*The Housekeeper, with her excited sense of the place, drops from her; the sense asserts itself as too personal for that, and she soars again at random to the noble spring of the roof.*) Just look at those lovely *lines!* (*They all bob back their heads, all but* CLEMENT YULE, *who, motionless in his place, never takes his eyes from the speaker; while several of the "party," subdued, overwhelmed, fascinated, elbow each other with strange sounds. She finds wherever she turns a pretext for breaking out.*) Just look at the tone of that *arras!* And at the gilding of that *leather!* And at the cutting of that *oak!* And (*throwing up her hands and dropping her arms again—it's so universal*) the dear old flags of the very *floor!* (*It keeps rushing over her, and the sense of having to part with it is, all despairingly, in the passion of the tribute she renders.*) To *look,* in this place, is to (*very big*) LOVE!

A VOICE. (*From some nudging member of the group; with an artless guffaw and probably a private pinch for one of the ladies.*) I say—so much as *that?*

THE PINCHED LADY. (*Excited to loud pertness.*) Won't it depend on who you *look* at?

PRODMORE. (*Responding in the highest spirits; making his profit of the simple joke.*) It certainly does depend, Miss! (*Delightedly expanding.*) Do you hear *that,* Captain? You must "look"—for the right *effect*—at the right person!

MRS. GRACEDEW. (*As if she at least has not been looking at the wrong; while she addresses* PRODMORE *quite as if the Party isn't there or doesn't in the least matter.*) I don't think Captain Yule dares. He doesn't do *justice*—!

YULE. (*While, in spite of her gay face, she falters and he waits; speaking very gravely.*) To what, Madam?

MRS. GRACEDEW. (*Boldly, but blandly.*) Well, to the value of your *house.*

YULE. (*Still watching her a moment.*) I like at least to hear you *express* it.

MRS. GRACEDEW. (*Fairly impatient; as if throwing it up.*) I *can't* "express" it! It's too inexpressible!

PRODMORE. (*Whom this suits down to the ground; cheeringly, soothingly, always with his patronising note.*) Do what you can for it, Madam. It would bring it quite home!

MRS. GRACEDEW. (*Communing with the genius of the place and taking another try.*) Well—the value's a Fancy-Value!

PRODMORE. (*Triumphant, exuberant, appealing to* YULE.) Exactly what I *told* you!

MRS. GRACEDEW. (*Developing, explaining, putting it in a nutshell.*) When a thing's unique, it's unique!

PRODMORE. (*Taking it for every bit he requires; casting it upon the echoes.*) It's unique!

A VISITOR. (*Taking it up, as with intelligent decision, for the general benefit.*) It's unique!

SEVERAL VOICES. (*Not to be left behind.*) Unique, unique!

MRS. GRACEDEW. (*Finding herself so sustained, but giving it essentially, and with all her authority, to the lawful heir.*) It's worth anything you *like!*

PRODMORE. (*Passing it on as the very truth he has contended for.*) Anything you like!

A VISITOR. (*Again, as from the effect of the pleasant discussion and the general interest.*) Twenty thousand now?

MRS. GRACEDEW. (*Down on him like a shot.*) I wouldn't *look* at twenty thousand!

ANOTHER PERSON. (*Taking courage.*) Thirty then, as it stands?

MRS. GRACEDEW. (*Pausing but an insant.*) It would be giving it *away!*

PRODMORE. (*Enchanted: taking and diffusing her word for it.*) It would be giving it *away!*

SOME VISITORS. (*Led on to positive sociability.*) You'd hold out for *forty?*

MRS. GRACEDEW. (*Requiring a minute to answer, while the whole place, in all the converging pairs of eyes attached to her, seems to hang on her words; which she addresses, however, specifically and responsibly to* YULE.) Fifty Thousand, Captain Yule, is what I *think* I should propose. (*And she accepts serenely the general impression made by this high figure.*)

PRODMORE *and* THE PARTY. (*Collectively taking it up; all of course with high relish and sympathy.*) Fifty Thousand! Fifty Thousand! (*Then* PRODMORE *speaks alone; reacting, with bright, assured reference to* YULE, *into a pledge, thus offered* MRS. GRACEDEW, *that no business transaction is dreamt of.*) You talk of "proposing"—but he'll never part with the dear old *home!*

MRS. GRACEDEW. (*Taking it from him as all she is in a position to want; yet as if, alas, it also dreadfully sounds for her the note of final rupture, which she still instinctively postpones.*) Then I'll go over it again while I've the *chance.* (*And to this end she immediately remembers again the Housekeeper at Castle Gaunt; marshalling, with a grand sweep, the compact Party.*) We now pass to the Grand Gallery.

YULE. (*Whose concentrated motionless attention during all the preceding finds a significant climax in the clear high tone in which he now for the first time speaks.*) Please let them pass *without* you.

MRS. GRACEDEW. (*Wondering but interested and, since he asks it, immediately, after another look at him, throwing up her game.*) Let them pass, let them pass!

YULE. Many thanks. (*Then to* CHIVERS, *in nervous impatience and with a free, comprehensive, imperative gesture.*) For Heaven's sake *remove* them!

CHIVERS. (*At once fluttering forward and taking up* MRS. GRACEDEW's *words.*) We now pass to the Grand Gallery. (*They all pass, the Party, led by* CHIVERS; *they huddle to the staircase, mounting it after him with their various signs and demonstrations, a general show of rising interest. Exeunt* CHIVERS *and Party.*)

YULE. (*As soon as* CHIVERS *has complied, to* MRS. GRACEDEW.) I should like to *speak* to you.

MRS. GRACEDEW. Here?

YULE. (*Seeing movement of* CORA; *disconcerted, still more impatient.*) Anywhere!

CORA. (*Who, visibly, anxiously, all through, has been watching her chance, and with whose design* YULE's *proposal seems to interfere; getting round to her friend with intensity.*) Mrs. Gracedew, *I* should like to speak to you!

PRODMORE. (*Watching and down on her*

straight while YULE, *put off by the girl's
pounce, turns sharply away, goes up.) After*
Captain Yule, my dear! *(He thus gives
the measure of his naturally wanting only
to promote those moments of conference
for* YULE *with the wondrous lady which,
through her enthusiasm for the place, may
work to his own advantage. He waves*
CORA *on to the staircase as if her natural
and very convenient place is in the. tour
of inspection under* CHIVERS.) Avail yourself now of the chance to see the *House!*

CORA. *(Delaying, resisting in spite of
him, and managing it through her failure
to draw her friend at once from an interesting attention to the restless discomposed manner of* YULE'S *retreat—his keeping his distance, as it were, till the field is
cleared of the* PRODMORES. *He reaches
again the door of the garden, where* MRS.
GRACEDEW'S *eyes keep him company
enough to leave the girl free for the instant, to plead with her father unnoticed.)*
She'll *help* me, I think, Papa!

PRODMORE. *(With all cheerfulness, without roughness now; only as knowing better still than* CORA *what is good for them.)*
That's exactly what strikes me, love, but
I'll help you too! *(He gives her, with gay
resolution, towards the stairs, a push pro-
portioned both to his authority and to
her quantity; and she has to mount a little,
climbing in the wake of the Party, while
he himself,* YULE *being, with his back always turned, more and more detached,
gets now at* MRS. GRACEDEW—*making his
point with her, in bright confidence, on
the basis of her recent opinions.)* Just pile
it *on!*

MRS. GRACEDEW. *(Her attention returning; though her eyes are still on* YULE,
*whose attitude while he gazes from his
doorway into the grey old court or whatever seems somehow to admonish her.)* He
isn't in *love*—? *(Then as* PRODMORE, *rather*

wincing, demurs.) I mean with the *House.*

PRODMORE. *(Clearer.)* Not half *enough.*
(Urgent.) Bring him *round.*

MRS. GRACEDEW. *(Her impression of the
young man's worried air combining with
this established fact to determine her.)*
Very well, I'll *bring* him.

CORA. *(From the stairs, renewing her
appeal, sending across a loud, distressful
quaver.)* Mrs. Gracedew, won't you *see*
me?

MRS. GRACEDEW. *(All kind response now,
but looking at her watch, while the note
of the girl's voice, acting on* YULE'S *condition, has made him, clapping his hand to
the back of his head, in expressive despair,
slip straight out of the doorway and pass
from sight.)* In ten minutes!

PRODMORE. *(Bland and assured, in fact
quite gallant; consulting his own watch.)*
You could put him through in *five*—but
I'll allow you twenty! *(Then with a flourish to* CORA *from where he stands.)* There!

*(*CORA *has but time to snatch from
her friend a mute understanding, a
compact* MRS. GRACEDEW *seals by
blowing over at her a kiss of radiant but vague comfort; for her father is already upon her to sweep
her to the region above. Exeunt*
CORA *and* PRODMORE *by the staircase; after which only* MRS. GRACE-
DEW *sees that* YULE *has vanished
and that she is alone. She has at
this an uncertainty—looks after her
as with a question. She stands hesitating as whether to follow him,
then moves as deciding to do so.
But she thinks better of this and
comes down again; still, however,
to meet afresh her doubt; all with
an effect charmingly droll. Quickly,
at last, as he still doesn't reappear,
she goes straight toward garden, the
Curtain falling while she moves.)*

ACT SECOND

*Still the old hall, a few moments later,
with* CAPTAIN YULE, *at rise of the curtain,
standing again in doorway of garden; but
now looking down at* MRS. GRACEDEW *who*

*is seated to right. Everything to conduce
during these first minutes to the effect of
the extreme brevity of the little interval;
and of its having presumably, inferentially,*

*happened that, before the break, she has
simply gone up to within view of the
outer region, the old grey court or garden,
or whatever, and seen there that, having
taken his restless turn, with time for the
PRODMORES to get off, he is on his way back;
on which, again, with the instinct of not
appearing to pursue him, she has quickly
come down again and dropped into a
chair, so that he shall find her there, and
even in a manner awaiting him. Already,
however, with his rather troubled, puzzled, drawn-out return, she has been there
moments enough to have lost herself, on
her own side, in sudden intense and interesting thought: which is why they are
thus before us, in silence, long enough for
us to take them well in—she, unconscious
for the minute and with her eyes fixed on
a point in the floor, and he watching her
first from the doorway and then as he
slowly comes nearer.*

YULE. (*Grave and with all courtesy, but
as if he is really a good deal puzzled.*) How
do you come to know so much about my
house?

MRS. GRACEDEW. (*Startled at first, but
just smiling as her attention comes back.*)
How do you come to know so little?

YULE. (*Very gently.*) Of course it must
strike you as strange. It's not my *fault*,
Madam. (*Then as if really wondering quite
how to put it.*) A particular complication
of odd—and rather unhappy!—things has
kept me, till this hour, from coming *within
a mile* of it.

MRS. GRACEDEW. Haven't you ever
wanted to come?

YULE. (*Still amused, for all his preoccupation.*) It was no use my "wanting." I
simply *couldn't*.

MRS. GRACEDEW. (*With a really quickened little yearning of interest.*) Why, you
poor *thing!* (*Then after considering him
a little in this melancholy light.*) Well,
now that you *have* come, I hope at least
you'll stay. (*And as if struck with his not
quite looking so.*) Do, for goodness' sake,
make yourself comfortable. Don't of all
things in the world, (*utterly repudiating
the thought*) mind *me!*

YULE. (*With a motion as for the oddity*

of it, and the sadness going a little out of
his smile.*) That's exactly what I wanted
to say to *you!* Don't mind *me!*

MRS. GRACEDEW. (*While something in
the tone of this amuses her too.*) Well, if
you *had* been haughty I shouldn't have
been quite *crushed*—should I?

YULE. (*The last remnant of his gravity
now, for the time, completely yielding.*)
Ah, I'm *never* "haughty." Never, never!

MRS. GRACEDEW. (*Cheerfully.*) Fortunately then—as I'm never crushed! When
I've taken a line I stick to it as you certainly must think I've done to-day.

YULE. Do you mean that of mistress of
this house? (*Then prompt and not in the
least attenuating.*) Yes—you do seem in
good possession.

MRS. GRACEDEW. (*With no pretence of
denying it and only thinking of him.*) *You*
don't seem in *any*—good or bad! (*Then as
to encourage him.*) You don't comfortably
look it, I mean. You don't look (*she develops it frankly, seriously*) as I *want* you
to.

YULE. (*As if it's when she's most serious
that she's funniest; but also as if it's when
she's funniest that she's most charming.*)
How do you "want" me to look?

MRS. GRACEDEW. (*As, while he looks at
her, trying to make up her mind, yet not
altogether succeeding.*) When you look at
me you're all *right*. (*Then candidly, but
as if she regrets it.*) But you can't always
be looking at *me*. (*Casting about as to test
him better.*) Look at that chimney.

YULE. (*After doing his best for it.*)
Well—?

MRS. GRACEDEW. (*Surprised.*) You mean
to say it isn't *lovely?*

YULE. (*Returning to it without passion;
then throwing up his arms as incompetent.*)
I'm sure I don't *know*. (*As more or less
putting himself in her hands.*) I don't mean
to say *anything!* I'm a rank *outsider*.

MRS. GRACEDEW. Is that why you've
stopped smoking?

YULE. (*Willingly producing another.*) I
thought perhaps I mightn't *here*.

MRS. GRACEDEW. (*Absolute again.*) You
may everywhere.

YULE. (*Bending his head gratefully to
the information.*) Everywhere.

MRS. GRACEDEW. (*Diverted at his docility and at their relation generally.*) It's a rule of the house!

YULE. (*Quite meeting her on it.*) What delightful rules!

MRS. GRACEDEW. How could such a house have any others? But now for the long gallery. Come right *up!*

YULE. (*Whom it doesn't suit to move and who has already, in sign of this, half seated himself on the angle of a smooth old table, only looking at her a moment and smoking.*) There's the Party "up."

MRS. GRACEDEW. (*Recognising.*) So *we* must be the Party down? (*Accommodating.*) Well, you must give me a *chance.* That gallery's the great thing about you and the principal one I came *over* for.

YULE. (*As if she's strangest of all when she, in her astounding serenity, explains.*) Where in the name of goodness did you come over from?

MRS. GRACEDEW. (*Immediate.*) Missoura Top, where I'm building— (*Then with consummate serenity.*) Just in this style. (*Imperturbable.*) I came for plans and ideas. I felt I must look right *at* you.

YULE. (*Wondering.*) But what did you know *about* us?

MRS. GRACEDEW. (*Keeping it a moment with a smile as if it's too good to give him all at once.*) Everything!

YULE. (*His wonder increased.*) At "Missoura Top"?

MRS. GRACEDEW. Why not? It's a growing place—forty thousand the last census. With nineteen schools. So you see we know things.

YULE. (*Staring; between diversion and dismay.*) Bless us—you've been to "nineteen"?

MRS. GRACEDEW. (*Promptly, but as if having quickly and candidly reckoned.*) Well, I guess I've been to Nine. And I *teach* in Six.

YULE. (*His amused curiosity growing.*) And what do you teach?

MRS. GRACEDEW. (*Smiling, serene.*) I teach Taste.

YULE. (*Wondering, echoing; as finding it a little vague for a course by itself.*) As a "subject"?

MRS. GRACEDEW. (*Cheerfully definite.*) Yes, just Taste. (*Amused even a little at herself.*) I'm "death" on Taste! But of course before I taught it I had to *get* it. So it was I got your Picture.

YULE. (*Again startled.*) Mine?

MRS. GRACEDEW. (*Signing with her head as to all the other aspect, and always amused at the way he receives the information in which he appears so deficient.*) A water-colour I chanced on in Boston.

YULE. (*With the same wonder.*) In Boston?

MRS. GRACEDEW. (*As if he is really too droll.*) Haven't you heard of Boston either?

YULE. (*Considering.*) Yes—but what has Boston heard of *me?*

MRS. GRACEDEW. It wasn't "you," unfortunately—it was your divine South Front. The drawing struck me so that I got you *up*—in the Books.

YULE. (*As if still, however absurdly, but half making it out, and as if even just suspecting her absolute literal veracity.*) Are we in the Books?

MRS. GRACEDEW. (*Who almost, for his blankness, gives him up.*) Did you never happen to *hear* of it? (*Then, from the impression of his face, for the real interest of his blankness.*) Where in the name of the "simple life" have *you* come over from?

YULE. (*Very definitely and gently, but as if scarce expecting her to follow.*) The East End of London.

MRS. GRACEDEW. (*As having followed perfectly, but as not quite satisfied.*) What were you *doing* there?

YULE. (*A little over-consciously, but very simply.*) Working, you see. When I left the army—which was much too slow unless one was personally a Whirlwind of War—I began to make out that, for a fighting man—

MRS. GRACEDEW. (*Taking him straight up.*) There's always somebody or other to "go For."

YULE. (*Considering her while he smokes; interested in her interest, and as if she may after all understand.*) The Enemy, yes —everywhere in force. (*Without a particle of flourish, very quietly.*) I went for *him.* Misery and ignorance and vice. Injustice and privilege and wrong. Such as you *see* me—

MRS. GRACEDEW. (*Understanding quickly and beautifully.*) You're a rabid Reformer? (*Then with a certain dryness of yearning.*) I wish we had you at Missoura Top!

YULE. (*As if regarding for an instant with a certain complacency his possible use there, but then remembering other matters.*) I fear my work is nearer home. I hope—since you're so good as to seem to *care*—to perform part of that work in the next House of Commons. My electors have wanted me—

MRS. GRACEDEW. (*In complete possession of it.*) And you've wanted *them,* and that has been why you couldn't come down.

YULE. (*Appreciating her easy grasp.*) Yes, for all this later time. (*Then as if deciding, in spite of his habit of reserve, to tell her more.*) And before that, from my rather dismal childhood up—

MRS. GRACEDEW. (*Breaking in; gentle but eager.*) Was your childhood "dismal"?

YULE. Absurdly. (*Then as if feeling with pleasure the sympathy and curiosity in her face, but not wanting too much to let himself go.*) But I must tell you about that—

MRS. GRACEDEW. (*Quick.*) Another time? Very good then—we must have it *out.* (*Smiling at him.*) I do *like* your dark pasts over here!

YULE. (*A bit sadly amused.*) Well, in *my* "dark past" there was another reason —for the ignorance I seem to find you here to *dispel.* (*Deciding to mention it.*) A family feud.

MRS. GRACEDEW. (*Clutching at the interest of this.*) Ah, how *right!* I *hoped* I'd strike some sort of a Feud! (*Expressing frankly her joy.*) That rounds it *off,* and spices it *up,* and—for the heartbreak with which I take *leave* of you—just makes the fracture *complete!* (*Then as if her reference to her taking leave suddenly brings her back to time and space, proportion and propriety, the realities and relations of things, she turns about with her instinct of not leaving or forgetting anything she may have bought or may take. This in turn, however, makes the sight of the staircase remind her.*) Must I really *wait*— to go *up?*

YULE. (*Who, watching her movement, has turned again to restlessness, shifting, coming round, tossing away unconsciously a cigarette but just begun and placing himself as if practically to bar her retreat; where he breaks out abruptly as if still so imperfectly satisfied.*) Only till you tell me this. If you absolutely meant a while ago there (*referring back to the scene with the Party*) that this old thing is so precious?

MRS. GRACEDEW. (*Pulled up; with amazement and quite with pity.*) Do you literally need I should *say* it? Can you stand here and not *feel* it? (*Then with all her conviction, a new rush of her impression.*) It's a place to adore! (*But casting about as for an expression intense enough.*)

YULE. (*So interested.*) To adore—yes?

MRS. GRACEDEW. (*With cumulative effect.*) Well, as you'd adore a Person! (*Then as if she can add nothing to this, which says all; and while some sound of voices or movements, some recall of the lapse of the hour, comes down from the "Party up" and makes her take a decision, she passes straight to the stairs.*) Good-bye!

YULE. (*Who has let her reach the stairs and has got to his distance while she does so; and who speaks now with an intensity, a sharpness of meaning he has not yet used; quite as if the point she has just made has brought them the more together.*) I think I "feel" it, you know; but it's simply *you*—your presence, as I may say, and the remarkable way you put things— that *make* me. (*Then as if it comes to him while she listens that it may help him a little to alarm her.*) I'm afraid that in your absence—!

MRS. GRACEDEW. (*Arrested, vague.*) In my absence—?

YULE. I may come back—! (*Smoking.*)

MRS. GRACEDEW. (*Echoing it almost sharply.*) "Come back"? I should like to see you *not!*

YULE. (*Still having smoked.*) I mean to my old idea—!

MRS. GRACEDEW. (*Wholly turning round on him now; as if he has created a vagueness.*) What idea are you talking about?

YULE. (*Letting her have it.*) Well—that one *could* give it up.

MRS. GRACEDEW. (*As if, after all she has done, aghast and bewildered.*) Give up Covering? *How,* in the name of sinful waste—or *why?*

YULE. (*Very definite.*) Because I can't afford to keep it.

MRS. GRACEDEW. (*Prompt, practical, as if his mountain is a molehill.*) Can't you *let* it?

YULE. (*Smoking first.*) Let it to *you?*

MRS. GRACEDEW. (*Laughing out as in triumph at the thought, and with her laugh bringing her nearer.*) I'd take it like a *shot!*

YULE. (*After an instant; while, taking her statement bravely and responsibly, he looks down, rather fixedly, in thought.*) I shouldn't have the face to charge you a rent that would make it worth one's while; and (*then after a break, raising his eyes*) I think even you, dear lady, wouldn't have the face to offer me one. (*He pauses, but with something that checks her now in any impulse to rush in; speaking as if he really can't but see the thing clear.*) My "lovely" inheritance is Dead Sea Fruit. It's mortgaged for all it's worth, and I haven't the means to pay the *interest.*

MRS. GRACEDEW. (*Who has hung upon his words till her hope goes; when she violently reacts.*) I never heard of anything so awful! Do you mean to say you can't arrange—?

YULE. (*Prompt and clear.*) Oh yes. An "arrangement"—if that be the name to give it!—has been definitely *proposed* to me.

MRS. GRACEDEW. (*All relieved.*) What's the matter then? For pity's sake, you poor thing, definitely *accept* it!

YULE. (*As if her sweet simplifications but make him wince.*) I've made up my mind in the last quarter of an hour that I can't. It's such a peculiar case.

MRS. GRACEDEW. (*Frankly wondering; her bias clearly sceptical.*) How peculiar?

YULE. (*Who finds the measure difficult to give.*) Well—more peculiar than *most* cases.

MRS. GRACEDEW. (*Not satisfied.*) More peculiar than mine?

YULE. Than "yours"? (*He looks at her,*

all candidly, as if he knows nothing about hers.*)

MRS. GRACEDEW. (*With a movement of her shoulders, as if it takes a Briton to "know nothing" after one feels that one has practically told him everything; yet indulgent, none the less, to this particular specimen, and deciding to be rudimentary.*) I forgot. You don't know mine. (*Then bethinking herself.*) But no matter. What *is* yours?

YULE. (*Bringing himself to the point.*) Well, the fact is—I'm asked to *change.*

MRS. GRACEDEW. (*Vague.*) To change what?

YULE. (*As wondering how he can put it, but at last simplifying.*) My—attitude!

MRS. GRACEDEW. (*With an amused reaction from her blankness.*) Is that all? Well, you're not a bronze monument.

YULE. No, I'm not a bronze monument; but on the other hand, don't you see? I'm not a whirling windmill. (*Then as making his explanation complete.*) The mortgages, I'm humiliated to confess, have all found their way, like gregarious silly Sheep, into the hands of one person—a devouring Wolf, a very rich, a very sharp, Man of Money. He has me, you see, in a cleft *stick.* He consents to make things what he calls "easy" for me, but requires that, in return, I shall do something for *him* that—don't you know?—rather sticks in my *crop.*

MRS. GRACEDEW. (*Following close.*) Do you mean something wrong?

YULE. (*As if it's exactly what he feels.*) Quite brutally wrong.

MRS. GRACEDEW. (*Turning it over like something of price.*) Anything *immoral?*

YULE. (*Promptly.*) Yes—I may certainly call it immoral.

MRS. GRACEDEW. (*After waiting for him to say more.*) Too bad to *tell?*

YULE. (*Throwing up his arms with a fidget, as if it's for her to judge.*) He wants me to give up— (*But he has a pause as if it is almost too bad to mention.*)

MRS. GRACEDEW. (*As wondering what it can be that is scarce nameable; yet naturally the more curious; pressing.*) To "give up"—?

YULE. Well, my Fundamental Views.

MRS. GRACEDEW. (*As with a drop.*) Oh-h! (*She has expected more.*) Nothing but—*that* sort of thing?

YULE. (*With surprise.*) Surely "that sort of thing" is enough when one has so very *much* of it! (*He develops for his justification.*) The surrender of one's opinions when one has (*he rather ruefully smiles*) so very *many*—

MRS. GRACEDEW. (*Down on him like a flash and with a laugh on the oddity of the plea.*) Well, I guess I've about as "many" as *anyone;* but I'd "swap," as they say out West, the whole precious collection—! (*With which she casts about the hall for something of the equivalent price, and then, as she catches it, points to the great cave of the fireplace.*) I'd take *that* set!

YULE. (*Scarce taking it in.*) The fire-irons?

MRS. GRACEDEW. (*Emphatic.*) For the whole "fundamental" lot! (*Nearer to these objects, she fondly values them.*) They're three hundred years old. Do you mean to tell me your wretched "views"—?

YULE. (*Amused, catching on.*) Have anything like that *age?* No, thank Goodness; my views—"wretched" as you please!—are quite in their *prime!* They're a hungry little family that has got to be *fed.* They keep me awake at night!

MRS. GRACEDEW. (*Appreciating that inconvenience.*) Then you must make up your sleep! (*Her impatience growing with her interest.*) Listen to *me!*

YULE. (*Admiringly ironic.*) That would scarce be the *way!* (*Then more earnestly.*) You must surely see that a fellow can't sacrifice his *politics.*

MRS. GRACEDEW. (*With a gesture that seem to say "Is that all?" while she reverts to the object she has just pointed out.*) I'd sacrifice mine for that old fire-back with your arms! (*Then while he scarce more than gapes at the fire-back; so that she's again impatient.*) See how it has *stood.*

YULE. (*While his spirit, at this, flares up.*) See how I've "stood"! You don't know what's behind the awkwardness—

MRS. GRACEDEW. (*As after trying to read in his face what this queer quantity would naturally be.*) What *is* behind it?

YULE. Why, my whole political *history!*

Everything I've said. Everything I've *done.* My scorching *addresses,* my scarifying letters—reproduced in all the *papers.* I needn't go into details, but, such as you see me here, dear lady, and harmless as I look, I'm a rabid, roaring, raving, Radical.

MRS. GRACEDEW. (*Making her question absolute and utter.*) Well, what if you *are?*

YULE. (*Moved to mirth by her so characteristic coolness.*) Simply *this*—that I can't therefore, from one day to the other, pop up at Gossage in the purple pomp of the opposite camp. There's a want of what I may call *Transition;* and, though I know that, in a general way, lovely women see no more *use* for Transition than the swallows atop of a cathedral-tower see for the winding stair that takes the panting tourist *up,* I should seem to need—as a mere wingless pedestrian, Madam—to be able to tell, at least, how I *came.*

MRS. GRACEDEW. (*As, pulled up a little at having to take him as he is, since she doesn't quite know what to do about it, she thinks hard a minute; meanwhile mechanically, with one hand, just pushing some object on a table or elsewhere straight, or smoothing down with her foot the corner of an old rug.*) Have you thought very much *about* it?

YULE. (*Rendered vague again by merely having watched her.*) Abóut what?

MRS. GRACEDEW. About what Mr. Prodmore wants you to do.

YULE. (*Disconcerted.*) Oh then you know it's *he?*

MRS. GRACEDEW. (*So preoccupied, so brave, that she's a bit dry.*) I'm not of an intelligence absolutely *infantile.*

YULE. (*Granting it amusedly.*) You're the sharpest Tory I've ever *met!* I didn't mean to mention my friend's *name* but (*with a shrug, giving up his scruple*) since *you've* done so—!

MRS. GRACEDEW. (*Already all there; pressing.*) It's *he* who's the devouring Wolf? It's *he* who holds your mortgages? Why doesn't he stand *himself?*

YULE. Well, like other devouring Wolves, he's not personally *adored.*

MRS. GRACEDEW. (*Eager at this.*) And you *are* personally adored? You'll be still more if you *stand?* (*Then as if herself answering her questions, seeing it clear, triumphantly making it sure.*) That's you poor lamb, why he *wants* you!

YULE. (*As if he can but honourably accept this account of the matter.*) I'm the bearer of my *name,* I'm the representative of my *family,* and to my family and my name—since you've *led* me to it—this countryside has been for generations indulgently attached.

MRS. GRACEDEW. (*Taking up as with instant passion the cause of the Lawful Heir; concluding from it for everything.*) You do, of course, what you *will* with the countryside.

YULE. Yes (*so far assenting*)—if we do it as genuine Yules. I'm obliged of course to grant you that your genuine Yule's a Tory of Tories. It's Mr. Prodmore's reasoned conviction that I should carry Gossage in that character, but in that character *only.* He thinks things are going too *far.*

MRS. GRACEDEW. (*With immense decision; taking a line and sitting straight down on it and on a hard chair.*) Well, they *are!*

YULE. (*Discomposed, as he thus stands before her, at her appearing again to fail him.*) Aren't you then a lover of Justice?

MRS. GRACEDEW. A passionate one! (*Sitting there as upright as if she held the scales.*) Where's the Justice of your losing this house? (*Then as with a high judicial decision.*) To keep Covering you must carry Gossage!

YULE. (*Bewildered, rueful.*) As a Renegade?

MRS. GRACEDEW. As a genuine Yule. What business have you to be anything *else?* (*She is perfectly convinced.*) You must *close* with Mr. Prodmore—you must stand in the Tory interest. (*Then rising as she makes it all out.*) If you *will* I'll conduct your *canvass.*

YULE. (*Almost distractedly fascinated.*) That puts the temptation *high!*

MRS. GRACEDEW. (*Impatient as of his manner; waving away the mere personal tribute; moved to eloquence.*) Ah, don't look at me as if *I* were the "temptation!" Look at this sweet old human home, and feel all its gathered memories. (*Urgent.*) Do you know what they *do* to me? (*Then*

as she takes them all in again.*) They speak to me for Mr. Prodmore.

YULE. (*As trying to do as she again instructs him; but as having also to take account of other things.*) Well, there are other voices and other appeals than these. One's "human home" is all very well—but the rest of one's humanity is better! (*She gives at this a charming wail of protest; she turns impatiently away.*) I see you're disgusted with me, and I'm sorry; but it's not my fault, you know, if circumstances and experience have made me a very modern man. I see something else in the world than the beauty of old show-houses and the glory of old show-families. There are thousands of people in England who can show no houses *at all,* and (*with the emphasis of sincerity.*) I don't feel it utterly shameful to share their poor *fate.*

MRS. GRACEDEW. (*Roused at this, but unwilling to lose ground, and moved to use, with a sad and beautiful headshake, an eloquence at least equal to his own.*) We share the poor fate of humanity whatever we do, and we do much to help and console when we've something precious to *show.* (*Then warming, with all charm, to her work.*) What on earth is more precious than what the Ages have slowly *wrought?* (*Specious, ingenious.*) They've trusted us— the brave centuries!—to *keep* it; to do something, in our turn, for them. (*Then in earnest, tender, pleading possession of her idea.*) It's such a virtue, in anything, to have lasted; it's such an honour, for anything, to have been *spared.* (*After which, for the very climax of her plea for charity.*) To all strugglers from the Wreck of Time hold out a pitying hand!

YULE. (*Moved, but with no retort to such dazzling sophistry quite ready at once, so that he throws himself, just chaffingly, on the first side-issue.*) What a plea for looking Backward, dear lady, to come from Missoura Top!

MRS. GRACEDEW. (*Shedding his irony; holding up her head; speaking with the highest competence.*) We're making a *Past* at Missoura Top as fast as ever we *can,* and (*with a sharp smile and hand-gesture of warning*) I should like to see you lay your hand on an hour of the one we've made! (*Then with her always prompt and easy humour.*) It's a Tight Fit, as yet, I grant, and (*all ingenious*) that's just why I like, in *yours,* to find room—don't you see?—to turn round. (*Then as knowing and able to say just what she thus intensely and appreciatively means.*) You're *in* it, over here, and you can't get *out.* (*Hence lucidly concluding.*) So just make the *best* of that and treat it all as part of the Fun!

YULE. (*Quite enjoying now the discussion.*) The whole of the Fun to me, Madam, is in hearing you *defend* it! It's like your defending Melancholy Madness, or hereditary Gout, or chronic Rheumatism—the things I feel aching in every old bone of these old walls and groaning in every old *draught* that must for centuries have blown *through* them.

MRS. GRACEDEW. (*As feeling no woman to be shakeable who is so prepared to be just all round.*) If there be aches—there *may* be—you're here to *soothe* them; and if there be draughts—there indeed *must* be!—you're here to stop them up. (*Then intenser.*) And do you know what I'm here for? If I've come so far and so straight I've almost wondered myself. I've felt with a kind of *passion*—but now I see *why* I've felt. (*Having moved about the hall with the excitement of this perception and separated from him at last by a distance across which he follows her discovery with a visible suspense, she brings out her vivid statement.*) I'm here for an act of Salvation. I'm here to avert a Wrong.

YULE. (*After they have stood a moment, while she glows, while she fairly shines, face to face across the distance.*) You're here, I think, Madam, to be a memory for all my *future!*

MRS. GRACEDEW. (*Taking it then at the worst for that and coming nearer ·while she sociably and subtly argues.*) You'll be one for *mine,* if I can see you by that hearth. Why do you make such a fuss about changing your politics? (*Then with a flare of gay emphasis.*) If you'd come to Missoura Top too you'd change them quick enough! (*But seeing further still and striking harder, she rises again to bright eloquence with the force of her plea.*) ·What do Politics amount to com-

pared with Religions? Parties and Programmes come and go, but a duty like this *abides.* (*Driving it home, pressing him closer, bringing it out.*) There's nothing you can break with that would be like breaking *here.* The very words are ugly and cruel—as much sacrilege as if you had been trusted with the key of the Temple. This *is* the Temple! (*Very high and confident.*) Don't *profane* it! Keep up the old altar kindly—you can't raise a new one as *good.* (*Reasoning, explaining, with her fine, almost feverish plausibility.*) You *must* have beauty in your life, don't you see?—that's the only way to make sure of it for the lives of others. Keep leaving it to *them,* to all the poor others, and heaven only knows what will *become* of it! Does it take one of *us* to feel that?—to preach you the *truth?* Then it's good, Captain Yule, we come right over—just to see, you know, what you may happen to be "up to." (*With her sense of proportion again, as always, playing into her sense of humour.*) We know what we haven't *got,* worse luck, so that if you've happily got it you've got it also for *us.* You've got it in *trust,* you see, and oh we have an eye on you! You've had it so for *me,* all these dear days of my drinking it in, that, to be grateful, I've wanted regularly to *do* something. (*With the rich assumption, the high confidence, of having convinced him.*) Tell me now I shall have *done* it—I shall have kept you at your *post!*

YULE. (*Highly reasonable.*) Of course I don't pretend, you know, that I don't *care* for Covering.

MRS. GRACEDEW. (*As taking this for a gain, though finding his tone almost comically ingenuous; and coming back to the chance for her that she has already two or three times all but grasped.*) You haven't even *seen* it yet! (*Then chaffingly, charmingly.*) Aren't you a bit *afraid?*

YULE. (*Bethinking himself; then perfectly candid, and amused also at having to say it.*) Yes—tremendously. But if I *am* (*more gravely*)—it isn't only Covering that *makes* me.

MRS. GRACEDEW. What else is it?

YULE. Everything. But it doesn't in the

least matter. (*As if, really, with every-thing in his case so formidably mixed, nothing in the least matters.*) You may be quite correct. When we talk of the house your voice comes to me somehow as the wind in its old chimneys.

MRS. GRACEDEW. (*For the drollery of this image.*) I hope you don't mean I *roar!*

YULE. (*Attenuating this awkwardness; as light about it as possible.*) No—nor yet perhaps that you *whistle!* (*Then keeping this up.*) I don't believe the wind does here—either. It only whispers (*he seeks gracefully to explain*) and more or less sobs and sighs—

MRS. GRACEDEW. (*Breaking in.*) And, when there are *very* funny gentlemen round, I hope, more or less shrieks with laughter!

YULE. (*Arrested by this, stopping now rather gravely before her.*) Do you think I'm a "very funny" gentleman?

MRS. GRACEDEW. (*Taking it from him while she sits; touched by it as an appeal more personal than any he has yet made; but hesitating.*) I think—I think—! (*Then going straight up and turning away.*) I think more things than I can *say!*

YULE. (*Watching her for the moment during which, as under the emotion sounding in her words, she keeps her back turned; then with abrupt emphasis and decision.*) It's all right.

MRS. GRACEDEW. (*Brought straight round.*) Then you promise?

YULE. To meet Mr. Prodmore? (*With his strained smile again, as he consciously thus disappoints her by delay.*) Oh, dear no! Not yet. (*Insistent.*) I must *wait.* I must *think.*

MRS. GRACEDEW. (*Who has at first one of her desperate drops of her arms for the check represented by this; but then seems to control herself to patience.*) When have you to *answer* him?

YULE. (*Very quickly; as with the intention of reassurance, but the effect of despair.*) Oh he gives me *time!*

MRS. GRACEDEW. (*His tone upsetting her again.*) *I* wouldn't give you time! (*Then with intensity.*) I'd give you a *shaking!* (*She moves about, as feeling the good minutes slip; then facing him again as if*

it's more than she can stand.) For goodness' sake, at any rate, (*waving him vehemently away*) go *upstairs!*

YULE. (*At a distance from her; aghast, not budging.*) And literally find the dreadful man?

MRS. GRACEDEW. (*As her eyes catch sight of* CORA, *who reappears at top of stairs, relieved, elated.*) He's coming *down!*

(*Re-enter* CORA *by staircase.*)

YULE. (*While* CORA'S *attention, as she descends, fixed only* MRS. GRACEDEW, *on whom, thus cautiously prowling down, she rests an undeviating glare; disconcerted, alarmed, ready for anything to escape the girl's range, and as he moves round, to give her a wide berth, seeing his best course in the direction from which she has come, and, when the stairs are clear, eagerly taking it.*) I'll go up! (*Exit* CAPTAIN YULE *by staircase.*)

CORA. (*Who has crossed with him, yet with visible avoidance of seeing him; and changing the pace at which she has stolen away from above almost to a leap and a bound as soon as the coast is clear; rushing to her wonderful friend.*) I've come *back* to you—I want to *speak* to you! (*Then in the pathos and the vehemence of her need.*) May I confide in you?

MRS. GRACEDEW. (*Wholly unprepared as yet for this, but immediately amused.*) You too? (*Then with her gay reflection.*) Why, it *is* good we came over!

CORA. (*Grateful, ingenuous.*) It is indeed! You were so very *kind* to me and seemed to think me so *curious.*

MRS. GRACEDEW. (*Responsive; liking her; believing in her honest type.*) Well, I loved you for it, and it was nothing moreover to what you thought *me!*

CORA. (*A little embarrassed, but candid.*) I loved *you.* (*Then generous; glowing.*) But I'm the *worst!* And (*as if it so much explains her*) I'm solitary.

MRS. GRACEDEW. (*Gay but positive.*) Ah, so am *I!* (*Then with one of her quaint effects of familiar generalisation.*) A *very* queer thing, I think, is mostly found alone. But, since we have that link, by all means "confide"!

CORA. Well, I was met here by tremendous *news!* (*Taking her plunge, produc-*

ing it with a purple glow.) He wants me to *marry* him!

MRS. GRACEDEW. (*Amiably receptive, but failing as yet to follow.*) "He" wants you?

CORA. (*So clear to herself.*) Papa, of course. He has settled it.

MRS. GRACEDEW. (*Still blank.*) Settled what?

CORA. Why, the whole question. That I must *take* him.

MRS. GRACEDEW. (*Just as much at sea.*) But, my dear, take *whom?*

CORA. (*As if surprised at this first lapse of her friend's universal intelligence.*) Why, Captain Yule, who just went *up.*

MRS. GRACEDEW. (*With a large full stare.*) Oh! (*Then with a sharper note, as the queer picture seems to break on her, looking straight away from* CORA.) Oh!

CORA. (*Almost apologetically explaining.*) I thought you'd probably *know.*

MRS. GRACEDEW. (*Considering her now humanely enough, but still speaking with clear emphasis.*) I *didn't* "know." I couldn't *possibly* "know." (*Then, in the light of this odd fact, looking the girl up and down, taking her in more and more, and moved to wonder, decidedly, by the odd fact itself.*) Has Captain Yule *asked* you?

CORA. (*Clear as a bell; not doubting of anything her father has settled with him.*) No—but he *will.* (*In complete possession of the subject now.*) He'll do it to keep the House. It's mortgaged to Papa, and Captain Yule buys it *back.*

MRS. GRACEDEW. (*As with a quick lurid illumination.*) By *marrying* you?

CORA. (*Instructed, to her cost; indoctrinated.*) By giving me his name and his position. (*Then with her lucidity even greater than her modesty.*) They're awfully great, and they're the *price*—don't you see. (*With all the effect of her substantial presence.*) *My* price. Papa's price. Papa *wants* them.

MRS. GRACEDEW. (*Hugely staggered and bewildered; piecing this together, yet finding gaps.*) But his name and his position, great as they may be, are his dreadful *politics.*

CORA. (*As helped, at once, by her being aware of them.*) Ah! You *know* about his

Dreadful Politics? (*Still perfectly clear.*) He's to change them—to get *me.* And if he gets *me*—

MRS. GRACEDEW. (*Like a shot; breathless.*) He keeps the House?

CORA. (*With lucid assent.*) I go *with* it. He's to have us Both. But only (*she duly demonstrates*) if he *changes.* (*With all her competence.*) The question is *Will* he change?

MRS. GRACEDEW. (*For whom the question is indeed so weighty; appearing profoundly to entertain it.*) I see. (*Taking it all in.*) Will he change?

CORA. (*With further lucid reach.*) Has he changed?

MRS. GRACEDEW. (*As if this possibility, so serenely uttered, is really a little too much for her now startled nerves; so that she speaks with abrupt impatience.*) My dear child, how in the world should *I* know?

CORA. (*Unconsciously piling it up; detached and judicial merely; terribly consistent.*) The thing is that he hasn't seemed to *care* enough for the House. *Does* he care?

MRS. GRACEDEW. (*Who moves away, passing over to the fireplace, where she stands a moment looking mechanically, without seeing them, at the fine features she has lately admired; then facing about with quite a new tone.*) You had better *ask* him!

CORA. (*Before her; unconscious of any irony and of the effect she produces; and almost as if entertaining* MRS. GRACEDEW's *suggestion, conclusive, logical, fatal.*) If he does care he'll *propose.*

MRS. GRACEDEW. (*Catching sight of* YULE *at top of stairs, just as she had shortly before, from opposite side of stage, caught sight of* CORA; *and making out from this fact of his rapid return that her own ardour has practically worked upon him, has taken such effect that he now comes down to act; but passing swiftly across to let the girl have it, in a quick whisper.*) He does care! He'll *propose.*

(*Re-enter* CAPTAIN YULE *by staircase.*)

CORA. (*Whom* MRS. GRACEDEW's *rush at her only has made aware; determined now instantly, by the young man's approach,* and still more by her friend's so confident appreciation of it; and moving to left as he appears to threaten an advance from the stairs to right and towards MRS. GRACE-DEW, so that she makes for garden door as easiest escape.) Oh dear, oh dear!

YULE. (Coming down, rather awkward at result of his return.) I drive Miss Prodmore away!

MRS. GRACEDEW. (As with instant presence of mind and taking fifty things in; smiling to ease them both off.) It's all right! (Then beaming at CORA as with full intelligence.) Do you mind, one moment? I've something to say to Captain Yule.

CORA. (Up at left, looking from one to the other.) Yes—but I've also something more to say to you.

YULE. (As if addressing her for the first time, he must be civil.) Do you mean now?

CORA. (Fluttered at his address and, as it were, receding from it.) No—but before she goes.

MRS. GRACEDEW. (All consideration.) Come back in a moment then—I'm not going. (With which she blows her afresh the same familiar kiss as on her last previous exit.)

(CORA at her distance, but still facing them, waits just enough to show, with a wondering look, some sudden fear or suspicion, her alarm at the possibility of her friend's urging on YULE to "make up" to her, to put himself on her father's side; after which she dashes out. Exit CORA to garden: while MRS. GRACEDEW, affected by her manner, addresses YULE.)

MRS. GRACEDEW. What in the world's the matter with her?

YULE. (Who waits a moment, watching her while she moves further from him, before speaking.) I'm afraid I only know what's the matter with me. (Then gravely and coldly.) It will doubtless give you pleasure to learn that I've closed with Mr. Prodmore.

MRS. GRACEDEW. I thought you said he gave you time.

YULE. Yes, but you produced just now so immense an effect on me that I thought

best not to take any. I came upon him up there, and I burnt my ships.

MRS. GRACEDEW. (In the same posture.) You do what he requires?

YULE. (Rather hard and grim.) I do what he requires. I felt the tremendous force of all you said to me.

MRS. GRACEDEW. (Turning toward him sharp on this; speaking with an odd quick curtness.) So did I—or I shouldn't have said it!

YULE. (With a laugh a little dry, as an effect of her tone.) You're perhaps not aware that you wield an influence of which it's not too much to say—!

MRS. GRACEDEW. (While he casts about as for how to put it strongly and vividly enough; and still with her strange sharpness.) To say what?

YULE. Well, that it's practically irresistible!

MRS. GRACEDEW. (Taking this in, having to accept it, and its consequence, as her own act; but not able to keep down a flare of feeling which rings out ironic.) You've given me the most flattering proof of my influence that I've ever enjoyed in my life!

YULE. (Wondering at her; so mystified that he is moved to a defence, with some spirit, of the act she appears now to regard so oddly.) This was inevitable, dear Madam, from the moment you had converted me—and in about three minutes, too—into the absolute echo of your raptures.

MRS. GRACEDEW. (With an extraordinary air of having forgotten all about them.) My "raptures"?

YULE. (Amazed.) Why, about my old home.

MRS. GRACEDEW. (Quitting the fireplace, moving to right, then at last recognising his allusion without the aid of looking at him.) Oh yes—your old home. (As coming back to it from far away.) It's a nice, tattered, battered old thing! (Looking round at it mechanically, coldly.) It has defects of course—there would be many things to be said. But (dryly, letting it go) there's no use mentioning them now.

YULE. (Who has crossed her, in his emotion, to left; really astounded at her change of tone, and not a little nettled.)

I'm bound to say then that you might have mentioned some of them *before!*

MRS. GRACEDEW. (*Consciously and ruefully perverse, but covering her want of logic, so far as she can, with a show of reason, though speaking also with a certain indulgence.*) If you had really gone over the house—as I almost went on my *knees* to you to do!—you might have discovered some of them yourself.

YULE. (*With heat at her injustice.*) How can you say *that* when I was precisely in the very act of it? (*Perfectly clear, making good what he has done.*) It was just *because* I was, that the first person I met above was Mr. Prodmore; on which, feeling that I must come to it sooner or later, I simply gave in to him on the spot—

MRS. GRACEDEW. (*Down to right, seeming to gaze from afar at some strange dim fact that she requires a minute to do justice to; though finally succeeding after a fashion in doing it.*) Let me then congratulate you on at last knowing what you *want!* There's no more to be said, therefore except that I leave you to your ancient glory as I leave you to your straight duty. Good-bye.

YULE. (*Throwing up his arms in real despair, in spite of her having done her work, while she moves.*) You don't mean to say you're *going!*

MRS. GRACEDEW. (*As in disciplined despair and resignation; accepting it.*) Why, I've got to go back *some* time!

YULE. (*As with the wonder and the question irresistibly rising; though not even yet quite understanding, himself, the full point of his desire for knowledge.*) But what is it—a—you go back to?

MRS. GRACEDEW. (*As a matter of course.*) Why, to my big beautiful Home—such as it is.

YULE. (*After an instant; ingenuously.*) Is it *very* beautiful?

MRS. GRACEDEW. (*Simply.*) Very. But not to be compared to this. To begin with, it's a mile too big.

YULE. (*As with a vain attempt to focus it; almost literal.*) A "mile"—?

MRS. GRACEDEW. (*Almost impatient—her house being so little in question.*) Well, for one person.

YULE. (*As suddenly struck.*) Are you only—a—one person?

MRS. GRACEDEW. (*With a short laugh.*) Why, do you think I look like Two? (*After an instant.*) I'm a lone, lone woman. (*After another instant, simply.*) Since my Husband died.

YULE. (*With a movement and a repressed vibration.*) Oh! (*Then again as if, for some difference it may make, his recognition is not repressible.*) Oh!

MRS. GRACEDEW. (*Always simply.*) I'm quite alone. (*As if there's nothing more to be said about it.*) So there it is!

YULE. (*Immensely and intensely taking it in.*) I see. There it is. (*Then as to conjure a certain awkwardness; to disguise the betrayal of too sharp an emotion at this.*) A great big Empty House.

MRS. GRACEDEW. (*Quietly prompt.*) A great big Empty Life! (*Then simply still yet also just a little vaguely and sadly.*) Which I try to fill—which I try to fill—!

YULE. (*Gently ironic.*) Which you try to fill with Taste?

MRS. GRACEDEW. (*Good-humoured, philosophic.*) Well, with all I've *got!*

YULE. (*Grave.*) You fill it with your Goodness.

MRS. GRACEDEW. It will be filled for the rest of my days, I think with my Success! (*Smiling.*) That is with Yours!

YULE. (*As but vaguely and remotely conscious of his own.*) Ah—"mine"!

MRS. GRACEDEW. (*Possessed only with her idea.*) Why what do you want More? (*As he makes a sceptical impatient gesture.*) If your House is *saved!*

YULE. (*His eyes on her as if intensely and excitedly thinking; then speaking with quick decision.*) I'll tell you if you'll *wait!* Don't go till I *see* you! (*Having jerked out his watch.*) I go back—under *promise*—to Prodmore.

MRS. GRACEDEW. Then don't let me for a moment more keep you *away* from him. (*Then as if it's beautifully and terribly a matter of course.*) You must have such lots to talk comfortably over.

YULE. (*Who, though he assents in form, looking at his watch again, keeps away from the stairs, gets further away, gets up to left and toward door of garden; where he remains as with an idea he's too paralysed to apply.*) I certainly feel, you know, that I must see him again. (*His watch in his hand, though not looking at it.*) Yes, decidedly, I *must!*

MRS. GRACEDEW. (*With light detachment and indicating garden, a perceptible effect of irony.*) Is he in *there?*

YULE. (*Coming straight away as at the possibility.*) No—I left him in the long gallery.

MRS. GRACEDEW. (*Flashing again into eagerness at this.*) You *saw* the long gallery then? (*All sincere.*) Isn't it divine?

YULE. (*Blank, incompetent.*) I didn't notice it. (*Then oddly plaintive.*) How could I?

MRS. GRACEDEW. (*His face so rueful that she breaks into a laugh, though with all her impatience for him.*) How *couldn't* you? Notice it *now* then! (*On which she turns away with a gesture of despair at him; but after a moment, while he only stands planted, divided, tormented, looking after her, she faces about, not hearing his step on the stair, and takes another tone, half imperious, half droll, at still finding him there.*) Captain Yule, you've got to (*insistent, emphatic, characteristic*) assimilate that gallery!

YULE. (*Still looking at her with a fixed strained, strange smile, almost a grimace of pain.*) Will you *wait* for me then?

MRS. GRACEDEW. (*Meeting his look an instant and then as if made uneasy, of a sudden, by something in it and in his tone, while she turns off and speaks with a note of sharper and higher admonition, of greater imperative curtness, than she has used at all.*) Ah, go up, sir! (*It affects him so that, with a start, reaching the staircase, he mounts briskly several steps, gets in fact half way, where again he has an arrest, an hesitation, and, while he looks down at her, descends again a step or two. She waits, motionless, for him to disappear; then, as aware of his pause, turns once more to make sure of him. A look seems to pass between them on this, which fairly settles him, so that with a gesture at once brave and desperate, he quickly decides and remounts—he does disappear. Exit*

CAPTAIN YULE *by the staircase. Satisfied of this after an instant, she addresses herself, with an immense almost articulate sigh of relief that is at the same time almost a wail of sorrow, to her own affairs; the great affair, that is, already three or four times defeated, of her getting away—but this even a bit vaguely and helplessly now; and breaking down, with a pause again, as soon as she has begun to move. The pang of what she has been left there to think of prompts her to brief, intense self-communion.*) Why didn't he tell me all? But (*throwing up her arms and letting them fall at her sides as in supreme renouncement*) it was none of my business! (*Yet it continues to hold her.*) What does he mean to do? (*Then as answering herself.*) What should he do but what he *has* done? And (*following up this sense of it*) what *can* he do, when he's so deeply committed, when he's practically engaged, when he's just the same as married—and as *buried?* (*With which, concluding, as for immediate, however melancholy, action.*) The thing for *me* to "do" is just to pull up short and bundle out: to remove from the scene they encumber the numerous fragments (*as she looks about her*)—well, of what? (*She has turned about, in her trouble, while she exhales these questions, and has caught herself up on this last at sight of* CORA PRODMORE, *who, returning from the garden, has reappeared in the doorway up at left. Re-enter* CORA *from garden. MRS.* GRACEDEW *has at this moment by the same token, spied near her, on some table or chair where they have been placed after the accident, the pieces of the vase smashed by* CHIVERS; *of which, accordingly, with · a happy thought, she avails herself to strike off a public solution of the appeal she has a moment before launched upon the air, and which* CORA *may have caught.*) Of my old Chelsea pot! (*She has, over the pathetic morsel, a gay, yet sad, headshake, and lays it down again, as having spoken for* CORA'S *benefit its little funeral oration.*)

CORA. (*Who has come down, staring in simple dismay at the signs of the smash and referring it as she refers everything, to her principal fear.*) Has he been *breaking—?*

Mrs. Gracedew. (*Laughingly tapping her heart.*) Yes, we've had a scene! He went up again to your father.

Cora. (*With a motion of regret, sorry; as if she may possibly have to pay for* Mr. Prodmore's *missing him.*) Papa's not there. He just came down to me the other way.

Mrs. Gracedew. (*With instant resignation.*) Then he can *join* you here. I'm going.

Cora. (*Pleading, made bold by her apprehensions.*) Just when I've come back to you at the risk of again interrupting— your conversation with Captain Yule?

Mrs. Gracedew. (*Letting this ball quite drop; with dry detachment.*) I've nothing to say to Captain Yule.

Cora. (*Surprised, rather resentful.*) You had a good deal to say ten minutes *ago!*

Mrs. Gracedew. (*Not perturbed; clear.*) Well, I've said it—and it's over. (*Plain, definite, tranquil.*) I've nothing more to say at *all!* (*Then, as quite relinquishing the subject, bethinking herself of a freer and brighter interest.*) What has become of my delightful Party?

Cora. (*Clear.*) They've been dismissed through the court and garden. But they've announced the probable arrival of a fresh lot.

Mrs. Gracedew. (*As with a sudden envious joy at hearing of this.*) Why, what times you do *have!* (*Then as generously, as quite sincerely interested for the girl.*) *You* must take the Fresh Lot—since the house is now practically yours.

Cora. (*Blank, not in the least accepting it.*) "Mine"?

Mrs. Gracedew. (*As surprised in turn at her stupidity.*) Why, if you're to marry Captain Yule.

Cora. (*In a flash and almost with a jump.*) I'm *not* to marry Captain Yule!

Mrs. Gracedew. Why the dickens then did you tell me but ten minutes ago that you *were?*

Cora. (*Only bewildered at the charge and intensely rebutting it.*) I told you nothing of the *sort!* (*In the highest degree positive; referring lucidly to what she has said.*) I only told you that the alliance— as Papa calls it!—has been *ordered* me.

Mrs. Gracedew. (*Breaking out in humour as from the force of her relief.*) Like a dose of medicine or a course of *baths?*

Cora. (*Not moved to mirth; serious, as to justify her expression.*) Well, as a remedy—!

Mrs. Gracedew. (*Quickly taking her up as she casts about; charming to her, delighted with her.*) Not, surely, for your being so nice and *charming?* (*Scouting everything.*) We don't want you cured of that!

Cora. (*With her just grievance.*) Papa wants me "cured" of everything. (*With the highest decision.*) But I won't listen to him!

Mrs. Gracedew. (*Risking it, for certainty, after an instant, even at cost of seeming to urge.*) Nor to Captain Yule himself?

Cora. (*With all her firmness, all her air, now, of knowing where she is and what she wants.*) I won't *look* at him!

Mrs. Gracedew. (*Instantly, though as with a wail, almost a sharp shriek, for lost time.*) Ah, my dear, then why didn't you let me *know?*

Cora. (*Perfectly straightforward.*) I was on the very point of it when he came in and *frightened* me!

Mrs. Gracedew. (*As struck with this; considering.*) You think him "frightening"—?

Cora. (*Perfectly logical.*) Why, when he wants to get *at* me!

Mrs. Gracedew. (*Considering her fondly.*) And you absolutely don't *want* him to get "at" you?

Cora. (*With a motion of her shoulders as if it's too unutterably a matter of course.*) Why, it's just to *tell* you so I'm here!

Mrs. Gracedew. (*As with supreme decision; taking it all on herself.*) Then, my dear, he shan't! (*Her emotion, over the difference made by this, over the clearance of her mistake, shows for the moment as almost too much for her; so that as if then suddenly conscious of the self-betrayal involved in this, and bethinking herself also of the little reparation she owes* Cora, *she explains, but almost pantingly.*) Pardon me—I misunderstood. I somehow took for granted—!

Cora. (*As she drops, from the impossibility of saying all she has taken for* granted.) You took for granted I'd *jump* at him? (*So pleased she has settled it.*) Well, now you can take for granted, *I won't!*

MRS. GRACEDEW. (*Drawn to her, enchanted with her, and, as for this reason wanting to express a further interest in her.*) You prefer not to be "cured"?

CORA. (*Lucid.*) Not by doctors who don't know what's the *matter* with me!

MRS. GRACEDEW. (*Amused at this turn, adopting it.*) Yet Doctor *Yule* seems remarkably clever!

CORA. (*Having turned this over, and in consequence almost bouncing about.*) Then why don't you marry him yourself?

MRS. GRACEDEW. (*As perfunctorily thoughtful; with a rise of her shoulders and a sort of happy philosophic sigh.*) Well, I've got *fifty* reasons! (*After an instant.*) I rather think one of them must be that he hasn't happened to *ask* me.

CORA. (*As doing justice to it, but more fully interested in her own.*) Well, I haven't got fifty reasons, but I *have* got one.

MRS. GRACEDEW. (*Sympathetic.*) I see. An older friend.

CORA. (*As starting a little at her quick divination, but also a little as at some warning sound or some possible check from the quarter of the garden; then recovering herself and coming quickly back to let herself go, to pour out her tale, while the coast is yet clear.*) I've been trying this hour, in my terrible need of advice, to *tell* you about him! (*Pantingly, and with all intensity.*) After we parted—you and I—at the station, he suddenly turned *up* there, my older friend; and I took a little quiet walk with him which gave you time to get here before me and of which Papa's in a state of ignorance that I don't really know whether to bless or to *dread!*

MRS. GRACEDEW. (*Immensely interested, but assuming a high gravity and making immediately the practical application of her confidence.*) You want me then to *inform* Mr. Prodmore?

CORA. (*Thus directly challenged, can only, in her predicament, feel her uncertainty and her fears; so that she seems mainly to cast about.*) I really don't know what I want! (*Unsupported, yearning,*

candid.) I think, Mrs. Gracedew, I just want *kindness.*

MRS. GRACEDEW. (*As if patient and tender with her, but necessarily definite.*) And how do you *understand* "kindness"?

CORA. (*Clear about that; honest.*) Well, I mean *help!*

MRS. GRACEDEW. (*As before.*) And how do you understand "help"?

CORA. (*Turning about in her embarrassment and her appeal; feeling it come down but to one thing.*) I'm afraid I only understand that I *love* him.

MRS. GRACEDEW. (*Still all serious and as if the information is valuable, but she has to think from step to step.*) And does he love *you?*

CORA. (*After a sturdy, honest pause, very simply.*) Ask him!

MRS. GRACEDEW. (*As weighing this practicability.*) Where *is* he?

CORA. (*As with a large confident look all over the place.*) Waiting.

MRS. GRACEDEW. (*Vague, and as, for action, requiring more.*) But *where?*

CORA. (*After an instant, as having just hesitated quite to bring out this detail of her duplicity.*) In that funny old grotto.

MRS. GRACEDEW. (*For but a moment vague; quickly recalling it.*) Half way from the Park gate?

CORA. (*Assenting, but with the impulse of pleading for it.*) It's ever so *nice!*

MRS. GRACEDEW. (*As turning it over; business-like.*) Oh, I know it!

CORA. (*Anxious.*) Then will you *see* him?

MRS. GRACEDEW. (*Inscrutable, for the minute; dry.*) No.

CORA. (*Taken aback.*) "No"?

MRS. GRACEDEW. (*As before.*) No. (*Then as amplifying.*) If you want help—

CORA. (*While she pauses as with the fullness of her thought.*) Ah, I do! I do!

MRS. GRACEDEW. (*In full possession.*) You want a great *deal!*

CORA. (*Responsive, throwing up her arms.*) Oh so awfully much! (*With this immensity all before her.*) I want all there *is!*

MRS. GRACEDEW. (*As having, with the highest responsibility taken her line.*) Well —you shall *have* it.

CORA. (*Delighted, convulsively holding*

her to it.) "All there is"?

MRS. GRACEDEW. (*Looking well at her before making the announcement; then sharply making it.*) I'll see your father.

CORA. (*Immensely grateful; overjoyed.*) You dear delicious lady! (*Then as for full assurance, MRS. GRACEDEW still looking thoughtful and grave.*) He's intensely sympathetic!

MRS. GRACEDEW. (*Surprised, sceptical.*) Your father—?

CORA. Ah, no—the Other Person. (*With candid enthusiasm.*) I *do* so believe in him!

MRS. GRACEDEW. (*Looking at her searchingly an instant; interested; then fully embracing her cause.*) Then I do too—and I like him for believing in *you.*

CORA. (*Encouraged, convinced.*) Oh, he does *that*—does it far more than Captain Yule; I could see just at one glance that, though *he*, poor man, may be trying his best to, he hasn't made much headway *yet.*

MRS. GRACEDEW. (*Interested now for herself.*) Ah, you think he hasn't made much headway yet?

CORA. (*Wondering; as if this may be, even now, a little disconcertingly, the note of dissent.*) What do *you* think?

MRS. GRACEDEW. Oh, my dear, how should I *know*? (*Innocent and blank, but bright.*) I'm so *out* of it all!

CORA. (*Denying this; not accepting such a tone; urgent and serious.*) Why, ain't we just exactly bringing you in?

MRS. GRACEDEW. (*Amused, then as deciding afresh.*) Well—I'll come in for *you!* Your father *forbids* you his Rival?

CORA. (*Only asking to tell, and perfectly definite.*) He *would*, of course, if he had more *fear;* but we've been so sure he'd hate it—we two—that we've managed to be awfully *careful.* He's the son of the richest man at Bellborough, he's Granny's godson, and he'll inherit his father's business, which is simply immense. (*After which all conclusively.*) I wouldn't have shown him I *care* for him if he hadn't been *nice.*

MRS. GRACEDEW. (*With a laugh.*) A man's always "nice" when you *do* show him you care for him!

CORA. (*Stimulated, more than meeting it.*) He's nicer still when he shows you he

cares for *you!*

MRS. GRACEDEW. (*Reasonably assenting.*) Nicer of course than when he shows you he *doesn't!* (*Stands a moment quite fixedly, yet at the same time absently, studying her, and then comes back abruptly to business almost as with an effect of sharp impatience.*) Then what's the *matter*—with the gentleman in the grotto?

CORA. (*Now for the first time faltering.*) The matter for *Papa* is his Name.

MRS. GRACEDEW. (*Surprised.*) Nothing but his name?

CORA. (*Whose eyes roll, in her embarrassment, from below to above and all over the place.*) Yes, but—!

MRS. GRACEDEW. (*Amused, yet inviting.*) But it's *enough*?

CORA. (*Fixing as in mild anguish a distant point.*) *Not* enough. That's just the trouble.

MRS. GRACEDEW. (*As with a delicacy to surmount, but kindly curious.*) What then is it?

CORA. (*Deciding to speak.*) Pegg.

MRS. GRACEDEW. (*Vague.*) Nothing else?

CORA. (*Serious, resigned.*) Nothing to speak of. (*Distinctly but sadly.*) Hall.

MRS. GRACEDEW. (*Still wondering.*) Nothing before—?

CORA. (*Calmly desperate and throughout this always looking at distances.*) Not a letter.

MRS. GRACEDEW. (*Formulating it, turning it over.*) Hall Pegg? (*Then as having winced at the sound, having recognised the inadequacy, but restraining indecent comment.*) Oh!

CORA. (*As having accepted the worst, but turning off with a renewed sense of what this is.*) It sounds like a hat-rack!

MRS. GRACEDEW. (*Who continues to study and sound it.*) "Hall Pegg"? "Hall Pegg"? Oh. (*She seems to wonder what may be done about it, but also, seeing no issue, to drop her arms a little in despair. But it occurs to her to ask.*) How many has Mr. Prodmore?

CORA. How many Names? (*Considering, but only to see it makes it worse.*) I believe he somehow makes out *five.*

MRS. GRACEDEW. (*Prompt, derisive.*) Oh, that's *too* many!

CORA. (*Conscientious, to meet all sides of the question.*) Papa unfortunately doesn't *think* so—when Captain Yule, I understand, has *six*.

MRS. GRACEDEW. (*Taken; with immense interest; candid.*) Six?

CORA. (*Clear.*) Papa, at tea there, told me them *all*.

MRS. GRACEDEW. (*Frankly wondering.*) And what *are* they?

CORA. Oh, all sorts. (*She begins to recall.*) "Marmaduke Clement—"

MRS. GRACEDEW. (*Cutting in; checking herself.*) I see. "Marmaduke Clement" will do. (*Consciously dropping that interest; coming back, with decision, to the point.*) But so will yours!

CORA. Mine? (*Rueful.*) You mean *his*.

MRS. GRACEDEW. (*Resolute.*) The same thing. What you'll *be*.

CORA. (*Emulating her optimism; trying it; ringing it out.*) "Mrs. Hall Pegg"?

MRS. GRACEDEW. (*With an inevitable shrug, as it falls flat in the noble space; but trying kindly to cover it up.*) It won't make you a bit less *charming*.

CORA. (*As if she has realised this, or at least hopes for it; making the best of it.*) Only for Papa!

MRS. GRACEDEW. (*Guaranteeing it.*) Never for *me*!

CORA. (*In the highest degree appreciative; gratefully caressing.*) You accept it *more* than gracefully. But if you could only make *him*—!

MRS. GRACEDEW. (*All attention, yet also all wonder.*) "Him"? Mr. Pegg?

CORA. (*Clear; resigned.*) No—he naturally *has* to accept it. But Papa.

MRS. GRACEDEW. (*Considering critically this large order; yet as if it belongs, after all, to what she has undertaken.*) Well, it will be a *job*. But I *will*. (*Then on another spasm of* CORA's *gratitude; sustained, inspired.*) And I'll make him *say* he does!

CORA. (*Yearning; as with the dream of it.*) Oh if I could only *hear* him!

MRS. GRACEDEW. (*Crystalline now; with a gesture of dismissal of that question decided.*) It will be enough if *I* do.

CORA. (*Appreciating her tone, satisfied.*) Yes then—I think it *will*. (*And as if now ready to go.*) I'll give you *time*.

MRS. GRACEDEW. (*As with the sharpness of her complete scheme.*) Thank you! But before you give me "time," give me something *better*.

CORA. (*Wondering, as if, having parted with her secret, she has parted with her all.*) "Better"?

MRS. GRACEDEW. (*Luminous.*) If I help you, you know, you must help *me*.

CORA. (*Ready but vague.*) But *how*?

MRS. GRACEDEW. (*Sharp.*) By a clear *assurance*. That if Captain Yule should propose to you you'll unconditionally *refuse* him.

CORA. (*As with the relief of it being only that.*) With my dying breath.

MRS. GRACEDEW. (*Holding her, intensifying.*) Will you give me even a *pledge*?

CORA. (*Solid and sound; looking about her as for a paper.*) Do you want me to sign—?

MRS. GRACEDEW. (*Immediate.*) No—don't "sign"!

CORA. (*At a loss.*) Then *what* shall I do?

MRS. GRACEDEW. (*Turning off as under an emotion; but after a few vague steps facing her again.*) Kiss me.

CORA. (*Responsive, in her arms; then as with all arranged.*) We meet of course at the Station.

MRS. GRACEDEW. (*While they hold each other.*) If all goes *well*. But where shall you *be* meanwhile?

CORA. (*Instant, surprised.*) Can't you guess?

MRS. GRACEDEW. (*Jumping to it.*) At that funny old *grotto*? (*Then clasping her again with the flourish of an arm; holding her, keeping her; hurrying her up to back.*) I'll *start* you to it!

With which, thus united, they quickly disappear into ante-room of main entrance, right, while Curtain falls.

ACT THIRD

The hall again after the lapse of a few minutes; with Mr. Prodmore *just appearing, at left, in doorway from garden. As he comes down briskly, on same side,* Mrs. Gracedew *who has at the same moment re-entered, at right, from the ante-room where she has been seeing* Cora *off through the Park, comes down as with a similar expression of no more time to lose; so that, though on his own entrance, he has not seen her emerge, but simply finds her there—a little fluttered, but carrying it off—they are confronted over the width of the stage. She has in her whole air the sense of a return now to the more immediate and sterner reality, and of having got, with all resolution, for this particular encounter, as quickly as possible under arms.*

Prodmore. *(As addressing the whole place, with his peremptory note, the instant he has. entered.)* My daughter's not here?

Mrs. Gracedew. *(A little blown, as if panting from her recent rapid transaction, and holding her hand lightly to her heart; but bracing herself, bright, ready for him.)* Your daughter's not here. But *(smiling bravely)* it's a convenience to me, Mr. Prodmore, that *you* are, for I've something very particular to *ask* you.

Prodmore. *(Who has crossed, on this, straight to right; at the door of the lower rooms.)* I shall be delighted to answer your question, but I must first put my hand on Miss Prodmore. *(Then, however, as he pauses at the sudden bright possibility.)* Unless indeed she's occupied in there with Captain Yule?

Mrs. Gracedew. *(Now at left; after keen consideration, with her eyes dropped, but raising them to him, as she speaks, with all her courage and with high distinctness.)* I don't think she's occupied—*anywhere!*—with Captain Yule.

Prodmore. *(Coming straight away from the door, his hands in his pockets; with a flash of wonder.)* Then where the deuce *is* Captain Yule?

Mrs. Gracedew. *(Highly diplomatic; guarding her manner; careful of each of her steps.)* His absence—for which I'm *(with a vague, nervous, cheery laugh)* responsible is just what renders the inquiry I speak of to you *possible.* *(Then as breaking ground, all debatingly, for the "inquiry.")* What will you take—? *(Hanging fire in spite of herself.)* What will you take—?

Prodmore. *(Feeling in it as yet only some odd, vague, but characteristic, general solicitude.)* "Take"? *(Distinct and curt.)* Nothing more, thank you—I've just had a cup of tea. *(Then on a second thought; remembering manners.)* Won't *you* have one?

Mrs. Gracedew. Yes, with pleasure—but not yet. *(Then casting about her as with the sense of what must come before this; at close quarters with her "job" and, instinctively, anxiously, a little painfully, pressing her light hand a moment to her eyes.)* Not yet.

Prodmore. *(As vaguely struck by this; making sure.)* You wouldn't be better for it immediately?

Mrs. Gracedew. *(Positive.)* No. *(Distinct again.)* No, I don't want to be "better." *(Then afresh with her nervous laugh.)* I'm beautifully *well!* *(On which, and on his motion of satisfied acceptance; though also as after a supreme roll of her eyes over the place; she comes back to her attack.)* I want to know how you'd *value*—

Prodmore. *(Instantly alert for that sweet word; putting himself as quickly in her place, that of a real connoisseur; so that he's already genial about it.)* One of these charming old things that takes your *fancy?*

Mrs. Gracedew. *(Looking at him, with one of her spasms of resolution, very straight now, and quite hard.)* They *all* take my fancy.

Prodmore. *(Enjoying it, with his noted geniality, as the joke of a rich person; the kind of joke he sometimes makes himself.)* "All"?

Mrs. Gracedew. *(As really and brilliantly meaning it.)* Every single one! *(Then as if this has already made a good*

Mrs. Gracedew Makes the High Bid
The High Bid (Act III).
Gertrude Elliot (Mrs. Gracedew)
and Edward Sass (Mr. Prodmore)

Sir Johnston Forbes-Robertson
(left) as Captain Yule and
Edward Sass as Mr. Prodmore
in *The High Bid* (1909).
From *The Sketch,* March 3, 1909

Henry James in 1900,
as captured in the celebrated portrait by Ellen Emmet

basis; taking familiarly for granted the ground they have covered at a stride.) Should you be willing to treat, Mr. Prodmore, for your interest in the whole nice thing?

PRODMORE. (Throwing back his head; struck; yet wondering here at some missing links.) Am I to take it from you then that you know about my interest—?

MRS. GRACEDEW. (With a conscious strained smile, but raising light and airy hands which just dispose, by a flourish, of any of the difficulties attending such a certainty.) Everything.

PRODMORE. (Accepting her knowledge then; but more reserved, and as for an important rectification.) Pardon me, Madam! (Explaining.) You don't know "everything" if you don't know that my interest—(pompous) considerable as it might well have struck you—has just ceased to—the least bit invidiously perhaps—predominate! I've given it up (with a confidential, an agreeable smile, as to soften the blow)—for a handsome equivalent.

MRS. GRACEDEW. (Not at all staggered; all there to meet it.) You mean for a splendid son-in-law.

PRODMORE. (As perfectly possessed of what he means, but with his constant responsibility to "form.") It will be by some such description as the term you use that I shall doubtless, hereafter, in the common course, permit myself to allude to Captain Yule. (Then as on a further genial vision.) Unless indeed I call him— (But he drops the bolder thought.) It will depend on what he calls me.

MRS. GRACEDEW. (After a moment, as with a still larger judgment of this.) Won't it depend a little on what your daughter herself calls him?

PRODMORE. (Considering the question, then settling it, radiantly, in the sense of the highest delicacy.) No. That mystery of their united state will be between the happy pair!

MRS. GRACEDEW. (Still advancing into the subject as with the flicker of all her light.) Am I to take it from you then—I adopt your excellent phrase!—that Miss Prodmore has already accepted him?

PRODMORE. (His head still in the air

and his manner seeming to signify that he has put his Fact down on the table, and that she can take it or not as she likes.) Her character—formed by my assiduous care—enables me to locate her, I may say even to time her, from moment to moment, (massive, clear-faced, watch in hand) with all but mathematical certainty! (Then as he complacently surveys his watch.) It's my assured conviction that she's combining inclination with Duty even while we sit here!

MRS. GRACEDEW. (Who, after having with a high, odd, but inarticulate sound, half an apprehensive groan and half a smothered joy "taken it from him" in all its fatuity and folly, gives way to her nervousness and moves up and round; invoking comfort and support, with all her eyes, from the whole picture, before speaking, abruptly on an effective change of tone.) Dear Mr. Prodmore, why are you so awfully rash as to make your Daughter afraid of you? (With increasing confidence, as she has broken this ice.) You should have taught her to confide in you. (Advisingly, soothingly, serenely.) She has clearly shown me that she can confide.

PRODMORE. (With a frown; pulled up by this new note.) She "confides" in you?

MRS. GRACEDEW. Well (facing him, smiling, laughing)—you may "take it from me"! (Then as if seeing her way now.) Let me suggest that, as fortune has thrown us together a minute, you follow her good example.

PRODMORE. Oh!

MRS. GRACEDEW. (She puts out a hand to check him; she knows what she's about; she takes her further step.) Tell me for instance the ground of your objection to poor Mr. Pegg.

PRODMORE. Pegg?

MRS. GRACEDEW. (Then as he starts at the name and remains blank, for excess of amazement, at her audacity; distinct, categorical, and as already with the sense of success.) I mean Mr. Pegg of Bellborough, Mr. Hall Pegg, the Godson of your Daughter's Grandmother and the associate of his father in their flourishing House: to whom —Miss Prodmore is devotedly attached.

PRODMORE. (Who has sunk in his dis-

may into the nearest chair, staring amazedly before him.) It has gone as far as *that?*

MRS. GRACEDEW. (*Triumphant now; towering above him.*) It has gone so far that you must let it go the rest of the way!

PRODMORE. (*Physically prostrate, but the solid gasping pretension, the habit of massive dignity of him, asserting themselves through everything, with deep resentment at having been "done."*) It's too monstrous of you to have plotted with her to keep me in the Dark!

MRS. GRACEDEW. (*Without insolence, only all candid and explanatory.*) Why, it's only when you're kept in the Dark that your Daughter's kept in the Light! (*Clear, completing, explaining, almost accommodating; as in the interest of the merest common sense.*) It's at her own earnest request that I plead to you for her Liberty of Choice. She's an honest girl—perhaps even a peculiar girl. And she's not a Baby. You overdo, I think—in your natural solicitude!—the Nursing! (*Then committing herself all the way.*) She has a perfect right to her *preference.*

PRODMORE. (*Helpless, overwhelmed; appealing with vain majesty from his chair.*) And, pray, haven't I a perfect right to *mine?*

MRS. GRACEDEW. (*Indulgent, kindly; but absolute, distinct, clear as a bell.*) Not at her Expense. (*Then as letting him know it fairly for his very own sake.*) You expect her to give up Too Much.

PRODMORE. (*Immediate, vehement.*) And what has she expected *me* to give up? What but the desire of my *heart* and the dream of my *life?* (*As if he has never heard of anything so fantastic; and has moreover, against* MRS. GRACEDEW's *game of opposition, this crowning card to play.*) Captain Yule announced to me but a few minutes since his uncontrollable *impatience* to get in his Bid!

MRS. GRACEDEW. (*Not at all upset by it, having her own reasons.*) Well, if he does get it in, I think he'll simply find—

PRODMORE. (*While she hangs fire as for effect and they look at each other hard.*) Find *what?*

MRS. GRACEDEW. (*Sharp, downright.*) Why, that she won't do Business.

PRODMORE. (*Whom it brings to his feet; erect, absolutely.*) She *will!*

MRS. GRACEDEW. (*With a gay undaunted headshake; insistent.*) She won't.

PRODMORE. (*Passionate, making for the staircase.*) She *shall!*

MRS. GRACEDEW. (*Getting there with a rush and a spring, before him; barring the way with her arms out; so that as a result of it they rise there confronted for the moment like real enemies.*) She shan't! (*Her movement, her attitude, her finer passion, check him and hold him thus as by their spell; during which she looks at him as a lady lion-tamer, at the circus, may look at one of the creatures she's accustomed to cow. After which, as having felt the spell work she comes back, on one of her sudden sharp changes of note, to their Real Question.*) Now tell me How Much!

PRODMORE. (*Giving way under it, yielding ground, turning off and coming down.*) How can I "tell" you anything so Preposterous?

MRS. GRACEDEW. (*Perfectly ready to show him how.*) Simply by computing the total amount to which—for your benefit!—this poor old estate is burdened! (*Then as, after moving away from her with a toss of impatience, he has paused for attention, his back expressively presented.*) If I've upset you by my proof—as I may call it!—that your speculation is built on the sand, let me atone for tḥat by my wish to take off your hands an investment from which you draw so little profit.

PRODMORE. (*In the same position; his attention still further held.*) And pray what profit will you derive—?

MRS. GRACEDEW. (*All cheerful, as with reasons, of a private nature, that suffice to her.*) Ah, that's my own secret! (*Then as if this ought to content him.*) I just *want* the nice old thing!

PRODMORE. (*Moving further away; with high decision.*) So do *I,* damn me! (*Stuffing into his breast-pocket, with a thrust of resolution, the crimson handkerchief taken out to mop his brow.*) And that's why I've practically *paid* for it!

MRS. GRACEDEW. (*Who waits a moment, all considerate, all perceptive, as taking in this; then brings out, as if her proposal*

is exactly and most reasonably, quite coaxingly, founded on all the facts of his
case.) I'll "practically pay" for it, Mr.
Prodmore—if you'll only tell me your Figure. As soon as you let me know it I cable
to Missoura Top to have the Money (with
an artless assumption of every facility)—
well, sent right straight out to you.

PRODMORE. (Highly superior; only dryly
amused at this fine feminine conception
of business.) You imagine that having the
money "sent right straight out to me" will
make you Owner of this Place?

MRS. GRACEDEW. (Her head on one side,
considering the question while, nervously,
she draws with one hand the end of her
scarf, draws her long gloves, or something
of that kind, through the grasp of the
other; and speaks as if it's rather a question for debate, for appreciation.) No—
not quite perhaps. But I'll settle the rest
with Captain Yule.

PRODMORE. (Planted there with his legs
apart now, his hands behind his coat-tails,
and with a superior sway of his upper
person to and fro a moment, so that he
looks down first, over his large white waistcoat, at his patent-leather laced boots,
with their bright tan-coloured tops, then
over the legs of his rather loud cross-
barred trousers, and finally, settling his
head in his florid blue neck-tie, up, with
sustained reserve at the roof.) Captain
Yule has nothing to sell.

MRS. GRACEDEW. (Blank, though sharply
ironic; infinitely surprised.) Then what
have you been trying to buy?

PRODMORE. (In whom this question,
ringing out clear, determines a sudden
quick and startled apprehension.) Do you
mean to say you're after that? (Then while
her face meets his intensity of emphasis
and the queer knowing grimace with which
it's accompanied; the effect of all of which
is to make her, under his eyes, turn away
with a mute comment, in her lightly raised
and dropped, her repudiating, disclaiming arm, on his perceptible vulgarity.)
You'll remember that you've yourself
given me the benefit of an estimate.

MRS. GRACEDEW. (As vague at first; then
understanding, but all candid about it.)
With those good people—when I showed

the place off?

PRODMORE. (Agreeably amused.) You
seemed to be taking Bids then. You ran it
up High—you said it's Magnificent—you
said it's supreme—you said it's unique—
oh you got in deep.

MRS. GRACEDEW. (As if the time he mentions is a long way to go back, yet as
making the effort and the journey; from
which she returns with an amused candid
recall.) Was I very grotesque?

PRODMORE. (This word on the contrary
not at all suiting him.) "Grotesque"?

MRS. GRACEDEW. (As really wanting to
know.) I mean did I go on about it?

PRODMORE. (Immediate, specific, vivid.)
"Go on"? You worked it up as, in the
course of a considerable experience, I've
never heard any auctioneer! You banged
the desk. You raved and shrieked.

MRS. GRACEDEW. (Lost as in the happy
but quite detached recognition.) We do
shriek at Missoura Top. (Musing, admitting.) Yes, and—when we like things—we
"rave." I raved just to please you.

PRODMORE. You said what you didn't
believe?

MRS. GRACEDEW. (With dignity, yet with
radiant, with supreme candour.) Yes. For
you.

PRODMORE. (Suspicious, vague.) For
"me"?

MRS. GRACEDEW. (Casting about her,
conscious under his eye; then finding as a
matter of course her other reason.) And
for those good people.

PRODMORE. Oh! (Sarcastic.) Should you
like me to call them back?

MRS. GRACEDEW. (Gay.) No. (Quite clear
about it.) I did what Housekeepers do—I
strained a point. "For the good of the
House"!

PRODMORE. (Taking it in, but unappeased, as at a highly suspicious story.)
Then if we ain't what you say (hanging
fire here, holding her with the question
very searchingly—all the more that while
he has this pregnant pause she consciously
looks away)—why the devil do you want
us? Why the devil (as she still says nothing
and takes, as it were, no notice) did you
say you'd offer Fifty Thousand?

MRS. GRACEDEW. (Brought round to him

as by the odd faint recall of this from far, far back; a little wan.) Did I *say that? (With a lithe expressive shrug, as if she can't imagine why.)* It was a Figure of Speech!

PRODMORE. *(Prompt, triumphant.)* Then that's the kind of Figure we're *talking* about! *(Then while she raises a vague though rather consciously ineffective, hand of protest, he sees* CHIVERS, *who appears at the door from garden, and at sight of whom* MRS. GRACEDEW *makes also a motion of relief and hope, getting further away from* PRODMORE *and letting the old man, whom her eyes fondly fix, come down between them. Re-enter* CHIVERS *from garden. The effect of this is that he draws to himself instantly* MR. PRODMORE'S *high displeasure.)* Have you seen Miss Prodmore? If you *haven't,* find her at once.

MRS. GRACEDEW. *(At whom alone* CHIVERS *has looked, from the first, and from whom, even under* PRODMORE'S *challenge, he doesn't take his eyes; speaking now as in full possession of all her wits; and as always to* CHIVERS, *very kindly, quite caressingly.)* You won't, my dear man, "find her at once"—you won't perhaps, very easily, *ever* find her again. *(Then bracing herself as for the supreme truth to* PROD-MORE, *and this time quite not flinching.)* Cora has gone with Mr. Pegg.

PRODMORE. *(Astounded.)* Pegg has *been* here?

MRS. GRACEDEW. *(Letting him, with the same high spirit have it all.)* He walked with her from the Station.

PRODMORE. *(Stupefied.)* When she arrived? *(Piecing it together.)* That's why she was so *late?*

MRS. GRACEDEW. *(Serene, even gay.)* Why I got here *first. (Then with her conscious habit of success, the sense of how it always floats her, and will in a manner float her now, into port, over no matter what shallows and after no matter what bumps.)* I think I get *everywhere* first.

PRODMORE. *(Aggravated, harsh, eyeing her as through menacing lids.)* Isn't the question, ma'am, rather where I shall expect to "get"—and *What? (Then as she meets this, keeping up her brave face, but*

in smiling inscrutable silence; peremptory, rude.) In which direction did they *go?*

MRS. GRACEDEW. *(Taking her time thus to make up her mind.)* I think I must let you find *out!*

PRODMORE. *(Pulled up, as unable, in the conditions, to deal with her; addressing himself wrathfully to* CHIVERS, *who has but stood bewildered and gaping.)* Call my carriage, you monster. *(Then while* CHIV-ERS, *starting in obedience as if fairly to dodge a brick hurled at him, shuffles up with all speed to the door to Park. Exit* CHIVERS *to Park,* PRODMORE *letting himself go so far as he dares at* MRS. GRACE-DEW.) So you abetted and protected this wicked, low intrigue.

MRS. GRACEDEW. *(Still taking her time; making some half-circle round and about, all thoughtfully and patiently, even a little pityingly, while she trails her dress down; now indifferent, above all, to any violence.)* You're too disappointed to see your Real Interest. Oughtn't I therefore in common charity to point it *out* to you?

PRODMORE. *(Facing her question all icily, yet so far as to treat it as one.)* What do *you* know of my Disappointment?

MRS. GRACEDEW. *(Perfectly frank, courageous and kind.)* I know Everything.

PRODMORE. *(Wrapt up in his wrong; as if not hearing her.)* What do you know of my Real Interest?

MRS. GRACEDEW. *(Perfectly gentle, reasonable, ready; also perfectly clear.)* I know enough for my purpose—which is to offer you a handsome condition. *Do* drive after them, if you *like*—but catch up with them only to *forgive* them. If you'll do *that*—

PRODMORE. *(As with a stimulated nose now for her possibilities.)* Well, if I do, exactly what it's odious to me to do—?

MRS. GRACEDEW. I'll pay your Price.

PRODMORE. *(With the same superiority.)* What do you call my Price?

MRS. GRACEDEW. *(As if it's too obvious.)* Why, the sum you just mentioned. Fifty Thousand.

PRODMORE. *(Stupefied; derisive, as if she's joking, while he settles his head in his florid neck-gear.)* That's not my Price— and never for a moment *was!* Besides *(his hands in his pockets, square and erect on his large patent-leather feet*)—My Price is up!

MRS. GRACEDEW. (*Disappointed, stricken; echoing it as with a long wail.*) "Up"?

PRODMORE. (*Fairly enjoying the sound of her.*) Up, *up,* UP. Seventy Thousand.

MRS. GRACEDEW. (*As, called on for so high a stake, she turns away overwhelmed.*) Oh-h—deary *me!*

PRODMORE. (*Up at right, as to gain his carriage; immutable, absolute.*) It's to take or to *leave!*

MRS. GRACEDEW. (*Who has at first seemed to look at it as out there before them in the middle of the hall in all its monstrous exorbitance, and thereby as if only to "leave"; changing, making, also at right, a quick restraining sign up to* PRODMORE *at sight of* YULE *on the staircase; who, arrested for an instant half way by finding them together, then comes down with decision and at left, looks from one to the other;* MRS. GRACEDEW *meanwhile watching him arrive and drawing from him a supreme inspiration.*) Seventy Thousand then!

(*Re-enter* CAPTAIN YULE *by staircase.*)

PRODMORE. (*Having during* YULE'S *entrance but glared at him from where he stands; and continuing to glare even while* MRS. GRACEDEW, *with her rapid, dissimulated nearer approach, right, has launched her desperate figure.*) Seventy Thousand. Done! (*Exit* PRODMORE, *with Bang of Door, to ante-room and park.*)

YULE. (*At left, astonished.*) He's gone? I've been *looking* for him!

MRS. GRACEDEW. (*Agitated, breathless, in fact quite heaving; but doing her best to dissemble, to keep herself together and spoil nothing now by a mistake, pantingly.*) I don't think, you know, you *need* him—now.

YULE. (*Mystified.*) "Now"?

MRS. GRACEDEW. (*Smiling, though a little blown; but trying to be plausible, more coherent.*) I mean that—if you don't mind! (*With a vague awkward laugh*)—you must treat with *me.* I've arranged with Mr. Prodmore to take it over.

YULE. (*Perfectly blank, his hands in his pockets.*) Take *what* over?

MRS. GRACEDEW. (*As wondering, in embarrassment, when it comes to the point, what she can call it; but casting about also as if she misses, or would like, a little more help from his imagination or his readiness.*) Why, your Big Debt.

YULE. (*Only, however, the less helpful and the more bewildered.*) Can you—without "arranging" with *me?*

MRS. GRACEDEW. (*Moving about, nervous, turning it over as if as much as possible to oblige him.*) That's precisely what I want to do. (*Then more brightly and sociably, as she thinks further.*) That is, I mean, I want you to arrange with *me.* (*Smiling at him, encouraging to his dimness.*) Surely you will—won't you?

YULE. (*His dimness persisting in spite of her brightness.*) But if I arrange with anybody— (*Not able to see.*) How do I perform my Engagement?

MRS. GRACEDEW. (*Considering it as if he might have fifty.*) The one to Mr. Prodmore? You don't perform it.

YULE. (*As requiring a moment to take it in; but then with the leap of a light to his face.*) He lets me *off?*

MRS. GRACEDEW. (*As delighted to give him the news.*) He lets you off!

YULE. (*Taking it in further, making it out, staring before him; but then wincing, pulling himself up, clouded again.*) Oh I see—I lose my House!

MRS. GRACEDEW. (*Shocked at his simplifications.*) Dear no—*that* doesn't follow! (*After an instant.*) You simply arrange with *me* to keep it.

YULE. (*Sincerely wondering.*) "Simply"? (*Not making it out.*) How do I arrange?

MRS. GRACEDEW. (*As cheerfully, sociably preaching patience.*) Well, we must *think.* We must wait. (*As if it's a mere detail, only the principle granted; fairly talking as if to a reasonable child.*) We'll find some way all right!

YULE. (*Quite willing to hope so, yet failing completely to see; and with an awkward nervous laugh for it.*) Yes—but what way *shall* we find? (*Then as if he can think only of the impossible ways, the ways that don't fit now.*) With Prodmore, you see, (*with a still greater awkwardness for his having even thus indirectly to refer to it*) it was—as you say—"simple" enough.

MRS. GRACEDEW. (*Thinking, demurring, downright.*) I never called *that* simple!

YULE. (*As wondering what, and how much, she knows; defining, however ruefully, his relation to the* PRODMORE *terms.*) It was at any rate clear. (*After an instant.*) I could marry his Daughter.

MRS. GRACEDEW. (*As in slow, conscious amazement, pointed irony, long-drawn and fine.*) *Could* you?

YULE. He put it in such a way that I had to—a—(*then rapid short*) pretend to think of it. (*Then as she takes this from him, in all its dreadfulness, as it were, only with the silence of her so feeling for him; sociably.*) You didn't *suspect* that?

MRS. GRACEDEW. (*As if these personal appeals from him really touch her too much; breaking off from him as by the effect on her nerves of her positive excess of interest.*) Don't ask me too many questions!

YULE. (*Looking after her now as if he wonders why.*) But isn't this just the moment for Questions? (*Not following her but, by a movement, a turn, rather more quiet and effective than quick or sharp, meeting and arresting her where she comes down, or round; and speaking for the first time as if a care for the appearance and the impression he may have made finally concern him.*) What *did* you suppose?

MRS. GRACEDEW. (*Brushing, without indifference, past him, not stopping to say it, saying it as she goes.*) Why, I supposed you were in *distress.*

YULE. (*Placed so that he now, at left or wherever, looks after her again while she moves right.*) About his Terms?

MRS. GRACEDEW. (*Who has seated herself again right, while her last movement and manner have kept him, as it were, left with the stage between them.*) About his Terms, of course! (*Then as quietly amused.*) Not about his Religious Opinions.

YULE. (*His gratitude too great even for such mild gaiety as that; his perception and admiration all growing now for the sureness with which her instinct and her intelligence have guided her.*) You really—

in your beautiful sympathy—*guessed* my fix?

MRS. GRACEDEW. (*Seated, serenely diverted, not viewing this as so very much a miracle.*) Dear Captain Yule, it stuck too immensely *out* of you!

YULE. (*His smile just a trifly sickly, while he wonders at the figure he may have cut.*) You mean I gasped like a drowning man?

MRS. GRACEDEW. (*Assenting then with decision to this interpretation.*) Till *I* plunged in!

YULE. (*Considering her for a moment from where he stands; she meanwhile not looking at him, but either only straight before her or, as occupied with her own thought, at some slab of the old floor; then, however, turning away and keeping up left before he speaks.*) You *saved* me!

MRS. GRACEDEW. (*As accepting it, but not insisting on it; only, in all happy lucidity and recognised responsibility concluding from it.*) What a pity, now, *I* haven't a daughter!

YULE. (*Who has moved, in his meditation, as far up left, say, as door of garden, or perhaps only has hovered before the great chimney-place; arrested by this odd expression of hers; thinking of it a moment with his back still turned to her; then facing about, blank, challenging, for the question.*) What on earth should I do with her?

MRS. GRACEDEW. (*Frankly ironic, sympathetically amused at his expense; the space between them not diminished.*) You'd *treat* her, I hope, better than you've treated Miss Prodmore.

YULE. (*Pulled up, distressed, not expecting this implication; as colouring with shame.*) Then have I been *base*—?

MRS. GRACEDEW. (*Only looking at him at first, always across their interval, as in admiration of his incurable candour and in compassion for her own small joke; then impulsively, as for her similar ejaculations of a few moments before.*) Oh you sweet simple man!

YULE. (*From the same place; relieved then; his momentary fear carried off; though his modesty once more a little compromised by her so wonderful quaintness* and directness.) Of course—I'm all *right*, and I feel but one Regret: which however is Immense. (*Putting it perfectly before her.*) I've nothing—nothing whatever, not a scrap of Service nor a thing you'd care for—to offer you in Compensation.

MRS. GRACEDEW. (*Slowly rising now; standing there a moment before she speaks; and even showing amusement for the highly definite way in which he has put it.*) I'm not, as they say, "on the make." (*Then gravely and a bit proudly, though not the least pompously.*) I didn't do it for Payment!

YULE. (*Also after an instant, still where he was; but as if by some idea of his own, he now "has" her.*) What then did you do it for?

MRS. GRACEDEW. (*Who has not moved, either from her position directly before her chair, casting about, looking up and over the place as for some plausible account of her motive; then suddenly finding it.*) I did it because I hated Mr. Prodmore.

YULE. (*Wondering, sceptical.*) So much as all that?

MRS. GRACEDEW. Well, enough for inspiration. So now—! (*Goes to him and shakes his hand.*)

YULE. (*Dejectedly.*) You really fly?

MRS. GRACEDEW. (*Smiling, appropriating the image.*) I *try* to. (*Then as if really to finish.*) Good-bye.

YULE. (*Who has already, with quiet concentration, and as absolutely having to, got between her and the door up right; where he stands as to ignore or postpone or defeat her farewell.*) I said just now I had nothing to *offer* you. But of course I've the House *itself*.

MRS. GRACEDEW. (*Down to left where she has come to pick up or recover something; wondering, brightly staring.*) The House? Why I've *got* it!

YULE. (*With a motion as if this has no sense.*) "Got" it?

MRS. GRACEDEW. (*Explaining.*) All in my head, I mean. (*Confident, satisfied; making light of any other relation to it.*) That's all I *want*!

YULE. (*Puzzled; studying her; mistrust-*

ful of this.*) Why, I thought you *loved* it so!

MRS. GRACEDEW. (*Prompt, sincere.*) I love it far too much to deprive *you* of it.

YULE. (*Unshaken.*) How in the world would it be "depriving"—!

MRS. GRACEDEW. (*Prompt again; definite.*) It's enough that it would be turning you *out*.

YULE. (*With raised voice, in full contradiction and derision.*) Why, dear lady, I've never been *in*!

MRS. GRACEDEW. (*Undaunted—none the less positive.*) You're "in" now at any rate—I've *put* you and you've got to *stay*! (*Then as he looks round too woefully, throwing up his arms in the expression of that's not suiting him a whit, from the moment she thus takes herself off; allowing for this, attenuating.*) I don't mean *all* the while, but long enough—!

YULE. (*Not at all taking it—*) Long enough for *what*?

MRS. GRACEDEW. For me to feel you're here.

YULE. (*Unappeased.*) And how long will *that* take?

MRS. GRACEDEW. (*As she considers for him.*) Well, I suppose I strike you as very "fast"—but when I'm doing what I really *want* it takes me half a *lifetime*! (*Then further to satisfy him.*) I told you just now that I had arranged you *lose* nothing. Shall my very next step then make you lose Everything?

YULE. (*Very serious now; passing to left to keep her down, then as she moves right doing the same thing there; consciously opposing her; and speaking with abrupt force.*) Why do you surrender your interests?

MRS. GRACEDEW. (*Pulled up; with a pang for her pride at having to say; and thereby begging the question.*) Weren't you ready to surrender Yours?

YULE. (*Before her; clearer; more dominant now than he has been about anything.*) I hadn't any—so that was Nothing. I hadn't paid for them.

MRS. GRACEDEW. (*While he holds her at bay, though she keeps her distance from him; prompt with her reply.*) Your Ancestors had "paid"—it's the Same

Thing! (*Then as the best statement of their case possible.*) You're just in a manner my Tenant.

YULE. (*Repeating the word as to test it.*) Your "tenant"? (*Blank.*) On what Terms?

MRS. GRACEDEW. (*As if this is but a detail.*) Oh, on *any* terms! (*Then moving, as to circumvent him, to right.*) You can write me about them! (*Cheerful and clear, as to put him off his guard.*) I go right Back. (*Then rapidly gaining left.*) Farewell!

YULE. (*His rapidity greater; his presence at left effectual; his manner still all courteous, but intensely earnest; his idea of what he wants to know now dominant.*) Just one little moment, please. (*Then while she's obliged to wait.*) If you won't tell me your own terms, you must at least tell me Prodmore's.

MRS. GRACEDEW. (*Not facing this; turning away from it; able only unpreparedly to echo it.*) "Prodmore's"—?

YULE. (*Not moving from her path; very emphatic.*) Yes, Prodmore's. (*Quite "categorical."*) How you did it. How you managed it. (*As if he quite expects her to tell him.*) You bought him *out?*

MRS. GRACEDEW. (*Giving way, turning off, before the barrier he thus erects for her; but with a motion of her arms that makes nothing of what she has done— seems to define it as a case of her having paid ninepence.*) I bought him *out.*

YULE. (*Not believing in the ninepence.*) For how *much?* (*Then as she now has turned her back; while he watches her move off; though keeping, guardedly, as it were, on a parallel line.*) You see I really must *know!*

MRS. GRACEDEW. (*Very determined, keeping away from him.*) You shall *never* know!

YULE. (*Equally emphatic; not seeing her face.*) I'll get it from *him!*

MRS. GRACEDEW. (*Throwing up and dropping her hands; very firmly but slowly and rather sadly shaking her head while she moves.*) Get it if you *can!*

YULE. (*Struck, with this while he watches her; sharply affected, but with an intense little pause before he speaks.*) He won't say because he *did* you?

MRS. GRACEDEW. (*Who has stopped, at this, in her slow movement, and then, after an instant's thought, turns round to him, shaking her head again in the same way.*) He'll never, *never* say!

YULE. (*Held there, the space between them being now considerable, by the expression of her face and voice, and by the sharper sense of what the whole thing, her determination not to speak in particular, may mean; then bringing it out with deep resentment.*) The Scoundrel!

MRS. GRACEDEW. (*Raising her two hands, holding them up, with authority, as if, for reasons of her own, to check that tone, which is in a manner an injustice.*) Not a bit a "scoundrel." A Victim. (*Then while she faces Yule.*) I was only too "smart" for him. (*After which as with a highly abrupt flare coming back to her purpose and moving upon him.*) So now let me go!

YULE. (*"All there" indeed now; impassable; his arms out, to prevent her, as if all across the hall; immensely protesting.*) With this heroic Proof of your Power, this Barren Beauty of your Sacrifice? (*Ardent, eloquent.*) You pour out Money, you move a Mountain, and to let you "go," to bow you stupidly *out* and close the Door *behind* you, is all my poor Wit can think of? (*His emotion trembling out of him like the stammer of a new language; but of which, in an instant, before her there, he is already master.*) You're the most Generous, you're the Noblest of women! (*Breathless.*) The wonderful Chance that brought you here—!

MRS. GRACEDEW. (*To whom he is now, in his ardour, so near that she has but to put her hand straight out—which she does, all beautifully—to grasp his arm and stay his words.*) It brought *you* at the same happy hour! (*Very simply and sincerely.*) I've done what I *liked* (*with an exquisite, a satisfied, accepting shrug*)—and the only way to "thank" me is to Believe it.

YULE. (*In full possession of his powers now.*) You've done it for a proud, poor man; who has nothing—in the light of such a magic as yours!—either to *give* or to *hope;* but whom you've made, in an hour of Mysteries and Miracles, think of you as he has thought of no Other Woman! (*Then while, under this final, this per-*

sonal possession of her, she has to take it from him, his eloquence, his coherency drop, and he can fall but to pleading.) Mrs. Gracedew—don't *leave* me! (*He signalises, with immense breadth, the whole place, glowing now with the more and more lovely hour.*) If you've made me care—!

MRS. GRACEDEW. (*Dropping sharply, his arm, which she has still been holding; interrupting him with a laugh of joy that disengages both of them; so that, as having got now all she has dreamt of, she can again put space between them.*) It was surely that *you* had made *me* first!

YULE. (*Accepting the space now; watching her, as she moves, as if no longer fearing her flight and completing the words she has launched upon the air; speaking as with a clear and definite vision gained.*) Then let us go *on* caring! (*Earnestly developing.*) When I begged you a while back to lay for me some simple plank across the dizzy gulf of my so sudden new Source of Credit, you merely put off the question—told me I must trust to Time for it. Well (*firmer and firmer*) I've trusted to Time so effectually that ten little minutes have *shown* me my wondrous Bridge: made of the finest, firmest, fairest material that ever spanned a deep Predicament. (*Keeping it up; gallant and clear with his image.*) If I've found where to *pass*—and how—it's simply because I've found You. (*Then for his fine climax; immensely definite.*) May I *keep* then, Mrs. Gracedew, *Everything* I've found? I offer you in return the only things I have to give—I offer you my Hand and my Life.

MRS. GRACEDEW. (*Holding off from him, across the hall, the entire space between them now, she decidedly left and he right; with an intensity of suspended response that may almost pass as a plea for further postponement, or even as a plea for mercy —in respect to so immediate a sequel to her deeds; though it is all a rich, deep, full response that comes out as she happily, expressively wails.*) Ah, Captain Yule—!

YULE. (*As she drops, and they both see* CHIVERS *up right; re-enter* CHIVERS *from ante-room, by whom his master is much*

disconcerted; veritably glowering.) What the devil *is* it?

CHIVERS. (*Characteristically pained at having to intrude, to nip in the bud, as it were, the fragrance that his fine old sensibility feels in the air; but only knowing his traditional duty.*) Another Party.

MRS. GRACEDEW. (*Instantly touched by this; in possession again of all her resources; delighted.*) The Party "up"? (*Resolute, rising to the occasion.*) Show them *in*! (*Exit* CHIVERS *to ante-room.*)

YULE. (*Astonished, alarmed; wailing across at her.*) You'll *have* them?

MRS. GRACEDEW. (*Sublime; tossing it back at him for all it's worth.*) Mayn't I be Proud of my House?

YULE. (*Radiant at this speech, raising up his arms from where he stands.*) Then you accept—?

MRS. GRACEDEW. (*Her arms, down at left, raised higher still, but with the fine spread, commanding, controlling movement by which a leader holds his big orchestra in check before the first note.*) Hush!

(*Re-enter* CHIVERS *in conduct again of a Party, ushering them down centre as he has ushered the previous, but making the most, this time, of more scanty material as to number, though more important and showy as to appearance and class: four or five persons of the eye-glassed, satchelled, shawled and hand-booked order that suggests a preponderantly American origin and a tourist habit; the appearance of a greater familiarity with remarkable houses and the general practice of behaving in them, when on view, rather as in the halls of big hotels, looking about with expert eyes and free sounds while they wait for rooms to be assigned.* YULE *gives way before them, instinctively edging off and, as he has been at right, passing impatiently behind them to get round and up to left and toward door of garden where he is furthest removed from them.* MRS. GRACEDEW, *on the other hand, in-*

stinctively does the opposite; awaiting them serenely in front of great chimney-place, whence she commands the clustered group, for which CHIVERS *has had his various immemorial motions and arrangements, several of which, as the taking from them of pointed instruments, sticks and umbrellas that they may dangerously poke at things, and the offering them of old catalogue-cards, on handles, like stiff fans, constitutes here a sufficient by-play. In these proceedings, though they are not too prolonged, but rapid, direct, and business-like, expressive of perfect expertness, detachment and world-weary automatism on* CHIVER'S *part,* MRS. GRACEDEW *frankly and unshrinkingly loses herself; the little business making a vivid interval during which the Tourists consider unreservedly the beautiful unperturbed lady, her person and her wonderful clothes, very much as if she's a part of the Show, one of the highly interesting Features; and she on her side returning their regard with a placid relish that expresses all the interest she promises herself now to extract from a future of these processions. It is after they have well taken her in, though glancing at their catalogues first as if she may really be mentioned in them, that, not finding her apparently "down" there, they address themselves to a reference to other objects;* CHIVERS *having, when he has marshalled them in row and properly supplied them, given them their cue by pointing, with a now-assumed wand of office, to the first in order of the dark pictures ranged on the most advantageous wall. The cue is immediately taken by one of the American gentlemen.)*

TOURIST. (*Catching in hand; very loud and familiar.*) The regular thing—fine old Family Portraits?

CHIVERS. (*Highly superior, ignoring familiarity and beginning, with a flourish*

of his wand, in the right place.*) Dame Dorothy Yule—who lived to a Hundred-and-Five.

TOURISTS. (*Together; much impressed.*) A Hundred-and-Five! Is that so?

TOURIST. (*With the habit of jocose comment.*) You must have a fine old Healthy Place!

MRS. GRACEDEW. (*From her position; uncontrollably; with the highest geniality and very rapidly.*) Yes, it's Fine, and it's Old, and it's Healthy—and it's perfectly Lovely!

CHATTY AMERICAN LADY. You tried it Long?

MRS. GRACEDEW. (*Prompt.*) No—but I'm trying it Now! (*Smiling at them sociably.*) You see we're not *all* a Hundred-and-Five. (*Then as* CHIVERS, *in his regular way, has raised his wand to the next portrait in order, her pointing arm directs their heads to it at the same time.*) John Anthony Yule; who passed away—poor Duck! in his flower!

(CAPTAIN YULE *has during this passage reached the garden door where he has restlessly turned about again, watching the scene and coming down, toward the chimney-place, left of* CHIVERS *and the Party; so that, irresistibly drawn back, he has approached* MRS. GRACEDEW *when the same inquirer speaks again.*)

CHATTY LADY. (*Indicating the portrait of the gentleman in the white trunk-hose, with the long legs, hung over door of garden; to whom* CHIVERS *has already raised his wand.*) And this *Funny* One—?

MRS. GRACEDEW. (*Who, with* YULE *close upon her now, is conscious only of him, and who takes his arm, drawing him beside her, as to present him, while she answers the* CHATTY LADY.) Oh, this Funny One's my Husband!

CHATTY LADY. (*Whose place is such that she is the first all sympathetically to take it, while she immediately imparts it to the Others, who stand in line down to right, each passing it to next, as in confidential Discretion and Interest.*) Her Husband. Her Husband. Her Husband.

YULE. (*Beside her, her arm in his, opposite to the Party, which he now addresses, while they smilingly and admiringly accept the presentation; while* CHIVERS, *centre staring at this announcement, yet instinctively straightens himself, his wand upright, his posture erect and official, his expression inscrutable; and while the Curtain is about to fall.*) And *this* Funny One's my Wife!

Rough Statement for Three Acts
Founded on

The Chaperon

1907

EDITOR'S FOREWORD

On November 12, 1907, James sent off to Forbes-Robertson his completed three act *High Bid*. Two days later, his interest in the stage now thoroughly revived, he re-read his old 1893 note on *The Chaperon* (*see* page 457) and dictated the "Rough Statement" which follows, breaking off in the middle and never returning to it. Miss Bosanquet's notes reveal that he decided it was more important to get on with a one-act curtain raiser to go with *The High Bid* which, despite its three acts, still did not fill out an evening.

This fragment of a scenario, which James calls also his "notes of Character and Design" can be taken as an example of the statements, notes, projects—he had different terms for them at different times—James set down for his plays, for his own use, during the 1890's. It is quite likely that the earlier ones were more succinct, since they ante-dated the period when James began to dictate his work directly to the typewriter. The "Rough Statement" in its manuscript form is "rough" indeed; apparently, since he never resumed dictating it, he never reread the sheets, and they survive as they fell from the typewriter, often unpunctuated and with the occasional lapses in style and grammar resulting from uncorrected dictation. The text has been printed here as it stands with only the insertion of a few commas as an aid to readability. In one of his short stories James described such scenarios as "the overflow into talk of an artist's amorous plan." The statement for *The Chaperon* takes its place with the notes for the unfinished novels *The Sense of the Past* and *The Ivory Tower*. It is quite distinct from the "projects" prepared by the novelist for magazines or publishers giving them the plan of his work (as in the case of the project for *The Ambassadors* or the outline for *The Bostonians*). The rough statement was intended for James's eyes alone and in the normal course of events would have been destroyed when it had outlived its usefulness.

James himself indicates the use to which he put it "step by step, inch by inch, one silver thread of the tangle handled at a time. . . ." The statement indicates how, in writing his plays, as in his novels, he accounted for every detail, "fixed" each person, gave each scene its plausible background and context.

The idea for *The Chaperon* in its original short story form was first noted by James at the Marine Hotel, Kingstown, Ireland on July 13, 1891, where he had gone to recuperate from a bad attack of influenza—the story of a young girl who decides to "chaperon" her mother (a woman with a "past"—she had left her husband and gone off with another man) and to reinstate her in her social position in London. Five days after his original note, he wrote to Horace

Scudder, editor of the *Atlantic Monthly,* that he would send him a "thing in two parts called *The Chaperon."* Two days later he had completed the first part, and eight days later the second. The story appeared in the *Atlantic* of November and December 1891 and was republished in *The Real Thing* in 1893.

ROUGH STATEMENT FOR THREE ACTS
FOUNDED ON
THE CHAPERON

Irresistible the pressure of inducement just to break ground, if nothing more, for a first go at the elements involved in this application of my idea; as nothing is done till one begins actively to grope, till one makes something in the nature of a start, however false, and with no matter how many steps to retrace and how many merely experimental *percées* into the vague or into the impossible one may make. This is the only way the possible comes; one must explore the country right and left, leaving no square foot of it untrodden or unsearched.

What I seem then to have got hold of, essentially, for the basis of my Exposition is the Occasion of the girl's—that is of Rose Tramore's—keeping for convenience the little names, provisionally, of the Tale—Birthday, or coming of age, or whatever; I mean the date at which, under the terms of her Father's will, her freedom of action practically begins. This seems to me very arrangeable, quite without difficulty; she simply comes of age, comes into her little money, which isn't very much, at twenty-one, quite as if she were a boy. The fact that an entertainment of some sort, of however mild an order, should commemorate this circumstance, may not on the face of it appear extraordinarily natural, but may be made so, quite easily, with moderate tact and ingenuity. It has only to by sufficiently *constaté* that the young Tramores, the three of them, have always, ever since their domiciliation with their Grandmother, enjoyed this little institution of the birthday-party, by an amiable family tradition, and by the epicurean humour in especial of their late Father, whose habit it has been to make up for a good deal of light and easy neglect of them (leaving them altogether to his Mother and Miss Tramore) by these three little commemorations or recreations in the year, one for each, for which he has provided conjurors, or fiddlers, or birthday cakes, or whatever, in the past; and for which he would now presumably do the thing more handsomely, were he alive to adorn with his presence this important date for his eldest child. What I am supposing is that he has been dead for rather more than a year, and that to-day is precisely a sign of the coming out of mourning, as it were, of the two Girls, who have practically stayed at home, so to speak, ever since; with the first appearances in the "world" of each of them, the first small social launching of the elder in particular, prematurely overdarkened by their bereavement, and above all by their highly sincere and decorous observance of it: an observance that has in Rose's case seemed rather excessive and overdone even to old Mrs. Tramore and to Julia T.; whom I see as somehow a bit irritated and ruffled in advance by this first symptom of the Girl's capacity for her own view and system and little private idea and conviction, firmly grasped and quietly, persistently applied, about everything. The boy is at his crammer's or wherever, and though probably present to-day, I make out no urgent use for him; the two others have then been living, in their old way, with their Grandmother, though of course, I must be careful to note, not absolutely buried; Rose having necessarily had to form the few social relations that immediately come into play: which, as this must be perfectly clear, I conceive her having formed during the year of her first "coming out"; the brief time between that event and her Father's death, during which she went about more or less under his easy and highly adequate protection, making the acquaintance of the sort of people he knew, "good" society, the best, essentially; into which her prettiness, cleverness, all the attributes it is necessary she should have, have made him quite happy and proud to be able to introduce her. It is from that time, for instance, that her acquaintance with Lady Maresfield dates, and the marking her for her own, then and there, by that lady, who has seen how beautifully she will probably do for the young up-growing, up-climbing, Guy. In connection with which remember that the little share of her patrimony that she comes into must be something of a respectable thing; the figure of it, with a thousand other items and values, to be fixed at closer quarters; as well as the very important matter of her further, though her wholly contingent, expectations from Old Mrs. Tramore; who can give or withhold quite according to her own pleasure and to the attitude taken by each of these young beneficiaries. It is highly conspicuous, of course, that she can "cut off" Rose at her discretion, if sufficiently displeased with her, and can divide everything between her unmarried middle-aged Daughter and her Son's two other children; who are such quite other affairs than Rose, and so comparatively plastic and, as it were, abject. But meanwhile, at any rate, Rose has enough of her own not only to "go on" with, but to make Lady Maresfield, not to speak of others, regard it as a "factor," a potential one, in an appreciable prospective income for Guy. It mustn't be presented as imperceptible to the other young man either, the young man who figures in the Tale as the rather priggish and precautionary, but really decent and sincere and loyal, Captain of Engineers, Bertram Jay; but whose profession, situation etc., I must now visibly alter to something more Contributive. I postulate that he will have met her first, and got his impression and so forth, during the year of her so distinctly successful little going-about before the subsequent sequestration; the continuity and consistency of which, *par parenthèse*, it would be admirable to be able to make salient as one of the many sharp, effective Notes of Character and Design, of intelligent choice and the Long View, on the part of my young woman. She has seen him since, but only three or four times, as she has seen also the youth presented in the Tale as Guy Manger; but has seen nothing much of anyone, as we definitely make out, and has really spent her time in nursing the conscious purpose and storing up the precious courage, to which it is the function of Act First to represent her as giving effect to in the most conspicuous and interesting and "dramatic" manner possible. Bertram Jay has had contact with old Mrs. Tramore, who approves and favours him and on whom—this being an Element of almost the first Value—she exactly counts to throw his weight, with Rose, on *her,* the old woman's side, in the conflict of judgment, opinion, in fine sharp and decisive action, which she has begun, though within a very short time, to see brewing and looming and darkening the domestic prospect, between herself and her Granddaughter. I make it out that Jay's function in this act is essentially to represent, to Rose, in common with Julia Tramore, the old woman's high and passionate, at any rate absolutely rigid and final view of the situation: I see him as yet, so far as I grope my way, for the time lucidly confined to that function. Her break with him is thus part and parcel of her break with her Grandmother, her Aunt, her Brother, and her Sister; her ultimatum to him part and parcel of her ultimatum to *them;* her making up her mind, luminously, insurmountably, to do without him so far as any further Discussion is concerned, but the other face of her preparedness, which I should like, I seem to make out, to be the subject of a little separate scene with each (save that here, at this stage, are of course abysses for further sounding) to do without most of the things that have made up her life hitherto. Salient, moreover, before I go further—and it bears on the question of her actual "means"—the high value of her definite "forfeit," as the price of her perversity: it being important for my purpose that she should forfeit something still more tangible than her place "in the Family" and the sympathy and esteem, the very intercourse, as it were, of the other members of it. She must forfeit money in some marked and eminent degree; she must bring money, in some degree or other, to her Mother—it is even one of her motives; yet I must reconcile this with her still having that which may still keep her in question for Lady Maresfield and such-like, during the period of her sacrifice and her ostracism. Apropos of which, at the same time, I recall that these designs of the Importunate are precisely to get her to give her Mother up, to renounce her missionary work, her quixotic campaign, as the bad job it is one of the Functions of Act Second to make it superficially appear; and so go back to the loaves and fishes, to the recovery and realisation of her possible prospects, that is, if she makes it up with the scandalised old woman before the latter dies disinheriting her. To put it simply and provisionally, just to get it down, Mrs. Tramore, the elder, has resources her share of which, conditioned on "good terms," may accrue to her; and Miss Tramore has the same—the latter and Bertram Jay being, with the Brother and Sister, indeed, if I "drag *them* in," (all, as yet here, however, preliminary darkness) the immediate expository mouth-piece of these stern realities. By which I probably mean, in fact, by which I still more prettily and interestingly mean, I daresay, that, after having had all the needful home-truths about her Step from the three others, it is she herself

who is the most, who charmingly becomes the most, authoritative exponent
of them to the more or less deputed and delegated, the earnest, the anxious,
the remonstrant, the supplicating, but the altogether baffled and discomfited,
Jay. It in fact rises before me Interesting that, face to face with this question of
Who the presented Agents here are limited or multiplied to; face to face with
the question of keeping them down in First only to such as may be Agents and
Values again in Second and Third; it glimmers beautifully, I say, that the
young man, here through may, more effectively than not, do the whole business of old Mrs. Tramore, by his acting, speaking, comporting himself, in her
name and at her behest; she having adopted him thus as her candidate and
solemnly laid it on him to do what he can. I see this is an Artful Simplification,
an accretion of value and interest for him; and as ministering, in fine, to my in
every way sublime Economy. The Brother and Sister, Eric and Edith, say,
have very conceivable uses wrapped up in them for Third; and Julia Tramore
not less, she being presumably of the first degree of Designation for First; on
the basis of involved sequences, later, finally, catastrophically, of all due vividness. Thus I get for the present Opposition the four persons thus named, with
the further Social Adjuncts to be gone into. Step by step, inch by inch, one
silver thread of the tangle handled at a time.

Old Mrs. Tramore, then, must be, I descry, conveniently, yet rather amply
and "handsomely" suburban; this the most workable basis, I piously, if not
presumptuously, judge, for my fundamental dispositions in Act First. What
I thus sketchily see, to begin with, is the bright and beautiful afternoon, early
in June, on which Rose's birthday-party is taking place, with people out from
town in carriages, in motors even, *supposons,* and by train, a number of people
sufficient to show the effort the fine old hostess has made to have a bright and
copious muster of old friends—on the basis of cards sent out three weeks before
and the further little fact that the high pitch of the Crisis (between herself and
Rose) has come only after the invitations have been issued: so that things have
been left as they are rather than cancelled—all the more that the old woman
doesn't really know the "length" to which Rose has, all the while, really been
going: the length, that is, of communication with her Mother already entered
into, though she has obeyed the letter of her Father's wishes and impositions,
by not yet having been to see her. She has only let her know, definitely, that
she comes, and comes to stay, the Hour she is Free. Technically speaking, perhaps, she is not free till the day has wholly elapsed; so that, giving her plan the
benefit of this doubt, she has determined to take her flight, to begin this new relation, only on the morrow. A part of the Function of Act First is to show this
patience as more or less violently modified, to show her Departure, to show the
Step in short, as dramatically precipitated. Wherewith, one promptly discerns,
one of one's first cares is to establish and set forth, as an almost prime preliminary, how much of a shadow, in the form of a shock, a scandal, a general and
particular flurry and chatter, this Coming Event has cast before it. Here spreads
itself precisely, therefore, one of those Visions of Beauty which consist of the

right, the felicitous and triumphant Determination of the March of the exhibited Case; the creation of the process or picture by which Clearness and Interest become complete; stage adding itself to stage, suspense to suspense, appearance to appearance, and the whole thing logically and dramatically developing.
It is of the essence, in other words, that the ground is first thoroughly laid, up
to the last point of excited expectation and curiosity, for our view of the
particular thing that is happening, as to which our knowledge grows minute by
minute; and that then from a given moment Rose's advent takes it all up,
where artful Preparation has left it off, simply stationing itself at the right
point to hand it over to her; and that *with* this appearance or irruption she takes
it completely in charge to climax. But the Preparation here will have to be of
the most consummate; which is but a reason, an inspiration and a value the more.

Roughly speaking, then, old Mrs. Tramore is out in the grounds, where the
beautiful day permits all the best of everything to go forward; and we have
the sufficient image of her reported, reflected, and borne in to us by a pointed
reference and echo, while our own immediate picture is constituted in the
Drawingroom of the house, open to the terrace, verandah, lawn and whatever,
and serving as a partial place of transit and arrest; also rendered comparatively
private and proper for my uses by the fact that everyone instinctively goes
further, has been "shown through," as it were; no one pausing, lingering, or
making use of it without such good reasons as our action brings into play and
makes them conform to. Admirably interesting and appealing, always, this
question of one's first "struck" note; the determination, really mathematical
in its logic, of the point furthest back and yet at the same time nearest to, at
which one's March must visibly, audibly, fruitfully begin; as with the concentrated germ of the Whole of the Rest folded up in it. There is always question of
the sufficiently Far Back for Clearness, and the sufficiently Near To for Straight-
ness and Immediacy. Well, I seem, till the contrary is proved, to clutch that point
here with the production of the two Young Men, as I call them, the youths who
figure, so very slightly, in the Tale as Eric Tramore and Guy Manger, but who
here immediately acquire an appreciable value. I seem to make out, for experiment, that, at rise of Curtain, the young Eric, coming in from the Grounds,
meets the Butler just introducing the young Manger, to whom he says—the
Butler does—that everyone is outside, but that he can pass through this way.
Important, evidently, that there must be the appearance of two Ways out to
where everyone is gathered; a way, and especially a course of Egress and Departure (always from the Grounds) more directly connected with the Entrance
to the House; so that there is the presumption, the indication, of coming and
going, but in particular of going, independently of this passage through the
Drawingroom; it being marked that the latter becomes thus the scene of such
passages, encounters and contacts as are specially motived and conditioned there.
Another point to make here instantly, further reflection shows me, is that the
Occasion, at rise of Curtain, is already waning to its close, though the long
June afternoon still is bright; and that the main movement is the ebb of

the tide, the stream of departure so that the latter part of the act, the whole Climax, finds the principal Agents free and unencumbered. Putting aside the three other persons I have here next to deal with (I mean after Eric and Guy), there can be no entrance, of any outsider, save for the purpose of getting away. What glimmers to me now, at any rate, is that the Butler *first* shows young Manger in, with an "Oh yes, sir, you can as *well* go this way: the Ladies receive in the Grounds" and that it is just as the visitor is about to pass across and out to the visible Terrace or whatever, that the young Eric comes in from that quarter, greeting him with an: "Oh yes, you're very late, but you can get *through*; though if you'll wait a moment I'll take you." This note of the youth's lateness is emphasised, with some reference to the fact that people are moving off; and with some occasion for Guy to ask if his Mother is still there; with the answer on the other's part as to Lady Maresfield's—Oh yes!— "sticking"; and perhaps even to the presence of the sister, Mrs. Vaughan-Vesey of the Tale, a Value, I assume, for later on; and part of the sign of the way the family have rallied. What is instant, at any rate, here, is Eric's motive for hurry-ing in, indicated by an immediate sign to the Butler to wait, even while he receives the other youth, with whom I conceive for him considerable identity of futile type, age, occupation, and vague state of preparation for some "smart" profession; presumably, on the whole, not military. Eric sends the Butler up to his room for a certain box of precious cigarettes—those Granny provides being (for young Manger) so beastly; producing ring of keys from his pocket and giv-ing him instructions where to look, so that some minutes are provided thus for the Butler's absence while the two young men wait; Guy indicating, for that matter, his preference and purpose to wait; with a good little touch of reinforcement in fact thus glimmering upon me. He carries in his hand a small, or indeed a rather ridiculously large, box done up in white paper and pink ribbon, a tribute in the form of chocolate-creams, marrons glacés, or whatever that he has brought in the form of a birthday offering to the young Rose; but that he has immediately become shy, self-conscious, and awkward about, on finding it a question of his sallying forth with it across the lawn and presenting it before a lot of people. I am not sure even—since one must thresh out every alternative—that he may not have an initial passage with the Butler before Eric appears; the Butler having relieved him of his parcel and, having, also, as we learn and see, introduced him into Drawingroom at his rather flurried and preoccupied request, and standing there with the beribboned object delicately held to await his indications.

All outside, sir: Mrs. Tramore receives in the Grounds.
Then could you—ah—carry that out for me?
(*Very grave.*) Leaving you to—a—follow sir?
Oh no, I'd go with you. But I don't like to take it myself.
Nothing to—a—go off, sir?
Oh dear no—(*then rueful*) unless chocolate-creams, in large masses, *do* explode

(*On which the* BUTLER, *who naturally has his business at the Door to attend to, availing himself impenetrably of this pretext.*) I had better perhaps place them here, sir—according to your first Idea.

(*The young* MANGER, *swayed by every breath, is constitutionally flurried, and agitatedly embraces this amendment.*) It *was* my Idea—where she'll see them; and perhaps wonder—!

In which case should I mention, sir—?

Oh yes, *do* mention; or (*as he sees* ERIC *come in*) perhaps, my dear chap, *you* kindly would! (*Then as* ERIC *takes in with surprise the very large beribboned box, with very big bows, that the* BUTLER *has now set down.*) Chocolate-creams— for Miss Rose!

ERIC. (*Who, entering from Terrace, has signed to* BUTLER *to wait, but is also amused at size of box.*) Half a Ton?

GUY. (*Complacent though flushed.*) For her Birthday!

ERIC. I'm afraid I should have to mention the Number as fatal. But do it yourself—they're all out there.

GUY. (*Who, by large open glass doors, has looked out, pulling himself up, rather, apparently, at what he sees; while the* BUTLER *approaches* ERIC, *who unhooks from left-hand pocket-button of his trousers a silver key-chain, with rings and several keys attached.*) I should like you to *take* me out!

ERIC. I *will*—with my Cigarettes. (*To* BUTLER, *who takes the keys from him.*) The *best* tin box in one of my locked drawers: search 'em *all* till you find it! I'll wait. (*After which, while* BUTLER *goes out and he turns to* GUY.) Granny's are too beastly!

GUY. (*Coming away from window; simple, surprised.*) Is Mrs. Tramore smoking?

ERIC. (*With fine youthful impatience and importance.*) For all I know—she has so lost her head!

GUY. (*Wondering, interested, but never anything if not simple.*) Through having such a Crowd?

ERIC. (*Prompt, sharp.*) Through having such a Grand-daughter.

GUY. (*As thinking quite to seize the point.*) Do you mean your so awfully successful Sister?

ERIC. (*Emphatic, resentful.*) I mean my Sister Rose, whose Success strikes me as mainly in setting us All—I mean all of us who have lived together here with Granny since Papa's Death: Aunt Julia and Edith and Me, you know—most awkwardly by the Ears; and in availing herself, for the purpose of this handsome Celebration—though I do say it!—of her Twenty First Birthday.

GUY. (*Anxious, alarmed.*) You don't mean to say she has gone and got Engaged?

ERIC. (*Youthfully superior; his thumbs in his waistcoat armholes; his eyes on the other a moment.*) There are more ways than that, old Chap, of making a Fool of yourself!

GUY. (*Gloomy, vague.*) And that's what she's doing—?

ERIC. (*Distinct, definite.*) What she's doing is to make some such Exhibitions of all of *us*—and above all such an Exhibition, as one may say, of the Character and Conduct of our late admirable Father who, in a most important particular, took pains to lay down the Right Line for us. From that Line Rose has just proclaimed it her intention to Deviate.

GUY. (*At sea, imperfectly following.*) "Proclaimed" it—before the Crowd?

ERIC. (*In his own manner.*) Before the Crowd assembled—but not in time, most unfortunately, to *prevent* its assembling.

GUY. (*Mystified but impressed.*) She's up to something, you mean, to put off a Party for?

ERIC. (*Like an approved man of character, and above all of action.*) I'd have put it off—if we had known it in Time. But she spoke but this Morning.

GUY. (*More and more anxious.*) What then did she speak of?

ERIC. (*Bringing it out with gravest effect.*) She spoke of Mamma.

GUY. (*Enlightened, relieved, even a little amused.*) Oh—I see!

ERIC. (*With the same high gravity.*) We don't speak of Mamma. (*Then for return of* BUTLER.) So hush! (*To* BUTLER.) Put them down.

GUY. (*While* BUTLER *places cigarette-box and goes out.*) But do you mean it affects *my* Chance?

ERIC. (*Who has gone to the table and taken out a cigarette; sniffing it.*) I didn't know you *had* a "chance"! (*Then as he passes him one.*) Will you have a Cigarette?

GUY. (*Distressed, though taking the cigarette.*) You haven't known about it all this Time?

ERIC. (*Impatient, lighting his cigarette, but, in his preoccupation, offering the other no light.*) Known about what?

GUY. (*Almost touchingly simple.*) Why, that—more than fifteen months ago— she Refused me.

ERIC. (*Smoking.*) Ah, fifteen months ago she Refused fifty fellows! That was before Papa's Death.

GUY. (*Definite.*) The year she came out—so tremendously Out! (*Ingenuous.*) She refused me twice.

ERIC. (*Dry.*) Do you want her to do it again?

GUY. (*Embarrassed, rueful, even slightly boobyish; scratching his thigh and looking askance at the big box.*) That wasn't what I brought those Sweets for!

ERIC. Hadn't you then better eat them yourself? I don't think it a particularly good moment for you to try again.

GUY. Oh! (*Then his eyes still a bit sheepishly and shamefacedly askance on his massive tribute.*) My Mother, you know, supposed that—with the Day and all, the charming Celebration and the happy Occasion it rather *would* be; and she directed me herself therefore to bring with me some nice little thing that would *please.*

ERIC. (*Amused.*) Ah, so that's your idea—? Well, you quite sufficiently "please" —yourself, my dear fellow,—however you come; please all of us together, I mean, so that I'm sure we're very glad to see you. But (*after an instant, with decision*) I think there's something you ought to know.

GUY. (*With a slight awkward hesitation, as from delicacy.*) Well, there are a lot of things that my Mother has told me!

ERIC. (*With a return of his dryness.*) It's your Mother then that takes the principal interest—?

GUY. (*All candidly.*) Why, isn't she here now—what she calls preparing the ground for me?

ERIC. She is here, I believe, and has been for the last couple of hours: I've encountered Lady Maresfield, I confess, at every turn of the Garden. But I doubt that she can have told you what she can't possibly *know;* and what I think, (*after further consideration, then with emphasis and importance*) I had better mention to you, without delay; to clear your mind—or at least to clear your Mother's!—of any fond hopes for which we might, later on, be held responsible!

GUY. (*Plaintively, conscientiously.*) Ah, but my Mother's mind *is* so terribly clear!

ERIC. (*Turning on him with a certain superior pity.*) Not, I take it, about the terms of my Father's Will—which have hitherto been nobody's business but our own, but which I think, from to-day, should really be, like Lost Articles, advertised to "Whom it may Concern."

GUY. (*With a foolish, awkward, yet amiable, laugh.*) It's at least her notion— if you press me!—that you're not, you know, half badly off!

ERIC. (*Throwing up his hands in sharp impatience, breaking off, taking a turn, but then facing round again as with importance and resolution.*) Do you know anything about Mamma?

GUY. (*Much of the space of the room between them; looking at him an instant and speaking not without a certain mild "point."*) You *do* speak of her then?

ERIC. (*Unperturbed.*) I never *have,* in the whole Course of my Days—but (*as justifying it to him completely*) Rose has now made it necessary we should do so One for All.

GUY. I've at least always heard that Mrs. Tramore is lovely.

ERIC. (*Very straight, grave and* digne.) So lovely that my Father was—at an early stage—forced to take Action.

GUY. (*Half confessing, half wondering.*) You mean there was a Row?

ERIC. (*Superior; not faltering.*) In the Divorce-Court—yes: when—by Papa's Decree, to say nothing of that of the Court itself *we* were too young to know. Since when we've never so much as seen her.

GUY. (*Artlessly but irrepressibly pleased at this advantage.*) *I* have—at the Opera.

ERIC. (*With high propriety.*) We've never—in view of that Danger so much as *been* to the Opera. (*Reconstituting, presenting, their young Annals, their past History.*) We made Papa that sacrifice—as we made him all those of which, as

I'm free to confess to you I think with all justice, he made, to the day of his Death, such an absolute point. We remained *his*—and I—for it sharply marks my Position—consider that we're His still; that we're in fact now His more than ever.

GUY. (*Impressed, interested, but slightly abashed and a good deal mystified.*) Do you mean that Mrs. Tramore—a—thinks—

ERIC. (*Breaking straight in.*) We've not the least idea what Mrs. Tramore thinks: it was settled in our Infancy that that was the *last* thing that was good for us. It was Papa's Arrangement that we were to live in Ignorance; and the Arrangement has perfectly *worked*. So we *have* lived—save for losing Him; "immune," as they say—till Rose takes this extraordinary occasion to start up and spoil All!

GUY. (*Following, but at a loss.*) But what does she want to do?

ERIC. (*As if it's so much more than enough.*) She wants to See her.

GUY. (*Wondering.*) And you consider that she *mayn't*—?

ERIC. Not if I can possibly prevent it!

GUY. (*After an instant; watching, as in suspense, his movements.*) Can you possibly prevent it?

ERIC. (*Arrested; his hands in his pockets, his shoulders up; after reflection.*) No. (*Then to explain.*) Rose is a Case.

GUY. (*As with, after all, his own opinion.*) She's a Brick—that's what I think, you know, she is!

ERIC. (*Dry, unmoved, ironic.*) You strike me as exactly expressing the Degree of her Sensibility! I mean, to the weight of Papa's high Example and Authority.

GUY. (*Yielding, conceding.*) Oh, of course she ought to mind—!

ERIC. (*Distinct, definite.*) She ought to mind her younger Sister, she ought to mind her elder Brother, she ought to mind her fine—and, I recognise, *firm*—old Granny, who has harboured us here from far back, and who remains the previous Vessel, as it were, of Papa's beautiful Influence. She ought, above all, to mind Public Propriety—and (*with significance*) a Lot more Things besides.

GUY. (*Who has taken this in as rather portentous; turning it over.*) Do you suppose my Mother's Appeal—

ERIC. (*Curt; sceptical; having quite, by his exhibition of his case, worked himself up to exasperation; so that he speaks, for the instant, indifferently and impatiently.*) You had better ask her!

GUY. (*Vague.*) Ask Miss Tramore—?

ERIC. Ask Lady Maresfield—if she thinks she can do any good. Only there are things that, in that case, she ought to know.

GUY. (*Interested.*) Things I may tell her?

ERIC. (*With a gesture, an impatience of assent.*) That Either of us who, under his Will, breaks its grand Provision—

GUY. (*As ERIC has paused as for positive pomp of effect.*) Loses a lot?

ERIC. (*With his effect.*) Loses Everything.

GUY. (*Impressed indeed.*) Everything?

ERIC. (*Making it unmistakable.*) Everything. But come out. I am conceiving at this point the Entrance, from the Terrace, of the personage not appearing at all in the Tale, but whom I make out as of high importance here—an importance I shall presently develop all the ground of; and whom I simply dub, to begin with, for convenience, the Colonel. In connection with which Entrance, as the two young men are about to leave, I immediately, suspending further detail, jot down roughly for benefit of memory the Concatenation of Sequences of the whole Act, the fine frame or mere osseous skeleton of it, as I from here experimentally view it. The Colonel arrives from the Grounds with of course, his abundant and vivid Motive; and I won't now tackle detail of the passage immediately taking place—the simple getting him in and getting the others out—beyond seeming to see that Eric shall have rung, just sharply pressed the bell, as he finally moves about, for Butler, and that on the latter's arriving he says to him, indicating the box of cigarettes on table, "Bring these." It is the Colonel who checks the Butler with his inquiry before the latter's Exit to Grounds and I thus promptly see that he mustn't have met the young men or crossed with them—a needless awkwardness—and that to this end, and probably certain other ends, though this alone would be enough, there must be a third easy Entrance to the Room. I have seen to the Left the Entrance from the Hall and main Passage of the House; which supposes the Diningroom where indoor Refreshments are liberally going on off in that quarter; which becomes a quarter of Reference. There is thus easily besides the Connection with Terrace and Grounds another Door or Passage to Right, as to a couple of other Rooms, smaller Sitting-room, Library, etc., upon which the Terrace also opens; so that they likewise may be entered from Garden. This is the way then the Colonel has come in, just as the young men go out and as the Butler, under orders, is about to follow them. He is instantly checked by the Colonel with the latter's question as to whether Lady Maud is there, whether he has seen her come or go, in fact whether the Colonel, who has passed through the other parts in search of her, is in time to get at her before she goes further. This is the Motive with which I bring him on; which he makes immediately vivid; and which gains further significance from the Butler's saying, that is becoming able to say, at sight of the person in question, just after the inquiry: "Here *is* her Ladyship";—and he may even announce her, true to his automatic habit, by her full name, as she appears at Entrance to Left. She and the Colonel thus instantly meet; the Butler goes out to Grounds, and they have their scene together. (Worth noting here, for remembrance, the small matter of a touch before the exit of the two young men. Eric has touched the button of the bell at the moment he says his second Everything; then he adds to his companion his "But we must go out." The Butler instantly appears, to whom he addresses his order to bring out the cigarettes, and makes his exit, while the Butler speaks to Guy. "*And* the chocolate-creams, sir?" On which I give a little the effect of the confidence about the girl's forfeiture of means just made him, by his hesitating, debating, while he just scratches his chin, and after a rueful glance at his massive tribute, decides and says "No!" He goes out after his friend, and then it is the Colonel arrives from Right in time to arrest the Butler. The moment there is of the briefest; the Colonel simply saying "Have you seen Lady M.?" and the man, one easily sees, on reflection, not uttering the superfluous word or two I imputed above, but simply with his look to the door Left as she appears there, announcing her by name; though indeed on reflection I see that as this is her first visit to the House he won't know her. Never mind; she has come in the moment before, while he was still outside, and he has heard her name herself to a footman. He simply hands it on, after the very momentary interruption caused by Eric's ring for him.) But I go into too many details that can wait so well till after I have finished, fully and simply stated, straight off, my present concatenation, as I have called it, of sequences. I shall come back, exhaustively, to the Function of the Scene between the Colonel and Lady Maud, as well as to the Function of each of these two individually; though I can't forbear just noting here even now that he tells her he has come to stop her off, as it were, and why—because, in three words, he thinks it's better, given something that clearly has happened in the House, though, mind you, he doesn't at all know yet *really* what this is, she shouldn't, so to speak, make so bold. She promptly replies that she has come by reason of an invitation straight from Rose herself—the nicest little note in the world that the Girl has been so good as to write her. The Colonel retorts to this that he knows, precisely, all about the nice little note— Rose having mentioned to him, out there in the Grounds just now, that she had taken this step and is hoping for the practical response. But none the less, the Colonel feels, it won't do—it won't at all do. And pray why won't it do?

Well, it will make a difficulty for her. There's thunder in the air—or there's powder—and I've been enough in the House, as an old soldier, to smell it. Something has happened—I don't quite know what; but Mrs. Tramore is as grim as a Death's head, and I don't advise you to go near her. He suggests, or appears to suggest, that he won't answer for it that in such an event there mightn't be a scene—out there before everyone; so that "My dear woman, just nip away again unobserved, and forgive me the crudity of my warning, for which I feel that you'll live to thank me. You see I know her, and you don't." Then for clearness: "I'm not talking of Rose herself, poor child—but who, you know, is a most interesting creature; I'm talking, my dear, and entirely for your benefit, of the terrible old woman."

LADY MAUD. (*Who has taken this with immediate interest and good humour, though with my idea of her listening to him and watching him quite amusedly and ironically while he speaks, as if she knows, as indeed she does, more than he of the very thing he is talking about, and has thus her card up her sleeve.*) You say my "showing" may make a difficulty for Rose. But mayn't it perhaps make, rather, a facility?

COLONEL. It will scarce make a "facility" for anyone that the Old Woman shall be rude to you.

LADY MAUD. (*With her smile and her air.*) People are never rude to me.

COLONEL. (*With his own similar resource.*) That, my dear, is because you always choose the right ones. With these people here you'd choose the wrong.

LADY MAUD. I haven't chosen—I'm called. Don't you understand, if you've talked with Rose, why she has sent for me?

COLONEL. (*A bit annoyed, as she looks so knowing.*) Why, because it's her coming of age, as she calls it,—and because, as she says, she has cast, for the occasion, a very wide net.

LADY MAUD. (*Amused.*) Is that the way she puts it?

COLONEL. I make use of her own sweet metaphor.

LADY MAUD. She's very clever.

COLONEL. Of course she's very clever. Too clever for any of them here.

LADY MAUD. (*Full of her knowledge.*) She's too clever for you, my dear—if you haven't guessed then, on the spot, what she's up to.

COLONEL. (*Struck, and even as with a sense of his own odd density, clapping his finger-tips to his forehead.*) She's going to her Mother?

LADY MAUD. (*As playing her card.*) She has practically sent for me—as Flora's best friend—to bring her.

COLONEL. (*Immensely startled.*) Lord o'mercy! (*Yet amused too and wondering.*) To snatch her up and run with her?

LADY MAUD. I mean that she three days ago let Flora know she may count on her.

COLONEL. (*Immensely interested, but vague.*) But count for What?

LADY MAUD. For Society.

COLONEL. (*Throwing up his hands.*) But—how and where?

LADY MAUD. At Home. She can come to her.

COLONEL. (*Still mixed.*) Flora can come here?

LADY MAUD. (*Enjoying it.*) Rose can come to us. She announces, my dear, that she Will.

COLONEL. (*Not even yet wholly catching on.*) Come to see her?

LADY MAUD. (*For her climax.*) Come to Stay. Come to Live. (*Highly serene.*) Always.

COLONEL. (*Now really astounded.*) You don't mean to tell me she's going to Chuck—

LADY MAUD. (*Taking him up, laying her hand straight on his arm and holding him an instant with her eyes on him.*) What *does* she in fact Chuck?

COLONEL. Why, by the rigour with which Tramore settled it, Everything.

LADY MAUD. (*Assured.*) Then she'll do it. She wants to chuck all she can.

COLONEL. (*Facing it, taking it in.*) I say, I say, I say!

LADY MAUD. (*Smiling, but with a certain reflection on his tone.*) Don't you like it?

COLONEL. (*Rubbing the back of his head with something of a grimace.*) We'll say I *admire* it!

LADY MAUD. (*Good humouredly.*) I admit it's Heroic.

COLONEL. (*Emphatic.*) It's Sublime! She gives up, poor dear, so much more than she Knows!

LADY MAUD. (*After an instant; as having, a little awkwardly for herself, to recognise this, but passing it off as with a slight sarcastic dig at him.*) Well, so long as she hasn't to give up You—!

COLONEL. (*As in possession, more and more, of what it means.*) Ah, Maud, I feel that—as the one old Friend of her Father's who, whether by the wisdom of the serpent or by the sweetness of the dove, whether for a sign of my constitutional "cheek" or only for a proof of my constitutional insignificance, has managed to remain, miraculously, with a foot in either Camp, has contrived the trick of still seeing Them Here while being known or suspected yet to see You, and above all *Her*, Elsewhere, of being loyal to my poor stiff old Friend and his Memory, in short, without undue prejudice to Sympathies less arduous, even though of course, as you'll allow, less Exemplary—I feel, I say, that as such a monstrous master of social Equilibruim, it will be a question not nearly so much of her giving me up as of her taking me quite systematically and comfortably *on*.

LADY MAUD. (*Impatiently.*) If what you want is to make me again remark to you that I don't know what, for so many years, we should have done without you, I decline to be dragged again through the Dust of that Abjection. I call your attention moreover to the fact that the Day of Deliverance for Flora has come, as it were, in spite of you.

COLONEL. (*Interested in this view.*) She regards it then, poor dear, *as* her Day of Deliverance?

LADY MAUD. (*Her shoulders up as for all there is, vainly, to say of it.*) Did you ever see Flora—

COLONEL. (*Instantly, comprehendingly taking her up.*) Depart from her glassy, her inimitable calm? I'm bound to say that, to the best of my recollection, and for the particular Charm we most value in her—Never!

LADY MAUD. Well then you'll see her Now! (*After an instant, almost with unction.*) It's Beautiful to see her!

COLONEL. (*Appreciative, as with the vision.*) You make me *want* to!—if her Ecstasy has gone the length of really deputing you—!

LADY MAUD. (*Prompt.*) "Deputing," my dear? She brought me every inch of the way.

COLONEL. (*Astonished, again, even alarmed.*) To this Door? (*Anxious.*) Then where *is* she?

LADY MAUD. (*Again enjoying her effect.*) In the victoria.

COLONEL. (*Quite aghast.*) And where's the victoria?

LADY MAUD. (*Serene.*) I told it to drive up and down.

COLONEL. (*As for the lurid vision.*) With May [1] Tramore *in* it?

---

[1] James, in dictating, has forgotten that his character's name is Flora, and is now calling her May.

LADY MAUD. (*Amused.*) If she hasn't—in her Ecstasy—tumbled out!

At which moment it is, I think, that the Butler, who of course has had time to do everything outside and get round and back into the House, effectively intervenes; appears at Left and announces to the two others "Mrs. Charles Tramore!" She is there upon them, upon the Colonel in particular—though I mark Lady M. as not prepared either for the *coup de tête* of this sudden portentous and dangerous irruption: I see her there upon them, as I say, with the most characteristic Entrance and Aspect possible; her extreme prettiness and ex-travagant·elegance of preserved youth, of immense care of herself, not really betraying the least departure from the glassy calm and the charming candid serenity that the Colonel has just appraised in her, and with the note, from the first and always, which is the prime note and value of her personality and effect through the whole play that though she expresses herself at moments with a certain innocent intensity of the superlative, and makes funny little statements about her emotions, opinions, conditions, her visible glossy, dainty, perfectly arranged and unperturbed state betrays at each moment, in the drollest way, the account she gives of herself. She stands there like a lovely large-eyed ex-pensive doll: she says something like: "I felt I *had* to come up—don't you think?" It's her note also that she's always placidly, tenderly, weakly—and one feels at bottom all indifferently—appealing. She proceeds with the sweetest, most fixed, least fluttered stare and smile: "I'm too awfully agitated to sit!" Meanwhile they're both upon her; talking together. "But, my dear May,[2] you really oughtn't, you know. But, my dear, this is dreadful! But, my dear May,[2] how reckless! But, my dear May,[2] You'll spoil all!"

I think this last will probably prove a good cue for her—for something in the way of: "Then she *will* come!"

LADY MAUD. (*In despair, with movements of precaution, while the* COLONEL *has gone to the window upon the Terrace, to the door Right etc.*) She won't come if you dish us!

COLONEL. (*Talking together with* LADY MAUD.) She won't come if you make a scandal!

MRS. TRAMORE. (*Absolutely unagitated by every sign, only looking about her with interest, as if taking in, in a perfectly detached way, the place, and its signs and tokens, her Daughter's habitation.*) She couldn't come to me here?

BOTH OF THEM TOGETHER. My dear woman, it's Madness!

MRS. TRAMORE. (*Smiling at them with her beautifully gloved and folded hands.*) But you don't know what it is to Wait!

COLONEL. (*Impatient, moving about, shrugging his shoulders, throwing up his hands.*) If you'd but take it from me what it may be for you *not* to Wait.

MRS. TRAMORE. (*Centre, looking straight before her with her beautiful fixed doll-like eyes.*) I've waited, you know, for Eighteen Years.

LADY MAUD. (*As ready to throw herself upon her to get her out.*) Then you might wait eighteen minutes.

---

2 P. 622, n.

Something is said, by her like Can't you let her know? which he echoes with: "Go out to her in the Grounds before everyone?"

Is she in the Grounds?

With all the rest of them?

With my other children?

With twenty Tramores!

Can I see her from there?

They both, as climax of short sharp scene get possession of her for retreat; the Colonel saying to Lady M.: "Take her, take her, take her—before anyone sees."

LADY MAUD. And not come back?

COLONEL. But don't you see? and, Lady M. then disappointedly assenting, Mrs. T., submitting, has yet an appeal to him:

MRS. TRAMORE. You don't back her? He throws up his arms: "I back her!"

LADY MAUD says: Then come to us! He replies: "to-night!" and hustles them off.

I see meanwhile, that I didn't jot down, in the above rough adumbration of possibilities, the Colonel's question to Lady M. as to "Why" it is that Rose wants to go to her Mother; the thing that brings Lady M.'s reply: "To do her good"; with, possibly, the Colonel's demand then of "What good?" and her retort, to this, of some contributive Value or other. She may only say perhaps: "Ah, you must ask her!"—that is ask Rose herself; which has the value and merit of putting in element of preparation for the so potentially interesting passage, the Climax of the Act between Rose and the Colonel. It drives in the little silver-headed nail for that. Also, there is no hint in the foregoing—as how should there be?—of what is almost the major indispensable of the scene, the provision required, so absolutely, so intensely, for the *placing*, the identification, in relation to the Girl and to her Mother, of each of these two. The passage required, for Value and Effect, that the vision of who and what each of the parties is, who it is, on one side and the other, that is talking thus, that some such perfectly definite little brief basis shall have been made firm and sharp. Exquisitely manageable, however, this; and by my making Lady M. "do" it about the Colonel, to himself; and making the Colonel "do" it, in the same degree, to Lady M., about *herself*. *C'est la moindre des choses*, as Difficulties go. So merely smeared a pictorial note, at any rate, does, I think, vividly justify my sense of this enormous importance of putting in the brief sharp vision, apparition, of Mrs. T., without a moment's more delay. No further reference to her has, or can have, required Value or Effect without the momentary *production* of her. Then the ground becomes firm, the spectator knows where he is; nothing, in other words, need, or can, prevent the March from being straight and strong. But I've tumbled into delay again as to memorising just here, before anything else, the order of my little successions. Let me parenthesise, all importantly, first, what I just above stupidly overlooked, that there is no reason for the Colonel's not himself immediately hustling off the two women, not himself departing with them in order to get them away, unless I give him his explicit motive for remaining; which is there, fortunately, in perfectly precious little form, and has only to be plucked in the manner of a full-blown rose from its stem. It comes his reason, his urgent ground for remaining, and his liveliest interest in doing so, exactly from the fact, about Rose's intention, that Lady M. has imparted to him—exactly from this fact in general, and above all from Mrs. Tramore's last word, her appeal about his "backing" the Girl in particular. "I'll back her," he says, and he *gives* it, with all due point and force, that this is exactly why he doesn't go away; why he remains there, waiting, wanting immediately to see Rose again, all eager to do so—both so that he shall serve Mrs. Tramore's anxiety and his own lively interest. So here is abundance of Provision; the carpet more and more smoothly laid and tightly drawn.

The two women then have no sooner gone than, at Right, the door to what I have called Library and so forth, the one by which the Colonel has himself come in, if I mistake not, Lady Maresfield appears; having passed in, by the same verisimilitude as the Colonel from the Grounds, and been ready, immediately, to explain her entrance. One would have liked to make her arrive from Left, for a particular reason; but this is impossible without the appearance of her crossing in that manner with Mrs. T. and Lady M.—a fatal stupidity; and the only thing I lose is my not being able to give her a word about her having come from the quarter that one postulates as the Tea-room. Her reason of presence is immediate—she is looking for Rose; with whom her business, she intimates, is urgent—just as the Colonel's is, we know, on his side; and since she is apparently by the line of Lady Maresfield's quest, not now in the Grounds, where at any rate the latter has missed her, it would have been mildly convenient for the Colonel to be able to say, with his own impatient interest, "Isn't she then in the Tea-room?" This, however, is nothing to waste words on—I mean for myself thus—and if I give him, immediately, "Won't she be— if she isn't outside—in the Tea-room?" it comes practically to the same thing. What is fundamental, and of the first importance here, is some formulation of the terms of acquaintance, of intercourse, of preliminary reciprocity, between these two—just to match, as it were, the perfectly constituted formulations of the preceding scene; but with the pressure of Time, of Space, going of course all the while crescendo; every inch, every instant and fraction of such, being, I needn't say, a precious stinted quantity before Rose's Entrance. Existing acquaintance, of a vague London order—but I won't go into that now; it is exactly what trips me up in this would-be mere bald statement of Sequences: I finish my statement first; then come back for real, consummate gouging everything out of everything. The passage between these two—suffice it—is constitutive according to its Function; and I may just note that it surely needn't draw itself out much, in fact can't do so, by reason of its thus discounting the scene that follows: all of Lady Mare.'s business being intensely reservable of course for the latter; with no clumsy leak in advance. Exquisite, really, for the Form this measure, this perfect sanctity and purity of the Passage or Part true consummately, ideally, to its Function, and keeping its edges as clear and sharp as steel from other muddlements and communities. So much, I say, for what awaits us between Lady Mares. and Rose; which we arrive at in its order. There is, however, valuably, importantly, or—to say the only word—constitutively—which I see the Colonel handling with her—beyond the mere little fact that they both "want" Rose. I can't help just worrying this Value here for a moment, in order to formulate it. What I do see, certainly, first of all, is that the very flurry and commotion, in either breast, which, on mention of Rose, betrays itself straightway by the holding back of neither, by their breaking ground on the Remarkable Matter or Startling News, they have just learnt, he from the women who have just left him, she from her Son, in the Grounds, on his going out there with his friend—I do descry this, I say, as a pictorial contributive Value. It gives the note of the consternation created; and really gives it the more strongly in proportion as the pair have not really had anything more (as they may so well, after all, not have been likely to have) than a mere sketchy, scrappy, casual London acquaintance. But more than this is wanted; and indeed, stupid that I am, I get it on the instant—it having been at the back of my head all the while; Lady M. becoming straightway for the Colonel, the sharp, high, vivid expression of the intensely shocked "worldly, conventional, social view," of Rose's projected action. She *gives* him this, of course; whereby I take it as figuring for him as a Determinant, in his own predisposed sense—that is as the sketch for the large formidable picture, to be hung up now in Chester Square, say, of the arrayed, the inimical, ignoring, cold-shouldering, dropping and cutting scandalised proper world. Moreover, as I instantly see, on exerting the smallest squeeze, I obtain here other Values, other little sharp, crisp Values, that neither of the two previous passages could give me, and that, though here just within the limit, are essentially of the sort that can't brook another moment's holding over. Not sharply, not possibly "formulated" yet, one immediately grasps, the Truth of the Peculiar Horror and Scandal, the Unprecedented Degree of the Commotion, surrounding poor Mrs. Tramore's Case 18 years before: the most important point in the world this, as I need scarcely state. The whole thing rests, as my little Tale in its way set forth, on the fact that all this *histoire* was prodigiously Exceptional—in the supposed Displeasingness of its features, an affair standing altogether by its dreadful, uneffaceable, unforgivable Self; so that the Attitude of Society has ever been in the same degree Exceptional, with not a muscle of its rigour relaxed, nor a symptom of the common inevitable eventual Condonation yet beginning to peep. Of the essence that this vital truth shall be established at the earliest possible juncture— whereby I had been taking for granted that it might just a little be dealt with between the Colonel and Lady Maud. There is, indubitably, some little place for it there; but it has to reckon there—being of course moreover wholly out of the question in the previous scene, which needfully stretches the nature of Eric's allusion to his Mother to the utmost length—with the sharp celerity of that encounter, which loses truth, on the spot, if it loses a certain breathlessness; accordingly these moments of this Scene Fourth *is* obviously my first moment of the golden opportunity; in conjunction with which it figures to me further, by the blessed law that the *squeezed* material, once it is real material, always gives out, as it were, the precious phosphorescent glimmer of what one needs—that here exactly pops in my germ of what I need the Colonel most particularly to "give" about the actual present facts of Mrs. T.'s position and existence (for herself) and, coincidently with this, of the form and habit of his own sustained Countenance of her, his continued, in short, friendship for her. He must make his little vivid statement with a sharp, effective radiation of rather droll, pitiful Picture in it, of what the current fact and features literally and familiarly (to him) are; not "discounting" even this, however, in view of what I reserve for him, at Climax, with Rose. He has facts to give her about her Mother; though, after all, as by that time her Determination will have been *wholly* taken, I seem to make out the case for their being most predominantly, quite most, administered to Lady Maresfield. She brings them on, as it were; promptly "voicing," as the newspapers say, the reprobation of the world, and forecasting it, though again, remember well, without discounting what I reserve for her with Rose. Her tone, her attitude, affect and aggravate the Colonel, who, given his idiosyncracies, is driven into sharper opposition by them; so that he positively "draws" her a little, into portrayal of the particular consistency and duration of the terms of the poor lady's outlawry—under the ban (pile this up) as London has never really seen a woman once well-connected before: all of which promotes what I want, for Clearness and Sharpness from the moment Rose comes on on the part of the Colonel. It is at the Climax then of Lady Maresfield's own "statement," as it were, in which her allusion to Mrs. T. as "that horrible woman," or something of that sort, rings out—it is at this juncture, I say, and quite as if she may have caught the expression as she stands there, that Rose appears: the Colonel seeing her first and raising a sharp hand of caution, an imperative "Hush!" as he becomes aware of her. She arrives up at Back from the Grounds and stands there a moment, in her birthday array, framed by the window-space and gravely looking from one to the other in a manner to suggest her guessing without difficulty to what this appearance of a somewhat heated passage between them refers itself, and who it is Lady Maresfield is in the act of denouncing. With which I immediately remember the stupid omission, in the immediately foregoing, of what I had in view definitely to note: the circumstance of Lady Mare.'s mentioning to the C., on her own entrance, not only that she has thought Rose might be in the room, but has thought she might be awaiting her, in consequence of her having mentioned to her, in the Grounds five minutes before—that is the older woman's having mentioned to the younger—that she would like so immensely a few minutes privately, as might be, with her. Yes, she has said this to the C., directly, for presentation of a motive; and she seems to convey that it is her habit to assume that when she has made such intimations of her desires, she mostly finds them promptly taking effect. This by itself is a note, for that matter, that just perceptibly aggravates the Colonel; he puts it quite forth, on his side, that he is staying on purpose for a word with the Girl; in connection with which I really seem to see the "fat on the fire," as it were, a little between them. To which, still further, let me note, just here, that it has glimmered before me as a little elementary effect that Lady Mare.'s denunciation, representation, misrepresentation, indignant evocation in fine, of Mrs. T., the parcel of monstrous colours, in fine, in which she brushes her off, gains for us, gains for irony and comedy, by the fact that we have just had Mrs. T. in our eye, in her habit as she so remarkably lives, survives and blooms; and that I also *constater* that Lady Mare. has never at all seen her, I mean in the multitude of London chances, which Guy has profited by; and that this marks the particular circle of revolution in which Lady M. goes round—all such chances being really out of her ken. She is really the dry hard kind of grim dragon of a British Matron; with the attenuation or aggravation of her characteristic desire to push her advantages and provide for her young. Rose, at any rate, is meanwhile there, as much "led up to" as can possibly be perpetrated; and with Lady M.'s instantly checking and recovering herself enough to greet her all eagerly with an "Oh, it's so sweet of you to have come!" Which Rose slowly advancing, after having completed at her ease, as it were, her look from the Colonel to the lady, and from the lady to the Colonel, receives with a reserve, or even with a vague protest that appears to indicate that she hasn't come for *this* formidable Visitor at all. In fact—I seize the conviction—she makes it clear, for my presently-to-be-realised advantage, that this is particularly not the case: she simply looks, keeps looking, like a sort of beautiful young Fate at the elder woman quite hard for a minute, and even disconcerting the latter's own fine hardness perceptibly by doing so, and by making no acknowledgement of the speech just addressed to her. I seem to want her to convey that the phrase, the tone "that horrible woman!" or whatever it is, continues to ring in her ears. Then, when her attitude has sufficiently conduced to this rather striking image, it is to the Colonel she speaks, and quite, for him, as an old and interesting, a valued and charming family friend.

ROSE. I'm so glad to find you—for three words. (*Then as she comes down, brushing past, as it were,* LADY MARESFIELD; *speaking only to the* COLONEL.) I was afraid you had gone without speaking to me. Lady Mare. instantly breaks in, before he has had time to do more than make a gesture, as with her prior claim: which bits only await treatment. The Colonel does the graceful thing, gives way, and there is an exchange or two during which Rose says nothing to their companion; only says to him that he must then come back to her—and that he had better meanwhile go and have his tea properly. He promises his return, and his exit to Left leaves her with Lady Maresfield; toward whom her attitude, not a little inscrutable, is that of not breaking silence till she is forced, as it were, of leaving the burden of approach, the inevitable floundering and embarrassment—if Lady M., has any delicacy—all on the other hands. Lady M., hasn't, in point of fact, any delicacy and immediately shows it: she straightway mentions to Rose that her Son Guy has just told her, just repeated to her—as it was his duty—what Eric Tramore has told him: viz. of her entertained, of her nourished, of her domestically imparted intention of "seeing" her Mother. I go on, with my Concatenation, straight from here; but again can't help just parenthetically noting, memorising, that this must quite definitely "give" that Lady Mare. knows it *only* from her Son; so that we have it definite that, as the Colonel has just been shown as knowing it only from Lady Maud, so, evidently and definitely, the thing hasn't as yet spread abroad. It is precisely in order to speak before it has had time to do so—and this exactly is the manner in which she puts it—that Lady Mare. now presents, announces, describes and images herself as rising there as the remonstrant, the warning Voice of Society. I give her this Function—the grand gist and essence of which is that if she does carry out her perversity Rose will simply find that she can't decently marry. Or she puts this at least for Climax, luridly presents first, the other things she forfeits; showing moreover that she hasn't needed to have, as yet, from old Mrs. Tramore the family view of her wicked course: she has gathered that sufficiently from her Son's echo of Eric's tone. A truce, however, to this immediate lingering; everything has to be come back to in such abysmal detail, and with such exhaustive thoroughness. Suffice it that the scene terminates with Bertram Jay's advent: he being announced by the Butler, Left, at exactly the right psychological moment. He is discomforting too, in his degree and manner to Lady Maresfield, thanks to the possibilities or presumptions as to his "carrying off" Rose, that cluster about him and some foretaste of which she has already had—as may well be involved, moreover, in the fact that if I don't get my "Preparation" for this Entrance between the two women in some way or other I don't get it at all. This highly vital fact, with its lesson to be extracted to the last drop; while I for the moment just now jot down that the Young Man determines Lady M.'s exit, that after this scene between the Others then, that is with its sequel, the "shank" of the Act, his exit is determined by the entrance of Julia Tramore, the aunt, from Grounds with request from her Mother, the old woman, still grimly encamped under her tree, that he will come out to see her. He goes, by Back after appealing to Rose for prospect of his seeing her again before leaving. Julia observes on this, conceivably if not monstrously, that perhaps after he has seen her Mother he won't want to see her niece, and then, on his exit, has her own highly important passage with the Girl. Into all the Values of this I don't pretend to go at this moment; suffice it that her exit is determined by Jay's return from Grounds, after his Interview with the old woman, and with his request to her Daughter that she will immediately go to her. Exit Miss Tramore; on which I get Jay's second and contrasted scene, his transformed attitude and appeal, to the Girl. He of course on his first entrance had arrived, late, straight from town; having heard nothing, knowing nothing. I get, I say, my Big Value for this encounter, which culminates then in the Colonel's return, as by his previous agreement; producing Jay's exit and departure. Then my Grand Climax, as it were, of the Situation of Rose and Colonel, culminating—well, in what I make it culminate in; and Curtain.

I am much moved to strain on to a preliminary rough ciphering-out of Second; but such a cloud of considerations still hangs about what I have here in hand that I must just worry with it a moment longer. All sorts of things come up; as for instance, in the light of future needs and opportunities, the whole of the future Situation, the question of the best Value for the Maresfield Young Man, as to whom my indication at the beginning of this Act is of course a mere vague hint, the survival of what was in the Tale; a form that will clearly take great bettering, in respect to what one may wish to get out of him, to do with him and use him for, in the further complexity. I see of course that the Tale really gives me nothing for him that is of special value here; and as one wants of course but to go in for Interest at any price, he must be conceived in the light of that interest; as to which I find myself just catching a considerable Glimmer, to be further caught, to be exhaustively worked out, further on. And then, as regards the foregoing, there are all sorts of things to be said about all my Values and possible, or rather and inevitable, Developments and Intensifications, from Rose's entrance on, she remaining on to Curtain, as the extremely interesting Agent and Centre of them all: to say nothing, for that matter, of those that precede her entrance—though I mustn't even accidentally speak as if the Whole thing were not one Intense and Continuous Fusion. On the degree to which the matter of the relation of my Young Woman and principal Young Man has to be, and will be, can't help, in my hands, becoming, richly and charmingly Interesting, I needn't Discant: there are so many things *in* it—*as,* for that matter, there are such innumerable workable and desirable things, right and left, at every turn, in all the rest. But this is my Horse-of-Battle, my High Ridge of Interest and to keep it so, vividly, from beginning to end, is of course the golden key to—well, to what I want. All this, however, goes so without saying. What I wanted particularly to note is that, as my rough adumbration stands, I get the Family Opposition to the Girl directly embodied only in her Situation with Julia Tramore, who represents thus, of course, represents officially and portentously, as it were, the Family, speaks for Them, for her august old Mother, the suggested Image of whom, invisible, but intense, and ruling the scene in spite of her absence from it, one wishes somehow to make felt, to make felt, to make appreciable, to cause, as it were, effectively and, I say, portentously, to play through. Miss Tramore represents, above all, and "voices" the dead Father and the view he would take of the case were he there; speaks for this, urges this, makes it definite, gives it all its Value; gives their Value, above all, to the facts, the sharp material facts that represent, collectively, the consequences and penalties, the losses and forfeitures, entailed by Rose's act. We must know with the most perfect clearness what these are, with what clearness they are present to herself, and with what clearness present to Bertram Jay, after his interview with old Mrs. Tramore has made them so. I want them present also—by which I mean *represented as* present to the Brother, and Sister; for whom, with these things, as I even thus roughly thresh them out, and therefore, evidently, still more, as I shall consummately cipher them in detail; for whom,

I say, the Climax of Act I strikes me, even under this light pressure, and as a consequence of this vague squeeze, as having more use and play than the foregoing scratches glance at. Yes, I want, all naturally, my Climax here *enriched* and, as it were, amplified as much as possible; and there are uses for the Brother and Sister in conducing to such enrichment and amplification. In the jottings, or as I say, the scratches, for they are no more, just perpetrated, *from* them, I say, this would result, that each of my Situations or cumulative passages, from Rose's Entrance to End would consist of two persons, practically; since the overlapping two or three times of a third doesn't count to speak of. This is very well, but I needn't in the least accept it as final; and I have my Brother and Sister all convenient, all contributive, all logically, and in fact indispensably, involved, for some small creation of the relief of Number. There Glimmer upon me the ways, the lights, in which They may fill out, animate and curiously, amusingly, ironically, illustrate, in the interest of fine Comedy, the Family Attitude exemplified by Miss Tramore—to which they give further body and colour. The simplest way to put it, and it immediately and dramatically imposes them, is that, as they profit handsomely by everything Rose relinquishes and forfeits, I must have them there to *do* so; have them there for the representation and picture of their doing it; with whatever features and illustrations of their partly priggish, partly rueful, in any case pictured and presented state of Conformity, of disciplined submission, of interested calculation (though not in the least heinous, or really ugly, of course) may be achievable for them. Beautiful and exquisite problems the very keeping of all this in the Tone, the right and bright and light, and always interesting, but never ugly, not overdone, nor in any way miscarrying or deviating, or, I needn't say, blundering, Ironic. The working in of Eric and Edith, or whatever their names may confoundedly be, is a part of the little goldmine that awaits me again to dig in; suffice it for the moment that I see them as presently reinforcing their Aunt in her Supreme Appeal, as, after a bit, associated with her in it; or perhaps even as kept in abeyance then, to be associated and admirably involved in my Climax Proper, as I must call it, the Situation of Rose and her invaluable old Family Friend and Man of the World, her old contributive Chorus and Critic and Precious General Agent, the Colonel. So many things crowd upon one in these widenings and intensifyings of Vision, that one scarce knows which first to clutch at, and one, for the moment, pushes in and overlies the next, driving it, driving them, out of one's head. Thus, for instance, the vital little truth of one's definitely seeing the Course of Action in the Girl *develope,* before one's eyes, under dramatic Determinations, from moment to moment and point to point: which is but a little way, precisely, of stating the very principle and meaning and beauty of Drama. It is a Concatenation of things visibly, appreciably, terribly or comically, at any rate logically and traceably determined within the frame of the picture before one's eyes; of every golden grain of applicable sense and force in which axiom I neither more nor less than propose that every inch of my March, and every touch of said Picture shall be a proof and an example. What I cling to is the Vision of her being *precipitated,* on the spot, and before us, to her Step; with everything that happens to her—and the whole of the Show, from her Entrance, is describable as a close succession of things happening to her—promoting the necessity, creating the inevitability, of her (so to speak) Deed. It grows there before us; all the others, that is, all save the Colonel, whose Function is a thing entirely apart, minister to its growth by the Fatuity (blest word—*that's* the comprehensive, vivid Idea I want) of their attempting just the opposite; so that really a lovely description of her line, of her situation and little history, is that it's a struggle, direct and intimate, with surrounding and appealing and would-be smothering Fatuity. Fatuous everyone, fatuous with the exception, all and always, the precious Colonel,—with whom the interest and charm of her tie is that *they* have in common *their* not being Fatuous. Fatuous in their respective ways the figures of 2nd and 3rd, fatuous Lady Maud, fatuous the young Maresfield scion, whose elder Brother, decidedly, dies, is killed by some hunting accident or something, between 1st and 2nd., so that his social and matrimonial value have gone straight up; and so that when in II I confront him, in the midst of Rose's Desolation, as I must call it, before Bertram Jay has played round and up, vulgarly speaking, I may confront him with the Girl as a temporarily thinkable Relief or Alternative or Solvent or Issue, or even slight Bribe; for I gather it to be a part of the complexity here that he really does care for her. The making right of his type entails of course a thorough and interesting working-out of his Mother's and of his curious and "amusing" relation with her. Fatuous, above all,—and this is just really, for irony and comedy and charm and grace and interest and pathos and Everything—fatuous above all is Bertram Jay himself; so that the drama of their relation, his and Rose's, the full extraction of meaning and picture from it is in the process of her reduction, conversion, transformation, clarification, illumination, of this element in him till his fine high-toned priggishness, with all sorts of good things beneath and behind it, becomes under her conscious and intelligent pressure, a "finer humanity"; a wider and kinder and brighter and more detached and amused sense of things, and of her situation and mission in particular; as to which I keep thinking of sidelights beautiful and valuable and helpful and droll, all the while on the part of the Colonel. The conversion of Jay, as well as the Bringing Out of her Mother, becomes thus the very description of what we see her actively and subtly and charmingly about, as consciously and fondly, even, capable of till she brings it to full Fruition; which full Fruition is the vague and remote and most embracingly general label for my Climax of Second—I come back to this just to note my sense, strong as one turns the matter over, that, very presumably, the Climax of the brief and rapid situation of the Colonel and the two women should be, over and beyond his vow to "back" Rose, her demanding of him this, that he let her Daughter know of her having been there, of his having waved her away, and of her having yielded on condition of his thus immediately telling Rose. She makes it [her] condition of going. He promises—then she goes.

ACT SECOND

I have to break ground here, I feel, from very far off indeed, to approach my place of Siege, by rather wide circumvallations, beginning with considerations quite general, and drawing closer drawing in, from these to the more particular and to the Centre. On the face of it one's subject here has the air of presenting rather more the aspect or category of the Difficult—as if, however, really, any thing appreciably worth doing, in these conditions were more Difficult than any other thing. What I mean is that, speaking, as I say most Generally, the Act, is, by its nature, in a large degree, or at all events in an appreciable one, the picture of a State or Status: full of character, full of colour, full of comedy, full in a word of *things,* including lively Interest (as I see and feel it all); but with the March and the Movement to be, doubtless, by due need, a little more artfully and ingeniously and scientifically extracted from it than in the case of what has preceded. What I most rudimentarily get, at any rate, is that I think, to begin with, a term of not much less than two years, in fact even a little more, has elapsed since the beginning of the last interval; two years that have run their course for Rose's Domestication with her Mother. Speaking again in an elementary fashion, all the warnings and vaticinations addressed to her in First bore on what she would be "in for," and in the most lurid, or at least intensely deterrent symbols: in spite of which she went her way. Well, now we have as first conditioned the picture of what she really *was* "in for"; what she has been, all this time, and still is, "in for." The time seems considerable, but I somehow don't make it out as less: it has to be considerable to present its meaning and bear its fruit. It becomes thus indeed a little longer than a term of two years, since I seem experimentally to disengage that they, the persons the thing gives me, are all together, toward the summer's end, gathered at some little foreign place to which Rose, now completely managing her Mother's life ("She believes in you," the Colonel says to the Girl with whom he is now an immense chum, "as she believes in the Preservation of her Figure, the Understanding of that Figure by her Paris Dressmaker"—or, experimentally, something of that sort; some shibboleth or superstition or sign and token, that passes with poor Mrs. Tramore for a rule of life, a Working Faith), has conducted her, in the absolute and unperturbed inveteracy of their ever being invited anywhere; anywhere, that is, that they will go—by which I mean that Rose, with her plan of campaign, her pious demonic subtlety, will consent to their going. Potentially exquisite, it gleams upon me here, the exhibition for their present situation, of this Generalship of exclusion, selection, discretion, precaution, high and delicate fastidiousness, as to their contacts and doings; even though it happens that, till something really worth while comes, the effect of it is to leave them all high and dry, utterly isolated, frequented, haunted, encompassed, for the nearer circle with no one but the Colonel and Lady Maud and young Maresfield and One Other Man, I seem speculatively to grope toward, a compromising man, a dreadful man, a man with amusement to give, a floating spar of Mrs. Tramore's great faraway shipwreck or crisis, who keeps imaging and symbolising and recording it, as for that matter Lady Maud does too, in her somewhat different way; though all under Rose's superior Control and Conduct and Compression: a part of the state of things that have ended in the absolute collective, grateful, plastic, comic, devout submission to her as their eventual Guide and Redeemer out of Bondage, if they will only be utterly good, and take the Law from her in every particular. There float before me Patches, as this most preliminary Process *is* but a floating before one of Patches—as of awfully characteristic and "comico-ironic" Exhibition of this high prudent system of vigilance, exclusion, selection, and all that sort of thing, on Rose's part, as for the organisation of her eventual victory: though just let me note here before I break off, that as each of my Acts essentially embodies a Crisis, and is, organically, the picture of the Crisis, so this one is partially, and for its start and beginning, a Crisis of Discouragement—presenting first the high bleak table-land, as it were, of the very Desolation of their general Propriety; which as yet has led to nothing at all—so that the March, here, can only be, all designated and indicated, as that of what it *begins*, under visible, vivid Determination, to lead to. It begins, I say; we see it so begin, as soon as the Desolation is duly and adequately presented and *constatée;* then the March is that of its further logical, and awfully dramatic and interesting, Development to a Climax.

The way I seem to see them is, as it were, at some last gasp of their high and dry state, their dreadful, desperate, fruitless propriety and respectability, reaching the vividest, drollest, blankest neutrality, as it were, in every direction and relation, on the part of Mrs. Tramore, and with the apparent failure of Rose's sacrifice, her devotion, her diplomacy, her wonderful behavior generally, to do anything for them—for I keep lumping Lady Maud *with* them, for the sake of the illustrative possibilities of "quaintness" of her,—in a worldly and social way, the particular way for which she has laboured. She has laboured, she has calculated and plotted, to float her Mother back into the innermost waters of the Harbour of Safety, and Mrs. Tramore, blandly and prayerfully passive, with her indefeasible superficiality and frivolity and amiability and juvenility, her utterly shallow, and serene passivity has sat, arrayed and hatted and gloved, ready to the last twist of a ribbon, to disembark, as it were, on the sacred strand; but with no summons whatever, no faint symptom of a call, an opportunity, a possibility, yet looming into sight. In short the situation depicted with all its foreshortened vividness in the Tale. My cue for Mrs. T.'s aspect and image throughout Act II is just the little figure that I think I used in the Tale; that of her sitting, as in the most temporary manner possible, on the edge of her chair, with "her things on," as waiting for the carriage which is to come and take her and drive her to some happy place to which she has not the faintest chance of going. Well, so things are—only with the faithful Colonel, always hovering, always revolving, always returning, and above all, always interested, intensely interested in Rose, always amused, amusing and tremendously Con-tributive. The particular Hour, as I feel it, is one at which the situation seems to "kind of" threaten to crack and give way as by excess of tension; as by having got, though to an extent they all loyally dissimulate, on all their nerves—espe-cially of course on Rose's, whose wound-up and overdone state, smilingly as she masks it, is in a manner the key of what we see happen. The Colonel comes and goes with *his* protected and privileged contacts and communities—he brings in reports of the outer life; he is, by function and character, their medium of communication and knowledge. If Rose has learned a short time before of the death of her Grandmother, and of what has happened at home since, as it were, that is of her own disinherited and further proscribed and condemned and branded state, it is all and only through the Colonel; as to which bereave-ment, moreover, I seem to see that she, as for perfect decorum, has put on light, perfunctory, though highly becoming, technically respectful and decorous mourning. Such is the image, that of very charming and simple qualified mourn-ing, a summer array of "tasteful" black and white, that she presents in this Act. Say we take her at the moment when it has really come up for her, under some Determination, quite supremely, whether she *can* "stand" it, any longer, the dreary *impasse* of her situation; whether she can stand it for another month, week, day or hour. Say they have gone to the little place, which I think of some-how as a pleasant, a beautiful and, as *might* have been propitious quiet resort in the Austrian or Bavarian Tyrol, on some calculation of her's, Rose's very own, worked out entirely by herself, that some "good," of a vague, sweet, blessed sort, would thereby come to them; say that they have taken rooms in a sort of chalet or Dependance of the main little hotel, which has its garden in common with the latter; the ladies being lodged together in the Dependance and the Colonel just a little way off at the hotel. Say, further, in conformity with this, that their presence has been somehow blighting, measurably detri-mental, in regard to a small circle, as it were, of English habitués, on whom the landlord largely counts, *has* counted, from year to year, for his month of Sep-tember or whatever; and say some effect, some consciousness, distinctly depress-ing and menacing, of this kind, is in the air on rise of Curtain, with our attesta-tions of it and of the other elements of the Case and Crisis rendered salient, amusing, interesting. Say we get it not only that they have Broken Down, but that this has somehow to-day got to be Recognised; say it comes up for them too unmistakably, and that the brunt of it is what Rose, trustedly, really quite unchallengedly, but all discouragedly, dejectedly, even all sceptically now at last, has to meet. They *have* it there, somehow—they have it before them that they can't "go on," as it were, unless something happens, since none of the things originally dreamed of have as yet in the least done so; and I want to give the note of Rose's Temptation, as it were, which she feels might become sharp on this, were it only to take the form of lurid Opportunity—the temptation, in other words, to throw up her sorry game, to "chuck" her vain speculation and clear out, saving at least her own skirts or skin. For she, above all, is Bored, poor Rose, to within an inch of her life; the society of the outlawed, of the supposedly "unspeakable," has come at last to excruciate her—that is her Mother's which is the real crux, has—by its desperate vapidity, vacuity and propriety. What I seem to clutch, as Constatations, in their order, or at any rate in their cluster (since the order requires, obviously, full threshing out) is that, perhaps first, of their appreciable Detrimentalism as to the little place they occupy; their having prevented this, that and the other annual visitor from coming, or having determined this, that or the other annual visitor, and his wife and daughters, prematurely to depart; their having, in fine, in some appreciable way exercised an uncanny and disquieting influence—which makes the landlord say, though appreciating *them* too, for the expense they are at, fidget and wonder and appear moved to bring the so odd matter to a head. *Mettons* that they have been there from rather early, having come on purpose, and with all their leisure—no late engagements or complications to keep *them* in town!— and so are encamped; with, after all, the Effect of their Presence, I hint to myself, a matter of Appreciation more by themselves, as an acute consciousness of their Detrimentalism, than a ground for the landlord's worriment—an element that, I see, wouldn't plausibly work, and that I don't really need. It's all a question with and for and roundabout Themselves; this, properly dealt with, making it quite a sufficient little silver-mine for all my Values. Their vision becomes thus a consciousness of everything as Negative; they haven't even the thrill or incident of shocking people and driving them away; they so create the desert about Them that, in the oddest, uncanniest, as well as drollest, way in the world, there *are* no People, to *be,* in any manner affected; all of which is a part of what is thrown up, appreciably diffused in the air, by the Break-down. I some-how seem to want to make some of the wrong people come, and I see thus that I do perfectly descry reason to be grateful for my Second Man, as I call him, the representative of the true Detrimental as distinguished from Themselves; the one whom they have never been able to get rid of, and whom in London, with whatever sneaking fondness for him still, they constantly have to try to suppress and relegate. I seem to see, as a happy value that, given their desperation now, they are only all too glad to have him again, with what he may have brought them from outside, from elsewhere, to relieve them of the burden of Themselves. I catch the tip of the tail of the idea that the three women are at the very first alone on the ground, at the place, together, and have been so for some little time, and that this ministers, in due course, to desperation—that is to despera-tion for Rose; who is the one for whom it most matters—matters, that is, to Us. The tip of this tail would seem to give me the successive arrivals, from elsewhere, of the four or five men: that is of my Second Man, as I call him, of the Colonel, of the Maresfield Scion, and of Bertram Jay. Each of these Contributive, each of these sharp Determinants. Besides, or rather *with* which, with everything to be disengaged from the richness, there flare at me the two images, as I thus parenthetically clutch at them, of what I call Lady Maud's Case, the case of her Demoralisation, for Rose to deal with; the case of her not Playing the Game (awfully precious this clue or note, for presentation of Rose, of her vigilance as to their Playing the Game;) and the case of the Awful Person, probably Impossible Woman, previously known and "shed," bearing down on them, and who must be as wildly waved away as the Colonel had to wave Mrs. Tramore at Wimbledon. Discussion, Discussion, the acute Discussion of their state, even as might be among Survivors on a Raft, casting about and differing as to what it is best to do. The waves of Discussion breaking against Rose's mask or armour of fortitude, but with such possible ironic amusement and interest in the presentation of it all. Everyone, that is each, is *shown* as demoralised, except Mrs. Tramore whose glassy surface of exquisite Ignorance never for an instant belies itself—though ah, the possibilities of all this crowd upon me almost too thick for discrimination. But steady and easy, step upon step: what I disengage for the instant, stated with the last crudity, is these differences in the two or three Demoralisations of which I see the Colonel as more or less the confidant. What I meant just now by Lady Maud's Case is her aspect and share in what I have called the frank Break-down. She does, all cynically give it up as a vain job; and though she makes Rose no "scene" (I see that as all inferior), Rose has it out with her, just as she would have it out with Rose if she dared, that Opportunity is all that is wanted for each of them somehow to collapse. Say Lady Maud wants, positively, cynically and admittedly, the Impossible Woman, their old pal—wants her for the simple change and relief and diversion and vulgarity she'll bring. "My dear, she's so delightfully vulgar—and we're just dying for want of that; with our perfect Distinction that has landed us on this sand-bank. Do let us have her, before we all become idiots!"—or something of that sort. Rose is "Disappointed" in her, and has to be austere and explicit about it; catching her, however—for I seem really to require it—in some *act*, some covert fact, of the course of subterfuge that I have called not playing Fair. And yet with, all the while, this hauntedness of her own by the sense . . . [the manuscript breaks off at this point.]

The Saloon
In One Act
1908

EDITOR'S FOREWORD

In his "rough statement" for *The Chaperon* Henry James speaks of the woman who "represents officially and portentously, as it were, the Family, speaks for them, for her august old mother, the suggested Image of whom, invisible, but intense, and ruling the scene in spite of her absence from it, one wishes somehow to make felt. . . ." Reduced to simpler terms, James here is speaking of the way in which the Spirit of Family—family duties, loyalties, ties, traditions—can rule a scene even when the parental or ancestral presences are absent from it. It is significant that he made this allusion at this time. For in casting aside *The Chaperon* on November 14, 1907 and deciding to do a one-act play instead, Henry James chose the one story of his in which the Spirit of Family is suggested in ghostly terms. Nothing is harder to put on the stage than a convincing ghost; yet this is exactly what Henry James decided to attempt. He selected his story of *Owen Wingrave* which he had published in the Christmas number of the *Graphic* in 1892 and republished in *The Wheel of Time,* a collection of tales, in 1893 in the United States, and in the collection *The Private Life* in England during the same year.

The figure of Owen has much in common with that of Guy Domville. Both are men of peace, both called to a life of action in the world. Owen would rather read poetry than be a soldier; Guy prefers the cloister to the world; both must answer the imperious claims of Family since both are the last of their line. Owen defies his family's military tradition but nevertheless is so much a part of it that in doing so he acts and dies like a soldier; young Wingrave wins his grave, and implicit in this is his renunciation of life. Guy finds the world cruel and sinister and renounces it for the monastery. In their renunciation both have had their revenge on their exacting ancestors. By their acts they make sure that the family line becomes extinct.

In writing the play James retitled it *The Saloon*—using the word *salon* in its old form. He set to work on it on December 1, 1907, dictating a brief sketch; then he worked at it alone in the evenings. Miss Bosanquet has described how plays, "if they were to be kept within the limits of possible performance," had to be written by hand. From his written manuscript he began dictating the play on December 22. He spent the last three days of 1907 completing *The Saloon* and it was probably to this play, as well as *The High Bid,* that he was alluding when he wrote to Edith Wharton on January 2, 1908, "I have passed here a very solitary and *casanier* Christmastide (of wondrous still and frosty days, and nights of huge silver stars,) and yesterday finished a job of the last urgency for which this intense concentration had been all vitally indispensable. I got the conditions, here at home thus, in perfection—I put my job through, and now—or in time—it may have, on my scant fortunes, a far-reaching effect."

During January he showed *The Saloon* to Harley Granville-Barker and from a letter written to the actor-dramatist we can gather that he was not completely satisfied with it. "The thing is tainted with its original vice—that of the little *tale*, of my own ancient telling, plausibly but treacherously and fallaciously offering itself as a theme under stress of conditions which made the fact that I already knew the thing, and had used it, a sort of false and misleading value. . . ."

On April 16, 1908, after the first night of *The High Bid* in Edinburgh, James amplified *The Saloon* in an effort to improve it: he had hopes that it would serve as a curtain-raiser for *The High Bid*, but the Forbes-Robertsons were not interested in it and the novelist laid it aside. Late that year, when it seemed unlikely that *The High Bid* would be produced in London, he was approached by the dramatist, St. John Hankin, who urged him to submit *The Saloon* to the Incorporated Stage Society which for some years had been giving subscription performances of meritorious plays that otherwise would never have reached the stage. James sent in his script. It was read by the members of the board and rejected by them at a meeting on January 12, 1909. The minutes of the board of that date say: "Mr. Bernard Shaw undertook to write to Henry James with reference to *The Saloon*." The letter is in Shaw's hand, as his first sentence indicates.

From G. Bernard Shaw to Henry James:

17th January 1909

My Dear Henry James
Shaw's writing—Bernard Shaw:
There is a play of yours called *The Saloon* in the hands of the Stage Society. My wife made me read it some time ago, and it has been sticking in my gizzard ever since.

What that play wants is a third act by your father. What do you want to break men's spirits for? Surely George Eliot did as much of that as is needed. Do you seriously think that you would have been beaten by that ghost? Are you more superstitious than Dr. Johnson, who said, "I, sir, should have frightened the ghost." In the name of human vitality WHERE is the charm in that useless, dispiriting, discouraging fatalism which broke out so horribly in the 1860's at the word of Darwin, and persuaded people in spite of their own teeth and claws that Man is the will-less slave and victim of his environment? What is the use of writing plays?—what is the use of anything?—if there is not a Will that finally moulds chaos itself into a race of gods with heaven for an environment, and if that will is not incarnated in man, and if the hero (of a novel or play or epoch or what you please) does not by the strength of his portion in that will exorcise ghosts, sweep fathers into the chimney corner, and burn up all the rubbish within his reach with his torch before he hands it on to the next hero?

It is really a damnable sin to draw with such consummate art a houseful of rubbish, and a dead incubus of a father waiting to be scrapped; to bring on for us the hero with his torch and his scrapping shovel; and, then, when the audience is saturated with interest and elated with hope, waiting for the triumph and the victory, calmly announce that the rubbish has choked the hero, and that the incubus is the really strong master of all our souls. Why have you done this? If it were true to nature—if it were scientific—if it were common sense, I should say let us face it, let us say Amen. But it isn't. Every man who really wants his latchkey gets it. No man who doesn't believe in ghosts ever sees one. Families like these are smashed every day and their members delivered from bondage, not by heroic young men, but by one girl who goes out and earns her living or takes a degree somewhere. Why do you preach cowardice to an army which has victory always and easily within its reach?

I, as a socialist, have had to preach, as much as anyone, the enormous power of the environment. But I never idolized environment as a dead destiny. We can change it: we must change it: there is absolutely no other sense in life than the work of changing it; and every young man who lays a ghost and puts his father in his proper place, in the second fighting line—not obstructive across the vanguard's path—is doing his bit of the job, and is delighted in (however secretly) by youth and the crowd.

You must write that third act, even if you have to lay your own ghost first. There is a fine play there; but it is like a king with his head cut off. As the thing stands now, it is very talented; but is it any better than Turgienef? People don't want works of art from you: they want help: they want, above all, encouragement, encouragement, encouragement, encouragement, encouragement and again encouragement until there is no more room on the paper. Yrs ever, G. BERNARD SHAW

Henry James to G. Bernard Shaw:

20 January 1909.

My dear Bernard Shaw,

Your delightful letter is a great event for me, but I must first of all ask your indulgence for my inevitable resort, to-day, to this means of acknowledging it. I have been rather sharply unwell and obliged to stay my hand, for some days, from the pen. I am, thank goodness, better, but still not penworthy—and in fact feel as if I should never be so again in presence of the beautiful and hopeless example your inscribed page sets me. Still another form of your infinite variety, this exquisite application of your ink to your paper! It is indeed humiliating. But I bear up, or try to—and the more that I *can* dictate, at least when I absolutely must.

I think it is very good of you to have taken such explanatory trouble, and written me in such a copious and charming way, about the ill-starred Saloon. It raises so many questions, and you strike out into such illimitable ether over the so distinctly and inevitably circumscribed phenomenon itself—of the little piece as it stands—that I fear I can meet you at very few points; but I will say what I can. You strike me as carrying all your eggs, of conviction, appreciation, discussion, etc., as who should say, in one basket, where you put your hand on them all with great ease and convenience; while I have mine scattered all over the place—many of them still under the hens!—and have therefore to rush about and pick one up here and another there. You take the little play "socialistically," it first strikes me, all too hard: I use that word because you do so yourself, and apparently in a sense that brings my production, such as it is, up against a lion in its path with which it had never dreamed of reckoning. Yes, there literally stands ferocious at the mouth of your beautiful cavern the very last formidable beast with any sop to whom I had prepared myself. And this though I thought I had so counted the lions and so provided the sops!

But let me, before I say more, just tell you a little how The Saloon comes to exist at all—since you say yourself "WHY have you done this thing?" I may not seem so to satisfy so big a Why, but it will say at least a little How (I came to do it;) and that will be perhaps partly the same thing.

My simple tale is then that Forbes Robertson and his wife a year ago approached me for the production of a little old one-act comedy written a dozen years or so previous, and that in the event was to see the light but under the more or less dissimulated form of a small published "story." I took hold of this then, and it proved susceptible of being played in three acts (with the shortest intervals)—and was in fact so produced in the country, in a few places, to all appearances "successfully"; but has not otherwise yet affronted publicity. I mention it, however, for the fact, that when it was about to be put into rehearsal it seemed absolutely to require something a little better than a cheap curtain raiser to be played in front of it; with any resource for which preliminary the F.R.'s seemed, however, singularly unprovided. The matter seemed to me important, and though I was extremely pressed with other work I asked myself whether I, even I, mightn't by a lively prompt effort put together such a minor item for the bill as would serve to help people to wait for the major. But I had distractingly little time or freedom of mind, and a happy and unidiotic motive for a one-act piece isn't easy to come by (as you will know better than I) offhand. Therefore said I to myself there might easily turn up among all the short tales I had published (the list being long) something or other naturally and obligingly convertible to my purpose. That would economise immensely my small labour—and in fine I pounced on just such a treatable idea in a thing of many years before, an obscure pot-boiler, "Owen Wingrave" by name—and very much what you have seen by nature. It was treatable, I thought, and moreover I was in possession of it; also it would be very difficult and take great ingenuity and expertness—which gave the case a reason the more. To be brief then I with consummate art lifted the scattered and expensive Owen Wingrave into the compact and economic little Saloon—very adroitly (yes!) but, as the case had to be, breathlessly too; and all to the upshot of finding that, in the first place, my friends abovementioned could make neither head nor tail of it; and in the second place that my three-act play, on further exploitation, was going to last too long to allow anything else of importance. So I put The Saloon back into a drawer; but so, likewise, I shortly afterwards fished it out again and showed it to Granville Barker, who was kind about it and apparently curious of it, and in consequence of whose attention a member of the S[tage] S[ociety] saw it. That is the only witchcraft I have used!—by which I mean that that was the head and front of my undertaking to "preach" anything to anyone—in the guise of the little Act—on any subject whatever. So much for the modest origin of the thing—which, since you have read the piece, I can't help wanting to put on record.

But, if you press me, I quite allow that this all shifts my guilt only a little further back and that your question applies just as much, in the first place, to the short story perpetrated years ago, and in the re-perpetration more recently, in another specious form and in the greater (the very great alas) "maturity of my powers." And it doesn't really matter at all, since I am ready serenely to answer you. I do such things because I happen to be a man of imagination and taste, extremely interested in life, and because the imagination, thus, from the moment direction and motive play upon it from all sides, absolutely enjoys and insists on and incurably leads a life of its own, for which just this vivacity itself is its warrant. You surely haven't done all your own so interesting work without learning what it is for the imagination to *play* with an idea—an idea about life—under a happy obsession, for all it is worth. Half the beautiful things that the benefactors of the human species have produced would surely be wiped out if you don't allow this adventurous and speculative imagination its rights. You simplify too much, by the same token, when you limit the field of interest to what you call the scientific—your employment of which term in such a connection even greatly, I confess, confounds and bewilders me. In the one sense in which The Saloon *could* be scientific—that is by being done with all the knowledge and intelligence relevant to its motive, I really think it quite supremely so. That is the only sense in which a work of art can be scientific—though in that sense, I admit, it may be so to the point of becoming an everlasting blessing to man. And if you waylay me here, as I infer you would be disposed to, on the ground that we "don't want works of art," ah then, my dear Bernard Shaw, I think I take such issue with you that— if we didn't both *like* to talk—there would be scarce use in our talking at all. I think, frankly, even, that we scarce want anything else at all. They are capable of saying more things to man about himself than any other "works" whatever are capable of doing—and it's only by thus saying as much to him as possible, by saying, as nearly as we can, all there is, and in as many ways and on as many sides, and with a vividness of presentation that "art," and art alone, is an adequate mistress of, that we enable him to pick and choose and compare and know, enable him to arrive at any sort of synthesis that isn't, through all its superficialities and vacancies, a base and illusive humbug. On which statement I must rest my sense that all *direct* "encouragement"— the thing you enjoin on me—encouragement of the short-cut and say "artless" order, is really more likely than not to be shallow and misleading, and to make him turn on you with a vengeance for offering him some scheme that takes account but of a tenth of his attributes. In fact I view with suspicion the "encouraging" *representational* work, altogether, and think even the question not an *a priori* one at all; that is save under this peril of too superficial a view of what it is we have to be encouraged or discouraged *about.* The artist helps us to know this,—if he have a due intelligence—better than anyone going, because he undertakes to represent the world to us; so that, certainly, if *a posteriori,* we can on the whole feel encouraged, so much the better for us all round. But I can imagine no scanter source of exhilaration than to find the brute undertake that presentation without the most consummate "art" he can muster!

But I am really too long-winded—especially for a man who for the last few days (though with a brightening prospect) has been breathing with difficulty. It comes from my enjoying so the chance to talk with you—so much too rare; but that I hope we may be able before too long again to renew. I am comparatively little in London, but I have my moments there. Therefore I look forward—! And I assure you I have been touched and charmed by the generous abundance of your letter.

Believe me yours most truly,

HENRY JAMES

G. Bernard Shaw to Henry James:

21 January 1909.

My dear Henry James,

You cannot evade me thus. The question whether the man is to get the better of the ghost or the ghost of the man is not an artistic question: you can give victory to one side just as artistically as to the other. And your interest in life is just the very reverse of a good reason for condemning your hero to death. You have given victory to death and obsolescence: I want you to give it to life and regeneration. Therefore, to oblige me, write that third act at once.

Nothing is commoner than for a man to begin amusing himself with a trifle, and presently discover that the trifle is the biggest thing he has ever tackled. Almost all my greatest ideas have occurred to me first as jokes. It is quite in keeping that your biggest play should be begun as a curtain-raiser.

In haste—I am in the thick of rehearsals—

Yours ever,

G. BERNARD SHAW

Henry James to G. Bernard Shaw:

23 January 1909.

My dear Bernard Shaw,

This is but a word to say No, I am not "evading," the least little scrap; though alas you will think I am when I say that I am still worried with work and correspondence put into sad arrears by my lately having been unwell and inapt. I am only conscious, I think, that I don't very well even *understand* your contention about the "story" of The Saloon—inasmuch as it seems to me a quarrel with my subject itself, and that I inveterately hold any quarrel with the subject of an achievable or achieved thing the most futile and profitless of demonstrations. Criticism begins, surely, with one's seeing and judging what the work has made of it—to which end there is nothing we *can* do but accept it. I grant of course that we may dislike it enough neither to criticise it nor to want to—only that is another matter! With which, too, I seem not to understand, further, what you mean by the greater representational interest of the "man's getting the better of the ghost," than of the "ghost's getting the better of the man"; for it wasn't in those "getting the better" terms on one side or the other that I saw my situation at all. There was only one question to me, that is, that of my hero's within my narrow compass, and on the lines of my very difficult scheme of compression and concentration, getting the *best of everything*, simply; which his death makes him do by, in the first place, purging the house of the beastly legend, and in the second place by his creating for us, spectators and admirers, such an intensity of impression and emotion about him as must promote his romantic glory and edifying example for ever. I don't know what you could have more. He wins the victory—that is he clears the air, and he pays with his life. The whole point of the little piece is that he, while protesting against the tradition of his "race," proceeds and pays exactly like the soldier that he declares he'll never be. If I didn't shrink from using the language of violence I would say that I defy you to make a man in a play (that shall not be either a comedy or an irony, that is a satire, or something like) proceed consistently, and go all lengths, as a soldier, and do his job, and *not* pay with his life,—not do so without exciting the execration of the spectator. My young man "slangs the ghost" in order to start him up and give him a piece of his mind; quite on the idea that there may be danger in it for him—which I would again defy you to *interest* any audience by any disallowance of. Danger there must be therefore, and I had but one way to prove dramatically, strikingly, touchingly, that in the case before us there *had* been; which was to exhibit the peril incurred. It's exhibited by the young man's lying there gracefully dead—there could be absolutely no other exhibition of it scenically; and I emphasise "gracefully"! Really, really we would have howled at a *surviving* Owen Wingrave, who would have embodied for us a failure—and an ineptitude. But enough—I think it is, really; and I don't and won't use the language of violence. You look at the little piece, I hold, with a luxurious perversity; but my worst vengeance shall be to impose on you as soon as possible the knowledge of a much longer and more insistent one, which I may even put you in peril of rather liking. But till then I am yours most truly

HENRY JAMES

Thus ended the light debate between Shaw who preached dramatic didacticism and James who did not believe art should serve social doctrine. It was a debate between a writer who dealt in psychological truths even when he disguised them in a ghost-play and a skilled dramatist whose art rested on satire and paradox as well as intellectual wit. Shaw told James that all his ideas began as jokes, by which he probably meant as paradoxes. James wasn't that frivolous. He preferred delicate irony. Shaw preached socialism and wanted to change the world and did not hesitate to endow his writings with propaganda. James took the world as he found it. There is no doubt that Shaw could have written a diverting play on James's subject but its message would have been "let's change the system." James was arguing for the artist's depicting human conflict and ambivalence. He wanted to show the plight of Owen Wingrave, caught between his family's rigidities and his profound pacifism.

The Saloon was laid aside again. James had two other plays in hand. He was also revising old travel sketches and assembling another volume of tales. Then came a severe bout of nervous illness and the critical illness of his brother. William James had come abroad in search of health, and the novelist returned to America with him and was with him at his death in August of 1910. He lingered in America into the winter and while there received a request for *The Saloon* from his agent. A note in his memo book of November 15, 1910, says, "Posted *Saloon* to Pinker." Six weeks later the play was produced in London.

The producer was Gertrude Kingston, an enterprising actress who had been on the London stage for some twenty-five years and who had recently built the Little Theatre in John Street (now John Adam Street), Adelphi. Her interest in *The Saloon* stemmed from her preoccupation with psychical research; she was attracted by the idea of the haunted room which James evoked in his play —a room in which there had been a "violent upheaval of passions" and which had become "a psychic repository of emotions." Like Shaw she recognized that the play was "the eternal story of the fight between the shibboleths of the old generation with the advanced theories of the new; Henry James clearly intended to convey the brooding Spirit of the 'House' (or Family) with its threat to the living."

The play opened on January 17, 1911, as curtain-raiser to Cicely Hamilton's *Just to Get Married.* The critics had decidedly mixed feelings about it. H. M. Walbrook in the *Pall Mall Gazette* called it "one of the most thrilling one-act plays produced in London of late years," whereas J. T. Grein in the *Sunday Times* queried: "Do people ever say such things and in such a manner?" The *Daily Chronicle* said it was "a distinct compliment to our stage," and the *Evening Standard* said the characters "spoke as no six people in a country house drawing-room ever spoke." On one thing the press was agreed: in its final moments the play was converted by the actors into ranting melodrama. They pitched the acting in so high a key that at the climax the stage was filled with shouting. The *Daily Chronicle* described it as "the shriek-and-darkness episode at the end of a sort of frenzied duet of soul analysis" and Walbrook said it was a "crude contest between a man yelling and a woman screaming, a sheer noise that afflicted the ear." It was to this that James alluded when he spoke of the "luckless little *Saloon*" and of "the evidently most massacred, by the duffers of actors, *Saloon*."

That Miss Kingston took some liberties with the text we know from a frantic cable dispatched by James on the day before the play opened. It was addressed to his friend, John Pollock, whose long-standing interest in the theatre and acquaintance with London players made him an ideal "ambassador" for the distant novelist. "Horrified at cut of two pages," cabled James to Pollock, "kindly maintain complete restoration." Pollock took the necessary steps of informing Miss Kingston and James's literary agent. There is no record whether Miss Kingston did restore the cut.

There is a record, however, of one important deviation from James's intentions. James had directed that the stage should be plunged into darkness at the crucial moment but gave no indication for the actual introduction of a ghost. He had been careful on this point in the story. The psychically-minded Miss Kingston, however, chose to materialize the ghost, and the spectators saw on the stage what one critic described as "the entry of a pale, dimly-seen figure."

From Henry James in New York to Gertrude Kingston in London: "I gather with real dismay that at the final crisis of *The Saloon* and during the momentary rush of black darkness, some object or figure *appears* on the stage—there is an attempt at the *showing* of the presence or monster that 'walks.' There is absolutely no warrant or indication for this in my text, and I view any such introduction with the liveliest disapproval. . . . Let me very earnestly request you then to suppress the 'figure'. . . ."

CHARACTERS

OWEN WINGRAVE, *young*
SPENCER COYLE, *forty-eight*
BOBBY LECHMERE, *twenty-five*
MRS. COYLE, *thirty-five*
MRS. JULIAN, *fifty*
KATE JULIAN, *twenty*

The Scene after dinner, and on late into the evening, an autumn night, at the country, the only, Home of old General Sir Philip Wingrave, K.C.B., etc.

THE SALOON

The large sitting-room, living-room, place of general assembly, in a plain but ample country-house of an October night; the date of this part of the house, the early Victorian stamp, sufficiently apparent. White woodwork, old pre-aesthetic papering; the pictures on the walls all engravings and all portraits of colonels, generals, military ancestors and greater celebrities still. The furniture rather scant and austere, though highly respectable and beautifully ordered and "kept": one of the principal articles a large glass case against one of the walls, containing precious military relics, old swords and shakos and epaulettes and field-glasses, a collection of family memorials; the other, balancing it, somehow in position, a spare, upright piano, of the old-fashioned "cottage" order, but with faded and fluted green silk in the front. Wide doors halfway down to right; another issue, more or less facing this, to left. The question of a chimney-place not important—this may be down front, out of sight; what is important being rather a highish clear window, not directly accessible from the floor, and not curtained, which must occupy the position most possible in relation to a third door, up at back, sketchily spoken of here as centre. The whole place betrays a little its having been a much older and formerly much lower, in fact quite low-browed "hall," more or less fundamentally renewed and modernised. The high window appears even a survival from some upper storey, perched aloft and alone, after the reduction of the two storeys to one. A large lamp, on a high stand, burns with an old-fashioned glass globe, but with no smart modern shade, up in the angle

left; another matches it on a table down at right. Near the door left is a small table on which, from an early hour of the evening has been set out a little array of old silver bedroom candlesticks; a couple of these indeed are fine old-fashioned flambeaux. Down at right is a larger table, showing, sparsely, a few objects of social use; a bowl of flowers, two or three books, MRS. JULIAN's little basket for her work and her keys. At rise of Curtain MRS. JULIAN, seated right of it, is in the act of taking it from the table to restore to it a roll of crochet or whatever, with which she has been occupied while waiting for the gentlemen to come in from dinner, and otherwise set it in order. She is a pale, sad, rather austere and slightly angular gentlewoman, dressed as in permanent black with high decency and propriety, but with a kind of elegance of frugality. MRS. COYLE, bright and fair and pleasing, much more obviously elegant, dressed in white, with a white fan, and just showing for the least bit bored, sits at the other side of the table, toward centre; further along from whom, at left, reigns a small stiffish unoccupied sofa. Up at the piano meanwhile, her back turned, sits KATE JULIAN, drawing from it a low thin music, but only as if vaguely preluding and playing to herself. She is not yet fairly in sight of us; we wait a little to see her. SPENCER COYLE and Young LECHMERE appear centre, joining, after dinner, the ladies who have been waiting for them; but KATE, from where she sits, is the first to see them; she greets them with a high bright challenge; as in the tone of a young person accustomed to speak not with any rudeness or pertness, but with a certain clear and even slightly proud firmness.

KATE. And poor old Owen? He doesn't care for us?

COYLE. (*Coming down, while* LECHMERE *addresses himself again, and with a youthful sportive flourish, to* KATE; *a slight, keen, alert man with a good, grizzled, intellectual head, a spare, clean-shaven, pedagogical, but eminently intelligent, acute and witty face, a pair of eye-glasses constantly worn, and the formal observance of evening-dress in the shape of his coat and in his black waistcoat, his prim little white tie, as if bought "made-up," and his three gold shirt-studs.*) He cares for us, I think—that is for us, I think—that is for us domestically and *personally*—as much as ever; but won't be able to indulge his passion till his Grandfather has done with him. He appeared to have been instructed, before dinner, to report himself Upstairs as soon as the ladies should leave the table.

MRS. COYLE. (*While she opens out and rather complacently considers her large "smart" fan, in the sense of possession of which she appears to take a certain desolate refuge.*) Sir Philip is well enough to see him then?—in spite of the dire effect Mr. Owen is described as having had on him?—and even though not well enough to have spared poor Miss Wingrave to *dine* with us?

MRS. JULIAN. (*Alert to make everything clear.*) She *was*, you know, to have left her Father—sadly shaken as he is!—long enough to come *down*. She *hoped* so—up to the last moment; and must deplore being reduced to doing so little for you: almost from the moment of your arrival. (*Explaining; as with the largest, most comprehensive reference.*) We scarcely know where we *are*!—under the shock that has made us so count on your sympathy.

MRS. COYLE. (*Amiable; adequate to the occasion.*) We've come, precisely—as I think Mr. Lechmere, on his side, (*looking at him as he descends at sound of his name*) has come—at Miss Wingrave's earnest *wish*: to help you all to *meet* the Shock, and to do you any other good in nature. But we understand your complication, and, with you and Miss Julian as hostesses, we're doing very well.

LECHMERE. (*Who has torn himself from* KATE JULIAN; *a blond young man, with the most ingenuous, open, cheerful countenance, and the most beautifully-appointed evening-rig of white waistcoat with gold buttons, of large white button-hole, and of superlative necktie that contrasts so with* COYLE'S.) Oh, I sprang to my arms, at Woolwich, at the first alarm that reached me—and they've been so good as to give me leave till to-morrow. And I'm not so much at home here—being but a fourth cousin, you know, and not a Wingrave at *that*—as not to have been awfully glad, this afternoon, when I got here to tea, to find the rest of you, just landed, so to speak, as new to the situation, and as fresh and keen about it, as *I* am. Awfully jolly, I seem to feel, to work *into* it with you!

COYLE. (*Who has, after first speaking, dropped upon the sofa at left, and there, throwing himself back so that his head, almost completely reversed, rests on the sofa top and his eyes scan the ceiling, while his fingers, on either side of him, drum in a nervous fidget, on the seat.*) I should like to remark to my gallant ex-pupil that it will be jollier still to work *out* of it with us!

LECHMERE. (*Between* COYLE *and his wife; candid, confident.*) Oh, we'll work out of it all right!

COYLE. (*Changing his posture; just a trifle dryly and pedagogically.*) Let us hope so! But I'm not "new," as a matter of fact—after two such intimate and interesting, two such happy seasons of him—to any of poor Wingrave's scruples, doubts, discoveries: beautiful high convictions on matters no one else—no one ever, before him, in the flower of his youth—has happened to think of.

MRS. COYLE. (*Smiling, complacent, as a fond wife, to the others.*) Of course any old Army Coach, and of course Spencer as so much the hardest-worked of them, is up to most of the tricks that even the cleverest young men can play him.

COYLE. (*While* LECHMERE *has pushed forward into same place a smaller chair; to his wife, good-humouredly.*) You may even say, my dear, that when those tricks are as "clever"—that is as much out of the common—as Owen Wingrave's, they give me a lot to *think* of.

MRS. JULIAN. (*Surprised; definitely dissentient.*) Do you *want* to think so much of a perverse youth who suddenly repays your unstinted faith by deciding to throw up in your face the noble profession you've prepared him for?

LECHMERE. (*Wanting to agree with everyone; falling in; leaning rather back in his chair, one ankle crossed on his knee while he rather complacently looks at the very high polish of his evening shoe.*) It *is* rather rum, Mrs. Julian, a fellow's finding out, when he has done what Owen has, that he doesn't "want" to go for a soldier!

MRS. JULIAN. (*Highly positive.*) And when he can do still what Owen so easily might! (*Full of her deeply-displeased conviction about it.*) I don't know what you mean by "rum"; but when such a thing occurs in such a House as this—when such a Case breaks out in such a Family!—it's very, very dreadful.

COYLE. (*In his place, always patient and a little detached.*) That proud old Sir Philip, and that wonderful Miss Wingrave, Deputy-Governor, herself, of the Family Fortress—that they, with their immense Military Tradition, and with their particular responsibility to his gallant Father, the Soldier Son, the Soldier Brother sacrificed on an Egyptian battlefield, and whose example—as that of his dead Mother's, of so warlike a race too—it has been their religion to keep before him: that *they* should take his sudden startling action hard is a fact I indeed understand and appreciate. But—I maintain it to you (*courteous but firm to* MRS. JULIAN)—I should deny my own intelligence if I didn't find our young man, at our crisis, and certainly at *his*, more interesting perhaps than ever!

MRS. JULIAN. (*Wondering, disapproving, slightly sarcastic.*) And is that what you've come so far to say to Sir Philip?

COYLE. (*Unperturbed.*) I've come, at Miss Wingrave's appeal, to project on my pupil's case, for Sir Philip's benefit, such light as I *may*. But I sha'n't *help* you, at any point, by being a Muff.

MRS. JULIAN. (*With some spirit and some*

dignity; also in clear sincerity.) No, nor by allowing *him* to be one. (*After which, on her feet, having gathered up her basket, to* MRS. COYLE.) I'm afraid I must go to Miss Wingrave—I leave you to my Daughter.

MRS. COYLE. (*Always responsive.*) Your Daughter's a Host in herself!

(KATE JULIAN, *at her Mother's mention of her, has ceased her vague, her softly-incoherent playing and left the piano; she comes down to left of* COYLE, *who rises to offer her the other seat on his sofa. She drops into the right half of it without marked acknowledgment, while he, passing behind it, takes his place again in the left corner.* KATE, *thus presented, is a handsome, dark-eyed girl in a vivid red silk dress which figures throughout the play, for the eye, as the only big patch of colour; the men and* MRS. JULIAN *being each in black, and* MRS. COYLE *all in white; the Saloon too all neutral and grey and severely faded, save for the dim glint of old gold and steel in the glass case of the relics; which colour of* KATE'S *may even vaguely figure a recall of the orthodox scarlet of the British Army. She wears it, as she wears three or four quaint ornaments, of no great value beyond their picturesqueness, a necklace-chain of Oriental beads, several time wound round, and sundry other effective trinkets, with a certain conscious assurance, a slightly amused, though also a slightly desperate defiance: all of which things mark her as a distinctly striking and original and not at all* banal *young person, who will be sure to take in all connections and on all occasions a line and a tone of her own; with the full, and not at all unbecoming or ungraceful, confidence of being able pretty well to keep them up.*)

KATE. We may be Hosts, Mrs. Coyle—but I'm afraid we're scarcely, as you called us just now, "Hostesses"! We're only visitors like yourselves. (*With her eyes on her*

Mother, while she has a nervous up-and-down pat of her foot, not unlike COYLE's *constant drum with his fingers.*) We're not even poor Relations; having but our title of Poverty—which isn't enough. Our visit indeed—thanks to that title!—has lasted five years.

LECHMERE. (*In his place; as from the habit and tradition of "chaff" with her; constantly more or less charmed by her, and never supremely wise.*) Jolly long visit, Miss Kate, certainly.

KATE. (*As for obligatory but indifferent retort, just to keep up the custom.*) Longer, you may quite feel, than I should have been likely to pay *you!*

LECHMERE. (*Aspiring to tease.*) It must have begun then when you were a very small child.

KATE. (*Prompt.*) Yes—and it won't end till you're a very great General.

LECHMERE. (*To keep it up on his side.*) You'll expect me then to arrive with my Staff to carry you off?

KATE. (*As not condescending to inform him of what she may now expect; reverting and confining herself to another point.*) I've been counting for that on Owen. But since he shows the white feather—!

MRS. JULIAN. (*Disapproving this; shocked and protesting.*) Ah my dear—not quite *that!*

COYLE. (*Taking it quietly and as if amusedly.*) Oh, I'm interested in Miss Julian's view.

MRS. JULIAN. (*Apologetic.*) My Daughter's views are very apt to be extravagant.

KATE. (*Clear, definite, unabashed; always perfectly self-possessed.*) Your Daughter's view, Mamma, is that of the Daughter of a Soldier—as *he* was the Son of so many before him. And it's not so different from the view of our Friend and Benefactor, Owen's Grandfather—grand grim old Warrior and Gentleman as we know and admire him—who's the Son and the Grandson and the Great-grandson, and anything else you *like,* of Soldiers; and who, as he was Father, till his loss, of one of the bravest and best, had hoped, up to this strange hour of a Break so unprecedented, that he might believe in the Temper of the Race to the last Generation.

LECHMERE. (*With spirit, optimistic; rallying to his kinsman and comrade.*) Ah, but you know, my Cousin has a Temper of his own!

KATE. (*Trenchant.*) It may be of his "own"—but it's not the old temper of the Wingraves!

COYLE. (*Smoothing the question down as with easy and cheerful tact while he looks at his watch.*) Whatever there is of it, all round, must be blazing away, upstairs then, I gather; and if we hold our breath a little we may perhaps hear, in spite of closed doors, the Boom of the Cannonade!

MRS. COYLE. (*Uneasy, not liking it; as with something between a shrug and a shudder of apprehension.*) I'm sure I want to hear Nothing. You make me among you too nervous.

COYLE. Ah, you yet knew, my dear, that you were coming to a Powder-Magazine!

MRS. COYLE. (*With some intensity.*) As a meek victim to your profession—with young men like Mr. Wingrave, poor dear, till three days ago, preparing, under us, for Horrors—I'm not new, certainly, to military houses. (*Then to* KATE JULIAN.) But I hope you don't mind my saying—what I shouldn't dare to say to Miss Wingrave—that this one gives me the "creeps."

KATE. (*Gravely and as with conscious effect meeting the statement.*) You're right —for the strange things that have been *done* in it.

LECHMERE. (*Gay, knowing, a little fatuous; as with a particular reference.*) Ah, we know all about *them!*

COYLE. (*Cool, restrictive, authoritative.*) On the contrary, Lechmere: acquainted as you are with the place, I yet *suspect* the profundity of your knowledge.

MRS. JULIAN. (*As to pass it off.*) There's really no call for "profundity." You'll be much better occupied with a game of Bridge, when Owen comes back—if (*to* KATE) you'll please see, in the Drawing-room, that the table and the lights are ready. (*To* MRS. COYLE, *explanatory.*) We don't play in the Saloon. We don't do anything in the Saloon.

MRS. COYLE. (*Wondering.*) Is this the Saloon?

KATE. (*Who has left her seat; throwing out her arms with an odd significant gesture of exhibition.*) This—for all it's worth—is the Saloon!

MRS. COYLE. (*To* MRS. JULIAN, *who has just shaken her hand informally, as for a brief separation.*) I sha'n't sit late.

MRS. JULIAN. (*At left.*) I come back. (*Exit* MRS. JULIAN, *left.*)

MRS. COYLE. (*To* KATE; *with a half-sad and all-impatient headshake of renunciation.*) I'm afraid of Bridge—I'm afraid of everything. I should *ruin* you.

LECHMERE. (*Gay, confident; offering himself to her partner.*) Blest, Miss Kate, if *I'm* afraid. *I'll* see you through!

KATE. (*Who has come to right; as keeping him in his place.*) Oh, *you* swagger!

COYLE. (*Conciliatory; falling in.*) Then Owen—who so absolutely *doesn't*—will play with *me.*

KATE. I'll make ready. (*Exit* KATE JULIAN, *right.*)

MRS. COYLE. (*Between her husband and* LECHMERE *now; still seated and appealing to the latter who has come round right.*) Do you mind telling me what's the matter with her?

LECHMERE. (*Judging as a man of the world.*) Why, he has gone back on her!

MRS. COYLE. (*Not seeing it.*) On *her?*

LECHMERE. (*Explaining it as he sees it; smiling.*) On her Profession—it comes to the same thing. They were brought up for each other, and now he's spoiled for her. Mrs. Julian's brother was poor Hume-Walker.

MRS. COYLE. (*Detached; without sympathy.*) And who in the world was "Hume-Walker"?

COYLE. (*Who, having risen when the two ladies have moved, has been turning about thoughtfully an instant, his hands in his pockets; but catching this question and "all there."*) Of the Artillery? He's dead, poor man: shot·through the head, years ago, on the Afghan frontier—to Jane Wingrave's permanent loss.

MRS. COYLE. (*More interested.*) Miss Wingrave was to have married him?

COYLE. (*Definite.*) So I've understood from Owen.

LECHMERE. (*As with high competence.*) Right you are!

COYLE. But all she could do, in her barren mourning—for cold comfort!—was to gather in at last, in *their* like trouble, his widowed sister and half-orphaned Niece; who without her protection, I conceive, wouldn't have had a penny in the world. (*To* LECHMERE.) Am I right?

LECHMERE. (*As before.*) Right you are! (*Completing the tale.*) So that as Sir Philip had taken home *their* Small Boy—

COYLE. (*Taking him up.*) There, at a tender age together, were the two young people—the little black-garbed Scions of Heroes loved and lost.

MRS. COYLE. (*Following; citing* LECHMERE'S *expression of a moment before.*) "Brought up for each other"—?

COYLE. (*Lucid about it.*) Almost as a matter of course.

LECHMERE. Old Jane—I beg her pardon, Miss Wingrave—would awfully have *liked* it. But (*smiling*) the Fat's on the Fire!

MRS. COYLE. (*For perfect clearness.*) Do you mean they're regularly engaged?

COYLE. (*As in perfect possession of it.*) More than regularly engaged. Regularly matched by their elders.

MRS. COYLE. (*Wondering.*) In spite of themselves?

LECHMERE. (*As from knowledge, from observation of the past.*) Oh, they thought it all right!

MRS. COYLE. But they find it all wrong?

LECHMERE. (*Making it out as* COYLE *has turned away.*) *She* does!

MRS. COYLE. (*Emphatic.*) Then she's horrid!

LECHMERE. (*Loud, positive.*) Oh, she's "rum"!

MRS. COYLE. (*Expressive, sincere.*) He's too good for her!

COYLE. (*Who, turning off during this exchange, has fidgetted up, falling again constantly into his own anxiety, his own preoccupation; and who has there, from centre, a view right and left; ·calling sharply down to them in warning.*) Look out!

(*Re-enter* KATE JULIAN, *right; enter* OWEN WINGRAVE, *left; where, pausing a moment, they stand confronted across the stage; each at first more conscious of the other than of the rest of the company; Mrs. Coyle and Lechmere being down and Spencer Coyle still up at centre.*)

KATE. (*Across to* Owen.) I've prepared for Bridge—will you play with *me?*

OWEN. (*Who has looked at her hard, visibly worried and with his handsome young face almost haggard, taking her in before he speaks.*) Ah, I don't know about Bridge! (*Then as he comes down left, pale, in his evening-jacket, with a black necktie, though still in general highly correct and, while addressing himself to the others too, rather sadly and inscrutably smiles.*) I'm engaged in another Game—and I don't know that I can play two at once!

MRS. COYLE. (*Addressing the remark to him.*) Then as I'm an idiot we sha'n't make up four! (*To* MISS JULIAN.) I'd much rather, if I may say so, listen to your beautiful Music.

KATE. (*Who has come down, and has* Mrs. Coyle *and* Lechmere *to her left and* Owen *to her right;* Coyle *remaining up centre.*) As you *like* then. But (*indicating the "upright" instrument*) it mustn't be on *that* low thing. I prefer the big piano.

OWEN. (*His preoccupation, his ravage, controlled and more or less dissimulated through all this, as practically throughout, by marked courtesy and attempted gaiety.*) She's great, Mrs. Coyle, on the Big Piano— she has often played to *me.*

KATE. (*Frank; irreverent.*) Wouldn't this be a chance again then—as David played to Saul?

OWEN. (*Smiling.*) Ah, wasn't that to smooth the old boy down? *You* find strange airs, Kate—that only ruffle me up!

MRS. COYLE. (*All kindness, and as meeting his gaiety.*) *I'll* smooth you down, Mr. Owen—you'll *see* if I don't!

COYLE. (*To his wife; coming down.*) In a moment, my dear—I've something to say to him first.

OWEN. (*Understanding* MRS. COYLE's *good intention.*) You've never been anything but kind to me, Mrs. Coyle—I'll join **you in a** *minute.*

LECHMERE. (*From his place, down, across to* KATE, *who has gone up with* MRS. COYLE.) May I come too?

KATE. (*Up right, after* MRS. COYLE *has passed.*) No. You don't *inspire* me!

(*Exeunt, right,* MRS. COYLE *and* KATE JULIAN.)

OWEN. (*Down centre, between* COYLE *and* LECHMERE, *to the latter of whom he speaks.*) If you don't "inspire" her to keep you on the jump, so much the better for *you!*

LECHMERE. (*Gay.*) Oh, you see, she isn't in love with *me.* That makes her let one off!

COYLE. (*As to turn it lightly.*) She strikes me as a young lady who doesn't let *anyone* off! (*Then after an instant's study of* OWEN's *face, while the young man, still between them, stares with his ill-concealed gravity.*) Have *they*—upstairs—(*indicating quarter, left*) at least had that patience?

OWEN. "Have they" let me off? (*After an instant.*) Yes—if you call it so!

COYLE. (*Interested, wondering.*) Accepted your plea?

OWEN. (*Dry, temperate; but as if feeling it.*) Accepted nothing. Didn't so much as *see* me.

COYLE. (*Surprised.*) After calling you up?

OWEN. (*Consistently grave.*) My Grandfather found when I got there that my presence makes him really too sick. (*Then while* COYLE *makes a gesture of regret.*) They want to see *you.*

COYLE. (*Alert.*) Now?

OWEN. (*Definite.*) They'll presently *send* for you.

COYLE. (*As with his dignity and his position.*) I *count* on it! (*Then reverting to the strangeness of the fact reported by* OWEN.) But I don't understand—

OWEN. (*Taking him up.*) Why I was kept so long, like a stranger or a beggar, or a small boy put in a corner—only to be told at last, at their closed door, by my Aunt's maid, that I couldn't be received at all? No more do *I* understand—unless it be that the Governor can't trust himself not to fly at my throat.

COYLE. (*Deprecating such a fancy; dismissing it.*) That's your gentle joke. And moreover—as you told me in our turn on the terrace after my arrival—he *has* seen you.

OWEN. (*Assenting, so far as that past statement goes.*) Yesterday—when I got here from Town.

COYLE. (*Consistently with this.*) My letter about you—after I had had it out with you in London—had of course prepared him.

OWEN. (*With emphasis; but without violence.*) Prepared him to treat me as a traitor and a sneak.

COYLE. (*Pained, but interested, and so far as possible attenuating.*) We must take into account his Type.

OWEN. (*With expression; ironic.*) Indeed we *must!*

COYLE. (*Following it up.*) But you told him, yesterday, your story?

OWEN. (*Candid and firm.*) I stated my case.

COYLE. (*As to help him out.*) Your "ideas"—crude as I must remind you I still feel them, but worked out for yourself; your convictions, your objections, your insurmountable scruples?

OWEN. (*Definite, clear, unflinching.*) The hatred and horror of War my time with you—and exactly by the ardent use of it you've *taught* me!—has step by step *led* me to. I presumed to express to him what I've come round to think.

COYLE. (*Rueful in his worriment; unable to keep it back.*) Ah, my dear Wingrave, if you only *didn't*, for a little while, "think"!

OWEN. (*Good-humouredly.*) I'm unfortunately a thinking animal—and it's scarcely for *you*, sir, who have *developed* my instincts, to reproach me with that effect of your high Example!

COYLE. (*Half-regretful, half-resigned.*) I've been too *proud*—to my shame!—of your possession of a Mind! (*Then desiring always the rest of* OWEN's *story.*) You betrayed to Sir Philip, at any rate, that you so unnaturally *have* one?

OWEN. (*Very simply.*) Why, it's what I came down here to do.

COYLE. (*As with the scene before him.*) You treated him to those flowers of meditation which you began some months ago

to drop into *my* lap?

OWEN. (*Reporting on it with perfect honesty.*) I told him how I feel—and that positively the more you "cram" me, the stronger the feeling grows.

COYLE. (*Smiling in spite of his uneasiness, and repeating here echoes of their discussions under his own roof.*) You remarked that "the perhaps too wide scope of your reading has itself opened your eyes"?

OWEN. (*Straightforward; falling directly in.*) That I find the ideals of War benighted, stupid, hideous; and find our tribute to those who wage it—when they wage it destructively enough—a worship of gods as false as the idols of savages.

COYLE. (*Reproducing as before.*) You "find the military Delusion, in short, a crass Barbarism"!

OWEN. (*Accepting serenely the paternity of these formulas, and completing it.*) The Scandal of History; the Dead Waste of Power; the Sin and Shame of the *World*.

COYLE. (*As ironically deferring to it.*) So that the study of the Campaigns to which I directed your attention—

OWEN. (*Taking him up.*) Had but for effect to make me reconsider my Position. I could but answer for myself, of course—

COYLE. (*Putting it in a nutshell.*) But you washed your hands of the Career.

OWEN. (*Acknowledging all.*) I left him no doubt that I preferred to embrace some Other.

COYLE. (*With a distressful grimace, while* OWEN, *his last point made, has, half-satisfied, half-restless, turned off; passing his hand over his head and rubbing, all wonderingly, the back of it.*) And you expected to escape with your Life?

OWEN. (*Turning round; clear.*) At least with my Honour. I put it as a matter of Conscience.

COYLE. (*His eyes on him; with a strained smile.*) And you're here—*after* it—to *tell* me?

OWEN. (*Quite ingenuous.*) Should I have been *afraid?*

COYLE. (*Looking at him still; then with a sharp gesture and a tone of admiring irony.*) Don't pretend to me you're not a Soldier!

OWEN. (*Smiling.*) Not a bit more than I can help!

COYLE. You can help *nothing*, luckily—for the immense opinion I have of you. But did he appreciate at least your nerve?

OWEN. (*Thinking it over.*) He glared.

COYLE. (*Wondering.*) Glared?

OWEN. (*Living through the passage again; seeing, evoking again the figure of his interview.*) Confined within his eighty iron years, his wondrous white bristles, his terrible stiff infirmities, as within the steel bars of a cage, he shows the strange gold-coloured eyes and the great white fangs he has still *left!*—like the man-eating Tiger they used to compare him to in India.

COYLE. (*Struck; rising to the strong picture.*) With your Aunt mounting guard as his Keeper?

OWEN. Ah, my Aunt—tall and tremendous as a Grenadier at his General's tent—only fixed on me her Medusa-mask of Deadly Disapproval.

COYLE. (*Taking it all in.*) Well, I don't want to "crow"—but you can't say I didn't *warn* you.

OWEN. (*Doing all justice to that.*) Oh sir, the very house betters your warning. I move about in this air as under the Ban. Strange Voices seem to mutter at me—to say dreadful things as I come. (*Then as explaining—with an odd intensity of expression.*) Keeping well before me, you know, the sense of what I'm doing.

COYLE. (*Rather unpleasantly affected; deprecating.*) Ah, but you mustn't let your imagination run away with you!

OWEN. (*With the same overwrought smile.*) Oh, I assure you it has regularly bolted! (*Then looking at him thus as with the strong veracity of it.*) I've started all the old ghosts. The very portraits glower at me from the walls. There's one in particular—on the second landing of the big staircase—that fairly stirs on the canvas, that just heaves as if to get *at* me, when I pass up and down.

LECHMERE. (*Who, during all this, at his distance, has been deeply and soundlessly attentive, almost awestruck by the full presentment of OWEN's attitude; not presuming to put in his oar, and moved to speech only by this last note.*) Do you mean your terrible Ancestor?

OWEN. (*Understanding.*) The Brute in the black Periwig—the subject of the awful Story.

LECHMERE. (*With his interest, to COYLE.*) Do you object to the awful Story?

COYLE. (*Prompt.*) Only before Ladies.

OWEN. (*Definite.*) Oh, he doesn't appear to Ladies!

COYLE. (*A little moved.*) Then he "appears"—?

OWEN. (*Kindly.*) Never to men as wise as *you!*

COYLE. (*Disclaiming the exemption.*) Oh, I don't want not to know—!

OWEN. (*Taking him up; as with a nervous need now to tell it.*) About the Boy they did to Death?

COYLE. (*Confessing to an imperfect impression.*) You allude to the grim legend of the child his Father corrected—

OWEN. (*Gravely, weightily making the point.*) It was his *Grand*father.

COYLE. (*Slightly embarrassed.*) Oh!

OWEN. (*Going on.*) He died, poor little beggar, of the Correction! (*Looking from one of his companions to the other.*) Administered on the same ground as Mine!

COYLE. (*Rather forcing the note of pleasantry.*) For refusing to go up to Sandhurst?

OWEN. (*Serious.*) For having refused to fight. It comes to the same thing.

COYLE. (*Wondering.*) But who on *earth* —as a Boy?

OWEN. Some other boy who had been put *up* to him. (*With a definiteness as of personal knowledge.*) He wouldn't. He didn't.

LECHMERE. (*At a loss.*) Do you mean he —a—*funked?*

OWEN. (*Consistently clear.*) I mean he —practically—declined the Career. Which closed for him the question of *any!*

COYLE. (*With frank horror-stricken interest.*) The monster beat him to death?

OWEN. He died that night of the beating.

COYLE. How horrible!

LECHMERE. (*Desirous to contribute.*) Ah, but the Monster *paid!*

OWEN. (*To COYLE, whose acute, attentive face asks for it all.*) He went in alone where the child was laid out. (*After an instant.*) But he never came forth again.

LECHMERE. (*With his zeal, to* COYLE.) As he *didn't,* you see, they entered the room.

OWEN. (*Quietly taking it from him.*) They found the wretch dead on the floor.

LECHMERE. (*To* COYLE; *impressive.*) Without traceable cause or wound.

OWEN. (*As if the cause is all evident.*) Stricken by the wrath of the gods.

COYLE. (*Duly affected.*) Lord, what a gruesome tale!

LECHMERE. (*Always to* COYLE.) Yes, for the Monster "walks."

COYLE. (*With a small, irrepressible start.*) Good God, where?

LECHMERE. (*Earnestly, to* OWEN, *who has turned away, with a slight start of his own, on the statement* LECHMERE *has just so frankly made.*) I say, Owen, *where?*

OWEN. (*Up at right; where he turns a moment with his eyes on them.*) Ah, we don't *speak* of it!

(*On which, with a vague but sharp motion of clearing the air of his ugly tale, he goes out abruptly to drawing-room. Exit* OWEN WINGRAVE, *right.*)

LECHMERE. (*Breaking out with expression after a pause during which he and* COYLE *have but gravely looked at each other.*) The Living and the Dead? Hang it, you know, sir, his cheeking them, it *is* Pluck!

COYLE. (*Understanding him.*) His *facing* them all so—and all for an Idea? (*With high emphasis.*) It's all the Blood of all the Wingraves!

LECHMERE. (*Who has moved up to right where, while he is arrested by it, a sudden gust of strange extravagant music, fantastic and exotic, reaches them from the drawing-room.*) Then the Blood of the Wingraves must dance! (*While they listen.*) I say, that Girl *does* play!

COYLE. (*Down left; taking it in.*) Wild, extraordinary Music!

LECHMERE. (*While it goes on; smiling quite excitedly down to* COYLE.) She can knock a chap!

COYLE. (*As to shake it off.*) Too hard— on top of that Story!

LECHMERE. (*Recognising; "knowing."*) It must be "Hungarian Gypsy"!

COYLE. (*Made too uneasy.*) Then it's more than I can *stand!* (*Impatient.*) For God's sake, *stop* her!

(*On which, while* COYLE *passes to right,* LECHMERE, *much taken, and with a gesture that is mainly a reassurance, a "Leave it to* me!" *with a little extra for a "Hush!" so as to lose nothing, bolts to drawing-room. Exit* LECHMERE, *right; after which* COYLE *alone a moment, with a vague gasp as for the sense, about him, of the queer place he has got into, becomes aware of* MRS. JULIAN, *who has appeared in doorway, left, and whom, with comparative relief, he immediately greets.*)

COYLE. Ah, you've *come* for me?

MRS. JULIAN. (*Coming down.*) I've seen Miss Wingrave. Will you please go up?

COYLE. (*Ready, gallant.*) With pleasure. Straight before me?

MRS. JULIAN. (*Who has left the door open.*) To the left at the top of the Stairs. She'll *meet* you. But before you go may I just say this?—that I assume of course you're undertaking to them that he shall still change back.

COYLE. (*A little pulled up and embarrassed, but smiling at her, though with a certain coldness.*) Does he strike you as so much of a Turncoat?

MRS. JULIAN. (*Anxious; grave.*) You think he'll brave it out?

COYLE. (*Still with his smile.*) "Brave" it may be the word!

MRS. JULIAN. (*Disconcerted; still more pained; almost with disgust.*) Is that then the comfort you've brought them?

COYLE. (*More stiffly, as thrown by her challenge upon his dignity.*) My "comfort," Madam, is, I'm afraid, my own affair.

MRS. JULIAN. (*With a movement of her arms that recognises that; yet, in her trouble, and with her eyes gravely dropped, barring his way still.*) I've no right—I know—to challenge you. But I appeal to you for my Daughter. (*Then raising her eyes to him.*) She was to have *married* him.

COYLE. (*After an instant.*) And now she *won't?*

MRS. JULIAN. (*Her eyes on him; sombre.*) He was to have been the Heir.

COYLE. (*Meeting her eyes.*) And the property's not entailed?

MRS. JULIAN. (*With a shrug of despair.*) No longer!

COYLE. (*Taking it in.*) So that if he *isn't* the Heir—?

MRS. JULIAN. (*As if it makes the matter dismally clear.*) She hasn't herself a penny.

COYLE. (*After a grave hesitation.*) How much does she love him?

MRS. JULIAN. (*Who has still stood erect and sombre, again looking down; but who, after an instant, abruptly, moves to right centre.*) Ask it of *her!*

(COYLE *goes left, her movement having cleared the approach, and there, at the door, stops another moment; during which, as she looks across at him, there appears to pass between them a mute troubled interchange; such as he can but take as adding to the difficulty of his own problem. Sharply then, as in recognition of this, with a vain decision, he throws up his hands and goes out. Exit* SPENCER COYLE; *and the next moment, right, re-enter* OWEN WINGRAVE; MRS. JULIAN *passing to left as* COYLE *disappears.*)

OWEN. (*Up at right an instant; more worried, a little more ravaged and "marked," as it were, than on his exit.*) Mr. Coyle's gone up?

MRS. JULIAN. This moment. (*Then as she takes him in; with a nod at the drawing-room.*) You can't stand it there?

OWEN. (*Coming down.*) Not when she plays *at* me so—astounding, you know, as I think her talent.

MRS. JULIAN. It shows you've a bad conscience. You can't bear Martial Music.

OWEN. (*Unabashed.*) Does such stuff strike you as "Martial"?

MRS. JULIAN. (*As in high appreciation of it.*) It sounds to me the Invasion of the Enemy's Country.

OWEN. (*Ironically, rather bitterly.*) Call it rather of the poor Friend's! But you do meet me, I confess, in Full Retreat. Only I so far differ from you about my "con-science" that I feel I retreat in Good Order.

MRS. JULIAN. If you find her Talent, at any rate, "astounding," allow her that advantage to persuade you of your mistake.

OWEN. (*With a certain detachment, but patiently again, as if used to the question now, and as courteously and helplessly resigned to her appeal.*) That's the way then, Mrs. Julian, that even *you* feel it?

MRS. JULIAN. (*With a high, wan, tragic spirit.*) Who in the world should feel it if not "we"? We're the Daughters of more Soldiers, Mr. Owen, than even those of *your* long Roll of Honour!

OWEN. (*Striving for the appearance at least of perfect good-humour.*) Oh, I do you justice—charming, candid guardians, as I've always known you, of the famous Esprit de Corps; Kate in particular the very Vestal of the Sacred Flame.

MRS. JULIAN. (*Intelligently accepting his image.*) We can at least certainly assure you that we've never seen the Sacred Flame extinct.

OWEN. (*Amusedly in his sombre way, but not unkindly.*) You've never been reduced to *blow* upon it—without rekindling a spark!

MRS. JULIAN. (*Looking at him, on this, as for the very strangeness of him.*) You speak as if you werè dead!

OWEN. What else is left a fellow so thoroughly *treated* as dead?

MRS. JULIAN. (*As after an hesitation; deciding.*) To let Kate see you alone, please: which she failed to do through those people—who, when she got back at tea-time from Brighton, were already on the spot.

OWEN. For all the *good* it has done them! (*Then not blinking her question.*) Hasn't she got me for Life?

MRS. JULIAN. (*Always grave.*) In what sense do you mean it?

OWEN. (*Standing there a moment as to attest his identity; his hands in his pockets.*) I mean here I am!

MRS. JULIAN. (*Dubious.*) "Here"? (*Marking frankly the restriction.*) You're here but on one Condition!

OWEN. (*Standing in the same way, but having to take it in; then as putting the thing to the touch.*) Does she give me up?

MRS. JULIAN. (*Up at centre; after an hesitation but then with decision.*) I *leave* her to you!

(*Exit* MRS. JULIAN, *centre; after which, left alone,* OWEN *still stands a moment, lost in thought; then, in his worried way, passing his hand all over his brow and head, wriggling his neck and shoulders a little, even, in their collar and coat, fidgets up restlessly again, getting to left and coming down, with the same preoccupation, on that side. Re-enter* MRS. COYLE, *right; watching him from near the door before he is aware of her.*)

MRS. COYLE. (*Struck with his being alone; struck with everything.*) And my Husband—?

OWEN. (*With an immediate change of face to a civil brightness; nodding at the door near him.*) He's *with* Them, Mrs. Coyle! (*Then as in humorous sympathy for what she has come from.*) *You* can't stand it either?

MRS. COYLE. (*Ingenuous.*) Miss Julian and Mr. Lechmere? Ah, "three," you know, "isn't company"! And I must go to Bed.

OWEN. (*Amiably, vaguely dissuasive.*) So very early?

MRS. COYLE. (*Positive.*) It isn't very early —it's very Late. I feel—I don't know why! —as if I had *never* sat up so late!

OWEN. (*With his desire not to be dreary for her.*) Isn't it perhaps because you've never been so *made* to "sit up"? I'm ashamed to be treating you to a Family Row.

MRS. COYLE. (*As if he needn't too much concern himself about that.*) Oh, your Aunt perhaps thought I'd pour oil on the waters.

OWEN. Ah, the waters are wild! (*Then smiling appreciatively.*) However, she knows your influence on me!

MRS. COYLE. (*Prompt.*) She doesn't know yours on *me!* (*Then with the frankest kindness.*) Seeing you so much in our house, I've never known a young man with less to be "ashamed" of. Will you take *that* from me?

OWEN. (*Touched, responsive.*) I think that from you, Mrs. Coyle—kind as you always were to me—I'd take *anything!*

MRS. COYLE. (*Earnest, sincere for his welfare.*) Then take *this* too—as a bit of expert advice: that in a "family row" there's but one safe place. Let me urge you to go to Bed.

OWEN. (*Amused, protesting.*) Ah, I assure you I never was *less* for Bed! Besides, I must see Mr. Coyle.

MRS. COYLE. (*After an instant; graver.*) What then is he doing for you?

OWEN. (*Smiling.*) Exposing his Life!

MRS. COYLE. (*Serious.*) He *would.* He *believes* in you.

OWEN. He forgives me. That's a great deal—for *him.*

MRS. COYLE. He says you're a Soldier of Soldiers.

OWEN. (*Gay, while at a small table on which the candles for the bedrooms are, in the old-fashioned way, set out, he lights one for her.*) A Soldier who fires in the air!

MRS. COYLE. (*With a sociable shrug.*) That's the kind I like best!

OWEN. (*Appreciative.*) Then here's our very best candlestick for you.

MRS. COYLE. (*As she takes from him the fine antique silver candlestick, admiring it.*) Too lovely! Good-night. (*As she goes up.*) Go to Bed as soon as you *can.*

OWEN. (*Going up a few steps with her; cheerfully assenting.*) As soon as I *can!*

(*Exit* MRS. COYLE, *centre; while he still goes up, and having at once relapsed into his visible uneasiness, comes down again, left, in the same way as after previous exit; restlessly pacing till he sees* LECHMERE *at right, for whose benefit he then straightway assumes again the smile of hospitality and gaiety.*)

OWEN. Clearly *none* of us can stand it!

(*Re-enter* LECHMERE *from drawing-room.*)

LECHMERE. (*Coming down.*) Do you mean "stand" *her?* How can I stand a person who packs me—like a Baby—to Bed?

OWEN. (*Struck; laughing.*) Ah, everyone seems to "pack" everyone *else!* But if Kate packs *you,* you've only to *go!*

LECHMERE. (*Rueful.*) But what are *you* doing?

OWEN. (*Definite; unembarrassed.*) Oh, I'm sitting up.

LECHMERE. (*Yearning.*) Late?

OWEN. As late as I dare!

LECHMERE. (*As if struck with his use of the term.*) As you "dare"?

OWEN. (*After an instant.*) In a house in which I've so markedly failed to please!

LECHMERE. (*On reflection; as if judging he ought to speak.*) It's Miss Julian who's down on you *most*—as I suppose you *know.*

OWEN. (*With a certain arrest, a certain dryness.*) Yes, I know.

LECHMERE. So will *she* sit up?

OWEN. (*Smiling.*) Probably. For a chance to "wig" me.

LECHMERE. (*Unsatisfied.*) I mayn't come back to smoke?

OWEN. (*Good-naturedly ironic.*) You mean, to protect me?

LECHMERE. (*Still not satisfied; smiling, more or less assenting.*) There's no smoke without *fire!*

OWEN. (*Having to recognise this; yet perfunctory; not really desiring his return.*) Yes, old man—if you very much *want* to.

LECHMERE. (*After a moment, looking at him.*) Thanks then.—I won't. (*With good-humoured sarcastic significance.*) I see Miss Julian smokes!

OWEN. (*Inadvertent, a little "off"; as if not having noticed that she has taken it up.*) *Does* she? On your principle then—that there's no fire without *smoke!*

LECHMERE. I understand. (*Yet hesitating still, as for something that* must *keep him.*) May I smoke in my *room?*

OWEN. (*Slightly surprised, but all easy about it.*) If you'll risk my Aunt's sniffing it!

LECHMERE. (*Struck; considering.*) Will her room be now near mine?

OWEN. (*Vague.*) I'm not quite sure how they've placed you.

LECHMERE. Oh, awfully well—with a four-poster and three windows and jolly old sporting prints; just where a passage comes out.

OWEN. (*Recognising.*) Under the round skylight? (*Confident.*) Oh no—you're all right *there.*

LECHMERE. (*Interested; with intention.*) *Really* all right?

OWEN. (*Reassuringly.*) My Aunt's in the other quarter.

LECHMERE. (*After an instant; bringing it out.*) But I don't mean only safe from Miss Wingrave, don't you know?

OWEN. (*Not catching on.*) Then from what else? The Governor's further still.

LECHMERE. (*Looking at him hard; then abruptly.*) It's not where that horror took place? (*After which, as* OWEN, *with a movement, meets his look; following it up.*) It's —if one *sleeps* there—not where your Monster "walks"?

OWEN. (*Astonished; at a momentary loss.*) He died in *that* room?

LECHMERE. Miss Julian says so.

OWEN. (*Still more surprised.*) She *speaks* of it?

LECHMERE. (*Seeing* KATE JULIAN *who has reappeared, right.*) She'll tell you what she speaks of!

(*Re-enter* KATE JULIAN *from drawing-room.*)

KATE. (*Who has caught, on her pause in doorway, at first unnoticed by them, both* OWEN's *question and the answer, and who comes down serene.*) Why shouldn't we *all* speak of a matter that so tests—all round— our Vocation?

OWEN. (*Pulled up; but rising to it gallantly.*) What do you call, Kate, *your* vocation?

KATE. (*Prompt, frank.*) What I don't call yours. The Military!

LECHMERE. (*Taking it straight on from her; referring to what she has said.*) That's it. It *shows*—such an experience—if a fellow's "game."

OWEN. (*Showing no wound from her thrust of a moment before, and as if amused now.*) If *you* are?

LECHMERE. (*Duly modest, but completing his idea.*) If I've got my Pluck.

OWEN. (*As having made up his mind; again at the little table with the lights.*) I think that what you had *better* have is your Candlestick!

KATE. (*Impatiently, dismissingly, while* LECHMERE *takes it.*) Good-night.

OWEN. (*With a kindliness and cheerfulness visibly intended for all reassurance; all easy rejection of the question just broached.*) Good-night, Bobby.

LECHMERE. (*After a long look of scrutiny from one to the other.*) Good-night, Owen. (*He goes up, stiff and straight, with his candlestick, as if to charge an entrenched enemy. Exit* LECHMERE, *centre.*)

OWEN. (*Earnestly, as soon as he is alone with* KATE.) It's surely not, by our horrible record, *there*—?

KATE. (*So that he shall be explicit.*) "There"—?

OWEN. Where they've put poor Lechmere. (*Then as she only looks at him.*) That my awful Ancestor used to be supposed to show himself.

KATE. (*Where she stands; impenetrable.*) What should *you* care—about that matter?

OWEN. (*Mystified by her tone; staring.*) Is there a particular reason, Kate, why *you* should? (*Then as, under this straight challenge, she temporarily gives way, turns off with a drop of her arms, as if she's more concerned than she's just yet ready to say, and so postpones the question.*) Isn't it just our advantage—in this age, after all, of less stupidity, and of greater decency—that we've stamped out the story and *exorcised* the Ghost: so that nobody, today, is in a position to *say?*

KATE. (*Facing him again; appreciating, weighing his question.*) Do you call it an Advantage?

OWEN. (*Confident, easy.*) Surely! To have cast out—(*his smile quite natural*) so far as we ever *can!*—the Foul Fiend!

KATE. (*As more or less lucidly considering.*) Then you make nothing of the high distinction—?

OWEN. (*Taking her up as if "twigging" her notion.*) Of our being able to brag of our Ancestor's continued Attention to us—?

KATE. (*Taking him up in turn.*) Of your enjoying, in your Exposure to it, a regular Touchstone, installed and enshrined among you—!

OWEN. (*While she waits, as from discretion, to develop further.*) A Touchstone for what?

KATE. (*As if she perfectly sees for what.*) Well for character.

OWEN. (*Turning it over; doubtful.*) "Character"?

KATE. (*Still with her clearness for herself.*) Well, for Virtue.

OWEN. (*More doubtful still—in fact quite derisive; as if the word, in the connection, is unexpected to him.*) "Virtue"?

KATE. (*Firm.*) In the fine old sense. (*Then immediately going on.*) I mean that —for all we know!—it may still sometimes act.

OWEN. (*Quite blank now in his failure to rise to this fine theory; losing even the thread of her argument; staring at the question.*) What *is* it, you hold, that "acts"?

KATE. (*With rising impatience.*) Why— on occasion—the Test I speak of!

OWEN. (*Still not apprehending.*) "On occasion"? On *what* occasion?

KATE. (*Cool.*) On occasions—if they come up!—of Doubt!

OWEN. (*Even yet vague.*) Of doubt of our Virtue? (*And then as she throws off, as almost with irritation at his remaining so out of it and at her having to explain so much, a gesture of assent.*) How the dickens does it "test"?

KATE. (*As if he's really now too "off" for patience.*) Don't you *know* then the central Legend of your House?

OWEN. (*Sceptical and sad.*) Ah, for all my "house," poor old thing, is worth *calling* "mine"!

KATE. (*Strenuous, not heeding this.*) Don't you know, and don't you value, your grandest superstition?

OWEN. (*As if fairly amused at her simplicity.*) Aren't Grand Superstitions, my dear, exactly what I'm buffeting? (*Then as she but repeats her movement of impatience.*) Besides, thank God, there are allusions that have always been, among us, "taboo."

KATE. So that you've preferred not to think of the Facts?—and will perhaps be shocked at one's having tried a little to face them *for* you?

OWEN. (*Affected a little by the meaning she appears to put into this.*) May I ask just how you've "faced" them?

KATE. (*Prompt, clear, as if seeing it perfectly for herself.*) By admiring, in the first place, the great Sense they have always *had* here. Which you don't even yet seem to me to understand! (*Then as he shows his own impatience.*) It's their having been *felt* so that makes them fine. (*Conceding, yet insisting; while her good faith about it overbears his dissent.*) It's horrible, yes—the story; the young scared Wingrave who wouldn't fight, and the older passionate Wingrave who couldn't *forgive* that; he paying, in the event, for his unholy passion, no doubt—as the poor boy paid for his want of pluck. (*Lucid and strong.*) Dreadful, pitiful the story in itself; but so grand—by what was to *come* of it—for the Spirit of you All!

OWEN. (*Who has taken this from her, as she has developed it, with a growing rigour of resistance.*) I should never have supposed anything so strange could have come of it as to hear you speak of it without Execration.

KATE. (*As if fairly at last amused at his benightedness.*) You're not up, Owen, to the height of your History! It has given you all the stiff consciousness that has *made* you soldiers. You've *faced* the tradition of the Plea for the Fighter. You've undergone—each of you at his hour—the Consecration. (*Completing the expression of this.*) It *becomes* one—must I explain—? that a Wingrave—when need is—shall have *seen* him.

OWEN. (*Still and always taking nothing from her as a matter of course.*) Seen him? Seen whom?

KATE. (*After an instant; holding off, at the last, from definitely naming.*) What has been seen.

OWEN. (*Rallying a little to the conception, as an effect of her tone; but with his interest even now of a detached kind, as for the mere ugly romance of the latter.*) The Shade of all the Shades? (*Then as her face, for the portentous thing, but dumbly and gravely assents.*) The Brute of all the Brutes? (*After which, as she but keeps her eyes on his own.*) To be met—"walking"? Where?

KATE. (*As really now in fair disgust at his voluntary density.*) Here!

OWEN. (*Nevertheless still questioning.*) Here?

KATE. (*Immensely emphatic.*) Here! (*Then going on at once with her demonstration.*) When the great thing has hap-

pened you know where you *are!*

OWEN. (*Still as with his density, wilful or natural.*) The "great thing"—?

KATE. (*Sticking to her story.*) If you're Good—*then!*—you've reason to know it.

OWEN. (*Still staring, none the less, and challenging; accepting at all no further than he sees or wants to.*) Good for what?

KATE. Good for Life!

OWEN. (*As after thinking a moment.*) But what do you *call* "life"–

KATE. (*Expressively, aggressively.*) Glory!

OWEN. (*His eyes on her; with sombre intensity.*) Rot! (*He takes a quick, disgusted turn away from her; but at once wheels round as with recovered self-control, piecing up her sense of a moment before.*) If we're "good," you say, we've reason to know it?

KATE. (*Splendidly clear.*) As the Knights of old knew it when they had passed their Vigil!

OWEN. (*With his hands in his pockets and his eyes on her; as if thinking of more things than he can say or than she'll understand.*) I feel—do you know, Kate?—as if this were *my* Vigil!

KATE. (*Blank.*) "This"?

OWEN. What you're putting me through.

KATE. (*With a shrug, a throw-up of her hands as for his notion of an ordeal.*) Oh—"I"!

OWEN. (*Good-humouredly.*) Well, I bear up! (*Then reverting.*) If you're *not* "good," at any rate—I suppose you mean to say—you've reason to know it even better!

KATE. (*As in entire possession of her case.*) They know it best who find you—as they found *him*: dead of the Death—

OWEN. (*Breaking in as too impatient for any but his own emphatic and entirely invidious way of putting it.*) Of the Bully, the Beast and the Murderer? (*Then while he has thus recovered it, taken it to himself as coming back from an old hearing; but with an immediate drop of any tension and a return to his high fine irony.*) The picture's really charming, and I thank you for bringing it *home* to me! But it's a case—when it happens!—in which the distinction, as you say, seems mainly for others than the Victim.

KATE. (*Matching her sarcasm to his own.*)

In the sense certainly that Others "distinguish"! If you survive the Shock, you're *not* a Victim, you see!

OWEN. (*As for amusement.*) Ah, then you may survive?

KATE. (*Definite; straight.*) You survive it if you've not been Afraid.

OWEN. (*As not, however, making it out.*) But if you're to survive, what is there to be afraid of?

KATE. (*Bethinking herself.*) You may be afraid of your own Fear.

OWEN. (*Following it, but objecting.*) You may in other words be in a preliminary Funk? Perhaps you *may* be! Some people are, no doubt, about everything. But if you're *not?*

KATE. (*Pulled up by this question; echoing it while she again thinks.*) "If you're not"—?

OWEN. (*Simply.*) I mean if you're afraid of Nothing. For you may be *that* too. (*Still simply.*) You see there *are* people—!

KATE. (*After an instant; giving it temporarily up.*) Yes—there are people!

OWEN. (*Pursuing it then in his own way.*) Who are afraid of nothing so much as a false—and a damnably vulgar!—conception of Honour! (*With a certain extra and more intentional coldness of irony.*) I don't mind telling you, you know, that I'm one of those. (*After another moment.*) I'd *take* the Chance—*that* way!

KATE. (*Not following.*) What way?

OWEN. (*Lighted with his thought.*) I'd redeem the Superstition.

KATE. (*Still at a loss.*) "Redeem" it?

OWEN. By treating it to a dose of *my* view of Honour—which is not to go in for the consecration of the Brute but for the affirmation of the Man and the liberation of the Spirit.

KATE. (*Understanding now enough to protest with a sharp retort.*) The people you call Brutes I call Heroes!

OWEN. (*Letting her have it back as sharp.*) The people you call Heroes I call Slaves! (*Then following this ardently up.*) Our legend, so stupidly, coarsely felt, has really no sense. It has meant, all the while, that if we *do* enjoy the privilege, as you call it, of the Test, we *should* be free Spirits. But we've never *risen* to that! If

we had we'd have made the End.

KATE. (*In deep but puzzled dissent.*) The "End"?

OWEN. (*Immediate.*) Of our tenth-rate view of Honour! We'd have routed—by our *contempt*—the Monster!

KATE. (*With a slow sad headshake; concluding to her own satisfaction, gravely, loftily, though just a little pityingly, on all this.*) You'll never rout him.

OWEN. (*As if he can afford to be amused.*) You mean he'll rout *me?*

KATE. It strikes me you *are* "routed." He doesn't recognise Failures.

OWEN. (*Brightly, rather extravagantly smiling.*) Ah, there you are with your low measure of Success. You want too much to live!

KATE. (*As agreeing to it with reserves.*) For Honour.

OWEN. (*Prompt, gay.*) Well, my dear, *I'm* ready to *die* for it.

KATE. (*As if these are easy words; impatiently.*) Oh!

OWEN. (*Sticking to his point and keeping it up.*) But—for *mine!* (*Then as he turns to the portraits, the old military engravings, more or less clustered on one of the walls.*) Not, you poor benighted old dears, for Yours! (*After which, as if grasping with his active play of thought still another connection of the matter, he faces again* KATE.) There's another thing, moreover, you know: even *they,* poor dears, (*with a nod at the gathered ancestors*) ended by funking. They did *that* when, sixty years ago, they altered the house.

KATE. (*With her detachment; but catching on.*) You mean when you built the Saloon?

OWEN. (*Definite.*) I mean when we built the Saloon.

KATE. (*As if all quietly and cleverly knowing better; not looking at him.*) You hold that that made the difference?

OWEN. (*Still as clear.*) I hold that it— practically!—*cleared* us. I hold that—to the relief of the nerves even of the Wingraves!—it cast out the Demon.

KATE. (*Always as with her deeper knowledge.*) You consider that he went "for good"?

OWEN. I consider that the work was done,

before my Father's time, exactly to the stiff *intention,* and the effective *promotion,* of his "going." This part—the fact sticks *out!*—is wholly, serenely, *modern.*

KATE. Don't you feel, nevertheless, that the Facts are all *round* us?

OWEN. The Facts?

KATE. Well, the scene, the old room of the Story.

OWEN. (*As not feeling it.*) In this space (*indicating the great extent, the ample form and the high ceiling of the place*) that swallows it up?

KATE. There was another floor, yes— *this* occupies the whole height. We stand *below*—but what happened happened but just *above.* So that if your great modern work—!

OWEN. (*While she hangs fire.*) Didn't *do* it—?

KATE. (*Almost triumphantly.*) The Demon *isn't* cast out!

OWEN. (*While he looks at her, wondering, as if she has produced in him a glimmer of doubt.*) If I *believed* that, my dear—!

KATE. Well, if you believed it—?

OWEN. (*Intensely, grimly.*) I *promise* you, I promise *him,* I'd "cast" him!

KATE. (*While he walks up as under the sudden stir of it; speaking dryly.*) It would probably be something of a job.

OWEN. (*As he returns.*) That's exactly why I should *like* it! (*Then pausing before her again.*) Better, Kate, than I like *your* deviltry!

KATE. "Deviltry"?

OWEN. Your "cheek" to poor Bobby— about *his* queer Room! You're the Arch-Tormenter of the Youth of England!

KATE. (*As not caring if she is.*) The Youth of England contains some Silly Specimens! Why did you invite him—at such a time?

OWEN. (*Charitably, cordially.*) He's the best little Sort going, and—for a third Cousin twice removed, on my Mother's side!—full of Family Feeling. Getting wind of the "time"—and just by *reason* of it— he offered himself. He *likes* Danger. (*Smiling.*) So you haven't scared him!

KATE. (*Quietly; coldly; without irritation.*) Then why did he *appeal* to you?

OWEN. (*Easy on it; smiling.*) Not for Fear. For Hope. (*Looking at her with his smile.*) So he'll be disappointed.

KATE. (*Who is now, in her own way, with the whole situation on her nerves, restless and preoccupied; even though her "own way" is so much to control it.*) Yes, he'll be disappointed. (*She looks vaguely into a book she has taken from a table, and puts it down again.*) I *wanted* to disappoint him.

OWEN. (*Looking at her as if at last really puzzled.*) You take a great deal of trouble!

KATE. (*Not looking at him; wandering off a little.*) You *give,* my dear Owen, a good deal! (*Then with an abrupt turn, as if putting it on the nearest score.*) I had three Changes, this afternoon—and three *Waits!*—on my way from Brighton.

OWEN. (*All adequately prompt.*) Then I feel your exertions, Kate—I recognise them fully. But remember I hadn't *called* you.

KATE. (*As if it comes almost to the same thing.*) Miss Wingrave "called" me—urgently *wrote* me: as soon as your Bomb had *burst!* But I wouldn't have come for *her* only. (*After an instant.*) I don't mind confessing that I came for my own relief.

OWEN. (*With the expression of what he misses.*) Ah, if you could tell me you're here for *mine*—!

KATE. (*Her head up—even to the rigour of a certain disdain.*) What do you want of "relief"? Who among *our* people has ever asked for it?—unless wounded in Battle?

OWEN. (*Standing before her, his hands in his pockets; looking down fixedly a moment, then raising his eyes to her.*) You don't consider that I'm pretty well wounded?

KATE. (*Not touched.*) While you can walk about and *complain* of it?

OWEN. (*Simply; quietly; with his slight shrug.*) Oh, I don't complain. (*With his stiff, dim, resigned smile.*) I accept my Fate.

KATE. (*Resolute.*) If you'll allow me to say so, I don't think you so much as *see* it—the fate of a Wingrave who has backed out!

OWEN. (*Who has turned away, without sharp impatience, only with extreme gravity and repressing sharpness as if from good taste; then, after four or five steps in which*

he works this off, has come down again.)
There are things I *regret*—several; though
I had *thought* of them well first. But do
you know what I regret *most*? (*Then as
she throws up her hands and drops her
arms as to indifference to the question.*)
I regret causing you all to take up with
such vulgar terms.

KATE. (*Stiff, not other than hard.*) The
way not to be described in vulgar terms
is not to do—vulgar things!

OWEN. (*Not wincing at this; taking it in
his own way; but looking at her a moment
with all his gravity.*) Do you know what I
really *thought?* I thought you might *understand.*

KATE. (*Less patient in proportion as
he's more so.*) Ah, you've had wonderful
thoughts!

OWEN. (*Shaking his head; repudiating
all excess.*) Not of the Others—no. But of
you.

KATE. (*Dry.*) There are things I don't
want to understand.

OWEN. (*Going on in his own way.*) You
used to be so kind; and never so much as
in that time here—which seems far and
short now, but wasn't it six months long?—
when you had come back from school, all
bristling with accomplishments and all
blooming with beauty, and I hadn't gone
on my fool's errand to London! You were
kind even at the hour I spoke to you—!

KATE. (*Giving way a little, and taking
him up and assenting, while he pauses
with the force of that reference.*) Of what
might happen for us some day—if, as we
said, you did *well.*

OWEN. (*Reconstructing, with this clarity,
their young recent past.*) On which—according to my lights, and to dear old
Coyle's I *did* "do well."

KATE. (*Accepting the picture.*) And I
waited.

OWEN. (*Filling the picture out.*) For a
year—till you went away.

KATE. (*Definite; contesting nothing of
it.*) To Brighton—for my poor relations;
and Abroad—for my French, for my
Music.

OWEN. (*With sharp, but not harsh
irony of reminder.*) Aye indeed—your
Music! which used, I remember, so to

charm me—as everything about you did!

KATE. (*Moved in a manner by this; in a
degree giving way, or at least breaking
out.*) Ah, when you talk of what "was"!
(*With sincerity.*) As if I *want* to do anything but "charm" you!

OWEN. (*His eyes on her while, flushed
with this avowal, she shines there before
him.*) Do you pretend, Kate, really to *care*
for me?

KATE. (*Going on with the same intensity.*) As if I've done anything—anywhere
—but *wait!*

OWEN. (*Upright before her; simply;
throwing up his hands as in an offer or a
surrender.*) Well, then, here I *am!*

KATE. (*Falling back again on her difficulty.*) "You"? How can I take it for *you?*

OWEN. (*With the same sad frankness.*) I
never was more than *now*—what I sincerely *am.*

KATE. (*After an instant; then as with
salutary resolution.*) Then do you *know*
what you are? You're—! (*But with the
sound checked on her lips by her sight of
SPENCER COYLE, left.*)

(*Re-enter SPENCER COYLE, left.*)

COYLE. (*Back from the interview upstairs, and catching her question before
either of them have seen him; standing
there a minute with it in his ears and
looking from one of them to the other.*)
I've come back to *tell* you what you are,
Wingrave—if you're prepared to *take* it
from me.

OWEN. (*Immediately gallant and cheerful.*) I had occasion just now to say to Mrs.
Coyle, sir, that I'd take *anything* from
either of *you!*

COYLE. (*Coming down; grave and troubled; repudiating all personal responsibility for his news.*) Ah, it's no judgment
of ours!

OWEN. (*Sounding COYLE's face with his
strained smile.*) But I *am* "judged"?

COYLE. You're sentenced! (*Then after
an instant.*) You're Disowned.

KATE. (*Loudly and irrepressibly, as with
the sharp harsh shock of it.*) Oh!

(*On which, as it makes the two
men turn their eyes on her—from
something almost sinister in the
sound of it—she bears their atten-*

tion but an instant and turns off, moving half-way up; where, as if stricken, yet motionless and stiff, her back presented, she remains during what next passes between them.)

OWEN. You mean of course (*smiling*)—substantially!

COYLE. (*Facing it.*) *And* morally! I mean you're Disinherited.)

OWEN. To the last penny?

COYLE. To the *last:* with the money all to go—!

OWEN. (*Taking him up.*) Oh I *feel* where the money's to "go"! To the Endowment of Research! Into New Explosives!

COYLE. (*With a rueful shrug; vaguely but sadly acknowledging.*) There are plenty of Organizations—!

OWEN. (*With gaiety.*) All more or less directly pegging away at them? (*With full assent.*) So many that even so clever a man as you couldn't play them *all* a trick!

COYLE. (*As having to accept this failure.*) Not, alas, to your advantage. Once before Sir Philip, I could—to *save* you—but say, with all my lungs, how much I *believe* in you. (*Then sombre, sick, with a despairing drop of his arms.*) But it's just *that* that damns you!

OWEN. (*Bright, with interest.*) By proving I'm not a Donkey?

COYLE. By attesting that you've a head!

OWEN. (*Clear, confident, grateful; frankly putting out his hand.*) Well, I shall *keep* my "head"!

COYLE. (*As to complete his report.*) And I promised them—in my wrath—that you'd fight!

OWEN. (*Who after giving a shake to* COYLE's *surrendered hand, has gone to the small table where the candlesticks stand; gay.*) I'd "fight"—any time—for Peace!

KATE. (*Who has finally turned round; coming down, at this, with her self-possession and assurance recovered.*) What more then did Marlborough?

COYLE. (*Meeting her as brightly as he can.*) Surely! We must *keep* old Marlborough!

OWEN. (*Coming to him with his lighted candle.*) Then may he guard your Dreams!

COYLE. (*Taking the candle from him,*

but uncertain and as if loth to leave him this way; interrogative.) Good-night?

OWEN. (*With decision.*) Good-night. You've earned your *rest.*

COYLE. (*Unappeased; with his light.*) I wish I could have earned Yours!

KATE. (*Strenuous; with "spirit."*) The Wingraves don't "rest"!

COYLE. (*Facing her an instant; uneasy.*) And don't even the Julians?

OWEN. (*Still with animation, but eager to get him off.*) Never from their Duty!

COYLE. (*Always with his candle; looking as with an effort of penetration from one to the other, yet feeling no liberty of interference.*) I leave you then to your Fate?

OWEN. (*Gallantly.*) My Fate is this young lady!

COYLE. (*Looking at her hard; which she meets, and then at* OWEN; *with high expression, sincerely.*) Soldier! (*Exit* SPENCER COYLE, *centre.*)

KATE. (*Down left, while* OWEN *is up centre, where* COYLE *has taken his good-night and left him.*) That lamp's going down.

OWEN. (*At the large lamp indicated, which is on a table or a stand of its own between centre and right.*) It should go *out.* (*He turns it out, so that the light in the room, which visibly shows but one other, is reduced by half—a marked difference; then comes down opposite* KATE, *with whom for a long minute of silence he is thus confronted. They remain in presence, vaguely, almost awkwardly moving, as if after the knowledge with which* COYLE *has left them there can be no "cheap" and immediate speech; each appearing to wait for what the other will say. It is* KATE *at last who speaks.*)

KATE. You can have it all *back*—with a word.

OWEN. (*So full of his own vision of his case that he seems at first scarce to understand her.*) "Back"?

KATE. All you've so horribly sacrificed.

OWEN. (*His eyes on her; apprehending.*) All the Property, you mean?

KATE. (*With the highest emphasis.*) All the precious old Place and all the precious old Honour.

OWEN. (*Considering this; putting it to*

her as with all his irony.) The precious old Honour it would seem then—when we really come to it!—*is* the precious old Place?

KATE. (*Not disconcerted; always consistent.*) The One is the symbol of the Other. You may call them the Same—for *me. (Then after an instant.*) But you hold them still in your hand.

OWEN. (*Reading what she means by this.*) If I return and kneel down and make submission? (*Then as she doesn't say it.*) If I promise I'm sorry and will never do it again—and take my thrashing to *prove* it?

KATE. (*Always hard, and with her hardness sharpened now by the irony of his own tone.*) Oh, you'd *have,* I think, to take your *thrashing!*

OWEN. (*Stands, at this, a moment longer, and then turns sharply off; moving up, afresh, in his trouble, while she watches him. Then he comes down and is again before her.*) Will you have me as I *am?*

KATE. (*Clear and without hesitation.*) It's not as you "are" I ever *dreamed* of you.

OWEN. (*As to put it to her, to make sure for himself.*) But *with* Everything as it was—?

KATE. (*Prompt, as clear as before.*) Yes! We should be again as *we* were!

OWEN. (*Quiet a moment; taking the full measure of it; then speaking with a certain dryness.*) You're not like dear old Coyle. *You* don't "believe" in me!

KATE. (*Firm, logical.*) I reply to that enough when I show you the way to *make* me.

OWEN. (*Who has once more moved off, to come back as before, while he looks at her as in sad, in positively mystified wonder for the consistency of her strangeness.*) You spoke a while ago of your wanting to "charm" me. (*Then going on before she shall answer.*) Your way then to charm me is to show me that all the while I thought only of *you,* you thought—!

KATE. (*As he pauses an instant, looking round him at the half-darkened room, almost sinister now, in the sleeping house, under its shade as of more than midnight, and she appears, irritated by his present note, sombre and sinister herself, to dare*

him to bring what he seems to be going to say home to her.*) Well, I thought—?

OWEN. (*As with what he has come to feel for everything about him breaking out, under this last acute impression, in a flare of resentful passion.*) Only of this evil Estate!

KATE. (*Stirred and put in the wrong by his clear sincerity, yet stirred the more to anger because of being put in the wrong; and collecting herself, while she glares at him, pale and dangerous, for her retort.*) You shirk then these stern shades only to shirk your Duty?

OWEN. (*Starting as if now reached, seriously, for the first time by this particular thrust or taunt.*) I "shirk"?

KATE. (*Carried further still by the passion of her retort.*) You talk of defying "tests," and can't even face your professional chances? (*Then intensifying her effect while he but straightens and gasps at the force of her assault.*) You break with everything here only to break with Courage?

OWEN. (*Echoing, blank and fairly appealing in his stupefaction.*) "Courage"?

KATE. (*Pursuing it without mercy to her climax.*) I grant it as much as you *like*— this house is no home for a Coward!

OWEN. (*Lashed as across the face; with a cry of pain and rage.*) A "coward"?

KATE. (*As with surprise for his surprise, of so strong and convincing a note; not sparing him as yet either, yet speaking in good faith.*) Does it only *now* dawn on you that that's what we all find you and how we all judge you?

(OWEN, *without reply, for a minute, raises his two hands to his head, passes them over it and his face, keeping them before his face as if to control this momentary convulsion. Then with a gesture as for the unspeakable consciousness and the odious revelation he has so of a sudden waked up to, he still again turns away and, still coming back, faces her still again; she, with the change in the situation, and in their acute relation, produced by his so genuine amazement at her charge, and so potent scorn of it, marked in her at present not looking at him, in her, on the contrary, herself moving away. He has, however, with his immense, intense effort, now so far controlled himself as to be able to speak quietly and coldly; to speak really, in fact, as with the icy chill of a positive detached curiosity.*)

OWEN. I care little for the wisdom of you "all"—and fortunately recognise Exceptions. But I'm to take it as *your* bright judgment—? (*Then as, still not looking at him—only wincing rather, with her eyes down, for the high, disdainful incision of his "bright"—she only waits.*) That I'm acting but to save my *skin?*

KATE. (*So much in the wrong, if she is really and utterly so, that she can't afford, thus on the spot, to recognise it—which the "icy chill" of his tone, as we easily see, makes precisely but the more difficult; and therefore, like the clever creature she is, finding her issue in an apparent mildness that may express for him the very candour of pity.*) "Save" it, my dear Owen, as much as you *like!* Good-night.

(*On which she goes up as to make her exit at centre, he making no answer; but she then pauses at centre and for a moment, unseen by him, takes him in as he stands upright and motionless, but brooding on the outrage and the stigma of which she has been the voice. At last then, as for reasons that have begun vaguely to ferment in her, she decides to speak again.*)

KATE. You sit up? (*After which, as he remains as if he has not heard her, she contends for a moment with her hesitation and her pride, and comes down, right, repeating her question.*) Do you sit up here?

OWEN. (*As coming back from a distance, from the depth of the deepest reflections and the wonder of the thoughts she has made him think, stares as across a wide abyss, speaking as in a voice she has never heard from him before.*) Why do you ask me *questions?* What have I to do with you now?

KATE. (*After an instant, checked, and as to her humiliation, by this tone that*

relegates her to her own distance; yet so far, in her stiffness, confessing to some need to account for herself.) Because I said just now—in *passion*—what I could hide no longer?

(OWEN, *moving about again before he speaks, in his still further intensified unrest, is again near the small table on which the candlesticks stand, and where at the time of lighting* COYLE'S, *before the latter's exit, he has also lighted a second one which has remained burning. This candle—as if struck with its being the right and simplest thing to do—he takes up and holds out to* KATE *without a word and without a look; the act operating merely, though most markedly, as a gesture of dismissal and a sign of the end of everything.* KATE, *at her distance, has, while she watches him, to recognise it as that; but, after this suspended stare for it, is so far coerced by the authority and, as it were, the dignity of the movement, that she comes over and receives from him the imposed object: with which then, he leaving the table, she waits as if practically at his disposition, and even a little under his spell, for what he may next say or do. He takes his time, but as having her own last word meanwhile fully present to him; then, still without his eyes on her, breaks silence as once for all and to have done with her for ever.*)

OWEN. What to me ever again shall be anything you've "said"—or *may* say?

KATE. (*Standing there with her candle; measuring, with eyes on him, the effect wrought and, as she may say to herself, "The way he takes it," and having to accept this and to act accordingly but then, as with her own grievance, flushing back into life, fortunately for her, under the sting of dismissal—he dismissing her; and so managing to speak as for her supreme justification.*) As little as to *me*, no doubt, your saying I but wanted your Money!

(*With which she goes again straight up, centre. Here, at place of* exit, she once more stands a moment, with her glimmering taper, looking down at him; then, as on this sight of him, he no more seeing her now than if she is quite gone, appears to change her mind and moves to the egress at left. *Exit* KATE, *left.* OWEN, *left alone, is steeped at first but in his unconscious brooding; after which, as waking up to his relation to the place itself, he looks about him and appears struck, as* KATE *has been struck, in the similar connection after* COYLE'S *visit, with the smell of the waning lamp, the mate of which he had then extinguished. He gives a vague sniff, then goes to the lamp and turns it out to have done with it; the effect of which is now that the room receives only the dim blue starlight of the high uncurtained window. He slowly revolves in the darkness thus vaguely tempered; with pauses, halts, uncertainties, vague surveys of the place, that indicate in him the balance of alternatives and the slow growth of a decision. These bring him, at last, however, all to the appearance of one; he goes back to the small table and there lights himself a candle; carrying which, without haste, yet as with a settled purpose, he proceeds to the door, left, and opens it and passes out, but without closing it. At the moment he so passes, re-enter* KATE, *right; reappearing in the doorway there, candle in hand. She returns as with the movement and the sense of the impossibility for her, of their separating and her leaving him on the horrible words they have last spoken; but is checked at her first step by the change to full darkness, and then, as she comes down, by failing to make out his presence. She pulls up so, in the middle of the great gloom, with her twinkling taper; she wonders.*)

KATE. (*Raising her voice to a slight quaver.*) Owen! (*Then as he doesn't an-*swer and as the door ajar, to left, doesn't strike her; again.*) Owen!

(*Re-enter* OWEN, *left. As he reappears, without his candle, in a longish Inverness cape and with a largeish soft brown hat which now looms black, the articles he has gone to some closet, or whatever, in the passage outside the room, to supply himself with, she gives, from tense nerves, a sharp, scared, smothered cry; in the shock of which she drops her candle, so that the light goes out, the gloom is again a shade deeper, and, thanks to that ambiguous medium,* OWEN *has presented thus muffled, as it were, for departure, a startling apparitional effect.*)

KATE. You're leaving the house? (*Then while he stands there arrested and incommoded by her return and making no answer save slowly and just disconcertedly to remove his hat, his visible intention of getting away works upon her; works with such force that her high-pitched irony of five minutes previous which we have seen measuredly drop before her exit, flares up again and she breaks anew, reverting, all her doubts rekindled, and as sincerely as at first, into the affront she has already launched.*) Truly then you can't face any-thing?

OWEN. (*Motionless; after an instant; with an indignation, a force of revulsion from whatever, from all, he may have felt in the past, of which we feel the rise and the ring.*) What creature has this poisoned air made of you—and kept you?

KATE. (*Always coming up when so directly challenged.*) It has made me harder than it has ever made you—for I've stayed and taken my chance. (*Then, keeping on, stationed there, planted before him, as with the intense need now, if he is going, of uttering, for her justification, the whole of her plea.*) That's what—since we part!— I've come back that you at least shall know. (*Then as utterly detached from her and indifferent to her now, he makes as to move past her in order to go up, she fronts him but the more resolutely, right and left, practically barring his way.*) I've seen— even I have!—and it has given me the right to *speak!* (*Thus persisting, virtually so heading him off that he can only hover, as in a grim patience, waiting to have it over and go. She brings out thus, breathlessly, in rapid but distinct sequences now, through the listening gloom, the point she has wished to make; he being kept by her as against his will and as putting her no question whatever, but only looking over her head, so to speak, through the same darkness, into the world of his own freedom of action, toward which—and the more just because so arrested—he yearns.*) A year ago to-night—on this spot—at this hour. I had stayed late *there*—(*with a nod back toward drawing-room*) and came through on my way to my room. (*After which, as if wanting or expecting him to press her further, while he doesn't do so, she can but give him the rest.*) I saw him as I see *you*—just about, as it happens, where you stand! (*Then as with the surging woeful sense within her of the way in which this may indeed, as she shall find, have turned for her to loss or sorrow.*) When one has done that—one's Different! (*To which she adds, as to complete this meaning.*) You see I've not been afraid. (*Then for her climax.*) To try to *save* you.

OWEN. (*Impressed, quite to credulity, by the claim he has kept still and irresponsive to let her thus convincingly make for her own portentous experience; but still holding on to his better and stronger light.*) You give me your "difference"—dreadful fact!—as a ground for your view of our Consecration?

KATE. (*With a flare, again, of her resolution.*) How can I not? (*With splendid cold audacity; throwing up her arms, as she stands before him, and letting them drop in expression of the majesty of what has happened to her.*) I'm consecrated!

OWEN. (*After a moment during which, with his eyes on her, he has faced and apprehended this; speaking with the fullest force of his own passion.*) You double then my joy that I'm not—to so stupid and hideous a god!

KATE. (*Her tone rising as his has done; and with alarmed admonitory hands.*) Take care how—*here!*—you blaspheme him!

OWEN. (*As if suddenly, quite gleefully,*

taken with this opportunity and breaking out as to the happy thought.*) By Jove, if I thought that would *hurt* him—!

KATE. (*As in the same degree made uneasy by this and looking under the sharper effect of it, about her.*) I suggest that you mind what you say!

OWEN. (*Struck with the sincerity of her warning.*) Then after all even *you* are afraid!

KATE. (*Meeting it as she must; making the best of what she has to reply; always with her austerity.*) Afraid—call it!—for *you!*

OWEN. (*Excited; smiling.*) You tremble, Kate, for my courage? (*Then as she doesn't answer.*) You tremble, Kate, for my *life?* (*After which, while she still, as under the growth of her nervousness, says nothing.*) Then as we've still the Horror upon us (*turning sharp again, and more and more excited, to the place of the dim array of portraits*)—you've all been afraid of *Something!*

KATE. (*Perceptibly affected now by the degree and nature of his excitement.*) Owen, Owen—!

OWEN. (*Moved to still sharper and more ironic explicitness by this; with the manner of that and the highest explanatory clearness.*) Our "privilege," you see, is that we've been *bullied!* Our shame, you see, is that we've *taken* it! (*Then as thinking, at his high and higher pitch, while he moves and looks about, and speaking with a decision to match.*) The great thing's to make an End!

KATE. (*Proudly and sacrificially, as it were, for herself; as from her own attested experience.*) The great thing's to have seen it through!

OWEN. (*Taking this from her as her own experience, the result of the encounter, the adventure he has accepted her statement of; but shining out more and more in his scorn.*) With all the abject honours—so that it shall only come *again?*

KATE. (*In supreme apprehension now.*) Owen, Owen—it *may* come again!

OWEN. (*Taking this from her as then, since she believes it, quite possible and, what is even better, from the point of view, and with the temper of his resolution, desirable; his pitch keeping up and up.) If it comes again, love—it shall come to a different welcome!

KATE. (With intensity.) Owen, Owen—I beseech you to hush!

OWEN. (Heedless and joyous.) If it comes again, love, it shall go—!

KATE. (As at a climax of nervousness now; breaking in, catching him up, as for deprecation, dissuasion, exorcism, and with a high movement of waving away and away.) Let it go, let it go, let it go!

OWEN. (All contentious, all bright with his idea.) Let it come, let it come, let it come—rather than that I shouldn't have spoken!

KATE. (In all her rueful distress.) But you have spoken—and I believe you now!

OWEN. (Smiling.) Believe I'm no use at all? (Laughing.) Thank-you for Nothing! (Then, however, as he more completely takes in her condition.) But, God forgive us, you're in Terror!

KATE. (As to get the better of it; as to conjure it all away.) Ah, let everything pass! I wasn't afraid for Myself.

OWEN. (As with a beautiful intelligence.) Afraid then, Kate, for him?—since (smiling again) you're all on the side of the Beast!

KATE. Owen, Owen, I'm on your "side." God knows I don't want you to pay!

OWEN. (With his cheerful gallantry.) But I do pay! It's quite my line to pay. What does one do without paying? The Beauty's in what one pays for!

KATE. (Passionate.) Ah, I won't have you pay for my Folly!

OWEN. Your Folly's a part of our Past, and I'm ready to pay for our Freedom! (With which, as suiting the action to the word, as proceeding to deliver himself with the force and to the express intent that have during all the latter part of the scene been gathering intensity in him, he turns to the portraits, dimly seen, on the wall; addressing them as his Family and his Contemners, and letting loose at them the full wave of his denunciation and defiance; which embraces thus the whole place, its inmates, its imputations, its immediate rather gruesome aspect, all its ugly actualities and possibilities, that bears him up and on to the end.) What do I care for

what you "see," if it makes you all Stupid and Cruel? What do I care for your narrow minds and your pitiful measure of Life?

KATE. (Keeping before him in the same way, but as if differently, extraordinarily, affected now by his thus striking out, as it were, at what bars him, and by the very sound of his voice, rolling through the haunted room; uttering his name almost as a denial of their rupture.) Owen! Owen!

OWEN. (Carried, as I say, further and further, by his surge of reaction, rebellion, repudiation, the passion that, come as it will, has to come now; and even himself affected, in this sense, by the echo of his tone.) What do I care for your Trash of "Tests" if you can't face the Test of knowing me?

KATE. (At left, before him, while he has moved left, and more and more under this quickened impression.) Owen, Owen—I like you now!

OWEN. (At right, while she still moves right, as to hold him.) What do I care for Voices of Visions that pretend to keep me a Slave?

KATE. (Hovering, pressing, imploring; yet as kept off too, with her clasped hands, by a sort of sacred terror.) Owen, Owen, I love you—but silence!

OWEN. (Crescendo.) What do I care for your fostered Horrors that prowl like Unclean Beasts?

KATE. (At the climax of an intense nervous apprehension now, at the same time as at that of her sense of listening to a new music; supplicating.) Don't, don't—and forgive me! Silence!

OWEN. (At his own highest resonant climax.) What do I care for the Demon himself (at which, as throwing herself back horror-stricken, KATE gives a piercing shriek) except for the joy of blasting—!

(But with the words, all but simultaneously with KATE's shriek, caught up and extinguished in a great quick Blackness of deeper Darkness, completely obscuring the cold light from the high window, which passes, like the muffling whirlwind of an Apparition, and has come and gone even as a great flash of light. Out of it has sounded, like a ringing cry of Battle, an immense, recognising "A—a—h!" the last breath of OWEN's gasping throat. When the Shade has passed the cold light of the high window again only reigns, in which we make out the young man smitten to the ground, at his length on his back, with KATE, thrown to her distance, staring at him in an immense recoil of wonder, terror, anguish.)

KATE. (*Coming to him.*) Owen, Owen—my Owen! (*But again thrown back, in the very act of kneeling to him, by the inrush and advent of* SPENCER COYLE.)

(*Re-enter* SPENCER COYLE, *still dressed as on his exit and with a light, who, not having been able, in his deep disquiet, to remain inactive in his room, has found himself, at the Crisis, within reach of* KATE's *high shriek. He rushes forward to where* OWEN *lies, holding high his light; while* KATE *shrinks, stricken again, at sight of the white exposed face, as with the movement almost of the red-handed slayer caught in the act.*)

COYLE. (*On his knees; aghast, horror-stricken, but not unimagining, and to that extent almost accepting; while he reaches with one hand to feel* OWEN's *heart and with the other keeps up his light, which catches and exposes* KATE's *face.*) Dead, dead?

KATE. (*Nearer at this, and then, after an instant, while she takes the sight all in—*COYLE's *light helping for it all our own vision as well—close enough to kneel, yet as for positive appalled pity at what she sees, and sees as her own work, not kneeling; only, all tremendously, recognising.*) Dead of the Death—!

COYLE. (*Who has put his light on the floor and springs up as, beside him, she speaks, grasping her wrist as in a vice of steel and sounding out, for her, as with the sternest highest authority and the curt hard blare of a trumpet the only word she or anyone shall dare to say for ever.*) Of the Soldier!

The Other House
In A Prologue and Three Acts
1908

EDITOR'S FOREWORD

There are few more exciting pages in the *Notebooks of Henry James* than those in which he set down the first glimmerings of the theme for *The Other House*. It was Christmas week of 1893 and he was in his De Vere Gardens study. He had three weeks earlier withdrawn *Disengaged* from Daly; *Guy Domville* was written and in Alexander's hands. He still had hopes of being produced—perhaps by Hare, by Comyns Carr, by Compton. . . .

> I have been sitting here in the firelight—on this quiet afternoon of the empty London Xmastide, trying to catch hold of the tail of an idea, of a 'subject.' Vague, dim forms of imperfect conceptions seem to brush across one's face with a blur of suggestion, a flutter of impalpable wings. The prudent spirit makes a punctual note of whatever may be least indistinct—of anything that arrives at relative concreteness. Is there something for a tale, is there something for a play, in something that might be a little like the following?

He then sketched the main outline of what became *The Other House*.

At the conclusion of this preliminary statement James wrote: "I seem to feel in it the stuff of a play of the particular limited style and category that can only be dreamed of for E.C." E.C. was, of course, Edward Compton. James seems to have set to work on a scenario almost immediately for he alludes in a note of January 23 to a "rough sketch" of *The Promise*—the tentative title he gave to the work; and in a further entry a year later speaks of it as *"The Promise, the donnée I sketched (I have it all) as a three-act play for poor E.C."* A letter to Auguste Monod of some years later reveals that he showed it to Compton alone, for he says *The Other House* was laid aside "after only one manager had read it." In a letter to Paul Bourget he speaks of it as *"un projet detaillé et abandonné de pièce en 3 actes."*

In 1896, having an opportunity to write a serial for a popular medium, the *Illustrated London News*, James bethought himself of his neglected scenario and felt that the theme was sufficiently melodramatic—it is his only story to contain a brutal murder—to "capture the public of the *Illustrated News*," even as it had seemed to him that it was suited for the country audiences of the Compton Comedy Company. *The Other House* appeared in thirteen instalments in the illustrated weekly during July, August and September of 1896.

What prompted Henry James to create the unusual figure of Rose Armiger? She is cruel, devious, sinister, perverse; she is, as James wrote of another stage heroine of the time, "various and sinuous . . . complicated and natural; she suffers, she struggles, she is human, and by that fact exposed to a dozen interpretations." This was James's account of Ibsen's Hedda Gabler after seeing

677

her interpreted by Elizabeth Robins in 1891. Hedda leads us to Miss Robins and Miss Robins to Rose Armiger. It was significant that James felt in his original plan for *The Other House* that it could "only be dreamed of" for Compton and yet assigned the major role to a woman. This is not, however, as curious as it may seem: Miss Robins was identified with *The American* and had played opposite Compton in it. In planning this work for Compton, the novelist probably cast Miss Robins in the feminine lead, duplicating in his mind the circumstances of his earlier play. Rose Armiger is an Elizabeth Robins role and by that fact an Ibsen role—and *The Other House,* of all of James's plays, can be said to be an "Ibsen play."

The original note had been entered at the height of the struggle for Ibsen in the London theatre. There had been an Ibsen season that year in which Miss Robins played Hedda Gabler, Rebecca West and Hilda Wangel. Between 1891 and 1897 James had devoted four critical articles to Ibsen's plays. He liked the "hard, frugal charm" of the Norwegian, his scenic economy, the manner in which he could confront the audience with the "clash of Ego against Ego and soul against soul." In *The Other House*'s provincial setting, the retrospective method employed in the prologue, the small cast, the use of Dr. Ramage as a family adviser (an Ibsen type recalling Judge Brack or Rector Kroll) and Mrs. Beever as the objective outsider, able to view the struggling characters with judicial calm, James has reproduced all the Ibsen externals. The plot has elements in common with *Rosmersholm,* with which James was familiar as far back as 1890 and which was played in London in 1893 when James made his note for his play. Both the James and Ibsen works are haunted by a dead wife: Beata's suicide in *Rosmersholm,* before the play begins, contributes a barrier of psychological guilt to Rebecca's and Rosmer's love, even as the promise Julia demands from her husband before her death interposes a barrier to Rose's love for Tony Bream, against which she acts with such violence.

For all its resemblances to Ibsen, *The Other House* stands on its own feet as a distinct Jamesian work. It is far removed in atmosphere from the gloom of *Rosmersholm.* Its action takes place in broad British daylight and the passions which explode in it with such force are acted out on disciplined lawns between stately British houses deriving their well-founded security from a banking fortune. *The Other House* is British in its motives and emotions.

In July 1908, after the Edinburgh production of *The High Bid* and the writing of *The Saloon,* James picked up his twelve-year-old novel of *The Other House* and began to study it with a view to turning it finally into the form for which it was originally intended. Miss Bosanquet noted that between September 3 and 5 he dictated a new scenario from the book and he continued to work on it during the remainder of that month. It is not clear for whom he intended the play at this time but we know that during the following spring he showed the scenario to Granville-Barker, with whom James had been discussing a play for Charles Frohman's repertory at the Duke of York's Theatre.

"But what we wanted from him was an original play, not an adapted novel," Granville-Barker wrote, overlooking the fact that this was originally a novelized dramatic work.

In June of 1909 James began to convert the scenario into a play for the repertory season that Herbert Trench, Anglo-Irish poet-scholar, was planning at the Haymarket. There followed the usual pattern: cuts against which James rebelled, difficulties in casting, disagreements with Trench and finally, with the collapse of the repertory, the return of the unproduced play to James who had received a £90 advance for his labors.

Nevertheless *The Other House,* in the technical problems it raised and which the novelist felt he had overcome, was regarded by him as "a divine little light" to walk by. It had been the first to demonstrate to him the way in which he could apply his play-scenario to the writing of fiction, and he regarded it as "a precedent, a support."

In one respect the play does not conform to the current murder-story tradition that the criminal must pay for his crime. James had given this problem careful thought when he was writing his precocious book reviews, in his early twenties. In *Orestes* or *Macbeth,* he wrote, the dramatic interest of crime "lay in the fact that it compromised the criminal's moral repose." In the novels of Wilkie Collins or Miss Braddon—as in most detective stories today—"the interest of crime is in the fact that it compromises the criminal's personal safety." In *The Other House* James remained true to his early critical distinction. He is concerned with Rose's "moral repose" and he makes it clear when she walks out "free" from "the other house" that her punishment will be greater than any the law can devise.

CHARACTERS

ANTHONY BREAM, *in Prologue thirty-five, in Play thirty-nine*
DENNIS VIDAL, *about the same*
PAUL BEEVER, *nineteen—twenty-three*
DOCTOR RAMAGE, *age of well-established country physician*
MRS. BEEVER, *forty-five—forty-nine*
ROSE ARMIGER, *twenty-five—twenty-nine*
JEAN MARTLE, *eighteen—twenty-two*
LITTLE EFFIE, *as small a child as conveniently possible*
MANNING, *Parlourmaid*
GORHAM, *Nurse*
THE BUTLER
A FOOTMAN

The scene in the little old country town of Wilverley, South or West of England; Prologue at the house of Anthony Bream, Country Banker; the three Acts at the "other" of the pair of houses, that of Mrs. Beever, his Partner in the Bank. In each case a long summer afternoon; the second one after an interval of four years.

THE OTHER HOUSE

PROLOGUE

The large bright, fairly modern, distinctly florid and rather provincially luxurious hall of Anthony Bream's house of Bounds, just conveniently within the little (Hampshire) town of Wilverley, with its grounds sloping to the small river on the other side of which, and with a private bridge and special communication between, stands the residence of Mrs. Beever, Eastmead; the going to and from between which two places is frequent and easy. The essence of the hall, for the Action, is its having no less than four places of entrance and exit; one of these through the wide window that on the beautiful summer Sunday stands open to the Garden, and so to the way to the Other House. The next principal passage is to the corridor and staircase leading to the room where MRS. BREAM *lies critically ill. Another leads to a part of the house on the same level, notably to the library and to a downstairs guestroom. Another, the main entrance, communicates with the exit from the house straight to the town.*

The hall at Bounds, with its four or five different communications; ROSE ARMIGER *in occupation and* JEAN MARTLE *arriving from the garden.* ROSE *has been seated at a table with her head buried in her arms, and the entrance has taken place without either's at first being aware of the other. Then* JEAN *has noticed the young woman, who at the same instant has looked up and, as quickly, risen to her feet and spoken; as with a consciousness of having been surprised in her slightly odd position.*

ROSE. Pardon my jumping out at you! I heard a sound—I was expecting a friend.

(Taking her in; guessing who she is.) And I dare say you've already heard of *me.*

JEAN. *(Smiling, interested.)* I haven't heard half as much as I want about anyone or anything—for, you know, I came to Mrs. Beever but last night. By way of making me feel at home, however, she has sent me over to ask if its really quite right we should come to luncheon. We came out of Church before the sermon, because of some people who were to go home with us. They're with Mrs. Beever now, but she told me to take straight across the garden —the short way.

ROSE. No way ever seems short enough for Mrs. Beever!

JEAN. Yes—isn't she wonderful?

ROSE. Wonderful! Did she direct you by chance, to enquire of *me!* I'm only here on a visit.

JEAN. *(Who has been struck with the great charming hall; pleased with everything.)* What a delightful house for that!

ROSE. I think indeed I shouldn't like yours so much—by which I mean Mrs. Beever's. Though each of course has its own strong points—which you've perhaps even already noticed she wishes each particularly to stick to!

JEAN. You mean she's so aware of hers—?

ROSE. *(Who has been taking more and more her charming measure.)* Now that she has *you* with her she must be so much more so than ever! But what I mean is that, facing each other in so friendly a way across their little river—bridged so charmingly for so easy an intercourse—the two houses are nevertheless about as different as possible, though, indeed, as pillars and props, on either side, of the Bank, it isn't as if

681

they could really have *afforded* ever to quarrel.

JEAN. (*Rising, as with charmed intelligence, to everything* ROSE *says and to the way she puts things.*) Ah yes—the Bank's everything!

ROSE. (*Rather amused.*) Well, if you feel it everything *there,* and I feel it everything here, we exhibit between us, I think, the state of mind of Wilverley; which is that Mr. Bream, as junior Partner perhaps, but as half proprietor and sole Manager, and Mrs. Beever, as senior Partner, and in particular as senior *Person,* representing her late husband's position and share, are quite the first people in this part of the world. Public opinion in the town—as you'll see if you stay awhile—is very funny about them.

JEAN. Isn't there something I heard imputed to it at home even before I started? —to the effect that though Mr. Bream may manage the Bank, Mrs. Beever manages Mr. Bream!

ROSE. So that it's she, in other words, who manages Everything?

JEAN. Well, so that's she's really what they call the moving force. But of course I know nothing about it.

ROSE. (*After a moment.*) I don't think they can know much about it either at— (*then at a loss*) where is it you come from?

JEAN. Oh I've been with Papa at Brighton.

ROSE. I remember. (*Then, as piecing together what she has heard about the girl, though as not quite sure.*) They've been friends from youth, your Father and she?— and your Father's out of health?

JEAN. Oh they really think him better now, and Mrs. Beever says my visit to her will be good for both of us.

ROSE. (*Amused.*) Good for you and herself?

JEAN. That *perhaps!*—but good in particular for Papa and me.

ROSE. Through your being *rid* of each other? I recognise her humour—but am I to recognise it still further in her having sent you with her message to *me?*

JEAN. To any one, I think, who would be here to tell me in case Mrs. Bream shouldn't be quite so well.

ROSE. (*As after just debating and deciding how definitely to state it.*) She isn't quite so well.

JEAN. Then ought I to be here?

ROSE. Have you a margin? I mean of time?

JEAN. (*As liking to stay, interested in* ROSE *and in this vision of her; but conscientious.*) Oh I can nip back!

ROSE. *Back here?*

JEAN. I meant back *there* (*with a nod off at the main entrance*). But here *too,* I hope—while I stay.

ROSE. I was speaking of *these* moments. But you *must,* for your visit at Eastmead, "stay"!

JEAN. Well, I've promised till Mr. Paul comes home. You know he's at Oxford, and his term soon ends.

ROSE. And yours ends *with* it? You depart as he arrives? Don't you like him?

JEAN. I don't know yet. It's exactly what she wants me to find out.

ROSE. Then you'll have to be very clear.

JEAN. But if I find out I *don't?*

ROSE. (*Laughing.*) I shall be sorry for you!

JEAN. Well, it will be then the only thing in this love 'of an old place that I *sha'n't* have liked!

ROSE. Do you like the Banker?

JEAN. (*Prompt, ingenuous.*) Mr. Bream? Oh immensely! But of course I only saw him for five minutes—yesterday at the Bank.

ROSE. We *know* how long you saw him— he has told us all about your visit. That is he told his poor dear little wife—who this morning told *me.* She understands his friendly way, and likes above all what she calls his grand spontaneity.

JEAN. (*All responsive.*) Then it must have been his grand spontaneity that made him tell me I shall see the Baby. He told me he shows her himself.

ROSE. (*Amused.*) He does indeed—to all and sundry!

JEAN. (*Simply.*) Is she very lovely?

ROSE. "Lovely"? Do you think small red squalling infants are *ever* lovely?

JEAN. (*Pulled up a little, embarrassed and rather snubbed.*) Well, those I've seen—!

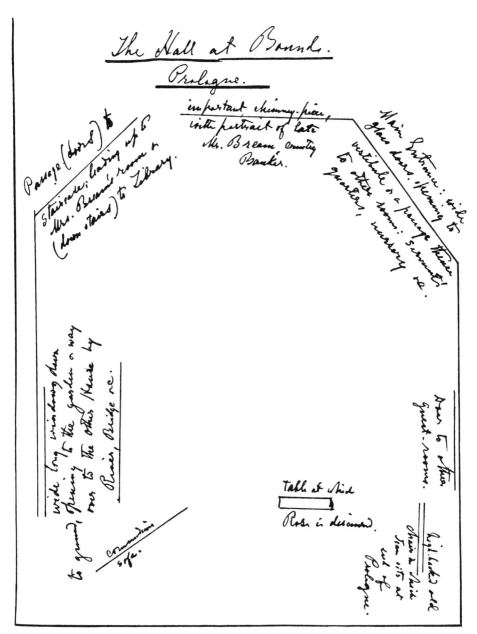

Henry James's Stage Plan for the Prologue to *The Other House*

Rose. (*Frankly.*) Those I've seen I've not adored. But if you'd like, all the same, to make Effie's acquaintance, I'll present you.

Jean. (*Artlessly.*) You won't terrify her?

Rose. Do I terrify *you?*

Jean. Oh *I'm* not six days old!

Rose. You mightn't, my dear, be more than two! But I won't destroy her.

Jean. Then do get her.

> (*Appearance, at the moment they speak, of* Mrs. Beever, *introduced at main door by* Butler. *Enter* Mrs. Beever *who hearing these last two speeches, comes down.*)

Mrs. Beever. (*With high decision.*) Not yet, not yet. The baby's of no importance. We've come over for the mother. (*Addressing* Rose *almost sharply.*) Is it true that Julia has had a bad turn?

Rose. I believe she feels rather down. But I don't imagine it's of the least consequence.

> (*On which the* Butler, *who has ushered in* Mrs. Beever *and has lingered a moment, comes down as for the importance of the thing.*)

Butler. (*To* Rose.) I may mention, Miss, that Dr. Ramage, who arrived some time ago, has not yet gone, and that Mr. Bream has been there with the Nurse this hour.

Rose. If you mean in Mrs. Bream's room, he's there as often as the Nurse allows him.

Butler. (*With his watch.*) She's allowing of him now, Miss, as never yet.

Rose. (*Prompt and logical.*) Then doesn't that just prove—?

Mrs. Beever. It proves that there can be no question of our coming to luncheon. (*Then to* Jean.) Go straight back to the Duggits, who will be at the house on the chance of being kept,—and tell them to hold their tongues. Then get rid of them; but come back here—as you *were* to have done—only if I send for you.

Jean. Yes Mrs. Beever. (*Then for a friendly break-off with* Rose.) I'm so awfully sorry. Please give her my love. (*With which she reaches the main entrance, whither the* Butler *has preceded her and where he lets her out, following her. Exeunt* Jean *and* Butler.)

Rose. Your young friend's as affectionate as she's pretty: sending her love to people she has never seen!

Mrs. Beever. She only meant the little girl. I thought we were going so straight.

Rose. I dare say we are. Only Nurse did tell me—early—that I mightn't see her at all this morning. It will have been the first morning for several days.

Mrs. Beever. You've enjoyed a privilege altogether denied to *me.*

Rose. You must remember that I'm Julia's oldest friend. It's my *footing*—the way she always treats me.

Mrs. Beever. Familiarly—of course. (*Very frank, as full in* Rose's *face.*) Well you're not *my* oldest—though it's very much the way I treat you too. You must wait with me here, at any rate, for more news, and be as still as a mouse.

Rose. Dear Mrs. Beever, I never made a noise in all my life!

Mrs. Beever. You will *some* day—you're so *clever.*

Rose. (*Moving about while* Mrs. Beever, *seated, watches her.*) I'm clever enough to be quiet! (*Then less gaily.*) I'm the one thing of her own dear Julia has ever had. Though I'm three years older we were brought together as girls by one of the strongest of all ties—the tie of a common aversion.

Mrs. Beever. (*All there.*) Oh I know your Tradition of *that!*

Rose. Perhaps you know then that her detestable Stepmother was, very little to my credit, my Aunt. If her Father, that is, was Mrs. Griffin's second Husband, my Uncle, my Mother's brother, had been the first. Julia lost her Mother; I lost both my Mother and my Father. It was then that Mrs. Griffin took me on: she had shortly before made her second marriage. She put me at the horrid school at Weymouth at which she had already put her Stepdaughter. But it's the only good turn she has ever done us.

Mrs. Beever. (*Critical; sceptical.*) Is she really such a Monster?

Rose. Don't ask me about her—I dislike her too much perhaps to be strictly fair. She didn't, however, find me an easy victim—I could take care of myself. I could fight. Julia bowed her head and suffered. Never was a marriage more of a rescue.

MRS. BEEVER. And yet Mrs. Griffin travelled all the way down from town the other day to make her a visit of a couple of hours?

ROSE. Ah, precisely! Why couldn't she let the poor dear alone? She came to "make peace," she said, but she only stirred up the wretched past and reopened old wounds.

MRS. BEEVER. She abused you a good deal, I presume!

ROSE. Shockingly, I believe—but that's of no importance to me. She doesn't touch or reach me now.

MRS. BEEVER. Your description of her is of a dreadful person. And yet besides her having got two honourable men to give her the last proof of confidence, she took you on, as you say, who were no real relation to her—she looked after you and put you to school. Wasn't that a service rendered?

ROSE. She took me to torment me—or at least to make me feel her hand. I didn't say she could let us alone—if she could she wouldn't have come here.

MRS. BEEVER. You make out a wonderful case, and if ever I'm put on my trial for a crimes—say for muddling the affairs of the Bank!—I hope I shall be defended by someone with your gift and your manner. (Quite blandly.) I don't wonder your good friends—even the blameless ones like this dear pair—cling to you as they do.

ROSE. If you mean you don't wonder I stay on here so long, I'm greatly obliged to you for your sympathy. Julia's the one thing I have of my own.

MRS. BEEVER. You make light, my dear young woman of our Husbands and Lovers! Haven't I had the pleasure of hearing of a gentleman to whom you're soon to be married?

ROSE. (Hanging fire a little while she opens her eyes rather wide—wondering and consciously.) Dennis Vidal?

MRS. BEEVER. (As for the tone of it.) Lord, are there more than one? Isn't it a definite engagement?

ROSE. (Who has been at a loss but for a miserable moment; looking up at the large clock of the hall.) Mr. Vidal—as it happens—will be here this morning. Ask him how he regards it.

MRS. BEEVER. (Alert, at the opening of the door to the rooms on the same floor.) Here he is perhaps! (Then as she sees DOCTOR RAMAGE.) Ah no!

(Enter DOCTOR RAMAGE from the library.)

DR. RAMAGE. (At once holding up to ROSE a sheet of note paper, covered with a prescription, that he carries in his hand.) This is to be made up instantly, please; I've already lost three minutes in the library—thinking and writing it out!

ROSE. (With the paper and after an intelligent glance at it.) I'll take it myself—for the walk: I'm too fidgetty to hang about. (Then explaining and excusing herself to MRS. BEEVER, though her more or less comprehending look at the prescription makes her also want to learn more.) My hat and jacket are in the vestibule—I put them there on the chance of Church: which, however (to the DOCTOR), I gave up when I saw that Mr. Bream did.

DR. RAMAGE. Excellent for you to go yourself—and repeat to their stupidity (pointing it out on the paper) my "Strong dilution." You're a very nice sharp obliging person.

MRS. BEEVER. She knows what she's about! (After which, with much expression, while ROSE, though under way, anxiously hangs on an instant.) But what in the world is Julia about?

DR. RAMAGE. I'll tell you when I know, dear lady!

MRS. BEEVER. Is there anything really wrong?

DR. RAMAGE. I'm waiting to find out!

MRS. BEEVER. Then you're not, I hope, going!

DR. RAMAGE. By no means, though I've another pressing call. (After which, to ROSE, who, checked by MRS. BEEVER's question of an instant before, has waited for the answer.) I must have that from you first.

ROSE. (Who has on this gone quickly to the main entrance, but again there with the appeal.) Is Mr. Bream still with her?

DR. RAMAGE. Very much with her! That's why I'm here. She prayed hard to be left five minutes alone with him.

ROSE. So Nurse isn't there either?

DR. RAMAGE. Nurse seized the occasion to pop down for her lunch. Mrs. Bream has taken it into her head that she has something important to say.

MRS. BEEVER. And pray what may that be?

DR. RAMAGE. She turned me out of the room precisely that I sha'n't learn.

ROSE. I think *I* know what it is.

MRS. BEEVER. (*Sharply.*) Then what, pray?

ROSE. Oh I wouldn't for the world *tell* you! (*Exit* ROSE, *hastily now, by main doors.*)

DR. RAMAGE. (*Studying his watch a little absently.*) Our young friend's exceedingly nervous.

MRS. BEEVER. Do you allude to that girl?

DR. RAMAGE. I allude to dear Mrs. Tony.

MRS. BEEVER. It's equally true of Miss Armiger; she's as worried as a pea on a pan. As for Julia, she *never* can have been a person to hold herself together.

DR. RAMAGE. Precisely—she requires to be held. Well, happily she has Tony to hold her.

MRS. BEEVER. Then he's not himself in one of his states?

DR. RAMAGE. I don't honestly!—quite make him out. He seems to have fifty things at once in his head.

MRS. BEEVER. When does he ever *not* have? But I had a note from him only this morning—in the highest spirits.

DR. RAMAGE. Well, whatever happens to him, he'll always have *them!*—I mean a hundred charming things to think of!

MRS. BEEVER. (*Who has kept her eyes on him an instant longer, and then rises, with decision, to her sharp challenge.*) Robert Ramage—since you say "whatever happens"—what *is* to happen to that character?

(*Before he has time to reply there rings out, as through the door of his entrance, a sudden sound, the practically near vibration, from* MRS. BREAM'S *room, of a smart, loud, new electric bell which has much of the effect of an answer to her question and which causes them*

both to start, holding their breath a moment. But the DOCTOR *quickly recognises.*)

DR. RAMAGE. (*Reassured and reassuring.*) It's for Nurse.

(*On which, however, as soon as he has spoken the bell sounds even more impatiently again.*)

MRS. BEEVER. (*Not reassured.*) Isn't it for *you?*

DR. RAMAGE. (*With a decisive headshake, but moving instinctively, while they listen, a few steps in the direction from which the sound has come.*) It's for Nurse. (*As he speaks the door is thrown open with vivacity to give passage to a tall good-looking, still young, or youngish, man, dressed as if, with much freshness, for Church, and wearing a large orchid in his buttonhole; whom the* DOCTER *instantly addresses.*) You rang for Nurse?

(*Enter thus* TONY BREAM, *from his wife's staircase, who stands looking from one of them to the other.*)

TONY. She's there—it's all right. (*Then while he passes his hand, with a vivid gesture of brushing away a sinister image, over a face of which the essential radiance is visible even through perturbation.*) But ah, my dear people—!

MRS. BEEVER. (*Anxious, eager.*) How's Julia now?

TONY. (*At once, on this, more easy.*) Much relieved, she tells me, at having spoken.

MRS. BEEVER. But spoken of *what,* Tony?

TONY. (*With the frankest expression of the effect of it for himself.*) Of everything she can think of that's inconceivable—that's damnable! (*Very nervously.*) Ramage, are you keeping something back? *Isn't* she safe?

DR. RAMAGE. (*Who has remained half Up, near the door* TONY *has left open, his watch, on which he keeps his eyes, in his hand.*) The dear lady's so convinced, you mean, that her very last hour is at hand?

TONY. So much so that if she got you and Nurse away, if she made me kneel down by her bed and take her two dear little hands in mine, what do you suppose it was to *say* to me?

DR. RAMAGE. Why, of course, that she's

going to perish in her flower.

TONY. (*Intensely urgent for reassurance.*) But she *isn't*, Doctor?

MRS. BEEVER. (*As knowing all about such cases.*) She has had her *chance* of perishing—but now it's too late.

TONY. But she says she *knows* it, you see. You surely know more than she, don't you, Ramage?

DR. RAMAGE. I know everything that can be known. I know that when, in certain conditions, pretty young mothers have acquitted themselves of that conviction, they turn over and go comfortably to sleep.

TONY. Then that's exactly what Nurse must make her do.

DR. RAMAGE. It's exactly what she's *doing!* (*Immediately after which, however,* MRS. BREAM'S *bell, now under the* NURSE'S *hand, sounds out for the third time.*) Excuse me. Nurse calls me.

TONY. (*Who has started up; checked as soon by the* DOCTOR'S *raised hand.*) And doesn't call me?

DR. RAMAGE. Not in the least. (*At his door; now with absolute professional authority.*) Stay where you are. (*Exit* DR. RAMAGE *to staircase.*)

MRS. BEEVER. Keep quiet and do as you're told!

TONY. I always do when it's you who tell me! And I shall do it better still if you'll stay to luncheon.

MRS. BEEVER. Why—I sent over Jean to to say that, all things considered, we had better not.

TONY. (*As if, while he fidgets about, still vague for the instant.*) "Jean"—?

MRS. BEEVER. My young visitor whom I brought yesterday to the Bank.

TONY. (*At once a shade brighter for this.*) Ah yes—that awfully pretty girl. Then she's here?

MRS. BEEVER. (*As with a certain snap for it.*) No—when I came I sent her home. Does she strike you as awfully pretty?

TONY. As pretty as a pretty song! I took a tremendous notion to her.

MRS. BEEVER. Why she's only a child— so don't for mercy's sake, show your notion too much.

TONY. I see what you mean. Of course I won't! Only, if you don't lunch—which

I regret!—is it what you call "showing" it too much to hope that she'll come back?

MRS. BEEVER. *Quite* too much—since Julia's so down.

TONY. It's just *because* Julia's so down— don't you see? A fellow can't *stand* it! (*And then as if her absence is an aggravation.*) Do you know what's become of Rose?

MRS. BEEVER. You want her to help you to stand it?

TONY. (*Pulled up a little, but ready and frank.*) Why yes—Rose helps!

MRS. BEEVER. (*Allowing it good-naturedly enough.*) She *does* then—she has gone over to the chemist's for the Doctor.

TONY. (*Frankly pleased.*) There it *is*— the comfort!

MRS. BEEVER. (*After an instant.*) Hasn't she been appointed to comfort somebody more in need of it? Who's this person who's coming today to marry her?

TONY. Oh—a very good fellow, I believe; and "rising." A clerk in some Eastern House.

MRS. BEEVER. "Rising"—yet has kept her so long waiting?

TONY. Well—he has been at Hong Kong, or some such place, trying hard to pick up an income. He's rising—but hasn't yet quite fully risen: "poor but pushing," Rose says. They've no settled means but her own two hundred.

MRS. BEEVER. Two hundred a year? That's quite enough for them!

TONY. Then you had better tell him so!

MRS. BEEVER. Well, if I do, I hope you'll back me up! How is it Miss Armiger knows what Julia wanted to say to you?

TONY. (*Taken by surprise and again a little vague.*) Just now? (*As trying to bethink himself; wondering.*) Does she know? (*Giving it up.*) I haven't the least idea! (*But then as* ROSE *reappears.*) Here she is.

MRS. BEEVER. Then—as I go—you can ask her.

TONY. Easily! (*Re-enter* ROSE, *in hat, jacket and gloves, from the quarter of her exit; whom he instantly addresses.*) So good of you to do these things!

ROSE. (*Between the others, coming down, taking off her gloves.*) They're to send it by the stroke of the hour. I *couldn't* wait—I was too impatient.

TONY. It's all right!

MRS. BEEVER. Let us hope so! Good-bye —till soon again.

TONY. (*With her to her exit.*) And you'll bring the pretty girl?

ROSE. (*Down while the other two are up; removing her jacket and apparently about to do the same to her hat.*) Yes—do bring the pretty girl! I'm so interested in her clothes!

TONY. (*Laughing.*) I'm so interested in the shade of her hair!

MRS. BEEVER. (*After having watched for an instant* ROSE *take up from the table a small ornamental glass and consult it as to the alternatives of removing or keeping on her hat; the visitor looking from her to* TONY *and back.*) Don't you think you've interest enough with what your situation here already offers? (*On which, without waiting for an answer, exit* MRS. BEEVER.)

TONY. (*In half-rueful, yet half-amused comment on their friend's characteristic asperity.*) Oh I say!

ROSE. (*Taking off her hat; good-humouredly.*) Isn't it a nasty one? Julia *has* been quiet?

TONY. (*Confident.*) Certainly—to all appearance. And (*not seeing why anyone should object to his saying it*) Miss Martle *is* pretty!

ROSE. (*Without reserve.*) Lovely!

TONY. So there you are. (*Then, however, promptly and restlessly reverting, while* ROSE *lays her jacket on chair, placing upon it her smoothed-out gloves and, carefully, her hat; so that his words have a certain effect of abruptness.*) Is it true that you *know* what Julia a while ago had the room cleared in order to say to me?

ROSE. Mrs. Beever repeated to you that I told her so? Yes then—I probably do know . . .

TONY. That she's dying?

ROSE. That she's dying. But she isn't!

TONY. Of course she isn't! But she has insisted on it to you too?

ROSE. She has done me that honour.

TONY. Done it you mean today?

ROSE. Today—and once before.

TONY. Yesterday?

ROSE. No—before your Child was born. Soon after I came.

TONY. She had made up her mind then from the first?—and you never *spoke* of it?

ROSE. To *you?* Why in the world should I? when she herself—take notice!—didn't. I took it perfectly for what it was—an inevitable but unimportant result of the nervous depression produced by her Stepmother's visit.

TONY. (*Who has fidgetted up and off and round again with his hands always in his trousers pockets.*) Damn her Stepmother's visit!

ROSE. (*Laughing.*) That's exactly what I did!

TONY. (*Disturbed, resentful.*) Damn her Stepmother too!

ROSE. (*Seeing the* DOCTOR *reappear.*) Hush!—we mustn't curse our relations before the Doctor!

(*Re-enter* DOCTOR RAMAGE *from staircase.*)

ROSE. (*To* DOCTOR.) They've promised to send it within the ten minutes.

DR. RAMAGE. (*Quick; under pressure of what he has next to do.*) Many thanks— I'll pick it up myself: we're quieter. (*To* TONY, *his hand reassuringly out.*) I *must* run to a bad case.

TONY. (*Taking his hand; keeping it.*) Quieter?

DR. RAMAGE. Quieter.

TONY. What was the loud ring that called you?

DR. RAMAGE. A stupid flurry of Nurse's. I blush for her!

TONY. Then why did you stay so long?

DR. RAMAGE. To have it out with your wife. She wants you again.

TONY. (*Promptly dropping his hand; all ready.*) Then I go!

DR. RAMAGE. (*With a protesting positive gesture.*) In a quarter of an hour—not before. (*Making him quite understand it.*) I'm most reluctant—but I allow her five minutes.

ROSE. (*Who has been attentive to this.*) It may make her easier afterwards.

DR. RAMAGE. (*To* ROSE, *as with rapid appreciation of her intelligence.*) That's precisely the ground of my giving in. (*Then to* TONY *again; with authority.*) Take care, you know—Nurse will time you.

TONY. (*While the* DOCTOR *goes up.*) So

many thanks. And you'll come back?

DR. RAMAGE. The moment I'm free. (*Exit* RAMAGE *by main entrance.*)

TONY. She wants to say it again. That's what she wants.

ROSE. Well, the more she has spirit to say it, the less it must be true. Besides, we can't have cared for her so only to lose her.

TONY. (*With an emphatic gesture and his way of instantly responding to cheer.*) I'll be hanged if we can! And such talk— if you can forgive me for it!—it's a vile false note in the midst of a joy like yours.

ROSE. (*Pulled up as she comes down, and exhibiting some vagueness.*) "Like mine"?

TONY. (*Amused, in spite of himself, at the odd effect of her stare of non-recognition.*) I hope that's not the way you mean to look at Mr. Vidal!

ROSE. (*A little sadly and as if she only now does catch on.*) Ah Mr. Vidal—!

TONY. (*Rather wondering at her ambiguous echo.*) Sha'n't you then be glad to see him?

ROSE. Intensely glad. But how shall I say it? There's gladness and gladness. It isn't love's young dream—it's rather an old and rather a sad story. We've worried and waited—we've been acquainted with grief. We've come a weary way.

TONY. I know you've had a horrid grind. But isn't this the end of it?

ROSE. Why—that's just what he's to settle.

TONY. (*Seeing* DENNIS VIDAL *as he appears preceded by the* BUTLER.) Happily I foresee! (*Cheeringly.*) Just look at him!

(*Enter* DENNIS VIDAL *by main entrance, ushered by* BUTLER.)

BUTLER. (*Announcing.*) Mr. Vidal. (*Exit* BUTLER.)

ROSE. (*Instantly all there, and moved moreover by the sight of her lover, who while still up, has faltered and paused a moment at the sight of her companion, throws up light, fluttered arms with the clearest cry and the frankest maidenly grace.*) Dennis, Dennis!

TONY. (*While* DENNIS, *not pretending to resist this, comes down all responsive, and the pair are locked an instant in an ardent embrace.*) I bless your reunion! (*Then, having gained the door to the other parts of the house, he waves across to* VIDAL *the friendliest salutation.*) I go to my wife— but am very glad to see you. (*Indicating* ROSE; *smiling.*) She'll make you at home! (*Exit* TONY BREAM *to staircase.*)

VIDAL. (*Covering* ROSE *with his gratified smile.*) My own dearest—you're still more so than one remembered!

ROSE. Still more what?

VIDAL. (*Laughing.*) Still more of a fright! (*With which he kisses her again.*)

ROSE. (*Free of him now, and a little off.*) It's you who are so wonderful, Dennis. You look so absurdly young!

VIDAL. If I looked as old as I feel, dear girl, they'd have my wizened mug in the illustrated papers. (*With which, she having the important sofa at left, behind her, he has come to her again to draw her down upon it beside him.*)

ROSE. (*Seated with him, yet in a manner detached too; so that she takes him in critically, though kindly.*) And yet it's not that you're exactly childish—or (*as to puzzle out, for her satisfaction, her impression of him*) so very extraordinarily fresh!

VIDAL. (*With a happy little jeer.*) "Fresh," my dear girl? (*Then having possessed himself of her hand and raised her wrist to his lips, holding it there as long as she lets him and looking at her hard.*) That's the freshest thing I've ever been more or less aware of!

ROSE. (*Who has repossessed herself of her hand and folded her arms; while she considers him still kindly but always with her habit of fine discrimination.*) You're worn—but you're not wasted! (*Then clear and positive.*) You're awfully all right, you know.

VIDAL. Yes I dare say I'm not all wrong! But don't "size me up" so! You make me nervous about what I may seem to amount to!

ROSE. I'm only thinking that you look young just as a steel instrument of the very best quality—no matter how much it is handled—often looks *new*.

VIDAL. (*Laughing.*) Ah if you mean I'm kept bright by use—!

ROSE. You're polished by life.

VIDAL. (*Still gay.*) "Polished" is grand of you!

ROSE. I'm not sure you've come back handsomer than you went—and I don't know if you've come back richer.

VIDAL. (*Prompt, frank.*) Then let me at once—on the latter head—assure you I *have!*

ROSE. Well, you're not splendid, my dear old Dennis—you're not dazzling, nor dangerous, nor even exactly distinguished. But you've a quiet little something that our long, tiresome time has made perfect, and that—just here where you've come to me at last—makes me immensely proud of you.

VIDAL. (*Touched by it.*) Thank you for *that*—only (*as he looks about him and rises*) haven't I perhaps come to you in a place and at a time that makes my coming at all rather awkward?

ROSE. (*Seated.*) For my friends here? Oh, when I answered your telegram everything seemed right.

VIDAL. I quite see how you must feel! But we have the advantage and the luck, haven't we? in case of any awkwardness!—that the essence of our own situation—by which I mean the end of your delay—is already in our hands.

ROSE. (*Disconcerted.*) Do you mean we're to go out and be married this minute?

VIDAL. (*Prompt; confident; taking out a pocket-book.*) Well, almost—as soon as I've read you a letter.

ROSE. (*While he seeks in the pocket-book.*) What letter?

VIDAL. The best one I ever got! (*While, having put back the pocket-book, he claps his hands on all his pockets.*) What the deuce have I done with it?

ROSE. From your own people?

VIDAL. (*While he continues the search.*) From the London House. It met me in town, and if it hadn't been Saturday afternoon—! (*Then wholly conclusive.*) But it makes everything possible.

ROSE. (*Quiet, just perceptibly unsuggestive; while he continues to hunt and fumble.*) Then it's certainly a thing for me to hear.

VIDAL. (*A little disappointed and even alarmed at not being able to produce it, slapping himself fruitlessly everywhere, he becomes aware of the* BUTLER, *who having*

reappeared by the Main Entrance, had approached him, discreet and perpendicular.*) But what the dickens—

(*Re-enter* BUTLER.)

BUTLER. Might I ask for your keys, sir?

VIDAL. (*With a light that makes him smite his forehead.*) Stupid—it's in my portmanteau!

ROSE. (*Who has seen* TONY *at the same door by which* BLACK *has entered; addressing* VIDAL.) Then go with Black and get it.

(*Re-enter* TONY *from staircase.*)

ROSE. (*To* TONY.) Do let Black take him. I want to speak to you.

TONY. (*Flushed, different from on his exit; with a smile for* VIDAL.) Will you excuse me then?

VIDAL. (*With compunction.*) Ah, the trouble I'm giving—!

TONY. (*Characteristically genial in spite of preoccupations.*) No trouble! (*Going up to him, his hand encouragingly on his shoulder; preceded by* BLACK.) Make use of Black!

(*On which* BLACK *ushers* VIDAL *out and follows him. Exeunt* VIDAL *and* BLACK *by main entrance.*)

TONY. Has he brought you good news?

ROSE. Very good. He's very well. He's all right.

TONY. (*His flushed face giving to the laugh with which he greets this almost the effect of that of a man who has been drinking.*) Do you mean he's quite faithful?

ROSE. (*As one who always meets a bold joke.*) As faithful as I! But *your* news is the thing. Is Julia still of the same mind?

TONY. She is of a much more extraordinary one. But I must get over it a little before I tell you.

ROSE. (*While she waits.*) You mean in insisting that she won't recover?

TONY. She treats her not recovering now as a mere detail.

ROSE. (*Wondering.*) Detail of what?

TONY. Well, of our situation—based on the view that she's sinking.

ROSE. (*As if fairly irritated.*) But *is* she, gracious goodness? Such a condition isn't a "view"—it's a fact or it's not a fact!

TONY. (*With resolute intensity.*) It's *not* a fact! How *can* it be when one has only to see that her strength hasn't failed?

What's the vehemence with which she expresses herself but a sign of sustained life? (*Reasoning it out as for his own reassurance.*) It's excitement of course—partly. But it's also striking energy. She takes an interest—asks questions, sends messages, speaks out with all her voice. She's delighted for instance to know that Mr. Vidal's at last come to you, and she tells me to let you know it from her, with her love, and to let *him* know it: to acquaint you both, in fact, how she rejoices that what you've so long waited for is now so close at hand. She asked me particularly about Mr. Vidal—how he looks, how he strikes me, how you met. She gives me a private message for him—private to spare your modesty! She wants him to know that she answers for you as the charmingest, cleverest, handsomest, in every way most wonderful wife that ever man will have had. But what do you suppose she wants me to *do*?

ROSE. (*Smiling as for suggestion's sake.*) Well—to allow her to name her successor?

TONY. Just the contrary! She wants me to promise she shall *have* no successor.

ROSE. (*Who instantly checks any show of the quick, perceptible impression made by this.*) I see. (*At a momentary loss.*) Then is your promising so difficult?

TONY. No, the idea's all right—God help us! But where the mistake comes in for me is in so acting as if her death *were* near and one were really taking leave of her. How can I lend myself in such a connection to such portentous death-bed solemnity?

ROSE. Does she wish it so—tremendous?

TONY. Oh *rather*! She's in dead earnest, poor darling. She wants a promise on my sacred honour. She wants a pledge of the most gruesome kind. How in the world can she dream I'm capable—? (*But he throws up his arms as without patience to finish his phrase.*)

ROSE. (*Competently finishing it.*) Of really taking a second wife? (*As with melancholy wisdom born of observation.*) Ah, your capability's another affair! We've nothing to do with that. Of course you understand poor Julia's feeling—what's at the bottom of her dread of your marrying again.

TONY. Assuredly I do! Mrs. Griffin, naturally—*she's* at the bottom. She has filled Julia with the vision of my perhaps giving our child a stepmother.

ROSE. There you are! And if you had known Julia's girlhood—as *I* knew it!—you'd do justice to the force of that horror. It possesses her whole being—she'd prefer the Child should die!

TONY. Well, I'd prefer neither of them should!

ROSE. The simplest thing then is to give her your word—just for the good it may do.

TONY. It may bring her round?

ROSE. It may bring her round—and before the Doctor returns. When he comes, you know, he won't let you go back to her.

TONY. (*Determined, with one of his quick, characteristic revulsions by these arguments; already almost at the door.*) Then I'll go now!

ROSE. Be very brief—but be very strong.

TONY. I'll swear by all the gods—or any other nonsense!

ROSE. Enter thoroughly into her idea—show her you understand it as she understands it herself. For the lifetime of your Daughter. If you should lose Effie, you see, the reason would fail—! But the thing is to *convince* Julia who will be much more deeply convinced if you strike her as really fixing your eyes on what you subscribe to.

TONY. (*With passionate vehemence and sincerity.*) I shall never, never, never, so much as look at another woman!

ROSE. (*Approving with the eager gesture of sending him to his act.*) You've *got* it, my dear Tony! Say it to her *that* way!

(*Exit* TONY *to the staircase while she speaks; and she turns to find herself face to face with* DENNIS VIDAL. *Re-enter* VIDAL *catching these words, from the quarter to which the* BUTLER *has ushered him out.*)

VIDAL. (*Smiling at her with his recovered, his exhibited, letter in his hand.*) What in the world has your dear Tony "got," and what is he to say?

ROSE. (*Disconcerted but for an instant.*) "To say"? Something to his wife, who appears to have lashed herself into an extraordinary state; giving herself up and declaring her end near. She's haunted with a morbid alarm on the subject, of all things, of his marrying again!

VIDAL. She would want him *not* to?

ROSE. She wants his positive promise about it. (*After an instant.*) She wants to have been the only one.

VIDAL. Well, I suppose that's the way ladies often feel. And doesn't the man *see* it?

ROSE. Absolutely. They're all in all to each other. But he's naturally much upset and bewildered. However, I'm as thoroughly nice to them both as they are to *me*.

VIDAL. I'm glad then you've such jolly friends—one feels, on this spot, that they must be charming people. It has been a great comfort to me lately to know that you were with them. (*He looks round him, conscientiously, at the bright, and beautiful hall.*) It *is* a good berth my dear—and it must be a pleasure to live with such fine things. They've given me a room up there that's full of them—a room like a Bond Street shop. (*He glances, as he turns about, at a picture or two; he takes it all more completely in.*) Do they roll in wealth?

ROSE. They're like all bankers I imagine. Don't bankers always "roll"?

VIDAL. Yes—they seem literally to wallow. What a pity *we* ain't bankers, hey?

ROSE. Ah, with my friends here their money's the least part of them. The great thing's just their personal goodness.

VIDAL. (*Who has stopped before a large photograph, a great picture in a massive frame, supported, on a table, by a gilded easel.*) To say nothing of their personal beauty! Mr. Bream, in all his glory, *does* show up!

ROSE. (*Who has recognised with an indulgent glance and sigh the characteristics of the florid image.*) Ah, poor Julia's taste!

VIDAL. (*Entering into it.*) Yes—one can quite see how he must have fetched her!

ROSE. I mean the gorgeous accessories—the *style* of the thing.

VIDAL. It isn't good, hey? Well, *you* know. (*Then, as he moves away from the picture.*) They'll be after that fellow.

ROSE. (*Not looking at him.*) The people she fears?

VIDAL. The women-folk, bless 'em—if he should lose her.

ROSE. I dare say. But he'll be proof.

VIDAL. (*Smiling.*) Has he told you so?

ROSE. In so many words. And he assures me he'll calm her down.

VIDAL. (*After a brief pause; he having opened his letter now and run his eyes over it; the letter that she all the while ignores.*) What a funny subject for him to be talking about!

ROSE. With *me*, do you mean?

VIDAL. Yes, and with his wife.

ROSE. My dear man, you can imagine he didn't begin it.

VIDAL. (*Humorously, whimsically; yet as if there's no other alternative.*) Did *you* then?

ROSE. (*After an instant; as with a humorous grace to match his humour.*) Yes—idiot!

VIDAL. (*Whom her manner has provoked as to a new demonstration of tenderness; which, however, she has as quickly arrested, so that he shall listen, on her seeming to have heard a sound from within the house.*) What's the matter?

ROSE. (*Who checks him; listening.*) Wasn't that a cry from Julia's room?

VIDAL. I heard nothing.

ROSE. Then it's only my nerves.

VIDAL. (*Who holds up his letter.*) Are they too bad for a moment's attention to this?

ROSE. (*Who takes in his letter as if she has become conscious of it for the first time.*) Ah, your letter?

VIDAL. It very intimately concerns our future. I went up for it so that you should do me the favour to read it.

ROSE. Then give it to me—but let me keep it a little.

VIDAL. Certainly. Only please remember that I've still to answer it; I mean referring to points. I've waited to see you because it's from the "Governor" himself—practically saying what he'll do for me.

ROSE. (*With the letter.*) Something very good?

VIDAL. Read and you'll see!

ROSE. (*Who has dropped her eyes to the*

open page, but after an instant while her left hand pats her heart, raises them to him with an odd strained expression.) I mean really good *enough?*

VIDAL. (*Laughing out.*) That's exactly what I want you to tell me!

ROSE. (*Aware of the* DOCTOR *again, putting down the letter; holding up her hand.*) I'll tell you when I've spoken to the Doctor.

(*Re-enter* DOCTOR RAMAGE *by main entrance.*)

DR. RAMAGE. (*Eager, rather out of breath.*) Our friend has not come back?

ROSE. (*As with a gracious intention for* VIDAL.) Mine has! (*Appealing to* DENNIS.) Let me introduce Mr. Vidal. (*Then while the men amicably bow; to* DENNIS.) The Doctor too thinks all the world of me!

DR. RAMAGE. (*To* DENNIS.) Oh she's a wonder—she knows what to *do!* But you'll see that for yourself.

VIDAL. (*Rueful; sincere.*) I'm afraid you won't approve of *me.* You'll think me rather in your patient's way.

DR. RAMAGE. No indeed—I'm sure Miss Armiger will keep you out of it! (*Then to* ROSE; *consulting his watch.*) Bream's not with her *still?*

ROSE. He came away—but has gone back.

DR. RAMAGE. (*Displeased.*) He shouldn't have done that!

ROSE. It was by my advice, and I'm sure you'll find it's all right. But you'll send him here again.

DR. RAMAGE. (*Emphatic.*) This instant! (*Exit* DOCTOR RAMAGE *to the staircase.*)

VIDAL. He's not at all easy!

ROSE. How do you know that?

VIDAL. By *looking* at him. (*Then after an instant, with his eye on her and an abruptness of emphasis.*) I'm not such a fool as you strike me, my dear, as wishing to make of me.

ROSE. (*As amazed; with a candid stare.*) As I strike you as "wishing"—? (*They look at each other hard and as if changing colour.*) My dear Dennis, what do you mean?

VIDAL. (*As coming to the point; deciding to bring out what he has begun to feel.*) I mean, Rose, that I don't quite know what's the matter with you. It's as if, unexpectedly, on my eager arrival, I find something between us.

ROSE. (*As if, since it's only that, she's relieved.*) Why, my dear boy, *of course* you do—poor Julia's between us—*much* between us. (*After which, all nervously, she breaks into emotion.*) I may as well confess it—I'm sharply, wretchedly anxious.

VIDAL. Yet you've quite denied to me up to this moment the gravity of Mrs. Bream's state.

ROSE. I've been doing that to deceive my very self! Think what these people *are* to me.

VIDAL. Oh I know that, enjoying their hospitality here, I should be conscious of all their merits. I *am* certainly, but I don't want you quite to sink the fact that *I'm* something to you too. (*Holding out his letter.*) Don't you call *that* a statement?

ROSE. (*Without eagerness.*) Ah your letter? (*She takes it from him mechanically and, as for the effort of going into it, drops again into a seat.*) Let's see then, let's see then—the great affair! (*While she turns over the leaf to see that there are no less than three large, close, neat, pages.*) He's a trifle long-winded, the "Governor"!

VIDAL. The longer the better—when it's all in *that* key! Read it quietly and carefully; take it *in*—it's really simple enough. (*He moves slowly about the hall, his hands in his pockets, whistling very faintly and looking again at the pictures; during which time her face, convulsed as with the constant effort not to betray the anguish of suspense in her, tells something of the story of her own inward drama. She has to pretend to be occupied with the letter, which she deals with, however, but as to gain time, her attention really hanging on the door through which* TONY *must at any instant return and make a break for her. Her silence accordingly, without sign or sound, so prolongs itself that* VIDAL, *struck with it and impatient for some symptom, at last comes down again.*) Don't you call that really meeting a fellow?

ROSE. I must read it again. (*She turns back to the beginning, and he again strolls away. Then she seems to go through it to the end; after which she folds it with tranquility.*) Yes—it shows what they think of you. As I said a while ago, you're a made man.

VIDAL. (*Cheered, gay.*) Then by the same token of course you're a made woman! You're really satisfied?

ROSE. For the present—perfectly.

VIDAL. You can face the music?

ROSE. (*Momentarily blank and absent.*) The "music"—?

VIDAL. (*Rather irritated again by her lapses.*) You have, my dear, the most extraordinary vacancies! The going *out* there —you accept that too?

ROSE. (*Looking brave; with a mechanical smile.*) Why it's only for two years. (*Then irresistibly and irrelevantly reverting.*) I can't make out why they don't send him back. The Doctor so little wanted him that something must have happened.

VIDAL. (*Bringing it out.*) Do you mean that the poor lady's gone?

ROSE. (*His question having run out so that she has a start of horror and speaks as to check him.*) Dennis! (*Then after an instant.*) God forbid!

VIDAL. God forbid too, I say. But may I nevertheless remind you of the great change that would take place in your situation if she *should* go. The way to provide against everything is—as I just remarked to you—to settle with me this minute the day, the nearest one possible, for our union to become a reality.

ROSE. The day to marry you?

VIDAL. The day to marry me of course! What else?

ROSE. I must settle it this minute?

VIDAL. When in the world if not now?

ROSE. You can't give me a *little* more time?

VIDAL. "More time"? (*His gathered stupefaction breaking.*) After giving you years?

ROSE. Ah, but just at the last here—this news, this rush, is sudden. You know I haven't hurried you—you've come because you *would.*

VIDAL. (*Grasping as with the amazement and the pain of it; his face as smitten and his eyes filling.*) You haven't *wanted* me?

ROSE. (*As trying to adjust things; putting what face on it she can.*) I'm delighted to see you, but I'm asking you—as I've asked you before—just to let me at such

a critical hour, turn round. I'm only suggesting you wait.

VIDAL. (*Catching her sternly up.*) Wait for *what?* (*As if to his indignation, it's all too obvious.*) It's because I've waited that I'm here. What I want of you is three simple words—that you can utter in three simple seconds. And you look at me like a stone. You open up an abyss. I arrive here with a *want* of you that words can't utter; and now I see—though I couldn't at once be sure—that you've been from the first constrained and unnatural. You're trying to gain time—that's what you're doing, and have only been doing it this hour. I don't know what it's *for*—you're *beyond* me; but if it's to back out I'll be hanged if I give you a moment! I'm here for you with all my soul, and I'm here for you now or never!

ROSE. Dennis—!

VIDAL. You do back out?

ROSE. (*After a moment; putting out her hand.*) Good-bye!

VIDAL. (*Who looks at her an instant as over a flood; and then, while he thrusts his hand behind him and looks about for the hat he has somewhere put down, moves blindly, like a man picking himself up from a violent fall.*) Good-bye.

(*Re-enter* TONY BREAM *from the staircase.*)

TONY. (*Coming down, but arrested as by a disappointment while the others stand separated by the width of the hall; speaking with the highest impatience.*) Mrs. Beever hasn't come back? (*To* ROSE.) Julia wants her—Julia must *see* her.

ROSE. (*While* TONY *comes to her and* VIDAL, *circling at his distance, struck and watchful, notes the manner in which he seems to throw himself upon her, and in which she's as immediately "all there" for their host as she has not been for himself.*) She has not come back, but if there's a hurry—!

TONY. (*Before she can finish.*) There *is* a hurry. Some one must go for her.

VIDAL. (*Perceptive, instantly deciding; acting before* ROSE's *rejoinder and at once taking, with an effort, the right tone.*) With your increasing anxieties, Mr. Bream, I'm quite ashamed to be quartered on you.

Hadn't I really better be at the inn?

TONY. (*As if in spite of everything he won't hear of it.*) At the inn?—to go from here? (*Even at this moment characteristically and sociably scoffing.*) My dear fellow, are you mad? (*With his smile of reassurance.*) Don't be afraid: we've plenty of use for you—if only (*with a laugh*) to keep this young woman quiet.

ROSE. (*Deciding and acting, on her side, as instantly as* VIDAL *has done.*) The servants are taken up—! (*Then looking at* DENNIS *as if not the shadow of a cloud is between them.*) Will you, Dennis, go over for Mrs. Beever?

TONY. Ah, we mustn't make him fetch and carry!

VIDAL. (*For his personal relief, catching at it.*) Do employ me, sir—to stretch my sea-legs! I'll do anything.

TONY. Since you're so kind then—and it's so near! Mrs. Beever's our best friend—and always the friend of our friends; and she's only across the river.

ROSE. (*Earnestly contributing.*) Just six minutes—by our short way. Bring her back with you.

TONY. Our short way is through my garden and straight out of it by the gate on the river.

ROSE. At the river you turn to the right—the little foot-bridge is *her* bridge.

TONY. You pass the old gate-house—empty and closed—at the other end of it, and there you are!

ROSE. Just *in* her garden—it's lovely. Tell her it's for Mrs. Bream—and highly important.

TONY. My wife's calling aloud for her. (*As to see him off; with relief.*) So!

VIDAL. (*Between them; for lucidity, taking it all from each in turn.*) It doesn't matter if she doesn't know in the least who I am?

ROSE. She knows perfectly—don't be shy!

TONY. (*Who gives him the friendliest pat on the back, going partly up with him, as to send him off.*) She has even something particular to say to you!

(VIDAL *has a moment's pause at the door to the garden, which he reaches, looking hard from* ROSE *to* TONY *and back again;* ROSE *having*

turned straight away on his fairly starting, but TONY *giving him a friendly smile and hand-waggle for send-off. It is this that determines* VIDAL's *departure without another word. Exit* VIDAL *to garden.*)

TONY. (*Going on to* ROSE.) She takes a great interest in his relations with you. She deprecates the idea of any further delay of your marriage and thinks you've quite enough to "set up" on. She in fact pronounces your means remarkably adequate.

ROSE. What does she know about our means?

TONY. No more, doubtless, than I! But it's the wish that's father to the thought; the result of her general good-will toward you.

ROSE. She has no good-will of any sort toward me. She doesn't *like* me.

TONY. My dear Rose—I think you're greatly mistaken! Mrs. Beever much appreciates you.

ROSE. (*After a moment.*) My dear Tony, I've never known anyone like you for not having two grains of Observation. I've known people with only a little—but that quantity's a poor affair. *You* have absolutely none at all—and that, for your character, is the right thing: it's magnificent and perfect.

TONY. (*Amused.*) I do enjoy a good square one between the eyes!

ROSE. Well, there's plenty of time for Mr. Vidal.

TONY. That means, I hope, that he's going to stay. I like his looks immensely. I like his *type:* it's the real thing—I wish we had him *here.* (*Then not attaching importance even to a small confused cry, an instinctive gesture of dissent, from* ROSE.) Upon my honour I do—he's just the sort of fellow I personally should have liked to *be.*

ROSE. (*Struck, even in her impatience, by the distinction he appears to make.*) You mean *you're* not the "real thing"?

TONY. (*Recognising the question as of a kind that his chronic good-nature and sociability, shining out almost splendidly through trouble, can always meet with princely extravagance.*) Not a bit. I'm bolstered up with all sorts of little appearances and accidents. (*Emphatic.*) Your friend there has his feet on the rock! (*But then, with a quick transition—this determined by a renewed impatient motion of* Rose's—*he reverts with the best conscience in the world to his point of just before.*) You must really, at any rate—as we were saying—do justice to Mrs. Beever, who I'm sure, never lifted a finger against you!

Rose. She *will!* You yourself have given me the proof—in telling Dennis she has told you of something she wants to say to him.

Tony. (*Blank at first: then recalling it but to make light of it.*) What she has to say is only what I myself have already said for the rest of us—that she hopes with all her heart things are now smooth for his marriage.

Rose. Well, what could be more horrid than that? What has she to do with his marriage? Why does she give opinions that nobody wants or asks her for? What does she know of our relation, or of what difficulties and mysteries she touches? Why can't she leave us alone—at least for the first hour?

Tony. (*All embarrassed and beautifully gaping, the unexpected having sprung upon him.*) Bless my soul, my dear child— you don't mean to say there *are* difficulties? (*Across the interval, as he speaks she suddenly faces round, and his view of her hereupon at once making him smite his forehead in his expressive penitent way. Something comes over him.*) What a brute I am not to have seen you're not quite happy, and not to have noticed that *he*—! (*He catches himself up: the face offered him is the convulsed face* Rose *has managed though only comparatively to keep from her lover. She literally glares at him; standing there with her two hands pressing down her agitated breast and something in all her aspect like the first shock of a great accident. What he sees, without at first understanding it, is the final snap of tremendous tension, the end of her wonderful false calm; which makes him instantly begin, dismayed and disappointed, to guess and spell out, as it were, quite misunderstandingly, the real truth of her*

situation. He thus springs at the idea that she has received a blow—a blow which her self-control up to within a moment only presents now as more touchingly borne. Her desire to get rid of* Vidal *becomes instantly a part of it for him: what has somehow happened flashes into vividness. Thus —giving her all the benefit of it—he pieces her case together.*) His eagerness to leave you surprised me—and yours to make him go! (*Then as it still more intensely comes to him, while even before he speaks her eyes seem to glitter it back.*) He hasn't brought you bad news—hasn't failed, for you, of what we hoped? (*Going nearer for compassion and tenderness.*) You don't mean to say, my poor girl, that he doesn't meet you as you supposed he would? (*Then as she drops at his approach, into a chair, where she bursts into passionate tears, and while she throws herself upon a small table, burying her head in her arms just as* Jean *has first found her, he stands over her, all wonder and pity, and feels helpless as she sobs.*) You don't mean to say he doesn't keep Faith?

Rose. (*Prostrate, sunk as under her wrong.*) Oh God, oh God, oh God! (*After which, as he turns off from her woe with a movement and confession of incompetence, she springs up as to brush away the gust of her passion; speaking through her tears, compunctious and ashamed.*) Don't mind me—I shall pull myself together. (*Reassuring; brave as for very decency.*) I shall be all right in a moment; only don't let Julia know—that's all I ask of you. Just give me three minutes, and I sha'n't show a trace.

Tony. Your bravery makes it too hard to help you!

Rose. Don't *try* to help me. Don't even *want* to. And don't ask any questions or tell any tales. (*Then with a complete change, seeing* Mrs. Beever, *while* Black *reappears, formal and punctual.*) Hush, hush!

(*Re-enter* Mrs. Beever *from the garden, re-enter at the same time* Black *by the main entrance.*)

Butler. Luncheon's served, sir. (*Exit* Black.)

Tony. Luncheon's all very well—but

who in the world's to eat it? (*To* MRS. BEEVER.) Before *you* do, there's something I must ask of you.

ROSE. (*With equal promptness.*) And something *I* must ask too. (*Serene and clear for* MRS. BEEVER's *inspection now.*) Didn't Mr. Vidal come back with you?

MRS. BEEVER. (*Characteristically incorruptible by any suavity.*) Indeed, he did. (*Sturdy.*) Mr. Vidal's in the garden of this house.

ROSE. Then I'll call him to luncheon. (*Exit* ROSE *to the garden.*)

MRS. BEEVER. (*Firing it off the instant she has gone.*) She has broken it off!

TONY. (*Wondering, demurring.*) "She"? How do you know?

MRS. BEEVER. I know because he told me so.

TONY. Mr. Vidal? Already? In these few minutes?

MRS. BEEVER. Of course I asked him first. I was on my way, and—meeting him at the bridge—saw at once he had had a shock.

TONY. (*With his totally different view.*) It's *Rose* who has had the shock! It's he who has thrown her over!

MRS. BEEVER. That's *her* story?

TONY. Practically—yes!

MRS. BEEVER. Then one of them lies.

TONY. It isn't at any rate Rose Armiger!

MRS. BEEVER. It isn't Dennis Vidal, my dear. I believe in *him.*

TONY. Your mental operations are rapid!

MRS. BEEVER. Remarkably. I've asked him to come to me. (*Then as* TONY *shows wonder.*) Till he can get a train—tomorrow. (*Mistress of her view and of the whole subject.*) He can't stay on here.

TONY. (*After an instant.*) I see what you mean. Is he very much cut up?

MRS. BEEVER. He's utterly staggered. He doesn't understand.

TONY. (*Puzzled at it; lost before it.*) No more do I! (*Then as for the moment throwing it up.*) But you'll console him.

MRS. BEEVER. I'll *feed* him—first. I'll take him back with me to luncheon.

TONY. How?—if Rose is bringing him in?

MRS. BEEVER. She isn't. She hasn't gone to him. That was for *me.*

TONY. Your mental operation, as I say, leaves me gasping! *I* found her—in my

stupidity!—under the unmistakeable effects of a blow.

MRS. BEEVER. I found her exactly as usual.

TONY. Well, that was also for *you!* (*Then more importantly, and as if, after all, it's for the moment his only point.*) Her disappointment's a secret.

MRS. BEEVER. (*Mercilessly ironic.*) Then I'm much obliged to you for mentioning it!

TONY. (*Earnest.*) I did so to defend her against your bad account of her. (*Then with a nervous revulsion, a sudden discouraged weariness.*) But the whole thing's obscure. I give it up!

MRS. BEEVER. *I* don't! I shall straighten it out. But I must see your wife first.

TONY. (*All there again; urgent at once for this.*) Rather! She's waiting all this while!

MRS. BEEVER. (*While he reaches the door to staircase and has already opened it for her; more deliberate.*) Shall I find the Doctor with her?

TONY. Yes—by her request.

MRS. BEEVER. Then how is she?

TONY. Maddening! I mean in her dreadful obsession—to which poor Ramage has had to give way and which is the direct reason of her calling you.

MRS. BEEVER. (*Who hears of this for the first time; interestedly wondering and putting it again sharply.*) What on earth are you talking about?

TONY. She'll tell you herself! (*On which, after another look at him, she disappears, and he takes, about the room, another of his restless turns; but in an instant, at the open door, she is back again.*)

MRS. BEEVER. Only a word to say that that child may turn up.

TONY. (*Far down and opposite at this moment a hundred miles off from it.*) What "child"—?

MRS. BEEVER. Oh if you don't remember—!

TONY. (*As it comes back to him.*) Oh your niece?—Certainly—I remember the shade of her hair!

MRS. BEEVER. She's not my niece and the shade of her hair's none of your business! But if she does come, send her straight home. (*Exit* MRS. BEEVER *to staircase.*)

TONY. Very good.

(TONY *has then alone in the hall, a considerable nervous anxious restless passage. It ends for him, after his brief and solitary, but in various ways significant scene, in the show of sudden lassitude under which he drops, as conscious of too many troublesome things, upon the sofa, where, with his head back, his eyes closed and his legs up, he seems to invite momentary slumber to overtake him. Thus it is that, quietly coming in by the main entrance,* JEAN MARTLE *finds him. Re-enter* JEAN MARTLE. *She almost steals in, for discretion, and has a movement of surprise to see the hall at first apparently empty. Then before* TONY, *through his doze, appears to become aware of her, she pulls up in sight of him, rather at a loss what to do. There follows a moment during which her figure, there before him, becomes to him not a dream-creature, but a reality; with the sense of it jerking him straight up to a slightly bewildered grasp of her identity, if not of her name. He springs to his feet.*)

TONY. Ah good morning. How d'ye do? Pardon my posture—I didn't hear you come in.

JEAN. (*Embarrassed, but happily animated and pleased.*) When I saw you apparently asleep I'm afraid I kept the footman from speaking. I came in because he told me Cousin Kate's here.

TONY. (*Alert, his wits all about him now.*) Oh yes—she's here. She thought you might arrive. (*Then as for a welcome as marked as his promise of a moment before to* MRS. BEEVER *has been marked in the other sense, and indicating to her a high Venetian chair.*) Do sit down.

JEAN. (*Compliant, taken, even though a little rueful for so instant a surrender; seated in the stately chair which helps to make a picture of her; where she finds herself moreover anxious to explain.*) I thought it better to come—as she wasn't there (*with a nod in the quarter of the other house.*) I had gone off to walk home

with the Duggits—I was gone rather long; and when I came back she had left the house. The servants told me she must be here.

TONY. (*On his feet, hovering and appreciating while she sits there.*) Oh it's all right—Cousin Kate's with Julia: that's my wife, you know. I wrote to you both to come to luncheon—when I found we couldn't meet at Church. I hoped so much you'd come. (*Then a bit rueful.*) But I'm afraid *she's* not staying!

JEAN. Ah then *I* mustn't!

TONY. Oh she'll be a little while yet. My wife has something to say to her.

JEAN. (*As breathing a little more freely at this; raising her eyes from the floor to look round her; generally a little more at her ease and casting about her as for something that will show him sympathy without freedom.*) I came an hour ago—and I saw Miss Armiger. She told me she'd bring down the Baby.

TONY. (*Interested, amused.*) But she didn't?

JEAN. No—Cousin Kate thought it wouldn't do.

TONY. (*Happily struck for the moment, and now under '*JEAN's *immediate influence, not at all minding* COUSIN KATE.) It *will* do! It *shall* do! (*As if they've already established the most amicable, in fact the most intimate, relation.*) You awfully *want* to see her?

JEAN. (*Smiling, rosy, responsive.*) Awfully! (*Then all earnestness.*) It's so kind of you!

TONY. (*All alert; rejoicing.*) I'll show her to you myself! (*He goes over to ring a bell, and then as he comes down.*) I delight in showing her! (*Extravagant.*) I think she's the wonder of the world!

JEAN. (*In the highest good faith.*) That's what babies always seem to me. It's so absorbing to watch them.

TONY. Absorbing!—isn't it, preposterously? (*With happy conviction.*) Wait till you've watched Effie!

JEAN. (*Only desirous to do this, above all in his company; but going on, a little embarrassed, while they do wait together for the response to his ring.*) I've a particular reason for my interest in her. I'm just the person to have it.

(*Enter* FOOTMAN *by main entrance.*)

TONY. "Just the person"—? (*Seeing* FOOTMAN; *urgent.*) Please tell Gorham to be so good as to bring down the Child.

(*The* FOOTMAN *bows and goes out.*)

JEAN. Perhaps Gorham will think it won't *do!*

TONY. Oh, she's as happy about her as I am! But if she *doesn't* approve I'll take you upstairs! That will be because, as you say, you're just the person. I haven't the least doubt of it—but you were going to tell me why.

JEAN. Because she was born on my day.

TONY. Your birthday?

JEAN. My birthday. The twenty-fourth.

TONY. Oh, I see! That's a most extraordinary coincidence—it makes a most interesting tie. Do therefore, I beg of you, whenever you keep your anniversary, keep also a little hers.

JEAN. I shall always send her something.

TONY. She shall do the same for *you!* You're her very first friend.

JEAN. (*Pleased, but wondering.*) Before she has ever seen me?

TONY. Oh, those *are* the first. You're handed "down."

JEAN. Why, I haven't seen her Mother either.

TONY. No, you haven't seen her Mother. (*All confident.*) But you *shall.* And you *have* seen her Father.

JEAN. (*In admiration.*) Yes, I "have" seen her Father.

TONY. Then shake hands with him on it! (*After which, however, as she has a little shyly but very prettily responded, so that he has taken her hand and held it a bit, losing himself in the sense of how charming she is, he pulls himself together with a quick realisation and a clap of his head.*) Do you know, however, I'm under a sort of dreadful vow to Mrs. Beever? (*Ruefully.*) She told me that if you should turn up I was to pack you off.

JEAN. Ah, I shouldn't have stayed!

TONY. You didn't know it, and I couldn't show you the door!

JEAN. (*With decision.*) Then I must go now.

TONY. Not a bit! I wouldn't have mentioned it—to consent to *that.* I mention it for just the other reason—to keep you here as long as possible. I'll make it right with Cousin Kate. I'm not afraid of her! You produce an effect on me for which I'm particularly grateful. I'm worried. I'm depressed—I've been threshing about in my anxiety. You keep me cool—you're just the right thing. Stay with me—stay with me!

JEAN. Ah, if I *could* help you!

TONY. (*As if really to show her how.*) Sit down again—sit down! (*Then seeing* GORHAM *with her charge; in full extravagance.*) Here's the wonder of the world!

(*Enter the Baby's* NURSE, *with the* CHILD, *both in full panoply, by the main door. Re-enter* DOCTOR RAMAGE *and* MRS. BEEVER *together at the same moment from the staircase, and are confronted with this unexpected apparition. Re-enter simultaneously* ROSE ARMIGER *and* DENNIS VIDAL *from the garden.*)

ROSE. (*Bright and responsible; as if acting in* JULIA's *absence as hostess.*) But luncheon, all the while? Served—spoiling —spoilt!

TONY. (*At once then gallantly supporting her and addressing* MRS. BEEVER.) Let us at last go in then! (*Repeating it to* JEAN *and* VIDAL.) Let us go in. Doctor, you'll come too.

DR. RAMAGE. (*Raising at once and as for general application a deterrent, authoritative hand.*) If you please, Bream—no banquet. (*Looking at* JEAN, ROSE, VIDAL *and* GORHAM; *grave and responsible.*) I take the house in hand. We immediately subside.

TONY. (*Instantly alert and anxious.*) Julia's worse?

DR. RAMAGE. (*Nervous, dry, sharp.*) No —she's the same.

TONY. Then I may go to her?

DR. RAMAGE. (*Imperative.*) Absolutely not! (*Grasping* TONY's *arm, linking it in his own, and holding him.*) If you're not a good boy, I'll lock you up in your room. (*Then again to the others.*) We immediately subside—we go our respective ways and we keep very still. The fact is, I require a hushed house. But before the hush descends Mrs. Beever has something to say to us.

MRS. BEEVER. (*On the other side of* TONY, *but not close to him, looking at her little audience:* ROSE *and* GORHAM *down together, and* JEAN *and* VIDAL *together opposite; the object in* GORHAM'S *ample arms has the air of a large white sacrifice, a muslin-muffled offering that seems to lead up to a ceremony.*) I've something to say to you because Doctor Ramage allows it, and because we're both under pledges—of the gravest sort!—to Mrs. Bream! (*Then proceeding after the high, competent, easy manner of a woman accustomed to deal with others, to preside at committees, to put through any business she may have in hand.*) I grant you it's an odd announcement for me to have on my hands; but I've just passed her my promise, in the very strictest manner, to make it, before leaving the house, to everyone it may concern—and to repeat it in certain other quarters.

TONY. (*With an ejaculation half pitying, half protesting, and all uncontrollable, for the element of the portentous in this.*) Oh I say! (*On which the* DOCTOR, *his arm round him instantly checks and pats him to silence;* MRS. BEEVER, *by the same sign, for the rest of her speech, markedly attaching her eyes to him.*)

MRS. BEEVER. She wishes it as generally known as possible that Mr. Bream to gratify her at a crisis of which I trust she exaggerates the gravity, has assured her on his sacred honour that in the event of her death, he'll not marry again.

DR. RAMAGE. (*Prompt and as for complete correctness.*) In the lifetime, that is, of her Daughter.

TONY. (*Again as for the extravagance of it.*) Oh I say!

MRS. BEEVER. In the lifetime—certainly! —of her Daughter.

TONY. (*As to humour impatiently the extravagance.*) In the lifetime, then, of her Daughter! (*Which succession of loud solemnities he takes as affecting the* CHILD *in* GORHAM'S *arms to the point of moving her to some sound that he has heard, this in turn creating a happy diversion and causing him to spring straight to his offspring, over whom he all tenderly and expressively bends, in* GORHAM'S *arms; putting down his face as if to press it there.*) So it *is,* my darling, my own, a shame and a scandal to be talking of "lifetimes"!

(MRS. BEEVER *and the* DOCTOR *meanwhile give the others the signal for instant withdrawal; the lady marshalling out* JEAN *and* VIDAL *as by a single stroke; which departure of her lover without a look at her, and under* MRS. BEEVER'S *convoy,* ROSE, *grave and pale, visibly watches. Exeunt* MRS. BEEVER, JEAN *and* VIDAL *to the garden.* ROSE *has already, however, on her own side, received her dismissal from the* DOCTOR; *exit* ROSE *to her own room, by the main entrance. Then the* DOCTOR *is alone with* TONY *and* GORHAM; *to which latter he instantly signals to retire with her charge. The two men are thus face to face, and* TONY, *still under the* DOCTOR'S *grasp, but not as yet conscious of the meaning of it, breaks out as for the personal relief of his irritation and distress.*)

TONY. How dreadfully ill she *must* be, Ramage, to have conceived a stroke in such awful taste!

DR. RAMAGE. (*Patient, significant, indulgent, as with news of the highest gravity, drawing him to the sofa and down upon it, where, in presence of his now completely roused suspicion, he lays his hand soothingly, pattingly on his knee.*) You must bear it, my dear boy. You must bear everything. (*Then while* TONY *fairly glares at him.*) Your wife's *exceedingly* ill.

ACT FIRST

The middle of a June afternoon, four years later, in the garden at Eastmead. The geography and topography, so elaborate, so difficult, yet so possible here, all to be lucidly worked out and presented. MRS. BEEVER *seated on her beautiful old velvet lawn by her tea-table, as in preparation for that pleasant repast. A large red rug, a large white tablecloth, sundry basket-chairs and, down to one side, a suspended hammock that sways in the soft west wind. She is occupied with a collection of parcels and pasteboard boxes that are heaped together near her, partly on the lawn close to her seat, partly on a low convenient stool. Of one of these parcels, enveloped in several layers of tissue-paper, she possesses herself and is about to proceed to uncover it. At the same moment enter* DOCTOR RAMAGE *from that portion of the house which we conceive as just visible, or presumable, rather up [1] to the right. He arrives as informally as if he's constantly in the habit of arriving; that is as the friend just now so much more than as the doctor.*

DR. RAMAGE. Guess whom I've just overtaken on your doorstep. The young man you befriended four years ago. Mr. Vidal, Miss Armiger's old flame.

MRS. BEEVER. (*Astonished.*) He has turned up again? For what in the world—?

DR. RAMAGE. For the pleasure of seeing a person of whose service to him he has clearly retained so grateful a sense.

MRS. BEEVER. "Service"? Why, I did nothing! Whatever I *might* have done, I had to let it alone.

DR. RAMAGE. Tony's condition on his wife's death—of course I remember—was *the* great call on you. But you gave this poor gentleman shelter that wretched day and night, and it was assuredly much to him to feel that, in the queer matter of his rupture with his young woman, you had

---

[1] Henry James wrote "down" but the stage plan indicates the house was to be situated on the upper right.

the right instinct for it and were somehow on his side.

MRS. BEEVER. I put him up for a few hours: I saved him by my prompt action; I admit, the embarrassment of finding himself in a house of death. But he took himself off the next morning early—bidding me good-bye only in a quiet little note.

DR. RAMAGE. A quiet little note which I remember you afterwards showed me and which was a model of discretion and good taste. It seems to me that he doesn't violate those virtues in feeling you've given him the right to reappear.

MRS. BEEVER. (*Struck to amusement with the way it has worked.*) At the very time, and the only time, in the long stretch, that his young woman, as you call her, happens to be again in the field!

DR. RAMAGE. That's a coincidence far too odd for Mr. Vidal to have dreamt of it.

MRS. BEEVER. You didn't tell him then?

DR. RAMAGE. I told him nothing save that you were probably just where I find you, and that, as Manning is busy with her tea-things, I'd come straight out for him and announce that he's there.

MRS. BEEVER. By "there" do you mean on the doorstep?

DR. RAMAGE. Far from it! In the safest place in the world—at least when you're not in it: in that austere monument to Domestic Method which you're sometimes pleased to call your boudoir. I took on myself to show him into it and to close the door on him. I reflected that you'd perhaps like to see him before anyone else.

MRS. BEEVER. You dear sharp thing!

DR. RAMAGE. Unless indeed—in so many years!—they've already elsewhere met.

MRS. BEEVER. She told me only yesterday they haven't.

DR. RAMAGE. I see. (*Then amusedly.*) However, as I believe you consider she never by any chance speaks the truth, that doesn't particularly *count!*

MRS. BEEVER. I hold on the contrary that a lie counts double!

DR. RAMAGE. (*Laughing, gallant.*) Then why have you never in your life told one? (*After which, as she but tosses her head.*) I haven't even yet quite made out why—especially with Miss Jean here—you asked Miss Armiger down.

MRS. BEEVER. (*As with her master-method for everything; lucid.*) I asked her for Tony.

DR. RAMAGE. Because he suggested it? Yes, I know that.

MRS. BEEVER. I mean it in a sense you think you *don't* "know." (*Then after a pause during which they intelligently look at each other.*) I asked her exactly on *account* of Jean.

DR. RAMAGE. (*Thinking, but as if this is a deeper depth than he can sound.*) I give it up—the more as you've mostly struck me as so afraid of every other girl Paul looks at.

MRS. BEEVER. Yes, I've always been; but I'm not so afraid of them as of those at whom *Tony* looks!

DR. RAMAGE. (*Rather pulled up.*) He's "looking" at Jean?

MRS. BEEVER. (*After a wait.*) Not for the first time!

DR. RAMAGE. (*As if it's a bit grave; fitting her pieces together.*) And do you think Miss Armiger—?

MRS. BEEVER. (*Taking him straight up.*) Miss Armiger's *better* for him—(*then with fairly sardonic humour*) since he must have Somebody!

DR. RAMAGE. You consider she'd marry him?

MRS. BEEVER. (*Assured; stating it for all it's worth.*) She's insanely in love with him.

DR. RAMAGE. (*Wincing as for the publication of it.*) Ay, Ay, Ay! (*Then as the cat's out of the bag; accepting it.*) Since you frankly mention it, she is indeed, poor thing, and I as frankly agree with you that I've never seen anything like it. And there's monstrous little I haven't seen! (*Then, however, as for their safeguard.*) But if Tony isn't crazy too—!

MRS. BEEVER. It's a kind of craze that's catching! He must *think* of that sort of thing.

DR. RAMAGE. It depends on what you mean by "thinking"! Do you imply that

the dear man, on what we all know—?

MRS. BEEVER. (*Taking him up again; with courage for what he can't phrase.*) Would break his Vow and marry again? (*She turns it over; superficially detached; busy with her little parcels; then she brings out with an effect of unexpectedness.*) Never in the world!

DR. RAMAGE. Then how does the chance of his thinking of Rose help her?

MRS. BEEVER. I don't say it helps *her*. I simply say it helps poor Me.

DR. RAMAGE. But if they can't marry—?

MRS. BEEVER. I don't care whether they marry or not!

DR. RAMAGE. (*Amused at her superior consistency.*) I don't know whether most to admire your Imagination or your Morality.

MRS. BEEVER. (*Perfectly clear and resolute for herself.*) I protect *my* girl.

DR. RAMAGE. (*Still more amused and as if choosing.*) Oh—I think—your Morality!

MRS. BEEVER. In doing so I also protect my Boy. That's the highest morality I know. I'll see Mr. Vidal out here.

DR. RAMAGE. So as to get rid of him easier?

MRS. BEEVER. My getting rid of him will depend on what he wants. He must take, after all, his chance of meeting any embarrassment. If he has plumped in without feeling his way—!

DR. RAMAGE. (*Taking her up.*) It's his own affair—I see. (*Then looking at his watch, getting up.*) I'll put it then to him—though (*laughing*) more gracefully than you do!—that you'll receive him in this place.

MRS. BEEVER. I shall be much obliged to you.

DR. RAMAGE. But before I go—where are all our friends?

MRS. BEEVER. I haven't the least idea. The only ones I count on are Effie and Jean.

DR. RAMAGE. (*With a gesture of happy remembrance.*) To be sure—it's their Birthday! That fellow put it out of my head. (*Entering fully into it.*) The Child's to come over to Tea, and just what I stopped for—

MRS. BEEVER. Was to see if I have your

Doll? (*Pulling away the papers of a muffled parcel in her lap and holding up the contents.*) Allow me to introduce the young lady!

DR. RAMAGE. (*Taking the doll, with all appreciation, into his hands.*) She's splendid—she's positively human! I feel like a Turkish Pasha investing in a beautiful Circassian! I feel too how right I was to depend, in the absence of Mrs. Ramage, on your infallible taste. (*Then restoring the effigy to the stool.*) Kindly mention how much I owe you.

MRS. BEEVER. Pay at the shop. They "trusted" me.

DR. RAMAGE. With the same sense of security that *I* have! Please then present the object and accompany it with my love and a kiss.

MRS. BEEVER. You can't come back to give them yourself?

DR. RAMAGE. (*Rueful, ironic at his own expense.*) What do I ever "give," dearest lady, but Physic?

MRS. BEEVER. Very good; the presentation shall be formal. But I ought to warn you that your beautiful Circassian will have been no less than the fourth. (*With a nod at the parcels on the stool.*) I mean the fourth doll the Child's to receive to-day.

DR. RAMAGE. (*Looking at them where they lie; amused.*) It's a regular slave-market—a perfect *hareem!*

MRS. BEEVER. We've each given her one. (*Bethinking herself.*) Each, that is, except Rose.

DR. RAMAGE. (*Interested.*) And what has Rose given her?

MRS. BEEVER. (*Simple, but a trifle dry.*) Nothing at all.

DR. RAMAGE. (*After an instant.*) Doesn't she *like* her?

MRS. BEEVER. She seems to wish it to be marked that she has nothing to do with her.

DR. RAMAGE. (*After another instant.*) I see. That's very clever.

MRS. BEEVER. (*Holding him a moment with her upward eyes.*) What do you mean—in the connection—by "clever"?

DR. RAMAGE. (*Standing an instant while he meets her eyes.*) I'll tell you some other time! (*Then as, before the display, missing*

something.*) There are no gifts for poor Jean?

MRS. BEEVER. Oh, Jean has *had* most of hers.

DR. RAMAGE. (*Further struck; clapping his head.*) But nothing from *me!* I'm quite ashamed!

MRS. BEEVER. You needn't be. She has also had nothing from Tony.

DR. RAMAGE. (*Surprised, wondering.*) Indeed? (*Then after an instant.*) On Miss Armiger's system? That of wishing it to be marked that he has nothing to do with her?

MRS. BEEVER. (*Busy for a moment at her table; then as if it says everything.*) He doesn't calculate.

DR. RAMAGE. That's *bad*—for a banker! (*After which, as for the great question.*) What then has she had from Paul?

MRS. BEEVER. Nothing either—as *yet*. That's to come this evening.

DR. RAMAGE. And what's it to *be?*

MRS. BEEVER. (*While they exchange the same longer look as a moment before.*) I haven't an idea.

DR. RAMAGE. (*Going, with a laugh.*) Ah, you can fib!

(*Exit* DOCTOR RAMAGE *to the house while* MANNING, *the parlourmaid, crosses him on her way out with a tea-tray.*)

MRS. BEEVER. (*Thoughtfully re-enveloping* DOCTOR RAMAGE'S *doll while the* PARLOURMAID *makes a place for three or four more of her articles on the table.*) Do you know, Manning, what has become of Miss Armiger?

MANNING. She went, ma'am, near an hour ago, to the pastry-cook's. She had heard you wonder, she told me, ma'am, that the young ladies' birthday-cake hadn't yet arrived.

MRS. BEEVER. And she thought she'd see about it? (*Impressed.*) Uncommonly good of her!

MANNING. Yes, ma'am, uncommonly good.

MRS. BEEVER. Has it arrived then now?

MANNING. Not yet, ma'am.

MRS. BEEVER. And Miss Armiger hasn't returned?

MANNING. I think not, ma'am.

MRS. BEEVER. (*Again struck; wonder-*

ing.) Perhaps she's waiting to bring it.

MANNING. Perhaps, ma'am—in a fly. (*Then with all detachment.*) When it comes, ma'am, shall I fetch it out?

MRS. BEEVER. (*Amused at her manner.*) In a fly too? I am afraid that after such an incubation it will really require one! (*Then more practically.*) I'll go in and look at it first. (*After which, detaining* MANNING, *who, her last touch to the table administered, is about, in her very stiff skirts, to rustle away.*) Mr. Bream hasn't been over yet?

MANNING. Not yet, ma'am.

MRS. BEEVER. (*Who has consulted her watch; concluding.*) Then he's still at the Bank.

MANNING. He must be indeed, ma'am.

MRS. BEEVER. And you haven't seen Miss Jean?

MANNING. (*Who has bethought herself.*) I believe, ma'am, Miss Jean is dressing. In honour of her birthday, ma'am.

MRS. BEEVER. I see—of course. And do you happen to have heard if that's what also detains Miss Effie—that she's dressing in honour of *hers?*

MANNING. (*After a perceptible wait.*) I heard, ma'am, this morning, that Miss Effie has a slight cold.

MRS. BEEVER. (*Surprised, a little disconcerted.*) But not such as to keep her at home?

MANNING. They were taking extra care of her, ma'am,—so that she might be all right for coming.

MRS. BEEVER. (*Alert, critical.*) Extra care? Then why didn't they send for the Doctor?

MANNING. (*After another slight wait and as if a bit conscious of her effect.*) They sent for Miss Jean, ma'am.

MRS. BEEVER. To come and look after her?

MANNING. They often do that, ma'am, you know. This morning I took in the message.

MRS. BEEVER. And Miss Jean obeyed it?

MANNING. (*Inexorable.*) She was there an hour, ma'am.

MRS. BEEVER. (*With a little slap almost of violence on her enveloped but unoffending doll.*) She said nothing about it.

MANNING. (*Relentless; with the word* sounding as tall as herself.*) Nothing, ma'am. (*She still just waits; after which, as a Parthian shot.*) Mr. Paul, ma'am—if you were wanting to know—is out in his boat on the river.

MRS. BEEVER. (*Tossing her doll with asperity back to its companions in the heap near her.*) Mr. Paul's never anywhere else!

MANNING. (*As for her merciless climax.*) Never, ma'am. (*Then as she sees* DENNIS VIDAL *appear; announcing.*) A gentleman, ma'am.

(*Enter* DENNIS VIDAL *from the house. Exit* MANNING *to the same.*)

MRS. BEEVER. (*Not getting up to meet him; but so friendly, none the less, as to be familiar; shaking hands with him where she sits, directing him to a chair and speaking with her characteristically immediate sense of the actual and the real.*) I feel I should tell you at once that Miss Armiger is with me. (*Then while as, so visibly pulled up at this as to show it for the last thing he has expected, he doesn't sit down, as he was about to do, but stands there in his surprise and disconcertment while she goes on for discretion's and safety's sake.*) She has gone out—but may reappear at any moment.

VIDAL. And if she does, will she come out here?

MRS. BEEVER. I dare say she'll change her dress first. That may take her a little time.

VIDAL. Then I'm free to sit with you ten minutes?

MRS. BEEVER. As long as you like, dear Mr. Vidal. It's for you to choose whether you'll avoid her.

VIDAL. (*Making the best of it, yet a little rueful.*) I dislike dodging, I dislike hiding; but I dare say that if I had known where she was—which (*as for* MRS. BEEVER'S *definite information*) I haven't at all known— I shouldn't have seen my way!

MRS. BEEVER. I feel hatefully rude—but you took a leap in the dark. The absurd part of it is that you've stumbled on her very first visit to me.

VIDAL. (*Seating himself; showing her indeed his need of illumination.*) These four years?

MRS. BEEVER. These four years. It's the

only time she has been here.

VIDAL. (*Hesitating but wondering.*) And how often at the other house?

MRS. BEEVER. (*Smiling.*) Not even once. I can quite say *that* for her.

VIDAL. To your certain knowledge?

MRS. BEEVER. To my certain and absolute knowledge. But *you*—where do you come from?

VIDAL. (*Simply.*) From far away. I've been out of England. After that time here I returned to my post.

MRS. BEEVER. And now you've returned with your fortune?

VIDAL. (*As liking to talk with her; but with his latent bitterness.*) Call it my misfortune! (*A bit grim.*) I've come back with *that*. It sticks to me.

MRS. BEEVER. (*Waiting a little, her eyes on him, as to spare him, all kindly, the hard truth of it; but too interested not then to put her question.*) You want her as much as ever?

VIDAL. I want her as much as ever. It's a chronic ache.

MRS. BEEVER. Which her treatment of you has done nothing to cure?

VIDAL. "To cure"? (*Absolute.*) It has done everything in life to aggravate it.

MRS. BEEVER. (*Thinking, but risking it.*) In spite of the particular circumstance—?

VIDAL. (*As she has hung, hesitating and considerate, on the note; perfectly understanding and taking it up.*) The particular circumstance of her chucking me because of the sudden glimpse given her, by Mrs. Bream's danger, of a possibility of a far better match? (*Then with a laugh drier than any of* MRS. BEEVER's *own; the ring of an irony from which long, hard thought has pressed all the savour.*) That "particular circumstance," dear madam, is every bit what's the matter with me!

MRS. BEEVER. You regard it with extraordinary coolness, but I presume to allude to it—

VIDAL. (*Breaking intelligently in.*) Because I myself made no bones of doing so on the only other occasion on which we've met?

MRS. BEEVER. (*At one with him.*) The fact that we both equally *saw*, that we both equally judged, was at that crisis really the only thing that had time to pass between us. It's a tie, but it's a slender one, and I'm all the more flattered that it should have had any force to make you care to see me again.

VIDAL. It never was to *cease* to be my purpose to see you—if you'd permit it— on the first chance. My chance has been precipitated—! I returned to England only last week, and was obliged two days ago to come on business to Southampton. There I found I should have to go, on the same matter, to Marrington. It then appeared that to get to Marrington I must change at Plumbury—

MRS. BEEVER. (*Lucidly concluding.*) And Plumbury reminded you that you changed there, that it was from there you drove, on that horrible Sunday.

VIDAL. It brought my opportunity home. Without wiring or writing you, without sounding the ground or doing anything I ought to have done, I simply embraced it. I reached this place an hour ago and went to the inn.

MRS. BEEVER. (*Regretfully, woefully.*) Poor dear gentleman!

VIDAL. I do very well. Remember the places I come from.

MRS. BEEVER. I don't care a button where you've come from! If Rose weren't here I could put you up so beautifully!

VIDAL. Well, now that I know it I think I'm *glad* she's here. It's a fact the more to reckon with.

MRS. BEEVER. You mean to see her then?

VIDAL. You must tell me two or three things first. Then I'll choose. (*Intensely thinking.*) I'll decide.

MRS. BEEVER. (*Who hands him now the cup of tea she has prepared for him.*) I must tell you frankly that if four years ago she was a girl most people admired—

VIDAL. (*Alert.*) She's still more wonderful now?

MRS. BEEVER. I don't know about "wonderful"—but she wears really well. She carries the years almost (*in friendly homage*) as well as *you* do—and her head better than any young woman I've ever seen. Life is somehow becoming to her. Everyone's immensely struck with her. She only needs to get what she wants. She has really a charm that I recognise.

VIDAL. (*Staring at the words as at a framed picture; the reflected colour of them making, so to speak, a light .in his face.*) And you speak as one, who, I remember, doesn't *like* her!

MRS. BEEVER. (*After an instant; but with characteristic frankness.*) No—I don't like her!

VIDAL. I see. May I ask then why you invited her?

MRS. BEEVER. For the most definite reason in the world. Mr. Bream asked me to.

VIDAL. Do you do everything Mr. Bream asks?

MRS. BEEVER. He asks so little!

VIDAL. Yes—if that's a specimen! (*But abundantly interested.*) Does *he* like her still?

MRS. BEEVER. Just as much as ever.

VIDAL. Do you mean he's in love with her?

MRS. BEEVER. He never *was*—in any degree.

VIDAL. Are you very sure?

MRS. BEEVER. Well, I'm sure of the present. That's quite enough. He's not in love with her now. I have the proof. His request in itself. (*Positive.*) If he were in love with her he'd never have made it.

VIDAL. You mean because he's completely held by his death-bed vow to his wife?

MRS. BEEVER. Completely held.

VIDAL. There's no likelihood of his breaking it?

MRS. BEEVER. Not the slightest.

VIDAL. (*Who, with a change of posture on this, as if it strongly affects him, exhales a low long breath of relief.*) You're very positive; but I've a great respect for your judgment. (*Then abruptly.*) Why did he wish her invited?

MRS. BEEVER. For reasons that, as he expressed them to me, struck me as natural enough. For the sake of old acquaintance—for the sake of his wife's memory.

VIDAL. He doesn't consider then that Mrs. Bream's obsession as you term it, had been in any degree an apprehension of Rose?

MRS. BEEVER. (*Clear for herself about it.*) Why *should* he? Rose, for poor Julia, was on the point—*all* on the point—of becoming your wife.

VIDAL. (*Harking back to it; ruefully.*) Ah, for all *that* was to prevent!

MRS. BEEVER. It was to prevent little enough, but Julia never knew how little. (*Then for as his full edification.*) Tony asked me a month ago if I thought he might without awkwardness propose to Miss Armiger a visit to the other house. I said "No, silly boy!" and he dropped the question; but a week later he came back to it. He confided to me that he was ashamed for so long to have done so little for her; and she had behaved in a difficult situation with such discretion and delicacy that to have "shunted," her as he said, so completely, was a kind of outrage to Julia's affection for her and a slur upon hers for his wife. I said to him that if it would help him a bit I'd address her a suggestion that she should honour *me* with her company. He jumped at that, and I wrote. *She* jumped, and here she is.

VIDAL. (*With a spring to his feet at this, as if* ROSE *is actually in sight.* MRS. BEEVER *has a laugh at him and a nod of negation for it; but he remains erect before her.*) This then is their first meeting?

MRS. BEEVER. Dear no—they've met in London. He often goes up.

VIDAL. How often?

MRS. BEEVER. Oh irregularly. Sometimes twice a month.

VIDAL. And he sees her every time?

MRS. BEEVER. (*Considering.*) "Every" time? I should think—hardly.

VIDAL. Then every other?

MRS. BEEVER. (*Not engaging for more than she's sure of.*) I haven't the least idea.

VIDAL. (*Looking round the garden.*) You say you're convinced that, in the face of his promise, he has no particular interest in her. You mean, however, of course, but to the extent of Marriage.

MRS. BEEVER. I mean to the extent of anything at all. He's in love with another person.

VIDAL. (*Promptly, on a first impulse, deprecating the confidence.*) Ah that's none of my business! (*Yet he closes his eyes an instant, pressing his right hand finger-tips upon them, as with the cool balm of it.*) But it makes a lot of difference.

MRS. BEEVER. (*As always easily touched by him, and while, now, on her feet, she lays a kind hand on his arm.*) Such a lot, I hope, then, that you'll join our little party! (*Then while he looks about him again, irresolute; to enlighten him and explain the nature of her queer parcels.*) Preparations for a birthday visit from the little girl at the other house. She's coming over to receive them.

VIDAL. (*Who at this, interested, impressed, drops again into a seat even though she stands there before him.*) At last, we've got to business. It's *she* I've come to ask about.

MRS. BEEVER. And what do you wish to ask?

VIDAL. How she goes on. I mean in health.

MRS. BEEVER. (*More amused than anything else at his question; yet bethinking herself.*) Not very well, I believe, just *today!* She's reported to have a slight cold. But don't be alarmed. In general she's splendid.

VIDAL. (*As to get the full measure and have only the truth of it.*) Then you call it a *good* little life?

MRS. BEEVER. (*Emphatic.*) I call it a dear little one!

VIDAL. (*To be absolutely right.*) You feel she won't pop off?

MRS. BEEVER. I can't guarantee that. But till she does—well, it's a comfort to see her. You'll do that for yourself.

VIDAL. I shall do that for myself. (*Then still settled in his basketchair.*) To be quite shameless—it was to do it I came.

MRS. BEEVER. (*Ironic; arch.*) And not to see *me?* Thank you! (*Then a bit indifferently.*) But I quite understand. You looked to me to introduce you. (*As to reward him.*) Well, make yourself at home and I will.

VIDAL. My shortest cut to that then seems to be to ask (*on his feet again*) if Miss Armiger is in love with Mr. Bream.

MRS. BEEVER. That's the one thing I can't tell you! You must find out for yourself.

VIDAL. (*Wondering hard; his eyes on her.*) How shall I find out?

MRS. BEEVER. (*Impatient.*) By watching!

VIDAL. Oh, I didn't come to do *that!*

(*With which, turning away, on his side, visibly dissatisfied, he checks himself at sight of* PAUL BEEVER.)

(*Enter* PAUL BEEVER, *a fair, robust, smooth-faced slightly corpulent and superficially heavy, but quite serene and bland young man in boating flannels, from the river; in whose presence, quickly deciding on a course,* VIDAL *simply addresses himself again to* MRS. BEEVER.)

VIDAL. May I think over what you've said to me and come back?

MRS. BEEVER. (*Taking account a little of her son's advent, though not to the point of introducing either party.*) I shall be very happy to see you again. (*Then at a momentary loss as to how to dispose of him.*) But, in this poor place, what will you do?

VIDAL. (*Taking in the river; then, as reassured and invited, appealing frankly to the young man.*) Will you lend me your boat?

MRS. BEEVER. (*Promptly but cheerfully interposing.*) It's my boat! (*Then as putting it so to* PAUL *by way of substitute for other forms and inviting him to assent.*) This gentleman—who has been with me on business—is perfectly welcome to it.

VIDAL. (*Closing at once with the chance; liking the idea of getting off on the stream.*) Then I'll take a good pull. (*Raises his hat to the two. Exit* DENNIS VIDAL *to the river.*)

PAUL. (*Quite conveniently accepting it; only wondering and a little uncertain, for civility.*) Hadn't I better show him—?

MRS. BEEVER. (*Prompt, authoritative; putting it out of the question and pointing to one of the basketchairs.*) You had better sit right down there! (*After which when he has compiled with the air of inveterate docility; making her transition prompt and sharp, and ignoring everything else.*) Pray, when in the world—with all your delays!—are you going to *give* it?

PAUL. (*Placid and imperturbable; having helped himself at once, instinctively and without looking, to a large bun from the tea-table; which he proceeds very deliberately to consume.*) When do you think I had better?

MRS. BEEVER. (*Sharper, throughout, in*

proportion as he's substantial and slow.)
Before dinner—distinctly. One doesn't
know what may happen.

PAUL. (*Quite unexcited.*) Do you think
anything at all *will*?

MRS. BEEVER. Nothing, certainly, unless
you take some trouble for it! You don't
seem to grasp that I've done for you all I
can do—and that the rest now depends
on yourself!

PAUL. (*Quite obligingly and reasonably.*)
Oh yes, Mother—I grasp it. (*Then after
another placid bite of his bun.*) Miss
Armiger has quite made me do that.

MRS. BEEVER. (*Interrupted in the preparation of his tea; pulled up, staring.*) Miss
Armiger? What in the world has *she* to do
with the matter?

PAUL. Why, I've talked to her a lot
about it. She takes just your view. I mean
the view that I've a great opening and
that I must make a great effort.

MRS. BEEVER. And don't you see that for
yourself? Do you require a pair of women
to tell you?

PAUL. (*Grave and impartial; masticat-
ing his bun while he stirs his tea.*) No,
not exactly. But Miss Armiger puts everything so well. She seems to make clear to
me what I feel.

MRS. BEEVER. (*Laughing out at this, in
her impatience.*) I'm delighted to hear you
feel anything. You haven't often *seemed*
to me to feel!

PAUL. (*Unperturbed.*) I quite feel that
Jean's charming.

MRS. BEEVER. Is that the tone in which
you think of telling her so?

PAUL. I think she'll take it from me in
any tone. (*Matter of fact; wholly unimagi-
native and uninflamed.*) She has always
been most kind to me. She asked me to
give her six months for a definite Answer—
and she likes me the more for having consented to do that. The time we have waited
has improved our relations.

MRS. BEEVER. (*Sarcastic.*) Well then they
must now have reached perfection! (*With
absolute maternal authority.*) You'll get
her definite answer therefore this very afternoon.

PAUL. (*As if always taking her orders.*)
When I present the Ornament?

MRS. BEEVER. When you present the Ornament. (*Then as she looks at his loose
array.*) You've got it safe, I hope?

PAUL. (*Having at this his first slight embarrassment; taking another bun.*) I imagine it's all right.

MRS. BEEVER. Do you only "imagine"—
with a thing of that value? What on earth
have you done with it?

PAUL. I've given it to Miss Armiger. She
was afraid I'd lose it.

MRS. BEEVER. And you weren't afraid *she*
would?

PAUL. Not a bit. She's to give it back to
me on this spot. She wants me too much
to succeed.

MRS. BEEVER. And how much do you
want *her*?

PAUL. (*Vague, blank.*) In what?

MRS. BEEVER. In making a fool of you!
(*Then as for the extreme importance of
it.*) Are you in love with Rose Armiger,
Paul?

PAUL. (*Conscientious; judicious.*) Not in
the least. I talk with her of nobody and of
nothing but Jean.

MRS. BEEVER. And do you talk with Jean
of nobody and nothing but Rose?

PAUL. (*As if really making an effort to
remember.*) I think I scarcely talk with her
at *all*. We're such old friends that there has
been for long almost nothing to say. But
do you doubt her recognising in a satisfac-
tory way that the time has come?

MRS. BEEVER. (*Looking hard an instant
into her teapot, then closing the lid with
a clap.*) No!

PAUL. Then what's the matter?

MRS. BEEVER. The matter is that if you
cherish—with no matter how bad a conscience—the vain dream that you've the
smallest real chance of making the smallest
real impression on anybody *Else*; all I say
is that you prepare for yourself very nearly
as much discomfort as you prepare disgust
for your mother. (*Then after a further instant, while his mild gape only irritates
her.*) How much freedom of fancy, I
should like to know, has Miss Armiger at
her command for your charms?

PAUL. (*As he sees* ROSE *arrive from the
House.*) Well, Mother if you'd like to know
it hadn't you better ask her? (*Enter* ROSE

ARMIGER, *from the house; bare-headed, in a fresh white dress, under a bright coloured parasol.* PAUL, *who has left his seat as she approaches and strolled to the hammock, into which he immediately drops; explaining his movement to his mother.*) She has come to give me up the Ornament.

ROSE. (*Who has not heard this; to* MRS. BEEVER, *all gaily and easily.*) The great Cake has at last arrived, dear Lady!

MRS. BEEVER. I'm much obliged to you for having gone to see about it.

ROSE. (*Bright and serene.*) It was an irresistible service. I shouldn't have got over, on such a day as this, the least little disappointment to dear little Jean.

MRS. BEEVER. (*Prompt and frank to match.*) To say nothing of course of anything so dreadful to dear little Effie!

ROSE. (*All responsive.*) It comes to the same thing—the occasion so mixes them up. (*With a gesture of her free hand, evoking the charming sight.*) They're interlaced on the Cake with their initials and their candles. There are plenty of candles for each—for their years have been added together. It makes a very pretty number!

MRS. BEEVER. (*Judicious and practical; not laughing.*) It must also make a very big Cake!

ROSE. Colossal!

MRS. BEEVER. (*With an eye to her already overcharged tea-table.*) Too big to be brought out?

ROSE. (*After consideration.*) Not so big, you know, as if the candles—added up!—had to be yours and mine! (*Then at once holding up to* PAUL, *as for perfect frankness and publicity, the "ornament," the object she has up to this time carried in her free hand, a small case in red morocco containing a pendant for a necklace.*) I surrender you my trust. (*With gay familiar decision, tossing it to him in his hammock.*) Catch! (*After which* PAUL *having happily caught and* MRS. BEEVER *noted the free relation, there is a moment of mute interchange between the two women, who look at each other hard while* ROSE *continues to smile; to smile as if in friendly loyal knowledge of what* PAUL's *mother really wants. It visibly determines her; so that, to express this assurance, she comes*

straight to her hostess and significantly kisses her. Then she gives her word.*) I'll polish him off!

MRS. BEEVER. (*Appearing to take it as it's meant; reassured and as to account for her departure to* PAUL.) Well—Mahomet must go to the mountain! (*Exit* MRS. BEEVER *to the house.*)

PAUL. (*Leaving the hammock; candid and simple as soon as she is gone.*) I was afraid dear Mamma would take me away!

ROSE. On the contrary, she has formally handed you over to me!

PAUL. (*With his plain but honest courtesy.*) Then you must let me perform her office and help you to some tea.

ROSE. (*Under the rich shade of her parasol; contentedly twirling it while she considers the table.*) I'll do it for myself, thank you—and I should like you to return to your hammock.

PAUL. (*Smiling at her.*) I left it on purpose—because, flat on my back that way, I'm at a sort of disadvantage in talking with you.

ROSE. (*Complete mistress, always, of her own idea or scheme.*) That's precisely why I make the request. (*Bright and peremptory, pointing again to the hammock.*) I wish you to be flat on your back and to have nothing whatever to reply. (*Then as to explain conveniently her own design— he having made the motion to offer her a chair, against which her gesture protests.*) I'll meanwhile walk about and do exactly as I like—and stand over you and bully you. (*He tumbles back then into his net, and she speaks from near enough to him to put out her hand.*) Let me see that treasure again. (*While he takes it from the pocket to which, before leaving the hammock, he has consigned it, she lowers her parasol, and then, with it under her arm, having received the box from him, opens the latter and stands a moment considering critically the mounted jewel that nestles in the white velvet. After which, closing the case with a loud snap, she restores it to him.*) Yes—it's very good. It's a wonderful stone, and Jean (*smiling*)—pampered little thing!—knows. But that alone, my dear, won't do it. (*She leans, facing him and the spectator, against the tense ropes of the hammock, while he, turned to her, looks up at her.*) You take too much for granted.

PAUL. That's just what I said to Mother you had already said when she said just the same.

ROSE. (*Staring at first; then smiling again.*) It's highly complicated—but I follow you! She has been waking you up.

PAUL. (*Sturdy and easy.*) She knows you advise me in the same sense as herself.

ROSE. She *believes* it at last—her having left us here together is a sign of that. I've at heart perfectly to justify her confidence —for hitherto she has been so blind to her own interest as to suppose that, in these three weeks, you had been so tiresome as to fall in love with me.

PAUL. I particularly told her I haven't at all.

ROSE. (*Moved to mirth by the way he says it.*) I hope you'll be more convincing than that if you ever particularly tell anyone you have "at all"! (*With which she gives a slight push to the hammock and lets it swing there gently while she turns away.*)

PAUL. (*Watching her while she goes to the table to pour out her tea.*) You mustn't ask too much of me, you know!

ROSE. (*Who, after drinking a little, puts down her cup and comes back.*) I should be asking too much of you only if you were asking too much of *her*. You're so far from that—and your position's so perfect. (*Almost wistfully.*) It's too beautiful, you know, what you offer.

PAUL. Well, if I'm good enough for Jean she has only to take me.

ROSE. You're good enough for the best girl in the world: so honest and kind, so sound and safe, that it makes any relation with you a real luxury and a thing to be grateful for. I shall always be glad and proud that you've been, if only for an hour, my friend!

PAUL. (*Who, under the action of this, turning out of the hammock, gets slowly and heavily to his feet, and then sitting in it, while he holds on to both sides, looks at her straight and long, before speaking; which he does with an effect of abruptness.*) Do you think I like what you do

to me?

ROSE. (*As if it's a sudden new note for her; but finding her quite ready.*) I don't care whether you like it or not! I only care that you should now make your appeal handsomely. Show her some tenderness, some eloquence; try some touch of that sort that goes home! Speak to her, for God's sake, the words that women *need.*[2] We all crave them, and we all feel them, and you can do nothing good without them. Keep well in sight that what you must absolutely do is to *please* her.

PAUL. (*As with docility.*) Please her and please *you.*

ROSE. It sounds odd—yes—lumping us together! But that doesn't matter—for the effect of your success *will* be that you'll unspeakably help and comfort me. (*Then after an instant.*) It's difficult to talk about —my grounds are so deep deep down. (*She hesitates, casting about her, asking herself how far she may go, and then deciding, as a little pale with the effort.*) I've an idea that has become a passion with me. There's a Right I must see done— there's a Wrong I must make impossible. There's a loyalty I must cherish—there's a memory I must protect. That's all I can say! (*But she stands there in her vivid meaning like the priestess of a threatened altar; she puts the thing finally at its clearest for him.*) If that girl becomes your wife —why then at last I'm at rest.

PAUL. You get—by my achievement!— what you want. I see. And please what do *I* get?

ROSE. You? Why, you get Jean Martle! (*Having looked at her a moment longer he turns away without a word, while, at the same instant, turning with him, she sees* JEAN *appear on the steps of the house. He comes round left, which is the side of the hammock, the side opposite the house, and as he, in his heavy troubled movement, faces up again, she meets him, reaches him; he again stopping short for her.*) If you give me the peace I pray for I'll do anything for you in life. (*After which she turns afresh, with a new recogni-*

---

[2] James changed this from "the words that women *like.* We like them, and we all feel them. . . ."

tion, to meet TONY, *who arrives from the other house.*)

(*Enter* JEAN MARTLE, *and enter simultaneously* TONY BREAM, *coming up from the short way across the river, the private bridge that abuts at its other end of his own place.*)

JEAN. (*While* TONY, *arriving, and still up, greets* ROSE, *who meets him; stopping short, disconcerted and anxious, at the bottom of the great square stone steps of* MRS. BEEVER'S *doorway.*) Isn't Effie well enough to come?

TONY. (*Cheerful, easy, no longer now in mourning: coming down between* JEAN, *right, and* ROSE, *left; while* PAUL *is further left.*) I've left the question, my dear Jean, in her Nurse's hands! She had been bedizened from top to toe, and then—on some slight appearance of being, by the mystic nursery measure, *less* fit—had been despoiled, denuded and disappointed. She's a poor little lamb of sacrifice. They were at her again, when I came away, with the ribbons and garlands, but there was apparently much more to come, and I couldn't answer for it that a single sneeze wouldn't again lay everything low! (*With a cheerful sigh.*) It's in the lap of the gods. I couldn't wait.

ROSE. (*Sympathetically suggestive.*) You were too impatient to be with dear delightful Us!

TONY. (*Responsive; straightening himself, with a successful air of very light comedy, for a gallant bow of recognition.*) I was too impatient to be with *you*, Miss Armiger!

JEAN. (*Always bright; with perfect serenity and gaiety.*) I'm glad that remark's not addressed to *me*—for I'm afraid I must at once withdraw from you the light of my society.

TONY. (*Conveniently resigned, yet perfectly pleasant.*) On whom then do you mean to bestow it?

JEAN. On your Daughter—this moment. I must go and judge for myself of her state.

TONY. (*A little more seriously: immediately alive to all propriety.*) Why, my dear child—if you're at all really troubled about her I'll go back with you. (*Then*

not insisting on this, but duly, but thoroughly appreciative.*) You're too beautifully kind—they told me of your having been with her this morning.

ROSE. (*With a slightly betrayed surprise, but above all as with a friendly interest; to* JEAN.) Ah, you were with her this morning?

JEAN. (*Standing there in her black dress and her fairy beauty and rather wondering at the question; yet with her wonder not of a sort to overcloud the extraordinary radiance of her youth.*) For ever so long. Don't you know I've made her my peculiar and exclusive charge?

TONY. (*Alertly and harmoniously—also as quite for the joke of it—completing* JEAN'S *sense and exclaiming to* ROSE.) Under the pretext of saving her from perdition! I'm supposed to be in danger of spoiling her—but Jean treats her quite *as* spoiled: which (*with mock gravity*) is much the greater injury of the two!

ROSE. (*Entering into the pleasantry.*) Don't go back, all the same—in spite of Jean's criminal weakness. (*Then in another tone; with frank, soft public persuasion.*) I really never see you, you know—and (*as with candid decision*) I want just now particularly to speak to you. (*After which, as* TONY, *with a genial gesture at once expresses submission, she, with a motion of her own, arrests* JEAN *who, at* TONY'S *assent to her own proposal, has turned off to take her way to the other house by the bridge. But while she thus checks* JEAN *she addresses* PAUL; *full as she is of the effect of what has just passed between them.*) Didn't you—on your side —just tell me of your wanting so awfully to get hold of Jean?

PAUL. (*Red, feeling the awkwardness, for him, of this pressure so publicly put upon him; but sturdily enough making the best of it and addressing the words to* JEAN.) Oh yes—I should rather like to speak to you, please.

JEAN. (*Who has paused half way up; candidly and kindly.*) Do you mean at once?

PAUL. (*As after a glance at* ROSE.) As soon as you've time.

JEAN. (*All accommodation.*) I shall have

time as soon as I've been to Effie. I want to bring her over. There are four dolls waiting for her.

ROSE. (*In familiar amused intervention.*) My dear child, over there (*with a motion of her head at the other house*) there are forty! (*Then in the same spirit to* TONY.) Don't you give her one every day or two?

TONY. (*Not heeding; too much, though all cheerfully, interested in* PAUL'*s arrangement with* JEAN, *to whom his attention is attached.*) Go then—to be the sooner restored to us! And do bring our little friend.

PAUL. (*As settling then with* JEAN.) I go in to change—but perhaps I shall presently find you here.

JEAN. (*Quite content.*) You'll find me, dear Paul—I shall be quick.

(*Exit* JEAN *rapidly by the way to the bridge; exit* PAUL *to the house.*)

ROSE. (*Who has meanwhile reached the tea-table, to* TONY.) Mayn't I give you some tea?

TONY. Decidedly, thanks.

ROSE. (*Ready with his cup; but full at him then, across the tea-table, with an effect of abruptness.*) Why have you ceased to call me "Rose"?

TONY. Have I, my dear woman? I didn't know—!

ROSE. When I was at Bounds four years ago you called me Rose and you called our friend there (*with a nod of her head in the direction* JEAN *had taken*) nothing at all. Now you call her by name—and call *me* nothing at all.

TONY. (*Still where he had stopped; turning it obligingly over.*) Don't I call you Miss Armiger?

ROSE. Is that anything at all? (*Then as to develop her criticism.*) You're conscious of some great Difference?

TONY. Between you and Jean?

ROSE. Oh, the difference between me and Jean goes without saying! What I mean is the difference my having been at Wilverley then and my being here now.

TONY. (*As if really quite at a loss about it.*) What have I called you when we've met in London?

ROSE. (*Behind her tea-table for him a little after the manner of a handsome barmaid behind her bar; with a slight pert-*

ness, as if even conscious of that.) Don't you even *know?* You've called me nothing. (*Just indulgently peremptory.*) Here's your cup—do sit down there with it. (*Then when, having taken it, he has sunk with it into one of the chairs.*) Have you by any chance been conscious of what I call *you?*

TONY. (*In his chair, with his tea—as well as with a sort of matter of course ruefulness.*) Doesn't everyone in the wide world call me the inevitable "Tony"? The name's dreadful—for a banker: it should have been a bar to me for that career! It's fatal to dignity. But then of course I haven't any dignity.

ROSE. (*Behind her bar; enjoying their talk.*) I think you haven't *much!* But, on the other hand, I've never seen anyone get on so well without it. And, after all, you *have* just enough to make Miss Martle recognise it.

TONY. (*With his constant candid wonder; then catching on.*) By calling me "Mr. Bream"? Oh, for her I'm a grey-beard, and I still address her as I addressed her when a child. (*Then as with a reflection, an intention, vaguely pacific.*) Of course I admit she has entirely ceased to be *that.*

ROSE. (*Behind her table, pushing toward him a muffin dish from which she has lifted the cover; also speaking ambiguously.*) She's wonderful!

TONY. (*As he submissively helps himself.*) She's a charming Creature.

ROSE. (*As to explain the sense of her praise.*) I mean she's wonderful about your little girl.

TONY. Devoted, isn't she? That dates from long ago. She has a special sentiment for her.

ROSE. (*Looking down at her tea-things after a small wait; very gravely.*) It's a little life to cherish—to preserve and protect! (*With a thoughtful sigh; a sort of exhalation of retrospect.*) Of course!

TONY. Why, to that degree that she seems scarcely to think the Child's safe even with its infatuated Daddy! (*With which, just impatiently, he puts down his cup.*)

ROSE. (*Across her table after an instant, with her eyes on him as under the effect of his words.*) Anything more?

TONY. (*Getting up.*) Nothing more. (*After which there ensues, as with a sort of conscious inevitability, a short effect of silence; a pause occupied by his a little nervously shifting his place; so as to be at the opposite side of the stage while* ROSE *comes round and down again from the table. He lights a cigarette; she watches him do it, while he reverts, as if something reminds him again, to their question of a moment before; looking at her frankly now through his light fumes after he has begun to smoke.*) I'll gladly call you, my dear Rose, any blest thing you *like!*—only you mustn't think, you know, that I've been capricious or disloyal. I addressed you of *old*—at the *last*—in the way in which it seemed most natural to address so close a friend of my wife's. But I somehow think of you here now rather as a friend of my own.

ROSE. (*Who has brought away her parasol from where she had previously rested it against the table and, having put it up, now twirls it again on her shoulder.*) And that makes me so much more distant?

TONY. (*Laughing; slightly confused for his rather extemporised plea.*) I seem to have uttered a *bêtise*—but I haven't! I only mean that a different title belongs somehow to a different character.

ROSE. (*Perfectly ready to reason it out amicably.*) I don't admit my character to be different—save perhaps in the sense of its having become a little intensified. (*As if it's all clear and high and fine to her.*) If I was here before as Julia's friend, I'm here still as Julia's friend now.

TONY. (*Amicably prepared to subscribe to any view of the matter she desires; highly cordial even though slightly illogical.*) Of course you are—from your own point of view. (*Only wanting to meet her as far on the way to a quiet honourable life as they can manage; and expressing this all tenderly for his wife's memory, though perhaps a little pointlessly for anything else.*) Dear little Julia!

ROSE. (*Loud and clear; addressing it three or four shades more directly to the memory of the unforgotten dead.*) Dear little Julia!

TONY. (*Irrelevantly and just a bit awkwardly.*) You don't *mind* my smoking? (*Then as she with a gesture signs that it's the last thing she's thinking of he moves across to the hammock with a recovery of ease.*) I'm not going to allow you to pretend you doubt of my having dreamed, these years, of the pleasure of seeing you here again—any more than of the diabolical ingenuity I exercised to enable your visit to take place in the way most convenient to both of us. You used to say the Queen-Mother disliked you. You see today how much.

ROSE. (*As if she sees everything perfectly.*) She has ended by finding me useful. That brings me exactly to what I told you just now I wanted to say to you. I mean about the interest I take in Paul Beever. I take the very greatest.

TONY. (*As struck by it; quite eager.*) Ah, if you only *would*, you know, my dear Rose!

ROSE. (*Pulled up a little by the very intensity of his response.*) Are you gracefully suggesting that I shall myself carry him off?

TONY. (*Conscious of a mistake and of his too great precipitation, but all ready at once to rectify and treating it as for their amusement.*) Not from *me*, my dear —never! I think a lot of him—and want, at the Bank, to keep my hand on him.

ROSE. You think he's safe then, and solid, and not so stupid as he strikes one at first?

TONY. "Stupid"? Not a bit! He's a statue in the block—a sort of slumbering giant. The right sort of tact will call him to life— the right sort of hand will work him out of the stone.

ROSE. And it escaped you just now—in a moment of unusual expansion—that the right sort are *my* sort? What do you think then of the difference of our ages?

TONY. Yours and Paul's? (*Smiling.*) Why, it isn't particularly worth speaking of!

ROSE. That's sweet of you—considering that he's only twenty-two. However I'm not yet thirty; and of course (*ironic, playing it on him*) to gain time one might press the thing hard. (*Then keeping it up; still more sarcastic.*) It's awfully vulgar, this way, to put the dots on the i's;, but as it was you, and not I, who began it, I may ask you if you really believe that if one should make a bit of an effort—?

TONY. (*While she invitingly pauses as to leave him to complete a question with which she's naturally too delicate to go on—showing that by this time he's rather watching for a trap—even though not particularly caring if the trap does catch him, and in consequence of this last sticking to the attitude of pleasantry.*) If you take, as you say, such an interest in him, you can calculate better than I the natural results of drawing him out. But what I can assure you is (*a shade more gravely*) that nothing would give me greater pleasure than to see you so happily "established," as they say—so honourably married, so affectionately surrounded, and so thoroughly protected.

ROSE. (*As for the charming wonder of it.*) And all alongside of you here?

TONY. (*Bravely, gallantly.*) It's precisely your being "alongside" of one that would enable one to see you.

ROSE. (*As if indulgently amused.*) It would enable one to see *you*—it would have that particular merit! But have you been supposing the great old question of Jean's making a match with Paul to be dropped?

TONY. I simply haven't heard much about it! The Queen-Mother used to talk about it! But she hasn't, I think—has she? —talked of late.

ROSE. She talked, my good man—and very hard indeed!—no more than half an hour ago.

TONY. (*Perceptibly wincing, but as with pleasant curiosity.*) Really? And what did she say to you?

ROSE. She said nothing to *me*—but she said everything to her son. She said to him, I mean, that she'll never forgive him if she doesn't hear from him in an hour or two hence that he has at last availed himself, with Miss Martle, of this auspicious day —as well as of the fact that he's giving her, in honour of it, something remarkably beautiful.

TONY. (*After a moment.*) What is he giving her?

ROSE. Shouldn't you suppose she'd show it you?

TONY. I dare say she will if she accepts it.

ROSE. And *won't* she accept it?

TONY. Only—I should say—if she accepts *him*.

ROSE. And won't she do that?

TONY. The thing will be for him to get her to.

ROSE. That's exactly what I want *you* to do.

TONY. Me? How *can* I?

ROSE. I won't undertake to tell you how —I leave that to your ingenuity. You think highly of Paul—

TONY. (*Seizing her sense; taking her up.*) And I think highly of Jean, and therefore I must see them through? I catch your masterly meaning. But have you—in a matter composed, after all, of ticklish elements—thought of the danger of one's meddling?

ROSE. A great deal. But I've thought still more of one's possible prudence—one's occasional tact. Have you really been supposing they've given it up?

TONY. (*Gaining time.*) Given up what?

ROSE. That Mrs. Beever and Paul have given up what we're talking about—the idea of his marrying Jean.

TONY. I haven't been supposing anything at all! (*Turning away, he goes up to within sight of the river.*) Here she is—on the bridge.

ROSE. (*Who is not in view of the river.*) Has she brought the Child?

TONY. I don't make out—with all the shrubbery. (*Then coming down.*) She may have her by the hand. Your idea is really that I should speak to her now?

ROSE. Before she sees Paul? I leave that to *you*—since you cast a doubt on the safety of your doing so. I leave it to your judgment—I leave it to your honour.

TONY. (*As wondering what this has to do with it.*) To my "honour"?

ROSE. My idea is only that, whether you speak to her or not, she will accept him. (*With intensity.*) She *must*, you know!

TONY. You take an immense interest in it!

ROSE. Take the same then yourself, and the thing will come off.

TONY. (*After meeting her eyes hard a moment.*) Then I'll speak. (*He goes up again a few steps, partly as if to meet* JEAN; *then as before she emerges into sight is down again.*) If she brings Effie will you *take* her?

ROSE. I'm afraid I can't do *that.*

TONY. Good God—how you stand off from the poor little thing!

ROSE. (*As* JEAN *reappears, but without the* CHILD; *turning away.*) I shall never take her from *her!*

(*Re-enter* JEAN MARTLE *by the way from the bridge.*)

JEAN. Would *you,* Miss Armiger, after a little, very kindly go over for Effie? She wasn't even *yet* ready—and I was afraid to wait after promising Paul to meet him.

TONY. He's not here, you see; it's he who most ungallantly makes *you* wait. (*Then all gaily and cheeringly.*) Never mind; you'll wait with *me.* (*Then frankly and pointedly, though still cheerily to* ROSE; *speaking across* JEAN *at centre.*) Will you go and bring the Child, as our friend here asks?—or is such an act as that also, and still more, inconsistent with your mysterious principles?

ROSE. (*With perfect good grace, to* JEAN.) You must kindly excuse me. I've a letter to write—now or never. I must catch the post.

TONY. (*Contentedly accepting it then, on this show of a good reason.*) Don't let us keep you then. I'll go over myself—as soon as Paul comes back.

ROSE. I'll send him straight out. (*Exit* ROSE *to the house.*)

TONY. (*Down opposite; having followed with his eyes this retreat of* ROSE's *in such good order.*) It's, upon my soul, as if she couldn't trust herself—! (*But with his remark going off, unfinished, into a snap of his fingers.*)

JEAN. (*Who has caught his exclamation.*) Trust herself for *what?*

TONY. (*After an instant; smiling at her.*) For nothing! The Child's all right?

JEAN. Perfectly right. It's only that the great Gorham has decreed that she's to have her usual little supper before she comes, and that, with her ribbons and frills all covered by an enormous bib, Effie has just settled down to that extremely solemn function.

TONY. Why shouldn't she have her supper here?

JEAN. Ah, you must ask the great Gorham!

TONY. (*Always with his cigarette.*) And didn't *you* ask her?

JEAN. I did better—I divined her. She doesn't trust our kitchen!

TONY. Does she apprehend poison?

JEAN. She apprehends what she calls "sugar and spice."

TONY. "And all that's nice"? (*Making the best of it.*) Well, there's too much that's nice here, certainly! (*Pleasantly benign.*) Leave the poor mite then, like the little Princess you all make of her, to her Cook and "Taster," to the full rigour of her royalty, and keep me company till Paul comes out. (*Looking at his watch and about at the broad garden where the shadows of the trees are quiet and the long afternoon has grown rich.*) This is remarkably peaceful—and there's plenty of time.

JEAN. (*Feeling the scene all as he does; under the charm of it and of* TONY *himself, and dropping into one of the basket-chairs, as if quite gratefully passive while she smiles her response.*) Plenty—plenty!

TONY. (*Before her as she sits; but having come to it as by a slight effort.*) Do you know what Paul wants of you?

JEAN. I *think* I do. And do *you?*

TONY. Yes—I've just heard.

JEAN. From Miss Armiger?

TONY. From Miss Armiger. She appears to have had it from Paul himself.

JEAN. Why has he told her?

TONY. Because she's such a good person to tell things to!

JEAN. Is it her at once telling them again that makes her so?

TONY. Well, if she hadn't spoken, you know, I shouldn't have known. And—of course!—I'm interested in knowing.

JEAN. But why is *she* interested in your doing so?

TONY. Well—she had several reasons. One of them is that she greatly likes Paul —and that, greatly liking him, she wishes the highest happiness conceivable for him. It occurred to her that as I, on my side, greatly like a certain young lady I might perhaps desire for that young lady a corresponding chance; and that, with a hint that she's really about to have it, I might by the same token see my way to put in a word for the dear boy in advance.

JEAN. How does she know whom you "greatly like"?

TONY. Why, I suppose I must have told her.

JEAN. And how many persons will *she* have told?

TONY. I don't care how many—and don't think *you* need! Everyone but she—from lots of observation—knows we're good friends, you and I; and it's because that's such a pleasant old story with us all that I felt I might frankly say to you what I have on my mind.

JEAN. About what Paul may have to say?

TONY. The first moment you let him.

JEAN. (*As he is about to go on again.*) How long have you had it on your mind? (*Then further at once; as if he strikes her as at a momentary loss—a bit embarrassed by her challenge.*) As it's only since Miss Armiger has *told* you, that you've known there's anything in the air.

TONY. (*Just visibly pulled up by it; but then meeting it with a laugh and a counter-appeal.*) You make me feel dreadfully dense —but do you mind my asking how long you yourself have known that what may be in the air is on the point of alighting?

JEAN. Why, since Paul spoke to me.

TONY. Just now—before you crossed the river? (*Then so that they may both be very clear.*) You were sure on the spot that that's what he wants?

JEAN. What else can he want? He doesn't want so much that there would have been many alternatives.

TONY. (*A little amusedly demurring.*) I don't know what you call "much"! (*But again before her and as wondering at her charming but rather inscrutable calm.*) And it produces no more effect on you—?

JEAN. Than I'm showing you now? (*With a fine sharp shrug for it.*) Do you think me dreadfully stolid?

TONY. No—because I know that in general what you "show" isn't at all the full measure of what you feel. (*In charmed appreciation.*) You're a great little mystery. (*He laughs for it; then blandly goes on.*)

Still, you strike me as calm—as quite sublime—for a young lady whose fate's to be solemnly sealed! Unless indeed you've regarded it as sealed from far away back.

JEAN. (*Always in her chair; with no answer for this but a short silence while she looks fixedly down. She raises her eyes again at the end of it as if consciously ignoring what he has said; she reverts simply and abruptly.*) You haven't answered my question—haven't told me how long you've had it on your mind that you must say to me whatever it is you wish to say.

TONY. Why is it important I should answer it? The question of Time doesn't signify—what signifies is one's sincerity. I want, without more delay, at any rate, to be definite to you about the really immense opinion I have of our friend. He's a young man of gold.

JEAN. (*Echoing it, in her sustained demureness, with punctual acceptance, yet as if it matters more for* TONY *than for herself that the description should be true.*) He's a young man of gold. (*Then after an instant; with quiet lucidity.*) It would be odd I should talk with you on a subject so personal hadn't I felt his attitude for so long past to have been treated as common property. He has felt that too, I think, poor boy; and, for good or for ill, there has been in our situation very little mystery and perhaps not much modesty.

TONY. Why *should* there be—of the false kind; when even the true has nothing to do with the matter? You and Paul are great people; he's the heir-apparent and you're the most eligible princess in the Almanac de Gotha. (*In vivid and humorous zeal.*) You can't be there and be hiding behind a window-curtain; you must step out on the balcony to be seen of the populace. Your most private affairs are affairs of State. (*Infinitely plausible now, and himself sincerely enjoying his plausibility.*) At the smallest hint like the one I just mentioned even an old dunderhead like me catches on—he sees the strong reasons for Paul's attitude. And he wants to make sure of your own.

JEAN. (*Very simply and as after final consideration.*) Then I think I ought to tell you I shall *not* do what you're so good as to represent everything as pointing to. I shall never marry him.

TONY. (*Frowning for the first time; quite as with a look of pain.*) In spite of knowing that you'll disappoint—(*after another instant*) the universal hope?

JEAN. (*As having taken the measure of everything.*) I know whom I shall disappoint. I shall disappoint the Queen-Mother.

TONY. Horribly.

JEAN. Horribly.

TONY. And poor Paul—to within an inch of his life.

JEAN. No, not poor Paul, Mr. Bream. Not poor Paul in the least. I know about poor Paul. It's all right about poor Paul. I should have liked it, if it *could* have been —the impossible. But it *never* could.

TONY. (*With a smile as strained as almost to look, in him, almost pitiful.*) Well, we've spoken of the disappointment to others, but I suppose there's no use in my attempting to say anything of the disappointment to *me*. *That's* not the thing that, in such a case, can have much effect on you.

JEAN. Do I understand you to put it to me that you really desire my marriage?

TONY. (*Facing her with an effort; bringing it out.*) I ask it of you—I ask it of you!

JEAN. (*While they thus front each other like a pair who, walking on a frozen lake, suddenly have in their ears the great crack of the ice.*) And what are your reasons?

TONY. I'll tell you my reasons when you tell me yours for having changed!

JEAN. I *haven't* changed.

TONY. (*Looking at her an instant longer, sounding her as if deeper and deeper; then abruptly turning away and speaking as beyond contradiction.*) You've changed —you've changed!

JEAN. (*Following him with her eyes an instant; then, on her side, turning away, so that as they are thus disjoined and distanced the silence of a minute seems to reign between them, terminated by a motion with which* JEAN *seems to give up, and with which she at last abruptly speaks.*) Wouldn't you much rather I should never come back?

TONY. (*Turning to her then; then as if frankly and confessedly.*) Ah rather! (*After*

which, however; with another tone.*) But you *will* come back?

JEAN. (*Taking it from him; reading, with her eyes on his own, and all intelligently, a meaning into it.*) So you think I had better come back—quite *different*?

TONY. (*His tenderness for her breaking into a smile.*) As different as possible. (*Then as they both see* PAUL *reappear.*) So take him—*take* him!

(*Exit* TONY BREAM *to the river. Re-enter* PAUL BEEVER *from the house.*)

PAUL. I've driven him away!

JEAN. It was quite time! Effie, who wasn't quite ready for me, must really come at last.

PAUL. (*Who has changed his dress and who drops his eyes on the small case which he carries and which contains the Ornament, while his hands turn it round and round in apparent and slightly awkward uncertainty as to whether he had better present it to her opened or shut.*) I hope you won't be as indifferent as Effie seems to the pretty trifle with which I've thought I should like to commemorate your birthday. It will give me great pleasure if you'll kindly accept this little Ornament.

JEAN. (*Unable not to take it from him —which she does mechanically too; and seeming helplessly to study it a moment while she speaks with a sort of despairing deprecation.*) Oh Paul, oh Paul!

PAUL. I thought you might care for the stone.

JEAN. (*Gaining time.*) It's a rare and perfect one—it's magnificent.

PAUL. Well, Miss Armiger *told* me you'd know.

JEAN. Did *she* kindly select it?

PAUL. No—Mother and I did. We went up to London for it; we had the mounting designed and worked out. (*Plainly simply and artlessly.*) They took two months. But I showed it to Miss Armiger and she said you'd spot any defect.

JEAN. (*Fairly amused at him over it.*) Do you mean that if you hadn't had her word for it you'd have tried me with something inferior?

PAUL. (*Grave.*) You understand what I mean.

JEAN. Yes, Paul—I understand what you mean. If Miss Armiger knows I'm a judge, it's because, as I think, she knows everything in the world—except a single rather important one, which I know better than she. I know *you*. I can't take your present. It's impossible.

PAUL. (*Not at all upset; with the jewel passively again in his big red fist.*) Not for your birthday?

JEAN. (*Shaking her head good-humouredly, though not gaily.*) It's too splendid for that—it's too precious. And how can I take it for that when it isn't for that you offer it? (*Putting the whole thing to him with quiet kind assurance.*) How can I take so much, Paul, when I give you so little? It represents so much more than itself—a thousand more things than I've any right to let you think I can accept. I can't pretend not to know—I must meet you half way. I want to do that so' much; to keep our relation happy—happy always, without a break or a cloud. (*Beautifully and infinitely confident and persuasive; almost gay now.*) It *will* be —be beautiful. We've only to be frank. (*As if charmed for her success, since he doesn't protest.*) We *are*—already: I feel it in the kind way you listen to me. If you hadn't asked to speak to me I should have asked it myself. Six months ago I promised I'd tell you—and I've known the time was here.

PAUL. Yes—it's the "time"; but don't "tell" me till you've given me a chance. I want so to please you—to make you take a favourable view. You know everything—you understand; but just let me repeat all that I am, all I have, all I can ever be or do—!

JEAN. (*Breaking in, but ever so kindly.*) Paul, Paul—you're beautiful! You're such a *gentleman*!

PAUL. That's the sort of fine thing I wanted to say to *you*!

JEAN. (*Smiling back at him.*) You've said far more to me than *that* comes to! I want you—oh I want you to be successful and happy! (*Her laugh for which, however, changing first to an ambiguous sob, develops then into a sudden burst of nervous tears.*)

PAUL. (*Watching her an instant as if, even though she quickly recovers herself, she has brought the tears into his own eyes.*) Oh, that's of no consequence! I'm to understand that you'll never, never—?

JEAN. Never, never. But it doesn't alter the fact that you risked your life, that you've been magnificent. And now—to make it perfect!—never let me see, or hear of, that expensive object again.

PAUL. (*Tossing the Ornament in its closed case, into the air and catching it again.*) They'll be tremendously down on us.

JEAN. On me of course. But why on you?

PAUL. (*Slipping the case into his pocket.*) For not having moved you.

JEAN. You've moved me immensely. We're better friends than ever. And we're happy!

PAUL. (*Looking at her as with deep wistfulness, with patient envy.*) You are!

JEAN. (*Seeing* TONY *reappear, but still without the* CHILD, *and at once thinking only of that and speaking to him, as he arrives disappointedly.*) Ah, you haven't brought her?

(*Re-enter* TONY *from the bridge, and at the same time re-enter* MRS. BEEVER *from the house; between whom and himself,* PAUL, *as if to evade the question from her of whether he has done what she desired promptly and visibly places the greatest distance.*)

TONY. (*Immediately answering* JEAN.) She'll *arrive*—but Gorham wouldn't let her walk. So they're coming round in the old pony-cart by the Town Bridge and at a snail's pace.

MRS. BEEVER. Well, even the old pony-cart wont hold the great Cake—which is blazing away there in the dining-room, where for want of transportation, it must remain.

JEAN. (*Eager, to* TONY.) May I go there then to receive her?

TONY. (*Very good-humoured.*) Yes, if you'll remember the reduced scale on which she's to partake.

JEAN. (*Laughing at him as she goes.*)

Oh, I'll eat her share! (*Exit* JEAN *to the house*.)

MRS. BEEVER. (*To* PAUL, *as if struck with his attitude of detachment.*) You don't go with her?

PAUL. (*After an instant during which his course hasn't been plain to him.*) I am going in.

MRS. BEEVER. (*As to keep him to it.*) To cut the Cake?

PAUL. (*Embarrassed, rueful, and with his little morocco case again nervously extracted.*) To speak to Miss Armiger.

MRS. BEEVER. (*Recognising the object in his hand; with high irony.*) To ask her to keep *that* again?

PAUL. (*With a flare of spirit.*) She may keep it for ever! (*Exit* PAUL *to the house, giving a toss-up to his little case as he goes, and catching it on the drop, while the two others watch him.*)

MRS. BEEVER. Heaven help us all—she has *refused* him!

TONY. Pray how do you know?

MRS. BEEVER. By his having his present to her left on his hands—a jewel a girl would jump at! (*Deeply disconcerted.*) I came back to hear it was *settled*—!

TONY. But you haven't heard it's *not*!

MRS. BEEVER. (*Confident: disgusted.*) That it's "not" sticks out of them! (*As if it stares them in the face.*) If she won't accept the gift, how can she accept the giver?

TONY. (*Blank for a moment; confounded; almost ridiculous in his vagueness.*) Why, she just promised me she *would*!

MRS. BEEVER. (*Struck; still further surprised.*) Promised *you*—?

TONY. (*Just hesitating.*) I mean she left me to infer that I had quite decided her. She was so good as to listen most appreciatively to what I had to say.

MRS. BEEVER. (*With high severity, all her disapproval of his meddling.*) And in the name of goodness what *had* you to say?

TONY. (*Embarrassed, disconcerted by her rigour.*) Well—(*rather rueful*) everything! I took the liberty of urging Paul's claim.

MRS. BEEVER. (*Staring; measuring this*

presumption.*) Very good of you! What did you think you had to do with it? [3]

TONY. (*With a sharper ring.*) Why, whatever my great desire she should accept him gave me.

MRS. BEEVER. (*Ironic, suspicious.*) From when does it date, your "great desire"?

TONY. (*As quite able to give an account of it.*) From the moment I really understand how much Paul had to hope.

MRS. BEEVER. (*Sarcastic, derisive.*) How "much"? (*With spirit.*) It wasn't so much that you need have been at pains to make it less!

TONY. (*After an instant, resentful.*) You accuse me of bad faith?

MRS. BEEVER. (*Prompt.*) Not even in my sore disappointment. But I accuse you of bad policy. You should have carefully let her alone.

TONY. (*Protesting, repudiating.*) Then haven't I common freedom—?

MRS. BEEVER. Not the least little mite!

TONY. But why I alone—?

MRS. BEEVER. (*Bringing it out with full emphasis.*) Because you alone are madly in love with her!

TONY. And your proof of that is my plea for your Son?

MRS. BEEVER. Your plea was not for my Son—your plea was for your own Danger!

TONY. (*Expressively shocked.*) My own "danger"? Need I inform you at this time of day that I've such a thing as a Conscience?

MRS. BEEVER. Far from it, my dear man! Exactly what I complain of is that you've too much of one. Your Conscience is as big as your Passion—and if both had been of a size less you might perhaps have held your tongue!

TONY. I felt a wish to testify to my great sympathy with Paul from the moment I heard—what I hadn't at all been clear about!—that this was the occasion when he was, in more senses than one, to present his case.

MRS. BEEVER. May I go so far as to ask

---

[3] The passage from this point to Mrs. Beever's speech below ". . . you alone are madly in love" was not in the earlier drafts of the play but was inserted at a later stage.

if your sudden revelation proceeded from Paul himself?

TONY. (*Thinking it over an instant.*) No—not from Paul himself.

MRS. BEEVER. And scarcely—I presume! —from Jean?

TONY. Not in the dimmest degree from Jean.

MRS. BEEVER. (*After an instant; all with her high, dry irony; not looking at him.*) Thank you. You've told me. (*Then before he can retort, can challenge her inference, whatever it is, she speaks as for something of the least importance.*) I've something to tell you myself—though it may not interest you so much. (*Then while her manner holds him wondering.*) Dennis Vidal is here.

TONY. (*With the most natural of starts and stares; casting about him.*) In the house?

MRS. BEEVER. On the river paddling about! (*After which, as his blankness grows.*) He turned up an hour ago.

TONY. (*Wondering.*) And no one may see him?

MRS. BEEVER. Ramage has seen him— and Paul. (*Then to explain.*) But Paul didn't know—with all my affairs he sees my people come and go, and he took Mr. Vidal for a vague man of business. The poor gentleman vanished when he heard that Miss Armiger's here.

TONY. (*Going from surprise to mystification.*) Not to come back?

MRS. BEEVER. On the contrary, I hope— as he took my boat!

TONY. (*Not yet catching on.*) But he wishes not to see her?

MRS. BEEVER. He's thinking it over.

TONY. (*Still at sea.*) What then did he come for?

MRS. BEEVER. (*Confirming it to herself; after a wait of meaning.*) He came to see Effie.

TONY. (*Blank.*) "Effie"?

MRS. BEEVER. (*Not faltering.*) To judge if you're likely to lose her.

TONY. How the devil does that concern him?

MRS. BEEVER. Hadn't I better leave you to think it out?

TONY. (*Already, with his bewildered face, more or less doing so.*) Then he still *wants* that girl?

MRS. BEEVER. Very much indeed! That's why he's afraid—!

TONY. That Effie may die?

MRS. BEEVER. (*With a shrug, embarrassed, yet facing it.*) It's a hideous thing to be talking about; but you've perhaps not forgotten who were present—

TONY. (*Immediate.*) I've not forgotten who were present! I'm greatly honoured by Mr. Vidal's solicitude; but I beg you to tell him from me that I think I can take care of my Child.

MRS. BEEVER. (*With particular point.*) You must take care of her more than ever! (*Then as* ROSE *appears on the steps of the house; earnest, sharp and for* TONY *alone.*) But don't mention him to *her*— much business as she clearly has with you!

(*Re-enter* ROSE ARMIGER *from the house; to whom as she comes down,* MRS. BEEVER *makes over the entertainment of* TONY.)

MRS. BEEVER. (*To* ROSE.) I leave you our friend!

ROSE. (*Smiling with her best grace.*) That's as I leave *you* your Son. I've just been with him—in the drawing-room. (*Then as to report further with complete exactitude for the discharge of her conscience.*) Miss Martle's in the dining-room.

MRS. BEEVER. (*Taking in these relations.*) And Effie?

ROSE. (*Prompt and smiling.*) Effie—of course!—must be where Miss Martle is.

TONY. (*Who, during this passage has lounged away as restlessly and consciously as if, instead of beaming on the lady of Eastmead* ROSE *were watching the master of the other house; but then turns before* MRS. BEEVER *goes.*) I say, dear Lady, you know—be kind to her!

MRS. BEEVER. (*Vague.*) To Effie?

TONY. (*Frank, sincere; not minding* ROSE.) To poor Jean.

MRS. BEEVER. I don't know why you call her "poor"! She has declined a beautiful settlement—but she's not in misery yet! (*Then to* ROSE.) I'll take Paul first.

ROSE. (*With a manner that detains her; pricking the point of her parasol, which she has brought out again with her, and*

Elizabeth Robins
". . . uncanny, distinguished, individual . . ."

Henry James in the garden of Lamb House,
October 1909, at the time of the writing of
The Outcry. From a snapshot taken by his
nephew, Edward Holton James

her play with which has now a certain shyness, into the lawn.) If you like, when you take Miss Martle— (*She pauses with her eyes on* TONY.)

MRS. BEEVER. (*With a new encouragement in her voice.*) When I take Miss Martle—?

ROSE. (*Fixing* TONY *still with her visible strangeness.*) Why, I'll come back and take the Child.

MRS. BEEVER. (*Alert; showing that this disposition of* EFFIE *will for the moment suit her.*) I'll send her out to you. (*Then, with high significance, to* TONY; *in allusion to her imminent overhauling of* JEAN.) It won't indeed be a scene for that poor lamb! (*Exit with high decision* MRS. BEEVER *to the house.*)

TONY. (*Under the effect of her manner; rather ruefully to* ROSE.) Does she propose to tear Miss Martle limb from limb?

ROSE. (*Prompt; and as with the air, for herself, of being again in possession of him.*) Do you ask that partly because you're apprehensive that it's what I propose to do to *you?*

TONY. (*Easy; as not, to his perturbation, apprehensive on that.*) By no means, my dear Rose, after your just giving me so marked a sign of the pacific as your coming round—

ROSE. (*Taking him straight up.*) On the question of one's relation to that little image and echo of her adored Mother? (*Then after an instant; as full of a purpose of her own.*) That isn't peace, my dear Tony. You give me just the occasion to let you formally know it's War. (*After which, as he throws up his hands all vaguely and irresponsibly*) But not on *you.* I pity you too much.

TONY. (*In the dark.*) Then on whom?

ROSE. (*After an instant; with high emphasis.*) On any one, on every one, who may be likely to find that small Child— small as she is!—inconvenient. (*Then while he stands with his eyes on the ground.*) Oh I know you'll say I come late in the day for this—and you'll remind me of how very short a time ago it was that I declined a request of yours to occupy myself with her at all. Only half an hour has elapsed, but—(*with full clear-*

ness and decision*) what has happened in it has made all the difference. That's what I hurried out to let you definitely know— in case you should be off without our again meeting. I told you before I went in how I "trusted" you—I needn't recall to you for what. But Mr. Beever soon appeared and told me Miss Martle had refused him. Then I felt that, after what had passed between us, it was only fair to say to you—

TONY. (*Taking her straight up; wondering.*) That you've *ceased* to trust me?

ROSE. By no means. I don't give to take back. (*As generous and indulgent for his mistake; therefore, after this fashion, still patient and easy with him.*) As I believe you did, in honour, what you *could* for Mr. Beever—well (*after an instant*) I trust you perfectly still.

TONY. (*As having followed; but to bring her to the point.*) Then what's the matter?

ROSE. (*After a moment; then bringing it out.*) I don't trust Miss Martle.

TONY. (*With precipitate derision.*) Oh my dear woman—!

ROSE. (*Holding her course with deliberation and distinctness.*) That's what has made the difference—what has brought me, as you say, "round"; round to a sense of my possible use, or rather of my clear obligation. Half an hour ago I knew how much you love her. Now I know how much she loves *you.*

TONY. And what is it that, in possession of this admirable knowledge, you see—?

ROSE. (*Who falters while he waits for her satisfaction at this appeal; but who, clearly, has not advanced so far simply now to make a botch of it.*) Why, that it's the obvious interest of the person we speak of not to have too stupid a patience with any obstacle to her marrying you.

TONY. (*Who, as he takes the full point of this in, draws up sharp as under the indignity of the implication.*) Pray why is it the "person's" obvious interest any more than it's yours?

ROSE. (*Prompt; not afraid of what she has done.*) Seeing that I love you quite as much as she does? (*Then perfectly ready with her answer.*) Because you don't love me quite so much as you love *her.* (*Then while he takes it and she turns triumphantly off;* DENNIS VIDAL *appearing from the river before she sees him.*) That's exactly "why," dear Tony Bream!

With which moving toward the house, she meets MANNING, *the parlourmaid, who appears on the steps, with a tray, or some sign of having come for the removal of the tea-things; with whom, there, her back turned both to the approach from the river and to* TONY, *she remains for an instant as in talk;* MANNING *naming to her in a discreetly subdued tone, it would seem, her domestic errand, and* ROSE *putting in return some question about the others of the party.* TONY, *after staring some seconds at the back she*

has presented with her last words, has on his side turned to left, with a gesture of despair, and has dropped thus distressfully, as if defeated of his best intention, into the nearest seat; where, also not conscious, from his position, of VIDAL's *advent, he sits gazing before him. Enter* DENNIS VIDAL. VIDAL, *on reappearance, stands arrested at sight of them both; each unaware of him and separated, all visibly disconnected, as if something sharp has happened between them, by the width of the stage. He hesitates, uncertain, appearing to consult the omens of their apparent relation; and while he thus remains in observation the Curtain falls.*

ACT SECOND

The Effect here, at rise of Curtain, compatible only with a brevity of "entr'acte" —an interval of some five or six minutes at most. The stage is the same save that it has been cleared of the tea-table and most accessories; while one of the maids just waits at the steps for some last object that the other, on making a final disposition of something, brings over to her; after which exeunt together to the house. ROSE, TONY BREAM *and* VIDAL *have meanwhile the air of having gone through mere formal recognitions and of discreetly waiting a little, to say more, till the maids shall have got out of the way. By this time, on the cleared stage, their positions are altered;* ROSE *is down at left,* TONY *at centre,* VIDAL *down at right; but the sense of the lapse of very little time must be marked.*

ROSE. (*Across to* VIDAL *and as in reply to some speech of his own already made; speaking herself with controlled astonishment.*) I understand then that you've already been here?

VIDAL. (*With the increase of assurance his last hour by himself has brought him.*) An hour ago—but I asked Mrs. Beever not to tell you.

ROSE. She obeyed your request to the letter. But—now that I've stretched the long arm of welcome, haven't I? across the desert of four cold years—may I know why in the world such sinister secrecy?

TONY. (*Before* VIDAL *can reply; and as for the benefit of both; also as for gay concilation.*) I should mention that Mrs. Beever did tell *me*—as a great sign of confidence!

ROSE. Ah I'm not speaking of *her* secrecy—I'm speaking of Mr. Vidal's.

VIDAL. (*Grave.*) Well, I can explain perhaps better why I've emerged again than why—after a little talk with our hostess— I sought cover!

ROSE. (*Not contentious; easy.*) You've emerged, I suppose, because you feel you want after all to see me. For I take for granted—(*after an instant*) you knew I was here.

VIDAL. At Wilverley? I think I took *that* for granted.

TONY. (*With his desire to keep things straight.*) I'm afraid it was really for Miss Armiger you came.

VIDAL. I would still *say* so—before her— even if it weren't!

ROSE. (*As entering into the pleasantry.*) Fortunately it must be true. So it saves you a fib!

VIDAL. It saves me a fib!

TONY. You're at all events *staying* a bit, I hope—and people don't come to Wilverley to go to the inn. Even if you've done *that*, I count on your coming to me.

VIDAL. Ah, you're very kind—!

ROSE. (*Breaking in; as to be very natural; to* TONY.) Why should you take him away from us, and why should he consent to be taken? (*Then to* VIDAL, *agreeably, amicably.*) Won't Mrs. Beever—since you're not snatching the fearful joy of a clandestine visit to her—expect you, if you stay anywhere, to give *her* the preference?

TONY. (*Dissentient, but all good-humouredly.*) Allow me to remind you, and to remind Mr. Vidal that when he was here before he *did* "give her the preference." Mrs. Beever made no scruple of removing him bodily from under my roof. I forfeited—I was obliged to—the pleasure of a visit from him. But that leaves me with my loss to make up and my revenge to take. (*Smiling.*) I repay Mrs. Beever in kind! (*Insistent, as if the more he looks at it the more he feels it will make for comfort all round; and putting it thus particularly to* DENNIS *himself.*) Don't you recognise the propriety of what I propose? I take you, and then deal with Mrs. Beever, as she took you, of old, and dealt with *me*. (*Really quite vividly urgent for his plan.*) Besides, your things haven't even been brought here, have they?—as they then had been brought to Bounds. I promise to share you with these ladies—and in especial not to grudge you the time you may wish to spend with Miss Armiger.

VIDAL. (*To* ROSE.) I think I had better go to Mr. Bream. There's a matter on which I want to talk to *you*—but (*looking at* TONY) I don't see that *that* need prevent.

ROSE. It's for you to determine! There's something about which I find myself, to you also, particularly glad of the chance of speaking.

TONY. (*To* ROSE.) Your chance then is here. Say your word now. (*To* VIDAL.) I've a little job in town; I must attend to it quickly; and I can easily stop at the hotel

and order the removal of your traps. All you'll have to do then will be to take the Short Way, which you *know* (*indicating the quarter across the River*), over the bridge there and through my garden to my door. We shall dine at an easy eight.

VIDAL. (*Very simply.*) Thank you.

ROSE. (*As* TONY *is starting for the town, not through the House, but so that he has to pass near it.*) You'll stop then on your way and tell Mrs. Beever—?

TONY. (*In haste; taking her up.*) Of my having appropriated our friend? Not this moment—I've to meet a man on business and shall only just have time. I shall if possible come back here, but meanwhile perhaps you'll kindly explain. (*Then to* VIDAL.) Come straight over, don't wait for me to return to you. (*He offers him a frank handshake on this, and then, as to make it square, offers one laughingly to* ROSE; *who, accepting it, retains his hand a moment as if she has more to say. So they stand an instant while* VIDAL *turns off as if they may have matters between them, and* TONY *covers up any small awkwardness there may be in this contention by adding, candidly, as if just remembering.*) There's something else I've got to do— I've got to stop at the Doctor's.

ROSE. To consult him?

TONY. To ask him to come over.

ROSE. I hope you're not ill.

TONY. Never better in my life. I want him to see Effie.

ROSE. (*Wondering.*) But since she's making her visit here she's not bad, surely?

TONY. She's not *right*—with the fright Gorham had this morning. So I'm not satisfied.

ROSE. Let him then by all means see her.

TONY. (*Waving his hand to* VIDAL, *who, as on the conclusion of his last passage, has faced about again.*) À bientôt (*Then to* ROSE *again.*) Let me hear from you— and from *him*—that in my absence you've been all right for our friend here.

ROSE. (*A motion on whose part, with her manner, even now still detains him; so that he takes what she says while* VIDAL *comes down again.*) I don't mind letting you know, Mr. Bream, in advance, exactly how "right" I shall be. It would be affectation on my part to pretend ignorance of your knowing—a little!—what once passed between this gentleman and me. (*Then going on as from a resolve now suddenly and intensely, but all courageously and remarkably taken.*) He suffered, at my hands, in this place, four years ago, a disappointment—a disappointment into the rights and wrongs, into the good reasons of which I won't attempt to go further than just to say that an inevitable publicity then attached to it. People *saw*, Mr. Vidal, the blight that descended on our long relations, and people believed—and I was at the time indifferent to their believing!—that it had occurred by my act. I'm not indifferent *now*—that is to any appearance of having been wanting in consideration for such a man as you. (*With the last nobleness of candour and humility.*) I've often wished I might make you some reparation—some open atonement. I'm sorry for the distress that I'm afraid I caused you, and here, before the principal witness of the indignity you so magnanimously met, I very sincerely express my regret and very humbly beg your forgiveness. (DENNIS VIDAL *stares at her—has turned dead white as she keeps it up; while the elevation, as it were, of her abasement has fairly brought tears to* TONY's *eyes. The effect she produces on* him *she thus more especially measures. For all her gravity, she still not invisibly enjoys this effect; and, after a moment's pause, handsomely and pathetically completes it.*) That, Mr. Bream,—since you just hoped I'd be "all right"—is the extent to which I'm *capable* of being!

TONY. (*Turning at once to* VIDAL, *who stands with his eyes fixed on the ground; as if he now quite sees a happier relation for these two.*) I change then my appeal—I make it, with confidence, to *you*. Let me hear, Mr. Vidal, when we meet again, that you've *risen* to this charming occasion. (*Then while* VIDAL, *clearly and deeply moved, but self-conscious and stiff, gives no sign of having heard him, and* ROSE, *on her side, turns off as if she had said her all, he still stands at centre a moment as if comparing their attitudes, but deciding also that these make for reas-*

surance.) Oh, you're *both* all right! (*With which he goes rapidly off.*)

(*Exit* TONY *to town.*)

VIDAL. Why did you do that?

ROSE. Do you really care, after all this time, *what* I do—or don't do?

VIDAL. (*Thinking only of the scene just over; not heeding her question; only persisting in his own demand.*) What business is it of his that you may have done this or that to me? What has passed between us is still between us. Nobody else has anything to do with it.

ROSE. (*Smiling at him as to thank him for being again a trifle sharp with her.*) He wants me—didn't you hear him?—to be nice to you.

VIDAL. (*Again even after his four years puzzled by her.*) You mean he wants you to do *that* sort of thing? (*Then having come nearer; but at a fresh stand.*) Do you care so very much what he wants?

ROSE. (*On the bench on which she has sat with* PAUL BEEVER *a while before; then, with a pleased patient smile, tapping the empty place.*) Come and sit down beside me, and I'll tell you how much I care. (*Then when, slowly and almost as with the precaution of approaching a creature strange and dangerous, he has but partly complied, to the extent, that is, of a few steps more; in another tone, abruptly.*) When did you come back?

VIDAL. (*On his feet still.*) To England? The other day—I don't remember which of them! I think you ought to answer my question before asking more of your own.

ROSE. No, no; there's an enquiry it seems to me I've a right to make of you before I admit yours to make any at all. What are you really here for? Has it anything to do with *me*?

VIDAL. I didn't know you were here. I had no reason to.

ROSE. Then you simply desired the pleasure of renewing your acquaintance with Mrs. Beever?

VIDAL. I came to *ask* her about you.

ROSE. How beautiful of you! Fancy your caring! As I understand you then you've had your chance—you've *talked* with her?

VIDAL. A very short time. I put her a question or two.

ROSE. I won't ask you what they *were*. But ask *me* what you like. I'll tell you everything.

VIDAL. You might then begin by telling me what I've *already* asked.

ROSE. Oh, why I attached an importance to his hearing what I just now said? Yes, yes; you shall have it. Only first—are you at all *jealous* of him?

VIDAL. That's a thing for you to find out for yourself!

ROSE. I see—I see. It would be too wonderful. Yet otherwise, after all, why should you care?

VIDAL. (*Before her there; yet not looking at her while she leans back with her eyes on him and waiting as with the sincerity of her question.*) I don't mind telling you I asked Mrs. Beever if you were still in love with him.

ROSE. (*Jerked forward; clasping her hands so eagerly that she almost claps them.*) Then you *do* care?

VIDAL. (*Moving off, turned away from her.*) She didn't give you away.

ROSE. It was very good of her! But I would tell you myself, perfectly, you know, if I *were*—(*after an instant*) what you say.

VIDAL. In love with him? You didn't tell me perfectly four years ago!

ROSE. Oh, four years ago I was the biggest fool in England!

VIDAL. Then what I asked Mrs. Beever—

ROSE. (*Catching him up.*) Isn't true? (*With a melancholy ironic shrug.*) It's an exquisite position for a woman to be questioned as you *question* me, and to have to answer as I *answer* you. But it's your revenge and you've already seen that to your revenge I minister with a certain amount of resolution. I'm *not* in love with Anthony Bream.

VIDAL. And *he* no longer cares—?

ROSE. For me? (*As with the final clearness of the deep sad truth.*) He never cared.

VIDAL. (*Sounding her.*) Never?

ROSE. (*Absolute.*) Never.

VIDAL. Upon your honour?

ROSE. Upon my honour.

VIDAL. But you had an idea—?

ROSE. I had an idea.

VIDAL. And you've had to give it up?

ROSE. (*As so detached now that she's quite frank.*) I've had to give it up.

VIDAL. (*As with a vague relief for the easing of his wound.*) Well, *that* does something.

ROSE. For your revenge? Surely it does everything. (*Then as she sees* GORHAM.) Miss Effie has come?

(*Enter* GORHAM *from the house, stopping on the steps at* ROSE'S *question.*)

GORHAM. (*In hat and jacket.*) It's just to let you know, Miss, that she's *there*—amusing herself and so *good!*—while I go to the Housekeeper for my tea.

ROSE. (*Wondering a little.*) Miss Jean's not with her?

GORHAM. Miss Jean's in the drawing-room.

ROSE. And Mrs. Beever?

GORHAM. In the drawing-room *with* Miss Jean.

ROSE. Very good then. I'll have an eye—!

GORHAM. I think she had better not come out, Miss.

ROSE. Then she *sha'n't*. I shall be going in—and you may even, if you prefer, go home.

GORHAM. (*Pleased.*) Well, Miss, as we're having *our* treat too—!

ROSE. (*Prompt, decided.*) Ah, go home and don't miss it!

GORHAM. (*Alert.*) Thank you, Miss. (*With which she is back at house.*)

ROSE. (*As she goes.*) You go by the town?

GORHAM. Just to *tell* her, Miss—and to see about *our* Cake.

ROSE. Lord, what a feast! But all right! (*Exit* GORHAM *to the house.*)

VIDAL. (*Who has attended with interest.*) And may *I* have an eye on Effie?

ROSE. We *both* will. (*On which they go up together to the window of the Dining-room,* ROSE *cutting in as they reach it.*) Here's a charming man, Effie, who wants to make your acquaintance.

VIDAL. (*Admiringly, at the window, seeing the* CHILD *within at play.*) Dear little Girl—dear *sweet* little Girl!

ROSE. (*Coming away.*) Oh her heart's in that Sailor-Boy Doll—she won't *jilt* him for you.

VIDAL. (*To the* CHILD *within.*) Good-bye

then! (*As he rejoins* Rose.) Oh, she's *lovely* —I think she'll *do!*

Rose. (*A trifle vague.*) "Do"?

Vidal. As an object of interest. She makes me remember!

Rose. (*Frankly meeting his reference.*) That extraordinary scene at the other house—poor Julia's message? You can fancy whether *I* forget it!

Vidal. You've more to keep it in mind.

Rose. I can assure you I've plenty!

Vidal. And the young lady who was also present: isn't she the Miss Martle—?

Rose. Whom I spoke of to Gorham? She's the Miss Martle. What about her?

Vidal. Does she also remember?

Rose. (*Wondering.*) Like you and me? I haven't the least idea!

Vidal. She's just staying here again— like *you?*

Rose. (*With gaiety and irony.*) And like *you?* No—not "like" either of us. (*As if it means a good deal.*) She's *always* here.

Vidal. And it's from *her* you're to keep the *Child?*

Rose. It's from *her.*

Vidal. (*After going up and standing at the window again as with his eyes on* Effie, *while he comes down.*) Would you leave her a little to *me?*

Rose. (*Surprised.*) To watch over? (*Then amused.*) Surely—if you like! (*On which* Vidal *returns to the window where he stands again a little as in sight of the* Child, *his back presented, while* Rose, *down left, waits; a situation that she ends by bringing out abruptly.*) What I said to Mr. Bream just now I didn't say *for* Mr. Bream.

Vidal. (*Without turning round.*) You said it for Mr. Vidal? He liked it, all the same, *better* than Mr. Vidal.

Rose. Of course he liked it—though (*as to have done with that*) it doesn't matter *what* he likes! (*Then after an instant, while he continues, at the window, still apparently occupied with* Effie.) As for *you*—I don't know that you're "liking" it was what I wanted.

Vidal. (*Always with his back turned.*) What then did you want?

Rose. (*Still down left; not looking at him now; her back turned to himself.*) That you should see me utterly abased— and all the more utterly that it was in the cruel presence of another.

Vidal. (*Slowly facing about at this and coming down.*) Why should that give me pleasure?

Rose. Why in the world shouldn't it? What's your Revenge but Pleasure?

Vidal. (*His hands in his pockets; impatient.*) Oh *damn* pleasure!

Rose. (*As in eager relief.*) It's *nothing* to you? (*Then shining at him as with the glimpse of a new hope.*) Then if it isn't, perhaps you pity me! (*Following it up before he can reply.*) I think you would if you *understood!*

Vidal. (*Looking at her hard, hesitating, but at last relenting and speaking as with a tired patience.*) Well, Rose—I *don't* understand.

Rose. Then I must go through it *all*— I must empty the cup. I'm simply at your feet. I'm yours to do what you will with— to take away or to cast away. Perhaps you'll care a little for your triumph— when you see in it the grand opportunity I give you. It's *your* turn to refuse now— you can treat me just as you were treated!

(*A deep motionless silence follows this speech; which leaves them confronted over his "opportunity," as if it has rather widened than bridged the separation. Before* Dennis *finds his answer to it, the sharp tension snaps, on the appearance of* Jean *at the door of the house, in the latter's clear earnest question. Enter* Jean Martle *from the house.*)

Jean. Oh, Effie isn't here?

Vidal. (*For immediate greeting to* Jean.) Perhaps you remember me, we were here together—

Rose. (*Breaking in.*) Four years ago— perfectly. (*All grace to* Jean.) Mr. Vidal and I were just talking of you. He has come back—for the first time since then— to pay us a little visit.

Jean. (*Promptly and easily understanding; all grace to* Rose *in return.*) Then he has things to say to you that I've rudely interrupted. (*To* VIDAL.) Please excuse me —I'm off again. I only came for the little girl.

VIDAL. She's at play there in the dining-room.

JEAN. (*All civility to him.*) Oh—with Gorham?

VIDAL. Gorham has gone home.

JEAN. Then I'll join Effie.

ROSE. I must ask you rather to leave her to *me*.

JEAN. But you're busy with Mr. Vidal.

VIDAL. Oh, I go over to Bounds. (*Then to* JEAN, *to take leave of her.*) I'm staying at the other house.

JEAN. It's no reason I should drive you away. You've more to say to Miss Armiger than I have. I'm only looking after Effie.

VIDAL. (*With a dry laugh.*) But you're *being* looked after too!

ROSE. I've indeed more to say to Miss Martle than I've now to say to you. I think that what I've already said to you is quite enough.

VIDAL. (*Falling in: only wanting now to go, to get off by himself again.*) Thanks, thanks—quite enough. I'll just go over.

ROSE. You won't go first to Mrs. Beever?

VIDAL. Not yet—I'll come in this evening. (*With which, raising his hat, exit* VIDAL *rapidly to the river.*)

ROSE. (*As losing no time now; as tackling at once any embarrassment presented there by her situation, by her tension, with* JEAN.) You must let me have the pleasure of making you the first person to hear of a matter that closely concerns me. I'm engaged to be married to Mr. Vidal.

JEAN. (*Astonished, but alert and interested, quite eager.*) Engaged?

ROSE. (*As if amused at her natural note.*) He arrived half an hour ago—for a supreme appeal; and it hasn't, you see, taken long! (*Then as if this is fully official and authoritative.*) I've just had the honour of accepting him.

JEAN. (*Really pleased; sincere.*) That's very *charming!* I congratulate you.

ROSE. It's "charming" of you to be so glad. (*Smiling as in her happiness.*) However, you've the news in all its freshness.

JEAN. (*Fully beguiled.*) I appreciate that

too. (*Then as if she rather owes an apology.*) But fancy my dropping in on a conversation of such importance!

ROSE. (*Gracious; as if this doesn't the least matter.*) Fortunately you didn't cut it short! We had settled the question. He had got his answer.

JEAN. If I had known it I'd have congratulated Mr. Vidal.

ROSE. You'd have frightened him out of his wits! He's so deplorably shy.

JEAN. (*Always in her good faith.*) Yes— I could see he was shy enough! But the great thing (*with all her candour*) is that he wasn't too shy to have come back to you.

ROSE. (*Who continues to take it as with bright ease.*) Oh, I don't mean with *me!* He's as bold with me as I am—for instance—with *you!* You'll think that says everything. (*Then with all the form of familiarity and confidence.*) I can easily imagine how you judge my frankness. But of course I'm grossly immodest—I always was!

JEAN. (*Wholly beguiled.*) I think you're a person of great courage—if you'll let me also be frank. There's nothing in the world I admire so much—for I'm afraid I've scarcely myself the spirit of a mouse! I dare say, however, that I should let you know just as soon if I were engaged.

ROSE. (*Smiling.*) Which, unfortunately, is exactly what you're not! Do you object to my speaking of *that* to you?

JEAN. (*Rather taken aback, but, in spite of her recent plea of timidity, facing it bravely enough.*) I don't know how much you know.

ROSE. (*Not in the least sparing her.*) I know everything. Mr. Paul has already told me.

JEAN. (*As with a flush for this prompt confidence of his to another girl.*) Mr. Paul already doesn't care!

ROSE. (*With spirit.*) That's fortunate for *you*, my dear! Will you let me tell you how much *I* do?

JEAN. (*Hesitating, embarrassed; not eager for this, yet not speaking ungraciously.*) I don't quite see that it's a thing you should tell me—or that I'm really obliged to hear. It's very good of you to take an interest—

Rose. (*Breaking in as with increasing spirit.*) But however good it may be, it's none of my business: is that what you mean? (*Then before* Jean *can attenuate.*) Such an answer is doubtless natural enough! My having hoped you'd accept Paul Beever, and above all my having rather publicly expressed that hope, is an apparent stretch of discretion that you're perfectly free to take up. But you must allow me to say that the stretch is more apparent than real. There's discretion and discretion—and it's all a matter of motive. Perhaps you can guess mine for having found a reassurance in the idea of your definitely bestowing your hand. (*Masterful and easy, as with the final relief of her chance and her frankness.*) It's a very fair and very charming hand, but it's possible happy action is out of proportion even to those things. It wasn't a question of meddling in your affairs—your affairs were only one side of the matter. My interest was wholly in the effect of your marriage on the affair of Others. Let me say, moreover, that it strikes me you hardly treat me with fairness in forbidding me an allusion that has after all so much in common with the fact, in my own situation, as to which you've no scruple in showing me your exuberant joy. (*With which she goes smoothly and inexorably on, while* Jean, *listening intently, draws shorter breaths, and looks away, as in growing pain, from the wonderful white mobile mask that supplies half the meaning of her words.*) You clap your hands over *my* being—if you'll forgive the vulgarity of my calling things by their names!—got out of the way; yet I must suffer in silence to see you rather more *in* it than ever!

Jean. (*Fairly appalled at what seems thus unexpectedly to open up to her; but calling all her pride and her presence of mind to her aid.*) You call things, certainly, by names that are extraordinary; though I follow you far enough to be able to remind you that what I just said was provoked by your introducing the subject.

Rose. (*Pulled up an instant by this retort, yet with a power to be effectively cool in exact proportion as her adversary is*

troubled.*) I introduced the subject for two reasons. One of them was that your eager descent upon us at that particular moment seemed to present you in the light of an inquirer it would be really rude not to gratify. The other was just to see if you'd succeed in restraining your glee.

Jean. (*Taking in this wonderful plea; less bewildered and speaking straight.*) Then your story isn't true?

Rose. (*With an impatient, an insolent laugh.*) There you are again! Do you know your apprehensions and your impatience are barely *decent?* (*Then having again, with great concentration, bethought herself; speaking with a still finer plausibility.*) I haven't, however, laid a trap with a bait at all make-believe. It's perfectly true that Mr. Vidal has again pressed me hard—it's not true (*not minding here at all her appearance of grand prevarication*) that I've yet given him an answer completely final. But as I mean to at the earliest moment, you can say so to whomever you like!

Jean. (*Quite strong and direct now.*) I can surely leave the saying so to *you!* (*Then really in possession of her comparatively modest powers.*) But I shall be sorry to appear to have treated you with want of confidence that may give you a complaint to make on the score of my manners—as to which (*with her own head at last well up*) you set me too high an example by the rare perfection of your own! Suffer me simply to let you know then—to cover every possibility of that sort—that I intend under no circumstance ever, *ever* to marry. So far as that knowledge may satisfy you, you're welcome to the satisfaction. (*With all the decision of which she is capable.*) I have therefore no apology whatever to make for my interest in Effie, and I beg you to understand that—since Gorham has gone—I propose myself to see her home.

Rose. You take my accommodation for granted, I suppose, because you've worked so long to produce the impression, which no one, for your good fortune, has gainsaid, that she's safe only in your hands. But *I* gainsay it at last—for her safety becomes a very different thing from the moment you give such a glimpse of your open field as you must excuse my still continuing to hold that you do give. My "knowledge"—to use your term—that you'll never marry has exactly as much and as little weight as your word for it. I leave it to your conscience to estimate that wonderful amount. You say too much—both more than I ask you and more than I can oblige you by prescribing to myself to take seriously. You do thereby injustice to what must be always on the cards for you—the possible failure of the great impediment. (*Then cumulative and overwhelming, as it were, in her high lucidity.*) I'm disinterested in the matter—I shall marry, as I've had the honour to inform you, without having to think at all of impediments or failures. That's the difference between us, and it seems to me that it alters everything. (*After which, quite supremely.*) I had a Delicacy—but now I've nothing in the world but a Fear.

JEAN. God forbid I should understand you; I only make out that you say and mean horrible things and that you're doing your best to seek a quarrel with me from which you shall derive some advantage that, I'm happy to feel, is beyond my conception. (*With which, turning off as to cut the dreadful situation short, she goes rapidly up to the house; where, at the window of the dining-room she stands looking in at the* CHILD *as* VIDAL *has done. Then she comes down again.*) I beseech you to make no scene.

ROSE. I'll consent to your taking her on one condition—that you deny to me on the spot that you've but one feeling in your soul. Repudiate and utterly renounce it—a fair and square bargain!—and you may then do what you like!

JEAN. (*After an instant; grave and sombre now, her weakness of the previous instant gone.*) I know what feeling you mean—and I'm incapable of meeting your condition. I "deny," I "renounce," I "repudiate" as little as I hope, as I dream, or as I feel I'm likely ever again to utter—! (*Throwing up her arms as for a drop that may speak for her better than words; yet only to bring out, the next moment, in her baffled sadness, though with so little*

vulgarity of pride that she seems to pity herself even as she says it.*) It's because of *that* that I want her!

ROSE. (*As if understanding but too well.*) Because you adore him—and she's his?

JEAN. (*Faltering, but too utterly launched now; with the repetition of her tragic gesture.*) Because I adore him—and she's his.

ROSE. (*Taking it in, and as now but the more completely seeing and embracing her own strong line and deciding on her own action.*) I want her for another reason—I adored her poor Mother, and she's *hers!* That's *my* ground, that's *my* love, that's *my* faith! (*With which she moves rapidly to the house, speaking out as to the* CHILD *while she goes.*) It's as your dear dead Mother's, my own sweet, that—if it's time—I shall carry you to bed.

(*Exit* ROSE *to the house by the long window of the dining-room; after which* JEAN *is alone for a moment on the stage. She has sunk upon a seat opposite, defeated and in horror of a public struggle, and remains there for the time, sick and weary, her face buried, as for the shame of the whole contention, in her hands. Re-enter then from the long window,* ROSE ARMIGER, *bearing the little girl triumphantly in her arms and passing rapidly with her straight to the way to the river. Exit thus* ROSE, *with* JEAN *roused and rising as by the sense of her quick passage and going up to watch her flight, at which she stands a minute sadly looking off. While* JEAN *is in this position enter* PAUL BEEVER *from the house. He comes down and, after a moment, aware of her, stands and watches her; at which, feeling him there, she raises her head, she sits up. There is a long pause between them; as if they now understand each other and can feel for each other better than while the obstacle cleared away by their last talk was still between them. It is as if all awkwardness has gone; so that he can speak his natural thought and the simple truth.*)

PAUL. I knew Miss Armiger had come back here—and I thought I should find her.

JEAN. She was here a few minutes ago—she has just left me.

PAUL. But not to go in?

JEAN. To go to the other house.

PAUL. With Mr. Bream?

JEAN. No—with his little girl.

PAUL. She's taken *her* up?

JEAN. Up—up—up: away up in her arms! She brought her out and fled with her—to get her *away* from me.

PAUL. Why should she wish to do that?

JEAN. I think you had better ask her directly. As you say, she has "taken *her* up." She's *her* occupation—from this time.

PAUL. Why—suddenly—from "this time"?

JEAN. Because of what has happened.

PAUL. Between you and me?

JEAN. Yes—that's *one* of her reasons.

PAUL. "One of them"? She has so many?

JEAN. She tells me she has two.

PAUL. "Two"? She *speaks* of it?

JEAN. She speaks of it with perfect frankness.

PAUL. (*Turning it over an instant.*) Then what's her second reason?

JEAN. That if I'm not engaged—(*just hanging fire, but at last bringing it out*) at least she herself is.

PAUL. (*Quite at sea.*) "She herself"?—instead of you?

JEAN. To you? No, not to you, my dear Paul. To a gentleman I found with her here. To that Mr. Vidal.

PAUL. (*Blank, staring.*) You found that Mr. Vidal with her? Where then *is* he?

JEAN. He went over to Bounds.

PAUL. And she went with him?

JEAN. No—she went after.

PAUL. (*Lost in it.*) Where the dickens did he drop from?

JEAN. (*Who has for herself given it up.*) I haven't the least idea.

PAUL. (*With sudden light.*) Why, I saw him with Mamma! He was here when I came off the river—he borrowed my boat.

JEAN. (*Wondering then.*) But you didn't know it was he?

PAUL. I never dreamed—and Mamma never *told* me.

JEAN. (*After an instant; piecing it together.*) She was afraid. (*With all confidence.*) You see *I'm* not!

PAUL. (*Now more pitifully wondering.*) She's "engaged"?

JEAN. (*Not attenuating.*) So she informed me.

PAUL. (*Looking at her suddenly aghast and stricken; then turning his eyes away and standing there all wondering and rueful.*) It's awfully odd!

JEAN. (*Who has risen to her feet as she measures this effect of her words on him; so that she stands there a moment rather helplessly pitying.*) I've had to *hurt* you. (*Very gently.*) I'm very *sorry* for you.

PAUL. (*His face away from her; failing of a convulsive attempt at a smile.*) Oh I don't mind it!

JEAN. (*After an instant.*) These are things for you to hear of—straight.

PAUL. (*Understanding.*) From her? (*Then as without the courage for it.*) Ah, I don't *want* to do that! (*After which, as to explain to her how he'll make the best of it.*) You see—of course—I sha'n't say anything. (*But he shows he is much moved and affected.*)

JEAN. Do you love her?

PAUL. I never mentioned it!

JEAN. Because you hadn't had your talk with *me*? (*Then as he doesn't answer.*) Dear Paul, I must say it again—you're beautiful!

PAUL. (*All honestly.*) But she knows it, you know, all the same.

JEAN. (*Very sincerely.*) I'm sorry for you.

PAUL. Oh it's all right! May I light a cigarette?

JEAN. As many as you like. But I must leave you.

PAUL. (*Who has struck a match, but pauses at this.*) Because I'm smoking?

JEAN. Dear no! Because I must go over to see Effie. I always bid her "Good-night." I don't see why—on her birthday, of all evenings—I should omit it.

PAUL. (*Taking for granted anything that may suit her.*) Well then, bid her "Good-night" for me too. (*Then as with a sudden other thought.*) Tony Bream puts him up?

JEAN. Mr. Vidal? So it appears.

PAUL. And she has gone over to *see* him?

JEAN. That may be part of her errand.

PAUL. (*Thinking further.*) They can't have lost much *time!*

JEAN. Very little indeed!

PAUL. (*Arresting her by a gesture as she again moves to go; bringing out his question with a certain intensity.*) What has he, what has the matter you speak of, to do with her cutting in—?

JEAN. (*Prompt while he pauses as in the presence of things rather queerly obscure.*) To the interest others take in the Child? Ah, if you feel as you do, don't ask *me.* (*Then decidedly going.*) Ask *her!*

(*Exit* JEAN *rapidly now to the way to the river.* PAUL *goes up as she disappears, and standing there in thought, while he smokes, seems to follow her with his eyes as she takes her course, out of all other sight, down to the stream, through a shrubbery which marks the path to the bridge and then across the rest of the bridge to the opposite bank. He appears to wait for a renewed final sight of her, but turns away, with a drop of attention, as if it has a little puzzlingly failed him. After which, looking at his watch and coming vaguely down and across, he is aware of his mother at the opposite side of the stage: Enter* MRS. BEEVER *from the house.*)

MRS. BEEVER. (*Who has come out as to look for something, is pulled up at the complete clearance of the lawn made at the beginning of this act; with which, seeing* PAUL, *she appeals to him.*) They've taken everything away?

PAUL. (*Vague, as if he hasn't noticed it.*) Apparently!—but haven't you had your tea?

MRS. BEEVER. (*Who has glanced at an empty chair or two that has survived the clearance.*) It isn't my tea—it's those precious puppets; which mustn't knock about.

PAUL. Effie's dolls? They'll have been taken in.

MRS. BEEVER. I didn't *see* them there—so I wondered; but if they're all right what has become of everyone else?

PAUL. (*Smoking; mildly ironic.*) I think we're *all,* Mammy dear, "Effie's dolls"; but

after the talk on which I lately left you I should think you'd know pretty well what had become of *me.*

MRS. BEEVER. (*After taking him in attentively.*) What on earth's the matter with you?

PAUL. (*Philosophic, ruminant.*) I've had my head punched.

MRS. BEEVER. Nonsense—for all you mind me. (*But still not satisfied.*) Are you ill, Paul?

PAUL. (*Resignedly.*) I'm all right.

MRS. BEEVER. (*After an instant during which she has further taken him in; speaking as with sudden sharp tenderness.*) Then kiss your old Mammy. (*Solemnly, silently he obeys her; after which, as he turns away, she gives him a smart tap.*) You're worth them all!

PAUL. (*Awkward for any compliment almost to ungraciousness, and harking, in his awkwardness, back to her question.*) I don't know where Tony is.

MRS. BEEVER. (*Prompt, sharp.*) I can do *without* Tony—but where's Tony's Child?

PAUL. Miss Armiger has taken her home.

MRS. BEEVER. (*Struck; quite pleased.*) The clever thing! (*Then as to have the full warrant for this.*) She was here when you came out?

PAUL. No—but Jean told me.

MRS. BEEVER. (*To that extent interested.*) Jean was here?

PAUL. No—but she went over.

MRS. BEEVER. (*Surprised, almost incredulous.*) Over to Bounds—after what has happened? (*Then fairly stern.*) What in the name of goodness possesses her?

PAUL. The wish to bid Effie good-night.

MRS. BEEVER. I wish to heaven she'd leave Effie alone!

PAUL. (*As out of his indulgence now, his kindly feeling and the cessation of his false position to* JEAN.) Aren't there different ways of looking at that?

MRS. BEEVER. Plenty, no doubt—and only one decent one! (*Then as the grossness of the girl's error seems to loom larger to her.*) I'm quite *ashamed* of her!

PAUL. (*Quiet; taking it easy.*) Well, I'm not!

MRS. BEEVER. (*With her rueful comprehension of the present terms of their peace.*)

Oh *you*—of course you excuse her! (*Then as in her irritation she turns, she almost flounces about, she has another of her quick propri :tary perceptions and transitions; her movement having brought her within sight of the descent to the river.*) Why, bless me, there's the boat!

PAUL. (*Naturally aware of this.*) Mr. Vidal has brought it back.

MRS. BEEVER. (*Facing round in surprise.*) You've *seen* him?

PAUL. No—but Jean told me.

MRS. BEEVER. (*Only staring the more.*) *She* has seen him? Then where on earth *is* he?

PAUL. (*Placid; sturdy.*) He's staying at Bounds.

MRS. BEEVER. (*Quite wonderstruck.*) He has got there already?

PAUL. (*Smoking a little, then explaining.*) It's not very soon—for Mr. Vidal. He puts things through. (*Then bringing his fact out the more quietly in proportion to its magnitude.*) He's already engaged to her.

MRS. BEEVER. (*Mystified, at sea.*) Engaged to Jean?

PAUL. (*With supreme tranquility.*) Engaged to Miss Armiger.

MRS. BEEVER. (*With a reaction, almost a disappointment; a quick shrug and a toss of her head.*) What news is *that*? He was engaged to her five years ago!

PAUL. (*Who seems for a moment to consider, and to have sadly to accept, this hard historic fact; yet always speaking dryly.*) Well, then he is *still*. They've patched it up.

MRS. BEEVER. (*On her feet with a bound.*) She has *seen* him?

(*Re-enter TONY BREAM from the town, whom MRS. BEEVER sees and addresses, eagerly, before PAUL can reply.*)

MRS. BEEVER. She has *seen* him—they've patched it up!

TONY. (*Breathless with curiosity, yet making but a bite of her news.*) It's on again—it's all right?

MRS. BEEVER. It's whatever you like to call it! I only know what Paul tells me.

PAUL. I only know what I had just now from Jean.

TONY. Oh but I dare say it's so, old man. (*Then explaining to MRS. BEEVER.*) I was there when they met, and I saw for myself pretty well how it would go.

MRS. BEEVER. Ah, then you were, as usual, sharper than I! It must have gone with a jump!

TONY. With a jump, precisely—and the jump was Miss Armiger's own! She's a most extraordinary girl and the effort she made there, all unprepared for it, was magnificent in its way—one of the finest things I've ever seen. Upon my honour she's cleverer—she has more domestic resources, as I may say—than—I don't care who!

MRS. BEEVER. (*Impatiently, as for the superfluity of this information.*) Oh, we all know, I think, how many cards she keeps up her sleeve!

TONY. I thought I did myself—but, by Jove, they came out in a regular cataract. (*To PAUL.*) She *told* you—with her grand coolness?

MRS. BEEVER. (*While PAUL doesn't reply—consciously and purposely occupied with another cigarette.*) Didn't you hear him say it was *Jean* who told him?

TONY. (*With a slight momentary drop at this.*) Oh, Jean? (*Wondering a little at it.*) She told *Jean*? (*With his gaiety, however, at this image, quickly coming back.*) That was charming of her!

MRS. BEEVER. (*Whom it leaves cold.*) Why in the world was it charming?

TONY. Oh, because there hasn't been much that *is* so between them—and it was a pretty mark of confidence. They're in the house?

MRS. BEEVER. Not in mine—in yours.

TONY. (*Surprised.*) Rose and Vidal?

PAUL. Jean also went over—went after them.

TONY. (*Bewildered.*) "After them"— Jean? (*To be clear about it.*) How long ago?

PAUL. About a quarter of an hour.

TONY. (*Not making it out.*) Aren't you mistaken? They're not there now.

MRS. BEEVER. (*Surprised at his surprise.*) How do you know—if you've not been at home?

TONY. (*Prompt.*) I *have* been at home— I was there five minutes ago.

MRS. BEEVER. (*Not fitting it together.*) Then how did you get here?

TONY. By the long way! I took a fly. I went back to get a paper I had stupidly forgotten and that I needed for a fellow with whom I had to talk. Our talk was a bore for the want of it—so I drove over there and got it, and as he had his train to catch, I then overtook him at the station. I ran it close, but I saw him off; and here I am. (*Positive.*) There's no one at Bounds.

MRS. BEEVER. Then where's Effie?

TONY. Effie's not here?

PAUL. Miss Armiger took her home.

TONY. You saw them go?

PAUL. No—but Jean told me.

TONY. Then where's Miss Armiger? And where's Jean herself?

MRS. BEEVER. Where's *Effie* herself? That's the question!

TONY. (*Pulled up, looking at the various alternatives; then breaking into a laugh.*) No! The question's Where's Vidal? *He's* the fellow I want to catch. I asked him to stay with me, and he said he'd go over, and it was my finding ten minutes ago he *hadn't* come over that made me drive on here from the station to pick him up.

MRS. BEEVER. Mr. Vidal can take care of himself; but if Effie's not at home, where *is* she? (*Then more peremptory to* PAUL.) Are you sure of what Jean said to you?

PAUL. (*In obliging thought; but attached to the testimony of his senses.*) Perfectly, Mamma. She said Miss Armiger carried off the little girl.

TONY. (*As struck with this; taking it in, doing it justice and making a movement of impatience for his own stupidity.*) That's exactly what Rose told me she meant to do. Then they're simply in the garden. They simply hadn't—when I was there—come *in.*

MRS. BEEVER. They've been in gardens enough! I should like to know that the Child's "simply"—as you call it—in bed.

TONY. So should *I!*—but I none the less deprecate the time-honoured custom of a flurry, I may say indeed of a first-class panic, whenever she's for a moment out of sight. (*Then to* PAUL.) You, at any rate, dear boy, *saw* Jean go?

PAUL. Oh yes—I saw Jean go.

TONY. And you understood from her that Rose and Effie went with Vidal?

PAUL. I think Mr. Vidal went first.

TONY. Thanks so much, old chap. They're all a jolly party in the garden together. I'll go over.

MRS. BEEVER. (*Who has gone up to where she may look off to river and have sight of the bridge, and now speaks with relief.*) Here comes Rose—she'll tell us!

TONY. (*Content, echoing her relief and her words.*) Oh then—! (*But now as with something he has all the while wished to ask of* PAUL.) You wouldn't object—a—to dining—?

MRS. BEEVER. (*Who has come down again, and, catching this, cuts in with her usual quickness of apprehension.*) To meet Mr. Vidal? (*Then with a flare of her humour.*) Poor Paul—you're between two fires! (*After which to* TONY, *as the best solution; as if her proposal practically settles it.*) You and your guest had better dine *here.*

TONY. (*Seeing this in a light.*) Both "fires" at once? (*Then smiling at* PAUL.) Should you like that better?

PAUL. (*Who, as his mother comes down, has gone up and is lost in the act of watching for* ROSE *at the point where he may first see her, and where he shakes his head absently for his friend's question.*) I don't care a rap!

TONY. (*Who has watched him a moment at his distance and seems to read his attitude.*) Poor lad—*I'll* bring him round! (*Then full of the other matter and with an abrupt transition.*) Do you mind if I speak to her of it?

MRS. BEEVER. To Rose—of this news? (*Then after a hard look at him, as quickly disapproving.*) Tony Bream, I don't know what to *make* of you! (*She is apparently on the point of making something rather bad, but* ROSE *is now already in sight,* PAUL *falling away a little as she arrives and comes down.*)

(*Re-enter* ROSE *from the river, meeting* MRS. BEEVER'S *instant inquiry.*)

MRS. BEEVER. You took Effie home?

ROSE. (*As pulled up and a little out of breath; wondering.*) Not I! She isn't *here?*

MRS. BEEVER. She's gone. Where *is* she?

ROSE. (*With all assurance.*) I'm afraid *I* don't know! I gave her up. (*Then while* PAUL, *the furthest up of the four, has turned short away at her first negation, and* TONY, *quite still, but with his eyes on her is left of* MRS. BEEVER; *she looks in the finest astonishment from one of her friends to the other.*) You're *sure* she's not here?

MRS. BEEVER. How *can* she be—when Jean says you took her away?

ROSE. (*Still a little panting, but staring at this and throwing back her head.*) "Jean says"—? (*Then looking round her as for this source of misrepresentation.*) Where *is* Jean?

MRS. BEEVER. She's nowhere about—she's not in the house. (*On which she challenges alike the two men;* PAUL *having now very quietly, almost softly, come down to far right.*) Where *is* the tiresome girl?

TONY. (*Answering* ROSE *across* MRS. BEEVER; *but as if it's very simple.*) She has gone to Bounds. She's not in my garden?

ROSE. (*At a loss—her shoulders and eyebrows up.*) She wasn't five minutes ago—I've just come out of it!

MRS. BEEVER. (*As not satisfied; with all her directness.*) Then what took you there?

ROSE. (*Not faltering an instant; bringing it bravely and clearly out.*) Mr. Vidal. (*After which she completes this statement with a smile at* TONY.) *You* know what! (*Then again for* MRS. BEEVER, *looking her full in the face, and as if her own matter is now all she thinks of.*) I've seen him. I went over with him.

TONY. (*In his optimistic, harmonising way.*) Leaving Effie with Jean—precisely.

ROSE. (*Completing the picture in this sense; explaining to* MRS. BEEVER.) She came out—she begged so hard. (*Then as to excuse her indulgent, her possibly indiscreet weakness.*) So I gave in.

MRS. BEEVER. (*Who has turned at this, in stupefaction, to* PAUL; *appealing to him for light.*) And yet Jean says the contrary?

ROSE. (*Struck with this; turning incredulous to* PAUL.) She said to *you*—anything so false?

TONY. (*Mystified by it and nervous; yet determined not to be and carrying it off*

with a laugh.) My dear boy, you simply didn't *understand!* Give me a cigarette.

PAUL. (*Whose eyes have been attached, while he smokes still harder, to* ROSE's *face. He has turned very red, and, instead of answering her, has come round, behind the others, and now, while he makes them wait, has reached* TONY's *left and enabling him to help himself from his cigarette-case. This has caused* ROSE, *in her lively astonishment, to move more to right; so that on* PAUL's *at last speaking the three others are more or less together, with a wideish interval separating them from* ROSE. PAUL *then brings out his reply.*) That was what I remember she said—that you had gone with Effie to Bounds.

ROSE. (*Across her interval; near the green bench; wonderstruck.*) When she had taken her from me herself—?

MRS. BEEVER. (*While* TONY *involuntarily gapes, referring her to what* PAUL *has already told them.*) But she wasn't with Jean when he *saw* her!

ROSE. (*Appealing, from her distance, to* PAUL.) You saw Miss Martle alone?

PAUL. (*Profoundly uncomfortable.*) Oh yes—quite alone.

TONY. (*Leaving* PAUL, *walking nervously up, as if these irreconcilabilities are too painful to him and speaking from centre.*) My dear boy—you simply don't remember!

PAUL. (*Where* TONY *has left him, and while* MRS. BEEVER *has dropped into a chair;* ROSE *being still before the green bench.*) Yes, Tony. I remember.

ROSE. (*Very grave now—as if only stupefied.*) Then what on earth has she done with her?

TONY. (*At centre, as if their confusion is too absurd.*) What she "had done" with her is evident: she had taken her home!

ROSE. (*Looking at it, but as if it doesn't see them any further.*) But if the Child's not there—?

MRS. BEEVER. (*Equally impatient, to* TONY.) You just told us *yourself* she ain't!

TONY. (*Still at centre, still publicly declining to be nervous, hunches his shoulders as if there may be many explanations.*) Then she's somewhere else. She's wherever Jean took her.

MRS. BEEVER. But if Jean was here without her?

TONY. Then Jean, my dear lady, had by that time come back.

MRS. BEEVER. Come back to lie?

TONY. (*Impatient, yet as if almost amused at her extravagance.*) Dear Queen-Mother, Jean doesn't "lie"!

MRS. BEEVER. (*With the highest spirit; bringing it roundly out.*) Then somebody does!

ROSE. (*Discomposed, but finding a brave smile for it.*) It's not *you*, Mr. Paul—I know. (*Then all categorical again.*) Was it you who saw her go over?

PAUL. (*At left, separated by the whole width of the stage.*) Yes; she left me here.

ROSE. How long ago?

PAUL. (*Looking as if fifty people were watching him.*) Oh not long!

ROSE. (*As more than ever in the dark; addressing the three.*) Then why on earth haven't I met her? She must explain her astounding statement.

TONY. (*With the highest emphasis and confidence.*) You'll see she'll explain it easily.

ROSE. (*As with growing resentment and as if her own anxiety isn't to be trifled with.*) Ah, but meanwhile where's your Daughter, don't you know?

TONY. (*As if he'll do anything if she'll not be absurd.*) I'm just going over to see!

ROSE. (*With intensity, almost peremptory; then breaking too in a nervous laugh, as to admit to the others that she is absurd, while she still glares at them, as for criticism of his inaction, with a white uneasy face.*) Then please go!

TONY. (*As if, in the first place, unused to being hustled; and then as really having something else to say and another point to make; on which he smiling insists.*) I want first to express to you my real joy. Please believe in it.

ROSE. (*As arrested in her preoccupation; thinking; seeming to come back from a distance.*) Oh, you *know?* (*Then to PAUL, as to account for TONY's coming by the knowledge.*) She told you? (*Impatiently, before he can answer, as not to waste time over it.*) It's a detail—for *the* question (*as coming incorruptibly back to that*) is the

poor Child. (*With which, as for TONY's not moving, she appeals again to PAUL.*) Will you go and see?

TONY. (*With an encouraging waggle of the hand to PAUL.*) Yes—go, boy!

MRS. BEEVER. (*Who has been giving much of her attention to ROSE, but now adds her voice for this.*) Go this moment.

PAUL. (*Having taken it from them both, but staying his own deliberate way for his own idea, and presenting to ROSE his unhappy, inscrutable face.*) I want *also* to express—

ROSE. (*Taking him up both with amusement and with impatience for his manner.*) Your real joy, Mr. Paul!

PAUL. (*With a dignity of his own; proof against any irony, and only the more formal for it.*) Please believe in that too. (*Exit PAUL to the river.*)

ROSE. (*Turning at once, as he goes, excitedly to the others.*) I believe in everything—I believe in everyone! But I don't believe—! (*She hesitates, however, as with a second thought; she checks herself.*) No matter. (*Then to MRS. BEEVER, with a pleading rueful smile.*) Can you forgive me?

MRS. BEEVER. For giving up the Child? (*Then after looking at her hard; bringing it out sharp.*) No! (*With which she turns straight away and goes up, as in her own restlessness, her own suspense, to where she can look off toward the river and the bridge and time her son's errand. Here, during what next passes, she frankly waits. She has had, on her coming out of the house, a book in her hand: as if it has been part of her motive to sit down with it for half an hour in the garden; which volume, retained during this last scene, she now, while she leans against the parapet, or whatever, that marks the picture here, vaguely opens as if to keep herself quiet.*)

ROSE. (*Going on straight, for TONY, in attenuation of what she has just referred to with MRS. BEEVER, her surrender of the CHILD.*) It was Dennis's coming, it made the difference. It upset me.

TONY. "Upset" you? Why, you were splendid!

ROSE. (*The light of what has happened in her face as she considers him.*) You are!

(*Then with her eyes to the ground an instant—raising them.*) But Dennis is finer than either of us.

Tony. (*As if this puts him, himself, immensely in the right.*) I told you four years ago what he is. (*Then with another glow of his always handy optimism.*) He's all right!

Rose. (*Inscrutably.*) Yes—he's all right. And *I* am—now. (*After which, as with a noble dignity.*) You've been good to me. (*She puts out her hand.*) Good-bye.

Tony. (*Surprised at this precipitation.*) "Good-bye"? You're going?

Rose. (*As if it's perfectly settled and arranged.*) He takes me away.

Tony. (*Genial; as almost scandalised at such unfriendly suddenness.*) But not to-night?

Rose. (*As accepting the hard necessity; making the best of it.*) Tomorrow early. (*Then as not meaning it at all in joke.*) I may not *see* you.

Tony. (*Taking it only for an extravagance; with a laugh.*) Don't be preposterous!

Rose. (*As resigning herself then against her conscience; exquisitely.*) Ah, well if you *will!* (*She stands a moment, again, looking down; and then still not meeting his eyes, brings out abruptly and in different, a lower, tone.*) Don't stand so *near* me. The Queen-Mother's waiting there (*as if he hasn't known she has stayed*)—and she's not reading; she's *watching* us.

Tony. (*Holding his ground and not turning about to see; as if in fact amused at her fine circumspection, while he yet accepts her hint of the lowered tone.*) How in the world, with your back turned, can you *see* that?

Rose. (*With quiet irony and as if enjoying even the momentary passage with him.*) It's with my back turned that I see most. (*Looking straight before her; facing the spectators.*) She's looking at us hard.

Tony. (*As, for the humour of the thing, confidently reckless now; smiling and really enjoying it himself.*) I don't care a hang!

Rose. (*With beautiful dignity.*) Oh, I don't say it for myself!

Tony. (*As if he has had hold of her hand and she has withdrawn it; putting his own*

straight behind him, and as for a change to real sincerity of accent.*) I hope you'll let me say to you—very simply—that I believe you'll be very happy.

Rose. (*As with no illusions about it, as having quite faced it.*) I shall be as happy as a woman can be who has abandoned her post.

Tony. (*Good-humouredly, soothingly; as if these are grand names.*) Oh, your post—! (*Then at once, as to make it all comfortable.*) Your post will be to honour us with your company at Bounds again; which, as a married woman, you see, you'll be perfectly able to do.

Rose. (*Sadly smiling at him.*) How you arrange things! (*Then with a musing headshake.*) We leave England.

Tony. (*All pleasant derision for it.*) How *you* arrange them! (*Then as for the real facts of it.*) He goes back to China?

Rose. (*After an instant.*) Very soon. (*Looking down.*) He's doing so well.

Tony. (*Frankly, gaily then.*) I hope he has made money.

Rose. A good deal. (*Then raising her eyes.*) I should look better—shouldn't I?—if he hadn't! (*Then resigned and philosophic.*) But I show you enough how little I care how I "look"! (*Not sparing herself; seeing herself as she is.*) I blow hot and cold; I'm all there—(*then with a melancholy shrug*) and I'm all off! (*But making the best of it.*) No matter! I accept your hopes for my happiness. It will be sufficient, no doubt, as soon as I learn—! (*But this drops with the return of her impatience, which is back upon her, and with which she faces again to the quarter of the approach from the other house.*)

Tony. (*Taking her straight up, while he is down at one side, she down on the other and Mrs. Beever far up, centre, as before.*) That Effie's all right? (*Then having taken a sign from Mrs. Beever, who has seen, from her position, what he hasn't, and has had for him an informing gesture.*) Here comes Paul to tell us.

Mrs. Beever. (*Coming down with great gravity, as if having moved off so as not to know anything bad too soon.*) It isn't Paul. It's the Doctor—without his hat.

Rose. (*Down right; at once; as if this is*

portentous.) "Without his hat"?

TONY. (*Cheerful and relieved, before he quite sees their good friend emerge from cover.*) He'll have it in his hand!

MRS. BEEVER. (*Dry, cold, contradictious, as* RAMAGE *arrives.*) He hasn't it in his hand.

(*Enter* DOCTOR RAMAGE, *breathlessly, from the waterside.*)

ROSE. (*All eagerness, as he pulls up at sight of them.*) Is Effie there?

DR. RAMAGE. (*Pausing there a moment, and then checking with an absolutely imperative gesture the great start, on the part of each, as for a rush to see for themselves, that his own indication, his disordered hair, his hard white face, his splashed wet clothes, his general revelation of some horror, have immediately provoked.*) There has been an accident.

TONY. (*All quick dismay.*) She's hurt?

MRS. BEEVER. (*As instantaneous, and going characteristically straighter.*) She's killed?

DR. RAMAGE. (*Centre, breathless, inscrutable for the moment, only bent, with his raised, authoritative arms, on checking them.*) Stay where you are! (*After which he heads off, he catches* TONY, *who has rushed up and made as to pass him; seizing the master of Bounds straight by the arm or wrist, jerking him powerfully round, and so holding him tight, while he closes his own eyes for this intensity of restraint.*) You're not to go. You're not to go.

TONY. (*As having leaped to the worst now.*) She's dead?

ROSE. (*Down right—she not having moved; but with a wail as of the fiercest need to know.*) Who's with her? Who was?

DR. RAMAGE. (*Recovering himself for lucidity and control.*) Paul's with her—by the water.

ROSE. (*With a shriek as of divination.*) By the *water*?

TONY. (*Down left, released by* RAMAGE; *with a cry of horror but not wanting now to see.*) My Child's *drowned*?

MRS. BEEVER. (*While* RAMAGE *is still centre; he having looked from one to the other, and now looks but at herself, who, instantly, admirably, with a strength*

quickly acknowledged by some mute motion in his expressive face, has stilled herself into the appeal of a blanched, breathless wait.) May *I* go?

DR. RAMAGE. (*Motioning her on—then off; making way for her.*) Go. There's no one else.

(*Exit* MRS. BEEVER, *with her rush, to the river.*)

ROSE. (*Still in her place; at once echoing.*) No one else? (*Then as with a frenzy of fierceness and of strange meaning.*) Then where's that girl?

TONY. (*To* DOCTOR, *who has come down toward* ROSE *with a repetition of his hushing, prohibitive gesture; speaking with quick quietness and as if only for the truth, whatever it is.*) Ramage have I lost my Daughter?

DR. RAMAGE. You'll see— be brave! (*Then with his immense, his repeated gesture of prohibition.*) Not yet. I've told Paul. (*For both of them.*) Be quiet. (*He has approached* ROSE *at first, as to stay her; but now moves to* TONY, *whose face has turned black and who stands rooted to the ground as by the very force of a long stare at* ROSE. *He lays his left hand on* TONY's *shoulder, as to impose a stillness, a vague hush, upon him; and so, close to* TONY, *he looks across at* ROSE *again for his question.*) Who, Miss Armiger, was *with* her?

ROSE. (*As if all her lividness wonders and she only wants to know the relations of time and place.*) When *was* it—?

DR. RAMAGE. (*Leaving* TONY *overwhelmed for the instant; more at centre.*) God knows! She was there—against the Bridge.

ROSE. (*Staring, glaring, wondering.*) "Against the Bridge"—where I passed but just now? (*As trying to fit it, with wide eyes of horror, and while* TONY *but dumbly closes his own.*) *I* saw nothing!

DR. RAMAGE. (*As to be clear as possible.*) I came over because, though I'd been called, she wasn't at the *house*, and— from the bank—*there* she was! I reached her—with the boat, with a push. She might have been half an hour—

ROSE. (*Breaking in as for what she vividly sees; instantaneous, plausible.*) It was half an hour ago she *took* her! (*Following it up.*) She's not *there?*

DR. RAMAGE. (*Looking at her hard.*) Of whom do you speak?

ROSE. (*As if it's too terribly obvious.*) Why, of Miss Martle—whose hands are never *off* her! (*Then turning from one to the other, with her mask that is as the mask of Medusa.*) What has become of Miss Martle?

DR. RAMAGE. (*Gazing, gaping, for this new issue; turning as from the irresistible force of* ROSE's *question to* TONY, *who stares before him now, wondering, seeming to see something, yet not to see it, with eyes that have not only opened but are half out of his head.*) What has become of her?

TONY. (*As to wonder how he should know.*) She's not there?

DR. RAMAGE. (*Definite; giving them the whole situation.*) There's no one there.

ROSE. (*Startled, bewildered.*) Not Dennis?

DR. RAMAGE. (*Staring for her question.*) Mr. Vidal? No, thank God—only Paul. (*Then, for all his pity inevitably pressing* TONY.) Miss Martle was *with* her?

TONY. (*As one in whom something strange and unspeakable is working; with a roll of his eyes as all over space.*) No—not Miss Martle.

ROSE. (*As with a clamour of almost fifty.*) But *somebody* was! (*As if it's too monstrous.*) She wasn't *alone?*

TONY. (*As moving his eyes with effort, after an instant, to meet her own; looking at her hard and simply repeating.*) Not Miss Martle.

ROSE. (*With all her vehemence.*) But who then? And where is she now?

DR. RAMAGE. (*As in the intensity of his wonder—his growing need to account for* JEAN; *to* ROSE.) It's positive she's not here?

ROSE. (*Absolute.*) Positive—Mrs. Beever knew. (*Then ringing out again.*) Where in the name of horror *is* she?

DR. RAMAGE. (*Again as under the effect of it, to* TONY.) Where in the name—? (*He pauses, however, as under the still greater effect of* TONY's *face.*)

TONY. (*While, with the width of the stage between them his eyes unspeakably sound* ROSE's *and hers blaze back; with*

his silence meanwhile and anguish, his face of convulsion; bringing it out in an altered voice.*) It isn't half an hour—!

DR. RAMAGE. (*As struck with his tone; catching him up.*) Since it *happened?* (*After which with a look at* ROSE, *he seems to blink at this sudden symptom, on their friend's part, of knowledge.*) Then when—?

TONY. (*Looking at him now straight; and as deciding, after an instant, to speak.*) When I was there.

DR. RAMAGE. And when was *that?*

TONY. After I called for you.

DR. RAMAGE. (*Fitting it.*) To leave word for me to go? (*Taking it in, for all it may mean; setting his face.*) But you weren't going home then.

TONY. (*After an instant.*) I did go—I had a reason. (*Then with his eyes again on* ROSE.) *You* know it.

ROSE. (*Wondering, thinking, not seeing as yet where he's coming out; but recalling what he alludes to.*) When you went for your business paper? (*Then as accepting this; yet still at a loss.*) But Effie wasn't there then.

TONY. (*As knowing himself now where, and all too horribly, he is coming out; as having mastered the relations and his way to put it.*) Why not? She was there—but Miss Martle wasn't *with* her.

DR. RAMAGE. (*As half, and yet all too portentously and terribly seeing what he means.*) Then, in God's name, who was?

TONY. (*After having made them wait a moment.*) I was.

DR. RAMAGE. (*Concentrated, sombre, incredulous, while* ROSE *has given a loud, inarticulate cry and turned off covering her ears with her hands.*) You?

TONY. (*Keeping it up; his eyes on* ROSE, *though she presents her back; watching her with a gaze that seems to count her respirations.*) I was with her—and I was with her alone. And what was done—*I* did. (*He pauses, and his pause has brought* ROSE *round; just as it holds* RAMAGE *gaping. Then he winds up with an effect of quietness and coldness.*) Now you know. (*RAMAGE has fallen back and up, as in his dismay and* ROSE, *passing round and coming down on the other side of him, seems to waver before speaking. But she is* checked by a fresh sound, in another tone, from TONY who fairly howls it out.) God forgive me! (He breaks into a storm of sobs; dropping up on a seat with his wretched face in his hands; while ROSE, with an answering passionate wail of equal violence, throws herself, appalled, her face down, on the ground; and the DOCTOR, in a colder dismay, looks from one prostrate figure to the other.)

ACT THIRD

Eastmead; MRS. BEEVER's drawing-room; the essence of the arrangement of which is two doors into other apartments more or less facing each other, still another, to the hall and a wide window to the terrace, if not a pair of such; so that one may be closed and the other only stand open to the early summer evening and show, after the sunset, the last glow of a patch of western sky. On rise of Curtain MANNING, the parlourmaid, is at the door from the hall, keeping her hand on the knob as if she has just quietly come in and softly closed it, while she looks about in expectation of somebody or something; somebody who then appears in the form of MRS. BEEVER, cautiously opening one of the doors from a contiguous room and looking in. At sight of MANNING she decides and enters, softly closing the door behind her; she thus for a moment looks hard at MANNING, as if with a question in her face, and comes down a little as if both hoping and fearing her servant may have something to tell her; which is in effect what MANNING understands.

MANNING. Yes, ma'am, Mr. Vidal. (Indicating the door opposite the one by which MRS. BEEVER has entered.) I showed him, as you told me, into the library.

MRS. BEEVER. (As between her relief and her fear.) Ah! (But then pulled up as with a further thought.) It may be wanted. I'll see him here. (Then again, as MANNING is back at door to hall.) Mr. Paul's in his room?

MANNING. (Clear for this.) No, ma'am, he went out.

MRS. BEEVER. (Wondering.) But a minute ago?

MANNING. Longer, ma'am. After he carried in—

MRS. BEEVER. (Staying the words on her lips and quickly supplying her own.) The dear little girl—yes. He went to Mr. Bream?

MANNING. (Definite.) No, ma'am—the other way.

MRS. BEEVER. (Considering, in her deep, stricken gravity; piecing together the situation of that moment.) But Miss Armiger's in?

MANNING. Oh yes—in her room.

MRS. BEEVER. She went straight?

MANNING. (Reflecting; after an instant.) Yes, ma'am. (Then after another instant.) She always goes straight.

MRS. BEEVER. (With subdued but full significance.) Not always. But she's quiet there?

MANNING. (Inscrutable.) Very quiet.

MRS. BEEVER. Then call Mr. Vidal.

(Exit MANNING to the hall, leaving the door open, while MRS. BEEVER, restless, infinitely anxious, yet ever so controlled turns vaguely about in her distress and approaches one of the windows from which she stares out at the dusk that slowly and faintly gathers. Enter DENNIS VIDAL from the hall, whom she hears, instantly turning round.)

VIDAL. (After he has closed the door, all anxiety, but as yet all bewilderment.) Something dreadful has happened?

MRS. BEEVER. Something dreadful has happened. You've come from the other house?

VIDAL. As fast as I could run. I saw Dr. Ramage there.

MRS. BEEVER. And what did he tell you?

VIDAL. That I must come straight here.

MRS. BEEVER. (Visibly troubled for him, but resolute.) Nothing else?

VIDAL. That you would tell me. (Yet as prepared for something bad.) I saw the shock in his face.

MRS. BEEVER. But you didn't ask?

VIDAL. Nothing. (*But as ready for any-thing—for the worst.*) Here I am.

MRS. BEEVER. (*With a muffled moan of relief, and a clasp of her hands against her breast; a gesture that practically reveals the worst.*) Here you are, thank God! I'm in dire trouble, and I venture to believe that if you came back to me today it was be-cause—

VIDAL. (*Taking her up eagerly.*) Because I thought of you as a friend? For God's sake, then think of *me* as one.

MRS. BEEVER. (*Pressing to her lips while she looks at him, dry-eyed, without tears, only with a now visible terror, the small tight knot into which her nerves have crum-pled her handkerchief.*) I've never appealed to one as I shall appeal to you now. Effie Bream is dead. (*Then at the instant horror in his eyes.*) She was found in the water.

VIDAL. (*Closing his eyes tight while he winces with the dismay of it, and so hold-ing himself a moment in silence, from any other show of the shock.*) The River?

MRS. BEEVER. Under the Bridge—at the other side. She had been caught, she was held in the slow current—by some ob-struction, by the pier itself. Don't ask me *how*—when I arrived she had, by the mercy of heaven, been brought to the bank. But she was gone. (*Then forcing herself on, with a motion of the head at the room she has quitted.*) We carried her back *there*. To think—to get more time. (*Vidal has stood a minute in his concentrated horror, and then, without a word, moving all too nervously away, has gone up and stood a minute looking out of the window where she has just stood; so that while his back is still turned though she has given him time as it were, she comes out with a ques-tion.*) How long were you at Bounds with Rose?

VIDAL. (*As if he has been lost in thought; turning away from the window and com-ing down, but not at once catching on.*) "At Bounds"?

MRS. BEEVER. When, on your joining her, she went over with you.

VIDAL. (*Thinking; putting things to-gether.*) She didn't go over with me. I went alone—after the Child came out.

MRS. BEEVER. (*Wondering.*) You were there when Manning brought her? (*Then as if the point's important.*) Manning didn't *tell* me that.

VIDAL. (*As for a perfectly lucid account of the matter.*) I found Rose on the lawn —with Mr. Bream—when I brought back your boat. He left us together—after very kindly inviting me to Bounds—and then the little girl came over. Rose introduced me to her out there—at your dining-room window; and I remained till Miss Martle appeared. Then I—rather unciv-illy—went off.

MRS. BEEVER. (*Who has attentively fol-lowed.*) You went off without Rose?

VIDAL. Yes—I left her with the little girl and Miss Martle. (*Then as seeing in her face a marked effect from this statement.*) Was it your impression I *didn't*?

MRS. BEEVER. (*Who, under the vision of matters given her by his speech has dropped into a seat and stares up at him.*) I'll tell you later. You left them in the garden with the Child?

VIDAL. In the garden—and with the Child at play just at hand.

MRS. BEEVER. (*As for absolute certainty.*) Then you hadn't taken her?

VIDAL. The Child? Not in the least. She apparently couldn't be dragged away, to come out to us, from the in-door attrac-tions you had prepared for her.

MRS. BEEVER. You went alone then to the other house?

VIDAL. Alone—but I turned off short. I *was* going; but if I had a great deal to think of after I had learned from you that Rose was here, the quantity was scarcely diminished, you can easily imag-ine, by our personal encounter. (*Then after an instant—as for what it may mean.*) I had seen her with him.

MRS. BEEVER. (*Intensely interested.*) Well?

VIDAL. (*As to remind her.*) Well—I asked you if she was in love with him.

MRS. BEEVER. (*Perfectly remembering.*) And I bade you find out for yourself.

VIDAL. I've found out.

MRS. BEEVER. (*Confidently waiting.*) Well?

VIDAL. (*As if it is even in this tighter ten-sion something of a relief to all his sore-*

ness to speak.) I've never seen anything like it—and (*with a significant comprehensive motion*) there's not *much* I've not seen!

MRS. BEEVER. (*Triumphant even though sombre.*) That's exactly what the Doctor says!

VIDAL. (*Who has stared an instant, but then speaks as from a natural need.*) And does the Doctor say Mr. Bream cares?

MRS. BEEVER. Not a farthing!

VIDAL. (*Assenting then; as from his own impression and conviction.*) Not a farthing. (*Then developing; as if the demonstration is even partly for himself.*) I'm bound to say I seemed to see for myself how well he has behaved. (*Then as, at this, restless in all her anxiety, she gives a smothered but audible wail that pulls him up.*) Don't you think that?

MRS. BEEVER. (*Postponing, reserving an opinion again; as if it's all too dark and deep.*) I'll tell you later. In presence of this misery I don't judge him.

VIDAL. No more do I. But what I was going to say was that, all the same, the way he has with a woman, the way he had with her there, and his damned good looks and his great happiness—

MRS. BEEVER. (*Breaking in with a movement of strong protest.*) His great happiness? God help him! (*Then as, with this baffling flare over the subject, she stands before him, all urgent, for more light.*) Where *were* you then?

VIDAL. After I left the garden? (*Fully explaining.*) I was upset, I was dissatisfied—I didn't go over. I lighted a cigar; I passed out of the gate by your little closed pavilion and kept on by the river.

MRS. BEEVER. By the river? Then why didn't you *see*—?

VIDAL. (*Taking her up.*) What happened to the Child? Because if it happened near the bridge I had left the bridge behind.

MRS. BEEVER. But you were in *sight*—!

VIDAL. For five minutes. (*The case plain to him.*) I was in sight perhaps even for ten. I strolled there, I turned things over, I watched the stream, and, finally—just at the sharp bend—I sat a little on the stile beyond that new smart boat-house.

MRS. BEEVER. (*Recognising and charac-*

teristic.) Yes—it's a horrid thing! But you see the bridge from the boat-house.

VIDAL. (*Considering.*) Yes, it's a good way—but you've a glimpse.

MRS. BEEVER. Which showed you nothing at all?

VIDAL. (*Echoing it; bethinking himself.*) Nothing at all? (*The question makes him turn again; it even carries him in his unrest to the window where he once more, for a little, stares out at the pale pink of the sky, now so cold that twilight has begun to fill the room. At last, while she only watches him, he faces about, returning down.*) No—I saw something. But I'll not tell you what it was, please, till I've myself asked you a thing or two.

MRS. BEEVER. (*Silent at first for this, while they stand face to face, across their interval, in the gathered dusk. She slowly then exhales a sigh of her anguish.*) I think you'll be a help.

VIDAL. (*Too dubious in his bitterness.*) How much of one shall I be to *myself*? (*Then, however, reverting with force to his statement.*) I went back to the bridge, and as I approached it Miss Martle came down to it from your garden.

MRS. BEEVER. (*With a deep start.*) Without the Child? (*And then again as he only looks at her.*) Without the Child.

VIDAL. (*True to his remembrance.*) Without the Child.

MRS. BEEVER. (*After another long stare at him.*) On your sacred honour?

VIDAL. On my sacred honour.

MRS. BEEVER. (*Who has dropped her face into her hands a moment, burying it in them as to hide a spasm of emotion; after which she looks up.*) You *are* a help!

VIDAL. (*As if utterly and loyally to satisfy her.*) Well, if it's being one to let you know that she was with me from that moment—

MRS. BEEVER. (*Catching him up; breathless.*) With you?—till when?

VIDAL. Till just now. When we again separated at the gate-house: I to go over to Bounds, as I had promised Mr. Bream, and Miss Martle—

MRS. BEEVER. (*Snatching the words from him in her emotion.*) To come straight in? Oh glory be to God!

VIDAL. (*Bewildered for what this may*

prove.) She *did* come—?

MRS. BEEVER. Yes—to meet this horror. (*Fully accounting for her.*) She's with Effie. (*Then as returning to what he has said for the very desire of the comfort of it again.*) She was *with* you?

VIDAL. (*Not fully following, but prompt and absolute.*) A quarter of an hour—perhaps more. (*At which* MRS. BEEVER *drops again upon her seat, her sofa or whatever, giving herself to the tears—now all of relief—that haven't sooner come. She sobs softly, controlling them; while he but watches her at first with his hard haggard pity. Then as to give her the whole thing more fully.*) As soon as I saw her I spoke to her—I felt how I wanted her.

MRS. BEEVER. (*On her sofa; her hands dropped now; as looking at him through a clearer medium, in which, however, there are still obscurities.*) You "wanted" her?

VIDAL. (*Explaining it as he can.*) For what she might say to me. (*Then as working this out for her.*) I told you, when we spoke of Rose after my arrival that I hadn't come to watch her. But while I was with them there (*jerking his head at the garden*) something remarkable took place.

MRS. BEEVER. (*On her feet again.*) I know what took place.

VIDAL. (*Struck.*) You "know" it?

MRS. BEEVER. (*Producing what she means.*) She told Jean.

VIDAL. (*Staring; not accepting this.*) I think not.

MRS. BEEVER. (*Wondering.*) Jean didn't speak of it to you?

VIDAL. Not a word.

MRS. BEEVER. She spoke of it to Paul. (*Then as to be more specific.*) I mean your engagement.

VIDAL. (*Silent at first; but after a moment, with a voice stranger than his silence.*) My engagement?

MRS. BEEVER. (*Knowing perfectly what she herself means.*) Didn't you, on the spot, induce her to renew it?

VIDAL. (*After a long troubled wait.*) Has she said so?

MRS. BEEVER. (*As if it's already notorious.*) To everyone.

VIDAL. (*After another wait.*) I should like to see her.

MRS. BEEVER. (*With a gesture of sharp demonstration as, the door opening from the Hall,* ROSE *appears.*) Here she *is!*

(*Enter* ROSE ARMIGER *from the hall.*)

ROSE. (*As already prepared for* VIDAL's *presence, and, as with a high tension, addressing him instantly and straight and ignoring* MRS. BEEVER.) I *knew* you'd be here. I must *see* you.

MRS. BEEVER. (*Before* VIDAL *can speak; passing at once to where* ROSE *has entered and, while she takes the two in together, letting her fifty years of order come out, before anything else, in her tone.*) Will you have lights?

ROSE. (*Immediate.*) No lights, thanks. (*Then as* MRS. BEEVER *is at the door.*) May I see Effie?

MRS. BEEVER. (*Fixing her, through the dusk, with a steady intense look.*) No! (*Exit* MRS. BEEVER *to hall.*)

ROSE. (*Immediate again to* VIDAL, *quite away from her now and at the opposite side of the stage.*) For what did you come *back* to me?—for what did you come *back?*

VIDAL. (*As having taken her in, across the dusky room, as a creature different now from anything she has ever been; moving away from her as she comes nearer; so that, through all the next passage, their distance is still preserved.*) To *you?*—to *you?* I hadn't the slightest notion you were here.

ROSE. (*At the highest pitch of the intensity of a planned attitude of her own; so that she speaks with quick authority, as having it all ready.*) Didn't you come to see *where* I was? Didn't you come absolutely and publicly *for* me? (*Then as he is jerked round again to the window with the vague wild gesture of a man in horrible pain, and in the greater pain now for having seen her face; without vehemence, but with clear deep cogency and plausibility.*) It was exactly when you found I was here that you did come back. You had a perfect chance, on learning it, not to show; but you didn't take the chance—you quickly put it aside. You reflected, you decided, you insisted we should meet. I hadn't called you; I hadn't troubled you; I left you as perfectly alone as

I've *been* alone. It was your own passion and your own act—you've dropped on me, you've overwhelmed me. You've overwhelmed me, I say, because I speak from the depths of *my* surrender. But you didn't do it, I imagine, to be cruel, and if you didn't do it to be cruel you did it to take what it could *give* you. (*Then as gradually, while she talks, he has faced round again, she stands there supported by the high back of a chair, which she has in front of her and either side of which she holds tight.*) You know what I *am*, if *any* man has known, and it's to the thing I am— whatever that is!—that you've come back at last from so far. (*Then as with the last lucidity and urgency.*) It's the thing I am— whatever that is!—that I count on you now to *stand by.*

VIDAL. (*Across his space.*) "Whatever that is"? (*With a slow ineffably sad and tragic headshake of negation.*) I feel, on the contrary, that I've never, never known!

ROSE. Well, it's before anything a woman who has such a need as no woman has ever had. (*Then after an instant.*) Why on earth did you descend on me if you hadn't need of me?

VIDAL. (*Who, after turning restlessly about, moving as in the dumb distress of a man confronted with the greatest danger of his life, has the effect both of keeping far from her, as already noted, and of revolving blindly round her. At last in his hesitation he pulls up before her.*) What makes, all of a sudden, the tremendous need you speak of? Didn't you remind me but an hour ago of how remarkably low, at our last meeting here, it had dropped?

ROSE. You can speak to me in harshness of what I did an hour ago? You can taunt me with an act of penance that might have *moved* you—that *did* move you? (*Then after the briefest intensity of pause with the force of her appeal.*) Does it mean that you've none the less embraced the alternative that seems to you most worthy of your courage? Did I only stoop, in my deep contrition just now, to make it easier for you to knock me down? (*With the finest bitterness of irony.*) I gave you your chance to refuse me, and what you've come back for then will have been only, most

handsomely, to *take* it! In that case you did injustice there to the question of your revenge. What fault have you to find with anything so splendid?

VIDAL. (*Who has listened with his eyes averted, meets her own again as if he has not heard; only bringing out his previous words with a harder and more wilful iteration.*) What makes your tremendous need?—what makes your tremendous need? (*Then as if he will do nothing and understand nothing till she gives him exactly her reason.*) I don't in the least understand why it should have taken such a jump. You must do justice, even after your act of this afternoon—a demonstration far greater than any I dreamed of *asking* of you—you must do justice to my absolute necessity for seeing everything clear. I didn't there in the garden see anything clear at all—I was only startled and wonderstruck and puzzled. Certainly I was "touched," as you say—so touched that I particularly *suffered*. But I couldn't pretend I was satisfied or gratified or even that I was particularly convinced! You often failed of old, I know, to give me what I really wanted from you, and yet it never prevented the success of your effect on—what shall I call it? (*He stops short, with a desperate gesture.*) On God only knows what baser, obscurer part of me! (*Then quickly going on.*) I'm not such a brute as to say that that effect was not produced this afternoon—!

ROSE. (*Promptly interrupting.*) You confined yourself to saying that it's not produced in our actual situation!

VIDAL. (*Staring at her an instant through the thicker dusk as if this is the strangest of challenges; then as if keeping his wits about him.*) I don't understand you! (*Then as she makes an almost amused ironic gesture.*) I do say that, whatever your success today may be admitted to consist of, I didn't at least then make the admission. I didn't at that moment understand you any more than I do now, and I don't recognise that I'm committed to anything that deprives me of the right of asking you for a little more light.

ROSE. Do you recognise by chance the horrible blow—?

VIDAL. (*Anticipating. her.*) That has fallen on all this wretched place? I'm unutterably shocked by it. But where does it come into *our* relations?

ROSE. (*Smiling as in exquisite pity; which has the air, however, of being more especially for herself.*) You say you were painfully affected—yet you really invite me to go further still! (*After an instant as of the noblest resistance to the last humiliation.*) Haven't I put the dots on all the horrid i's and dragged myself through the dust of enough confessions?

VIDAL. (*Who slowly and grimly shakes his head, doggedly clinging as to his only refuge.*) I don't understand you—I don't understand!

ROSE. (*As with a supreme effort to surmount her scruple against putting what she means into words.*) It would be inexpressibly horrible to me to appear to be free to profit by Mr. Bream's misfortune.

VIDAL. To appear, you mean, to have an interest in the fact that the death of his Daughter leaves him at liberty to invite you to become his wife?

ROSE. You express it to admiration.

VIDAL. Why—however I "express" it!—should you be in danger of that torment to your delicacy if Mr. Bream has the best of reasons for doing nothing to contribute to it?

ROSE. The best of Mr. Bream's reasons won't be nearly so good as the worst of mine.

VIDAL. (*Taking in her sense.*) That of your making a match with someone else? I see—I see! That's the precaution I'm to have the privilege of putting in your power.

ROSE. Your loyalty makes my position perfect.

VIDAL. And what does it make my own?

ROSE. Exactly the one you came to take. You *have* taken it by your startling presence; you're up to your eyes in it, and there's nothing that will become you so as to wear it bravely and gallantly. If you don't like it, you should have thought of that before!

VIDAL. You "like" it so much on your side that you appear to have engaged in measures to create it even before the argument for it had acquired the force of which you give so fine an account!

ROSE. Do you mean by giving it out as an accomplished fact? It was never too soon to give it out; the right moment was the moment you were there. Your arrival changed everything. It gave me on the spot my advantage—precipitating my grasp of it.

VIDAL. (*Wearily, jadedly, sceptical.*) You call your "grasp" the announcement—?

ROSE. (*Taking him up; ever so prompt and eager.*) My announcement *has* reached you? Then you know I've cut off your retreat! (*After which, as he turns again away from her, flinging himself on the sofa on which, shortly before, MRS. BEEVER has sunk down with a sob, and, as with the need of holding onto something, buries his face in one of the hard square cushions; she comes a little nearer, she goes on with her urgent lucid passion.*) So you can't abandon me—you can't. (*Standing over him—as giving him her last word.*) You came to me through doubts—you spoke to me through fears. You're *mine!* (*After which, as so leaving him, in a moment, to turn this over, she moves off and up to the door of* MRS. BEEVER's *exit and stands there a moment, all anxious and restless as the minutes ebb, to catch at any approach or any sound.*)

VIDAL. (*On the sofa, rousing himself, but leaning back as if more or less overwhelmed.*) What is it you look to me to *do?*

ROSE. (*As she comes away from the door.*) Simply to see me through!

VIDAL. (*On his feet again; as with no start; as only with the darkest conviction now.*) Through *what,* in the name of horror?

ROSE. Through everything. If I count on you, it's to support me. If I *say* things, it's for *you* to say them.

VIDAL. (*After a moment during which he has ever so wretchedly and yet so sternly, watched her.*) Even when they're black lies?

ROSE. What need should I have of you if they were only white ones? I thank you at any rate for giving so graceful a name to my weak boast that you *admire* me!

VIDAL. (*After again, for a concentrated*

moment and as for all he's worth, watching her.) Do you expect me—on that admiration!—to marry you?

ROSE. (*Throwing back her head as in sudden surprise, almost as in amusement; and then as but too glad to correct his mistake and right herself.*) Bless your innocent heart, no! For what do you *take* me? I expect you simply to make people believe that you *mean* to.

VIDAL. And how long will they believe it if I *don't?*

ROSE. (*Not an instant at a loss.*) Oh, if it should come to that, you can easily make them believe that you *have!* (*On which as he has started as with a shock from it, she takes for him a stride so rapid that it's almost a spring; she reaches him, lays her hand on him, and thus holding him by his shoulder, keeps him fast.*) So you see after all, dearest, how little I ask.

VIDAL. (*Who has stood passive, submissive, as with no movement but to close his eyes before the new-born dread of her caress. Yet he takes the caress when it comes—the dire confession of her hard embrace, the long entreaty of her stony kiss; takes it as a creature so trapped in steel that even after she has let him go he still stands at a loss as to how to turn. Then he finds something to open his eyes, to say it.*) That you went over with *me*—that's what you want me to say?

ROSE. (*Who has left him, turning at this, catching on.*) Over to Bounds? Is that what *I* said? (*Then as in her depths of need which are yet also depths of confused memory.*) I can't think? Thank you for fixing it. If that's it, stick to it!

VIDAL. (*Going on as before.*) And to our having left the Child with Miss Martle?

ROSE. Don't ask me—simply meet the case as it comes. I trust you as I trust the Bank of England—I give you a perfectly free hand.

VIDAL. You're very liberal—but I think you simplify too much.

ROSE. I can hardly do that if to simplify is to leave it to your Honour. It's the beauty of my position that *you* can't be doubted.

VIDAL. That then gives me a certain confidence in telling you that Miss Martle

was the whole time *with* me.

ROSE. (*Pulled up, wondering.*) Of what time do you speak?

VIDAL. The time after you had gone over to Bounds with Effie.

ROSE. (*Bethinking herself.*) *Where* was she with you?

VIDAL. By the river, on this side.

ROSE. (*Surprised; not making it out.*) You didn't go to Bounds?

VIDAL. Not when I left you for the purpose. I obeyed an impulse that made me do just the opposite. You see that there's a flaw in my Honour? You had filled my cup too full—I couldn't carry it straight. I kept by the stream—I took a walk.

ROSE. (*Still more at sea.*) But Miss Martle and I were there together.

VIDAL. You were together till you separated. In my return to the bridge I met her.

ROSE. (*Hanging fire an instant.*) Where was she going?

VIDAL. To the other house—but I prevented her.

ROSE. (*As trying to piece it together.*) You mean she joined you?

VIDAL. In the kindest manner—for another turn. I took her the same way again.

ROSE. (*As lost for a moment in thought.*) But if she was going over, why in the world should she have *let* you?

VIDAL. I think she pitied me.

ROSE. Because she spoke to you of me?

VIDAL. No. Because she didn't. But *I* spoke to her of you.

ROSE. And what did you say?

VIDAL. That—a short time before—I saw you cross to Bounds.

ROSE. You saw me?

VIDAL. On the bridge, distinctly. With the Child in your arms.

ROSE. Where *were* you then?

VIDAL. Far up the stream—beyond your observation.

ROSE. You were *watching* me?

VIDAL. I saw no more.

ROSE. (*Slowly rises again and moves back to the same window, beyond which the garden has now grown vague. She again stands there a minute, looking out; then, without coming away, turns her back to it, so that she shows her handsome head, with the face obscure, against the evening sky.*) Shall I tell you who did it?

VIDAL. If you feel that you're prepared.

ROSE. I've been preparing. I see it's best.

VIDAL. Who, then?

ROSE. Tony Bream—to marry Jean.

VIDAL. (*Protesting, amazed, loud, but barely articulate.*) Oh, oh, oh!

(*Which sound, however, irresistibly leaping from him is on the instant checked by the sudden opening of the door from the hall and a consequent gush of light. Re-enter MANNING from the hall, carrying a pair of tall candles in fine old high silver candlesticks. Re-enter DR. RAMAGE.*)

DR. RAMAGE. (*Who remains up while MANNING immediately places her candles and appears then about to proceed to the blinds and, in her imperturbable regular way, to the other duties of the moment.*) Leave the windows please—it's *warm*. That will do—thanks. (*After which, as she forbears, passing out while he holds the door open for her, he closes it again scrupulously and turns to face ROSE and VIDAL, from one to the other of which he stands looking.*)

ROSE. (*Who has quitted the window and speaks as on a quick intelligent selection and decision as to her best attitude.*) Do you want *me*?

DR. RAMAGE. (*While he looks at his watch and VIDAL watches her, as not before, in the light the candles throw on her altered aspect.*) I came in for Mr. Vidal, but I shall be glad of a word with you after I've *seen* him. I must ask you therefore (*nodding at the third door of the room*) kindly to pass into the library.

ROSE. You wish me to *wait* there?

DR. RAMAGE. If you'll be so good.

ROSE. (*Indicating VIDAL.*) While you talk with *him*?

DR. RAMAGE. While I talk with "him."

ROSE. (*After a pause during which she looks with long intensity across at VIDAL.*) I'll wait. (*Exit ROSE to library.*)

DR. RAMAGE. (*Addressing VIDAL at once and as for the most urgent business.*) I must appeal to you for a fraction of your time. I've seen Mrs. Beever.

VIDAL. I've done the same.

DR. RAMAGE. It's because she has told me of your talk that I mention it. She sends you a message.

VIDAL. (*As rather surprised at the indirectness.*) Where then is she?

DR. RAMAGE. With that distracted girl.

VIDAL. Miss Martle? (*Then as after considering.*) Miss Martle so greatly feels the shock?

DR. RAMAGE. (*As if surprised, on his side, at the question.*) "Feels" it, my dear sir? She has been made so pitifully ill by it that there's no saying just what turn her condition may take, and she now calls for so much of my attention as to force me to plead, with you, that excuse for my brevity. Mrs. Beever requests you to regard this hurried inquiry as the sequel to what you were so good as to say to her.

VIDAL. (*Thinking, guarded.*) I'm afraid that what I said to Mrs. Beever was a very small matter.

DR. RAMAGE. She doesn't think it at all a small matter that you say you'll *help* her. You can do so—amid the cruel demands our catastrophe make of her—by considering that I represent her. It's in her name therefore that I ask you if you're engaged to be married to Miss Armiger.

VIDAL. Please to say to her that—I *am*.

DR. RAMAGE. (*After looking at him hard an instant, draws out a key which he holds straight up.*) Then I feel it to be only right to say to you that this locks (*with a nod at the quarter to which ROSE has retired*)—the other door of the library.

VIDAL. (*His hands only in his pockets at first; looking at the offered key.*) You mean she's a prisoner?

DR. RAMAGE. On Mr. Vidal's honour.

VIDAL. But *whose* prisoner?

DR. RAMAGE. Mrs. Beever's.

VIDAL. (*Deciding to take the key, which he slips into his waistcoat; then as with inscrutable gravity.*) Don't you forget that we're here, all round, on a level—

DR. RAMAGE. (*Quickly taking it up.*) With the garden? (*With a gesture of reassurance.*) I forget nothing. We've a Friend on the terrace. (*Then as VIDAL, arrested, gives a questioning look as if he may mean*

TONY.) Mr. Beever. A friend of Miss Armiger's.

VIDAL. (*Completely inscrutable now, moves none the less restlessly a few steps, as if intently thinking, his eyes bent on the floor and his hands interclenched behind him.*) If I have this key, who has the other? (*Then as the* DOCTOR *is an instant at a loss.*) The key that confines Mr. Bream.

DR. RAMAGE. (*Who gives a sharp wincing gesture, none the less stands his ground.*) I have it. (*Then after an instant, his face searching* VIDAL'*s.*) She has *told* you?

VIDAL. (*As wondering which he means.*) Mrs. Beever?

DR. RAMAGE. (*Just sharply.*) Miss Armiger.

VIDAL. (*With a certain abysmal dryness.*) She has "told" me. But if you've *left* him—!

DR. RAMAGE. (*Taking it instantly up.*) I've *not* left him. I've brought him over.

VIDAL. (*Staring, at this; for all his hard collectedness.*) To see *me*?

DR. RAMAGE. (*Raising a solemn reassuring hand; but as in deep correction and speaking quite colouressly.*) To see his Child.

VIDAL. He *desires* that?

DR. RAMAGE. He desires that.

(*After which there is a pause as in an air charged with a consciousness of all that, between them, is represented by the unspoken. It is as if each is waiting to have something from the other first and as if* VIDAL, *presumably or evidently, is prepared to wait longest. He goes up, moving always all nervously, and* RAMAGE, *after watching him a moment seems to decide on something.*)

DR. RAMAGE. I do full justice to the difficulty created for you by your engagement. That's why it was important to have it from your own lips. Mrs. Beever feels, you know—all the same!—that it mustn't prevent our putting you another question —or rather our reminding you of the one you just now led her to expect you'll answer. From the bank of the river you saw something that bears on this remarkable performance. We appeal to your sense of propriety to tell us what you saw.

VIDAL. My sense of propriety is *strong;* but so—just now—is my sense of some *other* things. My word to Mrs. Beever was contingent. There are points *I* want made clear.

DR. RAMAGE. I'm here to do what I can to satisfy you. Only be so good as to remember that *time* is everything. Some action has to be *taken.*

VIDAL. You mean a declaration made?

DR. RAMAGE. Under penalty of consequences sufficiently—tremendous! There has been an accident of a gravity—!

VIDAL. (*At once taking him up; but still not looking at him.*) That can't be explained away?

DR. RAMAGE. (*Considers a moment and looks at his watch; then still thus holding it, applies the deep appeal of his face to* VIDAL.) You wish her presented as dying of a natural cause?

VIDAL. Why do you *ask*—if you've a supreme duty?

DR. RAMAGE. I haven't *one*—worse luck! I've fifty.

VIDAL. Does that mean you can keep the thing *quiet*?

DR. RAMAGE. Before I say, I must know what you'll *do* for me.

VIDAL. Hasn't it gone too *far*?

DR. RAMAGE. Well, I know *how* far; not so far, by a peculiar mercy, as it might have gone. There has been an extraordinary coincidence of chances—a miracle of conditions. Everything appears to serve. We'll call it a Providence and have done with it!

VIDAL. Do you allude to the absence of witnesses—?

DR. RAMAGE. (*With full alert assent.*) At the moment the Child was found. Only the blessèd three of us. And she had been there, poor mite—!

VIDAL. (*Breaking in as with an instant sick protest.*) Don't tell me how long! (*His hand over his throbbing head as with the anguish of thought.*) What do *I* want—? (*Then breaking off; all at once again to the practical.*) How do you meet the servants?

DR. RAMAGE. Here? By giving a big name to her complaint. None of them have *seen* her. (*Almost jubilant.*) She was carried in with a *success*—!

VIDAL. But the people at the other house?

DR. RAMAGE. They know nothing but that over here she has had an attack which it will be one of those fifty duties of mine I mentioned to you to make sufficiently remarkable. She was out of sorts this morning—this afternoon I was summoned. That call of Tony's at my house is the Salvation!

VIDAL. Hadn't she some fond Nurse—some devoted Dragon?

DR. RAMAGE. The great Gorham? Yes: the great Gorham didn't *want* her to come —in spite of the day and the apparently grand omens: she was cruelly overborne. There it *is*—but I must *face* the great Gorham. I'm already keeping her at bay —doctors are so luckily despots! They're blessedly *bullies*! She'll be tough—but it's *all* tough!

VIDAL. (*Who has turned away, all a prey to this last truth, again collapses at the end of a few steps with the confession, for the moment, that it's too horribly "tough" for him. He drops upon the sofa, all but audibly moaning; falling back in the despair that breaks through his false pluck.* RAMAGE *watches his pain as if almost with something to hope from it; but before he can speak* DENNIS *again sounds out.*) I don't in the least conceive *how!*

DR. RAMAGE. (*Alert.*) How it was *done?* Small *blame* to you. It was done in one minute; with the aid of a boat and the temptation—we'll handsomely call it!—of solitude. The boat's an old one of Tony's own—padlocked, but with a long chain. To see the Place is to see the Deed.

VIDAL. (*In horror covering his face with his convulsed hands.*) Why in Hell should I see it?

DR. RAMAGE. (*Who has slowly and considerately, tactfully as it were, approached him, sinks on the sofa beside him, and, going on with quiet clearness, really with tenderness, applies a controlling, soothing grasp to his knee.*) The Child was taken into the boat—and the boat was tilted. That was enough—the trick was played. (*VIDAL, motionless and dumb as with the*

fascination of the hideous fact, remains thus held, his eyes now on his companion's face, while the DOCTOR *completes the picture.*) She was immersed. She was held under water. She was made sure of. Oh, I grant you it took a hand—and took a spirit! But they were there. Then she was *left*. (*On his feet again, his demonstration achieved.*) A pull of the chain brought back the boat—and (*as he himself comes down, suiting his action to the words*) the author of the crime walked away.

VIDAL. (*As trying in spite of himself to understand.*) But how could she be *caught?*

DR. RAMAGE. (*Down at the side opposite the sofa, with a slight wince, or start, as for ambiguity; but then catching on.*) The poor little girl? You'd see if you saw the place.

VIDAL. I passed it to come back here. But I didn't *look*—for I didn't know!

DR. RAMAGE. (*Holding him as by the way, almost on discreet tiptoe, he comes back to him at this; seating himself again by him and again with the quieting pat of the knee.*) If you had known you'd have looked still less. She rose; she drifted some yards; then she was washed against the base of the bridge; and one of the openings of her little dress hooked itself to an old loose clamp. There she was *kept*.

VIDAL. And no one came by?

DR. RAMAGE. No one till—by the mercy of God!—*I* came.

VIDAL. (*Takes it in as with a long dry gulp; after which the two men sit looking at each other over it; the* DOCTOR *having laid his hand now on* VIDAL's *right and holding it as for the expression of his desire to see him through.* VIDAL *then gets up as with the sense of understanding this, while the* DOCTOR, *on the sofa, watches his movements.*) And yet the risk of anything but a straight course is hideous.

DR. RAMAGE. *Everything's* hideous. I appreciate greatly the gallantry of your reminding me of my danger. Don't think I don't know exactly what it is. But I have to think of the danger of others. I can *measure* mine; I can't measure *theirs*.

VIDAL. I can return your compliment! "Theirs," as you call it, seems to me such a fine thing for you to care for.

DR. RAMAGE. My dear man, I care for my Friends—the first of whom's Anthony Bream.

VIDAL. And what's *his* danger?

DR. RAMAGE. The danger we've been talking about.

VIDAL. Have we been talking of *that!*

DR. RAMAGE. You asked me, when you told me you knew—?

VIDAL. (*Taking him up as he recalls.*) Knew that he's accused—

DR. RAMAGE. (*Who has till now remained near the sofa; with a start at him as he comes down.*) Accused by *her* too?

VIDAL. (*Falling back as at his onset; staring.*) Is he by anybody else?

DR. RAMAGE. (*Fairly blazing with surprise.*) You don't know it *all?*

VIDAL. (*As if appalled.*) Is there any more?

DR. RAMAGE. (*Throwing up his arms as if it's the great fact.*) Tony cries on the housetops that *he* did it!

VIDAL. (*Blank and bewildered, overcome by this, drops into a seat on the left.*) *He* cries?

DR. RAMAGE. (*As if this other fact is but a shade less obvious.*) To cover Jean!

VIDAL. (*At seat.*) But if she *is* covered?

DR. RAMAGE. (*As having with a vengeance to put his dots on his i's.*) Then to shield Miss Armiger.

VIDAL. (*Gazing aghast; on his feet again; catching on.*) Who meanwhile *denounces* him? (*He moves up to the open window again; again he stands there while* RAMAGE, *only seeing him now in full comprehension, waits an instant in silence. Then* DENNIS *turns round.*) May I *see* him?

DR. RAMAGE. (*As if it is what he has most expected and desired, is already at the door to the hall.*) God bless you! (*Exit* DOCTOR RAMAGE *in high haste.*)

(VIDAL *has a passage now during which he is left alone. He stands so at first, rigid, in the middle of the room, immersed apparently in a stupor of emotion. Then, as if shaken out of it by a return of conscious suffering, passes in a couple of strides to the door of the library, the door of* ROSE's *exit. Here, however, with his hand on the knob,* he yields to another impulse which keeps him irresolute, listening, drawing his breath in pain. Suddenly then, at a movement of one of the opposite doors he leaves the spot—TONY BREAM *has come in. Enter* TONY *from the hall.*)

VIDAL. (*At once.*) If in this miserable hour I've asked you for a moment of your time, I beg you to believe it's only to let you know that anything in this world I can do for you—I'm ready, whatever it is, to do on the spot.

TONY. (*Who, his handsome face smitten, his reddened eyes contracted, his thick hair disordered and his black garments, hastily assumed, awry, has almost the handled, hustled look of a man just dragged from some riot or some rescue and only released to take breath. He may well appear to* VIDAL *as deeply disfigured as* ROSE, *but with a change more passive and tragic, less feverish and eager. His bloodshot eyes fix his interlocutor, and he has already raised his hands as in indication, absolute but courteous, of the vanity of* VIDAL's *assurance.*) I'm afraid there's nothing anyone can do for me. My disaster's *overwhelming*—but I must meet it myself.

VIDAL. Will it perhaps help you to think of something if I tell you that your disaster is almost as much mine *as* yours— and that what's of aid to one of us may perhaps therefore be of aid to the other?

TONY. It's very good of you to be willing to take upon you a grain of the weight of so big a burden! (*Then with a heavy headshake, and a gesture of warning still of his characteristically florid sort.*) Don't do that—don't do that, Mr. Vidal. Don't come *near* such a thing. Don't *touch* it. Don't *know* it. (*He straightens himself as with a long suppressed shudder; and then with a sharper and more sombre vehemence.*) Stand from *under* it! (*Then as speaking still more urgently in the sense of this.*) You came here for half an hour— for your own reasons, for your own relief: you came in all kindness and trust. You've encountered an unutterable horror, and you've only one thing to do.

VIDAL. Be so good as to *name* it.

TONY. Turn your back on it for ever—
go your way this *minute*. I've come to you
simply to say *that*.

VIDAL. Leave you, in other words—?

TONY. By the very first train that will
take you.

VIDAL. (*Appears to turn this over; then
speaks with a face that shows what he
thinks of it.*) It has been my unfortunate
fate in coming to this place—so wrapt, as
one might suppose, in comfort and peace—
to intrude a second time on obscure unhappy things; on suffering, and danger,
and death. I should have been glad, God
knows, not to renew the adventure; but
one's destiny kicks one before it, and I
seem to myself not the least part of the
misery I speak of. You must accept that as
my excuse for not taking your advice. I
must stay at least till you *understand* that.
(*After which he waits a moment; and then
abruptly and impatiently.*) For God's sake,
Mr. Bream, make use of the hand I hold
out to you.

TONY. (*After an instant, as unmoved.*)
You've come, I think, from China?

VIDAL. I've come, Mr. Bream, from
China.

TONY. And it's open to you to go back?

VIDAL. I can do as I wish.

TONY. And yet you're not off like a shot?

VIDAL. My movements and my inclination are my own affair. You won't accept
my aid?

TONY. (*With a sombre stare.*) You ask
me, as you call it, to meet you. Pardon me
if on my side I first inquire what definite
ground—?

VIDAL. On the definite ground on which
Doctor Ramage is good enough to do so.
I'm afraid there's no better ground than
my honour.

TONY. (*Whose stare is long and deep,
puts out his hand at last, which* VIDAL
takes, TONY *speaking while he holds it.*)
I understand you. Good-bye.

VIDAL. (*Still with his hand.*) Good-bye?

TONY. She's safe.

VIDAL. Do you speak of Miss Martle?

TONY. (*Who has drawn away his hand
and looks only before him.*) Not—of Miss
Martle.

VIDAL. Then *I* can. *She's* safe.

TONY. Thank—you!

VIDAL. And the person you do speak of—

TONY. As I *say*—is safe.

VIDAL. Then that's all I ask of you. The
Doctor will do the rest.

TONY. I *know* what the Doctor will do.
What will *you* do?

VIDAL. Everything but marry her.

TONY. (*Moved by this; with a large gesture that matches the flare of admiration
in his face.*) You're beyond me!

VIDAL. (*As with his emotion all spent
now and nothing but the hard truth itself
before him.*) I don't in the least know
where I am!—save that I'm in a black,
bloody nightmare; and that it's not I, it's
not she, it's not you, it's not anyone. I
shall wake up at last, I suppose, but meanwhile—!

TONY. There's plenty more to *come*? Oh
as much as you like!

VIDAL. For *me*—but not for you. For
you the worst's *over*.

TONY. "Over"? With all my life made
hideous?

VIDAL. (*Grimly philosophic; after a certain sturdiness of momentary silence.*) You
think so now—! (*Then more gently.*) I
grant you it's hideous enough.

TONY. (*Standing there lost again in the
horror of it, in the agony of the actual;
as with the tears welling into his hot eyes.*)
She murdered—she tortured my child. And
she did it to incriminate Jean.

VIDAL. (*As with it all dreadfully brought
back and made again vivid to him; after
an instant, with simple solemnity.*) The
dear little girl—the sweet kind little girl!
(*Nearer to* TONY; *with a sudden impulse
that, in the midst of this tenderness, seems
almost savage, he lays on his shoulder a
hard conscientious hand.*) She forced her
in. She held her *down*. She *left* her.

TONY. (*While the men seem to turn
paler as they look at each other.*) I'm infamous—I'm infamous.

VIDAL. (*After a pause so long that it's
almost like a strange assent from him;
bringing out his words at last, however,
with more of a suggestion of mercy.*) It was
her *passion*.

TONY. (*His eyes to the ground.*) It was
her passion.

VIDAL. She *loves* you—! (*Dropping with a throw-up of his arms, as before the lurid real, all vain terms for it.*)

TONY. (*His face reflecting the mere monstrous fact.*) She loves me—! (*Then after an instant, as seeing the whole of the tragic truth.*) It has made what it has made —her awful act and my silence. My silence is a part of the crime and the cruelty—I shall live to be a horror to myself. But (*resolute, settled, accepting the inevitable of the situation*) I *see* it, none the less, as I *see* it—and I shall keep the word I gave her in the first madness of my *fear*. It came to me—there it *is*.

VIDAL. I *know* what came to you!

TONY. (*Wondering.*) Then you've seen her?

VIDAL. (*After an instant.*) I know it from the Doctor.

TONY. I see. (*Then after a moment's thought.*) She, I imagine—

VIDAL. (*Taking him straight up.*) Will keep it to *herself*? (*With tragic comprehensive emphasis.*) Leave that to *me*. (*After which he offers his hand again.*) Good-bye.

TONY. You take her away?

VIDAL. (*As with his plan now all made.*) Tonight.

TONY. (*Still keeping his hand.*) Will her flight help Ramage?

VIDAL. Everything falls in. Three hours ago I *came* for her.

TONY. So it will seem prearranged.

VIDAL. (*In grim assent.*) For the event she *announced* to you. Our happy union!

TONY. (*While* VIDAL *released, reaches the door.*) There's nothing then I shall do for *you*?

VIDAL. It's done. We've helped each other.

TONY. I mean when your trouble has passed.

VIDAL. It will *never* pass. Think of that when you're happy yourself.

TONY. How shall I *ever* be—?

VIDAL. (*As he sees the door of* MRS. BEEVER'S *exit open and* JEAN MARTLE *appear.*) Ask *her*! (*Exit* VIDAL *to the library. Enter* JEAN MARTLE *by the opposite door.*)

JEAN. (*Faltering, pulled up near her place of entrance, at sight of* TONY *and his aspect further down at opposite side of stage.*) I must *speak* to you—I must *speak* to you! But how can you ever *look* at me? —how can you ever *forgive* me? (*In reply to which, taking deeply in her own aspect and woe,* TONY, *simply opens his arms wide, so that as if a gulf is bridged in a flash, she throws herself immediately into them. Thus they stand locked together for a minute in their misery, with no sound and no motion but her sobs; after which, through which, however, she presently speaks again—disengaging herself indeed as she does so.*) They tell me I'm ill, and insane; they want to shut me up, to give me things; they tell me to lie down, to try to sleep. But it's all to me, so dreadfully, as if it were *I* who had done it, that when they admitted to me that you were here I felt that if I didn't see you it would make me as crazy as they say. (*Then as all too vividly and horribly reverting to what has passed in the garden before her last exit.*) It's to have seen her *go!*—it's to have seen her *go: that's* what I can't bear—it's too horrible! (*She continues to sob; she goes on while* TONY *helplessly watches her and while they thus seem to hang over the thing together.*) I *let* her go—I *let* her go; that's what's so terrible, so *hideous*. I might have *got* her—have *kept* her; I might have screamed, I might have rushed for help. But how could I know or dream? How could the *worst* of my fears—? (*She breaks off; she shudders and drops; she sits and sobs while he comes and goes.*) I see her little face as she left me—she looked at me as if she knew. She wondered and dreaded: she knew—she *knew!* It was the last little look I was to *have* from her, and I didn't even answer it with a kiss. She sat there where I could see her, but I never raised a hand. I was close, I was *there*—she must have called for me in her terror! I didn't listen—I didn't come—I only gave her up to be murdered! And now I shall be punished for ever: I shall see her in those arms—in those arms! (*She must have dropped on the sofa; she throws herself down on it and hides her face while her smothered wild lament fills the room.*)

TONY. (*At centre, seeing everything she evokes and brings up, but only the more helpless in his pity.*) It was the only little minute in all the years that you had been forced to fail her. She was always more yours than mine.

JEAN. (*On the sofa.*) It was just *because* she was yours that she was mine. It was because she was yours from the first hour that I—! (*She breaks down, breaks off again; she tries to hold herself; she is again on her feet.*) What could I *do*, you see? To *you yourself* I couldn't be kind?

TONY. I don't see how you could have been kinder!

JEAN. Ah, didn't I try not to *think* of you? But the *Child* was a beautiful part of you—the *Child* I could take and keep.

TONY. She was a little radiant perfect thing. Even if she had not been mine you'd have loved her. If she hadn't been mine she wouldn't have been lying there as I've seen her. Yet I'm glad she was mine.

JEAN. (*As if to contend with him for almost all the responsibility for everything.*) She lies there *because* I loved her and because I so insanely *showed* it. That's why it's *I* who have killed her!

TONY. (*After a moment during which she has turned restlessly off and gone passionately up.*) It was *I* who killed her.

JEAN. (*As taking this at first for a mere self-torment like her own.*) We seem beautifully eager for the guilt.

TONY. (*Immediate, emphatic.*) It doesn't matter what anyone *else* seems. I must tell you *all* now. I've taken the act on myself.

JEAN. (*Bewildered.*) *How* have you taken it—?

TONY. To meet whatever may come.

JEAN. You mean you've accused yourself?

TONY. (*As if he has worked it all out and now abides by it.*) *Any one* may accuse me. Whom is it more *natural* to accuse? What had she to *gain*? My own motive is flagrant. There it *is*.

JEAN. (*As if this is but a fresh horror.*) You'll say you *did* it?

TONY. I'll say I did it.

JEAN. (*Aghast.*) You'll lie? You'll perjure yourself?

TONY. I'll say I did it for *you*.

JEAN. (*As if she has turned white; after an instant.*) Then what do you think *I'll* say?

TONY. Whatever you say will tell against me. (*Then as she wonders; as to explain.*) If the crime was committed *for* you.

JEAN. (*Blank.*) "For" me?

TONY. (*As if it would be evident.*) To enable us to marry.

JEAN. (*Stupefied—as in blighted horror.*) We—"marry"?

TONY. It won't be of any consequence that we sha'n't, that we can't; it would only stand out clear than we *can*. (*Then as after a halt of his sombre ingenuity; proving what he wishes to prove.*) So I shall save—whom I *wish* to save.

JEAN. (*With a fiercer wail.*) You wish to save *her*?

TONY. (*As if, awful though she may think it, it's a matter of course.*) I don't wish to hand her over. (*Then as taking in, however, her aspect and her natural resentment.*) But of course you can't *conceive* it!

JEAN. I? (*Then as casting about her for a negation not too unworthy of her hatred.*) I wish to hunt her to death! I wish to burn her alive! (*As if her emotion has all changed to utter failure to go with him here; as if the flame in her eyes has suddenly dried them.*) You mean she's not to *suffer*?

TONY. You want her to suffer—*all*?

JEAN. (*Ablaze with the light of justice.*) How can anything be enough? I could tear her limb from limb. That's what she tried to do to me!

TONY. (*In lucid concurrence.*) Yes—what she tried to do to *you*.

JEAN. (*With all the force of her challenge.*) And yet you *condone* the atrocity?

TONY. (*After a moment.*) Her doom will be to live.

JEAN. But how will such a fiend be *suffered* to live—when she went to it before my eyes? (*Staring as at her mountain of evidence; then eagerly.*) And Mr. Vidal—her very *lover*—who'll swear what he *knows*, what he *saw*!

TONY. (*With a stubborn headshake, as if wiser than this.*) Oh, Mr. Vidal!

JEAN. (*Only speaking as for her wrong.*) To make *me* seem the monster—!

TONY. (*Whose raised hand, as for a necessary statement, has checked her.*) She made it for the moment possible—

JEAN. (*Catching him straight up.*) To suspect me—?

TONY. I was *mad*—and you weren't there. (*Then as with a muffled, shuddering moan she sinks down again, covering her face with her hands.*) I tell you all—I tell you all. He knows nothing. He saw nothing. He'll swear nothing. He's taking her away.

JEAN. (*Starting as if he has struck her.*) She's *here?*

TONY. (*Surprised at her surprise.*) You didn't know it?

JEAN. (*Panting with amazement.*) She came *back?*

TONY. You thought she had fled?

JEAN. (*Who seems for the instant to hang there like a poised hawk.*) Where *is* she?

TONY. (*Who gives her with a grave gesture, a long, absolute look before which, gradually, her passion seems to fall.*) She has gone. Let her go.

JEAN. (*After a silence.*) But others. How will *they*—?

TONY. (*With a gesture that seems responsibly to extinguish them.*) There *are* no others. She would have *died* for me.

JEAN. (*Then after another pause.*) So you want to die for *her?*

TONY. (*As in full possession of his attitude now.*) I sha'n't die. But I shall remember. (*Then as she watches him; seeing it again.*) I must tell you all. I *knew* it—I always knew it. And I made her *come*.

JEAN. You were kind to her—as you're always kind.

TONY. No—I was *more* than that. And I should have been *less*. (*Then as his face seems to show a rift in the blackness.*) I remember.

JEAN. (*As if following in pain and at a distance.*) Do you mean you *liked* it?

TONY. I *liked* it—while I was *safe*. Then I grew afraid.

JEAN. (*Wondering still, but as a little soothed.*) Afraid of what?

TONY. Afraid of everything. You don't *know*—but we're abysses! (*With a long almost resigned groan; his hand to his head.*)

At least *I'm* one. (*And he seems to sound this depth.*) There are other things. They go back far.

JEAN. (*Raising her two hands gravely.*) Don't tell me—"all"! (*Then as if he has given her more than enough to think of with awe, and even a little at last with pity.*) What will *become* of her?

TONY. God knows. She goes forth.

JEAN. And Mr. Vidal with her?

TONY. Mr. Vidal with her.

JEAN. Because he still loves her?

TONY. (*After an instant, inscrutably.*) He still loves her!

JEAN. (*Blank for it.*) Then what will he do?

TONY. (*After another instant.*) Put the globe between them. (*And then after still another.*) Think of her *torture*.

JEAN. (*After looking for a moment as if she has tried; remaining rather vague as to what it may be sharpest about.*) Do you mean *that?*

TONY. (*His eyes on her; with a long, deeply significant, headshake of negation; meaning something different.*) To have only made us *free*.

JEAN. It's her *Triumph!*—that our freedom is *horrible!*

TONY. (*Who, giving a gesture of assent that is a confession almost of weariness, distinguishes now in the outer dusk PAUL BEEVER, who has appeared at the long window which in the mild air still stands open to the terrace.*) It's horrible!

JEAN. (*Who has not seen PAUL and has only heard TONY's answer, which touches again the source of tears, and the emphasis, again, of the truth.*) It's horrible! (*She breaks afresh into stifled sobs; and so, blindly, slowly, while the two men watch her, passes from the room by the door at which she has entered.*)

(*Exit* JEAN MARTLE. *Enter* PAUL BEEVER *by the long window from the terrace.*)

TONY. You're looking for me?

PAUL. I saw you through the open window, and I thought I'd let you know—

TONY. That some one wants me?

PAUL. She hasn't *asked* for you; but I think that if you could do it—

TONY. (*Breaking straight in.*) I can do

anything. But of whom do you speak?

PAUL. Of one of your servants—poor Mrs. Gorham.

TONY. Effie's nurse? She has come *over?*

PAUL. She's in the garden. I've been floundering about—I came upon her.

TONY. (*Wondering, as if the facts about her may considerably matter.*) What is she doing?

PAUL. Crying very hard—without a sound.

TONY. And without seeming to want to come in?

PAUL. Out of discretion.

TONY. You mean because Jean and the Doctor have taken complete charge?

PAUL. Yes—she yields to that. But she sits there on a bench—

TONY. (*As with the immediate vision of her.*) Weeping and wailing? (*Then on PAUL's mute assent.*) Poor dear thing—! I'll speak to her.

PAUL. (*Struck with this summary manner in which, gaining the long window, he appears about to leave the room.*) Hadn't you better have your hat?

TONY. (*Who has not brought it in; looking about him.*) Why?—if it's a warm night?

PAUL. (*Quiet, but significant.*) You never go out without it. Don't be too unusual.

TONY. (*After a stare.*) I see what you mean. I'll get it. (*With which he makes for the door to the hall.*)

PAUL. (*Again checking him.*) It's much better you should *see* her—it's unnatural you shouldn't. But do you mind my just *thinking* for you the least bit?—asking you for instance what it's your idea to say to her?

TONY. (*With the air of accepting this solicitude; yet meeting the inquiry with characteristic candour.*) I think I've no idea but to talk with her of Effie.

PAUL. As dangerously ill? That's all she knows.

TONY. Yes then—as dangerously ill. Whatever she's prepared for.

PAUL. But what are *you* prepared for? You're not afraid—?

TONY. (*Taking it up as he stops.*) Afraid of what?

PAUL. Of suspicions—importunities. Her making some noise.

TONY. (*As desiring to do the possibility justice; yet not otherwise than easily, with a slow headshake, making up his mind.*) I don't think—no!—that I'm afraid of poor Gorham.

PAUL. Everyone *else* is, you know. She's tremendously devoted.

TONY. (*As with—even at this hour—a degree of innocent and unconscious fatuity.*) Yes—that's what I mean.

PAUL. (*As if after sounding him a moment.*) You mean to *you?*

TONY. (*Excusable for not perceiving an irony so indulgent and on poor literal PAUL's part, mostly so rare.*) She'll do anything. We're the best of friends.

PAUL. Then get your hat!

TONY. (*In full concurrence now.*) It's much the best thing. Thank you for telling me. (*Then as with, always, so much of the ingenuous in him, that, with his habit of good-nature and his hand on the door, he yet lingers an instant as for poor PAUL's comfort and as even for the very tradition of sociability.*) She'll be a resource—a fund of memory. She'll know what I mean. I shall want some one. So we can always talk.

PAUL. (*As after having even in the short time thoroughly taken him in.*) Oh you're safe!

TONY. (*As if it has indeed completely come to him.*) I see my way with her.

PAUL. (*As a sort of melancholy and half-ironic tribute to him.*) So do I!

TONY. (*Fairly brightening through his gloom; at his place of exit.*) I'll keep her on.

(*Exit TONY to the hall; after which PAUL, left alone, is lost evidently in reflection of which ANTHONY BREAM is the subject. He exhales a long sigh that is clearly charged with many things; then as he casts about, turns about, his eyes attach themselves, as in sympathy with a vague impulse, to the door of the library; after which, deeply restless, he goes to take up the hat that, on coming in, he has laid on one of the tables; though he has kept it on for a few moments after joining*

TONY. *He is in the act of doing this when the door of the library opens and* ROSE ARMIGER *stands before him. She has, since their last meeting, changed her dress and, now arrayed for a journey, wears a hat and veil, the latter not yet pulled down, and a long dark mantle. For some time after she appears no word comes from either; but at last, entering only a step or two further, while the door closes behind her, she breaks the silence.*)

ROSE. Can you endure for a minute the sight of me?

PAUL. I was hesitating—I thought of going to you. I knew you were there.

ROSE. (*Coming, at this, a little further down.*) I knew you were here. You passed the window.

PAUL. (*With sombre assent.*) I've passed and re-passed—this hour!

ROSE. I've known that too, but this time I heard you stop. I've no light there (*indicating the room she has quitted*)—but the window on this side is open. I made out you had come *in.*

PAUL. (*As for what this may have exposed her to.*) You ran a danger of not finding me alone.

ROSE. I took my chance—of course I *knew.* I've been in *dread*—but in spite of it I've seen nobody. I've been up to my room and come down. The coast was clear.

PAUL. You've not then seen Mr. Vidal?

ROSE. Oh yes—seen *him.* But he's nobody. (*Then as conscious of the strange sound of this.*) Nobody, I mean, to *fear.*

PAUL. (*After a pause during which he appears to take in her whole portentous calm.*) What in the world is it *you* fear?

ROSE. (*As if really interested in his putting of the question.*) In the sense of the awful thing—that you *know*? (*Then as if ready to say; having considered.*) Here on the spot nothing. About *those* things I'm quite quiet. There may be plenty to come; but what I'm afraid of now is my Safety. There's something in *that*—! (*But she pulls up; she breaks down—as if there's more in it than she can say.*)

PAUL. (*Full always of his wonder at her;*

and as speaking also from his own anxiety.) Are you so *sure* of your safety?

ROSE. You see *how* sure. (*Very quietly.*) It's in your face. (*Then as with sincere feeling.*) And your face—for what it *says*—is terrible.

PAUL. (*As with whatever it says remaining there while he looks at her.*) Is it as terrible as yours?

ROSE. (*As if she has accepted this; with tragic detachment—all impersonally and fatally.*) Oh "mine"! Mine must be hideous—unutterably hideous for ever! Yours is beautiful. Everything—everyone here is beautiful.

PAUL. (*As almost gaping at her in honest awe.*) I don't understand you.

ROSE. (*As if it's indeed the last thing she expects.*) How *should* you? It isn't to *ask* you to do that that I've *come* to you.

PAUL. (*As with patience for her; waiting in his woeful wonder; speaking simply.*) For *what* have you come?

ROSE. (*As casting about a moment before she says; after an instant.*) You *can* endure it then—the sight of me?

PAUL. Haven't I told you that I thought of going to you?

ROSE. Yes—but you didn't go. You came and went like a sentinel; and if it was to *watch* me—!

PAUL. (*Interrupting her; quietly and simply.*) It wasn't to watch you.

ROSE. (*As quite for curiosity; but all gently.*) Then *what* was it for?

PAUL. (*With a sort of tragic ruefulness —a gesture as of his woe.*) It was to keep myself quiet.

ROSE. (*As with helpless compassion for him.*) But you're *anything* but quiet.

PAUL. (*Dismally allowing it.*) I'm anything but quiet.

ROSE. There's something then that may help you. It's one of two things for which I've come to you. And there's no one but you to care. You may care a very little—it may give you a grain of comfort. (*Then letting him have it all tragically and significantly while he waits.*) Let your comfort be that I've *failed.* (PAUL, *after a long look at her, turns away with a vague dumb gesture; as if it's a part of his sore trouble that, in his wasted strength, he has no out-*

let for emotion, no channel even for pain. She takes in the while his clumsy massive misery; then speaks as if it's the last accepted drop of bitterness of her humiliation and abjection.) No—you loathe my presence.

PAUL. *(Who stands a little in silence with his back to her, as if within him some violence is struggling up; and then with an effort, almost with a gasp, turns round, his open watch in his hand.)* I saw Mr. Vidal.

ROSE. And he told you too he'd come back for me?

PAUL. *(His watch still in his hand and his eyes on it.)* He said there was something he had to do, but that he would meanwhile get ready. He would return immediately with a carriage.

ROSE. That's why I waited. *(As showing herself as she is—all simplified now to what he sees before him.)* I'm ready enough. *(Then after an instant; as resignedly, as helplessly and stoically abandoned.)* But he won't *come.*

PAUL. *(As with his own dry confidence.)* He'll come. *(Yet with his equal sense of the awful nature of her crisis.)* But it's *time.*

ROSE. *(With a dreary shake of her head; as if she has quite made up her mind to this now.)* Not after getting off—not back to the horror and the shame! *(Explaining lucidly her tragic view.)* He *thought* so. No doubt he has *tried.* I do him justice. But it's *beyond* him.

PAUL. *(As if the very desolation of her tone almost convinces him.)* Then what are you waiting for?

ROSE. *(Casting about; as if wondering herself.)* Nothing—now. Thank you. *(She still looks about her—and as if she thinks of the window on the terrace.)* How shall I *go?*

PAUL. *(With his hand raised a moment as to check any precipitate or premature experiment, goes straight to the window, where he stands an instant listening.)* I thought I heard wheels.

ROSE. *(Listening too, but then shaking her head.)* There are *no* wheels. But I can go that way.

PAUL. *(Who turns back to her again heavy and uncertain, and stands wondering and wavering in her path.)* What will become of you?

ROSE. *(With absolute desolate sincerity.)* How do I know and what do I care?

PAUL. *(Before her still and bringing it out as if he hasn't heard her.)* What will *become* of you?—what will *become* of you?

ROSE. *(After an instant; as struck with the sincerity of his tone that she is moved with compassion almost to himself.)* You pity me too *much.* *(Then as from the need, and for the chance, supremely to explain herself.)* I've failed—but I did what I could. *(As even living it over again for herself; as seeing it almost as a passage or a picture of the history of another person.)* It was all that I saw—it was all that was left me. It took hold of me, it *possessed* me. It was the last gleam of a *chance.* *(Then, still, as if she sees a little that she makes him also comprehend it.)* I mean—to make him *take* her. You'll say my calculation was grotesque—my stupidity as ignoble as my crime. All I can answer is that I might none the less have succeeded. People *have,* in worse conditions. But I don't defend myself—I'm face to face with my mistake. I'm face to face with it for ever—and that's how I wish you to *see* me. Look at me, Mr. Paul—*well!*

PAUL. *(As if it's the only answer he can make.)* I would have done *anything* for you! Why didn't you *speak* to me—why didn't you tell me what you were thinking? There was nothing you couldn't have told me—nothing that wouldn't have brought me *nearer.* If I had *known* your abasement—!

ROSE. *(Taking him up as he breaks.)* What would you have done?

PAUL. *I* would have *saved* you.

ROSE. *(Consciously repeating it again as from the desire really to know.)* What would you have done?

PAUL. *(Very simply.)* Everything.

ROSE. *(Watching him while he goes again to the window, and speaking but after a moment of this.)* Yes, I've *lost* you—I've *lost* you. And *you* were the thing I might have had. *He* told me that, and I knew it.

PAUL. (*At the window; but having faced round.*) "He" told you?

ROSE. He tried to put me off on you. (*To let him have the benefit of it all.*) That was what *finished* me. (*Then after an instant; the transition all abrupt.*) Of course they'll marry.

PAUL. Oh yes—they'll marry.

ROSE. But not soon—I assume.

PAUL. Not soon. But sooner than they think.

ROSE. Do you know *already* what they think?

PAUL. Yes—that it will never be.

ROSE. Never?

PAUL. Coming about so horribly. But *some* day—it will come.

ROSE. It will come. And I shall have *done* it for him. That's more than even you would have done for *me!*

PAUL. (*As if strange inconsistent tears have forced themselves through his closed lids; and as if speaking, too, with an admiration still more perverse, more inconsequent and more at odds with his words.*) You're too horrible. You're too horrible. You're too horrible.

ROSE. (*Not resenting it; allowing now for everything.*) Oh, I talk only to *you:* it's all for *you.* Remember, please, that I shall never speak again. (*Then as if it's all over —looking about her and at the clock that's in view.*) You see he daren't come.

PAUL. (*As if afraid at last she may be right; looking again at his watch.*) I'll go *with* you.

ROSE. (*As doubting; challenging; not moving.*) How far?

PAUL. (*As if what he is prepared for is beyond any words; simply repeating it.*) I'll go *with* you.

ROSE. (*As believing it now of him; looking at him hard and as if in her eyes too there are tears; speaking then as if fairly awestruck at the lapse, at the drop, at the apparent extinction in these conditions, of her danger.*) My Safety—my Safety!

PAUL. (*Who has gone round now definitely for the hat that he was about to take up before her entrance.*) I'll go *with* you.

ROSE. (*As for a supreme scruple.*) Won't

he *need* you?

PAUL. Tony? (*Quite blank.*) For what?

ROSE. For help.

PAUL. (*After an instant; considering but dismissing it.*) He *wants* none.

ROSE. You mean he has nothing to *fear?*

PAUL. From any *suspicion?* Nothing.

ROSE. (*As entering into it then; as seeing, as understanding.*) That's his advantage. (*As putting it really in a nutshell.*) People *like* him too much.

PAUL. (*As in full dry assent.*) People like him too much. (*Then seeing DENNIS, at the open window, on the terrace.*) Mr. Vidal!

(*Re-enter, so far as the threshold of the long window, DENNIS VIDAL.*)

VIDAL. (*With a signal in the form of a short sharp peremptory gesture.*) Come! (PAUL, *at this puts down the hat he has taken up; he turns away to leave* ROSE *at liberty.* ROSE, *meanwhile, who has taken in, with a smothered revulsion,* VIDAL'S *fidelity, after all, to his vow, which breaks in upon* PAUL'S *offer has a moment of deep uncertainty; in which she approaches him while* VIDAL *waits; in which she lingers and wavers desperately as with a last word to speak. As* PAUL *but stands rigid, however, she falters, choking her impulse and giving her word but the form of a look; which holds her thus a moment with her eyes on him. At this* DENNIS *speaks sternly again from his half-seen station.*) Come!

ROSE *has another momentary struggle, her eyes always on* PAUL, *while the two men again stand motionless, only* PAUL *the more passive and detached; ending, thus, in her silent decision at last and her move up to the window. Here* VIDAL *puts forth an imperative strong arm and seizes her; they are seen to pass together quickly into the night.* PAUL, *left alone, again sounds a long sigh; this time it is the deep breath of a man who has seen a great danger averted.*

He approaches a table that stands more or less at centre, sinks into the chair beside it and then, with his

*arms on it, miserably drops his head
upon them and buries his face.*[1]

---

[1] The novel ended in a scene between Tony
and Paul. This was kept in one of the manuscripts of the play, then crossed out so that
the play ended with Paul alone on the stage.
In a second manuscript James wrote in a stage
direction for Tony, as follows: TONY BREAM,
*after a further movement comes back, and is
struck by the sight and attitude of* PAUL, *who
doesn't move.* TONY *comes nearer to him and
looks down at him for an instant as if to
speak; then understanding and thinking
better of it, changes his mind and softly and
significantly goes out, leaving him while the
Curtain falls.* In two other manuscripts the
play ends with Paul alone on the stage.

The Outcry

A Comedy In Three Acts

1909

EDITOR'S FOREWORD

Early in 1909 Charles Frohman, the American producer, began to lay plans for a repertory season in London at the Duke of York's Theatre. The moving spirit behind the repertory plan was J. M. Barrie. He enlisted the aid of those men who had contributed to the success of the repertory movement in England which, even before the turn of the century, had begun to breathe new life into the British stage. Harley Granville-Barker, whose management with John E. Vedrenne of the Court Theatre had played so large a role in establishing the reputation of Bernard Shaw and had introduced new playwrights to the British public (including Granville-Barker himself), joined their ranks. They engaged the discriminating services of Allan Wade, who had worked with Granville-Barker and who at the moment was in charge of the Abbey Theatre's season in London. Shaw, John Galsworthy, Granville-Barker, Somerset Maugham, John Masefield and Henry James were invited to write plays. Shaw wrote *Misalliance,* Galsworthy *Justice,* Granville-Barker *The Madras House* and Henry James *The Outcry.* Barrie contributed *The Twelve-Pound Look* and *Old Friends,* two one-act plays, and arranged George Meredith's unfinished comedy *The Sentimentalists* for the stage.

Frohman, in announcing the season, said that "whatever it accomplishes, it will represent the combined resources of actor and playwright, working with each other, a combination that seems to me to represent the most necessary foundation of any theatrical success."

This time the omens were decidedly favorable. James found himself dealing not with a "managerial abyss" but with fellow-craftsmen who appreciated his work and who were imbued with the same high ideals as his own for the British stage. He had met Granville-Barker earlier at the home of H. G. Wells and had been captivated by his personality. Granville-Barker was the man of the theatre *par excellence*—actor, manager, director, producer, playwright. Barrie, Galsworthy and Shaw were well established in their field. They drew James into their fellowship; he moved now, for the first time, in a veritable fraternity of dramatists and he found himself drawn, at this moment, into a very special "outcry" which these dramatists were raising over the British censorship of plays.

James joined in the "outcry" with spirit. There was sitting, during that summer of 1909, a Joint Select Committee of the House of Lords and the House of Commons hearing evidence of playwrights and men of letters in connection with the activities of the Lord Chamberlain, whose authority to license plays gave him full power to judge—and to suppress—works of art. James had been one of the signers of a protest in 1907 against the refusal to licence one of Edward Garnett's plays. Earlier, Shaw's *Mrs. Warren's Profession* had fallen under the axe of the Lord Chamberlain and now Granville-Barker's *Waste* had suffered a similar fate. There is a rare newspaper photo of James, in top hat, a massive figure beside the diminutive Barrie, arriving to attend one of the hearings. It was Galsworthy who read a statement by Henry James into the official record of the hearings during his evidence on August 12, 1909. James spoke out in terms that deserve resurrection from the official report in which they have been buried all these years:

> I answer your [the Commission's] appeal on the censor question to the best of my small ability. I *do* consider that the situation made by the Englishman of letters ambitious of writing for the stage has less dignity—thanks to the Censor's arbitrary rights upon his work—than that of any other man of letters in Europe, and that this fact may well be, or rather *must* be, deterrent to men of any intellectual independence and self-respect. I think this circumstance represents accordingly an impoverishment of our theatre; and it tends to deprive it of intellectual life, of the *importance* to which a free choice of subjects and illustrations directly ministers, and to confine it to the trivial and the puerile. It is difficult to express the depth of dismay and disgust with which an author of books in this country finds it impressed upon him, in passing into the province of the theatre with the view of laboring there, that he has to reckon anxiously with an obscure and irresponsible Mr. So-and-so, who may by law peremptorily demand of him that he shall make his own work square, at vital points, with Mr. So-and-so's personal and, intellectually and critically speaking, wholly unauthoritative preferences prejudices and ignorances, and that the less original, the less important and the less interesting it is, and the more vulgar and superficial and futile, the more it is likely so to square. He thus encounters an arrogation of critical authority and the critical veto, with the power to enforce its decisions, that is without a parallel in any other civilized country and which has in this one the effect of relegating the theatre to the position of a mean minor art, and of condemning it to ignoble dependences, poverties and pusillanimities. We rub our eyes, we writers accustomed to freedom in all other walks, to think that this cause has still to be argued in England.

There was thus a very real "outcry" in progress when James settled down that autumn to complete his play about another kind of outcry—the story of an American art collector's attempt to "raid" British treasures. It is not as curious a theme for James to have chosen as might be supposed; he had from far back witnessed the raids of wealthy Americans such as Mrs. John L. Gardner on the art riches of the Continent. In a note of July 15, 1895, he spoke of "the age of Mrs. Jack," as he familiarly called her, and added, "The Americans looming up—dim, vast, portentous—in their millions—like gathering waves—the barbarians of the Roman Empire." There is a similar thought in the play in which the Americans are likened to a "conquering horde" armed with check books. In a sense his theme for *The Outcry* was the reverse of *The High Bid*. In that play an American woman appears, more British than the British, to alert them against sacrificing their heritage; in *The Outcry* the voices are raised by Britons against the indifference of their fellow-countrymen who would allow their heritage to be carried off, piece by piece, by outsiders. The American, Brecken-ridge Bender, is a hard-headed and somewhat predatory Christopher Newman, not unfavorably drawn, neither villain nor hero, but a force and a Check Book, to be reckoned with. James himself saw in the theme a "larger morality"—the degree in which owners of precious works of art "hold them in trust . . . for the nation, and may themselves, as lax guardians, be held to account by public opinion."

James threw himself into the writing of this—his last play, as it proved—with all his old intensity and fervor. Allan Wade, who was play-reader for the enterprise, writes: "I remember very well the manuscript of *The Outcry* and my excitement in reading it, and my conviction that it would be far over the heads of our rather stupid audiences." He added: "It is true that James's dramatic sense was more in tune with the French than the English theatre of his day—but had he been given more occasion for actual and practical work *in* the theatre he would probably have been able to modify his tendency to excessive length and our theatre would have gained a really fine dramatist."

He began to work on the play during the early autumn of 1909. By that time he had drawn up a scenario and he wrote to Granville-Barker on October 16: "I can't . . . deny myself the pleasure of telling you that I feel myself ready to be getting on with *The Outcry* (if you'll kindly not mention the title!). . . . I have worked at it with great intensity and interest. I have got hold of it, I think, or it of me; but I shall need a small number of weeks more to finish it." He was in London in December 1909 working strenuously in his rooms at the Reform Club, sending great batches of manuscript to Lamb House to be typed by Miss Bosanquet. On December 2 he sent the greater part of the third act, writing to her: "London is mild and convenient and I shall *wholly* finish III before I stir. On my return we must do extra-time work of compression and re-copying." He added: "Haste and urgency are in the air." Two days later he sent another fifty pages of copy and a corrected earlier type-script. By December 17 the play was completed and in his notebook of that date, while elaborating the theme he later converted into *The Ivory Tower,* he wrote in a characteristic outburst: "More than ever then, at any rate, does it seem to me worth my while to cipher out the subject of this thing . . . after the manner of my late so absorbing and endearing plunge into the whole process of the *Outcry*. . . . The process of the *Outcry* has been of enormous benefit and interest to me in all this connection—it has cast so large and rich and vivid a light upon my path: the august light, I mean, of the whole matter of method."

He spent a cheerful Christmas in Rye close to his warm hearth, "a fine old Yuletide observance in general" but early in the new year began to experience extreme physical discomfort. On January 12 he revised Act I and in a message to Miss Bosanquet at her lodgings wrote: "I am not feeling very famous. . . ." He was in reality quite ill; digestive disorders, nervousness, a great sense of depression ("agitation, trepidation, black melancholia and weakness" was his own description of it). He took to his bed and remained there for weeks. There is little doubt that factors contributing to his depression were the failure of the New York Edition over which he had labored for more than three years and which now was having a highly restricted sale, as well as the intensity and anxiety with which he had written *The Outcry*. The cycle of rejection by the larger reading public had come full round: in the 1890's he had struggled for creative survival by essaying the drama and thereafter had released his anxieties into ghostly tales and stories of frustrated writers. Now at sixty-seven, in his isolated country retreat, after expending great resources of energy on *The Other House* and *The Outcry*, he quite suddenly collapsed. He remained an invalid throughout 1910 but, faced with the more serious illness of his brother, mustered strength for his American journey during that summer. Long before this all hope of producing *The Outcry* had been abandoned. There had been difficulties other than James's ill health and not the least of these was the casting of the play. Efforts were made to obtain the services of Sir John Hare for the role of Lord Theign; Gerald du Maurier, son of James's old friend, was sought for Hugh Crimble and Irene Vanbrugh, who had played a minor role in *Guy Domville*, for the part of Lady Grace. It had been planned to cast an American actor in the role of Bender.

Early in March, James's nephew and namesake, William's oldest son, came out to Lamb House to be with his uncle. The third Henry James, then a young lawyer, was able to minister greatly to his uncle's morale. "I am still having a very difficult and uphill time," James wrote in a pencilled scrawl to Miss Bosanquet in London, "with the one mitigation that one of my Boston nephews, the eldest, has just come out to be with me and is a blessed support. . . . There can be no production of *The Outcry* without my personal participation at preparation and rehearsal—and till there is a possibility of that no calculating. There can even be no casting of the piece without my presence in London. So all that is dark."

The third Henry James, remembered very well in later years James's preoccupation with *The Outcry* at this time. There was a day when the novelist, in bed, restless, irritable, bored, gave him a telegram to send off about the play—he seemed to recall it was to Granville-Barker—and upon the nephew expressing an interest, the ailing Henry began to speak of it: he outlined the plot, he recited speeches, he described the action, he sketched the form he hoped it would take on production, talking endlessly of it through the afternoon, animated with the re-creation of his work. It provided him, the younger Henry recalled, with some badly needed distraction.

Later, when he was up and about, having his good days and his bad, taking short motor rides and seeking relaxation ("I have had a perfect Hell of a Time—since just after Christmas—nearly fifteen long weeks of dismal, dreary, interminable illness," he wrote to one correspondent) there began the now-traditional ordeal of the cutting of the play. "He hated doing it, of course," Granville-Barker related, "and he had to be induced to part with first one bit; then after

awhile another. But it was really necessary. He was always good about it . . ."
Actually he bowed to the authoritative views of Granville-Barker and Barrie but
he inwardly resented the cuts. Later, when plans for production had been abandoned, he wrote to Miss Bosanquet asking her to re-type the entire play. He
wanted, he said, "a copy of it in which the *last* awful cuts (thousands and thousands of words slashed out loathingly, by me in May, sick and suffering, and
under Barker's and Barrie's even then urgent requisition) shall be embodied."

The collapse of *The Outcry* was followed by the collapse of Frohman's entire
repertory season with the death of King Edward VII on May 6, 1910. The
theatres closed down during the period of the funeral and national mourning.
This was the final blow to a season which, Granville-Barker said, Frohman had
been conducting "with great gallantry but—as it was his nature to—with rather
reckless extravagance." *The Outcry* had not been cast; Frohman paid a forfeit
to James of £200 and the novelist recovered his rights to the play.

During the next year James converted *The Outcry* into a novel and to his
astonishment it promptly ran into several editions. A year and a half after
James's death the play was produced by the Incorporated Stage Society. It was
at one of the two performances given July 1 and July 3, 1917 that Bernard Shaw
conducted the experiment he described in a letter to the *Times Literary Supplement* published on May 17, 1923:

"I experimented on my friends between the acts by repeating some of the
most exquisite sentences from the dialogue. I spoke fairly and distinctly, but
not one of my victims could understand me or even identify the words I was
uttering." Shaw came to the conclusion that "there is a literary language which
is perfectly intelligible to the eye, yet utterly unintelligible to the ear even when
it is easily speakable by the mouth . . . a writer who has always worked for
publication alone is likely to fail in direct proportion to his inveterate practice
and his virtuosity. . . . But the disastrous plays of James, and the stage failures
of novelists obviously much more richly endowed by nature and culture than
many of the successful playwrights with whom they have tried to compete,
suggest that they might have succeeded if only they had understood that as the
pen and the *viva vox* are different instruments, their parts must be scored
accordingly."

Granville-Barker, who had a more intimate knowledge of the text of *The
Outcry*, did not share Shaw's opinion, feeling that the problems presented by
James's dialogue in his final plays were no greater than those of the Restoration
comedies. The dialogue, he said, "is artificial—very; but that is legitimate. It
might be hard to speak but I think that most of it could be made very effective
once the right method had been found (I speak from memory of it). . . . Actors
certainly could not blend it with 'melodramatic' acting: this was probably
the fault with *The Saloon*—the incongruity. But I suggest to you to place it
beside a Congreve and a Wycherley. It may not be so good as the first but I
believe you'd find more style and bite in it than in the second."

CHARACTERS

THE EARL OF THEIGN, K.G., etc., *fifty-five*
LORD JOHN, *thirty-seven*
HUGH CRIMBLE, *twenty-nine*
MR. BRECKENRIDGE BENDER, *fifty-six*
BANKS ⎱
GOTCH ⎰ *Servants*
LADY SANDGATE, *mature*
LADY GRACE, *twenty-five*

The Action, highly contemporaneous, takes place in Act First at Lord Theign's House in the country; in the two others, after short intervals, at Lady Sandgate's in Bruton Street; from the Easter Holidays on.

THE OUTCRY

ACT FIRST

The hall at Dedborough Park. Entrance at left from the vestibule, main approach to the house, etc. Entrance centre from the terrace, gardens, park itself, etc. Entrance at right from other reception-rooms, "saloon," etc. BANKS, *the Butler, comes in from left, ushering* LORD JOHN, *and a minute afterwards* LADY SANDGATE *appears, entering from the terrace with a folded telegram in her hand.*

BANKS. No, my lord, no stranger has arrived. But I'll see if anyone has come in— or *who* has. (*Then as he perceives* LADY SANDGATE, *who has not heard the foregoing.*) Lord John, my lady. (*Exit* BANKS *to left.*)

LORD JOHN. I luckily find *you* at least, Lady Sandgate—they tell me Theign's off somewhere.

LADY SANDGATE. Only in the Park: open to-day for a schoolfeast from Dedborough —as you may have made out from the avenue; giving good advice, at the top of his lungs, to four hundred and fifty children.

LORD JOHN. (*Amused.*) Oh, he's so great on such occasions that I'm sorry to be missing it.

LADY SANDGATE. I've *had* to miss it—I've just left them. But he had even then been going on for twenty minutes, and I dare say that if you care to take a look you'll find him still *at* it.

LORD JOHN. Thanks—I should like to; but I came over partly to meet a friend who's motoring down by appointment, and about due now—whom I think I should be here to receive; and also a little, I confess, in the hope of a glimpse of Lady Grace—if you can perhaps imagine *that!*

LADY SANDGATE. I can imagine it perfectly—it quite sticks out of you. But you haven't then come from town?

LORD JOHN. No—I'm for three days at Chanter with my Mother; whom—as she kindly lent me her car—I should have rather liked to bring.

LADY SANDGATE. (*Before he can go on.*) But whom you doubtless had to leave, by her preference, just sitting down to Bridge! Ah yes—we know something of that!

LORD JOHN. You too then?

LADY SANDGATE. I mean in this house generally; where I'm so often made welcome, you see, and where—

LORD JOHN. (*Taking her up.*) Where your jolly good footing quite sticks out of *you*—perhaps you'll let me say!

LADY SANDGATE. You can't say more than I feel—and am *proud* to feel!—at being of comfort when they're worried.

LORD JOHN. And they're worried now, you imply, because my terrible Mother is capable of heavy gains and of making a great noise if she isn't paid?

LADY SANDGATE. Well, poor Kitty Imber has thrown herself, with her impossible big debt, upon her Father; whom she seems to think herself entitled to "look to" even more as such a lovely young widow, with a good jointure, than she did, formerly, as the mere most beautiful daughter at home.

LORD JOHN. And the ways and traditions of this place make it the place in England where one feels most the false note of a dishevelled and bankrupt charming elder daughter, breaking in with a list of her gaming debts—to say nothing of others!—

and wailing to have at least *those* wiped out in the interest of her reputation? Exactly so, and just *that,* I assure you, is a large part of the reason I like to come here—since I personally don't come with any such associations.

LADY SANDGATE. Not the association of bankruptcy—no; as you represent the payee. You represent the belief—very natural, I grant—that more than *one* perverse and extravagant flower will be unlikely on such a fine healthy old stem; and, consistently with that, the hope of arranging with our admirable host here that he shall lend a helpful hand to your commending yourself to dear Grace.

LORD JOHN. (*After an instant, as practically acknowledging.*) Then if I'm urgent you think he's likely to listen to me?

LADY SANDGATE. Well, the person he most listens to just now—and in fact at any time, as you know—is his imperative elder daughter.

LORD JOHN. Lady Imber's *here?*

LADY SANDGATE. She arrived last night; and—as we have other visitors—she seems to have set up a side-show in the garden.

LORD JOHN. Then she'll "draw," immensely, of course—as she always does. But where's Lady Grace?

LADY SANDGATE. Mightn't you go and see?

LORD JOHN. I would in a moment—if I hadn't got to look out for another matter. Meeting an American friend who motors down—

LADY SANDGATE. (*Interrupting him with surprise.*) You too have an American friend who motors down—?

LORD JOHN. (*In full assent.*) Mr. Breckenridge Bender.

LADY SANDGATE. You *know* my Breckenridge? Why, I hoped he was coming for *me!*

LORD JOHN. Had he told you so?

LADY SANDGATE. (*Offering him her loose telegram.*) He has sent me *that*—which, delivered to me in the Park, has brought me in to receive him.

LORD JOHN. (*Reading out.*) "Missing you in Bruton Street, start in pursuit and hope to overtake you about 4." Why, he has been engaged these three days to coincide

with *me* here, and not to fail him has been part of my business.

LADY SANDGATE. Then why does he say it's *me* he's pursuing?

LORD JOHN. Dear Lady Sandgate, he's pursuing expensive works of art. But what he arranged with me was that he should see the Dedborough pictures in general, and the great Sir Joshua [1] in particular—of which he had heard so much and to which I have thus been glad to assist him.

LADY SANDGATE. (*Struck.*) Does he want to *buy* Sir Joshua?

LORD JOHN. (*Struck in turn.*) Is that wonder for *sale?*

LADY SANDGATE. Not, surely, by any possibility. Fancy dear proud Theign—! (*Then as she sees the* BUTLER *reappear.*) But I judge your company is wanted.

(*Re-enter* BANKS, *centre, who hears this as he comes.*)

BANKS. By her ladyship, my lord, who sends to hope you'll join them below the Terrace.

LADY SANDGATE. (*To* LORD JOHN.) Ah, Grace hopes—there you *are!*

LORD JOHN. Then I rush! (*Exit* LORD JOHN, *centre.*)

BANKS. Will you have tea, my lady?

LADY SANDGATE. (*A little vague.*) Oh thanks—when they all come in.

BANKS. They'll scarcely *all,* my lady. There's tea in her ladyship's tent; but it has also been ordered for the Saloon.

LADY SANDGATE. Ah then Mr. Bender will be glad—!

BANKS. (*At right, seeing* BENDER *at left.*) Here he must be, my lady. (*Enter* MR. BENDER, *left, ushered by a* FOOTMAN *who silently retires, left. Exit also* BANKS, *right.*)

LADY SANDGATE. Welcome, dear Mr. Bender! Will you have tea—in the Saloon?

BENDER. (*Not immensely eager.*) Why, the very first thing?

LADY SANDGATE. (*Laughing, indifferent.*) Ah have it last if you like!

BENDER. You see your English teas—!

LADY SANDGATE. They're too much for you?

BENDER. Well, they're too *many.* I think

---

[1] Sir Joshua Reynolds (1723–1792) the most celebrated figure in the English school of painting.

I've had two or three on the road—at any rate my man did. I like to do business *before*—

LADY SANDGATE. (*Amused, gracious.*) Before tea, Mr. Bender?

BENDER. (*Genial.*) Before Everything, Lady Sandgate.

LADY SANDGATE. (*Almost affectionately appealing.*) Then you've *come* to do business? To tell me you *will* treat?

BENDER. (*Recalling, but only after an instant, what she means.*) For your Grandmother, Lady Sandgate?

LADY SANDGATE. My Grandmother's *Mother*, Mr. Bender—the greatest of all Lawrences; [2] as you acknowledged, you know, in our talk in Bruton Street. Your telegram made me at once fondly hope you'd be arriving to conclude.

BENDER. "Conclude"? You ladies want to get there before the road's so much as laid, or the country's safe! (*Then pausing before a smallish picture.*) Do you know what this *here* is?

LADY SANDGATE. Oh Mr. Bender you can't have *that*—and you must really understand that you can't have Everything! You mustn't expect to ravage Dedborough.

BENDER. I guess it's a bogus Cuyp [3]—but I know Lord Theign *has* things. He won't do business?

LADY SANDGATE. He's not in the least, and never can be, in *my* tight place; but he's as proud as he's kind, dear man, and as solid as he's proud—so that if you came down under a different impression—!

BENDER. I came on an *understanding*—that I should find my friend Lord John, and that Lord Theign would, on his introduction, kindly let me look round. But being before lunch in Bruton Street I knocked at your door—

LADY SANDGATE. For another look at my Lawrence?

BENDER. For another look at *you*, Lady Landgate—your Grandmother wasn't required. Informed you were *here*, and struck with the coincidence of my being myself

presently due, I dispatched you my wire, on coming away, just to keep up your spirits. Only meanwhile, to keep up mine, where's Lord John?

LADY SANDGATE. (*Who has become aware of* LADY GRACE *at centre.*) Lady Grace must know.

(*Enter* LADY GRACE, *centre.*)

LADY SANDGATE. My dear Grace, this is Mr. Breckenridge Bender.

GRACE. Of whom Lord John has told me and whom I'm glad to see. Lord John is detained a moment in the Park, open to-day to a big Temperance schoolfeast, where our party is mostly gathered; so that if you care to go out—!

BENDER. Are there any good *pictures* in the Park?

GRACE. (*Amused.*) We find our Park *itself* rather a good Picture!

BENDER. (*Smiling, dubious.*) With a big Temperance schoolfeast?

LADY SANDGATE. Mr. Bender's a great *judge* of Pictures.

BENDER. Will there be more tea?

GRACE. Oh there'll be plenty of tea!

BENDER. Well, Lady Grace, I'm after Pictures, but I take them "neat." May I go round right here?

LADY SANDGATE. Perhaps, love, you'll let me show him.

GRACE. A moment, dear. Do go round, Mr. Bender—at your ease. Everything's open and visible, and you'll have the place to yourself.

BENDER. I'll be in clover! And "The beautiful Duchess of Waterbridge"?

GRACE. (*Pointing off right.*) At the very end of *those* rooms.

BENDER. About thirty, *are* there? Well, I'll work right *along*. (*Exit* BENDER, *right.*)

GRACE. Lord John warned me he was "funny"—but you already *know* him?

LADY SANDGATE. (*Momentarily evasive.*) He thinks your little Cuyp a fraud.

GRACE. *That* one? The Wretch! But you've met him before?

LADY SANDGATE. Just a little—in town. Being "after Pictures" he has been after my Greatgrandmother.

GRACE. *She* must have found him funny! But he can clearly take care of himself—while Kitty takes care of Lord John, and

---

[2] Sir Thomas Lawrence (1769–1830), fashionable portrait painter of his age.

[3] Albert Cuyp (1620–1691), most famous member of a distinguished family of Dutch painters.

while you, if you'll be so good, go back and support Father—in the hour of his triumph: which he wants you so much to witness that he complains of your desertion and goes even so far as to accuse you of sneaking away from it.

LADY SANDGATE. But aren't you then failing him quite as much?

GRACE. Ah, I'm not at all the same thing; and as I'm the person in the world he least misses—!

LADY SANDGATE. You've been free to return and wait for Lord John?

GRACE. I've not come back to wait for Lord John. Kindly tell my Father that I'm expecting Mr. Crimble; of whom I've spoken to him even if he doesn't remember, and who bicycles this afternoon ten miles over, from where he's staying—with some people we don't know—to look at the Pictures, about which he's awfully keen.

LADY SANDGATE. Ah, like Mr. Bender?

GRACE. No—not at all, I think, like Mr. Bender.

LADY SANDGATE. May I ask then—if one's to meet him—who he is?

GRACE. Oh, Father knows—or ought to —that I sat next to him a month ago, in London, at dinner, and that he then told me he was working, tooth and nail, at what he called the "beautiful and wonderful new science of Connoisseurship"; that he was to spend Easter in these parts, and that he should like awfully to be allowed some day to come over and make the acquaintance of our things. I told him nothing would be easier; a note from him arrived before luncheon—

LADY SANDGATE. (Anticipating.) And it's for him you've come in!

GRACE. It's for him I've come in. If I sent for news of Lord John it was because Kitty insisted—though as soon as he appeared she pounced on him, and I left him in her hands.

LADY SANDGATE. She wants to talk of you to him. But what is she going to gain by it?

GRACE. Perhaps she's to gain a commission!

LADY SANDGATE. Is he in a position to pay her one?

GRACE. I dare say the Duchess is! If I

marry him she goes free.

LADY SANDGATE. She has her creditor's release?

GRACE. For every shilling!

LADY SANDGATE. And if you *don't* marry him?

GRACE. She of course throws herself more than ever on poor Father.

LADY SANDGATE. Then *could* you marry him? I mean if between them all—Lord John himself, Kitty, your Father *and* the Duchess—they should convince you that he cares for you.

GRACE. The Duchess will never convince me of anything but that she simply *wants* me; wants me for my Father's so particularly beautiful position, and my Mother's so supremely great people, and for everything we have been and have done, and *still* are and *still* have: except of course poor not-at-all-model Kitty!

LADY SANDGATE. For the general so immaculate connection.

GRACE. Well, we *haven't* had false notes. We've scarcely even had bad moments.

LADY SANDGATE. Yes—you've been beatific! (*Then seeing* HUGH CRIMBLE.) But this must be your friend.

(*Exit* LADY SANDGATE, *centre. Enter* HUGH CRIMBLE, *ushered by* FOOTMAN, *from left.*)

HUGH. (*A spare, intelligent, keen, clean-shaven young man, of a just slightly Bohemian air; his Bohemianism, however, rather corrected by his constant wearing of pince-nez.*) Awfully kind of you—in the midst of the great doings I noticed—to have found a *moment* for me.

GRACE. I left the great doings—which are almost *over!*—so that your precious time shouldn't be taken to hunt for me.

HUGH. You came in on purpose?—as kind to me as you were from that first moment! I haven't forgotten a bit of it, Lady Grace.

GRACE. Neither have I, Mr. Crimble. My neighbour on the other side wanted to talk to me of the White City!

HUGH. And I only to talk—or at least to hear—about *this.* My eye—I say, I say!

GRACE. Oh we've nothing particular in the Hall!

HUGH. (*Laughing.*) Nothing, I see, but

Claudes [4] and Cuyps! I *am* an Ogre—before a new and rare feast!

GRACE. Then won't you begin—as a first course—with some tea? (*And then before he can reply.*) If the other, that is—for there has been an Ogre before you—has *left* any!

HUGH. Some tea with pleasure—but when you talk but of *a* fellow-feaster I should have supposed that, on such a day as this especially, there would be a continuous *table d'hôte.*

GRACE. Ah, you can't work Sports in our Gallery and Saloon—the banging or whacking or shoving amusements that are all most people care for; unless perhaps your own peculiar one, as I understand you, of playing football—!

HUGH. (*Interrupting.*) With the name and signs and stories and "styles"—the so often vain legend—not to be *too* abusive! —of Author or Subject or School? (*Good-humoured.*) Ah, that's a game at which we can *all* play!

GRACE. But scarcely at which we can all *score!*

HUGH. (*Looking afresh about him a moment.*) Certainly no one can ever have scored much in *these* sacred places; which express so the grand impunity of their pride, their claims, their assurance!

GRACE. Ah, who knows—when you talk of our "assurance!"—whether even now Mr. Bender isn't pulling us to pieces?

HUGH. (*Struck as with a remembered name.*) Mr. Bender?

GRACE. The rich American who's going round.

HUGH. The Wretch who bagged Lady Lappington's Longhi? [5]—writing her his cheque there, before he left the house, for his infernal Eight Thousand!

GRACE. (*Smiling.*) Well, it's no use his writing *us* cheques—for Eight, or Eighteen, or even Eighty!

HUGH. Gracious goodness, I hope not!

The man doesn't surely *suppose* you'd traffic?

GRACE. I don't quite know what he supposes. But people *have* trafficked; people *do*—people are trafficking all round.

HUGH. Ah, that's exactly what deprives me of my rest—and, as a lover of our vast and beneficent art-wealth, poisons my waking hours. That art-wealth is at the mercy of a leak there appears to be no means of *stopping*. It's going out of our distracted country at a quicker rate than the very quickest—a century and more ago—of its ever coming *in!*

GRACE. Well, I suppose it came in—save for those awkward Elgin Marbles! [6]—mainly by *purchase*, didn't it? We ourselves largely took it away, didn't we? We didn't *grow* it all.

HUGH. We grew some of the loveliest flowers—and on the whole to-day the most *exposed*. We grew, for example, your famous, your splendid Sir Joshua.

GRACE. Yes—that *is* the one Mr. Bender seemed particularly "after."

HUGH. (*Sombre.*) Then he'd be capable of anything.

GRACE. Of anything, no doubt, but of making my Father capable—! And you haven't, at any rate, so much as *seen* the Picture.

HUGH. I saw it at the Guildhall—three years ago; and am almost afraid of getting again, with a fresh sense of its Beauty, a sharper sense of its Danger. (*Then as he takes in once more the so interesting place and things.*) I don't know what I mightn't want to *do* to Mr. Bender, on the chance—and yet it's not of my temptation to violence, after all, that I'm most afraid. It's of the brutal mistake of one's breaking—with one's priggish, precious modernity and one's possibly futile discriminations—into a *general* situation and picture so serene and sound and right. What should

---

4 Claude Lorrain, also called Claude Gellée (1600–1682), French landscape painter.

5 It is difficult to judge which Longhi James had in mind, Giuseppe Longhi (1776–1831), Pietro (1702–1762), Pietro's son Alessandro (1733–1813), Luca Longhi (1507–1580) and his daughter Barbara (1552–1619), all Italian painters.

6 The Elgin Marbles, "awkward" because they were brought to England from Greece between 1800 and 1813 by Lord Elgin, former British ambassador to Constantinople, who was accused by some of robbing Greece of its finest art. The Marbles were purchased from Elgin by the British Government in 1816 and are now in the British Museum. Some Britons still advocate return of the Marbles to Greece.

one do here, out of respect for that felicity, but hold one's breath and walk on tiptoe? The very celebrations and consecrations, as you tell me, instinctively stay outside. I *saw* that all—while we talked in London—as your natural setting and your native air, but then ten minutes on the spot have made it sink into my spirit. You're a case, all together, of enchanted harmony, of perfect *equilibrium*—there's nothing more to be done or said!

GRACE. (*After an instant, for all reply, directing his attention to the small landscape that* MR. BENDER *has looked at and reflected on.*) For what do you take that little landscape?

HUGH. (*Approaching it, interested.*) Why, don't you *know?* It's a jolly little Vandermeer.[7]

GRACE. It's not a base imitation?

HUGH. (*Looking again—then at a loss.*) An imitation of Vandermeer?

GRACE. Mr. Bender thinks of Cuyp.

HUGH. (*With sharp impatience.*) Then Mr. Bender's *doubly* dangerous!

GRACE. (*Laughing.*) Singly is enough! But you see you *have* to speak.

HUGH. Oh to *him*, rather, after that—if you'll *take* me to him!

GRACE. Yes, then! (*But then seeing, as she speaks,* LORD JOHN, *centre.*) But ah Lord John!

(*Re-enter* LORD JOHN, *centre.*)

LORD JOHN. (*Eagerly, and as having taken her exclamation, heard by him, for a greeting.*) Ah Lady Grace! I came back particularly to find you!

GRACE. (*Rather pulled up and a little at a loss.*) I was taking Mr. Crimble (*whom she has the manner of more or less introducing*) to see the Pictures. (*And then a little more pointed, as* LORD JOHN, *with his mere non-committal stare, doesn't appear at all to recognise the introduction.*) Mr. Crimble is one of the quite new Connoisseurs.

HUGH. (*Laughingly deprecating.*) Oh, I'm at the very lowest round of the ladder! But I aspire!

GRACE. You'll mount! (*Then as harmonisingly to draw in* LORD JOHN.) It's to

Lord John we owe Mr. Bender's acquaintance.

HUGH. (*After a look at* LORD JOHN.) Then do you happen to know, sir, what your friend means to *do* with his spoil? Can't he be induced to have a little *mercy?*

LORD JOHN. A "little"? How much do you *want?*

HUGH. Well, one wants somehow to be able to stay his hand.

LORD JOHN. I doubt if you can any more stay Mr. Bender's hand than you can empty his purse!

HUGH. Ah, the Despoilers!—but it's *we* who are base! (*But then instantly controlling himself with a turn to* GRACE.) Forgive me if I have it on the *brain!* And show me first of all, won't you? the Moretto of Brescia.[8]

GRACE. You know about the Moretto of Brescia?

HUGH. Why, didn't you tell me yourself?

GRACE. (*As she recalls.*) Clearly—yes—how I must have swaggered! (*To* LORD JOHN.) Will you also come?

LORD JOHN. I hoped you were at leisure —for something I particularly wish—!

GRACE. (*Taking a rapid decision and turning at once to* HUGH *with a smile.*) Let Mr. Bender then show you! And there are some things in the Library too.

HUGH. (*Looking at her hard a moment; then accepting her choice and the difference of his fate.*) Thank-you! (*Exit* CRIMBLE, *right.*)

LORD JOHN. Your friend seems remarkably hot!

GRACE. He has cycled twenty miles. But (*smiling*)—well, he *does* appear to care for what he cares for!

LORD JOHN. (*After an instant.*) Have you known him long?

GRACE. No—not long.

LORD JOHN. Nor seen him often?

GRACE. Only once—till now.

LORD JOHN. Oh! (*Then after another instant.*) Let us leave him then to cool! I haven't cycled twenty miles, but I've motored forty very much in the hope of *this*, Lady Grace—the chance of being able to assure you that I too, as you say, care

---

[7] Jan van delft Vermeer, also known as Jan van der Meer (1632–1675), Dutch painter.

[8] Il Moretto (1494–1554), Italian painter of the Brescian school.

very much for what I care for. I hadn't quite grasped in advance these immense revels; but since I've the great luck to find you alone—!

GRACE. (*While he just hesitates.*) Alone or in company, Lord John, I'm always very glad to see you.

LORD JOHN. Then that assurance helps me to wonder if you don't perhaps gently guess what it is I want to say. I've *tried,* all considerately—these three months—to let you see for yourself how I feel. (*Then as she still lets him go on.*) I feel very strongly, Lady Grace; so that at last—well (*giving up all shy circumlocution*), I regularly worship you. You're my absolute ideal. I think of you the whole time. Do you see what I mean?

GRACE. I believe you'd be perfectly kind to me.

LORD JOHN. (*Eager.*) Well, isn't *that* something to the good? Do tell me then that you see your way!

GRACE. (*Smiling.*) Shouldn't I have a little more first to see yours?

LORD JOHN. (*After a vagueness.*) Oh, what I have to look to in the way of a career? Well, your Father—dear delightful man!—has been so good as to let me understand that he backs me, for a decent deserving creature, and that I've noticed, as you yourself doubtless have, that when Lord Theign backs a fellow—!

GRACE. The fellow at once comes in for something awfully good?

LORD JOHN. I don't in the least mind your laughing at me—for when I broached to him the question of the lift he'd give me by speaking to you first, he bade me simply remember the complete personal liberty in which he leaves you. Yet if he does put it to you that he'd *like* it, as I believe he *will,* I may *see* you here again: mayn't I?

GRACE. You must have patience with me.

LORD JOHN. I *am* having it. But *after* your Father's appeal—and if even Lady Imber should wish to make another for me—?

GRACE. Will I listen to her? No, Lord John—Kitty's quite another affair, and I never listen to her a bit more than I can help.

LORD JOHN. (*As feeling that he mustn't too easily, in honour, abandon a person who has presented herself to him as an ally.*) I can't help thinking you're a little hard on her. Your Father himself—in his looser moments!—often takes pleasure in what she says.

GRACE. (*Not shaken.*) Oh, I know *that!* He began, long ago, with allowing her everything.

LORD JOHN. Yes—and he still allows her Two Thousand.

GRACE. (*Smiling.*) I'm glad to *hear* it—she has never told me how *much!*

LORD JOHN. Then perhaps *I* oughtn't!

GRACE. Well, you can't help it now!

LORD JOHN. You mean then he ought to allow *you* as much? I'm sure you're right—and that he *will;* but I want you to understand that I don't in the least care what it may be!

GRACE. You're very good to *say* so!

LORD JOHN. (*Who sees* LORD THEIGN, *centre, but speaks before he comes down.*) Will you let him tell you, at all events, how good he thinks me?—and then let me come back and have it from you again?

(*Enter* LORD THEIGN, *centre, fresh, festive and blooming, though as rather wiping from his bland and handsome brow the perspiration of recent benevolent and eloquent efforts. There is not a very marked appearance of practical disparity in number of years, nor any great air of inequality of attitude, between* LORD JOHN's *rather mature and well-worn five or six and thirty, and the sufficiently eminent Peer's beautifully preserved fifty-eight or sixty say.*)

GRACE. Lord John desires you should tell me, Father, how good you think him.

THEIGN. "Good" my dear?—good for what?

GRACE. I feel I must ask *him* to tell you.

THEIGN. Then I shall give him a chance —as I should particularly like you to go back and deal a little with those overwhelming children.

GRACE. Ah they didn't overwhelm *you,* Father!

THEIGN. If you mean to say I overwhelmed *them*, I dare say I *did*—from my view of that vast collective gape of six hundred painfully plain and perfectly expressionless faces. But that was only for the *time:* I pumped advice—oh *such* advice!—and they held the large bucket as still as my pet pointer, when I scratch him, holds his back.

GRACE. (*As with the habit of deferring, as a matter of course, to her father's wishes, but not eager.*) You work people up, Father, and then leave others to let them down.

THEIGN. The two things require different natures—! (*Then as used to authority, though without harshness.*) Go!

(LADY GRACE *yields to his practically peremptory gesture; only pausing an instant to look with a certain gathered meaning from one of the men to the other—after which she turns off with a faint sigh of resignation. Exit* LADY GRACE, *centre.*)

LORD JOHN. The nature that *can* let you down—I rather *like* it, you know! But she didn't want to go.

THEIGN. Then what's the matter with her?

LORD JOHN. (*After a moment.*) I think perhaps, a little, Mr. Crimble.

THEIGN. And who on earth's Mr. Crimble?

LORD JOHN. A young man who was just *with* her—and whom Lady Grace appears to have invited.

THEIGN. Where *is* he then?

LORD JOHN. Off there among the Pictures—which he seems partly to have come for.

THEIGN. (*Easy.*) Oh then he's welcome—on such a day!

LORD JOHN. (*As rather wondering.*) But hadn't Lady Grace told you—?

THEIGN. Not that I remember. (*But making nothing of this.*) You know the freedom I allow her. She has her friends, at this time of day, and I take them for granted. But where, by the way, is your *own?*—of whom I've just heard.

LORD JOHN. Oh off among the Pictures too—so they'll have met and taken care of each other. I mustn't (*as with all he*

has to think of) appear to Bender to have failed him; but I must at once let you know—before I join him—that, seizing my opportunity, I have just very definitely, in fact quite pressingly, spoken to Lady Grace. I've led her to expect—for our case—that you'll be so good, without loss of time, as to say a word yourself. (*Then as* LORD THEIGN *only appears to consider, saying nothing.*) The last thing my Mother did this morning was to remind me—with her fine old frankness—that she would like to learn without more delay where, on the whole question, she *is*, don't you know? Do we or *don't* we, decidedly, take up, practically, her very handsome offer—"very handsome" being, I mean, what *she* calls it; though it strikes even me too, you know, as rather decent.

THEIGN. (*After an instant, with considerable dryness, not unmixed, however, with irritated resignation.*) Kitty has of course rubbed well into me how decent *she* finds it! She hurls herself on me—successfully—for Everything; and it suits her down to the ground. (*Then going on as with the gallant, because the helpless, vision of his accumulated grievance.*) She pays her beastly Debt—that is, I mean to say, (*taking himself up a little*) discharges her monstrous obligations—by her Sister's fair hand; not to mention a few other trifles, for which I naturally provide.

LORD JOHN. (*At a loss but for a moment.*) Of course we take into account, don't we? not only the fact of my Mother's desire—intended, I assure you, to be most flattering—that Lady Grace shall enter our Family with all honours, but her expressed readiness to facilitate the thing by an undertaking over and above—!

THEIGN. (*Taking up what he leaves rather in the air.*) Over and above Kitty's release from her damnable payment? Of course we take *everything* into account—or I shouldn't, my dear fellow, be discussing with you at all a business one or two of whose aspects so little appeal to me; especially as there's nothing, you can easily conceive, that a daughter of mine can come in for by entering even your Family —or any other *as* a Family!—that she wouldn't be quite as sure of by just staying in her own. The Duchess's idea, at any rate, if I've followed you, is that if Grace does accept you she settles on you Twelve Thousand—with the condition—

LORD JOHN. (*Anticipating.*) Definitely, yes, of your settling the equivalent on Lady Grace.

THEIGN. And what do you call the equivalent of Twelve Thousand?

LORD JOHN. Why, tacked on to a value so great and so charming as Lady Grace herself, I dare say such a sum as Nine or Ten Thousand would serve.

THEIGN. And where the mischief, please, at this highly inconvenient and troublesome time, am I to pick up Nine or Ten Thousand? Into which of my very empty pockets will it be of the least use for me to put my hand?

LORD JOHN. (*Laughing with confidence.*) Oh, when a man has such a tremendous assortment of breeches—! (*Then seeing* BENDER.) But—if it's a question of pockets and what's *in* 'em—here's my friend!

(*Re-enter* BENDER *from the right.*)

LORD JOHN. (*Immediately greeting him.*) I've had awfully to fail you, Mr. Bender, but I was *coming!* Let me introduce you to our host.

BENDER: Happy to meet you—especially in your beautiful home—Lord Theign. (*Then while his host has accepted blandly, but without marked demonstration, his acknowledgement.*) I've been round, by your kind permission and the light of nature, and haven't required support; though if I *had* there's a gentleman there who seemed prepared to allow me any amount. A young, spare gentleman with eye-glasses— I guess he's a Writer. A friend of yours too, Lord John?

LORD JOHN. (*Prompt and positive.*) No, the gentleman is no friend of mine, Mr. Bender.

THEIGN. A friend of my Daughter's— whom I hope they're looking after.

BENDER. Oh, they took care he had *tea*— to any extent, and they were so good as to move something so that he could get on to a chair and see straight into the Moretto.

LORD JOHN. (*In general disapproval.*) On a chair?—I say!

BENDER. (*Cheerfully.*) Why I got right up myself—a little more and I'd almost have begun to *paw* it! He got me quite interested in that Moretto. But your biggest value, Lord Theign, I take it, is your Sir Joshua. Are you prepared, Lord Theign, to entertain a Proposition?

THEIGN. (*While his visitor has left these few words to speak for themselves, only meeting* BENDER's *eyes all serenely while he takes him up.*) To the effect that I part to you with the beautiful Duchess of Waterbridge? No, Mr. Bender, such a proposition would leave me intensely cold.

LORD JOHN. (*Irrepressibly.*) My dear Bender, I *envy* you!

BENDER. (*Imperturbably.*) I guess you don't envy me as much as I envy Lord Theign.

LORD JOHN. The beautiful Duchess of Waterbridge, Mr. Bender, is a golden apple of one of those great family trees of which respectable people don't lop off the branches whose venerable shade, in this garish and denuded age, they so much enjoy.

BENDER. (*Acutely regarding him.*) Then if they don't sell their Ancestors where in the world are all the Ancestors bought?

THEIGN. Doesn't it sufficiently answer your question for the moment that they're not bought at Dedborough?

BENDER. (*Cheerfully, patiently, even gaily, and always with his capacious candour.*) Why, you talk as if it were my interest to be *reasonable!* I'd be ashamed— with the lovely ideas I have—if I *were!* But (*with a sturdy smile for it all*) I guess I can *wait!*

LORD JOHN. (*With a jocose manner, but fixed, sustained look at* LORD THEIGN, *across* BENDER, *who has, of course, during the scene been between them.*) Mr. Bender's bound to *have* something!

THEIGN. (*After another look at him, and just a motion of nervousness, throwing it up and turning away.*) Then you may amuse yourself at my expense as you like!

LORD JOHN. (*Laughing.*) Oh I don't mean at *your* expense—I mean at Mr. Bender's! At any rate, Bender, I put you the question—of whether you'd care to acquire that Moretto.

BENDER. Well, the hitch about that Moretto is that it ain't what I'm *after*.

THEIGN. (*Easy, amused.*) Oh it isn't that we in the least *press* it, Mr. Bender!

LORD JOHN. (*As taking from* LORD THEIGN's *manner and face his cue for further humorous license.*) Ah, I beg pardon! *I* press it—very hard. You don't mean to say you don't feel the interest of that Moretto?

BENDER. Well, if you had seen me on that chair you'd have thought I did.

LORD JOHN. Then you must have stepped down from the chair properly impressed.

BENDER. I stepped down quite impressed with that young man.

LORD JOHN. Mr. Crimble—*his* opinion, really? Well, I hope he's aware of the Picture's value.

BENDER. He puts it at Ten Thousand.

LORD JOHN. Well, what's the matter with Ten Thousand?

BENDER. (*After deliberation.*) There's nothing the matter with Ten Thousand.

THEIGN. (*Smiling.*) Then what's the matter with *you*, Mr. Bender?

BENDER. The matter with me, Lord Theign, is that I've no use for a "Ten Thousand" picture. A picture of that rank is not what I'm after.

THEIGN. The figure isn't what you want to give?

LORD JOHN. The matter with Mr. Bender is that he wants to give *more!*

THEIGN. Well, there would be no difficulty about *that*, Mr. Bender! If you want an ideally expensive picture I'll make the Moretto as expensive as you like.

BENDER. Ah, but you can't do violence to the native modesty of a Moretto. (*And then as he sees* HUGH CRIMBLE *at right.*) But I guess this gentleman can *tell* you!

(HUGH CRIMBLE *has reappeared at entrance right in time to catch the beginning as well as the rest of* BENDER's *speech. Re-enter* HUGH CRIMBLE, *right.*)

HUGH. (*Who stands there a moment, flushed and smiling; evidently with a message or an idea that quite excites him, and that has impelled and sustained him in his return to the hall—or to the chance to report his impressions of what he has seen —which has a little the manner of an*

irruption. *He looks from one to the other of the three men, scattered a little by the sight of him, and fixes his eyes then recognisingly on* LORD THEIGN's, *whom he remains an instant longer communicatively smiling at. Then he takes up what he has first heard* MR. BENDER *say; but addressing his words to his host.*) I should say to *that*, Lord Theign, if you'll allow me, that the thing depends a good deal on just that question—of what *your* Moretto, at any rate, may be presumed or proved to "be." Let me thank you for your kind leave to go over your treasures.

THEIGN. (*Sufficiently affable, but with a shade in it of coolness for the slightly heated familiarity of the plain young man with the eye-glasses whom he sees for the first time.*) Oh, I've scarcely "treasures"— but I've some things of interest.

HUGH. (*As he comes down and enters the circle, as it were, full of what he has brought him.*) I think it possible, my lord, that you've a very great treasure—if you really have so great a rarity as a splendid Mantovano? [9]

---

[9] Henry James believed that he was creating a fictitious painter in naming his Italian master Mantovano—the Mantuan—(Tennyson thus hailed Virgil "I salute thee, Mantovano . . ."). After *The Outcry* appeared in novel form, a correspondent, Robert C. Witt, drew James's attention to the fact that there actually had been a Rinaldo Mantovano, a sixteenth century Mantuan, whose pictures were in the National Gallery. James replied on Nov. 27, 1912 "I am almost shocked to learn, through your appreciative note, that in imaginatively projecting, for use in *The Outcry*, such a painter as the Mantovano, I unhappily coincided with an existing name, an artistic identity, a real one, with visible examples, in the annals of art. I had never heard (in I am afraid my disgraceful ignorance) of the painter the two specimens of whom in the National Gallery you cite; and fondly flattered myself that I had simply excogitated, for its part in my drama, a name at once plausible, that is of good Italian type, and effective, as it were, for dramatic bandying about. It was important, you see, that with the great claim that the story makes for my artist I should have a strictly supposititious one—with no awkward existing data to cast a possibly invidious or measurable light. So *my* Mantovano was a creature of mere (convincing) fancy—and this revelation of my not having been as inventive as I supposed rather puts me out. But I owe it to you none the less that I shall be able—after

THEIGN. (*Struck, though mystified.*) A Mantovano?

HUGH. There have been supposed to be only *seven* known ones about the whole world; but if, by an extraordinary chance, you find yourself the possessor of a magnificent Eighth—!

LORD JOHN. (*Breaking in.*) Why, there you are, Mr. Bender!

HUGH. Oh, Mr. Bender—with whom I have made acquaintance—was present there when it began to work in me—!

BENDER. (*Anticipating him, amusedly, to their host.*) That your Moretto, after all, Lord Theign, isn't a Moretto at all! (*Then to* HUGH.) It began to work in you, sir, like *very* strong drink.

THEIGN. (*To* HUGH.) Do I understand you to intimate that my Picture isn't genuine?

HUGH. (*Facing his responsibility.*) As a picture, Lord Theign, as a great Portrait —one of the most genuine things in Europe. But it strikes me as probable that from far back—for reasons!—there has been a wrong *attribution;* that the work has been, in other words, long miscalled. It has passed for a Moretto—and I at first quite took it for one; and then, suddenly, I began to doubt—and then light flashed.

THEIGN. Flashed, you mean, from *other* Mantovanos—that I don't know?

HUGH. I mean from those I know myself —and I mean from fine analogies with *one* in particular. Yet I'm not so absolutely sure of that one, or of myself, I confess, as that I shan't be glad of a higher and wiser opinion—I mean than my own. It would be awfully interesting—if you'll allow me to say so—to have the judgement of one or two of the great men.

THEIGN. (*Finely—not grossly—ironic.*) You're not *yourself,* Mr. Crimble, one of the great men?

HUGH. Oh, I've too much still to learn —but I'm learning every day, and I shall have learnt immensely this afternoon.

THEIGN. (*Prompt, but smiling.*) Pretty well at my *expense,* Mr. Crimble—if you

I have recovered from this humiliation—to go and have a look at our N[ational] G[allery] interloper." (Lubbock ii 280–81).

demolish a name we've held so dear!

HUGH. (*With rising spirit.*) You may have held the name dear, my lord, but my whole point is that—if I'm right—you've held the Picture cheap.

BENDER. Because a Mantovano would come higher—to a purchaser—than a Moretto?

HUGH. Does Mr. Bender mean come to *him,* my lord?

THEIGN. (*After a moment, looking hard at* HUGH, *and then hard at* BENDER.) I don't know *what* Mr. Bender means! (*With which he moves away.*)

BENDER. Well, I guess I mean that it would certainly come higher to me than to any one! (*And then to* HUGH.) But how *much* higher?

HUGH. How much higher to *you?*

BENDER. Oh, I can size *that.* How much higher as a *Mantovano?*

HUGH. (*Hesitating; gaining time a little; full of his circumspection.*) Well, in view of the very great interest combined with the very great rarity, more than—well, more than can be estimated off-hand! But have I your permission, my lord, really to attempt to "find out"?

THEIGN. (*Gravely; as with a natural anxiety.*) What would it be your idea to *do* with my property?

HUGH. Nothing at all *here*—it could all be done, I think, at Verona. What besets, what quite haunts me is the vivid image of a Mantovano—one of the precious six or seven—in a private collection in that place. The conviction grows in me that the two Portraits must be of the same original. Will you let Pappendick—one·of the first authorities in Europe, a good friend of mine, in fact more or less my master, and who is mainly to be found at Brussels. I happen to know he knows your Picture, and he'll go and look again at the Verona one if I apply to him—he'll go and judge our issue in the light of certain new tips that I shall be able to give him.

BENDER. Well—how long will it take him to get there? I want him to start right away.

HUGH. (*Addressing his reply to* LORD THEIGN.) The day I hear from the great man you shall have the full report. And if I'm proved to have been unfortunately *wrong*—

THEIGN. You'll have caused me some inconvenience.

HUGH. (*In all easy candour.*) Of course I shall—like a meddling ass! But my conviction, after those moments with your Picture, was too strong for me not to speak—and, since you allow it, I face the danger and risk the test.

THEIGN. You make me in any event your proper charge.

HUGH. Oh, my charge won't be *high!*

BENDER. It ought to be handsome if the thing's marked *up!* (*Then with a look at his watch.*) But I guess I've got to go, Lord Theign—though your lovely Duchess does cry out for me again.

LORD JOHN. You'll find her then still there—and I'll join you in a moment.

THEIGN. I'll order your motor to the garden-front—you'll reach it from the Saloon; but I'll see you again first.

BENDER. (*At right.*) Well, if you're really ready to talk about anything *I* am! Good-bye, Mr. Crimble.

HUGH. Good-bye, Mr. Bender.

(*Exit MR. BENDER right.*)

HUGH. (*To LORD THEIGN, with the familiarity of confidence.*) As if you *could* be ready to "talk"!

LORD JOHN. (*To his host, while the two men exchange a look of surprise at what the irrepressible young outsider they find themselves with takes for granted.*) I've an idea you're quite ready to talk with *me.*

HUGH. (*Promptly then at this, but appealingly.*) Lady Grace spoke to me of things in the Library—!

THEIGN. (*Indicating left.*) You'll find it *there.*

HUGH. Thanks! (*Exit HUGH CRIMBLE, left.*)

LORD JOHN. (*Who has looked after him.*) Very *sharp*—but he wants taking down!

THEIGN. The people my Daughters—in the exercise of a wild freedom—*do* pick up!

LORD JOHN. Well, don't you see that all you've got to do—on the question we were dealing with—is to claim your *own* wild freedom? Surely I'm right in feeling you to have jumped at once to my idea that Bender is heaven-sent— Why look any-

where else for a sum of money that—smaller or greater—you can find with perfect ease in that extraordinarily bulging pocket?

THEIGN. The Moretto's too cheap—for a Yankee "on the spend."

LORD JOHN. Well, the Mantovano wouldn't be.

THEIGN. It remains to be proved that it *is* a Mantovano.

LORD JOHN. Well, go into it.

THEIGN. (*After an instant.*) Hanged if I won't! It *would* suit me—!!

LORD JOHN. A really *big* Yankee cheque?

THEIGN. It would suit me down to the ground! (*Then to his Daughter seeing her at centre.*) And the infant horde?

(*Re-enter LADY GRACE from the terrace.*)

GRACE. Marched off—in a huge *procession.*

THEIGN. Thank goodness! And our friends?

GRACE. All playing tennis—but those who are watching. (*Then as to explain her return.*) Mr. Crimble has gone?

LORD JOHN. He's in the Library—making Discoveries!

GRACE. Not I hope, to our disadvantage!

LORD JOHN. To your very great honour and glory. Your Moretto turns out a Mantovano.

GRACE. (*Astonished and elated.*) Our Moretto? Why then it's a *higher* Prize.

LORD JOHN. (*Confident.*) Rather—a higher, Lady Grace!

GRACE. And we shall owe it to Mr. Crimble?

THEIGN. Oh, I shall *pay* Mr. Crimble!

LORD JOHN. (*To GRACE, in rising spirits and friendly humour.*) Don't you let him stick it *on!*

THEIGN. (*Admonitory to LORD JOHN.*) Go *you* to Mr. Bender—straight!

LORD JOHN. (*Alert.*) Yes—till he goes. (*Then to LADY GRACE.*) But I shall *find* you here—shan't I?

GRACE. (*After an instant; definitely.*) I'll *wait* for you.

LORD JOHN. (*Waving his hand at her; happy.*) Then after a bit again—! (*Exit LORD JOHN, right.*)

THEIGN. (*A little nervously, but losing

no time.) He'll have told you I understand, that I've promised to speak to you for him. But I understand also that he has already broken ground.

GRACE. Yes, we talked—a while since. (*Smiling.*) Or at least *he* did.

THEIGN. Then if you listened—I hope you listened with a good grace.

GRACE. I should like to do what would *please* you.

THEIGN. Ah, what would please *me*—! (*Impatient.*) Don't put it off on "me"! Judge absolutely for *yourself*—in the light of my having consented to do for him what I always hate to do: deviate from my normal practice of not intermeddling? And to do so take your time.

GRACE. May I ask him then for a little *more?*

THEIGN. You know what he'll feel that a *sign* of.

GRACE. Well—I'll tell him what I mean.

THEIGN. Then I'll *send* him to you.

GRACE. Thanks, Father. (*Then arresting him.*) There's something else. (*With an effect of earnest abruptness.*) What does Mr. Bender want?

THEIGN. Mr. Bender? I think he must by this time want his car.

GRACE. Not then anything of ours?

THEIGN. (*Hesitating; self-conscious.*) Of ours?

GRACE. Why, if we've a new treasure—!

THEIGN. Oh, the Mantovano?

GRACE. I mean is *that* in danger?

THEIGN. How *can* it be—when he wants only Sir Joshuas?

GRACE. He wants *ours?*

THEIGN. Enormously!

GRACE. But you're not *discussing* it?

THEIGN. My dear child, for what do you *take* me?

(*Exit* LORD THEIGN, *right; after which* LADY GRACE *is for a minute alone, with the appearance of her having, suddenly, much to think of. She goes up; she stands for a minute at the open window to the terrace, looking off there; she comes down, she moves about, as if beset with an idea, with an anxiety. Then she sees* HUGH CRIMBLE *at left. Re-*

enter HUGH CRIMBLE *from the library.*)

HUGH. (*Radiant.*) What luck to *find* you! I must take my spin *back.*

GRACE. You've seen everything—as you wished?

HUGH. Oh, I've seen *wonders!*

GRACE. We've *got* some things.

HUGH. You've got five or six—

GRACE. (*Taking him up; disappointed.*) Only five or six?

HUGH. "Only"? (*Laughing.*) Why, that's *enormous*—five or six things of the first importance. Only—*par exemple*—a most barefaced "Rubens" [10] there in the Library.

GRACE. It isn't a Rubens?

HUGH. No more than I'm a Ruskin!

GRACE. Then you'll brand us—expose us for it?

HUGH. No—I'll let you off—if you go straight. I'll only hold it *in terrorem.* One can't be *sure*—in these dreadful days; so that if you don't go straight I'll come down on you with it. Only, to balance against that threat I've made the very grandest discovery. At least I *think* I have.

GRACE. (*After a moment.*) Of the Mantovano—hidden in the other thing?

HUGH. (*Almost wonderstruck—as if half believing it.*) You don't mean you've discovered that yourself?

GRACE. (*Graver than he.*) No—but my Father has told me.

HUGH. (*Eager.*) And is your Father greatly set up?

GRACE. I think he's immensely *pleased* —if you see your way to certainty.

HUGH. Well, it will be a question of the weight of expert opinion that I shall invoke. But I'm not afraid, and I shall make the thing, from its splendid rarity, the crown and flower of your Glory.

GRACE. It's awfully beautiful then— your having come to us so. It's awfully beautiful your having brought us, this way, in a flash—as dropping out of a chariot of fire!—more light and what you call more glory.

HUGH. Ah, the beauty's above all in your having *yourself* done it. If I've brought the

---

[10] Peter Paul Rubens (1577–1640), Flemish master.

"light" and the rest—that's to say the very useful *information*—who in the world was it brought *me?*

GRACE. (*With a gesture; making light of that.*) You'd have come in some other *way!*

HUGH. I'm not sure! I'm *shy*—little as I may seem to show it: save in Great Causes —when I'm preternaturally bold and horrid! Now, at any rate, I only know what *has* been! (*Looking after her as she turns away. She moves up a minute, restless and nervous as she has moved just before his re-entrance, and his eyes follow her as if he has suddenly received from her an impression that makes him a little graver.*) But does anything in it *trouble* you?

GRACE. (*Who has turned, further up, facing him across her wider space and speaking as with deep abruptness.*) What did you mean a moment ago by the chance of our not "going straight"? When you said you'd expose our false Rubens—in the event of a certain danger.

HUGH. (*Recalling, laughing; but frank and positive.*) Oh, in the event of your ever being bribed—!

GRACE. (*While he hangs fire, as from delicacy, an instant.*) Bribed?

HUGH. Why, to let anything—of your *best!*—ever leave Dedborough. By which I mean, really, of course, leave the country. (*And then as she says nothing, taking alarm.*) I hope you don't feel there *is* such a danger? I understood from you—when we first met here—that it was unthinkable.

GRACE. (*Very serious.*) Well, it *was*, to me, then. But if it has since come up?

HUGH. (*Wondering.*) "If" it has? But *has* it? In the form of that man? But Mr. Bender wants the great Duchess—

GRACE. And my Father won't sell *her?* No—he won't sell the great Duchess. But he greatly needs a certain sum of money— or thinks he does—and I've just had a talk with him.

HUGH. In which he has told you that?

GRACE. He has told me nothing—or, rather, told me quite other things. But the more I think of them the more it comes to me that he feels urged or tempted—

HUGH. (*Anticipating, looking round at the place in his dismay.*) To despoil and denude these walls?

GRACE. Yes—to satisfy, to *save* my Sister! Now do you think our state so ideal?

HUGH. But you terribly *interest* me. May I ask what's the matter with your Sister?

GRACE. (*Going straight on now.*) The matter is—in the first place—that she's too dreadfully beautiful.

HUGH. (*Sincere, serious.*) More beautiful than *you?*

GRACE. (*Sad, almost sombre, and without a shadow of coquetry.*) Millions of times. She has debts—great *gaming* debts.

HUGH. But to such *amounts?*

GRACE. Incredible amounts, it appears! And mountains of others too. She throws herself all on *him.*

HUGH. And he *has* to pay them? There's no one *else?*

GRACE. (*After an instant.*) He's only too afraid there *may* be—that's exactly how she makes him *do* it! (*Then as he stares, rather dismayed.*) You've made him aware, in the possible Mantovano, of a new value.

HUGH. Oughtn't I, at any rate before I go, to *speak* to Lord Theign?

GRACE. Is it your idea to *appeal* to him?

HUGH. It seems to me that I should *first* do that!

GRACE. He'll have to learn then that I've told you of my fear.

HUGH. And is there any good reason why he *shouldn't?*

GRACE. (*Deciding while she waits with her eyes on him; courageous and emphatic.*) No! (*With which she goes and touches an electric bell, then facing him again.*) But I think I'm rather sorry for you.

HUGH. Is the Sister you speak of, Lady Imber?

(GRACE, *seeing* BANKS *appear, right, raises her hand in caution. Re-enter* BANKS, *right.*)

GRACE. Please say to his lordship—in the Saloon or wherever—that Mr. Crimble must go.

(BANKS *bows. Exit* BANKS, *right.*)

GRACE. The Sister of whom I speak is Lady Imber.

HUGH. She loses heavily at Bridge?

GRACE. She loses more than she wins.

HUGH. And yet she still plays?

GRACE. What *else,* in her set, should she do?

HUGH. (*After an instant.*) So *you're* not in her set?

GRACE. I'm not in her set!

HUGH. Then I decidedly don't want to save her! I only want—

GRACE. (*Breaking in.*) I *know* what you want!

HUGH. So you're now *with* me?

GRACE. I'm now *with* you!

HUGH. Then shake hands on it!

(*He offers her his hand and she takes it. They stand a moment locked in the pledge of their grasp. Re-enter, so seeing them,* LORD THEIGN *from the right; on which they separate as with an effect of* HUGH's *leave-taking.*)

THEIGN. I'm sorry my Daughter can't keep you; but I must at least thank you for your suggestion about my Picture.

HUGH. (*As on a decision taken with a sense of possibly awkward consequences.*) May I—before you are sure of your indebtedness—address you rather a direct question, Lord Theign? (*And then while his host, as recognising the rather sharp note of this, has a stiff stare.*) If I contribute in my modest degree, to our establishing the true authorship of that work, may I have from you the assurance that that result isn't to serve as a basis for any peril —or possibility—of its leaving the country?

THEIGN. (*Pulled up, astonished and resentful, even though slightly embarrassed.*) You ask of me an "assurance"?

HUGH. (*Firmly, with his strained smile.*) I'm afraid I *must,* you see.

THEIGN. (*With a very grand manner.*) And pray by what right do you do anything of the sort?

HUGH. By the right of a person from whom you, on your side, are accepting a service.

THEIGN. (*With rising temper.*) A service that you half an hour ago *thrust* on me, sir—and with which you may take it from me that I'm already quite prepared to dispense!

HUGH. (*Controlling himself; with all courtesy.*) I'm sorry to appear indiscreet, I'm sorry to have upset you in any way; but I can't overcome my anxiety—

THEIGN. (*Taking the words from his lips.*) And you invite me—at the end of half an hour in this house!—to account to you for my personal intentions and my private affairs and to make over my freedom to your hands!

HUGH. I can only see the matter as I see it, and I should have been ashamed not to have seized *any* chance to appeal to you. I entreat you to think again, to think *well,* before you deprive us of such a source of just envy!

THEIGN. And you regard your entreaty as helped by the threat you're so good as to attach to it?

HUGH. I know nothing about threats, Lord Theign, but I speak of *all* of us—of all England; who would deeply deplore such an act of alienation, and whom, for the interest they bear you, I beseech you mercifully to consider!

THEIGN. (*With high and brave irony and decision.*) Understand then, please, that they'll show their interest *best* by minding their own business while I very particularly mind *mine.*

HUGH. (*After further thought, stating his conclusion very gravely.*) Then I'm to gather that you simply do what happens to suit you?

THEIGN. (*With ringing emphasis.*) In very distinct preference to what happens to suit *you!* (*Then very stiff, as to wind up their brief and thankless connection.*) So that I needn't longer detain you!

HUGH. (*Uncertain, unhappy, unsatisfied, looking about mechanically for the cap he has laid on a table on his first entrance.*) I apologise, my lord, if I seem to you to have ill-repaid your hospitality. (*After which, as with rather a wan smile.*) But my interest in your Picture remains.

GRACE. (*Breaking her strained watchful silence for the first time; coming down a little.*) And please let me say, Father that *mine,* also, grows and grows!

THEIGN. (*Surprised at her, and rather disconcerted and impatient.*) I'm happy to hear it, Grace—but yours is another affair.

GRACE. I think, on the contrary, that it's quite the same one—since it's on my *hint* to him that Mr. Crimble has said

what he has. I let him know what I supposed you to think—(*just hesitating under
the aggravated paternal glare*) of profiting
by the importance of Mr. Bender's
visit.

THEIGN. (*With high but partly dissimulated reprobation.*) Then you might have
spared, my dear, your—I suppose and
hope *well-meant*—interpretation of my
mind. Mr. Bender's visit will terminate—
as soon as he has released Lord John—
without my having profited in the smallest
particular.

HUGH. (*As all for* GRACE.) It was Lady
Grace's anxious inference—she will doubtless let me *say* for her!—that my idea about
the Moretto would add to your power of—
(*just a little embarrassed and awkward*)
"realising," advantageously on such a prospective rise.

THEIGN. (*Taking this in; to his Daughter.*) Understand then, please, that—as I
detach myself from *any* association with
this gentleman's ideas—whether about the
Moretto or about anything else!—his further application of them ceases from this
moment to concern us.

GRACE. (*On this, after a moment, with a
great successful effort, to* HUGH, *across her
Father who is between them.*) Will you
make your enquiry for *me* then?

HUGH. With all the pleasure in life!
(*With which he bows to them, together,
for departure so formally that it's almost
extravagant. Exit* HUGH CRIMBLE *rapidly,
right.*)

THEIGN. (*Indignant under the shock and
smart of what she has done.*) I denounce
the *indecency*, Grace, of your public defiance of me!

GRACE. (*Meeting his eyes hard, at her
distance, left, while she becomes aware of*
LORD JOHN *at right; then simply saying to
him.*) Lord John!

(*Re-enter* LORD JOHN, *right.*)

LORD JOHN. (*To his host.*) Bender's at
last *off*, but (*indicating the outer region*)
you may still catch him there with Lady
Sandgate.

(LORD THEIGN *stands a moment,
looking dark, flushed and uncertain,
from this visitor to his daughter
and back again; then decides, in silence, with a gesture of almost desperate indifference, and goes up.
Exit* LORD THEIGN, *centre.*)

LORD JOHN. What on earth's the matter
with your Father?

GRACE. What on earth *indeed*? Is he discussing with that man?

LORD JOHN. (*Taken by surprise; more
or less gaping.*) With Bender? (*Waving it
away.*) My dear, what do *we* care? I've
come for your kind *answer*—as your Father has told me to *hope*!

GRACE. I've no kind answer to *give* you.
I entreat you to leave me alone.

LORD JOHN. (*Deeply disappointed; quite
at sea.*) Why, what in the world has *happened*—when you almost gave me your
word?

GRACE. (*Only wishing to escape him.*)
What has happened, Lord John, is that
I've found it become impossible to listen
to you.

LORD JOHN. (*Utterly aghast; appealing.*)
That's all you've got to say to me—after
what has passed between us?

GRACE. (*Who has been, as it were, pursued by him till she gets up the exit to
left, where she holds him in a manner,
with her passionate denial, at bay.*) I've
got to say—sorry as I am—that if you *must*
have an answer it's *this*: that never, Lord
John, *never*, can there be anything *more*
between us. (*With a raised, utterly forbidding hand, as to check his further advance.*) Never—no, never! (*Then again as
she goes.*) Never, never, *never*!

Exit LADY GRACE *rapidly, left.
She leaves him thus desperately gaping, looking about him, appealing
to vacancy; then dropping upon a
chair or a sofa to go on staring at
his discomfiture while the Curtain
falls.*

ACT SECOND

The front drawing room at LADY SAND-
GATE'S *house in Bruton Street, with an
entrance right, straight from staircase and
upper landing and lobby, and a communication a good deal left of centre with the
back drawingroom, by the disposition and
glimpse of which latter the impression of
another entrance and exit within it, from
and to the rest of the house, is given.*
LADY SANDGATE *comes in right, meeting*
GOTCH, *her Butler, who comes out of the
back drawingroom; surprised at not immediately finding the visitor to whom she has
been called.*

LADY SANDGATE. But Mr. Crimble—?

GOTCH. Here he is, my lady.

(*On which* HUGH CRIMBLE
*emerges, entering from the back
drawingroom; in morning dress and
with a soft hat; while exit* GOTCH,
right.)

HUGH. I went in, with *his* permission,
to see your famous Lawrence—which is
splendid; he was so good as to arrange the
light. But I must look at her *again*, when
I've more time—for I'm here, frankly, at
this early hour, to ask your consent to my
seeing Lady Grace a moment, on a particular business—if she can kindly give me
time.

LADY SANDGATE. You've known then of
her being with me?

HUGH. I've known of her coming to you
straight on her leaving Dedborough—of
her wishing not to go to her Sister's, and
of Lord Theign's having gone, or being on
the point of going, abroad.

LADY SANDGATE. And you've known it
from having *seen* her?—these three weeks!

HUGH. Barely *met* her—two or three
times: at a Private View, the Opera, in the
Lobby, and that sort of thing.

LADY SANDGATE. Then she hasn't told
you that things have happened?

HUGH. Nothing but that she was *here*.

LADY SANDGATE. You've only talked—
when you've met—of "Art"?

HUGH. Well, art is "long"—!

LADY SANDGATE. Then I hope it may see
you through! But you should first know
that Lord Theign is presently due—not
having started yet, but coming up to take
the *train de luxe* this afternoon—for his
annual Salsomaggiore. With so little time
to spare, however, that to "simplify"—as
he wired me an hour ago from Dedborough—he has given *rendezvous* here to
Mr. Bender, who is particularly to wait
for him.

HUGH. And who may therefore arrive at
any moment?

LADY SANDGATE. (*Looking at her bracelet
watch.*) You'll have just your *chance*—!

HUGH. Thank goodness then. But what
is it you say has "happened"?

LADY SANDGATE. (*After an instant; deciding.*) Haven't you at least guessed that
she has fallen under her Father's *extreme*
reprobation?

HUGH. By her having asked me to act
for her about the Mantovano?—which I've
been doing. That's exactly what I've come
to *tell* her now at last—that I'm all impatience.

LADY SANDGATE. And you really haven't
made out the *other* effect of your hour at
Dedborough? (*Then as he clearly hasn't.*)
As soon as you had gone she turned off
Lord John. Declined, I mean, the offer
of his hand in marriage.

HUGH. (*Mystified but struck.*) He *proposed* there—?

LADY SANDGATE. He had spoken, that
day, *before*—before your talk with Lord
Theign, who had every confidence in her
accepting him. But (*as if she really believes herself there is something in it*) you
came, you went—and when her suitor reappeared, just after you *had* gone, for his
answer—

HUGH. She wouldn't *have* him?

LADY SANDGATE. She wouldn't *look* at
him! Her Father had his reasons for *counting* on her—and it has made a most painful crisis.

HUGH. I'm very sorry to hear it—but
where's the connection with *me?*

LADY SANDGATE. (*Gravely*.) I leave you to make out—but I'm all on Grace's side; for, if you'll keep the secret of everything I've said or say, I only *want* to make Bender impossible. If you ask me how I arrange that with my loyalty to Lord Theign—?

HUGH. (*Interrupting*.) I *don't* ask you—anything of the sort; and my own bright plan for doing what you say—!

LADY SANDGATE. (*Checking him as she again looks at her bracelet watch*.) You'll have time at the *most*, to explain to Lady Grace! (*She has reached an electric bell, which she touches; after which she comes down with an abrupt and slightly embarrassed change of tone*.) You do think *my* great Portrait splendid?

HUGH. (*Staring for the abruptness, but quickly remembering*.) Oh, your Lawrence there? as I said—magnificent!

(*Re-enter, interrupting,* GOTCH, *right*.)

LADY SANDGATE. Let her ladyship *know* —Mr. Crimble.

(*Exit* GOTCH, *right*.)

LADY SANDGATE. (*Resuming with the same rather awkward self-consciousness*.) Couldn't you, with your immense cleverness and power, get the Government to do something?

HUGH. About your picture? (*With his eyes on her a moment; smiling for reluctant interest*.) Mr. Bender's not after it?

LADY SANDGATE. Most intensely after it. But I'll never part with it to a bloated Alien!

HUGH. Then I applaud your patriotism. Only why not, carrying that magnanimity a little further, set us all an example as splendid as the object itself?

LADY SANDGATE. (*Shocked*.) Give it you for nothing? Because I'm an aged female pauper, and can't make *every* sacrifice! If I've told you precious things, mightn't you on your side—

HUGH. (*Sharply anticipating her*.) Estimate their value in cash? Ah, Lady Sandgate, I *am* in your debt, but if you *bargain* for your precious things I'd rather you took them back!

LADY SANDGATE. (*Becoming aware of* LADY GRACE, *left centre, makes him the*

sign of silence. Then brave and smiling*.) I won't bargain with the Treasury!

(*Exit* LADY SANDGATE, *right, while* LADY GRACE *appears at entrance from the other room. Enter* LADY GRACE, *left centre*.)

HUGH. (*As she shows him a light of welcome; full of his subject and going straight to business*.) I haven't been able to wait, I've wanted too much to tell you—that I've just come back from Brussels, where I saw Pappendick, who was free and ready, by the happiest chance, to start for Verona, which he must have reached some time yesterday. Allowing him time to have got into relation to the Picture, I've begun to expect his *wire*—which will probably come to my club; but my fidget, while I wait, has driven me to come to you here—in my fever, uninvited—and at least let you know I've "acted."

GRACE. (*Happy*.) Oh, I'm so glad to be acting *with* you! It's all I care for and think of now—and I've only wondered and hoped!

HUGH. Well, he was away from home at first, and I had to wait—but I crossed last week, found him and settled it. So at last I'm able to tell you how I feel the trouble I've brought you!

GRACE. What do you know—when I haven't *told* you—about my "trouble"?

HUGH. How can't I have *guessed*—with a ray of intelligence? You've sought asylum with this good friend—from the effects of your Father's resentment.

GRACE. "Sought asylum" is perhaps excessive. Yet I couldn't go, you see, to Kitty.

HUGH. I've set you adrift then—I've darkened your days. You're paying—with your comfort, with your peace—for having joined in my appeal.

GRACE. Why do you talk of it as "paying"—if it's all to come back to my *being* paid? I mean by your blest *success*—if you really do what you want.

HUGH. I have your word for it that our really pulling it off together will *make up* to you—?

GRACE. I should be ashamed if it didn't—for *everything*! I believe in such a Cause exactly as *you* do—and found a lesson, at Dedborough, in your frankness and your faith. I *see* our situation.

HUGH. And your Father only doesn't!

GRACE. He sees it—there's nothing in life he sees so much. But he sees it all *wrong!*

HUGH. (*Eagerly concurrent.*) Because my fond appeal the other day he took as a rude protest, and *any* protest—?

GRACE. (*Anticipating.*) He takes as an offence—yes. (*Smiling.*) It's his theory that he still has Rights—though he *is* a miserable Peer. He lives so in his own world.

HUGH. He lives so in his own, yes; but he does business so in *ours*—quite as much as the people who come up to the City in the Tube! (*And then as with a sharper recall to the intensely actual.*) And he must be here to do business to-day!

GRACE. You know he's to meet Mr. Bender?

HUGH. Lady Sandgate kindly *warned* me —and (*looking at his watch*) I've only ten minutes at best! The "Journal" won't have been good for him—which, if you haven't seen it, has a leader this morning a propos of Lady Lappington and her lost Longhi, and of Bender and his big hauls, and of the certainty—if we don't *do* something!— of more and more Benders to come: such a conquering horde as invaded the Old Civilisation—only armed now with huge cheque-books instead of spears and battle-axes. They refer to the current rumour— as too painful to *believe!*—of Lord Theign's putting up his Moretto; with the question of how properly to qualify any such dreadful purpose in him should the further report prove true of a new and momentous opinion about the Picture entertained by several high authorities.

GRACE. Is the article very aggressive?

HUGH. Well, it bells the cat. But how early do the papers get to you?

GRACE. At Dedborough? Oh, quite for breakfast.

HUGH. Then that's what has caused his wire to Bender.

GRACE. But how will such talk strike *him?*

HUGH. It will move him to absolute rapture. Mr. Bender—as he said to me himself at Dedborough of his noble *host* there—is "a very nice man"; but he's a product of the world of advertisement. That's really all he *sees*—and he lives in it as a fish in water or a saint in glory.

GRACE. But mayn't advertisement—after all!—in such a case turn against him?

HUGH. Oh, he rides the biggest whirl-wind—he has got it saddled and bitted.

GRACE. Then where does our success come in?

HUGH. In our *making* the beast, all the same, bolt with him and throw him! If— in such matters—all he knows is Publicity, the thing is to give him Publicity; and it's only a question of giving him *enough.* (*Abounding in his idea.*) Our policy therefore must be to *organise,* to that end, the Outcry. To organise Bender *himself*—to organise him to *Scandal!* He won't know it from a Boom! But may I come back to you from the club with my wire?

GRACE. Why *rather*—come back!

HUGH. (*Considering it; as important.*) Only waiting till your Father has left?

GRACE. (*Hesitating; then sharply deciding.*) Come when you *have* it!

(*Re-enter* GOTCH, *right.*)

GOTCH. (*As announcing that the visitor is mounting the stairs.*) Mr. Breckenridge Bender!

GRACE. Ah then I *go!*

HUGH. I'll stay myself—*three minutes!*

(*He goes up with her, alertly, to the other room to see her out, signalling to her, confidently, from the threshold as she disappears within. Exit* LADY GRACE, *left centre.* HUGH *has then an instant there by himself, still on the threshold and as if he has just come out; full of his possibilities, expectant and desirous of* BENDER *and of the chance of immediate action. Enter* MR. BENDER, *right, while the* BUTLER *also stands; who withdraws, however, then, closing the door.* MR. BENDER, *finding* HUGH, *throws up his hand as for friendly pleasure.*)

BENDER. Ah, Mr. Crimble, you've come with your great news?

HUGH. (*As if remembering but after a moment.*) About the Moretto? No, Mr. Bender, I haven't it *yet.* I knew it would take of course two or three weeks.

BENDER. Well, in *my* country it would take two or three *minutes!* Ain't you stirring them up?

HUGH. (*Goodhumouredly.*) I'm expecting, Mr. Bender—a report from hour to hour.

BENDER. So you'll let me have it right off?

HUGH. Well, frankly, Mr. Bender, if I myself had any *weight*—!

BENDER. (*Perceiving, anticipating.*) You'd put it in the scale *against* me? Why, what have I done that *you* should go back on me—after so working me up down there? The worst I've done is to refuse that Moretto—!

HUGH. (*Sincerely struck.*) Has it deplorably been *offered* you? (*And then as* BENDER *only looks at him hard, not, on second thoughts, giving* LORD THEIGN *away.*) Then why are you so keen on news from Verona? (*To which he adds as* BENDER *only continues to face him without replying, though smiling.*) Aren't you here, sir, on the *chance* of the Mantovano?

BENDER. (*Goodhumoured.*) I'm here because Lord Theign has wired me to *meet* him. Ain't you here for that too?

HUGH. (*After an instant.*) Dear no! I've but been in, by Lady Sandgate's leave, to see that Lawrence.

BENDER. (*Reminded, a bit rueful.*) Oh yes, she's very kind about it—one does "go in"! (*But then as if struck.*) Is any one *after* that Lawrence?

HUGH. (*Laughing.*) I hope not, Mr. Bender—unless you again, dreadfully, are!

BENDER. Ah, you know, Mr. Crimble, what I'm really after!

HUGH. The man in this morning's "Journal" does appear to have found out. But you must have talked *loud*—about the Sir Joshua!

BENDER. Well, I haven't so much talked as *raved*—for I'm afraid when I do want a thing I rave till I get it!

HUGH. You may easily get this one then —whatever it may prove to be; as you appear to have carried off your spoil, again and again, in the teeth of far greater people than I! But may I ask you for your word on *one* thing—very earnestly—as to any case in which that happens: that when precious things, things we are to lose, are

knocked down to you, you'll let us at least take *leave* of them, let us have a sight of them in London before they depart.

BENDER. (*With a grave, a longish face.*) Let them go, you mean, on exhibition?

HUGH. For three or four *weeks*—before they vanish forever.

BENDER. But won't that kick up a row?

HUGH. *Of course* it will kick up a row! You'll be, for the month, the best-abused man in England—if you venture to remain here at all!—except, naturally, in such a case as the present, Lord Theign, whom, however, if there should be too much of it all, for his taste or his nerves, it will cause to set his handsome face as a stone and never budge an inch. The strongest thing in such a type as his, is his resentment of a liberty taken; and the most natural thing is quite that he should feel almost anything you *do* take—uninvited—from the groaning board of his banquet of life—to *be* such a liberty.

BENDER. (*Having taken this picture of aristocratic sublimity in.*) Yes, I guess he has always lived as he likes—the way those of you who have got things fixed for them *do*, over here!—and to have to quit it on account of unpleasant remarks—! (*But he gives up trying to express what this must be; reduced to the thoughtful ejaculation:*) My!

HUGH. That's it Mr. Bender—he won't quit it without a hard struggle!

BENDER. (*At last giving himself quite gaily away as to his grand calculation of impunity.*) Well, I guess he won't struggle too hard for me to hold on to him if I *want* to!

HUGH. In the thick of the conflict then, however that may be, don't forget the claim of our public! But (*decidedly going*) good-bye—for another look *here!* (*With which he goes up to the left centre.*)

BENDER. (*Alert again at this; staying him, as by a gesture, for an appeal.*) How much is she really worth?

HUGH. "She"? (*Momentarily vague.*) Lady Sandgate?

BENDER. Her Greatgrandmother!

(*Re-enter, as he speaks,* GOTCH, *right.*)

GOTCH. (*As again not so much to announce as to mention the visitor to* MR. BENDER.) Lord John!

HUGH. (*At the threshold of the other room, but catching this.*) Ask *that* friend!

(*Exit* HUGH CRIMBLE, *left centre. Enter* LORD JOHN, *right.*)

GOTCH. (*Addressing both the visitors.*) Her ladyship will come. (*Exit* GOTCH, *right.*)

LORD JOHN. (*As he greets* BENDER.) Then he hasn't yet arrived. But his wire told me I should *find* you.

BENDER. He hasn't yet arrived—but what's the matter with him anyway?

LORD JOHN. The matter with him must be, of course, this beastly thing in the "Journal."

BENDER. (*Unenlightened and imperturbable.*) Well, what's the matter with *that* little piece?

LORD JOHN. (*Pulled up, surprised.*) Why, aren't you aware that the sharpest thing in it is a regular dig at *you?*

BENDER. (*Amused.*) If you call *that* a regular dig you can't have had much experience of the Papers. I've known them to dig much deeper. But what—if he feels the blot on his ermine—ain't *that* what you wear?—(*seeing* LADY SANDGATE, *who appears left centre, and at once eagerly greeting her with it*) what will Lord Theign propose, do you think, to do about it?

(*Re-enter* LADY SANDGATE *from the other room.*)

LADY SANDGATE. (*Smiling, unperturbed; but at first vague.*) To "do"—?

LORD JOHN. Don't you *know* about the thing in the "Journal"—so awfully offensive all round?

BENDER. (*Smiling at her.*) There'd even be a little pinch for *you* in it—if you were bent on fitting the shoe!

LADY SANDGATE. (*Meeting his allusion gaily, though with a firm look at him, as she comes down from her first arrest at* LORD JOHN's *challenge.*) Oh the shoes of such monsters as that are much too big for poor little *me!* (*And then to* LORD JOHN, *as to answer the challenge.*) I know only what Grace has just told me; but—since it's a question of "shoes"!—dear

Theign will certainly—what you may call —take his *stand!*

LORD JOHN. (*Finely confident.*) If I know him he'll take it splendidly!

BENDER. (*As with genial, though rather detached interest.*) And what—while he's about it—will he take it particularly *on?*

LADY SANDGATE. Oh, we have *plenty* of things, thank goodness, Mr. Bender, for such a man as dear Theign to take his stand on! That doesn't alter the fact, however, that we've evidently thus the first growl of an Outcry!

LORD JOHN. Ah, we've certainly the first growl of an Outcry!

BENDER. (*Aware of* LORD THEIGN, *who appears at right ushered and already announced by* GOTCH; *speaking as with a still finer shade than usual of unsophisticated humour.*) Why they tell me that what this *means,* Lord Theign, is the first growl of an Outcry!

(*Enter* GOTCH *and* LORD THEIGN, *right.*)

GOTCH. Lord Theign, my lady! (*Exit* GOTCH, *right.*)

THEIGN. (*A bit flushed perhaps, but splendidly unshaken and confident: in morning, or perfect travelling, dress, as already prepared for his closely impending journey abroad.*) I'm afraid I don't know what anything means to *you,* Mr. Bender —but it's exactly to find out that I've asked you, with our friend John, kindly to meet me here. (*And then to* LADY SAND-GATE.) For a brief conference, dear lady, by your good leave—at which I'm only too happy that you should yourself assist. The "first growl" of an Outcry, I may mention to you all, affects me no more than the last will—!

LADY SANDGATE. (*Taking him up.*) So that I'm delighted to gather you don't give up your so precious Cure.

THEIGN. (*Astonished and superior.*) "Give up"? (*After which, however, as by a jocose happy thought.*) Upon my honour, I *might* you know—that dose of the Daily Press has made me feel so fit! (*Then to the others, and more particularly to* BENDER.) I arrive, at any rate, with my decision taken—which I've thought may perhaps *interest* you. If that stuff *is* an attempt at an Outcry, I simply nip it in the bud. You will allow me to measure, myself, Mr. Bender, the importance of a gross freedom publicly used with my absolutely personal intentions and proceedings; to the *cause* of any definite report of which—in such circles!—I'm afraid I rather wonder if you yourself can't give me a clue.

BENDER. (*Taking the rather stately question in; after an instant.*) You rather wonder if I've talked of how I feel about your detaining in your hands my Duchess—?

THEIGN. (*Taking him up; amused; not too sharply resentful.*) Oh, if you've already published her as "yours"—with your *power* of publication—of course I easily trace the connection. My retort to that penny-a-liner, in any case, shall be at once to *dispose* of a picture. Only—once more and for the last time—you can't *have* our Duchess!

LORD JOHN. (*Sadly, sympathetically, ruefully.*) You can't have our Duchess!

LADY SANDGATE. (*As in amiable, sociable triumph.*) You can't have our Duchess!—and I wish he'd tell you, you dreadful rich creature, that you can't have anything at all!

THEIGN. (*More harmoniously.*) Ah what then would become of my retort?

BENDER. And what—as it *is*—becomes of my grievance?

THEIGN. Wouldn't a really big capture make up to you for that?

BENDER. Well, I take more interest in what I want than in what I have—and it depends, don't you see?—on what you *call* really big.

LORD JOHN. (*As with a bright idea.*) Wouldn't you like to go back there and *look*?

BENDER. (*Thinking; considering him as through narrowed eyelids.*) Look again at that old Moretto?

LORD JOHN. Well, it *may*, you know, be bigger than you thought!

THEIGN. (*With prompt intervention.*) It's more to the purpose that I should mention to you the rest of my little plan—which is at once to place the Picture on view: (*with a free, incisive, but elegant gesture*) on view as a thing disposed of!

With one of those fellows in Bond Street. (*Then as for the crushing climax of his policy.*) As a Mantovano.

LADY SANDGATE. But, my dear man, if it isn't one?

BENDER. Lady Sandgate, it's going to *be* one!

THEIGN. (*Gratified, to* BENDER.) You seize me? We *treat* it as one! I let *that* affirm my attitude.

BENDER. (*Complacently.*) Well, I guess it will raise some Discussion.

THEIGN. (*With high serenity.*) It may raise all it *will*!

BENDER. Oh, if *you* don't mind it *I* don't! You'll put it on view right off?

THEIGN. As soon as the proper arrangements—!

LADY SANDGATE. (*Anxiously interrupting.*) You put off your journey to *make* them?

THEIGN. (*Hesitating but an instant; appealing with gracious confidence to the others.*) Not if these friends will act—!

BENDER. (*In high satisfaction and decision.*) Oh, I guess we'll *act*—!

LORD JOHN. (*Interjecting with equal elation.*) Ah, *won't* we though?

BENDER. (*Going on to* THEIGN.) You understand I have an interest—?

THEIGN. I understand!

BENDER. And yet also have a freedom—?

THEIGN. I understand. The point is that *I* have a Show!

BENDER. Then *I'll* fix your Show! (*He waves an almost wild good-bye with his hat to* LADY SANDGATE.) Lord John—come right round!

LORD JOHN. (*Who is already at the door, which he has opened, while he lets* BENDER *pass out first; saying, behind him, in all glee, to the others.*) The fellow can do Anything Anywhere!

(*Exeunt* MR. BENDER *and* LORD JOHN, *right.*)

THEIGN. So much the better—for now I must see that Girl! I've three or four things to do—and I lunch with Kitty at one.

LADY SANDGATE. (*As accepting it, but disappointedly.*) Then—with Berkeley Square —you've no time. But I confess I don't quite *grasp*—your odd impulse to fly so in the face of Opinion!

THEIGN. "Opinion"? I "fly in its face"? Why, the beastly thing—as I'm taking my quiet walk—flies in *mine!* I give it a whack with my umbrella and send it about its business! (*Then with gravity and feeling.*) It's enough, my dear, to have been dished by Grace—without *your* falling away!

LADY SANDGATE. (*Sad; considerately pleading.*) It's only my great affection—and all that these years have been for us!—which make me wish you weren't so *proud!* Your surrenders to Kitty, at any rate, are your own affair—but are you sure you can *bear* to see Grace?

THEIGN. You suggest that I should leave the country with no sign of her explaining—?

LADY SANDGATE. (*Prompt.*) She *does* want to see you I know; but you must recall the sequel to that bad hour at Dedborough—when it was you who declined to see *her.*

THEIGN. (*Entirely reminiscent.*) Before she left the house with you, the next day, for *this?* What I recall is that even if I had condoned—that evening—her deception of *me,* I still loathed, for my friend's sake, her practical joke on poor John; played there apparently, out of the blue, for one of the wonderful friends she picks up: the picture-man introduced by her (what was his name?) who regularly "cheeked" me, as I suppose he'd call it, in my own house, and whom I hope, by the way, that under this roof, she's not able to be quite so thick with!

LADY SANDGATE. (*Evasive.*) Well, whatever your relations with others, dear friend, remember that I'm still here.

THEIGN. (*Sufficiently humane, but not moved to enthusiasm.*) That you're here, thank heaven, is of course a comfort—or would be if you *understood!*

LADY SANDGATE. Well, if I don't always "understand" a spirit so much higher than mine—and a situation so much more complicated, certainly!—I at least always defer, I at least always (*hanging fire an instant, but bringing it out with expression*) *worship!* (*Then as he remains not other than finely impassive.*) The old Altar, Theign—and a spark of the old Fire!

THEIGN. (*Who, without looking at her, has let her take his left hand.*) So I *feel!*

LADY SANDGATE. (*With considerable concentration.*) Do feel! (*She raises his hand to her pressed lips, drops it and goes up.*) Good-bye!

THEIGN. May I smoke?

LADY SANDGATE. Dear, yes!

THEIGN. (*While, having taken out his cigarette case, he looks about for a match.*) You must come to Victoria.

LADY SANDGATE. (*With intensity.*) Rather, dear! (*Exit* LADY SANDGATE, *left centre.*)

THEIGN. (*To himself as she goes.*) Poor nice Thing!

(*After which he has some moments alone, lost in thought, slowly and absently finding matches on a table and lighting his ciarette, and then, while he smokes, revolving and circulating in a manner that shows the degree of his preoccupation, till finally he sees* LADY GRACE, *who, having come to him through the other room, pauses in the doorway, whence she looks at him in silence. Re-enter* LADY GRACE, *left.*)

THEIGN. (*As he becomes aware of her.*) Oh!—I take for granted that you know I'm within a couple of hours leaving England under a necessity of health. (*And then as, coming down a little, she signifies, without speaking, her possession of this fact.*) Well then, I've thought that before I go I should—on this first possible occasion since that odious occurrence at Dedborough—like to let you know that if you had plotted and planned it in *advance*—from some uncanny motive!—you couldn't have arranged more perfectly to incommode, to disconcert, and, to all intents and purposes, make light of me and *insult* me. (*Then again, as with her eyes fixed to the ground now, she still lets him proceed.*) I had practically guaranteed to our excellent, our charming friend, your favourable view of his appeal—which you yourself *too,* remember, had left him in so little doubt of!—so that, having, by your performance, so egregiously failed him, I have the pleasure of their coming down on me for explanations and compensations—and for God knows what besides!

GRACE. (*As having taken it all in, though

not very much needing now to think it over again, while she raises her eyes.) I'm sorry indeed, Father, to have done you any wrong; but may I ask whom, in such a connection, you refer to as "they"?

THEIGN. "They"? (*Pulled up a moment by the question; but then with a brave, high assurance.*) Why, your own Sister, to begin with—whose interest in what may make for your happiness I suppose you decently recognise; and *his* people, one and all, the delightful old Duchess in particular, who only wanted to be charming to you—and who are as good people, and as pleasant and as clever, damn it, when all's said and done, as any *others* that are likely to come your way. (*After which, crescendo.*) Letting alone John himself, most amiable of men, about whose merits and claims you appear to have pretended to agree with me, just that you might, when he presumed, poor chap, gallantly to *urge* them, deal him with the more cruel effect that beastly blow on the mouth!

GRACE. (*Very grave, very patient, but not at all embarrassed.*) They so "come down" on you—I understand then, Father—that you're forced to come down on *me*? I interceded with you, earnestly, for our precious Picture—and you wouldn't on any terms, *have* my intercession. On top of that he blundered in—without timeliness or *tact*—and I'm afraid that, as I wasn't in love with him even *then*, he did have to take the consequence.

THEIGN. You recognise then that your reception of him *was* purely vindictive!—the meaning of which is that while you chatter about mistakes and blunders and about our charming friend's want of tact, what account have you to offer of the scene you made me there before that fellow—your *confederate*, as he had all the air of being?—by giving it to me with such assurance that if I had eminently done with him, after his remarkable display, *you* at least were but the more determined to see him keep it up.

GRACE. The only account I can give you, I think, is that I could speak, at such a moment, but as I felt—and that I felt very strongly—I feel in fact more than *ever* that

we shouldn't do such things. Even as my last word to you before you leave England, I'm ready to cry out to you that you oughtn't, you *oughtn't*, YOU OUGHTN'T!

THEIGN. (*Checking her, with raised eyebrows and raised imperative hand, as in an act really of violence.*) Hallo, *Hallo*, HALLO, my Daughter—no "crying out," if you please! (*After which, as arrested but unabashed, she still keeps her eyes upon him, he returns this examination for a minute, inwardly turning things over, making connections, taking a new strange measure of her; all to the effect of his then speaking with a difference of tone, a passage to a sharper irony.*) You keep bad company, Grace—it plays the deuce with your sense of Proportion. If you make this row when I sell a picture, what will be left to you when I forge a cheque?

GRACE. (*After an instant; grave.*) If you had arrived at the *necessity* of forging a cheque I should then resign myself to your selling a picture. (*Not disconcerted.*) Other People do such things, yes—they appear to have done them, and to be still doing them, all about us. But *we've* been so decently *different*—always! We've never done anything disloyal.

THEIGN. (*Echoing; as if frankly and almost interestedly amazed now.*) "Disloyal"? If it strikes you as happy to apply to your Father's conduct so outrageous a word, you must take from *him*, in your turn *his* quite other view of what makes "disloyalty"—understanding distinctly, by the same token, that he enjoins upon you not to set an odious example of it, in his absence, by discussing and deploring with any *one* of your extraordinary friends, any aspect or feature whatever of his personal conduct. When you have given me your word of honour in this sense I shall more cheerfully bid you good-bye.

GRACE. (*As if she has been for some time apprehending this and seeing where he must come out; but making him wait a moment.*) The only person to whom I have spoken—of your Sacrifice, as I suppose you'll let me call it?—is Mr. Crimble, whom you speak of as my "confederate" at Dedborough.

THEIGN. (*As with the relief of recover-*

ing the name.) Mr. Crimble—that's it!—whom you so amazingly caused to be present, and apparently so invited to be active, at a business that so little concerned him. You'll be so good as not to speak to Mr. Crimble again.

GRACE. Why, the question you forbid us is *the* question we care about—it's our very ground of conversation.

THEIGN. Then your conversation will please to dispense with a "ground"; or *you'll* please, better still—if *that's* the only way!—dispense with your conversation.

GRACE. (*After another pause, as weighing it.*) You require of me not to communicate with Mr. Crimble *at all?* (*Explanatory.*) You see, what we've set our hearts on is saving the Picture.

THEIGN. What you have set your hearts on is working *against* me!

GRACE. (*Very firm and straight and clean; but gently and without bravado.*) What we have set our hearts on is working for England.

THEIGN. (*In his amazement at her whole manner and assurance.*) And pray who in the world's "England" unless *I* am? What are "we" that you talk about, the whole lot of us, pray, but the best and the most English thing in the country; people walking—and riding!—straight; doing, disinterestedly, most of the difficult and all the thankless jobs; minding their own business, above all, and expecting others to mind theirs?

GRACE. Well, by "our" sense of what's due to the Nation—and what's characteristic of it, in such a case, I mean Mr. Crimble's and mine, and nobody's else at all. I express to you the way we feel. And I *know* how we feel—since I saw him here but half an hour ago.

THEIGN. (*Astonished.*) Saw him "here"? (*Indignant.*) He *comes* to you here—and Amy Sandgate didn't tell me?

GRACE. It was not her business to tell you—since, you see, she could leave it to *me*. And I quite expect he'll come again.

THEIGN. (*Immediate, authoritative.*) Then I simply demand of you that you don't see him. (*Then taking her expression of face in.*) You look at me as if I asked you to give up a fortune! (*Then as*

she only keeps her eyes on him as with gathering decision.) You're so wrapped up in him that the sacrifice is like *that* sort of thing?

GRACE. (*As if her choice is, with an effort, made.*) I'll wholly cease to see him, I'll turn my back on him forever, if, if, if—you'll withdraw the offer of our Picture to Mr. Bender—and never make another to any one else!

THEIGN. (*Really gaping at the size of it.*) If I'll obligingly announce to the World that I've made an ass of myself, you'll kindly forbear from your united effort—the charming pair of you!—to *show* me for one? (*Then as for cumulation; practically choking off any argument of her own.*) You give me a strange measure of what it costs you—

GRACE. (*Anticipating.*) To redeem the Picture?

THEIGN. To lose your tenth-rate friend!

GRACE. (*After they have stood sounding each other a long moment; before the end of which, however, she has become aware of the* BUTLER, *right.*) Well—I must *think!*

(*Re-enter* GOTCH, *right.*)

GOTCH. (*Announcing and ushering* HUGH CRIMBLE.) Mr. Crimble.

(*Re-enter* HUGH CRIMBLE, *right. Exit* GOTCH.)

HUGH. (*With a different face from that of his exit, and who stands a moment looking, under pressure of difficulty and effort, from* LADY GRACE *to her Father and back again; addressing himself, however, at first directly to* LADY GRACE.) Here I *am* again, you see—and (*bringing it out distressfully*) I've got my *news*, worst luck! (*Then to* LORD THEIGN, *more briskly.*) I learned you were here, my lord; but as the case is important I told them it was all right and came up. (*After which to* LADY GRACE *again.*) I've been to my club and *found* the beastly thing—!

GRACE. (*As he pauses an instant breathless.*) The news isn't good?

HUGH. (*Ruefully, but not abjectly.*) Not so good as I hoped. (*Then to* THEIGN.) For I assure you, my lord, I *counted*—!

GRACE. (*Breaking in; impatient to explain to her Father.*) It's the report from

Pappendick—about the picture at Verona.

HUGH. (*As* THEIGN *only glares at him, really familiar now again, as he himself becomes in his thought of nothing but the disconcertment he has to announce; together with the reviving possibilities, however, with which he has already begun to balance them.*) He has been able to get straight at *their* Mantovano, but he horribly wires me that he doesn't see my vivid, vital point—the absolute *screaming* identity of the two figures represented. I still hold that our man is their man and their man ours, but Pappendick thinks otherwise—and as he has so much to be reckoned with of course I'm awfully abashed! But I don't at all knock under, and I mean to appeal. (*To* LADY GRACE.) I've another shot in my locker—I had already written to Caselli—the great Caselli of Milan. For the Italians, I now feel, he must have most the instinct—besides of course his so *knowing* the Verona picture. As Pappendick went *there* for us I've asked Caselli to come here—(*then bethinking himself, with a turn*) if Lord Theign will be so good, that is, as to let him *see* the Moretto? (*He faces to that personage again, who, simply standing off and watching, in concentrated interest as well as detachment, this intercourse of his cool daughter and her cooler visitor, has clearly elected, as it were, to give them rope to hang themselves. Staring very hard at* HUGH, *he only meets his appeal in conscious and disconcerting silence; against which* HUGH, *however, bearing up, makes such head as he can. He offers his next words, that is, equally to his two companions.*) The Dedborough Picture seen *after* the Verona will perhaps point a different moral from the Verona seen after the Dedborough.

GRACE. How charming they should like so to work for you!

HUGH. Well, the thing, you see, is the ripping *interest* of it all—for (*again, with pertinacious amiability and now more and more recovered assurance, for* LORD THEIGN's *benefit,*) when we're really *hit,* over a case, we do almost anything in life! So give me *time*—!

GRACE. (*Breaking in, encouraging.*) How can we prevent your *taking* time?—or the

fact, either, that if the worst comes to the worst—

HUGH. (*Breaking in, in turn.*) The thing will always be at least the greatest of Morettos? (*So cheerily that it's still familiar.*) Ah, the worst shan't come to the worst, but the best to the best—my conviction of which it is that supports me in the deep regret I have to express (*to* LORD THEIGN *again*) for any inconvenience I may have caused you by my checked undertaking; for which I vow here before Lady Grace I will yet *more* than make up!

THEIGN. (*Who, after a continued hard blank stare at him, breaks for the first time the attitude of absolutely separate and invidious silence—compatible, however, with his air of having profoundly taken in everything that has passed—of which his latter part in the scene has effectively consisted.*) I haven't the least idea, sir, what you're talking about! (*On which he squarely turns his back and walks up to the door of the other room, where he stands a moment, thus averted, occupied with his own thought and ostensibly looking off at some object, the great Lawrence portrait or whatever within.*)

(*There ensues upon this an eloquent mute passage between* HUGH *and* LADY GRACE, *who, deeply divided by the width of the stage and looking up at their companion, only, thereafter, look again at each other in recognition of this unmistakable dismissal, at short orders, of* HUGH, *a dismissal for which the young man must immediately act.* LADY GRACE *throws up her arms and drops them helplessly again at her sides, as to convey that she has done all she can for him in his presence, however questionable as to its result, and that he must leave the rest to herself. The two communicate thus, for their full moment, without speaking; only with the long, the charged exchange of their gaze.* HUGH *has for an instant a show of hesitation, of the arrested impulse, with his eyes on the motionless figure, to utter another word to it before going. It is*

LADY GRACE's *raised hand and gesture of warning that check this possibility; he takes things in, and then deciding, after a last searching and answering look at her, goes noiselessly and rapidly out. Exit* HUGH CRIMBLE, *right. After which the stillness is prolonged a minute by the further wait of the two others,* LORD THEIGN *up and* LADY GRACE *down. It terminates at last in the former's turn about, as by his inferring from the silence that* HUGH *has withdrawn.*)

THEIGN. (*As he comes down.*) Is that young man your lover?

GRACE. (*After an instant.*) Won't your question be answered, Father, if you'll *think* a moment—without passion? (*And then as stiffly, and as probably seems to her, stupidly, he doesn't rise to it.*) If I offered not again to see him does that make for you the appearance—?

THEIGN. (*Staring, thinking.*) That you wouldn't see him, you mean, if I'd promised you not to sell—? I promised you nothing at all—

GRACE. (*Taking him up with emphasis.*) So I promised *you* as little! But that I should have been able to say so sufficiently meets your enquiry.

THEIGN. (*Impatient, quite as sharply, of any evasion.*) You risked it for the *equivalent*—over which you've so worked yourself up.

GRACE. Yes, I've worked myself up—that I grant you, and don't blush for! But hardly so much as to renounce my "lover" if—(*smiling*) I were so fortunate as to have one.

THEIGN. You renounced poor John mighty easily—whom you were so fortunate as to have!

GRACE. (*With the clearest, though not the cruelest, irony.*) Do you call Lord John my lover?

THEIGN. (*Highly declining to be gainsaid.*) He was your *suitor* at least—most assuredly—and as distinctly encouraged as he was respectfully ardent!

GRACE. Encouraged by *you,* dear Father, beyond doubt!

THEIGN. (*Not in the least baffled.*) Encouraged—er—by everyone! Because you were—yes, you *were!*—encouraging, and what I ask of you now is the plain straightforward truth—of whether you didn't turn him off because of your just then so stimulated views on (*just hesitating and then with an indication by his thumb to the place of* HUGH's *exit*) this gentleman.

GRACE. (*After an instant, as if moved to more things than she can say, though less in harshness than in trouble and yet in real compassion.*) Oh Father, Father, Father—!

THEIGN. (*As sounding her eyes for a searching moment, then giving way.*) Well then, if there's nothing—on your word of honour—of *that* sort between you, you can all the more drop him. I now accept your own terms for your doing so.

GRACE. (*Disconcerted at this—though as if she has also been fearing it.*) Not again to see him if you'd tell me the Picture's safe?

THEIGN. (*Prompt.*) The Picture's as "safe" as you please if you'll do what you just now said.

GRACE. (*As sharply troubled; after an intense inward debate; but having decided.*) I *won't* do what I then said. Because the case is different.

THEIGN. (*Echoing in indignant denial.*) "Different"?—*how,* different?

GRACE. He has *been* here—and that has done it. He knows.

THEIGN. (*Staring.*) Knows what I think of him, I hope—for a brazen young Prevaricator! But what else?

GRACE. What he will have seen—that I feel we're too good friends.

THEIGN. Then your denial's false—and you *are* infatuated?

GRACE. (*Very quietly and responsibly.*) I like him very much.

THEIGN. (*Passionately quick.*) So that your row about the Picture has been all a blind? (*And then, as, in her difficulty, she doesn't answer.*) And his a blind as *much* —to help him get *at* you?

GRACE. (*At left, separated from him by the width of the stage, he having reached the door right, after catching up his hat as in indignant supreme conclusion.*) He must speak for himself. I've said what I mean.

THEIGN. (*At the door.*) But what the Devil *do* you mean?

GRACE. (*After keeping him waiting a moment, their eyes on their eyes.*) Do what you like with the Picture!

THEIGN, *at this, holds her so, across the stage, a moment longer; then deciding, with a gesture of such passionate disgust for what her words seem to reveal that it's almost like a launched malediction, pushes the door before him and hurries out. Exit* LORD THEIGN, *right.* GRACE, *alone, stands a moment looking before her; then by a vague advance, held by a sense of what she has done, reaches a table at which she stands a moment lost in thought; only, however, after another moment, to fall into a chair close to it and there, with her elbows on it, yield to the impulse of covering her face with her hands while the Curtain falls.*

ACT THIRD

LADY SANDGATE'S *drawingroom; with* HUGH CRIMBLE *pacing, moving nervously about and waiting for* LADY GRACE, *to whom we see that his name has been taken and who comes to him after a little, left centre. There is no instant exchange of words; but they stand a moment looking at each other,* HUGH *more or less down right.*

HUGH. (*Then finding confidence.*) Am I right, Lady Grace, am I right?—to have come, I mean, after so many days of not hearing, not *trying*, not knowing. Whatever distress I may have created for you here a fortnight ago, there's something to-day that adds to my uncertainty too great a pang and that has made me feel I can scarce bear it as it *is*.

GRACE. Of what uncertainty do you speak? Your not having got yet the other Opinion—?

HUGH. Ah, *that* worries me—but you shall hear. My real torment, all this time, is that I've been in the dark, and feeling that I must leave *you* there; and now—just brutally *coming* again, under necessity and at any cost—I don't know if I most want or most fear what I may learn from you.

GRACE. Have you had—first of all!—any news yet of Caselli?

HUGH. He has *come*, as I hoped—like a regular good 'un; I've just met him at the station, but I pick him up again, at his hotel in Clifford Street, at five—leaving him meanwhile to a bath and a change and tea. *Then*, swooping down, I whirl him to Bond Street; where I guarantee you that his very first apprehension of the thing—clean and fine and wise!—will be the flash-light projected over the whole field of our question.

GRACE. (*All intense participation.*) That of the two Portraits but the one sitter.

HUGH. That of the two Portraits but the one sitter. So now you see my tension!

GRACE. While you, on your side, of course, keep well in view Mr. Bender's.

HUGH. Yes—I keep well in view Mr. Bender's; though of course these wretched days, you haven't known of Pappendick's personal visit here to explain. After that wire from Verona I wired him back defiance—

GRACE. (*Understanding.*) And that brought him on—? But only to stick then to his negative?

HUGH. To declare that, for *him*, our thing's a pure Moretto—and to declare the same, moreover, with all the weight of his authority, to Bender himself, who of course made a point of seeing him.

GRACE. So that Bender, as a consequence, is wholly off?

HUGH. (*In acute and humorous amendment.*) Bender, Lady Grace, lives like the moon, in mid-air, shedding his golden light on earth; but he *would* be in eclipse, as a peril, I grant—if the question could have struck him as really closed. Luckily the Press of our country—which is a pure heavenly joy, and now quite *immense* on it—keeps it open as wide as Piccadilly.

GRACE. Your great idea, you mean, has

so *worked?*—with the uproar *really* as loud as it has seemed to come to us here?

HUGH. All beyond my wildest hope!—since the *sight* of the Picture, flocked to every day by thousands, so beautifully *tells.* That we must at any cost *keep* it, hang on to it tight, is the cry that fills the air—air every breath of which is wind in our sails.

GRACE. I've been round there to *see* the thing; but I couldn't *stay*—for tears!

HUGH. Oh, we'll crow *yet!*—but *don't* those strange eyes of the fellow plead? The women, bless them, cling to him—and there's talk of a "Ladies' League of Protest" which all keeps *up* the pitch. So that the echo of the jolly row must certainly reach your Father.

GRACE. At far off Salsomaggiore? Possibly—but I don't hear.

HUGH. He doesn't write?

GRACE. He doesn't write. And I don't write either.

HUGH. And Lady Sandgate?

GRACE. I've asked her not to *tell* me—if he simply holds out.

HUGH. (*Making with interest the clear inference.*) So that as she *doesn't* tell you, he of course does hold out! (*Then as he looks at her hard.*) But your case is really bad.

GRACE. (*With a dim yet happy smile.*) My case is really bad.

HUGH. (*With a strong sense of impatience and contrition.*) And it's I who—all too blunderingly!—have *made* it so?

GRACE. (*With the same smile.*) Well, there it *is.* The last thing before he went I let the Picture go.

HUGH. (*Vague.*) You mean—a—gave up your Protest?

GRACE. I mean I gave up my protest. I told him he might do as he liked. I gave him my word I wouldn't help you. I see you against his express command.

HUGH. (*Immensely astonished and touched, but all jubilant.*) Ah, then thank God I *came!*

GRACE. Ah, but I *offered* him not to see you.

HUGH. (*Vague at first.*) Never again?

GRACE. (*As to go through with it.*) Never again!

HUGH. (*Understanding.*) If he'd stop the sale?

GRACE. If he'd stop the sale; but then he wouldn't. Just on that you came back—and after you had gone he would!

HUGH. And then you wouldn't?

GRACE. Then I wouldn't.

HUGH. (*As that scene is once more before him.*) You were too sorry for me?

GRACE. Those moments had put you before me—to say nothing of how they had put *him!*—in such a light that I couldn't grant his plea.

HUGH. Of my being too "low"?

GRACE. Of your being impossible.

HUGH. Not even when you're all such great people?

GRACE. (*As sparing him the invidious answer to this; turning it over and replying otherwise.*) "Great people," I've learned to see, mustn't do what Father's doing.

HUGH. It's indeed on the theory that they *won't* that we see—all the inferior rest of us!—in the *glamour* of their greatness.

GRACE. You won't see them in it for *long* —if they don't now, under such tests and with such opportunities, begin to take care!

HUGH. Lord Theign perhaps *recognises* some such canny truth! but "takes care" with the least trouble to himself, and the finest short cut, by finding "the likes of me" as his Daughter's good friend, out of the question.

GRACE. Well, you won't *mind* that—will you?—if he finds his Daughter herself, in any such relation to *you,* quite as much so!

HUGH. (*As in all the joy of what this seems to mean.*) "Mind" it?—when what he will have most done for us then is to keep us blessedly together!

GRACE. (*As really for conscience.*) Ah, but remember what I *did!* I told him to do what he *liked!*

HUGH. (*Coming back to that as with a stare and through a slight confusion.*) You mean you let the Picture slide? (*With a free brave laugh that accepts the whole inconsequence.*) Oh, I don't care a hang for the *Picture!* (*And then as she has let him closer, close to her at this, possess himself of her hands.*) We both only care, don't we? that we are *given* to each other thus! We both only care, don't we? that it has blessedly drawn us together!

GRACE. (*After they have for a moment held each other, by the hands, sounding and measuring and taking possession of each other ever so deeply and for the whole responsible future, as it were.*) Yes—let us *cleave* together.

HUGH. (*With deep ardour, taking her to his arms and his breast in the tenderest, completest embrace.*) Ah, forever and ever!

GRACE. (*While they, after the minute of her surrender, separate, though each still interlocking a hand; and as if she has heard a sound from the other room.*) Amy Sandgate!

(*They fall rapidly apart at this warning, though not too soon for* LADY SANDGATE, *who advances to the threshold, to appear to have got something of the impression of it and of what has taken place. Enter* LADY SANDGATE, *left centre, while* HUGH *and* LADY GRACE *reach, or have already reached, as she comes down a step further, opposite sides of the scene; whence, not having wholly recovered themselves, they give back, a shade awkwardly and consciously, the tolerably searching look that she directs from one to the other. This, however, not exaggerated, is the matter but of a few instants; and before these have all elapsed* GRACE *has again spoken, addressing herself to* HUGH.)

GRACE. (*In urgent reminder.*) But mustn't you go to Clifford Street?

HUGH. (*Coming back to it; all alert.*) At once! (*Then as he has recovered his hat, with which he gesticulates for farewell to* LADY SANDGATE, *reaching the door, right.*) Please *pardon* me! (*Exit* HUGH CRIMBLE, *right.*)

LADY SANDGATE. (*Who stands again for a moment silently confronted with* GRACE.) Have you freedom of mind for the fact that your Father's suddenly at hand?

GRACE. (*Much startled.*) He has come back?

LADY SANDGATE. He arrives this afternoon and appears to go straight to Kitty—

according to a wire that I found downstairs on coming in late from my luncheon.

GRACE. Brought back, you mean, by the Outcry—even though he so *hates* it?

LADY SANDGATE. Ah, hating still more to seem *afraid*, he has come characteristically to face the Music. Lest we should oppose him!—he hasn't even announced his start.

GRACE. (*Thinking, deciding.*) Then now that I've *done* it all, I shall never "oppose" him again!

LADY SANDGATE. (*As still under the impression she has received on entering.*) He'll only oppose *you*?

GRACE. (*After a little.*) Well, if he does we are two now to bear it.

LADY SANDGATE. Heaven save us then—your friend *is* clever!

GRACE. Mr. Crimble's remarkably clever.

LADY SANDGATE. And you've arranged—?

GRACE. We haven't "arranged"—but we've understood. So that, dear friend, if *you* understand—!

(*Enter* GOTCH, *right, interrupting* LADY GRACE.)

LADY SANDGATE. What is it?

GOTCH. Lord John, my lady—who has come on from Lady Imber's to know if his lordship's expected *here*, and whether, if so, he may come up.

LADY SANDGATE. (*To* GRACE.) May Lord John come up?

GRACE. As suits *you*, please!

LADY SANDGATE. (*To* GOTCH.) He may come up. His lordship's expected.

(*Exit* GOTCH, *leaving the door open.*)

LADY SANDGATE. You asked me just now if I "understood." Well, I do understand!

GRACE. Then you'll *excuse* me!

(*Exit* LADY GRACE, *left centre. Re-enter, as she disappears,* GOTCH, *mutely ushering* LORD JOHN, *and going out after his entrance.*)

LORD JOHN. (*As he greets his hostess; at the highest pitch of eagerness and tension.*) What on earth then do you suppose he has come back to *do*—?

LADY SANDGATE. I count on his doing nothing the least *foolish*—!

LORD JOHN. Ah but he can't have chucked everything for nothing; and can't not meet *somehow*, hang it, such an assault on his character as a great nobleman and a good citizen.

LADY SANDGATE. It's his luck to have become, with the public of the newspapers, the scapegoat-in-chief: for the sins, so-called, of a lot of people—!

LORD JOHN. (*Interrupting.*) Yes, the mercenary millions on whose traffic in their tuppenny values *this* isn't a patch! But I've been to Kitty's, and he was all right *so* far: he had arrived and gone out again—as Lady Imber wasn't at home.

LADY SANDGATE. Ah cool Kitty—!

(*Re-enter right, as she speaks, GOTCH, announcing.*)

GOTCH. Lord Theign!

(*Enter LORD THEIGN, right, in consummate afternoon dress. Exit GOTCH, right.*)

LADY SANDGATE. At *last,* dear Friend—but with Kitty not at home to *receive* you?

THEIGN. Oh, it was all right—I *dressed;* and I'm to find her at 5.30. But *Bender*—who came there before my arrival—he hasn't tried for me *here?*

LORD JOHN. I met him at the club at luncheon; he had had your letter and *knew*—which is the only way, my dear man, that *I* did. You'll *see* him all right—but I'm glad, if I may *say* so, Theign, to get hold of you *first.*

LADY SANDGATE. (*While LORD THEIGN looks hard, and as with a question, at this companion.*) You haven't come back, *have* you—to whatever clamour there may be!—for *trouble* of any sort with Breckenridge?

THEIGN. I've not come home for any "clamour," or to notice, for a minute, the delirium of insult—which, frankly, scarce reached me, out there; or which, so far as it did, I was daily washed clear of by those blest waters. (*Then once more to LORD JOHN.*) I've returned as an effect of a letter of Bender's, to which mine, as John mentions, was an answer—three pages about "Pappendick."

LORD JOHN. About his having suddenly turned up in person, yes—and, as Breckenridge says, "marked the Moretto down"! That *has* of course weighed on Bender—being confirmed apparently, on the whole, by the drift of public opinion.

THEIGN. (*Taking, with a movement of* impatience and irritation, a turn off, while he indicates, ironically, their companion to LADY SANDGATE.*) He has known me all these years and he comes here to talk to me about "the drift of public opinion"! (*And then with spirit to LORD JOHN.*) Am I to tell you again that I snap my *fingers* at the drift of public opinion?—which is but another name for the chatter of all the fools one *doesn't* know, in addition to all those—and plenty *of* 'em—that one does!

LADY SANDGATE. (*Soothingly.*) Ah you did *that*—in your own grand way!—before you went abroad!

LORD JOHN. (*To right himself.*) I don't speak of it, Theign, in the light of its effect on *you*—but in the light of its effect on Bender; who so consumedly wants the Picture, if he *is* to have it, to be a Mantovano, but seems unable to get it taken at last for anything but the fine old Moretto—of course!—that it has always been.

THEIGN. (*In growing impatience of the whole beastly complication.*) Well, isn't a fine old Moretto good enough for him—confound him?

LORD JOHN. (*Pulled up a little; slightly embarrassed.*) A fine old Moretto, you know, was exactly what he declined—for its comparative insignificance!—at Dedborough; and he only thought of the Picture when the wind began to set for the enormous rarity—

THEIGN. (*Anticipating.*) That that mendacious young cad who has bamboozled Grace tried to befool us into claiming for it? (*Completely now at the pitch of high impatience.*) My Picture, Moretto or Mantovano, is to take or to *leave*—and it's what I've come back here, if you please, John, to say to your friend to his face.

LADY SANDGATE. (*Again as with her best intention and as appealing to LORD JOHN.*) Yes—why in the world can't he choose *which?* And why does he write him, dreadful Breckenridge, such upsetting letters?

LORD JOHN. (*As with the air of something that has been working within him, rather vehemently, though cautiously too, as a consequence of THEIGN's tone and during this exchange: to which he has listened watchfully.*) I don't think I quite see, my dear man, *how* his letter was so upsetting.

THEIGN. Because he assumes on my part an interest in his expenditure of purchase-money that I don't feel, or pretend to! He doesn't want the Picture he refused at Dedborough; he *does* want the Picture that's on view in Bond Street; and he yet makes, with great emphasis, the stupid, ambiguous point that these two values haven't been "by now" proved different—as if I had engaged with him that I would myself so prove them!

LORD JOHN. (*After a moment's hesitation.*) He alludes to your hoping—when you allowed us to place the Picture with Mackintosh—that it would show, to all London, in the most precious light conceivable.

THEIGN. (*Staring as if mystified.*) Well, if it hasn't so shown what's the sense of this preposterous noise?

LORD JOHN. The noise is largely the noise of the people who contradict each other about it.

LADY SANDGATE. (*As to enliven the gravity of the question.*) Some—yes—shouting that it's a Mantovano, and others shrieking back at them that they don't know what they're talking about!

THEIGN. He may take it for whatever he likes if he'll but clear out with it and leave me alone!

LORD JOHN. What he'd *like* to take it for is something in the nature of a Hundred Thousand.

THEIGN. (*For astonishment.*) A Hundred Thousand?

LORD JOHN. Quite, I dare say, a Hundred Thousand.

LADY SANDGATE. (*Throwing off with promptness a momentary gape.*) Why, haven't you realised, Theign, that those are the American figures?

THEIGN. (*Looking at her fixedly a little; then looking in the same manner at* LORD JOHN; *then waiting a moment.*) I've nothing to do with American figures—which seem to me, if you press me, you know, quite beastly vulgar.

LADY SANDGATE. (*With extreme decision.*) Well, I'd be as vulgar as anybody for a Hundred Thousand!

LORD JOHN. (*To* THEIGN.) Didn't he let us know at Dedborough that he had no use, as he said, for lower values?

LADY SANDGATE. I've heard him say myself that he had no use for cheap pictures.

THEIGN. (*Highly objecting.*) Does he call the thing round the corner a cheap picture?

LORD JOHN. (*Throwing up his arms with a grimace of impatience.*) All he wants to do is to prevent your *making* it one!

THEIGN. I offered it, as it was, at a perfectly handsome estimate.

LORD JOHN. My dear reckless friend, you named no figure at *all*, when it came to the point—

THEIGN. (*Breaking in.*) It didn't come to the point! Nothing came to the point but that I put the Moretto on *view;* as a thing—(*at a reminding gesture of* LORD JOHN's) yes!—in which a rich American had an interest. That was what I wanted, and so we *left* it—parting each of us ready, but neither of us bound.

LADY SANDGATE. Ah, Mr. Bender's "bound," as he'd say—bound to make you swallow the enormous luscious plum that your appetite so morbidly rejects!

THEIGN. My appetite—as morbid as you like!—is my own affair and if the fellow must deal in enormities I warn him to carry them elsewhere!

LORD JOHN. (*As almost exasperated at the absurdity of this.*) But how can't you see that it's only a "plum," as she says, for a plum and an eye for an eye?—Since the Picture itself with this huge ventilation, is now quite a different thing!

THEIGN. (*Meeting it as with a perfect sharp clearness.*) How the deuce a different thing when just what the man himself confesses is that there's no at all *definite* ground—in spite of all the trumpery twaddle and the priggish pedantry!—for *treating* it as one?

(*On which, as having so unanswerably spoken, he turns off again in his high petulance and nervous, restless irritation; and goes up and away—the thought of something still other, and not yet quite at the surface, seeming to work in him beneath and behind all this. His companions meanwhile, right and left, watch him in uncertainty and with a reciprocal mute comment on his suddenly developed perversity and oddity:* LORD JOHN *giving a shrug almost of bored despair and* LADY SANDGATE *signalling caution and tact for it, by a finger waggled at her lips, and, immediately, taking tact and caution upon herself.*)

LADY SANDGATE. (*While* LORD THEIGN *is still up as in worried thought; having even taken up a book mechanically, which he then after an absent glance, tosses down.*) You're so detached from *reality,* you adorable dreamer!—and unless you stick to *that* you might as well have done nothing. What you call the priggish pedantry and all the rest of it is exactly what poor Breckenridge asks almost on his knees, wonderful man, to be *allowed* to pay you for; since even if they haven't settled anything for those who know—though who in the world, after all, *does* seem to know? —it's a great service rendered him to have started such a hare to run!

LORD JOHN. (*Abounding.*) Certainly his connection with the whole question and the whole agitation makes no end for his glory.

THEIGN. His "glory"—Mr. Bender's glory? Why, they quite *loathe* him—judging by the stuff they print!

LORD JOHN. Oh *here*—as a promoter of our Decay, even though they're flat on their faces to him, *yes!* But it's another affair over *there:* where he'll be, if you'll only let him, the biggest man of the hour. If he said of the thing, as you recognise, "It's going to be a Mantovano"—why "you can bet your life" it *is* somehow going to be some kind of a one!

THEIGN. (*Coming down, worked up by this unconsciously irritating insistence of the others to something quite openly wilful and perverse now.*) No kind of a furious flaunting one, under *my* patronage, that I can *prevent,* my boy! The Dedborough Picture in the market—owing to horrid little circumstances—is the Dedborough Picture, at a decent, sufficient, civilised Dedborough price, and nothing else whatever: which I beg you'll please take as my last word on the subject.

LORD JOHN. (*Hushed, with* LADY SANDGATE, *with whom he exchanges a helpless look, to silence for a moment; after which, however, he reasserts himself.*) May I nevertheless reply that I think you'll not be able to prevent *anything?*—since the discussed object will completely escape your control in New York!

LADY SANDGATE. And almost any discussed object is in New York—by what one hears—easily *worth* a Hundred Thousand!

THEIGN. (*Looking again from one of them to the other.*) I sell the man a Hundred Thousand worth of swagger and advertisement; and of fraudulent swagger and most objectionable advertisement at that?

LORD JOHN. It's the first time in all my life I've known a man feel insulted, in such a piece of business, by happening *not* to be, in the usual way, more or less swindled!

LADY SANDGATE. Theign is unable to take it in, you see, that—as I've heard it said of *all* these money-monsters of the new type—Bender simply can't *afford* not to be cited and celebrated as the biggest buyer that ever lived.

THEIGN. Ah, cited and celebrated at my *Expense*—!

LORD JOHN. (*Breaking in, going up, in his derisive impotence, and addressing the comment to* LADY SANDGATE.) The dear man's *inimitable*—at his "expense"!

THEIGN. Yes, at my expense is exactly what I mean—at the expense of my modest claim to regulate my own behaviour by my own standards! There you perfectly *are* about the man, and it's precisely what I say—that he's to hustle and harry me *because* he's a money-monster: which I never for a moment dreamed of, please understand, when I let *you,* John, thrust him at me as a pecuniary resource at Dedborough. I didn't put my property on view that *he* might blow about it—!

LADY SANDGATE. (*To help to harmonise.*) The only question perhaps is why doesn't he try for some precious work that somebody—less delicious than dear Theign!— can be persuaded on bended knees to accept a Hundred Thousand for?

LORD JOHN. (*Whom* THEIGN *has been*

more attentively watching.) "Try" for one? That was exactly what he did try for when he pressed so hard in vain for the great Sir Joshua. (*Then to* THEIGN.) Would you mind an agreement on some such basis as *this?*—that you shall resign yourself to the biggest equivalent you'll squeamishly consent to take, if it's at the same time the smallest he'll squeamishly consent to offer; but that, that done, you shall leave him free—

LADY SANDGATE. (*Taking it from him, rounding it off, as* THEIGN *only waits.*) Leave him free to talk about the sum offered and the sum taken as practically one and the same?

THEIGN. (*With the effect of an impulse that has intensely gathered force.*) You talk for him pretty well! You urge his case, upon my honour, dear chap, really quite as if you got a commission on the job. Has he *put you up* to that proposition, eh? *Do* you get a handsome percentage?

LORD JOHN. (*Rather visibly disconcerted and embarrassed, but not giving way.*) As he's to come to you himself—and (*looking at his watch*) I don't know why the mischief he doesn't come!—he will answer you that graceful question. (*After an instant, with spirit.*) I don't see why you should speak as if I were suggesting some abomination!

THEIGN. (*Facing about again.*) Then I'll *tell* you why! Because I'd rather give the cursed thing away outright and for good and all than that it should hang out there another day—in the interest of such Equivocations!

LADY SANDGATE. (*Quite amusedly wonderstruck.*) "Give it away," my dear friend, to a man who wants to smother you in gold?

THEIGN. (*Sharply impatient of her levity.*) Give it away—just for a luxury of protest and a stoppage of chatter—to some cause as unlike as possible that of Mr. Bender's splendid reputation; to the Public, to the Authorities, to the Thingumbob —to the Nation!

LADY SANDGATE. (*While* LORD JOHN *stands sombre and stupefied.*) Ah, my dear Theign, you have flights of extravagance—!

THEIGN. One thing's very certain—that the thought of the thing on view there does now give intolerably on my nerves— more and more every minute that I am conscious of it; so that, hang it, if one thinks of it, why shouldn't I have the Show immediately stopped? (*To each of them equally.*) It's *my* Show—it isn't Bender's surely? and I can do what I *like* with it. (*Then as with a sharp happy thought that relieves him.*) See here, John—do this: go right round there this moment, please, and stop it for me! Stop it *to-night.* Wind it up and end it: see? Have the Picture removed from view and the incident closed.

LORD JOHN. (*In extreme distress and displeasure.*) You really ask *that* of me?

THEIGN. (*Quite set now.*) Why in the world *shouldn't* I? It's a good deal less than you asked of me a month ago at Dedborough!

LORD JOHN. (*After a moment while they only look at each other.*) What then am I to say to them?

THEIGN. (*As if to have done with it.*) Say anything you please!

LORD JOHN. (*Still weighing it; then to* THEIGN *significantly, ominously.*) Those are your sentiments?

THEIGN. (*To get him off.*) Those are my "sentiments"!

LORD JOHN. (*Quite grimly taking his decision.*) Very well then! (*Then in final almost sinister consideration of* THEIGN.) Not one more day?

THEIGN. (*Waving it away.*) Not one more hour!

(LORD JOHN, *who has reached the door, indulges there in a motion of supreme chagrin and resentment, accompanied by another prolonged and decisive meeting of his friend's eyes; after which, clapping his hat quite resentfully and viciously on his head, he goes out. Exit* LORD JOHN, *right.*)

LADY SANDGATE. (*In sympathy.*) He can't bear, poor man, to do it.

THEIGN. I dare say not. But he goes too far, you see—and it clears the air. And now (*looking at his watch*) I must go to Kitty.

LADY SANDGATE. Won't you at any rate wait for Bender?

THEIGN. (*Curtly.*) What have I to do with him now?

LADY SANDGATE. Why, surely, if he'll accept your price—!

THEIGN. (*Thinking, wondering; then as if fairly amused at himself.*) Hanged if I know now what *is* my price! (*After which he goes for his hat.*) But there's *one* thing. Where's my unnatural Daughter?

LADY SANDGATE. I'll send and find out if you like.

THEIGN. (*Checking her.*) Not now. But does she *see* that fellow?

LADY SANDGATE. Mr. Crimble? Yes, she sees him.

THEIGN. (*His eye on her.*) How far has she gone?

LADY SANDGATE. (*Hesitating; a little embarrassed.*) Well, not even yet, I think, as far as they want.

THEIGN. They want to marry?

LADY SANDGATE. (*Evasive, after an instant.*) What should you say to it?

THEIGN. Why, that it lets us so beastly down—down from what we've always been and done; down, down, down! Why in the name of goodness *have* I such children? What on earth has got *into* 'em?—and is it really the case that when Grace offers me for proof of her license and a specimen of her taste such a son-in-law—as I understand you it comes to *that*—am I just helplessly and abjectly to *put up* with it?

LADY SANDGATE. (*After an instant.*) Do you find Mr. Crimble so very impossible?

THEIGN. I found him on the two occasions before I went away in the last degree offensive and outrageous;

(*Re-enter* GOTCH, *as he speaks, right.*)

GOTCH. (*Interrupting, mentioning, not announcing.*) Mr. Breckenridge Bender.

LADY SANDGATE. (*While* LORD THEIGN *makes a movement of sharp impatience.*) Coming up?

GOTCH. If his lordship will see him.

THEIGN. Oh, he's beyond his time—I can't see him now!

LADY SANDGATE. (*Gracefully urgent.*) Ah, but *mustn't* you—and mayn't *I* then? (*And then to* GOTCH *again, while* LORD THEIGN *stares, with a gesture of reluctant accommodation, as rather wondering at the*

point she makes of it.) Let him come.

(*Exit* GOTCH, *right.*)

LADY SANDGATE. (*Then going on to her companion.*) Does the kind of relation you would have with Mr. Crimble let you "down, down, down," as you say, more than the kind you've been having with Mr. Bender?

(*On which, however, seeing* GOTCH *reappear, she raises her hand with a "Hush!" of warning. Re-enter* GOTCH *introducing* MR. BENDER, *who comes in. Exit* GOTCH, *right.*)

THEIGN. (*Sharply immediate and frank.*) I've but a moment, to my regret, to give you, Mr. Bender; and if you've been unavoidably detained, as you great bustling people are so apt to be, it will perhaps still be soon enough for your comfort to hear from me that I've just given orders to close our Exhibition. (*And then as* BENDER, *astonished, pulls himself up, looking at him hard.*) From the present hour on, Mr. Bender.

BENDER. (*In spite of his surprise unruffled as ever.*) Why, do you really mean it, Lord Theign?—removing already from view a work that gives innocent gratification to thousands!

THEIGN. Well, if thousands have seen it I've done what I wanted, and if they've been gratified I'm content—and invite *you* to be.

BENDER. (*Vague at first; then with a bright light.*) In other words it's *I* who may remove the Picture?

THEIGN. (*After a moment.*) Well—if you'll take it on *my* valuation!

BENDER. But what, Lord Theign, all this time, *is* your valuation?

THEIGN. (*With a final hesitation; then, at door, with his eyes on* LADY SANDGATE'S, *deciding.*) Lady Sandgate will tell you! (*Exit* LORD THEIGN, *right.*)

LADY SANDGATE. (*Smiling at* BENDER, *while, in his surprise at their friend's whole proceeding, he stands, rather blankly enquiring and appealing.*) He means that yours is *much* too shockingly high.

BENDER. But how can I know *how* much —unless I find out what he'll take? Is he crazily waiting for the thing to be proved *not* what Mr. Crimble claims?

LADY SANDGATE. You mean it's at the worst the biggest bone of artistic contention—?

BENDER. (*Anticipating her.*) Yes, that has come up for quite a while, I guess I can do with it for *that.*

LADY SANDGATE. (*After a moment; serene, assured, gay; as if having now made out her way.*) Well, if it's the biggest bone of contention I won't touch it; I'll leave it to be mauled by my betters! But since his lordship has asked me to name a price, dear Mr. Bender, I'll name one; and as you prefer big prices I'll try and make it suit you. Only it won't be for the Portrait of a person that nobody is agreed about. The whole world is agreed, you, know, about my Greatgrandmother.

BENDER. (*Moving off with a gesture of now at last really ruffled patience.*) Oh shucks, Lady Sandgate!

LADY SANDGATE. You've been delivered into my hands—too charmingly; and you won't really pretend now that you don't recognise it and feel it?

BENDER. (*Who has faced about to her again in stupefaction—though not without its characteristic goodhumour—at the way the case, or at least this particular part of it, appears to be turning out for him.*) Do you mean that those uncanny words (*indicating quarter of* THEIGN's *exit*) were just to put me off? (*And then as she but smilingly and appealingly shrugs, repudiating responsibility.*) Look here, Lady Sandgate, aren't you honestly going to help me?

LADY SANDGATE. (*Gaily and sincerely.*) Mr. Bender, Mr. Bender, I'll help you if you'll help *me!* That's all *I* ask!

BENDER. (*Echoing.*) "All"? (*Then while he thinks.*) How does it foot up then?

LADY SANDGATE. Ah, isn't it in these matters always a question of what you *give?*

BENDER. Do you mean how little—?

LADY SANDGATE. Yes, how "little"—you dear sharp rich thing!

BENDER. Well, let's see. How will you *have* it?

LADY SANDGATE. Will you write a cheque?

BENDER. Yes—if you want it right away. But (*clapping vainly a breast-pocket*) my cheque-book's down there in my car.

LADY SANDGATE. At the door? (*While she touches the bell.*) Then Gotch can *get* it! It's so sweet your "flying round" with your cheque-book!

BENDER. It flies round pretty well with *me!*

(*Re-enter* GOTCH, *right.*)

LADY SANDGATE. Mr. Bender's chequebook—in his car.

BENDER. (*To* GOTCH.) You'll find in the pocket a large red morrocco case.

GOTCH. Very good, sir. (*To* LADY SANDGATE.) But Lord John wants to know—

LADY SANDGATE. (*Breaking in.*) Lord John's *there?*

GOTCH. (*As aware, by the open door, that* LORD JOHN *is coming up.*) Here he *is,* my lady.

LADY SANDGATE. (*To* BENDER; *as now, all resignedly, to be very open.*) It's he who went round to Bond Street.

BENDER. (*Staring, but taking it quickly in.*) To stop the Show? (*Then without violence, as* LORD JOHN *re-enters.*) You've stopped the Show?

(*Re-enter* LORD JOHN, *right. Exit* GOTCH.)

LORD JOHN. (*Hurried, flurried, breathless; quite other than on his exit.*) It's "on" more than ever! (*Excitedly to* LADY SANDGATE.) But Theign should be here—I announce to you a call from the Prince.

LADY SANDGATE. (*Half aghast, half enchanted.*) The Prince? He's coming?

BENDER. (*As if rising in a flash to the advantage, for his own reverberations and victories, of this auspicious possibility.*) Is the *Prince* after the thing?

LORD JOHN. (*Conscious of nothing but his errand.*) He was there with Mackintosh—to see and admire the Picture; which he thinks, by the way, a Mantovano pure and simple!—and did me the honour to remember me. When he heard me report to Mackintosh in his presence the sentiments expressed to me here by our friend and of which (*to* LADY SANDGATE *very particularly*), embarrassed though I doubtless was, I gave as clear an account as I *could,* he was so delighted with it that he said they mustn't think then of taking this thing off, but must keep it tremendously on, and he would come round and congratulate and thank Theign and explain to him his reasons.

LADY SANDGATE. Why, Theign's at Kitty's, worse luck! He calls on him *here?*

LORD JOHN. He calls, you see, on *you,* my lady—at 5.45; and desired me so to put it to you!

LADY SANDGATE. He's awfully kind—but I'm not even *dressed!*

LORD JOHN. You'll have *time*—while I rush for Theign to Berkeley Square. And pardon me, Bender—though it's so near— if I just take your car.

LADY SANDGATE. (*With the extremity of zeal.*) That's it, that's it—take his car! The Prince wants to "congratulate"?

LORD JOHN. On Theign's decision, as I've told you—which I announced to Mackintosh, by Theign's so extraordinary order, *before* him, and which he took up like a shot!

LADY SANDGATE. (*As it flashes upon her what* LORD JOHN *must have done; all to cover and evade this issue.*) The decision to remove the Picture?

LORD JOHN. (*Also ignoring what she evades.*) He wouldn't hear of such a thing —says it must stay stock still; so there you are!

BENDER. (*Clamorous.*) But what in thunder has the Prince to do with Theign's decision and what sentiments did you report he had expressed here?

LORD JOHN. (*At the door, without scruple.*) Lady Sandgate, *you* tell him! I *rush!* (*Exit* LORD JOHN *rapidly, right.*)

LADY SANDGATE. (*Determined not to recognise or to give the case away.*) They put everything on *me,* my dear man—but I haven't the least idea. Lord John's so agog that he doesn't know *what* he says!

(*Re-enter* GOTCH, *right, bearing on a salver the object he has been sent for.*)

GOTCH. The large red morocco case.

LADY SANDGATE. (*With a radiant welcome for it; to* BENDER.) Your cheque-book! (*To* GOTCH.) Lay it on my desk. (*And then to* BENDER *again, as* GOTCH, *having put down the case, goes out, right.*) Mightn't we conclude before he comes?

BENDER. (*Preoccupied.*) The Prince? (*Then coming back with a certain vague-*ness of effort to her purpose, from which his imagination has strayed.*) Will *he* want your Greatgrandmother?

LADY SANDGATE. Well, he may when he *sees* her! And Theign, when *he* comes, will give you, on his own matter—I feel sure— every information! (*Then at her writing table, to which he has come, with no great rapidity, at her persuasive gesture, and while with much deliberation, he seats himself there, his back turned to us; she having opened out the case to his use, so that he has but to help himself.*) Shall I fish it out for you? What *enormous* cheques! *You* can never draw one for two-pound-ten!

BENDER. (*Before his cheque, while he considers.*) That's exactly what you deserve I *should* do!

LADY SANDGATE. (*Gaily; coming away.*) Well, I *leave* it to you!

(*Re-enter* GOTCH, *right.*)

GOTCH. (*At the door.*) Mr. Crimble—for Lady Grace.

LADY SANDGATE. (*Surprised and disconcerted.*) Mr. Crimble?—*again?*

BENDER. (*At his cheque.*) Mr. Crimble? Why he's a man I want to *see!*

GOTCH. (*As* HUGH *has reached the landing.*) Here he *is,* my lady.

LADY SANDGATE. Then tell her ladyship.

GOTCH. (*While* LADY GRACE *appears, left centre.*) She has come down.

(*Re-enter* HUGH CRIMBLE, *right. Re-enter* LADY GRACE *in hat and gloves, etc., prepared to go out, from the other room. Exit* GOTCH, *right.*)

GRACE. (*Eagerly; straight across to* HUGH *as soon as they see each other.*) I was listening—for your knock and your voice.

HUGH. (*Breathless, but jubilant and radiant.*) Then know, thank God, it's all right!

GRACE. (*Divining, delighted.*) A Mantovano?

HUGH. (*Proud and happy.*) A Mantovano!

LADY SANDGATE. (*Echoing; also carried away.*) A Mantovano!

BENDER. (*Who has jumped up, all eagerness, from his table.*) Mantovano! (*All intensity of interest to* HUGH.) A sure thing?

HUGH. (*Smiling.*) I've just left Caselli, who hasn't the shadow of a doubt and is delighted to declare it!

BENDER. Will he declare it to *me?*

HUGH. (*Amused.*) Well, you can *try* him!

BENDER. (*All impatience to act at once and as making for his hat.*) But try him *where?* Where *is* he?

LADY SANDGATE. (*To* BENDER.) You won't wait for the Prince? (*And then anxiously to* LADY GRACE *before he can reply.*) My dear, are you *ready* for him?

GRACE. Is he *coming?*

LADY SANDGATE. At five-forty-five. (*With which she looks at her bracelet watch; but only to utter almost a scream of alarm.*) Ah, it *is* that—and I'm not dressed! (*With which she hurries out through the other room. Exit* LADY SANDGATE, *left centre.*)

BENDER. (*Then to* HUGH.) It's Caselli I want first—I'll take the Prince after!

HUGH. (*Goodhumouredly.*) Then I left him at Long's Hotel.

BENDER. (*Optimistically.*) Why, right near—I'll come back! (*Exit* BENDER *rapidly, right.*)

HUGH. (*As soon as he is alone with* LADY GRACE.) Why does the Prince come, and what in the world is happening?

GRACE. My Father has suddenly returned!

HUGH. (*Under the sudden shadow of a surprise that becomes an anxiety.*) To give us his final curse?

GRACE. I don't know and I don't care; I don't care, so long as you're right, and that the greatest light of all declares you are.

HUGH. Well, there before the holy thing, and with the place, by good luck, for those great moments, practically to ourselves—without Mackintosh to take in what was happening, or any one else at all to speak of—it was but a matter of ten minutes: Caselli had come, he had seen, and *I* had conquered!

GRACE. (*Anticipating.*) Then your reputation blazes out and your fortune's made?

HUGH. (*Doing a happy violence to his modesty.*) Well, he adores intelligence—and takes off his hat to me.

GRACE. So you need take off yours to nobody! But I should like to go and take off mine to *him;* which I seem to have put on—to go away and get *out*—on *purpose* for that!

HUGH. (*Amused and delighted.*) You *must*. We'll go forth together and you'll come there *with* me!

GRACE. (*With a sombre second thought.*) The only thing is that our awful American—

HUGH. (*As he sees the door right open; warning her with a raised hand.*) Not to speak of our awful Briton!

(*Re-enter at right* LORD THEIGN, *who at sight of his Daughter and her companion, pulls up and stands looking very hard and very stiffly, from one of them to the other; during a silence broken, however, by* HUGH's *after a little very gallantly and undauntedly addressing him.*)

HUGH. If you find me again in your path, my lord, it's because I have a small but precious document to deliver to you, if you'll allow me to do so; which I feel it important myself to place in your hand. (*With which he draws from his breast a pocket-book, extracting thence a small unsealed envelope; retaining the latter a trifle helplessly in his hand while* LORD THEIGN *still only stares at him. But he goes bravely on.*) I mentioned to you the last time we—somewhat infelicitously!—met that I intended to appeal to another, and probably higher, artistic authority on the subject of your so-called Moretto; and I in fact saw the Picture, half an hour ago, with Caselli of Milan, who, there in the presence of it, did absolute, did *ideal*, justice, as I had hoped, to the claim I've been making. I then went with him to his hotel, close at hand, where he dashed me off this brief and rapid, but quite conclusive Declaration, which—if you'll be so good as to read it—will enable you perhaps to join us in regarding the vexed question as settled.

(LORD THEIGN, *having listened to this address, stares again hard at* HUGH, *hard at the note in his hand, hard at the floor; and then turns off and goes ambiguously and inscrutably up, his head a good deal in the air, while* HUGH *and* GRACE *exchange together a decidedly hope-less look. Then* GRACE *speaks.*)

GRACE. If you won't take it from Mr. Crimble, Father, will you take it from *me?* (*And then as, turning, he comes down.*) It may be long again before you've a chance to do a thing I ask!

THEIGN. (*With a high, cold, dry emphasis.*) The chance will depend on yourself! (*On which, however, he holds out his hand for the note which* HUGH *has given her, and which she approaches him with; they stand separated, as it were, by a long silent mutual gaze while he slowly accepts the missive. She then turns away on one side, as* HUGH *has turned on the other;* LORD THEIGN *draws forth the contents of the envelope and broodingly and inexpressively reads it; after which, as gravely thinking it over, he gives it back to* LADY GRACE, *who has turned again to take it. She restores it to* HUGH, *while her father fidgets once more up, coming round and down and meeting* HUGH, *who now again holds out the letter for him to receive it back.* THEIGN *has on this with him a similar passage to the one he has previously had with* GRACE; *they look at each other hard—then he decides to accept the document, which he accordingly receives and slips into his breast-pocket. After which he speaks sharply, shortly, distinctly.*) Thank you, sir! (*Under the eyes of the others he bethinks himself—then he addresses his daughter.*) I must let Mr. Bender know—

HUGH. (*Anticipating him.*) Mr. Bender, my lord, *does* "know." He's at the present moment with the author of that note—at Long's Hotel.

THEIGN. (*After another ambiguous look at him.*) Then I must now write him.

GRACE. (*Indicating* LADY SANDGATE'S *desk, at which* BENDER *has been seated.*) Will you write *there?*

THEIGN. (*Who at this, with a movement of decision, has gone to the desk and sat down; uttering the next moment, as he appears to help himself to paper and ink, and on taking up the cheque that* BENDER *has left lying there, a startled cry.*) Hullo!

GRACE. (*Who is down on one side while* HUGH *is down on the other.*) You don't

find things?

THEIGN. On the contrary! (*But suppressing his surprise, he hastily indites a few words, still under the eyes of his silent companions, and then, having put them into an envelope and addressed it, comes away with it.*)

HUGH. If you like I'll *go* with it.

THEIGN. (*Weighing, wondering.*) But how do you know what's *in* it?

HUGH. I *don't* know. But I risk it.

THEIGN. (*After an instant longer; deciding, giving him the note, as finally to wash his hands of the whole question.*) Then you'll learn.

GRACE. (*To her father as* HUGH *has stood a moment with the note, and with his eyes mutely appealing to her.*) And may *I* learn?

THEIGN. You?

GRACE. May I go *with* him?

HUGH. (*As* THEIGN *hangs fire a little, as if facing it without enthusiasm.*) With me, my lord.

THEIGN. (*After a short further delay, to* GRACE; *with a tone and manner as of chucking it all up.*) You may do as you like!

(*At this* LADY GRACE, *with a movement that seems supremely to present her choice as made, reaches the door, which* HUGH, *who has been down right, opens for her. Here she pauses as for another, a last look at and from her father; and then she goes out.*)

HUGH. (*At the door, to* LORD THEIGN, *for farewell.*) Thank you then! (*Exit* HUGH CRIMBLE, *right.*)

THEIGN. (*Alone, in a moment's thought; with impatient irony.*) Tit for tat! (*After which, quickly bethinking himself, he goes back to the table at which he has written his note; coming away from it again the next instant with* BENDER's *forgotten cheque in his hand. This he again scrutinizes, in much wonderment.*) What the Devil—! (*But he checks himself as he becomes aware of* LADY SANDGATE, *who has appeared through the other room; and awaits her there with the cheque thrust into his waistcoat-pocket.*)

(*Re-enter* LADY SANDGATE, *left*

centre; having changed her dress for something still smarter and more appropriate to receiving Princes.)

LADY SANDGATE. Ah, you're alone?

THEIGN. I've just parted with Grace and Mr. Crimble.

LADY SANDGATE. (*As if it's ambiguous.*) "Parted" with them?

THEIGN. Well, they've gone forth together.

LADY SANDGATE. But surely to come back!

THEIGN. I haven't the least idea. I don't *understand* it at all—I dislike it too completely.

LADY SANDGATE. (*Optimistically, cheeringly.*) You'll get *used* to it!

THEIGN. That's just what I'm *afraid* of—what such dreadful doings *make* of one!

LADY SANDGATE. (*As before.*) The recipient, at the *worst*, you see, of royal attentions!

THEIGN. Oh, it's as if the gracious Personage were coming to *condole*!

LADY SANDGATE. (*Impatient of the lapse of time; assuring herself again of the hour.*) Well—if he only *does* come!

THEIGN. John—the wretch!—will take care of that: (*mastering more and more his vision of the manner of it*) I had come between him and some profit that he doesn't confess to, but that made him, viciously and vindictively, serve me up there, as he caught the chance, to the Prince—and the People!

LADY SANDGATE. By saying that you had remarked here that you offered the People the Picture—?

THEIGN. As a sacrifice—yes!—to morbid, though respectable Scruples.

LADY SANDGATE. (*After an instant; bravely and boldly taking her line.*) Ah, you had reacted against Bender—but you didn't go so far as *that*!

THEIGN. (*Keeping it altogether before him.*) I had reacted—like a gentleman; but it didn't thereby follow that I *acted*—or spoke!—like a Demagogue; so that there only flushes through my conscience the fact that he has forced my hand.

LADY SANDGATE. (*After an instant; soothingly.*) Well, even if he did so spitefully commit you, you still don't want—do you? —to back out.

THEIGN. (*Shocked at the suggestion; his head very high.*) When did I ever in my life back out? The Picture, none the less, has just been pronounced definitely priceless! (*And then to meet her inquiring gaze.*) Mr. Crimble's latest adviser, who clearly proves it a Mantovano and whose practical affidavit I now have.

LADY SANDGATE. (*As he takes from his waistcoat the ample cheque found by him on her table and which he has stuck away on her entrance.*) Is that the affidavit?

THEIGN. This is a cheque to your order for Ten Thousand Pounds.

LADY SANDGATE. (*Catching it up; immensely struck.*) Ten Thousand—?

THEIGN. Drawn by some hand unknown—

LADY SANDGATE. (*In the flush and confusion of her wonder; strangely echoing.*) "Unknown"—?

THEIGN. Which I found there (*nodding at the table*) a moment ago, and I thought best, in your interest, to rescue from accident or neglect—even though it be, save for the single stroke of a name begun, unsigned.

LADY SANDGATE. (*In complete embarrassment.*) "Unsigned"? Then it isn't good—?

THEIGN. It's a Barmecide feast! (*With his eyes sharply on her.*) But who is it who writes you colossal cheques?

LADY SANDGATE. (*Recovering herself by a great and brilliant effort; facing him bravely while she smiles and bethinks herself.*) And then leaves them lying about? Why, who can it have been but poor Breckenridge too?

THEIGN. (*Still sharply watching her and wondering.*) "Breckenridge"? What in the world does he owe you money for?

LADY SANDGATE. (*After an instant; magnificent in the revolution she then successfully performs.*) Not, you dear suspicious thing, for my Greatgrandmother! (*Then while he stares perplexed.*) He makes my life a *burden* to me—for the love of my precious Lawrence.

THEIGN. (*In superior surprise and reprobation.*) Which you're letting him *grab*?

LADY SANDGATE. (*Shaking her head now as in bland compassion for such an idea.*) It isn't a Payment, you goose—it's a *bribe*!

I've withstood him, these weeks, as a rock the tempest; but he wrote that and left it there to tempt me, to *corrupt* me!

THEIGN. (*Unsatisfied: turning the cheque over again.*) Without putting his name?

LADY SANDGATE. (*Bethinking herself, with an effort, for this anomaly; then sincerely accounting for it.*) He must have been interrupted in the act—he sprang up, with such a bound, at Mr. Crimble's news. Then he hurried off—leaving the cheque forgotten and unfinished. (*Then smiling, her eyes fascinated by the morsel of paper which her companion still handles.*) But of course on his next visit he'll add his great signature!

THEIGN. (*With passionate decision.*) No he won't! (*He tears the cheque into several pieces which flutter to the floor.*)

LADY SANDGATE. (*With an irrepressible but humorous wail.*) Ay, ay, ay—!

THEIGN. (*His eyes fixed on her again.*) Do *you* want to back out? (*And then for clearness.*) I mean from your noble stand.

LADY SANDGATE. (*After an instant, with an heroic effort; to banish all suspicion.*) I'd rather do even what *you're* doing—offer my Treasure to the Thingumbob!

THEIGN. (*With a different look at her now; moved by this.*) Will you then *join* me in enriching the National Gallery?

LADY SANDGATE. (*Her breath taken away.*) Ah, my dear friend—!

THEIGN. (*Insistent, persuasive, appealing.*) It would convince me.

LADY SANDGATE. (*Feeling it; affected; drawing nearer him.*) Ah, ah—!

THEIGN. It would comfort me.

LADY SANDGATE. (*Nearer still.*) Ah, ah, ah—!

THEIGN. (*Now as in frank homage.*) It would captivate me.

LADY SANDGATE. (*Close to him; as fluttered by all her hope.*) It would captivate you?

THEIGN. Well, one needs *help*, you see—to be consistently heroic!

LADY SANDGATE. Oh I'm very certain that *I*, at such a rate, shall need it!

THEIGN. Then we'll bring it off *together* —and (*while he takes her hand*) it will make us incorruptibly *one!*

LADY SANDGATE. (*With gay courage.*) Well—I dedicate my one ewe lamb, I confirm my sacrifice.

THEIGN. And keep your poor old friend up! (*With which he kisses her hand in earnest consecration of this agreement; but drops it as he sees* LORD JOHN *at the door and she moves away.*) The Prince?

(*Re-enter* LORD JOHN, *right.*)

LORD JOHN. (*As in the manner of a call to arms.*) The Prince!

THEIGN. (*Who has reached the door.*) I meet him below!

LADY SANDGATE. (*Demurring, wondering.*) But oughtn't *I*—in my house?

THEIGN. (*Weighing it for an instant, but with a smile.*) You mean he may *think—?* (*Then deciding, with a kiss of his hand to her.*) He shall think the Truth! (*Exit* LORD THEIGN, *right.*)

LADY SANDGATE. (*As* LORD JOHN, *who has stared in some surprise at this exchange, is, with eagerness, about to follow; addressing him with an authority she has not before used.*) Lord John, be so good as to stop! (*And then, as looking about as at the state of the room, she sees on the floor the fragments of the torn cheque.*) And please pick up that litter! (*To compliance with which sharp order we see him, after another surprised stare, bend his extreme elegance, while the Curtain descends.*)

Monologue
Written for Ruth Draper
1913

EDITOR'S FOREWORD

The monologue for Ruth Draper, written by Henry James in 1913, is outside the main stream of his dramatic writing. It is essentially a *jeu d'esprit* and was his tribute to Miss Draper's art as a *diseuse* long before she had achieved her distinguished international reputation. When James first saw her do some of her characterizations and sketches she had not yet embarked upon her professional stage career; she had appeared in London in a few private salons, always writing and developing her own material. Miss Draper talked to James of her plans. She wondered whether she should go on the stage in plays, devote herself to writing or do the unique type of sketch she later made famous. She has quoted James as saying to her, "My dear child . . . you . . . have woven . . . your own . . . very beautiful . . . little Persian carpet. . . . Stand on it!"

That she had produced a deep impression is shown in the fact that he wrote the monologue even though she assured him it was not her habit to use material other than that written by herself. He sent her his first rough draft, keeping no copy for himself, and wrote to her on December 4, 1913, "perhaps you may find it more or less to your purpose. . . . I seem definitely to 'visualize' you and hear you, not to say infinitely admire you, very much in it. It strikes me, going over it again, as a really practical, *doable* little affair. . . ." He pleaded for complete anonymity and gave her permission to cut it "if you find anything *can* be spared." He expressed doubt on that score, however, "because it seems to me so *close* already, for comprehension and clearness; for adequate *expression*, I mean, of its idea."

Miss Draper felt that to have done the monologue without revealing its authorship, as James suggested, was impossible. For one thing it "bore his peculiar stamp." She felt she certainly could not do it as written by herself, and consequently she never produced it. "I think he was disappointed, but I never learned it or tried it on anyone," she said.

Readers of Henry James's novels and tales will recognize the theme of the monologue. It expresses "the acute case of Queenship" which he felt to be too prevalent among certain American women of his day. James had written all his life about American women, representing them in his fiction either as supremely gifted heiresses of all the ages, or as predatory creatures, or as creatures such as Daisy Miller, simple, naive, possessed of a New World freshness and insouciance unaware of complex forces at play around them. He liked the courage, independence and individuality of the American woman; but on the negative side of their new-found freedom he saw some of them as aggressive, demanding, masculine. Spoiled by doting husbands or parents, they walked across the American-European stage, hard and imperious, graceless and exacting. In a series of articles written for *Harper's Bazar* in 1907 on the speech and manners of American women, reflecting his impressions of his rediscovery of America after his long residence abroad, he clearly expresses his disappointment that the American woman's enviable social position did not seem to carry with it a feeling of *noblesse oblige*.

He wrote: "The world about the American woman has not asked of her . . . that she shall have definite conceptions of duty, activity, influence; of a possible grace, a possible sweetness, a possible power to soothe, to please, and, above all, to exemplify. It has simply . . . taken her for granted as a free, inspired, supreme thing, nobly exempt . . . there is nothing the American woman socially less resembles than a second fiddle. It is before her, and her only, that the score is open, while, without any hesitation, and with a play of elbow all her own, she brandishes the bow."

It is in this context, as in the context of *The Bostonians* with its ironical treatment of suffragettes, faddists, the "do-gooders" of James's time, the socially and politically ambitious female, that this little monologue must be read.

MONOLOGUE WRITTEN
FOR RUTH DRAPER

The Secretary of Embassy, who has called, is there in her sitting-room at the hotel or wherever, but she is clearly disappointed as to what he has had to say.

Do you mean to say, Mr. Lynch, that you've come to tell me my Presentation isn't even yet arranged, after all the time I've given you—with my writing on from Florence? Why, I've got to go over to Paris for at least three weeks on the 23rd; so this next Drawing-room is just the one I want, as I can't possibly be here for the one after, and still less wait if there's to be another; I want to get the good of it— I should think you'd understand!—before I'm about ten years older. You didn't come to tell me anything about it—is that what you suggest, but just for my sweet society and to talk over friends in New York? Well, then, you shall have all of my society you want as soon as this thing is fixed—but I won't talk over anything till you can let me know it is. I have the Ambassador's promise—that is, I have your colleague's assurance, which I hope you understand I *take* for a promise—that the Ambassador wants me to be put right through. Why, he told me so himself last week, when I asked him what you're all here for, in such style, at our expense, unless to back us up and protect us. Your colleague, as your superior, is responsible?—and he must be attending to it; is that what you mean? Well, I want you to go right to that telephone—just step across the hall there, you'll see, and ring them up about it, and come back in about three minutes and tell me my name's down for the 9th. What will I do for you

if you see about it? Why, I'll just tell you with my sweetest smile that I'm glad to see you do feel what you were sent out here for; it seemed to me at the Embassy lunch that you didn't quite feel it. Don't you know you were sent out to act, for our benefit—not to talk about it, but just to do it: for which I'm giving you such a splendid chance. Yes, you shall have tea at five if Sir Robin Adair doesn't come in before—I'm staying in for him on purpose, but he's usually before his time, and rather awful, too, if he finds anyone else. He mostly does, as I couldn't live in solitude for him, poor man, even if I wanted to; but I told them to let in nobody *but* you—just to have from you what I've been waiting for. (*With the opening of the door.*) Here he *is.* (*To her maid, who ushers in* SIR ROBIN.) *Faites voir à Monsieur le téléphone.* How are you, dear Sir Robin? You know Mr. Lynch, our Second Secretary?—who's arranging my Presentation for the 9th. (*Then as the two men have bowed and the maid waits, waving* MR. LYNCH *off.*) Remember the 27th won't do a wee *speck.* . . (*The door closed, she is alone with* SIR ROBIN.) Why yes. I've got to go to Paris for about three weeks—oh don't be afraid, you won't lose me for long, and I expect you'll come over too! So it simply *has* to be this first one. And it's always my rule, too, everywhere, to have my Presentation fixed for the very first date, don't you see?—so that I come in for whatever else I want. You can *do* all sorts of things with Them then —or at least *we* can; but I suppose you know. I lost about a month at Berlin last year—they seemed too *helpless,* and at last I practically did it myself. But I can assure you our man there heard of it—as they shall hear of it here too (*with smiling and pleasing decision*) if I have to waste my precious days. (*Then, as if he has spoken amusedly.*) I seem to make them do what I want? Why, what in the world *should* I make them do? I agree with you—one ought to help them on their way. Then if they don't understand, poor dears, it isn't at least one's fault; and I don't at all subscribe to the pushing and fighting and rowing that *your* women seem to find necessary. The only way *I* can see it is that we should always be perfectly charming. We *have* it all—what we want—over there, have it as our *right;* we don't have to scream and scratch and kick for it. It comes to us of itself—by the natural chivalry of our men, who just *keep* us on the pedestal where we belong —at our nicest!—in any society that has a right to call itself civilised. Why, I had never really had to ask for anything in all my life till I struck that state of things in Berlin. *Their* women are abject—they grovel to the men; and our Embassy, with the sight of it all round them, seemed to have lost their own sense! Don't I miss it here then—since yours grovel too? Don't I miss our native pedestal and the lovely way we just float on? (*She looks at him a moment with beautiful bland archness.*) Well, no, Sir Robin—I don't think I miss anything with *you,* because I seem to recognise that you feel the *charm*—oh no (*with a laughing protest against the too personal application*), I don't mean mine more than any other, you poor dear dense delightful Englishman; I mean that of our beautiful response to the way we're treated in general—when we're really nice: the effect on us of being treated as Queens is that we have the grace and dignity and outlook of a class *expected* to receive homage sweetly. We get so much of it that we *have practice*—we know *how;* and that's why (*more and more charming to him*) I have the confidence just to accept all yours. It's the way to make you comfortable—don't pretend to tell me it isn't. I know how to make people comfortable, and (*as she sees her maid reappear*) I don't

mind telling you that my husband over there is the person in all the world I make *most so! Un télégramme? Merci.* (*With the missive, holding it up as a trophy.*) A cable —à propos!—just to show how he feels I trust him; and probably not even his regular remittance; since he knows by instinct when I want a little extra, and it's just laid then, with his compliments, at the foot of my Throne. *Bien,* Marie. You allow me? (*She has opened her envelope, but her face shows dismay as she reads.*) Well, I declare—of all the coolness! It isn't a remittance? No, it isn't a remittance. (*Taking in the disconcerting difference.*) It's only a Liberty! Then they do take them with us, you say? Possibly—(*throwing up her head with spirit, with decision and disgust*)—Men are capable of anything anywhere! But this is quite the *first* Mr. Tuff has ever taken—and (*with still higher decision*) I nip it in the bud. What I *call* a Liberty? I call *that.* (*Thrusting her cable at him, the words of which she repeats.*) "Think of sailing Saturday— want change." (*With rising impatience.*) Well, then, *I* don't—change is the very last thing that would suit me now: except—yes —in the sense in which, as you say, he doesn't send it! To be sure! Your wit is homely, Sir Robin, but that *is* exactly what I'd prefer—that he should stay at home and *make* change!

(*On which* MR. LYNCH *reappears.*) Oh, Mr. Lynch—well then? Your "confounded colleague"? Well, if you've been talking with him what does he say? "He's talking now with the Ambassador, who's at home." (*Surprised, displeased.*) Does it take such floods of talk? (*To* SIR ROBIN.) About my poor little Presentation! Rather—"they ought to jump at me"! (*To* MR. LYNCH *again, holding up her cablegram.*) Well, then, while they're sitting in judgment and you're doing nothing, just telephone, please, to the Cable Office: "Cipher, New York. Don't Sail. Await remittance. Cora." No—don't muddle it, please; it isn't *I* who don't sail—I never meant to! *He* doesn't. Nor he who awaits remittance. *I* do. There —just that. And right off, please. But for goodness' sake, too, keep hold of your colleague. (*To* SIR ROBIN *again, as poor helpless* MR. LYNCH *is off.*) Yes—as I was explaining; that's how it is: we're Queens because you just *make* us so. That is, not *you* in particular, because we come to you ready made—and you wouldn't be capable even if we didn't! But you all feel our difference—even when you don't know, poor things, what to do with it: yes, except to be just abjectly under the charm. You struggle—because you think you ought to and can't help it; but I do you justice—you *are* all the while nice and abject. You see it *gives* us something, and that carries us: our unique position—which wouldn't be anything, no, perhaps, if we didn't know how to take it. But we do know how to take it, you see—and that's why we reign! Why, I'd be just as ashamed to abdicate—with our power for *good*—as Queen Victoria would have been; who was about the only one of your women, anyway, who has *had* our position. (*Smiling at him for the bewildered way he takes this.*) You don't know what to think of my comparisons—but that's just why I fascinate you! (*As* MR. LYNCH *reappears.*) Well, have you sent it? Then *that* at least is a mercy! And have you got your colleague back? "Seems a difficulty"—with your Chief? What difficulty? On the part of your colleague? What has he to do with it, anyway? Can't you talk to the Ambassador straight? If you really can't, you know, *I* can! (*Then as for the benefit of both of them, as if* SIR ROBIN *has spoken.*) "I did in Berlin"—yes, very straight indeed—and I guess it's on the records! (*Then all to* MR. LYNCH, *who has spoken to her in astonishment.*) The difficulty's about Mr. Tuff—where he *is*? (*Really amazed.*) What has *that* got to do with it? The Ambassador wants to know? (*With resolution.*) Then tell him it's none of his business! (*To* SIR ROBIN.) Oh—"I go too far"? Not in the least!—I go but the full length of the American woman's right! (*To* MR. LYNCH *again.*) Tell your Chief I ask him where the Ambassadress is. (*Echoing.*) "She happens to be just now in New York"? (*As with triumph.*) Well, then, that's just where Mr. Tuff happens to be. (*In continued surprise as* MR. LYNCH *goes on.*) "He isn't due, then, to arrive before—?" Before

what? Before the Drawing-room? (*Then to* SIR ROBIN, *while* MR. LYNCH *hangs fire embarrassed.*) And as you say, indeed, when I just stopped him!—though (*with amusement*) I guess if he was thinking of coming it wasn't for the Drawing-room. Mr. Tuff isn't much on Drawing-rooms. (*Yet explicitly, for the benefit of both.*) Mr. Tuff is a *very* nice man—and a very *fine* man; but he has no call at all to London; and (*to* MR. LYNCH) I *must* ask you to get on, please, with my business. I can do *my* part alone—without Mr. Tuff. (*Exit* MR. LYNCH; *with her surprise at the apparently desperate manner of it.*) What in the world's the matter with him—throwing up his hands like that. (*Then as after some shrug from* SIR ROBIN.) It does, indeed, seem another case of Berlin—and if our people down there aren't simply stupid about it, why your old monarchs over here want looking after; and if they don't take care I'll just go for them. Perfectly—as you say—one regular Royalty is as good as another; when Royalty is what we claim! (*But renewed surprise again for* MR. LYNCH'S *reappearance with a question.*) "Can't I get him?" Mr. Tuff? Get him for *you*,—poor dear busy Alvin! "Get him for the Lord Chamberlain"? (*At her climax of bewilderment.*) What does *he* want all of a sudden—? (*She looks in sincere challenge and wonder from one of the men to the other; then, in impatience, almost in pity, for so much queer clumsiness; addressing* MR. LYNCH.) Yes, you strange ineffectual thing, please say I want to understand and should very much like to *know!* (*Exit again* MR. LYNCH; *followed by her stare of an instant at* SIR ROBIN, *in whom she sees criticism, amusement or whatever.*) I "scare" him—"out of his wits?" (*In perfect good faith.*) How can I?—when I'm so clear and reasonable, if *they*'d only be! (*Quite bland and earnest to* SIR ROBIN *as if really for explanation.*) We don't scare—how ridiculous!—with our position, and our grace; and our men know how to take us—that's the way they understand it. (*With a nod towards* MR. LYNCH'S *whereabouts.*) He's all right, except that he's not as *bright* as we really ought to have them, you see. But I shall have done him good. I'm not sorry that you should see, in a sort of way, what you told me the other day you wanted so—"how our institutions work." (*But as if a bit pulled up by something he answers.*) Our "social" ones—yes; I'm not talking about our political—though (*as with the duty of showing spirit*) I guess they're about as good as yours anyway. You'll see how *this* will work—if I just sit tight—even if your Lord Chamberlain *has* gone off at such a tangent. If they can have *me*, why such a clamour for Mr. Tuff? Alvin's nice, as I say—and if he *were* here I guess he'd be interested, but that's just what he just is in *my* being! Therefore, why drag him in? (*Amused.*) Don't you think you might—as your province—find out what's the matter with them? (*With* SIR ROBIN's *having, as he shows, his idea.*) "You think you know—and wonder I don't guess?" Well, if I don't, it's perhaps because over there on our side we're not used to be kept guessing. When we don't know we're informed. (*As he has, to her amusement, taken her up.*) "But we generally know"? Yes, I think we generally know—because I think we happen to have instincts. "And here (*as he has imputed*) my instinct fails"? Well, I'm not obliged to have one for the mysteries of your machinery—so let me enjoy the sensation of feeling my mind a blank! (*Highly good natured.*) "I make you so often feel yours one"? Then we'll call it quits—and (*as the door again opens*) let Mr. Lynch perhaps at last explain! (*But she sees only her maid with an open note.*) Il est parti? (*Taking the note.*) Qu'est-ce donc? (*With the note, mystified; but first to* SIR ROBIN.) What are you laughing at? (*Wondering at his answer.*) He's in a "funk"? Well, *I'm* not! (*With her eyes only now on the contents of her note, which she reads out.*) "Lord Chamberlain wants *Husbands*—to

account for you all; and draws the line at four of you, in the six of our submitted list, without apparently half-a-one between you! Too few, he says, to the dozen. Requires at least one—so fear it's for *you* to produce him. No song, no supper! Lynch." (*She stands quite arrested and astounded; it's really a revelation, requiring time for her to take it in.*) Well, of all the feeble arguments! (*But she sees her visitor convulsed with his amusement.*) Yes—and as funny as you like! (*She has a pause, a long one, quite a silence, of deep consideration—her first mystification beginning to pass gradually, while she gazes before her into the recognition of her practical necessity. This passage represents her fine little capacity for understanding, after all; and shadows forth in her, with its light on the practical, her possession of the famous "American adaptability." She must make it very pretty and interesting— as she easily can; and, in its visible process, very intelligible. She is after a moment before the table, facing her public, on which writing materials stand, and there, thoughtful, reads over again* MR. LYNCH's *revelation. Then, as with a comprehensive decision, to* SIR ROBIN, *her maid having left before.*) Please ring them up for me. No— not the Embassy. To *cable*. (*More definitely launched in action now, taking the cable advertisement, with its telephone indications, from the table, and holding it out to him.*) Their number. (*Then as he has come back for it, she reads it out.*) "Come right over; King wants us both, Cora." (*Then to* SIR ROBIN.) That, please. (*Alone again, after his exit with the paper, she mechanically straightens out two or three things while she thinks; then she is on her feet again—with a sort of uplifting vision of everything.*) I'm so glad Alvin's nice!

A Note on the Texts
Notes
Index

A NOTE ON THE TEXTS

In assembling the plays of Henry James for publication, over a period of two decades, the editor was able to collate thirty-three texts of six of the seven hitherto unpublished plays (the seventh being *Summersoft* of which only one text appears to be extant). The corrections and emendations were such as occur in the progress of a modern play from the dramatist's desk, through the production office into the theatre. James was called upon to revise his plays many times; typed copies were multiplied, each with different cuts and alterations. The very abundance of the texts testifies to the consistency—as well as the persistency—of his struggle within the dramatic form.

How arrive at a text Henry James would have deemed "definitive"? One could always produce a variorum edition, but neither the dramatist, nor the plays, nor the textual problems arising from collation, warranted such a procedure. Some middle course obviously was indicated that would satisfy the demands of scholarship—that is of truth, fidelity to text and to the writer's intentions— while meeting the general purpose which publication of these plays would serve: that of demonstrating their role in Henry James's half-century of creation and of providing a basic text of each play to permit students and public alike to read them and perhaps—if the fancy of some producer might be caught in the process—provide the means for the appearance of at least some of them on the American stage. I therefore directed my editing to this end.

It seemed to me that a variorum edition of at least one of the plays was justified, so that the reader might follow the problems James encountered and sought to overcome in the creation of a play. *The American* was ideally suited to this purpose, since there existed the original typescript of the Southport production with James's alterations in his own hand, and the printed prompt books of the London production, two of them from James's own library, as well as other copies with corrections and stage directions inserted by him or by the actors. It was thus possible to give the mutations of James's first important effort in the theatre, including a variant fourth act.

As regards the other plays, a simple principle was applied. Henry James invariably resisted the cutting of his texts. Therefore the plays had to be published in their longest, fullest form, with all the cuts restored; in a few minor instances there were cuts followed by alterations and where these were in James's hand they were accepted as his final reading; where there were simply cuts, these were put back so long as they were consistent with the rest of the text. Where later revisions made re-inclusion of any portion impossible, it was deemed wiser to adhere to the ultimate changes. No generalizations, however, can cover the problems encountered in such a multiplicity of texts and in a number of instances arbitrary editorial discretion had to be exercised; where deemed advisable, the alternate readings have been given.

There was one exception from the general rule of the fullest possible text. This was in the case of *The High Bid.* Having access to the Forbes-Robertsons' typescripts of the play, I decided that it would be of interest to publish the text as actually performed on the stage in 1909, which James had approved, despite a number of alterations and cuts. This play can thus be studied in its three versions: as a one-act play never performed; as the short story *Covering End* and in the final form it took when it reached the stage.

While James went over most of the manuscripts of his plays, making corrections and verbal changes, or inserting new portions, he did not pay close attention in certain instances to spelling or punctuation. There are inconsistencies from play to play and inconsistencies within the plays as well. Where no changes in meaning were involved, punctuation and spelling have been made consistent *within each play* but have been allowed to stand inconsistent from play to play. Such inconsistencies as Newman's alternately referring to "Valentin" and "Valentine" are retained as in the text as well as James's highly personal and likewise inconsistent method of obtaining emphasis or meaning through capitalization and italicization. In some of the texts the names of the characters were abbreviated before each speech; these have been spelled out as an aid to readability.

Readers seeking bibliographical information concerning the five published plays and the two rare prompt-books of *The American* and *Guy Domville* will find these fully described in LeRoy Phillips's *Bibliography of the Writings of Henry James* (New York, 1930), pp. 26–27, 46–47 and 115–16.

A listing and evaluation of the texts collated for this edition follows:

The American:

(1) The Lord Chamberlain licensed *The American* for production at the Winter Gardens Theatre, Southport, on December 12, 1890. The typescript submitted to the Lord Chamberlain's Office appears to have been Edward Compton's. It contains many corrections and several inserted pages in James's hand as well as his indications of action and pronunciation for Edward Compton.

(2) The printed prompt-book for the London production, set up by William Heinemann, but never published. This differs in a number of instances from the Southport typescript. Speeches have been tightened and rendered more colloquial. The stage directions have been retained and elaborated and the exact position and movements of each actor are indicated. In a number of instances speeches in the original text have been made to serve as stage directions in the revised text—where James had used words which had, in production, been supplanted by action and stage business. The prompt-book is set up in the same style as the published plays, with the names of the characters centered over the speeches. It is clear from the care taken in the setting that James intended to have this type used for an edition of the play, had it proved a greater success. The following copies were examined:

(a) A copy from Henry James's library, now in the Houghton Library, interleaved with corrections inserted in his hand. This copy contains a number of changes in Act IV, apparently those made for the "second edition" of the play on the fiftieth night of the London run.

(b) A copy formerly in the James Collection of the late Paul Lemperly of Cleveland, Ohio now in the Colby College Library, Waterville, Maine, with Henry James's signature on the cover and containing a number of corrections in James's hand.

(c) A copy from Henry James's library now in the Houghton Library, with his autograph on the front cover. On the fly-leaf, in James's hand are pencilled notes, apparently reminders to himself—the word "girl" and under it "Mme. de B's getup" and under this "Music before 3rd Act." This copy contains a number of changes similar to those in (b) as well as some other emendations.

(d) Elizabeth Robin's copy containing a few of her notes on the role of Madame de Cintré. The copy is dated in her hand Sept. 10, 1891, clearly the day she received it, since James wrote to her on Sept. 9, 1891, "I hope to be able to send you *today* the printed prompt-book."

(e) A copy in the possession of John L. Balderston, who dramatized *Berkeley Square* from James's unfinished novel *The Sense of the Past*. There are no corrections.

(f) A copy in the archives of Messrs. Heinemann, publishers, London, containing no corrections.

Guy Domville:

(1) The typescript of the play is in the Houghton Library.

(2) The printed prompt-book follows closely the typescript with only a few minor alterations such as, "Leave him with me," changed to read, "Leave me with him," and substitution of a few phrases and words to improve clarity. The prompt-book is not printed with the care of *The American* and the names are to the left of the speeches instead of being centered over them. The following copies of the prompt-book were examined:

(a) A copy in the Lord Chamberlain's office, containing no alterations and marked as licensed for production on Dec. 10, 1894.

(b) A copy in the Houghton Library. This was Henry James's and contains a number of corrections in his hand. At the Houghton there is to be found a sheaf of manuscript in James's hand, individual sheets containing a series of corrections and alterations made by the novelist. These were copied into the prompt-books, apparently by a copyist or secretary at the theatre, and this explains the fact that other copies which have turned up in the rare book market are interleaved and contain numerous textual changes.

(c) A copy in the Henry E. Huntington Library, San Marino, California, interleaved and containing the corrections and alterations of the loose sheets described in (b) written in by three hands, one of them James's. The majority of changes, however, are not in James's hand but in a handwriting resembling that of other similar copies. James's autograph changes are on pp. 18, 19, 26, 31, 53, 55, 78, 79.

(d) Marion Terry's copy, interleaved and corrected in a similar fashion to (c), now at the Colby College Library, Waterville, Maine.

The text of *Guy Domville* published in this volume includes all the alterations in Henry James's copy as well as those contained in the miscellaneous manuscript sheets at Harvard and in addition such alterations as are in the Huntington Library copy which do not occur elsewhere.

The High Bid:

(1) The Lord Chamberlain's copy of the play was licensed as *Covering End* March 9, 1908 for production at Edinburgh. The text corresponds, with a few minor alterations, to the Forbes-Robertson copy. Typescript.

(2) Sir Johnston Forbes-Robertson's copy at the Houghton Library, each act bound in black cardboard and signed "J. Forbes-Robertson, 22 Bedford Sq. W.C." Contains a number of cuts and alterations including some inserts in the actor's hand. Act I does not have the part of the "Young Man" later written in by James. Typescript.

(3) Gertrude Elliott's copy, in her possession, contains all the cuts and changes of the Forbes-Robertson copy, with the part of the "Young Man" written in. This text is reproduced here.

(4) Three acts, each separately bound in red, at the Houghton Library, with the "Young Man" inserted in Act I. Typescript.

(5) A single-volume copy, bound in blue, at the Houghton Library, containing the label of James's literary agent, J. B. Pinker. This is an uncut, unaltered typescript of (4).

The Saloon:

(1) The Lord Chamberlain's copy, a typescript; licensed Jan. 23, 1911. The text described under (3) below.

(2) First typescript of the play, loose sheets, at the Houghton Library, marked "draft copy" containing corrections and changes by James.

(3) Second typescript, also at the Houghton Library in which some scenes have been extended and clarified and the dialogue sharpened.

(4) A clean typescript of (3) at the Houghton Library. This text has been reproduced in this volume.

The Other House:

(1) Three acts and a prologue, at the Houghton Library, each act and the prologue bound in blue. This is the longest typescript, following closely the novel except for (a) the first scene, (b) the scene with the child.

(a) In the novel the connection between the two houses and Jean's position is narrated by the author. In the play this has been incorporated into dialogue.

(b) In the novel the child appears and speaks. In the play this has been eliminated. At this point, in the manuscript, Henry James's corrections, written in his hand, have been pasted over the typewritten sheets.

This typescript has been corrected several times. Most of the corrections are in Henry James's hand and they seem to have been made at different times, in blue pencil and in different shades of ink. There are also some corrections in Theodora Bosanquet's hand. This version has been reproduced in this volume.

(2) A second blue-bound copy, at the Houghton Library, each act bound separately. The Prologue contains a stage plan in James's hand. Act I has a stage plan drawn by Theodora Bosanquet. The text is a cut version of (1). After (2) was typed further changes were made in the Prologue and Act I of (1) which are not included here.

(3) A carelessly-typed uncorrected copy of (1) at the Houghton library, incorporating all corrections marked therein. Acts II and III are the same as in (2).

(4) A copy submitted to the Incorporated Stage Society similar to (2).

The novel ends in a scene between Tony and Paul. This was reproduced in (1), then deleted so that the play ended with Paul alone on the stage. In (2) Henry James wrote in an exit and re-entrance for Tony. In (3) the play ends similarly to the corrected (1), i.e. Paul alone on the stage.

The Outcry:

There are five typescript versions of *The Outcry* in the Houghton Library. Each act of each manuscript is typewritten and bound with the exception of one version (5) in which each act has paper covers.

(1) Brown covers. This is the longest and probably the earliest version of the play.

(2) Red covers. This is a cut version of (1) and contains extensive deletions and emendations. The second half of Act I, after page 30, contains deletions made by Henry James while Acts II and III contain deletions made by James and some by Granville-Barker.

(3) Brown covers: but distinguishable from (1) since the number of each act printed on the cover is in thinner lettering. Pages 1 to 30 in (2) have been cut down and retyped forming here pages 1a to 17. The remainder of this act (Act I) is the same as Act I of (2). Corrections apparently were copied into this version by James from (2). This was probably Miss Bosanquet's copy—she having a separate one to refer to when James was in London and she in Rye.

(4) Green covers. This is the version compiled by Theodora Bosanquet from versions (2) and (3) re-incorporating all the parts deleted "under Barker's and Barrie's . . . urgent requisition." This version seems to be the one James considered as the definitive version of the play and is the text reproduced here.

(5) Paper covers, marked "Miss Dickens' Typewriting Office." This version was copied from (2) and (3) as cut by James and Granville-Barker and is the shortest version of the play.

(6) A copy sent to the Incorporated Stage Society consisting of Act I of (1) and Acts II and III of (2).

There exists also at the Houghton Library a red-covered Act I which is the same as Act I of (1) except for a few minor changes. The novel appears to have been written from (1) with some references to (2) and (3). Some passages omitted in the latter versions are restored in the novel. Some changes made in them are also included in the novel in which a few completely new speeches have been inserted.

NOTES

Abbreviations

ASB ....*A Small Boy and Others*, London and New York, 1913
NSB ....*Notes of a Son and Brother*, London and New York, 1914
N ....*The Notebooks of Henry James*, London and New York, 1947
(U) ....Unpublished document
T&F ....*Theatre and Friendship*, London and New York, 1932
HJ ....Henry James
WJ ....William James
AJ ....Alice James
AJJ ....*Alice James, Her Brothers, Her Journal*, New York, 1934
L ....*The Letters of Henry James*, London and New York, 1920
Ed ....The editor of this volume

FOREWORD

9   Preface to The Awkward Age, N.Y. Edition, IX, xiii.

9   "After the Play," in *New Review* (June, 1889), reprinted in *Picture and Text* (New York, 1893). James wrote two other essays in dialogue form: "Daniel Deronda: A Conversation" in *Atlantic Monthly* (Dec. 1876), reprinted in *Partial Portraits* (London, 1888) and "An Animated Conversation" in *Scribner's* (March, 1889) reprinted in *Essays in London* (London and New York, 1893).

10   HJ to H. G. Wells, L., I, 298–99.

10   *Theatre-stuff* . . . HJ to Martin Secker, 17 June 1913 (U). The letter was communicated by Mr. P. S. O'Hegarty of Dublin, Ireland.

11   HJ to J. R. Osgood, 5 May 1883 (U). This letter is in the Yale University Library.

NOTES AND ACKNOWLEDGMENTS

13   Edward Compton's father was born a Mackenzie but took the name of Compton for his stage career in 1826 from his paternal grandmother, Susannah Compton. See Compton Mackenzie, *My Life and Times*, vol. 1: 1883–1891 (London, 1963).

14   "*it is the play*" . . . HJ to Edward Compton, May 2, 1893 *Letters*, ed. Leon Edel (Cambridge, Mass., 1980), III, 410–12.

14   "*an impossible couple* . . ." HJ to William Dean Howells, March 30, 1877 *Letters* (1975), II, 104–7.

14   Preface to *The American* N.Y. Edition, II, xvi–xxi.

15   HJ to Edward Compton, May 16, [1893], holograph letter (Texas). See also Mackenzie, *My Life and Times*, vol. 2, appendix, 310–12.

15   George Bernard Shaw, *The Diaries, 1885–1897*, 2 vols., edited by Stanley Weintraub (University Park, Pa., 1986, I, 121. The full entry reads: "Wrote paragraphs for DR. Went to Psychical in the evening. Podmore suggested that I should sleep at a haunted house. I agreed, hurried home and sent off my copy, and stayed very late. Went by train to South Kensington and walked the rest of the way. Found Leonard, Goodman and Fountain at the house. Slept there. Terrific nightmare." Weintraub adds that "Shaw wrote about the adventure in an unsigned essay, PMG, 6 November 1885," but on researching this, at my request, he found only the brief, unattributed Shavian allusion which I quote.

16   *Owen Wingrave* first appeared in *The Graphic* (November 1892) and was published in book form in *The Private Life* (London, 1893).

16   I have transcripts of four other letters from James to Granville-Barker sent to me by the late Allen Wade, who was an assistant to Granville-Barker at the time. These are dated January 10 and 22 and February 7, 1908, as well as one dated October 16, 1909 which belongs to the Princeton sequence. There also exists a letter from James to Granville-Barker dated March 21, 1914, in the Johns Hopkins Library, which was written at Carlyle Mansions. In it James responds to a suggestion, made by Granville-Barker, that the Moscow Art Theatre might be interested in *The Outcry*. James rejects the idea on the ground that the Russians would not be interested in the theme, namely, that of a valuable painting leaving England for another country: "The Moscow theatre is evidently remarkable, but can't be as remarkable as that!" He adds, "Trust the fond author to have liked this amusement, if he *could!*"

THE DRAMATIC YEARS

19   "*the dramatic way* . . ." N., 347–48. L., I, xix–xxi.

19–20   HJ at the theatre: H. M. Walbrook, "Henry James and the English Theatre," *Nineteenth Century* (July, 1916). Elizabeth Robins, T&F, 128–29. Mary Anderson's reminiscence, letter to Ed., 23 July 1930. See also L., I, 328–30, HJ's artful inscription in her autograph album, hinting he would have liked to write a play for her.

20–24   HJ's childhood playgoing, ASB, 75, 78–80, 100, 101, 103–20, 131, 133, 154–71, 316, 323, 354–62, 382–85, 404, 405. See also *Annals of the New York Stage*, edited by Odell, Vols. V, VI.

22   "*Paternal discrimination* . . ." *William Wetmore Story and His Friends* (Boston, 1903), II, 259–60.

then altered it to the third. On *Le Demi-Monde,* see Preface to *The Siege of London,* N.Y. Edition, XIV. On Coquelin in London, N., 38–39. Coquelin to HJ, letter of 12 May 1891 (U).

Journal, 1881. In alluding to "journal" I have followed a distinction made by HJ between notebooks and journals. James considered an author's journal to be the record of day-by-day trivia or such incidents as he wished to note for future reference. The notebook served the more specific function of the "working out pen in hand" of stories he was writing or planned to write. This distinction has not been made in the published *Notebooks* which contains a number of "journal" entries. See Sidney E. Lind, letter to *Times Literary Supplement* (27 Nov. 1948).

The Tragic Muse, N.Y. Edition, VII, VIII. The conversation relating to the theatre is in Chap. iv of Book First, and the visit to the Théâtre Français in Chap. xx of Book Fourth. See also *The Ambassadors,* N.Y. Edition, XXI, Book Second, Chap. i.

"To be read 200 years . . ." Unsigned paper by HJ in the *Nation* (9 Jan. 1873), reproduced in *The Scenic Art.*

"Impatient . . . to . . . work . . . for the stage." HJ to WJ, 23 July 1878 (U).

"most cherished of all my projects . . ." N. (26 Dec. 1881), 37–39.

Rents from Albany and Syracuse. Many letters from HJ to WJ contain acknowledgments of sums sent him by WJ derived from property owned by the James family.

"One must go one's way . . ." L., I, 170.

Dramatizing of *The Portrait of a Lady.* To Lawrence Barrett, 11 Aug. [1884] (U).

To Julian R. Sturgis, 20 Sept. [1886] (U).

To Howells. L., I, 135.

"The Private Life," in *The Wheel of Time and Other Tales* (New York, 1893). "Benvolio," in *The Madonna of the Future* (London, 1879).

The conflict at Dane Hall. See *The Ghostly Tales of Henry James* edited by Leon Edel (New Brunswick, N.J., 1949), Preface to the story "The Great Good Place," pp. 567–70.

Edward Compton and Virginia Bateman, N., 99 and from information supplied Ed. by the late Mrs. Compton and her son, Compton Mackenzie.

Gabriel Nash's outburst. *The Tragic Muse,* N.Y. Edition, VII, 66–67.

Mercenary reasons. From a letter to AJ a portion of which appeared in L., I, 166–68. To WJ, 9 Dec. 1890 (U).

WJ to HJ, 4 June 1890 (U).

Secrecy. HJ to WJ, 24 Jan. 1894 (U).

To Stevenson. L., I, 176–77, 182. To WJ, L., 180

Payment for *The Tragic Muse.* Letter to T. B. Aldrich, 3 March 1888 (U).

"massacred little play . . ." HJ to WJ, 1 Sept. 1891 (U), 4 Feb. 1895 (U).

A Most Unholy Trade, Letters on the Drama by Henry James (Cambridge, Mass., 1923; privately printed), p. 15.

Rehearsal at Portsmouth: HJ to WJ, 7 Nov. 1890 (U).

The question of time. HJ to WJ, 1 Sept. 1891 (U).

Allusions to plays in progress are to be found in a series of HJ letters to WJ of the 1890's as well as in AJJ and T&F.

Oscar Wilde. Described by HJ to Henrietta Reubell, letter of 25 Feb. 1892 (U).

Reviewer in the *Daily Chronicle.* Colonel C. Archer, brother of William

Since HJ's death two highly successful plays have been adapted from his work. John Balderston and J. C. Squire wrote *Berkeley Square* based on *The Sense of the Past;* Ruth and Augustus Goetz dramatized *Washington Square* under the title *The Heiress*. *The Turn of the Screw* and *The Aspern Papers* were adapted by Allan Turpin and *The Tragic Muse* was adapted by Hubert Griffith. *Berkeley Square* and *The Heiress* were filmed, and *The Aspern Papers* was screened in a virtually unrecognizable form as *The Lost Moment*. A number of HJ's novels and short stories have been broadcast as radio dramas both in England and America among these *The Turn of the Screw, The American, The Ambassadors* and "Four Meetings."

PYRAMUS AND THISBE

STILL WATERS

DAISY MILLER

THE AMERICAN

PAGE

and Sketches (London, 1912). See also HJ's preface to Balestier's posthumous volume, *The Average Woman* (New York, 1892). Tributes to Balestier appeared in the *Pall Mall Gazette* (7, 17 Dec. 1891) and in *The Speaker* (19 Dec. 1891).

181   To William Archer, 27 Dec. 1890 (U). This and other letters to Archer were supplied by his brother and literary executor, Colonel C. Archer.

181   To Urbain Mengin, 3 Jan. 1891 (U), supplied by M. Mengin. James wrote a fluent, easy French retaining in it his characteristic style. He wrote to Mengin: "*Comme vous pensez bien, c'est la soif de l'or qui me pousse dans cette voie déshonorante. . . .*"

181   To Edmund Gosse, L., I, 172. See also Jules Jusserand, *What Me Befell* (London, 1933), p. 102. I am indebted to the late M. Jusserand for reminiscenses of HJ in the 1890s.

182   ". . . *is it going?*" To Mrs. Hugh Bell, L., I, 173.

183   The Southport Cast: Newman—Edward Compton; Marquis—Sydney Paxton; Valentin—Clarence Blakiston; Deepmere—Dudley Wilshaw; Nioche—Young Stewart; Claire—Mrs. Compton; Marquise—Miss Elinor Aickin; Noémie—Miss Sidney Crowe; Mrs. Bread—Alice Burton; De Marignac—Harrison Hunter.

183   Supper after the play . . . HJ's account in preface to Balestier, *The Average Woman* (New York, 1892), pp. 31–32.

184   WJ to HJ, 4 Jan. 1891 (U). Also *New Letters of James Russell Lowell* (New York, 1932), p. 346.

185   Balestier to Howells, 17 Jan. 1891 (U).

185   Wolverhampton-Stratford. From an account in the stage journal *Era*, 17 Jan. 1891. Accounts of the provincial tour in letter to Francis Boott, 24 March 1891 (U); *Dramatic Review*, 25 April 1891; letter Mrs. Compton to HJ, dated "Friday night, Theatre Royal, Greenock" (U). AJJ, 196. HJ to WJ, 23 March 1891 (U).

186   Elizabeth Robins. HJ to Mrs. John L. Gardner, 7 June 1891 (U). I am indebted for this to Mr. Morris Carter of the Isabella Stewart Gardner Museum (Fenway Court), Boston. See also Lady Bell, *Landmarks* (New York, 1929), pp. 107–13; also HJ, "On the Occasion of *Hedda Gabler*," and "On the Occasion of the *Master Builder*," published respectively in the *New Review* (June, 1891), and *Pall Mall Gazette* (17 Feb. 1893), reprinted in *The Scenic Art*, pp. 243–60. For Miss Robins's account of *The American*, see T&F, Chap. ii.

186   Preparations for the London production. HJ to Grace Norton, 22 Sept. 1891 (U). An interview with Compton appeared in the *Pall Mall Gazette*, 26 Sept. 1891.

188   Miss Woolson, in a letter to Katherine L. Mather, 20 Oct. 1891, reproduced in *Constance Fenimore Woolson* by Clare Benedict (London, [no year]; privately printed), pp. 371–72. I am indebted to Miss Benedict for this and other material made available to me.

189   First night and the critics. Notices and news items appeared in *The Referee* and *The Observer*, 27 Sept. 1891; *Times, Daily News, Evening News and Post, Morning Advertiser, St. James Gazette, Star, Echo, Daily Chronicle, Daily Telegraph, Pall Mall Gazette*, 28 Sept.; *Woman*, 30 Sept.; *Stage*, 1 Oct.; *The Speaker, Dramatic Review, Era, Vanity Fair, Illustrated Sporting and Dramatic, Athenaeum, The Academy, Illustrated London News, Gentlemen's Magazine*, 3 Oct.; *Weekly dispatch, Sunday Times*, 4 Oct.; *The Theatre*, 4 Nov. The *Atlantic Monthly* account appeared in the December 1891

issue. The N.Y. *Times* carried a dispatch on 27 Sept. Sixty-five critics were
invited to the first night.

189–90   The London run: HJ to G. W. Smalley, 7 and 19 Oct. 1891 (U); to Henrietta
Reubell, 13 Dec. 1891 (U); to Grace Norton, 16 Nov. 1891 (U); to George
du Maurier, 11 Nov. 1891 (U). See also "Personal Recollections of Henry
James" by E. S. Nadal, *Scribner's* (July, 1920); "Renaissance of the Stage,"
by David Christie Murray, *Contemporary Review* (Nov., 1891). Allusions to
The American were made, during its run, in *The Critic* (24 Oct.), *Era*
(7 Nov.), *Echo* (16 Nov.). See also AJJ, 245–46. Miss Daphne du Maurier
made available to me HJ's letters to her grandfather.

190   Prince of Wales. AJJ, 246. HJ to WJ, 21 Oct. 1891 (U).
190   The "Second Edition." Noticed *Echo, Daily News, Evening News and Post,*
16 Nov.; *The World* (Archer), 18 Nov.; *Illustrated Sporting and Dramatic,*
Era, The Speaker (A. B. Walkley), 21 Nov.
190   "*Honor is saved . . .*" HJ to WJ, 3 Dec. 1891 (U).
190   Balestier's death. AJJ, 244.
190–91   AJ's death. HJ to WJ, 6 and 9 Mar. 1892 (U).

THE NEW FOURTH ACT

241   Audience's reception: HJ to WJ, 15 Nov. 1892 (U). See also T&F 77.

THEATRICALS: TWO COMEDIES

254   HJ to Howells, 28 May 1876 (U).
254   T&F, p. 152.
254   *Theatricals: Two Comedies* was reviewed in *Athenaeum;* 17 Nov. 1894;
Sunday Times, 13 Jan. 1895; *Pall Mall Gazette* and *Daily Chronicle,* 16
June 1894. In the United States in *Nation,* 28 June 1894; *Literary World,*
30 June; *Dial,* 1 Sept.; *Critic,* 12 Jan. 1895.

TENANTS

257   HJ to WJ, 9 Dec. 1890 (U).
257   HJ to Mrs. Bell, 7 and 11 Dec. 1890; 27 Jan. 1891 (U).
258   Play Number 2. HJ to WJ. This quotation is from an unpublished portion
of the letter of 6 Feb. 1891, reproduced in L., I, 179–81.
258   HJ to Mrs. Bell, 13 April 1891 (U).
258   AJJ, 222.
258   "*Irrepressible delays . . .*" HJ to WJ, 1 Sept. 1891 (U).
258–59   Oscar Wilde . . . T&F, 112–14, 121, 124.
259   Modjeska . . . Although HJ wrote to Modjeska "in the very strictest confidence," a long paragraph on the correspondence appeared in the column
"The Lounger" of *The Critic* (19 Dec. 1891). I am indebted to Mr. James
Gilvarry for the HJ letter to Modjeska of 17 Nov. 1891 (U). Modjeska
replied to HJ on 26 Nov. 1891 and wrote to him again 24 Jan. 1892 (U).

DISENGAGED

295   Fanny Kemble's anecdote. N., 95–96.
295–96   Ada Rehan—Daly. HJ's letters to Augustin Daly, in which the progress of
Disengaged can be followed from the play's inception to its withdrawal by
James, are in the Theatre Collection of the Harvard University Library. A
copy of Daly's final reply is also to be found with this correspondence.
295   "*vainly dissimulated . . .*" Joseph Francis Daly, *The Life of Augustin Daly*
(New York, 1917), pp. 552–54.

made available to me by Lady Alexander. See also A. E. W. Mason, *Sir George Alexander and the St. James's Theatre* (London, 1935).

465   The "germ," and list of names. N., 126.

466   *A Foregone Conclusion* . . . HJ reviewed Howells's novel in the *North American Review*, Jan. 1875 and *Nation*, 7 Jan. 1875. Howells dramatized this novel during the same period as James's dramatization of *Daisy Miller*. Howells in letters to James of 10 March, 12 May, 26 Aug. and 5 Dec., 1873, kept his friend informed of the writing of the book. In "A Roman Holiday" (*Atlantic*, July, 1873), reprinted in *Transatlantic Sketches*, as "From a Roman Notebook," James described his impressions of a young priest kneeling before the altar in a Roman church as "a supreme vision of the religious passion —its privations and resignations and exhaustions, and its terribly small share of amusement . . . his seemed a grim preference, and this foreswearing of the world a terrible game—a gaining one only if your zeal never falters; a hard fight when it does."

467   Alexander's terms. HJ to Alexander from Ramsgate, undated, 1893 (U).

467   Preparations . . . HJ to WJ, 19 Oct., 29 Dec. 1893 (partially reproduced L., I, 210–11), 24 Mar., 28 May, 7 Sept., 27 Oct., 8 Dec., 22 Dec. 1894 (U). Allusions to the impending production were made in the theatrical gossip Columns, *Referee*, 21 Jan., 13 May, 29 July 1894; *Athenaeum*, 18 Nov. 1893, 8 Aug., 17 Nov. 29 Dec. 1894; *Illustrated Sporting and Dramatic*, 15 July, 9 Dec. 1893, 27 Jan., 4 Aug., 3 Nov., 24 Nov., 8 Dec. and 15 Dec. 1894; *The Sketch*, 13 Dec. 1893, carried an interview with Mr. and Mrs. Alexander, "A Chat With George Alexander." HJ also alluded to plans for the play in a letter to Francis Boott, 15 Dec. 1894 (U) and to Henrietta Reubell, 31 Dec. 1894 (L., I, 225–27). See also T&F, 137–39 and all of Chap. viii.

468   *"tremulous hours . . ."* HJ to Gosse, 3 Jan. 1895, from a letter partially reproduced in Simon Nowell-Smith, *The Legend of the Master* (London, 1947, New York, 1948), pp. 62–63. Kipling wrote to HJ, 15 Dec. 1894, from Vermont to wish him well on his behalf and his wife's. Mrs. Kipling was the former Caroline Balestier, sister of Wolcott.

468   The telegram . . . Its text was reproduced in *Westminster Gazette*, 9 Jan. 1895, "upon really good authority." Edward F. Spence, who wrote the notice of the play for the *Gazette* was in touch with James and Alexander. James describes the telegram incident in a letter to Miss Robins, T&F, 166–67.

468   Letters to friends and relatives . . . HJ to WJ is dated "Saturday January 5th 5.45 p.m." (U). Among the friends to whom he wrote—and in prophetic vein—was Mme. Bourget who was in Cannes (U): "It is 5 o'clock in the afternoon and at 8.30 this evening *le sort en est jeté*—my poor little play will be thrown into the arena—like a little white Christian Virgin to the lions and tigers."

468   The Wilde play. HJ to WJ, L., I, 232–36. HJ's opinions of Wilde are to be found in a letter to Henrietta Reubell, 25 Feb. 1892 (U), and in *Letters of Mrs. Henry Adams* (Boston, 1936), pp. 328, 333, 338.

469   The account of the appearance of the theatre and of those present is based on the editor's inspection of the theatre and the theatre gossip and society columns of the time.

470   Shaw and Wells. See H. G. Wells, *Experiment in Autobiography* (New York, 1934), pp. 450 ff.

471   Arnold Bennett's account *Things That Have Interested Me* (London, 1921), in which he included a reprint of his review published in *Woman* of 16 Jan. 1895. He also amplified one or two details in a letter to Ed. of 29 July 1929.

PAGE

Bernard Shaw's review appeared in *Saturday Review* of 12 Jan. 1895 and was subsequently reprinted in the first volume of *Dramatic Essays and Opinions* (New York, 1928). Wells's review, never reprinted, appeared in the *Pall Mall Gazette*, 7 Jan. 1895; William Archer's in *The World*, 9 Jan.; Clement Scott's in *Daily Telegraph*, 7 Jan. A. B. Walkley wrote three reviews, *The Star*, 7 Jan., *The Speaker*, 12 Jan. and "Guy Domville, An Appreciation" in *Harper's Weekly*, 2 Mar. 1895.

472–82   Notices and comment on the play appeared in the following newspapers and journals: 6 Jan. 1895—*Daily Graphic, Referee* (also 13 Jan.), *Observer, Sunday Times;* 7 Jan.—*Times, Daily Chronicle, Daily News, Westminster Gazette* (also 8, 9, 10 Jan. [letters to editor]), *St. James Gazette, The Star, The Sun, The Morning, Manchester Guardian,* 8 Jan.—*Westminster Gazette;* 9 Jan.—*The World, Westminster Gazette;* 10 Jan.—*Stage, London Figaro, Westminster Gazette* (letters to the editor); 11 Jan.—*Catholic Herald;* 12 Jan.—*Era* (also 19 Jan., 9 Feb.), *Athenaeum, The Speaker, The Graphic, Today* (also 19 Jan.), *Illustrated London News, Illustrated Sporting and Dramatic, Saturday Review;* 13 Jan.—*Weekly Dispatch;* 16 Jan.—*Vanity Fair, The Sketch* (scenes from the production), *Woman,* 19 Jan.—*Punch;* 1 Feb.—*The Theatre.*

In the United States, in addition to Walkley's appreciation, the N.Y. *Tribune* carried a full-length dispatch from G. W. Smalley, 20 Jan. and *The Critic* an article by Arthur Waugh, 26 Jan. The New York *Times*, 13 Jan., carried a dispatch by Harold Frederic, as well as an editorial, "Henry James as a Playwright."

Apparently HJ did not read many of the reviews, most of which were favorable and sympathetic, for he wrote to WJ (L., I, 228), "The 'papers' have, into the bargain, been mainly ill-natured and densely stupid and vulgar; but the only two dramatic critics who count, W. Archer and Clement Scott have done me more justice." HJ sent a bundle of his "fan-mail" to WJ, dotting some of the letters with footnotes, such as one from Mrs. Montague Crackanthorpe of 24 Jan. 1895, who told him the play was neither for gallery nor for stalls "in their entirety but for the few scattered about, thank goodness, everywhere." HJ's footnote was "What I tried so heroically to make it for." WJ's opinion, formed after examining this evidence, was expressed in a letter to Howells, "other extracts and letters show the exact facts about HJ's play, which was evidently exquisite in texture, but which let human action die away at the end and give up and disappear in the sand—a thing at which any audience has a right to get mad."

Among HJ letters extant on the play are—in addition to those addressed to WJ in L., I, 227–29, 232–36 and to Howells *ibid.*, I, 230–2—one to Sir George Henschel, 15 Jan. 1895 (in Leon Edel, *Henry James: Les années dramatiques*, Paris, 1931) and in L., I, 229–30; to Henrietta Reubell, 10 Jan. 1895 (U); to W. Barclay Squire, 8 Jan. (U); to Henry Arthur Jones, 15 Jan. published in the catalogue of a book sale at the Union Art Gallery, New York City, 27 Feb. 1934; to Marion Terry, 15 Jan. (U), "that ill-starred second act—which broke down under the accumulation of its misfortunes"; to Edward F. Spence, 8 Jan. (U); to W. Morton Fullerton, 9 Jan. (U); to Elizabeth Robins and Mrs. Bell, T&F, 166–68; to Gosse, 13 Jan. (U).

472   Willie Elliot . . . W. G. Elliot, *In My Anecdotage* (London, 1925), p. 56.
473–74   Mrs. Saker's crinoline . . . Robertson, *Life Was Worth Living*, pp. 268–69.
474   The drinking scene: HJ's essay "The Théâtre Français" in *French Poets and Novelists* (London, 1878), pp. 424–25.

475   The voice from the gallery: from information supplied by Dame Irene Vanbrugh and Franklyn Dyall of the cast, H. M. Walbrook and an anonymous ticket seller at the St. James's.

475-76   The walk from the Haymarket. HJ to WJ, L., I, 232-36.

475-79   Backstage and hissing: information supplied by members of the cast. Accounts of the hissing and other details are to be found in the following volumes among others: Douglas Ainslie, *Adventures Social and Literary* (London, 1922); Mason, *Sir George Alexander;* Walter Sichel, *The Sands of Time* (London, 1923); Edmund Gosse, *Aspects and Impressions* (New York, 1922); F. Anstey (Thomas Anstey Guthrie), *A Long Retrospect* (London, 1936); H. G. Hibbert, *Fifty Years of a London Life* (London, 1916); George Moore, Preface to *The Heather Field* (Edward Martyn) (London, 1899); Robertson, *Life Was Worth Living;* Robins, T&F; Clement Scott, *The Drama of Yesterday and Today* (London, 1899); Alfred Sutro, *Celebrities and Simple Souls* (London, 1933); *Letters of George Meredith* (London, 1912); W. L. Courtney, *The Passing Hour* (London, [no year].)

478   HJ on hissing, *Nation,* 11 Mar. 1875.

478   *"Alick lost his head."* Bernard Shaw to Ed. 25 June 1929.

479   Epilogue. Quoted in a letter from the Ranee of Sarawak to Gosse, 16 May 1929 (U).

482   Shortly after *Guy Domville* HJ wrote two letters to Robert Underwood Johnson, an editor of the *Century* (and later U.S. ambassador to Italy) which, while colored perhaps by the fate of his play, nevertheless expressed his strong feeling about stage-folk. Johnson, a great admirer of Eleanora Duse, had asked HJ to write an article about her. HJ replied 5 May 1895 ". . . I can't write any more about theatrical people—and I don't *want* to! I think the whole periodical press takes a vastly disproportionate view of the importance and interest of mountebanks and mimes . . ." On 24 June 1895 he returned to the subject ". . . I am . . . woefully weary of the (today) all-invasive theatre, with its cheapness of criticism, its over-estimated art, and vulgarity of air . . . the ridiculous abandonment of all proportion and perspective in the worship of the *actor and actress,* the deification of their little third rate personalities, the colossal inflation of them by the gigantic bellows of the Press—which, in our English-speaking countries, the total absence of dramatic authors (worth speaking of) contributes to by establishing no measure of their relativity, their merely servile office. In France, where the drama is primarily the Author, the case is infinitely less bad: the actors are kept more in their places. (I shall not forget Alphonse Daudet's stupefaction the other day at John Kemble and Mrs. Siddons— by statue—in Westminster Abbey)." I am indebted to Mr. James Gilvarry for communicating these letters to me from his collection.

482   Fifteen years after *Guy Domville,* HJ talked to H. M. Walbrook, drama critic of the *Pall Mall Gazette,* of the play's failure and wrote to him, 8 July 1912 (U): "I have dreamed of reviving him [Guy Domville]—but only on the basis of making his 3 acts into 4. That was his weakness (for he *had* one), that he was the victim of my ideal of a certain supreme technical perfection—whereby I made a unity, for unity's sake, of what should have been two sequent steps in the drama, and so compressed my matter into an economy too drastic and of which no single sapient creature understood the beautiful, the compositional intention and interest. But this is stirring old wan ghosts—say of the murdered. . . ." I am indebted to the late Mr. Walbrook for details of his discussion of the drama with HJ.

483   HJ to WJ, 8 Jan. 1895 (U).

PAGE

SUMMERSOFT

519   See T&F, Chap. xi.

519   HJ on Ellen Terry, unsigned article, "The London Theatres," *Scribner's*, Jan. 1880; reprinted in *The Scenic Art*.

519   *Mme. Sans-Gêne.* N., 128–29, 185–87.

520   The journal entry, dated Rye, Thursday, 30 July 1914, not included in the published *Notebooks*, begins: "Identified yesterday the date of sending Ellen Terry the little one-act play (afterwards *The High Bid*) from Osborne Crescent, Torquay, as August (toward end of) 1895—nearly 19 years ago."

520   The country house. Letter to Countess of Jersey, L., I, 192. See also The Dowager Countess of Jersey, *Fifty-One Years of Victorian Life* (London, 1922).

521   Story anecdote. HJ, *William Wetmore Story and His Friends*, I, 12–13.

522   The MS of *Summersoft* remains in the envelope in which HJ placed it to return it to Elizabeth Robins. It bears the postmark, 13 Nov. 1899, Rye, Sussex. Across the inner envelope HJ wrote the words, "One Act" and "E.T."

523   New Century. T&F, 211. Miss Robins made available to me the text of Archer's report.

THE HIGH BID

549   Sir Johnston Forbes-Robertson, *A Player Under Three Reigns* (London, 1925), pp. 246ff.

549   HJ to Elizabeth Robins, 9 Oct. 1907 (U).

549   HJ to Mrs. W. K. Clifford, 20 Oct. 1907 (U), also 21 March 1908 (U). The work dates were supplied by Miss Bosanquet.

550–51   HJ to Edith Wharton, 23 March 1908 (L., II, 94–95). Other letters on the same subject to Howard Sturgis, 23 April 1908 (U); to Jocelyn Persse, 30 Jan., 22 Feb. and 24 March (U); to Howells, 10 March 1908 (U). See also T&F, 269. The Edinburgh production was reviewed in the *Edinburgh Evening News* and *The Scotsman*, 27 Mar. 1908 and in *Era*, 28 Mar.

551   Ellen Terry's claim. HJ to Mrs. W. K. Clifford, 6 April 1908 (U).

551   "*a great . . . success . . .*" HJ to his nephew Henry, L., II, 96–97.

551   Gertrude Elliott to HJ, undated autumn 1908 (U). HJ's reply is of 22 Oct. 1908 (U).

552   The alterations were sent with two covering letters of 31 Dec. 1908 (U), and 1 Jan. 1909 (U).

552   Notes on the Forbes-Robertson MS give the following differences in the timing of the Acts between the road production at Glasgow and the London performance: Act I, Glasgow 48 minutes; His Majesty's 47 minutes. Act II, Glasgow 47; HM 41. Act III, Glasgow 18; HM 15.

552   The London cast: Yule—Forbes-Robertson; Prodmore—Edward Sass; Chivers—Ian Robertson; A Young Man—Alexander Cassy; Mrs. Gracedew —Gertrude Elliott; Cora—Miss Esme Hubbard.

552–53   Max Beerbohm's review appeared in *Saturday Review*, 27 Feb. 1909, and was reprinted by him in *Around Theatres* (New York, 1930), II, 698–703. The unsigned review in the *Times* (A. B. Walkley) was of 19 Feb. Other reviews appeared on that date in *Pall Mall Gazette, Evening Standard, Daily Chronicle, Daily Telegraph* and in *The World*, 23 Feb. (H. Hamilton Fyfe).

552   See also Montrose J. Moses and Virginia Gerson, *Clyde Fitch and His Letters* (Boston, 1924), p. 337 and Royal Cortissoz *The Life of Whitelaw Reid* (New York, 1921), II, 421.

PAGE

ROUGH STATEMENT FOR "THE CHAPERON"

607 Idea for *The Chaperon*. N., 106–8.

608 HJ to Horace Elisha Scudder, 18 July 1891 (U). HJ's correspondence with Scudder was made available to me by Mr. Donald Brien, who also furnished from his invaluable collection the photograph of 34 DeVere Gardens reproduced in this volume.

608 At the time of the success of *The High Bid* HJ published his short story "The Velvet Glove" in the *English Review* (March 1909). Its hero is a novelist who has successfully dramatized one of his works and has "tasted in their fulness the sweets of success." The story was republished in *The Finer Grain* (London and New York, 1910).

THE SALOON

641 For an account of the origin and the writing of the story of "Owen Wingrave" see *Ghostly Tales*, pp. 311–15.

641 HJ to Edith Wharton, L., II, 91.

642 HJ to Granville-Barker, 22 Jan. 1908 (U).

642 Mr. W. S. Kennedy, chairman of the Incorporated Stage Society, made available to me the Board's minutes of 12 Jan. 1909.

642 I am indebted to Bernard Shaw for permission to publish his letters to HJ and for making available to me HJ's replies. Across the copies of the letters to James, Mr. Shaw wrote in his characteristic hand: "Mr. Leon Edel is authorized to quote these two letters in full in his edition of Henry James's dramatic works. But he must on no account print my name with a George. Professionally I am Bernard Shaw. Privately I am G.B.S. I am NEVER George except from the pens of pirates. G. Bernard Shaw, 7th May 1937."

648 "*duffers of actors . . .*" HJ to Theodora Bosanquet, 14 May 1911 (U). Miss Bosanquet made available HJ's letters to her as well as other material relating to this period.

648–49 From an interview with Miss Kingston in 1937 and a memorandum supplied to Ed., 9 June 1937.

648 The play was reviewed by the late H. M. Walbrook in the *Pall Mall Gazette*, 18 Jan. 1911, and reprinted in *Nights at the Play* (London, 1911), p. 115. HJ's letters to Walbrook acknowledging the book and discussing the drama were published in the London *Mercury* (Oct., 1929), "Three Letters and a Monologue." J. T. Grein's review appeared in the *Sunday Times*, 22 Jan. 1911, and the *Saturday Review* notice, signed "P.J.," appeared 21 Jan. 1911. The London dailies reviewed the play on 18 Jan. 1911.

648 The cast: Kate Julian—Dora Barton; Spencer Coyle—Halliwell Hobbes; Mrs. Coyle—Frances Wetherall; Mrs. Julian—Mary Stuart; Bobby Lechmere —Owen Nares; Owen Wingrave—Everard Vanderlip.

648 HJ to Miss Kingston, 31 Jan. 1911 (U). HJ discussed *The Saloon* in two letters to Louis Shipman, 26 Jan. 1911, and 22 Feb. 1911, published in the *Colby College Library Quarterly* (Waterville, Maine), June, 1943, on the occasion of the James centenary.

THE OTHER HOUSE

677 For an account of the writing of the novel from the scenario see Leon Edel, Introduction to *The Other House* (New York and London, 1948). For an early adumbration of the situation in the play see HJ's "The Romance of Certain Old Clothes" (*Atlantic Monthly*, Feb., 1868) reprinted in *A Passionate Pilgrim* (Boston, 1875). See also *Ghostly Tales*, pp. 3–4.

765   Frohman's forfeit. From an unpublished letter, HJ to J. B. Pinker, kindly supplied to Ed. by Simon Nowell-Smith.

765   Earnings of the novel: HJ to Edith Wharton, L., II, 209.

765   The letter to the *Literary Supplement* carries the heading "Mr. Shaw on Printed Plays."

765   Granville-Barker's views: from an undated memorandum to Ed.

MONOLOGUE FOR RUTH DRAPER

811   From information supplied by Miss Draper. See also Simon Nowell-Smith, *Legend of the Master,* p. 73.

811   HJ to Ruth Draper, 4 Dec. 1913. The letter was published with the monologue in the London *Mercury* (Oct., 1929).

812   American Women: "The Speech of American Women" and "The Manners of American Women," *Harper's Bazar* (Nov.–Dec. 1906, Jan.–Feb. and April–July 1907).

INDEX